Abnormal Psychology

Understanding

Human Problems

Second Edition

Philip C. Kendall
Temple University

Constance Hammen
University of California, Los Angeles

Houghton Mifflin Company   Boston New York

To Sue, Mark, and Reed

To Amy and B.R.

Sponsoring editor: David Lee
Senior associate editor: Jane Knetzger
Senior project editor: Rosemary Winfield
Senior production/design coordinator: Sarah Ambrose
Senior designer: Henry Rachlin
Senior manufacturing coordinator: Marie Barnes

Cover designer: Harold Burch, Harold Burch Design NYC.

All other credits appear on page A-1, which constitutes an
extension of the copyright page.

Printed in the U.S.A.

Library of Congress Catalog Card Number: 97-72499

ISBN: 0-395-75491-7

23456789-VH-0100 99 98

Brief Contents

Special Features

Contents

CHAPTER 12   Sexual Dysfunctions and Disorders   368

CHAPTER 13   Personality Disorders   404

Preface

In our roles as teachers, scientists, therapists, and members of families and communities, we are confronted daily not only with "normal" behavior but also with the many forms of human disorder and dysfunction—and the ways in which they affect our lives and those of people around us. We wanted to make this reality—that normality is broadly defined and that psychological disorders are common, pervasive, and woven into the threads of everyday lives—the central theme of the Second Edition.

Humanizing Abnormal Psychology

Abnormal behavior is not about the exotic and the rare; it is about common—sometimes severe—human problems that affect not only the individual but also family, friends, and the community as a whole. Our goal is for this book to help students recognize and understand human disorder, as well as appreciate the scientific and social policy applications in this field. To emphasize our central theme, we have added a subtitle to the book: *Understanding Human Problems*. In addition, several features in each chapter explore the theme further.

Those Among Us   Each chapter begins with a series of short new vignettes that refer to experiences students are likely to have had either directly or indirectly, whether experienced by themselves, friends, relatives, coworkers, neighbors, or acquaintances. These vignettes not only bring the material close to home but also frame some of the questions to be addressed in the chapter.

What's Normal?   The "What's Normal?" feature in each chapter addresses our central theme by asking what is the line between typical, frequent, everyday experiences and disorder, and it demonstrates that such a line is often only a matter of degree.

Family Matters   The "Family Matters" section in each chapter (formerly called "Focus on the Family") further discusses research on families' experiences with disorder, their contributions to disorder, or their efforts that may alter the course of disorder.

Consider the Following   The new critical-thinking feature at the end of each chapter, called "Consider the Fol-

lowing," places students in a realistic scenario that requires forming some judgment or opinion based on the material presented. Many of these scenarios involve complex ethical, legal, or interpersonal issues. This feature reinforces the idea that "abnormal psychology" will have a place in students' lives as individuals, parents, and citizens.

Changes in This Edition

In addition to the greater emphasis on the theme of disorder and everyday life, further changes are reflected in this edition. Suicide is no longer a separate chapter, having been integrated into the Mood Disorders chapter. We have expanded coverage of gender and multicultural issues throughout and included greater coverage of new information on topics such as eating disorders in Chapter 15, borderline personality disorder in Chapter 13, the biology of violence in Chapter 14, the genetics of schizophrenia and mood disorders in Chapters 8 and 9, and effects of managed care in Chapter 18. There is more on gay families, homelessness, spousal violence, and other topics of contemporary public interest. Moreover, every section of every chapter has been updated with information from the latest research studies.

Features Retained in This Edition

As before, the book is research-focused, with the goal of presenting the most up-to-date research methods and findings. We strive to stimulate students' understanding and appreciation for scientific investigation of complex human problems and to provoke critical thinking about both practical and theoretical implications of research on human disorders.

Also, as in the previous edition, we present diverse theoretical perspectives on the causes and treatments of disorders. The book continues to give weight to several approaches that contemporary empirical investigations support: biological, cognitive-behavioral, and social-familial approaches. The book presents more biological data than do many comparable textbooks, reflecting the current state of the field and the fact that important developments in genetics, brain functioning, and neuroendocrine functioning help us to more clearly delineate the contributions of psychological and social factors.

We continue to emphasize the gender, cultural, and historical/political factors that influence definitions and expressions of disorders. More than ever before, researchers are investigating disorders in diverse populations both within the United States and around the world, and we have attempted to include the latest work in these developing fields.

There is also ample coverage of contemporary, empirically based investigations of childhood experiences and developmental processes as they affect psychopathology and treatment.

We retain several special features in each chapter from the first edition, including

What's Normal? As described above, the "What's Normal?" feature continues to explore the continuum on which abnormal behavior lies. This edition includes new material, such as "Is Abnormality Normal?" (Chapter 1); "Sometimes a Little Depression Is Not a Good Thing" (Chapter 8), and "Normality Changes Over Time" (Chapter 12). For a full list of "What's Normal?" features, consult page iv.

Focus on Research The feature "Focus on Research" appears in each chapter and presents an in-depth look at a particular topic or method and how scientists formulate questions and proceed to answer them. Some of the new topics include "Does Culture Influence Children's Disorders?" (Chapter 1); "What Predicts Safer Sex Among Youth at Risk for AIDS?" (Chapter 12), and "Can We Prevent Depression in Children?" (Chapter 18). A full list of titles appears on page iv.

Family Matters As noted above, the "Family Matters" feature was formerly entitled Focus on the Family. Among the new topics are "The Importance of Family in Mental Health" (Chapter 1) and "Children of Homeless Mentally Ill Mothers" (Chapter 18). For a complete list, see page iv.

What Lies Ahead? Emphasizing that the field is far from stagnant, the "What Lies Ahead?" feature that concludes each chapter identifies issues or controversies that require further study—or highlights future developments that are on the horizon. The feature underscores that this is a changing field and that no topic or question is truly resolved.

Case Vignettes Each chapter contains case materials to illustrate key disorders or treatments. Many are based on expanded descriptions of the "Those Among Us" vignettes at the opening of each chapter. Though relatively brief, the cases attempt to highlight key issues. Many are drawn from the authors' experiences as clini-

cal psychologists, with appropriate camouflage to protect confidentiality. Additional case material is available with this text, as described below under "Ancillaries."

Pedagogical Support As before, we have aimed to include pedagogical features that facilitate students' ability to process a large amount of material and complex information. For instance, the *illustration program* has been expanded, using graphic and other visual methods to emphasize important points. We have added *sticky notes* to many of the graphs and illustrations to highlight key results. There is also a *new list of key terms* at the end of each chapter, along with a *summary* of essential points. As before, each chapter opens with a detailed *chapter outline*.

Organization and Coverage

Our text includes eighteen chapters that cover all the basic and necessary topics in abnormal psychology. It begins with a series of five chapters that represent general themes, theories, and tools, then proceeds to chapters covering specific disorders and problems, and concludes with a chapter that takes a broad perspective on legal and social issues facing the field.

The opening chapter defines abnormal behavior and emphasizes the role of context in defining disorders, including historical, cultural, age, gender, and situational factors. The important themes of the influence of culture and gender on mental disorders are revisited in each subsequent chapter. Chapters 2 and 3 cover *Models of Psychopathology* and *Approaches to Treatment*. These chapters introduce basic conceptual models: biological, cognitive-behavioral, psychodynamic, humanistic, and social-familial. The models chapter weighs the pros and cons of the various approaches and introduces essential concepts that are relevant to more disorder-specific coverage in subsequent chapters. The treatment chapter discusses not only theoretical models but also individual, family, couple, and community interventions. Key tools for evaluating the effectiveness of treatments are introduced. Individual chapters also present disorder-specific treatments, but this chapter introduces more general conceptual foundations and considerations that may give a broader perspective than that contained in specific chapters.

Chapters 4 and 5 cover *Assessment and Diagnosis of Psychological Disorders* and *Research Methods*. Both introduce conceptual issues pertaining to measurement, hypothesis-testing, and key tools used by clinicians and scientists. Numerous examples of methods and research studies attempt not only to give background for fuller understanding of subsequent chapters but also to capture the flavor of the research process that permits complex human problems to be studied systematically.

Twelve chapters present coverage of specific disorders or common human problems. Five of these present some of the "traditional" topics in abnormal psychology: *Anxiety Disorders* (Chapter 6), *Somatoform and Dissociative Disorders* (Chapter 7), *Mood Disorders and Suicide* (Chapter 8), *Schizophrenia* (Chapter 9), and *Substance-Related Disorders* (Chapter 11). We attempt to cover these topics with presentation of phenomenology and case materials, plus the latest in research on factors that cause and influence the disorder. Each of these chapters also covers treatment approaches that are specific to the disorder, presenting methods and analyses of their effectiveness.

Several chapters' coverage is not limited to specific diagnostic categories but rather refers more broadly to problems in living. These include *Psychophysiological Disorders and Behavioral Medicine* (Chapter 10), *Sexual Dysfunctions and Disorders* (Chapter 12), *Personality Disorders* (Chapter 13), and *Antisocial Personality and Violent Conduct* (Chapter 14). Each of these chapters discusses common—or rare—human problems that do not always fit neatly into diagnostic categories. Psychophysiological disorders reveal the role played by psychological processes in the onset or exacerbation of medical conditions, allowing examination of newly emerging findings on the relationship between stress, the immune system, and health. Sexual dysfunctions and disorders are both intriguing and painful personal topics to many—and issues concerning gender identity and sexual preference are of interest to most students. Many abnormal psychology texts do not cover personality disorders as extensively as does this book, and yet this is a field of growing importance both in research and clinical practice. Similarly, few abnormal psychology books devote an entire chapter to violence, and yet this is a major national preoccupation—and one that commonly affects every individual either directly or indirectly.

Two chapters are relatively specific to childhood disorders, *Behavioral and Emotional Disorders of Childhood and Adolescence* (Chapter 15) and *Mental Retardation and Developmental Disorders* (Chapter 16). Additionally, however, many other chapters discuss manifestations of adult disorders that may appear in childhood. At the other end of the age spectrum, Chapter 17, *Cognitive and Neuropsychiatric Disorders*, has a significant focus on psychological disorders associated with aged populations, but other chapters also present information about manifestations of psychopathology among the elderly.

We believe that no abnormal textbook is complete without considering far-reaching legal and social issues, including barriers to treatment, alternatives to traditional treatments, including prevention, and ethical issues that affect service delivery. These are covered in the final chapter, *Legal, Ethical, and Social Issues in Mental Health* (Chapter 18).

Ancillaries

This text is supported by a rich set of supplementary materials designed to enhance the teaching and learning experience. Several new components make use of new instructional technologies.

Instructor's Resource Manual Each chapter of the *Instructor's Resource Manual* includes learning objectives that are repeated in the test bank and the study guide, a detailed chapter outline keyed to recommended activities and resources, lecture and discussion topics, student activities and handouts, and lists of recommended videos and readings.

Test Bank The heavily revised *Test Bank* features 100 multiple-choice questions per chapter, keyed to answer, learning objective, text page reference, and whether the question emphasizes facts, concepts, or application of knowledge. Essay questions have also been added in this edition.

Computerized Test Bank The test questions are also available on disk with a software program that allows instructors to add or edit questions and create tests. An online testing option and a grading system are included.

Study Guide Each chapter of the student *Study Guide* contains learning objectives, a chapter overview, a review of key terms, and three sets of multiple-choice questions—factual, conceptual, and applied. The answer key explains why each incorrect answer is incorrect.

Transparencies The sixty color transparency acetates that accompany the text provide a balance of charts, tables, graphs, and anatomical images from the text and other sources.

Power Presentation Manager This new instructional slide presentation software, available for PC or Macintosh platforms, comes fully loaded with over 150 tables and figures from the text and other sources, including all 60 transparencies. Also included are several dozen instructional Powerpoint sequences, a set of editable chapter outlines, and a guide to relevant videoclips and images from Houghton Mifflin's *The Psychology Show* laserdisk. With this simple software, instructors can preview and select images, add their own, and sequence them to create dynamic customized lecture presentations.

Psychology Web Site Houghton Mifflin's Psychology web site can be reached by pointing to the Houghton Mifflin home page at http://www.hmco.com and going to the College Division Psychology page. This location provides access to additional useful and innovative teaching and learning resources that support this book.

Casebook A new casebook entitled *Case Studies in Abnormal Psychology*, by Clark R. Clipson and Jocelyn M. Steer, is available for shrinkwrapping with our text. This supplement examines sixteen cases, each representing a major psychological disorder. After a detailed history of each case, critical-thinking questions prompt students to formulate hypotheses and interpretations based on the client's symptoms, family and medical background, and relevant information. The case proceeds with sections on assessment, case conceptualization, diagnosis, and treatment and outlook. A final set of thought-provoking questions for discussion and writing concludes each case.

Reader An innovative new reader called *Abnormal Psychology in Context: Voices and Perspectives*, by David N. Sattler, Virginia Shabatay, and Geoffrey P. Kramer, is also available for shrinkwrapping with our text. This unique collection features forty-five first-person accounts and narratives written by individuals who live with a psychological disorder and by therapists, relatives, and others who have direct experience with someone suffering from a disorder. These vivid and engaging narratives are accompanied by critical-thinking questions and a psychological concept guide that indicates which key terms and concepts are highlighted by each reading.

Multimedia Policy A wide variety of videos is available to adopters. Consult your Houghton Mifflin sales representatives for further information.

Acknowledgments

Numerous external reviewers were solicited by the publisher and kept anonymous during our revision and rewriting process. These colleagues provided the input that clearly enhanced both the overall scholarship and the readability of specific sections. We appreciate the time and expertise that the following people gave to the task:

Joann Bachorowski, Vanderbilt University

Cole Barton, Davidson College

Joe S. Bean, Shorter College

Peggy R. Brooks, North Adams State College

Joyce L. Carbonell, Florida State University

Amy Claxton, Fort Hays State University

Frank L. Collins, Oklahoma State University

Rosemary Cox, Confederation College, Ontario

Keith Crnic, Penn State University

Paul J. Frick, University of Alabama

Heidi M. Inderbitzen, University of Nebraska at Lincoln

Jerald J. Marshall, University of Central Florida

Art Olguin, Santa Barbara City College

Dimitri Papageorgis, University of British Columbia

Michele Cooley Quille, George Mason University

Douglas Wardell, University of Alberta at Edmonton

Many people must function as a team to produce a book of this size and complexity. We appreciate the encouragement of David Lee, Sponsoring Editor, and his help in fine-tuning the aims of the Second Edition. Our senior associate editor, Jane Knetzger, attended the birth of the first edition, and her keen judgment, experience, and organizational skills have kept us on track and in focus in this second edition. Rosemary Winfield, our project editor, has managed, with poise and dedication, the complexities of keeping the parts together while having an eye on the whole. Marcy Kagan, our photo researcher, entered our world and helped us to realize visually the excitement as well as the poignancy of the topics we wanted to depict. These hard-working professionals put themselves into the effort and care about the end results as much as we do. Without their skill, humor, and encouragement, we wouldn't dare to undertake a textbook—and certainly they have made the process as close to pleasurable as a second edition can be.

Our families, students, and friends have provided the encouragement and supported flagging confidence when needed. Phil very much appreciates the tolerance and flexibility offered by his spouse, Sue, and the energy and scholarly interest of his sons, Mark and Reed. He also appreciates the discussions with, and assistance from, numerous graduate students in clinical psychology at Temple University. Connie is grateful for the patience and cheerleading skills of her family and students. They gave space when needed and turned off the computer when that was needed also. Special thanks to Amy—and to Molly, Patrick, and Lisa, who particularly appreciate what the effort means. Also thanks to Phil's students at Temple and to Connie's students at UCLA, who—after all—are really the point of all this.

Philip C. Kendall
Constance Hammen

About the Authors

Philip C. Kendall, Ph.D., ABPP, is professor of psychology and head of the Division of Clinical Psychology at Temple University, in Philadelphia, where he currently serves as editor of the *Journal of Consulting and Clinical Psychology*. In 1977, and from 1980 to 1981, he was a fellow at the Center for Advanced Study in the Behavioral Sciences, Stanford, California.

The author of numerous research papers, Dr. Kendall has also coauthored *Clinical Psychology: Scientific and Professional Dimensions* (with Julian Ford) and *Cognitive-Behavioral Therapy for Impulsive Children* (with Lauren Braswell) and coedited *Cognitive-Behavioral Interventions* (with Steven Hollon), *Anxiety and Depression: Distinctive and Overlapping Features* (with David Watson), and *Psychopathology and Cognition* (with Keith Dobson).

Dr. Kendall is a fellow of the American Psychological Association and the American Association for the Advancement of Science and a past president of both the Association for the Advancement of Behavior Therapy and Section III of the Division of Clinical Psychology of the American Psychological Association. In 1996/97, he was a recipient of Temple University's prestigious "Great Teacher" Award.

His interests lie in the integration of the science and practice of clinical psychology, the development and evaluation of psychological treatments, especially with youth, and the study of the nature and causes of psychological disturbances. He has lectured throughout the United States, Canada, and Australia and in Europe and South America.

A former surfer (the result of distance from the waves), Dr. Kendall currently enjoys participating in athletics, coaching youth sports (JV basketball), renovating his home, and raising his two sons with his wife, Sue. He looks forward to the appearance of this book, marking its completion, and the chance to return to these other interests and activities.

Constance Hammen, Ph.D., is professor of psychology and chair of the clinical psychology program at the University of California, Los Angeles. She also has a professorship in the Department of Psychiatry and Biobehavioral Sciences and is associate director of the Affective Disorders Clinic at the UCLA Neuropsychiatric Institute.

Dr. Hammen's research interests include the field of psychopathology—the study of the nature and causes of mental disorders. Her particular interest is in mood disorders such as depression and bipolar illness. Her work explores psychological issues in mood disorders, including cognitive, stress, interpersonal, and family aspects. She has written several books, including *Depression Runs in Families* (1991), *Depression* (1997), and *Psychological Aspects of Depression: Toward a Cognitive-Interpersonal Integration* (1992, with Ian Gotlib). She has written numerous research articles and book chapters with her students and colleagues.

Dr. Hammen serves on the editorial boards of various professional journals. She was president of the Society for Research in Psychopathology (1995–1996) and a member of the W. T. Grant Foundation Consortium on Depression in Children and Adolescents.

Dr. Hammen is an enthusiastic traveler and enjoys visiting with colleagues in various countries. She also likes to write—including textbooks. At the present time she is collaborating on a research project that frequently takes her to Queensland, Australia. Her other interests include cooking and gardening and keeping in touch with family members spread across the country. Although it's not exactly a pastime, she also enjoys her clinical practice, specializing in treatment of emotional disorders.

CHAPTER 1

Abnormal Behavior in Context

Those among us...

- Marina works in your office, a wonderful, outgoing woman. But in the eleven months since she was attacked and nearly raped, her personality has changed; she has become irritable, jumpy, unfriendly, and suspicious of any stranger.

- You read with horror in the local newspaper that a young Japanese immigrant woman drowned her two young children in the ocean.

- Your roommate Jonah told you he has started therapy, but he seems perfectly normal to you.

- Your uncle Joe can't stop drinking once he has started — and he drinks almost daily. He says he knows it isn't good for him, but he hasn't been able to stop.

- In the neighborhood where you grew up, Mrs. Jones next door firmly believed that she had seen flying saucers on several occasions.

What's the line between normality and mental disorder? Are people always considered abnormal if they drink too much, or can't get over a bad event, or go into therapy, or see things that others do not see?

Are some mental problems like "diseases" in that people can't help having them?

Do the same mental problems happen all over the world? Are men and women likely to have the same psychological difficulties?

Psychological abnormality has many faces and affects all of us directly or indirectly. This book is about psychological abnormality, its description, causes, treatments, and the research methods used to study these topics. We know psychological abnormality by many technical as well as slang terms: insanity, mental illness, deviance, psychological dysfunction, maladjustment, nervous breakdown, crazy, nuts, whacko, bonkers, looney. Many of these terms are meaningless, or even misleading, as ways to describe what this book is about. So we begin with a discussion of the complex issue of what we mean by *abnormality*.

MYTHS AND DEFINITIONS OF PSYCHOLOGICAL ABNORMALITY

People are curious, alarmed, disgusted, intrigued, and mystified by human behavior that goes beyond personal definitions of normality. However, defining psychological abnormality is difficult and involves explaining not only what it is but also what it is not.

Myths and Misunderstandings

There is no single, definitive, widely accepted truth about what constitutes psychological abnormality. But there are guidelines for defining abnormality and practical standards for the formal diagnosis of disorders. Today's definitions have evolved over the centuries and have changed even within the past few years. The process continues as new information and new methods of evaluation replace misconceptions about people with psychological disturbances, and as cultural conventions change.

What are the myths and misconceptions that people have associated with psychological abnormality? Table 1.1 introduces some of the most common ones. As the book unfolds we will replace these faulty beliefs with scientifically supported fact and reasoned speculation.

Most people would admit to some confusion about what psychological abnormality is. Consider some of

---

Table 1.1 Misconceptions About Mental Illness

The following are erroneous beliefs associated with psychological abnormality that people in Western cultures frequently express.

1. *A person who has been mentally ill can never be normal.*
   False. Psychological disturbances are often temporary, lasting only days or weeks, followed by lengthy periods — maybe even a lifetime — of psychological health. Even persons with recurring problems are not maladjusted all of the time.

2. *Even if some mentally ill persons return to normal, most don't, and chronically ill people remain crazy.*
   False. It is not true that most persons with psychological disorders fail to return to normal. Although people with severe problems may have lifelong difficulties, with good support from families and communities, psychological counseling or therapy, and medications, even many chronically mentally ill persons can lead productive lives and make positive contributions to society. Studies show that about one-third of individuals with mental disorders get better even without treatment.

3. *Persons with psychological problems are unpredictable.*
   False. After recovery, most persons will be as consistent in their behavior as they were before their episode of disorder. Some disorders do involve unpredictable behaviors when the person is experiencing the symptoms, but this pattern is certainly not true of all disorders.

4. *Mentally ill persons are dangerous, and they could go berserk at any time.*
   False. Unfortunately, news accounts that feature past disturbances may contribute to this misconception. Headlines such as "Former Mental Patient Attacks Neighbor" confirm people's unwarranted fears. Headlines describing the most typical scenario — "Former Mental Patient Lives Quiet, Uneventful Life" — never appear in the news. Research studies have shown that people formerly hospitalized for psychological disorders do not have higher rates of arrest for violent behavior than people in the general population; their rates of arrest may even be lower, unless they had a history of violence before hospitalization. Former patients who do commit violent crimes also tend to be those who had criminal records before they were hospitalized (Monahan & Steadman, 1984). Finally, among hospitalized patients, incidents of violence or aggression are much more likely to be caused by situational factors (e.g., conflict, crowding) than by internal precipitants such as delusions (Bjorkly, 1995).

5. *Mentally ill people are deadbeats and misfits.*
   False. Many highly intelligent, creative, and well-functioning people who have enriched society have had periods of severe psychological disturbance — Abraham Lincoln, Winston Churchill, many famous writers, poets, and composers, not to mention gifted movie stars and entertainers. People with major disorders commonly return to their previous level of functioning and are perfectly intelligent, rational, and capable of contributing to society based on their previous skills, talents, education, and opportunity.

the criteria that people sometimes erroneously believe define abnormality.

Does Infrequency Define Abnormality? If normality is what is typical, then abnormality must be what is atypical or rare — right? Yes and no. It is true that some of the disorders described in this book occur infrequently, such as multiple personalities or seeing things that do not exist. And it is certainly true that if almost everyone had panic attacks or if most people had extreme mood swings, then we might consider these experiences normal. Statistical infrequency, however, is a poor criterion for defining abnormality.

Consider, for example, two very rare qualities — genius and sainthood. Although only a few people like Albert Einstein or Mother Teresa have ever been born, we do not consider his extraordinary intellectual ability or her uncommon charity to be psychologically abnormal. Therefore, rarity cannot serve as the sole basis for defining psychological abnormality. By the same token, some very frequent behaviors are disruptive and distressing — depression and alcoholism, for example.

Does Suffering Define Abnormality? Perhaps abnormality has to do with personal distress and suffering. After all, if a person is miserable or feels persecuted and tormented by voices, then there must be something psychologically abnormal about that person's life. Indeed, personal distress is one of the reasons that people define themselves as having a psychological problem and decide to seek treatment.

Yet distress alone is not a satisfactory criterion for defining abnormality. Many persons who are considered mentally ill do not appear to suffer at all, such as an extremely euphoric manic person or a child molester who experiences no remorse.

Does Strangeness Define Abnormality? Perhaps abnormality is the same as bizarreness or strangeness. From this point of view, abnormality could be defined in terms of departures from normal sensory experience. It is certainly true that seeing or hearing things that others do not may constitute what mental health professionals call a psychotic experience.

Such experiences in and of themselves do not necessarily signal psychological abnormality, however. Recall Mrs. Jones, from your neighborhood, who reported seeing flying saucers. You always wondered if she was a little "off," but she has no other unusual beliefs or behaviors. And now research confirms that many people have odd or unusual experiences, as Table 1.2 indicates (Roper Organization, 1992). They appear to be temporarily "possessed" when overcome with religious ecstasy, sometimes speaking in tongues that are unintelligible to others. They report visions, hallucinations, out-of-body experiences, or communication with dead relatives or from past lives. But rarely would any of these

Table 1.2	**Unusual and Bizarre Beliefs**
Experience	**Percentage of Adult Americans Who Said Yes**
Seen a ghost?	11
Felt that you were actually flying through the air?	10
Seen unusual lights or balls of light without knowing what caused them or where they came from?	8
Seen a terrifying figure — monster, witch, devil, or other evil figure?	15
Felt as if you left your body?	14
Seen a UFO?	7

Source: Roper Organization (1992).

Weird experiences are not all that unusual. The above figures are from polls conducted in 1991 by the Roper Organization in three representative U.S. samples (total sample = 5,947 persons). These are the percentages of the total who said that the event had happened to them at least once.

people be considered by themselves or others to be abnormal or psychotic.

Conversely, a great deal of what experts consider to be psychological abnormality is not at all strange or bizarre. In fact, it is commonplace: excessive fears, overwhelming sadness and dejection, sexual dysfunctions, the decline of cognitive capabilities in old age. All of these conditions occur, at least in mild forms, among the majority of people at some point.

Does the Behavior Define Abnormality? Some behavior is so disgusting or shocking to human sensibilities that it might seem the behavior in and of itself constitutes psychological abnormality. But consider such horrendous behaviors as murder, incest, and cannibalism. In most circumstances, murder and mutilation represent abnormality; and yet under conditions of combat, such acts are common, and aggressiveness is expected and rewarded. Incest, which is typically considered abnormal, was once accepted in some rural communities in the United States as the privilege of a father. And then there's cannibalism. In a few well-known cases — such as the soccer team whose plane crashed in the Andes in 1972 and the members of the Donner expedition

"Abnormal behavior" is common. According to recent surveys, nearly one-half of all U.S. adults have met diagnostic criteria for at least one psychological disorder in their lives.

decimated by snowstorms as they crossed the mountains into California in the winter of 1846 — cannibalism was a last-resort act of survival. Thus, the meaning of a behavior depends on its context. Behaviors themselves cannot be judged abnormal apart from the situations and historical periods in which they occur.

Is Normality a Guideline?   Perhaps we could define psychological abnormality as a departure from normality. If we know how a person is supposed to behave and feel, then deviations from such norms would help identify abnormality. An auto mechanic knows how a car is supposed to run; when it doesn't run right, the mechanic can generally find the defect and figure out how to repair it. Unfortunately, we do not have the same knowledge of human behavior. As we see in Chapter 2, there are many theories of abnormality — models of the causes and mechanisms of human dysfunction. But efforts to define normality have not generated wide acceptance.

WHAT'S NORMAL?

Is Abnormality Normal?

In each chapter of this book we ask the question "What is normal?" Our aim is to distinguish between common human experiences and clinically significant dysfunction. The line is sometimes difficult to draw and fairly arbitrary. Often the definition depends on how much the person is impaired.

One big problem in defining abnormality is that psychological difficulties are so common, and these difficulties, and individuals' responses to them, are well within the range of normality. It's easy to believe that psychological abnormality affects only other people. In reality, possibly half of all adults (in the United States) admit to having problems at some point in their lives that would meet official criteria for a diagnosis. This statistic comes from **epidemiological surveys,** or surveys in which researchers have interviewed large numbers of people who represent all segments of the population — different sexes, ages, races, socioeconomic statuses, and geographic locations — using standard, consistent methods of interviewing. The most recent epidemiological survey covered forty-eight states and was conducted in 1990–1992 on people aged fifteen to fifty-four years (Kessler et al., 1994). It found that 48 percent of the population had at least one of the disorders covered, at some point in their lives. Additionally, the study found that 60 percent of those with a disorder actually had two or more disorders.

Not only are *lifetime* rates exceedingly high, but up to 30 percent of those surveyed had met diagnostic criteria either at the time of the interview or within the past six to twelve months (Kessler et al., 1994). As we will see in later chapters, there is increasing evidence that some disorders are even more frequent today than they were ten or twenty years ago.

For readers of this book — college students — there is good news and bad news. On the one hand, epidemiological surveys have found that people with college educations and backgrounds of greater affluence are less likely to experience psychological disorders. On the other hand, young adults are at relatively higher risk for disorders than are older adults.

What about children? To date there has been no comparably large direct-interview epidemiological survey of children. However, several studies suggest that the rates of psychological disorder are high — and that they increase with age. A large-scale study by Elizabeth Costello and her colleagues (1988) of American youngsters (aged seven to eleven) attending clinics for routine medical checkups revealed that 22 percent had one or more diagnoses. This figure is remarkably comparable to that for Ethiopian children (Mulatu, 1995) and Spanish children (Gomez-Beneyto et al., 1994), though it is somewhat higher than the finding in a recent survey of French children (Fombonne, 1994). Children's rates

of disorder appear to increase with age, and persons with childhood-onset disorders usually have poorer outcomes (Newman et al., 1996).

Deciding what's "abnormal" is further complicated by the possibility that some people present themselves as healthy when they really are not. This difficulty is most likely to arise when symptoms of disorder are surveyed by questionnaires for which there is no check on the accuracy or validity of responses. In a series of studies, Shedler, Mayman, and Manis (1993) compared subjects' scores on symptom measures (such as "neuroticism" or depression) with clinicians' ratings based on self-reports from the subjects about their lives and early experiences. Grouped into three categories — genuinely distressed, genuinely healthy, or having "illusory mental health" (that is, exhibiting no symptoms but judged by the clinicians as being mentally unhealthy), these subjects were then compared on heart rate and blood pressure reactivity while performing stressful mental and psychological tasks in the laboratory. Figure 1.1 demonstrates coronary reactivity during these tasks for the illusory and genuine mental health groups. The results suggest that the illusory mental health subjects were more distressed than they reported themselves to be. According to the authors, these and related findings indicate that some people are psychologically "defensive" — often unconsciously denying the existence of problems that they really have.

What do all these findings mean? They mean that psychological difficulties are extremely common; in all likelihood, nearly everyone is affected, directly or indirectly. They mean that within every family there is probably someone who has such difficulties. They mean that nearly everyone has at least one friend whose life is somewhat impaired by psychological problems. They mean that at times you may find it difficult to function well, or that your relatives, bosses, teachers, coworkers, and neighbors might sometimes have problems. They mean that sometimes people are even hiding their emotional difficulties, or unaware that they have them.

This brings us back to the question of how to define psychological abnormality. If it is not a matter of infrequency, suffering, strangeness, deviant behavior, or departure from agreed-on normality, then what is it?

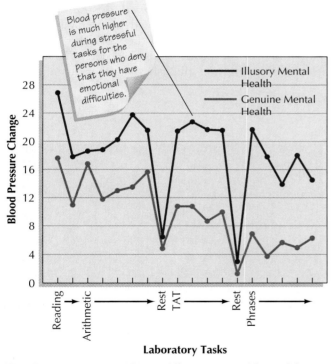

Blood pressure is much higher during stressful tasks for the persons who deny that they have emotional difficulties.

Figure 1.1   Genuine or Illusory Mental Health

Normal students and staff at a university were classified as having genuine or illusory mental health on the basis of the agreement between their self-reported symptoms on a questionnaire and a clinician's review of their recollections about their early life experiences and reactions to themselves and others. Measures of coronary reactivity (blood pressure) during several stressful laboratory tasks appear to indicate greater distress for those judged to have illusory mental health. After finding similar results in three such studies, the authors concluded that some people who present themselves as psychologically healthy are really displaying defensive denial of actual emotional difficulties.

Source: Shedler, Mayman & Manis (1993).

Behavior in Context: A Practical Approach to Abnormality

Professionals generally use two practical guidelines to define abnormality. First, they take into account the person's behavior, the context in which it occurs, and its appropriateness for that context. In other words, they consider whether the person's behavior causes impaired functioning. Second, they consider whether the person displays a consistent set of maladaptive feelings or behaviors that have been defined by experts as constituting psychological abnormality. These judgments are reflected in the *Diagnostic and Statistical Manual of Mental Disorders*. After discussing these two guidelines, we propose a working definition of psychological abnormality.

Impaired Functioning   The practical approach to abnormality involves, first, a judgment about whether the behavior or experience causes **impaired functioning** — difficulty in performing appropriate and expected roles. Judgment about functioning or impairment can be made only in reference to the person's context — that is, the setting of the behavior, the person's age and sex, and the historical, social, and cultural background of the behavior. For example, a person might display considerable sadness, loss of appetite, excessive crying, and gloomy thoughts; but if the person's spouse or child recently died, we would not consider this behavior to be abnormal. Similarly, a single instance of drunk and disorderly behavior at a New Year's Eve party would not be considered a psychological problem; but someone who drinks to excess regardless of the occasion and who suffers job, family, and legal problems as a result would be

diagnosed as having an abnormal state of alcohol abuse and dependence. Consider another example:

> *Jack burst into the room, wearing nothing but a bedsheet tied around his waist with a belt. The young man's eyes darted from person to person. Finally, he ran out of the room, muttering to himself. It sounded like he said, "I'll get you."*

Is Jack a paranoid schizophrenic? A weird eccentric? Not really. Although it is both strange and rare to wear nothing but a bedsheet, Jack had just been the victim of a college prank. His roommate had hidden all of his clothes while he was in the shower, and Jack grabbed the nearest covering he could find.

The Diagnostic and Statistical Manual   A second practical guideline for determining abnormality is whether a person's behaviors fit expert professionals' rules for specific diagnoses. These rules are stated in the *Diagnostic and Statistical Manual, 4th Edition* (called **DSM-IV** for short), the most widely accepted system in the United States and around the world for classifying psychological problems and disorders. The World Health Organization publishes another manual used

Unusual or strange behavior, appearance, and language are not necessarily signs of abnormality, if they occur in an appropriate context. Walking on hot coals is not abnormal if you are Dr. Martin Hart, conducting a fire-walking seminar illustrating the influence of

mind over physical matter, and wearing aluminum cans is not abnormal if you are Can Man, making a statement about recycling at an Earth Day rally.

worldwide, the *International Classification of Diseases* (ICD), which in many respects is similar to the DSM.

To be diagnosed with a disorder according to the DSM, a person must exhibit multiple behaviors that fit a defined pattern, the behavior must cause dysfunction or subjective distress in the person's typical context, it must be present for a specified duration, and it must not be due to some other explanation or disorder. The nature and use of this manual, and the ways in which the diagnostic rules have been determined, are discussed more fully in Chapter 4. The following example illustrates how a judgment might be made to consider someone's behavior abnormal:

> *Marina was a conscientious and reliable executive secretary in a business office, typically cheerful and easy-going. In the past months, however, she has missed many days of work and has to force herself to go to the office at all. She is tense, irritable with coworkers, and refuses to be alone in the office suite. At home she is distant from her husband and teenage children, preferring to be left alone rather than participate in family activities that used to give her much pleasure. She has nightmares and awakens screaming. Her behavior is clearly impaired compared to her typical functioning.*
>
> *Marina's family and coworkers are somewhat baffled. They know that this is unusual behavior for her. They also know that nearly twelve months ago when she was working late in the office after everyone had gone for the day, a stranger entered the building, found her alone, robbed her at gunpoint, and was attempting to rape her when he was scared off by sounds of someone coming into the office. Although friends realize that she was traumatized by the event, they think that she should have recovered by now, and wonder if she is exaggerating her distress.*
>
> *Eventually Marina consulted a mental health professional who explained to her that she displayed symptoms of posttraumatic stress disorder, and that this disorder may be accompanied by prolonged or even delayed symptoms following an unusually traumatic event. To be diagnosed with this disorder, the person who has experienced a major trauma must display three characteristics. One is that the person repeatedly reexperiences the trauma in memories, dreams, situations that remind the person of the event, or "flashbacks" that vividly re-create the trauma. A second feature required for diagnosis is that the person avoids anything that might remind him or her of the event or that might arouse intense feelings of any kind. Such behavior might include avoiding thoughts of the traumatic event or situations that recall the event. Avoidance may also include a general deadening or numbing of emotional experiences and detachment from others. Finally, for a person to be diagnosed with posttraumatic stress disorder, he or she must appear to be physiologically aroused, as shown by sleeplessness or lack of concentration or being easily startled or very watchful.*
>
> *Because Marina displays impairment in her typical functioning and also shows evidence of all of the major diagnostic features, she is diagnosed as having a psychological disorder — posttraumatic stress disorder.*

A Definition of Psychological Abnormality Many people sometimes — or even most of the time — display behaviors and attitudes that most of us would find obnoxious and objectionable or eccentric and different. Does that mean that those people are mentally ill or have a psychological disorder? Probably not. A person can be irresponsible and immature; he or she can have unusual preferences or tastes, and can appear to be foolish or clueless about things that others consider mildly inappropriate. However, having a different lifestyle or being eccentric does not in itself define mental disorder.

Rather, **psychological abnormality** is defined as impaired functioning over a period of time with respect to expected performance suitable for the person in a relevant context. Relevant context includes consideration of the situation in which the behaviors occur as well as gender, age, cultural values, and historical perspective. We therefore typically use the term *psychological abnormality* interchangeably with *psychological disorder* when a person fails to behave appropriately according to his or her context and displays a pattern of experiences and behaviors that experts have defined as a diagnosable psychological condition. We may sometimes use another term, **mental illness,** although, as we see in Chapter 2, there are difficulties using the term *illness,* which implies that all disorders are "medical" problems. (In fact, very few of those listed in the DSM are truly medical disorders.) In general, then, we prefer the term *psychological abnormality* or *psychological disorder* over *mental illness.* We will also be using the term **psychopathology,** which refers to the scientific study of psychological disorders.

CHANGING HISTORICAL VIEWS OF PSYCHOLOGICAL ABNORMALITY

> *The old woman can be seen at night, wandering the dark streets of her village, muttering meaningless phrases. Her clothes are torn and she is dirty. Sometimes she'll cry out as if she's being attacked, commanding the unseen intruders to go away.*

This scene recurs throughout civilization. Such people — men or women — could be found in Mycenaean

Greece, in ancient India, or in tribal Africa. They could be seen walking the streets of medieval England or imperial China — or colonial Salem, Massachusetts, or today's Venice Beach, California. But depending on when and where they lived, their plight would be viewed very differently.

Ancient texts from most cultures contained clear descriptions of major psychological disorders that we would recognize today: depression, manic-depression, schizophrenia, Alzheimer's disease, anxiety states, and more. Three major interpretations of psychological disorders have been seen in all centuries and cultures: supernaturalistic, naturalistic, and psychoneurotic. In some eras people were thought to be possessed by gods or demons; they were innocent victims of malicious and capricious spirits or deserving of their fate because they failed to conform to the community's standards of acceptable attitudes and behaviors. In other places and times people were understood as suffering from bodily imbalances; they displayed aberrant behavior because the elements of their biological functioning were diseased and lacked equilibrium. Their imbalances were seen as a result of failure to follow appropriate habits involving moderation in eating, drinking, personal conduct, and possibly spiritual attitudes. And in yet other eras people were viewed as suffering from some deep, inner turmoil of a psychological nature, possibly caused by overwhelming current stress or by childhood experiences that left them psychically scarred.

Corresponding to their views of causes of aberrant behavior, societies have reacted by punishing the person or attempting to exorcise the demons; by providing magical or medicinal remedies to help restore the balance within the person; or by ensuring comfort, rest, and protection to the person to aid in recovery from psychological distress.

In each culture and in different eras, views of psychological disorder paralleled views of other aspects of human nature and the natural order. Not surprisingly, dominant views of psychologically dysfunctional people commonly reflected more comprehensive theories that helped explain the entire world. We next survey viewpoints from a few representative cultures that have contributed to our current concepts of psychological disorder.

Greek and Roman Contributions to Understanding Mental Illness

Twelve centuries of Greek and Roman culture (from about 700 B.C. to the fifth century A.D.) provided some of the fundamental concepts of mental illness that persist in one form or another into modern times (Ducey & Simon, 1975). The Greeks, in particular, explored two influential themes: the relationship between mental dis-

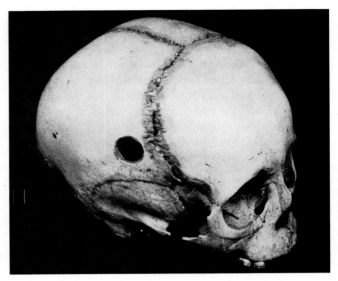

Stone Age skulls display the earliest evidence of a surgical attempt to alter abnormal behavior. Scholars presume that the holes were made to release demons suspected by ancient societies of causing madness. The process, called *trephining,* was a forerunner of the views of Hippocrates who, centuries later, taught that mental illness is caused by the brain — a view that continued in the Middle Ages and that continues to be prominent in modern explanations of disorder.

order and psychological conflict, and mental disorder as a physical illness with biological causes.

Homer's *Odyssey* and many of the Greek tragedies clearly depict examples of psychological disorder. They often portray mental disturbance as resulting from psychological conflicts, which people attempted to relieve with food, wine, drugs, songs, storytelling, and prayer. Twenty-five centuries before Freud, Greeks developed views of the *psyche* and how the mind works. Plato and others were aware that adults are shaped by childhood experiences, family life, and education. These concepts reflect an emphasis on individual experience and development and a recognition of psychological factors apart from bodily functioning. Indeed, they represent some of the foundations of Western thought.

At the same time, the ordinary ancient Greek citizen tended to believe that mental illness was primarily due to possession by demons and gods who had been angered (for example, the Furies). Accordingly, disturbed people were often objects of fear, awe, or ridicule — and the burden of their care fell on their families.

A very different contribution from ancient Greece is evident in this excerpt, typically attributed to Hippocrates, written five centuries before the birth of Jesus:

> Men ought to know that from the brain, and from the brain only, arise our pleasures, joys, laughter

and jests, as well as our sorrows, pain, grief, and tears. . . . It is the brain which makes us mad or delirious; inspires us with dread and fear, whether by night or day; brings sleeplessness, mistakes, anxieties, absentmindedness, acts that are contrary to our normal habits. These things that we suffer all come from the brain, including madness. (From *Sacred Disease*, cited in Ducey & Simon, 1975, p. 15)

Hippocrates considered psychological abnormality a disease caused in the same ways as other bodily illnesses — by an excess of one of the humors. In fact, he originated the view of humoral (fluid) balance as the basis of health. According to the **humoral theory**, the body is composed of four fluids produced by various organs — blood, phlegm, yellow bile, and black bile. Diseases were believed to develop as a result of excesses or imbalance of these substances from internal or external causes. For example, an excess of black bile was considered the cause of melancholia, or deep depression. Treatments of mental and physical illness thus consisted of attempts to restore the proper balance, using drugs and folk medicines and diet.

Hippocrates' views were extended and elaborated in the second century A.D. by the Greek physician Galen. Galen proposed purification remedies such as diet and exercise to restore bodily imbalances. His medical observations and hypotheses were influential throughout much of the world until the seventeenth century.

Asian and African Views of Psychological Disorders

Although Western societies tend to trace their heritage to classical Greek and Roman origins, current views of psychopathology also owe much to cultures from Asia and Africa.

Chinese Views of Mental Health   The earliest descriptions of mental illness go back to fourteenth century B.C. China. According to historian Vivian Ng (1990), mental disorder was recognized as an illness since at least the first century A.D. and, like other maladies, was considered a disruption of natural processes or of the balance between *yin* and *yang* (Kao, 1979). For the Chinese, **yin and yang** represent the dual forces within the universe — good and bad, male and female, dark and light, positive and negative. Normal and healthy functioning requires a balance between these forces, achieved by following the prescribed ways of nature and society and by adhering to moderation of thought and deed. Excesses of yin or yang and their complex relations with other systems of the body were blamed for certain kinds of behavioral and mental disorders. Accordingly, remedies for physical and mental problems consisted of methods for restoring the natural balance — herbal medicines, acupuncture, and folk remedies. For example, a person suffering from *kuang*, or mental and emotional difficulties believed to be caused by an excess of yang, might be treated with cooling liquids to help reduce inner heat and thus restore bodily harmony and balance.

Because mental disorders were considered physical imbalances, no particular stigma was attached to any madness that was attributed to such causes. Families protected their ill members and were expected to attempt to find healers and provide remedies for the disorder.

Coexisting with the physical imbalance approach were other explanations of madness that involved the supernatural order: possession by spirits or retribution for sinful deeds. Belief in spirit possession included the notion that madness was caused by the spirits of ancestors, by an angry or restless soul (or one not properly buried), or by other superhuman beings. The victim might be singled out for no apparent reason, and families and communities were fairly tolerant, seeking the services of shamans and folk healers. If the disturbances were attributed to sinful deeds, however, sufferers and their families might be castigated and expected to make retribution for the alleged misdeeds. Eventually, Chinese medicine moved toward criminalization of the mentally ill with stringent laws established in the eighteenth century (Ng, 1990).

Gradually, in the twentieth century China adopted many of the attitudes and procedures of Western psychiatry, but with a difference: Current practices are extraordinarily eclectic and provide a mixture of traditional remedies, modern psychotherapy, and pharmacological treatment. During the Cultural Revolution of the midtwentieth century, even revolutionary politics played a role in the treatment of the mentally ill, as illustrated in the following excerpt on the treatment of schizophrenia from a medical text written in the 1970s:

> *Preventing recurrence: For patients who have been cured of schizophrenia, it is necessary to help them to learn Chairman Mao's works with specific problems in mind in order to correctly resolve the various factors that have caused the disease in the first place. Use heroic figures as examples to help the patient to improve his awakening in class struggle. (Cited in Kao, 1979, pp. 131–135)*

Middle Eastern Cultures and Mental Illness   Mental disorders were recognized in ancient Palestine, Babylonia, Egypt, and other nations of the Mediterranean and Near East. In the Bible, mental disorder is portrayed as an impulsive, uncontrolled, and unreasonable condition inflicted by supernatural powers — God, demons, or evil spirits — usually as punishment for sins (Rosen, 1968).

The cure for mental disorder was to make amends, soothe and charm the evil spirits, or have the demons cast out. The Bible refers to the use of music and songs to soothe inner demons, and both the Bible and the Koran teach that obedience to God's laws is the main source of health. Religious and folk healers were called on to exorcise demons — Jesus is depicted as casting out evil spirits in people possessed by demons. Madmen who were not violent were allowed to roam the streets and roadways, but they were sometimes followed by children and adults who mocked and abused them or threw stones at them (Rosen, 1968).

As the cultures became more influenced by the Greeks and Romans, they generally adopted the humoral theory. Later, the great Hebrew philosopher and physician Maimonides (twelfth century) emphasized the influence of emotion on bodily function. Folk medicine, healing practices developed and handed down by the common people, and magic practiced by healers who used charms and incantations, continued well into the Middle Ages. Eventually, the influence of European concepts and forms of treatment replaced the folk ways.

African Views of Mental Disorders Traditional African societies in past centuries attributed both physical and mental disorders to enemies, to malicious spirits, or in some cases to offended ancestors. Some traditional African communities also believed that illnesses resulted from natural (physical) causes. Because their beliefs varied, they pursued diverse remedies. Nevertheless, most African societies — today as in the past — share two attitudes toward mental health and illness. First, they attach relatively little social stigma to psychological disorders, and they are relatively tolerant of disturbed members — especially in rural areas. Families and community residents provide contact and support as well as shelter and physical care for individuals with disorders. Often, severely disturbed persons find acceptable roles in their communities (as beggars, for example). A second attitude characteristic of African societies is that folk healers serve an important function in treating those with both psychological and physical disorders. Healers are skillful observers and diagnosticians of psychological disorders, and they may use healing rituals and exorcism as well as herbal remedies to alleviate distress. Communities also use "group therapies" such as dance, music, and trance states to relieve psychological distress and prevent malevolent powers from causing disorder.

Colonialism and Christian missionary efforts in Africa introduced alien viewpoints in many arenas including mental illness. As vast and diverse cultures in transition, African communities have sometimes adopted religions synthesized from Christian missions and folk beliefs in which spiritual and healing systems are combined (Lambo, 1975). Today, as in most of the developing world, Western European traditions of medicine may exist side-by-side with more traditional folk practices.

Cultures vary widely in their views of the causes and treatments of mental and physical disorders. A Chinese apothecary, for example, can play an important role in providing natural remedies for maintaining or restoring natural balances in the body that some Chinese believe to be essential for mental and physical health.

For several centuries — reaching a peak in the 16th and 17th centuries — Europe and the New World were preoccupied with a fear of witches. Thousands of persons were believed to be possessed by the devil — and probably many of their behaviors that were interpreted as signs of the devil were really forms of psychological disorders. The fear of such people, chiefly women, caused great hysteria and persecution, with countless trials and executions. This women is being examined for "marks of the devil."

European Traditions of Understanding Mental Illness

Between the fifth and twentieth centuries, European beliefs about mental illness gradually evolved from witchcraft and **demonology** (the study of the influences of demons) — for which the treatment was punishment — to scientific study and humane treatment.

Witchcraft and Demonology   From the fall of the Roman Empire in the fifth century A.D. until the Renaissance of the fifteenth and sixteenth centuries, Europe was swept by tides of invasions, conquests, and rapidly changing political and social conditions. In addition, storms, fires, poor sanitary conditions, epidemics, and other natural and manmade disasters constantly threatened lives and stability. The Church was a central influence in peoples' lives, and through much of this period people widely believed in the coming of the end of the world and were greatly preoccupied with fear of hell and of the devil.

By the end of the fifteenth century, the extent of these beliefs had reached frightening proportions. For the next three centuries, following church directives, Europe and its overseas colonies experienced witch hunts and mass executions intended to rid the populace of heretics and the devil (Rosen, 1968). Unknown thousands of persons, chiefly women, were prosecuted as agents of the devil; they were burned, hanged, and drowned in an effort to save their souls. Women may have been victims because they were easy targets of scapegoating for the vast problems of the time. This persecution and killing of many people who were possibly mentally ill stand in sharp contrast to the relatively benign approaches to madness of the earlier Greeks, Romans, Arabs, Chinese, and Hebrews.

Witchcraft trials reached their peak in the sixteenth and seventeenth centuries. In 1692, in the town of Salem, Massachusetts, nineteen women and men were accused by suggestible teenagers and hanged as witches. Eventually, as social conditions changed and rationality began to prevail, some of those accused of witchcraft were recognized as mentally ill and were even transferred to hospitals. Interest in the mentally ill reemerged as a subject of scientific discipline, and communities began to discover other explanations or solutions for their mentally ill members. The scapegoating of witches came to an end.

Public Treatment of the Mentally Ill   Mentally ill persons believed to be insane and not possessed by the devil were cared for in prisons throughout medieval Europe. Those who did not have families or who were considered too dangerous or disruptive to be confined at home were likely to be cared for at public expense. Although some of the first mental hospitals, or **insane asylums,**

From Hippocrates through much of the middle ages, many believed that mental disorders and personality temperaments resulted from the predominance or deficiency of one of four bodily fluids (humors). Choler (yellow bile) was associated with anger and irritability; melancholy (black bile) with depression and a negative outlook; (phlegm) with lethargy and sluggishness, and sanguinity (blood) with optimism and cheerfulness.

were built in Europe in the Middle Ages, they provided little in the way of humane and comforting care. For example, the Hospital of St. Mary of Bethlehem in London, founded in 1247, was known from records at least since 1402 to house mental patients, among others. "Bedlam," as the hospital was known, eventually became a word for describing chaos and noisy confusion, reflecting the condition of the hospital and its inhabitants. Patients were typically chained and provided with little treatment. Londoners could buy tickets to view the spectacle in the wards of Bedlam.

In eighteenth-century England, private madhouses were prevalent and highly profitable. They provided such poor care that the government eventually intervened to control them. Increasingly, the government began to support public facilities that offered less harsh treatment. Though sometimes still chained, patients were also likely to receive treatments thought to be useful, such as bloodletting, purgatives, and emetics to resolve imbalances of humors.

A growing concern with the welfare of mental patients led to public inquiries. Parliamentary investigations uncovered a dismal picture of overcrowding, inadequate staff, harsh restraint, incarceration of the poor, and many other injustices, prompting reforms that continued to modern times (Howells & Osborn, 1975). A turning point in care of the mentally ill was the establishment in England in 1796 of The Retreat by William Tuke with the support of the Society of Friends (Quakers). Using minimal restraint, caregivers treated patients like guests with unusual freedoms and courtesies.

Other reformist voices also spoke out for the humane treatment of the mentally ill. Among them was Frenchman Philippe Pinel, credited with removing the chains from the patients at the asylum in Paris that he headed after the French Revolution. He observed patients' behavior with and without restraints. The absence of violence when they were unchained convinced him that restraints were unnecessary. Removal of patients' chains ushered in an era of enlightened and humane treatment of the hospitalized mentally ill. Pinel's method, often called **moral treatment,** included treating the patients kindly and respectfully, offering guidance and support, and encouraging fresh air and activity. At about the same time, the American Benjamin Rush, a signer of the Declaration of Independence, instituted reforms in the treatment of mentally ill patients in the United States, where he is known as the father of psychiatry. Later, a Boston schoolteacher named Dorothea Dix crusaded for reforms in care of the mentally ill, and successfully pushed for laws and public hospitals serving mentally ill people in the years from 1841 to 1881.

Growth of Scientific Concepts of Mental Disorder As reflected in the change in treatment of the mentally ill, medical and scientific knowledge about mental illness increasingly replaced demonology, magic, and folk treatment during the seventeenth, eighteenth, and nineteenth centuries in Europe. The general public as well as scholars came to recognize that mental disorders were often the result of physical states or personal and social conditions. Writers and playwrights depicted madness and mental disturbance resulting from guilt, passion, grief, and other stressful circumstances and experiences of human life. In the 1620s, English physician Robert Napier reported that four kinds of stress were most common as sources of illness: troubled courtship, marital problems, bereavements, and economic problems (tabulated by MacDonald, 1981). His records show a keen understanding of the psychological origin of many mental afflictions, and his systematic observations of types of stressors associated with disorders heralded a scientific approach to the study of disorders.

Until the early 1800s in Europe, the mentally ill were housed in "insane asylums" where inhumane conditions were typical. The French reformer, Philippe Pinel, removed the chairs from inmates in Bicêtre and encouraged respectful, supportive treatment — ushering in the era of what was called moral treatment of the mentally ill.

The tradition of scientific observation and exploration of the psychological basis of disorders continued in Europe, leading to such developments as the diagnostic classification system of Emile Kraepelin (1855–1926); Sigmund Freud's (1856–1939) theory of personality and method of **psychoanalysis,** a talking-based treatment using principles from Freud's theories; and modern experimental psychology and psychiatry. These topics are discussed extensively in Chapter 2.

Mental Illness in the Late Twentieth Century

Systematic observation and scientific analysis of psychological and biological causes of mental disorders continue to the present. During the twentieth century we have seen important developments in knowledge of the causes and treatments of mental illness, based on both biological and psychological factors. In this century we have also witnessed major changes in the quality of care for seriously mentally ill patients and the development of extensive legal protections, as discussed in Chapters 3 and 18. Professions specializing in the treatment of psychological disorders have developed in this century as well.

In contemporary Western society there is a strong emphasis on exploring the biological basis of psychological disorders as well as on social behaviors acquired through learning. As we see in later chapters, research into brain functioning, genetic transmission of disor-

This century has witnessed enormous advances in the understanding and treatment of mental illness. Former first ladies, Rosalynn Carter and Betty Ford — and most recently, Tipper Gore (shown here), wife of Vice President Gore and herself a daughter of a mentally ill mother — testified before Congress in support of health care coverage for the treatment of mental disorders and substance abuse.

Table 1.3 Therapist Training and Professional Degrees

Profession	Education and Training
Clinical psychologist	Ph.D. in psychology (sometimes Psy.D. — Doctor of Psychology) B.A. degree plus five to six years of graduate school in psychology, research methods, assessment, and therapy; Ph.D. thesis. Supervised clinical experience of about two years, plus a one-year full-time clinical internship.
Psychiatrist	M.D. B.A. or B.S. plus four years of medical school; three or four years of residency (specialty) training in medical practice, use of psychotropic medications, diagnosis, and psychotherapy.
Clinical social worker	Usually M.A. B.A. degree plus typically two-year program of master's level graduate training in social work methods and psychotherapy.
Marriage, family, child counselor	Usually M.A. B.A. degree plus typically two-year program of master's level training in counseling and psychotherapy.

There are many types of mental health professionals whose programs have emerged in this century. People sometimes have difficulty knowing how one therapist differs from another. Apart from differences in their beliefs about the fundamental causes of psychological disorders, these professionals differ mostly in their education and training. All professional therapists must be licensed in their states based on completion of required professional education plus examination to demonstrate competence.

ders, and biochemical changes has come to the fore. Other investigators emphasize that maladaptive ways of thinking and behaving — often acquired as a result of family and social influences — are sources of psychological difficulties. Correspondingly, the development of **psychotropic medications** to control severe symptoms of mental disorder and to reduce distress associated with psychological problems in the early 1950s was a major breakthrough in treating disorders. A variety of scientifically validated psychotherapy procedures is now also available to treat different kinds of psychological disorders. Coupled with the development of legal safeguards to protect the rights of patients, these new and successful treatments represent tremendous advances in the quality of care for those who suffer from psychological disorders.

The twentieth century has also witnessed the emergence of mental health care professionals who specialize in treating persons with psychological disorders. Table 1.3 briefly notes the training and emphases of these different professions. Many others provide related counseling services in schools, religious organizations, and specialized treatment settings. Research professionals who study mental disorders typically have M.D. degrees or doctorates in fields such as psychology, sociology, or public health.

Despite considerable advances in knowledge of causes and treatments, some cultures and subcultures continue to believe that mental and emotional health depends on avoiding the displeasure of God or ancestral spirits, or on avoiding evil and demonological sources of retribution. In many groups, mental health is viewed as an outcome of keeping a state of balance or harmony in physical, spiritual, and behavioral matters.

Professionals and scientists as well as ordinary people have diverse perspectives and opinions. Recurring issues are whether disorders have biological or **psychogenic** (originating from psychological factors) causes, and whether the individual is merely a victim of outside forces or the source of his or her own disorder. Chapter 2 reviews the various contemporary perspectives on causes of disorders.

CULTURAL FACTORS IN PSYCHOLOGICAL ABNORMALITY

Just as accounts of mental illness have changed throughout history, cultural contexts have greatly shaped views of normal, adaptive behavior. Cultural experiences determine what is expected from people, and ethnic and cultural differences influence their exposure to stressors or protective environments that in turn influence the development of disorders — even if biological factors are also involved. Finally, of course, cultural factors influence the consequences of having disorders.

Only recently have researchers and practitioners begun to pay attention to the vast implications of multicultural (and intracultural) experiences on mental health and illness. As nations become more interdependent and multicultural, cross-cultural issues are taking on increasing importance and practicality. They represent an emerging, evolving emphasis in contemporary studies of mental health. Because this is a relatively new emphasis, however, research about cross-cultural issues is scanty.

Cultural Issues in the Experience and Meaning of Psychological Disorders

Some of the fundamental assumptions of Western thought about psychological states differ radically from those of the majority of people in the world. As anthropologist Arthur Kleinman (1991) stated, it is characteristic of Western culture to separate the emotional and physical components of a disorder (such as depression) and give primacy to the emotional aspects. In other cultures, where internal emotional experiences are not thought to be separate from bodily experiences, people might focus on physical ailments instead of psychological distress. For instance, a Chinese person (or an Asian American) might complain of a stomachache or back pain rather than depression and seek a physical remedy.

Even apart from the Western mind-body duality, across cultures there are notable differences concerning which emotions can appropriately be expressed and in what ways. Some groups and subcultures place great value on openly showing feelings, at least under certain conditions, whereas others emphasize containment and reduced outward emotional expression. Western cultures, though they vary from one another, tend to permit display of emotional reactions whereas many non-Western cultures encourage minimal outward display of feelings.

Another assumption of Western thinking is that mental illness is caused by psychological conditions and can be treated by psychological processes. In other cultures, by contrast, religious or spiritual causes of mental illness are emphasized or symptoms are believed to be the result of character weaknesses. A Caribbean black person or a devout Catholic Italian American, for example, might seek a religious or spiritual solution to a psychological problem. In many cultures, going to a mental health practitioner would seem an irrelevant pursuit at best or a humiliating admission of personal weakness at worst (e.g., Koss-Chioino, 1995).

A third assumption of Western thought is the sense of an individual self, ideally experienced as whole, continuous over time, distinct and unique from that of others, and oriented toward self-expression and autonomy. Many psychological disorders are viewed as disruptions of this natural, desirable process, and individuals might experience symptoms and distress as a result of inadequacies in the sense of an autonomous, distinct self. Other cultures, however, place far greater emphasis on the family, community, or society than on the self. In these cultures, experiences that bring shame to the family or reflect disrespect for authority would be particularly troublesome personally (e.g., Lewis-Fernandez & Kleinman, 1994).

Consider the following case, illustrating vast cultural differences in the meaning of suicide:

> *A young Japanese woman living in Los Angeles was distraught over discovering that her husband was having an affair. She had no work skills, spoke no English, and felt worthless and helpless. She became increasingly depressed and dysfunctional. One spring day she took her infant and four-year-old to the beach, bought lunch, and then walked into the ocean with the children to commit family suicide. Passersby witnessed the act and were able to summon help. The woman survived, but both children drowned. Although she was jailed and accused of murder, the Japanese American community, sympathetic to her effort to resolve her dilemma through a suicide that included her children, rallied to her support. They argued that in traditional Japanese communities the family is the unit, not the individual, and they called it Japanese suicide, not American murder. (Group for the Advancement of Psychiatry, 1989)*

Related to the emphasis on the self in Western culture is a relatively narrow tolerance for departures from agreed-on physical reality. Many other cultures have a much more fluid view of the self and reality. As Kleinman (1991) noted, for example, a Plains Indian who hears the voice of a recently deceased relative calling from the afterworld would view the experience as normal. But a European American person who hears the voice of a dead relative might see the experience rather differently — possibly as an auditory hallucination. Similarly, many cultural groups sanction trancelike states, often associated with religious ecstasy or ritual —

Cultural values play a significant role in shaping both the pressures and the reactions that contribute to psychological disorder. In U.S. society, for example, individuality is greatly valued, and a view into a classroom of youngsters captures the emphasis on self-expression, perhaps at the expense of order. In other cultures, the classroom may reveal entirely different values, such as order and the submersion of individuality in favor of broader social norms.

as might be observed at a revival meeting in the United States. Yet altered states of consciousness occurring outside of ritual might be labeled as "dissociative states," psychopathological conditions that we discuss in Chapter 7.

Cultural meanings shape what is considered normal or abnormal in many ways. Consider, for example, the extent to which contemporary Western society has "created" certain kinds of psychological disorders. Western society places great emphasis on the inner, private experiences of individuals. Freud and his followers revolutionized our views of human beings by suggesting that everyone has certain basic urges that can lead to internal, psychological conflict if they are not resolved satisfactorily. Because these urges are at war with the conventions and constrictions of modern society, conflicts and "neuroses" are expected to be commonplace.

Even more striking than the expectation or "discovery" of neuroses is the recent emphasis on self-fulfillment, self-actualization, and the pursuit of personal meaning and happiness. As people in the industrialized

West became more affluent and liberated from the search for basic necessities, they increasingly turned toward intangible, psychological goals. As a result, more and more people have become highly conscious of their inner lives, the gap between what they think they should feel (happiness, fulfillment) and what they actually feel (frustration, unhappiness, nervousness, anger). The situation described in the following case would seem quite unacceptable to many people from non-Western cultures:

Jonah is seeing a therapist once a week to discuss his problems, which appear to have resulted from a lack of fulfillment in his life. Despite a well-paying and prestigious job, good health, and numerous friends, he is unhappy. He believes that he should be more independent from his family, having recognized that some of his discontent stems from a vague sense that he is a disappointment to his highly critical father. Jonah also believes that he ought to be more creative, or make a more meaningful contribu-

tion in life. He is plagued by worries that he is not rich enough, attractive enough, or successful enough, and that he lacks an inspiring relationship. He suffers from mild depression and anxieties, and often feels awkward in social situations with women.

In many other cultures — and, indeed, perhaps in Western culture a few decades ago — seeking therapy for such experiences would be judged as self-indulgent, disrespectful of the family, and a waste of time and money. But what this case also demonstrates is that the values of modern life have created more or different disorders. Some forms of mental illness that involve outright madness, such as schizophrenia, dementia, mania, and other forms of psychosis, have apparently continued since the dawn of civilization. Now, however, we have "added" internal, private disorders that interfere with contemporary standards of high functioning.

In short, ethnic and cultural diversity provide contexts in which behavior is understood, and the differences across cultures range from the basic ways of understanding the nature of human beings to the specific meanings of individual behaviors. These differences pose tremendous challenges not only to the people directly affected but also to mental health professionals.

Cultural Issues in the Expression of Psychological Disorders

Despite the fact that certain psychological disturbances occur in every culture, different cultures seem to be associated with different frequencies of specific disorders — probably because a culture's values shape the behaviors of its individuals and define what is appropriate and what is not. Consider the example of suicide, which varies across cultures in terms of the meaning attached to it and the rate at which it occurs. Both Catholicism and Islam consider suicide a sin, and there are relatively low rates of suicide in Catholic countries such as Italy and Spain and in Moslem countries such as Iran — due not only to prohibitions against it but also to the reluctance of authorities to "detect" it. As we note in Chapter 8, in many westernized countries suicide is an escape from physical illness and psychological pain; in Japan it is an honorable solution to perceived shame or disgrace.

Alcoholism also is markedly affected by cultural beliefs and practices, as discussed in Chapter 11. In some cultural groups the use of alcohol is strictly forbidden, and in others its use is restricted to certain ceremonial or social situations where excess use is not tolerated. Cross-national studies indicate wide differences in definitions of excessive use, according to amount and the setting in which it is consumed (e.g., Bennett, Janca, Grant & Sartorius, 1993). For example, some cultures stress the use of large quantities of alcohol under conditions such

as male socializing and bonding. John Helzer and his colleagues (1990) compared rates of alcohol problems in various cities using standardized methods. The results, presented in Figure 1.2, indicate considerable cross-national variability; in all sites, rates for women were consistently low.

Sometimes cultural values create disorders that might not otherwise exist or that have a very low incidence rate in other countries, perhaps including attention deficit disorder in children, or dissociative identity (multiple personality) disorder. For instance, eating disorders — stemming from the extreme preoccupation with thinness as an ideal for women — are nearly nonexistent in much of the world except in westernized upper middle classes (Hoek, 1993). Supporting these patterns, one study examined evaluations of male and female

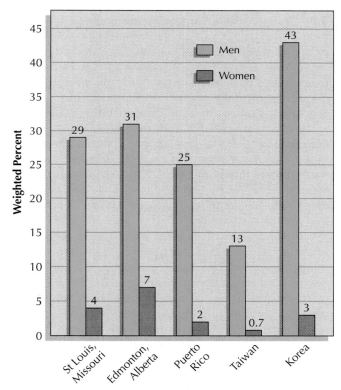

Figure 1.2   Lifetime Prevalence of Alcoholism by Location and Gender

Investigators sampled rates of alcohol dependence in St. Louis, Canada, Puerto Rico, Taiwan, and Korea. They gave standardized interviews to randomly selected citizens who represented the various ages, sexes, and socioeconomic statuses in their cities. Lifetime rates of alcohol disorders for men and women ranged from 13 percent among Taiwanese men to 43 percent among Korean men. Note that Korean men spend considerable time socializing in bars with business associates, whereas excessive use of alcohol is discouraged among Taiwanese men.

Source: Helzer et al. (1990, p. 316).

body shapes by British and Ugandan students. The African students expressed considerably more tolerance and preference for heavier female figures than did the British (Furnham & Baguma, 1994). Research has also uncovered culturally specific forms of disorder that are unique to particular groups. For example, *koro,* a panic state that occurs among men in some Asian countries, results from a fear that the genitals will retract into the abdomen and cause death. And in other cultures, states of *possession* have been reported, involving trance-like conditions and personality changes stemming from the belief that the person has been taken over by spirits.

FOCUS ON RESEARCH

Does Culture Influence Children's Disorders?

John Weisz of UCLA and his colleagues hypothesized that culture helps to shape the forms that psychological problems will take. On the assumption that youngsters are strongly affected by culturally determined values and expectations that influence how their parents and teachers treat them, they embarked on a series of studies of children and adolescents in different cultures. Their general model predicted that cultural values determine the threshold for parental distress over children's problems, influencing what problems are considered serious and what actions should be taken. Not only do cultures differ in their level of tolerance for various behaviors, but they might also differ in the specific kinds of behaviors that are likely to arouse concern.

Weisz and his colleagues tested these predictions across various cultures in several ways: by assessing the frequency of psychological problems, by measuring adults' reactions to hypothetical cases of children's problems, by evaluating the nature of referrals for clinical treatment, and by actually observing children's behavior in standard settings such as the classroom.

In randomly selected families from these various cultures, parents were interviewed about their child's behavior (Weisz et al., 1987b). A standardized checklist developed in the United States but translated into different languages permitted the measurement of the same behaviors across different samples. Because U.S. parents are tolerant of aggressiveness and self-expression in their children, greatly valuing and encouraging independence and assertiveness (especially in boys), Weisz and his colleagues wondered whether the cultural values of the United States might encourage excessive "undercontrolled" behaviors (aggression, impulsivity, distractibility). Conversely, the Buddhist tradition in Thailand emphasizes peacefulness and nonaggression, and children there are taught to be polite, modest, and deferential toward others. Given that outward emotionality and

aggressiveness are prohibited by this tradition, and quiet, controlled behavior is emphasized, are Thai children at risk for developing "overcontrolled" problem behavior?

To answer these questions, Weisz and associates (1987b) randomly selected nearly one thousand normal (not in treatment) children in the United States and Thailand, and administered standardized checklists to their parents. Confirming their prediction, they found that Thai parents reported significantly higher levels of overcontrolled problems in their children than U.S. parents did in theirs. This research was subsequently verified in a sample of Thai adolescents (Weisz et al., 1993), who exhibited significantly more overcontrolled behaviors (shyness, fearfulness) than American teenagers. Although the Thai and U.S. samples did not differ on *total* undercontrolled behaviors, the American teens displayed more direct, interpersonally aggressive problems such as fighting and bullying, whereas the Thai youth exhibited more indirect undercontrolled behaviors such as sulking.

These findings were expanded to include comparisons with African children (Weisz, Sigman, Weiss & Mosk, 1993). Embu children in Kenya were compared with Thai and U.S. children (both Caucasian and African American) from similar rural communities. As Embus greatly prize politeness, respect, and obedience in their children, the researchers predicted a high level of overcontrolled symptoms among them compared to U.S. children. Figure 1.3 presents the comparisons between these four groups. The results generally confirm the prediction that in cultures emphasizing self-control and obedience, children exhibit higher levels of internalized or overcontrolled symptoms.

Using a different methodology, Weisz and associates also asked adults of different cultures to rate their reactions to written vignettes describing hypothetical children who were displaying either disruptive, undercontrolled behaviors or fearful, overcontrolled behaviors. For instance, Lambert and Weisz et al. (1992) compared Jamaican and American samples. They hypothesized that Jamaican parents, as descendants of British-owned slaves from Africa, would combine the British emphasis on respect for authority with the African emphasis on respect for one's elders. Accordingly, they expected Jamaican children to be polite, obedient, and unaggressive. In contrast, American youth are permitted to be brash and nonconformist. As predicted, culture did have an important effect: Jamaicans were more tolerant of children's problems overall, but also more worried than U.S. parents about undercontrolled problems.

Finally, Weisz and associates (1995) explored the question of whether teachers have different levels of tolerance for problem behaviors, given different cultural values. They trained observers to rate children's behav-

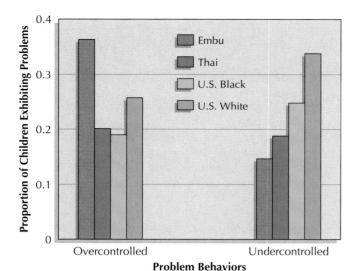

Figure 1.3   Cultural Influence of Overcontrolled and Undercontrolled Behaviors

Embu children exhibited significantly higher levels of overcontrolled problem behaviors than did each of the other cultural groups, and levels of undercontrolled behaviors among U.S. white children were higher than those among Embu and Thai youngsters. Note, however, that a substantial number of the overcontrolled problems among Embu children concerned somatic symptoms such as aches and pains, headaches, nausea, vomiting, and sleeping less. When such symptoms were omitted from consideration, the groups did not differ greatly. The source of these physical problems is not known; the Embu children may truly have been medically more sick, or they may have tended to emphasize somatic expressions of psychological distress.

Source: Weisz, Sigman, Weiss & Mosk (1993).

iors in classrooms in both the United States and Thailand. Whereas Thai teachers who were given standard checklists about children's behavior tended to *report* higher levels of behavior problems than American teachers did, the results were very different when the actual behaviors were observed. The Thai children were far less disruptive than the American youngsters (that is, out of their seats and talking 10 percent of the time versus 23 percent, respectively). Thus, the teachers from the two cultures had very different standards for what they considered to be problem behaviors among their pupils.

This series of studies suggests that children's psychological disorders are, to some extent, in the eye of the beholder. An individual, influenced by the values and expectations of his or her culture, will tend to perceive behaviors as problems according to these cultural patterns. Keep in mind, however, that cultural factors are not the only contributor to children's disorders, and that such factors may be more relevant to some kinds of disorders than to others. Indeed, throughout this book we discuss further research that attempts to determine individual and environmental causes of disorders among children and adults of the same culture. Culture is but one of many pieces of the puzzle when it comes to understanding disorders.

Consequences of Cultural Differences in the Expression of Symptoms

Because cultural groups differ markedly in how they experience and express psychological abnormality, it is not surprising to find differences in what happens to a person who has a disorder. For instance, **help-seeking** (entering treatment for a disorder) varies considerably from group to group. Some cultures encourage individuals to hide or deny their problems, whereas other cultures show great tolerance for psychological difficulties and even encourage people to seek professional help. Accordingly, research has shown major differences in the extent to which ethnic groups use mental health services. Compared to European Americans, for example, Hispanics and Asian Americans use services less, whereas African Americans use services more (e.g., Sue, Chun & Gee, 1995). These differences appear to reflect cultural attitudes about psychological problems and where to turn for help.

The effectiveness of services to different groups also varies. Psychotherapy based on talking and delving into childhood experiences may be of little use or interest to persons who are facing terrible poverty or who believe that their problems are due to physical imbalances (e.g., Dwairy & Van Sickle, 1996). Cultural differences in the effectiveness of mental health treatments are discussed more fully in Chapter 18.

In addition, the course of a disorder may be greatly affected by cultural differences in the recognition, meaning, and response to the problem. Social factors influence whether the disorder (even one with biological causes) will be mild, recurrent, or chronic. For example, in tolerant and supportive cultures, families, and communities, individuals with severe disorders such as schizophrenia may function better than in those less tolerant circumstances.

Biases Due to Cultural Factors in Psychological Disorders

Cultural differences in the experience and expression of symptoms must be taken into account when assessing or diagnosing disorders. Failure to consider appropriate culturally sensitive factors may result in bias in the diagnostic system itself, in clinician judgments, in the evaluation of symptoms, and in research based on samples that exclude multicultural representation (e.g., Dinges & Cherry, 1995).

Consider one example of the possibility of bias in the current diagnostic system. Medical anthropologists examined studies of mental health across samples of Puerto Rican people living in U.S. cities and in Puerto Rico (Guarnaccia, Good & Kleinman, 1990). Over many years and in many different kinds of studies, these researchers consistently found higher rates of symptoms and disorders among Puerto Ricans in U.S. cities than in other groups, including other economically disadvantaged groups. Some of the differences may be due to the presence of actual disorders resulting from hardship or to Puerto Ricans' greater willingness to admit to symptoms. Investigators have speculated, however, that much of the apparent excess of disorder stems from *misdiagnosis*. Puerto Ricans have a unique way of reacting to highly stressful events and losses — *ataques de nervios*, which include symptoms such as heart palpitations, faintness, and brief seizurelike episodes. These episodes are not considered abnormal by Puerto Ricans (especially among women and older, less-educated persons). But interviewers may misinterpret these symptoms and mistakenly think that they represent various diagnostic conditions, with the result that Puerto Ricans are labeled as more disturbed than they really are. Guarnaccia and his colleagues argue that current diagnostic methods typically fail to recognize such unique expressions of distress and instead try to fit diverse people into preexisting categories that may not be valid.

When cultural considerations are ignored, bias may also occur in clinician judgments and use of diagnostic systems. Critics have charged that bias may lead to the attribution of certain symptoms to schizophrenia rather than to alcohol or drug abuse in African American men (Dinges & Cherry, 1995). And social commentators have speculated that when African American men exhibit aberrant behavior they are likely to be treated as criminals and sent to prison rather than to be diagnosed as mentally ill and needing psychiatric treatment. These controversial issues have often elicited more rhetoric than research, but they highlight the need for culturally appropriate diagnostic guidelines.

Bias may occur in the tests and assessment procedures that characterize psychological abnormality. Test items may be specific to the culture in which they were developed, and, even when translated into different languages, the wordings of symptoms may be unfamiliar or fail to accurately characterize psychological experiences.

Finally, when cultural factors are disregarded, bias can result from generalizing about mental health and psychological distress from samples that are predominantly white and middle class. Most research on psychological abnormality and treatment has been based on primarily European American samples. The full implications of this practice are unclear because multicultural research is only now beginning to bridge some of the gaps in our knowledge.

GENDER AND PSYCHOLOGICAL ABNORMALITY

Joey is six years old and has always been a handful to manage. He's noisy and active, and he never seems to sit still or play quietly. He teases his younger brother and sometimes gets into fights at school. He's cute and bright, but sometimes he is aggressive about getting his own way. He interrupts in class, takes toys away from other children, and would much prefer to be outside playing sports instead of reading a book at his desk in school.

What are your reactions to this child? Many people might think that "he's all boy," that "he's a normal, active boy." Suppose, however, that we change the pronouns from male to female and tell this same story about Susie. Read the vignette again; what do you think this time? Perhaps your impression of the child has changed. Perhaps now you think that "she's got problems" or "her behavior is not normal."

Consider the following vignette:

Mary has been coming into work late this week, and her eyes are puffy and she looks miserable. She tries to do her work, but mostly she sits at her desk weeping. When you ask her what's wrong, she says that her husband is leaving her and she doesn't know how she'll survive. She feels that her life is worthless without him.

What is your reaction to Mary? Perhaps you feel sympathetic and want to help her. But suppose that the person weeping at the desk is Bill. Reread the scene with Bill in mind. Do you have a different reaction? Many people would think that "he's weak," "he's overreacting," or "it's hard to respect him." In a study conducted by one of the present authors (Hammen & Peters, 1977), similar vignettes were given to a group of college students: Half received stories about a man and half received the same stories about a woman. When the stories depicted a man experiencing depression, judgments and reactions were much more negative than when the character was a woman.

These descriptions illustrate that most people expect men and women to behave and react differently. We expect girls to display feminine qualities and boys to display masculine qualities. Because American society particularly values masculine characteristics, however, we are somewhat more tolerant of girls who are "tomboys" than of boys who are "sissies." Accordingly, people might be quick to label a boy who isn't active in sports and likes to play with girls as having a psychological problem, whereas girls who enjoy rough-and-tumble activities and don't like to wear dresses are expected to "outgrow it." Clearly, sex roles shape decisions about what is acceptable and what isn't. By the same token, men and women are subjected to various freedoms or restraints that in turn shape decisions about what is abnormal.

To some extent, then, it is appropriate to take gender into account when diagnosing abnormality. When a person deviates sharply from expected gender behavior, a problem may actually exist. Socialization and biology lead to notable differences between the sexes in the experience and expression of psychological disorders. However, gender differences can also create bias.

Sex Differences in the Experience and Expression of Psychological Disorders

Men and women experience and express psychological disorders in different ways. Figure 1.4 shows gender differences in several disorders, based on large-scale community surveys. These differences may reflect the ways that men and women are taught to express their conflicts and upsets. As we noted, most societies have different standards and expectations for the behaviors of men and women. In U.S. culture we expect men to be strong, dominant, independent, rational, and in control of situations and emotions; we expect women to be emotional and dependent, and to require help and protection by men. This difference in expectation gives women greater freedom to express emotions and neediness.

Different gender patterns of disorders might also reflect society's tolerance or even encouragement of certain behaviors, at least in their milder forms. For instance, women are urged to be extremely conscious of their weight and body image; men are encouraged to be dominant and aggressive in pursuit of their goals. Here's another example of a disorder highly shaped by gender roles:

Your Uncle Joe and his older brother, your father, were raised in a small rural community. Joe was always a bit rebellious. In high school he would sneak out at night, meet his friends, and have a few six-packs of beer. His father always said "boys will be boys." After he graduated from high school and went to work, each day ended with a trip to the tavern to hang out with the guys and have a few drinks. When his girlfriend left him, he drank heavily — just like in the country-Western songs he'd hear at the bar. He finally joined the Army, which surrounded him with even more men who thought it was a "male" thing to get drunk. By the time you were in junior high, you could see pretty clearly that visits from Uncle Joe usually ended with someone having to drive him home because he'd become so intoxicated. He was a fun-loving man, and a good story-teller, but he never seemed to be able to hang out with people

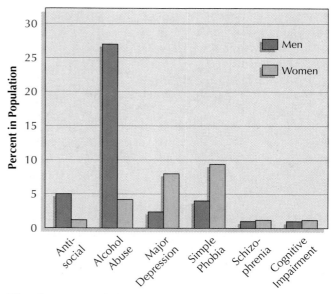

Figure 1.4   Gender Differences in Disorders
Many surveys show that women are more likely to have "emotional" disorders such as anxiety and depression, whereas men are more likely to have "behavioral" disorders such as drug and alcohol abuse and antisocial conduct. "Biological" disorders such as schizophrenia and dementia (cognitive disorder) typically do not show gender differences. This figure shows rates of various lifetime diagnoses based on a community study in a large American city.

Source: Robins et al. (1984).

unless he had a drink in his hand. His alcoholism has now cost him two marriages.

Biases Due to Gender Differences

The fact that men and women exhibit different rates of certain disorders does not necessarily reflect bias. Such differences could validly reflect differences in biology, **gender socialization** (the process of learning expected feminine and masculine behaviors and attitudes), and experiences. At least four sources of potential bias are, however, based on gender.

First, the diagnostic system itself may encompass disorders that differentially lead to the stigmatization of one sex or another. Indeed, some critics assert that the DSM includes, or is being pressed to include, diagnoses that are unfair to women and that it labels as a disorder certain symptoms that women experience but men do not. For example, late luteal phase dysphoric disorder (a severe form of premenstrual distress or PMS) was proposed for inclusion in the two most recent versions of the DSM. Opponents of the diagnosis insist that it stigmatizes women and that the disorder should be considered not mental but medical or endocrinological in nature. And feminist scholars have argued that the DSM should include a parallel diagnosis for problems

Gender shapes the experiences, behavior, and expectations of men's and women's behavior, influencing both normal and disordered patterns. As sex roles change, we are beginning to see more of behaviors previously not "expected" such as aggressive, violent females — as in the Girl Bloods Gang.

associated with male hormones, such as testosterone aggression syndrome (Tavris, 1992).

Second, there may be bias in the ways that clinicians label disorder. The question is, Do they erroneously apply the diagnostic criteria for a disorder to one sex more than to the other? Studies suggest that they do. For example, the same symptoms called "overwork" in a man might be called "depression" in a woman. Another illustration is provided by Maureen Ford and Thomas Widiger (1989), who prepared hypothetical case vignettes for two disorders: histrionic personality disorder (HPD), characterized by traits such as excessive emotionality, flamboyance, and attention-seeking, and antisocial personality disorder (APD), defined as a history of callousness, disregard for others' rights and feelings, and illegal conduct. Ford and Widiger worded each vignette in one of three ways: The person described was male, female, or sex unspecified. They then contacted hundreds of clinicians and asked them to read the

vignettes and make diagnostic ratings. The clinicians were significantly more likely to diagnose the female cases as histrionic than as antisocial personality disorder — even when the cases explicitly described the latter. The investigators concluded that clinicians were overdiagnosing HPD in women because emotionality was more "typical" of women, whereas men were "expected" to display aggressive, inconsiderate, and antisocial behavior.

Third, bias may result from methods for measuring disorder, such as questionnaires and interviews. In general, women tend to be more willing than men to admit to symptoms involving feelings and emotions. Thus, many interviews or questionnaires that call for acknowledgment of negative emotions might result in higher scores for women than men simply because women are more willing or able to disclose feelings.

Finally, gender bias may occur in **sampling,** the process of selecting populations for study. Until relatively recently, most of our information about mental disorders was based on people in treatment. As noted, however, men and women differ in their willingness to admit problems and to seek help for them. Women are significantly more likely than men to seek treatment for emotional and mental health problems (and even for medical problems). Accordingly, mental health statistics that are based on "treatment-seeking" populations in clinics and hospitals might create the misleading impression that men are "healthier" than women. On the other hand, women tend to be underrepresented in certain kinds of treatment settings such as prison facilities and Veterans Administration (VA) hospitals. A great deal of research has been conducted on VA patients over the years, and until recently much of what we knew about schizophrenia was based on male patients only.

Overall, gender notably shapes beliefs and expectations about the meaning and appropriateness of a person's behavior. Such contextual information may be necessary for correctly interpreting someone's behavior, but it can also create biases in our understanding of abnormality.

AGE AND PSYCHOLOGICAL ABNORMALITY

Judgments about psychological disorder must also take age into account. We expect people of different ages to behave somewhat differently, and we evaluate their actions accordingly. For example, children are assumed to have certain fears and to need adult reassurance. But what would we think of a grown man who is scared and cries on his first day at work? Or an adult woman who is afraid of being away from home? We would probably consider their behavior abnormal and impairing for the context in which it occurs.

Age Differences in the Experience and Expression of Psychological Disorders

Children and adults differ in the ways they express and cope with distress, and these differences can lead to age-related psychological difficulties. For example, a man who is socially fearful or who has difficulty expressing anger may turn to alcohol to loosen his fears and release tension. But a child who is socially fearful and angry might "act out" — start fights, break things, and disobey adults.

Researchers are now studying children's disorders more than ever before, but there is much to learn. Childhood depression is a good example of how our knowledge has increased and changed. Until fairly recently theorists believed that children could not be depressed — both because childhood was assumed to be a happy time and because children lacked the psychological capacity for depression. Some clinicians believed that youngsters could experience only "depression equivalents" such as stomachaches, bedwetting, or conduct problems rather than depressive symptoms such as guilt, hopelessness, and loss of pleasure. But researchers have discovered that children as young as preschoolers can experience major depressive reactions with many of the same symptoms that characterize adult depression. Indeed, new information is emerging about a host of age-specific disorders; much of this information is reviewed in Chapters 15 and 16. We know far less, however, about disorders that might be specific to older ages. Those specifically related to brain changes sometimes associated with aging are reviewed in Chapter 17.

Age Trends and Sources of Bias in Psychological Disorders

In addition to determining how a person's age modifies our concepts of psychological disorders, we need to consider what age patterns can tell us about causal factors and what potential biases or misunderstandings may be related to age.

Age and Causal Factors The ages at which disorders are more likely to occur provide important clues about the disorders themselves. For example, Figure 1.5 illustrates the *age of onset* of major depressive episodes for males and females. Note that among young women between fifteen and nineteen years of age, depression rates skyrocket; the rates are lower for young men. Also note the big jump in onset of major depression among the very old. What happens during those years? The answers to this question might help us to understand, treat, and even prevent such disorders. In addition, among both men and women the median age of onset is between thirteen and twenty-five for the following disorders besides depression: bipolar disorder (manic-depression), panic disorder, obsessive-compulsive disorder, phobias, drug abuse, and alcohol abuse (Burke, Burke, Regier & Rae, 1990). Other studies have indicated that the years between late adolescence and early adulthood are also the peak age of onset for schizophrenia and antisocial personality disorder.

Figure 1.5 Age of Onset of Major Depression

In a random community survey, adults who were diagnosed with major depression at some point in their lives reported the age at which the disorder first occurred. Note the extreme jump in the rate of depression between ages 15 and 19 for women.

Source: Burke, Burke, Regier & Rae (1990).

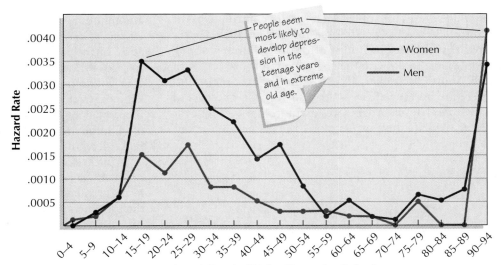

Age at Onset of Major Depressive Episode

The family is the primary source of mental health or illness, transmitted by genetic or parent-child experiences — or both. The family is a concept that has changed radically in recent years, including single parents or blends of biological and step-relatives. In some communities, families include gay and lesbian domestic partners and their children, as is shown in this photo and the photo on page 27.

The striking conclusion about age-of-onset information is that late adolescence and early adulthood are indeed periods of high risk for the development of psychological disorders. There seem to be fewer psychological disorders in older adulthood than in the young and middle-adult years. Does this mean that older people have different ways of expressing their distress, or that they are less distressed? Maybe young people are simply more willing to admit that they have problems, even though they don't really have more problems than older people. Or perhaps the most disturbed people simply do not survive to older ages.

Another possibility is that these findings are valid and signal a tremendous strain on today's young people, and that severe stressors faced by youth contribute to the occurrence of disorders. Some researchers have speculated that increases in rates of disorders among young people have to do with the changing family, so let's turn to a short discussion of why families are important. There are no easy answers for resolving the question of why rates of disorders are extraordinarily high for young people, but we explore this issue in various chapters.

FAMILY MATTERS
The Importance of Family in Mental Health

Family life is the key formative experience for the shaping of personality, transmission of values, and acquisition of language and reasoning skills. Along with genetic transmission of predisposition to certain forms of mental disorder, family experiences fundamentally determine mental health and adjustment. Thus, when essential characteristics of the family change, there are important implications for mental health.

Dramatic changes in family structure have occurred in modern industrialized countries. The main change is the huge proportion of children who are now being raised by a single parent, usually the mother. In the United States, nearly 40 percent of marriages end in divorce, typically resulting in the placement of children under their mothers' care or in reconstituted stepfamilies. Moreover, nearly one-third of all U.S. births occur among unmarried women. The teenage birthrate in the United States is the highest in the industrialized world, at 57 births per 1,000 teenage girls.

Overall, this means that nearly one in three dependent children are being raised by single mothers in the United States (in Great Britain the ratio is one in five [Haskey, 1994]). Among African Americans, 55 percent of children are raised in single-parent families (O'Hare, Pollard, Mann & Kent, 1991).

Unfortunately — though not inevitably — children raised by single mothers may be seriously impaired in terms of adjustment and mental health — not because of their mothers' unmarried status but because of the stressors that often accompany being single. For instance, divorce and family disruption are significant risk factors for maladjustment (e.g., Barbarin & Soler, 1993; Coie et al., 1993), although the effects vary greatly according to

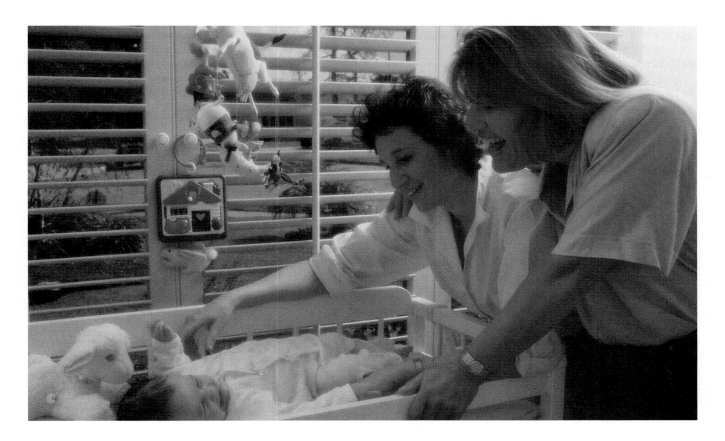

the age of the children and individual family circumstances. Poverty is often another culprit, exposing children to adversities that overwhelm their coping skills and impede healthy development.

The grim consequences of family breakdown on children's mental health are explored in various chapters of this book. However, it is important to emphasize that being raised by both a mother and a father is no guarantee of emotional health. Conversely, children raised by an effective and caring single mother who has adequate resources can certainly be healthy and happy. Also, there are many adaptive alternatives to the traditional two-parent family — including extended family groups, child-rearing by grandparents, and the like. Indeed, recent research verifies that alternative family structures headed by caring and competent adults, including gay and lesbian parents, result in healthy children (Bailey, Bobrow, Wolfe & Mikach, 1995; Flaks, Ficher, Masterpasqua & Joseph, 1995; Golombok & Tasker, 1996; Patterson, 1992; Tasker & Golombok, 1995).

Age-related Biases The same questions raised for gender and ethnicity can apply to age as well: Is the diagnostic system itself biased? Are clinicians biased in their views of psychological disorder in people of different ages? Are assessment methods biased? Is our knowledge

biased by failure to study all age groups? These issues, too, must be addressed, even though definite answers are not currently available.

There is no clear evidence of bias in the diagnostic system as it currently stands; but because of gaps in data about children and older adults, the system is incomplete. Just as erroneous assumptions about children's capacity for depressive experiences delayed the "discovery" of childhood depression, we can expect further clarification and "discovery" of childhood disorders in the future.

Until fairly recently, research also neglected the psychological experiences of the elderly. Most studies and epidemiological surveys systematically excluded people more than sixty-five years old. More generally, the experiences of older adults have been considered uninteresting to our youth-oriented society. Stereotypes of the elderly abound in the media; older characters — if they appear at all — are often portrayed as useless, senile, and feeble. But our society can no longer afford this point of view because people are living longer, healthier lives than ever before, and within the next decade or two the population of older adults will increase dramatically as a proportion of the population. When researchers begin to study the lives of older people more fully, they might find that their unique experiences produce unique disorders. Currently, however, because senility is what is expected of older adults, senility is what clinicians may "see" when elders seek treatment. Fortunately, as we explore in Chapter 17, scientists are beginning to expend considerable effort to understand the biological causes of Alzheimer's disease.

Currently there is intense interest in learning more about the experiences of those at both the younger and older ends of the spectrum. The more we learn about normal development in these age groups, the more we will be able to characterize unique experiences of psychological disorder and their consequences in children and elders.

What Lies Ahead?

For more than 2,500 years, cultures have been defining and explaining psychological deviance and disorder. This process will continue into the future as we "discover" new forms of psychological maladjustment and learn more about the universal disorders that have been acknowledged since the beginning of civilization. The impact of historical, cultural, gender, and age factors on psychological disorders is enormous — and this is true even for disorders considered to have a biological component.

At present, the process of discovery and definition of abnormality is based on scientific principles of obser-vation and systematic study. Science itself occurs in a political, historical, economic, and social context, however, and that context determines what society believes to be true and important. When a culture believes that certain attitudes and behaviors are threatening to its goals, it is not tolerant of those attitudes and behaviors. It identifies some behaviors as illnesses, some as immoral behaviors, and some as criminal acts. Our brief review of the history of mental illness provides many such examples. But the process of defining and explaining persists today. For instance, U.S. society is presently ambivalent about whether certain behaviors (such as alcoholism, homosexuality, and antisocial conduct) reflect biological predisposition, moral weakness, or psychological causes. Changing social norms will doubtless contribute to future changes, refinements, and definitions of these and other psychological conditions.

The scientific study of psychological disorder has also not fully grappled with the potential biases in matters of gender, culture, and age. Moreover, there are gaps in our knowledge of the effects of age, culture, and gender on psychological disorders — gaps that need to be filled. Because of changing cultural and social experiences, there is reason to expect changes in the patterns of disorders displayed by groups differing in these characteristics.

KEY TERMS

DSM-IV (8)
demonology (13)
epidemiological surveys (6)
gender socialization (23)
help-seeking (21)

humoral theory (11)
impaired functioning (8)
insane asylums (13)
mental illness (9)

moral treatment (14)
psychoanalysis (15)
psychogenic (16)
psychological abnormality (9)

psychopathology (9)
psychotropic medications (16)
sampling (24)
yin and yang (11)

SUMMARY

Myths and Definitions of Psychological Abnormality

There are many misconceptions about *psychological abnormality,* including confusion over how to define it. Various individual yardsticks all have certain limitations. Instead, we use two practical guidelines: First, does the behavior cause impaired functioning with respect to expected performance suitable for the person in a relevant context? Relevant context includes considerations of the situation, the historical perspective, and the person's gender, age, race, and cultural values. Second, does the person's behavior fit experts' rules set forth in the *Diagnostic and Statistical Manual, 4th Edition* (DSM-IV)? A psychological abnormality exists, then, if a person fails to behave appropriately according to his or her context and displays a pattern of experiences and behaviors that experts have defined as a diagnosable psychological condition.

Changing Historical Views of Psychological Abnormality

From ancient times to the present, three themes have characterized how cultures view the meaning of psychological abnormality. One view identifies the causes as demon possession or punishment by supernatural forces. Another points to physical abnormality (such as imbalances of bodily fluids or brain changes). Yet another has to do with psychological disturbances owing to conflict, stress, or moral weakness. Depending on the dominant view of a particular culture and era, these views might lead to acceptance and tolerance of the person, or to fear and persecution. Accordingly, treatments have consisted of attempts to exorcise the demons or punish the afflicted person, to restore physical balance, or to resolve psychological difficulties. *Insane asylums* were large institutions for the mentally ill, but only with the rise of *moral treatment* did more humane forms of caretaking develop, eventually including psychotherapy, *psychoanalysis,* and medications. Scientific observation characterizes present efforts to understand mental disorders.

Cultural Factors in Psychological Abnormality

Cultural experiences are also contextual factors that shape our understanding and definition of abnormality. Western ways of thinking about human nature and psychological disorders emphasize concepts that other cultures may not. For example, Western thought distinguishes between mind and body, emphasizes natural causes (including psychological ones), and deemphasizes supernatural causes. Western thought also emphasizes the individual self, whereas other cultures emphasize unity with the social or natural order. As a result of these differences in meaning and expression of psychological states, diagnostic labels may be misapplied or the unique experiences of individuals may not be properly recognized and understood.

Culture also influences *help-seeking* and views about the relevance or effectiveness of different kinds of treatments.

Gender and Psychological Abnormality

Males and females experience and express psychological symptoms somewhat differently, and the society expects some-what different behaviors from them. Consequently, there may be differences in the rates of disorders for men and women and in the ways specific patterns of behaviors are judged. These differences could validly reflect differences in biology, *gender socialization,* and experiences. Four sources of bias are based on gender: The diagnostic system may reflect cultural values about the different roles of men and women; clinicians may "see" and label the same behaviors differently in men and women; assessment methods may not validly reflect the experiences of both sexes; and bias may exist in our knowledge due to samples that do not inlcude both sexes equally.

Age and Psychological Abnormality

Age is clearly an important consideration in identifying and understanding abnormality because we have different standards for conduct in children and adults. However, study of children's disorders is relatively new. Researchers have also neglected the experiences of older adults. Strong age-related patterns of major disorders compel us to try to understand their causes. Greater attention to age factors in *mental illness* will help shed further light on the meaning, causes, and consequences of various psychological disorders.

Consider the following. . .

D'Andre, a nine-year-old African American from the inner city, has been assigned to the cabin in which you are a summer camp counselor. He is here on scholarship because his mother, raising him alone, cannot afford such luxuries as camp fees as she struggles to manage with four young children; in contrast, most of the white kids attending camp have never lacked for either attention or material goods. You've discovered that D'Andre will start fights if he feels threatened, that he stole some snacks from the cabin, and that he is sometimes defiant toward authority figures (like you). The other counselor in your cabin says he's bad news, that he's on his way to being classified as having "conduct disorder" (a childhood behavior disorder reflecting antisocial tendencies), and that he'll end up in jail. But what alternative explanation can you suggest, given the culture of D'Andre's community? Keep in mind that his behavior is being evaluated from different perspectives — and consider how teachers, police, and maybe other professionals both within and outside his community might assess him. What outcomes are likely over his lifetime, depending on how his behavior is evaluated?

Imagine that you are the new parent of a baby girl. In dreaming about her future, ask yourself how you would respond to her in each of the following situations: when you shop for her clothes or comb her hair, when she falls down and hurts herself, when she decides to walk to school by herself, when she wants a skateboard, when she gets angry at you, when you list some chores for her to help with, when someone at school bullies her, and when she goes to the toy store. After you have thought about how you would respond in these situations, consider the implications of your choices. Do some of the choices emphasize or minimize gender differences? Do some of the choices have long-term implications for her view of herself, what she considers important, how she deals with problems, and her emotional expression? In other words, will her mental health reflect your emphasis on gender socialization?

CHAPTER 2

Models of Psychopathology

Those among us . . .

■ Matt, an acquaintance who worked at the local convenience store, had been yelling at and arguing with customers. You learn that he was recently hospitalized. When you ask, "Why, what happened?" you get several different answers. Your dad said, "He was a confused man, always struggling within himself." Your friend said, "Matt lost curiosity in things after the car accident," quietly adding, "I think the accident caused a nervous breakdown."

■ You learn that your friend Andrew has conduct disorder. You aren't surprised; you've known of his bullying and fights at school and his having set fire to a building. Unintentionally, you overhear his mother and someone from Andrew's school discussing the problem. "Well," says his mom, "he did fall on his head when he was very young." After a pause she continues, "And he does like to play rough sports. . . . He looks like his uncle, and his uncle has been in trouble with the law, too."

■ You enjoy mystery novels by Hennie Robinson and eagerly await his next book. But it doesn't appear. Despite Hennie's accomplishments, he has been frustrated and dissatisfied with his life. He discounts his successful book as "last year's work" and chides himself by saying "What have I done lately?" Currently, he struggles to write, feels worthless, has a poor appetite, and experiences sleep problems. In everyone else's eyes, Hennie is a success — so how can we come to understand his being depressed?

What sorts of problems and stressors lead some people to experience what has been called a "nervous breakdown"? Is it due to some inherent weakness in them, something beyond their control, or a bit of both?

Does head injury or genetics explain the origins of conduct disorder?

What causes depression? Is it due primarily to a biochemical imbalance in the brain? Is it caused by faulty thinking? Does this disorder particularly afflict people who have certain characteristics or life styles?

How can we learn more about abnormality? Once we have some information, how can we organize it to guide future studies and applications? Students and professionals in abnormal psychology need a guiding framework — a **model** or **paradigm** — to help conceptualize and organize the available information about the onset and development of maladaptive behavior. They also need a way to test assumptions and hypotheses. Models stimulate hypotheses, and research tests the validity of assumptions. In this chapter and the next three, we discuss the models and methods pertinent to the treatment, assessment, and study of abnormal psychology.

A model is a general orientation to the field of abnormal psychology that includes assumptions about what drives human behavior, hypotheses about how disorders develop, and prescriptions for how disorders can be treated. Thus, models help identify factors involved in psychological disorder and therapy, and provide a context into which new information can be integrated.

In this chapter, we introduce five major models of contemporary psychology: the biomedical, behavioral, cognitive, psychodynamic, and humanistic models (see Table 2.1). Because psychological disorders are so numerous and so varied, and because their causes are often multiple and interactive, no one model can explain

them all satisfactorily. But a blend of several models, as in **eclecticism**, may provide an adequate framework for understanding a specific disorder. Toward this end, *empiricism* plays an important role, guiding research evaluations of the proposed models. Psychologists today recognize that elements of the major models can be integrated; later in the chapter, we discuss these emerging integrative approaches.

THE BIOMEDICAL MODEL: PSYCHOLOGICAL DISORDERS AND BIOLOGICAL CONDITIONS

The **biomedical model** suggests that the symptoms of psychological disorders are caused by biological factors. This model is variously referred to as the medical, organic, biological, or disease model, but only slight differences are implied by these terms. Overall, the biomedical model identifies brain defects, infectious transmission, biochemical imbalances, and genetic predispositions as possible sources of psychological disorders. Recall Hennie, the depressed writer we mentioned at the start of the chapter. We return to this case as we discuss each of the major models of psychopathology. From a biological perspective, Hennie's depression is the result of a genetic predisposition and of problems with

Table 2.1 Major Models of Psychopathology

Model	Causal Factors	Select Descriptive Terms for Disorder	Treatment and Treatment Goals
Biomedical	Diseases; organic, biochemical, genetic factors; brain defects	Symptoms, syndromes, diseases	Medications, hospitalization, surgery, shock treatment; therapist seeks symptom remission
Behavioral	Maladaptive learning	Deficient or excessive behavior, influence of environment and the behavior of others	Therapist provides performance-based experiences to foster new learning
Cognitive	Maladaptive views and interpretations of the world	Irrational beliefs, illogical thinking	Therapist modifies client's interpretations of the world
Psychodynamic	Internal psychic conflict	Fixated personality development, anxiety, defensiveness	Psychoanalysis; therapist fosters emotional insight via interpretations
Humanistic	Frustrated personal growth; false presentation of self	Disorganized, frustrated, false presentation of self	Therapist sets the stage for client to work toward self-care

This table lists, in overview form, the causal factors, descriptive terms, and treatment goals used by each of the major models of psychopathology. The differences in emphasis are evident in this summary.

his body's neurotransmitter substances. Other forces may be involved, but underlying biological factors are seen as primary.

Historically, the identification of syphilis as the cause of one psychological disorder — general paresis — gave a strong impetus to the biomedical model. General paresis was a serious mental illness of past centuries, producing symptoms such as delusions of grandeur (unfounded beliefs in extreme self-importance) and paralysis, in many cases leading to death. Scientists discovered that general paresis was a physical disease caused by syphilitic infection of the cerebral cortex of the brain. Early in the twentieth century, scientists identified the bacteria that cause syphilis and developed a test to diagnose the presence of the organism in the blood.

Clearly, the biomedical perspective applied to general paresis. If a person infected with the syphilis bacteria remained untreated, his or her emotional and physical behavior eventually became abnormal. The person's blood contained indicators of the organism's presence, and the brain displayed deterioration from the causal agent. Extrapolating from the example of syphilis, experts suggested that other psychological disorders, too, could be the result of physically determined maladies.

The Role of the Brain in Psychological Abnormality

As we consider the role of physical maladies in psychological adjustment, an obvious place to start is the brain. Two major factors suspected of producing abnormalities are the *structure* of the brain and *communication* between brain structures.

Anatomy of the Brain   Of all body parts, the brain is the most complex. Billions of cells — neurons (nerve cells) and glial (support cells) — make up the brain. Different collections of neurons, in different regions of the brain, are responsible for certain functions.

The outer layer of the brain — the **cerebral cortex** — is primarily responsible for sensory processing, motor control, and higher mental functioning involving complex information processing, learning, memory, planning, and judgment, among other activities. The cerebral cortex has four regions: the frontal, parietal, temporal, and occipital lobes. Figure 2.1 shows these regions. The *frontal lobes* — located near the front of the brain — contain the motor cortex, a region that controls the more than six hundred muscles of the body. The frontal lobes are also involved in the higher mental functions such as thinking and planning. The *temporal lobes*, located near the temples on the side of the brain, are involved in processing language as well as in memory and perception. The *parietal lobes* contain the

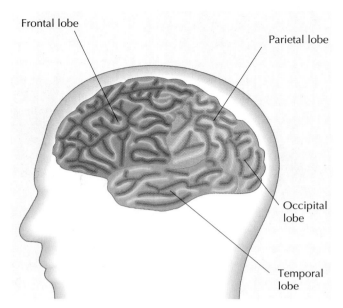

Figure 2.1   Regions of the Cortex
Each hemisphere of the cerebral cortex can be separated into four regions or lobes. The frontal lobes contain the motor cortex and are also involved in the higher mental functions such as thinking and planning. The temporal lobes are involved in processing language as well as in memory and perception. The parietal lobes contain the somatosensory cortex, a region that receives information about pain, pressures, and body temperature. The occipital lobes contain the visual cortex, where vision is processed.

somatosensory cortex, a region that receives information about pain, pressures, and body temperature. The *occipital lobes*, at the back of the head, contain the visual cortex, where vision is processed. Damage to the occipital lobe can result in impaired vision or blindness.

Another way to examine the brain is to consider its three sections: the forebrain, the midbrain, and the hindbrain (see Figure 2.2). It is in the forebrain that the two cerebral hemispheres, the thalamus, and the hypothalamus are located. The **thalamus** is important in the processing and relaying of information between other regions of the central nervous system and the cerebral cortex; the **hypothalamus** regulates hunger, thirst, sex drive, and body temperature. The **limbic system** — which includes parts of the cortex, the thalamus, and hypothalamus — provides homeostasis, or constancy of the internal environment, by regulating the activity of endocrine glands and the autonomic nervous system. All of these structures play critical roles in emotions and drives (Kalat, 1995).

Below the forebrain is the midbrain, a way station that coordinates communications between the forebrain and the region just below it called the hindbrain. The hindbrain contains the pons, medulla, and reticular activating system and is connected to the spinal cord. The pons is involved in sleeping, waking, and dreaming; the

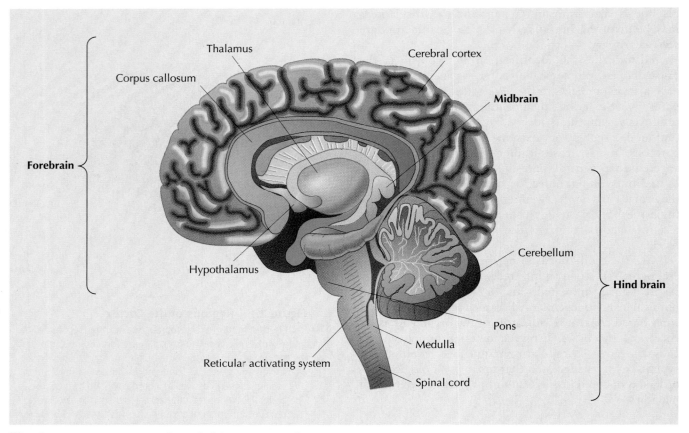

Figure 2.2 Cross-section of the Human Brain

This view of the brain shows the *forebrain,* with its two cerebral hemispheres, thalamus (relays between the CNS and cerebral cortex), and hypothalamus (regulates hunger, thirst, sex drive, body temperature); the *hindbrain,* with the pons (involved in sleeping, waking, dreaming), medulla (regulates breathing, heart rate), and reticular activating system (screens incoming information, arouses other areas of the brain); and the *midbrain,* coordinating between forebrain and hindbrain.

medulla regulates breathing and heart rate. The pathways from other regions of the brain pass through the pons and medulla. The reticular activating system is a network of neurons that screens incoming information and arouses other areas of the brain.

Abnormalities in these structures can arise in numerous ways. A person might be born with an abnormally small or oddly formed brain structure. Or an injury resulting from complications at birth or a severe blow to the head might disturb some part of the brain. More subtle processes such as prenatal exposure to toxins — whether drugs, alcohol, environmental pollutants, or viruses — can also alter the development of the brain. Whatever their source, anatomical abnormalities have been linked to certain psychological disorders. Recent interest in the biomedical model of psychopathology has focused not only on abnormalities in the structure of neurons but also on how these neurons communicate (Rosenzweig, Leiman & Breedlove, 1996).

Communication in the Brain: Neurotransmitters
Neurons transmit electrical impulses to other neurons by means of **neurotransmitters** (Dunant & Israel, 1985). Neurotransmitters are essential for the effective functioning of the neurons and play a major role in transmitting information in the brain. Individual neurons typically consist of several parts: a cell body, dendrites, and an axon (see Figure 2.3). The point of contact between one neuron and another is the synapse, and the space between neurons is called the synaptic gap or synaptic cleft (see Figure 2.4). These structures and substances coordinate efforts to send signals within the brain (Sejnowski, Koch & Churchland, 1988).

A neuron receives a chemical signal or message in the form of a neurotransmitter and transforms it into an electrical impulse. The axon is the long fiber that, along with the shorter dendrites, conducts the electrical impulses generated in the cell body. When a signal reaches the end of the axon, it prompts the cell to release neurotransmitters; these cross the synaptic cleft at the synapse and thereby pass on the signal to the next cell.

Thus far, scientists have discovered more than fifty types of neurotransmitters in the brain; different neurotransmitters serve different regions of the brain. Several

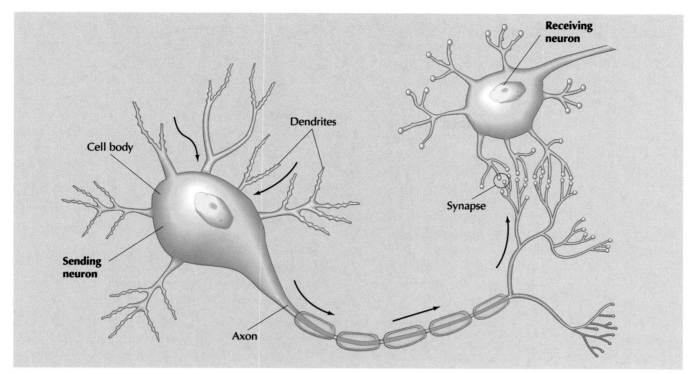

Figure 2.3   Neurotransmission

Neural impulses travel from the axon of one neuron to the cell body of another neuron. The point at which the communication takes place is the synaptic cleft, and neurotransmitter substances communicate between neurons by crossing this cleft (gap).

of these are important to psychopathology — in the study of depression, for example. The relationships between certain neurotransmitters and psychological disorders are described in the chapters that cover these disorders.

Neurotransmission can go awry in many ways because the processes governing both the release and the reabsorption of a particular neurotransmitter substance are highly complex. Neurotransmission problems can involve (1) the amount of the neurotransmitter, (2) the neurotransmitter receptors, (3) the presence or absence of neurons that inhibit neural connections, and (4) the interrelationships between the different neurotransmitters. Such problems in turn can contribute to psychopathology. Behavior may also be affected when environmental forces such as stress inhibit synaptic transmission, or when medications used to treat the symptoms of certain mental disorders disrupt the neurotransmitter process.

Arousal and Overarousal

Rosalyn and Brad have been married for two years. Brad, age thirty-five, has had two previous marriages; Rosalyn, age thirty-three, has had one. Both are self-employed musician-artists with an unusual lifestyle: They live on a relatively low income in a small home they built themselves in a canyon.

Rosalyn and Brad have a tempestuous marital relationship. Rosalyn is emotional; Brad says he is rational. Both have a great deal of difficulty understanding and accepting the other's point of view. During their frequent loud quarrels each feels like giving up the relationship. The quarrels involve intense emotion — shouting and crying — and both Rosalyn and Brad have reported increased heart

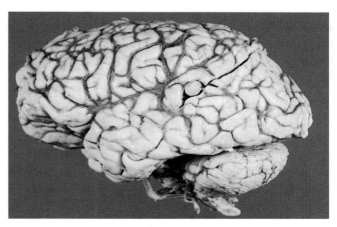

The human brain — the central computing, processing, and storage mechanism — weighs about three pounds. Itself a fragile substance, it is well protected by the skull.

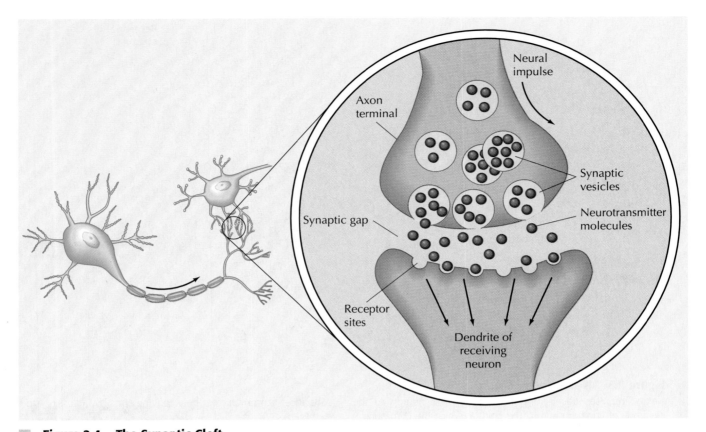

Figure 2.4   The Synaptic Cleft
Neurotransmitter substances leave the synaptic vesicles in the axon terminal of one neuron, cross the synaptic gap, and bind to recep-tor sites on the receiving neuron. One neuron may have synaptic connections with hundreds or thousands of other neurons.

rates, rapid increases in breathing, and occasional bursts of energy.

When a quarrel begins, smiles fade, lips tighten, and the two exchange long, sharp gazes. Cues for anger emerge — raised voices, sarcasm, and loud and abrupt barbs intended not to resolve the situation but to provoke the other person. The focus of conflict changes from one topic to another. The couple is quickly lost in the heat of these emotionally charged quarrels. (See Retzinger, 1991, for an analysis of the verbal exchanges of this couple, described as Roxanne and Brian.)

Although Rosalyn and Brad's quarrel is highly provocative in itself, physiological arousal plays a part as well. Disorders may be rooted in how our bodies respond to the situations we face. Any response involves not only the brain but a complicated series of physical reactions that are regulated by the **autonomic nervous system.** The autonomic nervous system regulates the motivational and emotional states of the body and monitors its basic physiology. It consists of two branches, the sympathetic and the parasympathetic systems. The **sympathetic system** mediates the body's response to stress, speeding up the heart rate, increasing blood pressure, and generally preparing for action. This preparation has been called the fight-or-flight response, and it is usually accompanied by an increased flow of adrenaline. After the threat or the need for the physical response has passed, the **parasympathetic system** calms the nervous system down, working to conserve the body's resources and restore homeostasis; it slows the heart rate, reduces blood pressure, and prepares the body for rest. Sometimes these two systems work together, and sometimes they work in opposition.

When the brain perceives an event as stressful, a series of reactions begins. First, the hypothalamus releases hormones that stimulate portions of the pituitary gland, which in turn releases hormones that are transported in the blood to the adrenal cortex, where they activate secretion of the hormone cortisol. Cortisol has a broad range of effects, such as increasing energy availability and modulating emotions. When the sympathetic nervous system is activated, as during a heated quarrel, the adrenal glands are stimulated; a burst of energy from the adrenals affects the body's overall arousal, including the muscles; and, if the parasympathetic system does not calm the system down, excessive unwanted emotional arousal can interfere. Both personal adjustment and interpersonal relationships can suffer. For example, some cases of violent outbursts have been linked to hyperarousal, and problems such as essential hypertension (high blood pressure) and panic disorder involve physiological responses.

Genes and Their Expression

Why would some people respond to stress in a way that makes the situation worse? One possibility is that these people are simply born with a system that overreacts; they inherit a biological predisposition to be easily over-aroused and highly emotional. The idea that mental disorders might be inherited is a very old one, but recently scientists have gained new information about exactly what people may inherit from their parents and how biological inheritance occurs. Indeed, current research suggests that certain traits, temperaments, and even specific disorders can have a genetic component (Bouchard et al., 1990).

Chromosomes carry codes for the potential expression of characteristics in their basic units, **genes.** Each human cell normally contains twenty-three pairs of chromosomes. Genes control innumerable characteristics such as eye color, hair color, male baldness, and colorblindness, to mention only a few.

In later chapters we discuss genetic contributions to psychological disorders. For now, let's use the color of the coat of Labrador retrievers to take a closer look at genetic transmission (see Figure 2.5). Labrador retrievers are typically black or yellow: The color of the coat is inherited. The black coat is the dominant characteristic, and yellow is the recessive characteristic. Black Labradors carry either two dominant genes for black or the black-dominant gene in tandem with a recessive gene for yellow. The coat color of the progeny of two black Labradors depends on the genetic background of the parents. If both parents carry paired genes for black (are pure for that color), all puppies will also be pure for black. If one of the parents carries a recessive gene for yellow, the puppies will all be black, but one-half of them will have the genetic makeup of one parent — pure for black — and one-half will have the genetic makeup of the other parent — appearing black but carrying one dominant and one recessive gene. The color of the coat is determined by the combination of dominant and recessive genes. Keep in mind that the fractions used in discussions of genetic probabilities apply on the average and are only approximations in any given mating.

Is human behavior like the color of Labradors? Do genes carry a code for psychological disorders? Clinicians have long known that some forms of psychological disorder run in families. Researchers have also noted that **monozygotic** (identical) **twins** who share the same genetic makeup are more likely to share the same

Figure 2.5   Genetic Transmission

The basic operation of genetic transmission is apparent in the color of the coat of Labrador retrievers. The first litter is solid black, with no yellow genes. In the second litter, one parent carries the yellow gene; all puppies are black, but two carry the yellow gene. In the third litter, both parents carry the yellow gene, and one of the offspring has a yellow coat. When one parent is yellow and the other is black — as in litters 4 and 5 — the coat depends on whether the black parent carried a gene for yellow. When both parents are yellow, the puppies will be yellow.

disorder than are **dizygotic** (fraternal) **twins** who share only 50 percent of their genes — like any other sibling pairs. For example, the average rate for schizophrenia in the full population is 1 percent. Yet studies have shown that when one monozygotic twin has schizophrenia, in about 40 to 50 percent of the cases the other twin will also have schizophrenia. Under these same circumstances only 5 to 15 percent of dizygotic twins will have the disorder (Gottesman & Shields, 1972; Gottesman, McGuffin & Farmer, 1987).

The data on schizophrenia are informative, but will scientists find alterations of gene functions or unique combinations of genes that help account for other forms of disorder? Will a single gene or multiple genes be found responsible for some psychological disturbance? In Chapter 5 we describe in more detail the search for clues to genetic transmission.

Biological Predispositions and Interactions with the Environment

In the schizophrenia example just cited, notice that the predisposing genetic factors do not account for all of the cases of schizophrenia. If the disorder were entirely genetic, then both members of an identical twin pair would receive an identical diagnosis. In fact, nongenetic factors, such as sociocultural influences and stress, also play a role.

Sociocultural Influences   Biology does not operate in a vacuum. According to the sociocultural view, psychopathology, as well as an individual's personality, reflects the larger society. Proponents of this view consider many influences: societal values and norms, economic status, discrimination, and technology.

Cultures have their own established and sanctioned patterns of behavior. Most members of a culture share certain behavior patterns, and cultural forces actively shape members' responses to the environment. Consider the example of authority figures. In most cultures, authority figures are given respect and compliance. Some subcultures, however, perceive authority figures as enemies and condemn cooperation with them. As another example, note that people are often unaware of the influence of their culture until they come into contact with people from another culture. For example, when Americans meet someone, they usually expect that the person will be friendly and outgoing. In contrast, when members of the Oriental culture meet someone, they expect that person to be restrained and deferential.

According to the most extreme sociocultural perspective, cultural relativity, one cannot apply the same standards and criteria for abnormality to all societies. Although this stance is not widely held, sociocultural factors cannot be disregarded. Some influences on our adjustment do indeed seem to be tied to the culture in which we live. Consider the situation of a child who is raised in a war-torn city amid constant bombings, threats, and exposure to violence and death. She is escorted to and from school and not allowed to play outside. Compare this social context to the social context of a middle-class American child who has a secure home and rides her bicycle to and from school and her friends' houses. The experiences of these two youths could lead to very different levels of psychological adjustment in adulthood. Contemporary models of psychopathology do not directly attribute disorders to social or cultural factors, but they recognize the role of sociocultural influences and encourage the study of psychopathology in differing cultures and with diverse ethnic groups.

The Diathesis-Stress Model   The **diathesis-stress model** proposes an active interaction between genetic and other biological predispositions and stressful environmental influences. **Diatheses** are predisposing vulnerability factors, which include biological determinants and characteristic manner of responding. **Stress** is the current environmental factors that can, but do not always, contribute to the development of abnormal behavior. Common stressors may include school, work, or marital failures; loss of loved ones; accidents; and simply taking on too much responsibility. According to this model, diathesis and stress are complementary; neither is sufficient by itself to cause abnormal behavior (National Advisory Mental Health Council, 1995). Over the years psychologists have remained interested in such issues as the relative potency of environmental and biological factors and whether the biological side of the human organism can be modified (Lerner, 1984).

Applying the diathesis-stress model to schizophrenia, we find that predisposing factors are involved, but they do not account for all of the data. Indeed, development of this abnormality also depends on the contribution of stresses and related environmental influences. Recall Matt, the convenience-store clerk mentioned at the outset of the chapter. As it turned out, he had a family history of mental disorder and was himself at risk for psychopathology. The car accident he was involved in, as well as his daily conflicted relationships with customers, combined to produce the stress that preceded his need to be hospitalized. As noted diathesis-stress theorist Paul Meehl described in 1962, only those persons with a genetic makeup conducive to schizophrenia can develop the disorder, but they will become schizophrenic only if exposed to a detrimental learning environment and stressful life experience. Thus, complex interactions between the individual and the environment shape the behavior of the person — sometimes in dysfunctional ways that contribute to psychological disorders.

FOCUS ON RESEARCH

Can the Role of the Environment in Development Be Experimentally Shown?

Research on the interaction of genetic and environmental influences often employs animals as research subjects. Consider the important work reported in *Science* by C. K. Govind and Joanne Pearce (1986) of the Life

Three generations of an Indian family. Can you recognize a familial similarity? One component of the biomedical model is the argument that there is a genetic contribution to human behavior.

Sciences Division at the University of Toronto. The topic of the research was lobsters and the function of their claws — but the findings have intriguing implications for humans as well.

Govind and Pearce were aware that lobsters have two claws and that these claws are identical in the early stages of life: The claws as well as the muscles that close them are symmetric. Both claws look like cutters and both have a central band of fast muscle fibers sandwiched between slow muscle fibers. But later in development the two claws separate into different types of claws: (1) a stout crusher claw with slow muscle fibers and (2) a slender cutter claw with largely fast fibers. What determines which claw becomes a crusher and which becomes a cutter? Will the right-hand claws be crushers and the left-hand claws cutters? Is the destiny of each claw preprogrammed, or can the environment influence development of a crusher or a cutter?

The researchers raised some lobsters in a plastic tray without materials to manipulate and exercise their claws; the claws on these lobsters did not differentiate and remained symmetric. Among lobsters raised in an environment that did allow exercise, the claws developed asymmetrically. Evidently the materials that allowed exercise provided the needed opportunity for developing distinct claws and different claw functions.

To further test the hypothesis that environmental opportunity for activity contributed to claw differentiation, the researchers hand-held some lobsters and gave them added opportunities to exercise a specific claw. Usually, the exercised claw became the crusher. But when both claws were exercised, no differentiation took place. Thus, it is the relative level of activity of one claw over the other that determines its eventual status. The claw on the side with the greatest activity becomes the crusher; the claw on the side with less activity becomes the cutter. Exercise was essential to the differential claw development.

The upshot of these crusher-versus-cutter studies is that both genetic and environmental factors contribute to development. On the one hand, genetic predispositions set certain restrictions on environmental influences (the environment does not seem capable of producing claws that clap, for instance). On the other hand, the environment determines which claw will be a cutter and which will be a crusher, or whether the claws will differ at all. Among humans, too, genetic predispositions set boundaries for the influence of the environment.

Pros and Cons of the Biomedical Model

Proponents of the biomedical model have identified how infectious agents, structural abnormalities, biochemical imbalances, and genetic predispositions might produce psychological disorders. Schizophrenia, for example, has a biological component. Indeed, important discoveries have linked disturbed functioning and biological malfunctions.

In addition, the biomedical model of psychological disorder has stimulated advances in medical treatments that have had enormously positive effects. As we explore in the chapters on specific psychological abnormalities, psychoactive medications have helped countless people better manage their schizophrenia, depression, and manic-depression.

As biological influences become newly identified, however, it is important that they not be deemed the sole causes of disorder. Instead, they must be recognized as merely some among *several* causal factors. Accordingly, throughout this book we emphasize the need for integrated models linking biological predisposition with social and psychological factors that lead to disorder in some individuals but not in others.

The biomedical model also has several potential shortcomings. First, it appears to be more relevant to some problems than to others. A widespread and exclusive focus on biological processes could lead therapists to ignore or downplay the contributions of, say, personal learning histories, ongoing interpersonal conflicts, or cognitive misperceptions in the search for defective genes.

A second area of concern is gender differences. A shortcoming of the biomedical model is that it does not, with few exceptions, explain (or address) gender differences. There is little information, from the biomedical perspective, on gender differences. To what degree do cultural values and social pressures contribute to these differences? And — important for the biological approach — are there physiological factors that contribute to the observed gender differences?

Third, the scientific status of biological factors as causal agents in disorder is far from established. The discoveries of neurochemical or other biological differences between people with disorders and normal people, for example, do not indicate whether these differences are causes or merely by-products of the disorder. Ethical considerations prevent controlled experimental studies with human beings in which some people are subjected to biological damage. Therefore, much of the scientific research on biological processes must infer a causal relationship that may not be accurate. Similarly, the success of medications in treating disorders is not itself evidence that the disorders arose from biological causes. We can successfully treat a fever with aspirin, for example, but that does not mean that the lack of aspirin was the underlying cause of the fever or that aspirin treats the actual underlying microorganism that is causing the body to create the fever.

BEHAVIORISM: THE LEARNING MODELS

One of the most rapidly growing approaches to the study of abnormality since the 1960s concerns the manner in which behavior is acquired or learned. Psychologists had long studied the processes involved in learning, but the application of the learning process to the understanding and modification of disturbed behavior is a more modern occurrence.

Behavior occurs as a consequence of its having been learned in the past. Regarding Hennie's case, for example, behaviorally oriented psychologists would underscore the role of reinforcement, pleasant events, and Hennie's learning history, as well as the role of the current social and interpersonal environment, as forces contributing to his depression.

The **behavioral model** emphasizes the observable behavior of the person and the environmental factors that maintain the action. Behaviorists believe that when other influencing factors are constant, the differences that exist among people are the result of differential learning. These learned behavior patterns, both normal and abnormal, are influenced greatly by the existing environment, and changes in the environmental influences will change the behavior pattern (Masters, Burish, Hollon & Rimm, 1987; O'Leary & Wilson, 1987). Three forms of learning associated with psychological disorders are classical conditioning, operant conditioning, and observational learning.

Classical Conditioning

Classical conditioning is a basic form of learning in which once-neutral stimuli come to evoke involuntary responses. Classical conditioning involves both conditioned (learned) and unconditioned stimuli and responses. If you found yourself stuck in a dangerous location, such as on the yellow lines dividing traffic on a major highway, then your being afraid would be perfectly normal. However, people can learn to be afraid of things and situations when it is not normal to be fearful. Classical conditioning can help us understand the development of these fears.

A Russian physiologist named Ivan Pavlov (1928) discovered what we currently refer to as classical conditioning. Serendipity played a role in Pavlov's discovery. While investigating salivation in dogs, Pavlov and his associates gave them meat powder, and the dogs salivated naturally. Soon, however, they noticed that the dogs began to salivate as the researchers were about to provide the meat powder. Soon after, the dogs salivated at the sight of the researchers and the sound of their footsteps. The dogs had learned to anticipate the meat powder. Pavlov described the salivation as conditioned or learned, marking the discovery of the classically conditioned response.

A realistically dangerous situation produces fear without prior learning or conditioning. Because this fear occurs without learning or conditioning, the dangerous *situation* is called an **unconditioned stimulus (UCS)** and the *reaction,* fear, is the **unconditioned response (UCR)**. They occur naturally. A neutral stimulus alone does not

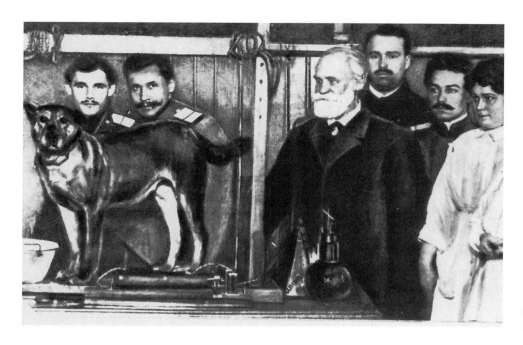

Pavlov used dogs and the salivation response to study the process of conditioning.

produce a response. But a neutral stimulus repeatedly paired with a dangerous situation becomes a **conditioned stimulus (CS)** that in itself can lead to the UCR, fear. When the neutral situation thus becomes capable of producing fear, the fear it produces is called a **conditioned response (CR)**. Conditioned (learned) responses are what particularly interest researchers in psychopathology. For example, a specific piece of music played repeatedly in a dangerous situation becomes itself capable of producing fear. Think of the two-note theme from the movie *Jaws*. This music is a CS because it has acquired fear-producing properties via conditioning, and the fear it produces is a CR (see Figure 2.6).

Researchers have conducted thousands of experiments with animals and human beings to document how conditioning takes place. Recent theory suggests that the learner acquires actual knowledge about relationships among events (Rescorla, 1988). One oft-cited study of the classical conditioning of emotions was conducted more than seventy-five years ago (Watson & Rayner, 1920). Though by today's research standards the study lacks rigor and is ethically questionable, it remains important as a classic case of conditioned emotional reactions.

In this classic study, an eleven-month-old boy — Little Albert — acquired a conditioned fear. Albert was first introduced to a tame white rat and was reported to show no fear. Just as he reached out to touch the rat, however, an experimenter struck metal to metal and produced a loud noise. The noise startled Albert. When he again reached toward the animal, the experimenter again created the loud noise. Soon Little Albert was afraid of the white rat. In this instance, the loud noise was a UCS, which led to startle and fear — the UCR.

After repeated pairings, the white rat itself led to the startle and fear and became a CS for the conditioned fear response (CR). Now, when shown the rat, Albert quickly moved away from it; he also showed some fear to stimuli that resembled the white animal. Via classical conditioning, Albert acquired an emotional reaction to a stimulus that previously had not produced a reaction.

Through conditioning processes, each of us has developed fears, preferences, and other reactions. Many researchers have used classical conditioning to explain the development of psychological disorders such as phobias, which are fears of specific objects or situations (see Chapter 6).

Classical conditioning can help explain otherwise perplexing phenomena. Consider the following case. A mother brought her infant to a hospital for a routine operation. The infant had been breastfed from birth. The hospital staff asked the mother to shift to bottle-feeding at the start of the hospitalization — a reasonable request because breastfeeding was difficult while the child was in the hospital. The child was reluctant to take the bottle — an understandable reaction in a new environment with the mother not present — and the hospital staff began to use a feeding tube. Repeatedly, when the bottle was presented but not readily taken by the child, the feeding tube was inserted into the child's mouth. The bottle, initially a relatively neutral stimulus, had come to be associated with the aversive insertion of the feeding tube. The child became classically conditioned to reject the bottle.

Fortunately, classical conditioning can also be applied in an effective treatment. In this case, a music box was used as a cue for the child: When the music

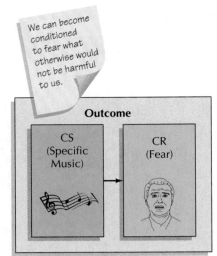

We can become conditioned to fear what otherwise would not be harmful to us.

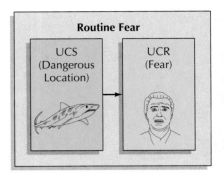

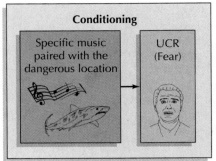

Figure 2.6 **The Classical Conditioning Process**

In the classical conditioning process, a once-neutral stimulus comes to acquire the properties of an unconditioned stimulus and produces conditioned responses.

played there was no forced feeding. Gradually, during the music, the bottle was introduced and eventually accepted by the child — another case of classical conditioning. Within two weeks the child was feeding quite well.

Operant Conditioning

Unlike research in classical conditioning, which focuses on the effects of *pairings of stimuli* on behavior, **operant conditioning** is concerned with the *consequences of behavior* — with the probability that a response will be increased or decreased when it is followed by reinforcement or punishment. One of the founders of the operant approach was Edward Thorndike (1874–1949). Like Pavlov, Thorndike (1898) used animals to study the acquisition of behavior.

In Thorndike's classic work, a cat was placed in a box fitted with a lever that would open the door. The cat was deprived of food, and a piece of fish was placed outside the closed box. Thorndike recorded the time it took the cat to escape from the box, noting that the cat's initial irregular pattern of escape soon became regular and prompt. The cat had developed the ability to push the lever and escape from the box to receive the food. Thorndike believed that the learning was produced by the consequence — getting the desired food.

When responses lead to satisfying consequences, the responses are strengthened and more likely to occur in the future. Conversely, when responses lead to unsatisfying consequences, they are not strengthened and are less likely to occur again in the future. This, then, was Thorndike's *law of effect*.

B. F. Skinner (1904–1990) further developed the study of behavioral consequences. Skinner (1953) used the principle of *reinforcement* to describe how behavioral consequences can strengthen the probability of a behavior's recurrence. Numerous contingencies have been described and researched (some of these are listed in Table 2.2), and Skinner's operant conditioning has had significant effects on psychological research and theory (see *American Psychologist*, special issue, 1992).

Punishment occurs when a response leads to a negative outcome. Consider the dog who jumps on a guest and is swatted on the rump, or the misbehaving student who is corrected in front of peers in class. Each of these examples illustrates the principle of *punishment*: Following an unwanted behavior with a negative outcome reduces the likelihood that the unwanted behavior will occur in the future. Although punishment can have desirable effects, it can also be detrimental. Indeed, when harsh or excessive, it can cause serious inhibitions. A child who is punished too often may become overly withdrawn, unwilling to do anything, and potentially depressed.

When positive consequences follow a behavior, the behavior is *positively reinforced* (rewarded) and becomes more likely to occur again in the future. Maladaptive and desirable behaviors alike can be acquired through their consequences. When a child screams for a toy in the toy store, she may get her way because the parent simply wants to quiet her. However, the child is also learning that the screaming behavior produces rewards.

Complex behaviors need not be directly reinforced for the behaviors to be learned. Consider the process of rewarding successive approximations, called **shaping**. This process does not require the learner to produce an entirely new response pattern to receive the reinforcement. Rather, shaping is gradual, providing reinforce-

Table 2.2   Avoidance Learning and Other Contingencies

Punishment	A response leads to a negative outcome.
Reward	A response leads to a positive outcome.
Escape	A response stops a negative condition.
Avoidance	A response prevents a negative condition.

As an outgrowth of the operant conditioning approach, the role of contingencies in learning is now better understood by psychologists. Here are select examples of contingencies.

ment for several interim steps. As the learner masters a new step, reinforcement shifts so that it is provided only after this new last step. Thus, for example, an individual does not learn all at once to be loud and vulgar — the undesirable behaviors and actions can be the result of a shaping process that has taken years to complete.

Reinforcements buttress behavior, but more reinforcement is not necessarily better. In fact, behaviors that are followed by **partial reinforcement,** or reinforcement given only some of the time, are actually more persistent than behaviors that have been maintained under conditions of continuous reinforcement. It may take longer for a behavior to be acquired through partial reinforcement, but once acquired, the behavior is more likely to continue. Behaviors that are continuously reinforced go away more quickly when reinforcement is discontinued.

Behaviors that are maladaptive may become more persistent over time as a result of partial reinforcement. For example, people who gamble do not know when the reward will occur. They may rarely win and lose money overall, but — operating by partial reinforcement — they continue to gamble. A behavioral analysis of pathological gambling rests on the notion than an occasional win — partial reinforcement — can maintain maladaptive and even self-defeating behavior.

Both the shaping of behavior and the persistence of behavior resulting from partial reinforcement have important implications for child development (Gewirtz & Pelaez-Nogueras, 1992) and abnormal psychology. For instance, complex, disturbed behaviors need not themselves be reinforced; rather, it can be shaped over time as small portions of the maladaptive pattern are reinforced. An overall pattern of aggression, for example, might be shaped by rewards for successive approximations of violence.

Mike sat quietly, slumped in a chair and gazing out a window, as the principal dialed his mother's work phone number. It was his third visit to the office for disciplinary action, and he knew that he was about to be suspended from school for a fight in the hallway. His junior year in high school was not going well — his grades were poor, he didn't make the varsity football team, and he wasn't exactly popular — but he really didn't care.

Although there were many and varied reasons for Mike's situation, and many factors that contributed to his aggressive behavior pattern, a few of the early learning experiences described by his mother, Carol, stood out. It seems that Mike, as early as age three, was being encouraged and taught by his father, Jerry, to "fight for his rights." Carol noted that when, at age seven, Mike was roughed up by a neighborhood boy who was a year older, Jerry was really upset and taught Mike to fistfight. Carol also recalled that Jerry wouldn't discipline Mike or try to limit his fighting; instead, he would pat him on the back for being tough. Mike wasn't a very thoughtful boy and couldn't express his emotions well — instead, he had learned that fighting was the solution to problems.

A second type of reinforcement is **negative reinforcement,** in which the likelihood of a behavior is increased by the removal of a negative (unpleasant) stimulus or situation. For example, if you politely ask a roommate to turn off the television so you can study, and your roommate does so immediately, the likelihood of your making a similar polite request in the future is increased. The polite request is reinforced by the removal of the unwanted (aversive) television distraction.

Additional stimulus-response relationships include escape and avoidance. An *escape response* stops a negative condition, whereas an *avoidance response* prevents a negative condition. Consider the following example:

Sue was up late the night before and is now sleeping with an alarm clock set to go off at 7 A.M. When the loud and aversive alarm rings, Sue reaches out of bed and hits the snooze button (an escape response). The snooze button turns off (stops) the alarm for ten minutes. Sue returns to sleep but notes that the alarm will sound again at 7:10. When it does she slaps the snooze button a second time (another escape response) for an additional ten minutes of sleep. The alarm is now programmed to go off at 7:20, only this time Sue looks at the clock at 7:19 and presses the snooze button to prevent it from sounding at all (an avoidance response).

In this case, the avoidance response worked and was sensible; however, people can also learn avoidance responses that are not functional. They make responses that they believe will prevent an aversive situation but that, in fact, do not. The avoidance response offers a remarkable explanation for some of the anxiety disorders. Consider the case of an adolescent girl who attends a school dance and is teased by a group of students. The teasing soon becomes harshly delivered ridicule, and it badly hurts her feelings. To stop the pain, she leaves the dance (an escape response). Because of this experience,

Seminal behavioral researcher B. F. Skinner.

in the future she is more likely to run away from potential ridicule and, perhaps, to avoid the presence of her peers. Eventually, staying away becomes associated with anxiety reduction — an avoidance response that prevents the experience of unwanted emotions. The avoidance response may continue even when fellow students are no longer likely to tease and ridicule her. Patterns of behavior such as these are the result of **avoidance learning.** They occur, for example, in avoidant personality disorders and social phobias, leading individuals to avoid feared social or performance situations even though these behaviors may interfere with social and work relationships. Avoidance responses are persistent; unfortunately, individuals who have acquired such habits often continue to use them when they are no longer needed.

Modeling

Why was I embarrassed when my then five-year-old son dunked his croissant in a glass of milk at a somewhat formal brunch? The answer: I know where he learned to dunk breakfast pastry! Dunking is not genetic, nor did I ever reward him for dunking. He has simply watched me dunk various pastries into my morning coffee and, through observation, has learned to do the same.

Stanford University psychologist Albert Bandura pioneered the analysis of **observational learning,** or **modeling,** which is the process of learning behavior by observing others (Bandura, 1969). This learning occurs without any direct rewards or reinforcement — it is learning through imitation. A tennis trainee who watches the coach demonstrate (or model) the desired motions of a serve and then practices what she has seen is using observational learning.

Many behavior patterns can be traced to observational experiences. For instance, how little or how much alcohol a person consumes can be influenced by the drinking behavior that the individual observes in others.

In one study, alcoholics who observed several confederates consume wine at high or low rates adjusted their own wine consumption according to the models' consumption (DeRicco & Neimann, 1980).

Experiments by Bandura and his colleagues (e.g., Rosenthal & Bandura, 1978) suggested that aggressive behavior can result from observing aggression. Adult models punched and abused a "Bobo doll" while children watched. These children were then given an opportunity to play with the doll and, unlike children who observed adults behaving nonaggressively, were found to display the violent aggressive behavior that the adult had modeled. No direct instructions or external rewards were offered; rather, the observation of aggressive actions led to similar aggression (Bandura, 1973).

Observational learning ties in with **social learning theory** (Bandura, 1986), which proposes that behavior is the product of both external stimulus events and internal cognitive processes. An individual's social context is important because it provides many opportunities for behaviors to be observed and imitated. When researchers report that certain disorders run in families, it is often difficult to separate the effects of genetics from the

Observational learning is a powerful component of the behavioral perspective. Like someone instructing you in how to tie your shoelaces, this Cherokee elder teaches about arrowheads using demonstration. By attending, rehearsing to herself, and practicing, the observer can learn complex behaviors and skills.

effects of the shared social learning environment. Recall Andrew, the boy with conduct disorder mentioned at the outset of the chapter. Social learning explanations would discount his head injury and downplay his genetic inheritance, underscoring instead the role of behaviors that have been modeled for and observed by him. Having spent time with his uncle who has been arrested several times, Andrew has been exposed to and learned a troublesome pattern of behavior.

Pros and Cons of the Behavioral Model

The behavioral approach has produced voluminous research, explanations for the development of abnormality, and specific methods for treating psychological disorders. Because the model focuses on the person's environment, it is especially sensitive to cultural and social factors. Similarly, because it deals with the learning history and environment of individuals, it is implicitly concerned with ethnic and gender influences.

Learning explanations of psychological disorders, however, have been criticized as oversimplified and unrealistic. For instance, behavioral studies of aggression and violence often rely on a count of aggressive acts. But aggression, critics argue, is more than the frequency of specific actions: It results from complex causes including biological, familial, and cultural factors, and to explain them solely in terms of prior learning is too delimiting. Science requires that human behavior be reduced to small units that can be measured, but this reduction has been criticized as distorting the complexities of real human behavior.

A second criticism of behaviorism is that its attempt to explain maladaptive behavior without considering the unobservable aspects of human existence downplays the role of cognition in the onset and treatment of abnormality. This criticism, however, has been addressed by an emergent integrative model — cognitive behaviorism — that we will discuss later in this chapter. Cognitive behaviorism holds that human information processing can be studied scientifically along with observable behavior, thus acknowledging the richness of human thought and its role in human action.

THE COGNITIVE MODEL: DISORDERED THOUGHT PROCESSING

Contemporary psychology is very much concerned with human cognition — how human beings perceive, recognize, attend, reason, and judge. These aspects of cognition have come to play important roles in attempts to

Two perspectives on the sleeping dog. The cognitive model of psychological adjustment emphasizes one's cognitive processing regarding people and events. One sleeping dog, whose behavior is unknown, is seen from two diverging cognitive perspectives. (Artist: Peter J. Mikulka)

understand the development of psychological disorders. The **cognitive model** emphasizes that cognitive functioning contributes to emotional or behavioral distress.

Misperceptions of social situations, a tendency to think negatively without sufficient data, and a habit of inaccurately blaming oneself for mishaps are examples of dysfunctional cognitive processing. The cognitive model emphasizes the individual's perceptions, reasoning, and thinking — and, for example, would see faulty thinking as contributing to Hennie's depression.

Cognition is best understood in terms of cognitive structure, cognitive content, cognitive operations (processes), and cognitive products (Ingram & Kendall, 1986). **Cognitive structures** refer to the internal organization of information, and **cognitive content** is the actual material that a person is processing, including the things that we say to ourselves. **Cognitive processes** are the operations or manner of operation by which the system inputs, stores, transforms, and governs the output of information. **Cognitive products** are the conclusions that people reach after processing an event. This terminology provides one way to relate the various cognitive functions to the causation, maintenance, and modification of dysfunctional processing of information.

Jonathan is a 24-year-old man who is unemployed, lives with his mother, has few friends, and stays in his home most of every day. Jonathan has developed a characteristic way of evaluating the world — a cognitive structure. The theme of this structure is the potential of threat. Jonathan can't seem to do anything without worrying about threat and danger. Like most anxious individuals, he sees threat and impending danger (Beck & Emery, 1985) in even the most innocuous and appealing activities. As a result, he perceives as threatening situations and events that are not stressful for most people. When Jonathan is introduced to someone, he views the experience not as a chance to make a friend but, rather, as a risk that puts him in jeopardy. In such situations Jonathan frequently says to himself, "What will he think of me or do to me? Will he try to hurt me?"

As another example, note that most of us think of dogs as pets and evaluate them in terms of their breed, how well behaved they are, what tricks they can do, and the potential companionship they can provide. But people with a fear of dogs are anxious when near them and view dogs on only one dimension — how ferocious they are (Landau, 1980). According to the cognitive model, cognitive structures such as these influence the perceptions of situations, the people in such situations, and the likelihood of events to follow.

Cognitive content is the actual material that the person is processing, including the self-talk that an individual engages in. Characteristic of an anxious person's self-talk are questions such as "What's going to happen?" "What am I going to do now?" "How can I get out of this situation?" and "Why does this happen to me?"

Anxious persons process information differently from normal persons. For example, they often misperceive the demands of the environment. The anxious person may hear a routine conversation and process the information in a distorted way. If the conversation is about the latest fashions, for example, a comment such as "Do you believe what some people wear these days?" may then be processed inappropriately by the anxious person. Being highly self-focused, the anxious person could think that the comment was about him — "That person does not like the way I dress."

Cognitive products, the conclusions that people reach, include attributions, the way people explain the causes of behavior. Most people recognize that there are many causes of behavior, only some of which are in their control. But the anxious person may conclude from the previous comment about fashions that he has to dress differently to please other people. He may conclude that he isn't generally liked or accepted. He may also conclude that he has to try exceptionally hard, or may worry endlessly that he really doesn't have what it takes to be socially successful. Ultimately, the anxious person may conclude that he must do more to succeed. He attributes the need for this extra work to a personal lack of ability, a conclusion that may be based on faulty processing.

A further aspect of cognitive functioning is the distinction between cognitive distortions and cognitive deficiencies (Kendall, 1993). **Cognitive deficiencies** refer to an absence of thinking — as when an individual's responses and emotional states do not benefit from careful thinking or planning. In contrast, **cognitive distortions** refer to thought processes that are dysfunctional, such as active misperceptions and misconstruals of the environment.

Cognitive distortions have been implicated in depression (Beck, 1976; Ingram, 1984), schizophrenia, and several other abnormalities (see Dobson & Kendall, 1993; Ingram, 1986). And cognitive deficiencies, such as the interpersonal problem-solving deficits and information-seeking deficits of impulsive children, have been confirmed by research in child psychopathology.

Cognitive Distortions and the Emotional Disorders

Two major systems within the cognitive model of abnormality are Albert Ellis's (1962) rational-emotive view and Aaron T. Beck's (1967) cognitive theory of depression. Ellis offers his notions about rationality and emotions as a general explanation of emotional maladjustment, whereas Beck's cognitive theory is a theory of depression. In both models, emotional and behavioral distress is linked to distorted ("faulty") cognitive processing.

Irrational Beliefs Ellis believes that maladaptive behavior results when people operate on misguided and inaccurate assumptions, or **irrational beliefs,** such as "the idea that one should be thoroughly competent, adequate, and achieving in all possible respects if one is to consider oneself worthwhile" (Ellis & Harper, 1975). The eleven irrational beliefs originally catalogued by Ellis in 1962 are said to be linked to the misery in the lives of many people (see Table 2.3).

The misery derives not only from the lack of validity of the beliefs but also from their imperative "demanding, commanding" nature, which Ellis has characterized as "*must*urbatory ideology" (Ellis, 1977). More recently, Warren and Zgourides (1991) also noted that a central feature of the list of irrational beliefs is their "must" quality [italics in original]:

1. I *must* perform well and/or win the approval of others, or else it's awful, and I am inadequate or worthless as a person.

2. You *must* treat me fairly and considerately and not unduly frustrate me, or it's awful, and you are a rotten person.

3. My life conditions *must* give me the things I want easily and with little frustration and must keep me from harm, or else life is unbearable, and I can't be happy at all.

According to Ellis, it is not the event itself that causes distress and produces psychological dysfunction but, rather, the manner in which the person interprets the event. This basic postulate of the theory is expressed in Ellis's A-B-C model in which private *beliefs* (B) about particular *activating events* or situations (A) determine the emotional *consequences* (C) that are experienced

Table 2.3   Irrational Beliefs: Ellis's Core Cognitive Problems

1. It is a dire necessity for an adult human being to be loved or approved by virtually every significant person in his community.

2. One should be thoroughly competent, adequate, and achieving in all possible respects if one is to consider oneself worthwhile.

3. Certain people are bad, wicked, or villainous, and they should be severely blamed and punished for their villainy.

4. It is awful and catastrophic when things are not the way one would very much like them to be.

5. Human unhappiness is externally caused, and people have little or no ability to control their sorrows and disturbance.

6. If something is or may be dangerous or fearsome, one should be terribly concerned about it and should keep dwelling on the possibility of its occurring.

7. It is easier to avoid than to face certain life difficulties and self-responsibilities.

8. One should be dependent on others and need someone stronger than oneself on whom to rely.

9. One's past history is an all-important determiner of one's present behavior, and because something once affected one's life, it should indefinitely have a similar effect.

10. One should become quite upset over other people's problems and disturbance.

11. There is invariably a right, precise, and perfect solution to human problems, and it is catastrophic if this perfect solution is not found.

Source: Ellis (1962, pp. 60–88).

Ellis (1962, 1971) designed rational-emotive theory on the principle that psychological problems result from irrational beliefs. Living one's life with irrational assumptions can result in unwanted consequences. This is the original list of irrational beliefs that he linked to emotional problems.

(see Figure 2.7). Although individuals are generally acutely aware of their affective responses at point C, they frequently fail to attend to the beliefs that mediate and determine them. When these silent assumptions are inaccurate and framed in absolute or imperative terms, psychological maladjustment is likely to result.

For instance, imagine that a man believes that it is a dire necessity for an adult human being to be loved or approved by virtually every significant other person in his community. Imagine also that this man meets a woman who lives several houses down the block and who complains that the fence he recently built in his yard doesn't fit or belong in the neighborhood. What is he to do? If he believes that he must be loved and accepted by all, then he is likely to be upset by the neighbor's disapproval of his fence. He may then give the neighbor's comment added attention and worry about whether to keep the fence and what he should have done to check that no others would be upset by the fence. In situations such as these, psychological distress, even marked anxiety and depression, can result from holding an irrational belief. It is as if the adage "I'll believe it

when I see it" has been rearranged as "I'll see it when I believe it!"

Cognition and Depression   According to Beck (1967, 1976, 1987), psychological problems "are not necessarily the product of mysterious, impenetrable forces but may result from commonplace processes such as faulty learning, making incorrect inferences on the basis of inadequate or incorrect information, [and] not distinguishing adequately between imagination and reality" (Kovacs & Beck, 1978). Beck suggested that early in life individuals begin to formulate rules about how the world works, and that, for depressed persons, these rules are based on erroneous ideas. An individual continues to distort experience through characteristic errors in perceiving and thinking about event outcomes, personal attributes, and interpersonal relations. These features define the *cognitive model of depression*.

In depression, thought content centers on the experience of major loss, the anticipation of negative outcomes, and the sense of being inadequate. Depressed persons, according to Beck, possess a negative cognitive

Founder of rational-emotive therapy Albert Ellis.

Prominent cognitive theorist Aaron T. Beck.

triad (Beck, 1967; J. Beck, 1995; Beck, Rush, Shaw & Emery, 1979; Hollon & Beck, 1979): "They regard *themselves* as deprived, defeated, or diseased, *their worlds* as full of roadblocks to their obtaining even minimal satisfaction, and *their futures* as devoid of any hope of gratification and promising only pain and frustration" (Hollon & Beck, 1979, p. 154; italics in original). Because these perceptions distort reality in unnecessarily fatalistic ways, Beck called them **negative distortions.** For example, a depressed person who drives to the store and finds it closed may say to herself "I'm a jerk, I should have known the store was closed. I can't do anything right." Because of these cognitive processing features, depressed persons perceive the world and event outcomes in terms of their own personal weaknesses and limitations.

Pros and Cons of the Cognitive Model

Although Ellis's unidirectional A-B-C model has been considered simplistic, albeit clinically useful (Arnkoff & Glass, 1982), some basic tenets of his theory have received a degree of empirical support. The evidence indicates a correlation between the presence of a variety of symptoms and disorders, on the one hand, and the tendency to endorse irrational beliefs on written surveys, on the other (Alden & Safran, 1978; Goldfried & Sobocinski, 1975). Other investigations have yielded mixed results, however (Craighead, Kimball & Rehak, 1979; Sutton-Simon & Goldfried, 1979), and Ellis (1989) has recently made several revisions to his formulations based on the theoretical and empirical advances made by others.

Nevertheless, the cognitive model has its critics. Some, for example, have noted that "thought" is only part of the complex system in which people exist; what about the biological and interpersonal factors that influence peoples' lives? Others (e.g., Coyne, 1982) have commented that it is not yet clear whether cognitive fac-

tors are causally linked to disorder: Perhaps cognitive dysfunctions are consequences or correlates of disorder rather than causes. These criticisms have led cognitive researchers to examine the role of dysfunctional thinking as a vulnerability factor: People with maladaptive cognitive processes are at risk for psychological disorder.

Critics of the cognitive model also point out that many psychologically disturbed people live under objectively horrible life circumstances that are not easily reduced to "irrational" thinking. Another concern voiced about cognitive factors has to do with the difficulty of verification. People can readily report their thoughts, but reporting their beliefs is fraught with difficulties (Smith & Allred, 1986). A person who holds irrational beliefs, for instance, may not be aware that they are irrational. These criticisms deserve further attention.

The Cognitive-Behavioral Model

The cognitive-behavioral model emphasizes learning process and the influences of the environment, while underscoring the importance of cognitive-mediating and information-processing factors in the development and

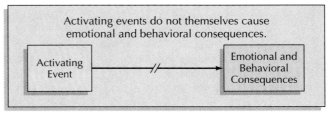

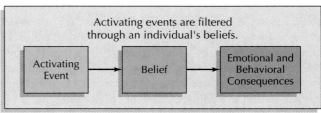

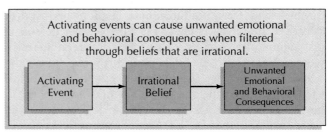

Figure 2.7   The ABCs of the Rational-Emotive Model

The ABCs of the rational-emotive model illustrate that emotional and behavioral consequences are caused not by activating events per se but by the mediating beliefs that are held by the person.

treatment of psychological disorders (Kendall, 1993). Accordingly, this model proposes treatments aimed at modifying the client's perceptions, evaluations, and processing of events, while employing behavioral performance–based procedures, modeling, and rewards (see Chapter 3).

The cognitive-behavioral model is therefore an integrated model (Alford & Norcross, 1991). Cognitive behaviorism is the result of movement from two perspectives (Kendall & Hollon, 1979): Behavioral theorists have shown increased interest in the cognitive aspects of psychopathology, and psychodynamic and cognitive theorists have shown greater concern for the performance-based learning aspects of psychological disorders. Not all members of each camp have come together, but both sides have shifted toward a middle ground; indeed, the cognitive-behavioral model has served as a functional vehicle to encourage such integration (Mahoney, 1977, 1993; Meichenbaum, 1977, 1993). For example, Ellis (1996) has retitled his approach from rational-emotive therapy (RET) to rational-emotive behavior therapy (REBT).

The increased acceptance of cognitive-behavioral approaches is evident in the impressive number of mental health professionals who describe themselves as cognitive-behavioral. As early as 1980 (Smith, 1980), many survey respondents identified with this label. More recently, these self-identifications have grown in number, with cognitive-behavioral ranking second only to eclecticism (the practice of drawing from various therapeutic viewpoints) as a preferred self-identification. The increasingly popular cognitive-behavioral model has made great strides toward integrating the seemingly conflicting theories that had previously dominated the study of psychopathology.

PSYCHODYNAMICS: AN INTRAPSYCHIC MODEL

In the section on the biomedical model, we saw how behavioral disorders, such as Hennie's depression, could be the result of biological factors. But what if Hennie's depression is not biologically based? A very different explanation for Hennie's depression points to conflict within the individual: A psychodynamically oriented psychologist might argue that the depression is a result of Hennie's anger turned inward.

Toward the end of the nineteenth century, Sigmund Freud broke new theoretical ground. Those before him had attributed abnormal behavior to magic or unfounded biological notions. Freud's lifetime efforts resulted in the first truly psychological theory of normal and abnormal behavior and development (Freud, 1913,

1914, 1917). This approach — labeled the **psychodynamic model** — emphasizes the role of internal mental processes and early childhood experiences.

Elements of Freud's Theory

The core elements in Freud's theory include analysis of mental structures in conflict, levels of consciousness, defense mechanisms, and stages of psychosexual development.

Mental Structures in Conflict Freud's theory is termed psychodynamic because it is based on the belief that personality and psychological disorders are the outcome of a dynamic interaction among mental structures. According to Freud, the human psyche consists of three mental structures — the ego, id, and superego. Thoughts, attitudes, and behaviors result from conflict among these structures, which Freud called **intrapsychic conflict.**

Suppose that you're employed part-time at a clothing store and have the opportunity to steal an expensive jacket that you couldn't otherwise afford. This situation might activate a variety of reactions and ideas. On the one hand, you might feel a strong urge to own the jacket and want to simply take it. You imagine how good you'll feel wearing it and how good you'll look to your friends. On the other hand, you may recoil from the idea of stealing because it is wrong and you will lose your self-respect for engaging in that behavior — and, furthermore, you might get caught. While you agonize between what you want and what you should do, you might begin to work out some other way of obtaining the jacket. Perhaps you could devise a savings plan, make a gradual-payment arrangement with the store, or ask several family members to chip in and get it for you as a birthday present.

The part of you that wants the jacket and would do anything to obtain it immediately is what Freud called the id (see Figure 2.8). The **id** is an unorganized reservoir of wishes and passions related to our basic sexual and aggressive drives; it strives for immediate gratification that bypasses the demands of reality, order, and logic. In the unrealistic world of the id, when it wants something it wants it now, without regard to consequences other than obtaining pleasure.

The part of you that would prohibit stealing the jacket Freud designated the superego. The **superego** is the storehouse of moral and ethical standards taught by parents and culture (what we generally think of as "conscience"). When these standards are violated, the superego generates guilt.

That you find a realistic means to resolve such conflicts — for example, by obtaining the jacket in an acceptable way — Freud attributes to the ego. The main function of the **ego** is to mediate the wishes of the id, the demands of reality, and the strictures of the superego. The ego attempts to achieve realistic gratification for the

The noted theorist Sigmund Freud.

id within the bounds of what is allowed by the superego. By regulating internal conflict and stress, the ego promotes adjustment. But, according to Freud, when the ego is not mediating effectively, conflict erupts and psychological abnormality emerges.

Levels of Consciousness The conflicts Freud described may occur at various levels of awareness. *Conscious* material is that which we are aware of at any given time, and it changes constantly. *Preconscious* thoughts are those that are easily made conscious by the effort to remember or by the spark of a related idea. You are now probably conscious that you are reading a book and, with a prompt, you could become conscious of the placement of your right foot. Some thoughts or memories are less accessible than others, but all preconscious thoughts can potentially become conscious. According to Freud, the ego and superego function at various levels of consciousness (see Figure 2.9).

A major portion of mental activity such as the id is **unconscious** — that is, mental activity outside a person's normal awareness. Thoughts and ideas that are unconscious, according to Freud, press for expression; but they may be withheld from consciousness because they are unacceptable to the ego or the superego. Sometimes, the ego is unable to gratify id impulses or even unwilling to allow them access to consciousness. When these impulses press for gratification or consciousness, the ego experiences intense anxiety.

Similarly, guilt may result from conflicts between the superego and id. The superego is constantly evaluat-

ing thoughts and behavior. Because part of the superego is unconscious, like the id, the superego can anticipate the activation of id impulses it finds unacceptable and flood the personality with feelings of guilt or even suggest self-punishment (Holzman, 1970). This unconscious activity of the superego may explain otherwise inexplicable guilt as well as feelings of worthlessness and subsequent depression.

Freud suggested that unconscious processes such as these may produce external behavior in addition to anxiety and guilt. *Conversion disorder* (see Chapter 7) is an example. Briefly, conversion disorder is a symptom that appears to be physical — for instance, a hearing loss — but has no physical cause. According to Freudian theory, the symptom (hearing loss) reflects the conversion of an unconscious psychological conflict into a physical complaint.

In short, Freud believed that unconscious thoughts and ideas profoundly affect thinking, emotions, and behavior. The implication is that we have motives we are not aware of and would probably not recognize or believe if they were pointed out to us. "Unconscious motivation" has been viewed both as one of Freud's greatest theoretical contributions and as an unverifiable and therefore weak component of the model.

Defense Mechanisms When the ego experiences discomfort induced by the superego, defense mechanisms emerge. **Defense mechanisms** are unconscious processes that try to protect the ego from anxiety or guilt provoked by unwanted or unacceptable impulses. These

Figure 2.8   Hypothetical Conversations Among the Id, Ego, and Superego

According to the psychodynamic model, the interactions of the id, ego, and superego are important in behavior. In these hypothetical conversations, the prototypic characterization of each psychic structure is described.

processes are defensive because they defend the self. By avoiding our unwanted feelings we avoid appearing unacceptable and having our security undermined; we make ourselves look better and put ourselves in a more flattering light. Yet these mechanisms may not be true to reality or even true to another observer.

One defense mechanism is **repression,** the unconscious but purposeful exclusion of painful thoughts or unacceptable desires or impulses from consciousness. A person might, for example, fail to recall — or repress — being mistreated as a child. Repression is often regarded as the primary defense mechanism.

Table 2.4 describes various defense mechanisms. According to Matthew Erdelyi (1985), defensive processes are the foundation on which the structure of psychodynamic theory rests. But experimental research on defense mechanisms has produced ambiguous results. For example, Erdelyi's review of the evidence regarding repression concluded that a person can experience selective rejection of information from awareness, that organisms tend to avoid aversive stimuli and to defend themselves against pain, and that some psychological processes can occur outside of a person's awareness. However, although each of these separate features of repression has some support, there still is no clear-cut demonstration of the entire phenomenon taking place all at once. Thus, although psychological studies have helped us understand complex mental processes, unconscious defensive processes remain a challenge for research.

According to Freud, if a person's defense mechanisms are unable to reduce or prevent unwanted anxious arousal, a neurosis may result. The term *neurosis* is no longer used to label disorder, but it is still used to describe the conflicts seen in some persons. Neurotic individuals are said to exhibit intense infantile wishes

Figure 2.9 Levels of Consciousness
According to Freudian theory, consciousness, that part of the mind about which we are aware, is but a small part of mental life. In the preconscious there is a glimmering of awareness, and increased awareness is possible. The largest segment, the unconscious, is not easily accessed, yet it gives rise to important needs and drives that influence current behavior. Defense mechanisms are unconscious processes that function to protect the individual from unacceptable needs and drives.

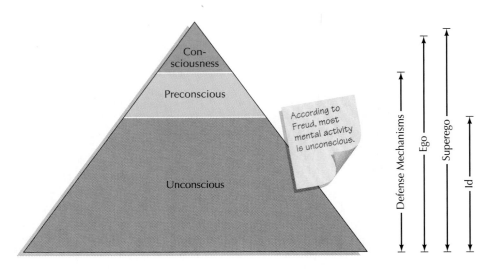

and impulses. These impulses are so strong that they drive the individual to excessive and rigid use of defense mechanisms to contain them. Excessive repression, for example, keeps facts from awareness and can intensify personal conflict and interpersonal distress.

Keep in mind that moderate use of numerous defense mechanisms is not abnormal. They help us avoid our own unwanted feelings, and they keep us from seeming less acceptable. Their use becomes abnormal only when a few defenses are relied on excessively or extensively.

Stages of Psychosexual Development   For Freud, the idea of sexuality includes all sensual striving and satisfactions (Brennan, 1955). As a person develops from infancy to young adulthood, the focus of sexual or sensual pleasure changes from the mouth to the anal area and then to the genitals. In his theory of personality development, Freud proposed five phases for **psychosexual development.**

In the *oral stage,* during which the major source of pleasure is the mouth, the infant seeks gratification through sucking, biting, and feeding. The oral stage covers the first year of life. According to some adherents of Freudian theory, persons whose development was **fixated** — stifled or stuck — at the oral stage attempt to satisfy oral needs and are prone to disorders such as alcoholism.

The *anal stage* extends from one to about three and a half years of age, through the period of toilet training. During this phase the child derives pleasure from the retention and expulsion of feces. An individual who experiences conflict during the anal stage may become fixated on this issue and continue to have problems surrounding excessive neatness, stinginess, and strict adherence to rules.

Boys and girls differ in their experience of the next phase, the *phallic stage.* From about three and a half to

five or six years of age, the child's interest centers on the genitals and on masturbatory activities. Borrowing from the theme of the Greek tragedy *Oedipus Rex,* Freud proposed that the phallic-aged boy develops a sexual attachment to his mother and views his father as his rival — the *Oedipal dilemma.* He wishes to see his father gone, and fears that his father wishes the same toward him. These wishes and fears conflict with the young boy's genuine love for his father. An adjusted individual resolves this dilemma by renouncing his desire for his mother and identifying with his father.

The phallic-age girl experiences an analogous situation with her parents — *the Electra dilemma* — but Freud believed that girls are less motivated than boys to resolve their dilemma. According to Freud, a girl's shift away from mother and toward father is facilitated both by her belief that it was her mother who deprived her of a penis and by her subsequent development of what Freud called *penis envy.* The theory holds that if the child — either boy or girl — is unsuccessful in resolving these dilemmas, the conflict will linger unconsciously and form the basis of maladjustment in adulthood.

At six or seven to eleven years of age, the child then enters a *latency stage,* during which the sexual drives seem to be inactive. The next phase, the *genital stage,* begins with puberty. This period is characterized by a reawakening and maturation of the sexual drives.

With each successive phase, functioning is increasingly mature. The experience of inordinate gratification or frustration at any given phase can cause psychological difficulties at a later stage. A person may become fixated to someone or something that is appropriate to an earlier level of development. Or a person may **regress,** or revert, to an earlier and thus more immature form of behavior, usually as the result of some external stress or in response to internal conflict. Regression can occur in both normal and disturbed persons.

Table 2.4   Ego Defense Mechanisms

Defense Mechanism	Description	Example
Repression	Unconscious but purposeful exclusion of painful thoughts or unacceptable desires or impulses from consciousness.	You fail to recall mistreatment by your mother when you were young.
Regression	Reversion to an earlier, more immature, form of behavior; acting childish in a situation when the proper, but as yet unmastered way to cope would be a mature solution.	A 21-year-old displays a temper tantrum.
Reaction formation	Endorsement of a conscious attitude or wish that is the opposite of the individual's unconscious wish or impulse; a reversal of motives.	A woman who hates her father and sees him as untrustworthy cannot accept such a view and, instead, is excessively loving and caring toward him, thus disguising her true attitude.
Projection	Attribution of one's own unacceptable impulses or thoughts to others.	During an exam you want to copy answers from your neighbor's paper. The anxiety created by the desire to cheat leads to your saying to the instructor, "You better put empty seats between people during this exam, as some kids are cheating." The unacceptable impulse is blamed (projected) on someone else.
Rationalization	A constructed, socially acceptable explanation for some behavior that is socially unacceptable.	When seen by someone you know at an X-rated movie, you create the explanation that you are doing research for a class project.
Denial	The act of not admitting that a threatening idea or feeling might apply to oneself.	A heavy smoker, you learn of a family member who died of lung cancer. A friend asks you if you are going to quit and you reply, "Me, heck, no, I'm in good shape."
Displacement	Reassignment of aggressive impulses or desires onto an object that is not the source of the discomfort; substitution of a different object against which to aggress.	Your instructor tells you to redo your paper; you can't aggress toward your instructor, so you displace and yell at your younger sister.

According to Freud, the ego uses defense mechanisms when it experiences discomfort. These defenses, which are unconscious, protect the individual from unwanted anxiety associated with unacceptable impulses.

Neo-Freudian Reconsiderations

Freud's views have been stimulating and provocative, attracting a large number of followers. Nevertheless, some supporters, the neo-Freudians, made changes to his original theory. Like Freud's theory, neo-Freudian views are based on intrapsychic conflict. But whereas Freud saw sexual impulses as the basis for neurotic anxiety, the neo-Freudians drifted from their mentor when considering the role of sexuality. For example, Carl Jung (1875–1961) emphasized a more positive, spiritual, and expanded role for the unconscious. In addition to a personal unconscious, he conceived of individuals as having a **collective unconscious,** comprising a collection of primitive ideas and images that are inherited and shared across the human race.

Alfred Adler (1870–1937) believed that humans are social beings, motivated more by social needs than by sexual drives. He saw that individuals suffered from feelings and fears of basic inferiority, along with an urge to compensate for these feelings by striving for power and superiority over others. With normal development, Adler proposed, the child's striving evolves from selfish

Carl Jung, prominent theorist who introduced the idea of a collective unconscious.

Alfred Adler downplayed instinctual urges and emphasized social urges.

to social goals. Harry Stack Sullivan (1892–1949) believed that the basic human need is for security in a potentially hostile world; he emphasized interpersonal relationships as crucial to personality development. Karen Horney (1885–1952) also emphasized security. She believed that environmental factors are central, but she argued that childhood relationships are the most important factor in secure psychological adjustment.

One modern spin-off from psychodynamic theory is **object relations** theory (Kohut, 1977; Kernberg, 1976; Mitchell, 1988). This perspective, which is derived from the idea that people are often the object of others' drives, deemphasizes impersonal forces and counterforces and instead focuses on the influences of early interpersonal relationships. Accordingly, object relations theorists are concerned with the role that human relationships play in the development of psychological abnormality. They believe that the early mother-child relationship is crucial to the child's development, self-concept, and conceptions of others — indeed, crucial to the quality of human relationships. Severe disturbances in early relationships can result in poor, if not chaotic, interpersonal relationships. Thus, the child's early interactions and impressions greatly influence later object relations.

Pros and Cons of the Psychodynamic Model

The contributions of Freud and his followers to our understanding of psychological disorders are enormous. Despite their impact, however, many psychodynamic ideas have not stood the tests of time and scientific study. After considering the enduring contributions we note several of the weaknesses.

Enduring Contributions Some of Freud's observations were powerful and accurate. He was the first to recognize that a child's early experiences — especially relationships with parents — influenced his or her adult behavior. He was also correct in noting that internal conflict is an important source of psychological difficulty. Indeed, although his ideas about the dynamics of the conflict have been questioned, there is widespread acceptance that human dysfunction arises from stress and conflict that a person cannot cope with effectively.

Perhaps Freud's most enduring contributions were his identification of the unconscious and his proposal that unconscious motives may play a role in human behavior. (When he was asked "Do you believe in the unconscious?" a smile came to his face as he remarked "Not that I am aware of!") Yet despite considerable agreement that human beings engage in behaviors that appear to reflect processes they are not aware of, exploring unconscious processes presents special problems for researchers. First, such processes are nonobservable. Second, they are, by definition, not accessible to the subject. Because we can't see the unconscious, we must rely on verbal reports to indicate the information that is in awareness — and these verbal reports may be biased. A classic study reported in 1949 by E. McGinnies illustrates the problem of report bias. McGinnies quickly flashed a variety of words before the subjects' eyes. Some words were neutral and had no emotional tone — *apple* and *house*, for example. In contrast, other words were considered taboo — *penis, Kotex*. The researchers recorded the subjects' delay in recognizing the words while gradually increasing the amount of time that the words were exposed. According to the results, taboo words required longer exposures before participants could correctly identify them. McGinnies also used the galvanic skin response (GSR) — a measure of skin conductance that is influenced by sweat — to measure each subject's emotional reactions. Interestingly, the GSRs were higher for the taboo words. In addition, during exposures presumably too brief to allow recognition of taboo words, participants' emotional reactions indicated that the words were being processed nevertheless.

Theorist Karen Horney emphasized the social and cultural aspects of abnormal behavior.

But what about report bias? It may simply be that the subjects were able to identify the taboo and neutral words with equal accuracy but, in an effort to avoid being embarrassed, they held back identifying the taboo words until they were more certain. The findings, then, would be evidence of a bias in reporting taboo versus neutral words, not evidence of the unconscious.

Researchers are continuing to study complex cognitive processes and their association to psychological disorders (Dalgleish & Watts, 1990). But today they refer not to unconscious processes, as Freud did, but to nonconscious processes. *Nonconscious processes* have to do with the ways our learned experiences function beyond awareness (Kihlstrom, 1987). In other words, our well-learned and practical behaviors become automatic, and we may organize and implement our expectations, beliefs, and even memories without fully understanding or being aware of them.

Unsupported Ideas Several aspects of Freud's original model have not been verified. Consider, first, his contention regarding the universality of sexual and aggressive instincts as the basis for all human behavior: Although these biological motives are powerful, we now know that *learned* motives are powerful as well. Second, there is no evidence that human development unfolds according to Freud's psychosexual stages. Third, there is an absence of evidence to support the claim that the hypothesized psychic structures (id, ego, and superego) do not optimally explain the nature of human disturbance.

Freud's theory was based on a sample of 20- to 45-year-old upper-middle-class women living in Vienna at a time when sexual expression was discouraged. But because his studies lacked the representativeness required for a comprehensive model of human behavior, many have questioned whether his theory can be applied universally. In addition, Freud's views have been criticized as sexist (Lips, 1988). He not only depicted women as inferior but also theorized (in the context of penis envy) that a girl's belief she had been castrated would produce feelings of inferiority in subsequent psychological development. Yet, as critics have been quick to point out, Freud was not in a position to know what developing girls think as he did not study children — only the retrospective reports of frustrated adult female patients. Interestingly, when his theory is revised in a modern feminist fashion (Chodorow, 1978), some of its strengths can be separated from its inherent sexism.

Certain disorders, perhaps those most closely resembling the characteristics of Freud's original clientele (such as conversion disorder or histrionic personality disorder) can be explained in psychodynamic terms. Other disorders, however, are more typically explained by other models. In addition, although the psychodynamic model is not as influential today as in the past, some of its principles can be and have been integrated into contemporary models of psychopathology.

HUMANISM: SELF-FOCUSED VIEWS

In contrast to the psychodynamic view, the humanistic approach rejects psychic determinism. Humanists, most active in the mid-twentieth century, accept only a minimum of determination by prior events and experiences. They are concerned with the positive aspects of life, choice, and self-determination. A basic principle of the **humanistic view** is the emphasis on each individual's values, free choices, and personal sense of purpose. The notion of the self plays a central role, and the nature of human needs and personal growth experiences are essential components of this model. Adequate adjustment requires accepting responsibility for one's own thoughts and actions. Abnormality is said to result from the refusal to accept personal responsibility for one's actions and their impact on others in the social environment. A humanist would explain Hennie's depression as follows: As part of the human condition, we are faced with many choices in our lifetime. These choices are burdensome, and the continual pressures of choice can take a toll. Coupled with feelings of alienation and confusion, an inability to handle choice caused Hennie's depression.

In contrast to contemporary psychopathology, humanists typically oppose the practice of diagnosing abnormal behavior. According to humanists, diagnostic labeling pays insufficient attention to the inner suffering and unhealthy experience of the client and as a result fails to address the crucial consideration, which is the person's inner experiences and sense of self. Two of the leading proponents of humanism are Carl Rogers (1902–1987) and Abraham Maslow (1908–1970).

Rogers's View of the Self

Debbi telephoned the clinic and, in her calm, self-effacing style, asked if she could possibly get an appointment to see a psychologist. Over the last several years she had become increasingly frustrated by her work and disappointed in her life. Despite her credentials and her salary, she felt unappreciated at work and unattractive to potential mates. Her career was now a chore, dating had become unfulfilling, and interpersonal relations were generally unsatisfying.

Debbi had a long history of defining herself in terms of what other people thought of her. As a younger woman, she had been extremely dependent on her parents for direction and encouragement. In the early days of her career, she found herself striving for approval from supervisors. Later, it became clear that Debbi felt trapped in her job. She wanted to try new ideas, develop her skills as a leader, and "branch out," but she was being forced to stay in her entrenched submissive role. It was especially troubling to her that her male counterparts at work were being allowed to change and expand their responsibilities — options that were not afforded to her.

Debbi felt trapped: Her choices were limited, and she reported feeling unable to determine for herself how her future would unfold. Her inner experiences caused distress. Carl Rogers (1961) was deeply concerned with the quality of a person's inner experience. He believed that the source of individual motivation is within the self — a drive toward the fulfillment of individual potentials. According to Rogers, Debbi, or any person, can achieve fulfillment by exploring and accepting the self, its needs, and its responsibilities.

Rogers's view values **personal authenticity,** living in a way that reflects awareness and care of one's self and others. Being spontaneous, open to new experiences, self-directed, and accepting of personal responsibility are also part of an authentic self. A genuine person achieves a balance between personal ideals and environmental restrictions. Disorders occur when a person lacks self-acceptance and relates to others in a manner that is not authentic to the self.

Rogers's humanism plays little part in research on psychological disorders. Instead, Rogers is most noted for his client-centered approach to therapy, which emphasizes the importance of the self and self-determination. As we discuss in Chapter 3, in client-centered therapy, the therapist establishes conditions for clients to make progress and grow, but the clients work out the solutions to problems on their own.

Maslow's Self-Actualization

Another major proponent of the humanistic view is Abraham Maslow (1943, 1968), who described a **hierarchy of human needs** (see Figure 2.10). At the bottom of the hierarchy are the basic human needs such as food, drink, and sex; at the top is the need for **self-actualization,** which is an ongoing fulfillment of personal potentials and missions, a fuller acceptance of one's intrinsic nature, and a willingness to be oneself yet share fully with others.

According to Maslow, a person must meet the basic physiological needs for food, drink, and sex before trying to meet the higher needs. Once these basic physiological needs are satisfied, the person proceeds to resolve the need for safety and security. The role of a warm and

Carl Rogers was a significant contributor to the humanistic perspective on abnormal behavior.

Abraham Maslow's proposed humanistic approach emphasized how people strive for self-actualization.

accepting family can fulfill the basic need for love and belongingness, and close relationships are necessary before a person can move toward achievement of more advanced needs. When the physiological needs are met and a sense of security is established, the individual strives for belongingness; it is at this time that the absence of friends, family members, or children becomes a source of much conflict. Until the need for love and acceptance is met, the person cannot proceed toward fulfillment of the need for self-esteem. According to Maslow, when needs are not met, conflict emerges, and individuals arrange their lives around attempts to resolve each of these stages of conflict over need fulfillment.

Maslow and the followers of this model believe that fulfillment of the more basic needs is not enough. Failure to meet the higher needs can result in psychological stress, which in turn can cause or exacerbate a wide variety of psychological and physical disorders.

Pros and Cons of the Humanistic Model

The humanistic model inspired a focus on interpersonal group encounters in which the intent is to facilitate clients' ability to understand themselves and reach their full potential. This emphasis on human growth, and the practice of group therapy itself, has endured. Additionally, the model's special focus on each individual engenders sensitivity to cultural, gender, and ethnic diversity, although the model does not explicitly emphasize this sensitivity.

In other ways, however, the influence of humanism has diminished. For example, the humanists' rejection of diagnostic practices was influential in past years, but today this influence has dissipated as the acceptance of diagnoses has increased. Indeed, with the exception of Rogers's studies of the effects of therapy, the rejection of the methods of science as a proper approach to under-

Figure 2.10   Maslow's Hierarchy of Human Needs
According to Maslow, an individual must meet the needs listed at the bottom of the pyramid before trying to meet the higher-order needs. When needs are not met, conflict emerges.
Source: Maslow (1943, pp. 370–396).

standing and treating human problems is a limitation of humanistic views. In general, the study and treatment of severe psychological disorders and research on abnormality are relatively uninfluenced by the humanistic model.

FAMILY MATTERS

Models of Family Functioning and Psychopathology

Most models of psychological functioning address the individual patient. But what about models of ongoing systems of people? The behavioral and psychodynamic perspectives, for example, have advanced our understanding of how a primary social system — the family — might contribute to psychological abnormality. Yet, despite the differences between these perspectives, they concur that the locus of pathology is not within the individual, who is designated the "patient," but within the family members' interrelationships.

Behaviorists emphasize the environment as a controlling and contributing factor in human behavior and identify the family — especially the parents — as one of the most important environments (Braswell & Bloomquist, 1991; Forehand & McMahon, 1981; Patterson & Bank, 1989). Behaviorally, parents can be influential in several ways: (1) through their own behavior, as models; (2) through their selective rewarding of activities within the family; and (3) through their cre-

ation of a social climate, inasmuch as parents may be hostile and rejecting or warm and accepting. Indeed, as central players within the family system, parents wield a great deal of influence.

With less emphasis on parents' behavior but more emphasis on interpersonal relations, the psychodynamic model also sees pathology as occurring within the context of family relationships. One example of a psychodynamic family model addresses the eating disorder *anorexia*. Briefly, anorexia involves a preoccupation with "feeling fat" along with efforts to lose weight — sometimes to the point of starvation. The disorder typically occurs among female adolescents (see Chapter 15). Operating from the Philadelphia Child Guidance Clinic, Salvador Minuchin and his colleagues (Minuchin, Roseman & Baker, 1978) described the characteristics of the family system with an anorexic child as enmeshed, rigid, overprotective, and tending to lack skills for conflict resolution.

Note that *enmeshment* in a family system refers to a situation in which no member can have a separate identity; everyone in the family must be together, with a resulting absence of privacy. *Rigidity* is evident in an unwillingness to tolerate change. *Overprotection* is characterized by expressions of concern at the least sign of discomfort. And finally, when a family denies that conflict exists, or changes the topic of conversation to avoid it, conflict is not resolved. Minuchin's family systems view of anorexia places the abnormality within the family: The female adolescent cannot achieve separation from the family, is denied privacy, feels overcontrolled, and strives for independence by controlling her eating. In short, the anorexia isn't her disorder!

The family systems approach is beginning to receive research evaluation and to be included in integrated models of psychopathology. According to this approach, an individual does not have a disorder; instead, he or she has a problem with patterns of interaction within the family. Because the family is defined as the primary social network, it is the interaction pattern within the family that is seen as dysfunctional. In fact, this interaction pattern is often the target for change in family therapy.

WHAT'S NORMAL?

What the Models Have to Say about Healthy Functioning

We have considered several models of psychopathology in this chapter. Whereas they all contribute to an understanding of abnormality, most deal somewhat less directly with normal functioning (see also Strack & Lorr, 1994). Accordingly, we now take a brief look at

Children shopping for food with their father. Many opportunities for interpersonal interaction are provided in these shared experiences, and children learn a great deal from parents about how people interact.

"normality" within each of the models and then consider an overall model of positive mental health.

Since the biomedical model suggests that psychological disorder is linked to underlying physical and chemical imbalances, we can infer from the model that healthy psychological functioning is linked to healthy physical functioning whereby the brain structures are intact, neurotransmitter substances are operative and in balance, and the nervous system is without serious flaw. In other words, psychological functioning implies a proper biochemical and physical functioning.

An interesting principle of the behavioral model is that learning itself is not good or bad; it is not abnormal or normal. Thus, since the same learning process underlies both adaptive and maladaptive behaviors, it is not the behavior itself but judgments made about the behavior that determine whether it is normal or psychopathological.

The cognitive model describes various maladaptive features of the information processing in disturbed individuals, whereas it assumes that such processing is logical and rational in normal persons. In addition, normal cognitive activity is not determined by biased or dysfunctional beliefs.

The psychodynamic model suggests that when serious intrapsychic conflict is absent, when the individual has proceeded through the stages of psychosexual development without major trauma, and when the ego is adequately operating on the reality principle, the individual is functioning within the normal range. According to object relations theory specifically, a secure mother-infant attachment provides the foundation for healthy adult functioning.

Finally, the humanist model does not employ diagnoses and hence does not emphasize the differentiation of abnormal from normal. Rather, it considers every person to be essentially good and motivated to do good. Thus, an individual's choices, acceptance of personal responsibility, and self-determination affect the quality of psychological adjustment.

In this context, note that self-actualized persons are not necessarily happier, wealthier, or more popular than the average person; however, as Maslow argued, they do tend to be more caring, spontaneous, curious, tolerant, and accepting of themselves and others than are most people. In addition, such persons are creative, self-directed, independent, and ethical; and though open to new experiences, they are also capable of finding great joy in common events. Above all, perhaps, self-actualized persons are accurate in their view of themselves and others, capable of solving interpersonal problems, and willing to struggle to understand others' points of view without compromising their own perspective. An important message advanced by the humanistic view is that life is a constant struggle, one that occurs at different levels, involves different people, and deals with different needs. As such, it requires a reserve of psychological health through which the individual can meet its inevitable challenges.

Maria Jahoda (1953, 1958) was one of the few authors to directly tackle the question of what is normal in terms of positive mental health. She argued that positive psychological adjustment is directly related to interpersonal problem-solving skills. She also proposed that the core of healthy adjustment consists of a specific sequence of problem-solving steps: Recognize and admit the problem, reflect on possible solutions, make a decision, and take action. Although Jahoda did not label her theory as integrative in nature, it was a forerunner of models that blend multiple perspectives. Specifically, Jahoda combined cognitive and behavioral notions in her theory of positive mental health.

What Lies Ahead?

It is precisely because psychopathology is so complex an area of study that several different models have emerged to help explain abnormal behavior. But intrapsychic explanations contrast with learning models, and the biological approach diverges from humanism. How can we best deal with these multiple points of view? Can one perspective be argued as superior to all others? Should it be? And should empirical research dictate which models survive?

Historically, models of psychopathology have sought to explain all of human personality, pathology, and adjustment. One need not go beyond Freud's model to see an example of this effort to be all-encompassing — as if, to be valuable, a model must explain all disorders, for all human beings. Such thinking is no longer being advanced. Rather, grand theories are now viewed as being so broad, and entailing so many mini-theories and sub-theories, that they can never be tested as a whole. Modern approaches to the development of a model of psychopathology do not expect universal applicability.

As the field moves away from mega-models, researchers are increasingly proposing micro-models — models that strive to explain individual disorders. As this chapter makes clear, certain models have been more or less successful in explaining some but not other disorders. (Note that models specific to individual disorders are discussed in subsequent chapters devoted to those disorders.) The tendency to develop disorder-specific models is likely to increase.

Another noteworthy trend is that models are becoming integrated. Although a comprehensive and universally accepted integration has not yet appeared, recent trends support the view that integrative efforts are reasonable and desirable. Both the diathesis-stress model and the cognitive-behavioral model, already widely accepted themselves, illustrate this integration. With the increased recognition that an individual may suffer from more than one disorder (a phenomenon known as comorbidity), an understanding of psychopathology may require even further integration of models.

Models of psychopathology have been offered as explanatory systems broad enough to hold true for men as well as women and for majority as well as minority ethnic groups. Future developments, however, will likely witness greater gender and ethnic specificity. For example, given the biological differences between men and women, should we not expect differential incidences of certain disorders? Soon to be gone, perhaps, are the days of a universal single-minded model of all forms of psychopathology for all varieties of peoples.

KEY TERMS

autonomic nervous system (36)
avoidance learning (44)
behavioral model (40)
biomedical model (32)
cerebral cortex (33)
classical conditioning (40)
cognitive content (45)
cognitive deficiencies (46)
cognitive distortions (46)
cognitive model (45)

cognitive processes (45)
cognitive products (45)
collective unconscious (53)
conditioned response (CR) (41)
conditioned stimulus (CS) (41)
cognitive structures (45)
defense mechanisms (50)
diatheses (38)
diathesis-stress model (38)

dizygotic twins (37)
eclecticism (32)
ego (49)
fixation (52)
genes (37)
hierarchy of human needs (56)
humanistic view (55)
hypothalamus (33)
id (49)
intrapsychic conflict (49)
irrational beliefs (46)

limbic system (33)
model (32)
modeling (44)
monozygotic twins (37)
negative distortions (48)
negative reinforcement (43)
neurotransmitters (34)
observational learning (44)
object relations (54)
operant conditioning (42)
paradigm (32)

SUMMARY

Psychologists use *models,* or *paradigms,* as guiding frameworks to organize information. The biomedical, behavioral, cognitive, psychodynamic, and humanistic models have been influential in abnormal psychology. Currently, integrative models such as the diathesis-stress and cognitive-behavioral models are receiving increased attention.

The Biomedical Model: Psychological Disorders and Biological Conditions

The *biomedical model* is concerned with the role of disease, individual biochemistry, and human genetics in psychological disorders. Thus, it examines ties between psychopathology and structures of the brain. The biomedical model also examines how *neurotransmitter* substances (which carry messages between the neurons) and the *autonomic nervous system* (which consists of the *sympathetic* and *parasympathetic* systems) influence behavior. Both the biological predispositions that we inherit and the manner in which these predispositions influence how we interact with the world are also part of the biomedical model.

The *diathesis-stress* model is a model of combined influences. *Diatheses* and *stress* interact. Diatheses are predisposing factors, whereas stress occurs as a result of current environmental factors. Thus, the diathesis-stress model emphasizes the interaction between predispositions and environmental stress in psychological disorder.

Behaviorism: The Learning Models

Behaviorists emphasize the observable behavior of the person and the environmental factors that maintain the action. The *behavioral model* of psychopathology is centrally concerned with maladaptive learning and use the outcomes of laboratory research on *classical conditioning, operant conditioning,* and *modeling* to advance this understanding. Classical conditioning describes how a behavior called a *conditioned response* is acquired through the pairing of *unconditioned* and *conditioned stimuli.* Operant conditioning refers to the strengthening of responses that occurs when they are followed by rewarding experiences. Modeling refers to observational learning, which takes place when an individual's behavior is influenced by having observed and imitated the behavior of someone else. *Social learning theory* asserts that behavior is the product of both external events and internal cognitive processes.

Applauded as scientific and rigorous, the behaviorist model has been criticized for not reflecting the complexities of human existence. Earlier learning models ignored cognitive functioning, whereas contemporary behaviorism attends to cognitive functioning.

Family systems models suggest that an individual is disordered as a result of a disturbed family system. For behaviorists, learning paradigms operate within the family. For psychodynamic theorists, interpersonal dynamics are what contribute to maladjustment.

The Cognitive Model: Disordered Thought Processing

The *cognitive model* emphasizes the contribution of cognitive factors to emotional or behavioral distress. *Cognitive structures* refer to the internal organization of information, and *cognitive content* is the information that is in our heads. *Cognitive processes* are the ways that we operate on the information, and *cognitive products* are the conclusions that we reach after processing information. All of these aspects of our cognitive functioning influence psychological maladjustment. *Cognitive deficiencies* include lack of forethought that would otherwise be useful, and *cognitive distortions* are dysfunctional thought processes.

Ellis tied irrational beliefs to psychological distress; Beck's cognitive model of depression emphasizes the *negative distortions* seen in the cognitive processing of persons with depression. Although cognitive models are sometimes difficult to assess, data suggest that cognitive functioning is associated with various psychological disorders. The cognitive-behavioral model is integrative, emphasizing both the process of learning behavior and the cognitive information-processing factors that influence such learning.

Psychodynamics: An Intrapsychic Model

Freud's groundbreaking theory suggests that psychological disorders result from conflict over needs and satisfactions among three intrapsychic structures: the *id, superego,* and *ego.* This theory places important weight on the *unconscious* causes of behavior.

Early modifications to Freud's *psychodynamic model* by the neo-Freudians included Jung's notion of the *collective unconscious,* Adler's concept of basic inferiority, and Sullivan's and Horney's theories based on security. Contemporary revisions of psychodynamic theory include the *object relations* approach, a theory that refers to persons as objects of drives and that places greatest emphasis on interpersonal relationships and their role in individual psychopathology. One of Freud's lasting contributions was his identification of the unconscious. However, the nonrepresentativeness of his original subjects and the nonempirical features of his theory have been sources of concern.

Humanism: Self-Focused Views

The *humanistic view* emphasizes each person's values, choices, and purposes and suggests that distress results from failure to accept personal responsibilities. This view rejects both determinism and diagnosis. Examples of the humanistic approach are Rogers's notions of *personal authenticity* and the need for personal growth, and Maslow's *hierarchy of human needs*, including the need for *self-actualization*. Strong in its subjective understanding of the person, the humanistic model is weak in its promotion of the scientific knowledge of disorders.

Consider the Following. . .

Although you aren't sure if it was because of your dad's advice ("You'll always need to be able to give speeches") or your roommate's inside information ("Everybody gets an A or a B"), you are preparing a speech for your communications class; your topic is "the government's role in mental health." The premise of your assignment is that the government has set aside a large budget to improve mental health. You must argue how best to spend that money and why. Given what you have learned in this chapter, what model might guide you in making your arguments? Are some models more suggestive than others about where money is best spent?

You've chosen psychology as a major and now, in your senior year, you are considering graduate schools. How might the diversity of models you have read about in this chapter affect your search for the perfect school for you? What model(s) guides your thinking about psychopathology? Do you think it is important for you to match your orientation with that of your future graduate school? What might be the pros and cons either way — matching or not matching?

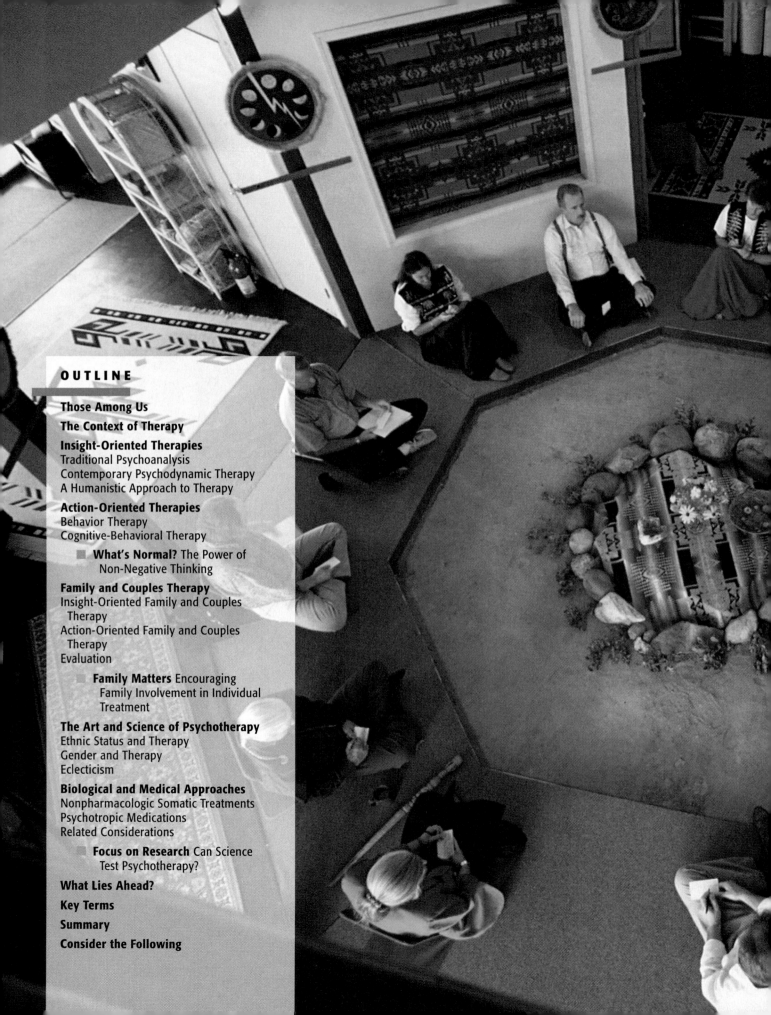

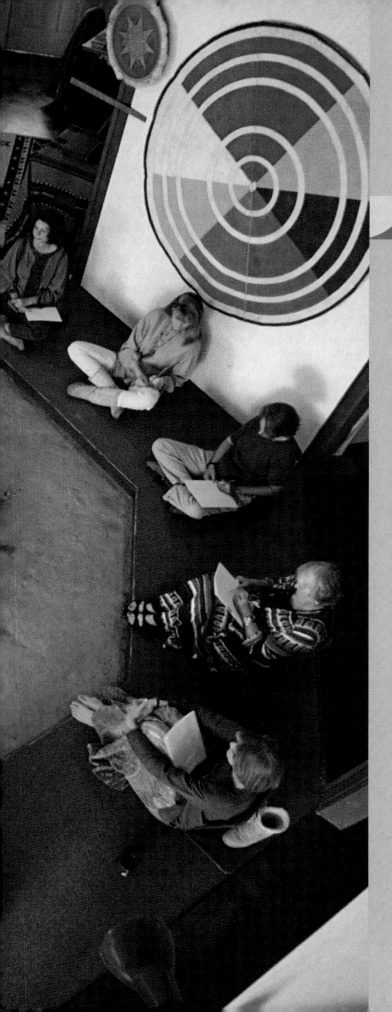

CHAPTER 3

Approaches to Treatment

Those among us...

- Lani, a twice-married daughter of a neighbor, has been in psychodynamic therapy for several years, attending three fifty-minute sessions per week for eleven months of the year. In therapy, Lani often describes her dreams and discusses her relationship with her mother. Over the years, Lani has told you that she is distressed, believes she is unloved, and feels a sense of aimlessness.

- It's Sunday morning and you and a friend are off to brunch. As you stroll toward the restaurant, you pass a clean-cut, well-dressed man in his mid-forties. It's a neighbor, Mr. Berg. His face is covered with lather, he holds a razor in hand, and he is shaving while peering at his reflection in the picture window. Believe it or not, this is part of his therapy.

- You are at a shopping mall, about to meet your friends to go home. As you wait by the main door, a young man approaches and introduces himself as Rameen. He says that, in the past, he has been very fearful of people and crowds, and that, for him, just being at the mall is a real accomplishment. Following this brief conversation, someone comes up and thanks you for helping.

- During a part-time summer job you meet and become friends with Jerry. Though his behavior seems just fine to you, Jerry does admit that he is on medication to control his delusions. As the return to school nears, Jerry begins to act erratically. He tells you that he thinks he is being followed by a secret foreign-government force.

Must therapy require so much time — three appointments per week for years? Or are there effective, brief treatments available? How can shaving in public or walking up to strangers and beginning a staged conversation possibly be part of therapy?

When individuals are taking medicine for mental disorders, does the effectiveness of the medication change over time? What might lead someone on medication to behave erratically?

These examples have obvious differences, but they are similar in that they all describe therapists' efforts to help their clients or patients. Lani's therapist, for instance, is seeking to increase her self-understanding. In other, more action-oriented therapies, the therapist and client work together to identify the client's problem and design an assignment to facilitate a solution to the client's problem. Mr. Berg, the public shaver, was a highly anxious and controlling man who was such a perfectionist that he insisted on redoing handwritten notes until they were perfect. He always wore pressed and starched clothes, and he rarely spoke about anything but work-related topics. For him, shaving in public has provided a valuable experience: Even after doing something he thought was "shameful," he understands that some things can be laughed at, that people aren't perfect, and that the world isn't overly critical. His experience has been an eye-opener for him. And Rameen, the person at the mall, was agoraphobic — that is, he was afraid of open spaces — and he was completing part of an assignment involving increasingly difficult tasks designed to help him overcome his fears.

THE CONTEXT OF THERAPY

Throughout most of this century, being in a hospital was considered therapeutic for those with psychological disorders. Few other treatments were offered, biological or otherwise. Hospitalizations were often prolonged — even lifelong — and may even have *contributed* to the problems they attempted to treat. Public-supported care for the chronically mentally ill in the United States relied on large state mental hospitals, earlier called *asylums*. Often these institutions were underfunded and overcrowded, with insufficiently trained and poorly supervised staffs.

In the mid-twentieth century, the introduction of antipsychotic medications (discussed later in the chapter) revolutionized the treatment of major mental illnesses. These medications controlled the worst of the symptoms, and the sedated patients could then be exposed to treatments such as vocational rehabilitation and various forms of psychological therapy. But the post-drug era brought new problems, including overmedication, improper medication, and insufficient attention to disabilities that were worsened by drugs or by institutionalization itself.

Increasing public awareness brought another revolution in the treatment of severe mental disorders. In 1963 the U.S. Congress passed the Mental Retardation Facilities and Community Mental Health Center Construction Act. The goal of this legislation — **deinstitutionalization** — was to replace the huge mental hospitals that often served an entire state with local facilities that enabled patients to become more fully integrated into their own communities. Indeed, all communities in the United States are now served by **community mental health centers** that include facilities for short-term hospital care as well as follow-up outpatient services (Garfield & Bergin, 1994). Severely mentally ill patients who cannot live independently are cared for through arrangements such as halfway houses, with treatment provided by outpatient services, day treatment facilities, or programs that facilitate occupational and social rehabilitation.

Institutions, such as this English "madhouse" (circa 1735), held disturbed persons in confined settings without providing treatment. Today, there are far fewer mental institutions, and those that remain offer a wide variety of therapeutic experiences.

Before the passage of the Mental Retardation Facilities and Community Mental Health Center Construction Act in 1963, the chronically mentally ill were placed in large state mental hospitals, or asylums, which were often overcrowded and undersupervised.

The policy of deinstitutionalization was successful in one sense: From 1950 to 1990 the number of patients in public mental hospitals dropped from more than 500,000 to approximately 100,000. In spite of worthy ideals, however, deinstitutionalization has unleashed a host of unintended and negative consequences. Not only are vast numbers of mentally ill people now lacking adequate treatment for their disorders, but they are also homeless. Indeed, from a sociological perspective, a large proportion of the homeless population consists of mentally ill persons who may once have been sheltered by mental institutions. In Chapter 18, we consider why the original goals for deinstitutionalization have not been realized.

What about those who *do* receive treatment? Most individuals in treatment do not require hospitalization: Those with mild, moderate, and sometimes even severe psychological problems typically receive outpatient care. Although the relationship between the therapist and client is important in all cases, the type of treatment given is guided by different theoretical orientations. Psychologists, psychiatrists, social workers, and other helping professionals treat mental health problems in hospitals, institutions, and community and private clinics. And the treatment sessions themselves may focus on an individual client or on the client and significant others.

A common form of treatment is **individual therapy**, in which the goal is to remedy personal adjustment problems and enable the client to function autonomously. In some instances, therapists decide that an individual is best treated if the person's partner or family becomes involved in therapy. For example, in **couples therapy**, also referred to as marital therapy, the therapist works with two people who share a long-term relationship. Couples therapy often focuses on the structure and communication patterns in a relationship.

A central assumption underlying **family therapy** is that disturbances in relationships or the social context influence individual adjustment, and that when one member of a couple or family develops a problem, the others are likely to be affected as well. Family therapists treat the entire family as the client, downplaying the problem of an individual and emphasizing the problem as belonging to the family system.

In **group therapy**, a therapist brings together previously unacquainted individuals for the purpose of resolving personal problems. As part of the treatment, the group develops an interpersonal system, within which the therapist works to improve the quality of adjustment for each of the individuals.

In contrast to institutionalization, patients can receive treatments in a group home setting. Some contemporary living arrangements foster independent living and self-care. Staff provide supervision and support as patients learn from staff and from each other how to adjust to a community-based setting.

Recall the different theoretical models described and discussed in Chapter 2. Each of these can guide therapists toward therapeutic programs designed to treat specific child and adult psychological disorders (see Table 3.1). Although the various therapies — biomedical, behavioral, cognitive, psychodynamic, and humanistic — are different in major ways, they also share some important features (Goldfried, 1980). For instance, all therapies are designed to be corrective and helpful, all involve an interpersonal relationship between therapist and client, and all aim to increase the client's adaptive and autonomous functioning. On the basis of these commonalities, and guided by their theoretical model and the needs of the client, therapists employ additional procedures and strategies to alleviate specific psychological disorders. These procedures are discussed in the sections that follow.

INSIGHT-ORIENTED THERAPIES

Insight refers to a person's ability to understand the basis of his or her thinking, behavior, emotions, and perceptions. Some therapists believe that clients' insights into the causes of their disorders lead them to change problem behavior. Helping the client gain insight is a goal of both psychodynamic and humanistic therapies.

Psychodynamic therapy addresses the mental mechanisms established in childhood and their effects on adult adjustment. It is the therapeutic outgrowth of the psychodynamic model described in Chapter 2, and it has two branches: traditional psychoanalysis and contemporary psychodynamic therapy. Both branches focus on searching for the underlying causes of maladaption and seeking insight as a path to improved adjustment.

Traditional Psychoanalysis

Psychoanalytic theory maintains that clients since childhood have reduced anxiety by overusing defense mechanisms, which enable them to avoid rather than confront the conflicts that produce anxiety. These conflicts, therefore, are banished to the unconscious. It is the task of the psychoanalytic therapist to facilitate the client's insight into the conflicts. According to Freud (1917), through the process of **psychoanalysis,** the therapist's interpretations of client behavior enables these unconscious feelings, thoughts, and needs to become conscious. Lani, described earlier as feeling unloved and aimless, was receiving this form of treatment.

What strategies does the therapist use to bring conflicts into awareness? We can gain a basic understanding of how psychoanalysts work by examining their main treatment techniques: free association, interpretation, dream analysis, resistance, and transference.

Free Association Psychoanalysts allow clients to disclose their unconscious impulses and defenses in a safe,

Table 3.1 Therapeutic Approaches of the Major Theoretical Models

Model	Examples of Treatment Techniques	Sample Therapies	Treatment Goals
Psychodynamic	Interpretation, free association	Psychoanalysis, object-relations therapy	Client insight
Humanistic	Active listening, accurate empathy	Person-centered therapy	Client self-satisfaction
Behavioral	Conditioning, modeling	Systematic desensitization, token economies	Foster new learning
Cognitive-behavioral	Collaborative empiricism, changing self-talk	Cognitive therapy for depression, problem-solving therapy	Altering client's cognitive processing of events
Family and couples	Communication training	Family systems therapy	Change the interpersonal system or family context
Biomedical	Medication, surgery	Benzodiazipine, lobotomy	Symptom remission and corrected biochemical imbalances

Various treatment techniques are used to reduce psychological disorders. This list, organized by the major theoretical models, provides examples of treatment techniques used by different therapies.

nonjudgmental therapy situation. In **free association**, a client expresses thoughts and feelings as they come to mind and without fear of censure. One popular image of psychotherapy is that the client lies on a couch and says anything that comes to mind, while the therapist remains relatively silent. Although the therapist appears to be sitting passively, however, he or she is actually working toward gaining an understanding of the client, the problem, and the situation — an understanding that later guides the therapist in providing interpretations.

Interpretations According to psychoanalytic theory, both intentional and unintentional behaviors hold meaning and provide clues to unconscious conflicts. Suppose that a young man with a shaved head asks someone for change for a dollar. The person fumbles in his pockets, eventually locates some coins, but drops a few coins in the process. He then comments, "Sorry, but I've had a really hairy morning." Why did he choose the word *hairy,* when he could have chosen a number of other words (*bad, hectic, lousy*)? Freudians would argue that, at an unconscious level, the man's bald head had caught his attention and although he didn't want to be openly critical, his word choice did provide an ever-so-slight interpersonal jab.

Interpretations are statements made by the therapist that identify features of something the client has said or done, of which the client had not been fully aware. In our example, a psychoanalytic therapist might provide an interpretation by saying, "You didn't like the shaved head, but you didn't want to be direct about it." The therapist's job is to pay close attention to the client's expressions and behaviors and to interpret their meaning for the client to increase the client's self-understanding. Slips of the tongue, expressions of anger, being late for therapy sessions, and even being overly cooperative in therapy sessions are aspects of the client's behavior that are open to the therapist's interpretations.

Sitting In on Psychoanalytic Therapy In this transcript notice how careful timing helped produce increased insight.

CLIENT: We had a salesmen's meeting, and a large group of us were cramped together in a small room, and they turned out the lights to show some slides, and I got so jumpy and anxious I couldn't stand it.

THERAPIST: So what happened? (*Question*)

CLIENT: I just couldn't stand it. I was sweating and shaking, so I got up and left, and I know I'll be called on the carpet for walking out.

THERAPIST: You became so anxious and upset that you couldn't stand being in the room, even though you knew that walking out would get you into trouble. (*The therapist is providing a clarification.*)

CLIENT: Yeah. . . . What could have bothered me so much to make me do a dumb thing like that?

THERAPIST: You know, we've talked about other times in your life when you've become upset in close quarters with other men: once when you were in the army and again in your dormitory at college. (*The therapist's comment is a confrontation.*)

CLIENT: That's right, and it was the same kind of thing again.

THERAPIST: And if I'm correct, this has never happened to you in a group of men and women together, no matter how closely you've been cramped together. (*Further confrontation*)

CLIENT: Uh . . . yes, that's right.

THERAPIST: So it appears that something especially about being physically close to other men, and especially in the dark, makes you anxious, as if you're afraid something bad might happen in that kind of situation. (*Interpretation*)

CLIENT: (*Pause*) I think you're right about that . . . and I know I'm not physically afraid of other men. Do you think it might be sexual, that I might get worried about something homosexual taking place? (Weiner, 1975, p. 142)

Analysis of Dreams Just as psychoanalysts examine the meaning of behavior, they also make sense of dreams. According to Freud (1913), dreams have both manifest and latent meanings. The content of the dream as it is recalled by the dreamer is the **manifest dream.** Telling of a dream about a drive in the country, a puzzling road map, and an unmarked fork in the road would be the manifest content. The **latent content,** on the other hand, contains repressed conflictual material in a disguised form. The psychoanalytic therapist interprets the latent content of the dream. For example, the dream of a drive in the countryside might suggest that the client is at a decision point in life and must make a difficult choice. Similarly, the fork in the road and the confusing map may represent the client's perception of his current conflicted place in life. This example is clear-cut; most dreams and dream meanings are not as transparent.

Resistance Have you ever noticed that people are sometimes hesitant to listen to advice — even good advice? On occasion, even the best advice is ignored because it may be too sensitive, too potent, or too distressing for the listener. Roadblocks such as these occur in therapy as well and are called **resistance** — the client's unwillingness to express true feelings, divulge actual thoughts, or accept the therapist's interpretations. An insight-oriented understanding of resistance suggests that it involves the client's unconscious efforts to actively oppose attempts to explore symptoms that serve a defensive function; it further involves processes to resist change. But if the therapist's interpretation is wrong (a possibility seldom discussed within psychoanalysis), the client's response would constitute not resistance but a logical response.

Transference: Reliving Relationships As the therapist and client work closely together, a special relationship develops. This relationship provides the raw material for probing the unconscious and its defenses. A major part of this relationship is **transference,** a process by which the client reexperiences the thoughts and feelings that were experienced in childhood when relating to an authority figure such as a parent. At an unconscious level, these relationships are relived through transference, thus replaying the client's internal conflicts — conflicts that often go back to childhood and lie at the root of the current symptoms (Luborsky et al., 1985; Westen, 1988). **Countertransference** refers to the therapist's feelings about the client.

According to Butler and Strupp (1991), "Analysis of the transference is the sine qua non of dynamic therapy" (p. 523). Psychoanalysts interpret how the therapist serves as an authority figure and how the client reenacts unresolved earlier conflicts. For example, if the client's father had humiliated him, the client may see the therapist as humiliating him. The client, with the guidance of the therapist, then "works through" the transference relationship. **Working through** refers to the process by which the client accepts formerly unconscious experiences and comes to relate to the therapist and, by extension, to the parent in a positive way.

Evaluation What's the current thinking about the benefits of traditional psychoanalysis? Trained psychoanalyst Matthew Erdelyi (1985) conducted studies evaluating specific psychoanalytic hypotheses. For example, he studied memory to compare the memory-enhancing effects of three "strategies" that resemble the therapy techniques of free association, recall under hypnosis (another treatment strategy sometimes employed within psychoanalysis), and focused concentration (whereby the therapist provides direct prompts and questions). Which strategy actually augments memory best? In one study (Haber & Erdelyi, 1967), free association was found to enhance recall, but it was not possible to determine whether this hyper-recall was an enhancement of correct recall or simply evidence that the subjects were reporting more. Erdelyi pointed out that although free association does increase recall, the recall isn't necessarily more accurate; subjects are simply saying more. Later, Erdelyi (1985) reported results indicating that focused concentration did enhance recall, whereas free association did not produce hyper-recall beyond that obtained by focused concentration alone.

Not all aspects of psychoanalysis have been so carefully studied. Indeed, a frequent criticism of psychoanalysis is that its hypotheses have not been adequately examined and its outcomes have not been adequately tested. Psychoanalysts may not agree with this criticism, however, because they typically do not adopt the methods of science when evaluating therapy. In short, although treatment-outcome studies are lacking and its practice is declining, psychoanalysis continues and may be best suited for the verbal and intelligent person with mild psychological problems.

Contemporary Psychodynamic Therapy

A large number of practicing psychotherapists hold a contemporary psychodynamic perspective — emphasizing the unconscious determinants of behavior, seeking to acquire insight about their clients, using interpretations, and striving to make sense of transference to foster the development of client insight. However, in contrast to psychoanalysts, whose treatment may last for extended periods of time (perhaps years), today's psychodynamically oriented therapists are more likely to employ briefer, more time-limited forms of treatment. Some psychodynamic approaches (e.g., Luborsky, 1984; Strupp & Binder, 1984) have generated some favorable research evaluations (e.g., Henry, Strupp, Schacht & Gaston, 1994) and spawned new theoretical directions (e.g., Grenyer & Luborsky, 1996).

Ego Psychology Unlike their psychoanalytic predecessors, **ego psychologists** are more concerned with the functions of the ego than with the superego or the id (Hartmann, 1939). Hartmann stressed the conflict-resolving functions of the ego and identified perception, planning, memory, and problem solving as functions of the ego that are important targets for treatment. Although their treatment strategies often follow psychodynamic theory, ego psychologists' focus on conflict resolution and related cognitive processes matches the general trend in contemporary psychotherapy toward more time-limited therapy.

Object Relations As noted in Chapter 2, object relations theory is one modern spin-off from psychodynamic theory (Cashdan, 1988; Kernberg, 1976; Kohut, 1977). But unlike psychoanalytic therapy, which focuses on internal drives, **object relations therapy** takes an interpersonal approach that emphasizes the role human relationships play in the development of personality. Object relations therapists seek to gain insight about internal representations of significant others and developmental changes in the child's way of viewing interpersonal relations. The mother-child relationship is particularly important in the theory, and transference and countertransference issues are central in the therapy.

The aim is to understand childhood interpersonal relations and how these patterns are repeated in adult life. As one aspect of the therapeutic relationship, the therapist can experience the client's "evoking style," which comprises an individual's characteristic ways of interacting with people that evoke more or less specific counter-responses from other people (Anchin & Kiesler, 1982).

Consider, for example, the *borderline personality,* which is an adult disorder defined by extreme difficulty in establishing stable interpersonal relationships (see Chapter 14). According to object relations theorists such as Otto F. Kernberg (1976), this disorder results from troubled early interpersonal experiences. The child internalizes objects (that is, individuals) that have highly conflicting attributes — caring and rejecting, affection and abuse — and as a result develops his or her own internal conflict. Object relations therapists suggest that because of these unstable childhood relationships, such an individual is unable to develop a consistent sense of self and will have trouble forming stable adult relationships and leading an integrated life.

Interpersonal Therapy Harry Stack Sullivan was an early interpersonal theorist who believed that many psychological disorders were social phenomena, with roots in the parent-child relationship. In **interpersonal therapy** (Kiesler, 1991; 1996), the therapist's essential task is to disrupt the client's vicious cycle of self-defeating interpersonal interactions. In contrast to traditional psychodynamic therapists, interpersonal therapists are more directive and active: They use their own experience with the client to identify the client's maladaptive actions and communications. These interpersonal markers (Safran & Segal, 1990) then become the target for treatment. Note, however, that not all interpersonal psychotherapy has a psychodynamic tradition. In fact, several interpersonal treatments for depression (e.g., Gotlib & Colby, 1987; Safran & Segal, 1990) are interpersonal and cognitive in focus.

Interpersonal approaches have been applied to the treatment of depression (Weissman & Klerman, 1990) because studies have shown that depression can result from and/or lead to difficulties in interpersonal relationships (Gotlib & Hammen, 1992). Weissman and Klerman's interpersonal psychotherapy (IPT) strives to reduce depressive symptoms by educating the client about the nature and course of depression (though medications may also be used). It also seeks to alter clients' interpersonal functioning by encouraging them to express their emotions, to communicate more clearly with significant others, and to explore their own interpersonal functioning.

Evaluation Compared to psychoanalysis, contemporary psychodynamic therapies are more concerned with interpersonal issues and less concerned with stages of

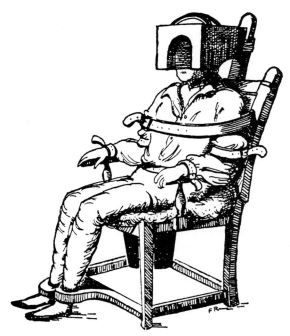

Benjamin Rush's tranquilizing chair restricts stimulation and activity. Perhaps a precursor of modern tranquilizer medications, the intent was to restrict the patient and maintain a state of tranquility. Although minimal restriction may still be required today, the tranquilizer chair is no longer used as a treatment for psychological disorder.

psychosexual development or with sex as a primary drive. They are also more likely to have been influenced by advances in other fields, such as the action-oriented therapies, discussed later in this chapter.

Although many psychologists are withholding judgment pending further evaluation of research, some have offered general praise for the interpersonal focus of contemporary psychodynamic therapies. Current data suggest that interpersonal psychotherapy reduces depression (Elkin et al., 1989; Elkin et al., 1995), but research evaluations are still under way for other disorders.

A Humanistic Approach to Therapy

Humanistic therapy emphasizes that each person has an inherent tendency toward growth and reaching one's full potential. The humanistic therapist believes that each individual is motivated and able to change and improve. But how can self-exploration and personal growth be facilitated? The goal of the humanistic therapist is to set the stage for clients to improve *themselves* — to facilitate self-exploration and to aid self-change. Unlike the psychodynamic therapist, the humanistic therapist does not interpret the client's behavior or thoughts, but instead works to establish a close and accepting relationship with clients that will encourage them to pursue their own therapeutic change. Humanistic therapy is perhaps best understood through a detailed consideration of one version of humanistic therapy — person-centered therapy, developed by Carl Rogers.

Person-Centered Therapy Originally referred to as client-centered therapy, Rogers's (1951) **person-centered** approach emphasizes the client's own self-perceptions, experiences, and personal understandings. The therapist does not tell the client what to do, does not interpret the client's actions, and does not offer solutions to the client's problems. To do any of these would be directive, and person-centered therapy is *non*directive: The therapist listens to the client's problems and is nonjudgmental and accepting, thus creating what is thought to be an optimally facilitative environment.

Just what constitutes a facilitative environment? Under what conditions will people take a careful and honest look at themselves and their interpersonal relationships? According to the person-centered approach, the therapist establishes the conditions for the client to improve by (1) being genuine, (2) providing accurate empathy, and (3) showing unconditional positive regard. Therapists exhibit **genuineness** by allowing their true inner feelings and thoughts to emerge honestly and openly — not by acting or playing a role, but by experiencing genuine feelings for and with the client. The therapist provides **accurate empathy** by coming to see and understand the world the way the client experiences it. The therapist then shares this understanding of the client's situation and the emotions associated with it. This sharing is accomplished in a relationship based on **unconditional positive regard** — an active acceptance, without judgment, of the client as a valued person and of the client's own interest in and ability to improve.

The person-centered therapist is an active listener who reflects and clarifies the client's stated thoughts and feelings. In active listening, the therapist acknowledges and accepts, and then echoes and refines, what the client has said. It requires a great deal of practice and patient understanding.

Sitting in on Person-Centered Group Therapy. The following transcript illustrates the role of the person-centered therapist. Because person-centered therapy has had a marked influence on the practice of group therapy, we include in this transcript a portion of the first therapy hour with six university students.

JANE: One thing I might say is my particular feeling that I want to work on a problem of the concept of dependence and independence in marriage. I've been married about a year and married to — he's a law student — who is primarily an unemotional person, and I would say there's a good deal of lack of understanding between us.

An artist's impression of a dream produced while under the influence of ether. Dreams have a magical and mysterious quality, and it is not surprising that the use of dream analysis has played a role in theories of psychopathology and psychotherapy.

LEADER: It's not wholly satisfactory to you now.

JANE: No, it is not a satisfactory relationship, but I do think there's a good deal of possibility of its being a satisfactory relationship.

BETTY: (*Pause*) I think most of my trouble is not having enough confidence in myself to assert myself when I am with others. I feel confidence in being able to do things, but when I'm in a social group or in a classroom, I more or less withdraw and let everybody else do the talking and thinking.

LEADER: You feel rather confident of your ability, privately or as an individual, yet when you work with people you tend to devalue yourself.

BETTY: That's right. I tend to evade issues or withdraw instead of meeting them face on.

LEADER: Yes.

JANE: Does that happen in small groups as well as large ones — amongst — uh, intimate family and social relationships?

BETTY: With a small group of good friends that I've known for some time, I don't have that feeling, but in a classroom or with my family groups, when we have relatives in, or just a gathering of family friends, I stick in the background.

LEADER: You have to feel pretty strongly supported by a small group of people before you feel free to be yourself. (Rogers, 1951, pp. 280–282)

Evaluation The harshest critics of person-centered therapy have called it simple-minded — as if all the therapist has to do is repeat what the client says. This criticism is unfounded. Like all therapeutic approaches, person-centered therapy, when done properly actually requires a great deal of training and practice as well as an understanding and patient therapist.

Person-centered therapists acknowledge the use of the scientific method for the study of the process and outcome of therapy. Indeed, Rogers and his colleagues (Rogers, Gendlin, Kiesler & Truax, 1967) were among the pioneers of therapy evaluation. One of their early findings was that patients whose therapists exhibited high levels of genuineness, empathy, and unconditional positive regard showed significant positive behavior change, whereas clients of therapists who offered low levels of these conditions showed deterioration in personality and behavioral functioning.

There have been criticisms, however. For instance, many studies of the effects of empathy have used trained observers to listen and score the degree to which the therapist was being empathic. The critics are quick to point out that the important consideration is not the observer's ratings but, rather, the client's ratings of the therapist's empathy; yet these were not the ratings used in most of the studies.

Subsequent evaluations of person-centered therapy have also yielded mixed findings. Reviewers (such as Orlinsky & Howard, 1986) continue to acknowledge that genuineness, accurate empathy, and unconditional positive regard by the therapist aid the client's search for understanding. But these conditions may not be sufficient for therapeutic gain or optimal for certain types of psychological abnormality. Although a person-centered approach might be appropriate for relatively healthy individuals who would profit from a better understanding of their interpersonal relationships, practitioners would probably not rely on it to treat a client with a severe anxiety disorder.

ACTION-ORIENTED THERAPIES

In the last forty years, action-oriented approaches to therapy have become a major force within the mental health field. Therapies with an action orientation encourage the client — child or adult — to change behavior and ways of thinking. They downplay aspects of the human condition that are nonobservable, such as the unconscious, and they emphasize the client's observable actions and reactions, measuring and evaluating the resulting changes in behavior. According to this approach, a client's perfectionism, phobic behavior, or depression *is* the problem, not merely a symptom of an unseen problem. The action-oriented therapies — behavior therapy, cognitive therapy, and problem-solving approaches to therapy — emphasize the use and practice of adaptive skills in the client's present situation.

Behavior Therapy

Behavioral explanations of psychological abnormality rely heavily on the principles of learning (see Chapter 2). A basic assumption of **behavior therapy** is that human action is acquired through the learning process (Salter, 1949). Understanding the factors that influence learning (such as rewards, punishments, and the environment) and providing opportunities for guided practice are central concerns of the behavioral therapist.

Applications based on classical conditioning, operant conditioning, and observational learning have had a meaningful impact on treatment (see Emmelkamp, 1994; Kazdin, 1994; O'Leary & Wilson, 1987). Indeed, many behavioral techniques are based on the principles of learning (see Table 3.2). In this chapter we look at only a few of these techniques; later, we examine more of them, and in greater detail, when we discuss their application to specific disorders.

Systematic Desensitization A therapy based on classical conditioning, called **systematic desensitization,** was developed by Joseph Wolpe at Temple University (Wolpe, 1958). In this approach the therapist assumes that the client is capable of adaptive responding but is hindered by debilitating anxiety. To reduce anxiety, systematic desensitization uses *counterconditioning,* a process in which the client is gradually taught to replace an undesirable response — the anxiety response — with one that is incompatible with the undesirable response — the relaxation response. Indeed, Wolpe (1973) described relaxation and the **anxiety hierarchy** as the two central features of systematic desensitization.

Because relaxation is the incompatible response that will replace anxiety, the client must be taught to recognize the presence of tension and to produce a state of relaxation. Systematic desensitization entails very gradual and systematic steps to achieve relaxation. Often, the first several sessions are devoted to building a relaxation response. To teach clients how to relax, therapists give them relaxation tasks to practice and audiotapes to listen to at home.

The anxiety hierarchy is an important component of desensitization. As Wolpe describes it, "An anxiety hierarchy is a list of stimuli, on a theme, ranked according to the amount of anxiety they evoke" (1973, p. 108). First, the therapist acquires detailed information about the client's anxiety and situational factors that contribute to it. Once the sources of unwanted anxiety are identified,

Table 3.2   Behavior Therapy Techniques

Type of Therapy	Description
Modeling	The process of learning (behavior and ways of viewing the world) by observing others
Role-play exercise	A procedure that utilizes staged practice opportunities to help develop interpersonal skills.
Systematic desensitization	A process based on classical conditioning in which fear responses are paired with relaxation. Often, images of feared situations are presented while the person relaxes.
Token economy	A system for improving behavior in which patients earn tokens (rewards) for accomplishing desirable behavior and the tokens can be exchanged for privileges or items of value to the person.
Homework activities	Out-of-session assignments that the client completes and monitors, and that the client and therapist evaluate collaboratively.
Exposure	A procedure for reducing anxiety that involves exposing the client to features of a feared situation so that the client experiences anxiety and has an opportunity to use new skills to manage the anxiety.

Behavior therapy is not a single approach to the treatment of psychological problems but, rather, a wide variety of treatment strategies and techniques that are applied in diverse settings and for a wide range of disorders. This list illustrates a sample of the many types of behavior therapy.

they are classified into themes and rank-ordered according to the level of anxiety associated with each.

Roger was twenty years old when he sought treatment. Unmarried, he lived with his parents and several siblings in a small house near the center of a large city. He completed three years of high school, worked part-time, and spent his free time hanging out with friends at a neighborhood tavern. He rarely ventured very far. Because he had an intense fear of riding in a car, getting around town on foot was his only means of transportation. The following is a brief illustration of a hierarchy appropriate for Roger, based on his and his therapist's collaborative ranking of the activities.

- *Discovering that food needs to be purchased at the store*

- *Anticipating an approaching holiday when visiting is expected*

- *Planning a trip out of town*

- *Sitting in the front seat of a sedan*

- *Sitting in the front seat of a small sports car*

- *Driving a car*

- *Driving a small car*

The sheer anticipation of having to be in an automobile was sufficient to produce mildly distressing anxiety. Actually being in a car produced greater distress. Also of note, the size of the car mattered for this client: A small sports car was more distressing than a larger sedan.

In the desensitization process, the client — in a state of complete relaxation — is asked by the therapist to first imagine the least-provoking situation. If the client can stay relaxed, the therapist moves up the hierarchy, asking the client to imagine the next situation. When the client experiences unwanted anxiety, he signals the therapist, the relaxation is reintroduced, and the client imagines a scene that was not anxiety provoking. Gradually, perhaps after only three to five situations per session, the therapist moves the client up the hierarchy until he can remain relaxed while imagining the highest situation on the hierarchy.

Although a wide range of research studies have indicated that systematic desensitization can reduce unwanted anxiety associated with specific situations or things, the extent to which the effects spread to other situations and the way that desensitization works are unclear. Research has suggested that exposure — whereby patients confront the once-feared objects or situations — is an active component of treatment (Barlow, 1988). By facing and not avoiding the fearful situation, the person learns that the situation can be faced without catastrophe. Recall Rameen, from the beginning of the chapter: Having to face his interpersonal fears by meeting people at the mall, he was able to overcome those fears.

Operant Procedures Experiments based on the work of B. F. Skinner and others (Skinner, 1953, 1969; see also special issue of *American Psychologist,* 1992) have shown that reinforced behaviors are more likely to recur. Furthermore, if behaviors that are closer and closer approximations of the desired behavior are reinforced, then these adaptive behaviors can come to replace maladaptive ones. These facts form the basis for **operant conditioning procedures,** which seek to alter problem behaviors by applying positive and negative reinforcements and by shaping through successive approximations. In a treatment of depression, for example (Lewinsohn, Biglan & Zeiss, 1976), clients develop "menus" of pleasant events to use later to reinforce self-enhancing behaviors that will reduce depression. Rewards can be linked to exercise, maintenance of social relationships, participation in work activities, or any desirable behavior.

Another application of operant procedures is a reinforcement system called a **token economy** (Atthowe & Krasner, 1968; Kazdin, 1994). This approach uses tokens much like money is used in an economic system. The therapist makes explicit the desirable behaviors and the number of tokens administered for their performance. For example, a token economy was designed for a ward in a California mental hospital where patients were not engaging in interpersonal interactions and not participating in ward activities. The economy identified as desirable certain behaviors relevant to personal hygiene (bathing), ward maintenance (chores), social interaction (conversations), and attendance in self-improvement classes (therapy). A patient who completed a desired behavior was credited with tokens that were later exchanged for reinforcers — snacks, special events, or special hospital privileges. Many token economy programs, in a variety of settings, have been successful in altering behavior and improving the overall level of client functioning (Lovaas, 1987).

One classic illustration of a token economy is Achievement Place, a homestyle rehabilitation program for delinquent boys (Phillips, 1968). The boys at Achievement Place earned tokens for desired behavior and lost them for inappropriate behavior (see Table 3.3). Data gathered to evaluate this token economy suggested that it was a successful intervention technique for "speaking aggressively" (for example, "I'll kill you if you get in my way"). As shown in Figure 3.1, three boys exhibited a marked reduction in aggressive statements

In a token economy, desirable behaviors earn points or tokens, and undesirable behaviors lose points. Here are examples of ways that points can be earned or lost at Achievement Place, a homestyle rehabilitation program for delinquent boys.

Table 3.3 Earning and Losing Points in a Token Economy

Behaviors Earning Points	Points
1. Watching news on television or reading the newspaper	300 per day
2. Cleaning and maintaining neatness in one's room	500 per day
3. Reading books	5–10 per page
4. Aiding houseparents in various household tasks	20–1,000 per task
5. Performing homework	500 per day
6. Obtaining desirable grades on school report cards	500–1,000 per grade
7. Turning out lights when not in use	25 per light

Behaviors Losing Points	Points
1. Failing grades on the report card	500–1,000 per grade
2. Speaking aggressively	20–50 per response
3. Forgetting to wash hands before meals	100–300 per meal
4. Disobeying	100–1,000 per response
5. Being late	10 per minute
6. Displaying poor manners	50–100 per response
7. Stealing, lying, or cheating	10,000 per response

Source: Phillips (1968).

after receiving fines that resulted in the withdrawal of tokens.

Today, operant procedures are not used by themselves as a method of treatment. Rather, they are combined with many behavioral and other forms of therapies (e.g., Ammerman & Hersen, 1995). For instance, a student in a special school might experience a token economy in the classroom; attend an individual, person-centered, weekly therapy session; and participate in a community meeting where students and staff provide each other with social support and discuss problems that emerge in the school.

Observational Learning Action-oriented therapists often use the principles of **modeling,** or learning that occurs through observing a desired behavior in others. Modeling is effective in a broad range of behavior problems. Shy and withdrawn youths may overcome social avoidance behavior by participating in a small group, adults may initiate more independent and assertive behavior following a therapist's or peer's demonstration, and individuals lacking in response options may see a world of opportunity by watching an effective problem solver in action.

Numerous studies of modeling have been conducted and reported, largely in the 1970s and early 1980s (see Masters, Burish, Hollon & Rimm, 1987). The results point to a fairly consistent conclusion: Exposing someone to a model who demonstrates desired behaviors increases the likelihood that observers will perform similarly in the future. Unassertive individuals become increasingly more assertive (Kazdin, 1974), dog-phobic youths are able to approach dogs (Bandura, Grusec & Menlove, 1967), and sexually anxious women modify their sexual behavior and attitudes (Everaerd & Dekker, 1982).

In treatment applications, certain features of the model and the observer can contribute to the effectiveness of modeling. For instance, models are likely to generate imitative behavior if they are distinctive and capture the attention of the observer, if they are powerful and associated with the dispensing of rewards, if they are similar to the observer, and if they are already admired by the observer. Moreover, modeling is most likely to be effective when the observer is emotionally comfortable, motivated, and paying attention.

Therapists can choose from three modeling procedures: filmed modeling, live modeling, and participant modeling, which involves live modeling by a therapist who guides the client through the fearful situation. Therapists can also choose to model either mastery or coping behavior. Consider, for example, a client who is trying to overcome fearful behavior. A *mastery model* would demonstrate ideal (fearless) behavior. In contrast, a *coping model* would initially demonstrate apprehension but subsequently model strategies to overcome the fear and eventually act fearlessly. Coping models seem to be more effective than mastery models in helping clients

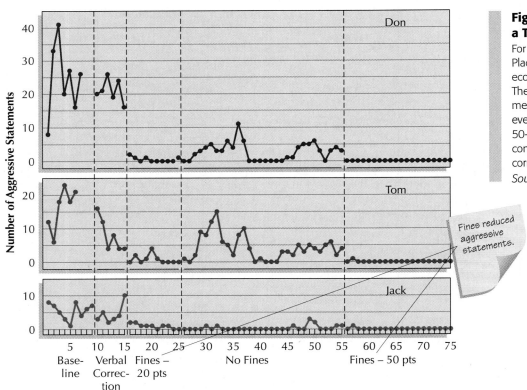

Figure 3.1 The Effects of a Token Economy

For three youths at Achievement Place, the use of fines in a token economy had beneficial effects. The number of aggressive statements declined dramatically or even stopped in the 20-point and 50-point fine conditions when compared to the baseline, verbal correction, and no-fine conditions. *Source:* Phillips (1968).

overcome avoidance (Ginther & Roberts, 1982; Meichenbaum, 1971), perhaps because the coping models are more similar to the observing clients themselves.

Research into the process of modeling has suggested that clients alter their sense of self-efficacy as they develop newly acquired responses. *Self-efficacy* is confidence in one's ability to cope with difficulties (Bandura, 1977). Observers who witness models successfully coping with various situations often experience an increased sense of their ability to cope with difficulties.

Modeling is typically not a solo intervention. Rather, modeling procedures are integrated with other behavioral strategies such as rewards and relaxation. Treatments that have been evaluated in research often integrate applications of modeling within the treatment. Observational learning has influenced therapy because therapists now pay attention both to what they demonstrate and to what clients observe.

Evaluation   Behavioral therapists score high marks for their conscientiousness in scientific evaluation, but the scientific side of behavior therapy has been a double-edged sword. Some critics have described behavior therapy as mechanical in its application and as limiting the benefits of treatment to changes in observable behavior. Others note that clients engage in the desired behavior while in therapy but do not necessarily generalize the desired behaviors to other settings over time.

Behavior therapy was criticized early on for downplaying the role of human thoughts, or cognition, in psychological maladjustment. For contemporary behavioral therapists, however, modeling as well as classical and operant conditioning procedures constitute only part of a comprehensive intervention. Indeed, behavioral therapists are concerned with the therapeutic relationship and with clients' relationships with significant others in their lives, and they incorporate behavioral strategies with this clinical sensitivity in mind. Behavioral therapists are also careful to attend to their clients' cognition — what they are saying to themselves — while they partake of behavior therapy. In treatments involving modeling, for instance, therapists are interested in the client's cognitive activity while the client is watching the model, when the modeling is over, and while the client is trying the new behaviors. In fact, cognitive factors have been integrated into many of the action-oriented behavior therapies.

Cognitive-Behavioral Therapy

As suggested by the label, **cognitive-behavioral therapy** combines behavioral performance-based interventions with strategies that address the client's thinking. In cognitive therapy, clients are encouraged to examine and challenge their automatic thinking, replacing distorted thoughts with realistic understanding. This process encourages the clients to become more active, to engage

in rewarding experiences, and to tackle the problems contributing to the distressing mood (Beck, 1995). Basic to the treatment is **collaborative empiricism,** whereby the client and therapist work together to identify problems, design and execute tests of specific hypotheses, and reexamine beliefs. Ideally, the data generated by the client provide the instigation for adaptive change (Hollon & Beck, 1979). Combining behavioral and cognitive strategies is currently a preferred approach among the action-oriented therapies.

The following principles (adapted from Mahoney & Arnkoff, 1978) capture the basic tenets of cognitive-behavioral interventions:

1. People respond to how they *think* the world is, rather than to how it actually is.

2. Thoughts, feelings, and behaviors are causally interrelated. No one domain is primary; they all influence each other.

3. The cognitive activities of clients are central to producing, predicting, and understanding effects of therapeutic interventions, and cognitive therapies try to clarify and alter the way people think about themselves and their worlds.

4. Cognitive processes can be integrated with behavioral paradigms, and it is both possible and desirable to do so.

One distinctive feature of cognitive-behavioral therapy is that client and therapist work together to evaluate problems, generate potential solutions, try out plans of action, and evaluate the effects. In the context of this collaborative empiricism (Hollon & Beck, 1994), the client participates actively in suggesting ideas, trying out new behaviors, and reporting back to the therapist. Using action and practice, and employing sound principles of reasoning, client and therapist strive together to alter behavior, emotion, and cognitive processing.

One way to get a flavor of the cognitive-behavioral approach and see how it differs from the insight-oriented approach is to consider how each looks at and handles a client's resistance. Psychoanalytic theory, for instance, suggests that resistance reflects unconscious processes; cognitive-behavioral theory focuses not on intrapsychic processes but on the noncompliance itself. Note that the strongest influence on how cooperative a client will be is the client's beliefs about the therapeutic process. Private monologues about the progress of the therapy, the attitudes of the therapist, the feasibility of change, and the meaning of setbacks may all lead to treatment impasses (Cameron, 1978; Lazarus & Fay, 1981; Meichenbaum & Gilmore, 1982). For example, if a client says to himself, "I'm not going to listen to this woman; she dresses like a slob, and she keeps a really messy office," then his performance will probably reflect these negative attitudes toward the therapist. Another client who thinks that nothing will help is unlikely to be an involved or motivated client. Conversely, a client who believes in the treatment is more apt to succeed.

Cognitive-behavioral therapists are more likely than their insight-oriented counterparts to focus on specific procedures for preventing resistance and modifying its effects. They apply strategies directly to influence treatment adherence (e.g., Meichenbaum & Turk, 1987). To forestall resistance, the therapist might conduct thorough analyses of the client's problems, skills, and goals to select appropriate procedures. Before implementing the procedures, the therapist might offer a clear rationale for them, emphasize the gradual nature of change, and use Socratic dialogue and hypothesis-testing techniques. When resistance does occur, the cognitive-behavioral therapist treats it as an opportunity for engaging in the same kind of cognitive analysis that is applied to other material: Like anomalous data for the scientist, resistance can provide additional occasions for exploring the nature of the client's thoughts, feelings, and behavior. Is this approach appealing to clients? Evidently so; one study indicates that, of five different therapies, the cognitive-behavioral orientation was most preferred by clients (Wanigaratne & Barker, 1995).

Included in the cognitive-behavioral approach are rational-emotive therapy (Ellis, 1962), cognitive therapy for depression (Beck, Rush, Shaw & Emery, 1979), and problem-solving approaches to therapy (Kendall & Braswell, 1993). We now consider each of these therapies in turn.

Rational-Emotive Therapy An early example of the cognitive-behavioral approach was articulated more than thirty years ago by Albert Ellis (1962). Departing from his psychoanalytic background, Ellis advanced the premise that psychological disturbances result from cognitive distortions that he labeled *irrational beliefs* (see Chapter 2). Based on the belief that human beings habitually filter their perceptions through the beliefs that they hold about themselves and the world, **rational-emotive therapy (RET)** teaches clients to identify and change the illogical notions that underlie their distressing symptoms.

Rational-emotive therapy focuses on changing pervasive patterns of irrational thinking rather than on target symptoms. Although it incorporates behavioral techniques, as Ellis explains, RET "largely consists of the use of the logico-empirical method of scientific questioning, challenging, and debating" (1977, p. 20). Therapists train clients to replace maladaptive thoughts, such as "I can't stand it" or "It shouldn't happen," with more rational responses, such as "It is unpleasant, but I can tolerate it" or "I wish it hadn't happened" (Lipsky, Kassinove & Miller, 1980). The goal is to promote a "new philosophy" that will enable clients to view themselves and others in a more sensible, rational manner.

RET may also include rational role reversal, in which the patient guides the therapist through a problem using the "A-B-C" model (see Chapter 2). Another frequent technique of RET involves "shame exercises," in which clients are encouraged to perform embarrassing activities deliberately to challenge their need for conventionality and to demonstrate that the consequences of carrying out socially prohibited acts are rarely catastrophic. Shaving in public, for Mr. Berg, was an example of this strategy.

Sitting In on Rational-Emotive Therapy The following dialogue, between an RET therapist and a client with a posttraumatic stress disorder (see Chapter 6) and extreme anger, addresses the client's relationship with her spouse after an accident.

THERAPIST: So, Carol, if I understand you correctly, you feel extremely angry at Ted for not being more understanding and caring about your condition.

CLIENT: I get so mad at him I could wring his neck!

THERAPIST: Would you say that your anger at Ted is helpful, or is it getting in the way?

CLIENT: I don't know, I guess it really doesn't help. Ted just withdraws and then I feel worse, like I'm really all alone.

THERAPIST: So it sounds like if there were some way that you could not feel so angry, and perhaps figure out some way to get Ted to be more supportive, that would be best for you.

CLIENT: Right, that's what I really want.

THERAPIST: Well, perhaps if we can work on the anger first, then we can do some problem solving on how to get Ted to be more supportive.

CLIENT: All right.

THERAPIST: Fine, now remember how we've talked about how your thoughts and beliefs affect your emotions. Let's then try to figure out how your thinking might be connected to your anger at Ted. Any ideas about what goes through your mind when you're most angry at Ted?

CLIENT: (*Pause*) Well, I just keep thinking that if he really cared, he would be more understanding of my needs. Because he's my husband, he should understand better than anyone else how my anxiety since the accident affects me.

THERAPIST: So it seems that Ted more than anyone else should realize how the accident has affected you.

CLIENT: Right, but when I startle so easily, he just gets irritated. He doesn't understand why I now avoid driving on freeways.

Severe fear of flying motivates television sportscaster and former Oakland Raiders football coach John Madden to travel to his assignments not by airplane but in a custom-made luxury bus.

THERAPIST: I think that you've hit on it with the belief that he should understand. It sounds like more than just wishing or preferring he would be more understanding.

CLIENT: Right.

THERAPIST: So, I think it's the *should* that really keeps the anger going. If that's the case, what do we need to do to reduce the anger?

CLIENT: Well, not think in terms of *shoulds,* I guess.

THERAPIST: Right. Now, to do that, we need to understand why the *should* may not be so reasonable. See any problems with the *should?*

CLIENT: Well, I'm demanding that he be more understanding.
(*And later . . .*)

CLIENT: I just wish he did understand. I could really use his support.

THERAPIST: Of course you do. And as long as you stick to wishing and not demanding, will you feel so angry?

CLIENT: I suppose not. (Adapted from Warren & Zgourides, 1991, pp. 159–160)

Continuing Concerns Conceptual criticisms of RET theory include questions about Ellis's identification of a core set of specific irrational beliefs and his tendency to equate rationality and adaptiveness (Smith, 1989; Zettle & Hayes, 1980). Ellis has suggested that a therapist "can easily put almost all [the] thousands of ideas [expressed by clients] into a few general categories" (1977, p. 5), but Diane Arnkoff and Carol Glass (1982) of the Catholic University of America argue that "there is no 'correct' list of irrational beliefs that can be decided on for all people on an *a priori* basis." Arnkoff and Glass have also expressed a preference for the characterization of beliefs as "maladaptive" or "dysfunctional" rather than "irrational." They contend that a functional view of "rationality" must take into account the utility of each client's beliefs, recognizing that "irrational" ideas can sometimes be effective and desirable, whereas "rational" ones may prove maladaptive in certain situations. Although the notion that beliefs influence emotion and behavior has both an empirical basis and fairly widespread acceptance, RET's extrapolations from this premise have been questioned philosophically and experimentally (see Bernard & DiGiuseppe, 1989; Mahoney, Lyddon & Alford, 1989; Rorer, 1989).

Practical problems with RET center on two issues: (1) The method gives little attention to diagnostic issues, and (2) it has yet to provide comprehensive analyses of and therapeutic strategies specifically designed for different forms of psychopathology. The procedures of RET are put forth as appropriate treatment for a wide variety of disorders, ranging from anxiety to substance abuse, yet few of these procedures include specific prescriptions for tailoring therapeutic strategies to the target problems.

Cognitive Therapy for Depression   Not all psychological disorders are alike, so it is essential that a treatment for a precise disorder pay attention to the features specific to that disorder. Aaron Beck's **cognitive therapy for depression** provides an example of just such an approach. Derived from Beck's (1963) cognitive formulation and description of the nature of depression, this treatment approach (Beck, Rush, Shaw & Emery, 1979) seeks to modify depressive emotional states by altering the client's cognitive functioning. In particular, the therapist and client work together to test and change the client's inaccurate and maladaptive thoughts and assumptions.

Beck's cognitive therapy is an active, structured, and usually time-limited approach to treatment. As part of his conceptualization of depression, Beck believes that maladaptive beliefs and illogical thinking habits are tied to depressed states. Maladaptive beliefs give rise to negative self-verbalizations, which Beck calls *automatic negative thoughts* — statements that clients make to themselves without testing their accuracy. Consider the example of Denise, who was attending a small group meeting at work. The group was discussing ways to improve efficiency in the office. Denise made a suggestion. When the group did not immediately agree that it was the best idea, Beth thought, "My idea was terrible; I'm no good." Her self-statement, a harsh and overly critical commentary on her idea, went untested. That is, she didn't make the effort to evaluate the accuracy of the automatic negative thought.

Beck's therapy typically includes both behavioral and cognitive techniques. The behavioral procedures recommended are daily self-monitoring of both activities and mood levels, activity scheduling, graded task assignments, and role-playing exercises. Activity scheduling means doing something rather than nothing, which is one of the most powerful antidepressants available to us. The treatment also includes extensive self-monitoring of cognition and related mood on a structured data form. In this procedure, clients are guided by therapists to formulate specific predictions related to their dysfunctional beliefs. They then design and carry out experiments that bear on these predictions and, at a later time, reevaluate their original hypotheses. In short, the clients gather data to test specific hypotheses and typically bear witness to evidence that their beliefs were inaccurate and dysfunctional (see also Salkovskis, 1996).

Sitting In on Cognitive Therapy for Depression The following transcript involves a woman who complained of headaches and who stated that "My family doesn't appreciate me; I'm worthless."

CLIENT: My son doesn't like to go to the theater or to the movies with me anymore.

THERAPIST: How do you know that he doesn't want to go with you?

CLIENT: Teenagers don't actually like to do things with their parents.

THERAPIST: Have you actually asked him to go with you?

CLIENT: No, as a matter of fact, he did ask me a few times if I wanted him to take me . . . but I didn't think he really wanted to go.

THERAPIST: How about testing it out by asking him to give you a straight answer?

CLIENT: I guess so.

THERAPIST: The important thing is not whether or not he goes with you but whether you are deciding for him what he thinks instead of letting him tell you.

CLIENT: I guess you are right but he does seem to be inconsiderate. For example, he is always late for dinner.

THERAPIST: How often has that happened?

CLIENT: Oh, once or twice. . . . I guess that's really not all that often.

THERAPIST: Is he coming late to dinner due to his being inconsiderate?

CLIENT: Well, come to think of it, he did say that he had been working late those two nights. Also, he has been considerate in a lot of other ways. (From Beck, Rush, Shaw & Emery, 1979, pp. 155–156)

As it turned out, the patient discovered that her son would go to the movies with her. It is important that the therapist did not accept the client's faulty conclusions and inferences but, instead, persisted in checking their accuracy.

Evaluation   The research evaluations of Beck's cognitive therapy for depression are discussed in Chapter 8. It is worth noting here, however, that studies have found the treatment to be effective (Hollon & Beck, 1994), and recent studies have assessed and compared the effectiveness of Beck's therapy to the effects produced by antidepressant medications. (These medications are discussed later in the present chapter.) An early report (Rush, Beck, Kovacs & Hollon, 1977) provided evidence that the psychological treatment was comparable in effectiveness to the treatment with medications, and more recent reports provide similar findings (see also Elkin et al., 1989; Hollon et al., 1992). For example, in one study using subjects' self-reported state of depression and in another using clinicians' ratings of patients' mood, clients showed significant improvement over the course of both cognitive therapy and medications (see Figure 3.2).

But what happens after treatment is completed or medications are discontinued? Are patients cured? Studies indicate that, whereas medication effects dissipate once the medications are discontinued, the effects of cognitive therapy are potent in preventing relapse (the recurrence of depression). Consider the following data: Within four months after medications were discontinued, 50 percent of patients experienced a relapse of depression. In contrast, only 10 percent of cognitive therapy patients relapsed four months after treatment, and only 21 percent relapsed after a full two years (Evans et al., 1992).

Based on a review of twenty-eight studies, Keith Dobson (1989) concluded that cognitive therapy compared favorably to control conditions and to other forms of psychotherapy. Although it is not the only useful treatment for depression, data suggest that it can be effective.

Critics of research on cognitive therapy have raised some interesting questions. For example, when different therapies produce comparable results, how can we know whether clients are improving because of something specific to cognitive therapy or as a result of some nonspecific mechanisms common to other psychological therapies? And what treatment effects can be expected in cases involving *comorbidity,* in which clients who are depressed also have other psychological problems such as alcoholism or drug abuse?

Critics of the practice of cognitive therapy have asked about the origins of maladaptive cognitive functioning (Sarason, 1979). For instance, how and where do depressive styles of thinking originate? These critics

suggest that cognitive therapy could be enhanced through attention to the sources of the dysfunctional thinking. Finally, cognitive therapy has been challenged on the erroneous grounds that it is a simple promotion of the power of positive self-talk.

WHAT'S NORMAL?
The Power of Non-Negative Thinking

Perhaps you are wondering about your own thinking. Do you find yourself making harsh judgments about your performance? If you sometimes think negatively, are you abnormal or maladjusted?

Negative thinking is self-critical (for example, "I can't do anything well"), whereas *positive thinking* is upbeat, coping-oriented, and self-enhancing (for example, "I can handle it"). One way researchers examine thinking is by tapping an individual's ongoing self-talk through measurements based on thinking aloud, thought listing, and questionnaires. Everyone, at times, has negative thoughts. In fact, some negative thinking is normal. However, persons who are well adjusted show lower levels of negative thinking when compared with persons who are less well adjusted. Indeed, the presence of excessive negative thinking not only separates normal persons from distressed persons but also diminishes noticeably following successful therapy (e.g., Kendrick, Craig, Lawson & Davidson, 1982; Treadwell & Kendall, 1996).

What is the proper balance between positive and negative thinking? Some nonprofessionals proselytize about the power of positive thinking and claim that you can accomplish any goal if you just commit to telling

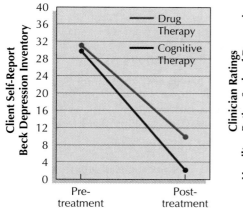

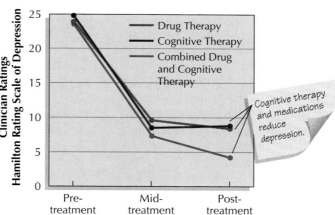

Figure 3.2   Outcomes from Treatments for Depression

(A) As measured by the Beck Depression Inventory (BDI), the self-reports of clients who received cognitive therapy for depression and those who received medication (imipramine) showed a meaningful decrease in depression over the course of a three-month treatment period (Rush, Beck, Kovacs & Hollon, 1992). **(B)** As measured by clinicians' ratings of patients' mood on the Hamilton

Rating Scale of Depression (HRSD), a meaningful reduction in patients' depression occurred at both midtreatment and posttreatment (Hollon et al., 1992). These studies, and others, give weight to the claim that cognitive therapy can be as effective as medication in the treatment of depression.

"Sorry, no water. We're just a support group."

yourself that you can. Is such completely positive thinking the ideal? Research and theory (Kendall, Howard & Hays, 1989; Schwartz & Garamoni, 1986) have suggested that psychological adjustment is associated with an optimal ratio of 66 percent positive thinking to 34 percent negative thinking. Although these numbers aren't magic, they emerged from studies that assessed the frequency of both positive and negative self-talk and the presence or absence of psychological maladjustment. In the absence of maladjustment, the positive-to-negative ratios were 63:37 in one study and 64:36 in another. But in the presence of increasing maladjustment such as depression, the ratio was closer to 50:50. Of course, there is variability around this optimal ratio, but it is approximately 2:1 positive-to-negative thinking.

In short, psychologically healthy thinking is not 100 percent positive. It includes some negative thinking, but not enough to outweigh or dominate the positive thinking. A therapist who is working to help a woman improve her self-esteem would not encourage the client to tell herself, "I am the greatest. I can do anything!" On the contrary, a healthy self-esteem is more likely to approximate the following self-talk: "I'm not perfect, but I have many good qualities." Successful treatment produces a favorable balance between positive and negative thinking.

Problem-Solving Approaches to Therapy   Consistent with other cognitive-behavioral therapies, the **problem-solving therapist,** working in collaboration with the client, generates a variety of hypotheses and systematically assesses the merits of alternative solutions to personal problems. But unlike rational-emotive therapy and cognitive therapy for depression, in which the therapist works to correct clients' *distorted* thinking, problem-

solving treatments are useful to help clients overcome *deficiencies* in thinking.

The cognitive aspect of problem solving addresses the thinking steps that help to resolve the problem; the behavioral aspect enables the client to practice the desired behavior and earn the desired reward. Unlike the insight-oriented therapies, in which the therapist might infer an underlying problem from the observed symptoms, problem-solving approaches identify specific problems that need attention and focus the treatment on a careful and reasoned solution to them.

A number of researchers have described the process of problem solving and its relevance to therapy (D'Zurilla, 1986; Kendall & Braswell, 1993; Nezu, Nezu & Peri, 1989; Weissberg, Caplan & Harwood, 1991). Typically, the problem-solving process is divided into five steps:

1. Identify the problem.

2. Generate alternative solutions.

3. Anticipate the behavioral and emotional consequences.

4. Make a decision.

5. Implement and evaluate the plan.

The first step is to identify the problem that needs to be solved. This involves discussing the problem and defining it as specifically as possible. A well-defined problem is likely to lead to an appropriate and effective plan of action; therapeutic efforts at a solution to a poorly defined problem may be misguided. When a client reports more than one problem, it is the therapist's task to discern which problem is the most important for this client at this particular time.

Having identified a problem in need of a solution, the therapist and client collaborate to generate many ideas about possible solutions, but without judging the merits of these ideas. Premature judgments tend to hinder, not advance, the process of thinking creatively. It is useful to anticipate the behavioral and emotional consequences of possible plans and solutions.

Decision making, or making a plan of action, involves discussing how to implement the various alternatives that were generated, and also considering the likelihood that the most appealing alternative solutions might actually be beneficial. Then, the client can try out solutions to see if they are effective. Hence, decision making, and the next stage, implementation and evaluation, have a combined impact on the eventual solution.

The problem-solving approach has been applied to a variety of psychological disorders, including impulsivity in childhood (Kendall & Braswell, 1993), adult depression (Nezu, Nezu & Peri, 1989), and marital distress (Margolin, 1987). This approach has also been applied in **preventive treatment** — targeting clients at risk for the later development of disorders. In New Haven, Connecticut, Roger Weissberg and his associates (Caplan et al., 1992; Weissberg, Caplan & Harwood, 1991) provided a problem-solving intervention for children at risk for drug abuse, delinquency, and unwanted pregnancy. The program consisted of a series of lessons, delivered as part of a social problem-solving curriculum in the schools. It resulted in improved teacher ratings of conflict-resolution skills, impulse control, and peer relations as well as in students' self-reports of substance-use intentions and excessive alcohol use.

Critics of the problem-solving approach argue that problem-solving skills can be learned and used in one setting but do not always generalize to other contexts. One way to increase generalization, however, is to involve significant others in the problem-solving process.

FAMILY AND COUPLES THERAPY

The family, or couple, is a crucial interpersonal system in every person's life. It is where individuals learn to interact, where psychological disorders are displayed, and where therapeutic change can be facilitated. Several approaches to the treatment of the family (Bowen, 1978; Minuchin, Lee & Simon, 1996) and couples (Margolin, 1987; Alexander, Holtzworth-Munroe & Jameson, 1994) are based on the notion that the source of psychological disorder is within the system, not within the individual.

Both insight- and action-oriented approaches can be applied when more than one person is in treatment. In general, however, family therapists are systems therapists. Each family has its own set of rules, communication patterns, and expectations for its members, and

these combine to form the interpersonal system. When there is evidence of abnormality, family therapists change the system.

Insight-Oriented Family and Couples Therapy

Insight-oriented therapists working with families tend to focus on the disturbed relationships that the therapist identifies within the family and on the resolution of hidden or unconscious sources of conflict. For example, in his chapter on psychoanalytic family therapy, Nichols (1984) provided an example of how intrapsychic conflict can be displayed in a family. Consider the following case. An important goal in insight-oriented family therapy is for the parents to gain an understanding of the family situation.

> *The J family sought help controlling fifteen-year-old Paul's delinquent behavior. Arrested several times for vandalism, Paul seemed neither ashamed nor able to understand his compulsion to strike out against authority. As therapy progressed, it became clear that Paul's father harbored a deep but unexpressed resentment of the social conditions that made him work long hours for low wages in a factory, while the "fat cats didn't do shit, but still drove around in Cadillacs." Once the therapist became aware of Mr. J's strong but unexpressed hatred of authority, they also began to notice that he smiled slightly when Mrs. J described Paul's latest exploits. (Nichols, 1984, p. 194)*

The acting-out of this fifteen-year-old son brought the parents to treatment, but the father's role in the boy's behavior was a sign of a disturbed family system.

Action-Oriented Family and Couples Therapy

Action-oriented family and couples therapists emphasize active and direct involvement in the interpersonal system to produce change. An important goal of this approach is to improve social skills and communication among the participants.

Action-Oriented Family Therapy One of the founders of family therapy, Virginia Satir (1964), stressed the need to revise the interaction patterns that develop among family members. Her approach, **conjoint family therapy,** requires that all members of a family be seen together in therapy as a single group. Because the goal is to change their dysfunctional patterns of communication, the therapist is active and direct in pointing out any observed communication difficulties.

Among family therapists, Salvador Minuchin's (1974) work with anorexic youths is often cited. Traditionally, *anorexia,* a dysfunction manifested by a discontinuation of food intake (and resulting weight loss), has been difficult to treat. Minuchin's family

In couples therapy, individuals learn to interact effectively under the guidance of a trained therapist, who acts as both facilitator and referee.

treatment approach targets the parent-parent and parent-child relationships. In the following example, the anorexic is Laura, but Minuchin has the entire family attend the session — the parents, Mr. and Mrs. R, Laura (age fourteen), Jill (age twelve), and Steven (age ten) (Aponte & Hoffman, 1973). Laura's eating disorder was the identified problem, and Minuchin's plan included having the family eat lunch together during the therapy session.

Before the actual lunch began, family members were asked to discuss the problem. Minuchin observed that although there were disagreements among family members, the mother denied that anyone in the family disagreed with anyone else. Although not stated openly, the mother's behavior revealed her belief that all members of the family should think alike and agree on everything. Minuchin noted the parental control and speculated that privacy and independence were taboo in this family.

As the session progressed, it became clear that Mr. and Mrs. R had no relationship with each other outside of their role as parents. Minuchin initiated a direct dialogue that involved having them talk to each other instead of to the children. Stressing the importance of an independent adult relationship for the parents, he rearranged the seating so that mother and father sat together. Minuchin challenged the parents, now seated as a unit, and stressed that they seemed to want Laura to be just like her siblings although she was fourteen years old. Without blaming Laura, Minuchin reframed the

eating problem as being related to the parents' need for their own relationship and to Laura's need for developmentally legitimate self-assertion. This scenario points to an abnormality that is not within the individual but within a disturbed family system.

Family therapists who follow behavioral and cognitive-behavioral theories use the various strategies already discussed to address family problems. As an illustration, consider how these theories and strategies can be applied to conduct problems in children.

Persistent difficulties with aggression, stealing, disobedience, truancy, and related conduct problems among youths have been labeled as *conduct disorder* (see Chapter 17), and they are often attributed to the unfavorable influence of a dysfunctional family. One or both parents may be ill-equipped to raise their offspring owing to a lack of parenting skills, the presence of a personal psychological disorder, a lack of time or energy because of demands from work, or some combination of untoward influences. Not surprisingly, treatments for conduct disorder often involve the entire family.

In action-oriented family therapy, parents learn skills for the management of their children (Forehand & McMahon, 1981; Webster-Stratton & Herbert, 1994; Patterson, Chamberlain & Reid, 1982). The therapy includes teaching parents how to use principles of social learning — rewards, ignoring, and time-out procedures — to modify their child's behavior. Parents practice using their new skills with the guidance and feedback of the therapist. Throughout the therapy, the child's behavior is monitored to provide data for an evaluation of the outcomes.

Action-Oriented Couples Therapy   Couples therapy emerged from the need for interventions to rectify relationship problems such as marital discord. Even when neither member of a couple qualifies for diagnosis of a disorder, their relationship may nevertheless be a source of serious concern and distress. The therapist sees the couple together and focuses treatment on the relationship issues.

Action-oriented couples therapy has often been called *behavioral marital therapy* (BMT) because most early applications involved married couples. Currently, however, the therapy is geared toward the relationships of couples whether married or not. BMT is labeled behavioral because of its use of skills training and homework assignments as well as in-session practice. But like the whole field of behavior therapy, BMT has become increasingly concerned with cognitive functioning. In current BMT practice, cognitive intervention strategies are widely used (Baucom & Epstein, 1989; Epstein & Baucom, 1993; Fruzzetti & Jacobson, 1991). Such strategies include correcting spouses' negative attributions about their partners, reducing unrealistic expectations, and changing spouses' negative self-talk about their partners.

BMT also focuses on communications and problem solving (Jacobson & Margolin, 1979). In fact, the problem-solving process described earlier readily applies to couples treatment. Consider the case of a couple whose relationship has evolved into a distant and verbally abusive exchange. The problem to be solved is that the husband has long relied on negative tactics for control — threats, criticisms, and aggressive language. Although his efforts to control initially suppressed unwanted behavior in his spouse, they have become overused and excessive. Soon the wife, too, is resorting to threats and demands. Stuck in a cycle, the couple will be unable to create a different pattern of interaction unless they come to recognize the original problem and take steps to solve it.

BMT and BMT plus cognitive therapy have been found to be effective in improving marital adjustment (e.g., Baucom & Lester, 1986). Interestingly, both BMT and BMT plus cognitive-behavioral therapy were better than waitlist, and the effectiveness was similar for both the men and the women involved in the treatment (see Figure 3.3).

Several couples therapies address communications problems, but the action-oriented approach applies systematic training procedures, including specific instructions, evaluative feedback, and opportunities for behavioral rehearsal. In other words, couples cannot just talk about communicating more clearly; they must

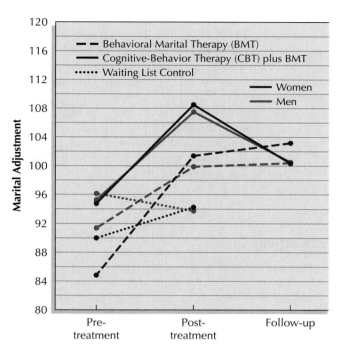

Figure 3.3   Action-Oriented Couples Therapy
Evidence of treatment efficacy. For men and for women, behavioral marital therapy (BMT) and BMT plus cognitive-behavioral therapy were superior to a wait list control condition in improving marital adjustment.
Source: Baucom & Lester (1986).

interact in front of the therapist and have their performance evaluated. Accordingly, therapists use modeling, coaching, and role playing to improve communications.

The therapist teaches actual skills that include active listening, validating, and expressing positive and negative emotions. **Validating** is one person's acknowledgment that he or she understands what the other person just said; it does not necessarily mean agreeing or disagreeing with what was said. For example, the wife says, "Look, he may be a teenager, but that doesn't give him the right to take over the house. He uses anything he wants but doesn't clean up. He comes and goes as he pleases, and his mouth is full of gutter talk." A reply from the husband like "Yeah, you did the same thing when you were a teenager; just ask your mother," or "Yeah, he is a creep, and you helped make him that way" would not validate the communication. Rather, a validating comment would be "I can tell you are really angry and upset with our son." Validating can be of use in any interaction, especially when distress and heightened emotionality are present.

Action-oriented couples therapists strive to change partners' attributions about their significant other. It is interesting to note that individuals in distressed couples more often attribute negative states to stable and general personality features of their partners than do individuals in nondistressed couples (Holtzworth-Munroe & Hutchinson, 1993). For instance, instead of seeing a negative episode as temporary — as the result of a bad day or a frustrating experience — a member of a distressed couple is more likely to attribute the negative situation to a trait — to laziness, say, or lack of interest in providing for the family. In such cases, the therapy identifies examples of this problematic attribution pattern and provides feedback and opportunities for practicing alternative explanations for partner behavior. Altering the attributional process has been found to favorably influence the quality of the relationship.

Evaluation

Although it makes a great deal of sense to involve family members in an individual's treatment, not all family therapies have had the benefit of research evaluation. For example, psychodynamic family therapy has received less research evaluation than BMT or approaches that emphasize altering interpersonal communications. Where research has been conducted, however, the results provide supportive evidence (Alexander, Holtzworth-Munroe & Jameson, 1994). Also, many family therapy evaluations occurred when the initial target was a child with an identified problem and when the family system was seen as part of the child's problem.

Action-oriented family therapy for child disorders has also been evaluated favorably: The treatment is better than no treatment, home-based programs have sometimes helped produce child behavior gains in the classroom, and the deviant behavior of siblings of the identified child client have also shown noteworthy reductions. In contemporary applications, action-oriented family therapies directed at youths with behavior problems have expanded to include methods to address parental disorders, needed social support for the family, and the availability and use of agency programs that can provide activities for the at-risk youths as well as continued contacts for the struggling parents.

From a research perspective, less is known about the use of family therapy for diagnosed adult disorders. But data do support the use of action-oriented couples therapy for treating depressed women (Jacobson et al., 1991). In particular, these clients have been taught communication and problem-solving skills for use in resolving conflicts, with significant positive effects on the marital relationship.

FAMILY MATTERS

Encouraging Family Involvement in Individual Treatment

Psychological disorders affect individuals, but these individuals live in social environments, and others in those social environments affect and are affected by these same individuals. The family is a central social environment. The severely depressed spouse who can no longer go to work, maintain a conversation, or carry out the responsibilities of a household has a profound impact on those around her. How can her family members be involved most appropriately and effectively? Psychological therapies can take several approaches toward a solution: family members as (1) co-clients, (2) collaborators, and (3) consultants.

One direct path to the goal of family involvement is family therapy, whereby all members of the family are *co-clients*. There is no one disordered person; instead, there is a family with a problem. In some cases, family members are invited to participate in the therapy; in other cases, family members are required to attend sessions. Getting all family members to become involved in treatment, or to see its personal value if they are not themselves suffering, can be difficult. In our hurried world of busy schedules, family members often complain that they shouldn't have to attend therapy when someone else has the problem.

Family members can contribute to beneficial treatment even when they are not themselves clients. As *collaborators*, they are informed about the treatment, cooperate in its implementation, and provide a consistent and supportive environment for the emergence of client improvements. For example, some treatments for seriously disturbed individuals are directed toward the patient (as when medications are given to persons with schizophrenia), but family members are concurrently taught how best to relate to and express affect toward the patient. The expectation is that when the person returns to the home, the family will interact differently — and more effectively.

Family members can also be involved in individual treatment by serving as *consultants*. When, for example, a young adult is in treatment, parents can provide information about their son or daughter's developmental history, family background, and experience with prior efforts to cope with difficulties. Then, as treatment proceeds, family consultants can apprise the therapist of progress.

Using any of the various approaches to effectively treat psychological abnormality requires the cooperation of those in the person's social environment. That cooperation may involve encouraging the client to continue personal gains, fostering self-acceptance by refraining from criticism, or using new strategies to instill self-determination. But regardless of the specifics, family members are persuasive people in the client's social environment who can have a powerful influence. To varying degrees across the different therapies, family members thus contribute to treatment outcome. Nevertheless, research is needed to inform practitioners of the optimal involvement.

THE ART AND SCIENCE OF PSYCHOTHERAPY

Can therapy be evaluated using the methods of science? Can clients serve as participants in an experiment? Many mental health professionals endorse the position that careful and controlled investigations can and do provide useful information for the practice of therapy. Without such research, we would be uninformed about the relative effectiveness of the different treatments for various disorders. (In Chapter 5 we describe how this research is conducted.)

Research on the effects of therapy has had a rather brief history — less than fifty years — yet this research has revealed a great deal. For instance, we know that several forms of therapy are better than no treatment, that certain types of therapy may have preventive benefits, that no one known treatment is always best, that no one treatment works for all disorders, and that, for several specific disorders, some forms of treatment are better than others. In our discussions of specific disorders in later chapters, we review studies that have examined the effectiveness of different types of therapies for those disorders.

Other health professionals argue that therapy is an art and that its results depend on each therapist's intuitive skills as well as on the relationship between therapist and client. They maintain that many of the beneficial features of therapy are in fact lost through the rigid application of treatment techniques and that these features cannot be revealed by narrow measures of improvement. Although the debate continues, progress toward better research and service is evident in two areas. Those who study therapy scientifically have acknowledged and begun to evaluate the role of the therapist-client relationship and other factors in outcome. And those who were once opposed to measuring therapy outcome are beginning to implement measures of psychological adjustment before and after treatment.

In this section we examine three issues related to the art and science of psychological therapy: the role of ethnic status, the role of gender, and eclecticism, or how treatment techniques can be combined.

Ethnic Status and Therapy

Do some ethnic groups make more or less use of therapy services than other ethnic groups? Are there differential effects of therapy for members of different cultural and ethnic groups? The client's ethnic and cultural background may need to be considered when making decisions about the treatment of choice (Aponte, Rivers & Wohl, 1995; Sue, Zane & Young, 1994).

For example, Asian Americans are more likely than Caucasians to believe that mental health problems are caused by physical factors and that mental health is associated with will power, discipline, and maintenance of positive attitudes. As a result, it is very stigmatizing for these people to seek help because treatment-seeking suggests personal weakness. In contrast, some Hispanic Americans view mental health problems as burdens to bear, or they seek religious or folk remedies. Additionally, different ethnic groups may hold standards of conduct that are at variance with the middle-class Anglo culture. For example, an Asian American man may have great respect for authority, or an African American woman might value having children even in the absence of an obligated father. Unfortunately, some segments of society may hold negative attitudes toward these values — a situation that could create boundaries between potential clients and mental health services. Situations such as these suggest that, because of different beliefs, some groups may not find existing mental health services to be useful or meaningful.

According to some reports, minority groups underutilize the available mental health services (Snowden & Cheung, 1990; see also Mays & Albee, 1992); others suggest that members of minority groups often quit therapy or experience less effective outcomes. Two major studies, conducted in the same city more than a decade apart, have provided useful information about ethnic minorities and mental health services.

Based on a study of nearly 14,000 clients in the Seattle area, Stanley Sue (1977) found that various ethnic minorities differed in their use of mental health services and in their pattern of termination of use. For example, Asian Americans and Latinos underutilized services, whereas American Indians and African Americans overutilized services in comparison with their respective populations. Moreover, the study showed that all ethnic minority groups dropped out of treatment quickly: Ethnicity was a significant predictor of premature termination, even when other factors were controlled. Another study (Sue et al., 1991) that examined five years of service utilization data on thousands of clients in the Los Angeles area reported that, in comparison with local populations, Asian Americans and Mexican Americans underutilized services and African Americans overutilized services.

What about the outcomes from the services that were provided? Using scores based on each client's attainment of desired goals, Sue and associates (1991) reported that "Mexican Americans, Whites, and Asian Americans exhibited greater improvement after treatment than did African Americans" (p. 539). In addition, African Americans attended fewer treatment sessions, suggesting that African Americans enter the system but terminate quickly and show little improvement. But before trying to understand these data, we should note that the goal-attainment score is a narrow measure of improvement and that different results may emerge when other aspects of treatment outcome are measured.

Also, it may be that African Americans sought help but terminated early because of the absence of ethnically similar therapists to provide treatment. This latter point is supported by Sue and associates (1991), who reported that ethnic match (that is, ethnic sameness between client and therapist) was a meaningful predictor of the duration (length) of treatment. Given that most therapists are nonminority members (Jenkins & Ramsey, 1991), one (or both) of two strategies needs implementing: training nonminority therapists how to work with minority clients (Lopez et al., 1989) or training minority therapists. Indeed, given an increase in the number of minority therapists, members of similar minority groups seeking therapy may stay in therapy longer and benefit more.

As this chapter makes clear, therapy is not one form of intervention but a variety of approaches. As issues of ethnicity take hold within the field, it is not surprising that considerations of ethnic factors in dynamic therapy (Wohl, 1995), family therapy (Wilson, Phillip, Kohn & Curry-El, 1995), and cognitive-behavioral therapy (Treadwell, Flannery & Kendall, 1995) have increased.

Gender and Therapy

To what extent do client characteristics — age, race, social class, and gender — influence treatment outcome (Garfield, 1986)? Among these, the therapist's gender and the match between client's and therapist's gender have not only received research attention but also prompted lively discussion. For example, should a male client have a male therapist — and a female client, a female therapist? Should the female therapist be a feminist (Chrisler, 1993; Rothblum et al., 1993)?

In the 1970s, feminist therapy grew in response to perceptions of a once male-dominated psychological and medical profession. Politically active women objected to sexism in therapy and, independent of the theory or format of therapy, worked to raise the professional consciousness with regard to women's issues. Today, the mental health field has a visible and vocal contingent of women and continues to address the issue of sexism. As yet, however, there are no data regarding any special or significant effects solely from a feminist approach to therapy.

Clients often make judgments about a therapist's status on the basis of highly visible features such as gender. Moreover, a review of the relevant literature (Beutler, Machado & Neufeldt, 1994) suggests that gender similarity is associated with positive client perceptions of the treatment relationship (e.g., Jones, Krupnik & Kerig, 1987). Indeed, gender similarity is a demographic characteristic most strongly preferred by clients, often enhancing their perception of the therapist's understanding and empathy as well as their liking for the therapist.

Yet, according to Beutler and associates (1994), the effects of gender matching are quite modest when compared to other influences on therapy outcome. In addition, even these modest effects may be more attributable to the therapist's flexibility of attitudes toward sex roles than to gender per se. For example, some gender-matching studies suggest that therapists' flexibility and acceptance of diversity in female roles contribute to client satisfaction and growth regardless of whether the therapists are male or female (e.g., Beutler et al., 1994).

Eclecticism

As we have seen, no one method of psychotherapy has emerged as the single remedy for all psychological disorders. Different therapies take different approaches and thus apply, in varying degrees, to some but not all disorders and clients.

Because there is no one panacea, or cure-all treatment, therapists may choose to specialize in a particular form of therapy and work with those clients whose specific disorders can be adequately treated using that therapy. Conversely, they might choose to work with a more diverse group of clients and adopt an eclectic strategy (Garfield, 1995; Goldfried, 1995; Norcross & Goldfried, 1992). *Eclecticism* involves using different treatments for clients with different disorders or using a rational combination of various treatments for the same client, and it is a dominant force in the field today (see Figure 3.4). Indeed, psychotherapy integration is a popular trend among practitioners.

Practitioners who employ different therapeutic approaches for different clients might also use individual, couples, and family formats as they deem appropriate and optimal for specific cases. For instance, a psychologist working in a counseling center at a university might adopt a person-centered approach for a graduate student who is in conflict about career choices, since this approach would allow for self-determination without excessive self-focus. For a married client suffering from depression, the same psychologist might rely on the research data and choose a cognitive-behavioral couples therapy. And to treat an undergraduate troubled by excessive conflict with his parents, the therapist might call the parents or the entire family into the treatment sessions and implement an action-oriented approach focusing on improving communications among family members.

Eclecticism or psychotherapy integration is common in the treatment of specific disorders as well. Many eclectic clinicians combine cognitive and behavioral, humanistic and cognitive, and psychodynamic and cognitive approaches in their professional practice (Norcross & Prochaska, 1988). In the treatment of depression, for example, features of already developed and evaluated treatments — cognitive therapy and inter-

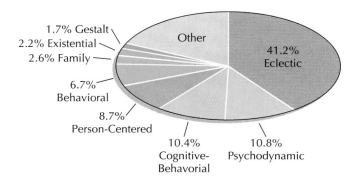

1.7% Gestalt
2.2% Existential
2.6% Family
Other
41.2% Eclectic
6.7% Behavioral
8.7% Person-Centered
10.4% Cognitive-Behaviorial
10.8% Psychodynamic

Figure 3.4 Theoretical Orientations of Therapists
According to a survey of clinical and counseling psychologists (members of the American Psychological Association), the majority of practitioners describe themselves as eclectic. The two dominant theoretical systems are cognitive-behavioral and psychodynamic.
Source: Smith (1982).

personal therapy — can be integrated (Safran & Segal, 1990). In such cases, therapists work to modify both dysfunctional thinking patterns and dependent interpersonal styles. Although integrative therapies have received research attention only recently, their components are known to be effective, both separately and in combination.

Another important illustration of eclecticism is the combination of psychological approaches to treatment with psychoactive medications. Although psychologists do not themselves prescribe medications, they often work in conjunction with physicians (for example, psychiatrists); thus, some of their clients are also receiving pharmacological intervention. In these circumstances, the psychologist must be well informed not only about several psychotherapeutic approaches but also about biological and medical interventions.

BIOLOGICAL AND MEDICAL APPROACHES

Ellen was relatively normal throughout high school, although more introverted and shy than many young women of her age. She wrote enchanting poems and short stories and hoped to study creative writing in college. Hearing voices and believing she was possessed, she had a psychotic episode during her first year at college. After a period of several weeks on antipsychotic medications, she reported that the voices and strange ideas had diminished, and eventually she was able to leave the hospital and reenter school. Months later, she was doing fairly well, but if she forgot her medications or resisted taking them for a few days, she would feel the first signs of psychotic experiences returning.

As this case indicates, medications are effective. Indeed, they can be an important component of the treatment of psychological disorders. But biological and medical approaches can also include nonpharmacologic procedures such as shock treatments and psychosurgery.

Nonpharmacologic Somatic Treatments

In the early 1930s, several major somatic (medical) therapies were developed: (1) insulin and other chemical shock treatments, (2) electroconvulsive therapy, and (3) psychosurgery. These procedures attracted considerable attention, mostly positive, and spread rapidly between Europe and the United States. The media and the public were enthusiastic, and widely read publications such as *Time, Newsweek,* and *Reader's Digest* endorsed the procedures, uncritically accepting the studies that purported to demonstrate their effectiveness. The explanation for this enthusiastic reaction is that there was nothing at that time to offer the severely mentally ill besides mental hospitals and straitjackets.

Insulin Shock Therapy **Insulin shock therapy** emerged accidentally when Manfred Sakel, a physician in Berlin, gave an insulin overdose to a diabetic patient who also had a morphine habit. An overdose of insulin deprives the brain of glucose and induces a coma. When the woman regained consciousness, her craving for morphine was apparently gone. Soon, Sakel was giving insulin overdoses to all the drug addicts in his practice. Another of his patients was not only an addict but also a psychotic; following an insulin-induced coma this patient appeared to be more rational. Eventually Sakel tried his methods on schizophrenic patients. An early report claimed an incredible 88 percent success rate with his insulin shock (coma) method.

The use of insulin shock therapy (and related coma-inducing chemicals) continued until the early 1950s, when it was supplanted by the new antipsychotic medications. But the extent to which it was used does not necessarily mean that it was successful: Although it reduced some disturbance, it was hardly a cure and had temporary effects at best.

Electroconvulsive Therapy About the same time as the accidental discovery of insulin shock therapy, Italian physicians Ugo Cerletti and Lucio Bini formulated the theory that naturally occurring convulsions in epileptics produced some apparently positive effects. From experiments with rats, they eventually discovered that by placing two electrodes on a rat's head, they could induce convulsions without running the current through the animal's heart (which would kill it). They treated their

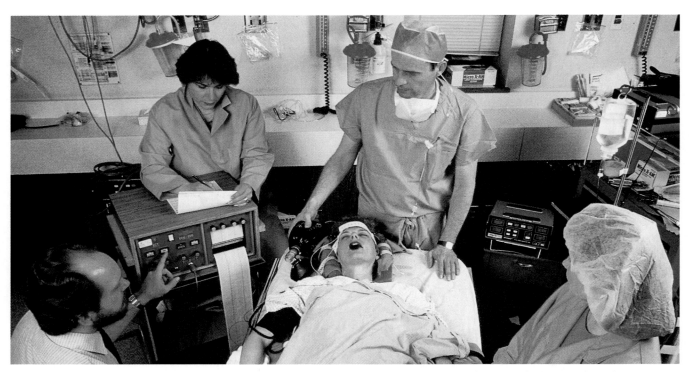

A severely depressed patient who was nonresponsive to alternate treatments receives electroshock therapy. Although controversy has surrounded shock therapy, and our knowledge of the mechanisms of its action are limited, this biomedical approach can be effective for some patients.

first human in 1938 and reported decreases in psychotic symptoms.

Like insulin shock therapy, **electroconvulsive therapy (ECT)** spread rapidly and was heralded by the popular press as a breakthrough. Unfortunately, the procedure was misused; applied to many patient groups without evidence of effectiveness, it caused physical damage or even death to some. Consequently — and concomitant with the rising popularity of psychoactive medications — the use of ECT declined markedly. ECT did not disappear entirely; it is still used in the treatment of certain kinds of severe, otherwise untreatable depression.

Many of the difficulties with ECT stemmed from the effects of the convulsive seizures on the bodies of patients. Occasionally, limbs were broken or dislocated; even deaths occurred, though very rarely. To make the procedure physically safer, practitioners introduced a number of improvements. Today muscle relaxants and anesthesia are administered, and the amount of current used is kept at the lowest level that induces a seizure. Electrodes deliver current on either one or both sides of the patient's head. Unilateral treatment to the patient's nondominant side of the brain is associated with less verbal memory impairment, but there is controversy over whether unilateral or bilateral treatments have the best outcomes. The typical course of treatment involves a total of about six sessions, at the rate of two or three per week.

One possible side effect of ECT is memory loss of events occurring immediately before and after treatment; but long-term memory loss is rare (Lader & Herrinton, 1990). For instance, patients sometimes experience a period of brief confusion after the treatment. One study using magnetic resonance imaging (MRI) found no evidence of damage or change to brain structures from ECT (Coffey et al., 1991). Despite this reassuring result, a few patients do experience notable cognitive deficits. The other potential danger of ECT is death, usually from cardiac complications. Nevertheless, the risk of mortality is quite low. Although some practitioners are satisfied with the effectiveness of ECT in treating depression, as scientists we are frustrated because we do not fully understand how ECT works.

Psychosurgery The origin of **psychosurgery** — the practice of operating on the brain to alter the symptoms of a severe psychological disorder — is attributed to the Portuguese neurologist, Egas Moniz. Three months after attending an international conference on the frontal lobes, and without benefit of experiments to perfect the safety of the technique, Moniz operated on the frontal lobes of a schizophrenic woman (Valenstein, 1986). He drilled two holes in her skull and injected alcohol into the holes to damage the underlying frontal lobes, which he believed to be the source of her madness. Soon thereafter, he changed his technique, using a knife to sever the nerve fibers to the frontal cortex. This latter procedure was called a **lobotomy.**

Moniz's theory was based on the idea that the frontal lobes are the seat of psychic activity, and that serious mental illness was due to maladaptive nerve-fiber connections. Therefore, the goal was to destroy these abnormal pathways. Moniz's procedure was widely used. Although in many patients the damage to other mental capacities was substantial, the public was enthralled with this latest scientific development. Sources have estimated that about 10,000 lobotomies per year were performed in the United States between the late 1940s and early 1950s.

What actually happened to the patients on whom lobotomies were performed? In 1947, *Life* magazine stated that 30 percent were able to return to their normal lives, 30 percent benefited greatly, a few died, and the rest were unchanged. According to modern reviews (Valenstein, 1986), these are highly doubtful and overoptimistic figures.

The effects of lobotomies were not clear. The lobotomies did seem to reduce the emotionality of anxious and depressed patients in select cases, but at some cost in terms of reduced capacity for higher mental functioning. Tooth and Newton (1961) surveyed the records of more than 10,000 lobotomized patients in Great Britain between 1942 and 1951. They observed that two-thirds of persons receiving treatment were schizophrenics; about one-fourth had affective disorders. Their records indicated that only 18 percent of the schizophrenics had "good" outcomes, compared with about 50 percent of the depressed patients.

At the height of enthusiasm for psychosurgery, Moniz was awarded the 1949 Nobel Prize in medicine, along with Walter Hess. Subsequently, however, the procedure declined in popularity with the increased availability of psychoactive drugs and the growing awareness that lobotomies were not as successful as claimed, that failures were not being reported, and that instead of being the treatment of last resort, lobotomies were being used indiscriminately. Prompted in part by Ken Kesey's book and the 1975 movie, *One Flew Over the Cuckoo's Nest,* the anti-psychosurgery cause led many states to greatly restrict the conditions under which psychosurgery could be performed.

Today, a few highly experimental procedures are performed under controlled medical and ethical conditions. For example, between 1962 and 1986, 465 psychiatric patients underwent psychosurgery at Massachusetts General Hospital. Modest conclusions were drawn from a long-term follow-up of 33 of those patients receiving the treatment for severe obsessive-compulsive disorder in which no previous treatment worked (Jenike et al., 1991). The investigators noted that 25 percent of the patients were improved with few side effects.

Psychotropic Medications

The discovery and development of medications to alter psychiatric conditions — collectively called **psychotropic drugs** or **psychopharmacology** — have revolutionized the treatment of severe mental illness. There has been a tremendous effort to develop drugs to treat a wide variety of less severe psychological disorders as well (Klerman et al., 1994). In this section we mention some of the categories of these medications (see Table 3.4). Additional information about the medications that are effective for specific psychological disorders appears in the chapters that deal with those disorders.

Three common types of psychotropic medications are antipsychotics, antidepressants, and antianxiety drugs. Although **antipsychotics** reduce the intensity and frequency of hallucinations, delusions, and other psychotic behaviors, they are not a cure. Chlorpromazine (Thorazine) is an antipsychotic sometimes used as one part of the treatment for psychotic disorders. **Antidepressants,** such as imipramine (Tofranil), elevate mood and increase activity. In many cases, however, they produce no long-term benefits; relapse often occurs when the medication is discontinued. The **antianxiety drugs** reduce muscular tension and have a calming and soothing effect on the emotions, but they can cause drowsiness and lethargy.

How Do the Drugs Work?   For the most part, we know what the drugs do chemically in the body — but we do

Table 3.4   Common Psychotropic Medications

Medication	Generic Name	Brand Name
Antipsychotics	Chlorpromazine	Thorazine
	Thioridazine	Mellaril
	Trifluoperazine	Stelazine
	Haloperidol	Haldol
Antidepressants	Imipramine	Tofranil
	Amitriptyline	Elavil
	Nortriptyline	Pamelor
	Fluoxetine	Prozac
Antianxiety drugs	Alprazolam	Xanax
	Chlordiazepoxide	Librium
	Diazepam	Valium
	Lorazepam	Ativan

Several types of medications are used for treating the diversity of psychological disorders. Antipsychotics reduce the intensity and frequency of psychotic behaviors, antidepressants elevate mood, and antianxiety drugs reduce muscular tension and calm and soothe the emotions. Listed here are common drugs of each type.

not know precisely why they have the effects that they do. Recall from Chapter 2 the discussion of neurotransmitters, which are substances that function as chemical messengers between neurons across the synaptic cleft. Although there are many neurotransmitters in the brain (and not all have yet been discovered), most of the emphasis in psychiatric treatment is directed only to a few, such as dopamine, serotonin, norepinephrine, and GABA. These particular neurotransmitters are thought to be especially important because they appear to be related to the regulation of mood, sensory experiences, and thinking.

Psychotropic medications affect neurotransmitters in one of several ways (Gitlin, 1990):

The medication binds to the receptor site, either causing a reaction or blocking the effect of a naturally occurring substance.

The medication causes the release of more neurotransmitters, thereby increasing the effect of the neurotransmitter.

The medication blocks the reuptake of the neurotransmitters back into the presynaptic neuron, thereby increasing the amount of the neurotransmitter substance.

The medication alters the neurotransmitter receptors, either by changing the number of receptor sites or by changing their sensitivity to neurotransmitters.

The medication alters the metabolism of a neurotransmitter, thereby changing the amount available for release.

The medication affects the amount of precursor ingredients necessary to make the neurotransmitter.

Several of these processes may be active at once, the processes may interact, and the effects may vary over time. We know that the medications can be effective, but we simply have not yet identified the exact mechanisms that are changed by medication. Jerry, your friend from the summer job, was able to successfully reduce and control his delusional thoughts by taking his prescribed antipsychotic medications. Clearly, such medications play an important role in the treatment of severe psychological disorders, but much more research is needed before we fully understand the underlying physiological processes that are being influenced.

Side Effects   In addition to their described effects, medications often have unwanted effects — **side effects** — that must be weighed when considering the benefits of the medications. As noted, possible effects from antianxiety medications include drowsiness or lethargy. Possible side effects from imipramine for depression are dry mouth, blurred vision, and drowsiness. More serious side effects are linked to the antipsychotic medications. The most feared, yet common side effect of antipsychotic medications is **tardive dyskinesia (TD)**, which, though not life threatening, is irreversible even if medication is discontinued. Manifestations of TD include involuntary facial movements such as grimacing, tongue thrusting, lip smacking, and motor activity in the hands and feet.

Medications can have other unwanted effects. When taken with alcohol, the effects of medications may be dangerously intensified. *Toxicity* — resulting in unsteadiness, sedation, and impaired psychomotor behavior — can occur when dosages are too high or when medications are taken with other drugs or alcohol. Some medications, such as benzodiazepines, can cause *tolerance* — the need for increased dosages to experience the same effects — and even *dependence* — a condition in which drugs must be taken to prevent withdrawal symptoms. Brief medication usage may result in minor withdrawal, but severe withdrawal symptoms are associated with longer use, higher dosages, and more abrupt withdrawal. In studies of patients taking antianxiety medications (Rickels et al., 1988; Rickels, Schweizer, Case & Greenblatt, 1991), only 43 percent were able to tolerate discontinuing the medications for even one week before going back on them.

Perceptions About Medications   Psychotropic medications do not cure a disorder the way an antibiotic can cure an infection. But psychotropic medications can treat symptoms. Sometimes the symptoms are themselves the cause of a client's problem. In other cases, the symptoms are a response to some underlying process — whether physical, psychological, or an interaction of the two. Thus, antidepressants may truly be helpful when the symptoms of the depression syndrome are themselves problems, as when low motivation, low self-esteem, and a sense of futility prevent a person from taking steps toward improvement. In other cases, however, even when the symptoms are reduced there are still difficulties in the person's life that need to be resolved or else they may cause further emotional dysfunction. Symptom relief may be vitally important, but viewing the disorder as a disease that a pill can cure is often an exercise in wishful thinking.

An additional misconception about psychotropic medications is that the doctors who prescribe them are experts in diagnosis and treatment of mental disorders. Indeed, this is not necessarily the case. The National Center for Health Statistics (NCHS) surveys office visits to physicians, and so it probably represents the most extensive database available for estimating aspects of medical practice. According to NCHS records kept

The technician is using MRI to scan the patient's brain. In the future, as more information is gathered about brain functions, MRI data may be useful to the mental health professionals' diagnosis and treatment planning.

between 1980 and 1981 (Beardsley, Gardocki, Larson & Hidalgo, 1988), primary care physicians (usually general practitioners and internists) provided a larger percentage of prescriptions for all classes of psychotropic drugs (except lithium) than did psychiatrists. This situation persists today: For example, primary care doctors prescribe a far greater proportion of antianxiety drugs compared to psychiatrists.

Even when prescribed by psychiatrists, medications have often been prescribed improperly. In the 1950s and 1960s there was considerable overuse of antipsychotic medications, and a more recent study suggests that this practice is continuing (Reardon et al., 1989). In the same study, which reviewed the treatment records of patients in three typical settings (general hospital psychiatric ward, community mental health center, and state hospital), neuroleptic dosages were computed for the years 1973, 1977, and 1982. The investigators found a significant increase in dosages over time and at all three settings (Reardon et al., 1989). However, they expressed the concern that there is no evidence that higher dosages work better.

It was also during the 1950s and 1960s that antianxiety drugs were given freely to people complaining of various physical and emotional difficulties, and many people became addicted to Valium and related drugs. They commonly suffered severe withdrawal symptoms and the return of anxiety when the medications were discontinued.

Psychotropic drugs may also be overprescribed. A recent study examined prescription records from a nationwide sample of pharmacies and found that the total dollar costs were significantly higher than anticipated (Zorc, Larson, Lyons & Beardsley, 1991). Based on 1985 records, the investigators determined that of the $1.45 billion spent on outpatient psychotropic medications, 60 percent was earmarked for antianxiety and sedative medications.

What do these high cost figures suggest? At best, they mean that lots of people (and their physicians) are turning to mind-altering drugs. At worst, they mean that some people (and their physicians) overrely on medications for dealing with problems of life, that others are overmedicated, and that still others need alternative kinds of services.

Related Considerations

Despite the concerns just raised, medications are an oft-used and reasonably effective method for the management of psychological disorders. Often they are only one facet of treatment — typically provided along with psychotherapy — but they are highly visible and provocative. Several related considerations deserve attention.

The Treatment-Etiology Fallacy Consider the following question: If ECT helps relieve depression, and if medicine helps reduce psychotic symptoms, isn't the implication that the depression and psychosis have a biological cause? The common conclusion is that if the medicine worked, the original cause must have been biological. This is flawed thinking, however. As such, it exemplifies the **treatment-etiology fallacy,** an error of logic in which the treatment mode is assumed to imply the mechanism of the original cause of a disorder. In fact, the method by which a treatment works may have no relation to original etiology.

Consider an everyday example: aspirin as a treatment for headache. Just because aspirin reduces headache pain does not imply that the cause of the headache was the absence of aspirin. Similarly, although antidepressants regulate certain neurotransmitter actions in the brain that serve as the biological manifestation of depression, that fact does not rule out the possibility that a psychological event gave rise to the depressive reaction of which neurotransmitter changes were a result.

Can We Afford Our Enthusiasm for Medical Breakthroughs? If there is a single historical pattern that emerges in our account of modern medical treatment for psychological disorders, it is this: Each new widely heralded advance has generated enormous optimism that has eventually proved unfounded and/or been diminished by reports of serious side effects. For example, ECT, certain medications, and psychosurgery have contributed to important improvements in the lives of many people; yet they all promised more than they delivered, and for some people the outcomes of their use were tragic. Antipsychotic medications have been successful in controlling symptoms but, as we have learned, they may even accentuate negative symptoms. And benzodiazepines have been prescribed for everything from homemaker blues and undergraduate worries to agoraphobia — but it turns out that they can be terribly addicting, and discontinuing them may lead to even worse anxiety than the patient originally experienced, not to mention severe withdrawal effects.

In short, although biological and medical approaches have provided advances in the treatment of psychopathology, as a society we seem to be enamored of medical science, and we expect enormous accomplishments from it. We are also enamored of chemically induced altered states of consciousness, as evidenced by the huge portions of the population who use alcohol, drugs, and mood-altering medications. When it comes to mental disorders, do we expect too much from chemicals and from medicine?

For all forms of therapy — biomedical and psychological — we need to be increasingly careful about the scientific requirements *before* public use. And we need to be increasingly attuned to the ethical issue of informing patients about all possible disadvantages of treatment. No matter what new advances are written and spoken about in the media, we need to assume that time and careful research are needed to tell the whole story.

FOCUS ON RESEARCH

Can Science Test Psychotherapy?

As we will note throughout this text, some treatments have been subjected to scientific evaluation (that is, they have been empirically tested), with results that indicate positive gains for clients. Other treatments, however, have not been validated as yet and their effects, scientifically speaking, are unknown. How do we judge whether treatments have been adequately evaluated, and what is the current status of those treatments that have been found to be reasonably effective?

Consumer Reports, a popular magazine that evaluates products such as appliances and cars, published a study of several thousand subscribers' experiences with therapy. Those who participated in the survey reported on their satisfaction with the mental health services they had sought and received. As reported in November 1995, 75 percent of those who sought help saw a mental health professional and almost everyone got some relief from the problems that brought them to a therapist. These survey results are favorable and suggest that therapy can make a difference. But there are limitations associated with survey data (see Chapter 5), such as lack of representativeness among the respondents: Perhaps only those who improved sought to respond to the survey. Other methodologies are thus preferred.

The empirical evaluation of therapy is an important theme — so much so that the American Psychological Association (APA) convened a task force to address the question. One of the core outcomes of this task force is a set of criteria against which to judge whether a treatment has been shown to be effective (e.g., Chambless & Hollon, 1997). Using criteria that reflect methodological strengths, several authors reported a summary of effective treatments for a variety of psychological disorders. Many of these treatments are the very ones we discuss in forthcoming chapters devoted to the respective disorders.

Taking a scientific stance, some psychologists have argued that *only* those empirically evaluated treatments that have shown to be effective should be provided to clients and taught in graduate training programs. "How," they ask, "can someone educate professionals in a treatment that hasn't yet been tested when an already tested and supported treatment is available?" Others disagree, arguing that such a stance would prematurely close the door to potentially effective treatments and ultimately foreclose on the option to evaluate alternate forms of treatment.

We also need to consider those who are paying for the treatment. Do they have the right to expect and/or require that any treatment for which a fee is paid first be found effective? The topic of empirically evaluated treatments is controversial, and there are enormous implications for the practice of psychological therapy, professional training, reimbursement from insurance companies, and research undertakings. The findings of the reviews of empirically evaluated treatments, as well as commentaries from supporters and detractors, can be found in a Special Section of the *Journal of Consulting and Clinical Psychology* (1997).

Overall, psychotherapies can exert powerful influences on the course of psychological disorders. Only careful science can help untangle what their true effects might be.

What Lies Ahead?

Historically, many and varied efforts are associated with the treatment of psychological disorders. Diverse and sometimes conflicting psychological therapies as well as a range of drastic medical treatments have been used. Yet treatments for psychological disorder are also ongoing, and the field is in the midst of several trends. What lies ahead for psychological and medical treatments?

Increasingly, psychological treatments are becoming the focus of needed research attention. Treatment outcome studies, described in later chapters, provide evidence for the effectiveness of several approaches. No longer will the field rally behind and be led by the founder of a single form of therapy or by the richness of a theory. On the contrary, emerging standards increasingly require that treatments be supported by research data.

Related to this research trend is the movement toward development, evaluation, and provision of treatments designed for specific disorders. Knowledge about the nature of different disorders allows for a variety of treatments that address specific types of psychological problems to be developed. The managed-care movement, in particular, has become active in providing guidelines for determining which treatments can be applied for which disorders.

Current professional practice emphasizes the need for integrative treatments. Specific psychological therapies, in combination with medications and programs for the client's family and social supports, are often the approach of choice. But each component of an integrated approach to treatment must first be documented as effective in well-controlled research studies.

Ultimately, we must all face the question — not just as students and scientists but also as citizens — of what kind of society we want and how we should address the problems of mental illness.

KEY TERMS

accurate empathy (70)
antianxiety drugs (89)
antidepressants (89)
antipsychotics (89)
anxiety hierarchy (71)
behavior therapy (71)
cognitive-behavioral therapy (75)
cognitive therapy for depression (78)
collaborative empiricism (75)
community mental health centers (64)
conjoint family therapy (81)
countertransference (68)
couples therapy (65)

deinstitutionalization (64)
ego psychologists (68)
electroconvulsive therapy (ECT) (88)
family therapy (65)
free association (67)
genuineness (70)
group therapy (65)
humanistic therapy (69)
individual therapy (65)
insight (66)
insulin shock therapy (87)
interpersonal therapy (69)
interpretations (67)
latent content (67)
lobotomy (89)

manifest dream (67)
modeling (74)
object relations therapy (68)
operant conditioning procedures (73)
person-centered therapy (70)
preventive treatment (81)
problem-solving therapist (80)
psychoanalysis (66)
psychodynamic therapy (66)
psychopharmacology (89)
psychosurgery (88)
psychotropic drugs (89)
rational emotive therapy (RET) (76)

resistance (67)
side effects (90)
systematic desensitization (71)
tardive dyskinesia (TD) (90)
token economy (73)
transference (68)
treatment-etiology fallacy (92)
unconditional positive regard (70)
validating (83)
working through (68)

SUMMARY

Therapy for psychological disorders can follow a variety of approaches, both psychological and medical; it can also utilize a variety of formats. These formats include *individual, couples, family,* and *group therapy.* Medical therapies, such as

treatment in mental hospitals, have shifted over time — from asylums and milieu therapy to *deinstitutionalization* and *community mental health centers.*

Insight-Oriented Therapies

Insight, the ability to understand the causes of one's own behavior, is a goal of contemporary *psychodynamic therapy* and *psychoanalysis*. *Ego psychologists* emphasize the conflict-resolving features of the ego. Contemporary psychodynamic therapy (such as *object relations therapy*) and *interpersonal therapy* emphasize the role of interpersonal relationships in psychopathology and psychotherapy.

Humanistic therapy relies on the therapist's acceptance, active listening, and nondirective interactions with the client to promote client development. *Genuineness, accurate empathy,* and *unconditional positive regard* are the three therapist conditions said to most benefit the client's personal growth.

Action-Oriented Therapies

Behavior therapy, which takes an action orientation, includes such treatments as *systematic desensitization* for phobias (an application of counterconditioning), *operant conditioning procedures* in which rewards are arranged and applied systematically, and *modeling* to demonstrate the use of strategies for adjustment.

Cognitive-behavioral therapy integrates action-oriented approaches and hypothesis-testing exercises, with efforts to alter the client's dysfunctional ways of thinking. This approach often uses *collaborative empiricism,* in which the therapist and client work together to examine and actively test some of the notions that the client believes to be true. Clients' irrational beliefs are disputed through the activities and discussions involved in *rational-emotive therapy (RET),* and *cognitive therapy for depression* combines behavioral and cognitive strategies to alter automatic negative thoughts and thereby modify depressive thinking. Contrary to the popular self-help notion about power in positive thinking, psychological adjustment is not linked solely to positive thinking but, rather, entails a 2:1 ratio of positive to negative thinking.

Problem-solving approaches to therapy involve the therapist and client working together to identify the problem, generate alternative solutions, anticipate consequences, make a decision, and implement and evaluate the plan. These approaches are used in preventive treatment and have been adapted for a variety of psychological disorders.

Family and Couples Therapy

With an emphasis on the system, family and couples therapists change interpersonal expectations, rules, and communication patterns. Both insight- and action-oriented approaches have been applied. In the action-oriented therapies, such as behavioral marital therapy, clients are provided communications (*validating*) training and problem-solving training.

The Art and Science of Psychotherapy

Trends in the field include the continuing struggle to ensure scientific study of psychological therapy, an increasing awareness of the need to be sensitive to ethnic and gender issues, and the widespread acceptance of eclecticism.

Biological and Medical Approaches

Nonpharmacologic somatic treatments include shock and surgery. Modern *electroconvulsive therapy (ECT),* used to treat severe depression, may have untoward effects on memory. Reactions to *psychosurgery* (such as *lobotomy*) have ranged from extreme praise to public outrage; the procedure is practiced only rarely.

Psychotropic drugs are an often-used component of multifaceted treatment. *Antipsychotics* control severe symptoms; *antidepressants,* such as imipramine, elevate mood; and *antianxiety drugs,* such as the benzodiazepines, are widely prescribed. *Side effects,* such as *tardive dyskinesia,* can be serious. Tolerance and dependence can also result.

Despite the effectiveness of psychotropic drugs in reducing symptoms, the drugs themselves do not solve personal problems in living. Other dilemmas include the fact that psychoactive medications are typically prescribed by nonpsychiatrists and, even when prescribed and monitored carefully, have potentially serious side effects. Although biomedical treatments can be effective, one would be committing a *treatment-etiology fallacy* to assume that the original problem must have been biologically caused.

Today there are far fewer mental institutions than before, and those that remain offer a wide variety of therapeutic experiences. Patients can also receive treatments in a group-home setting. Some contemporary living arrangements foster independent living and self-care.

Consider the Following. . .

Suppose that your Aunt Tildy has been seeing a therapist who is an advocate of a controversial new treatment for anxiety. Over the years, your aunt has been to a number of therapists, none of whom helped her overcome her fears. But this therapist at last seems to be helping. Ironically, your aunt's health care plan covered the costs of all the therapists who were unsuccessful with Aunt Tildy, but they won't cover the costs of this new therapist because they say that the treatment has not yet been found to be effective. What guidelines should be used to determine if a particular psychological therapy should be covered by health insurance or not, and who should determine those guidelines? How might new therapies that are not yet proven effective be introduced and tested most efficiently? What kind of role should health organizations have in this process?

Suppose that you are a therapist treating a client who suffers from depression. The client's managed health care system covers a maximum of ten therapy sessions. Your client is clearly in need of additional treatment, but you know that this particular HMO will not budge on their maximum number of sessions. You know that your client's financial resources are strained. What should you do? Stop his sessions? Assure him that he can take his time paying his bill? Treat him at a reduced rate or for free? Considering the many treatment strategies you have read about in this chapter, what would be your immediate advice and strategy for your client and for you?

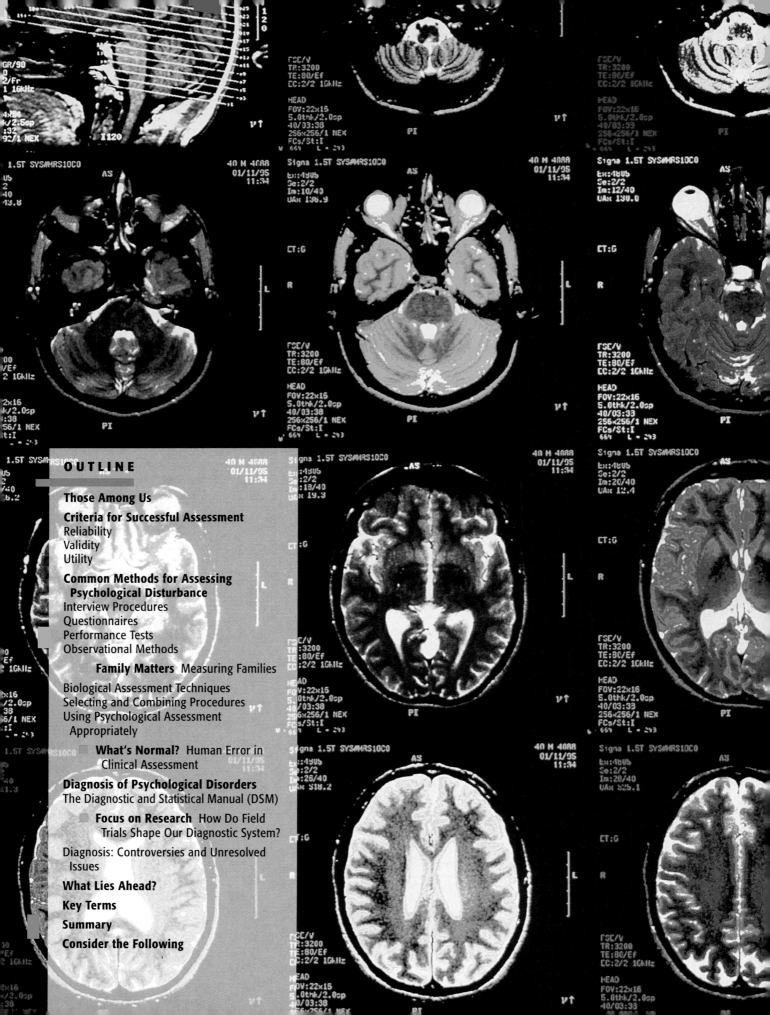

CHAPTER 4

Assessment and Diagnosis of Psychological Disorders

Those among us . . .

■ Your roommate experiences sensations that make her believe she is having a heart attack — difficulty breathing, pounding heart, and tightness in her chest. She went to the emergency room and was told the problem was psychological. How can we be sure?

■ You are concerned about your Aunt Martha; she has continued to mourn your uncle's death long after you expected her to return to normal. How depressed is she, and how much grieving is normal?

■ Donald is convinced that he has a brain disease causing mental deterioration, but he is also severely depressed. How can we figure out the source of his memory problems?

■ A teacher observes Mickey, a child who is disruptive at school and unpopular with his peers. What might be going on, and how should the problem be treated?

How can we know whether a problem is medical or psychological, or a combination of both?

How can we measure "how much" of a feeling or psychological condition a person has?

How can we decide what treatment is needed and whether it is effective?

How can we distinguish among different forms of psychological disorder?

These are among the countless questions that arise when we study psychological disorders. In short, the tasks in the mental health field are to *describe, classify, explain, select, predict, plan,* and *evaluate.* To do these tasks, we need procedures to measure and define disorder. In this chapter we focus on some of the important issues and processes involved in the measurement, or assessment, of human mental functioning. We also describe and discuss the diagnosis, or classification, of mental disorder.

Previous chapters explored the concepts of mental illness, models of psychopathology, and the theoretical and practical factors that help define what is abnormal. In this chapter, we focus on the tools that psychologists use to translate these abstract concepts into specific decisions about individuals. For example, we might have a general sense that depression is abnormal when it lasts longer and is more pronounced than expected after certain distressing conditions. We might also have biological and psychological theories about the causes of depression. But what we need is a way to measure depression and determine whether it should be treated, and if so, what form of treatment would be most effective. Similarly, measurements recorded after depression is treated can help determine whether the treatment really was effective or needs to be changed.

CRITERIA FOR SUCCESSFUL ASSESSMENT

Assessment is the systematic collection and analysis of information about a person's characteristics and behaviors. Assessment procedures — such as interviews, questionnaires, and performance tests — are essential for describing people's behavior, classifying their psychological problems, explaining the causes of their problems, selecting treatments to match with people or people to match with treatments, predicting the future course of a disorder, planning treatments and programs, and evaluating the results. Each of these issues may require somewhat different methods and standards.

Establishing the criteria for effective assessment is further complicated by the variety of behaviors and characteristics we want to measure and how much we need to *infer* about the presence and meaning of a particular behavior or characteristic. For example, a clinician may want to measure an overt behavior that can be quantified simply by direct observation or sampling of the behavior (as when determining how much anxiety a person is displaying, how frequently a child gets out of his seat in the classroom, or how accurately someone can perform arithmetic problems). At other times, however, a characteristic cannot be measured directly and requires some abstraction and inference (for example, the level of a person's self-esteem, the presence of a learning disability, or the likelihood that someone will commit repeat offenses if released from prison). The more we use assessment procedures to draw inferences about aspects of the person that cannot be measured directly, the more evidence we require of a valid link between what we measure and what we conclude.

Sometimes the characteristics we measure concern temporary conditions called *states,* and sometimes we measure enduring and unchanging characteristics called *traits.* States such as depression, delirium, test anxiety, and marital conflict usually raise assessment questions of whether the conditions can be measured accurately right now and whether the states change when conditions change. By contrast, measuring traits, such as sociability, conscientiousness, psychopathy, or compulsiveness, requires evidence of their existence across a variety of settings, time, and situations — and of their relation to behaviors.

Three criteria are commonly used to evaluate assessment procedures: reliability, validity, and utility. They are interrelated, but for particular questions and characteristics, one may be more essential than the others.

Reliability

Measurement procedures repeated under similar conditions should yield the same results. **Reliability** refers to the consistency or repeatability of results. Reliability is computed by various statistical procedures that evaluate the extent of agreement between test results on different occasions, between different raters, or between different sets of items within a test. Reliability is represented as a matter of degree, usually on a continuum from 0 to 1, where 1.0 means perfect reliability (extremely rare). The degree of reliability that is considered necessary depends on how the assessment procedure will be used. For research purposes — to explore new ideas, hypotheses, and measures — we might allow lower reliability than for clinical judgment about a person's life. There are three types of reliability: test-retest reliability, internal consistency reliability, and interrater reliability.

Retest reliability is the consistency of a test's results over time. A questionnaire or an interview designed to measure the experience of self-concept, for instance, should yield the same results regardless of whether a person completes it on Tuesday or on Thursday. This form of reliability is especially important when the characteristics being measured — say, compulsive behaviors — are expected to be fairly stable in the absence of a treatment intended to change them. A characteristic like anxiety, on the other hand, might fluctuate, and high test-retest reliability over a long period would not be expected. Figure 4.1 presents test-retest reliability information regarding the Diagnostic

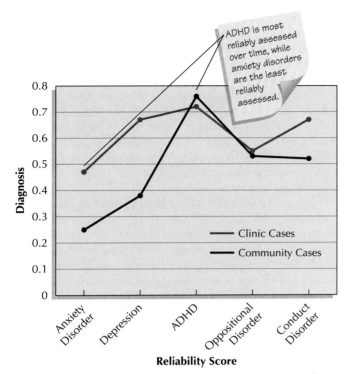

Figure 4.1   Retest Reliability of the Diagnostic Interview Schedule for Children

Illustrated here are retest reliabilities over two to three weeks for an interview assessment of children's symptoms conducted in New York. (The most perfect agreement would be close to 1.0; lower scores indicate less reliability.) This assessment, called the Diagnostic Interview Schedule for Children (DISC), has been under development for more than ten years in an attempt to improve its reliability and validity. The figures are considered to represent reasonably solid reliability, although many researchers believe that they are not strong enough to serve as a basis for estimates of disorder in the community. Note that the figures are highest for disorders that are considered to be more severe (as in clinic cases) and more stable (as with attention deficit hyperactivity disorder). *Source:* Jensen et al. (1995).

should be consistent. Internal consistency of an instrument is likely to be low when the concept being measured is not well defined, when the assessment procedure includes too many diverse or extraneous items, or when it contains only a few items.

A third kind of reliability is **interrater reliability,** or consistency among scorers or observers. Independent judges observing a person's behavior ought to come to the same conclusions. This kind of reliability evaluates the agreement between two raters administering the same interview, rating the same videotape of a person's behavior, or observing a person's behavior in a particular setting. High interrater reliability is important because it increases confidence that the procedure is really measuring what it is supposed to measure. For example, it is important to have reliable diagnostic criteria so that different interviewers agree on how to classify a person's problem behaviors. Similarly, we expect the scoring system of an assessment procedure to be reliable; in other words, we expect that independent users of a particular test will score it in the same way.

In each of these examples, it is clear that an instrument must have high reliability if we are to draw accurate conclusions from it. For instance, if a test of intelligence (a trait we expect to be fairly stable) demonstrates low test-retest reliability, we probably should not claim that it measures intelligence. Yet an instrument can yield high reliability and still not be accurate. Two observers might watch a child in a classroom and agree on exactly how many times he got out of his seat; calling this a measure of hyperactivity, however, would not necessarily be accurate, or valid. Validity requires more than just reliability.

Validity

The **validity** of a measuring procedure means that it measures what we say it measures. Just because a researcher or clinician says that an assessment procedure measures a certain characteristic does not mean that it does. A doctor claiming that she has developed a blood test to detect future Alzheimer's disease, a school psychologist saying that he has a personality questionnaire that identifies people prone to alcoholism, or a psychiatrist labeling your child as having attention deficit disorder *must* base these conclusions on valid procedures. Not just assertion but scientific evidence is required to back up claims of validity of a particular procedure.

A procedure may be valid for one purpose but not another. For instance, a positron emission tomography (PET) scan may be a valid measure of brain activity, but it is not valid as a test of intelligence. Likewise, a questionnaire valid for predicting future psychosis is not valid as a test for creativity.

Validity, like reliability, is a matter of degree. However, unlike reliability, which can usually be

Interview Schedule for Children (DISC), an interview assessment of children's symptoms.

A second kind of reliability is **internal consistency,** or correspondence between test items. In a questionnaire intended to measure potential for child abuse, for example, we expect that all of the items on the questionnaire contribute to identifying this potential. But if some of the items are irrelevant or not meaningfully related to potential for child abuse, they would affect the internal reliability of the questionnaire, inflating its scores and erroneously suggesting that someone is at risk for abuse who really is not. Statistical techniques evaluate internal consistency reliability; the higher the level of reliability, the more likely that the items on the instrument measure a similar concept. The same principle applies to different versions of the same questionnaire or test: Their content represented as a statistical computation, validation is a process, typically based on research. Any given test, according to the American Psychological Association, should exhibit three forms of validity: content validity, criterion-related validity, and construct validity, although high levels on all three are not needed. Let's examine these three forms of validity.

Content validity means that the items of an assessment device represent true examples of what the test is targeting. A questionnaire for measuring anxiety, for example, is expected to include all of the relevant experiences that most people mean by anxiety. Direct-observation tasks, as when couples' communication conflict is observed, may be especially high in content validity if couples are asked to discuss a topic that they disagree about.

Face validity, related to content validity, refers to whether the items on a test *appear* to measure what the test purports to measure. A test for fear of flying, for example, would be face valid if it contained items about attitudes toward air travel. However, a measure can have face validity by appearing to measure relevant content, yet not actually be valid for its stated goals. For example, a magazine questionnaire on marital compatibility might ask how much both partners enjoy breakfast in bed — but similarity of tastes and habits does not necessarily predict marital happiness.

Neither content validity nor face validity by themselves are requirement for a good test, since some assessment procedures measure a hidden or underlying tendency that may not be obvious from the content. For instance, an inkblot (Rorschach) test may be valid for measuring qualities such as defensiveness or ego strength, even though the apparent content of the test may not reveal that capability. On the other hand, content validity is often highly relevant when the measurement procedure is intended to sample a concept's attributes directly, as when depression is being assessed.

To establish the meaning and usefulness of assessment procedures, researchers need to use additional forms of validation. One of the most convincing validation methods is to compare the scores on a procedure with a criterion for the actual behavior being predicted — that is, with an existing standardized measure of the behavior. This form of validity, **criterion-related validity,** involves either *current* or *future* agreement with the criterion. For example, suppose that researchers developed a way to measure men's sexual arousal in response to a videotape depicting child molestation and claimed that this measurement indicated the likelihood that prisoners convicted of molestation would repeat the offenses outside of prison. For the sexual arousal procedure to be considered valid for predicting future sexual offenses, the researchers would need to demonstrate that high-aroused men commit molestation after release from prison more than low-aroused men do. Thus, there would have to be an association between the test results

and future behavior. Studying future agreement with a criterion, as in this example, involves **predictive validity**.

Concurrent validity compares the results of an assessment with some criterion that is obtained at about the same time (instead of in the future). For example, if a test of Alzheimer's disease uses brain imaging to indicate damage to a particular region of the brain, the procedure could be validated by demonstrating that the results agree with independent evidence of Alzheimer's disease based on diagnostic interviews and tests of intellectual functioning. Obviously, for criterion-related validity, the criterion itself must be valid.

For **construct validity,** test results must be related to the theoretical construct (or concept) that the test is attempting to measure. This form of validity is especially appropriate when the construct to be measured is abstract and lacks specific indicators or criteria against which it can be compared — as when self-esteem or ego strength is being assessed. In such instances, the process of validating the measure of the concept is actually the process of testing a theory. Indeed, construct validation is a means of demonstrating that measures of the construct are related to findings predicted by a theory. For example, if you have a theory that bulimia (an eating disorder involving binge eating followed by purging) is due to inner emptiness, you might devise a scale to measure inner emptiness. But it would not be sufficient validation to demonstrate that bulimics score higher than nonbulimics on inner emptiness. (After all, they might score higher on many negative traits and those traits might be the result, rather than the cause, of their disorder.) Also, a high score does not mean that the scale measures just inner emptiness. Accordingly, you might specify that inner emptiness is related to (but not the same as) loneliness, low self-esteem, fear of being alone, and boredom. Positive correlations with scales measuring these related concepts would then further the process of construct validation. This process involves specifying predictions from the theory of the construct and collecting research data to test the predicted patterns. Construct validation thus depends on the degree to which the pattern of results is consistent with the predictions.

Many circumstances can interfere with the reliability and validity of an assessment instrument. Certainly one important issue is the extent to which conclusions based on the assessment procedure are *applicable* to the person in question. For instance, tests that have been validated on adults may not apply to children, and procedures validated on whites do not necessarily apply to African Americans. Further, questionnaires may be too short or too complicated; the questions may be ambiguous or reflect temporary conditions such as mood, energy level, and motivation that can affect the results. Such conditions increase the chance that people will give different answers on different occasions. Also, scoring methods may affect validity. For example, if most of the items on a questionnaire are scored on the basis of the respondent's *agreement* with them, the questionnaire might actually be reflecting a yea-saying bias in which the person tends to agree regardless of the content. Or if the items contain material that the respondent is reluctant to admit, they may elicit replies that are socially desirable and represent the respondent in an artificially favorable light. Clearly, such **response biases** would impede not only the reliability of a test but also its validity, or accuracy.

Similar problems interfere with the reliability and validity of behavioral observations: If the behaviors to be rated are not defined clearly, then different observers might interpret them differently. For example, if nurses in an in-patient ward are asked to monitor whether a patient is suicidal, one nurse might think he was suicidal every time he stood near the window, whereas another might consider as suicidal only the patient's verbal statements of wanting to die.

Utility

A final criterion for deciding that an assessment procedure is worth employing is **utility,** or whether it is useful. To be useful, the assessment procedure should give valid and reliable information that cannot otherwise be obtained more simply, more cheaply, or more promptly, such as from routine procedures (Meehl, 1959). For example, we might develop elaborate questionnaires to determine whether a person has bulimia or some other disorder. But if interviewing clients about their experiences is simpler and cheaper and equally valid, then the questionnaires lack utility.

For some clinical decisions, utility must also be weighed in terms of the cost of making mistakes — especially given that no measurement procedure is perfect. All such procedures result in a certain number of *false positives* (which imply that a condition exists when it does not) and *false negatives* (which fail to detect a condition that is actually present). Consider as an example a test that is used to predict the risk that certain children will become arsonists. The test may erroneously label some youngsters as high risk and ignore others who are truly at risk. So, to determine whether a test is useful, we need to weigh the cost of false positives — of misclassifying and possibly stigmatizing clients — versus the cost of not detecting a problem.

Errors are especially likely to occur if the trait or condition being assessed has a low **base rate** — another way of stating that its occurrence in the general population is relatively rare (Meehl & Rosen, 1955). Consider the example illustrated in Figure 4.2. A company decides to use a lie detector to eliminate dishonest staff. Let's suppose that the base rate of dishonesty in the population is only 5 percent and the accuracy of the test is 80 percent. If 1,000 persons are screened, there will be 200 errors of classification: 190 honest persons will be falsely accused and 10 dishonest persons will not be

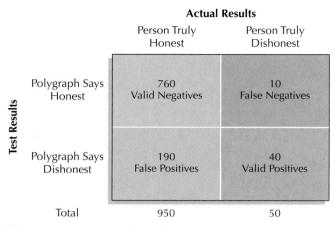

Actual Results

	Person Truly Honest	Person Truly Dishonest
Polygraph Says Honest	760 Valid Negatives	10 False Negatives
Polygraph Says Dishonest	190 False Positives	40 Valid Positives
Total	950	50

(Test Results)

Figure 4.2   Misclassification Because of Low Base Rates

The issue of utility concerns not only whether an assessment procedure is useful but also the costs of using it despite errors. This example illustrates that, due to measurement inaccuracy, some honest persons will be falsely accused and some dishonest ones will not be detected. A similar situation could arise if we use a procedure to detect a disease or a child's risk for future problems. Attempts to detect relatively low base rate (i.e., rare) conditions tend to increase the rates of error.

detected. If the company had simply decided to assume that everyone is honest, and thus had used no polygraph, it would have made only 50 errors of misclassification. Would the testing in this case be considered useful?

Unlike reliability, which can usually be reflected in statistical calculations, or validity, which requires scientific evidence of predicted associations between variables, utility involves a practical or even ethical judgment. Like both reliability and validity, however, utility is a matter of degree. Ultimately, all three criteria for evaluating the soundness of assessment devices are important and interrelated, but different tasks and goals may require emphasizing one criterion more than the others.

In the following sections we explore some of the major forms of assessment methods and further elaborate on their advantages and disadvantages.

COMMON METHODS FOR ASSESSING PSYCHOLOGICAL DISTURBANCE

To diagnose and understand human behavior, people have used everything from astrological forecasts to bumps on the head to magnetic resonance imaging. We present a few examples of some of the most common methods, grouped for convenience into five categories: interview procedures, questionnaires, performance tests,

Structured interviews are one of the most direct means of assessment of people's attitudes, beliefs, and behaviors. Modern technology, such as the hand-held computer, facilitates use of such procedures in natural settings.

observational methods, and biological assessment techniques. In reality, some of these categories may overlap.

Interview Procedures

When in doubt, ask. Oral means of collecting information from someone — interviews — have many advantages: They can cover topics of direct relevance to the targeted issue; they can be sensitive and flexible so that if the person misunderstands a question it can be clarified; and if a response raises additional important issues those issues can be explored. Interviews can be highly efficient at getting to the heart of the matter or at identifying topics that need to be explored more deeply.

Unstructured interviews are open-ended; since they do not follow a particular format, two interviewers might obtain very different information. When the reliability and validity of conclusions need to be increased, interviews can also be structured or semistructured. In both formats, the same questions are asked in the same way, and they follow the same order. But the *structured interview* allows for very little deviation from the format, whereas the *semistructured interview* method permits the interviewer to explore certain areas as needed.

Extensively used for diagnostic evaluations and clinical research in psychopathology are the Diagnostic Interview Schedule, or DIS (Robins, Helzer, Ratcliff & Seyfried, 1982), and its modification, the Composite International Diagnostic Interview (Kessler et al., 1994), and the Structured Clinical Interview for DSM-III-R, or SCID (Spitzer, Williams, Gibbon & First, 1990). Table

4.1 shows excerpts from both the DIS and the SCID. Illustrated here are the symptoms of panic disorder, the kinds of symptoms possibly experienced by your roommate, as described at the beginning of the chapter.

> *Your roommate was standing in a crowded line at the movies one night, and suddenly her heart began to pound, and she felt as though a heavy weight on her chest was making it hard to breath. She felt dizzy and faint — all for no apparent reason. Terrified that she was having a heart attack, she took a taxi to the hospital. After checking her in the emergency room, the doctors found no physical problem and asked her a lot of questions (similar to the ones in the interviews excerpted in Table 4.1). The doctors suggested that she had experienced a panic attack. She was mystified because it came out of the blue and she hadn't been aware of any psychological problems.*

The DIS is a structured interview that has been used in large-scale epidemiological community surveys; it is the basis for much of the information concerning frequency of disorders that is presented throughout this text. The DIS is relatively simple and requires little decision making by the interviewers; in fact, it can be used by people who have no professional training in mental health but are trained in the specific use of this interview. A version of the DIS known as the DISC (see Figure 4.1) is also available for children (Costello, Edelbrock & Costello, 1985; Jensen et al., 1995).

The SCID requires that the interviewer have clinical experience and be able to make certain judgments about the meaning of responses provided by the interviewee. Its semistructured format includes general probes and then specific follow-up questions. If a person reveals no disorder on the probe questions, the interviewer skips to the next section. The SCID and its forerunners such as the Schedule for Affective Disorders and Schizophrenia, or SADS (Endicott & Spitzer, 1978), are widely cited in research studies reported in this book.

Many other interview procedures are used for research and clinical purposes. The goal of some interviews is to diagnose specific disorders or types of disorders or to evaluate the nature and severity of specific types of symptoms, such as level of depression or anxiety. Other interview procedures have been developed to fulfill specific research and clinical goals, such as evaluating marital satisfaction, the attitudes of family members toward their schizophrenic relative, or experiences of early childhood.

Despite numerous advantages, interviews are not always the best way to obtain information. They may be time consuming, and their effectiveness often depends on an interviewer who is skilled and carefully trained as well as on a respondent who is cooperative and willing to answer the questions truthfully. Numerous studies have shown that gender, race, and age differences between interviewer and respondent may affect the information that is disclosed (e.g., Buros, 1988). And sometimes it is simply more efficient and less costly to put questions in the form of a questionnaire.

Questionnaires

A **questionnaire** — a written set of questions to which a person provides written replies — has the potential to provide a great deal of information in the assessment of psychological problems. Indeed, questionnaires can be tailored to specific content, and they are easily and cheaply administered.

Consider the measurement of depression — this time, as it applies to your Aunt Martha, who is described at the beginning of the chapter. Questionnaires, combined with interview procedures, might be used to assess the extent of Martha's depressive symptoms. Table 4.2 presents several examples of these questionnaires that measure experiences of depression. These examples illustrate just some of the many formats that can be used in questionnaires.

Aunt Martha, for example, feels low in energy, cries a lot, thinks the future looks bleak, sleeps poorly, and doesn't enjoy pleasurable activities as much since her husband died. These are all reactions that define what we mean by depression. If she were administered a questionnaire such as the Beck Depression Inventory, her

score would probably fall into the range considered to indicate moderate levels of depressive symptoms at the time of testing. A clinical interview might further indicate how much impairment Martha experiences because of depression, how long and consistently she displays depressive symptoms, and how appropriate they are to the situation of her mourning. Taken together, both forms of information provide a basis for determining whether your Aunt Martha needs to be treated for depression.

Many questionnaires measure not only symptoms and psychological conditions but countless other experiences relevant to psychological disorder such as marital satisfaction, sex role attitudes, unusual perceptual experiences, beliefs about personal control, and alcohol use. Recently, questionnaires have also been devised to assess dysfunctional cognitions, or thoughts and interpretations about one's self and circumstances. Questionnaires that tap such inner experiences have helped in the study of vulnerability to psychological disorders as well as in the planning and evaluation of treatment.

Questionnaires may cover a single domain of functioning and offer a direct approach requiring little inference, or they might be complex and multifaceted and attempt to represent more hidden or inferential aspects of the person. Among the best-known examples of the latter are **personality inventories**. Mental health professionals often use personality inventories to derive an elaborate picture of a person's overall *personality* — the traits, characteristics, tendencies, and styles that are thought to underlie behavior.

Like questionnaires, personality inventories vary in terms of the way they are derived. They utilize three principal methods: rational, empirical, and statistical. In the *rational* method, items are based on theory or experience. (This is sometimes called the "armchair" method because the developer sits and thinks about what the items ought to be.) The *empirical* method includes and retains after empirical analyses items that have been shown to distinguish between groups with known characteristics. For instance, many items might be included initially but only those that distinguish between a group of people who are known to be extraverts and a group known to be introverts might be retained to form a scale of introversion-extraversion. The entire personality inventory might consist of a number of such empirically derived scales. A questionnaire derived by the *statistical* method includes items that have been shown to cluster together, using complex mathematical procedures to determine patterns in the ways that people respond to a large pool of items. For example, from an initial 100-item questionnaire, a specific group of 23 items might emerge to define a particular subscale, given statistical analyses showing that a certain group of people have tended to be very consistent in the way they answered these items.

Table 4.1   Examples of Structured Diagnostic Interviews

Diagnostic Interview Schedule (These sample questions come from the section on panic disorder.)

CODE

1 = no	4 = medical explanation
2 = below criterion	5 = yes
3 = due to drugs or alcohol	

61. Have you ever considered yourself a nervous person?

No . . . . (GO TO Q. 62) 1
Yes . . . . (ASK A) 5

A. At what age did this nervousness begin? (IF R SAYS "WHOLE LIFE": ENTER 02)

ENTER AGE AND
GOT TO Q. 62:

62. Have you ever had a spell or attack when all of a sudden you felt frightened, anxious or very uneasy in situations when most people would not be afraid?   1   2   3   4   5

63. During one of your worst spells of suddenly feeling frightened or anxious or uneasy, did you ever notice that you had any of the following problems? During this spell: (READ EACH SYMPTOM AND CODE "YES" OR "NO" FOR EACH. <u>REPEAT</u> THE PHRASE "DURING THIS SPELL" FOR EACH.)

		No	Yes
A.	were you short of breath — having trouble catching your breath?	1	5
B.	did your heart pound?	1	5
C.	were you dizzy or light-headed?	1	5
D.	did your fingers or feet tingle?	1	5
E.	did you have tightness or pain in your chest?	1	5
F.	did you feel like you were choking or smothering?	1	5
G.	did you feel faint?	1	5
H.	did you sweat?	1	5
I.	did you tremble or shake?	1	5
J.	did you feel hot or cold flashes?	1	5
K.	did things around you seem unreal?	1	5
L.	were you afraid either that you might die or that you might act in a crazy way?	1	5

Source: Robins, Helzer, Croughan & Ratcliff (1981).

Two types of structured diagnostic interview are the Diagnostic Interview Schedule, or DIS, and the Structured Clinical Interview for DSM-IV, or SCID (First, Spitzer, Gibbon & Williams, 1997). The example on page 104 is from the DIS. It asks screening questions, which, if answered yes, are followed by a series of precise questions. Interviewers are trained to give the interview but are not clinicians, and scoring does not permit the interviewers to make judgments about the significance of reported symptoms – only about whether they occur or not. The example on page 105, from the SCID, includes questions that a trained clinical examiner asks about panic disorder. In the SCID, if the answer to the initial screening question is no, the examiner skips to a later section of the interview. Each item is scored using the scale at the bottom of the table. (The items have been updated for DSM-IV.) Interviews like these permit clinical information to be obtained in the same way by different interviewers while still yielding reliable diagnostic decisions.

One of the most widely used personality inventories is the *Minnesota Multiphasic Personality Inventory,* or MMPI (Hathaway & McKinley, 1948). The MMPI was originally derived largely by the empirical method, comparing the responses of groups of patients diagnosed with disorders such as depression, antisocial conduct, paranoia, schizophrenia, and mania to the responses of normal, nondiagnosed individuals. Its revision, the MMPI-2, includes new comparisons between ethnically diverse groups from numerous U.S. locations and has derived current norms for the different scales (Butcher et al., 1989). Some items that were originally written in the

Table 4.1 (cont.)

Structured Clinical Interview for DSM-IV Axis I Disorders (Version 2.0)	Panic Disorder		Anxiety Disorders F.1

F. ANXIETY DISORDERS
   PANIC DISORDER

PANIC DISORDER CRITERIA

Have you ever had a panic attack, when you *suddenly* felt frightened or anxious or *suddenly* developed a lot of physical symptoms?

   IF YES: Have these attacks ever come on completely out of the blue—in situations where you didn't expect to be nervous or uncomfortable?

   IF UNCLEAR: How many of these kinds of attacks have you had? (At least two?)

A. (1) recurrent unexpected panic attacks

? 1 2 3   F1

GO TO *AWOPD,* F.7

After any of these attacks . . .

Did you worry that there might be something terribly wrong with you, like you were having a heart attack or were going crazy? (How long did you worry?) (at least a month?)

   IF NO: Did you worry a lot about having another one? (How long did you worry?) (at least a month?)

   IF NO: Did you do anything different because of the attacks (like avoiding certain places or not going out alone)? (What about avoiding certain activities like exercise?) (What about things like always making sure you are near a bathroom or exit?)

(2) at least one of the attacks has been followed by a month (or more) of one of the following:

   (a) worry about the implications of the attack or its consequences (e.g., losing control, having a heart attack, "going crazy");

   (b) persistent concern about having additional attacks;

   (c) a significant change in behavior related to the attacks

? 1 2 3   F2

GO TO *AWOPD,* F.7

When was the last bad one? What was the first thing you noticed? then what?

   IF UNKNOWN: Did the symptoms come on all of a sudden?

   IF YES: How long did it take from when it began to when it got really bad? (less than ten minutes?)

During that attack . . .

B. The panic attack symptoms developed abruptly and reached a peak within ten minutes

? 1 2 3   F3

. . . did your heart race, pound, or skip?	(1) palpitations, pounding heart, or accelerated heart rate	? 1 2 3	F4
. . . did you sweat?	(2) sweating	? 1 2 3	F5
. . . did you tremble or shake?	(3) trembling or shaking	? 1 2 3	F6
. . . were you short of breath? (have trouble catching your breath?)	(4) sensations of shortness of breath or smothering	? 1 2 3	F7
. . . did you feel as if you were choking?	(5) feeling of choking	? 1 2 3	F8
. . . did you have chest pain or pressure?	(6) chest pain or discomfort	? 1 2 3	F9
. . . did you have nausea or upset stomach or the feeling that you were going to have diarrhea?	(7) nausea or abdominal distress	? 1 2 3	F10
. . . did you feel dizzy, unsteady, or like you might faint?	(8) feeling dizzy, unsteady, lightheaded, or faint	? 1 2 3	F11
. . . did things around you seem unreal, or did you feel detached from things around you or detached from part of your body?	(9) derealization (feelings of unreality) or depersonalization (being detached from oneself)	? 1 2 3	F12
. . . were you afraid you were going crazy or might lose control?	(10) fear of losing control or going crazy	? 1 2 3	F13
. . . were you afraid that you might die?	(11) fear of dying	? 1 2 3	F14
. . . did you have tingling or numbness in parts of your body?	(12) paresthesias (numbness or tingling sensations)	? 1 2 3	F15
. . . did you have flushes (hot flashes) or chills?	(13) chills or hot flashes	? 1 2 3	F16

? = inadequate information   *1 = absent or false*   *2 = subthreshold*   *3 = threshold or true*

Source: First, Spitzer, Gibbon & Williams (1997).

Table 4.2 Examples of Depression Questionnaires

Measuring Depressed Mood

1. Depression Adjective Check List (DACL): check those that apply right now.

_____ Blue	_____ Glad
_____ Hopeless	_____ Interested
_____ Rejected	_____ Strong

2. Visual Analogue Scale: draw a line in the scale that represents how you feel right now.

Worst I ever felt   Best I ever felt

Measuring Depression Symptoms

3. Beck Depression Inventory (BDI): consists of twenty-one items; subjects circle 0, 1, 2 or 3. Here are two examples:

0 I don't cry any more than usual.

1 I cry more now than I used to.

2 I cry all the time now.

3 I used to be able to cry, but now I can't cry even though I want to.

  0 I have not lost interest in other people.

  1 I am less interested in other people than I used to be.

  2 I have lost most of my interest in other people.

  3 I have lost all of my interest in other people.

4. Center for Epidemiological Studies–Depression Scale (CES-D): consists of twenty items; items describe how the person felt in the last week:

	Rarely 0	A little 1	Moderate 2	Most 3
I felt sad.	____	____	____	____
My sleep was restless.	____	____	____	____
I did not feel like eating.	____	____	____	____

Source: DACL: Zuckerman & Lubin (1965); BDI: Beck et al. (1961); CES-D: Radloff (1977).

Four different formats and types of content are illustrated as examples of questionnaires assessing depression: (1) The Depression Adjective Check List measures the client's current mood state using adjectives; (2) the Visual Analogue Scale measures current mood state using a simple line; (3) the Beck Depression Inventory measures the various symptoms of depression, not only mood state; and (4) the Center for Epidemiological Studies–Depression Scale measures various symptoms of depression.

1940s and are now considered inappropriate or objectionable (such as "Sometimes at elections I vote for men about whom I know very little") have been eliminated or rephrased for this revision. The MMPI-2 now contains 567 items, scored "true," "false," or "cannot say." Respondents are asked to read and respond to the test items, and the questionnaire may be scored by hand or computer. Sample items are presented in Table 4.3.

The MMPI measures psychological disorder and personality, and it features ten content scales as well as scales for detecting sources of invalidity such as carelessness, defensiveness, or evasiveness on the part of the respondent. Many statistically derived subscales have also been identified for use in specific clinical or research situations. The MMPI does not simply diagnose a person; it attempts to present a profile of scores across all of the major scales, presented as deviations from general population norms. The normal scale score is a T score of 50; the higher a scale score, the more likely is the presence of disorder. Although a single scale can be informative, MMPI experts typically interpret the pattern of relative scores from the entire profile. In the hands of a trained and experienced clinician, the relative elevations of different scales present a complex picture of the personality being assessed. Figure 4.3 presents a profile of MMPI results, along with some of the interpretations that might be derived from the profile. Over the years, thousands of research studies have examined the reliability and validity of the MMPI scales and their interpretations (e.g., Butcher, Graham & Ben-Porath, 1995; Butcher & Spielberger, 1995).

Table 4.3   Sample Items from the MMPI-2

1. I like automobile magazines.	T	F
2. I have been worried about things that most people don't worry about.	T	F
3. I wake up with lots of energy most mornings.	T	F
4. Sometimes my thoughts are broadcast over the radio.	T	F
5. I am easily startled by loud noise.	T	F

Source: MMPI-2 (Butcher et al. 1989). Copyright © 1942, 1943 (revised 1970), 1989 by the Regents of the University of Minnesota. Reproduced by permission of the publisher.

These are simulated examples of the more than five hundred items of the MMPI-2. Participants answer true or false, as applicable to them. Each item is scored for one or more of the subscales of the personality inventory, and the results are plotted relative to a standardized score of 50, as shown in Figure 4.3.

Personality inventories can provide a great deal of useful information obtained relatively easily. But they have disadvantages as well. For example, conclusions might be drawn that have not been validated, and interpreting the inventories requires considerable clinical training. An enormous amount of research has been performed in an effort to validate some of the most notable personality tests for specific purposes. However, these tests are often used to make "clinical" inferences (such as "He has a deep distrust of women"), which do not constitute an empirically validated use of the tests. Therefore, while they can be extremely useful and are frequenty well-validated for certain uses, conclusions drawn from such tests are not always valid.

Performance Tests

Performance tests involve the completion of tasks believed to indicate cognitive abilities. They include both physical tasks (such as solving puzzles, copying designs, and naming objects) and mental tasks (such as defining words, solving mental arithmetic problems, and recalling items from a memory test). The most widely used performance tasks are tests of intelligence and cognitive impairment. We also discuss personality tests that require the person to perform tasks such as completing a story.

Tests of Intelligence   *Intelligence* is a controversial concept that has yielded many different definitions and assessment methods. Indeed, it is often defined somewhat circularly as "whatever IQ tests measure." Tests of intellectual functioning, often called **intelligence (IQ) tests**,* are most widely used to place children in academic settings or to screen adults for occupational placement. They may also help address questions regarding psychological abnormality. For instance, a teacher may

wish to determine whether a youngster's difficulty in school is due to underlying intellectual limitations or other problems. And in the case of a man returning to work after a head injury who finds that he cannot perform the necessary tasks as well as before, intellectual testing may help determine whether this deficit is due to the injury. In fact, intelligence tests are commonly included among a larger battery of neuropsychological performance tests of cognitive functioning. Their results help researchers determine, for example, whether a child's IQ score affects the outcome of his or her conduct disorder, whether a special treatment program alters the intellectual functioning of children born to crack-addicted mothers, and whether electroconvulsive treatment for depression affects long-term intellectual performance.

Numerous intelligence tests are currently in use. Among the most widely administered and studied are the Wechsler Intelligence Scale for Children–Third Edition, or WISC-III (Wechsler, 1989); the Stanford-Binet (Terman & Merril, 1960), also for children; and the Wechsler Adult Intelligence Scale–Revised, or WAIS-R (Wechsler, 1981). All of these are individually administered and consist of multiple subscales. One set of subscales includes verbal tasks (such as verbal reasoning or vocabulary) and another set includes performance tasks (such as assembling blocks or puzzle pieces); all items range from easy to difficult. The three tests are used in various countries and, with appropriate modifications where necessary, can be scored similarly (e.g., Crawford, Gray & Allan, 1995).

An individual's ability to solve increasingly difficult items within a given amount of time is summed across the different tasks, and his or her performance is compared with that of others of the same age. Based on this comparison, an IQ score may be derived for the verbal and performance sections as well as for the overall test, with 100 as the average score. Typically, the numeric scores are of less importance to assessment questions than is the identification of a person's relative strengths and weaknesses across various intellectual tasks.

---

*IQ stands for "intelligence quotient."

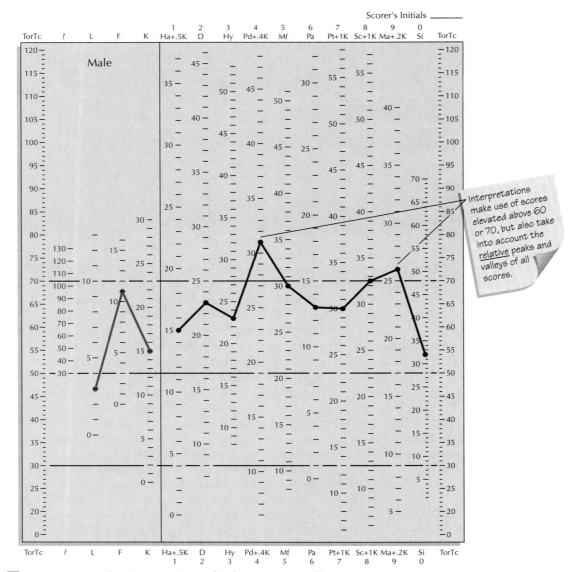

Scorer's Initials _____

Interpretations make use of scores elevated above 60 or 70, but also take into account the relative peaks and valleys of all scores.

Figure 4.3   The Minnesota Multiphasic Personality Inventory

This man's overall profile indicates significant departure from normal scores (a T score, indicated by "TorTc," of 50 is average) on most of the 10 clinical scales. (Each scale is the source of interpretations about an area of functioning; thus, scale 4 [Psychopathic Deviance] refers to antisocial conduct and conformity to conventional standards of behavior and values.) The scores might be interpreted as indicating personality traits and likely behaviors. An interpretation might consist of both description and hypothesis: This patient is callous and manipulative, with little respect for the rights of others or interest and trust in other people. His tendency for explosive rage may make him dangerous under conditions that threaten his weak sense of masculine identity. He is not likely to respond well to verbal psychotherapy but might profit from structured, behavioral problem-solving programs to deal effectively with anger. *Source:* MMPI (Hathaway & McKinley, 1948). Copyright © by the University of Minnesota 1942, 1943 (revised 1970). This profile from 1984, 1976, 1982. Reproduced by permission of the University of Minnesota Press.

Among the factors that can affect performance on IQ tests are motivation, persistence, ability to control anxiety, fatigue, and familiarity with the examiner. Therefore, the examiner must be skilled in observing, interpreting, and controlling these factors. Although performance on intelligence tests changes somewhat over time, these tests yield highly reliable results when administered properly. Intelligence tests are considered valid for uses such as predicting school performance or suggesting a person's current level of intellectual functioning. They are not valid, however, for judging a person's innate capacities or for predicting success in life, so their use for these purposes has been highly controversial. Still unresolved is the question of whether these tests measure an *innate capacity* as opposed to *achievement* of certain skills and knowledge; whether they tap a single, global quality or distinct abilities; and whether the tests are fair and accurate for all segments of society.

The *fairness* issue, which has stirred the greatest controversy of all, centers on the significant differences between the mean IQ scores of Anglo and African American school children. But the issue is much larger.

This second-grader is taking the Wechsler Intelligence Scale for Children, a set of subtests individually administered by a psychologist with special training in the procedures.

Critics have charged that the standard IQ tests do not adequately represent the experiences of African American children, that such children are therefore at a relative disadvantage, and that decisions made on the basis of such testing may result in bias whether at the level of school placement, employment, or military service.

Heated public and scholarly debates over fairness and bias have led to both improved content of standardized tests and to greater care in applying the test results. Indeed, considerable efforts have been made to rid IQ and achievement tests of items that are *culturally biased* and to include a balanced distribution of ethnic groups in samples used for standardization of scoring.

Tests of Cognitive Impairment   An increasingly useful and sensitive approach to cognitive assessment is **neuropsychological assessment,** which tests numerous types of cognitive functioning. If a person has suffered brain injury or if neurological disease is suspected, such testing is used along with medical examinations to identify the nature and extent of possible impairment — and sometimes even to identify the location of neurological damage. Neuropsychological assessment can be useful in diagnosis (for example, when a practitioner is trying to determine whether a problem is psychological or medical or whether it is symptomatic of schizophrenia or brain damage) as well as in planning and evaluating treatment.

Sometimes neuropsychological assessment can identify subtle neurological impairment that is not detectable by medical examinations, including neuroimaging techniques. Because different regions of the brain are involved in different functions, a wide variety of tasks may be used to identify the type of impairment. The use of multiple tests also permits confirmation of important patterns based on various sources. Typically, an intelligence test is given to determine overall intellectual functioning

as well as particular areas of deficit or adequate performance, followed by tests administered to assess short-term and long-term memory functioning, speed and accuracy of performance on visual and spatial tasks, auditory and tactile perception, and language performance. A complete battery might take six or eight hours to complete. Figure 4.4 gives an example of one commonly used neuropsychological test.

Among the batteries of neuropsychological tests available are the Luria-Nebraska test (Luria, 1973) and the Halstead-Reitan test (Reitan & Davison, 1974). A profile comparing actual performance with expected normal performance can yield information on the nature, severity, and possible location of brain dysfunction. As we learn more about the specific functions of different areas of the brain, the development of tests that locate possible damage and assess its severity will become increasingly possible.

Projective Tests   One type of performance test, the **projective test,** seeks to reveal the underlying personality of individuals by measuring how they handle an ambiguous task. In projective tests the examiner is interested in both the verbal responses and the test-taking behaviors of the person. The best-known projective test is the *Rorschach inkblot test,* in which the participant is presented with a series of ten standardized inkblots and asked to describe what he or she "sees." In the *Thematic Apperception Test (TAT)* the participant is presented with a series of photographs and asked to tell a story about each one. Figure 4.5 shows a Rorschach-like inkblot and a TAT.

The theory behind projective tests is that a person given an ambiguous task or stimulus will *project* onto the task his or her unconscious motives, feelings, defenses, and personality characteristics. The assessor interprets

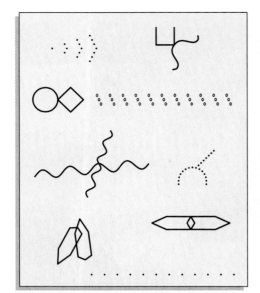
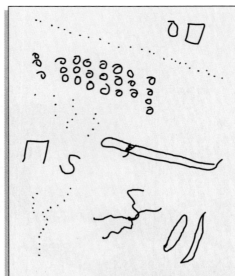

Figure 4.4 The Bender-Gestalt Test

The Bender-Gestalt test (Bender, 1933; Hutt, 1969) is a widely used measure of sensorimotor construction skills. On the left are the Bender-Gestalt items. The participant is instructed to reproduce nine two-dimensional figures on a blank sheet of paper. The figures are presented one at a time. Patients with brain damage may reproduce figures that are rotated to varying degrees or are missing sections of the stimulus figure. When asked to recall the figures after testing is completed, brain-damaged participants show evidence of memory deficits. On the right are the drawings copied by a child with a brain tumor. The pattern of poor ability to reproduce the figures suggests considerable perceptual-motor difficulties, consistent with a tumor in the right cerebral hemisphere.
Source: Sattler (1990, p. 709).

the subject's responses, either by a systematic scoring system or through inferences based on clinical judgment. For example, the Rorschach test may be scored according to formal attributes of responses, such as presence of human or animal movement and quality of form, color, and shading (e.g., Exner, 1990). Research has validated some clinical applications of projective tests; for instance, inanimate movement responses (as when the subject reports seeing a flag waving, flames leaping, leaves falling) are said to reflect the experience of external stress over which the person feels little control. Thus, trainees on the day before a first parachute jump and hospital patients the day before surgery show more inanimate movement responses than they do at less stressful times (see Erdberg & Exner, 1984).

The degree of comfort that a professional feels with respect to projective methods depends on his or her acceptance of the underlying theory and of the reliability and validity of the uses of these techniques. Originally developed on the basis of psychodynamic assumptions, the Rorschach and other projective tests might now also be used by clinicians who subscribe to cognitive-behavioral models. For instance, cognitively oriented psychologists might find such methods useful in revealing a person's beliefs about the world and the self: "This client repeatedly saw malevolent figures or attributed hostile and threatening intentions to characters, which suggests that she experiences herself as vulnerable to danger from other people and expects to be harmed in her relationships with others." Projective techniques can also be used to give samples of language and thought that can help detect schizophrenic thought disorder. Hundreds of studies with different methods and scoring systems have suggested that projective tests are valid for certain purposes. Most commonly, they are used to aid clinicians in forming hypotheses about the personality of clients, perhaps revealing information that clients cannot or will not report directly. However, projective techniques are also often used to confirm preexisting clinical hunches without empirical validation of their accuracy.

Observational Methods

The interview, questionnaire, and performance test disclose segments of a person's behavior. But sometimes questions concerning whether a disorder exists, what its causes and characteristics are, and how it should be treated are best answered through more direct **observational techniques** — by actually watching what a person does in a particular setting. A child, for instance, is usually not able to report that he has trouble sustaining attention in settings where there are distractions, or he may erroneously report that he hits other children only when they hit him first. A person brought to the emergency room may deny that he has hallucinations because his illness involves a lack of insight. Or a wife might tell the interviewer about her husband's faults but be unaware that he criticizes her during a conversation only when she ignores or demeans him.

Figure 4.5   A Rorschach-Like Inkblot and a Thematic Apperception Test

(A) The Thematic Apperception Test (TAT) involves presentation of cards containing photos or paintings. The examinee is asked to tell a story about what he or she sees, and the assumption is that the individual "projects" his or her psychological conflicts, needs, and defenses onto the story in a way that can be interpreted by the psychologist.

(B) This is an example of an ink-blot "projective" test, in which the participant tells what he or she "sees." Projective tests assume that the individual reveals inner, or hidden, information about the self by "projecting" onto an unfamiliar or ambiguous stimulus.
Source: Sundberg (1977, p. 212).

Thus, on many occasions it is helpful to have specific information about a problem behavior in the context in which it actually occurs and unbiased by what people are able or willing to report.

Behavioral observations are commonly an assessment method of choice when the clinician's theoretical orientation emphasizes overt behaviors and their contingencies. For example, a behavioral or cognitive-behavioral model holds that the problem behavior (including dysfunctional cognitions) is itself the problem rather than a sign of underlying inner conflict. From this point of view, the goal of assessment is to find out what people do rather than what they have (Mischel, 1968). Accordingly, behavioral observation may contribute not only to assessment and diagnosis but also to planning, implementing, and evaluating treatment.

Behavioral observations may be *structured* — as when a therapist asks a married couple to discuss a controversial topic — or they may be *naturalistic* — as when a therapist observes a child on the playground or an unresponsive patient in the dayroom of a mental hospital. The targeted behaviors must be carefully defined in advance, and they can be counted in various ways: how many times the behavior occurs in a certain period,

whether it occurs after a particular stimulus, or what sequence of behaviors occurs during an interval of observation.

> *Mickey is seven years old, and his teacher reports that he is disruptive in the classroom and that he bothers the other children. Based on her reports, he may display signs of attention deficit disorder with hyperactivity, a childhood dysfunction that can often be treated successfully with a combination of medication and behavioral techniques. His mother, however, says that he's just a typical boy and just has lots of energy. She adds that Mickey's father left the family a few months ago and that the child is upset; so if he is overactive at school, it might be temporary.*

The task of assessment in this case is to determine whether Mickey's behavior is unusual compared to other children. Observation would also help to determine the specific disruptive behaviors he displays, and whether different behaviors occur in several different settings.

Figure 4.6 presents a coding sheet for classroom observation of one element of Mickey's behavior. The observer, a trained teacher's aide, might watch his

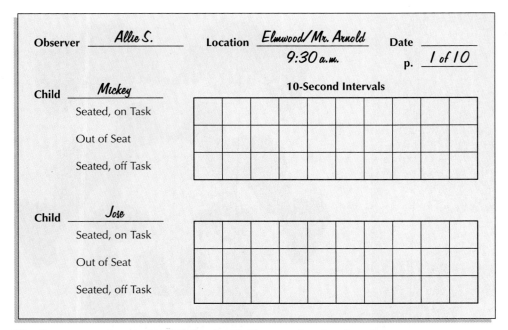

Observer _____Allie S._____ Location _____Elmwood/Mr. Arnold_____ Date _____
9:30 a.m.   p. _I of 10_

Child _____Mickey_____   **10-Second Intervals**

Seated, on Task

Out of Seat

Seated, off Task

Child _____Jose_____

Seated, on Task

Out of Seat

Seated, off Task

Figure 4.6 Example of Behavioral Observation Scoring Form

Mickey, the target child, is being observed to determine if his difficulty in sitting still and working quietly is different from the "typical" behavior of other children (e.g., Jose). The setting is the classroom during a period of quiet desk work. An observer makes a check mark for each occurrence of a behavior during the time interval (every 10 seconds). The categories are mutually exclusive. Different kinds of rating systems could be devised to answer different questions.

behavior and that of a comparison child during a twenty-minute period once a day for a week and record whether a specific behavior occurred during that interval. Combined with other kinds of observations and interviews with his teachers and parents, this information may help to determine the best course of action to help alter Mickey's disruptiveness.

Sometimes, determining the most meaningful behaviors to observe is difficult. Unless the targeted behaviors are carefully defined, reliability of observations may be impaired. However, even when good reliability (especially interrater reliability) is achieved, validity can be compromised if the individual is observed under conditions that are contrived or do not represent typical situations. Thus, observational methods sometimes suffer from lack of generalizability to real-life situations. Also, reliability and validity may be diminished if those who are being observed behave atypically because they know that they are being watched. This problem, called **reactivity,** raises the issue of whether the assessment itself changes people's behaviors — an issue that arises in many forms of psychological assessment.

Observational methods also permit the assessment of people's behaviors in a social context: children with peers, couples or families, or groups. Unlike traditional methods of interviewing or administering questionnaires, which are geared toward individual behavior and experience, behavioral observation is especially suited to obtaining information about interactions between individuals.

FAMILY MATTERS

Measuring Families

Both traditional psychodynamic and contemporary cognitive-social learning theories emphasize the influence of the family on development. Indeed, throughout this book we cite numerous studies of abnormal behavior associated with maladaptive childhood and family experiences (such as abuse, neglect, family disruption, and deviant role models). Surprisingly, however, most of this research is based on reports of events that happened in the past, called *retrospective reports,* which are limited by bias, memory, and accuracy.

Questionnaires that assess the characteristics of families and of parent-child interactions are perhaps less well developed or less extensively used than are those that measure individual experiences and personal characteristics (see Touliatos, Perlmutter & Straus, 1990). A few questionnaires appear frequently in family studies. For instance, the Family Adaptability and Cohesion Evaluation Scales, abbreviated FACES, contain twenty items on which to rate cohesiveness (closeness) and adaptability, or ability to change (Edman, Cole & Howard, 1990; Olson, Portner & Lavee, 1985). The Family Environment Scale, or FES (Moos & Moos, 1986), is a true-false questionnaire for rating a variety of dimensions of family life such as organization, cohesion, and independence. Other scales have been used primarily to assess adults' perceptions of their childhoods. For

Although direct observation is desirable to understand how families function, complex processes, such as a mother interacting with two young children, are challenging to measure. Does she behave the same way when observed as when unobserved? What are the most useful behaviors to measure, and can results be applied to other settings? Such issues illustrate why questionnaires (self-reports) are often overused to the relative neglect of behavioral observations.

example, the Parental Bonding Instrument assesses dimensions of affection and control (Kendler, 1996; Parker, Tupling & Brown, 1979; Weich, Lewis & Mann, 1996).

Certain difficulties with measures of families limit the potential value of questionnaires. One problem is the possible contamination of ratings and perceptions by a family member's current mood and distress or by other factors that limit the accuracy of the ratings as reflections of what really goes on in the family (Gerlsma, Emmelkamp & Arrindell, 1990). A person who is currently depressed, for example, might rate her parents and family life more negatively than if she were in a good mood. Another problem is that the ratings often combine views of mothers and fathers who might in fact be very different. Conversely, different measures that have the same labels (such as "cohesiveness") might actually assess somewhat different qualities — a situation that leads to confusion when the results of multiple studies are compared. And certainly one of the most important problems of all is the lack of clarity as to which dimensions of family functioning are most important to assess.

Some of these shortcomings can be addressed in part by direct observation of family functioning. Indeed, a particular hypothesis may result in measurement of a specific behavior during an observation period. For example, Gerald Patterson and his colleagues (1982) at the Oregon Research Institute have developed a standardized method of observing the interactions between parents and their children with conduct disorders (the Family Interaction Coding Scale). Like many observational coding methods, this one not only counts the occurrence of certain events but also analyzes their sequences and patterns. This study and others have demonstrated dysfunctional patterns in which (1) par-

ents and children escalate each other's negative behaviors, and (2) parents typically fail to reinforce children for positive behaviors (e.g., Patterson, 1996).

Another example of family assessment that has been used in research on the course of schizophrenia (though not for routine assessment) is called Expressed Emotion (Vaughn & Leff, 1976). Investigators first ask a close relative to describe the schizophrenic patient; they then count, among other factors, the frequency of critical comments (such as "He's lazy and won't lift a finger to help his mother around the house"). In families with relatives who express the highest levels of criticism, patients tend to experience a more rapid return of their schizophrenic symptoms after release from hospital treatment (reviewed by Mintz, Liberman, Miklowitz & Mintz, 1987). Numerous other investigators have observed distressed marital couples, depressed mothers with their children, and parents with their manic-depressive offspring, to name just a few examples. Such studies provide accurate information about factors that may shape disorder.

Unfortunately, observational procedures also have some drawbacks. For example, each research team tends to develop its own coding system, so that there are few widely used procedures that permit comparisons across multiple studies. In addition, the problem of reactivity may limit validity if the families behave differently while being observed than they do while alone — or if, like individuals, they simply behave differently in different settings. Finally, as with questionnaires, family observation assessments are limited by our lack of knowledge about which dimensions of family interactions are particularly critical for understanding normal and abnormal development. This gap is an important one that researchers are working to fill.

Self-monitoring is a behavioral observation procedure in which individuals observe themselves in certain contexts. It is useful in cases where detailed information is needed about the frequency of a behavior or the circumstances surrounding its occurrence, but where an observer cannot follow the subject around all day. Under these conditions it is simply more efficient to ask the person to do the observing.

> *Susan had bulimia. The therapist, wanting to learn more about what triggered her eating binges, asked Susan to keep a detailed diary of her feelings and the circumstances associated with urges to eat. After reviewing the records over a week or so, the therapist discovered that Susan's binges seemed to start with feelings of loneliness and boredom in circumstances when she was alone. The treatment, therefore, focused specifically on changing these feelings and circumstances: reducing the loneliness, altering the thoughts that led to eating, and developing new responses to eating-related cues.*

Other self-monitoring techniques are also effective. A person might be asked to count the frequency of a problem behavior, such as self-critical or fearful thoughts, by using a wrist-counter. Or, as part of a treatment for marital difficulties, each partner might be asked to keep a record of the other person's pleasing behaviors such as expressing affection, being helpful, and making supportive comments. Self-monitoring methods do require a clear rationale and careful definition of the targeted behavior, but they are limited only by the ingenuity of the therapist or assessor and the individual. It is important to note that self-monitoring may create reactivity, such that the assessment procedure itself actually alters the behavior. If the goal is to change a problem behavior, this is not a limitation; nevertheless, in situations where careful and accurate information about the problem behavior is needed, reactivity may be an issue.

Biological Assessment Techniques

Both diagnostic assessments and research into the causes and attributes of various disorders increasingly use biological assessment techniques. In principle, if the biological causes of disorders are clearly established, biological measures would be the predominant assessment technique. Thus, just as one form of psychosis was found to be caused by syphilis, the presence of which is established through a blood test, in the future there may be definitive tests for diagnosing neurotransmitter deficiencies, structural brain abnormalities, or genetic defects. However, since research is far from establishing such direct causal links, most physiological assessment currently supplements other diagnostic methods or is employed as a research tool to further understand a disorder and its causes. The two major types of biological assessment methods are neuroimaging techniques and psychophysiological techniques.

Neuroimaging Techniques **Neuroimaging techniques** are methods of viewing the living brain, based on computerized synthesis of images that are far more sensitive than x-rays. They are used both for medical diagnoses and for research studies, and we will see numerous applications in later chapters. In *computerized axial tomography (CT)* scans, a radioactive ray passes through bone and tissue. The different densities of these substances determine how much of the radioactive particles get through to the detector and show up as images of different shades. A computer synthesizes the numerous images viewed from different angles and forms a two-dimensional picture.

Positron emission tomography (PET) scans are unique in that they show actual brain activity. The technique is based on the fact that the areas of the brain that are doing the most work at a given time consume the most glucose in the blood and cause a rise in the flow of blood carrying glucose to these areas. Water containing a small amount of radioactive substance is injected into the bloodstream so that blood flood can be monitored, and a radiation detector placed around the head measures the amount of radiation (positrons) appearing in different regions of the brain. The different amounts of blood flow are transformed into images with different colors (wavelengths) representing different levels of activity. In Figure 4.7 the brighter colors indicate regions of higher levels of activity.

Nuclear magnetic resonance imaging (NMR or MRI) is an advanced technique for evaluating brain structure that produces sharp images but does not require radioactive substances. In this procedure the person is placed inside a circular magnet. The magnetic field alters the movement and electromagnetic field of atoms in the molecules of the body. A computer synthesis of the movement produces excellent images of the structure of the brain or other body parts for use in both medical and psychological studies. Recently, *functional MRI (fMRI)* has been developed to provide views of even briefer changes in brain activity, and with better resolution, than those measured by PET scans. Functional MRI also does not require injection of radioactive material.

Psychophysiological Techniques **Psychophysiological techniques** are used to measure certain aspects of the autonomic nervous system. The assessment instruments are based on the assumption that emotional states involve changes in autonomic nervous system function such as heart rate and sweat gland activity (see Chapter 2). The principle of one such instrument — the polygraph, or lie detector — is that people undergo certain physiological changes when they lie. These physiological changes can be detected as electrical impulses that are recorded as tracings on paper. Although lie detectors have not been

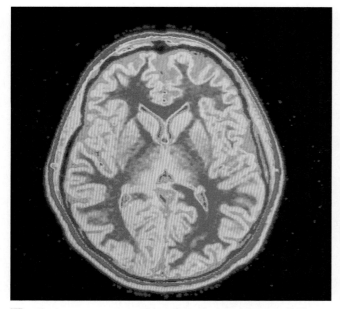

PLACEBO

HALOPERIDOL

nonresponder   responder

Figure 4.7   Examples of Brain Imaging Techniques
(Left) Magnetic resonance imaging (MRI) provides a view of brain structure made up of a computer-synthesized image based on type of tissue, where red is the most dense and blue the least dense. It provides a highly detailed type of x-ray.

(Right) Positron emission tomography (PET) is a view of blood flow and glucose metabolism; yellow and red indicate areas of higher metabolic rate than areas of green and blue.

found to be valid for detecting falsehoods or illegal behavior (e.g., Kleinmuntz & Szucko, 1984; Lykken, 1984), measurement of psychophysiological processes has many useful research applications. For instance, we will see its use in studies of antisocial personality disorder (e.g., Raine, Venables & Williams, 1995), children's temperament, sleep abnormalities in depression, and sexual functioning (e.g., Adams, Wright & Lohr, 1996) in later chapters.

Selecting and Combining Procedures

There are many formats for systematic measurement of psychological conditions. Each method has its own set of advantages and disadvantages. Table 4.4 summarizes some of the major uses and advantages of each type of assessment; it also notes any particular limitations.

Because of the limitations in any one form of assessment, a combination of procedures is commonly used in clinical evaluations, research investigations, treatment planning, and outcome measurement. In such instances, the assessor attempts to draw conclusions from patterns of responses rather than from a single source. Consider the following example of assessment used to answer clinical questions concerning evaluation and treatment planning.

Donald is a sixty-year-old man who, as we learned at the start of the chapter, is severely depressed. He complains of notable memory loss, trouble concentrating, hopelessness, loss of energy,

and many other signs of depression. He has taken a leave from work because of his impaired functioning. Convinced that he has a brain disease that is causing deterioration of his mental capabilities, Donald insists that he is depressed because of loss of intellectual functioning and the expectation of further deterioration and death. Medical examinations have revealed no evidence of disorder, and doctors now recommend psychological evaluation — though Donald is convinced that medical tests have simply failed to find the underlying problem.

A psychologist is consulted. Interviews with Donald and his wife confirm that his memory is poor and that he gets lost when driving alone. The psychologist's interview further confirms diagnosable depression, and additional procedures are administered to learn more about what is going on. Both the scores and actual observations based on a Wechsler Adult Intelligence Scale reveal that Donald is not mentally impaired, especially as indicated by subtests that are relatively resistant to depression (such as those assessing vocabulary and verbal reasoning). A memory test consisting of various performance tasks suggests that Donald's concentration is more likely the problem than his actual memory; when pressed to concentrate and do his best, Donald responds relatively well. Furthermore, the MMPI suggests that Donald tends to focus on physical problems rather than to acknowledge psychological problems, and that he is a highly conscientious worrier who gets overwhelmed in the face of stress. Based on this

Table 4.4   Major Types of Assessment Procedures

	Uses and Advantages	Limitations
Interview	Probes specific content; observes behaviors	Needs skill and training; outcome can be affected by interaction
Questionnaire	Covers specific content; easily administered	Subject to bias; limited to what is asked and what can be reported
Performance task		
Intellectual	Samples relevant behavior	May be generalized inappropriately
Projective test	Provides access to "internal" processes and information	Interpretations may not be valid
Observation	Samples behavior in relevant context	Labor-intensive; may be generalized inappropriately

All of these assessment procedures require evidence of reliability and validity, and all can be validly used only for some purposes and not others. All procedures except questionnaires require skill to administer and score. Because different methods are used for different purposes, several procedures are often combined to explore a clinical or research question.

information, the psychologist suspects that Donald is experiencing depression (which in turn is causing his cognitive symptoms), specifically because of some stress that he has failed to acknowledge as a problem. Further interviewing reveals that he was passed over for a hoped-for promotion given to a younger man. Even though Donald has told himself it doesn't matter because he will retire soon, the psychologist concludes that the experience, plus its psychological meaning to Donald, has triggered a major depression. She recommends treatment for the depression based on her assessment.

Using Psychological Assessment Appropriately

Even when assessment instruments are reliable and valid, potential misuses and abuses must be guarded against. One potential misuse, *invasion of privacy,* is less prevalent now because safeguards to privacy are stronger than in previous decades. Individuals seeking psychological evaluation and treatment can generally assume that their records will remain confidential. And those who participate in research projects must give *informed consent,* which is agreement to participate only after the procedures and their risks are fully disclosed, and after the investigator has promised to provide confidentiality for any records and results obtained.

Much of the misuse of assessment stems from applying the procedures to unsuitable situations or groups and from drawing conclusions beyond the information given. Consider the following example. You work in a pediatric clinic where cases of suspected child sexual abuse are evaluated using an interview method based on studies of white males. But children referred to the clinic from certain Asian and Hispanic subcultures are more likely to be reticent about discussing sexual experiences

than are those from other groups. Therefore, the current interview may be inappropriate, and you may need to develop different procedures to accommodate both sexes as well as diverse ethnic groups. This situation illustrates a question that will arise throughout the book: Do the procedures — the tests, diagnostic instruments, interviews, and so on — adequately represent the experiences of different groups? Do the results lead to unbiased decisions about both males and females of diverse ages, ethnic background, and socioeconomic status? Differences in language, education, and status may indeed affect a person's performance on an assessment task.

More generally, an assessment instrument should be applied only to the uses for which it has been validated. Typically, the interpretation of an assessment result involves some degree of inference or generalization — a matter of going beyond the result to predict a person's characteristics or behaviors in different situations. Some interpretations involve only small inferences. For example, a score on a depression inventory taken in a therapist's office probably predicts how a person will be feeling that day even when not in the office. Other interpretations involve large leaps — and these are perilous. Consider the following hypothetical interpretations and the conclusions actually justified by research:

What the tester infers	*What research justifies*
The polygraph shows that this person is dishonest and should not be hired.	This person may (or may not) have told a lie, but the test can't tell if the person *often* lies.
The Rorschach test indicates poor controls coupled with aggressive fantasies; the person may become violent.	The best predictor of violence is past history of violence in similar situations.

Psychophysiological measures of heart rate, respiration, and sweat gland activity are among variables used in research to understand the link between thinking and bodily responses. When used in the form of a polygraph (lie detector), as in this scene, their reliability and validity for purposes of detecting deceit are matters of controversy.

The MMPI suggests that this person has deep-seated doubts about his masculinity.

This person endorses interests and attitudes not stereotypically masculine, but lack of masculine interests does not in itself mean maladjustment.

None of these inferences have been validated by the research that is available. Given that they all involve important personal outcomes for the individuals in question, validation is more than just a nicety or a matter of routine.

Moreover, people tend to misinterpret the *source* of problems revealed by assessment procedures. If an adult scores poorly on a memory task, if a schizophrenic patient is apathetic during an observation in the hospital, or if a person's scores on a personality test indicate high levels of disturbance, we usually conclude that something about the person is causing the scores. This conclusion may or may not be true. When people explain the behavior of others, they generally underestimate the influence of situations and overestimate the influence of personality traits; this tendency is called the **fundamental attribution error** (Ross, 1977). In fact, situations can be very influential. The person scoring poorly on a memory test may lack the energy and interest to perform well because he is currently depressed; the schizophrenic patient may be apathetic because there is nothing that she likes to do in the dayroom of the hospital. Clearly, then, it is important to try to understand the situational determinants of a person's performance rather than automatically attributing all data solely to underlying traits.

Indeed, mental health professionals themselves may often be the source of error in assessment. Some of the difficulties involved in interpreting assessment results are normal human errors made while drawing conclusions from complex information.

Human Error in Clinical Assessment

Contrary to current clichés, the human mind does not resemble a computer. Unlike a computer, it makes a lot of mistakes. Many such errors are based on mental shortcuts used by human beings when they are trying to process complex information rapidly. The following mental shortcuts can actually interfere with accurate clinical judgment. They are "normal" in the sense of being typical ways that people process information, but unfortunately they can lead to errors in conclusions based on assessment.

1. *Confirmatory bias.* Several decades of research indicate that incoming information is often filtered through *schemas,* or mental templates or filters based on experience that help us process information rapidly. Schemas shape how information is attended to, interpreted, and recalled. But information that is inconsistent with a person's schemas may be ignored or distorted. In ambiguous situations people fill in the gaps based on what they expect to find. Thus, an interviewer who hypothesizes that the person being interviewed is manic-depressive is likely to notice and remember information that agrees with this belief and to ignore information that does not fit. Similarly, an investigator observing a child who is reported to be aggressive may fail to count the times that the child is cooperative. The confirmatory bias thus helps sustain stereotypes. In some sense, all psychological theories may lead to confirmatory

bias — and that is why the scientific method teaches us specifically to look for disconfirming information.

2. *First impressions.* The confirmatory bias is one testament to the potency of first impressions. These impressions provide the basis for a theory or bias, which people then use to anchor subsequent observations. For example, a clinician may find a client to be initially charming and apparently sincere, yet subsequently minimize evidence that the client lies and is irresponsible.

3. *Illusory correlation.* Both trained clinicians and naive judges tend to interpret certain responses on a Rorschach or other projective task as indicating certain characteristics, even after they are told that there is no valid basis for those interpretations — a tendency known as illusory correlation (Chapman & Chapman, 1967, 1969). In one instance, a person who reported seeing "eyes" in the inkblot was labeled suspicious; in another, a person who reported seeing male genitals was labeled homosexual. There was absolutely no truth to these interpretations, but the judges kept making them — because of strong perceptual or meaning associations. (In the first example above, they may have drawn a strong association between eyes and suspiciousness, or watchfulness.) Such preexisting associations may lead to illusory correlations that are very resistant to change. Stereotypes also give rise to erroneous interpretations, such as the assumption that people with big foreheads are intelligent.

4. *Availability bias.* Suppose that a clinician is asked to diagnose a boy who has peer problems and discovers that the youngster likes pornographic magazines. The clinician recalls that years ago she evaluated a boy who had been brought in for treatment because he fondled the dead bodies of young men in funeral homes — and he also had peer problems and read pornographic magazines. Bingo! The clinician now looks for all possible parallels and forms the theory that this youngster is a potential necrophiliac. Her reasoning illustrates the availability bias: When people select a hypothesis or propose a solution, they are likely to choose whatever evidence is most "available" to their memory (Tversky & Kahneman, 1973). And often what people recall most easily is a function of how vivid, personally meaningful, or colorful the memory is.

These are only a few of the errors that researchers have identified in human information processing (for others, see Nisbett & Ross, 1980). The point is that the reliability and validity characteristics of a measurement method are not sufficient to ensure that the method will be properly used; indeed, clinical (human) judgment is also needed to interpret and combine information.

DIAGNOSIS OF PSYCHOLOGICAL DISORDERS

Assessment typically involves collecting various sources of information to form a thorough picture of a person. Often a goal of assessment is **diagnosis,** or determining the constellation of symptoms and how they fit the classification system for mental disorders. Consider the following case:

> *You've seen Ellen in the women's gym at all hours; she seems to be working out for many hours a day, and is very thin and muscled. Her friends have also started to notice that she picks at her food, seeming to eat very little — and that when she's out to dinner she will order only salads no matter what else is on the menu. When her closest friend tried to express concern, Ellen was angry, and denied that she was too thin. "I'm not anorectic" she said. "I am just trying to be healthy."*

As the case of Ellen illustrates, diagnosis is important for three major reasons. First, diagnostic classification has implications for understanding and treating a problem: What is going on? Is there a psychological disorder? Once the key problem is defined, research and clinical experience about the nature of the problem may provide understanding about its likely causes and course as well as indicate available treatment options. Second, diagnosis permits communication among professionals and thus facilitates a shared basis of knowledge. Diagnostic classification offers a shorthand way of conveying information and aiding professionals in organizing knowledge that helps them learn and communicate more effectively. Third, in scientific study, diagnosis is essential in terms of defining a sample of people for investigation and providing a basis for characterizing the nature of a particular disorder as distinct from other disorders.

Suppose that interviews and psychological evaluation reveal that Ellen's basic diagnosis is an eating disorder called *anorexia nervosa.* The clinician speculates that it results from her excessively perfectionistic standards about body image and an extreme need to control her environment, leading to excessive weight loss and impairing her health and personal life. Treatment options include psychotherapy, medication to control the intense perfectionistic strivings, or both. These treatment options might be very different from those recommended if Ellen were diagnosed as having a drug-abuse problem or experiencing a schizophrenic episode causing internal disorganization.

Diagnosing mental disorders also involves potential difficulties, many of which center on the classification system. For example, imagine trying to devise a classification system for vegetables. Some are hard, some soft; some are green, some yellow; some are big, some small; some have strong flavors, some bland; some grow above ground, some below; some have thin skins, some thick. Within all this diversity, how do we figure out the essential differences that might provide the organizing framework of a classification system? Do you focus on starch content? Healthiness? Molecular structure? Size? And what system would lead to putting each vegetable in only one category? What about "borderline" cases? If size is a key feature, for example, where do potatoes go? The choices are endless.

If we consider psychological disorders instead of vegetables, the task is even more complicated. What elements are essential, and how are the elements related to each other? Should we use broad or narrow categories? Any system of classification compels us to decide between "splitting and lumping" — between having very narrow distinct categories or broader more inclusive ones. If the categories are too narrow, we may end up treating closely related conditions as different disorders; if the categories are too broad, our experimental groups may be too heterogeneous to be practical for research and clinical decision making. If several conditions share similar symptoms (as, say, irritability, poor concentration, and agitation do), where should the boundaries be drawn? And when is a condition severe enough to qualify for diagnosis?

Another complexity in building a diagnostic system is the question of *who decides*? Initial efforts to develop diagnostic manuals for widespread use were often based on the theoretical persuasions and even political positions of just a few clinicians. Later, opinion surveys of members of the American Psychiatric Association were used to decide what should be included in such manuals and what the criteria should be. In the following sections we explore these issues and current procedures used for diagnosis.

The Diagnostic and Statistical Manual (DSM)

For several thousand years, virtually every culture has recognized differences among madness (loss of contact with reality), melancholia (deep depression), dementia (impairment of memory and mental function from brain injury or advanced age), and criminality. Yet only in the last fifty years has further classification of mental disorders emerged as a major goal of mental health professionals. In 1948, for the first time, the World Health Organization included mental disorders in the sixth edition of its *International Statistical Classification of Diseases, Injuries, and Causes of Death* (ICD). And in the early 1950s the American Psychiatric Association decided to prepare a uniform manual of diagnoses. The result was the *Diagnostic and Statistical Manual–Version I* (DSM-I), which appeared in 1952 and has sub-

sequently been revised. The current version is DSM-IV. (See the inside front cover of this book.)

Features of the DSM   The most recent versions of the DSM include some features not present in earlier versions. DSM-IV (1994), in particular, uses scientific evidence to resolve controversies about the categories of disorders and the criteria for diagnosing them. Indeed, research has been used to establish boundaries between disorders and their key defining features. For example, based largely on research, manic-depression and depression have come to be viewed as distinctly different disorders, with the former now included as a bipolar affective disorder, and the latter as unipolar depression — differing in course and treatment. Increasingly, the research relied upon to guide revisions of the DSM consists of careful reviews of existing studies; reanalyses of existing data to try out different criteria; and field trials, which are research projects specifically aimed at testing particular diagnostic questions by examining relevant populations. Theory and clinical judgment also continue to play a major role in the process of refining the diagnostic system, but research is increasingly being used to resolve diagnostic issues.

Another new feature of the DSM is its **multiaxial** format; that is, it provides for evaluations on five different scales, or axes, representing different aspects of the person's life. Such assessment reflects the recognition that all of the person's life circumstances need to be taken into account. Together, the different ratings provide much more complete information for planning treatment and predicting the course of a disorder than could result from diagnosis alone.

Axis I refers to the disorder with which the client is currently diagnosed. That's as far as diagnostic systems usually go, but DSM-IV also includes Axis II for diagnosing personality disorders and mental retardation that are thought to be chronic and stable patterns of impaired functioning that may underlie Axis I disorders. Of the three additional measures of current functioning, Axis III concerns physical conditions, Axis IV reports current psychosocial stressors (rated on a six-point scale), and Axis V concerns the global level of functioning (a hundred-point scale). Table 4.5 presents the Global Assessment of Functioning Scale.

Consider an example of multiaxial diagnosis based on Donald, described earlier, who is depressed and anxious, although he believes he is suffering from medical problems.

> *Axis I: 296.23 (major depression–single episode, severe without psychotic features) and 300.02 (generalized anxiety disorder)*
>
> *Axis II: 301.40 Obsessive-compulsive personality disorder (possible)*
>
> *Axis III: None (no medical conditions)*

Axis IV: 3 (job problems)

Axis V: Current GAF 60 (overall functioning scale); highest GAF past year 75

Another feature of DSM-IV is that it defines disorders in terms of descriptive, observable characteristics rather than variables that are assumed to cause the dis-

order. For example, the diagnosis of *neurosis* in the original DSM was based on Freudian theory and its assumptions about personality dynamics; but since then, a more theoretically neutral and descriptive term, *anxiety disorders,* had been substituted. Axes I and II of DSM-IV describe the characteristics of symptoms with a precision never before provided. For example, according to

Table 4.5	**Global Assessment of Functioning (GAF) Scale: Axis V**
Code	(Note: Use intermediate codes when appropriate, e.g., 45, 68, 72.)
100 | 91	Superior functioning in a wide range of activities, life's problems never seem to get out of hand, is sought out by others because of his many positive qualities. No symptoms.
90 | 81	Absent or minimal symptoms (e.g., mild anxiety before an exam), good functioning in all areas, interested and involved in a wide range of activities, socially effective, generally satisfied with life, no more than everyday problems or concerns (e.g., an occasional argument with family members).
80 | 71	If symptoms are present, they are transient and expectable reactions to psychosocial stressors (e.g., difficulty concentrating after family argument); no more than slight impairment in social, occupational, or school functioning (e.g., temporarily falling behind in school work).
70 | 61	Some mild symptoms (e.g., depressed mood and mild insomnia) OR some difficulty in social, occupational, or school functioning (e.g., occasional truancy, or theft within the household), but generally functioning pretty well, has some meaningful interpersonal relationships.
60 | 51	Moderate symptoms (e.g., flat affect and circumstantial speech, occasional panic attacks) OR moderate difficulty in social, occupational, or school functioning (e.g., no friends, unable to keep a job).
50 | 41	Serious symptoms (e.g., suicidal ideation, severe obsessional rituals, frequent shoplifting) OR any serious impairment in social, occupational, or school functioning (e.g., no friends, unable to keep a job).
40 | 31	Some impairment in reality testing or communication (e.g., speech is at times illogical, obscure, or irrelevant) OR major impairment in several areas, such as work or school, family relations, judgment, thinking, or mood (e.g., depressed man avoids friends, neglects family, and is unable to work; child frequently beats up younger children, is defiant at home, and is failing at school).
30 | 21	Behavior is considerably influenced by delusions or hallucinations OR serious impairment in communication or judgment (e.g., sometimes incoherent, acts grossly inappropriately, suicidal preoccupation) OR inability to function in almost all areas (e.g., stays in bed all day; no job, home, or friends).
20 | 11	Some danger of hurting self or others (e.g., suicide attempts without clear expectation of death, frequently violent, manic excitement) OR occasionally fails to maintain minimal personal hygiene (e.g., smears feces) OR gross impairment in communication (e.g., largely incoherent or mute).
10 | 1	Persistent danger of severely hurting self or others (e.g., recurrent violence) OR persistent inability to maintain minimal personal hygiene OR serious suicidal act with clear expectation of death.
0	Inadequate information.

Source: DSM-IV. Reprinted with permission from *The Diagnostic and Statistical Manual of Mental Disorders,* Fourth Edition. Copyright © 1994 American Psychiatric Association.

Consider psychological, social, and occupational functioning on a hypothetical continuum of mental health–illness. Do not include impairment in functioning due to physical (or environmental) limi-

tations. This scale from the DSM gives an overall rating of functioning and impairment, as part of the multiaxial diagnostic process.

DSM-IV, major depression may include "significant weight loss or weight gain when not dieting, e.g., more than 5 percent of body weight in a month or decrease or increase in appetite nearly every day."

Still another feature of DSM-IV is that it is based on *prototypes*. That is, definitions of disorders reflect the assumption that, despite considerable variability in the specific symptoms displayed by persons with the same diagnosis, they share certain *essential,* defining characteristics. DSM-IV therefore indicates which features are essential and which ones may vary. For most diagnoses, it lists (1) typical symptoms of which the person must show a certain minimum number but which will vary from person to person and (2) specific conditions that cannot be present. Also, the criteria usually specify how long the symptoms must have been present. Table 4.6 shows an example.

In sum, DSM-IV has four key features: The diagnostic categories and criteria are empirically validated to a considerable extent; the diagnostic system is multiaxial; the criteria for disorders are based on observable, descriptive features; and the system attempts to indicate essential and variable features of disorders.

Major Categories of the DSM The DSM-IV lists more than two hundred mental disorders and the specific clinical criteria needed for each diagnosis. It also provides basic information on the known features, clinical course, predisposing factors, and demographic characteristics of each disorder. Following are some of the major categories of disorders that will be described in detail later in the book.

Disorders of Infancy, Childhood, or Adolescence. These disorders are usually diagnosed during childhood and include emotional, behavioral, intellectual, language, and physical disorders that begin in early life. Some are lifelong (such as mental retardation or learning disorders); others typically disappear by adulthood (such as elimination disorders and separation anxiety disorders). Sometimes children develop disorders that are most commonly seen in adults (such as depression or schizophrenia).

Cognitive Impairment Disorders. These disorders are caused by known or suspected brain disease or injury or by medical conditions affecting brain functioning. Among them are delirium (clouding of consciousness) and dementia (impairment of memory, learning, and judgment). Alzheimer's disease is a common type of dementia.

Substance-Related Disorders. This is one of the most common diagnoses in the adult population. Substance-related disorders refer to the frequent or regular use of drugs or alcohol to the extent of personal and social impairment and unpleasant or dangerous physical effects. These disorders are subclassified by the substance being used (such as alcohol, amphetamines, hallucinogens, or opioids) or by whether multiple substances are involved.

Schizophrenia and Other Psychotic Disorders. Schizophrenia is the most common form of psychosis, a class of disorders involving loss of contact with reality. Psychoses often include hallucinations (sensory experiences with no basis in reality) and delusions (bizarre and unfounded beliefs) and may also involve disorganization of language and unusual or impaired emotional and social functioning.

Mood Disorders. Depressive disorders are among the most common psychological diagnoses, involving not just sadness but also negative views of the self and the future and physical and behavioral changes that impede enjoyment and activity. Bipolar disorders are mood disorders that include periods of depression alternating with its opposite — mania (or a milder form called hypomania).

Anxiety Disorders. Disorders that involve excessive fear, anxiety, or apprehension are included in this category. A person may have a phobia, or fear of a specific object or situation, that typically leads to avoidance of the feared stimuli. Or the anxiety may take the form of panic attacks, in which the person is usually not able to identify a specific situation that triggers the reaction. Excessive worries are characteristic of generalized anxiety disorder.

Somatoform Disorders. In this broad category are disorders that include physical symptoms or bodily preoccupations that arise from psychological causes. One form is conversion disorder, in which a psychological problem is manifest as a physical complaint that has no medical basis, such as sudden-onset blindness or paralysis of a limb. Another form is somatization disorder, in which the patient has frequent, multiple medical complaints and seeks treatment, either when there is no medical basis or when the complaints and impairment are not warranted by the extent of the physical disorder.

Dissociative Disorders. These disorders involve psychologically based disturbances or changes in the experiences of identity, memory, or consciousness that normally give a person a sense of wholeness or integration. If the dissociative disorder occurs in memory, the person cannot recall important personal events, as in cases of dissociative amnesia. If it occurs in the realm of identity, the person's usual identity is forgotten or displaced by other identities, as in cases of dissociative identity disorder (formerly called multiple personality disorder).

Sexual Disorders. This broad category includes disorders of sexual functioning and unusual sexual

Table 4.6 Example of Diagnostic Criteria from the DSM: Bipolar Disorders

Manic Episode

A. A distinct period of abnormally and persistently elevated, expansive, or irritable mood, lasting at least one week (or any duration if hospitalization is necessary)

B. During the period of mood disturbance, at least three of the following symptoms have persisted (four if the mood is only irritable) and have been present to a significant degree:
   (1) Inflated self-esteem or grandiosity
   (2) Decreased need for sleep (e.g., feels rested after only three hours of sleep)
   (3) More talkative than usual or pressure to keep talking
   (4) Flight of ideas or subjective experience that thoughts are racing
   (5) Distractibility (i.e., attention too easily drawn to unimportant or irrelevant external stimuli)
   (6) Increase in goal-directed activity (either socially, at work or school, or sexually) or psychomotor agitation
   (7) Excessive involvement in pleasurable activities that have a high potential for painful consequences (e.g., the person engages in unrestrained buying sprees, sexual indiscretions, or foolish business investments)

C. The mood disturbance is sufficiently severe to cause marked impairment in occupational functioning or in usual social activities or relationships with others, or to necessitate hospitalization to prevent harm to self or others

D. Not due to the direct effects of a substance (e.g., drugs of abuse, medication) or a general medical condition (e.g., hyperthyroidism)

Note: Manic episodes that are clearly precipitated by somatic antidepressant treatment (e.g, medication, electroconvulsive therapy, light therapy) should not count towards a diagnosis of Bipolar I Disorder.

Source: DSM-IV. Reprinted with permission from *The Diagnostic and Statistical Manual of Mental Disorders,* Fourth Edition. Copyright © 1994 American Psychiatric Association.

DSM-IV provides specific, reliably applied behavioral descriptions that allow for different patterns of symptomatology, provided that essential defining features are present. Here are the criteria for mania.

behaviors. Sexual desire or arousal disorders and orgasm disorders, for example, reflect persisting problems that men and women may experience during otherwise normal sexual functioning. Disorders called paraphilias refer to sexual fantasies and practices involving unusual, bizarre, or illicit activity. Examples include exhibitionism (displaying genitals to an unsuspecting stranger) and sexual sadism (experiencing sexual pleasure from inflicting pain, suffering, or humiliation on another).

Eating Disorders. Eating disorders involve a loss of normal eating patterns that may result in severe, even fatal, health consequences. The two most common kinds of eating disorders are anorexia nervosa and bulimia nervosa. Anorexia nervosa involves a preoccupation with thinness and dieting to the point of excessive weight loss and refusal to maintain normal body weight. Bulimia nervosa involves episodes of binge eating followed by efforts to counteract weight gain by purging, excessive exercise, or dieting.

Personality Disorders. Certain patterns of stable traits that are maladaptive and inflexible, and that create difficulties in a person's relationships and life adjustment, are called personality disorders. DSM-IV lists ten specific personality disorders that may be diagnosed either as a person's central problem or as a chronic disorder underlying a more temporary disorder. Examples include narcissistic personality disorder (excessive sense of self-importance), and antisocial personality disorder (callous disregard for the rights of others and chronic antisocial conduct).

FOCUS ON RESEARCH

How Do Field Trials Shape Our Diagnostic System?

One cornerstone of the empirical basis of DSM-IV — as well as that of DSM-III (1980) and the upcoming tenth edition of WHO's International Classification of Diseases and Disorders (ICD-10) — is the use of field trials. Some field trials commonly focus on the reliability of a diagnosis (that is, on how well different interviewers using the criteria agree that a particular disorder is present); other field trials aim to test the validity of certain diagnostic categories or refine the criteria.

Field trials for DSM-III focused largely on reliability because previous versions of the manual had such poor reliability. Clinicians were invited to participate and to use existing patients for the trials. Altogether about 12,667 patients were evaluated by 550 clinicians (Widiger et al., 1991). The clinicians used various draft versions of proposed diagnostic categories. In some cases, two clinicians interviewed a patient together; in others, clinicians interviewed a patient independently; in yet others, judges made diagnoses based on written case studies. Then, comparisons were made to determine how closely pairs of clinicians agreed on the patients they rated, and results were tabulated for different diagnoses. In general, the field trials for DSM-III helped establish good, though not perfect, agreement in the use of the major diagnostic categories.

The reliability field trials for DSM-IV were even more systematic in scope, involving approximately 3,000 clinicians who diagnosed patients seen in videotaped interviews. By using tapes, and by including patients who varied in their characteristics, these field trials yielded results that not only indicated the reliability for diagnostic categories but also clarified which features of cases are not reliable.

Similarly, in preparation for the publication of the ICD-10, a document called the Diagnostic Criteria for Research was submitted to nearly 1,000 clinicians in thirty-two countries, who conducted nearly 12,000 individual assessments of patients. Interrater reliability was found to be high for most major diagnoses (Sartorius et al., 1995).

Validity has been considered as well. Two additional field trials attempted to refine the criteria for specific diagnoses, evaluating how valid certain features of the disorder are and whether they should be included in the diagnostic system. One study specifically addressed concerns about the validity of the frequently criticized criteria for *antisocial personality disorder,* a pattern of irresponsibility, lack of remorse, and antisocial behavior dating from childhood. Complex results led to the modification and simplification of these criteria in DSM-IV (Widiger et al., 1996). Another study examined *obsessive-compulsive disorder,* an anxiety disorder marked by disruptive behavioral rituals or intrusive thoughts. The authors examined characteristics of over 400 patients and, on the basis of their findings, recommended several changes in the criteria so that they would more validly reflect the actual features of the disorder (Foa & Kozak, 1995). One change, for example, led to the inclusion of mental rituals (such as counting patterns) as compulsions; accordingly, compulsions were no longer restricted to overt behaviors.

Field trials were also used in the preparation of DSM-IV to evaluate the validity of proposed new diagnostic categories. Robert Spitzer of the New York State Psychiatric Institute and his colleagues (Spitzer, Williams, Kass & Davies, 1989) conducted a field trial to determine the validity of a new category of personality disorder termed "self-defeating personality disorder," which involves a pattern of self-sacrificing; choosing people and situations that lead to failure, disappointment, or mistreatment; and avoiding offers of help or opportunities for pleasure. Critics of the proposed inclusion of this alleged disorder argued in part that it labeled as sick those women who were simply meeting society's ideal of women. (See Tavris, 1992, for a discussion of the history of this controversy.)

In the first part of the study, Spitzer and his colleagues mailed questionnaires to psychiatrists asking for their opinions about the proposed diagnostic criteria — a procedure that in the past might have been the sole basis for determining whether to include a diagnosis in the DSM. Additionally, however, the investigators asked for descriptions of one client who displayed self-defeating patterns and of another client with a personality disorder that was not self-defeating, thereby providing a basis for systematic analysis of the validity of the new category. Half of those surveyed did not think that a new diagnostic category was needed. Although the characteristics that the therapists listed as examples of a self-defeating personality were similar to those in the proposed new category, they overlapped considerably with characteristics of clients with other personality disorders, thus indicating that the new category lacked validity as a distinct condition.

In the second part of the study, Spitzer and his colleagues asked several thousand psychiatrists to consider a patient with a personality disorder and to rate that individual on thirty-two characteristics. The thirty-two items included criteria for the proposed self-defeating personality disorder as well as for other established personality disorders. This study also confirmed the tremendous overlap between the criteria for the self-defeating personality and those for personality disorders already in the DSM. Thus, the field trial provided important evidence of the questionable validity of the proposed category. Though not included in the DSM, it was placed in the appendix as an example of a proposed category needing further study.

These examples illustrate how field trials have contributed to the empirical basis of the DSM, specifically by encouraging research to refine the understanding of mental disorders. But field trials have accomplished even more: They have helped generate the expectation that diagnostic standards change. No longer do researchers and clinicians view diagnostic categories as fixed copies of reality. Instead, they see these categories as approximations of the truth that may need to be amended as knowledge is refined.

The DSM is now used in many countries for both clinical and research applications. DSM-IV was published in 1994. Meanwhile, the International Classification of Diseases and Disorders has been revised several times. With the forthcoming publication of ICD-10, the two systems will be very similar.

Diagnosis: Controversies and Unresolved Issues

Despite widespread use and practical utility, the current diagnostic system has shortcomings that various critics have identified.

In Search of the Perfect System In an ideal diagnostic classification system, a person would receive a single diagnosis that captured the essentials of his or her problems (unless of course the person actually had two independent disorders). There would be clear boundaries and no overlap between different conditions. Unfortunately, however, it appears that human nature — or at least human mental disorder — is not neatly organized into discrete, clear categories. Instead, we have had to *impose* order. As a result, some of our choices of classification rules are problematic.

One potential difficulty is extensive diagnostic **comorbidity,** the tendency of persons to have more than one condition. Among adults and children, and in the context of many, perhaps most, diagnoses, a person who has one disorder probably has others as well (e.g., Kessler et al., 1994; Hammen & Compas, 1994). For example, depression, antisocial personality disorder or conduct disorder, anxiety disorders, and substance-abuse disorders are all more likely to occur with other conditions than alone. Comorbidity may not be an inherent problem of a diagnostic system if in fact most people really do have multiple disorders. On the other hand, it could be a sign that our diagnostic categories are too narrow or include too many overlapping symptoms. In this case, what may look like separate co-occurring disorders could be a result of flaws in the way that the disorders are conceptualized.

A second difficulty, and the source of frequent criticism, is the possibility that our system forces categorization into different diagnoses even when "mixed" conditions are valid and distinctly separate categories in themselves. An example is the apparent overlap between depression and anxiety disorders. Traditionally, clinicians had to decide which one was the "basic" disorder, or if there were two "separate" disorders. But there is now growing recognition of a possible third condition — namely, a mixture of anxiety and depression features (Clark & Watson, 1991).

The problem of mixed disorders is related to another issue as well: whether to use categories or dimensions.

Indeed, disorders sometimes appear to occur not as distinct categories but as clusters of characteristics or dimensions that range in severity. Thus, there are overlapping symptoms and indistinct boundaries between disorders. As we explore in more detail in Chapter 13, some critics argue that, for some disorders at least, we should abandon classification in favor of using ratings of severity along dimensions of personality traits. To date, however, no widely accepted set of dimensions has been validly used.

It May Be Reliable, But Is It Valid? The quest for reliable diagnoses has been a preoccupation of the modern DSM because previous systems failed to enable different clinicians to reach the same conclusions as one another. As we note in our discussion of assessment, however, excellent interrater reliability and poor validity are possible at the same time: Clinicians may define diagnostic criteria in ways that emphasize the features that are easiest to observe and agree on, but exclude important features that are difficult to characterize. For example, the criteria for major depressive disorder are reasonably easy to identify, and there is excellent interrater reliability for this category. Clinicians recognize, however, that the category encompasses extremely heterogeneous forms of depression. Maybe there are important, valid subtypes of depression that have not yet been clarified because their defining features are obscure (as in depression owing to serotonin deficiencies, early childhood losses, genetic predisposition, sensitivity to criticism, and hopelessness).

Some have argued that we are a long way from establishing the validity of many of our diagnostic categories. Often, validity is judged against a criterion of clinician judgment, but obviously we have to decide if clinician judgment is correct in the first place. Other criteria for validation, such as biological variables, characteristics of the course of the disorder, or genetic factors, may provide useful data for verifying the accuracy of diagnostic decisions. Validation of diagnoses is a matter of degree, and while we consider our current categories to be valid, additional research may improve their validity or suggest alternative criteria.

Labeling and Reification An unfortunate by-product of the diagnostic procedure is that once a person is assigned a diagnosis, we come to think of the person as having the disorder. And we are likely to think of the disorder as an "it," treating a useful abstraction as if it were an object. This process is called *reification*. Remember that, unlike diagnosing a medical disorder (which means discovering an underlying illness), diagnosing a psychological disorder is a process of describing features and imposing a classification system. Of course, advances in research on biological mechanisms of psychological disorders may eventually reveal that some psychological disorders are diseases, and research in human develop-

These modern women illustrate how different cultures may be in their visions of female beauty. Such differences are a sharp reminder that views of what constitutes abnormal or maladaptive behaviors cannot be assumed to be universal, and that cultural variations must be taken into consideration when we apply diagnostic criteria.

ment may further clarify the nature of dysfunctional psychological adjustment. But for many of the current diagnoses, we are essentially describing useful but hypothetical processes.

Labeling may also be a problematic outcome of diagnosis when the person is viewed as if he or she is the diagnosis. The label often becomes permanent and may eventually overshadow other aspects of the person's identity. Consider the frequency of such reports as "Former mental patient snatches purse" or references to someone as "an alcoholic" or "a schizophrenic," rather than to a person suffering from alcoholism or a person with schizophrenia. In such cases, labeling is not only stigmatizing; it is also dehumanizing.

Cultural and Gender Bias Critics have argued that although major disorders appear to be universal, cultures experience and express the disorders in different ways as we discuss in Chapter 1 and at various points in this book (see also Brown & Ballou, 1992). Some conditions may be specific to particular cultural groups, such as eating disorders in Western industrialized societies (or cultural groups identified with Western ideals) that have resulted from extreme preoccupation with appearance and thinness (e.g., Furnham & Baguma, 1994). Other conditions appear to be culture-specific expressions of disorders that we recognize as psychological but that do not directly correspond to DSM-IV criteria. For example, *koro,* which is a panic state resulting from a fear that the genitals will retract into the abdomen and cause death, occurs only in Asian countries. Research has also revealed many culture-specific

versions of *possession,* a belief that one's body has been taken over by a spirit, leading to an altered state of consciousness resembling a trance and to temporary personality changes.

The compilers of DSM-IV made a concerted attempt to prepare guidelines for appropriate applications of the manual to diverse populations. Accordingly, it urges clinicians and researchers to recognize that different cultural meanings and expressions of distress are attached to symptoms that, in turn, need to be explored and understood.

Gender bias in diagnoses has also generated a great deal of controversy. Diagnoses of the personality disorders, in particular, have been criticized for giving a diagnostic label to behaviors that society often teaches women to display, such as submissiveness, devotion to the needs of others, and dependency. According to another argument, there is an inherent male definition of normality against which departures are considered abnormal (Tavris, 1992).

Efforts to establish a data-based diagnostic system have met with much success. Indeed, during the past forty years we have moved from minimal diagnosis to a system based on votes and surveys to an internationally accepted and comprehensive system based on extensive empirical research. Still, the quest for the validation of diagnoses continues.

What Lies Ahead?

There is a tremendous need and demand for good assessment procedures to fulfill clinical and scientific goals concerning psychological disorder. We place great faith in the ability to measure, and therefore to predict, human behavior. In recent years we have made considerable progress not only in developing new methods but also in maintaining standards of reliability and validity. Indeed, we can expect to see further developments, such as technological advances in biomedical instrumentation and medical testing, as well as increasing sophistication in the application of statistical and sampling procedures. Unfortunately, however, scientific soundness does not ensure that all our tests are being used appropriately, so continuing attention to fairness is needed — in terms of both applying the results of tests and overcoming a narrow cultural focus.

Interest in and research on diagnostic issues has increased dramatically in the past fifteen or twenty years.

The DSM no longer defines homosexuality as abnormal, nor does it include references to neuroses. Critically important distinctions between manic-depression and unipolar depression have emerged, and "new" problems — such as eating disorders, generalized anxiety disorder, and posttraumatic stress disorder — have been carefully defined. There is every reason to expect that refinements in existing diagnoses will continue and that new disorders will be identified.

Further versions of the DSM and ICD may yet add and refine diagnoses. However, the task of verifying the meaning, origins, correlates, and outcomes of disorders remains as important as ever. Perhaps future editions will specify not only the criteria for diagnosis but also information on predisposing factors, recommended treatment, and predicted responses to treatment.

KEY TERMS

assessment (98)
base rate (101)
comorbidity (124)
concurrent validity (100)
construct validity (100)
content validity (100)
criterion-related
  validity (100)
diagnosis (118)

face validity (100)
fundamental attribution error
  (117)
intelligence (IQ) tests (107)
internal consistency (99)
interrater reliability (99)
multiaxial (119)
neuroimaging techniques
  (114)

neuropsychological
  assessment (109)
observational techniques
  (110)
performance tests (107)
personality inventories (103)
predictive validity (100)
projective test (109)

psychophysiological
  techniques (114)
questionnaire (103)
reactivity (112)
reliability (98)
response biases (101)
self-monitoring (114)
test-retest reliability (98)
utility (101)
validity (99)

SUMMARY

Criteria for Successful Assessment

All of the tasks involved in the *assessment*, treatment, and scientific study of psychological disorder require measurement. We use several criteria to evaluate measures. *Reliability* refers to the repeatability of results under similar conditions. Ways of assessing reliability include *test-retest reliability, internal consistency,* and *interrater reliability.* Unless a procedure is reliable, its results cannot be assumed to be valid. *Validity* means that the measure actually accomplishes the purpose for which it is intended. Procedures may be valid for one use but not another. The type of validation may vary from one task to another, including *content* or *face validity, criterion-related validity* (*predictive* or *concurrent*), and *construct validity.* Many circumstances can interfere with a test's reliability and validity, including *response biases. Utility* is also an important practical guideline for evaluating an assessment procedure.

Common Methods for Assessing Psychological Disturbance

Interviews are direct and rich methods of collecting a lot of information, and they are widely used for many purposes. However, certain types of interviews may require extensive training, may be costly to administer, and may obtain only the information that a person can or will disclose. A cheaper and simpler technique than the interview is the *questionnaire,* which can be tailored to a very particular content. One drawback, however, is that it may be limited by what people can and will divulge and, indeed, people often wish to present themselves in a certain light. Questionnaires may also contain ambiguous items, leading to error. *Personality inventories* are elaborate, lengthy questionnaires that aim to uncover information about attributes of the personality.

Performance tests sample actual behaviors to make a more general prediction about an individual's functioning. These are most commonly used to evaluate intellectual and cognitive performance, as in *intelligence (IQ) tests* and *neuropsychological assessment.* Neuropsychological tests may involve not only intelligence tests but also a large battery of tests of specific cognitive functions. A profile comparing patterns of performance strengths and weaknesses can yield information about both the degree and nature of neurological impairment. The *projective test* is a kind of performance test in which the person's solutions or responses to an ambiguous task are believed to be "projections" of the underlying personality or ways of thinking about the world and the self. Such procedures are most likely to be used by those who subscribe to psychodynamic theories.

Observational techniques involve directly watching the person's behavior and systematically scoring or counting relevant actions. Such procedures may be time-consuming and difficult to arrange either in the laboratory or in natural settings. However, they are particularly useful when the relevant behaviors cannot be understood without seeing their actual details in the setting, or when they cannot be reported by the individuals in questionnaires or interviews. *Self-monitoring* is a behavioral observation procedure in which individuals observe and keep records of their own experiences and behaviors. It plays a useful role in collecting private or not easily available information.

Biological assessment is playing an increasingly prominent role in both diagnosis and research. *Neuroimaging techniques,* for instance, make extensive use of technologies that permit noninvasive glimpses of brain structure or even brain metabolic activity. *Psychophysiological techniques* permit recording of a variety of bodily processes, such as heart rate, electrodermal (sweat gland) activity, respiration, sleep patterns, brain waves, and even sexual arousal.

It is common to combine the various types of assessment methods to form a more complete picture of the person.

Misuse of testing can occur when assessment instruments are biased by cultural content or are applied in situations that result in unfair decisions. Privacy and labeling are additional concerns about psychological assessment. Even if the assessment procedures have established reliability and validity, errors may arise if investigators draw inferences and conclusions that are not supported by the available data or misinterpret the cause of a problem. Especially when complex information from different sources must be integrated, errors of interpretation may arise due to normal human information-processing.

Diagnosis of Psychological Disorders

Diagnosis is the act of classifying a disorder, and classification is useful for conveying information about the disorder. Diagnosis is also an essential scientific tool. The present system used for diagnosis is the Diagnostic and Statistical Manual (DSM-IV), which provides defining features and diagnostic criteria for scores of disorders. The criteria are based on both clinical experience and research, and field trials are increasingly being used to determine the best definitions of disorders and to characterize their features. DSM-IV provides a highly reliable system with a *multiaxial* format.

Any classification system must struggle with finding the optimum breadth or narrowness of categories and dealing with cases that do not fall neatly into a single category. The DSM system, as a result of its emphasis on relatively narrowly defined diagnoses, implies significant *comorbidity,* the tendency of patients to have more than one disorder. On the other hand, some conditions may be truly "mixed." Another controversy is whether some disorders might be best defined in terms of degrees of particular traits rather than by categories. Opponents of diagnosis argue that labeling often dehumanizes and stigmatizes patients. The diagnostic system has also been criticized for its focus on Anglo-European conditions and for having an inherently male basis for judging normality and abnormality.

Consider the following. . .

Suppose you are a parent who has just enrolled your child in kindergarten. A notice is sent home indicating that all children in kindergarten and first grade are to be tested for "delinquency prone-ness," and that those at risk for developing delinquent patterns will be eligible for a special preventive treatment program to reduce such antisocial conduct. Based on what you now know about psychological assessment, can you identify the advantages and disadvantages of such a testing program? What information would be essential to determine the value of this assessment? Even if the assessment is based on highly valid methods, are there other issues that might affect whether you would support it?

Suppose you are the human relations manager at a large company and want to make hiring decisions based on mental health (as well as ability to perform the job). What kind of assessment would you devise to weed out the mentally unfit? Which methods would be ideal? What possible methods would you use if you had a limited budget and limited time per person, and if you were the one who had to make the evaluations? What are the pros and cons of different methods of assessment? What are reasonable goals for assessment?

CHAPTER 5

Research Methods

Those among us . . .

■ Your older brother has suffered from depression for years, and today you found out that your grandfather has been diagnosed with Alzheimer's disease. You wonder why this bad news had to come the day before you must declare your major. Then again, perhaps it's a "sign." Maybe you should major in psychology, with the goal of becoming a researcher who finds the answer to what causes and, better yet, prevents Alzheimer's or depression.

■ Each morning you overhear your neighbors, the Joneses, in chaotic exchanges of angry accusations and loud and excessive arguments. The children have been truant from school, and the police have visited the home several times because the children are suspects in a rash of fire settings.

■ In 1950, your uncle, Mel, at age twenty, was hospitalized for extremely troublesome behavior. Soon after, while living at home, Mel spent all day alone in his workshop, often claiming that he was inventing a new computer and getting financing for a new company. In reality, he puttered around in a garage full of old diode tubes from broken television sets. Your grandfather, Mel's father, was eager to treat the disorder and quickly gave permission for a lobotomy. Mel underwent the operation. Afterward, he was calmer. But the lobotomy did not alter his lifestyle, help him gain employment, or improve his interpersonal functioning.

What approach to research might best address the question of the causes of psychopathology?

What is likely to happen to depressed teenagers? Delinquent teenagers? What research methods could be used to better understand their present situation, predict their future, or evaluate a program to reduce their current distress?

How can research on treatments be conducted in such a way to ensure that treatment is more than a stop-gap, that it is truly beneficial to the patient?

The popularity of books and television programs about detectives, private investigators, and mysteries attests to our widespread interest in snooping and seeking the facts. Science, too, is a kind of snooping, in that scientists aim to discover the facts or laws that operate in their discipline. Psychologists, who are scientists interested in the facts about human behavior, want to know what criteria can be used to identify psychological disorders. What factors cause these disorders? How do an individual's biological, cognitive, and familial influences contribute to psychological problems? What can be done to rectify psychological dysfunction?

To answer questions like these, psychologists conduct research studies based on scientific methods. This chapter is about those studies and methods; it focuses on the strategies of science and their place in abnormal psychology. We begin with a brief description of the scientific process and then examine the strengths and weaknesses of various methods used for research into abnormal psychology. After discussing several key research questions, we close with a consideration of the ethical principles that should guide any psychological research.

SCIENCE AND PSYCHOPATHOLOGY

According to the dictionary definition, *science* is "the observation, identification, description, experimental investigation, and theoretical explanation of natural phenomena" (*American Heritage Dictionary,* 1985, p. 1099). The methods of science are based on *empiricism,* an assumption that the world can be known through careful observation. Observation sets the stage for identifying and asking questions, and questions lead to *hypotheses* about the answers — that is, to opinions that are open to verification. Some hypotheses are suggested by previous research findings, such as those published in research journals. Other hypotheses emerge from *theory* — an organized system of assumptions and principles that purport to explain a psychological phenomenon. Investigators then use the scientific methods of inquiry to test or verify the hypotheses.

Note that the letters of the word *science* (see Table 5.1) provide an acronym for the steps in scientific inquiry: *s*pecifying the problem; *c*ollecting information; *i*dentifying possible causes or patterns; *e*xamining options; *n*arrowing the options by experimenting; *c*omparing the data; and *e*xtending, revising, and further testing (Mahoney, 1980). Thus, the overall strategy of science calls for careful observation, elimination of rival hypotheses, and repeated testing.

Table 5.1 The Steps in Scientific Inquiry

Specifying the problem
Collecting information
Identifying possible causes or patterns
Examining options
Narrowing the options by experimenting
Comparing the data
Extending, revising, and further testing

Source: Mahoney (1980).

At each step of the inquiry, scientists aim for precision and repeatability. They must document their procedures so others can reproduce the findings, and they must carefully define the concepts being studied and specify how observations will be conducted. Ambiguity is one enemy of precision and repeatability. To reduce ambiguity, scientists use *operational definitions,* which define a concept by the operations (steps) used in measuring it.

As an example, let's assume that a researcher is interested in the effects of sugar on the activity level of hyperactive children. *Hyperactivity* is a popular term for a disorder called *attention-deficit hyperactivity disorder,* or ADHD (see Chapter 15), of which the primary symptoms can include inattention, impulsiveness, and excessive motor activity. To do a proper study, the researcher must operationalize the *quantity of sugar* that will be studied and the *activity level* of the participants, all of whom have been diagnosed with ADHD. Accordingly, the researcher manipulates the quantity of sugar ingested by giving different types of cookies to different groups of children. All of the children consume three cookies each, but the children in one group receive sugar-free cookies, those in another group receive regular cookies, and those in a third group receive cookies that are loaded with extra sugar. The variable of interest, sugar, is thus operationalized in terms of the quantity of sugar in the cookies given the children.

How will the researcher measure activity level or attention span to determine the effects of sugar? One possibility is that she could arrange a selection of toys on a black-and-white checkered floor, creating a grid pattern. Observers could then record the number of times each child with ADHD crosses from one part of the grid to another, the number of different toys each child plays with, and the number of times each child switches from one toy to another. The frequency of the children's grid crossings or toy switches, for instance, could then be examined to see if there are systematic differences between the children who consumed large amounts of sugar and those who had consumed small amounts.

Internal and External Validity

To avoid flaws in scientific investigations, researchers aim to meet certain standards. As noted in Chapter 4, validity is a concept important to psychological assessment. Two important standards are internal and external validity.

Internal validity is the extent to which a study's methodology allows the researcher to draw strong conclusions. A study that is not open to alternate explanations of the results is said to be internally valid. In addition, if its results can be interpreted clearly, the study is said to be free of confounds. A **confound** is a factor that might have affected the dependent variable. When a confound is present, the investigator cannot know whether it or the independent variable was responsible for the results. Suppose that you developed a treatment for severe anxiety, applied it to a group of anxiety sufferers, later measured their emotional adjustment, and concluded that your treatment was a success. How do you know that the treatment caused the outcome? In this instance, you do not. Instead, perhaps major stresses in the participants' lives were somehow reduced during your treatment, and the reduced stress, not your treatment, was responsible for the reduced anxiety. Because the research design did not measure or control extraneous influences, the results have many possible explanations, and the study lacks internal validity.

Among the threats to internal validity are simultaneously occurring outside events, natural maturation, the effects of testing, and statistical regression (Campbell & Stanley, 1963; Kazdin, 1992). Consider the case of a 32-year-old divorced woman who complained of depression. She lived alone near her family and former in-laws, worked in a stable position with several close associates, and sought help to overcome an increasing sense of worthlessness. The therapist provided psychological therapy, and several months later the woman reported that she was feeling much better. Did the therapy produce the improvement? Rival explanations include the following:

- *Simultaneously occurring events.* Simultaneous events that occur outside the treatment may explain the observed effects. In this case, the fact that the client won the lottery and got back together with a former lover at about the time her treatment began might have accounted for the temporary alleviation of depression.

- *Natural maturation.* Because the passage of time can influence psychological functioning, maturational changes can explain observed changes. It is possible that the client's depression lifted as time passed and she matured.

- *Effects of testing.* If a person takes a test twice, the second score may be different from the first simply because the person has taken the test before. Similarly, this client's score on a questionnaire may indicate less depression the second time she completes the questionnaire simply because she believes that she has already expressed her concern about her low mood.

- *Statistical regression.* Extreme scores on tests are more likely to regress toward the mean than to become more extreme. In other words, people with extremely high or extremely low scores on a first testing will probably score less extremely on a second testing. The less extreme scores on the second test can give the impression of improvement. But in actuality, if a client scores extremely high on the first measure of depression, there is little room for the client to report feeling worse on the second measure.

In addition to internal validity, researchers must aim for **external validity,** which is the degree to which research findings can be generalized to situations, persons, or locations beyond those employed in the study. For instance, results that are externally valid can be generalized to persons who were not in the study. If a study examines the television viewing habits of violent youth, researchers cannot draw conclusions about the relationship of television viewing and violence in children in general because violent youth are not representative of youth in general. **Representativeness** is the degree to which important characteristics of the sample of persons studied match these characteristics in the population. When a study uses only male participants, the conclusions cannot be extended to all males and females; when a study does not represent ethnic and cultural diversity, external validity is again compromised. We cannot assume that the findings from studies of white American college females apply to all people. What we know depends on the questions we ask, how we ask them, to whom we direct them, and how our participants respond. If science is to make important progress, then, our studies must address gender and ethnicity by including a diversity of participants. Throughout this text, we refer to studies that have proper gender representation and a multicultural perspective. Because issues of internal and external validity are so important, we discuss them in connection with each of the research methods covered in this chapter.

WHAT'S NORMAL?

Researchers Struggle with the Question

Research into the nature of psychological abnormality inevitably touches on questions about normality. Are normal and abnormal behavior related? One way to consider this question is to think about the selection of subjects who will participate in a study. If a researcher is interested in studying the psychology of distressing levels of anxiety, should the research participants be persons who have been diagnosed with anxiety disorders, or should the investigator study otherwise normal persons who are currently experiencing anxiety? In other words, is abnormal behavior separate and distinct from — that is, discontinuous from — psychological normality? Or are normal behavior and abnormal behavior simply degrees of — or continuous with — the same behavior?

According to the **continuity theory**, psychological dysfunctions and normal behavior form one continuum, ranging from normal behavior to mild disturbance to severe disturbance. Normality and abnormality are different, but the difference is a matter of degree. In contrast, the **discontinuity theory** states that mild and severe psychological dysfunction are distinct from each other and from normality; they stem from different causes and follow different courses. Normality and abnormality are quite different, with nonoverlapping members (see Figure 5.1). If the continuity theory has merit, then studying anxious individuals from the normal end of the continuum can provide important information about the nature and experience of clinical anxiety, and the results of a study with moderately anxious persons can be extrapolated to persons with severe anxiety. But if individuals with anxiety disorder are distinct from normal persons and from mildly anxious persons, then extrapolating from a less severe condition to a severe

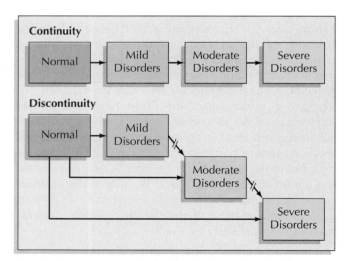

Figure 5.1   Continuity and Discontinuity in Normality and Psychological Abnormality

Are normal and abnormal behavior patterns on the same continuum? The continuity model answers yes: Psychological abnormality and normal behavior form one continuum, from normal to mild to severe disturbance. The discontinuity model, however, suggests that mild dysfunction and severe dysfunction are distinct from each other and from normality, and have different causes and courses.

one is unwarranted, or at best risky. Thus, the researcher using a discontinuity model would be less interested in moderately distressed normal persons and more likely to focus research on those persons who have been diagnosed.

Because research evidence both supports and refutes the continuity and discontinuity theories, scholars have begun to consider that each of these models might apply to different disorders. This *specificity* suggests that models for psychopathology research (including a place for normality) are distinct for separate disorders. For instance, the anxious aroused state of otherwise normal college students may inform us of factors that influence more extreme, nonnormal variations in anxiety. Accordingly, anxiety may be seen as occurring on a single continuum from mild to severe. With respect to multiple personality disorder, however, researchers prefer to study diagnosed persons, suggesting that a discontinuity model is more appropriate. In short, researchers must make decisions about the participants they choose for their studies, and these decisions have implications for the location of normality within models of psychopathology.

Designing Research

The principles and rules of the scientific method permit many and varied procedures. One important choice that researchers must make when selecting a procedure is that between data-gathering techniques and research methods.

Data-Gathering Techniques   The careful gathering of meaningful data is a cornerstone of quality science. Typical approaches to data gathering include questioning participants, requiring participants to respond to specific tests or tasks, inducing specific moods, and recording psychophysiological data (see Chapter 4). Consider, for example, some of the ways researchers have gathered information to study depression.

- Jack Hokanson and his associates at Florida State University (1989) used interviews and questionnaires to compare depressed college students, college students who displayed other forms of psychological abnormality, and normal students. Several times during a nine-month period they interviewed the students and administered questionnaires about their relationships with their roommates. The results suggested that low social contact with roommates, low enjoyability of these contacts, and high stress were associated with current depression.

- Laboratory tasks, such as the Stroop test (Stroop, 1938; Williams, Mathews & MacLeod, 1996), are often used in the study of depression. In the Stroop test, participants are asked to name the ink color of various printed words, while ignoring the meaning of the words (see Figure 5.2). Researchers have found that people cannot completely ignore a word's meaning. As the difficulty of ignoring the meaning of the word increases, the time needed to name the color also increases. Depressed persons exhibit longer latencies on the color-naming task when the words are related to depression.

- At Cambridge University in England, John Teasdale has used mood-inducing procedures to study memory in depression (Teasdale & Russell, 1983). For example, by having participants listen to certain music and read specific self-referent statements, Teasdale induced his subjects to experience either an "elated" or "dysphoric" (sad, mildly depressed) mood. Participants in the induced depressed mood recalled fewer positive memories and a greater number of negative ones than did participants in the induced elated mood.

- Electroencephalograph (EEG) tracings — records of electrical activity in brain-wave activity — were taken of formerly depressed patients, who have been found to display a distinctive pattern of electrical brain activity (Henriques & Davison, 1990). Specifically, compared with never-depressed persons, formerly depressed people show less activation of the left-side anterior and right-side posterior of the brain. Because the activity patterns of the brain are similar in formerly and currently depressed people, this brain pattern may be an indicator of, or *marker* for, the presence of depression.

Sometimes psychologists must use less direct methods of gathering information, such as analogue research. An **analogue** is a facsimile of reality, a scaled-down version that contains certain basic characteristics of the real thing in a simplified and controlled manner. The game Monopoly is an analogue for the world of finance and real estate. A researcher who wants to study the problem-solving abilities of people with depression may bring people together to observe them solve a problem that resembles the type of problems of interest to the disorder. For example, they might discuss how to schedule pleasant activities.

On other occasions, when research cannot be conducted with human beings, lesser animals have been employed in analogue tests of hypotheses. For example, Martin Seligman's (1975) *learned helplessness* model of depression resulted from initial studies of the effects of electric shock on dogs. In these studies, beginning in the late 1960s (Overmier & Seligman, 1967), dogs were exposed to between sixty and eighty somewhat painful (but not physically damaging) shocks. Important for the research, the shock was *un*controllable: It was administered at a predetermined rate that was entirely indepen-

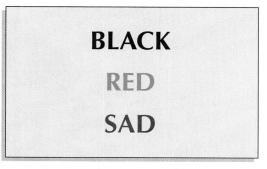

Figure 5.2   Items from the Stroop Test
The Stroop test has been used to study depression. Individuals are asked to name the ink color of each printed word but to ignore the meaning of the word. In this example, depressed people would take longer to name the ink color for the third word.

dent of the actions of the dogs. After this experience, the dogs were then placed in an apparatus where shock *could* be avoided. Although they exhibited brief activity initially, the dogs who had received prior uncontrollable shock did not try to escape the shock. But the dogs who did not have such prior experience learned to make responses to escape and avoid shock. As Seligman (1975) described it, there is a motivational deficit in learned helplessness, an absence of effort to learn to escape unpleasant circumstances. Even when the researchers later tried to teach the animals the usefulness of certain responses to avoid shock, those dogs with uncontrollable shock in their prior experience did not readily learn. Seligman drew parallels between these results and the human condition: Depressed persons, like the animals who had learned helplessness, lacked motivation and did not readily learn responses needed to avoid negative situations. This analogue approach prompted research with human beings and influenced several later approaches to the prevention and treatment of depression (see Chapter 8).

When ethical and technical issues prevent researchers from conducting certain studies, analogue research often provides opportunities for reasonably sound tests of hypotheses. Such research offers high levels of control of variables as well as technical accuracy, often contributing to high internal validity. External validity suffers, however, since we cannot be certain that analogue procedures are generalizable to real behaviors and situations of interest.

Research Methods   Researchers often have different goals, and they may choose different research methods to try to achieve these goals. Descriptive methods (such as surveys), correlational methods, and experimental methods are the major options available to researchers in psychopathology. For example, an investigator interested in the number of new cases of depression during

Dr. Penny Patterson and Koko using sign language. Nonhuman animals are sometimes used in research, as in this analogue study of language development and communication ability.

the past year might opt for a survey method, whereas a researcher evaluating the effects of treatment for depression would most likely choose the experimental method.

DESCRIPTIVE METHODS

The science of abnormal psychology began with the careful description of symptoms and the arrangement of these symptoms into categories; today, descriptive studies continue to provide a foundation for the study of psychological disorders. **Descriptive approaches** are general procedures used to summarize and organize samples of data. They take two main forms: case studies and surveys. The case study focuses on a single individual, whereas the survey seeks to describe a population.

Case Studies

A **case study** examines and describes in depth an individual's current feelings, thoughts, and behaviors. Historically, one need go no further than Sigmund Freud and Emil Kraepelin to see the merits of case studies. Freud's case studies provided valuable descriptions of his early theory of the development of disorders; Kraepelin's observations of cases helped him construct the first system for the classification of abnormal behavior.

Today, when an innovative approach to treatment is being developed, a case study may be the first step toward testing its effectiveness. In fact, for almost all major forms of therapy, early reports of their effects dealt with single cases. The case study approach also has

particular value for examining rare disorders. When a disorder occurs at a very low frequency, such as 1 in 10,000 cases, data on such a large number of cases is next to impossible to gather. But the detailed description of a single case, in a case study, can contribute to knowledge about the disorder. Multiple personality, a disorder that receives much media attention but is in fact quite rare, has often been described in a case study format. Similarly, defendants using the insanity defense are rare but well publicized and, as such, are prime targets for detailed case analysis. (Later in the book, specifically in the dissociative disorders section of Chapter 7, we present an actual case study of an individual who was described as having multiple personality and who used the insanity defense against charges of repeated rape.) The case study approach can indeed provide relevant information, in as reliable a fashion as possible, when there simply aren't enough such cases to allow more rigorous investigations.

Cheryl, age seventeen, was 5'6" tall, weighed 115 pounds, had shoulder-length brown hair, and was middle-class. She appeared quite typical, except for her mild retardation and her visual complaint: She stated that her vision was restricted to a very narrow area shaped like a tunnel. She cooperated with her father when he suggested that she see an optometrist.

At the optometrist's office Cheryl participated in careful testing using sophisticated equipment. On all physical tests, her eyes worked normally. But when she was tested for the boundaries of her visual field, the results — an oddly shaped area of restricted vision — could not be explained on the basis of existing knowledge about the eye. Her tunnel vision was thought to be psychological, a hypothesis that was consistent with the fact that she was a highly conflicted woman who had been abused and who would not talk about her problems. Could she have converted psychological distress into a physical problem? (In this connection, see the discussion of conversion disorders in Chapter 7.)

After psychological consultation, Cheryl was told that her restricted vision could be remedied by a neon arrow that would "hook" the rim of her visual field and draw it to wider boundaries. A three-foot neon arrow was placed in front of her as she faced a grid used for assessing visual field. Gradually, as the arrow moved outward, she reported that her visual field was "expanding," and, in the end, she stated that her vision was back to normal. Although the procedure worked, it had no physiological explanation. Cheryl had a rare conversion disorder — tunnel vision — that appeared as a physical symptom but was actually the result of a psychological problem. (Berman, 1979)

The most important contributions of the case study approach are generally historical, largely because this method has important limitations. First, variables that may potentially influence the data cannot be controlled in case studies. **Variables** are specific aspects of a person, group, or setting that are measured for purposes of a study. Second, the cases examined are not necessarily representative, and the data gatherer for a given case study is typically the individual's therapist, who may not be objective about the case. Third, the data and evaluations in case studies may not be gathered systematically.

In short, case studies lack both internal validity (methodological controls) and external validity (representativeness). Thus, although the case study method can be valuable for examining rare disorders and for evaluating innovative treatments, it has important methodological shortcomings. A related method, the single-subject design, is discussed later in this chapter.

Surveys

Unlike case studies, which focus on the rare and innovative, **surveys** provide information about the nature and scope of mental health problems across large populations or regions, often yielding clues as to the causes of disorders. Surveys are thus an important tool in **epidemiology**, which is the study of the incidence and prevalence of disorders in a specified population. **Incidence** refers to the number of new cases of a disorder reported during a specified period of time, and **prevalence** means the overall frequency of a disorder in the specified population. In one national survey, for example, more than eight thousand noninstitutionalized people aged 15 to 54 were questioned about the occurrence of psychological disorders (Kessler et al., 1994). The report produced estimates of both lifetime and 12-month prevalence rates of various disorders, presented separately for men and women. Some of these data are shown in Figure 5.3.

Epidemiological data can help identify the causes of disorder, as occurred in the now-classic example of a cholera outbreak in London during the last century. At the time, no one knew how the disease was spreading. But as data on the incidence and location of cases were gathered and examined, researchers noticed a pattern and hypothesized, correctly, that the source was contaminated water. When a recent cholera epidemic began in January 1991, data on the incidence of the disorder were gathered throughout the world (*Morbidity and Mortality Weekly Report*, 1992). The incidence data, along with

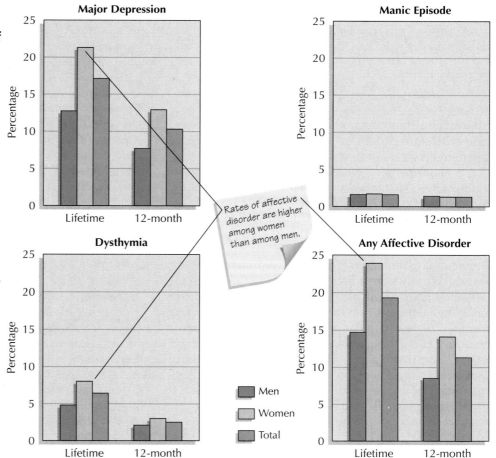

Figure 5.3 Survey Results: Lifetime and 12-Month Prevalence Rates of Affective Disorders

Kessler and associates (1994) reported lifetime and 12-month prevalence rates from a national sample of 15- to 54-year-old noninstitutionalized people. The figure combines the data for participants of different ages and presents these data as percentages. Like many surveys, this one has provided useful information about psychopathology. For example, major depression occurs at a higher frequency than mania, and rates of affective disorder are higher among women than among men. *Source:* Kessler et al. (1994).

In 1990, Anna Fisher was found to have ovarian cancer. Her grandmother died of "female cancer" in the 1940s. When Fisher was 5 years old, her mother developed breast cancer. Ten years later, her mother died from cancer. A maternal aunt had ovarian tumors and five cousins contracted breast cancer. As this case study illustrates, Ms. Fisher has cancer as part of her pedigree. Fisher's oncologist proposed a once unthinkable step: a preventative double mastectomy. To date, however, no controlled studies have evaluated the survival rate for such a procedure. A controlled experiment is needed.

information about international travel patterns, enabled researchers to determine that this cholera epidemic began in Peru (see Table 5.2).

A major concern for the survey researcher is external validity — in particular, the representativeness of the sample studied. If a survey is based solely on, say, the responses of women from the affluent section of a city, the results cannot be generalized to the entire population of the city because the participants are not representative of the full population. To ensure representativeness, researchers most often use one of two methods. On the one hand, they might use random sampling. In **random sampling,** regardless of the size of the sample, every member of the population of interest has an equal chance of being included. On the other hand, researchers might seek participants who match a predetermined "picture" of the demographic characteristics of the population. For example, if 57 percent of the total population is female and 43 percent is male, then the researcher surveys a sample with a similar ratio of females to males. In either case, the desired goal is exter-

nal validity, which is achieved by ensuring that the sample is representative.

One obstacle to representativeness is that subjects may refuse to participate. Suppose a stranger approaches you at a shopping mall and asks about your preferred laundry detergent or mealtime habits; would you supply the information? If a large number of people refuse, the survey might not be truly representative. After all, the individuals who participate may differ in some meaningful way from those who choose not to comply.

A second obstacle is that not all subjects who agree to participate provide accurate information. Participants may intentionally distort their answers for any of a multitude of reasons. For example, persons asked about the mental health of their family members may paint a brighter picture than actually exists.

A third obstacle is that the wording of survey questions can influence the answers and detract from the internal validity of the survey. Yet despite these and related problems, which survey researchers try to overcome, surveys can be especially useful when planning for mental health needs, developing programs for the prevention of maladjustment, or evaluating budgets at governmental mental health agencies. Indeed, the results of surveys often provide the basic data for knowledge about the incidence, prevalence, and distribution of psychologically meaningful phenomena.

FAMILY MATTERS

The Changing American Family

One demonstration of both the importance and the limitations of surveys comes from recent controversy about the American family. Pundits of all ideologies have been declaring that the United States is in a state of decay and that the decline in the American family is the cause. More important for our purposes, researchers as well as social critics have argued that families wield a powerful influence over the development of psychological disorders. Just what is the American family like? Is it changing? And if it is, are those changes likely to have an effect on psychopathology in the United States? Data from surveys provide a first step toward answering questions like these.

Surveys conducted by the U.S. Census Bureau provide ample evidence that the nature of the American family is indeed changing (see Figure 5.4). The number of single-parent households has almost doubled over the past two decades. The increase is widespread across racial and ethnic groups, but the total number of single-parent households is far greater among African Americans than among whites. This information is important for researchers who study single-parent households; they need to know the racial distribution of the population in

Table 5.2   Sample of Epidemiological Data

Country	Cases 1991	Cases in 1992	Total Deaths
Peru	322,562	162,152	626
Ecuador	46,320	29,431	194
Brazil	2,101	15,925	195
El Salvador	947	6,433	38
Colombia	11,979	2,168	23
Mexico	2,690	1,826	15
Panama	1,178	947	14
Argentina	0	451	15
Honduras	11	222	10
United States	28 (8)[1]	96 (7)[1]	1
Canada	1[1]	0	0

[1]Not related to the Latin American epidemic.

Source: Morbidity and Mortality Weekly Report (1992).

Cholera cases in the Western Hemisphere were reported to the Pan American Health Organization in August 1992. This table provides a sampling of the incidence data that helped locate the source of the 1991 cholera outbreak. Researchers recorded the dates of the reported cases and traced prior travel, basically working backward from the known cases. Patterns in the travel records emerged, thereby suggesting sources for the epidemic.

order to select a sample of families that match the overall percentages of cases by race. Also, once they know the differences among the various races, they need to ask why they exist.

Consider this stunning fact: More than one-half of all children born in the United States in 1980 will probably spend some time living in a single-parent household before they reach the age of eighteen (Lewin, 1992). Will this social-familial change affect the adjustment of these children or their own relationship preferences? And what would it mean for theories of psychological adjustment if such dramatic changes have little or no effect on children's adjustment? Future research will address these questions.

Another interesting aspect of the increase in single parenting is how these people became single parents. The majority of single-parent households still result from separation, divorce, or widowhood, but the number of never-married single parents is on the rise. This trend, too, is seen across all groups studied, although it is most pronounced among African Americans. Past research may need to be reinterpreted as we learn more about the reasons that people became single parents. We also need to investigate — first with surveys and later

U.S. Census Bureau surveys have documented the widespread increase in single-parent households, which have almost doubled over the past two decades. Researchers are studying the effects of these changes on the mental health and adjustment of both children and adults.

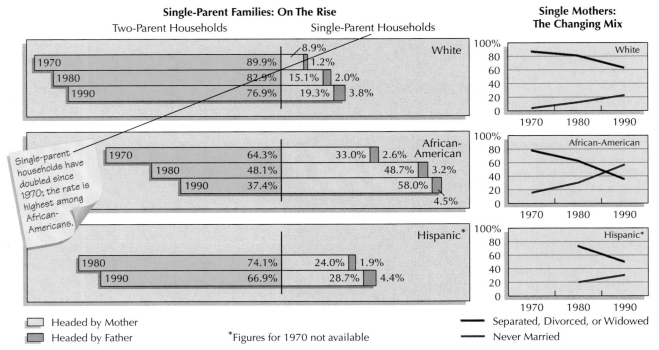

Single-Parent Families: On The Rise

Two-Parent Households / Single-Parent Households

Single Mothers: The Changing Mix

☐ Headed by Mother
☐ Headed by Father

*Figures for 1970 not available

— Separated, Divorced, or Widowed
— Never Married

Figure 5.4   The Changing American Family

Data from the U.S. Census Bureau have documented the increasing number of single-parent households. These survey data allow us to recognize the differences across the three ethnic groups studied. *Source:* Lewin (1992).

with experimental studies — possible explanations for the racial differences in the reasons for single-parent families.

Surveys have clearly documented changes in what constitutes "the family." But survey data have limitations, as we have seen, so additional research methods are sometimes needed to answer important questions. Consider the following examples.

- Recall from Chapter 2 that several of the major theories of psychopathology emphasize the importance of early childhood experiences. Will children growing up with single parents suffer psychologically? Conversely, if single parenthood is not detrimental, what does that say about our theories of psychological disorder? For answers to both questions, longitudinal research methods are needed to identify and follow children from different family backgrounds while assessing the presence of psychopathology.

- Are children's psychological needs met in two-parent families that aren't satisfied in single-parent families? Here, studies that compare single-parent and two-parent families, or studies that use correlational methods, are needed.

- What might we learn about the role of fathering in child psychopathology from research that compares never-married, single-parent mothers with separated or divorced mothers and with married moth-

ers (Phares & Compas, 1992)? Certainly, experimental methods and genetic research methods are appropriate to this issue and likely to yield valuable information.

- Do cultural factors, specific to certain ethnic and racial groups, influence an individual's choice to be a single parent? More in-depth studies of the groups in question are needed before we can describe the causes underlying the observed pattern of racial differences.

Beginning with a survey-based documentation of the important shift that has occurred in family structure, researchers can use a variety of additional research strategies to address these and other questions that have emerged.

CORRELATIONAL METHODS

Neither case studies nor surveys can determine the degree to which variables are related; correlational studies can. **Correlational studies** focus on the relationship (covariation) among variables. When two variables are highly related, knowledge about one variable can be used to make predictions about the other variable.

As an example, consider the problem of alcohol abuse. People have varying expectations about how alcohol will affect them, and people themselves vary in the extent to which alcohol use creates problems in their lives. Are their expectations and their problems related? Sandra Brown (1985) used a correlational approach to study the relationship between these two variables. Brown's sample consisted of college students. She assessed their alcohol consumption and distinguished three patterns. *Heavy drinkers* consumed large quantities of alcohol and frequently experienced physical distress from drinking. *Problem drinkers* also consumed large quantities of alcohol with high frequency, but in addition they had had some contact with authorities for problems associated with drinking. *Context-determined drinkers* consumed alcohol only in select settings, such as at home or with friends at a bar. Brown also measured each subject's expectancies about the effects of alcohol. In other words, what did the participant believe to be the positive or negative effects of consuming alcohol? Using a ninety-item questionnaire, she assessed several expectations including social and physical pleasure, sexual enhancement, tension reduction, and sense of power. The results showed that certain expectations about the effects of alcohol and problem drinking were significantly correlated. Specifically, individuals who held high expectations that alcohol would dramatically reduce tension were likely to be problem drinkers.

Because Brown's participants were college students (and thus not a truly representative sample), the results of her study have limited external validity. Research with working adults, clinical patients, and other samples of people (see Goldman & Rather, 1993; Smith, Goldman, Greenbaum & Christiansen, 1995), however, confirmed that the correlation between expectations and problem drinking can be generalized to the larger population. Unfortunately, this correlation does not tell us the cause of the alcohol consumption or, for that matter, the cause of the expectations.

Assessing Correlations

Correlational research involves measuring at least two variables and analyzing the degree of relationship between them. The data can be displayed in **scatterplots** (see Figure 5.5), in which values of one variable are shown on the horizontal axis and values of the other variable are shown on the vertical axis. If measurements are available for two variables, the direction and magnitude of the relationship between them can be calculated and represented by the **correlation coefficient.** It is denoted by the letter *r*, and its value ranges from +1.0 to −1.0.

The closer the correlation coefficient is to +1.0 or −1.0, the stronger the correlation and the greater the confidence that can be placed in the predictiveness of the

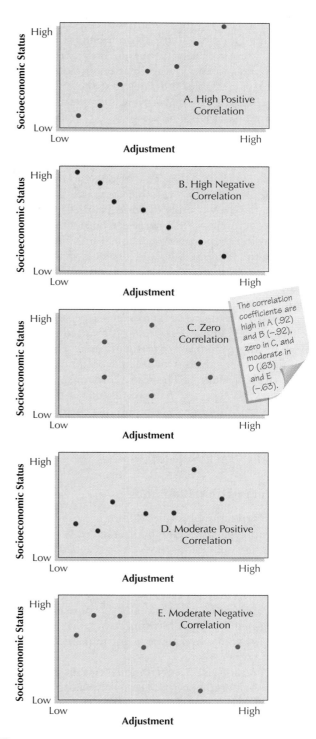

The correlation coefficients are high in A (.92) and B (−.92), zero in C, and moderate in D (.63) and E (−.63).

Figure 5.5   Patterns of Correlation

These scatterplots depict five of the possible correlations between two variables — in this case, socioeconomic status (SES) and level of education. In the positive correlations (A: high positive; D: moderate positive), an individual with a high degree of education is associated with a higher SES. In the negative correlations (B: high negative; E: moderate negative), a high degree of education is associated with a lower SES. When the correlation is zero (C), the two variables are unrelated.

relationship (see Figures 5.5a and 5.5b). Thus, correlations in the range of .20 to .30 are not as strong as correlations greater than .50, nor do they carry as much predictiveness. A very low correlation, or no correlation, between two variables indicates that there is no recognizable relationship between the two variables being investigated (see Figure 5.5c).

The sign of the correlation coefficient — another way of saying whether it is positive or negative — indicates the direction of the relationship. *Positive correlations* indicate that as the value of one variable goes up, the value of the other variable increases as well. For example, the Brown study discussed earlier found a positive correlation ($r = +.51$) between expectations of dramatic tension reduction and problem drinking. As these expectations increased, so did problem drinking. In a *negative correlation,* the value of one variable increases as the value of another variable decreases. For example, the intensity of religious beliefs and suicide attempts are negatively correlated: The more intense a person's religious beliefs, the less likely that person is to attempt suicide.

Not all correlations are significant. A **statistically significant** correlation is one that would not occur as a result of chance alone. The researcher must apply a statistical test to correlations to determine if the relationship is significant. It is generally accepted that for a result to be significant, the statistical test must indicate that this result is beyond a result that could have occurred in fewer than 5 of 100 instances by chance alone.

Using Correlational Methods

Because correlational studies do not use random assignment of participants and do not directly manipulate variables, the deductions that can be reached are limited. Specifically, correlations alone do *not* provide evidence for cause-effect conclusions. However, it is possible for a correlation to represent a cause-effect relationship when such a relationship has already been experimentally demonstrated. By itself, a strong correlation means only that two variables are related, *not* that one necessarily causes the other.

One reason why correlations cannot be used to make causal arguments concerns the problem of the **third variable.** When two variables are correlated, a third, as-yet-unknown variable may be responsible for both other variables. Consider that in the northern United States and Canada, a positive correlation exists between the amount of ice cream sold and the frequency of burglaries. Does the sale of ice cream cause burglaries? Would a ban on ice cream reduce burglaries? Both of these outcomes are highly unlikely. Instead, a more reasonable explanation is that a third variable covaries with and influences the others. Weather is the third variable. As warm weather predominates, ice cream sales rise; at the same time, homeowners are more likely to leave their windows open and criminals are more likely to be outdoors than they are during the very cold northern winters, so burglaries are more feasible. Still, we cannot say that weather *causes* burglary, only that the two are related.

Similarly, in psychopathology research, correlations cannot always be assumed to inform us about causality. For example, a correlation exists between homelessness and the presence of mental illness, yet homelessness does not *cause* mental illness. Perhaps having a mental disorder interrupts routine work and contributes to a downslide into homelessness. The third-variable problem exists in research on alcohol as well. For example, suppose an investigator observes that the problematic alcohol consumption of teenage males is correlated with the presence of alcoholism among the youths' fathers. One interpretation might be that the relationship is causal, owing to the shared genetics between father and son. However, a third variable — the fact that these two males shared the same living environment for eighteen years — might also be a reasonable explanation. (Interestingly, from a genetic standpoint, the explanation of alcoholism as a result of shared social environment would be seen as faulty — since the third variable in this instance would be the genetic similarity.) From a single correlation, reaching conclusions about what caused what simply isn't possible.

Another reason why correlations cannot inform us about causality has to do with the problem of **directionality:** Which variable caused the other? If variables A and B are correlated, did A cause B, or vice versa? For example, data support a relationship at the start of adolescence between increased hormone levels and increased conflict with certain adults. People had long assumed that the hormonal changes cause the conflict. But because the data are correlational, it is also possible that increased conflict influences hormonal activity. So, rather than assuming that hormonal changes create adolescent-adult conflict, one could consider the more provocative idea that increased conflict stimulates hormonal changes. The point to emphasize here is that a correlation informs us of the degree of a relationship, but it does not inform us about the direction of causality.

Despite these limitations, correlational methods are appropriate in abnormal psychology within many areas of investigation. They are particularly appropriate if the investigator cannot directly manipulate variables of interest or wants to know how variables covary naturally — that is, without the influence of the investigator. Consider the possible relationship between distress among family members and an individual's depression. An experimenter could not intentionally cause familial distress just to study whether a participant becomes depressed! Rather, families in which distress has occurred naturally can be investigated to determine if depression is associated with the distress. Thus, correlational analyses allow us to investigate areas in which experimental manipulation would be inappropriate.

Studies may be correlational in design even when they do not use correlation coefficients. For example, researchers commonly compare a group of patients who are *classified* a certain way, on the one hand, with a group of normals who are not so classified, on the other. This use of **classification variables** has also been applied to **quasi-experiments** — where membership in a class or category, and not random assignment, determines the experimental and comparison groups. For instance, a researcher investigating the relationship between brain activity and severe psychological disorder might conduct positron emission tomography (PET) scans on the brains of severely disturbed schizophrenic patients and normal persons. Such a study would be considered quasi-experimental because its participants are not randomly assigned to the schizophrenic and normal groups but, rather, are grouped according to their actual classification as either schizophrenic or normal. As another example, consider a researcher who wants to compare suicidal and nonsuicidal clients. Clearly, the researcher does not directly influence the likelihood of suicide; rather, he classifies the clients as either suicidal or not (using, say, an interview or questionnaire format) and then compares the two groups.

EXPERIMENTAL METHODS

Note that a major difference between the experimental method and other research strategies is that in an **experiment** the researcher directly influences — or manipulates — one or more of the variables. The variable that the researcher manipulates to investigate its effects is called the **independent variable**. One or more **dependent variables** are used to assess the effects, if any, of the manipulated independent variable. The value of the dependent variable *depends* on the value of the independent variable. That is, the researcher manipulates the independent variable to see what happens to the dependent variable. For example, type of therapy can serve as an independent variable in abnormal psychology. The researcher manipulates the independent variable — type of therapy — by assigning clients with identified disorders to one type of therapy or another. Randomly assigning participants to the treatment or the control group is also essential. The dependent variables, then, would be measures that indicate improvement, such as ratings by independent clinical judges, clients' self-reports, tests scores, and observations of behavior.

In experimental research, as noted, the independent variable is manipulated *directly* — as when the researcher

An observer watches children and a teacher in a classroom. Once trained and reliable, the observer can record the behaviors of the class participants. Securing data on the behavior of subjects in the natural environment is valuable: subjects may not know or pay attention to the fact that they are currently being observed and the observations are therefore likely to be representative of the participants' typical behavior.

determines that two types of therapy will be provided to the groups of clients. However, since direct manipulation is not always possible or ethical, researchers often rely on independent variables that are manipulated by selection. This approach — involving the use of classification variables — was discussed earlier.

The experimental approach to research has certain advantages over descriptive and correlational methods. Most notably, experimental studies permit statements of cause and effect. When a manipulated independent variable produces effects that do not occur in the absence of the manipulation, causal status can be assigned to that independent variable. A descriptive or correlational study might suggest such a conclusion, but only an experimental study can definitively reach it.

Even so, the proper conduct of an experiment requires careful control of extraneous variables as well as assurance of both internal and external validity. These considerations are examined in the sections that follow.

Controlling Variables

Researchers want to isolate the effects of the independent variable and determine its effects on the dependent variable; but to do so, they need a control group. A **control group** is a group of participants exposed to all features of the experiment with the exception of the independent variable. The experimental group is exposed to the independent variable, and the responses of the control group and the experimental group on the dependent variable are then compared. As an example, consider the following question: Does the induction of a dysphoric mood influence memories? To study this question, you could design an experiment in which participants in the experimental group are exposed to conditions that induce low mood and then are asked to report recollections from memory. The participants in the control group would be treated in the same way as those in the experimental group, but without the mood-induction procedure.

Variables other than the independent variable manipulated by the experimenter may influence the dependent variables. In studies of adults with serious psychological disorders, for instance, medications can affect the dependent variable. Many of the patients in mental health centers are receiving medications, the effects of which can distort or otherwise influence the dependent variables and interfere with accurate conclusions about the effects of the independent variable. Thus, proper control groups are needed. For example, a researcher concerned about unwanted effects of medications on the dependent variable would include separate groups of medicated and nonmedicated patients in her study. Then, by comparing these groups, she could isolate the medication effects.

Recall the earlier example in which the sugar intake of children diagnosed with ADHD was operationalized in terms of the sugar content of cookies provided by the researcher. Sugar, however, is not the only factor that could be responsible for the behavior of these hyperactive children: Their activity levels could instead be related to gender or to the amount of exercise the children had before participating in the study. Researchers employ various procedures to control the unwanted influences of extraneous variables, including randomization, matching, counterbalancing, and placebo control groups. They can also use statistical tests to assess the significance of the effects of the independent variable.

Randomization When researchers assign participants to a condition in an experiment purely by chance — by flipping a coin or using a table of random numbers — they are employing **randomization.** In the sugar study, for example, the children would not be asked to volunteer for one of the three conditions because some precondition in the children might influence both the decision to volunteer and the dependent variables. For instance, a child who jumps up and volunteers for the sugar-dense cookies may already be an overactive child. To prevent such confounding, the researcher would instead randomly assign the ADHD children to the three cookie conditions, thereby reducing any existing differences across the groups.

Matching Matching is the attempt to ensure that the participants in all conditions are comparable — first, by defining the important ways that people could differ from one another and, then, by placing an equal number of persons of each type in each group. In our sugar study, for example, participants might differ in their initial levels of activity. Researchers could measure initial levels of activity and assign the children to groups so that each group includes children who scored low, medium, and high on that measure. They might also want to assign an equal number of boys and girls to each condition.

Counterbalancing Whenever different aspects of an experiment are sequentially presented to participants, it is important to consider the order of the presentation. Because the sequence of events could influence the dependent variables, it needs to be controlled. For instance, a researcher interested in the effects of sugar on children's activity level would want to avoid a situation in which some youths are running around before entering the experimental room while others are arriving fresh and rested. One way to control unwanted sequence effects is by **counterbalancing,** or presenting research events to participants in different orders. In a study of the effects of exercise on activity level, for example, some children in each of the conditions would be given

access to exercise equipment twenty minutes before their participation in the research, whereas the remaining children would exercise after the experiment. The researcher could then examine the data and test to see whether the order had an effect.

Placebo Control Groups A **placebo** is an inert substance in pill form; it has no therapeutic effect. For example, if patients with headaches are given a placebo and told that it will relieve the pain, some patients may report relief, even though the pill contains no medicine. Indeed, research participants may report reduced symptoms or improved health simply as a result of their being given something that they believe will be helpful. This outcome — called the **placebo effect** — is caused by the expectation of relief, not by the treatment.

Because the placebo effect can interfere with the study of the effects of treatment for psychological disorders, it is necessary to use placebo control groups. For example, in a study of the effects of medications on depression, researchers might have a genuine medication condition in which participants are given an active medication (such as imipramine), a placebo control condition in which participants are given placebos, and a wait-list or no-treatment condition in which participants are assessed but given neither active treatment nor the expectation of having received a treatment (Hollon, DeRubeis & Evans, 1987). If patients who are led to expect improvement — the placebo condition — change as much as those who receive the putative active medication, then researchers cannot conclude that the med-

ication is effective. For the medicine to be deemed effective, the improvements need to be greater for those receiving the active ingredient than for those receiving only the placebo and for those receiving no treatment.

It is easy to design research with placebo controls when the investigation concerns medications, but what about placebo comparisons in psychotherapy research? In the placebo groups in such research, the clients see a therapist, but the therapist provides attention only. Yet the therapist must provide a convincing rationale for the procedure, thereby activating the client's expectation that this "therapy" will be effective — much as taking a pill activates the client's expectation that pain relief is on the way. Many of the better rationales actually resemble forms of psychotherapy. For instance, being a reflective listener as a therapist in a placebo condition would, for those who follow Carl Rogers, be similar to providing a form of client-centered therapy.

Researchers face additional concerns in designing placebo controls for studies in psychotherapy and pharmacotherapy. For instance, they may have difficulty maintaining a positive expectancy over the duration of the placebo treatment. Indeed, this duration is problematic from an ethical standpoint because clients are essentially going untreated. Clearly, then, although placebo conditions are often necessary to control extraneous influences, they must be used cautiously and judiciously.

Statistical Significance For experiments, as for correlational studies, researchers must analyze the role of chance in producing the observed results and determine whether those results are statistically significant. **Inferential statistics** provide the methods for determining the probability that the effects of an experiment are explained not by chance but by the variable being investigated. The number of participants, the variability in their scores, and the distribution of scores are among the factors that determine whether a result is significant.

Internal and External Validity in Experimental Studies

As an illustration of how researchers address the concerns we discuss in this section, consider a study conducted and reported in 1966 by Gordon Paul (see also Emmelkamp, 1995). Paul compared two different forms of therapy for anxiety: systematic desensitization and insight-oriented psychotherapy. The participants in his study were college students who experienced anxiety when speaking in public. They were randomly assigned either to one of the treatments or to one of two control conditions: an attention-placebo control and a no-treatment control. The therapists recruited for the study were experienced in providing therapy and received procedural manuals for the different treatment conditions. The treatments were provided over a specified number of sessions, and all participants completed several measures before, during, and after therapy. Being in the treatment or control condition was the independent variable; scores on the measures before, during, and after therapy were the dependent variables. An illustration of the results appears in Figure 5.6.

Does this study have internal validity? Can we be confident that changes in the dependent variable were solely the result of the independent variable? Does the study have external validity? Can we generalize to other samples? Paul took several steps to address issues of internal validity. Procedural manuals were used to ensure that the treatments were provided properly. Participants were assigned to conditions randomly. Control groups were used; those in the attention-placebo control received attention and completed the measures but did not receive the specific treatment, and those in the no-treatment control completed the measures before and after a period of time similar to the duration of treatment. Each of these steps, and others, added confidence that the results were not undermined by unwanted influences and thus were internally valid.

The external validity of the study was another matter. Can a therapist who works with real patients expect the results of a study with college students to be helpful? Are college students and clinical patients sufficiently similar? It could be argued, for instance, that clinical patients typically seek help for their problems, whereas the students in Paul's study were sought out to participate in the research. In addition, clinical problems are

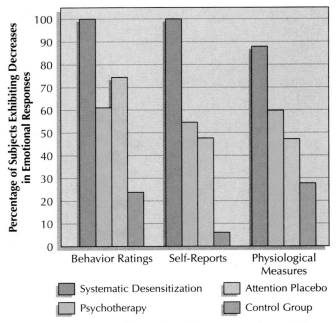

Figure 5.6   Paul's Study of Treatment for Public-Speaking Anxiety

In Gordon Paul's 1966 study, different treatments for public-speaking anxiety (the independent variable) produced different outcomes on various dependent variables: behavior ratings, self-reports, and physiological measures. Illustrated here are the percentages of people showing decreases in anxiety as measured by these dependent variables. *Source:* Bandura (1969).

more severe than student problems. Did these factors eliminate the study's external validity? No, external validity was not eliminated, although it was limited by the sample used. Studies of the process and outcome of therapy, even with volunteers, can help identify the factors that are most beneficial. Internally valid studies are necessary to draw solid conclusions, and often the steps necessary to achieve control of many variables can best be taken with nonclinical participants. So, in this case, some degree of external validity was sacrificed for the sake of added internal validity. What remains is for the practitioner to apply the findings to clinical cases and determine the appropriateness of generalizations from the initial findings.

When Paul decided how to conduct his experiment, he emphasized its internal validity and thus the confidence that could be placed in its findings. For example, Paul's decision to provide treatment over a specified number of sessions created a situation dissimilar from clinical practice — which involves variable numbers of sessions — but it allowed for greater control of extraneous factors. In this as in all experimental research, there is a trade-off between internal and external validity.

Remember Mel, who underwent a lobotomy at age twenty, yet is still poorly adjusted as an adult. In retrospect, his father's permission for the operation may seem unjustified. However, at the time it was performed, there was no research — certainly nothing as clean and crisp as the Paul study — on which to make an informed decision. Quality studies, on the other hand, offer consumers a basis for making such decisions about their loved ones.

SINGLE-SUBJECT DESIGNS

We have already discussed case studies and concerns about their adequacy. **Single-subject designs** are research designs in which the effects of an intervention can be evaluated using a single case. Like case studies, single-subject designs are based on individual participants, but they are both less vulnerable to the criticisms directed toward case studies and more likely to identify factors involved in a disorder, its course, and its treatment.

Basically, single-subject designs involve comparing the naturally occurring frequency of a target behavior — called a **baseline** — with the frequency of the same behavior under other conditions. An initial period of observing and recording the natural frequency of a problem provides the standard against which to judge any treatment-produced changes. Then the clinical researcher alters the conditions, examines the resulting behavioral frequencies, and asks the question: Did the altered conditions (the intervention) influence the rate of the problem's occurrence?

If the frequencies of the target behavior change, the treatment may be the cause, but it is also possible that other, rival influences have had an effect. These influences are *threats to internal validity,* as we discuss earlier in the chapter. Procedures aimed at controlling rival influences are important ingredients of a single-subject design. Two of these procedures are the A-B-A-B design and the multiple baseline design.

The A-B-A-B Design

The **A-B-A-B design,** also called a *reversal design,* assesses the effects of an intervention by demonstrating that the problem behavior changes systematically with the provision and removal of treatment. "A" refers to the baseline conditions and "B" to the treatment. In an A-B-A-B design, the baseline and treatment conditions are alternated. In the second A phase, treatment is terminated. The treatment is then reapplied in the second B phase. If the problem improves during the two B phases, the investigator can assume that the treatment is responsible for the improvements. But if the problem does not revert to pretreatment levels after treatment is termi-

nated in the second A phase, then the intervention may not be responsible for the changes. For the treatment to be seen as effective, the client's problem must vary systematically with the conditions of treatment and no treatment.

Consider the case of a four-year-old cerebral palsied child who engaged in excessive *bruxism* — nonfunctional gnashing and grinding of the teeth. The researchers (Gross & Isaac, 1982), using an A-B-A-B design, sought to evaluate the effects of a treatment that involved (1) having the child engage in forced-arm exercise and (2) rewarding the child for behavior other than bruxism. Daily observations of the child were made for fifteen minutes at 10:15 A.M. During consecutive twenty-second intervals, all incidents of bruxism, during the baseline and treatment phases, were recorded by a trained observer. To reduce unwanted influences, the observer was blind to (uninformed about) when the baseline and treatment conditions were in effect. The frequency of bruxism was markedly reduced by the treatment, returned to unwanted levels when the treatment was temporarily discontinued, and was again reduced when treatment was reapplied. The A-B-A-B design allowed the researchers to conclude that the treatment was effective (see Figure 5.7).

The second A phase, the return to baseline, can be difficult to accomplish. If serious problems have eased, the investigator may be hesitant about implementing this reversal. Also, both the client and persons in the client's environment may not want to revert to earlier conditions. And even if they are willing to do so, it may be difficult, or possibly unethical, to re-create the original baseline situation after a treatment has been implemented. Without the second A phase, however, it is impossible to conclude that the treatment, and not some other variable, caused the desired change in the behavior. For these reasons, researchers may choose to utilize other single-subject designs, such as a multiple baseline design.

The Multiple Baseline Design

Unlike the A-B-A-B design, the multiple baseline design does not require removing treatment. In a **multiple baseline design** two or more baselines of different durations are recorded simultaneously, and the intervention is applied for only one of the baselines. The multiple baselines can be different behaviors by a single person, the same behavior by different persons, or one behavior in different situations. The logic of this design is that if the treatment is responsible for changes, then these changes will be evident on the baselines that are treated and not evident on the untreated baselines.

As an example, consider Philip Saigh's (1986) use of a multiple baseline design to evaluate treatment for a

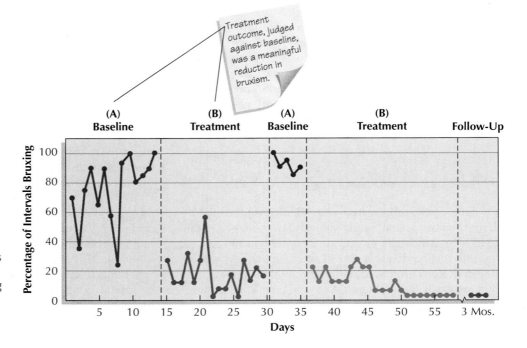

Figure 5.7 Evaluating Changes in Bruxism Using an A-B-A-B Design

A child with cerebral palsy was treated for bruxism, and the treatment was evaluated using an A-B-A-B design. *Source:* Gross & Isaac (1982), The Haworth Press.

six-year-old boy, Ron, who suffered a posttraumatic stress disorder, or PTSD (see Chapter 6). Ron was exposed to a bomb blast in a war zone where he had lived and, characteristic of PTSD, had a detrimental reaction to this stressful event. He reexperienced the blast; avoided situations that reminded him of it; and suffered sleep disturbances, nightmares, and depression. Saigh used an imagery-based desensitization (see Chapter 3) to treat Ron. Scenes related to the trauma were developed, and the treatment was applied following baselines of different durations. After the therapist taught him to be relaxed, Ron was asked to imagine the various scenes. Throughout, Ron's discomfort level was measured. Each time the treatment was applied to a different scene, the distress dropped (see Figure 5.8). Incidently, Saigh reported that Ron's depression and school performance also improved after the treatment.

Cautions Regarding Single-Subject Designs

Single-subject designs have certain advantages over the descriptive case study, but they also have shortcomings. For single-subject designs, as for case studies, the generalizability of the findings is limited. Will the treatment that was effective for one subject be effective for someone else? The procedures must be repeated with a different client and the findings replicated before the researcher can attempt to generalize beyond the single case.

Evaluations using single-subject designs may be limited for other reasons. Consider, for instance, an A-B-A-B design in which the target behavior changes repeatedly with the alternation from treatment to base-line conditions. This outcome shows that the treatment produced the changes, but does it not also show that the changes were transitory?

Multiple baseline designs have an additional problem: What happens when the effects of treatment "spill over" to the other baselines — that is, when the treatment effects are so strong that they influence more than the one baseline? In our earlier example involving Ron, the treatment might have been so effective that the application of scenes 1 and 2 had a positive impact on the other scenes. Although this general reduction of distress is a desirable result of treatment, it nevertheless undermines the logic of the multiple baseline design and reduces the confidence that can be placed in the findings.

Despite their shortcomings, single-subject designs are advances over the less rigorous case study method (Hersen & Barlow, 1989; Kazdin, 1982). Though still somewhat linked to the behavioral approach, these designs are relevant to a variety of researchers who are interested in the specific data of an individual case.

FOCUS ON RESEARCH

What Can Be Learned from Different Approaches to Studying a Particular Behavior?

Not all researchers make the same decisions about how to go about their science. A wide variety of approaches are used in studies having to do with the same form of

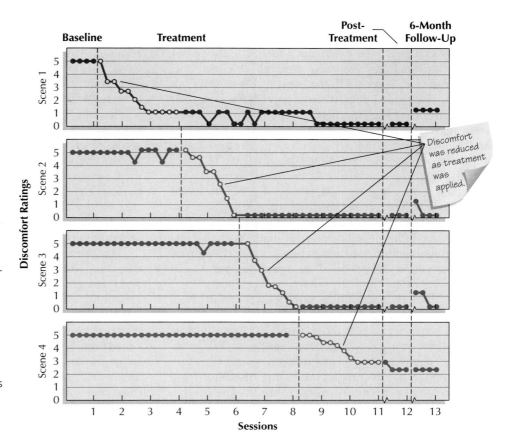

Figure 5.8 Evaluating Changes in Ratings of Discomfort Using a Multiple Baseline Design
Illustrated are the results of treatment for posttraumatic stress disorder using a multiple baseline design. The participant rated his distress on a scale of 5 (maximum discomfort) to 0 (no discomfort). The treatment, an imagery-based exposure procedure (graphed as open circles), reduced distress systematically as it was applied to different distress-producing scenes. *Source:* Saigh (1986).

abnormal behavior. Antisocial behavior, for example, is seen in children and adolescents described as conduct disordered (such as juvenile delinquents), as well as in adults diagnosed with antisocial personality disorder. Some researchers interested in the childhood predictors of adolescent and adult criminal activity might choose to survey and interview adults about their childhood experiences, while others might select a longitudinal design and take many measurements on the participants beginning in childhood and then in subsequent years of their lives. Because only a few of the research participants will actually commit crimes, large numbers of participants must be sampled. Still other researchers interested in the psychology of already-identified antisocial individuals might choose an experimental strategy and, with proper controls, test specific hypotheses. Let's look at some examples of these decisions.

Lee Robins and Rumi Price (1991) examined the data from an epidemiological survey involving more than 19,000 people. Among other questions, the participants were asked to report on their current psychological state as well as on their childhood behavior. The researchers focused on the answers to these questions to see if there was a meaningful predictive relationship between childhood conduct problems, such as truancy, cruelty, and fire setting, and the presence of adult disorders. Recall the Joneses' children from the start of this chapter: Are they on an identifiable path? As it turns out, there is a predictive relationship: Robins and Price found that childhood conduct problems are associated with numerous adult disorders, including antisocial personality and alcohol abuse. Interestingly, the predictive power of conduct problems is similar for males and females. The Jones family may need immediate intervention.

The Robins and Price study was strong in representativeness. It included persons of both genders from New Haven, Baltimore, St. Louis, Durham, and Los Angeles as well as members of white, African American, and Hispanic groups. However, it also had potential limitations. First, the data were based entirely on participants' self-reports — and these can be inaccurate. The study would have been more internally valid had the data been corroborated by external sources. Second, the retrospective nature of these self-reports raised the concern that a participant's willingness to admit a history of childhood conduct problems may have been associated with a willingness to admit adult problems. And third, by studying only adults, the researchers were uninformed about participants who died before adulthood.

In a longitudinal investigation, Terri Moffitt (1990) studied the developmental trajectories of the same children from ages three to fifteen. (Longitudinal research is discussed in detail in a subsequent section.) Her sample included all consecutive births between April 1, 1972, and March 31, 1973, in the city of Dunedin, New Zealand. Of the 1,139 eligible births, Moffitt reported on antisocial behavior problems across childhood for 435 boys assessed at two-year intervals (for example, ages three, five, seven). On the basis of her many findings, she concluded that there are predictors of later antisocial behavior. Specifically, those children who were aggressive and involved in illegal acts in childhood and who had received a diagnosis of attention-deficit hyperactivity disorder, or ADHD (see Chapter 15) were found likely to be persisting in antisocial action at age fifteen. Will they be criminals as adults? Moffitt's longitudinal study has not yet reached the point where she can report on adult outcomes, but data from other research have suggested that individuals with ADHD and aggression continue their acting-out behavior problems into young adulthood (Farrington, Loeber & van Hammen, 1993).

The fact that Moffitt's sample was from New Zealand raises the question of external validity: Can her findings be generalized to other countries? It is noteworthy that the sample was predominantly of European ancestry (less than 2 percent Polynesian) and therefore quite comparable to samples consisting of whites from other English-speaking Western cultures. The study's generalizability to more urban groups or to ethnic minorities, however, remains in question.

Another example concerns adult *psychopaths,* who have an antisocial personality disorder. This condition is characterized by a pattern of behavior including violation of the rights of others, cheating, stealing, and inability to engage in close interpersonal relationships. Psychopaths typically do not respect authority and often experience conflict with the law. (See Chapter 14 for more details about antisocial personality disorder.)

The findings of previous research indicate that psychopaths are relatively poor at learning to inhibit behavior. At the University of Wisconsin, Joseph Newman and David Kosson (1986) were interested in discovering whether there are differences between psychopathic and nonpsychopathic prisoners in terms of their ability to inhibit responses. They chose a mixed-design research tactic that combined the use of a classification variable with an experimental strategy.

More specifically, Newman and Kosson used the classification variable to see if the learning of psychopathic and nonpsychopathic inmates was influenced differentially by the types of incentives provided to motivate learning. The experimenters directly manipulated one independent variable — type of incentive. Receiving or losing chips, worth ten cents each, served as the reward and punishment, respectively. One group performed the learning task with competing incentives — namely, opportunities for both reward and punishment. The second group had only the opportunity for punishment.

The learning task was a computer-based discrimination task in which participants had to learn when to respond (by pressing a button) and when not to respond to various stimulus numbers. Responding to an incorrect stimulus was of particular interest because it reflected a failure to inhibit a response. According to the results, the psychopaths made more errors than the nonpsychopaths when the task contained competing goals (reward and punishment), but they performed as well as the nonpsychopaths when only avoiding punishment (see Figure 5.9). Apparently, psychopaths are relatively poor at learning to inhibit reward-seeking behavior that results in monetary punishment. Nonpsychopaths, in contrast, appear to take punishment more seriously and inhibit themselves accordingly.

The Newman and Kosson study (1986) used counterbalancing to control for the order of the several learning tasks presented to the participants. Participants were randomly assigned to complete the tasks in different orders. Later, statistical tests documented that the differences in learning were beyond those that would be expected by chance alone. Newman and Kosson followed an appropriate experimental methodology and used proper methods of data analysis. We can thus be confident that their findings are meaningful; in other words, it is quite likely that psychopaths are poor at learning to inhibit reward-seeking behavior. This important finding has direct implications for the criminal justice system — particularly for facilities designed to rehabilitate criminals. Treatment programs may be especially beneficial to the extent that they focus on and succeed at teaching psychopaths when to inhibit responding.

Experimental Conditions

	Reward and Punishment	Punishment Only
Psychopathic Inmates	13.80	14.70
Nonpsychopathic Inmates (controls)	8.52	15.78

Figure 5.9 Mean Error Rates for Psychopathic and Nonpsychopathic Inmates Under Two Different Conditions

This research used the experimental method, including the direct manipulation of two different reward/punishment conditions and the application of procedures to control for other unwanted influences. As shown, psychopaths made more errors than nonpsychopaths when the task contained competing goals (reward and punishment) but performed as well as nonpsychopaths when the task contained only punishment. *Source:* Data provided by Newman & Kosson (1986).

Research is an ongoing activity, using multiple strategies and varied data sources. Ultimately, we learn not from a single study but from a series of investigations. Though varied, the studies discussed here nevertheless present a clear picture of the persistent troubles associated with antisocial behavior.

PERENNIAL THEMES: SOME KEY QUESTIONS FOR RESEARCH

Behind the differences in research designs that we have discussed lie variations in the approaches and topics pursued by researchers. A researcher who is trying to evaluate a treatment for depression, for example, uses different techniques than a researcher who is interested in determining the prevalence of this disorder in various countries. The first might turn to the multiple baseline design discussed in the preceding section and follow it with an experimental study of the effects of treatment. The second might turn to surveys. Each research study would reflect a unique mixture of related choices concerning topic, approach, and design. The study of abnormal behavior is indeed a broad and far-reaching enterprise.

Still, among the countless topics pursued by researchers in psychopathology, we can isolate a few important recurring questions that emerge from the scores of studies performed each year: What is the nature of a disorder? How widespread is the disorder? And what effect, if any, does treatment produce? Earlier in the chapter we discuss examples of research aimed at answering these questions. In this section we consider how researchers look for answers to four additional questions.

1. What course does a disorder follow?

2. What role, if any, does genetics play in this disorder?

3. Are the effects of treatment meaningful?

4. How do all these findings fit together?

Identifying the Course of Disorders: Longitudinal Research

Perhaps the single most frequently asked question in abnormal psychology is some variation of the following: What will happen next? In other words, what can we say about the future of a person now suffering from a disor-

der? The question assumes that a disorder develops over time, and this assumption is held by most mental health scholars and practitioners. One way to examine the course of a disorder is through **longitudinal designs,** which allow researchers to study changes and stability over time by repeatedly measuring the same participants at select intervals (see Friedman & Haywood, 1994). In contrast, **cross-sectional studies** examine the same characteristics in different individuals at different ages. For instance, symptoms of a disorder might be assessed at one particular time in children, adolescents, and adults.

Investigators use several types of research designs to try to track a disorder. The longitudinal approach is evident in **follow-up studies** that identify patients at a particular point, such as when they are first diagnosed, and study these vulnerable persons again at a later time. **Follow-back studies** identify adult patients and examine their earlier records at schools or treatment agencies. **High-risk studies** look at vulnerable children who are exposed to conditions that are thought to contribute to disorder (such as having a depressed mother or living in poverty). In cases where these children are then followed to see if they do develop problems, these high-risk studies take on the advantages of the longitudinal approach.

One compelling longitudinal report by Leo Kanner (1971) described eleven children (eight boys and three girls) who, from an early point in life, did not relate to people the way other children did (Kanner, 1943). The children showed an obsessive desire for the preservation of sameness, preferred to be alone, had many stereotypic behaviors (such as repeated wrist waving), and did not progress normally. These behaviors are now seen as features of *autism* (discussed in Chapter 16). What would these children be like as adults?

To find out, Kanner conducted a longitudinal follow-up study and found an interesting range of adjustment. Some of the children, as adults, had seizures, were hospitalized, and remained in the care of the state. Others were isolated, lived alone, and were unemployed, but they were able to perform simple chores moderately well. Two of these autistic children were success stories: After special training one of them, as an adult, became a regularly employed bank teller, and the other began operating duplicating machines. Thus, although the majority of the children provided evidence of the need for lifelong interventions, the examples of successful self-help and employment described by Kanner provided longitudinal evidence that some autistic children can achieve a modest level of adjustment.

Indeed, longitudinal studies in abnormal psychology are quite useful in several ways. They permit causal inferences, identify precipitating factors, assess diagnostic stability, describe the course of a disorder, and identify predictors of outcome. Kanner's study demonstrates not only the usefulness of longitudinal designs but also

Best friends at ages 5-8, 12-15, and 14-17. Longitudinal studies, when the same subjects participate over several years, can provide answers to questions that are not accessible from other research methods (e.g., cross-sectional designs).

one of their important drawbacks: They take a very long time. Two other difficulties are also noteworthy: Longitudinal studies are expensive, and participants may drop out of them for various reasons, thereby shrinking the number of observations. When too many participants drop out, we can no longer be confident about the representativeness of the sample. For these reasons, longitudinal designs, although they are increasingly being used in contemporary research, remain relatively rare.

Studying Genetic Transmission of Psychological Disorders

If a person has a psychological disorder, what are the chances that someone else who is genetically related will have the same disorder? Do the chances change systematically with changes in the degree of genetic relatedness? What psychological disorders, if any, are inherited? Are predispositions or vulnerabilities to certain disorders transmitted genetically?

Each individual receives a certain amount of genetic information in the form of chromosomes from both father and mother. This information is a person's genotype (see Table 5.3 for definitions of terms used in genetics research). Chromosomes contain genes that transmit a biochemical code responsible for determining the structure and activity of the body's proteins. At the biochemical level, differences in this genetic code lead to individual physiological and physical differences. Some physiological differences, such as colorblindness, are the result of a single gene. Some physical differences, such as height, are the result of a number of different genes. Everyone, except for monozygotic (identical) twins, has a unique genetic and biochemical makeup.

Genetics research is growing rapidly, yet ethical concerns limit how researchers can address the many fascinating genetic questions. For example, scientists would not conduct experiments requiring that assumed carriers of a disorder reproduce in order to test the presence of a disorder in the offspring. However, researchers can study the role of genetics in psychological disorders through the methods that are summarized in Table 5.4. These methods are suitable only for certain questions and conclusions, and each of them has several limitations.

Family Studies **Family studies** address the question of whether a disorder runs in families. In particular, they attempt to verify whether the frequency of a particular disorder is higher among family members than in the general population. The investigator first identifies patients with a particular disorder and a comparison group without the disorder. The next step is to obtain information about each close relative of the participants both with and without the disorder — either by directly interviewing them or, if that is not possible, by asking

Table 5.3 Terms Used in Genetics Research

Term	Definition
Genotype	The genetic characteristics a person inherits. For example, someone may inherit a genetic predisposition for a disorder, but the genotype may or may not result in the disorder.
Phenotype	A person's observed behavior and trait patterns. A disorder may be inherited but it is the phenotypic expression of the genotype that is seen.
Dominant gene	A gene whose hereditary characteristics prevail in the off-spring.
Recessive gene	A gene whose hereditary characteristics are seen only when paired with another identical gene.
Single dominant gene	A single gene whose expression prevails in the offspring (for example, colorblindness).
Multiple genes	Several genes whose expression prevails in the offspring (for example, height).
DNA fragment	A portion of a gene; DNA stands for deoxyribonucleic acid, the principal component of genes.

Genetics research has provided important findings regarding psychopathology, and it will continue to do so.

each participant or someone else in the family about the relatives. Finally, the researcher compares the rates of the disorder to see if these rates are higher among the relatives of patients with the disorder than in the control group representing the general population.

An example is provided by William Grove of the University of Minnesota, who used the family study method to examine schizophrenia. Grove and his colleagues (1991) administered structured interviews, questionnaires, and tasks to seventeen schizophrenic patients, sixty-one first-degree relatives, and eighteen normal control subjects. The schizophrenic patients scored abnormally on essentially all of the measures, and their relatives scored significantly more in the abnormal direction than did the normal control subjects. Grove and his colleagues concluded that the characteristics measured in their study seem to run in families. Thus, the family study approach allows researchers to conclude that the disorder has a familial pattern; it does not, however, separate what is due to genetic factors (nature) and what is due to a shared environment (nurture).

A variant of the family study is the *high-risk method,* in which the child of a parent with the identified disorder is studied. The investigator closely watches the child's development over time, trying to identify what factors influence development of the disorder. In other words, by comparing the development and even-

tual outcomes of a child of a disordered parent with a child of normal parents, the researcher hopes to learn about the extent of the child's risk for developing the disorder and the factors that might contribute to that risk. Note, however, that although a high-risk study can illuminate the psychological mechanisms contributing to the risk for disorder, it cannot isolate the role of genetics, and its findings cannot be generalized to other populations. For example, high-risk studies have shown that a child of a depressed mother is more likely than a child of a nondepressed mother both (1) to be depressed and (2) to experience conflict with the mother (Hammen, 1991). Thus, we might hypothesize that being the child of a depressed mother creates a risk for developing depression, and that part of this risk, beyond any genetic contribution, comes from characteristics of the parent-child interaction.

Twin and Adoption Studies To answer the question of whether a disorder is genetically transmitted, we need methods that separate the influence of nature from the influence of nurture. Twin studies and adoption studies represent "experiments of nature" that help researchers come close to isolating these forces.

In **twin studies,** researchers determine the extent to which both twins experience a disorder that one twin has (e.g., van den Oord, Verhulst & Boomsma, 1996). If

Table 5.4 Methods, Goals, and Limitations of Genetics Research

Method	Question to be Answered	Limitations
Family study	Does the disorder run in families?	Cannot separate genetic and environmental effects
High-risk study	What factors influence development of the disorder?	Cannot separate genetic and environmental effects, although it can characterize the impact of specific effects; results generalizable only to similar high-risk populations
Twin study	Is the disorder inherited?	Rare examples; environmental factors uncontrolled
Adoption study	Can we separate genetic and environmental contributions?	Difficult to get accurate information on biological parents or to control confounding factors
Pedigree analysis	What is the nature of inheritance?	Requires large inbred families with the disorder
Linkage analysis	Where is the gene located?	Best with disorders controlled by a single dominant gene

Genetics research, as is true for all research, must select from among several methods the one approach that provides the optimal data to answer a given question. Because each method has limitations, combinations of studies using different methods can provide more compelling evidence.

both have the disorder, they are said to be *concordant*. Researchers then compare the concordance rates for monozygotic (identical) twins, who have the same genetic makeup, with the rates for dizygotic (fraternal) twins. For monozygotic twins, the extent of genetic similarity is 100 percent; for dizygotic twins, 50 percent. Therefore, if a disorder is genetically transmitted, we expect the concordance rates for monozygotic twins to be higher than the concordance rates for dizygotic twins, who are no more alike than any two brothers or sisters.

Drawing conclusions from twin studies, however, is complicated by uncertainty about just how similar the environmental influence is. For instance, if identical twins are treated more similarly than nonidentical twins are, the higher concordance for disorders for monozygotic twins might result from that more similar environment.

Researchers also face difficulties in carrying out twin studies. It is extremely difficult to find samples of people with psychological disorders who have a twin. And can a researcher who knows the status of one twin be truly objective in evaluating the other? **Adoption studies** provide another way of studying genetic influence, and they go beyond twin studies in separating genetic and environmental influence.

In an adoption study, researchers compare the rates of disorder among adopted children whose biological parents had diagnosable conditions with the rates among adopted children whose biological parents did not have disorders. In a variant known as **cross-fostering**, researchers study the children of normal biological parents who have been adopted and raised either by normal or disordered parents. Another variant is the *family study of adoptees,* in which the researcher first identifies a group of adopted people who are disordered and a group of adopted people who are not and then compares the psychological status of the biological parents of the two groups.

Presumably, genetic transmission is at work if a child develops the same disorder as that affecting his or her biological parent even though the child is being raised by other people. However, adoption studies cannot eliminate the possibility that the prenatal environment influenced development of a disorder. Furthermore, it can be difficult to ensure that adopted children have not had contact with their biological relatives, that their adoptive parents do not have disorders themselves, and that their adoptive homes do not present other risk factors for the disorder. In short, adoption studies do not provide as clean a separation of biology and environment as was once hoped. Nevertheless, such studies, especially when the degree of environmental similarity can be measured and taken into account, do provide useful information to help unravel the cause of psychological disorders.

Are the Effects of Treatment Meaningful?

Researchers use statistical tests to determine if chance alone could account for their observations. However, statistically significant changes, or changes that are beyond chance, are not always clinically significant. An emotionally distressed man who is angry and hostile toward his family might show treatment-produced improvement that is beyond chance, yet still be more hostile than normal and too hostile for the well-being of his family. In this case, the reduction in hostility might be statistically significant but not clinically significant. Indeed, **clinical significance**, after statistical significance, is an important standard: Is the client no longer clinically distressed? How can we study the clinical significance of treatment effects?

Several approaches to clinical significance have been described (Jacobson, 1988). One approach, involving **normative comparisons** (Kendall & Grove, 1988), requires that for a treatment to be clinically significant, clients after treatment must be indistinguishable from a representative nondisturbed group. An example is provided by a study (Kazdin, Siegel & Bass, 1992) that used normative comparisons to evaluate the effects of two cognitive-behavioral treatments for antisocial behavior in children. In addition to statistical tests, which documented that the treatments produced significant changes, the researchers in this study compared the posttreatment functioning of the treated children to normative levels of child functioning. As shown in Figure 5.10, the treated children were no longer outside the normative limits as a result of the interventions. In this study and others, evidence of clinical significance clearly added to the evaluation of reported outcomes.

Meta-Analysis: Integrating Research

The approaches taken by researchers are indeed varied. Accordingly, scientists and students alike must integrate diverse findings to learn more about the causes and optimal treatment of maladjustment. Journals such as the *Psychological Bulletin* make this job easier by publishing reviews of the literature on specific topics. These reviews might include descriptions of individual studies, comments about their methodological strengths and weaknesses, and summaries and conclusions. But for those who are dissatisfied with this kind of evaluation, a recently developed technique called meta-analysis offers a quantitative method for integrating a body of literature.

Meta-analysis is a technique for comparing the effects found in different studies as well as for examining the relationship between certain features of specific studies (variables) and the outcomes of these studies. In conducting a meta-analysis, the researcher first calculates an effect size for each dependent variable reported in each study. Typically, the **effect size** is calculated as the difference between the means of an experimental and control condition divided by the standard deviation of

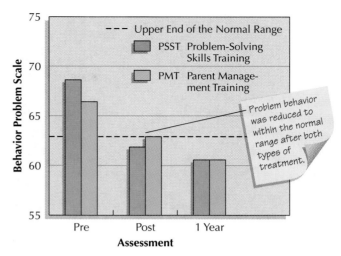

Figure 5.10 Normative Comparisons as a Test of Clinical Significance
When normative comparisons were used to evaluate the effects of two different treatments for antisocial behavior in children, researchers found that both treatments successfully reduced the average total behavior problems to within the normal range.
Source: Kazdin, Siegel & Bass (1992).

the control condition (Kazdin, 1994). In studies of psychotherapy, for example, the effect size refers to the degree to which the treated group improved with respect to the control group. Next, the researcher categorizes (or codes) features of the individual studies and tries to determine if any of these features are associated with larger effect sizes.

In one major application of the meta-analytic method, Mary Smith and Gene Glass (1977) examined the outcomes of nearly four hundred studies of the effects of psychotherapy. Because most of these studies used several dependent measures, Smith and Glass's meta-analysis calculated 875 effect size scores. Using these effect sizes, the authors concluded that clients in psychotherapy seem to be able to improve some areas of adjustment more than others. For example, they reported large effect sizes, which indicated improvement, for measures of fear or anxiety and self-esteem. In addition, Smith and Glass used effect sizes to compare different types of psychological therapy (see also Rosenthal, 1995; Weisy et al., 1995). We report some of the results of the 1977 study and other recent meta-analyses in later chapters dealing with treatments for specific disorders.

Meta-analyses are increasingly appearing in the literature. Such analyses provide a useful technique for combining and comparing studies and for gauging the relative potency of research manipulations (see Rosnow & Rosenthal, 1996). The technique is not entirely quantitative, however, since the researcher must

Will the real Dolly please stand up? Many people question the ethics of cloning Dolly, the seven-month-old sheep produced in the laboratory of a group of Scottish scientists. Can human cloning be far behind? Who will regulate this technology, and how?

make judgments about the studies that are included and about the coding of these studies. Accordingly, although meta-analysis is often seen as an advance, critics point to the subjectivity of certain of its aspects as a source for concern.

RESEARCH ETHICS

Imagine that as you approach your psychology instructor's office, a cartoon on the door catches your eye. The cartoon depicts an ominous castle atop a dark hill; surrounded by a wall, it is accessible only through an imposing gate. A sign on the lawn near the closed gate warns: "Trespassers will be experimented upon." It seems playful and humorous, but still you wonder.

Relax. Trespassers will not be used against their will. Researchers are guided by a series of ethical principles designed to prevent scientific inquiry from infringing on the rights of participants — be they human or animals (American Psychological Association, Committee for the Protection of Human Participants in Research, 1990). These principles include the following:

- Researchers must determine that participants will not experience unjustifiable or extreme *risk* by agreeing to participate. Any risk, even if minor, must be weighed against the potential gain that could come from the investigation. For example,

researchers wishing to use human beings in their research must first receive approval from committees that are arranged for the protection of human participants.

- Before participating, subjects must give their **informed consent.** They must be told about the study and give their permission to be involved. In describing what participants are likely to experience during the study, researchers need not include every detail; but all aspects of the research that might reasonably be expected to influence a person's willingness to participate must be disclosed. Suppose that a researcher is planning to study the emotional effects produced by visiting a state institution for the criminally insane. Would you volunteer to participate? Think for a moment. Suppose that the visit will last three days. It would be unethical for researchers not to inform potential participants about the duration of the visit. Caution and forethought in obtaining informed consent are especially important when research involves participants with psychological disorders. If their psychological conditions prevent people from making informed decisions about participating in research, an agent of their hospital or other supervisory personnel may act on their behalf.

- When information must be withheld from participants in order to test an experimental hypothesis, the researcher must subsequently **debrief** all participants, or provide them with a clear statement of the rationale and methods of the study when their participation is completed.

- Participants in psychological research must also be informed that they can terminate their involvement in the study at any time and that disengagement will not harm them in any way.

- Research participants also have a right to **confidentiality;** that is, their responses to psychological tests or tasks are not open to the public. Researchers routinely assign each participant a number and use this number rather than the participant's name as the means of identification.

- If a subject reports distress as a result of participating in the study, even if all ethical guidelines were followed, the researcher is responsible for removing or correcting the unwanted consequences. In addition, contact with a clinical psychologist and possibly therapy must be available to participants who have become emotionally upset.

Do these guidelines constrain research? Yes, but the constraints are necessary. Indeed, human beings are potentially influenced by so many experiences that it is especially important that researchers in abnormal psychology adhere to ethical principles.

What Lies Ahead?

Each year, hundreds of research journals publish the findings of thousands of studies using the methods described in this chapter. Four trends are evident in current research. First, with the continued interest in the causes of psychological disorders, research is expanding in such areas as the function of familial factors, the contribution of genetics, and the role of human cognition in the onset and expression of psychological disorders. Though time consuming, longitudinal studies are also on the rise.

Second, interest in evaluating treatments of disorders is increasing. These treatments use the results from studies about the nature of specific disorders to inform the therapy. For example, when studies found interpersonal problems among depressed persons, a new focus was directed to interpersonal issues in several treatments for depression. Faced with the issue of cost containment, researchers are more closely examining psychological treatments and their effectiveness.

Third, researchers are now more aware of the need to examine diversity and thus are increasingly studying the influence of gender, age, race, and culture on the development, expression, and treatment of psychological disorders. It is no longer tolerable to claim that the description, symptoms, cause, or treatment of a disorder is always the same for all people. The representativeness of samples of participants and the external validity of studies are important issues concerning diversity.

Last, new research methods are being developed, such as advanced statistical procedures for testing complex theoretical models. These advances will permit increased sophistication in our efforts to understand psychopathology.

The field of abnormal psychology progresses each time the results of published research are integrated into the knowledge base. This knowledge steers both future research and the ongoing practice of psychology. Indeed, the content of the remaining chapters of this book is guided more by published research findings than by any other single force.

KEY TERMS

A-B-A-B design (145)
adoption studies (152)
analogue (133)
baseline (145)
case study (134)
classification variables (141)
clinical significance (153)
confidentiality (155)
confound (131)
continuity theory (132)
control group (142)
correlational studies (138)
correlation coefficient (139)
counterbalancing (142)

cross-fostering (152)
cross-sectional studies (149)
debrief (154)
dependent variables (141)
descriptive approaches (134)
directionality (140)
discontinuity theory (132)
effect size (153)
epidemiology (135)
experiment (141)
external validity (131)
family studies (150)
follow-back studies (149)
follow-up studies (149)

high-risk studies (149)
incidence (135)
independent variable (141)
inferential statistics (144)
informed consent (154)
internal validity (131)
longitudinal designs (149)
matching (142)
meta-analysis (153)
multiple baseline design (145)
normative comparisons (153)
placebo (143)
placebo effect (143)

prevalence (135)
quasi-experiments (141)
randomization (142)
random sampling (136)
representativeness (131)
scatterplots (139)
single-subject designs (145)
statistical significance (140)
surveys (135)
third variable (140)
twin studies (151)
variables (135)

SUMMARY

Science and Psychopathology

Psychologists who study abnormal behavior use the scientific method to test hypotheses about the causes, patterns, and treatments for psychological disorders. Two main concerns facing researchers are internal and external validity. The *internal validity* of a scientific study is the degree to which the research method supports strong, specific conclusions. *External validity* is the degree to which the findings of a given study can be generalized beyond that study.

Researchers also struggle with the question of how to define normality and abnormality. Some define normality according to the *continuity theory,* which states that psychological abnormality and normal behavior form one continuum, from normal to mild to severe disturbance. In contrast, the *discontinuity theory* states that mild and severe psychological dysfunction are distinct from each other and from normality.

Descriptive Methods

The careful description of symptoms is important to the study of psychopathology. *Descriptive approaches* take two main forms: *case studies* and *surveys.*

Correlational Methods

Correlational studies focus on the relationships among variables. Correlations can be displayed visually in *scatterplots.* The higher the *correlation coefficient,* independent of the sign, the greater the degree of relationship. A *statistically significant* correlation is one that would not occur as a result of chance alone.

Experimental Methods

An *experiment* involves random assignment of subjects (participants) and the purposeful manipulation of a variable to assess its effects. The researcher manipulates the *independent variable,* while controlling for the effects of extraneous variables, to evaluate the effect on chosen *dependent variables.* To conduct an optimal test, researchers strive to control all extraneous variables using *control groups, randomization, matching,* and *counterbalancing.* To test the effects of treatments, researchers weigh the merits of *placebo* control

conditions. *Inferential statistics* are used to gauge the significance of the findings of an experiment.

Single-Subject Designs

When researchers want to go beyond the case study method, yet still conduct a detailed study of a single person, *single-subject designs* may be used. In an *A-B-A-B design,* baseline and treatment conditions are alternated to determine if systematic parallel changes have occurred in the targeted behavior. In a *multiple baseline design,* two or more baselines are recorded simultaneously, and the intervention is applied to only one. Useful in several ways, single-subject designs are nevertheless subject to a number of criticisms.

Perennial Themes: Some Key Questions for Research

Among the many questions addressed by abnormal psychology, some continue to receive widespread attention. The one asked perhaps most frequently — What will happen next? — is often answered through *longitudinal designs,* which examine changes and stability over time. *Cross-sectional studies* examine the same characteristics in different individuals at one point in time. *Follow-up* and *follow-back studies* often target the causes of psychological disorder. *Family studies* are used to study the genetic transmission of mental disorders. And *twin studies,* which play an important role in family studies, inform researchers of the degree to which genetics contributes to mental health.

Researchers are beginning to ask not only if the effects of psychotherapy are statistically significant but also if they are clinically meaningful. *Clinical significance* can be defined as the ability of a treatment to move participants who were once diagnosed as having a disorder to within the limits of normal behavior. *Normative comparisons* are used to evaluate this outcome. In addition, researchers are beginning to combine the results of many studies, often using an approach called *meta-analysis,* to assess treatment effects across studies.

Research Ethics

In psychological research, certain ethical guidelines exist to protect participants. The code of ethics prepared by the American Psychological Association includes requirements that researchers obtain the *informed consent* of participants, *debrief* participants if necessary, and provide *confidentiality.*

Consider the following. . .

Suppose that medical scientists have identified a new form of heart disease. Several expert physicians have been consulted, but they haven't yet reached a consensus about what to do since medical research has not yet determined the optimal treatment for the disease. The physicians are considering medications, surgery, or diet modification. Participants are needed for research to compare these treatments, but some participants will get treatments later found to be less effective than others. Is this research ethical? Would you participate? Do the same standards and concerns apply to research on psychological treatments? What type of study would you design?

Suppose that you're planning to apply to graduate school and you know that standardized test scores are important for gaining admission. Your scores in the past haven't been bad, but you recall reading an ad for a Preparation Course claiming success in increasing exam scores. What data would you want to see regarding the effectiveness of this program before you spend your money on it? Can you think of ways in which the advertising could be accurate even if the course is ineffective?

CHAPTER 6

Anxiety Disorders

Those among us . . .

- Your roommate Cheryl is a nineteen-year-old college sophomore. The two of you share an interest in music and have gone out together as friends. Sometimes she's fun; at other times she dwells on her fears, which are excessive and troubling. "You know," she says, "I just can't ride in cars, buses, elevators, airplanes — anything that moves. It drives me crazy." You used to listen, but now the complaints are wearing your relationship thin.

- You always thought of Uncle Bob as one of the successes in your family. As a corporate executive, he has a big home, a fancy car, and financial security. Little did you know that Bob has social phobia: He experiences intense fear of doing something embarrassing, and it is a serious obstacle in his life.

- Suppose your mother fit the following description — a middle-aged woman who has always been fussy and house-proud. You, too, like a neat house, but lately you've noticed that mom checks each chore several times to be certain that it was completed. She also checks the front door three times to convince herself that it is locked, parks the car in a specific spot at the store, and never stays out past mealtime.

Why does Cheryl feel so terribly anxious in everyday situations?

Why doesn't Bob just get over his fears? Can he be helped by medications or psychological treatment?

Why does your mother check things so often? What is the problem, and can it be changed?

Cheryl, Uncle Bob, and your mom are experiencing emotional difficulties. The three cases have obvious differences but also a common thread: They are laced together by the theme of anxiety. The extreme discomfort, tension, and distress felt by each person are anxiety-related symptoms associated with one or another of the several anxiety disorders.

The experience of anxiety is quite complex. Symptoms include a racing heart and disturbed breathing, behavioral discomfort and nervous gesturing, cognitive distraction, and perhaps even preoccupation with unwanted thoughts. Thus, the bad news is that behavior, emotion, cognition, and physiology are all affected by the state of anxiety. **Anxiety disorders** involve symptoms of anxiety and avoidance behavior that cause clinically significant distress or impairment of functioning in social and work situations. The good news, however, is that, since the early 1980s, research on anxiety disorders has dramatically increased (Cox et al., 1995; Norton, Cox, Asmundson & Maser, 1995).

Psychologists have described the features of anxiety disorders, categorized several types of anxiety disorders (see Table 6.1), provided theories about the causes of anxiety, and developed treatments to reduce anxiety and

The anxiety disorders are all characterized by excessive feelings of anxiety and behavioral avoidance. Symptoms of anxiety can include racing heart, disturbed breathing, behavioral discomfort, nervous gesturing, cognitive distraction, and possibly preoccupation with unwanted thoughts. The person's social and work situations are often impaired.

Table 6.1   Anxiety Disorders

Anxiety Disorder	Description and Symptoms
Generalized anxiety disorder (GAD)	Excessive anxiety and worry that occur on most days for a period of six months about events and activities such as work or school; symptoms include restlessness, fatigue, difficulty concentrating, irritability, muscle tension, and sleep disturbance.
Specific phobia (sometimes called simple phobia)	Persistent, excessive, and unrealistic fear triggered by the presence of a particular situation or object.
Social phobia	Persistent and marked fear of one or more social or performance situations.
Agoraphobia	The fear of experiencing the symptoms of fear and the fear of being in places from which escape might be difficult. (It is also possible to experience agoraphobia without panic.)
Panic attack	A discrete period of intense fear or discomfort that appears abruptly and unexpectedly and peaks within ten minutes; symptoms include pounding heart, shaking, trembling, shortness of breath, sweating, abdominal distress, lightheadedness, and fear of losing control. Panic attacks can occur with or without *agoraphobia*.
Obsessive-compulsive disorder (OCD)	May be defined by either obsessive or compulsive symptoms; *obsessions* are recurrent and persistent thoughts or images that cause distress and are experienced as intrusive and inappropriate, and *compulsions* are repetitive behaviors that the person feels driven to perform.
Posttraumatic stress disorder (PTSD)	The persistent reexperiencing of a traumatic event (e.g., in images or dreams) and the avoidance of stimuli associated with the trauma; symptoms include sleep disturbances, difficulty concentrating, angry outbursts, or an exaggerated startle response.
Acute stress disorder	Resembles PTSD, but symptoms persist for at least two days but less than four weeks.

Source: DSM-IV. Reprinted with permission from *The Diagnostic and Statistical Manual of Mental Disorders,* Fourth Edition. Copyright © 1994 American Psychiatric Association.

alleviate anxiety disorders. In this chapter we survey the many facets of anxiety, looking closely at the different manifestations shown in the opening vignettes and other illustrative cases.

WHAT'S NORMAL?

Just How Mellow Should We Be?

Almost everyone can recall at least one episode of anxious arousal and fear — an experience of worry, tension, a racing heart, sweaty palms, or an upset stomach. Indeed, anxiety and fear can serve an adaptive function: Anxious arousal tells us to take special action, to fight what is threatening us or to flee. The fact that most of us experience some degree of anxiety suggests that it is a part of normal functioning.

Although anxiety and fear frequently occur together, they are sometimes differentiated. When they are, fear is said to be associated with a specific discernible object, such as fear of heights, whereas anxiety is viewed as a diffuse and vague feeling of dread or apprehension. **Fear,** then, is a reasonable and rational reaction to a genuinely alarming situation. Being afraid to stand atop a tall building in a wind storm is both reasonable and rational. In contrast, **anxiety** is uneasiness over an anticipated situation or object that typically would not produce discomfort in rational individuals (such as standing atop a book). Awareness is another factor that distinguishes between fear and anxiety. People who have fears can usually identify what they are afraid of, whereas anxious people are often not aware of the reasons for their discomfort.

Is being entirely anxiety-free normal or even desirable? If we are "super-mellow," are we better off? The answer is no. Very low levels of anxiety, like high levels, can be detrimental to performance: With few exceptions, we perform best when we experience mild levels of anxiety (see Figure 6.1).

At different points across the life span, there are common sources of fear or mild anxiety. Infants show fear and anxiety reactions to loud noises, strangers, and heights. Toddlers demonstrate normal fears and anxieties associated with separation from their primary caregiver. Children might experience anxiety in the presence of strangers whom they perceive as "bad," during severe storms, or when separated from known and comfortable settings. Preteens and teens may experience social distress tied to social events or peer evaluations. Young adults can experience distress associated with sexuality and intimacy. And for the elderly, death can be a source of anxiety. These anxiety-provoking situations are all aspects of normal development, and successful coping at any one point along the way can be helpful in successfully adjusting to later challenges. In short, stressors affect everyone, and there is nothing inherently wrong with experiencing moderate anxious arousal.

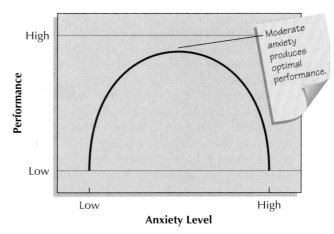

Figure 6.1   Anxiety and Performance
As you can see from this "inverted U," people perform most effectively at moderate levels of anxiety, whereas high anxiety and low anxiety result in suboptimal performance.

However, when the experience of anxiety is prolonged, intense, distressing, and unwanted, and when it interferes with the individual's life, it becomes an anxiety disorder. Common complaints linked to the anxiety disorders are persistent tension, nervousness, heart palpitations, sweating, trembling, dizziness, and problems with concentration.

One young male client, Robert, who was diagnosed with an anxiety disorder, reported the following:

"I sometimes can't talk to people because I'm busy thinking about what to say and trying to get it just right. By the time I feel like I know what I want to say, it's too late. As I think about it, I get sweaty and my mouth feels dry. I worry too much about what to say, and I end up not saying anything. Usually, I walk away and feel like I disappointed myself."

PEOPLE AND PLACES: THE INTERACTION OF PERSON AND SITUATION IN ANXIETY

Does anxiety come entirely from within the person? Is it the result of a chemical imbalance or of maladaptive thinking? Or is it caused by environmental conditions? As we have seen, areas of the brain affect and are affected by different neurotransmitter systems, some of which, in turn, play an important role in the experience of fear and anxiety. But environmental forces also activate fear and anxiety, and the way these events are interpreted by the person is important in the shaping of anxiety disorders. In the final analysis, then, a model of anxiety disorders must include biological vulnerabilities that affect arousal and activation in interaction with personal, psychological, and environmental characteristics. The *diathesis-stress model* (see Chapter 2) is one offshoot of this **interactional perspective,** which holds that individual dispositions (diathesis) and situational influences (such as stress) interact to create and maintain psychological disorders (Magnusson & Ohman, 1987).

To understand the interaction of person and situation in anxiety, consider the following scenario. Suppose your instructor randomly selects someone from your class to go to the front of the room and, as part of a demonstration of the critical role of life experiences, describe the first sexual experience that he or she can remember. When the chosen student walks to the front of the room, it is obvious that he is extremely anxious. His voice cracks, he is wringing his hands, and he starts to pace erratically. Is the anxiety the result of a **trait** — the person's tendency to behave in a certain way across various situations? Or is it a consequence of the particular situation he faces?

Before you answer, consider a second illustration. This time your instructor informs the class that someone will be randomly selected to collect the written summaries of the assigned reading. As the end of class approaches the instructor appears to have forgotten, and no one is selected; the assignments go uncollected. You then overhear someone say, "Whew, what a relief. I was terrified that I might be called on." Is the anxiety the consequence of the person's traits or the situation?

Controversy between psychologists who argue that individual traits explain variability in behavior (Cattell, 1965) and others who hold that situational influences are dominant (Mischel, 1968) has stimulated considerable research. The two examples above seem to support either the trait or situation side of the debate. In the first example, the situation was so strong, we could argue, that anyone would become anxious. In the second situation, although most people would not become anxious, we would lean toward a trait explanation to understand those who do. Experimentation has suggested that a more reasonable explanation of anxiety is that *both* personality and situational influences interact to produce the differences we observe among people.

Is there a general trait that makes people susceptible to anxiety, or are there traits that make people vulnerable to anxiety in particular situations? To study this question, Kendall (1978) used separate measures to assess (1) the general trait of anxiety and (2) anxiety traits that are specific to types of situations. The measures were compared for their ability to predict who

The Scream, by E. Munch. In anxiety, there is tension, apprehension, physiological arousal, and distress. The anxiety disorders have as their basis interfering and maladaptive anxious arousal.

would experience an increased **state** of anxiety (how anxious a person feels *right now*) in two different situations. The first situation, a test of intelligence, provided a threat that a person might feel upon being evaluated; the second situation, a car-crash film shown before subjects drove home, provided a threat of physical danger. Kendall found that the situation-specific measures were better predictors of a subject's experiencing anxiety than was the measure of the general trait of anxiety. In other words, a subject's level of anxiety produced by the situations was best predicted by measures that took the situation into account. So too with anxiety disorders: Individual predispositions and situational factors have been found to interact.

Neither traits nor situations by themselves completely explain anxiety and the anxiety disorders. Predisposing features of the person, such as genetic makeup and aspects of personality, and features of the situation interact constantly not only in the development and experience of anxiety but also in the contexts of resilience and reduced vulnerability to anxiety disorder (e.g., Sutker, Davis, Uddo & Ditta, 1995). In the following section we examine specific predisposing and situational factors that might contribute to the development of anxiety disorders.

THEORIES ABOUT ANXIETY DISORDERS

Each of the following theoretical perspectives — biological, cognitive, behavioral, and psychodynamic — has generated extensive literature on anxiety and the development of anxiety disorders. In addition to the interactional (diathesis-stress) perspective just described, we consider how these four major perspectives explain anxiety and anxiety disorders.

Biological Theories

Anxiety and the anxiety disorders are often linked to the body's physical systems of arousal. In times of heightened distress, our bodies react. When we turn a corner in our neighborhood and see the smoke of a burning home, when we receive a phone call from a hospital late in the evening, or when we see but can't stop a toddler who is wandering in a busy parking lot, our bodies do indeed react.

The autonomic nervous system carries messages between the brain and major organs of the body — the heart, stomach, and adrenal glands (see Figure 2.5). In turn, the adrenal glands release a hormone, adrenaline (or epinephrine), that activates this system. When signals of distress are legitimate, adrenaline galvanizes the individual to action. In the absence of crisis, however, excessive adrenaline can cause anxious distress.

Fright is a physical response of enormous evolutionary usefulness. Human beings and animals are born with the capacity to react to threatening situations in adaptive ways — flight or fight. Accordingly, some investigators assume that anxiety disorders represent biological malfunctions or excesses in the normal processes of reacting to the presence of danger and then calming down in its aftermath.

Causes The biological perspective considers the roles of genetic and constitutional factors, biological reactivity, endocrinological and neurotransmitter factors, and brain anatomy and functioning in the development of anxiety and anxiety disorders. These causal roles are examined in the sections that follow.

Genetic and Constitutional Factors. One argument for a biological basis of anxiety disorders comes from ideas about simple phobias (specific pathological fears). If people "learn" phobic reactions as a response to frightening objects, why aren't more people phobic about guns, bicycles, electric sockets, or other potentially harmful objects? In fact, although individual phobias could potentially develop for nearly all objects, the great majority of people with phobias are fearful of just a few items such as large animals, snakes, heights, spiders, and closed spaces. The term **selective association** has been used to account for the finding that humans are apparently more easily conditioned to some stimuli than to others (Garcia & Koelling, 1966). Based on these observations, one hypothesis holds that humans and many animals are "prepared" to learn fears as a result of evolutionary natural selection. Thus, phobias may be learned, but it may also be the case that evolution has prepared us to be especially sensitive around certain objects. Clever research illustrates this point: Monkeys can learn to be fearful of snakes by watching other monkeys show fear of snakes, but the same process does not happen when the monkeys observe other monkeys behaving fearfully around artificial flowers (Cook & Mineka, 1989). Are the monkeys somehow prepared to become phobic of some stimuli but not others?

Data from research with animals and humans buttress the notion that anxiety disorders may be present from birth. In one study, for example, researchers showed that certain animals can be bred to show the trait of "nervousness" or emotionality, believed to resemble human anxiety (e.g., Kendler, Heath, Martin & Eaves, 1986). In other research, Jerome Kagan and his colleagues at Harvard University studied toddlers and identified some as displaying social inhibition, or avoidance of interactions with others (Kagan et al., 1988; Reznick et al., 1986; Kagan, Reznick & Snidman, 1987; Kagan, Reznick & Gibbons, 1989). Seven years later, the same children were still exhibiting this behavior, so the social inhibition was found to be relatively stable. Although these particular subjects have not yet been followed for a sufficient duration, some researchers have speculated that socially inhibited youth are the ones most vulnerable to anxiety disorders in adulthood.

Studies of the genetic contributions to anxiety have increased in complexity and rigor. Most of the reported findings indicate significant, though modest, heritability. One anxiety disorder — panic disorder — has been found to occur in nearly 25 percent of close relatives of patients with panic disorder, compared with about 2 percent in a control population (Crowe, Noyes, Paul & Slymen, 1983). Research on twins also suggests the heritability of panic disorder. In one study, 31 percent of the monozygotic twin pairs, but none of the dizygotic twin pairs, were concordant for panic disorder (Torgersen, 1983).

The heritability of another anxiety disorder — generalized anxiety disorder (GAD), discussed later in this chapter — is in question, as some research has suggested little genetic transmission. In a large-scale study of more than one thousand female twin pairs, 30 percent of whom were concordant (Kendler et al., 1992a), GAD was found to be only modestly familial. Simple phobias, however, run in families to a greater extent, as examinations of close relatives (Fyer et al., 1990) and female

Everyone experiences fear at one time or another: it is a normal response to a threatening situation. One characteristic of a phobic response, however, is that the fear is irrational and disproportionate to the actual danger inherent in the situation. In this photograph, the girl manifests an extreme response, given that the dog is on the other side of a tall stone and iron fence and is also not displaying any aggressive behavior toward her.

twin pairs (Kendler et al., 1992b) have shown. Kendler and associates (1992b) also interpreted their complex statistical analyses to suggest that agoraphobia (fear of open places where escape could be difficult) has an even larger genetic component, with social phobia in between. Thus, the anxiety disorders are not at all alike in terms of the degree to which the disorders are genetically caused (Kendler et al., 1995). According to these analyses, a substantial environmental component also plays a role.

Overall, the evidence has suggested a moderate degree of family transmission of anxiety disorder. Some questions remain unresolved, however. First, is there specificity of transmission, such that social phobia is specifically related to relatives' social phobia or any other disorder? (see Fyer et al., 1993). Second, since familial patterns do not necessarily reflect genetic transmission, are there psychological factors in the family that could account for anxiety disorders? Children of parents with anxiety disorders are more likely than other children to display anxious and inhibited behavior (Biederman et al., 1990), and the relatives of children with anxiety disorders are more likely themselves to have anxiety disorders than are relatives of children with no disorder or with a different disorder (Last et al., 1991). But these children may have *learned* the anxiety. For example, a mother greatly afraid of dogs may well instill the same fear in her children. In short, although evidence supports the presence of a genetic component in at least some anxiety disorders, psychological factors are clearly implicated as well.

Biological Reactivity. Do anxious persons have a highly reactive autonomic nervous system? This popular and long-standing hypothesis has been studied using laboratory "challenge" situations in which a person is exposed to certain substances or conditions that have a temporary effect on physiology (as when sodium lactate is injected, hyperventilation is induced, or carbon dioxide is inhaled). (See the related discussion in Focus on Research, later in this chapter.) People with panic disorders are considerably more likely to have a panic attack than are normal subjects undergoing the same challenge condition (reviewed in Barlow, 1988; Gorman, Liebowitz, Fyer & Stein, 1989). Despite these reliable findings, though, the biological overreactivity hypothesis is not always confirmed. For example, people who experience panic attacks in daily life are no more likely than normal persons to have panic attacks when exposed to other kinds of stressful events in the laboratory such as pain experience or mental arithmetic (Roth et al., 1992).

Endocrinological and Neurotransmitter Factors. Years of research on numerous fluids and hormones have provided little clear evidence of a biological marker of anxiety disorders. But the discovery of receptors in the brain that are specific to benzodiazepines (the chemical compounds found in many drugs used to treat anxiety) has led researchers to speculate that there might be a naturally occurring substance in the brain that binds to these sites. Perhaps anxious people lack sufficient quantities of this substance. Meanwhile, researchers have hypothesized that an inhibitory neurotransmitter, gamma-aminobutyric acid (GABA), relates to anxiety disorders. GABA must be present at the receptor for benzodiazepines to function. At such times, then the benzodiazepines enhance the inhibiting effects of GABA. This is a promising area in neuroscience, but additional research is needed.

Among Vietnam war veterans, posttraumatic stress disorder (PTSD) has been linked to altered neuroendocrine functioning in the form of lowered plasma cortisol (Boscarino, 1996). And in obsessive-compulsive disorder (OCD), a neurotransmitter system — the serotonergic system — has been implicated. The research focus on serotonergic functioning in OCD has been greatly influenced by the apparent success of medications that block the reuptake of serotonin, such as fluoxetine (Prozac) and clomipramine (Anafranil). This process is discussed further in Chapter 8.

Brain Anatomy and Functioning. There has been considerable interest in the structure and functioning of various parts of the brain that might be implicated in anxiety disorders (Charney et al., 1992) — the frontal lobes, basal ganglia, brainstem, limbic system, and others (see Figures 2.1 and 2.2). Recent research on brain functioning in anxiety disorders has used neuroimaging techniques to observe the living brain, but these methods are not without their limitations.

Medical Therapies Manufactured tranquilizers have included barbiturates, nonbarbiturate sedatives, benzodiazepine substances, and other, newer compounds. Barbiturates are addictive and can be lethal if taken in overdose. Although nonbarbiturate sedatives such as meprobamate (Miltown) and benzodiazepines such as diazepam (Valium) have some advantages over barbiturates and sedatives, they are not free of problems. In this section we focus primarily on the benzodiazepines because they are the most widely used antianxiety drugs today.

Benzodiazepines. Benzodiazepine drugs (see Table 6.2) inhibit the central nervous system. These medications are called *anxiolytic* because they reduce anxiety, lessen nervousness, and have an overall calming effect. They are the most commonly prescribed drugs for treating psychiatric symptoms. An astonishing 9 to 10 percent of the population use benzodiazepines occasionally over a one-year period. As Gitlin (1990) has noted, this means that lots of people go around with a Valium or Xanax in their pockets or purses, ready to be used as desired.

Researchers have also estimated that between 1 percent and 2 percent of the adult population use benzodiazepines regularly for a year or more (Salzman, 1991). These drugs are widely prescribed — not just by psychiatric specialists but by family doctors and others — presumably because they are highly effective at reducing mild symptoms of anxiety, muscle tension, and insomnia. Benzodiazepines are most commonly used for specific anxiety-provoking situations, insomnia, GAD, and panic disorder.

Data have supported the effectiveness of benzodiazepines to treat panic disorder, especially alprazolam, or Xanax (Schweizer, Rickels, Weiss & Zavodnick, 1993), although other benzodiazepines may also have antipanic properties. Investigators studying the medication treatment of panic speculate that benzodiazepines may restore to the brain the proper level of neurotransmitter substances and, relatedly, reduce the panic symptoms.

How do benzodiazepines work? As we have seen, researchers (Mohler & Okada, 1977) discovered a specific receptor site on the surface of neurons to which benzodiazepines bind. The "tightness" of the binding to the receptor site is related to the clinical effects of the medication. The discovery of this specific receptor site suggested that there is a naturally occurring substance in the brain, a natural "tranquilizer." Attempts to synthesize this chemical, however, have not yet proven successful. In addition to binding to the receptor site on the surface of the neurons, benzodiazepines increase the activity of the neurotransmitter GABA, which has general inhibitory effects in the brain. People who take medications that have an inhibitory effect report feeling calmer and less agitated.

The benzodiazepine drugs vary in terms of how fast they work and how long they remain in the bloodstream (short or long half-life). Therefore, the choice of drug for a particular person depends on the need. For instance, if the medication is to be used to control anxiety for a flight-phobic person who has to take an airplane for a business trip, the appropriate drug would be one that clears the bloodstream fairly quickly (so as not to reduce the person's mental alertness over a prolonged period). The rate of elimination from the bloodstream is also related to issues of withdrawal. As discussed later in the section, the prolonged use of such medications is not recommended because of potential tolerance and dependence.

What are the side effects of benzodiazepine? Because these drugs diminish psychophysiological arousal through both sedating and tranquilizing effects, they may cause slowing of physical movements and cognitive functioning as well as drowsiness or lack of

Table 6.2 Antianxiety Drugs: Benzodiazepines

Generic Name	Brand Name
Alprazolam	Xanax
Diazepam	Valium
Lorazepam	Ativan
Flurazepam	Dalmane
Triazolam	Halcion

These medications affect the central nervous system, lessening nervousness and anxiety and producing an overall calming.

alertness to the point of interfering with learning and motor performance. When benzodiazepines are taken with alcohol, these effects may be dangerously intensified. The effects of toxicity — which occurs when dosages are too high or when the drugs are mixed with other sedatives or alcohol — include unsteadiness, sedation, and impaired psychomotor behavior. In these circumstances, the person may be at risk of cognitive impairment, falling, or reduced driving skills.

Benzodiazepines cause **tolerance,** which means that dosages need to be increased over time to produce the same effects. More important, they cause **dependence,** which is manifested as physical withdrawal symptoms that can range from such common experiences as anxiety, irritability, tremor, insomnia, and tingling sensations to the rarer but more extreme experiences of grand mal seizures, paranoia, and severe depression. More severe withdrawal symptoms are associated with longer use, higher dosages, and more abrupt withdrawal. For example, as shown in a study of abrupt discontinuation after treatment lasting for at least one year, patients taking short half-life antianxiety medications exhibited the most rapid onset and severe withdrawal symptoms. In fact, only 43 percent were able to tolerate the discontinuation for even one week before going back on the drugs, and only 38 percent of those using short half-life medications stayed off the drug for five weeks (Rickels, Schweizer, Case & Greenblatt, 1990). Perhaps this situation is due to **rebound effects,** whereby the anxiety symptoms appear to be worse when the medication is stopped.

Physicians gradually reduce the antianxiety medications their patients are taking, rather than stopping them suddenly (Abelson & Curtis, 1993). Even tapering off, however, may cause withdrawal reactions and a desire to continue taking the drugs. Investigators found that 90 percent of patients who tapered off still reported mild to moderate withdrawal symptoms, and 42 percent of the users of short half-life benzodiazepines were unwilling to remain drug-free — a figure only somewhat higher than that for long half-life drugs (Schweizer, Rickels, Case & Greenblatt, 1990).

Other Medications for Anxiety Disorders. Because anxiety symptoms often co-occur with depression, it should not be surprising that some of the antidepressants also reduce anxiety. Data have suggested that antidepressant medications such as clomipramine (Mavissakalian, Turner, Michelson & Jacobs, 1985) and the monoamine oxidase (MAO) inhibitors (Insel et al., 1983) can reduce certain anxiety symptoms.

Panic disorders, in particular, respond relatively well to antidepressants. According to one published report, 60 to 90 percent of such patients display significant improvements when treated with antidepressants (see also Ballenger, Burrows & Dupont, 1988). In some cases

of posttraumatic stress disorder, researchers have claimed that antidepressants are effective as well (Davidson et al., 1990).

Cognitive and Behavioral Theories

Cognitive Causes   The basic idea underlying cognitive approaches is that anxiety results from dysfunctional efforts to make sense of the world. We all try to understand the events and experiences that we are a part of, but those persons whose cognitive activities proceed in distorted ways may then suffer unwanted anxiety.

As discussed in Chapter 2, Ellis posited that people with unhealthy emotional lives are also victims of cognitive irrationality — they view the world based on self-defeating assumptions. To become afraid on a camping trip when you are disoriented in unfamiliar territory is rational. To be unwilling to participate in a new game for fear that you won't be the absolute best player is irrational. Irrationality is based on extreme and inflexible beliefs that require, rather than allow, behavior. The troubled person is telling himself that he "must" do this or "should" do that, or else something outrageous and catastrophic will happen.

Research reported by Deffenbacher and associates (1986) confirmed the strong relationship between irrational beliefs and anxiety. More than five hundred subjects were studied, and the patterns were similar for males and females: Holding beliefs reflecting overconcern, personal perfectionism, and catastrophizing were predictive of high levels of persistent anxiety.

Anxiety has been associated with other cognitive functions as well. For example, anxious individuals are more likely than nonanxious persons to expect future negative events (MacLeod & Byrne, 1996), to show interference on cognitive tasks (McNeil et al., 1995), and to pay selective attention to physical threat (Ehlers & Breuer, 1995).

Research on schema concepts suggests that it is the individual's memories — both the content of prior experiences and the ways in which these memories are stored — that lead to anxiety. According to Beck and Emery (1985), an "anxious schema" reflects the themes of danger, harm, or threat. For example, the perceived threat may be the possibility of negative evaluation by others or the belief that certain physical sensations are indicative of a heart attack. Any well-articulated schema carries with it a mental template for viewing the world, and this template filters what is seen and how it is processed. Accordingly, individuals with threat schemata carry a heightened sense of threat and are overly sensitive to perceptions of danger to the self.

Dog lovers, when approached by a dog, might perceive the dog in any of several ways — in terms of attractiveness, breed, grooming, or posture. But people with a dog phobia (an excessive fear of dogs) have a narrow and negative view of dogs, seeing them in terms of their size and ferocity. They never see the dog's tail wagging; they see only teeth (Landau, 1980).

Consider the following example of cognitive influences in the experience of deleterious anxiety. Sam is waiting for his mother to pick him up after school. Most of the other children have already gone home. Sam thinks to himself, "Why isn't she here?" In itself, this thought is not detrimental; many children in the same situation might ask themselves the same question. Sam also thinks to himself, "What will happen if she doesn't show up? What will I do?" He continues to think about her being late, and he continues to worry. Rather than using the time to complete a homework assignment or talk with friends or teachers, the anxious youngster engages in task-irrelevant thought. A child with a schema for rejection might erroneously conclude that his mother is late because "she doesn't love me." But a child not preoccupied with processing the world around the theme of rejection, though he may question why she is late, would be more apt to attribute his mother's lateness to traffic congestion or car trouble.

Interestingly, the self-talk that characterizes anxious individuals often takes the form of an automatic questioning process (Kendall & Ingram, 1989). This internal dialogue not only focuses on questions about their adequacy but also seems to be highly future oriented, encompassing concerns about impending situations, possibilities, and potential consequences. Anxiety, then, appears to be linked to misperceptions of environmental demand, self-focused preoccupation, and cognitive content laced with questions about the future.

Anxiety disorders have multiple causes and multiple expressions. As we discuss, several forces interact in the development of disorders of anxiety, and not all expressions of these disorders are the same. Indeed, several different types of anxiety disorder appear in contemporary classification schemes.

Behavioral Causes   Behavioral explanations of anxiety emphasize the processes involved in the acquisition of anxiety responses. Behaviorists hold that persons who suffer distressing levels of anxiety have learned to behave in an anxious manner through classical conditioning, operant conditioning, or modeling.

Recall from Chapter 2 that in *classical conditioning* an initially neutral stimulus may become aversive after it is paired with an aversive stimulus. Emotional responses, such as anxiety, are readily learned through classical conditioning. For example, a child will show an unconditioned emotional response when a loud aversive noise is delivered. The noise is the unconditioned stimulus (UCS), and the emotional response is the unconditioned response (UCR). If a dog is present at the first instance of the noise, the child, after repetition of this combination, will show the emotional response to the dog — even before the noise occurs. The dog becomes a conditioned stimulus (CS) that will produce a conditioned emotional response. Evidence has suggested that traumatic social conditioning experiences and shyness are associated with social phobic disorder: Among persons with specific social phobia, approximately half have reported traumatic conditioning experiences.

Operant conditioning involves the development of behavior patterns as a result of reinforcements. People can learn to make a response that prevents a feared situation from occurring — called an *avoidance response.* The relief of avoiding something unpleasant serves as a positive reward. Consider the case of an adolescent girl who is being teased by a group of students at a school dance. The teasing soon becomes harsh ridicule. To stop the painful ridicule, the teenager leaves the dance (an *escape response*). In the future, say behaviorists, she will be more likely to run away from peers and potential ridicule, and will perhaps leave the presence of peers sooner. Eventually, staying away becomes associated with reduced anxiety. To avoid the feared emotional pain, she avoids going to other dances; that is, she makes an avoidance response that prevents the unwanted emotions from being experienced. Many anxiety disorders are marked by behaviors that look like avoidance responses.

Modeling, also called vicarious learning or observational learning, is another behavioral explanation for anxiety responses. Unlike conditioning, modeling produces learning without personal experience with a situation or object. Thus, an individual can develop an emotional response after watching someone else experience an aversive emotional condition. Recall our earlier example. An adolescent boy who observed the adolescent girl receive the ridicule from peers might stay away from those same peers hoping to avoid similar teasing and rejection. He didn't experience the rejection directly, but he observed it and learned to avoid it from the vicarious experience.

FAMILY MATTERS
Witnessing Someone Else's Fear

As we have seen, one person can acquire abnormal behavior by observing another person's reactions and behavior patterns. Often, when we speak of familial influences on psychopathology we are referring to what is observed by the offspring within the context of the family.

What are the effects of witnessing fear? Can this question be tested? Correlational research strategies can be used, but as we note in Chapter 5, a third variable might be present and the direction of the relationship may thus be uncertain. To provide a meaningful test of the modeling hypothesis, researchers need to employ an experimental research strategy. Some children would have to be exposed to an environment in which fear was modeled by their parents, and others would have to be exposed to a similar environment but without the modeling of fear. Then, researchers would monitor and record the fearful behavior of the observing children. Ethically, this valuable test of a model of the development of fear should not be conducted — researchers can't intentionally expose children to unfavorable conditions. They can, however, test the hypothesis with nonhuman subjects.

Susan Mineka, a psychologist at Northwestern University, conducted a series of studies investigating the acquisition of fear responses among rhesus monkeys (Mineka, Davidson, Cook & Keir, 1984). Because monkeys are similar to human beings, Mineka's research with monkey families can serve as an analog for the human family. The first study found that young monkeys, raised by parents who have a fear of snakes, do not acquire this fear if they have not had any specific experience with snakes. The mere fact of being born to fearful parents — that is, without being exposed to their fearful reactions — was not sufficient to produce fear in the offspring. These data suggest that if anxiety runs in families, its cause is not simply genetic.

In the second study, offspring of wild-reared parent monkeys were allowed to observe their parents showing fear reactions to real snakes and to toy snakes. As a result of the observations, five of six young monkeys acquired an intense and persistent fear of snakes. The fear reactions were learned rapidly (after eight minutes of observation), and the acquired fear was persistent: After three months, it had not diminished significantly. Also, the fear reactions were not situation-specific. In other words, although the fear behavior was observed and displayed in one situation, the observer monkeys also displayed the fear behavior in another situation. As Mineka and her colleagues noted, these results support the hypothesis that fear can be acquired through observation. They further suggest that attention — the degree to which the observer attends to the model — may be central to the acquisition of fear.

Imagine that a child has witnessed, on multiple occasions, a parent being fearful of interacting with others. Would this experience not likely contribute to the child's own fearfulness?

Therapies Procedures such as systematic desensitization and exposure treatments are examples of behavioral therapies that have received widespread application in both research and practice. Accordingly, many studies of the treatment of specific anxiety disorders include behavioral intervention features.

Contemporary behavioral programs typically emphasize the client's cognitive functioning and are described as cognitive-behavioral.

There are several versions of cognitive-behavioral therapy (recall Chapter 2), each designed or considered appropriate for a specific disorder. Among those for anxiety disorders are cognitive therapy for anxiety (Beck & Emery, 1985), the rational-emotive therapy (RET) developed by Ellis (see Warren & Zgourides, 1991), stress inoculation therapy (Meichenbaum, 1985), and a structured version of RET known as systematic rational restructuring, or SRR (Goldfried, 1988). Beck's cognitive therapy approach is covered in detail when we describe therapy for depression (Chapter 8), and stress inoculation therapy is discussed in the chapter on stress (Chapter 11). Here, however, we examine some variations of cognitive-behavioral therapy as applied to specific anxiety disorders.

Cognitive-behavioral strategies have been found beneficial in the treatment of generalized anxiety (e.g., Borkovec & Mathews, 1988), social phobia (e.g., Heimberg, 1989), and panic disorder (e.g., Salkovskis, Jones & Clark, 1986). The outcomes of these programs are described when we discuss treatments for specific anxiety disorders.

Psychodynamic Theories

Psychodynamic explanations of anxiety are important both as a part of the history of efforts to understand the troubling experience of anxiety and as a backdrop against which to view the newer and more research-based theories. Freud defined anxiety as an unpleasant emotional state, and he differentiated three types of anxiety: objective, moral, and neurotic. In *objective anxiety,* the source of the unpleasant emotion is in the outside world, such as someone with a loaded gun. Objective anxiety is similar to what we today call fear. In *moral anxiety,* the superego is the source of the individual's sense of threats of and worry about being punished for doing or thinking something that violates an accepted standard of behavior. Finally, in *neurotic anxiety,* the threat is a sense of being overwhelmed by an uncontrollable urge to engage in some thought or behavior that might prove harmful or socially unacceptable.

Thus, neurotic anxiety, or simply "anxiety," is an unconscious concern about the consequences of expressing one's own impulses or instincts. Repression is the defense mechanism that is said to keep from awareness these instinctual urges and to reduce the unwanted arousal associated with them. Freud believed, however, that repressed material retains its arousing properties and continues to seek conscious expression. As discussed in Chapter 2, anxiety emerges from internal conflict between ego and id regarding the expression of these urges or impulses. And, according to Freud, anxiety is the core problem in all neurotic disorders (Freud, 1936).

Causes Modern psychodynamic theory relies less on *intra*personal and more on *inter*personal influences. Hence, it is not so much the id-ego-superego conflict as the early mother-child relationship that sets the stage for later interpersonal relations. Parental separation, divorce, death, and marital conflict are examples of stressful life events that can disrupt parenting and cause separation from the mother (e.g., Bowlby, 1961). Although data support the notion of separation's disruptiveness, separations themselves do not routinely lead to an identifiable anxiety disorder. Critics (e.g., Gittelman, 1986) have pointed out that many separation-anxious children have not actually experienced unwanted separation in their homes.

More generally, there is still the possibility that a person with a social-phobic anxiety disorder is reliving an early anxiety-laden mother-child relationship. Other parent-child relationships, too, may contribute to child and later adult anxiety. Although research has not yet adequately tested these contemporary psychodynamic hypotheses, many consider the psychodynamic trend toward interpersonal factors to be a positive step.

Therapies Psychodynamic therapists seek to reduce anxiety by increasing their clients' insight. Both psychoanalytic and modern psychodynamic therapists use interpretations and an analysis of the client-therapist transference to foster this insight, but there are differences. In contrast to psychoanalysts, for instance, psychodynamically oriented therapists are likely to employ briefer forms of treatment (that is, short-term psychodynamic therapy), and some have described their therapy in the form of a manual (Strupp & Binder, 1984).

Based on a comprehensive review of studies reported between 1978 and 1988 — in which the majority of the subject samples were generally depressed, anxious, or personality disordered — Svartberg and Stiles (1991) concluded that psychodynamic treatment for clients described as neurotic were effective. Time-limited psychodynamic treatment appears to be superior to no treatment and reasonably effective for certain neurotic patients. With reference to specific anxiety disorders and to outcomes of longer-term psychodynamic treatment, however, there is an unfortunate absence of data.

Humanistic and Existential Theories and Therapies

Although the person-centered approach is not likely to be used for the treatment of severe anxiety disorders, it may apply to milder anxiety-related problems. Its effectiveness in this area merits careful evaluation in outcome studies.

Unlike most other psychological therapies, **existential therapy** is not a set of approaches, strategies, or techniques. Rather, it is a philosophy (Fischer, 1991). Frankl (1960), a distinctive existential therapist, developed a method called *logotherapy*, which is geared toward clients' acceptance of their attitudes toward their symptoms. One component of Frankl's logotherapy is paradoxical intention, which focuses specifically on anxiety and phobic disorders. Frankl viewed anxiety disorders and phobic reactions as the result of excessive anticipatory anxiety, whereby the severity of the anticipation contributes to the appearance of an unwanted symptom. A **paradoxical intervention** encourages the client to intend or wish for exactly what is feared. The treatment consists of reversing the client's attitude toward the symptom (see also Efran & Caputo, 1984). According to Hunsley (1988), paradoxical therapists believe that people's attempts to solve their problems often cause them to maintain the very problems they are trying to solve. The paradoxical therapist thus provides directives that are designed to help clients give up their "problem-maintaining solutions" (p. 554).

What is the current status of paradoxical intention as a therapeutic approach? (see also Weeks & L'Abate, 1982). Although limited, research has studied the effects of paradoxical prescriptions for various problem areas, including agoraphobia, insomnia, procrastination, stress, and depression. In an evaluative review of twelve studies of paradoxical interventions, Shoham-Salomon and Rosenthal (1987) concluded that paradoxical interventions, though not significantly more effective than nonparadoxical procedures, did produce beneficial changes that were of a magnitude comparable to those produced by other therapies. Treatment-outcome research is expanding and, in the future, will likely further our understanding of this intriguing paradoxical treatment.

CLASSIFYING AND TREATING ANXIETY DISORDERS

"Neuroses Are No Longer a Psychological Problem!" If this fictional newspaper headline had appeared in the newspaper, it would have been technically accurate, because, as discussed in Chapter 4, revisions for DSM-III eliminated the classification of disorders known for so long as "neuroses." Unfortunately, as you may have suspected, the disorders themselves were not eliminated; only the names changed. The DSM system abandoned the use of terms and categories that were associated with certain theories about the causes of disorders and replaced them with classifications that refer to disorders by the features that describe them. For example, phobic neurosis is now called specific phobia or social phobia, and obsessive-compulsive neurosis became obsessive-compulsive disorder.

Anxiety disorders are among the most prevalent of all mental disorders, affecting approximately 15 percent of the population. Using facts about the situations that produce anxiety and the types of symptoms that are displayed, psychologists have subdivided the anxiety disorders. Our coverage here includes generalized anxiety disorder, phobias, panic disorder, obsessive-compulsive disorder, and posttraumatic stress disorder. In addition, symptoms of anxiety are seen in several other disorders, covered in subsequent chapters. Among the anxiety disorders, comorbidity is common; that is, a person may suffer from more than one anxiety disorder at a time or experience anxiety disorder along with other psychological disorders. For example, DiNardo and Barlow (1990) reported that 27 percent of their patients with social phobia were diagnosed with another anxiety disorder as well. Anxiety and depression also are often seen together (Kendall & Watson, 1989).

Generalized Anxiety Disorder (GAD)

Katherine, a single parent, worried about her young son's health and adjustment. She took him to the physician frequently, experienced distress when a schoolday didn't go exactly as preferred, and worried about each and every detail of his well-being. "Should he play baseball at recess? What if he gets hit with the ball? But if he doesn't play, will he be left out of his peer group?" Such questions are not unreasonable if they lead to a decision and life moves forward. Katherine's concern about baseball was only one of many, however, and she could neither decide nor get this concern out of her mind. Her worry was so intense that it undermined her performance at work. On occasion, she would tremble with uncertainty, experience shortness of breath, and have trouble swallowing. She was described by a friend as being "keyed up" and "preoccupied with this 'baseball thing.'"

In fact, Katherine had been worried about baseball for several weeks, but for several months before that she was worried about something else, and before that something else. Her intense apprehension has lasted for well more than a year. She often finds herself tossing and turning in bed, troubled both by a desire to anticipate what will happen next and by a need to relive what already happened the previous day.

Katherine's chronic, persistent anxiety — or **anxious apprehension** (Barlow, 1988) — is characteristic of **gen-eralized anxiety disorder (GAD)**. This disorder is marked by unrealistic or excessive anxiety and worry that do not appear to be linked to specific situations or external stressors. Because of this "free" quality, GAD is sometimes called *free-floating anxiety.*

Clients with GAD exhibit major emotional, physical, and cognitive symptoms. They may describe themselves as feeling tense, nervous, and on edge, as if something bad were going to happen (Deffenbacher & Suinn, 1987). Persistent tension and uneasiness dominate their emotional state. They are also likely to experience physical symptoms such as a racing heart, a sinking stomach, and signs of motor tension such as shakiness. In cases where the disorder goes untreated, health-related difficulties such as headaches, ulcerative colitis, and insomnia may occur. Other symptoms include pervasive worrying (Rapee, 1991), a bias for negative information (Bradley et al., 1995), and impeded ability to focus on the tasks at hand.

Before GAD can be diagnosed, several criteria must be met. According to DSM-IV, the excessive and unrealistic anxiety and worry must be present more days than not, for a minimum of six months; they must be experienced as difficult to control; and they must be associated with at least three of the following symptoms:

Restlessness, feeling keyed-up or on edge

Easily fatigued

Difficulty concentrating or mind going blank

Irritability

Muscle tension

Sleep disturbance (difficulty falling or staying asleep, or restless and unsatisfying sleep)

Although 98.6 percent of GAD patients meet the criterion of three out of six symptoms, a large percentage of patients with other anxiety disorders also fulfill this criterion. Raising the criterion to four or more symptoms increases diagnostic accuracy (Brown, Marten & Barlow, 1995).

Who Is Affected with GAD? Generalized anxiety disorder occurs twice as frequently among women as among men, and at a slightly higher frequency among black than nonblack groups. Estimates of the prevalence of GAD vary, but preliminary data have suggested that 4 percent of the population is affected (see Rapee, 1991). GAD occurs across cultures and in all ages, but it is likely to appear first before the age of thirty.

Causes of GAD If someone in your family has GAD, are you at greater risk of developing GAD than someone from a non-GAD family? The results of two studies (Cloninger, Martin, Clayton & Guze, 1981; Davidson et al., 1985) that have investigated family members of persons with GAD suggest that familial transmission is "negligible" (Torgersen, 1988, p. 162).

One explanation of GAD focuses on the role of worrying. The client with GAD worries excessively — and most often about social evaluation (Borkovec, 1985). Because social evaluation can happen almost anywhere and at any time, the anxiety in GAD is pervasive. But why does the client with GAD worry? One possibility is that he or she fears a loss of control, and worrying helps the client avoid this anxiety-provoking situation. By being cognitively vigilant (worrying) the GAD sufferer gains a false sense of control. Thus, the person with GAD wants to be in control and deems vigilance and cognitive preparation as necessary for attaining that control. When feeling out of control, the GAD sufferer worries further rather than acts.

Thomas Borkovec and his colleagues uncovered a phenomenon that reinforces this interpretation of GAD (e.g., Heide & Borkovec, 1984). Keep in mind that relaxation, produced through deep muscle relaxation training or through meditation, is a common procedure for reducing anxiety. But Heide and Borkovec found that, for the patient with general anxiety disorder, the process of inducing relaxation paradoxically produced anxiety and tension! This phenomenon has been called **relaxation-induced anxiety.** For example, more than half of the patients with anxiety disorder being treated with meditation reported increased tension.

Why would a procedure designed to produce relaxation bring on anxiety and tension? One possible explanation is that a state of relaxation requires a relinquishing of control, and any impending loss of control creates anxiety for the client with GAD. Thus, becoming relaxed, which can also be seen as relinquishing vigilant efforts to be in control, is a situation that can cause anxiety for some individuals with GAD.

Treating GAD   Borkovec and his colleagues have provided some interesting information about the ability of clients to learn how to manage their worrying. In one study (Borkovec, Wilkinson, Folensbee & Lerman, 1983), clients reported that worry consumed approximately 50 percent of each day and caused them major problems. During an intervention, the clients participated in a program that included (1) establishing a specified half-hour period (same place, same time) for daily worrying, (2) identifying negative thoughts and task-relevant thoughts, (3) postponing worrying until the allotted time, and (4), at the time assigned for worrying, engaging in intense worry and problem solving. After four weeks, the treated subjects showed a reduction in the percentage of time they spent worrying. In a second study (Borkovec & Costello, 1993), in which the subjects were instructed either to write down their thoughts or to worry mentally, the results were again positive. Indeed, both of these stimulus-control procedures resulted in meaningful reductions not only in the per-

centage of time subjects spent worrying but also in their reports of tension. Apparently, providing a time and place for worrying (stimulus control) reduces its pervasiveness and its detrimental effects.

As more is learned about the nature of the anxious distress that characterizes GAD, specific treatment programs can be developed and evaluated. Borkovec and Costello (1993) have reported an evaluation of three different treatments for GAD that incorporate strategies targeting specific aspects of the disorder. Because the environmental triggers for anxiety are not always obvious among clients with GAD, these treatments relied on clients' self-observation to identify the onset of the process of anxiety. The three treatments compared in the study were (1) nondirective therapy (an exploration of life experiences in a quiet and relaxed atmosphere), (2) applied relaxation, and (3) cognitive-behavioral therapy. Although all three treatments produced gains, the relaxation and cognitive-behavioral treatments were superior to the nondirective therapy. Figure 6.2 illustrates the changes that occurred in clinicians' ratings of client anxiety as a result of these three treatments.

Another interesting comparison, this time between psychological and pharmacological treatments for

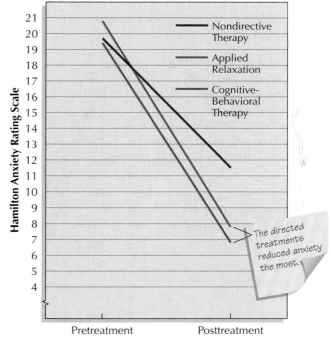

Figure 6.2   Comparing the Effectiveness of Treatments for GAD

Borkovec and Costello (1993) compared the effectiveness of three treatments for GAD, based on clinicians' ratings of their clients' level of anxiety both before and after the different therapies. Although improvement was evident among all participants, those in the applied relaxation and cognitive-behavioral treatments showed superior gains. *Source:* Borkovec & Costello (1993).

GAD, was conducted in Scotland (Power, Simpson, Swanson & Wallace, 1990). The subjects in this investigation — 101 persons diagnosed with GAD — were randomly assigned to one of several conditions: cognitive-behavioral therapy, medication, placebo, cognitive-behavioral therapy plus medication, or cognitive-behavioral therapy plus placebo. All of the treatments lasted ten weeks. Subjects receiving the cognitive-behavioral treatment were given a combination of relaxation training, exposure to feared situations, and training to modify their automatic thoughts and irrational assumptions. A wide range of measures, including both clinician assessments and subjects' self-reports, revealed that all of the cognitive-behavioral therapy conditions — especially cognitive-behavioral therapy alone and cognitive-behavioral therapy with medication (diazepam or Valium) — brought about superior outcomes. Interestingly, treatment with medication alone (a fixed low dose) was no more effective than the placebo. Figure 6.3 illustrates the differential effectiveness of these treatment approaches, based on changes in clinicians' assessments of client anxiety using a structured rating scale.

As is evident, various interventions are used for treating GAD. The cognitive methods aim to modify the ways that clients perceive and process the world and to reduce their negative thinking and worrying. Relaxation training can be effective in reducing the physiological components of GAD, but given the possibility of relax-

ation-induced anxiety, practitioners must be cautious in their use of such training. Ultimately, both research and theory have suggested that a combination of relaxation procedures and cognitive restructuring are particularly effective in reducing anxiety among patients with GAD.

Phobias

Unlike GAD, phobic disorders are tied to specific objects or situations. **Phobias** are intense, recurrent, and irrational fears that are disproportionate to the actual situation. **Claustrophobia,** the fear of closed spaces, is a common example of a phobia.

Most of us have some discomfort or fear associated with fire, disease, snakes, and being in small and enclosed places. Urban dwellers may avoid using certain segments of the mass transit system late at night out of fear, youngsters have been known to avoid walking near an abandoned "haunted house," and college students may avoid biology courses because they are uneasy about the blood that is rumored to be a part of the lab work. To a degree, these fears are rational. Phobic reactions, however, lack the rational, realistic qualities that characterize nonphobic fear. Consider Claire, a female college student.

Claire had never actually touched or even been close to a live snake, and she stated that she didn't really expect to see one in the urban envi-

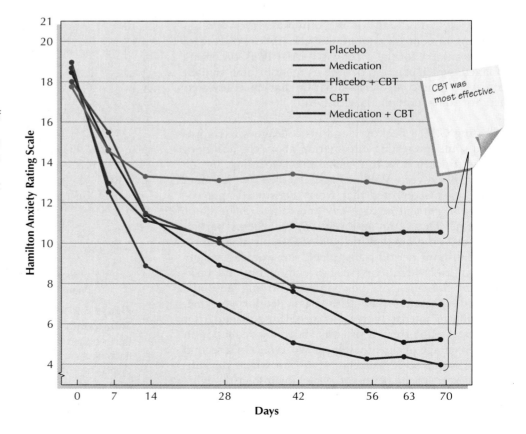

Figure 6.3 Comparing the Effectiveness of Psychological and Pharmacological Treatments for GAD
Power and associates (1990) compared the effectiveness of several treatments for GAD and reported that the greatest amount of positive changes in anxiety was produced by the cognitive-behavioral treatment (CBT) — both alone and in combination with medication.
Source: Power, Simpson, Swanson & Wallace (1990).

ronment in which she lived. Nevertheless, she was fearful, and she worried about what she would do if she ever did see a snake. Just how worried could she have been? How can a fear of snakes interfere with urban living?

The extent of Claire's fear became evident during one of her visits to the clinic; although the event was unplanned, it provided valuable information. Claire arrived for her appointment and, with her therapist, walked to a small private room. On a wall in the room, a carpenter had used a blue chalkline to mark off the area where a new one-way window would be installed. An error in the chalkline was crossed out with a black wavy line. Claire apparently perceived the wavy line as a snakelike image, became very upset, and had to leave the room. Later the therapist learned that she could not eat spaghetti, as it, too, resembled snakes and caused her great discomfort. She may not experience live snakes in her day-to-day life, but her snake phobia was bothersome nonetheless.

Phobias involve specifiable fear reactions — fear that is cued by the anticipation or presentation of a specific object, animal, or situation. Exposure to the phobic stimulus reliably provokes an anxiety response. In one study, phobic participants showed an anxious response even when the feared stimulus was masked and they did not recognize it (Ohman & Soares, 1994).

Many clients with phobias recognize that their fears are excessive and unreasonable, and they work to avoid the phobic stimulus. Symptoms such as headaches, dizziness, stomach pains, and other general physical complaints are often reported in association with phobias. Lack of self-confidence, mild depression, and doubting may also accompany phobic conditions. Fainting has been reported in phobics exposed to the feared situation or object (such as the sight of blood), but these reports are not as prevalent as once thought. Some phobias, such as those provoked by small animals, are present in early childhood, but phobic disorders typically begin in adolescence or early adulthood.

Who Is Affected with Phobias?   Phobic disorders are the most common of the anxiety disorders, with a lifetime prevalence of 14.2 percent of the population (Eaton, Dryman & Weissman, 1991). Early estimates of phobic disorder (.5 per thousand) were based on a count of the number of people receiving treatment. These estimates were probably low because they included only people whose phobias were severe enough for them to have sought and found treatment. Using current diagnostic criteria, and sampling from more than eight thousand people from noninstitutional households, Magee and associates (1996) reported lifetime prevalences of 13.3 percent for social phobia, 11.3 percent for specific

The wolf spider. It is not uncommon for people to show a preference not to interact with spiders. However, spider phobic persons show a persistent and unreasonable fear that interferes with their personal, social, and occupational functioning.

phobia, and 6.7 percent for agoraphobia. (See Table 6.3 for percentages by gender.)

Among groups of phobic clients, women generally outnumber men 2 to 1 (Eaton, Dryman & Weissman, 1991). The initial symptoms usually appear during early adolescence (at about age thirteen). The lifetime prevalence rates for African Americans (see also Neal & Turner, 1991) and Hispanics is three times higher than for whites, and this higher frequency holds across all levels of education.

Recent classification has identified three phobic disorders: specific phobia (previously known as simple phobia), social phobia, and agoraphobia.

Specific (Simple) Phobias   **Specific phobias** are pathological (excessive and unrealistic) fears of specific animals, objects, or situations. Common examples include needles, elevators, dogs, snakes, storms, blood, dentists, and tightly enclosed spaces (see Table 6.4). Although the phobic individual may be reasonably well adjusted when not directly faced by the phobic stimulus, he or she

Table 6.3   The Epidemiology of Phobias

Type	Men	Women	Total
Social phobia	11.1	15.5	13.3
Specific phobia	6.7	15.7	11.3
Agoraphobia	4.1	9.0	6.7

Source: Magee et al. (1996).

These percentages indicate the frequency of social phobia (fear of social or performance situations), specific phobia (fear of a particular object, animal, or situation), and agoraphobia (fear of being in closed places where escape might be difficult, with or without panic) in the United States.

experiences anticipatory anxiety when aware of an impending situation that could force a confrontation with the object of fear. When the phobic individual is actually exposed to the phobic stimulus, there is almost invariably an intense and immediate anxiety response. For example, the person with needle phobia who comes in contact with a needle will report sweating, difficulty breathing, and a racing heart. The phobic stimulus is viewed as powerful indeed, as this second example illustrates. In an experiment conducted in the Netherlands (de Jong, Merckelbach & Arntz, 1995), women with phobias were shown various slides of phobic stimuli and given very mild shock. Even though the researchers ensured that there was no relationship between the slides and the shock, these women nevertheless overestimated the covariation: They believed that the shock had been paired with the phobic-stimulus slides. The researchers concluded that because phobic stimuli cause such discomfort, they are routinely avoided rather than faced directly and endured.

Specific phobias are more often diagnosed in women than in men, although women's phobias do not have an adverse effect on marital quality (McLeod, 1994). Comorbidity, especially with other anxiety disorders, is high among persons with specific phobias. And among children, specific phobias may remit with time, but those that persist into adulthood generally require treatment.

Social Phobias   Being asked to perform before an audience will produce some anxiety in almost all of us. The thought of having nothing to say or of saying something inappropriate causes us to become self-conscious and nervous. These are normal, rational fears. **Social phobias,** however, involve a persistent fear of being in a social situation in which one is exposed to scrutiny by others and a related fear of acting in a way that will be

humiliating or embarrassing. As self-focus increases, so too does the anticipation of anxiety (Woody, 1996). Phobic and nonphobic individuals have comparable concerns, but the intensity, extremeness, and irrationality of the reactions of social phobics set them apart from their nonphobic counterparts (Heimberg, Liebowitz, Hope & Schneier, 1995). Examples of social phobias include irrational reactions to eating in public places, using public restrooms, or speaking in front of large groups of people. Like the specific phobic, the social phobic experiences marked anxiety when anticipating the phobic situation and therefore usually avoids it. This avoidance interferes with the person's daily routine and can potentially ruin his or her career.

Recall Uncle Bob, the corporate chief executive officer described at the outset of this chapter. Now forty-eight years old, Bob had risen from midlevel management to the top of the firm, where he was faced with the challenge of public-speaking requests, announcements to the board of directors, and reports delivered at stockholders' meetings. Bob's social phobia interfered notably with his job performance. When an opportunity for a television interview precipitated an intense anxiety reaction, he finally recognized the need to seek help. His treatment combined graduated exposure and modification of inaccurate expectancies and cognitive appraisals. Eventually he overcame the social phobia, as evidenced by his ability to appear on national television and fulfill numerous speaking requests.

Social phobia can co-occur with an avoidant personality (Tran & Chambless, 1995). It may also resemble shyness, but there are differences. Whereas shyness occurs in 40 percent of people (Zimbardo, 1977), the prevalence rate for social phobia is only about 2 percent. People are shy for a variety of possible reasons: They may prefer to do things alone, they may lack self-confidence or social skills and feel at risk for embarrassment, or they may be concerned with carefully monitoring their own behavior to ensure that they don't violate cultural rules. One characteristic that distinguishes shyness from social phobia is the degree of impairment. Shy individuals, like social phobics, may experience anxiety in social situations, but they do not become so distressed that their academic, interpersonal, or occupational functioning is impaired.

Agoraphobia   The term *agoraphobia,* which is derived from the Greek word *agora,* meaning marketplace, was originally used to refer to a pathological fear of open or public places. At present, **agoraphobia** is considered a marked fear of being alone or of being in public places where escape is difficult or where help is not readily available in the event of a panic attack that the person fears would be overwhelming. The agoraphobic might

Table 6.4 Examples of Specific Phobias

Label	Fear
Acrophobia	Heights
Aichmophobia	Pointed objects
Algophobia	Pain
Arachnophobia	Spiders
Astraphobia	Storms; thunder and lightning
Claustrophobia	Closed spaces; confinement
Gephyrophobia	Bridges
Hematophobia	Blood
Hydrophobia	Water
Nyctophobia	Darkness
Ophidiophobia	Snakes
Pyrophobia	Fire
Thanatophobia	Death
Xenophobia	Strangers

Specific phobias involve excessive fear of certain animals, objects, or situations. Reactions to the feared stimulus include sweating, difficulty breathing, racing heart, and perhaps a sense of panic. One additional example that we wouldn't want to omit is arachibutyrophobia, or the fear of peanut butter sticking to the roof of the mouth.

experience intense fear in shopping malls during the holidays, in crowds at concerts or sports events, and in tunnels, bridges, or public vehicles. Agoraphobia also occurs within an interrelated and overlapping cluster of phobias, such as a phobia for cars, buses, planes, and trains. As a result of agoraphobia, the sufferer restricts travel or requires a companion when away from home.

The primary characteristics of agoraphobia include severe phobic anxiety and phobic avoidance of the feared situations. Many clients report a prior experience during which they were restricted to their homes (Michelson, 1987). There are even reports of people who were roombound because of their fear and required a close and trusted companion to accompany them as they moved from one room to another in their own homes.

Psychological disorders may not be as obvious to the sufferer as they are to the professionals who work with them, and self-diagnoses are not typically correct. Consider the case of a 22-year-old woman who sought help from a psychologist for "self-diagnosed" agoraphobia. The woman called and made an appointment for herself, stating that, like her mother before her, she was agoraphobic and needed cognitive therapy. She lived an hour's drive from the psychologist's office and was only slightly familiar with the highways that she would have to take. She was sent a map and given a 7:00 P.M. appointment for a day later the same week.

The client arrived on time, having driven across a bridge, negotiated a crosstown traffic jam, and followed the map of relatively unfamiliar roads — all during rush hour! When she entered the office she was not visibly upset, nor was she worn out from the travel ordeal. Instead, she was enthusiastic and eager. Given her performance in getting to the appointment, does her problem fit what is known about agoraphobia?

As it turns out, the self-diagnosis was incorrect. The woman did experience extreme fears, but the therapist discovered that these were associated with her second husband's business trips. She had divorced her first husband because of his repeated extramarital affairs, which took place when he was out of town on business. Now, plagued by fears, she sought help for "agoraphobia," but she was actually suffering from fears that her second husband might also be unfaithful.

The mean age of onset of agoraphobia is approximately twenty-eight years (Chambless, 1982). Cultural and gender factors may also play a role in the incidence of this disorder. In the United States and Western Europe, for example, the ratio of female to male agoraphobics is 4 to 1, whereas in Japan there are no gender differences (Shioiri et al., 1996). And in India, where agoraphobics are predominately male, women are not expected to venture out of the home by themselves, so a woman who is homebound is not considered abnormal.

Although 50 percent of agoraphobics are not diagnosed with another disorder, the remaining half do receive at least one other secondary diagnosis (Barlow, 1985). In the United States, depression and panic disorder often accompany agoraphobia; in Japan, however, comorbidity is low (Shioiri et al., 1996).

Causes of Phobias Phobic disorders have been explained in several ways, according to the various models of psychopathology (Merckelbach, de Jong, Muris & van den Hout, 1996). For example, the psychodynamic explanation of phobia is that the anxiety expressed toward the phobic object or situation is displacement of an internal anxiety. From this perspective, then, a snake phobia is more than a fear of snakes — it represents some other underlying anxiety. The phobia is seen as having arisen because the patient lacks understanding

about this underlying anxiety and uses displacement as a defense mechanism.

Some evidence of a genetic predisposition for phobic disorder exists (Torgersen, 1983). First, regarding incidence of behaviors that are relevant to the study of social phobia (such as eating in public, being observed at work), monozygotic twins are more alike than dizygotic twins. Second, parents of children who are diagnosed with a childhood phobic disorder are themselves more likely to meet the criteria for this disorder. Although these findings suggest a familial pattern, they do not tell us whether the pattern is genetic or learned.

Contemporary explanations of phobias also rely heavily on the notion of faulty learning. According to this model, the person with a phobia has learned a maladaptive anxious avoidance as a way to attempt to cope with distressing situations. As we have seen, conditioning and modeling explanations for phobias are supported by research.

Consistent with the general trend in psychopathology, cognitive influences, too, have become increasingly relevant to an understanding of phobias. For example, researchers have suggested that social phobias develop from a heightened attention to or focus on the self (Heimberg, 1989). This excessive self-focus, in turn, can lead to thoughts that interfere with task performance and intensify emotional reactions (Hope, Gansler & Heimberg, 1989). It isn't surprising, therefore, that persons with social phobias are characterized by fear of negative evaluation and self-deprecation (Turner & Beidel, 1989).

One model of the development of agoraphobia specifically includes cognitive and behavioral processes (Craske & Barlow, 1988; Mathews, 1985). The features of this model are as follows.

1. *Anticipation of panic.* A "fear of fear," also seen in panic patients, is an aspect of agoraphobia.

2. *Anxiety sensitivity.* **Anxiety sensitivity** is the belief that anxiety experiences have negative implications. Persons with agoraphobia hold biased emotional expectations; they expect unwanted emotional arousal, are overly alert to cues that signal anxiety, and are highly motivated to avoid anxiety-provoking stimuli (Reiss, Peterson, Gursky & McNally, 1986).

3. *Uncontrollability.* In persons with agoraphobia, an unwillingness to approach or to try to master stressful situations is accompanied by a sense of loss of control.

The same model suggests that, after an anxiety experience, the agoraphobic might misattribute his or her acute arousal to threats in the environment. This misattribution of internal physiological events (changes in breathing, heart rate) may then result in further negative processing. For example, one study (Marks et al., 1991) reported that catastrophic thoughts are directly related to threat-relevant anxiety-provoking symptoms. With distorted thinking, the person becomes increasingly dependent and non-self-reliant and continues to avoid anxiety-provoking situations. This avoidance is negatively reinforcing and thus maintains the pattern.

Another approach to agoraphobia, the family systems model, looks for sources of this disorder in a dysfunctional marriage or family interaction pattern. For example, agoraphobia may be a way for a controlling spouse to manipulate his or her mate. In accordance with the theory, couples in which one spouse is agoraphobic would be expected to experience more psychological misery than other couples. Research comparing couples with and without an agoraphobic partner, however, has not found meaningful differences either in the ways that such couples describe their marriages or in the degree of marital distress (Arrindell & Emmelkamp, 1986).

Treating Phobias Specific phobias have been successfully treated with **systematic desensitization,** which alleviates anxiety by pairing relaxation with imagined (or real) scenes involving the client in anxiety-producing situations. Systematic desensitization is a behavior therapy procedure developed at Temple University by Joseph Wolpe (1959, 1982), who has described it as a counter-

Relaxation can counter the tension and distress linked to anxiety disorders, and relaxation training involves having clients visualize calm and tranquil settings, such as this view of Banff National Park, Alberta.

conditioning process. In counterconditioning, old maladaptive associations are replaced by newer, more adaptive ones.

Favorable results from early research evaluations (see Davison, 1968) led to the generally accepted conclusion that desensitization is an effective treatment approach. After more than twenty-five years of research, the bulk of the evidence has confirmed that desensitization is effective in treating phobic disorders. More recent research is attempting to identify the essential ingredients in the therapy. Researchers agree that it works but actively debate how and why it does so.

Generally, the most effective procedures for the treatment of phobias rely on systematic exposure to the actual feared situation (Borkovec, 1982). **Exposure —** which involves placing the client in the context of the feared situation — seems to be an important ingredient in a successful outcome. Note that exposure can be either maximal or gradual. In **flooding,** the client experiences maximum anxiety; in gradual exposure, the anxiety-producing situations are presented in a hierarchy of progressively greater intensity.

How does exposure work? Does it cause subjects to habituate to the feared stimuli? Are the stimuli actually counterconditioned? The psychological process underlying the positive changes is not clear. For example, the pairing of fear cues along a hierarchy while the patient is relaxed has been considered the essence of systematic desensitization, yet the same effects have been produced without the relaxation component, without the hierarchy, and without the pairing of hierarchy items with relaxation (Kazdin & Wilcoxon, 1976). What, then, is taking place during the desensitization process that could account for these therapeutic gains?

Perhaps cognitive factors can help explain the positive outcomes produced by desensitization. It could be, when clients are exposed to feared situations in the form of imagery, that this **imaginal exposure** is the active treatment ingredient. Another possibility has to do with clients' cognitive expectancy for gains: If clients are provided with a convincing rationale and an enthusiastic and confident therapist, then their expectancy for success could be heightened and the eventual outcome positively influenced. Behavioral exposure treatments, both flooding and desensitization, do provide evidence of clients' newly acquired knowledge and ability to manage anxiety. As the clients come to experience and accept the ability to cope with once-feared situations, self-efficacy increases and remains with the clients as part of their newly acquired sense of mastery over prior phobia. To paraphrase a familiar maxim: Nothing succeeds like a belief in success.

Cognitive-behavioral treatments for agoraphobia have also been described and empirically evaluated. One treatment program (Michelson, Mavissakalian & Marchione, 1985) focused on teaching clients how to change their habitual anxiety and avoidance. An important component of this program was self-directed, graduated, prolonged exposure in real situations. Clients entered phobic situations and remained there until their anxiety and discomfort decreased. Outcomes were quite favorable in terms of improved measures of cognition, psychophysiology, and behavior. For instance, at the end of the treatment program subjects were able to complete a one-mile walk during which they encountered a crowded urban environment and a congested bus stop.

In vivo practice, which involves exposure in the real environment, has emerged as an important component in the treatment of agoraphobia. In one study, Lloyd Williams of Lehigh University (Williams & Rappaport, 1983) compared subjects receiving in vivo practice alone to subjects receiving in vivo practice along with cognitive training. The two groups showed comparable improvements, but neither method was consistently found to be superior to the other. Reviewers (e.g., Michelson, 1987) have questioned the degree to which the addition of cognitive procedures could be expected to have beneficial effects, given the brief nature of the cognitive training that was provided in this study. Indeed, further research is needed to investigate more fully the important question of the benefits of exposure treatments plus cognitive training.

Panic Disorder

The term *panic* originated with Pan, the Greek god of fertility, who was said to be a happy but ugly man: He had the horns, ears, and legs of a goat. When in a bad mood, he enjoyed scaring away unwary travelers — hence the word *panic* (Ley, 1987). Experiences that may

Useful distress-reducing strategies sometimes can be as simple as this teddy bear technique used by one state trooper. The donated toys in this photo are used by state police officers to soothe children at the scenes of accidents.

well be called panic have been around for a long time, but it was not until recently that consistencies across research findings and clinical practice led to the identification of panic disorder as a separate type of anxiety disorder.

A person suffering from **panic disorder** is vulnerable to frequent **panic attacks** — discrete instances of fear or discomfort. Panic attacks are unexpected in the sense that they do *not* occur in a predictable context or immediately before a situation that almost always causes anxiety reactions; they are *not* the result of evaluation of the person or of scrutiny by others. In these ways, panic disorder is differentiated from specific phobia and social phobia, which do involve situational determinants.

To warrant a diagnosis of panic disorder, according to DSM-IV, a person must experience recurrent unexpected panic attacks, with one or more attacks being followed by a period of at least a month during which the person has a persistent concern about (1) having another attack, (2) the implications of the attack or its consequences, or (3) changing behavior related to the attack.

Panic attacks, and the associated symptoms, involve a sudden onset of intense apprehension that usually lasts for a period of minutes and only rarely lasts as long as an hour (see Barlow, Brown & Craske, 1994). To meet the criteria of DSM-IV for a panic attack, sufferers must report at least four associated symptoms from the list in Table 6.5. In most cases that have been studied, persons with panic disorder have developed some of the symptoms of agoraphobia. As a result, a person can be diagnosed as having panic disorder with or without agoraphobia. Without proper treatment, the prognosis is poor: Over a one-year follow-up, nearly all panic patients (92 percent) continue to experience panic attacks (Ehlers, 1995).

Who Is Affected with Panic Disorder? Panic attacks occur in panic disorder, but they are also sometimes reported in patients with phobias, substance-abuse disorder, and mild depression. In one study, researchers interviewed 1,306 residents of San Antonio, Texas, and found that 5.65 percent reported panic attacks, but only 3.8 percent met criteria for panic disorder (Katerndahl & Realini, 1993). Panic disorder in women typically occurs at more than twice the frequency of panic disorder in men. However, research conducted in Australia determined that, in terms of symptoms, age of onset, cognition, and duration, there are no significant differences between male and female patients with panic attacks (Oei, Wanstall & Evans, 1990).

According to a second study, lifetime prevalence rates for panic disorder are lower among both African Americans and Hispanics than among whites (Eaton, Dryman & Weissman, 1991). However, a third study (Horwath, Johnson & Hornig, 1993) suggests a comparable prevalence among African Americans and whites (1.4 percent and 1.2 percent, respectively). Two addi-

Table 6.5   Symptoms Experienced in Panic Attacks

1. Palpitations, pounding heart, or accelerated heart rate

2. Sweating

3. Trembling or shaking

4. Sensations of shortness of breath or smothering

5. Feeling of choking

6. Chest pain or discomfort

7. Nausea or abdominal distress

8. Feeling dizzy, unsteady, lightheaded, or faint

9. Derealization (feelings of unreality) or depersonalization (feeling detached from oneself)

10. Fear of losing control or going crazy

11. Fear of dying

12. Paresthesias (numbness or tingling sensations)

13. Chills or hot flashes

Source: Adapted from DSM-IV. Reprinted with permission from *The Diagnostic and Statistical Manual of Mental Disorders*, Fourth Edition. Copyright © 1994 American Psychiatric Association.

A diagnosis of panic (a discrete period of intense fear or discomfort) requires that at least four of these symptoms be present, develop abruptly, and reach a peak within 10 minutes.

tional studies suggest that age of onset and symptom severity for African Americans and whites are comparable (Friedman & Paradis, 1991; Horwath, Johnson & Hornig, 1993).

Among 300 college students studied, 5% reported panic symptoms (Craske & Krueger, 1990). But a sample of homeless individuals showed symptoms at 8 times the rate of regular residents of the same region (Koegel, Burnam & Farr, 1988).

FOCUS ON RESEARCH

Are Panic Attacks Biological?

Are panic attacks specifically associated with biological vulnerabilities? Proponents of a biological model cite studies showing that panic patients responded distinctively to a variety of "challenges" they faced in the laboratory. Other proponents of a biological model have

suggested that patients with panic disorder have a dysfunctional heart. Let's look at some of the data.

Biological explanations of panic have been based, in part, on research in which volunteers, through various means, are induced to experience marked changes in physiological activity. Recall that the challenge situation can be produced in any of several ways: by injecting sodium lactate, inducing hyperventilation, or having the patient inhale carbon dioxide. One early study (Pitts & McClure, 1967) examined the effects of lactate infusion on subjects with panic disorder as compared to subjects with no history of panic. In the former group, the lactate infusion caused a panic attack; in the latter group, it was not as likely to do so. Indeed, researchers have typically reported that 65 to 100 percent of patients with panic disorder respond with panic attacks, whereas control subjects rarely do so (Dager, Cowley & Dunner, 1987). Still other studies, which compare the frequency of panic attack for patients with panic disorder to that of patients with other disorders, have suggested that the response to sodium lactate is relatively specific to panic disorder. Biologically minded scholars have suggested that injecting lactate into the blood begins a chain of chemical reactions that trigger a panic attack.

Upon reexamining the original Pitts and McClure data, Ley (1986) found that lactate infusion produced uncomfortable symptoms for *both* categories of subjects, but that the panic patients were more sensitive and catastrophic in their interpretation of the discomfort. Whereas a person in the control group might sense and report "arousal" or "discomfort," the panic patient might report "having a heart attack." The lactate prompted reactions in all subjects, but it was the nature of the individual interpretations of the physiological reactions that determined whether panic was reported.

How best to further study this phenomenon? Researchers have been able to discover how panic sufferers interpret their bodily arousal by examining responses to hyperventilation. When subjects breathe at a rate of sixty breaths per minute for three minutes, they experience hyperventilation, which in turn produces physiological reactions similar to those that occur naturally in panic attacks (Clark, Salkovskis & Chalkey, 1985). Using hyperventilation as a challenge situation, researchers have manipulated and studied the effects of subjects' expectancies on the experience of panic attack. For example, Jurgen Margraf and Anke Ehlers (1989), at Philipps University in West Germany, studied reactions to hyperventilation in patients with panic disorder and in normals. To test the influence of the subjects' expectancies, the researchers manipulated the instructions. Some subjects (panic patients and normals) were told that they were participating in a "biological panic attack test," whereas others were told that it was a "fast-paced breathing task." The results revealed that the level of panic sufferers' anxiety and arousal depended on what they were told. Among these patients, the expectation that they were taking a panic test produced physiological reactions and self-reported elevations in anxiety and arousal. In contrast, the manipulation of the instructions and expectations had no effect on the responses of the normal subjects. This outcome would not have been expected if the patients' reactions were due to a biological vulnerability (Margraf & Ehlers, 1989).

In addition to subjects' reported emotional reactions, research has examined the physiological changes that occur when panic attacks are induced in patients with panic disorder and in normals. According to several reports, the biochemical and psychophysiological changes that occurred were similar for both patients and controls, although self-reported anxiety and arousal were higher for the panic patients (Margraf & Ehlers, 1989). This finding is *in*consistent with the hypothesis that panic results from an underlying biological vulnerability.

Additional evidence has recently suggested that the biological model of panic disorder may be incorrect. Carter, Hollon, Carson, and Shelton (1995), of Vanderbilt University, had each panic patient inhale carbon dioxide either with or without an accompanying safe person who was chosen by the patient. The researchers surmised that if the panic process were solely biological in nature, a person's presence should have a minimal effect. In fact, their findings indicate that panic patients without a safe person reported greater distress, more catastrophic cognition, and more physiological arousal than did panic patients who had a safe person present (see Figure 6.4).

Does this mean that physiological reactions are unimportant in panic disorder? Probably not. A study of agoraphobic clients by Ley (1985) reported that they experienced physiological symptoms *before* they felt fear; thus, it was the sharp and sudden onset of somatic arousal problems, for which the clients could identify no cause, that gave rise to their reported panic. Stated differently, sudden changes in breathing and heart rate frightened the subjects.

In short, panic is a fear response to unexpected and unexplained somatic events (Clark, 1989). It is as if changes in bodily functions that can't be easily explained (such as a sudden change in breathing) prompt the panic sufferer to anticipate the worst and to experience fear and panic (see also McNally & Eke, 1996). According to Clark (1986), misinterpretation of the arousal cues is causally linked to panic. Thus, although persons with panic attacks in their history and those without such a history both experience similar arousal (as a result of, say, hyperventilation), only the subjects with panic disorder view these physiological cues as indications that a catastrophe is forthcoming. Somatic complaints precede the fear, and the somatic changes are frightening to the panic sufferer (see Figure 6.5). In general, research has supported the idea that panic attacks result from the client's fear response to certain bodily sensations.

A more natural kind of "challenge" might be a dysfunctional heart. Researchers have speculated that the experience of panic attack is related to a cardiac condition called mitral valve prolapse (MVP), in which the mitral valve bows back into the left atrium during functioning. To examine the relationship of MVP and panic, researchers have studied the frequency of MVP among panic patients, the frequency of panic among MVP patients, and the frequency of MVP among other (nonpanic) patients and normals. Margraf and Ehlers (1989) reviewed seventeen studies of the prevalence of MVP in panic patients and found that the average was only 18 percent. Normal persons, too, have a similar percentage of MVP. Studies of MVP patients have failed to find elevated frequencies of panic, but studies of patients with other disorders (GAD, eating disorders, bipolar disorder) have found elevated frequencies of panic. Although these data are inconsistent, they suggest that MVP does not appear to be a strong precursor of panic attack.

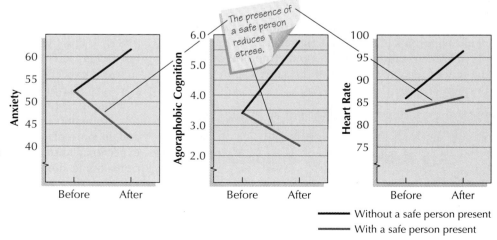

Figure 6.4 Psychological Factors in Panic Disorder

Carter and associates (1995) measured emotional, cognitive, and physiological reactions of panic patients both with and without the presence of a safe person, and before and after a laboratory "challenge." Their results indicated that the panic process is not solely biological in nature. *Source:* Carter, Hollon, Carson & Shelton (1995).

The presence of a safe person reduces stress.

—— Without a safe person present
—— With a safe person present

Figure 6.5 A Model of Panic Disorder

"Challenges," such as lactate infusion and hyperventilation, produce changes in bodily functions and physiological arousal. The aroused individual then interprets these physical changes. The person's interpretation of the arousal is what determines the likelihood of panic. Persons with panic disorder interpret such physiological changes as indications that a catastrophe is imminent; normal persons do not.

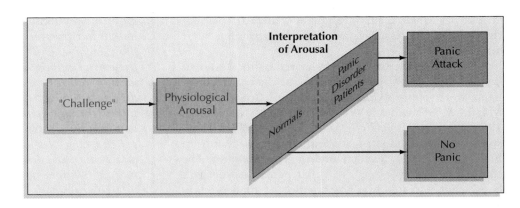

Having symptoms caused by an irregular heart (as in MVP) can prompt health concerns in anyone. It should not be surprising that some people — including patients with panic disorder — will interpret the symptoms as potentially catastrophic. MVP may not be specific to panic, but its symptoms can nevertheless prompt a panic patient to interpret the experience in a manner that causes a panic attack.

The panic patients' reactivity is certainly physical, and it may be inherited; however, it is also controlled by what the person is thinking. Cognitive activity focused on threat or danger is therefore an important element of high levels of arousal. Thoughts of losing control when physiological arousal or change is experienced may be especially implicated in panic attacks. What gives rise to these attacks, then, is not so much the challenge itself as the person's misperceptions about the bodily reactions to that challenge.

Why do some patients with panic disorder develop avoidance behavior (as in agoraphobia), whereas others do not? (Clum & Knowles, 1991). The data have indicated that cognitive-expectational variables, such as the general expectation of a panic attack in a certain situation, are related to subsequent avoidance behavior. Ratings of anxiety and worry about panic increase the day after an unpredicted panic (Craske, Glover & DeCola, 1995). Also, those who do develop the avoidance are more likely to be depressed and more likely to be women. As we noted earlier, panic disorder and agoraphobia often co-occur. Evidence to date has suggested that agoraphobic avoidance develops from a panic sufferer's fear of panic in certain situations (Clum & Knowles, 1991).

Treating Panic Disorder Consider the following transcript of a therapist's session with a person suffering from panic disorder. In this case, the therapist helped to change the patient's view of his symptoms — to alter his misappraisal of his bodily sensations.

THERAPIST: Tell me a little about the attack. How did it begin?

PATIENT: I'm not sure. I was just sitting there and listening to the sermon, when all of a sudden I couldn't catch my breath, my heart began to pound, and I just had to get out.

THERAPIST: Why did you *have* to get out? What would have happened if you had stayed?

PATIENT: I don't know; I probably would have suffocated.

THERAPIST: That's a pretty strong word, suffocated. How likely do you really think it was that you would have suffocated — have you ever suffocated before?

PATIENT: Of course not. I guess I wouldn't actually have suffocated, it was just so frightening to not be able to catch my breath.

THERAPIST: Again, look at the probability of what you are saying. Do you mean that you weren't breathing?

PATIENT: No . . . I don't know . . . I suppose I was just puffing a lot.

THERAPIST: And even if you were puffing a lot, what's the worst that could happen?

PATIENT: Well, I know I wouldn't suffocate and I have never passed out before . . . I guess it just felt uncomfortable. (Rapee & Barlow, 1989, p. 252)

To date, the findings regarding therapies for panic disorder are quite encouraging. Consistent with the defining features of panic, many of the effective programs combine cognitive and behavioral treatments. In particular, interventions focus on teaching relaxation skills in conjunction with more rational evaluations of bodily arousal, as when clients are taught that heart palpitations are not necessarily proof of an impending heart attack.

At a conference in 1991 sponsored by the National Institutes of Health, several studies of the treatment of panic were reported and reviewed (e.g., Craske, 1991; Magraf & Schneider, 1991; Michelson & Marchione, 1989; Ost, 1991; Salkovskis & Clark, 1991). These studies were conducted in four different countries: England, Germany, Sweden, and the United States. The cumulative evidence suggested that panic disorder can be effectively treated by a combination of applied relaxation, exposure to feared situations, and modification of cognitive misinterpretations. Initially, the panic sufferers who participated in this study exhibited significant impairment of their quality of life. But the treatment provided relief from this impairment, and this relief was shown to have been maintained for six months (Telch et al., 1995). Longer (twenty-four month) follow-up data are also fairly supportive (Brown & Barlow, 1995). Clark's (1991) summary stated that 75 percent to 95 percent of clients become panic-free after three months of cognitive-behavioral treatment.

Obsessive-Compulsive Disorder (OCD)

Have you ever found yourself humming an inane commercial jingle — a tune that stays in your mind longer than you want it to? In a small way, this experience is like an obsession. **Obsessions** are persistent and unwanted thoughts, ideas, or images that a person does not intentionally produce. Rather, the unwanted thoughts are perceived as invading the person's thinking. The recurring thoughts are troublesome, unnecessary, and distracting, and the person tries to be rid of them.

Do you know someone who mows the lawn each week on the same day and in exactly the same direction? Or someone who insists that a catastrophe will happen if the toilet paper roll dispenses sheets from over the top rather than from under the bottom? These examples suggest the discipline, orderliness, precision, and rigidity that characterize **compulsions**. For a behavior pattern to be truly indicative of a compulsive disorder, however, the person must feel compelled or driven to act a certain way, and the drive to perform the action must feel alien to the person. Compulsive behavior is more than a display of singlemindedness or persistence; it is more than an energetic concern about occupational success or a commitment to excellence in leisure pursuits (de Silva & Rachman, 1992; Reed, 1985). True compulsions are not ends in themselves, but avoidance behaviors. The following case illustrates maladaptive obsessional thinking.

Robin, a middle-aged, successful banker, sought psychological help pending a career decision. She was considering several options: taking a promotion at another firm where she would receive more money immediately; waiting for a promotion within her present bank, which could provide even more income; or setting out on her own in an entrepreneurial opportunity that could make her either wealthy or broke. As she put it, "I'm not sure what to do and I thought it would help to have someone to talk it through with." On the surface, the problem was simply a career choice. In reality, Robin was experiencing obsessional thinking; the related stress and strain was affecting her physical well-being, her marital relationship, and her on-the-job functioning.

The ruminative pattern was apparent in Robin's sleep habits. Bedtime was typically around 11 or 11:30 P.M., and her alarm was set for 7 A.M. Regularly, around 4 A.M., Robin would awaken to a rush of ideas about how to proceed and what the possible consequences of her job choices might be. (Insel and associates [1982] found that obsessive-compulsive patients sleep poorly, with many awakenings.) Robin wanted to be asleep, but could not return to sleep without taking medication. She wanted to rest, but was unable to turn off her seemingly constant focus on what to do. Although troubled by the ruminating, she behaved as if she believed that by thinking about her situation more she could understand all the options completely and thereby be guaranteed of making the one and only correct choice.

Spending time planning and pursuing financial success is altogether rational, and making a major career change without some forethought, planning, and discussion is short-sighted and impulsive. But struggling with the options for months and months, even beyond the time when the options expire, is unwise, fruitless, and self-defeating. Robin, to her own distress, could not let go of the intricacies of each and every possibility. Here is an example of her obsessional thoughts:

"If I change jobs, then the new personnel department is going to do a background check, I just know it." When questioned about the problem with a background check, Robin replied, "I once smoked marijuana and lived with a group of political radicals while in college." She went on to add that she "knew she would be fired if they were to find out." She was convinced that as part of a background check, potential employers would contact former acquaintances who might relish the opportunity to dredge up some of her old antics. She proceeded to confess to "stealing food from the college cafeteria, being intimate with her boyfriend in the football stadium, and turning in someone else's paper for a 'crib' course." She recalled the names of people who were involved in these events and felt certain that "things would become common knowledge and lead to the end of her career." The problem lay not so much in the fact or fallacy of her college-day behavior, or even in the reality of her vulnerability, but

rather in her being overcome with and troubled by nearly continuous thinking about what to do. Her spouse did not want to hear about it any longer, and her supervisor at work had noticed her preoccupation. Moreover, she herself no longer wanted to think about it, but she simply could not clear her mind.

Other examples come from clients in our clinical practices. For instance, one man was so driven by a fear of electromagnetic rays that he wouldn't use electric appliances, a woman was afraid that she would forget how to talk, and a young adult was obsessed with the thought that she had killed some creature on the open road and felt compelled to drive back to the spot repeatedly to check.

Features of OCD   The content and form of normal and abnormal obsessions are similar. Abnormal obsessions, however, are more frequent, more intense, and of longer duration; they produce more discomfort; and they are more associated with compulsions than are normal obsessions (Salkovskis & Harrison, 1984). Is heightened emotional intensity possibly an important aspect of the intrusive quality of obsessions? (Clark & de Silva, 1985). The studies to date, using nonclinical cases, support this hypothesis and suggest that reducing the frequency of any negative cognition will increase the client's ability to dismiss such thoughts.

Descriptions of clients with obsessive-compulsive disorder typically highlight either the obsessive or the compulsive aspect of the disorder. Obsessives are described as worriers and doubters, as people with excessive insecurity and a persistent focus on details who nevertheless miss or never get to the point. They feel that

danger is imminent and that they need to be in control. Their excessive concern with the nearly endless number of possibilities leaves family and friends tired and unwilling to listen to any more "talk." Obsessive qualities are often revealed in sorting tasks. For example, when asked to sort potatoes into two pots, one for small potatoes and another for large potatoes, most people will perform the task with reasonable speed and accuracy. The obsessive, in contrast, will ponder the size of each potato, create several intermediate-size categories, and labor excessively over the few potatoes that don't seem to fit exactly into any of these categories. In short, their obsessions interfere with performance of the task. Researchers Persons and Foa (1984) found that obsessive-compulsive patients — compared to other patients who did not meet the criteria for obsessive-compulsive disorder — made finer distinctions among items in a card-sorting task.

What thoughts typically persist and dominate obsessive thinking? The most frequently reported clinical obsessions have to do with fears of being contaminated. Approximately 55 percent of obsessive-compulsive clients, in both England (Rachman & Hodgson, 1980) and India (Akhtar et al., 1975), described obsessions about contamination and dirt. One woman feared that she was contaminated whenever she came in contact with her hometown or certain objects associated with it (Foa & Steketee, 1984). Her obsession with contamination prevented the woman from visiting her family. Another example is provided by Howard Hughes, who made a fortune in the aircraft and movie industries but spent the later part of his life captured by his obsessive-compulsive disorder. He developed an obsession with germs that led him to have his windows and doors sealed. He used paper towels to insulate his touching of objects or people. Even his food had to be wrapped in tissue. Overcome by his inordinate efforts to be germ-free, he was alone and miserable. Interestingly, despite such efforts, he lived out his later years in what others would label a filthy environment.

Although compulsions appear to be purposeful behaviors, they are essentially nonfunctional and ritualistic. The compulsion reported most often is checking, which results from pathologic doubt linked to repeated attempts to "make sure" (see Table 6.6). An obsessive-compulsive person might fear that the front door was left unlocked and so repeatedly return to the door to check that it is locked. Other common examples of compulsive checking include repetitions intended to determine that gas and water taps are shut and lights and appliances are off. Still other cases highlight a need for organization — checking that kitchen utensils are properly aligned, cupboard contents are correctly arranged, and closets are organized in the "right" order. Some common rituals include repeatedly putting clothes on and taking them off; hoarding items such as newspapers, mail, or boxes; and repeating certain actions such as going through a doorway.

Compulsive hand washing is linked to a preoccupation with dirt and contamination and may be tinged with reports of disgust regarding urine, feces, or semen. Compulsive hand washers avoid public restrooms, doorknobs, shaking hands, and money, all of which are viewed as contaminated. Patients may wash as many as eighty times a day, often causing damage to their skin.

Who Is Affected with OCD?

How common are obsessive-compulsive disorders? An early estimate of the prevalence of OCD was .05 percent — low enough for it to be considered rare — but more recent epidemiologic studies tell a different story. Data from Myers and associates (1984) have indicated a six-month prevalence of 1 percent to 2 percent. According to Regier and associates (1990), the lifetime prevalence for obsessive-compulsive disorder is 2 percent to 3 percent, or about 4 million persons out of the total population (see also Emmelkamp, 1990). Regarding comorbidity, Crino and Andrews (1996) reported high lifetime comorbidity rates with other anxiety disorders: 54 percent with panic/agoraphobia, and 31 percent with GAD. OCD also co-occurs with depression in between 20 percent and 66 percent of patients (Edelmann, 1992).

Whites are more likely than African Americans or Hispanics to be diagnosed with OCD (Karno & Golding, 1991). And unlike many of the other anxiety disorders, OCD affects a fairly equal number of males and females.

The usual age of onset for OCD is early adulthood (ages eighteen to twenty-four), although OCD can occur in childhood (Rapoport, 1986). If OCD is untreated, the

---

Table 6.6 Sample of People with Compulsive Checking Habits

Mr. A., a 41-year-old cafe manager, suffered pronounced feelings of inadequacy and worries about his business. Among several compulsive symptoms was his excessive checking of locks and switches, both at home and at work.

Mr. N., a 25-year-old clerk, suffered from compulsive doubts and fears. He could not retire to bed without checking all the household bolts, locks, and switches, a task that took at least an hour each night.

Mrs. F., a 28-year-old typist, suffered from an increasingly obsessional fear regarding the spread of illicit drug abuse. She found it necessary to compulsively check with hospitals, police, and newspapers to assure herself that no local drug-related catastrophe had recently occurred.

Mr. D., an 18-year-old student, suffered from continual obsessional ruminations about the possibility that he had murdered two elderly neighbors. He compulsively checked the whereabouts of the "victims" to assure himself that they were unharmed.

Source: Reed (1985).

Compulsions are ritualistic and repetitive behavior patterns. Compulsive checking, which is manifested in many ways, can interfere with social, academic, and occupational functioning. The checking is not functional but, rather, serves to prevent or postpone other actions.

---

problems associated with it become increasingly severe and detrimental to functioning.

Causes of OCD

Each of the theoretical models we describe in this book addresses the causes of OCD. A biological explanation is illustrated in certain positron emission tomography (PET) scan studies, which have found elevated cerebral glucose metabolism in the brain, especially the frontal regions, of persons suffering from an obsessive-compulsive anxiety disorder (e.g., see Baxter et al., 1989). Researchers have speculated that the obsessions and compulsions reflect fixed-action patterns that are "wired" into the brain (for reasons having evolutionary significance). When stressful conditions stimulate the person's perception of danger, these fixed action patterns may be inappropriately activated. Normal individuals cease performing an action when their senses tell them that the action has been completed, whereas, according to the theory just described, persons with OCD become helpless victims of their repeating patterns (see Rapoport, 1989).

Are obsessions and compulsions inherited? Using the family history method, which involves interviews about the presence or absence of psychological disorder in clients' families, researchers have reported a prevalence for obsessive-compulsive disorder of approximately 1 percent to 10 percent in first-degree relatives (see Carey & Gottesman, 1981). And in studies of twins, researchers have found a concordance rate for OCD of 50 percent to 60 percent (e.g., Hoaker & Schnurr, 1980). However, since the large majority of twins studied were reared together, and since imitation and identification occur as monozygotic and dizygotic twins develop alongside one another, the twins shared much more than genes. Indeed, they experienced similar environments, similar families, and similar learning histories. Accordingly, although more data are needed, OCD is not currently considered a genetic disorder; the learning and cognitive influences are viewed as more plausible explanations.

Treating OCD   The impatient friend of an obsessive person advises, "Just don't think about it." But the person's unwanted thoughts persist nonetheless. The spouse of a compulsive checker shouts, "We're going to be late. Stop that damn checking." But the checking continues. The experience of nonprofessionals is that obsessive-compulsive disorder is very resistant to direct instructions. Indeed, obsessive patients have thought and thought about matters that they feel are major, and they frequently do not respond to the suggestions of others. Compulsive persons, too, are said to be resistant to advice. What techniques might be helpful for persons with OCD?

One technique involves psychosurgery. Between 1962 and 1986, 465 psychiatric patients underwent this procedure at Massachusetts General Hospital. Most had a form of **cingulotomy,** or interruption of the cingulate bundles of the brain performed by passing current through precisely placed electrodes. A long-term follow-up was conducted on 33 of those patients for whom no previous treatment had worked (Jenike et al., 1991). Outcomes were modest: The investigators argued that at least 25 percent of the patients were substantially improved with few side effects.

Psychosurgical procedures are used in only a limited number of cases; medication remains the most widespread biological treatment for OCD. Research suggests success with the antidepressant known as clomipramine, or Anafranil (DeVeaugh-Geiss, Landau & Katz, 1989). Clomipramine achieves its effects by altering the activity of serotonin, a neurotransmitter chemical in the brain. Several studies provide evidence that this medication is more effective than a placebo (e.g., Leonard & Rapoport, 1989).

Because the reduction of obsessive-compulsive symptoms is associated with changes in serotonin, some have suggested that obsessive-compulsive disorder may be linked to abnormal levels of serotonin. Remember,

however, that the relationship between the medication and treatment effectiveness does not confirm the initial cause of the symptoms or disorder. Another medication—sertraline—has also been found to be helpful with OCD patients (Griest et al., 1995a), but clomipramine is even more effective (Griest et al., 1995b).

The improvement rates when medications are used alone have indicated an average decrease in symptoms of 28 percent to 34 percent, leading investigators Turner and Beidel (1988) to recommend that the most effective strategy might be a combination of medication and behavior therapy.

Support groups for patients with OCD and their families can also be helpful. Particularly when family members learn more about OCD, they are able to be more supportive of the improvements that can result from individual therapy. One support group for OCD uses a slogan with a double message: "Every member counts."

Behavioral techniques have also been used to remediate obsessive-compulsive disorder. These techniques have changed somewhat over the years. Early behavioral interventions were typically either (1) exposure procedures to reduce anxiety or (2) blocking or punishing procedures to decrease the obsessions or compulsions (Foa & Steketee, 1984). The more contemporary approach involves exposure and response prevention, whereby the client is placed in the real feared situation and the compulsive behaviors are blocked (Turner & Beidel, 1988). For instance, the treatment of a client who fears contamination from contact with the bodily fluids of other people would include gradual exposure to these very substances. In an initial session the client might be required to hold the doorknob of a public restroom. In later sessions the client would come in contact with other people's sweat and touch toilet seats. Though not pleasant to think about, exposure of this nature has been found effective in the treatment of people with obsessive-compulsive disorder.

According to Marks (1981), behavior therapy produces the largest changes in rituals such as compulsive cleaning or checking, but does not achieve changes in obsessive thoughts quite as readily. Response prevention may be temporarily distressing to compulsive checkers; but when required *not* to check, they are often surprised that nothing happens. In actual clinical practice, response prevention translates into allowing compulsive checkers to check once — to make one check that the door is locked or one check to determine that the oven is turned off.

Current research suggests that, with the implementation of behavioral strategies, obsessive-compulsive disorder is more treatable than once thought. Interestingly, behavioral treatment of OCD not only reduces unwanted obsessions and compulsions but also has been reported to effect changes in brain activity (caudate

The immensely wealthy and successful Howard Hughes, here at midlife, later became an extreme recluse with severe obsessive-compulsive disorder. Having moved to an apartment where he would not interact with others except through his staff, he displayed many obsessive-compulsive symptoms. For example, he would not touch an object or person without a tissue: he often sat naked in a chair with tissues between himself and the seat.

glucose metabolism) (Schwartz et al., 1996). Yet despite this improved picture of treatment outcomes, there are instances of treatment failure, particularly among clients who have obsessive-compulsive disorder complicated by interfering depression.

Cognitive-behavioral methods have also been used effectively to treat patients with obsessive-compulsive disorder. Generally, cognitive-behavioral therapy strives to correct faulty thinking and beliefs through self-monitoring, creating real experiences to test dysfunctional beliefs, and rehearsing new thinking styles and skills. Given that the basic schema for obsessives is one of threat and danger — including the belief that the threat is real and the danger is imminent — helping clients to test their dysfunctional beliefs and to reappraise situations more realistically may be particularly useful. In essence, then, a successful cognitive-behavioral therapy may require reeducating clients to steer away from catastrophic, overgeneralized conclusions that are based on limited and overvalued events. When applied to Dutch

patients diagnosed with OCD, one such intervention was found to reduce anxiety, improve scores on a measure of obsessive-compulsive behavior, and reduce depression (Emmelkamp, Visser & Hoekstra, 1988).

A prominent behavioral explanation is learned avoidance. An initially neutral event, closely linked in time with discomfort and fear, eventually produces discomfort itself. Escape and avoidance behaviors are then undertaken to reduce the anxiety.

Cognitive hypotheses about the development of obsessive-compulsive disorder suggest that the behavior pattern is acquired through experiences with the environment and through maladaptive cognitive processing of these experiences. In short, an obsessive-compulsive person has learned to engage in certain cognitive-processing patterns that are ineffective and repetitive, yet serve to satisfy the internal need to be mentally vigilant and attentive (e.g., McFall & Wollersheim, 1979).

Once the front door is checked and found to be locked, why does the compulsive checker return to check it yet again? Researchers have speculated that compulsive checkers may check repeatedly because they forgot that they have already checked. Do compulsive checkers have a poorer memory for prior actions than noncheckers? Or can a difficulty in **reality monitoring,** or distinguishing real from imagined events (Johnson, 1985), help explain compulsive checking? When compulsive checkers are confronted with the question "Did I lock the front door?" they may be biased toward believing that the memory of checking the door was only imagined. And if they have difficulty recalling whether an action has actually taken place, they will engage in checking behavior. Yet one study of OCD patients found no support for a deficit in reality monitoring (Brown et al., 1994).

According to psychodynamic theory, underlying conflicts not in the client's awareness are the causal agent in OCD. A woman who compulsively checks her baby's food is seen as conflicted about the child: She does not know whether she is happy to be a mother or terribly bothered by the many new inconveniences. Concealing a wish to harm the child — a wish she cannot express directly, for it would be morally unacceptable and shameful to her — she checks carefully and regularly to make sure that the child's food is not contaminated. According to psychodynamic theorists, she is checking to be certain that she has not accidentally contaminated the food herself.

Posttraumatic Stress Disorder (PTSD)

Psychologically speaking, what is similar about the experiences of rape, torture, military combat, airplane crash, earthquake, a disastrous fire, and the collapse of a large building? Each can cause severe trauma. **Posttraumatic stress disorder (PTSD)** is a cluster of psychological symptoms that can follow a psychologically distressing event. Stressors that produce PTSD would produce marked distress in almost anyone, and they are outside the range of normal, common stressors such as chronic illness, marital separation, or business failure. Although not all disasters result in psychopathology (Rubonis & Bickman, 1991) — indeed, some people seem invulnerable to the distress — certain individuals do develop severe disorders related to trauma.

The typical symptoms of PTSD occur following a recognizable stressor (traumatic event) that has involved intense fear and horror. They include reexperiencing of the traumatic event, persistent avoidance of any reminders of the event, numbing of general responsiveness, and increased arousal. To warrant a diagnosis of PTSD, a client must experience these symptoms for at least one month. **Acute stress disorder,** a recent addition to DSM, refers to PTSD-like reactions that persist for at least two days but less than four weeks.

Clients with PTSD may have recollections or recurring dreams of the event, feelings or thoughts that the event is recurring, or a sense of reliving the experience against their will. They also actively avoid any reminders, real or symbolic, of the trauma. For instance, a man who was tortured in a log cabin thereafter stayed away from rooms with wood paneling, and women raped in elevators report that they have to take the stairs to their office.

Serious psychological problems are also related to traumatic military histories such as this one.

Mr. K., a 43-year-old Vietnam combat veteran, was the second-oldest child from a working-class family dominated by a harsh father. Although he did well in school, he dropped out at the age of seventeen to join the Navy. He earned a GED and married the first woman he ever dated. After leaving the Navy he had difficulty finding suitable employment, so he joined the Army. Then, after six years in the Army, he was sent to Vietnam as a staff sergeant in charge of a vehicle maintenance team.

His tour of duty was punctuated with frequent traumatic combat experiences, including the death of a close friend, shooting an enemy soldier at close range, witnessing the death of a workmate, finding the crew of a tank burned inside its cockpit, and seeing the demolition of an enemy village. The death of his close friend by sniper fire in a "safe" area was particularly traumatic — Mr. K. felt personally responsible.

When he returned from Vietnam, his marriage ended in divorce and he began drinking heavily. He received several military disciplinary actions, usually for being AWOL (absent without leave). After three years, he again volunteered for military duty. Following this discharge, his functioning again deteriorated. He had two short marriages, lived in five different states, and worked a long series of various

jobs. He began having Vietnam-related nightmares and flashbacks. (Adapted from a case history reported by Foy et al., 1987)

Who Is Affected with PTSD? According to recent epidemiological data (Kessler et al., 1995), the estimated lifetime prevalence of PTSD is 7.8 percent. The trauma most commonly associated with posttraumatic stress disorder among men is combat exposure, which is rated the most upsetting trauma for 28.8 percent of men with PTSD. Among women, rape is most commonly associated with PTSD; it is rated most upsetting by 29.9 percent of women with PTSD. Fifty-eight percent of battered women also report high rates of PTSD (Astin, Ogland-Hand, Coleman & Foy, 1995).

Military-combat-produced PTSD is not new; writers described its occurrence after the Civil War, World Wars I and II, and the Korean War. Early reference was made to "shell shock" or "battle fatigue" to refer to an array of symptoms seen in men whose military experience included exposure to artillery fire, attack, and bombings. In the United States, the Centers for Disease Control conducted a four-year epidemiological study of approximately 15,000 Vietnam veterans and reported that 15 percent suffered from combat-related PTSD since their discharge (Roberts, 1988). African American veterans of Vietnam experienced a somewhat higher frequency of symptoms of postwar stress (Neal & Turner, 1991). Although more research is needed, some data support the idea that it is not the war zone itself but the person's perception of threat that contributes to eventual PTSD (King, King, Gudanowski & Vreven, 1995).

For victims of rape and torture that involve willful acts by others, the experience of PTSD can be especially tormenting (Steketee & Foa, 1987). Catastrophes such as aircraft disasters, tornadoes, and fires can also produce widespread and serious emotional problems. An aircraft crash at a major airport can cause emotional stress reactions in any of the surviving passengers or flight crew as well as in witnesses to the crash, in members of the families or work associates waiting for passengers to arrive, and in the airport employees who are asked to assist in the emergency services and crash cleanup. Only some of those involved actually suffer diagnosed PTSD or acute stress disorder, but case reports nevertheless indicate widespread distress. After mobilizing energies and working cooperatively during the immediate time of the emergency, people soon tire. When the event has passed and is no longer the topic of conversation, people report loss of sleep, a reliving of the experience, and fearful dreams.

Understanding PTSD Although traumatic military experience is only one cause of post traumatic stress disorder, it serves as a prototype for the many factors that contribute to the onset of PTSD. For example, the combat situation involves exposure to injury and death, abusive violence, and perceived threat (King, King, Gudanowski & Vreven, 1995). The many close calls that are experienced produce increased feelings of threat and anxiety, and the emotional impact can be worsened when members of the combat group do not allow these feelings to be expressed. The soldier is expected not only to kill, but to kill repeatedly. Add to these feelings and experiences the fact that most people do not have a desire to kill others and are never really prepared for it when they do have to kill someone, and the result is a set of circumstances that can make even the trained combat soldier vulnerable to psychological distress.

Using the Minnesota Multiphasic Personality Inventory (MMPI) test responses of one hundred Vietnam combat inpatients and one hundred nondistressed contemporaries, Fairbank, McCaffrey and Keane (1985) found that the two groups could be reliably distinguished. Features of MMPI-identified disorder that separated the two groups included anxiety, depression, and social isolation. The scales of the MMPI that tap emotional adjustment confirmed the traumatic stress reactions of the combat inpatients.

Researchers have suggested that it was not the combat duty but, rather, some aspects of the soldier's premilitary adjustment that accounted for the maladjustments. Foy and his colleagues (1984) provided data to address this question. In a study involving forty-three Vietnam veterans who had sought psychological help, Foy and colleagues applied PTSD criteria and divided the veterans into PTSD-positive and PTSD-negative groups. They then examined the relative contribution of premilitary adjustment, military adjustment, and extent of combat exposure to the development of PTSD. Their findings supported the notion of a trauma-produced psychopathology. Combat exposure and, to a lesser degree, military adjustment were significantly related to PTSD symptoms. Premilitary adjustment was not significantly related to PTSD. These results are consistent with other studies of veterans (e.g., Roberts et al., 1982) and with the findings of studies of natural disaster victims. The data underscore the primacy of traumatic exposure among the causal factors in PTSD.

PTSD veterans also suffer losses in **social support** — the network of individuals with whom a person has social or personal contact within a certain time, providing especially the support related to emotional well-being (Keane et al., 1985). This finding corroborates the suggestion that PTSD veterans need access to others as part of their struggle for adjustment, preferably other veterans who had undergone similar ordeals.

In one case not related to military combat, Hispanic and African American students were exposed to a sniper attack at an elementary school as classes were being dismissed; one child was killed and thirteen people were injured (Pynoos et al., 1987). Interviews one month after the incident indicated that the children who were closest to the attack had the greatest number of PTSD symptoms; those on the playground when the gunfire began experienced more symptoms than children in classrooms, on the way home, or on vacation. The children's symptoms included reported nightmares, fears of the event's recurring, intrusive images, and reduced interest in typical pleasures.

PTSD, like the other anxiety disorders, affects physiological, behavioral, and cognitive response systems. Accordingly, an understanding of its causes requires a consideration of each of these areas. Physiologically, responses in PTSD resemble biochemical changes that occur as a result of inescapable and unavoidable shock (Van der Kolk, Boyd, Crystal & Greenburg, 1984). Exposure to trauma causes exaggerated neurotransmitter activity and is related to hypersensitivity, lively startle responses, and aggression. In short, biological factors are no doubt involved. Yet a solely biological model fails

These Hispanic refugees are being housed in temporary shelters in the aftermath of a devastating earthquake. Several of these victims will later experience the cluster of psychological symptoms known as post-traumatic stress disorder.

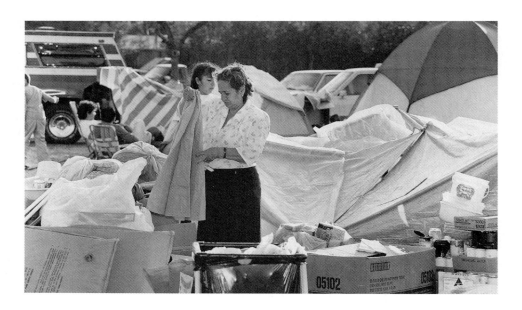

Victims of the fighting in the former Yugoslavia. Not all victims die in war. This woman and child are homeless after having fled their residence. Psychological disorders such as PTSD can be an untoward outcome of life under conditions of war.

to explain why some people suffer PTSD in response to trauma and others do not, and also why some PTSD reactions occur long after exposure to the trauma.

Behavioral explanations of PTSD emphasize conditioning. Persons exposed to traumatic events are seen as having become conditioned to show distress to a variety of neutral stimuli that were present at the time of the trauma. Other explanations rely on cognitive concepts regarding information processing. Cognitive information-processing models identify biased processing of threat cues (Bryant & Harvey, 1995; McNally, Amir & Lipke, 1996) and invoke the notions of controllability and predictability. With time, life provides a certain degree of control and predictiveness. After trauma, however, cues prompt reliving the experience — a state that is perceived as far less controllable and predictable, and thus parallels chronic fear. Still other explanations can have psychodynamic overtones. Finally, psychodynamic cognitive explanations, such as that described by Horowitz (1986), refer to the distress experienced in PTSD as a result of the person's inability to integrate the traumatic event into his or her sense of self. Since rethinking the traumatic event overwhelms the individual's coping mechanisms, this "numbing" of the individual is seen as defensive and protective.

Together, the various perspectives suggest that exaggerated neurotransmitter activity, conditioned reactions to trauma stimuli, perceptions of uncontrol and unpredictability, and inability to integrate the trauma characterize the onset of PTSD. Interestingly, despite the diversity of these explanatory systems, psychologists have reached the consensus that further exposure to the trauma along with some form of corrective therapy can alleviate the long-term negative consequences of PTSD.

Treating PTSD   The psychological treatment of clients with posttraumatic stress disorder has generated interest and enthusiasm. The research literature is young, however, because PTSD did not appear as an identifiable form of disorder until 1980. An early and practical first step was Operation Outreach, a program designed specifically for Vietnam combat veterans. At Operation Outreach, any veteran can find a needed outlet for his or her emotional distress.

Early treatment efforts for PTSD include cognitive-behavioral and psychodynamic approaches. In a cognitive-behavior treatment reported by Keane and Kaloupek (1982), a PTSD veteran client was asked to repeatedly recall all of the details of the trauma that he could remember and focus on the event for extended periods of time. This repeated exposure resulted in meaningful reductions in his subjective and physiological arousal. In contrast, a particular psychodynamic treatment (Horowitz, 1989) begins with the establishment of a relationship and aims at increasing the clients' degree of self-awareness, through recognizing and accepting the traumatic event and the thoughts associated with it. Although the language used by Horowitz differs from that used by Keane and Kaloupek, both approaches focused on reducing trauma-linked distress through repeated exposure to thoughts and feelings tied to the trauma.

A similar approach has proved effective in the management of PTSD among rape victims. Edna Foa and her colleagues (1991) reported that a cognitive-behavioral treatment (as measured at the end of treatment) and a prolonged exposure treatment (at follow-up) were more effective in reducing PTSD symptoms than either an alternate treatment or a wait-list control condition.

These findings are promising, as are more recent outcomes (Foa, Hearst-Ikeda & Perry, 1995; Echeburua, deCorral, Sarasua & Zubizarreta, 1996). But a related fact also deserves mention: Many of the rape victims who were offered treatment declined to participate. This may be related to rape victims' tendency to avoid confrontation of the rape memory, a tendency that is symptomatic of PTSD. In addition, some rape victims may not show symptoms of any disorder or may not see themselves as patients in need of treatment. Nevertheless, cognitive-behavioral and exposure treatments seem to be helpful to PTSD sufferers, whether veterans or rape victims.

What Lies Ahead?

The anxiety disorders are common and persistent. They represent the largest domain of psychological disorder in the United States and other countries, and they persist if untreated. Accordingly, the anxiety disorders have been and are likely to remain an active topic for research.

Each model of psychopathology has addressed anxiety and the anxiety disorders. From the early psychodynamic explanations of "neuroses" to the more recent emphasis on biological and cognitive features of specific anxiety disorders, anxiety has played a central role in theories of psychological abnormality. Traditionally, these models were seen as rivals; more recent trends evidence a movement toward theoretical consolidation of biological, behavioral, and cognitive approaches (Barlow, 1988).

The sheer bulk of contemporary research on the anxiety disorders is impressive (Cox et al., 1995; Norton, Cox, Asmundson & Maser, 1995); indeed, two new research journals specifically address studies of these disorders. Because the journals are not restricted to advocates of any single theory, readers are likely to see research on all aspects and features of the disorders. Unfortunately, most studies of the causes of anxiety disorders have failed to use prospective longitudinal designs. Until we are able to follow children from youth into adulthood, we cannot adequately confront questions of causality.

Yet the anxiety disorders provide ample opportunity for optimism — because many of these disorders are treatable. Indeed, a number of psychological therapies are at their best when directed to the amelioration of anxious distress. Current emphasis has been on the development of treatment programs for specific anxiety disorders. Given the high frequency of comorbidity, however, the treatment guidebooks designed to address aspects of co-occurring conditions will require sophisticated modifications in the years to come. Medications are also effective in reducing anxiety, but the potential for unwanted side effects remains a concern. Perhaps future researchers will pay increased attention to the proper therapeutic use of combinations of medications and psychological therapy.

KEY TERMS

acute stress disorder (187)
agoraphobia (174)
anxiety (161)
anxious apprehension (170)
anxiety disorders (160)
anxiety sensitivity (176)
cingulotomy (185)
claustrophobia (172)
compulsions (182)
dependence (166)

existential therapy (169)
exposure (177)
fear (161)
flooding (177)
generalized anxiety disorder (GAD) (170)
imaginal exposure (177)
interactional perspective (162)
in vivo practice (177)
obsessions (182)

panic attacks (178)
panic disorder (178)
paradoxical intervention (169)
phobias (172)
posttraumatic stress disorder (PTSD) (186)
reality monitoring (186)
rebound effects (166)
relaxation-induced anxiety (171)

selective association (163)
social phobias (174)
social support (188)
specific phobias (173)
state (162)
systematic desensitization (176)
tolerance (166)
trait (162)

SUMMARY

Psychological disorders associated with pervasive and persistent anxiety are referred to as *anxiety disorders*. *Fear* is considered a reasonable and rational reaction to a genuinely alarming situation, whereas *anxiety* is viewed as a diffuse and vague feeling of apprehension.

People and Places: The Interaction of Person and Situation in Anxiety

The *interactional perspective* holds that individual dispositions and situational influences interact in a causal way in the development and maintenance of psychological disorders. An offshoot of this perspective, the diathesis-stress model, attributes disorders to interactions between predisposing forces and environmental contexts. An enduring personality feature, or *trait*, may contribute to an anxious state.

Theories About Anxiety Disorders

Biological contributions (diatheses) to the anxiety disorders include genetic and constitutional factors, biological reactivity, endocrinological and neurotransmitter factors, and brain anatomy and functioning. Cognitive approaches emphasize the phenomenon of *anxious apprehension*, whereas behavioral explanations refer to learning processes such as classical conditioning. Psychodynamic explanations of anxiety differentiate among *objective anxiety, moral anxiety,* and *neurotic anxiety.*

Classifying and Treating Anxiety Disorders

Generalized anxiety disorder (GAD) is marked by unrealistic or excessive anxiety and worry that do not appear to be linked to specific situations or external stressors. In contrast, *phobias* are tied to specific objects or situations. They involve intense, recurrent, and irrational fears that are disproportionate to the actual circumstances. *Specific phobias* are pathological fears of specific animals, objects, or situations. *Social phobias* involve a persistent fear of being in a social situation in which one is exposed to scrutiny by others and a related fear of acting in a way that will be humiliating or embarrassing. Clients with *agoraphobia* have a marked fear of being alone or being in public places where escape might be difficult or where help may not be readily available. Persons with an anxiety disorder may experience *anxiety sensitivity,* the belief that anxiety experiences have negative implications.

A person suffering from *panic disorder* is vulnerable to frequent *panic attacks* — discrete instances of fear or discomfort. Panic attacks are unexpected; they are not the result of evaluation of the person or of scrutiny by others. *Obsessive-compulsive disorder (OCD)* involves both obsessions and compulsions. *Obsessions* are persistent thoughts, ideas, or images that the person does not want, does not intentionally produce, and perceives as invading his or her thinking. *Compulsions* are ritualistic and repetitive behavior patterns.

Stress can contribute to anxiety disorders. *Posttraumatic stress disorder (PTSD)* is a cluster of psychological symptoms that can follow a psychologically distressing event. *Acute stress disorder* involves PTSD-like reactions that persist for at least two days but less than four weeks.

Existential therapy is more a philosophy than a specific approach to treatment, yet one strategy, *paradoxical intervention,* is associated with the existential approach. Medications (such as benzodiazepines) can be effective, but there are concerns about *tolerance* and, more important, about *dependence.* There are also concerns about *rebound effects,* whereby the anxiety symptoms appear to be worse when the medication is stopped.

The current trend in the treatment of anxiety disorders is toward the development of psychological therapies that are specific for each type of disorder. *Systematic desensitization* has been used to treat phobias, as have *exposure* and *flooding* procedures. With the increased use of cognitive strategies, use of *imaginal exposure* is becoming more widespread. Many of the contemporary treatments for anxiety disorders combine cognitive and behavioral approaches, such as treatments for GAD that address client expectational and apprehensive concerns during *in vivo exposure.*

Cognitive-behavioral treatments have also been used effectively with PTSD and are recommended for panic disorder. Although psychosurgical treatments have been used to treat OCD, current practice emphasizes both cognitive-behavioral and medication treatments.

Consider the following...

Suppose that you are a member of the community school board and the principal has asked you whether or not to require all 7th- and 8th-graders to participate in the school's speech contest. Participation involves writing and presenting a three-minute speech before the entire student body. Given what you now know, do you think that all students should be required to participate? Or can some students request to be excluded, and, if so, would distressing anxiety be a valid excuse? If everyone does participate, could the experience prove helpful to fearful students? What would you recommend?

Suppose that a friend of yours, when confronted with anxious arousal, becomes distressed and opts to avoid the stressful situation altogether. You know that medications can ease the symptoms of some anxiety disorders and that, for others, psychological interventions requiring exposure to the feared situation are effective in increasing active coping and reducing unwanted anxiety. Should your friend be forced to face his fears? Should mental health clinics, often funded by government resources, be required to provide exposure treatments to your friend, or are there reasons for which alternative approaches to treatment should be offered?

CHAPTER 7

Somatoform and Dissociative Disorders

Those among us . . .

■ Although you haven't babysat for years, you agree to help out your Aunt Estelle, whose scheduled sitter just called in sick. Estelle is a 45-year-old accountant, proud of her two young children but not of her health: She complains regularly about such a variety of ailments that people no longer listen and no longer sympathize. That night, while helping the children brush their teeth before bed, you notice that Estelle's bathroom cabinet and adjacent shelves are full of medicines — some old and some new. Nosily, you look them over and recognize that they were prescribed by different doctors, for different problems. In addition, some have passed their expiration date.

■ Scanning the newspaper as you sip your morning coffee, you read about Ben and his son Roberto, now seven, who was only five years old when his father "disappeared." The article states that after seventeen years on the police force and nineteen years of marriage, Ben did not show up for work one day, nor did he return home. It turns out that, unknown to others, Ben had driven more than six hundred miles into the next state, taken a job as a security guard, and rented a room alone in a boarding house. Ben has no knowledge or memory of his family.

■ Your pen pal in China has won a prestigious fellowship to a British university. Chang is thoroughly excited about having been selected. The day before his departure, however, he becomes paralyzed from the neck down. Multiple visits to several hospitals fail to identify any physical reason for Chang's paralysis. Soon after the option to take the fellowship expires, the paralysis lifts and he regains full mobility.

■ You read in your psychology textbook about a rise in the number of cases of multiple personality (dissociative identity) disorder. An acquaintance claims to have multiple personalities, and says that the disorder is the result of child sexual abuse. Can her claim be true?

Do some individuals really need a cabinet full of medicines to deal with their many ailments, or might they benefit more from psychological counseling?

Is it really possible to so forget your past that you have no recollection of your family at all?

Do we sometimes respond physically — for example, by becoming paralyzed — to psychological stress?

Is sexual abuse a cause of multiple personality (dissociative identity) disorder? And is it true that there are more cases today than ever before?

The disorders discussed in Chapter 6, on anxiety disorders, were conceptually linked: They all involved the experience of unwanted and distressing anxiety. Anxiety and other distressing emotions can be a part of several other disorders as well, including the somatoform and dissociative disorders — the disorders to be considered in this chapter. However, in contrast to people with anxiety disorders, those with somatoform and dissociative disorders frequently do not report feeling underlying, unwanted emotions and psychological conflicts.

SOMATOFORM DISORDERS

The mind and the body interact in many ways, both adaptively and maladaptively. When mind-body interactions are maladaptive, a somatoform disorder may result. **Somatoform disorders** involve physical symptoms for which, based on current knowledge of physical functioning, there is no adequate explanation. (*Soma* means body, and *somatoform* means "bodylike.") One patient with a somatoform disorder may report being blind yet, according to medical tests, have normally functioning eyes. Other patients may display hypochondriacal behavior — that is, be continually concerned that they have any number of serious illnesses. Somatoform disorders include somatization disorder, hypochondriasis, and conversion disorder (see Table 7.1).

Somatization Disorder

A person with **somatization disorder** may not claim to have a specific physical disability, but usually displays a long history of complaints regarding physical ailments, beginning before the age of thirty. Although the pattern of complaints can vary, it often involves pain, gastrointestinal functions, sexual or reproductive issues, or the senses. Indeed, the DSM requires a specific number of complaints in each of these areas for a diagnosis of somatoform disorder: four pain symptoms, two gastrointestinal symptoms, one sexual symptom, and one pseudoneurologic symptom (see Table 7.1). The symptoms must be severe enough both to warrant medical attention or treatment and to impair social and occupational functioning.

The medical history of patients with somatization disorder is often long and complex, and the patient typically sees multiple physicians for the variety of somatic complaints, as was the case with Estelle in the opening vignette. The search for relief takes the patient from physician to physician and involves describing symptoms in a vague, exaggerated, or dramatic fashion. In a study of persons engaging in "doctor shopping" behavior, Sato and associates (1995) found a high frequency of somatization disorder. Although the symptoms seem to be a genuine source of concern for the sufferer, they do not fit together neatly into an identifiable category of physical disorder.

Aside from health-related concerns, the patient with somatization disorder often reports personal distress in the form of anxiety and depression (Brown, Golding & Smith, 1990). In addition, as Rost, Akins, Brown, and Smith (1992) reported, 60 percent of somatization patients have at least one personality disorder (see Chapter 13). Occupational and marital difficulties are also common among these patients — a finding that is not surprising, as their persistent physical complaints strain interpersonal relationships.

■ *Carla grew up in a small town where everyone, it seemed, knew everyone else. Throughout grade school, she was known as "the frail child." Her parents ran a general store, where the majority of townspeople purchased most of their supplies. As was sometimes necessary during tough economic times, her parents would barter their goods for needed services. From an early age, often as a trade or favor to her father, the local physician frequently checked Carla's health. Her parents, who were not well educated, were easily enamored of medical terminology and expertise.*

At age thirty-one, Carla was diagnosed with somatization disorder. Even at this young age, her medical file was quite thick: She had a history of visiting physicians with numerous physical complaints. For example, early in her first marriage, Carla sought help for the pain she reported experiencing during intercourse and for her unsuccessful efforts to get pregnant. She visited all of the local physicians, and

Table 7.1   Somatoform Disorders

Disorder	Diagnostic Criteria
Somatization disorder	A history of significant physical complaints (pain, gastrointestinal disorder, sexual dysfunction, neurologic problems) that result in treatment for impaired social and occupational functioning. According to DSM-IV a diagnosis of somatization disorder requires that the complaints began before age thirty and that they occurred for several years. Also required are 1. Four pain symptoms: Pain must be related to at least four different sites or functions (e.g., head, back, joints, extremities, chest, or during intercourse, menstruation, or urination) 2. Two gastrointestinal symptoms (other than pain) such as nausea, diarrhea, bloating, or vomiting (other than during pregnancy) 3. One sexual symptom (other than pain) such as sexual indifference, erectile or ejaculatory dysfunction, irregular menses, or vomiting throughout pregnancy) 4. One pseudoneurologic symptom or deficit suggesting a neurological disorder (e.g., impaired coordination or balance, double vision, deafness, seizures, difficulty breathing, or loss of consciousness other than fainting)
Hypochondriasis	Based on misinterpretations of bodily reactions, the sufferer is preoccupied with fears of having a serious disease. Though not a delusion, the fear persists despite medical evaluations. The preoccupation causes clinical distress of at least six months' duration.
Conversion disorder	One or more symptoms or deficits affecting voluntary sensory or motor functioning that cannot be explained by a neurological or general medical condition (after appropriate investigation) and is not a culturally sanctioned behavior. Psychological factors (though not intentional) are judged to be involved because symptoms are exacerbated under stress and the symptoms are useful for the patient's avoidance of stress. The symptoms or deficits cause clinically significant distress or impairment in social, occupational, or other important areas of functioning.
Body dysmorphic disorder	(Although body dysmorphic disorder is not described in the text, it is listed here because it is included in DSM-IV.) Preoccupation with an imagined defect in appearance that causes clinically significant distress or impairment in social, occupational, or other important areas of functioning.

Source: Adapted from DSM-IV. Reprinted with permission from *The Diagnostic and Statistical Manual of Mental Disorders,* Fourth Edition. Copyright © 1994 American Psychiatric Association.

Somatoform disorders involve physical symptoms that have no organic basis, that are not produced voluntarily, and that are associated with psychological conflicts and stress.

even traveled to a major city for further evaluations. She complained regularly of nausea and diarrhea and of sensitivity to spicy foods. She also visited several different physicians with complaints about headaches and difficulty breathing and swallowing as she tried to go to sleep at night. Childless, she and her second husband divorced after two years.

According to Edelmann (1992), somatization disorder is the tendency to experience and communicate psychological conflict and distress in the form of somatic symptoms, with the person misinterpreting symptoms as indications of serious illness and tending to make many unfounded somatic complaints. Perhaps it is because of difficulties in expressing psychological needs or addressing other personal conflicts that the sufferer reports physical complaints and seeks physical solutions.

Who Is Affected with Somatization Disorder?
Somatization disorder, which was once known as Briquet's syndrome, occurs in about .67 percent to 1 percent of the population. Accurate accounts of the prevalence of this disorder are difficult to obtain because the definitions of several of the somatoform disorders within the DSM system have changed. Historically, the identified cases were almost entirely women. That the symptoms of somatization disorder are described as "hysterical" in nature is no doubt tied to earlier notions of hysteria (in DSM and elsewhere) as a female condition. (The word *hysteria* is derived from *hystero,* which means uterus.)

Traditionally, somatization disorder in men was thought to be rare. Research today suggests that this is not the case (Wool & Barsky, 1994). By studying the diagnostic status and other characteristics of 30 men and 117 women who were referred for multiple unexplained somatic complaints, Jacqueline Golding and her colleagues at the University of Arkansas (Golding, Smith & Kashner, 1991) were able to address the issue directly. Their data indicated that 12 men and 68 women met the diagnostic criteria for somatization disorder. Although generalizing from such a small sample has limitations, the disorder apparently does occur in men, although at a lesser frequency than in women. Interestingly, both the men and women with the disorder showed similar clinical characteristics.

Somatization disorder occurs among members of different ethnic groups and across various social classes (Janca, Isaac, Bennett & Tacchini, 1995). However, according to one large-scale study conducted in four cities (Swartz, Hughes, Blazer & George, 1987), identified cases were more likely to be nonwhite, less educated, and poor. Gender differences were again found: The female-to-male ratio was 10 to 1.

Course of Somatization Disorder Somatization disorder, by definition, involves a long history of complaints that begin before the age of thirty. Thus, it is a chronic condition that does not dissipate over time. Among patients with this disorder, there are fluctuations in the frequency of reports of physical complaints; but it is rare for a year to go by without at least one physical complaint that requires medical attention.

Somatization disorder often begins in the teen years; for a girl, complaints and concerns associated with the menstrual cycle are often the earliest symptoms.

Cause of Somatization Disorder The classification of somatization disorder grew out of extensive clinical experience with medical patients who voiced complaints about being unhealthy but who were typically found not to have specific physical problems. Studies of the families of persons with somatization disorder have indicated that it is more common among female relatives of women with the disorder — in fact, ten times more common than in the general population (Guze, Cloninger, Martin & Clayton, 1986). Walker, Garber, and Greene (1994) studied children whose parents varied in terms of somatic complaints and family distress. At a one-year follow-up, children reporting high levels of somatic complaints had fathers — and, to a lesser extent, mothers — who had reported high levels of somatic complaints. In another study, children in families of adults with somatization disorder were associated with significantly more emergency room use, suicidal behavior, and missed school days (Livingston, Witt & Smith, 1995). These data suggest that the disorder runs in families, but they do not yet separate the contribution of genetics from that of family environment.

Indeed, parents can serve as powerful models for how to address physical difficulties, stressful life events can exacerbate the likelihood of physical complaints, and a person's social competence may help reduce the effects of parents and/or stress. Walker, Garber, and Greene (1994) also evaluated these factors and reported that high levels of negative family life events (family stress, loss of a job, child-care problems) were associated with increased somatic complaints among children assessed as being low in social competence (see Figure 7.1).

Treating Somatization Disorder Patients with somatization disorder — given their repeated visits to multiple physicians — are costly to the health-care system (Labott, Preisman, Popovich & Iannuzzi, 1995), but reducing this expense is no simple matter. Such patients, when told that their problems are not physical, usually reject the suggestion that they may be psychological and seek the opinion of another physician. In those rare instances when psychotherapy is sought, a variety of approaches can be applied — as discussed below. Unfortunately, however, research on the treatment of somatization disorder is scant, and optimal procedures for treatment have yet to be determined.

Insight-oriented therapists strive to bring into clients' awareness the knowledge that their symptoms are not physical and that personal conflicts underlie the physical complaints. This goal may be sought through the cautious interpretive approach or even through confrontational interventions. Some case studies of the cautious interpretive approach exist, but the data are insufficient to make conclusive statements about its effectiveness. Even less data are available for the confrontational approach; clients involved in this form of therapy typically leave it quickly (against professional advice) and often experience an unwanted increase in resistance to treatment.

Nonconfrontational efforts, too, may be worthwhile. Because patients with somatization disorder tend to contact multiple physicians, an effective strategy may be to inform physicians about the management of such patients. In one study, Smith, Rost and Kashner (1995) reported sending a letter to practitioners informing them not to tell patients with somatization disorder that the problem "is all in your head" but, rather, to regularly schedule brief appointments that include brief physical examinations. Ultimately, this intervention reduced annual medical care charges by nearly $300 — a 33 percent reduction. Group therapy has also been found to reduce health-care charges (Kashner, Rost, Cohen & Anderson, 1995).

Treatment approaches with a behavioral basis, such as response prevention, also have potential application. In **response prevention**, clients are deflected from mak-

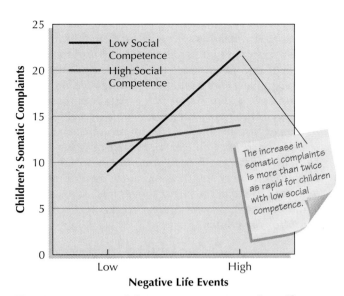

Figure 7.1   Social Competence, Negative Life Events, and Somatic Complaints

Studies have shown that, as negative life events increase, somatic complaints rise more rapidly among children with low social competence than among those with high social competence. *Source:* Adapted from Walker, Garber & Greene (1994).

ing the dysfunctional avoidance response. For instance, they may be prevented from persisting in the search to find a physical disorder to explain current distress. Once the response has been prevented, and the clients have recognized that disaster does not result, their search for a disease is expected to dissipate.

In short, psychological treatment is appropriate for genuine cases of somatization disorder. As the result of a misdiagnosis, however, someone with a *real* physical problem could end up being told that the disorder is in the head. This cloudy diagnostic situation makes the study and treatment of somatization disorder quite difficult.

Hypochondriasis

Being afraid of disease and tending to misinterpret physical signs have been linked to hypochondriacal behavior patterns. **Hypochondriasis** is a preoccupation with the fear or belief that one has a serious medical condition. According to the diagnostic criteria for this disorder, a physician's assessment does *not* support the sufferer's self-diagnosis of a disease. Yet the person with hypochondriasis, despite the physician's negative findings, continues to believe that the disease exists and persists. Reassurance is not helpful (Salkovskis & Warwick, 1986).

Hypochondriacs often express vague physical complaints and are preoccupied with their bodily functions. Cognitively, they are focused on their own health and predisposed to make erroneous interpretations of their

physical well-being. They are certain that they are ill and often disappointed when a physician does not confirm their beliefs. Note, however, that although they receive attention for their complaints, they are not faking a disease to be relieved of work or family responsibilities.

You may already be speculating about the contents of the medicine cabinet and the recreational reading habits of an individual with hypochondriasis. If you expect to find many bottles of old and new medications, with prescriptions written by many different physicians, you would be right. If you expect to find numerous magazines that deal with the latest "popular" medical diseases, again you would be right. Sometimes, as students read about symptoms they may think that they have the disorder being described. Hypochondriacs, on the other hand, are extremely inclined to believe they have the diseases that they read about.

Gillis, a 37-year-old married man with a 7-year-old daughter, was referred for treatment by his employer, an overnight delivery service. He had a tenth grade education and a poor history of holding employment. His current job was the fifth in only ten years: His dismissals were due to his erratic attendance, which in turn resulted from his many presumed medical problems.

For example, while playing with his daughter one day, Gillis felt a "jump" in his chest. He was convinced that his glands were overworked and that his heart was beating irregularly. He spent inordinate amounts of time visiting multiple hospitals and private physicians, repeatedly demanding treatment. Uniformly, the physicians found no physical problem, so Gillis sought a specialty clinic. The plane trip back from the clinic provided Gillis with hours of reading time — which he spent poring over medical books and journals. Although he learned several technical terms, his descriptions of his symptoms remained incomplete and inconsistent with the results of the medical assessments. During his initial interview with a psychologist, he was pleasant and cooperative. His only intense emotions came when he expressed deep concern about his health.

Differentiating somatization disorder from hypochondriasis can be challenging, because the distinction is not always clear cut. In theory, however, a person with hypochondriasis is more likely than one with somatization disorder (1) to be focused on a single disease rather than on a profuse set of symptoms, (2) to be concerned with the disease rather than the experience of symptoms, and (3) to have experienced the onset of the disorder after age thirty. Additionally, although the hypochondriac's physical symptoms are not explained by a known physical disorder, there is no evidence that they serve a psychological purpose. In practice, this distinction is often difficult to verify. Equally difficult is the determi-

Counting and checking pills. Necessary medications require monitoring, but hypochondriasis often includes an excessive concern with various over-the-counter pills thought to be needed for a variety of physical complaints.

nation of the possibility of an undiagnosed physical illness. The diagnostic procedures and criteria are not fault-free, and care must be taken to weigh the costs and benefits of each possible diagnosis.

Somatization disorder and hypochondriasis are considered unintentional, in that persons with either condition are not deliberately faking physical symptoms. When symptoms *are* being faked deliberately, the disorder is considered factitious. **Factitious disorders,** which are more common among men than among women, involve the intentional production (feigning) of physical or psychological signs or symptoms, motivated by the desire to assume the "sick role." Factitious disorder is different from **malingering,** in which signs and symptoms are faked but external incentives such as economic gain or the avoidance of work or legal responsibility are also present.

 "Charles Magic Johnson," he said when I asked his name.
"And what brought you here today, Mr. Johnson?"
"Well, I hear voices, and they tell me to jump." I requested more information. "What do the voices tell you?"
"They tell me to jump off the bridge by the highway, right onto the highway, with all the cars and all."

This brief dialogue took place at a mental health facility where Mr. Johnson walked in off the street. Although it was not clear at first, it soon became

apparent that he wanted to be hospitalized. In fact, staff who had been working at the mental health center for several years recognized Mr. Johnson. In the words of one senior staffer, "Oh, him . . . he comes here every year just as it starts getting cold up north. He comes here and claims he's gonna commit suicide and stays in the hospital for a couple of weeks. Then he moves further south." Mr. Johnson was malingering: He knew that danger to himself or others was a sufficient reason to detain him in the hospital, and he purposefully reported this made-up symptom to be admitted. He was abusing the mental health system to avoid having to pay for a place to stay as he traveled south for the winter.

Malingering can also include a patient's faking an increased severity of symptoms to avoid being transferred to a different, less desirable facility, or faking symptoms to collect insurance payments or to avoid standing trial. The key aspect of malingering is the intentional production of symptoms for recognizable gains that are obvious once identified.

Who Is Affected with Hypochondriasis? Of the somatoform disorders, hypochondriasis is one of the most common. Prevalence estimates for hypochondriasis range from 3 percent to 13 percent (Kellner, 1985). Hypochondriasis is present in 14 percent of general medical patients. The peak ages of onset are adolescence, ages thirty to fifty, and after sixty.

Hypochondriasis is equally prevalent among men and women. Members of different social classes and ethnic groups are also well represented among those diagnosed as hypochondriacs.

Course of Hypochondriasis Considered a chronic condition, hypochondriasis typically emerges in persons between twenty and thirty years of age. Symptoms must be present for six months for a diagnosis of hypochondriasis. Indeed, hypochondriacal symptoms have temporal stability: Patients who were hypochondriacal at one assessment were hypochondriacal at another assessment an average of twenty-two months later (Barsky, Cleary, Sarnie & Klerman, 1993).

Cause of Hypochondriasis Data on the cause of hypochondriasis are limited. Though unsupported by data, explanations are nevertheless suggested by various theories. According to learning theorists, for example, patients receive certain reinforcements for their "sick role." Physicians and nurses are trained to be responsive to and supportive of patients' concerns, and family members may, at least initially, be equally responsive and concerned. Excuses from work and avoidance of other responsibilities may also reward the person who plays the "sick role." Relatedly, parental modeling may be involved in the disorder. When parents reward reports of illness with solicitous attention, they may be contributing to hypochondriacal beliefs. Even more directly, parents may have demonstrated to children their own tendencies to be both preoccupied with bodily reactions and overly concerned with minor variations in health status.

Psychodynamic explanations suggest that repressed conflict is at the source of hypochondriacal behavior, whereas the family systems approach emphasizes the role of family members in maintaining the symptom reports of the target individual. Until research findings from these areas are reported, however, our understanding of the cause of hypochondriasis will remain descriptive and relatively uninformed by data.

The one area in which recent research has been reported underscores the importance of cognitive factors. Specifically, cognitive theorists identify misperceptions and misinterpretations of bodily functions as being at the core of hypochondriasis. When asked to explain an ambiguous bodily symptom, how do hypochondriacal subjects respond? Hitchcock and Mathews (1992) provided data indicating that subjects (college students) with high hypochondriacal concern were more likely than normal counterparts to endorse an illness interpretation of an ambiguous bodily sensation. Let's say that stiffness is reported in the upper shoulder: What is wrong? Whereas nonhypochondriacs might suggest a sports injury, hypochondriacal people are more likely to attribute the sensation to an illness process. A contemporary phrase used to describe this situation is **somatosensory amplification.** Without longitudinal studies we cannot be certain that such amplification causes the dis-

order; however, it is clear that hypochondriasis involves misperceptions of bodily sensations.

Treating Hypochondriasis Persons with this disorder are often offended when physicians suggest that their problem may be psychological and not medical. As a result, they frequently refuse referral for mental health care and are not often seen in mental health settings.

A college student, Kamala, sought help from the campus medical clinic for her "cramps, aches, belching, and weak stomach." After some initial questioning, it was clear that Kamala spent hours every day keeping track of her bodily functions. For example, she cooked her own meals and ate alone so that she could record any cramping or belching that resulted. If belching occurred, she tried to avoid those foods in the future. She also examined and recorded her bowel movements, again avoiding foods that were associated with discomforting stools. She was referred to the psychological services center.

After a few sessions with her psychologist, Kamala reported that she didn't need to be there. "I have a real problem, a messed-up stomach, not a messed-up head." Kamala did not recognize that her preoccupation with her bodily functioning was isolating her from friends and preventing her from developing close relationships. In fact, Kamala would not admit that her wedding plans were canceled by her fiance because of her worries about her health, nor would she acknowledge that her worries were excessive. Despite medical assessments and a competent therapist, Kamala left treatment without changing

"Basically, there's nothing wrong with you that what's right with you can't cure."

her habits and without recognizing that they inter-fered with her life.

Despite the relative infrequency of hypochondriasis within the mental health system, some treatment outcomes have been reported. At the Institute of Psychiatry in London, Warwick and Marks (1988) studied hundreds of treated cases and identified seventeen patients whose primary concern was an illness phobia or hypochondriasis. Although their report lacked control groups and rigorous diagnostic procedures, the authors' clinical experience suggested that exposure to the feared stimuli (as when patients visited hospitals) and response prevention (as when therapists banned patients' efforts to seek reassurance) were effective in significantly reducing patients' reported distress. Six single-case studies, reported by Visser and Bouman (1992) of the Netherlands, also suggested that exposure and response prevention are useful procedures for reducing hypochondriasis.

Given the hint that behavioral procedures can be useful, as well as the view of hypochondriasis as involving somatosensory amplification, researchers have suggested combining cognitive strategies with behavioral ones. Paul Salkovskis, at Warneford Hospital of Oxford University in England, has developed a cognitive-behavioral treatment for hypochondriacal clients (Salkovskis & Warwick, 1986). Part of the treatment involves modifying clients' thoughts about pain and bodily sensations; another feature of the treatment alters reinforcers — such as inactivity and spousal support — that are seen as maintaining the hypochondriacal pattern. When the clients' preoccupation with bodily sensations was lessened, their exercise was increased, and spousal acceptance of their symptoms was removed, their hypochondriacal behavior pattern was reduced. This promising approach deserves additional study.

Comorbidity of Hypochondriasis   Since there are several areas of overlap among the somatoform disorders, differentiating them can be challenging. Unraveling these disorders from within a mix of comorbid conditions is equally taxing. For example, adults with somatoform symptoms also commonly display anxiety and depressive symptoms (Barsky, Wyshak & Klerman, 1992). Patients with schizophrenia may have somatoform symptoms, and many patients with somatoform disorders qualify as having a personality disorder as well. Avoiding the misdiagnosis of an as-yet-unidentified medical condition is especially demanding in this area. Not only input from medical professionals but also reliable applications of diagnostic procedures are essential to assessments of somatoform disorders.

Conversion Disorder

Conversion disorder involves a loss or alteration of physical functioning that appears to be physical but is an expression of a psychological problem. The criteria for a diagnosis of conversion disorder, according to DSM-IV, include the following: (1) One or more symptoms affecting motor or sensory functioning suggest a physical problem, (2) the symptoms are not produced intentionally by the person, and (3) psychological factors are judged to be associated with the physical symptoms.

Conversion disorder can simulate almost any known disease and involve any of the senses. For example, patients with **glove anesthesia** report that they cannot feel anything in the hand over an area that resembles a glove. We understand enough about the physiology of nerve endings, however, to know that it is not possible to have sensitivity that conforms to a glove-like pattern — this simply isn't the way the body is arranged (see Figure 7.2).

Research tasks can be useful in assessing conversion disorder, as evidenced in the following case. The client was a 33-year-old white man (whom we will call David) with a seven-year history of treatment at a veterans hospital. His problem began when he was hit in the right eye with the butt of a rifle during military training. He reported seeing only shapes and silhouettes of objects in his right eye. He later reported that he could not see anything with his right eye. David was given intensive ophthalmological assessment that revealed normal ocular mobility and pupillary reactions. Neurological assessment (such as a CAT scan) also indicated normal functioning. The diagnosis was visual conversion disorder.

Richard Bryant and Kevin McConkey (1989), in Sydney, Australia, designed a visual information task to

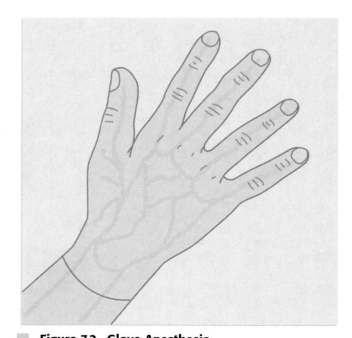

Figure 7.2   Glove Anesthesia
Nerve endings do *not* stop at a line that creates a "glove" shape. Yet clients with glove anesthesia have reported that they do not feel anything in the hand.

further study David's visual conversion disorder (see Figure 7.3). They used equipment that presented a visual cue and an oral cue. The visual cue was three triangles illuminated in different orientations; it also emitted a tone. A switch below each triangle could be used to turn off the tone. The task was to identify the triangle that was oriented differently from the others and to flip the switch under that triangle to turn off the sound. On some occasions the visual cue (the lighting of a triangle) was provided; on other occasions it was not. David's good eye was covered; in fact, he never saw the machine without his good eye being entirely covered. After many trials on the task — turning off the sound using the switches — the researchers determined that David was processing the visual information. Specifically, he performed better on the task (provided more correct responses) when the visual information (cue) was provided. Although David was unaware of his behavior, it betrayed the conversion disorder aspect of his visual dysfunction. Importantly, this case also documents the usefulness of laboratory research paradigms in the clinical assessment process.

Now let's examine the case of Marty — which may or may not involve conversion disorder. You consider the evidence.

Marty was a 32-year-old serviceman whose job in the military was to translate from the German language. He came from a very poor, dysfunctional family and was the only member of his family to graduate from high school and college. In fact, learning the German language, and becoming a translator, was his ticket out of his deprived home environment. He was assigned to a U.S. military post in Germany, where he translated high-priority matters for upper-level officers. The military made him feel successful.

Marty met a woman while in Germany. She was an elegant woman, the daughter of an influential military leader. They were romantically swept away, and the relationship developed rapidly. Soon, marriage seemed a certainty. When Marty's woman friend asked to go back to the United States with him to meet his family, however, Marty began to experience **aphonia** — *an inability to speak above a whisper. Marty was examined by the best physicians, but they concluded that there was nothing physically wrong with him. He was returned to the United States for further medical (and psychological) testing.*

Was Marty suffering a conversion reaction? Go back and check the diagnostic criteria against the information in this case. You will likely decide that, yes, Marty did have conversion disorder. Let's review why. First, the dominant symptom suggested a physical problem, but the medical tests failed to confirm a physical problem. Second, psychological factors were involved:

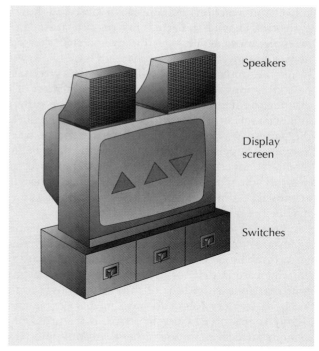

Figure 7.3 Clinical Assessment of a Visual Conversion Disorder
This apparatus was used in an experiment to study the conversion disorder of David, who reported visual impairment in his right eye. The apparatus presented three triangles illuminated in different orientations; it also emitted a tone. Below each triangle was a switch that could be used to turn off the tone. David's task was to identify the triangle that was oriented differently from the others and to use the switch under that triangle to turn off the tone. The visual cue (the lighting of a triangle) was provided sometimes, but not always. David's good eye was covered during the entire experiment. After many trials on the task, it was determined that David was using the visual information. Although David was unaware of his behavior, it betrayed the conversion disorder quality of his visual dysfunction. *Source:* Bryant & McConkey (1989).

The symptom appeared at a time of intense conflict, and it enabled Marty to avoid an unwanted situation.

Although conversion disorder is relatively rare, Marty had a true case of it. The aphonia appeared just as a major conflict was developing in his life; it prevented him from doing his military translating and required that he return alone to the United States, thus avoiding the embarrassment of having his elegant friend meet his family. Does this all seem to fit together too easily? Does it make you question whether Marty was displaying the symptom on purpose to get out of Germany? In fact, conversion reactions are not intentional. Unknown to Marty, his aphonia was a physical expression of an underlying psychological problem. We return to Marty's case below.

Traditionally, the *behavior* of the sufferer was thought to indicate the possibility of conversion disorder. That is, when trying to separate a real physical symptom from a conversion reaction, the physician observed how the patient's behavior reflected his or her attitude. For example, most people who discovered that they could not speak above a whisper, or that they were blind, would be terribly upset. Yet those whose disorders were said to be conversions showed a nonchalant and matter-of-fact attitude, limited concern about any pain or suffering, and relatively little distress about their disability. In fact, the pattern was observed so frequently that it became known as **la belle indifference.** Currently, la belle indifference is not considered a diagnostic indicator because it is only sometimes evident and because researchers have acknowledged that in certain cases the patient's attitude may be the result of a stoic approach to illness.

Because some studies have suggested that the misdiagnosis of conversion disorder is somewhat frequent (e.g., Fishbain & Goldberg, 1991), clinicians must take extreme care in diagnosing conversion disorder. In one four-year follow-up, four of thirty-two conversion disorder cases were found to have medical explanations (Kent, Tomasson & Coryell, 1995). If the problem is a genuine medical condition rather than conversion disorder, the patient may suffer unduly and there may be legal ramifications.

Who Is Affected with Conversion Disorder?
Historically, conversion disorder was included in the diagnostic system as a "hysterical" disorder. As mentioned, *hysteria* is a term related to a woman's womb, and its past use in psychiatry was associated with repressed sexual energy. Hence, a diagnosis of hysterical conversion disorder implied that the woman's complaint of a loss of physical functioning was the result of her repressed sexuality. Since sexual energy is no longer a part of the diagnostic criteria, however, the label "hysterical" has been removed. Indeed, men as well as women experience conversion disorder, although women are diagnosed with it twice as often as men.

Course of Conversion Disorder Although an exact course for conversion reactions is unknown, they typically first appear in adolescence or early adulthood. In addition, they have been reported to occur with increased frequency in military medical wards, especially during wartime.

Cause of Conversion Disorder The question of what causes conversion disorder still piques psychological interest. Psychological factors are judged to be involved in the development of symptoms (1) when there is a temporal relationship between a psychological conflict that demands attention and the initiation or exacerbation of the symptoms, (2) when the symptoms enable the person to avoid an unwanted activity, and (3) when the symptoms enable the person to gain support from the environment. The physical symptoms are said to be conversions of psychological problems into physical ones.

Such an explanation lends itself to the psychodynamic perspective, which maintains that repression and the unconscious alteration of psychological conflict into medical symptoms are factors in conversion disorder. Equally persuasive, however, are the learning, family, and cognitive explanations, each of which uses its own terminology to describe the process whereby conflict and distress are transformed into symptoms that are "safer" for the client to describe and report. In contrast, the medical model offers little meaningful information with regard to conversion disorder. Owing to the infrequency of the disorder and the limited data on its causes, the majority of theoretical positions remain largely untested.

Treating Conversion Disorder Consistent with the limited empirical information available about the cause of conversion disorder, studies of its treatment are equally uncommon. Accordingly, we must learn from existing case reports.

One such report, now classic, was that of Anna O., a case that is often described as a foundation for Freud's theory of psychoanalysis. Anna O. had several symptoms — paralysis, trances, sporadic deafness, speech and visual problems — that appeared to be physical but were deemed psychological. Ellenberger (1972) took a closer look at the case of Anna O. and revealed some interesting questions.

The initial report of Anna O. appeared in 1895, yet she was actually treated between 1880 and 1882. In the 1895 report by Joseph Breuer, the successful treatment of Anna O. was attributed to his having hypnotized her; under hypnosis she was returned to an original underlying traumatic event and her symptoms disappeared. Breuer referred to the treatment as "catharsis," although Anna O. chose to call it her "talking cure." Freud paid close attention to Breuer's report, which had a strong influence on talking therapy (free association) and the notion that underlying experiences must be relived to produce psychological relief.

An investigation at the hospital where Anna O. had been placed uncovered a report written in 1882, at the actual time of her treatment. Details about Anna's family in the newly discovered report strongly suggest that it pertained to the same case. The report mentioned that her symptoms were reduced with therapy, but it made no reference to the psychological treatment, only to the use of morphine and other medications. Questions raised about the validity of the case of Anna O. have sparked debate, yet psychoanalytic practitioners discount the negative aspects of the controversy.

The treatment of Marty's aphonia, described earlier, began when his case was brought to the attention of a psychological therapist. The psychologist prepared a behavioral treatment program in preparation for meeting Marty. Marty, however, wanted nothing to do with mental health professionals. He was convinced that he had a medical problem and wanted to be examined by additional expert physicians. The therapist remained patient, meeting with Marty several times without introducing the treatment program. Even though their communications were restrained by Marty's having to whisper, they did begin to develop a working relationship. During this time the therapist learned that Marty loved to sing and that he had been an active member of the Christmas Chorale while in Germany. Because it was mid-December, the therapist asked Marty to sing a holiday song in German. Marty began to sing at full volume. With a surprised look, he quickly reverted to a whisper. It was as if he changed to a whisper as soon as he realized that his full voice was broadcasting. He explained the situation as a brief return of his voice, but was so disquieted by the experience that he never returned for another therapy session.

DISSOCIATIVE DISORDERS

Individuals with a dissociative disorder experience a severe disruption or alteration of their identity, memory, or consciousness. Ben — the policeman who abandoned his family, described at the beginning of this chapter — has a dissociative disorder. Three types of **dissociative disorders** are discussed in this chapter: dissociative amnesia, dissociative fugue, and dissociative identity

disorder. Although dissociative disorders typically involve disruption of identity, dissociative amnesia can involve loss of memory without loss of identity. Table 7.2 summarizes these disorders (see also Michelson & Ray, 1996).

Until recently, the term *psychogenic* was used in the names of these disorders — as in psychogenic amnesia and psychogenic fugue — to indicate that the fugue or memory loss is not physically caused. The dissociative disorders include psychologically caused difficulties associated with some aspect of the person's identity.

Dissociative Amnesia and Fugue

Dissociative Amnesia Each of us, throughout our lives, has forgotten certain things — a person's name, a friend's birthday, the need to stop at a store on the way home. Forgetfulness, however, is not the same as memory loss. The person with memory loss is unable to recall important personal information too extensive to be viewed in terms of forgetfulness. When there is actual damage to the brain, from injury or disease, the information that isn't recalled is lost forever. But in dissociative (psychogenic) amnesia, the memory system is not physically damaged, yet there is selective psychologically motivated forgetting. Often, what has been forgotten is traumatic for the individual. It can sometimes be retrieved from memory.

There are two main types of amnesia: selective and generalized. In cases of **selective dissociative amnesia**, a

Jane Doe. Host David Hartman chats with a victim of amnesia. She did not know her name and could not recount the events that led to her being found naked and near death in a Florida state park. Following TV coverage of her case, she was identified as the daughter of a suburban Chicago couple.

Table 7.2 Dissociative Disorders

Disorder	Diagnostic Criteria
Dissociative amnesia	Different from ordinary forgetfulness, this disturbance involves one or more episodes of an inability to recall important personal information, usually of a stressful or traumatic nature.
Dissociative fugue	Sudden and unexpected travel away from the home or place of work, with an inability to recall one's past. There is confusion about personal identity, and a new identity is assumed.
Dissociative identity disorder (multiple personality disorder)	The presence of two or more distinct personalities in one person, each with its own relatively enduring pattern of perceiving, relating to, and interacting with the environment. At least two of these personalities recurrently take control, and the patient's inability to recall important personal information is too extensive to be explained by ordinary forgetfulness.
Depersonalization disorder	(Depersonalization disorder is not described in the text but is included in DSM-IV.) Persistent and recurring experiences of being detached from, or an outside observer of, one's own mind and body. The depersonalization causes clinically significant distress and impairment in important areas of functioning.

Source: Adapted from DSM-IV. Reprinted with permission from *The Diagnostic and Statistical Manual of Mental Disorders*, Fourth Edition. Copyright © 1994 American Psychiatric Association.

Dissociative disorders involve severe disruption or alteration of identity, memory, or consciousness. These symptoms are not due to the direct effects of substance use or general medical condition.

person forgets some but not all of what happened during a certain period of time.

Ed and Gary rode motorcycles together almost every weekend for several years; it was the basis of their friendship. One day, while riding alone, Gary had a traumatic accident. He was hit by a driver who turned in front of his motorcycle while he was traveling at 55 miles per hour. It took 8 weeks for Gary to recover from the physical injuries he sustained.

Interestingly, although Ed was not involved in the accident, he showed symptoms that appeared just after Gary's collision. Ed could recall his name, identify his family, and locate his residence. He could even talk about an assortment of past events associated with Gary and motorcycling. What Ed could not do was describe the day or two before the accident, nor could he recall anything about the accident per se. His amnesia was selective; he forgot only the events preceding Gary's traumatic event.

In contrast to the selective nature of Ed's amnesia, Shakai suffered **generalized dissociative amnesia,** which is the forgetting of one's entire life history.

Shakai, a homeless person in an urban environment, was brought into a hospital by volunteers for treatment of her health needs. When asked her name, she knew only "Shakai," the name given her by her friends on the street. She couldn't recall the names of her family members, where she was born or where she had lived, or any of her childhood experiences. Her history, as she reported it, didn't exist. Consistent with dissociative amnesia, Shakai could not, when shown pictures, recognize her parents or identify her childhood home. Interestingly, however, her basic habits and abilities continued to operate in a normal fashion. She continued to smoke cigarettes, buying the same brand and lighting them with a characteristic flick of the match. She spoke English, using the words she had learned earlier. And she used a complicated portable telephone, also a skill she had acquired before the onset of amnesia.

WHAT'S NORMAL?

Recovering Memories: How Accurate Are We?

What did you eat for breakfast today? When is your birthday? These questions do not tax our memory system and appear easy to answer. When you read a textbook but struggle to answer exam questions, you might complain that you just "can't remember." Why?

Forgetting happens as a routine part of life, and there are several explanations for why you forget. *Decay*

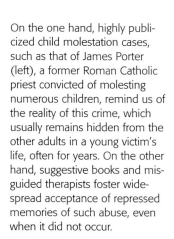

On the one hand, highly publicized child molestation cases, such as that of James Porter (left), a former Roman Catholic priest convicted of molesting numerous children, remind us of the reality of this crime, which usually remains hidden from the other adults in a young victim's life, often for years. On the other hand, suggestive books and misguided therapists foster widespread acceptance of repressed memories of such abuse, even when it did not occur.

theory maintains that loss of memory is a result of disuse and the passage of time; if information is not used or rehearsed it fades over time. *Interference theory* suggests that memory has a limited capacity; when its capacity is reached, you are susceptible to confusion and forgetting. When you are first given information to remember and then given a new set of facts, the new facts interfere with the recall of the old information. Another theory suggests that forgetting occurs when there is failure in the *process of retrieving information.* The information is there, stored away, but it appears to have been forgotten because you cannot retrieve it.

Although each of these explanations for everyday forgetting has received research support, they are not the same explanations used to understand clinical cases of fugue and amnesia. Recall from Chapter 2 the notion of the unconscious. For Freud, there was a reason why people forget certain things — repression. An unwanted and unpleasant event can be lost from memory because a person wants to forget it. *Repression,* then, is motivated forgetting, or the burying of unwanted memories in the unconscious where they stay largely inaccessible. Research tests of repression are limited by the methods used and by the very nature of the phenomenon being studied. Nevertheless, it is not difficult to imagine that a distressing, or traumatic, experience could be blocked from memory as a way to help the person cope. With regard to childhood sexual abuse, there is the possibility that early abuse leaves a traumatic psychological scar — a scar that is not in one's memory but nevertheless has unwanted effects.

Recently, there has been a rise in reported memories of childhood sexual abuse that were allegedly repressed for many years (Loftus, 1993). In one 1989 case, a 27-year-old woman began to have recollections about having been molested by her father as a child; she had no recollections of the molestation until therapy and counseling lifted her repression. She sued her father for damages — both emotional and physical. But, you might ask, what about the statute of limitations? Until recently, the statute provided protection against surprise claims that were allowed to wither while evidence was lost, but current thinking has allowed the statute to be suspended in cases of child sexual abuse. In many U.S. states, legislation now permits once-repressed memories to form the basis of lawsuits.

Are the reports of formerly repressed memories authentic? Elizabeth Loftus (1993), of the University of Washington, examined a variety of sources and reviewed the issues. Loftus reported that many therapists believe in the authenticity of the recovered memories that are described by their clients. However, therapists should be suspicious of recovered memories, for at least two reasons: suggestive popular writings and the use of leading questions by therapists.

Certain popular writings, which are advertised as a resource for survivors of sexual abuse, promote the notion that abuse has occurred. Consider Loftus's description of *The Courage to Heal,* by Bass and Davis (1988):

> Readers who are wondering whether they might be victims of child sexual abuse are provided with a list of possible activities ranging from the relatively benign (e.g., being held in a way that made them feel uncomfortable) to the unequivocally abusive (e.g., being raped or otherwise penetrated). Readers are then told "If you are unable to remember any specific instances like the ones mentioned above

but still have a feeling that something abusive happened to you, it probably did" (p. 21). (Loftus, 1993, p. 525)

The message of this book is blatant: Any current personal problems can be traced to earlier sexual abuse, whether or not the person has a current memory of the abuse. That the book has played a role in recent cases is evident from the results of a survey taken in 1992. In that year, Wakefield and Underwager reported that, among several hundred family members accused by persons with no-longer-repressed memories, the book was implicated "in almost all cases" (1992, p. 486). Are the readers of this book actually recovering truly repressed events, or do they believe the written message that abuse occurred even in the initial absence of a memory of it?

The second reason to be suspicious of recovered memories involves the therapist's behavior. Not all therapists ask leading questions of clients, but there are examples in the repressed-abuse literature to implicate at least some therapists. For example, Loftus (1993) noted that some therapists persist in intrusive probing as a way to uncover early traumatic memories, while others provide examples of leading questions as a way of describing their work:

> You know, in my experience, a lot of people who are struggling with many of the same problems you are have often had some kind of really painful things happen to them as kids — maybe they were beaten or molested. And I wonder if anything like that happened to you? (Forward & Buck, 1988, p. 161)

With leading questions, is it any wonder that clients are increasingly reporting prior incidents? And yet, the question of accuracy remains.

Some of the therapists who attempt to uncover repressed trauma are undoubtedly well-intentioned. Yet their referrals to suggestive books and their use of leading questions can unwittingly promote cases of inaccuracy. Because no studies as yet have scientifically examined the validity of repressed memories, it may be wise to avoid the uncritical acceptance of them as causes of current psychological problems.

Dissociative Fugue The fugue state involves physical retreat; during a fugue, the individual suddenly and unexpectedly departs. Two important features for diagnosing **dissociative (psychogenic) fugue** are listed in DSM-IV: a sudden unexpected travel away from home or work with an inability to recall one's past, and confusion about personal identity. Marked confusion about personal identity interferes with routine daily activities, so, in an effort to adjust and relate to others, the person assumes a new identity. Despite the new assumed identity, characteristics of the "old self" are recognizable. Often, complicated behaviors are carried out during the fugue. A victim may drive a long distance, find a place to live, obtain employment, and begin a new life.

Browny, as his friends called him, was a scuba diver off the coast of Florida. He spent his time searching for sunken treasures, but made a modest living by hiring himself out for search and recovery missions. He assisted the police in retrieving bodies and cars from accidents that ended up in the water, and he did some work on bridge supports for the state department of transportation. When he didn't return home for several weeks, his family assumed that he must have died in a diving accident.

Nine years later Browny called his wife on the phone and told her that he was working as a swimming instructor in California and that he had just remembered his name. He had a memory of his recent past, but he still could not retrieve the details of his life ten years earlier. Memories came back to him as his wife mentioned the names of his children and activities that they had enjoyed together. At first, Browny's wife was extremely pleased to learn that her husband was alive. Soon, however, her emotions turned to anger and upset: She did not understand dissociative fugue and began to question the truth of Browny's story.

The psychological processes of dissociative amnesia and fugue are seen as the same. Hence, they are discussed together in the following sections.

Who Is Affected with Dissociative Amnesia and Fugue?
Both dissociative amnesia and fugue are rare. Reports of cases suggest that these disorders can appear at any point in the life span, though less among the elderly. Amnesia is most frequent among adolescent and young women, but its incidence increases slightly among men during periods of military conflict. Oquendo (1995) has described *ataque de nervios*, a culturally condoned expression of distress among Hispanic women that resembles dissociation, but there are few other data on ethnic differences in the prevalence of dissociative amnesia or fugue.

Owing perhaps to the limited number of individuals who experience dissociative disorders, as well as to the intrigue and appeal of the psychological processes involved, researchers have begun to study dissociation among college students. For example, Rauschenberger and Lynn (1995) administered a questionnaire by which they identified fantasy-prone college students who also reported dissociative experiences and symptoms. According to the results, more high-level fantasy-prone than medium-level fantasy-prone students met the criteria for having dissociative experiences. These results are

"I DON'T KNOW WHO RUNS IT, NO ONE EVER SHOWS UP TO OPEN THE DOOR..."

interesting, but they do not necessarily indicate a direct link between the tendency to fantasize and the incidence of dissociative disorders — especially given that the high-level fantasizers also had a higher frequency of past diagnoses of depression. Furthermore, it should be noted that there is nothing inherently wrong with fantasy, nor are all fantasy-prone persons at risk for dissociation (Kihlstrom, Glisky & Angiulo, 1994).

Course of Dissociative Amnesia and Fugue Most instances of dissociative amnesia or fugue are short-lived, lasting only hours or days and involving fleeting travel. More extended memory loss and travel (as in Ben's case, described in the chapter opener) occur infrequently. Recovery from amnesia and fugue is typically rapid, with a full return of memory; and individuals who have suffered amnesia or fugue are *unlikely* to have a second episode.

Cause of Dissociative Amnesia and Fugue Consistent with the basic notion that amnesia and fugue are psychogenic, episodes often follow severe psychological stress associated with extreme marital conflict, distressing military conflict, natural disasters, or numerous personal rejections. Those affected experience extreme distress and anxiety for which there is no apparent solution. Memory loss or moving away from the situation enables them to avoid the distress that could not, in their mind, be handled any other way. Avoidance, therefore, plays an important role in the development of the symptoms seen in these anxiety-related disorders. Thus far we have discussed psychological amnesias, but disruptions in memory can also be caused by biological and neurological factors (see Chapter 17).

Treating Dissociative Amnesia and Fugue Not surprisingly, a person in an amnesic or in a fugue state who is unaware of important facts about his or her own identity is often equally uninformed about the need for therapy. Typically, dissociative amnesic and fugue patients do not seek treatment themselves but, rather, are referred to a therapist after an episode has occurred. The therapy itself often addresses clients' need for more adaptive ways to manage personal distress and conflict.

Stress management programs, such as stress inoculation (described in Chapter 10), may be used to treat dissociative amnesia and fugue. That is, to the extent that dissociative disorders emerge as a consequence of a person's inability to handle stress, interventions that provide stress management skills can be effective. In these programs, clients are taught first to identify the conflicts in their lives and then to use problem-solving strategies to address rather than avoid these conflicts, thereby undermining and diminishing the psychological causes of the dissociation.

Treating dissociative amnesia with preventive methods — intervening before the onset of the disorder — is contraindicated because the disorder occurs so rarely that even a large-scale prevention effort (which would also be very costly) would likely affect only a very small number of cases. Applications of preventive strategies for identified cases would also be senseless because dissociative amnesia and fugue rarely recur.

Dissociative Identity Disorder

Dissociative identity disorder (DID), formerly known as multiple personality disorder, involves the alteration of a person's memory, consciousness, or sense of identity. The person may either lose his or her sense of identity or assume a new identity. DID has received considerable public attention, but where does it fit among the many different types of psychological disorders? Readers may wonder whether it is related to the *personality disorders* (see Chapter 13). It is not: Unlike DID, personality disorders involve clusters of behavioral traits that are excessive, maladaptive, lifelong, and pervasive. Also, although DID may resemble a "split mind," which is the literal translation of the word *schizophrenia* (see Chapter 9), it is not a psychotic disorder. Indeed, although dissociative identity disorder and schizophrenia are commonly confused with one another in the media and popular press, they are *not* the same.

Typified in the popular press by "Sybil," a girl with sixteen personalities (Schreiber, 1974), DID is characterized by the presence of two or more distinct personalities or personality states within one individual. Each of the personalities has unique behavior patterns, memories, and relationships, perceiving itself and the world differently from the other personalities. Some patients have only a few distinct personalities; others have many (up to a hundred have been claimed). The different personalities recurrently take full control of the person's behavior, and the transition from one to another is usually abrupt. In some cases, the personalities are aware (and might even be friends or foes) of each other; in other cases, the basic personality is unaware of the existence of the others. The differences between the personalities can be quite dramatic: One is a shy recluse, another is a flamboyant party-goer; one is left-handed, another is right-handed; one is heterosexual, another is gay. The personalities may also differ in IQ scores, gender, or ethnic identity.

In 1954, Thigpen and Cleckley published *The Three Faces of Eve*, which describes a client whose three different personalities were virtual opposites in terms of their emotional and behavioral patterns. Eve White was the quiet, polite, hard-working, and conservative mother of a young daughter. Eve Black was seductive, impulsive, risk-taking, and adventure-seeking. Jane, the third personality, was a confident and capable woman. Interestingly, it was Eve White who sought therapy, Eve Black who emerged first during therapy, and Jane who appeared after eight months of treatment.

Perhaps because of the popularity of Thigpen and Cleckley's book or that of the movie depicting the case (starring Joanne Woodward in an Oscar-winning role), or as part of her personal therapy, the real person behind the alias, Chris Costner Sizemore (1989) wrote her own book entitled *A Mind of My Own*. Sizemore described many personalities — several more than were depicted by Thigpen and Cleckley — and wrote about how they emerged and then disappeared. By her own account, Sizemore experienced the integration of her diverse personalities at the age of forty-six.

The case of Billy Milligan provides another informative illustration of this intriguing disorder.

Based on hundreds of meetings and conversations with Billy Milligan and interviews with sixty-two persons whose lives touched his, Keyes (1981) wrote The Minds of Billy Milligan. *The story covers the life of the man who, in the 1970s, was the first person in U.S. history to be found not guilty of major crimes by reason of insanity because he possessed multiple personalities. Keyes reported gaining access to the many sides of Billy Milligan from the fused Milligan — when Billy's many selves came together at one time, with clear recall of the different personalities and their actions. Each had its own history, private feelings, and behavior patterns. Keyes also had access to videotapes of Billy's therapy sessions.*

Here are descriptions of the ten personalities that were brought to the attention of the courts. Keyes (1981) described an additional fourteen, suggesting a total of twenty-four.

- *Billy was the original core personality — a high school dropout with blue eyes and brown hair.*

- *Arthur was a rational, emotionless Englishman who spoke with a British accent and could read and write in Arabic. He saw himself as a capitalist and an atheist, and he wore glasses.*

- *Roger Vadascovinich was Yugoslavian, spoke English with a Slavic accent, and could read and write Serbo-Croatian. He was an expert in karate and munitions, and he was an atheist and communist. He had been involved in crime. He had a drooping mustache and, being colorblind, did drawings in black and white.*

- *Alan was a manipulative con man who was into making deals. He played the drums, smoked cigarettes, parted his hair on the right, and, of all the personalities, was the only right-handed one.*

- *Tommy was antisocial. He was skilled in electronics and was an escape artist. He played the saxophone and painted landscapes.*

- *Danny was afraid of men. He painted still lifes.*

- *David was highly sensitive and suffered from the pain caused by the other personalities.*

- *Christene was a bright little English girl who liked to draw flowers and butterflies, but had to stand in the corner at school.*

- *Christopher spoke with a British accent, played the harmonica, and was Christene's brother.*

- *Adalsua was a shy, lonely, introverted lesbian who wrote poetry, liked to cook, and did household chores.*

Billy Milligan came to the attention of police and of the local public — and eventually the nation — when he was arrested as a suspect in a series of crimes. In 1977, for instance, three rape-abductions occurred at Ohio State University. One victim remembered that the suspect wore gloves, handcuffed her to the inside of the car door, and drove her into the country. Another victim said her assailant had an oily stain on his hands, wore sunglasses, and took down the names of her relatives whom he said he would harm if she identified him. A third victim was forced into a car and required to drive to an open country area. Two of the victims identified a mug shot of William Milligan as the assailant, and a fingerprint found at one of the crime scenes matched his.

Billy was arrested by a SWAT team pretending to deliver a pizza. When he opened the door and saw their guns drawn, Milligan looked shocked. He kept saying he wasn't *Milligan. Then a SWAT officer saw some paintings and asked, "Did you do those?" "Yes," Billy replied. They were signed Milligan. One of the officers mentioned the rapes, and Milligan said, "Did I do that?"*

The accumulating evidence was impressive; found in his apartment were handcuffs, charge cards belonging to the victims, paper with a victim's name and address on it, and an automatic revolver and other weapons. Eventually the local paper reported the arrest of a suspect and printed Billy's picture — much to the concern of the police, who feared that it would prejudice the forthcoming line-up. Events proceeded rapidly: The evidence mounted, Billy attempted suicide, and his public defender suggested an insanity plea. The evidence pointed to Billy Milligan, and yet, over time, discrepancies in the crime reports seemed to be consistent with a multiple personality disorder. Eventually he was tried and found not guilty by reason of insanity. Many of those who met Milligan at different times and as different personalities seemed to think he was a very disturbed man, but others thought he was a liar.

Was Billy Milligan a genuinely disturbed person, or was he a fake? Either he lived a desperately troubled life, or he duped society and escaped from a prison term that was warranted by his crimes. Should persons with DID be held responsible for the consequences of their actions? Although there is evidence of impaired awareness in connection with this disorder, some have argued that, yes, they should be. (Deahrs, 1994; see also Applebaum & Greer, 1994)

The topic of DID is quite controversial. Some professionals claim that the disorder does not exist in nature but, rather, is an unwanted effect of therapy. For example, Spanos (1994) has argued that therapists both suggest the presence of and legitimize multiple personalities and then proceed to shape and reward the client for engaging in behavior associated with different personalities. In a counterargument, Gleaves (1996) contends that most of the research does not support Spanos's position. But the controversial aspect of DID is clear: In a national survey of mental health professionals conducted in the United States, 24 percent of the respondents expressed moderate to extreme skepticism about DID (Hayes & Mitchell, 1994); and 27 percent of Canadian psychiatrists agreed that media publicity and psychiatrists' own beliefs affected the prevalence of DID (Mai, 1995).

FOCUS ON RESEARCH

Has Dissociative Identity Disorder Really Increased?

Dissociative identity disorder was long considered extremely rare — occurring in fewer than two hundred documented patients. Though controversial, some research on the disorder now suggests that it may not be as rare as once thought (Putnam, 1989). What has happened to account for this presumed increase in the frequency of cases?

Some practitioners argue that improved diagnostic procedures have facilitated the accurate identification of patients. Others argue that the criteria are too inclusive (Piper, 1995). Still others assert that as the search for cases has increased, so has the number of reports, but that many cases are false-positive — not genuine multiple personalities. Recent research conducted in Europe, Asia, Canada, and United States, using a variety of methods, has provided some interesting information to consider.

In the Netherlands, Suzette Boon and Nel Draijer (1993) used structured interviews to describe seventy-one Dutch patients earlier identified as having DID (then called multiple personality disorder) and compared them with U.S. patients with DID. Their results indicated that the Dutch patients' symptoms included amnesia, depersonalization, derealization, and identity confusion — much the same as among the U.S. patients. (Similar findings were also found in Turkey by Tutkun, Yargic, and Sar, 1995.) These data led the authors to conclude that patients with multiple personality disorder exhibit a consistent core set of symptoms worldwide.

Boon and Draijer did not, however, verify the accuracy of the initial diagnoses of the seventy-one Dutch patients. In fact, these patients reported many different symptoms and, before the study, had received numerous diagnoses other than DID. The implication is that they possibly had a variety of disorders but nevertheless reported symptoms resembling those related to DID.

Thus, although Boon and Draijer's findings suggest that the symptoms of the seventy-one Dutch patients paralleled those reported by the U.S. patients with DID, the methods of their study do not permit the conclusion that all seventy-one had confirmed diagnoses of DID.

The survey method has also been used to study the prevalence of dissociative identity disorder. For example, in 1992 (again, at a time when DID was called multiple personality disorder), Jiri Modestin used this method to gather data in Switzerland. Swiss psychiatrists were sent copies of the DSM diagnostic criteria along with questionnaires, 770 of which were analyzed. Three percent of the psychiatrists reported that they were treating someone who met DSM criteria for DID, and 10 percent reported that they had seen DID at least once in their careers. Based on the survey, Modestin calculated that DID occurs in 0.05 percent to 0.1 percent of patients seen by Swiss psychiatrists. What we do not know, however, is how many people with DID are seen by other mental health professionals, or how many are outside the mental health system altogether. Because neither question is answered by the survey method, DID may occur more frequently than we think. Still other surveys — conducted, for example, in France (Darves-Bornoz, Degiovanni & Gaillard, 1995) and in Ireland (Aldridge-Morris, 1995; Saks, 1995) — have reported that DID is rare.

An interesting fact that bears on the question of prevalence concerns the disproportionate identification of DID patients by individual professionals. That is, the patients identified as having DID by the Swiss psychiatrists (Modestin, 1992) were not equally distributed across these psychiatrists: Three of them reported seeing a much higher number of patients with DID than did hundreds of other professionals. When disproportionate identification occurs (Merskey, 1994), researchers have reason to be concerned about the degree to which diagnoses are, in effect, in the eye of the diagnostician. Note that estimated prevalence should also be questioned when diagnoses are not independently confirmed — again, as in the Modestin (1992) study.

Canadian researchers (Ross, Anderson, Fleisher & Norton, 1991) used a screening procedure, followed by a diagnostic interview, to assess the frequency of DID among in-patients. A total of 299 patients completed the screening procedure, and 80 received the structured interview. The researchers determined that 10 of the in-patients had DID. This systematic screening and diagnostic interviewing methodology is superior to the methods used in other studies because it permits a greater degree of confidence in the results. Indeed, based on their calculation that 3.3 percent of the in-patients met diagnostic criteria for DID, the researchers were able to conclude that DID does occur more frequently than once believed.

Another promising avenue in the search for ways to separate false versus real cases of DID involves the use of physiological measurements. For instance, in one study (Putnam, 1984) the brain waves of patients diagnosed with authentic DID were found to be much more varied than the brain waves of persons who were simply asked to pretend to be multiple personalities. To the extent that measurements other than self-report continue to be used, further advances in the accurate determination of DID are likely.

Who Is Affected with DID? DID has been found to occur many times more often in women than in men (estimated rates are three to nine times higher in women). The most common explanations offered for this variance are that women are typically more exposed to sexual abuse, women may handle their psychological traumas in "internal" ways whereas men may "externalize" their problems in ways that do not come to the attention of mental health professionals, and, finally, women tend to seek help more than men do.

Course of DID A systematic survey of individuals who had been diagnosed with multiple personality disorder (Ross, Anderson, Fleisher & Norton, 1991) identified several common experiences. For instance, many of the patients had reported unusual perceptual experiences such as hearing voices coming from inside the head, experiencing another person inside the body, and feeling under the control of another person. Such symptoms can contribute to alternate diagnoses, including schizophrenia, substance abuse, mania, and anxiety disorders. In fact, nearly 64 percent of the subjects studied by Ross and associates (1991) had been diagnosed with borderline personality disorder, and more than 90 percent had current major depressive disorders. As this study shows, the symptoms of multiple personality disorder are difficult to separate from other diagnoses, and people with this disorder exhibit high rates of other psychiatric problems as well.

The data of Ross and associates (1991) also indicated that many of the patients with DID (more than 65 percent) reported flashbacks, blank spells, being told of unremembered events, or being told that they are known by strangers. The high frequency of these experiences led the authors to propose that they be added to the diagnostic criteria for multiple personality disorder. In the absence of confirmations from other research, however, the presence of these symptoms in one group of DID patients is not sufficient to modify the diagnostic criteria. The authors suggested that if clinicians knew more of the right questions to ask, they would detect a much higher frequency of multiple personality disorder among their patients. Unfortunately, expansion of these criteria would increase the likelihood of false-positive cases — a problem that is already a source of concern.

Childhood amnesia has also been described in the context of DID. Experimental psychologists who study

Chris Sizemore, the real subject of the *Three Faces of Eve.* Ms. Sizemore suffered from multiple personality disorder (MPD; dissociative identity disorder). Currently, she is one person — a suburban housewife.

memory (Schacter, Kihlstrom, Kihlstrom & Berren, 1989) compared the frequency of autobiographical memories in a woman with multiple personality disorder and in appropriate comparison groups of normal subjects, using several standard memory tasks. The most striking finding was the woman's total inability to recall personal events before the age of ten, with only poor recollection between the years ten and twelve. The researchers hypothesized that such blockage, or dissociation, of memory was related to her traumatic sexual abuse. Another interesting study involves the case report of a woman with DID. Bryant (1995) found that one personality was able to recognize only half of the memories reported by the other. This result led Bryant to conclude that a patient with DID reports different autobiographical memories across personalities.

FAMILY MATTERS
DID and Childhood Physical and Sexual Abuse

Case studies and research have repeatedly indicated that dissociative disorders in general are caused by traumatic experiences. Amnesia, fugue states, and depersonalization have all been found to occur under conditions of combat or exposure to severely stressful events. For example, after the earthquake in San Francisco in 1989, the frequency of dissociative symptoms among a non-clinical sample was found to have increased (Cardena & Spiegel, 1993).

The hypothesized origin of DID is defense against intensely painful and frightening experiences in childhood. The individual uses — to an extreme degree — the normal capacity to shut out conscious experiences or to detach from them, thus blocking out trauma, separating it from awareness in memory, and employing fantasy to experience positive or compensatory states. In time, some of the dissociative states may be elaborated into alternative "selves" that presumably serve to protect the otherwise helpless child from overwhelming feelings about and memories of the traumatic situations. This sequence may be especially likely to occur in children experiencing trauma in families that do not provide healthy ways for the children to contain or regulate emotional experiences or to promote a cohesive sense of self. In contrast, healthy families are more likely to respect individual autonomy, to refrain from inhibiting independence, and to provide warmth and support (Darling & Steinberg, 1993).

One commonly reported association is that between DID and childhood physical and sexual abuse. For instance, Ross, Anderson, Fleisher, and Norton (1991) found that 95.1 percent of the nearly one hundred patients with DID they studied had a history of childhood abuse. The researchers also reviewed other studies, which revealed that between 68 percent and 86 percent of patients with DID had reported childhood or adolescent sexual abuse and that 60 percent to 82 percent acknowledged past history of physical abuse.

As further evidence of the possible link between dissociative states and traumatic childhood events, Sanders and Giolas (1991) administered a Dissociative Experiences Scale to a group of hospitalized adolescents in treatment for a variety of psychiatric problems. They also had the youngsters complete questionnaires about the extent of physical abuse or punishment, psychological or sexual abuse, neglect, and negative home environments they had experienced. As predicted, there was a significant relationship between reported abuse and family discord and dissociative experiences. This study points out that dissociative experiences can co-occur with many types of psychiatric problems, and that multiple personality disorder may be only one outcome associated with childhood exposure to abusive situations. Indeed, according to Walker, Bonner, and Kaufman (1988), a significant history of child sexual abuse has been found among prostitutes, child molesters, and rapists as well as among those suffering personal distress, in the form of depression, substance abuse, and eating disorders.

Two caveats are in order here. First, not all abused youngsters develop DID. Second, at this relatively early stage of research in DID, retrospective reports of childhood experiences have provided only preliminary ideas and hypotheses. And as we mention in our earlier discussion of uncovered repressed memories, retrospective reports can be inaccurate. In short, there is a need for *prospective* research in which both abused and nonabused patients are examined to see who does and does not develop DID or other psychological abnormalities.

Treating DID Among many patients, DID remains undetected for a long time. Because of the high frequency of comorbidity with other psychological problems, such patients may be treated with therapy or medications for these other disorders. (Antidepressants and antianxiety drugs would be the medications commonly used in these circumstances.) Once DID *is* detected, however, the typical treatment involves psychotherapy aimed at helping replace the patients' internal division with a unity of personalities (Putnam, 1989).

Traditionally, hypnosis has frequently been used as a technique for helping to bring out and integrate the memories of traumatic experiences. Yet despite the finding that persons with dissociative disorders score higher on measures of hypnotizability (Frischholz, Lipman, Braun & Sachs, 1992) and are therefore viewed as good candidates for hypnosis, scientific evaluations of the effectiveness of hypnosis for dissociation are notably absent.

Psychodynamic therapy has also been applied as treatment for DID. The goal is to help the person gain insight and process experiences in a more meaningful and constructive way than by dissociation. In other words, it strives to free the individual from "needing" the alternate selves so that feelings and conflicts can be integrated in a psychologically sound fashion. Thus, the psychodynamic approach emphasizes techniques that assist the person in recalling, recognizing, and coming to terms with the traumatic basis of his or her problems. To date, there are no systematic controlled studies of treatment outcome with DID, but case studies appear frequently in the clinical literature. These cases indicate that psychotherapy can be successful in dispelling the "other" personalities and strengthening the core, integrative personality. Caution is mandated, however, as some cases also reveal that once-"treated" patients exhibit persistent problems after the reported cure.

What Lies Ahead?

It is a simple fact that the mind and the body interact. Yet the pattern of interrelationships is quite complex and often not well understood. Different professionals focus on different aspects of similar problems; for example, medical professionals focus on bodily disease, and psychological professionals and psychiatrists focus on mental disorders. Although the artificial boundaries between these associated interests will likely never be removed entirely, the future may nevertheless bridge some of them. Emerging trends include increased collaborative research as well as a more holistic approach to treatment. Both provide an impetus that will advance our understanding.

Data on the prevalence and descriptive features of the somatoform and dissociative disorders have helped debunk beliefs about the gender-specificity of at least some of these disorders. But there are precious few studies of their cause. Additional attention must be paid to the factors that contribute causally to the development of these disorders. Several topics likely to receive increased attention include family factors, such as parenting styles and the modeling of explanations for ambiguous bodily sensations; early traumatic events, such as the occurrence of childhood sexual molestation or emotionally charged "medical" experiences; cognitive factors, such as an individual's manner of processing bodily sensations as a predisposition to somatoform disorders; and biological factors, such as the underlying physiological changes that take place in somatoform and dissociative disorders. This research arena is far from stale: Many avenues are worthy of pursuit.

Until recently, treatment studies have been limited by the rarity of identified cases. With new diagnostic procedures and more widespread assessment efforts, additional cases are being recognized. The resulting increase in sample sizes will allow for the progression from case studies and single-case designs to more controlled comparisons of the efficacy of different treatments.

KEY TERMS

aphonia (201)
conversion disorder (200)
dissociative disorders (203)
dissociative identity disorder (DID) (208)

dissociative (psychogenic) fugue (206)
factitious disorders (198)
generalized dissociative amnesia (204)

glove anesthesia (200)
hypochondriasis (197)
la belle indifference (202)
malingering (198)
response prevention (196)

selective dissociative amnesia (203)
somatization disorder (194)
somatoform disorders (194)
somatosensory amplification (199)

SUMMARY

Somatoform Disorders

Somatoform disorders involve physical symptoms that have no organic basis, that are associated with psychological conflicts and stress, and that are not produced voluntarily. Three types of somatoform disorders are somatization disorder, hypochondriasis, and conversion disorder.

Patients with *somatization disorder* have a long history of physical complaints that result in treatment for impaired social and occupational functioning. In cases of *hypochondriasis*, the sufferer is preoccupied with fears of having a serious disease. The patient seriously misinterprets bodily reactions and, as a result of the preoccupation, experiences a clinical level of distress. Other conditions must also be considered: *factitious disorders*, in which the patient intentionally produces (fakes) the symptoms to assume the role of a sick person; and *malingering*, in which the symptoms are intentionally faked for reasons involving an external incentive. The presence of *somatosensory amplification* has been implicated in hypochondriasis.

Conversion disorder involves one or more symptoms or deficits affecting voluntary functioning that cannot be explained by a neurological or general medical condition. In the past, the attitude of the patient was used to determine the presence of conversion disorder: *La belle indifference* was the label given a nonchalant and matter-of-fact attitude that seemed to reflect a lack of concern about the suffering or disability. Although attitude may be informative, one must also consider the possibility that patients are being stoic in their approach to an illness.

Women are twice as likely as men to be diagnosed with conversion disorder, and the types of conversion reactions differ for the genders. For all sufferers, conflict and stress, as well as familial, learning, and cognitive factors, are implicated in the onset. The limited incidence of the disorder has slowed research on treatment outcome.

Dissociative Disorders

The *dissociative disorders* are characterized by disturbance or alteration of the integrative functions of identity, memory, and consciousness. Three types of dissociative disorders are amnesia, dissociative fugue, and dissociative identity disorder. In cases of *selective dissociative amnesia* a person forgets some but not all of what happened. The forgetting of one's entire life history is called *generalized dissociative amnesia*. Theories of forgetting include decay theory, which holds that memory loss is a result of disuse and the passage of time; interference theory, which suggests that memory loss is a result of the memory system having reached its capacity and become susceptible to confusion; a theory that points to problems in the process of retrieving information, whereby forgetting is linked to a person's inability to retrieve stored information. Also implicated in psychopathology is the notion of repression, in which unwanted memories are kept out of the person's awareness.

Dissociative (psychogenic) fugue involves sudden and unexpected travel away from one's home or place of work with an inability to recall one's past and, often, the assumption of a new identity. In cases of both amnesia and fugue, sufferers are unlikely to have a second episode. Recovery is frequently rapid, with a return of memory. Our understanding of both the cause and treatment of these disorders is limited.

Dissociative identity disorder (DID), one of the most popularized disorders, is relatively rare. It involves the presence, in one person, of two or more distinct personalities, each with its own relatively enduring behavior pattern. DID is not the same as schizophrenia, nor is it a personality disorder. New approaches to assessment have suggested an increased frequency of cases. Unfortunately, in many instances, we are not able to determine if these are true or false-positive cases. DID occurs more often in women, has been identified worldwide, and is thought to be associated with traumatic early childhood sexual experiences. Treatment often takes a psychodynamic perspective, which seeks to uncover and unravel underlying conflicts.

Consider the following...

Suppose that a local mental health professional was being interviewed for a call-in television program and claimed forcefully that every patient he has seen in his years of clinical practice who had DID had been sexually abused — and he claimed to have seen over 200 patients with this disorder. Why might the professional be making this claim? Is there a genuine increase in the incidence of DID? If not, what could account for the rise in the number of identified cases? Put these specific questions aside for a moment and ask who selects the professionals to be on "talk shows" and does anyone have the responsibility to check their assertions for accuracy or credibility?

Suppose that you are the employer of a small home-repair company. One of your workers injured his back on the job and has been receiving worker compensation while recuperating. Initially, the doctors had predicted that recovery could take two months; but it has now been seven months since the accident, and your employee is still complaining of pain and has not returned to work. You, of course, are concerned that the worker may be malingering — that is, faking his continued pain in order to continue to collect benefits. What should be done in cases where there is no visible physical injury? Should psychological factors be taken into account? What if the injury and pain are not real, yet the person is not intentionally faking — as in conversion disorder?

CHAPTER 8

Mood Disorders and Suicide

Those among us . . .

- Donna lives down the hall in your dorm. She recently had to drop out for the semester because of depression. She became upset when her boyfriend ended their relationship, getting to the point where she wouldn't come out of her room and could not keep up with her course work.

- Arlene is a cheerful young woman who works as a cashier at your supermarket. You always enjoy chatting. Last week she told you she was pregnant, after trying for a long time; then she burst into tears. You've since heard that she took a leave from the job because of depression.

- Tony is a close friend of your brother. You've always known him to be outgoing, but over the past few weeks he has been acting outrageously — talking a mile a minute, spending far too much money, telling you about some plans he has that he thinks are brilliant but you think are a bit off the wall. Then, rather abruptly, he's become extremely depressed.

- Jerry, a middle-aged man who was your supervisor at work, is found in a hotel room where he'd carefully laid out a sheet and shot himself to death. You had no idea that suicide was on his mind.

How can people get seriously depressed about things that are seemingly not that negative or devastating or even sometimes positive?

What causes people to go into an intensely positive mood state and then switch into the opposite, a deep depression?

Do people make "rational" choices when they commit suicide? How can seemingly reasonable and healthy people take their own lives?

Depression is widely misunderstood. It is commonly thought of as a state that people should "snap out of" through will power and effort. Its onset is often puzzling and paradoxical. People who don't seem to have any reason to be depressed — who are wealthy or successful or have good families — still get depressed. And people sometimes stay depressed even after others incorrectly assume that they "should" recover from their problems. Depressed individuals often seem irrational, exaggerating their shortcomings or misfortunes. Sometimes they wish to die — and many actually commit suicide. Even mild or moderate levels of depression may drain people's energy and impair their ability to generate or sustain activity. But as much as someone may want to refuse to acknowledge depression, denying it will not make it go away.

Depression is one of the most common psychiatric disorders, affecting all segments of society. It is a **mood,** or **affective, disorder,** defined by intense emotional states as well as related behavioral, cognitive, and physical symptoms. Figure 8.1 shows the common forms of mood disorders, which are grouped into two main categories: unipolar depression and bipolar disorder. See also the DSM-IV classification on the front endpapers. In this chapter we review the features, causes, and treatment of these disorders, and then discuss suicide, sometimes a fatal result of mood and other disorders.

FEATURES OF UNIPOLAR DEPRESSION

"I was really depressed when I got a B instead of an A on my midterm." "This weather is so depressing." "She looks depressed — must be having a bad day." As these examples illustrate, people often use the word *depression* casually to mean a normal mood state that lasts for several minutes, hours, or days — a temporary negative mood that usually follows an unpleasant, disappointing, or upsetting experience. But the *syndrome* of depression, the entire set of symptoms that define depressive diagnoses, is far more than just a bad mood.

Clinical Characteristics of Unipolar Depression

Clinically significant depression, in contrast to normal mood depression, is a condition that persists for weeks or months. It is not just a disorder of mood but also a disorder of the way people think, their physical state, and their behaviors. To be diagnosed as such, a depression must involve multiple accompanying symptoms, persist over time, and cause impaired functioning — as we discuss in the following sections. When depression occurs without the extreme positive mood known as

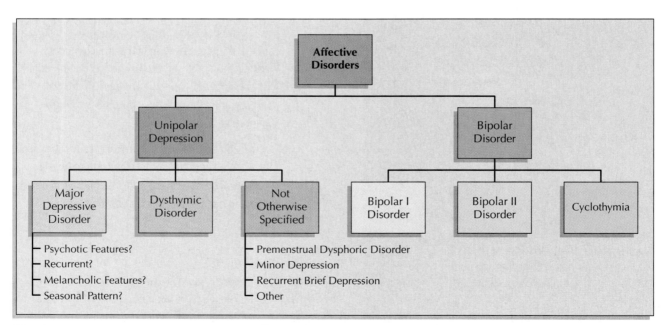

Figure 8.1 Common Forms of Mood Disorders

Mood, or affective, disorders are psychological problems defined by notable mood changes and related symptoms. Unipolar depression consists of two main subtypes that vary in severity and chronicity, plus depressive disorder not otherwise specified (NOS). When the mood disorder involves shifts between depression and extreme high moods called mania, it is identified as bipolar disorder. Bipolar disorder also varies in the patterning and intensity of mood swings.

mania, the disorder is called **unipolar depression.** As Figure 8.1 indicates, unipolar and bipolar disorder are different diagnoses; but the depression may be identical in both, possibly leading to misdiagnosis. In a later section we discuss how to tell these disorders apart.

Mood Symptoms   Being down, sad, or blue is often the dominant feature of the syndrome of depression. What many people feel, however, is the sense that everything is dull, gray, and flat. Nothing is enjoyable, and the ability to experience pleasure is lost. A depressed man might feel apathetic about his job and his family. He might go through the motions of his daily routine but derive no enjoyment from his accomplishments or family interactions. Irritability is also a common expression of depression.

Cognitive Symptoms: Depressive Thinking   Another hallmark of depression is negative thinking. A depressed person seems to pay attention only to negative information or to minimize the positive while exaggerating the negative; Table 8.1 gives some examples. When people are in a depressed mood, they perceive and interpret themselves as inadequate and the world as rejecting. They are pessimistic. As a result of their bleak outlooks or expectations that only bad things will happen, they feel, "What's the use?" and their motivation becomes impaired. To the extent that depressed people view the future negatively, they might also become *hopeless* — a cognitive style that is strongly related to suicidal feelings. If they believe themselves incapable of dealing with a situation, they feel helpless and give up. And if they feel undesirable or incompetent, they are likely to believe that others do not like them or want to be around them. When no longer depressed, however, people display a more balanced perspective.

As you can imagine, the negative thinking of depression makes people feel worse. It also generates some of the irrational aspects of the disorder that are so baffling to those around depressed people. Consider, for example, the executive who gets promoted to her lifelong

Depression has many faces — quiet sadness, blankness and absence of pleasure, intense suffering and despair.

dream of being a vice-president but becomes depressed because she feels she really does not deserve the job and will fail miserably for all to see.

Clinical depression is also marked by difficulties in cognitive activities such as concentration, memory, and decision making. The more severe the depression, the more the person complains about difficulties in remembering or concentrating or even carrying on a conversation. Decision making becomes very difficult, whether it involves choosing an item from a restaurant menu or deciding how to solve an important problem.

Physical and Behavioral Symptoms   Depressed people often find it difficult to initiate activity because they cannot imagine that it will give them pleasure or satisfaction. A loss of energy and feelings of fatigue are also very common. Depressed people report feeling heavy and lifeless. Their persistent tiredness may be accompanied by aches, pains, stomach problems, and other physical symptoms. Although some depressed people continue with their daily schedules, others are unable to get out of bed or merely go through the motions of daily life. Changes

Mood has a powerful influence on thinking. A person selectively interprets events more negatively when depressed than when not depressed. As these examples show, depressive thinking may cause a person to construe minor, ambiguous, or positive everyday events in a negative light. Events that are negative are seen as extreme catastrophies. These tendencies toward negative thinking contribute to even more depression.

Table 8.1   Examples of Depressive Thinking

Everyday Events	Thoughts
My boyfriend didn't call me.	He's out with someone else. He will leave me.
Our son's teacher wants to discuss his performance.	I've failed as a parent.

Major Negative Events	Thoughts
I'm getting a divorce.	No one will ever love me.
I've been laid off my job.	I'm a failure. I'll never get another job.
I'm seriously ill.	I'll never be happy again.

in psychomotor activity occur. Depressed persons may be slowed down; they may move more slowly, talk with less animation, show less facial expression, and sigh often. Conversely, they may be agitated and restless, unable to sit still, pacing, and wringing their hands.

Changes in sleep and appetite also accompany clinical depression. In one common pattern, the person wakes up in the middle of the night or early in the morning and is unable to go back to sleep. In another pattern, the person with depression sleeps more than usual. Appetite, too, may increase or diminish. Some depressed people eat more and gain weight. Others lose weight because they don't feel like eating; their sense of taste and enjoyment disappear, and their stomachs feel like lead.

Finally, social withdrawal is common among people with depression. They want to stay at home or in their rooms, believing that there is no enjoyment in being around other people or that others don't want to be around them.

Living with Depression: Impaired Functioning As we've noted, depression is far more than just a mood

problem. Compounding the emotional pain is the extent to which depression disrupts people's lives and possibly worsens their circumstances: People experience a vicious cycle of depression and impairment that is particularly debilitating for those whose depression is chronic or recurring. The person's typical activities — as student, parent, employee, family member, friend — suffer greatly.

Interpersonal difficulties often result from depression. In fact, depressed people are difficult to be around, sometimes eliciting rejection and negative moods in others. James Coyne and his colleagues (1987) found that adults and spouses reported facing many burdens as a result of living with a depressed person, and many needed treatment themselves. Relationships between depressed parents and their children are also impaired (reviewed in Hammen, 1991). Depression appears to lower women's tolerance for their children's demands, sometimes causing them to become withdrawn and disinterested in the children's activities and critical of their shortcomings. The depressed person's relationships even with roommates or strangers may be negatively affected, because others generally don't like to be around "down" people (e.g., Hokanson et al., 1989).

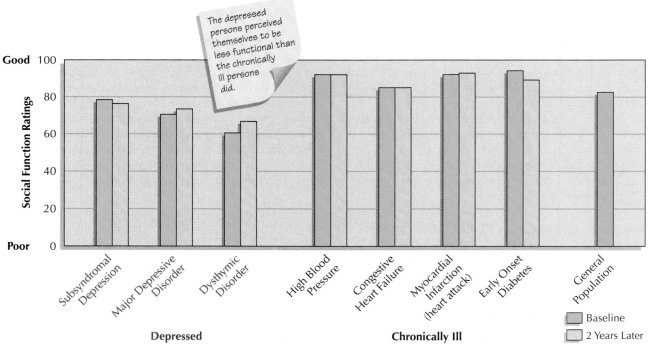

Figure 8.2 Social Functioning in Depressed Versus Medically Ill Adults

This figure shows patients' ratings of their social functioning (the extent to which health problems interfere with their social activities with family, friends, and others). Note that the three groups of depressed people rate themselves lower in social functioning than did those with chronic medical ailments and the general popula-tion. Although these three groups improved over a two-year period, the changes were not substantial. Also note that even the patients with mild chronic subsyndromal depression reported more impair-ment than the chronically medically ill patients. *Source:* Hays et al. (1995; adapted from Table 3).

Studies show that the extent of overall impairment associated with depression is surprising. In one investigation involving more than 11,000 patients (Wells et al., 1989), depressed people were compared with those who had hypertension, diabetes, coronary artery disease, angina, arthritis, back problems, lung problems, and gastrointestinal disorders. All patients were given a questionnaire that asked about (1) their physical, social, and role functioning (that is, their ability to conduct work, go to school, etc.); (2) the number of days they had spent in bed during the last month because of their condition; and (3) their perceptions of their own health. On nearly every measure, the depressed persons perceived themselves to be worse off than people who had significant chronic medical problems. When a subset of the original sample was followed up two years later, those with depression continued to perceive their lives as less functional than those of patients with chronic medical conditions, as Figure 8.2 indicates (Hays et al., 1995).

Due to seasonal patterns of depression, researchers have come to suspect that some mood disorders may be related to the amount of daylight the person is exposed to. This is a daytime scene in winter in Barrow, Alaska — and we might expect that there are more depressed people here than in Miami in the winter.

Diagnosing Unipolar Depression

Clinically significant depression is widespread. Because of its frequency we suspect that there are many different forms of depression. As shown in Figure 8.1, two major subcategories of unipolar depression appear in DSM-IV: major depressive disorder and dysthymic disorder. These two classifications may be further characterized by certain descriptive features. To warrant a diagnosis of unipolar depressive disorder, a person must never have had a manic or hypomanic episode (which we describe in the section on bipolar disorders). Thus, clinicians must evaluate the person's past experiences as well as his or her current condition.

Major Depressive Disorder Major depressive disorder refers to a distinct period of moderate-to-severe symptoms called *major depressive episode*. According to DSM-IV, diagnosis of this condition is contingent on a period of at least two weeks during which at least five of the following symptoms occur most of nearly every day: depressed mood or loss of pleasure in typically enjoyable activities; significant weight gain or loss or change in appetite; insomnia or too much sleep; fatigue, loss of energy, or psychomotor changes (either slowed down or agitated) that can be recognized by others; feelings of worthlessness or excessive guilt; diminished ability to think, concentrate, or make decisions; and recurrent thoughts of death or suicide.

Major depressive disorder may be characterized by other features as well. *Psychotic depression*, for example, may involve severe symptoms plus departures from reality such as hallucinations (sensory experiences for which there is no physical basis, as when a person hears voices) or delusions (beliefs that go beyond reality, as when a person thinks he is Jesus Christ). The hallucinations and delusions sometimes have a depressive content, such as voices telling oneself to end it all because one is not worthy of living, or the belief that one is responsible for all of the evil in the world. Unlike schizophrenia, which is a disorder involving disturbed thoughts and perceptual experiences often marked by little emotionality, psychotic depression is characterized by a depth of negative emotion and other features of the syndrome.

Researchers have speculated that some of the features of depressive episodes reflect biological disturbances of bodily functions. Nowadays, these are called *melancholic* features, referring to a severe depressive experience in which the person has lost pleasure in almost all activities or is unresponsive even when something good happens. Melancholia may also include certain distinctive *physical* symptoms, such as waking up early in the morning, marked psychomotor change, worse mood in the morning, and significant weight loss. Two additional indicators of melancholia may be excessive or inappropriate guilt and a quality of the depressed mood that makes it feel different (to the person) from emotions that would be experienced after the death of a loved one. Nonmelancholic depressions display fewer of these distinctive patterns of symptoms. Research continues to explore whether melancholic depressions have unique biological causes and whether they respond better to biological as opposed to psychological treatment.

A subcategory of major depressive disorder, called **seasonal affective disorder (SAD)**, refers to the time of year when depression occurs. In both the Northern and Southern hemispheres the most common pattern involves fall or winter depressions, which remit in the spring; some individuals, however, experience regular summer depressions. The seasonal pattern has been observed in 15 percent of patients with recurrent mood disorders, including both unipolar and bipolar illness (Faedda et al., 1993). Many individuals, children and adolescents among them, report mild symptoms of depression and associated impairment in the dark winter months, even though they do not meet the full criteria for major depression (Kasper et al., 1989; Madden, Heath, Rosenthal & Martin, 1996; Swedo et al., 1995). There is some evidence that seasonal changes in mood and behavior run in families, suggesting a genetic predisposition to SAD (Madden, Heath, Rosenthal & Martin, 1996). The characteristic symptoms of both clinical and subclinical seasonal depressions include low energy, excessive sleeping, overeating (often with a craving for carbohydrate foods), and weight gain.

Dysthymic Disorder Major depression, which is relatively brief and severe, contrasts with the mild, prolonged form of depression known as dysthymia or **dysthymic disorder**. To be diagnosed with this disorder, a person must have symptoms that persist for two years or more (one year for children and adolescents). During this period, the person, though not necessarily depressed every single day, must be symptomatic more days than not, and altogether does not have more than two symptom-free months. And in addition to depressed mood (or irritability in children or adolescents), the person must have at least three of the nine symptoms that characterize dysthymia: low self-esteem, pessimism or hopelessness, general loss of pleasure, social withdrawal, chronic tiredness, guilt or brooding about the past, irritability, decreased activity or productiveness, or diminished concentration, memory, or ability to make decisions.

The Heterogeneity of Depression Since depressions can take many forms, research and treatment may be hampered by including diverse groups who might actually have somewhat different versions of the disorder, possibly with different causes. Over the years clinicians have drawn many diagnostic distinctions — reactive versus endogenous, neurotic versus psychotic, and others. None of these has proven to be valid or useful in the sense of delineating distinctive features, course, or causal factors. Nevertheless, it is highly likely that not all depressions stem from the same causes or respond to the same treatments, and therefore the search for useful subtypes continues.

Meanwhile, the current diagnostic system makes subtype distinctions solely on the basis of symptoms. For example, as Figure 8.1 indicates, depression not other-

wise specified (NOS) is a residual category including *minor depression* (at least two weeks of depressive symptoms but less than the five symptoms required for a major episode) and *recurrent brief depression* (involving periods of depression that occur at least monthly and are intense but brief — two to fourteen days in duration — and are not associated with the menstrual cycle).

A controversial addition to the NOS category is *premenstrual dysphoric disorder*, in which depressive symptoms occur during the last week of the luteal phase of the menstrual cycle and are severe enough to cause notable impairment in the woman's typical roles. We discuss this disorder later in the chapter.

Comorbidity Depressive disorders often co-occur with other kinds of illnesses, both medical and psychiatric. On the one hand, depressive symptoms can be caused by medical problems (such as certain viral infections) or their treatments, endocrinological disorders (such as thyroid problems), neurological problems (such as certain types of stroke), and certain kinds of cancer (such as pancreatic cancer). A person who feels depressed over a period of time should therefore have a thorough medical evaluation to rule out physical causes. Conversely, a person who complains to a doctor about fatigue, loss of appetite, poor sleeping, or aches and pains that don't seem to improve may actually be experiencing depression. And, of course, medical problems may contribute to depression, just as depression may exacerbate medical symptoms and disability.

On the other hand, depression often co-occurs with other psychological problems. A recent community survey found that, among the total number of people who currently had major depressive disorder, 56 percent also had another diagnosable condition (Blazer, Kessler, McGonagle & Swartz, 1994). Alcoholism and anxiety disorders, for instance, are frequently seen in people with depressive disorders, and depression often develops after previous psychological problems have begun — possibly as a result of the consequences of other disorders. In addition, many people suffering from anxiety disorders become depressed. And personality disorders — which we discuss more extensively in Chapter 13 — occur in 30 percent to 70 percent of the outpatients diagnosed with depression (Farmer & Nelson-Gray, 1990). Even in children, depression rarely occurs by itself; mixtures of conduct disorders, attention deficit disorder, or anxiety disorders co-occurring with depression are common (Hammen & Compas, 1994). We discuss childhood depression further in Chapter 15.

Having described the various manifestations of depression, its symptoms, and its diagnoses, we now revisit the issue of the line between normal and unhealthy depression.

Sometimes a Little Depression Is Not a Good Thing

Since many disorders vary in degree, people with a low level of symptoms may be considered normal, yet acquire a diagnosis at some higher level of symptoms. Depression, however, is a disorder for which "low" may not mean healthy.

Normally, people are relatively happy and contented — or at least somewhat satisfied. In the scores of studies that have asked people to rate themselves on scales of subjective well-being, the majority of individuals report a positive level of well-being. This finding holds up for nearly every country surveyed — and, perhaps surprisingly, is true even of most of the people we would expect to be unhappy with their lives: the multiply handicapped, poor and nonwhite people, and the elderly (reviewed in Diener & Diener, 1996). Moreover, research on twins suggests that level of happiness may be substantially less associated with life circumstances than with genetic factors (Lykken & Tellegen, 1996). Thus, a *positive mood* is normal — and may be more a matter of what we are born with than of good or bad fortune.

Of course, depressed mood is such a common part of life in response to everyday hurts and disappointments that having *brief* periods of depressive reactions is also normal. It is equally normal to have sustained periods of grief or distress following loss. However, it turns out that even low scores on depression measures — for example, poor self-esteem, lack of enthusiasm, a pessimistic outlook, or a tendency to be easily hurt or discouraged — can signal a state that is not mentally healthy *if* those symptoms persist. The following paragraphs describe circumstances under which even low, mild, nondiagnosable symptoms of depression are not normal or healthy.

1. Mild symptoms may be a precursor to later depressive episodes. One longitudinal study showed that people with mild, subclinical symptoms of depression were 4.4 times more likely to develop major depressive episodes over a one-year period than were those without symptoms (Horwath, Johnson, Klerman & Weissman, 1992). A similar study found that 10 percent of all individuals who showed minor depression went on to develop a major depressive episode within one year (Broadhead, Blazer, George & Tse, 1990). We cannot predict why a mild persisting depression might become a major depressive episode, but people in an already depressed state might be especially vulnerable if negative events befall them.

2. Mild symptoms may be associated with significant impairment. As Figure 8.2 indicates, even people with mild chronic subsyndromal depression reported more social impairment than did persons suffering from chronic medical illnesses. Work, family relationships, and perceptions of overall health may also be affected by mild symptoms of depression.

Mild symptoms may be associated with other adverse outcomes as well. A community survey found that those who showed even low levels of symptoms, compared to nondepressed persons in the general population, were more likely to burden their community's resources with visits to emergency rooms, suicide attempts, and lost work days, as indicated in Figure 8.3 (Johnson, Weissman &

Figure 8.3 Adverse Outcome as a Function of Depression Status

A survey of 18,000 representative U.S. adults examined the link between depression, use of services, and impairment. The researchers found not only that those with diagnoses of major depression or dysthymic disorder differ from nondepressed people, but also that those with even *mild,* nondiagnosable symptoms differ from the nondepressed. For example, mildly depressed people made significantly more use of emergency services for emotional problems, attempted suicide more often, experienced more work absence for more than one week due to emotional problems, and used tranquilizers more frequently. These figures suggest that since mild symptoms of depression are fairly common in the population, they may account for a sizable cost to their communities through use of emergency services and work loss. *Source: Johnson, Weissman & Klerman (1992).*

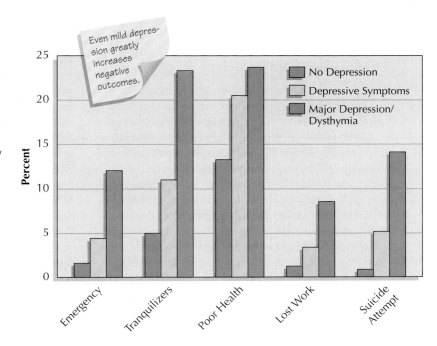

Even mild depression greatly increases negative outcomes.

Abraham Lincoln is one of several historical figures who suffered from depression. He wrote, "I am now the most miserable man living. . . . I awfully forbode I shall not be better."

Contemporary public figures, like television journalist Dan Rather, have also acknowledged suffering from — and being treated for — severe depression.

Klerman, 1992). Finally, given that depressive symptoms often co-occur with other psychological disorders, we should not be surprised by the following results. A large-scale study that assessed mood symptoms in the U.S. population discovered that, when the participants were followed up sixteen years later, those with initially elevated depression scores — even mild, subclinical levels — were significantly more likely than nondepressed people to have been hospitalized for some psychiatric disorder (Zonderman et al., 1993).

3. Mild symptoms may indicate a *depressive personality.* Researchers have long speculated that some people have stable personality traits that resemble depression; specifically, such people are pessimistic and incapable of fun, introverted, self-critical, critical of others, highly conscientious, worrying and preoccupied with feelings of inadequacy. For example, Klein and Miller (1993) surveyed college students and found that, although many of them who scored high on these traits had depressive disorders, a full 39 percent had no diagnosable depression — just the traits. Morever, those with high scores on depressive personality traits showed significantly more impaired personal and social functioning than

did those with only few of the traits. In short, the presence of depressive personality seemed to predict both susceptibility to depressive disorders and impaired functioning.

Who Is Affected with Unipolar Depression?

Depression occurs so frequently in the population that it has earned the label "common cold of psychological disorders." According to a review of epidemiological studies throughout the world, current *major depression* occurs in 5 percent to 7 percent of adults (Smith & Weissman, 1992). In the United States, the figure is about 4.9 percent (Blazer, Kessler, McGonagle & Swartz, 1994). Another 2 percent to 4 percent of the world population currently have dysthymic disorder (Smith & Weissman, 1992). Across their *lifetimes,* Americans have a 17 percent chance of having a major depressive episode (Blazer, Kessler, McGonagle & Swartz, 1994).

These are overall averages, and they are high. Some segments of the population exhibit even higher rates. But no segment of the population escapes depression. It afflicts not only the poor and disadvantaged but also the wealthy, the privileged, and the talented.

Depression as a Disorder of Women One of the most consistent findings in research on depression is that women are more than twice as likely as men to be depressed (e.g., Weissman & Olfson, 1995). As Figure 8.4 shows, this gender difference occurs in all countries. It is not seen in young children, but first becomes well established in adolescence (Angold & Rutter, 1992).

Women not only exhibit higher rates of depression; they also appear to have more severe disorders. Longitudinal research indicates that they are more likely than men to experience recurrences of depressive episodes, especially younger women and those with younger onset of depression (Lewinsohn et al., 1994; Winokur et al., 1993). Women's depressions may also last longer (e.g., Sargeant, Bruce, Florio & Weissman, 1990).

How can we account for these gender differences? Hormonally linked biological differences in depression rates have been cited as one possible explanation. However, most theories emphasize psychological and sociological issues, which we discuss later.

Recall Donna, the college student introduced at the start of the chapter. Her case is fairly typical of the nature and expression of major depressive disorder. It emphasizes many of the key symptoms of the depression syndrome, including depressive thinking. The combination of certain personal characteristics and a stressful event is a common triggering mechanism for depression, as we also explore later.

> *Donna developed a major depression following her break-up with Jeff, and because she was withdrawn, lacked energy, and couldn't command the motivation to continue school, she dropped out for the semester. You had seen her mood get worse and worse over a few weeks, to the point where she often didn't get out of bed in the morning and slept many hours. She seemed to require a big effort just to take a shower and get dressed. Her appetite also vanished; although you and others urged her to eat, she said she didn't feel like it. Finally, someone called her parents, who came to see her and decided she needed treatment. Her doctor thinks she has a good prognosis for recovery, so she can return to school later if she wishes. You've always known her as someone lacking in confidence, a bit shy with people. When Jeff ended their six-month relationship, she was convinced that no one would ever be interested in her again, and that she'd be alone forever. When you tried to reassure her, she thought you were just "putting up" with her and didn't really care. She said*

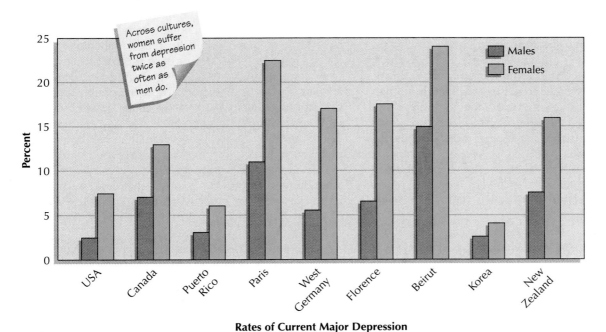

Rates of Current Major Depression

Figure 8.4   Rates of Current Major Depression
Weissman and Olfson (1995) examined large-scale international studies of depression. Although the overall rates differ somewhat from country to country, every nation showed a significant gender difference: Depression affects more women than men. (On average, the ratio is 2:1.) Any valid theory of the causes of depression must therefore explain why it is more prevalent among women. *Source:* Weissman & Olfson (1995).

she felt like a burden on everyone and just wanted to stay by herself. She had always seemed a very nice person but didn't have a lot of friends. Her parents appeared to be caring people, although she'd sometimes said they were pretty wrapped up in their own lives and were glad she was away at college. You and the others on the dorm floor have been very worried about her and are glad that she got into treatment. Still, everyone wondered why she was so upset over a relationship that hadn't lasted that long anyway.

Cultural and Ethnic Differences in Depression

As we have seen, major depression occurs in all cultures and in all segments of society. In the United States, epidemiological surveys have generally indicated that major depressive episodes occur with about equal frequency in African American and white groups (Blazer, Kessler, McGonagle & Swartz, 1994; Brown, Ahmed, Gary & Milburn, 1995) and at a somewhat higher frequency among Hispanics (Blazer, Kessler, McGonagle & Swartz, 1994). These rates are also influenced by gender and age.

Nevertheless, there are important cultural differences in the expression of depressive disorders. For instance, as we note in Chapter 1, Western industrialized societies make a distinction between mind and body as well as between emotional and somatic symptoms. In many non-Western or nonindustrialized cultures, however, depressive symptoms may be reported as bodily symptoms. Because this emphasis on somatic symptoms may be misunderstood, some cultural groups, using Western-based criteria, may not be appropriately diagnosed or treated. Hence, culturally patterned expressions of disorder must be increasingly acknowledged and emphasized by diagnosticians. For instance, Koreans and Korean Americans recognize a syndrome called *hwa-byung*, characterized by various physiological and psychological symptoms such as fatigue and depressed mood. When Korean Americans who said they had suffered from *hwa-byung* were interviewed using standard DSM criteria for major depression, researchers found a significant overlap between these two conditions, suggesting that *hwa-byung* may represent a culturally patterned way of expressing major depression (Lin et al., 1992).

Young People: The Epidemic of Depression

A decade or two ago, depression was often characterized as a disorder of middle age; children and youth were not considered to be at risk for depression. But two trends have recently come to the attention of behavioral scientists: the apparently increasing rates of depression among young people, and the early onset of depressive disorders.

Because current instruments and procedures for measuring depression were not available in past decades, we have only indirect evidence that rates of depression are increasing among young people. This evidence comes largely from studies of people of different ages who are interviewed about their past experiences with depression. Several preliminary studies suggesting higher rates among people born more recently led to a cross-national investigation conducted by researchers in different countries. Percentages of lifetime depressive diagnoses for different birth cohorts (categorized by decade of birth) are shown in Figure 8.5. Although the countries vary somewhat in terms of age patterns, all but Italy show higher rates by age twenty-five for the group born after 1955 than for any other cohort, as well as generally higher rates for younger subjects (Cross-National Collaborative Group, 1992). Within the United States, evidence points to increasing rates even during the past few years. For example, investigators who conducted a large community survey of adolescents in Oregon found that rates of major depression for adolescent females aged fourteen to nineteen were higher among those born between 1972 and 1975 than among those born between 1968 and 1971 (Lewinsohn, Rohde, Seeley & Fischer, 1993).

The second trend, which is related to the first one, concerns lower age of *onset* of depression than that observed in previous clinical studies. The initial experience of major depressive episode is now most likely to occur between the ages of fifteen and nineteen among both men and women, based on surveys of five U.S. communities (Burke, Burke, Regier & Rae, 1990). Not long ago, typical onset was more likely to occur during the thirties or older.

Why are the rates of clinically diagnosable depression so high for young people? Maybe young people have become more willing to report depressive symptoms. However, depression rates reflect not just subjective complaining but also increased incidence of hospitalization and suicide. Another possible explanation concerns memory: Perhaps older people who are interviewed simply forget that they were depressed earlier in their lives. Note, however, that studies comparing peoples' reported symptoms with other sources of information about their symptoms, such as treatment records and relatives' reports, have shown that depressed people up to age eighty are fairly accurate and reliable reporters of actual depression (reviewed by Klerman & Weissman, 1989).

Although the true causes of increased depression rates are not fully known, investigators have suggested that various factors contributing to risk for depression have become more salient. These include social and demographic changes that both intensify depression and reduce the effectiveness of coping resources, such as the changing structure and composition of the family, increased mobility and urbanization, increased disengagement from the community, increased exposure to stressors, and decreased access to desired goals. Later in this chapter we examine how these and other factors contribute to depression.

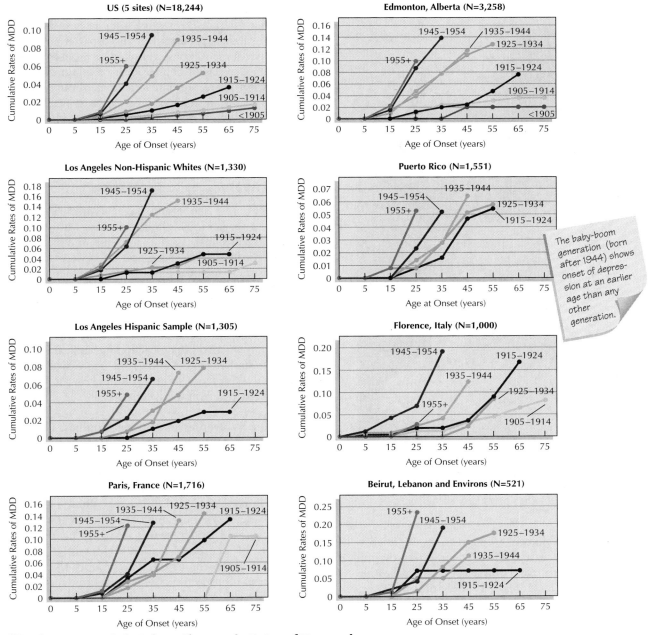

Figure 8.5   Birth Cohort Changes in Rates of Depression

Investigators in several countries interviewed individuals representing different birth cohorts about their histories of depressive experiences. In nearly every case (except Italy), those born in 1955 or later exhibited the highest rates of major depression by age twenty-five. Most of the countries show higher rates for those born in younger birth cohorts. *Source:* Cross-National Collaborative Group (1992).

The baby-boom generation (born after 1944) shows onset of depression at an earlier age than any other generation.

Course of Unipolar Depression

The good news is that, whether treated or untreated, major depressive episodes nearly always subside within a few months. In addition, episodes appear to be self-limiting, with more than 50 percent of depressed people recovering within six months and about 70 percent recovering within a year (Coryell et al., 1994).

The bad news, however, is that most people who experience a major depressive episode will have more than one — and many have recurrent depressions. Indeed, Keller (1988) reported that within a five-year period 76 percent of depressed patients experienced a recurrence, and an international study sponsored by the World Health Organization found that depressed patients experienced an average of 2.7 major depressive episodes over a ten-year period (Thornicroft & Sartorius, 1993). Another negative outcome is *chronic*

Although for most women a joyous occasion, childbirth is commonly followed by "baby blues" or even by clinically diagnosable major depression in a smaller number of women. Both biological and psychological factors may trigger such depressive reactions.

depression. About 25 percent of depressives experience persisting depression, in the form of either dysthymic disorder or failure to recover completely from depressive episodes (e.g., Depue & Monroe, 1986; Sargeant, Bruce, Florio & Weissman, 1990). Unfortunately, studies consistently show that depression predicts depression: Prior episodes predict recurrence, and long periods of depression predict further depression (e.g., Winokur et al., 1993).

CAUSES OF UNIPOLAR DEPRESSION

Consider some of the facts about depression: It is fairly common, it is a disorder not only of mood but also of thinking and bodily reactions, it is more frequent in women and young people, and past depression predicts future depression. Depression is often an understandable reaction to adversity, and yet it can also occur in the apparent absence of an important negative event. Add to these another finding: Depression runs in families. Can a biological model explain all of these patterns? What about an environmental or psychological model? Do we need different models of depression to explain different circumstances? There are many theories about the origins of depression; in this section we discuss the biological and psychological approaches. Included among the latter are the psychodynamic, cognitive-behavioral, and diathesis-stress perspectives.

Biological Approaches to Depression

Several facts about depression have pointed investigators toward a search for biological causes. Many of the symptoms are physical, such as appetite and sleep disturbances and loss of pleasure and energy. And as we note earlier, many medical illnesses produce depression. In addition, medications that are known to deplete certain neurotransmitters cause depression, and drugs that increase their availability reduce depression. As we explore the meaning of these patterns, the question to keep in mind is whether biological findings indicate *causal* factors, or whether they result from depressive symptoms themselves or from some additional factor such as response to environmental adversity.

Genetic Studies   Depression runs in families. Later in the chapter we discuss the psychological meaning of this pattern, but here we explore the possibility of genetic transmission. Twin studies give a clear indication of heritability by comparing those who are genetically identical (monozygotic twins) with those who share only half of their genes (dizygotic twins). In one recent study, researchers located British twin pairs from hospitalization records of depressed patients (McGuffin, Katz, Watkins & Rutherford, 1996). They found 46 percent concordance in monozygotic twins, compared to 20 percent concordance in dizygotic twins. An earlier large-scale U.S. twin study similarly concluded that the patterns suggest both genetic transmission and environmental influences on depression (Kendler et al., 1992).

Numerous other studies also show familial patterns: If one person is depressed, close relatives of that person tend to reveal more depression than is true of the general population (reviewed in Goldin & Gershon, 1988; see also Figure 8.9 later in the chapter). In one of the largest such studies, the rate of severe major depression involving hospitalization or incapacitation was 10 percent among close relatives of depressed patients, compared with about 5 percent among the relatives of healthy controls (Winokur et al., 1995). About 40 to 50 percent of the children of depressed mothers also show evidence of depressive disorders (Hammen, 1991).

Recent developments in molecular genetics using recombinant DNA techniques have provided new tools

for trying to locate genes for mood disorders. However, genetic linkage methods will probably not prove particularly useful for studying unipolar depression because such methods work best with clearly defined disorders that follow simple patterns of genetic transmission by way of a single major gene. Indeed, as unipolar depressions are quite heterogeneous disorders, it is highly unlikely that single gene locations are involved (Blehar, Weissman, Gershon & Hirschfeld, 1988).

As usual, given suggestive evidence of at least modest genetic contributions to unipolar depression, we must pose the question "What is inherited?" This question remains unanswered, although, as we next explore, there are several possibilities.

Neurotransmitter and Neuroendocrine Functioning

Considerable research has focused on the speculation that the small subset of neurotransmitters called **monoamines** (largely norepinephrine, dopamine, and serotonin) play a central role in depression. The monoamine neurons, known to be important in the limbic system of the brain, are widely distributed into other areas, affecting and integrating emotional, psychomotor, and biological functions. Initially, antidepressant medications were believed to produce their effects by increasing the availability of monoamine neurotransmitters (especially norepinephrine), principally by blocking their reabsorption back into the presynaptic neurons and thus leaving more available in the synapse. An earlier theory of the biology of depression, therefore, hypothesized that depression resulted from too little of such neurotransmitters (especially norepinephrine and serotonin) and that mania resulted from too much (Schildkraut, 1965).

The original theory was much too simple, however: Antidepressants not only alter amounts of monoamines but also change the complex interactions among various neurotransmitter systems and the receptors that respond to them. A new model of depression has since emerged that emphasizes the *dysregulation* of neurotransmitter systems, defined as the instability, desynchronization, and abnormal reactivity of the monoamine neurotransmitter system, causing depression (Siever & Davis, 1985). Although dysregulation appears to be an accurate description, the question now is whether this condition captures the essential problem of vulnerability to depres-

sion, or whether it is part of a larger problem or even the consequence of a more fundamental dysfunction.

Consider another piece of this complex puzzle. Recall that the neurotransmitters are involved in communication; they relay messages between areas of the brain serving different functions. The neurotransmitters serotonin, dopamine, and norepinephrine are especially important in the functioning of the limbic system (comprising the amygdala, hippocampus, hypothalamus, and associated structures) in that they regulate instinct, emotion, and drive. Through the hypothalamus, important *neuroendocrine systems* (complex interconnections among the brain, certain hormones, and various organs) are regulated by neurotransmitters. One of these systems, the **hypothalamic-pituitary-adrenal (HPA) axis,** is believed to play an especially important role in depression. This system is highly relevant to the body's mobilization in the face of stress. A person's perception of stress activates a complex chain of events in which a hormone is synthesized and secreted by the hypothalamus and transported to the pituitary gland. Portions of the pituitary release additional hormones that stimulate the adrenal glands; these in turn produce the hormone **cortisol,** which physiologically prepares the body for response to the stress. Cortisol inhibits further production of the hormones produced by the hypothalamus and pituitary, thus permitting the stress reaction to "switch off" so that the body can return to a normal state when the stress has passed. Elevated cortisol and abnormal daily rhythms of cortisol level are consistently found among acutely depressed people, compared with people who are not depressed. Also, many depressed people have abnormal cortisol reactions, continuing to create cortisol instead of showing the normal switching off reaction. When no longer depressed, most people return to normal cortisol functioning (Gold, Goodwin & Chrousos, 1988a).

Clearly, therefore, the human stress response involves complex interactions among neurotransmitters, neurohormones, and brain areas controlling different functions and their association with other physiological systems. Philip Gold and his colleagues (1988b) postulated that some forms of depression arise from situations in which the body, following exposure to acute generalized stress, fails to return to a normal state when the precipitating conditions are no longer present. They also speculated that defective stress mechanisms may involve genetically transmitted dysfunctions, and that severe early childhood stress reactions potentially sensitize and damage the activation and operation of the HPA system, resulting in vulnerability to severe depression in the face of stressors.

Biological Rhythm Dysfunction   The human body normally demonstrates regular daily cycles of changes, called **circadian rhythms,** in functions such as sleep-wake cycles, neuroendocrine activity including the HPA axis, and body temperature. These cycles usually follow the day-night patterns of light. Depressed people, however, experience disruptions in certain elements of the cycles, suggesting the intriguing idea that depression may be a disorder of abnormal regulation of the circadian rhythms.

Because the sleep-wake cycle is one of the principal rhythms of the body, investigators have long pondered the meaning of sleep disturbances in depression. Not only do patients report difficulties in staying asleep or waking up too early in the morning, but electroencephalographic (EEG) measures of brain waves during different stages of sleep (see Chapter 4) also indicate abnormalities in depressed patients. David Kupfer and his colleagues, among others, have reported that depressed patients in sleep laboratories demonstrate abnormal patterns, particularly reduced time to the onset of the rapid eye movement (REM) sleep stage after the beginning of sleep. Called *reduced REM latency,* this pattern appears to be relatively specific to depressed patients, does not necessarily change when they are no longer depressed, and may predict subsequent risk for relapse (Kupfer & Reynolds, 1992; reviewed by Benca, Obermeyer, Thisted & Gillin, 1992). The importance of sleep abnormalities in causing or exacerbating depression is further emphasized by the finding that partial sleep deprivation may be an effective, though not enduring, treatment for depression (Wu & Bunney, 1990), as we discuss later in the section on treatment.

What do these sleep patterns mean? One speculation is that recurrent mood disorders, including depression, reflect a defect in the mechanisms for keeping the different circadian rhythm processes synchronized. This topic of study requires intense focus on complex neuroregulatory processes, involving many levels of analysis from behavioral patterns associated with seasons of the year all the way down to intracellular mechanisms.

The Role of Hormones   Much energetic debate has been waged over the link between moods and the female hormones known as estrogen and progesterone. Some researchers have proposed that the prevalence of women among depressed people can be explained in part by hormonal processes (reviewed in Nolen-Hoeksema, 1987). Disorders such as premenstrual syndrome (PMS), post-partum depression, and menopausal depression (involutional melancholia) do suggest that changes in female hormones underlie mood changes. Unfortunately, separating fact from fiction in this area is very difficult.

Consider postpartum depression, for example. Within a few days after giving birth, women experience a dramatic drop in estrogen and progesterone levels. The majority of women may undergo brief spells of crying, sadness, anxiety, and upset, but these do not constitute depression in the clinical sense; indeed, they might best be called *postpartum blues.* Possibly one to two women per thousand experience postpartum psychosis, which can be severe enough to lead to the mother's attempted suicide together with an attempt to kill her baby. In between postpartum blues and postpartum psychosis in severity are the depressive episodes called postpartum depression. Clearly, therefore, dramatic hormonal shifts as such do not lead to depression inasmuch as the majority of women do not have major depression when experiencing biological changes such as childbirth. When women do experience major episodes of depression, these episodes could be attributed to stressful circumstances or to preexisting depressive disorders.

Researchers are uncertain about the meaning of premenstrual syndrome, or PMS (Gitlin & Pasnau, 1989). Interpretation of research on this topic has been hampered by biases against women, feminist politics, and poor methodologies — but mostly by overly simplistic theories. Whether PMS is primarily a hormonal problem, a psychiatric problem related to preexisting psychological conditions, a type of response to stressful circumstances, or a combination of these factors is a matter of debate. Previous versions of the DSM did not resolve the controversy. But DSM-IV, despite its failure to clarify the cause or meaning of PMS patterns, for the first time includes *premenstrual dysphoric disorder* as a diagnosis under the residual category of Depressive Disorders Not Otherwise Specified.

Overall, considerable support exists for biological features of depressive episodes. As noted, however, most of this research does not establish causality. Depression — a severe disruption of normal behavioral and physical function that often occurs as a response to stressors — may be accompanied by biological changes (given that all behavior is represented as physical processes), or it may be the *cause* of disrupted biological patterns. The next question to pursue is why some people get depressed under dire environmental conditions and others do not.

Psychological Perspectives on Depression

For most people, common sense dictates that depression is a reaction to something bad happening, such as the loss of an important relationship or the loss of a source of self-esteem. What goes beyond common sense, however, is the question of why depression persists, why it is

For many people, the immediate cause of depression is a personally meaningful event with negative implications and consequences. This jobless man at the unemployment office is depressed because loss of his job in his mind represented personal failure and lack of a source of self-worth, as well as economic difficulties he feels unable to cope with.

so extreme in some people, and why it sometimes occurs even in situations that most people would not consider very stressful. The centrality of this question is such that nearly all psychological models of depression take a *diathesis-stress* approach, which assumes that a negative, stressful event is the immediate trigger but that some kind of psychological predisposition (or combination of psychological and biological factors) is also implicated.

The Psychodynamic Perspective   Freud and his associates argued that depression is like grief, in that both often follow the loss of an important relationship. Unlike a grieving person, however, a depressed person displays low self-esteem and a tendency to blame and devalue the self as worthless and incompetent.

Freud and others suggested that the source of the self-deprecation was an ambivalently loved person, such as a mother, who died or withdrew love. The child internalizes the lost "object" (relationship), but the anger directed toward it is now directed toward the self. This "anger turned inward" creates a lasting vulnerability to the experience of depression when subsequent losses are experienced over the years. Later theorists expanded on these basic ideas. Although the early psychodynamic models about mechanisms of depression (such as intrapsychic aggression) have not been substantiated by research, they were accurate in their observation that loss experiences — and the way these are interpreted by the person — are powerful instigators of depression. The same themes have been pursued in very different forms by modern theorists, who consider the role of cognitive

appraisals, especially those related to a person's feelings of worth and competence; the importance of social and family relationships in supporting and maintaining a positive sense of the self; and the impact of negative life events such as losses. Each of these approaches is pursued in the following pages.

Cognitive Vulnerability   Recall the discussion of Aaron Beck's cognitive-behavioral perspective in Chapter 2. Beck, a psychoanalytically trained psychiatrist, listened to his patients' complaints and was struck by their profoundly self-critical, despairing, and pessimistic thinking (see Table 8.1), which he considered to be distortions of reality. He proposed that most depression is as much a disorder of thinking as of mood, and he hypothesized that some people may be susceptible to depression because of their **cognitive triad,** or characteristic negative ways of thinking about the self, the world, and the future (Beck, 1967, 1976). According to this perspective, stressful situations — but even minor or neutral events as well — result in depression because the person interprets them as reflections of personal inadequacy, feels a sense of futility about resolving problems, and exaggerates misfortune. Thus, an event activates negative thinking, which causes depressed mood — and depressed mood in turn stimulates even more negative thinking, prolonging or deepening the depression.

Moreover, according to Beck, underlying negative beliefs, or **depressive schemas,** cause people to *distort* information — to select interpretations that fit their beliefs while ignoring or reinterpreting information that does not fit. The result is a self-perpetuating system of beliefs. For example, a person with a negative self-schema who gets a B on a midterm may conclude, "I'm a failure" (consistent with the schema), instead of thinking that "a B is a pretty good grade; maybe if I work harder I can improve" (an interpretation inconsistent with the negative view of the self and the world). Beck's approach to depression vulnerability thus emphasizes schemas relevant to self-worth. From this perspective, depression occurs to the extent that a person's interpretations result in beliefs about worthlessness and incompetence.

Beck's model has been especially useful in several ways. (1) It was the first to focus on the negativism of the depressed person as more than just an incidental symptom. In short, it holds that negative thinking causes or intensifies depressive reactions. (2) Beck's model helps explain why some people get depressed and others do not, even when awful events befall them, or why some people are depressed even when others believe they have no "reason" to be depressed. (3) The emphasis on negative cognition encourages a view of depressed people not as willfully resisting change or stubbornly holding onto obviously irrational beliefs, but as having a disorder the essence of which is negative schemas and negative thinking. Thus, it isn't that depressed people just refuse to "snap out of it"; rather, they honestly, though unrealistically, do not believe that their efforts will make any difference. (4) As we discuss in the section on treatment, the model has direct and highly effective implications for treating depression.

How does Beck's model stand up under scientific scrutiny? Ample evidence has supported the idea that people who are currently depressed think in pessimistic, self-critical, and hopeless ways (reviewed in Gotlib & Hammen, 1992; Segal & Ingram, 1994). When they are no longer depressed, moreover, their interpretations, expectations, memories, and beliefs resemble those of nondepressed people, yet remain dormant and ready to be activated by an event that triggers negative interpretations. Research has also demonstrated that, as predicted, people are more likely to experience depression when negative events befall them in the specific areas they have identified as vital to their self-worth, such as relationships or achievement (reviewed in Gotlib & Hammen, 1992; Hammen, Marks, DeMayo & Mayol, 1985; Robins, 1990). Sometimes the vulnerability is such that even seemingly positive events can trigger depression, as the following case illustrates.

Arlene, described at the outset of the chapter, is your favorite checker at the supermarket. When she becomes depressed upon finding out that she is pregnant, you're baffled because you know that she's been trying for a long time. Although you aren't close friends, you call her at home when you find out she's taken some time off because of depression. She tells you that she was just as surprised as you were

that finding out about this happy event should cause her to become gloomy, sad, and down. She explains further that thinking about having a baby caused her to start thinking a great deal about her own childhood. She'd had parents who were abusive and even cruel — clearly preferring her two older brothers, belittling her accomplishments, and making fun of her failures. She'd also had a traumatic experience with the next-door neighbor, a man who molested her repeatedly for about a year when she was around eight years old. Finally, she told her mother, who responded, "You must have been asking for it; don't say anything to the neighbors or we'll all get into trouble." After that, Arlene felt even more frightened and guilty; but she also came to believe that mothers and their daughters can only be distant, mistrustful rivals. Arlene realizes that because of her own bad childhood experiences she longs for a loving mother that she'll never have, while also fearing that she won't be able to be a good parent to her own baby. Fortunately, Arlene has been visiting a therapist. She now recognizes that her depression stems from a belief that all of her worst thoughts, fantasies, and memories about herself are true.

Another cognitive vulnerability model, the **learned helplessness** approach, was articulated by Martin Seligman (1975) and his colleagues. Originally applied in animal analogue studies, learned helplessness was the term used to describe the erroneous expectation that one has no control over important outcomes and therefore takes no action even though action might be successful. When people believe that they are helpless to change an unwanted situation, Seligman argued, they become depressed and give up. This model has undergone two revisions. One emphasizes that depression results not just from perceived helplessness over undesirable events but also from one's negative interpretations of *why* the event occurred. To the extent that people believe that bad events occur because of something negative about themselves that is enduring and affects many parts of their lives — a *negative explanatory style* — they are vulnerable to depression (e.g., Abramson, Seligman & Teasdale, 1978; Peterson & Seligman, 1984). For instance, a student who gets a poor grade on an exam but believes that it was caused by insufficient study (something that can be changed) would not be depressed, whereas a student who attributes the cause of a poor grade to low ability (an internal, general, and pervasive factor) would be depressed.

The other revised model, called the *hopelessness theory* of depression, attempts to include additional cognitive and environmental features; it is meant to apply to a subgroup of persons whose thoughts are characterized by hopeless interpretations (Abramson, Alloy & Metalsky, 1988; Alloy, Lipman & Abramson, 1992). According to this perspective, hopelessness is a direct cause of depression, occurring among those who have negative explanatory styles in interpreting events and who believe that their own characteristics prevent them from wielding influence over important events in their lives.

Cognitive models of depression have been hugely successful in stimulating research on a topic previously neglected. In addition, they acknowledge the importance of people's conscious experiences — not just the hidden, intrapsychic, symbolically expressed conflicts long emphasized by psychodynamic models. These cognitive models have been applied widely to other forms of psychological disorder (as we review in other chapters), but they had their origins in depression theory.

Stressful Life Events   When bad things happen, some people become depressed. Modern research has greatly broadened the psychodynamic idea of loss and its association with depression, explaining it in very different terms — as a function of stress. Indeed, life stress triggers many unwanted reactions, both medical (see Chapter 10) and psychological. Clinicians and researchers were quick to observe the apparent link between depression and stress, and many studies have since examined the association of stressful life events and depressive symptoms among community residents as well as in clinical samples. As Figure 8.6 illustrates, seven such studies uniformly found significant associations between the recent occurrence of negative life events and depression (Brown & Harris, 1989): The majority of people who became significantly depressed had experienced at least one major stressful event in the prior six months.

The mere occurrence of negative events is not enough to predict depression, however. If it were, then nearly everyone would be depressed at some point. In fact, most people do not become clinically depressed even when awful things happen — such as the death of loved ones, separations and losses, financial hardships, and work problems. They limp along, facing whatever pain and distress they have to deal with, but without becoming clinically depressed. Most contemporary stress theorists agree with Beck that *cognitive appraisals* (ways of thinking about or interpreting stressors) are critical. When trying to determine whether depression or some other negative psychological reaction is occurring in the face of significant stress, researchers thus need to understand how the negative events are viewed by the individual. One person's disaster is another person's challenge. Indeed, according to cognitive models, even positive or neutral events (such as having a baby or getting promoted) may trigger depression if they are interpreted negatively.

Another approach to depression vulnerability in the face of stress suggests that individuals vary in terms of biological susceptibility. Although few studies have actually tested this model, a recent genetic study is noteworthy. When Kendler and associates (1995) studied the occurrence of depression in the past year in a sample of more than a thousand female twin pairs, some monozygotic and some dizygotic, they found that onset of major depression is significantly associated with the occurrence of a major stressful event in the preceding month. Moreover, as Figure 8.7 illustrates, they demonstrated that the tendency to respond to a stressor with

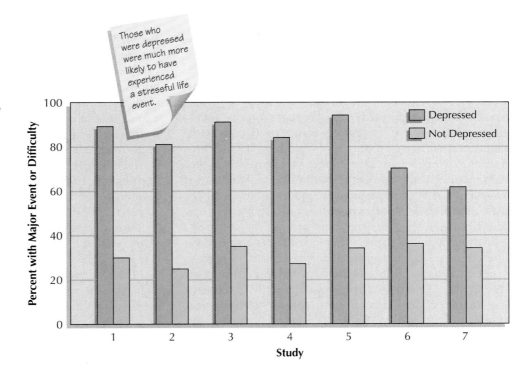

Figure 8.6 Life Events and Onset of Depression

Brown and Harris (1989) reviewed seven studies of community samples of women who were intensively interviewed to determine depression status and occurrence of stressful life events. As the results of this review clearly indicate, each study found that major, personally meaningful life events were highly likely to have occurred in the six months before onset among the women who had experienced an episode of depression — but such events were less prevalent among those who did not get depressed. *Source:* Brown & Harris (1989).

Those who were depressed were much more likely to have experienced a stressful life event.

Figure 8.7 Genetic Vulnerability to Depression and Life Events

In this genetic modeling study of adult female twins, investigators found that depression was more likely to occur among those who experienced a severe negative event in the prior month and had greater genetic vulnerability to depression. Genetic vulnerability was scaled according to whether a depressed woman was an identical or fraternal twin, and whether the twin sister herself had a previous history of major depression. The findings indicate that risk for depression in response to a severe stressor was most likely in women who had an identical (monozygotic) twin who also had previously experienced depression. Precisely which vulnerability factor was genetically transmitted is not yet known. *Source:* Adapted from Kendler et al. (1995).

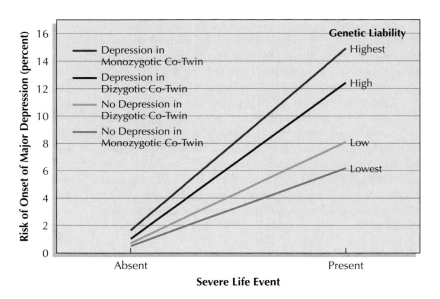

depression is affected by genetic factors. That is, a person who has a depressed *identical* twin is more likely than one who has a depressed *fraternal* twin to develop major depression following a stressful event.

An additional factor that influences whether stressful circumstances cause depression is the person's ability to *cope* with the negative events. In particular, having supportive relationships with other people seems to help reduce the impact of unwanted events — thus reducing the likelihood of depression (e.g., Sherbourne, Hays & Wells, 1995). Unfortunately, many depressed people do not have such relationships, or they believe that their relationships with other people are not supportive (e.g., Gotlib & Lee, 1989; reviewed in Barnett & Gotlib, 1988).

The issue of coping with stressful life events is potentially relevant to the question of why more women than men are depressed. Some researchers have argued that this gender difference is simply a by-product of women's greater openness to admit psychological symptoms. Others have argued, however, that women experience more stress and are less able than men to cope with that stress (reviewed in Nolen-Hoeksema, 1990). For instance, women may face greater stressors associated with restricted employment opportunities and job status as well as less education, income, and social support. To the extent that depression is an outcome of negative life circumstances, then, women who are poorly educated, who must raise and support children alone, or who have limited access to high-paying or prestigious jobs may experience higher rates of depression. Also, according to studies by Susan Nolen-Hoeksema (1991; Nolen-Hoeksema, Morrow & Fredrickson, 1993), women exhibit a "ruminative" style of coping. They tend to overanalyze their problems, focus inwardly, think about their feelings, and emphasize emotional expression — all of which are coping methods that can actually intensify

or prolong depression. In contrast, men tend to use action- or "avoidance"-oriented methods of coping with stress, such as engaging in physical activity or trying to take their minds off their problems. Some observers have also speculated that men resort to escapist coping methods such as drugs and alcohol to a much greater extent than women do.

Thus far in our discussion of the psychological approaches to depression, we have examined the ways in which people think about and cope with negative events. Now we consider another important factor: the possible *origins* of dysfunctional cognitions and coping resources in early family experiences.

Parent-Child Relations in Childhood Depressed patients often reveal childhoods marked by family disruption, conflict, and unhappiness. Do unhappy childhoods predispose a person to depression? In systematic studies of different kinds, depressed adults have been asked to evaluate their relations with their parents, depressed children's interactions with their parents have been observed, and the impact of current negative family relationships on depressed adults' depression has been examined (reviewed in Hammen, 1996; Gotlib & Hammen, 1992). According to one such study (Brown & Harris, 1993), early childhood adversity in the form of poor parent-child relations, as well as sexual and physical abuse, is linked to vulnerability to depression (see also Chapter 14).

Bear in mind that negative parent-child relationships can be associated with many disorders besides depression. Nevertheless, researchers from Freud onward, including John Bowlby (1980), have theorized that the early parent-child attachment bond is crucial to the formation of a positive view of the self. **Attachment** refers to the quality of relationship resulting from the degree of warmth, responsiveness, and caring expressed by parents. A parent or primary caretaker who is rejecting, uncaring, unavailable, or inconsistent may foster a negative self-concept in the child. And if a negative self-concept is a potential cognitive vulnerability factor for depression, as just discussed, then a poor parent-child relationship may cause a child to become vulnerable to depression later in life — possibly in response to negative events that the child believes are reflections of his or her value.

Thus, what children learn to believe about themselves and others in their own families gives rise to schemas and other cognitive patterns that determine how they interpret themselves in their worlds. Considerable research in the fields of child development and developmental psychopathology has documented the link between the quality of parental attachment and children's later adjustment. In particular, this research indicates that depressed parents have difficulties in their relations with their children. Indeed, to the degree that being depressed interferes with one's ability to be a loving and attentive parent, depression may be transmitted to children by psychological, rather than just genetic, means.

FAMILY MATTERS

Children of Depressed Parents

Depression runs in families. Although this assertion has genetic implications, research indicates that the psychological reality of living with depressed people can also contribute to depression (Hammen, 1991). From large-scale studies using clinical interviews (Weissman et al., 1987) to relatively intensive small-scale studies (e.g., Gotlib & Lee, 1990; Hammen, 1991), the results are consistent: Between 50 and 80 percent of youngsters with a depressed parent have diagnosable conditions, and most of these disorders involve depression.

Many psychological factors influence this pattern. For one thing, stress and depression often go hand in hand: Stress produces depressive reactions, and depressive syndromes create ongoing stressful marital, occupational, and financial difficulties. In addition, stress and depression undermine parents' ability to function warmly, positively, consistently, and responsively — as indicated by considerable research based on observations of parent-child interactions (e.g., Burge & Hammen, 1991; Cohn, Campbell, Matias & Hopkins, 1990). Marital conflict itself can be very upsetting to children (Downey & Coyne, 1990). Not only might depressed parents be stressed, but children also experience their own stressors. And in families with a depressed mother, a stressed child may not find the support needed to buffer the effects of the stress (Hammen, Burge & Adrian, 1991).

As noted, depressed parents may interact negatively with their children. According to studies based on systematic behavioral observations as well as questionnaire self-reports of parent behavior and child self-esteem, a child's self-esteem suffers when the mother or father is disinterested and critical. In short, the child may feel unloved and unwanted. Such negative perceptions of the self have been shown to correlate very strongly with depression symptoms in children of depressed mothers (e.g., Jaenicke et al., 1987).

The mother-child interaction is certainly not a one-way street, however: Children of depressed women may themselves have major behavioral problems and present difficulties for the mother. Indeed, one study showed that depressed women who had normal children interacted with them more positively than did depressed women whose children behaved dysfunctionally (Conrad & Hammen, 1989). Depression may make a parent feel overwhelmed and unable to cope with the difficult child, contributing to a vicious cycle of discord and symptoms.

Although severe or recurrent depressive disorders in parents may contribute to family dysfunction that puts children at risk, negative outcomes are not inevitable. Some youngsters may be **resilient,** showing no ill effects in the face of negative circumstances. Preliminary results from a family depression study suggest that several qualities of the child (positive self-concept, good academic achievement) and characteristics of the family (good relations with the mother, low family chronic stress, availability of a healthy father) are associated with good outcomes for the children (Conrad & Hammen, 1993). Such findings are consistent with the idea that when a parent has a major affective disorder, the whole family may be affected — but when the family maintains relatively healthy functioning, children can adapt successfully.

In the future, the best models for understanding the causes of depressive disorders will undoubtedly involve the *diathesis-stress* approach, because a variety of factors appear to be important and no single model can account for all of the patterns of depression that have been observed. To date, however, few models have truly integrated biological and psychological factors or clearly addressed the interrelationships between environmental and personal factors. Interestingly, studies of nonhuman primates provide a good example of the prospects for research that combines multiple levels of analysis.

FOCUS ON RESEARCH

What Can Monkeys Teach Us About Depression?

As Stephen Suomi (1991a, 1991b, and 1991c) has long observed, in both controlled laboratory conditions and natural settings, monkeys form deep attachments to

Researcher Steve Suomi has found that some baby monkeys exhibit intense reactions resembling depression when separated even briefly from their mothers. Studies of such animals have permitted controlled tests of both biological and psychological models of human depression.

each other; when separated, they display distress and despair that resemble human depression. Suomi's studies of the impact of even briefly separating infant monkeys from their mothers have suggested that primate research can shed light on biological and psychosocial processes in human depression. First of all, rhesus monkeys have a complex social structure that parallels human social organization in certain ways. Second, monkey studies permit experimental controls in the laboratory that are not ethically possible with human beings. And, third, studies of natural behaviors in colonies of free-ranging monkeys provide a humane method of testing hypotheses over a much more rapid course than would be possible with human children.

Suomi drew on theories and studies of human depression to pose several questions. Do young monkeys show individual differences in their reactions to separation from their caretakers? Do depressive reactions to separation vary according to characteristics of the infant-caretaker relationship? Are monkeys' reactions to separation accompanied by biological changes that resemble those associated with human depression?

A number of Suomi's laboratory trials employed brief separations. Initially, each infant monkey was housed for four days in an individual enclosure before being reunited with the mother. (These separations were analogous to naturally occurring separations in monkey colonies, as when the mother leaves to engage in courtship and mating or the birth of a sibling.) One pattern was repeatedly observed in the trials: Although most of the infant monkeys did not display much long-term reaction to the brief separations, about 20 percent of them displayed persistent, severe behavioral and emotional reactions such as despair, agitated behavior, and vocalization (Suomi, 1991a).

Next, Suomi measured biological changes from blood drawn from the infants. The most distressed monkeys exhibited lower levels of norepinephrine and related metabolic changes along with indications of activated hypothalamic-pituitary-adrenal axis reactions such as increased cortisol. When the young monkeys were reunited with their caretakers, they returned to normal behaviors, but some remained "clingy" (reviewed in Suomi, 1991a). This 20 percent subgroup of young monkeys might be considered at high risk for depression in view of their exaggerated behavioral and biological reactions.

To address the question of the influence of different child-rearing conditions, Suomi (1991c) compared infant monkeys who were raised by their mothers with those who were separated at birth and reared with a group of four to six peers. When later observed at the age of six months, the mother-raised and peer-raised monkeys showed comparable development and relatively few differences in social interactions. Dramatic differences emerged, however, when the two groups were subjected to the brief social separation experiences. The peer-raised monkeys showed significantly higher levels of behavioral and neuroendocrine reactions than did the mother-raised monkeys, suggesting that some factor provided by the natural mothers was protective against stress (Suomi, 1991c). Borrowing from the theories of Bowlby (1980) concerning the effects of consistent, responsive mothering on quality of attachment, Suomi speculated that peer-raised monkeys were *less securely attached* than mother-raised monkeys and therefore at greater risk for emotional distress when separations occurred.

In another trial designed to learn more about depression and quality of mothering, Suomi designed a cross-fostering method of studying high-risk (highly reactive) monkeys in comparison with normal monkeys. Infant monkeys were raised either by typical monkey mothers or by monkeys known through previous observation to be highly experienced and exceptionally nurturant (Suomi, 1991c). Observation of the young monkeys indicated that the high-risk monkeys were similar to the normal monkeys in most ways, but those raised by nurturant mothers were seemingly *better* developed in terms of behavior and exploration skills than all of the other groups. When briefly separated from their foster mothers at six months of age, however, the highly reactive monkeys displayed more severe behavioral and physiological reactions than the low-risk monkeys, regardless of their mothering. In a related study, Suomi (1991a) noted that specific early rearing experiences may have different effects on long-term development, but none of these experiences appear to eliminate the reactivity of the high-risk group.

Suomi has suggested that this high-reactivity pattern may in part be genetically transmitted, based on observed similarities in response to separations between biological fathers and sons (even when they were reared apart) as well as between half-brothers and the same fathers. He has also experimented with the use of antidepressant medications with highly reactive monkeys. The antidepressant drug imipramine appears to reverse many of the negative behavioral and physiological correlates of separation (Suomi, 1991a).

Taken together, these studies provide an intriguing glimpse into the biological predispositions to depressive reactions in high-risk samples, demonstrating that, for some primates, separation from an intimate caretaker relationship is highly likely to elicit depressive reactions. Suomi is continuing his work in an effort to more fully characterize the role of biological mechanisms and early loss experiences in such predispositions, to identify the results of specific antidepressant treatments, and to design psychosocial treatments that ease depressive reactions in monkeys. This research is consistent with studies of human depression that implicate quality of parent-child attachment as well as biological predisposition.

For individuals who suffer from significant seasonal mood disorders, light therapy (exposure to bright light for an hour or so per day) may provide significant — though temporary — relief.

TREATMENT OF UNIPOLAR DEPRESSION

Fewer than half of those who develop depressive disorders seek treatment for their depression, despite the fact that it causes substantial impairment (e.g., Coryell et al., 1995b). Among those who do seek treatment, some look to primary care in medical settings, often greatly inflating health costs (e.g., Simon, Ormel, VonKorff & Barlow, 1995). Resistance to seeking help specifically for depression may stem in part from depressive futility ("What's the use"?) and in part from others' negative attitudes about depression ("Pull yourself together and don't let things get you down"). Until recently, moreover, there were few resources that depressed people could turn to; indeed, traditional psychotherapy was the only officially recognized treatment for depression, and it did not work very well. Among other difficulties, therapists were often discouraged by their clients' negativism and did not relish working with such difficult patients. Fortunately, two highly effective options are now available to help with this debilitating disorder: antidepressant medications and psychotherapies designed specifically for depression.

Antidepressant Medications

Over the past decade, the use of **antidepressant medications** has increased to an astounding degree (Olfson & Klerman, 1993). Antidepressants (like many other medications) require a medical doctor's prescription, and

most are prescribed by physicians in general medical practice — although more severe or complex cases of depression are typically treated by psychiatrists. As psychologists cannot prescribe drugs, those who treat depression with psychotherapy may refer clients to a psychiatrist for medication evaluation either in combination with the psychotherapy or as an alternative to it, if such treatment appears warranted.

Like many medical advances, the discovery of antidepressant medications was fortuitous: Drugs being tested for other purposes were found to reduce depression. Two classes of drugs were thus introduced in the United States in the 1950s: the tricyclic antidepressants (named for their chemical structure) and the monoamine oxidase inhibitors (MAOIs). Recently, several new-generation, or heterocyclic, drugs have also been introduced. The tricyclic antidepressants alter functions of the norepinephrine, dopamine, serotonin, and related neurotransmitter systems, whereas many of the newer antidepressants work more selectively — for instance, by blocking the reuptake of serotonin so that more is available in the synaptic cleft. And as their name implies, MAOIs block the effects of substances that break down the monoamine neurotransmitters, increasing their availability. The effects of antidepressants are more complex than a mere increase in the amount of a neurotransmitter, however; if they weren't, the results of these drugs would be more rapid than the two weeks or more that are typically required for therapeutic effectiveness. Some probably work by altering the densities and sensitivities of certain receptors in the brain (McNeal &

Cimbolic, 1986). Table 8.2 lists seven of the more than twenty currently available antidepressants. (Additional ones are being developed every year.)

Use of Antidepressants Antidepressants are especially recommended for moderate to severe levels of depression, although they may also be useful for mild cases (Hellerstein et al., 1993). Some of these medications are initially taken at low dosages and build up to a therapeutic level over time, adjusted for the person's needs and reactions; others, especially the newer drugs, involve a standard dosage for everyone that starts immediately. Positive effects are usually not seen for two weeks or more, so depressed people need to be informed that they will not recover immediately.

Once the acute symptoms have diminished, **continuation treatment** at the same dosage is recommended for at least sixteen to twenty weeks; then the medication is discontinued through a tapering off of the dosage. If medication is withdrawn too soon after remission, the likelihood of relapse is relatively high. Also, abrupt discontinuation may cause unpleasant side effects. For individuals who have a history of recurrent episodes of depression, **maintenance treatment** is recommended; in such cases, medication is continued at a level sufficient to prevent recurrence (American Psychiatric Association, 1993).

As all of the current antidepressant medications are about equally effective, the consideration of which drug to take depends on the person's previous response to medications, specific symptoms, and life circumstances (Gitlin, 1996). Furthermore, some of these medications are stimulating, whereas others are sedating. And some are lethal if taken in an overdose; thus, suicidal risk may be a consideration.

Type of depression may also determine which medication is prescribed. For example, MAOI drugs are often preferentially used to treat atypical depressions that involve considerable anxiety or personality disorders. In some cases, combinations of antidepressants are used; in others, antidepressants are combined with lithium, a drug known to be effective in reducing the likelihood of recurrences of affective episodes.

Side effects are also a consideration in choice of medication. Some antidepressants cause dry mouth or blurry vision. Some, as noted, are sedating (causing drowsiness or a feeling of being slowed down), whereas others are stimulating (causing anxiety, tremor, rapid heart beat, insomnia). Weight gain and sexual dysfunction (such as erectile difficulties) are also common side effects. At the most serious extreme, a few medications cause seizures (rarely) or cardiac irregularities. MAOI drugs, in particular, are associated with a potentially life-threatening side effect: Suddenly increased blood pressure, stroke, or even death may occur if the person taking such medications also ingests foods or other drugs con-

Table 8.2 Chemical and Brand Names of Some Antidepressant Medications

Generic Name	Brand Name
Tricyclic antidepressants	
Imipramine	Tofranil
Amitriptyline	Elavil
Clomipramine	Anafranil
Heterocyclic antidepressants	
Fluoxetine	Prozac
Bupropion	Wellbutrin
Sertraline hydrochloride	Zoloft
Monoamine oxidase inhibitor	
Phenelzine	Nardil

Antidepressants work in various ways that are not fully understood. Most of the older tricyclic antidepressants affected availability of neurotransmitters such as norepinephrine and serotonin by altering the activity of specific receptors. Some of the new-generation drugs block the reuptake of serotonin.

taining tyramine. (Tyramine is an amino acid found in many aged foods such as cheese, smoked or pickled fish or meats, and red or fortified wines.) Constant medical evaluation is thus important.

The new-generation drugs have become popular because they have relatively few side effects. In particular, fluoxetine (Prozac) has attracted considerable attention as a potential "wonder drug" (although there is no evidence that it is any more effective than other antidepressants), with some individuals claiming that it has changed their personalities and their lives. A few years ago the media spotlighted Prozac because of reports that it sometimes caused suicidal feelings and behaviors. Anti-Prozac publicity became widespread, apparently promoted in part by antipsychiatry groups such as the Church of Scientology. However, the Federal Drug Administration's Psychopharmacological Drugs Advisory Committee concluded that there was no evidence of a causal relationship between use of the drug and suicidal behavior (see also Mann & Kapur, 1991). Experts have argued that most alleged cases of suicidal behavior might have been due to prior history of suicidality. But because most antidepressants are prescribed by general physicians who lack specialized training in psychiatric disorders (Beardsley, Gardocki, Larson & Hidalgo, 1988), there may be a risk of inadequate assessment of patients' suitability for medication treatment.

Effectiveness of Antidepressants How effective are antidepressants in the treatment of depression? Numerous studies comparing the medications to placebos in controlled blind trials (in which neither patients nor doctors know whether the pills administered are active or placebo) have reported effectiveness in the reduction of acute depression at between 65 percent and 75 percent, compared with about 33 percent for placebos (e.g., Prien, 1988).

Although the effectiveness of continuation and maintenance treatments have been less thoroughly investigated, recent reviews of drug studies confirm that relapse is less likely if the person is continued on antidepressants for a few months after symptoms decrease (e.g., Hirschfeld, 1994). In addition, long-term studies support the effectiveness of maintenance of antidepressants among those with recurrent depression (Fava & Kaji, 1994; Kupfer et al., 1992).

Can we tell who will respond well to antidepressants? Currently no indicator predicts treatment response. Some research supports the idea that depressed persons with more of the *physical* symptoms of depression — such as appetite and sleep changes, psychomotor retardation, and loss of energy and fatigue — respond best to antidepressants (Rush & Weissenburger, 1994). But there is no evidence that depressions that seem to have been precipitated by psychological causes such as negative life events respond less well to antidepressants than do allegedly biological depressions.

Individuals with very severe depressions, agitated depressions, and depressions with psychotic features do not seem to respond well to antidepressants alone and may require additional treatment with hospitalization and, possibly, electroconvulsive therapy (ECT). Likewise, persons with certain kinds of atypical depressions, depressions involving major personality disorders, and severe histories of repeated or prolonged episodes do not appear to respond well to the standard antidepressants. Finally, although chronic depressions may be effectively treated with antidepressants to *reduce* the severity of symptoms, these drugs may not eliminate symptoms entirely (e.g., Hellerstein et al., 1993).

Other Biological Treatments for Depression

Electroconvulsive therapy (ECT), which involves passing electric current through the brain sufficient to cause a seizure, usually strikes people as a barbaric, inhumane treatment that should be entirely abolished. Indeed, in past decades it was misused, was applied to many patient groups without evidence of effectiveness, and caused physical damage to many persons (see Chapter 3). Accordingly, and also because of the increased use of antidepressants, ECT's use declined markedly as a primary treatment of major depressions. ECT has not *disappeared*, however, for one very good reason: It is effective in treating certain kinds of severe, otherwise untreatable depressions (Sackheim & Rush, 1995). In fact, it may be considered the treatment of choice for persons with prominent psychotic or melancholia features of depression, in cases where severe depression has

"Before Prozac, she loathed company."

not responded to medication, and in life-threatening situations when rapid response is needed. It is currently administered under medically safe conditions (with minimal electrical stimulation), limiting its side effects such as temporary memory loss. Numerous studies conducted on its cognitive side effects have generally concluded that there is no evidence of long-term memory loss or other undesirable cognitive changes (e.g., Devanand et al., 1994). We do not know precisely how ECT works; but the fact that it requires a seizure state to be effective suggests that resulting changes in neurotransmitters and other neurobiological mechanisms may be responsible for its antidepressant effects (Nobler et al., 1994).

Light therapy, exposure to bright light for a prescribed period during the day, is a treatment for the seasonal affective disorder subtype of depression. Recognizing that persons with SAD do not respond well to antidepressant medications, and speculating that the disorder may be a hibernation-like response resulting from circadian rhythm dysfunction during diminished exposure to light during winter, investigators reasoned that increasing exposure to light might reverse the depressive symptoms. The effectiveness of light therapy has been established in controlled studies (e.g., Wirz-Justice et al., 1993). But because its positive effects seem to be relatively temporary, lasting only a few days, depressed people with SAD need to receive continuing treatments during the low-light months of the year.

Sleep deprivation is an experimental treatment in which depressed patients are kept awake during part of the night. Its use is based on the association between sleep disturbances and depression, as well as on the discovery of atypical rapid eye movement (REM) sleep patterns in some depressives. More than one-half of the patients treated with sleep deprivation showed remarkable mood improvement (Wu & Bunney, 1990). However, the positive changes are temporary, possibly disappearing after a night's sleep or even after naps. So far, most of the research on this treatment has been methodologically weak (Leibenluft & Wehr, 1992). Nonetheless, the effects of this low-cost, harmless procedure suggest that it is worthy of further study as a brief or occasional intervention.

Psychotherapies for Depression

Although antidepressant medications work well for many depressed persons, they obviously do not alleviate the problems that might have caused the depression in the first place. Pills cannot improve the bad marriages, unhappy work situations, or family conflicts that preceded the depression. Therefore, many depressed people benefit as well from psychotherapies designed to help them cope with the difficult life circumstances or personality vulnerabilities that put them at risk for depression. Psychotherapy is sometimes also the recommended treatment for people who have medical conditions (such as pregnancy and some heart problems) that preclude the use of medications.

As we saw in Chapter 3, certain forms of therapy do effectively treat depression. Cognitive-behavioral therapy for depression (Beck, Rush, Shaw & Emery, 1979) and interpersonal therapy (Klerman, Weissman, Rounsaville & Chevron, 1984) are two relatively short-term focused psychotherapies that have demonstrated effectiveness with depressed patients.

Characteristics of Cognitive-Behavioral Therapy Aaron Beck's cognitive-behavioral therapy (CBT) focuses on reducing depressive symptoms and resolving the life problems and personal vulnerabilities that contribute to depression. Helping clients become more actively engaged in pleasurable or productive activities (such as mastery and pleasure assignments determined by their own preferences) often improves depressed mood, low energy, and lack of motivation. Also, clients are taught to observe the extent to which their thoughts are unrealistic and have a negative quality that often intensifies the depression. By learning to challenge these thoughts, clients become better able to deal with themselves and their problems constructively. One procedure for teaching these methods is called the *three-column technique,* illustrated in Table 8.3. After identifying the automatic negative thoughts associated with an upsetting event, the person probes each negative thought to see if it is accurate, is based on evidence, or can be viewed in a more reasonable, less distorted way. The technique,

practiced as a homework assignment, becomes a common tool to counter depressive negative thinking. Over time, persons with depression also learn to identify and challenge the underlying maladaptive assumptions or schemas that contribute to their depression. In addition, they undertake behavioral changes as needed to resolve specific problems such as finding a good job, meeting new people, and improving communication in a relationship.

Characteristics of Interpersonal Therapy Interpersonal therapy (IPT), also designed specifically to treat depression, is a short-term therapy that focuses on the interpersonal issues related to the individual's depression. Based on psychodynamic principles, it was developed by Gerald Klerman, Myrna Weissman, and their colleagues, whose backgrounds have included extensive research in mood disorders (Klerman, Weissman, Rounsaville & Chevron, 1984). Through such psychodynamic techniques as discussion, reflection, support, interpretation, and encouragement by the therapist, the depressed person attempts to explore relevant issues having to do with current relationship problems, conflicts, communication difficulties, social relatedness, and family dysfunction. Like cognitive-behavioral therapy, IPT attempts to reduce depressive symptoms as well as to address problems in the interpersonal context.

Effectiveness of Psychotherapy for Depression Overall, cognitive and behavioral treatments of depression have proven to be effective in reducing acute symptoms (Robinson, Berman & Neimeyer, 1990). In addition, studies have found that outcomes of psychotherapy for depressed people are at least comparable to those of antidepressant drug treatments (e.g., Jacobson & Hollon, 1996). Most of the recent outcome research on treatment effectiveness with depressed patients has focused on cognitive-behavioral therapy or interpersonal therapy. For example, CBT has been evaluated in dozens of controlled therapy studies (Dobson, 1989; Hollon et al., 1992; Nietzel, Russell, Hemmings & Gretter, 1987). It has been shown to be effective in reducing depressive symptoms in adolescents as well as adults (Lewinsohn, Clarke, Hops & Andrews, 1990), the elderly (Beutler et al., 1987), and inpatients (Miller, Norman & Keitner, 1989). CBT also appears to be successful — possibly even more so than antidepressants — in reducing the likelihood of relapse (Clarkin, Pilkonis & Magruder, 1996; Hollon, Shelton & Davis, 1993).

Studies have also found IPT to be effective in reducing acute symptoms. Its effectiveness is comparable to that of tricyclic antidepressants (reviewed in Weissman & Klerman, 1990, 1992). And like CBT, IPT may be even more effective than maintenance tricyclic antidepressants in reducing relapse over time — provided that patients receive continuing treatment (Frank, Kupfer & Perel, 1989).

Table 8.3   Beck's Cognitive-Behavioral Therapy: Three-Column Technique

Event	Automatic Negative Thoughts	Rational Replies
My boyfriend didn't call on Friday.	He's losing interest in me. He'll leave me.	*What's the error?* I can't read his mind or foretell the future. *What's the evidence?* He doesn't call as much as he used to. However, he's been very busy at work. *Could I collect more information?* I could ask him how he thinks our relationship is going. *Is there another way to look at it?* He's probably just busy and couldn't call. Even if he is losing interest, however, that doesn't mean he'll leave me. Maybe we can improve things. *So what?* Even if the worst is true and he did leave me, I guess I could survive. I've been on my own before, and even if it was hard at the time, it wasn't impossible.
	I feel rejected. It means I'm undesirable. No one will ever love me. I'll always be alone.	(Ask the same kinds of questions as those listed above, and try to come up with more realistic thoughts.)

Beck invented the three-column technique for cognitive-behavioral therapy of depression. It provides a tool to help clients learn to observe their automatic negative thoughts, and then to challenge the accuracy and effectiveness of those thoughts. By "deautomatizing" their negative thinking, depressed clients become better able to select adaptive ways of dealing with their real-life problems and to recognize that depression, not reality, affects how they interpret the world.

For many people, the combination of antidepressants and CBT or IPT might be most effective (e.g., Hollon et al., 1992; Hollon, Shelton & Davis, 1993; Weissman, Sholomkas & John, 1981). In a large-scale comparison of CBT and IPT conducted by the National Institute of Mental Health Treatment of Depression Collaborative Research Program (TDCRP) over a period of several years, 250 carefully diagnosed patients at three research sites were randomly assigned to one of four treatments: CBT, IPT, imipramine, and pill placebo. The two pill conditions included clinical management — that is, contact with a doctor who provided support, advice, and review of symptoms. All the treatments ran for approximately sixteen weeks, with patients assessed at the beginning, at the end, and at follow-ups up through eighteen months. The results indicated that both of the psychotherapies and the imipramine were about equally likely to reduce symptoms (Elkin et al., 1989). Interestingly, the placebo condition also reduced symptoms. The most severely depressed patients tended to do better with medication and IPT than with the placebo treatment, whereas the initially less depressed patients experienced reduced symptoms with all treatments. Clearly, the clinical-management component of treatment had important effects at least for the less depressed patients.

Figure 8.8 illustrates the results of the eighteen-month follow-up of this study (Shea et al., 1992). Although the CBT and IPT treatments were somewhat superior to antidepressants in preventing relapses, many patients in all groups deteriorated. The authors emphasized that sixteen weeks of treatment may be insufficient for most patients to achieve and sustain full recovery.

Overall, however, psychotherapy was found to be as effective as medication. Moreover, some studies have suggested that psychotherapies do a better job of preventing relapse. In particular, continuing, or maintenance, psychotherapy, as well as maintenance medication, may be needed to help prevent recurrences of depression.

FEATURES OF BIPOLAR DISORDER

Much rarer than unipolar depression, **bipolar disorder** involves not only depression but also mania or hypomania. Individuals cycle between periods of elevated or depressed mood and normal mood. **Mania** is in many ways the opposite of depression. It is a disorder marked by grandiose or irritable mood; increased

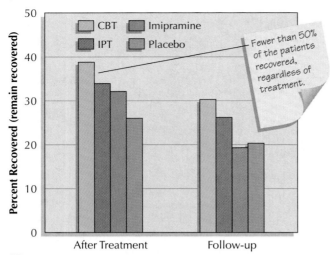

Figure 8.8 Psychotherapy Versus Medication

These figures indicate the proportions of patients with major depression who no longer showed significant depressive symptoms following treatment and then remained well for eighteen months of follow-up. The follow-up figures are based on the sample for whom complete follow-up data were collected over the entire period. Notice that, although these figures show a slight superiority in the effectiveness of the two psychotherapy conditions, the differences were not statistically significant. More important, they indicate that the majority of patients who started the treatment program did not recover and remain well. Clearly, despite relatively successful treatments, the long-term outcomes are not excellent. In short, sixteen weeks of treatment, with no maintenance phase, may not be adequate for those suffering from recurrent depression. *Source:* Shea et al. (1992; adapted from Table 1, p. 784).

energy, activity, and distractibility; and excessive engagement in pleasurable behaviors that may lead to painful consequences. **Hypomania** is a mild version of mania. Bipolar disorder, previously known as *manic-depression,* and unipolar depression are very different in their features, presumed causes, and available treatments.

Clinical Characteristics of Bipolar Disorder

The symptoms and experiences of depression that we describe in the sections on unipolar depression also apply to bipolar disorder. The same diagnostic criteria for a major depressive episode apply to both. Without information about a person's previous experiences with mania or hypomania, a clinician is unable to tell whether the person has a unipolar or bipolar disorder. We therefore emphasize the clinical characteristics of mania and hypomania in this section. Like depression, these states are defined by changes in cognitive functioning, physical state, and behaviors as well as by changes in mood. In a later section on the course of bipolar disorder, we discuss the patterns or cycles of mood change associated with this condition.

In a *hypomanic state* a person might have a pronounced sense of either well-being — feeling exhilarated, outgoing, confident, and enthusiastic — or irritability. The emotional state is excessive and different from a normal good mood. It may persist for days or sometimes even months. In the *manic state* the mood is even more extreme. The person is elated, expansive, or extremely irritable and angry. Sometimes, in a *mixed state,* the person has many symptoms of a manic episode but also displays a pronounced negative mood and emotional distress.

In addition to these mood symptoms, hypomania and mania are characterized by inflated self-esteem. People experiencing mania and hypomania believe that they have unusual abilities, talents, powers, and skills. Hypomanic persons feel that they can succeed at all they try. Manic individuals exhibit grandiosity, sometimes to the point of delusions, and may therefore concoct outlandish business ventures, start to write novels, or describe fabulous inventions. At the same time, thought processes speed up and the mind races from one idea to the next, and the person may be unable to stay focused on one thing at a time. At the most extreme, manic individuals may feel overwhelmed and bewildered by the thoughts that seem to race through their minds beyond their control. In milder, hypomanic states, the experience may resemble heightened creativity and quickness of thinking.

Not surprisingly, these grandiose beliefs and rapid thought processes are commonly accompanied by overactivity, increased energy, and a decreased need for sleep. The manic or hypomanic individual talks more and faster, and feels pressed to keep talking; in extreme manic states the person may be incoherent. The individual might start one project after another, trying to manage multiple activities without finishing any. Some people in a hypomanic state might become more productive at work, with a rush of ideas and plans; others might become more outgoing, charming, and fun. In addition to being more talkative, the person makes funny quips and jokes and becomes the center of attention — often to the point of being obnoxious. In more pronounced manic states, an individual becomes dysfunctionally active, going out on several dates in a day, trying to juggle too many projects, driving too fast, spending too much money, or engaging in promiscuous sexual activities. Because of their grandiosity or irritability, people in manic states may also get into barroom brawls, get arrested for traffic violations, cause bankruptcies, or become involved in social, political, or sexual activities that shame or embarrass their families.

In the most severe stages of mania, some individuals are physically restless and out of control, delusional, and incoherent; they experience hallucinations and are unable to sleep, eat, or take care of other physical needs.

The actress Patty Duke is one of many famous and creative people who have been diagnosed with bipolar disorder. She has written of her bouts of suicidal depression alternating with manic episodes that made her life a rollercoaster before she was accurately diagnosed and treated. Margot Kidder the actress recently came to public attention for a bizarre episode of homeless wandering; it was later revealed that she suffers from bipolar disorder.

In most such cases, hospitalization is clearly needed, as the following example illustrates:

> *Tony had always been an outgoing, sociable young man, but recently even his friends noticed a change: He seemed excited and talked more rapidly and loudly than usual, and had long and animated chats with people he barely knew. It wasn't that he was just feeling good and being more extraverted and confident than he had been previously. Rather, he was obnoxious and irritating; he interrupted people and cracked sometimes-inappropriate jokes. It was hard to follow his conversations; his mind seemed to jump from topic to topic, and the slightest distraction derailed his train of thought. He told everyone he was hatching plans for a vast new business venture, and he stayed up most nights working on that and related projects; he barely slept a few hours a night. He ran up thousands of dollars worth of bills on his parents' credit cards, buying clothing and taking people out to dinner to impress them.*
>
> *One day he suddenly headed for the airport and said he was going to fly to New York to talk to business leaders about his wonderful ideas. He assumed they'd give him millions of dollars to invest in his ideas. His erratic behavior attracted security police at the airport, and he attacked them when they tried to stop him for questioning. They could readily see that he needed mental health care immediately. He was hospitalized with help from his family, but within a few days he seemed to suddenly "crash" and become morbidly depressed to the point where all he did was lie silently in bed. It turns out that he had had one previous manic episode when he was about eighteen. Now at twenty, he has friends and family wondering how often this is going to happen to him.*

Diagnosing Bipolar Disorder

In the past, although manic-depressive illness was often described in terms of swings between mania and depression, the label was also applied to people who had only recurring depressions. Thus, in earlier decades, a person with what we now think of as recurring unipolar depression might have been diagnosed with manic-depression. It was not until the late 1960s that the importance of distinguishing between the unipolar and bipolar forms of mood disorder became clear. Only since the early 1970s have diagnostic criteria been developed to differentiate bipolar disorder more clearly from other disorders.

In fact, countless people with bipolar mood disorders have been misdiagnosed over the years. Many errors probably occurred because clinicians considered only the present episode rather than the entire pattern of mood swings. In particular, because some schizophrenic people have delusions of grandeur, it is very likely that people with bipolar disorder were sometimes labeled as suffering from schizophrenia if they were diagnosed during a psychotic manic state.

When seen during a person's depressed state, bipolar disorder may be difficult to distinguish from unipolar depression. In fact, misdiagnosis as unipolar depression is more likely if the person has only hypomanic episodes or if the person's first bipolar episode is major depression. Researchers have estimated, for example, that 10 percent to 15 percent of people initially diagnosed with unipolar depression will subsequently have manic or hypomanic episodes (Akiskal et al., 1995; Coryell et al., 1995a). Thus, the overlap among symptoms of unipolar, bipolar, and schizophrenic disorders has caused diagnostic problems over the years, often with negative consequences for treatment.

Diagnostic Criteria for Bipolar Disorder In order to diagnose bipolar disorder, the therapist needs to examine the entire history of a client's episodes. As discussed, the person may currently be in either a manic or a depressive episode. No matter how often or severely a person may be depressed, the individual is diagnosed as bipolar if he or she has *ever* had a manic or hypomanic episode that was not attributable to psychoactive drugs or a medical condition. On rare occasions, an individual will have only manic episodes and no apparent history of depression. This person would still be diagnosed as bipolar.

The criteria for episodes of mania or manic episodes specify that pronounced euphoria or irritability must last at least one week. During this period the person must experience major impairment of functioning in his or her usual roles, activities, or relationships and exhibit at least three additional symptoms. The symptoms include inflated self-esteem (grandiosity), decreased need for sleep, increased talkativeness or a feeling of being pressed to keep talking, racing thoughts, distractibility, increased activities and projects (or agitation), and excessive involvement in pleasurable activities that have a high potential for bringing harmful consequences. The criteria for hypomania are similar, except that the actual experience of a symptom may be milder, cause less impairment, and be briefer in duration than with mania. (Regarding duration, the elevated or irritable mood must last at least four days.)

DSM-IV includes three basic subcategories of bipolar disorder: bipolar disorder with manic episodes (bipolar I), bipolar disorder with hypomanic episodes (bipolar II), and cyclothymic disorder, or cyclothymia. **Cyclothymic disorder** is a bipolar disorder involving mild and frequent mood swings. The criteria for cyclothymia specify that the pattern of frequent ups and downs must have lasted more than two years. During the mood changes, the person displays mild versions of the symptoms associated with a depressive episode or hypomania but does not meet the criteria for a major depressive or a manic episode.

Comorbidity As many as 61 percent of individuals with bipolar disorder meet the criteria for drug or alcohol abuse or dependence at some point, seeming to self-medicate or to experiment with drugs and other substances that may exacerbate their mood syndromes and become problems in their own right (Regier et al., 1990). The presence of substance abuse greatly complicates the diagnostic picture and treatment. Personality disorders (described in Chapter 13) are also common among patients with bipolar disorder and, again, pose both diagnostic and treatment difficulties.

Who Is Affected with Bipolar Disorder?

Unlike unipolar depression, bipolar disorder is relatively infrequent. Community surveys suggest that only about 1.2 percent of the U.S. adult population have experienced bipolar disorder in their lifetime (Weissman et al., 1988). Of these, about two-thirds, or 0.8 percent of the population, experienced bipolar I disorder (with mania). Cross-cultural studies that use current diagnostic criteria are rare, but most such research supports the observation that the rate of bipolar disorder in the world's population is about 1 percent.

Ethnic differences within the United States have not been noted in epidemiological surveys (Karno et al., 1987; Robins et al., 1984). On the other hand, although men and women are about equally likely to meet the diagnostic criteria, there are important gender differences. Women are thought to experience bipolar II disorder (with hypomania) more frequently than men, to be more likely to have a predominantly depressive course, and to undergo more rapid cycling (reviewed in Goodwin & Jamison, 1990; Leibenluft, 1996). Reasons for these possible gender differences in symptom patterns are not known.

One element of the population does appear to have an elevated risk for bipolar disorder: persons with greater socioeconomic status. Of thirty-four studies conducted in the United States and other Western industrialized countries, the majority reported that more bipolar patients came from *higher* socioeconomic groups and none of the studies found the reverse (Goodwin & Jamison, 1990). Diagnostic and treatment biases might have influenced these results, however. It is possible, for example, that some poor people affected by bipolar disorders were misdiagnosed as schizophrenic, a stigmatizing label that more affluent patients may have avoided. Or perhaps some aspect of the personalities and behavior of those with bipolar disorder was linked with creativity and accomplishment and thus with greater socioeconomic status.

In fact, some researchers have argued that mood disorders in general and perhaps bipolar disorder in particular are associated with creativity and accomplishment. Mood disorders, especially bipolar disorder, can contribute to the creative state by increasing the speed, fluidity, and flexibility of a person's thinking; by generating high energy and productivity; and by providing intense emotional experiences as a basis for creation (Goodwin & Jamison, 1990).

Many writers, statesmen, artists, and musicians have been known to experience severe mood states or mood swings. We cannot actually diagnose most of these individuals, but historians have provided suggestive evidence. For instance, William Blake, Lord Byron, Samuel Taylor Coleridge, Edgar Allan Poe, Wolfgang von Goethe, Herman Melville, Ernest Hemingway, F. Scott Fitzgerald, Virginia Woolf, and William Saroyan are among the many writers apparently afflicted with severe mood disorders. The composers Tchaikovsky, Mahler, Handel, and Schumann as well as political figures such as Lincoln, Churchill, Napoleon, and Cromwell also experienced marked mood swings or mood states (Goodwin & Jamison, 1990). When Kay Redfield Jamison (1989) interviewed a sample of contemporary English writers and artists whose awards marked them as the most eminent in their fields, she found that one-third had histories of severe mood swings and one-fourth had histories of extended elated states.

Despite these interesting links, it is important that we not romanticize mood disorders. After all, it may be that only those individuals whose symptoms are fairly well controlled or not too severe can fully realize their creative potential. Further research is needed to clarify the associations and mechanisms involved (Andreasen, 1987; Richards et al., 1988).

Course of Bipolar Disorder

For the vast majority of affected people, bipolar disorder is a lifelong disorder with multiple episodes of depression and mania. Most individuals experience their first diagnosable episodes in early adulthood (e.g., Burke, Burke, Regier & Rae, 1990). But researchers are finding increasing evidence that the disorder may begin in adolescence and even childhood (e.g., Strober & Carlson, 1982). In previous decades such early bipolar episodes may have been misdiagnosed as schizophrenia or even attention deficit hyperactivity disorder.

The Pattern of Episodes   The total number of episodes over a lifetime is difficult to gauge. The vast majority of studies have indicated great variability in the number of depressive and manic episodes, with one long-term, naturalistic study finding that the *median* number was seven to nine episodes — meaning that one-half of the affected individuals experienced more than that (Angst et al., 1973). About 15 percent to 20 percent of bipolar patients are described as *rapid cyclers* because they experience four or more episodes of depression or mania each year. In general, the best predictor of future episodes is the number of previous episodes. Once a person experiences a first episode, the cycles start occurring closer together. Then, after three to five episodes, the cycles may become more regular (reviewed in Goodwin & Jamison, 1990).

What about patterns of depression and mania? Is depression always followed by mania, or the reverse? Each individual has a different pattern. One may exhibit a pattern in which either a manic or depressive episode is followed by normal mood. Another may experience a cycle such as depression followed by mania. Yet another may experience a triphasic cycle such as short depression followed by long mania followed by long depression. In some people these mood shifts have irregular patterns, whereas in others they cycle with clocklike regularity. The majority of people with bipolar disorder undergo periods of relative normality between episodes, although some experience fairly continuous symptoms.

Outlook for Adjustment   As with most major mental illnesses, research on the outcome of bipolar disorder brings both good and bad news. The good news is that many individuals can be treated with lithium or other mood stabilizers (as discussed in the section on treatment of bipolar disorder) and experience relatively effective control of major mood episodes. Between major episodes, many bipolar patients also function relatively well. For others, however, bipolar disorder is a very debilitating experience. The bad news is that recent longitudinal studies indicate relatively poor outcomes for most patients, with more than half experiencing significant episodes within one or two years — regardless of whether they were treated with lithium (e.g., Goldberg, Harrow & Grossman, 1995; Gitlin, Swendsen, Heller & Hammen, 1995; Keller et al., 1993). Moreover, despite symptomatic recovery, many bipolar patients experience continuing difficulties in the social, marital, and work adjustments (e.g., Coryell et al., 1993; Gitlin, Swendsen, Heller & Hammen, 1995; Goldberg, Harrow & Grossman, 1995). These results stand in sharp contrast to the somewhat rosy picture of high rates of successful treatment of bipolar disorder that emerged in recent years. Even with the help of lithium, individuals who have a chronic or recurrent pattern of severe mood shifts face great disruption in their lives.

CAUSES OF BIPOLAR DISORDER

Current research is based on the hypothesis that bipolar disorder is primarily biological in origin, particularly as in recent years it has become more clearly distinguished from unipolar depression.

Biological Perspectives on Bipolar Disorder

As with most areas of modern psychopathology, biologically oriented research on bipolar disorder examines possible genetic factors and neurotransmitter dysregulation. In addition, bipolar episodes have been approached as disruptions in biological rhythms or as alterations in brain functioning — topics we explore in more detail below.

Genetic Studies   The evidence for heritability of bipolar disorders is strong, even if confusing. Twin studies show significantly higher concordance for bipolar disorder in monozygotic twins than in dizygotic twins (Gershon, 1990). Family studies also paint a consistent picture of genetic influence. Figure 8.9 shows the results of eighteen studies of diagnoses of the family members of unipolar and bipolar patients (Gershon, 1990). High rates of unipolar depression were found in the families of both groups, but only among the bipolar patients' relatives were the rates of bipolar disorder elevated beyond those expected in the general population (see also Winokur et al., 1995).

For a time, *genetic linkage* studies of bipolar disorder provided the strongest evidence in all of psychopathology for genetic transmission. The early work in the late 1980s generated tremendous enthusiasm for the possibility of identifying specific genes for bipolar disorder (e.g., Baron et al., 1987; Egeland et al., 1987). However, this research was not replicated in other populations (e.g., Hodgkinson et al., 1987; Kelsoe et al., 1989), suggesting the possibility that more complex processes, multiple genes, or multiple forms of the disorder are involved. Investigators continue to pursue the search for a "bipolar gene" (e.g., Smyth et al., 1996).

Neuroregulatory Processes   Proposed neuroregulatory mechanisms of bipolar disorder need to account for the cyclicity of moods — why there are ups as well as downs, how some people switch from one mood to another, and why the episodes recur. The earlier catecholamine hypothesis, that depression results from too little norepinephrine and mania from too much, has proven too simplistic, as we discuss on page 227. Recently, *dopamine* has been the focus of a theory that bipolar disorder may be caused by a dysfunction in the

Figure 8.9   Studies of Families of Bipolar and Unipolar Patients

Findings from the two sets of studies of (A) families of patients with unipolar depression and (B) families of patients with bipolar disorder illustrate familial patterns. Overall, rates of mood disorder are higher in these families than in the general population. Although unipolar depression is the most common mood disorder in both samples of families, bipolar patients are far more likely to have bipolar relatives than are the unipolar patients. These patterns suggest heritability of bipolar disorders — but they may also indicate that genetic liability includes risk for either bipolar or unipolar disorders. *Source:* Gershon (1990).

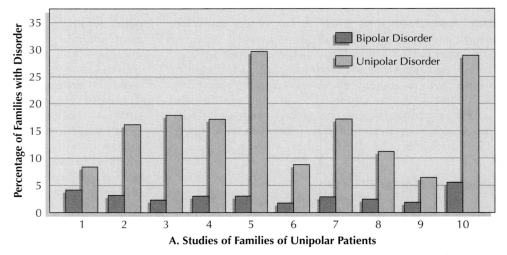

A. Studies of Families of Unipolar Patients

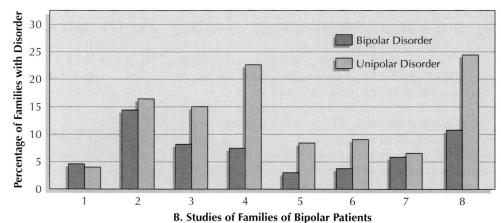

B. Studies of Families of Bipolar Patients

behavioral facilitation system, areas of the brain regulated by dopamine that guide active engagement with the environment (Depue & Iocono, 1989). The segment of the dopaminergic system that modulates motivational processes and goal-directed behavior may be the particular site of dysfunction (possibly as the result of a genetic defect), where behavioral and emotional reactivity is switched off (leading to depressive symptoms) or excessive reactivity is caused (bringing about the symptoms of mania). This intriguing model of bipolar disorder is supported indirectly by animal studies such as laboratory experiments with rats, but it awaits further exploration in human beings (Depue & Iocono, 1989).

Robert Post (1992) offered a theory that focuses on the recurring nature of episodes. He hypothesized that repeated episodes of mood disorder actually alter the brain, possibly resulting in increased *sensitivity* in neurotransmitter and neurohormonal regulation. In other words, the brain becomes increasingly responsive to stimuli that trigger mood swings. Specifically, he argued that the brain becomes sensitized to the effects of precipitating stressful events, so that less and less stress triggers relapses and the episodes eventually become virtually spontaneous. Post drew from his research on processes known as *behavioral sensitization* and *kindling,* which refer to experimentally induced brain and behavioral changes in animals (Post, Rubinow & Ballenger, 1984). Human studies have yet to demonstrate the validity of this hypothesis. However, due in part to Post's research on kindling (stimulation of animal brains leading to the development of spontaneous seizure phenomena), clinicians have increasingly turned to anticonvulsant medications to treat bipolar disorder, as we discuss later. Recent research on brain structure using MRI techniques, also influenced in part by Post's hypotheses, suggests that, indeed, bipolar disorder is sometimes accompanied by neuroanatomical abnormalities, possibly reflecting changes in the brain (e.g., Altshuler et al., 1995; Dupont et al., 1995). The nature and significance of these changes are not currently understood, however.

Chronobiological Dysfunction Another approach to the biological origins of bipolar disorder (as well as seasonal affective disorder) postulates underlying disturbances of the circadian rhythm systems — again, as with unipolar depression, presumably caused by a genetic defect (Goodwin & Jamison, 1990). Many manic episodes, for example, seem to be triggered when bipolar patients don't get enough sleep, possibly resulting in disruptions of circadian rhythms (Wehr, Sack & Rosenthal, 1987).

How do disturbed circadian rhythms relate to the cycles of mania and depression? The answer has to do with the strong relation between circadian rhythms and seasons of the year. Recall that the circadian rhythm is driven to a great extent by day-night light patterns, which are, of course, greatly affected by seasonal factors. In short, periods of the rhythm are highly sensitive to light. Animals (and, indeed, many humans) show profound behavioral and physiological alterations associated with changes in light and temperature. Researchers have argued that symptoms of depression and mania are like exaggerations of these normal seasonal variations. In human beings a disturbance in the circadian rhythm could be associated with a disturbance in light sensitivity resulting in further circadian rhythm disruption affected by the season of the year. In fact, as research has documented, more manias occur during the summer months and more depressions during the fall and winter months in the northern hemisphere (Goodwin & Jamison, 1990; Silverstone & Romans-Clarkson, 1989). Certainly not all patients show clear seasonal patterns of bipolar disorder, but enough do to suggest some link between these chronobiological patterns and the mechanisms of mood shifts.

Overall, there are many promising leads to pursue in understanding the biological bases of bipolar disorder — but as yet, no theory clearly explains the illness. Do psychological factors play a role? We turn to that question next.

Psychological Perspectives on Bipolar Disorder

Today's largely biological emphasis on the origins of bipolar disorder contrasts sharply with the psychoanalytic perspective taken during the first half of this century. Adherents of this perspective hypothesized that depression expressed inner-directed anger over the loss of an important person or source of self-esteem, and mania was viewed as a *defense* against depression. The psychoanalytic perspective is rarely accepted today. Nonetheless, interest has returned to the psychological factors that might affect the *course* of bipolar disorder. These factors mostly involve stress and coping.

Stressful life events have been found to trigger not only unipolar depression but episodes of bipolar depression and mania as well (e.g., Ellicott et al., 1990; Hammen & Gitlin, 1997; Hunt, Bruce-Jones & Silverstone, 1992). While not a primary cause of bipolar disorder, stressors may affect the timing of episodes. Some patients with bipolar disorder may generate high levels of stress in their lives, due to disruptive behaviors, thereby potentially contributing to frequent relapses.

Difficulties in family relationships may be both a trigger and a consequence of manic-depressive episodes. David Miklowitz and his colleagues (1988) determined that relapse in young patients with bipolar disorder could be significantly predicted by the level of negative family attitudes. (Expressed emotion, a concept particularly studied in families of schizophrenics, is described more fully in Chapter 9.) Negative relations with others are also associated with poorer adjustment overall (O'Connell et al., 1991).

Though limited, research on psychological issues more generally points out the relevance of social circumstances for understanding bipolar disorder. Such research also has important implications for treating bipolar disorder.

TREATMENT OF BIPOLAR DISORDER

Until the 1960s, relatively little could be done to treat the extreme mood swings and disruption associated with bipolar disorder. Early on, hospitalization for containing the acute symptoms was common, and psychotherapy was sometimes attempted, based on psychoanalytic principles, but without wide success. Then, in the 1940s **lithium carbonate,** a naturally occurring salt sometimes used for industrial purposes, was suspected to have antimanic properties. Eventually used in Europe, it was finally approved for use in the United States in the 1960s. Lithium represented a virtual revolution in the care of bipolar disorder — even though the mechanism by which it has its effects was (and is) not fully understood. Today, lithium is the treatment of choice for all bipolar patients, although additional medications and psychotherapy may also be recommended.

Characteristics and Effects of Lithium

Lithium produces two major effects: It reduces acute manic and hypomanic symptoms, and it prevents (or at least diminishes the frequency and intensity of) manic and depressive episodes (Goodwin & Jamison, 1990). Because bipolar disorder invariably involves multiple episodes over a lifetime, the majority of persons with this condition should be maintained indefinitely on the medication for its *prophylactic* properties. During acute episodes, manic patients may need to be hospitalized. Treatment of acute manic and depressive symptoms may also require antidepressants and antipsychotic medications called neuroleptics. Caution is required with antidepressants, however, because they may induce manic or hypomanic reactions or precipitate rapid cycling of depression and mania (American Psychiatric Association, 1993).

Initially, research suggested a 70 percent effectiveness rate for lithium in preventing relapse, but recent studies have lowered that rate to around 50 percent (Smith & Winokur, 1991). As we noted earlier, despite the use of lithium, many patients continue to have episodes and poor functioning, though some may do very well as long as they continue to use lithium. Patients with frequent episodes and comorbid substance abuse are least likely to benefit from lithium (Calabrese & Woyshville, 1995).

Side effects of lithium include thirst, weight gain, excessive urination, and fatigue. Many patients also report cognitive effects such as diminished concentration and memory or a feeling of "dullness." The most severe side effect is *toxicity.* Lithium is not metabolized; instead, it is filtered by the kidneys and excreted unchanged. Any condition that alters the patient's kidney functioning can therefore alter lithium level — and a high lithium level can damage the kidneys and thyroid. Therefore, its level in the blood must be closely monitored. Pregnant women should not take lithium because of potential damage to the developing fetus.

A major problem for bipolar patients taking lithium is *noncompliance* — the tendency to refuse medication or to fail to take it regularly in the prescribed amounts. Studies show that 18 percent to 53 percent of patients report failure to take the lithium prescribed for them (Goodwin & Jamison, 1990). Although these rates may not be higher than for other psychological medications, bipolar patients are unique in reporting that they sometimes don't take lithium because they like the "highs" associated with their symptoms (Jamison, Gerner & Goodwin, 1979).

Anticonvulsant Medications as Mood Stabilizers
Because many bipolar patients show no or few positive responses to lithium, additional medications have been tried. In particular, two anticonvulsants, carbamazepine (Tegretol) and sodium valproate (Depakote), have been used to successfully reduce acute manic symptoms (Post, 1988). Researchers already knew that anticonvulsants — medications used to treat individuals with seizures — have some mood-stabilizing properties. Although mania does not involve seizures, the reasoning behind the use of anticonvulsants is that they seem to decrease the excitability of areas of the brain that might be involved in emotional regulation (Post, 1987). Controlled studies indicate that anticonvulsants are successful in acute treatment, but their effects on long-term maintenance of mood stability have not been adequately demonstrated in double-blind trials (Solomon et al., 1995). Nevertheless, they appear to hold considerable promise as alternatives to, or in combination with, lithium.

Psychotherapy for Bipolar Disorder

Whereas lifelong medication is considered the best treatment for bipolar disorder, psychotherapy may be needed as a supplement. The goal of psychotherapy is to provide support to the patient in coping with a chronic and disruptive illness, and perhaps to reduce or prevent stressful experiences that could precipitate episodes. To date, no systematic outcome studies have evaluated the usefulness of psychotherapy as an adjunct to medication. Several such studies are under way at present, however, and their results will soon provide clues about the effectiveness of this approach.

SUICIDE

Suicide often occurs in the context of depression, but it is more complex than that. Suicide is paradoxical. It is both familiar and foreign. Many persons think about it but believe it happens only to "other people." Suicide is variously viewed as an understandable response to certain life disasters or as the decision of a troubled mind. It may be a systematic, carefully planned act, or the tragic outcome of a momentary impulse. In some cultures it is considered a shameful act; in others, a noble one. Often it is the end of pain for one person but the beginning of lifelong pain for others who knew that person.

Meaning and Context of Suicide

Suicide, whether attempted or actual, reveals numerous motivations. Ronald Maris (1992) suggested that suicidal phenomena fit into one of five motivational types:

1. *Escape.* The most common motivation for suicide is escape from psychological pain because of circumstances that are perceived to be intolerable.

2. *Revenge.* Maris (1992) estimated that 20 percent of suicides are motivated by anger, retribution, and manipulation of others. Murder-suicides, for example, frequently reflect the anger and hurt of a jealous, depressed husband who kills his wife (and maybe children) and then takes his own life (e.g., Rosenbaum, 1990).

3. *Altruism.* Dedication to higher goals as a motivation for suicide was suggested by French sociologist Emile Durkheim (1897/1951). Martyrdom, military suicide missions, and *hara-kiri* are examples of this rare form of suicide.

4. *Risk-taking.* Suicides that occur in the course of games or suicidal ordeals, such as Russian roulette, generally do not have death as the primary goal; the motivation is to have a stimulating rather than a long life.

5. *Mixed.* No doubt some suicides are motivated by a mixture of these considerations.

Figure 8.10 presents some actual suicide notes written by teenagers, reflecting a variety of these motivations. Most suicide victims do not leave notes, however. According to one study, notes are left by only 12 percent to 15 percent of people who kill themselves (Leenaars, 1992).

Sometimes, of course, the person seeks not death but some other outcome, such as communicating severe distress, changing the feelings or behaviors of another person, or punishing others. Thus, the intent might be a **suicide attempt,** not actual suicide.

Dr. Jack Kevorkian is pictured with two terminally ill Michigan women who requested his assistance in taking their own lives — and who did, just before the governor of the state signed into law a bill banning assisted suicides. The controversy over Kevorkian's activities reflects society's deeply divided attitudes about suicide; it is always wrong, bad, or sick versus people have the right to take their own lives and for some people under some circumstances, it is the "reasonable" choice.

```
            I'm
so sorry I let you
all down so much -- Please
don't be angry with me.
I love you all very
much
Now that I sit and
think about it, I know
I don't want to go but
I guess deep down I
realize there's no other
way
I feel so alone. I
never ever felt this pain
before
```

```
          , yes you have
hurt me  Everyone who
tryed to help me thank you,
but I'm apparntly a LOST
cause. I'm sorry but
I guess I belong no
where except off this earth.
Either with God or somewhere
else with whoever.
Mom & Dad, it's now 3:00 am.
I'm not drunk, don't worry.
I have decided something
that's not my decision to make
I guess that doesn't make
sense.
I know I don't have the
right to destroy my
life but inside I'm so
confused I don't feel I
have any other choice. I'm
sure there must be one
but I don't know it.
```

```
I know I was at your
apt. that night. I know
what happened & so do
you. How you explain
it, even though you
don't have to, is on
your conscience forever


          I
hate you!
so much that
even the devil
cant tell you
how much!
```

```
          I have run out of
hope. I prayed last night
for help. But there must
not be any more fore
me.
God knows that I have
trid my hardest. But, where
I'm going to go, it's got
to be better than the hell I
live
in now. Please don't
feel guilty about what
I'm going to do. I
have wanted to find
peace for a long time
          love you always
```

```
I DIDN'T MEAN
TO HUR ANYONE
BUT I CAN'T
GO ON LIVING
IN A WORLD WHERE
I'M ALWAYS
          GETTING
               HURT.
```

```
I'M CRYING
I'M CRYING
I'M CRYING


I'M MUCH TO SAD
THOUGH I CAN'T
LIVE WITH OUT YOU
I'VE EXPERIENCED TRUE
LOVE, LOVE I'LL NEVER
AGAIN EXPERIENCE HERE
ON EARTH
```

Figure 8.10 Suicide Notes

These notes are actual messages from adolescents who took their own lives. All identifying information has been omitted, but the notes are reproduced here exactly as written. They reflect the enormous variety of intense emotions and motives that contribute to suicidal acts. Thanks are expressed to suicide researcher Dr. Barry Garfinkel, who provided these samples.

As noted, suicides can range in motivation from escape to impulsive risk-taking like Russian roulette. It can also take the form of self-administered euthanasia in terminal illness. Except for murder-suicides in families, it is usually a solitary act, although occasionally there are *suicide pacts* among individuals or groups. And in recent years we have become aware of **cluster suicides,** multiple individual suicides committed in imitation of the publicized suicide of a famous person (even a fictional character) or of other publicized events such as teenage suicides (Gould et al., 1990; Phillips & Carstensen, 1988).

As the following case illustrates, suicide is sometimes baffling — as well as anguishing for those who are left behind:

Jerry, your supervisor at work, appeared to be a well-adjusted guy, so his suicide is a great mystery to all in the office — and everyone is agonizing over the thought that they should have seen or heard something about his behavior that might have helped. Slowly, you learn more information, and discover he'd left a suicide note for his sister. A single gay man, Jerry had a lover of many years who died of AIDS just a couple of months earlier. Everyone had known how hard it was for Jerry, but outwardly he seemed to cope pretty well. Now it appears that he couldn't get over his grief and felt that he really couldn't talk to many people about the depth of his pain. Though successful at work, he no longer seemed to get pleasure from it and didn't see any new challenges in the future. He worried that, as a middle-aged man, he was unlikely to develop a close and meaningful relationship with someone new. But perhaps most frightening of all, he believed that he had probably been infected with the AIDS virus — although he didn't go for testing. He couldn't bear the thought of suffering the way his partner did and, even worse, going through the agony of the disease alone. To Jerry, suicide seemed a logical choice — but to his distraught family, friends, and co-workers, it was anything but reasonable.

Who Commits Suicide?

Each year in the United States approximately 30,000 persons take their own lives. The true number is proba-bly considerably larger because circumstances often prevent the true manner of death from being recorded. In addition, although the overall rate of suicide deaths has been relatively stable over the last few decades in the United States, the figures are misleading because of vast differences in suicide rates not only among segments of the population and but also among historical trends. These patterns underline the complexity of the motives and circumstances associated with suicide.

Cultural Variations in Suicide Suicide is virtually universal and has occurred throughout all periods of history. Yet, as revealed by prevalence rates across countries and eras, it is highly shaped by culture. Rates of suicide by age group in several major industrialized countries reflect important differences (see Figure 8.11). For example, Japan and several other countries exhibit higher rates than the United States, particularly among older age groups.

Comparing the United States with *nonindustrialized* countries reveals further differences. The overall U.S. rate in 1980 was 11 per 100,000, compared to a rate of 10 in Taiwan, 7.8 in India, 5.6 in Iran, and 4.9 in Thailand (Headley, 1983). The meaning of these differences is complex, involving cultural variations in the acceptability of suicide, accuracy of official counts of suicide, and social conditions that prompt use of suicide as a method of dealing with difficulties.

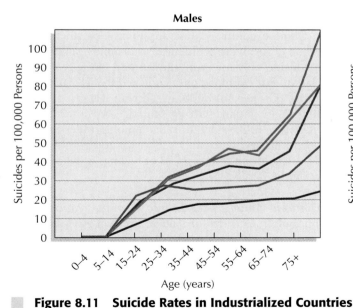
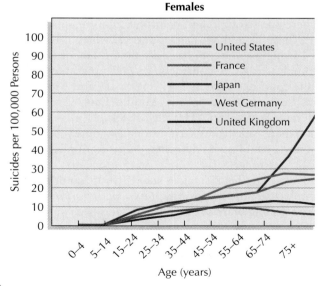

Figure 8.11 Suicide Rates in Industrialized Countries
Nations differ considerably in rates of suicide owing to cultural factors that define the acceptability of suicide, socioeconomic conditions that contribute to distress, and methods of recordkeeping. In most countries men exhibit higher rates than women, and rates of self-inflicted death tend to increase with age. What these figures do not show, however, are recent rapid increases in suicides among young people, especially males, in many industrialized countries. *Source:* Rockett & Smith (1989).

Suicide is usually seen, tragically, as a solution to unbearable misery—but often it is a baffling and irrational "solution." For example, Marilyn Monroe was one of the most beautiful and famous women in the world, with all the wealth and adoration one could ever want, but her psychological problems prevented her from finding solace in her good fortune. Though known to be troubled by drugs, Kurt Cobain also seemed to have every reason to live—fame and fortune, marriage, and a new baby.

There are strong religious prohibitions against suicide, in Catholic and Moslem countries, where it is considered a sin; in some countries, attempted suicide is also a criminal offense. Accordingly, certain predominantly Catholic countries such as Italy and Spain and Moslem nations such as those in the Middle East have low reported rates of suicide (Headley, 1983).

In Japan, suicide was traditionally approved as a solution to certain social dilemmas — for example, as an altruistic act to preserve honor or to atone for disapproved acts. Sacrificial suicides such as those committed by kamikaze pilots and the *seppuku* or *hara-kiri* that occurred among warriors or nobility, and even suicidal love pacts, were part of the tradition. In a culture that emphasizes being useful to one's family and society, individuals who believe that they have brought dishonor or who feel worthless may turn to suicide as a way of clearing their names. In modern times, relatively high rates of suicide among Japanese youngsters who have failed their college entrance exams reflect the ongoing social acceptance of suicide (Tatai, 1983).

Chinese culture is less supportive of suicide as a method of resolving problems. Accordingly, suicide rates are considerably lower in Taiwan and Hong Kong than in Japan. For example, data collected in 1989 indicate a rate of 9.8 per 100,000 in Taiwan versus 17.8 per 100,000 in Japan (Group for the Advancement of Psychiatry, 1989). High rates among older Chinese women, however, possibly reflect an acceptance of suicide as a solution to loneliness or feelings of being a burden on the family.

Variations Among U.S. Ethnic Groups Among U.S. subpopulations, rates of suicide are highest for Native Americans and whites, moderate for Mexican Americans, and lowest for Chinese Americans, Japanese Americans, and African Americans. These overall figures, however, obscure several important trends. There are increasing rates of suicide among young black men, low rates among young black women, high rates among Native American men, and high rates among elderly Japanese American women and, especially, Chinese American women. Rates among white males have been and continue to be the highest of all groups overall except for Native American males.

The rise in suicide rate among young African American men has been especially dramatic. Between 1960 and 1987, it increased from 4.1 per 100,000 to 12.9 per 100,000 among black males fifteen to twenty-four years old (Berman & Jobes, 1991). Though still lower than that of young white men, the rate among young black males has increased more than that of any other group. One possible explanation is that both homicide and suicide have increased among young black males, who are resorting to violence because of greater accessibility of firearms together with more frequent experiences of powerlessness and alienation (see Baker, 1990; Berman & Jobes, 1991).

Despite these differences between groups, we must not lose sight of the fact that an overwhelming 72 percent of all suicide deaths in the United States involve white males (National Center for Health Statistics, 1992).

Suicide and Gender As Figure 8.11 indicates, in almost every country, men are significantly more likely to kill themselves than women are. Numerous explanations for this gender difference have been proposed. For example, men's and women's purposes may differ, with women wishing to communicate distress more than they wish to die. In fact, women are three times more likely than men to make nonfatal suicide attempts. (Each year, an estimated 225,000 women attempt suicide, compared to about 75,000 men.) Women are typically less socially isolated than men — especially older men — and are willing to turn to others for support. Alcoholism rates are much higher in men than in women, and, as we discuss shortly, alcoholism is an important risk factor for suicide. And, finally, men are more likely to use lethal means of death such as guns, hanging, or jumping from high places, whereas women are more likely to use pills, poisons, and gas, which are less immediately fatal and so have a greater possibility of discovery and rescue (Group for the Advancement of Psychiatry, 1989).

Age Patterns in Suicide At different ages, people face different risks and challenges and have different resources to deal with them. It is hardly surprising, therefore, that there are important age-related aspects of suicide. Suicide is more common among older than younger persons (see Figure 8.11) — and it is especially frequent among older white men. However, in recent

Older white men, especially those who are alone, may be at particular risk for suicide under certain conditions — such as poor health, lack of meaningful roles, or alcohol abuse.

years we have seen a dramatic increase — apparently nearly worldwide — in suicide deaths among young people.

Among the elderly, widowhood and divorce are associated with higher rates of suicide. Indeed, social isolation has been cited as a major cause of suicide among older adults (reviewed in McIntosh, 1992). Although poor health may also be a factor, only a small percentage of all suicides involve terminal illness (Clark & Fawcett, 1992). Since 1933 a sharp decrease has occurred in suicide deaths among the elderly, possibly due to the improved economic security and better health care associated with Social Security and Medicare.

In the United States, the suicide rate among adolescents has quadrupled since 1950. The rate among the younger group of fifteen to nineteen year olds has also continued to rise (Berman & Jobes, 1991). These increases have touched off national concern about the causes of suicide, resulting in extensive efforts to reduce the rates. In fact, the rate of violent, self-inflicted death among teens parallels the increased rate of homicide death in the same age group — as well as increased rates of teen pregnancy, AIDS, and motor vehicle accidents. Similar in many ways to adult suicides, adolescent suicides are associated uniquely with factors such as impulsiveness, access to guns, and alcohol and substance abuse. Adolescent suicidal behavior is also marked by high rates of *suicide ideation* and *nonlethal attempts*. For instance, according to a nationwide survey of ninth through twelfth graders, 27 percent said that within the past year they had thought seriously about suicide and 8 percent made an actual attempt (Centers for Disease Control, 1991) — rates much higher than for the general population.

Suicide in childhood is quite rare, with about 250 deaths per year in the United States among children younger than fourteen. That it occurs at all, during a period of life that we assume should be carefree, is startling. Suicide is more common among boys than girls, and children from all backgrounds and socioeconomic levels appear to be vulnerable (Joffe & Offord, 1990). However, although young children may know what suicide is, they might not fully understand the consequences of their acts and thus lack the ability to understand that death is final (Sokol & Pfeffer, 1992). Among children and adolescents who do take their own lives, there is usually a considerable history of family turbulence, including physical abuse as well as stressful events occurring at the time of the suicide (de Wilde, Kienhorst, Diekstra & Wolters, 1992), poor family relationships, and parental dysfunction involving abuse, substance use, and mental illness (reviewed in Berman & Jobes, 1991). As a result of family problems, suicidal children and adolescents often have long-standing and ongoing problems of psychological maladjustment, social isolation, and academic difficulties.

Causes of Suicide

To understand the causes of suicide, psychologists have tried to understand the minds of victims — or, more precisely, to understand the predictors or correlates of suicide and thereby indirectly infer the causes.

Suicide as an Illness A growing body of evidence suggests that the vast majority of suicides occur in the context of diagnosable mental illness. Thus, suicide may be an abnormal reaction that occurs during an impaired state of mind. Many studies have reconstructed the thoughts, motives, and behaviors of suicide victims in the days before death. According to a review of these studies from various countries, major psychiatric disorders were present in at least 93 percent of the suicides (Clark & Fawcett, 1992).

Diagnosable depressive disorders have been implicated in 40 to 60 percent of suicides (e.g., Clark & Fawcett, 1992). About 15 percent of persons with a diagnosis of major depression or bipolar disorder will eventually kill themselves (Clark & Fawcett, 1992; Goodwin & Jamison, 1990). The second most frequent diagnosis among suicides is alcoholism, associated with approximately 25 percent of suicide deaths (Murphy, Wetzel, Robins & McEvoy, 1992). Although the proportion of alcoholics who commit suicide is relatively low (approximately 2 to 3 percent), the presence of depression along with alcoholism is a particularly severe risk factor for suicide (Murphy, Wetzel, Robins & McEvoy, 1992). Anxiety disorders (such as panic disorder) and schizophrenia (a severe disorder involving thought disorder and delusions and hallucinations) are also implicated in a substantial number of suicides (e.g., Weissman, Klerman, Markowitz & Ouellette, 1989).

A recent study found that 90 percent of children and adolescents who committed suicide had psychiatric disorders — a proportion similar to that among adults (Shaffer et al., 1996). Especially among adolescents, *impulsiveness* is believed to be a factor in the majority of suicides. Depression in combination with antisocial behaviors, conduct problems, substance abuse, and difficulties in impulse control are considered especially risky for suicide among adolescent males (e.g., Shaffer et al., 1988).

These facts do not mean that mental illness *causes* suicide; indeed, the majority of people with diagnosable disorders do not kill themselves. But they do strongly suggest that the decision to commit suicide and the actions taken toward that end may be influenced by psychological conditions that impair a person's judgment. Recall, for example, that depression often involves *hopelessness,* an often-distorted perception that the future is bleak and that circumstances are unchangeable. Hopelessness can be measured on questionnaires assessing individuals' outlooks about themselves and their future. Several studies have found that eventual suicide victims scored high on hopelessness measures during previous periods of depression (Glanz, Hass & Sweeney, 1995; Beck et al., 1990).

Risk Factors for Predicting Suicide   Table 8.4 summarizes findings from numerous studies of the correlates (predictors) of suicide. Note that these factors reflect both psychological issues and demographic characteristics. They don't so much "explain" suicide as indicate the variables that are often found in the backgrounds of suicidal individuals. For instance, suicidal talk does not cause suicide; indeed, a common myth holds that if people talk about it, they won't do it. But an estimated 80 percent of suicides *are* preceded by some kind of warning, either direct ("I think I'm going to kill myself") or indirect ("sometimes I don't think life is worth living") (Shneidman, 1987).

We also know that older white males who are alcoholic, isolated from their families, and unemployed are particularly at risk for suicide — especially if they are depressed. Perhaps these factors converge to create a sense of futility and meaninglessness that feels beyond the person's power to change. Being isolated and lacking the support of positive relationships may well limit that person's access to resources that would otherwise counteract the hopelessness.

Are prior suicide attempts an accurate predictor? As it turns out, most suicide victims did not previously attempt suicide; according to research estimates, only 18 to 38 percent of suicides were preceded by an attempt (e.g., Fawcett et al., 1987; Rich, Young & Fowler, 1986). Nevertheless, a small but significant number of attempters — 7 percent to 10 percent — eventually succeed (summarized in Clark & Fawcett, 1992). Other estimates are as high as 15 percent (Maris, Berman, Maltsberger & Yufit, 1992).

Finally, a note on *lethal methods*. At the simplest level, this issue means that people who use, say, firearms are more likely to complete a suicide than those who use pills. But at another level, it is possible that increased availability of firearms contributes to increased rates of suicide. Several studies have suggested an association between availability of guns and suicide (e.g., Killias, 1993; Lester, 1993; Sloan et al., 1990). One in particular (Carrington and Moyer, 1994) shows that both gun-related and overall suicides decreased in Ontario, Canada, after the passage of gun-control laws. Gun availability among youths, in combination with impulsivity and intoxication, presents a disastrous formula for increased suicide rates in young males (e.g., Brent et al., 1988).

Treatment of Suicide Risk

The person who is known or suspected to be at risk for suicide urgently needs evaluation and intervention. A

Table 8.4   **Predictors of Risk for Suicide**
1. Depressive illness, mental disorder
2. Alcoholism, drug abuse
3. Suicide thoughts, talk, preparation
4. Prior suicide attempts
5. Lethal methods
6. Isolation, living alone, loss of support
7. Hopelessness, cognitive rigidity
8. Older white men
9. Modeling, suicide in family, genetics
10. Work problems, economics, occupation
11. Marital problems, family pathology
12. Stress, life events
13. Anger, aggression, low serotonin
14. Physical illness
15. Combination of factors, suicidal "careers"

Source: Maris (1992).

These are some of the most common correlates of suicide, replicated in numerous studies. Although they provide important clues to the understanding of suicide, they neither predict who will commit suicide nor explain individual deaths.

trained professional can attempt to judge the seriousness of the risk. In the most critical cases, where there is a need to protect the person from imminent harm, psychiatric hospitalization may be recommended as the safest way to contain and monitor the person. When the person refuses voluntary treatment, involuntary commitment may be advised. Although involuntary admission to a psychiatric facility is permitted by law for a limited time (usually three days), it requires certification by a mental health professional that the person is a danger to himself or herself.

If the individual does not appear to be at immediate risk for self-harm, therapy or crisis intervention may be recommended to deal with currently pressing concerns. Diagnosable conditions are commonly treated with medications or psychotherapy (or both) to resolve the symptoms that might have contributed to the suicidal crisis. Symptoms that can be treated to relieve suicidal danger include (1) the grave misperceptions of reality that lead patients with unipolar depression or bipolar disorder to exaggerate the hopelessness of the situation, (2) schizophrenic delusions, and (3) impaired judgment and impulsiveness heightened by alcohol and drugs. On the one hand, outpatient treatment might attempt to determine and resolve the life circumstance problems that precipitated the suicidal behavior, often using such methods as cognitive-behavior therapy or interpersonal psychotherapy. On the other hand, **crisis intervention**, involving brief therapies conducted either as inpatient or outpatient treatment, may attempt to identify and quickly resolve the immediate crisis by drawing on the person's own resources, including support from friends and family. Occasionally a suicide attempt in itself "solves" the individual's problems by dramatically drawing attention to the need for help and support.

Suicide Prevention Unfortunately, either many suicidal individuals do not communicate their intentions to others, or they and others lack the resources, knowledge, or willingness to seek individual therapy or crisis management. For example, in a survey conducted at a major university, freshmen were asked about suicidal thoughts, behaviors, and help-seeking. Ten percent of the students said they had made a suicide attempt in their lives, but only 3 percent of all students ever sought medical attention for their injuries (Meehan, Lamb, Saltzman & O'Carroll, 1992). Thus, with respect to many people with life-threatening urges and behaviors, the treatment task is to provide preventive services that do not require them to be in the patient role. Also, adolescents and others who are restricted in their access to services without family involvement may be especially receptive to preventive services.

Since the 1960s a massive effort has been undertaken in nearly every community in the United States to provide **suicide prevention centers** (organizations providing service to suicidal people), commonly involving **telephone hotlines** that people can call to receive immediate supportive services. Typically, these services are staffed by volunteers trained to offer listening and support. They provide anonymity, are available twenty-four hours a day, and can help guide individuals to appropriate mental health care if needed.

Few data about the effectiveness of suicide prevention centers are available. Effectiveness is difficult to test because clients are anonymous and because those who call in would have to be compared with those who are equally in crisis but do not call. One potential method of overcoming this methodological problem is to compare suicide rates in communities before and after they established suicide prevention centers. One study that summarized a number of such investigations came to the conclusion that the presence of these centers did not significantly reduce suicide rates overall (Dew, Bromet, Brent & Greenhouse, 1987). Bear in mind, however, that this study examined overall patterns and did not focus on the prevention of individual deaths. Preventing even some deaths validates the worth of such centers and crisis hotlines. Moreover, these services are commonly used by people in turmoil, so counting suicide deaths is only

one way to evaluate whether they are helpful. As a testament to their utility, most communities continue to offer such services.

In 1991 the Centers for Disease Control published a proposal to reduce violence and abusive behavior, with the specific goal of reducing suicidal deaths among youths between fifteen and nineteen years of age (Berman & Jobes, 1991). This proposal, involving a Task Force on Youth Suicide, recommended several prevention strategies for providing services. One such ongoing effort involves *school-based prevention programs* — that is, educational programs integrated into the curriculum that teach teens about the circumstances and myths of suicide, warning signs, and resources for helping with problems). Some of the programs include communication and problem-solving skills training.

Are these programs useful? Do they work? Opinions are mixed. Some critics have charged that school-based prevention programs that try to "normalize" suicide in an effort to destigmatize it may instead glamorize suicide and misrepresent the strong link between suicide and psychological disorder. Other critics have argued that knowing about suicide doesn't prevent it and that the teens most at risk are least likely to attend suicide prevention programs (Berman & Jobes, 1991). Ultimately, however, the school setting is the most logical place in which to help teens recognize suicidal risk in themselves and others. More empirical studies are needed to determine which methods are most helpful, and whether school-based programs actually prevent teenage suicides.

What Lies Ahead?

Our understanding of mood disorders has changed enormously since the 1970s. The finding of a basic distinction between unipolar and bipolar forms, the sophisticated genetic and psychosocial research being conducted on causal factors, and the development of effective treatments are all relatively recent. Yet these breakthroughs not only stimulate new ideas and findings; they also raise new questions.

Among these questions are the following. Why are children and youth displaying more depression, and what can we do about it? Is there a gene for manic-depressive disorder — and if so, can we prevent development of the disorder? Are there subtypes of depression with different causes and cures? Do early childhood losses or traumas actually alter the brain in ways that create susceptibility to depression? And given the success of psychotherapies for depression, how can we disseminate them so that more people can actually be treated for this disorder?

Suicide, of course, raises many troubling issues for the future. Another important question, then, is How can we prevent it? Or, for that matter, can our society ever resolve its considerable ambivalence about the right of people to take their own lives? Will changes in social programs such as welfare and Medicare and Social Security have an impact on suicide rates, altering individuals' perceptions of available resources to help cope with their lives. Finally, given the increase in youth violence — and in the availability of guns — will we continue to see elevated rates of suicide among teens and children?

KEY TERMS

affective disorder (216)
antidepressant medications (235)
attachment (232)
bipolar disorder (239)
circadian rhythms (228)
cluster suicides (248)
cognitive triad (229)
continuation treatment (236)

cortisol (227)
crisis intervention (254)
cyclothymic disorder (242)
depressive schemas (229)
dysthymic disorder (220)
hypomania (240)
hypothalamic-pituitary-adrenal (HPA) axis (227)
learned helplessness (230)

light therapy (237)
lithium carbonate (246)
maintenance treatment (236)
major depressive disorder (219)
mania (239)
monoamines (227)
mood disorder (216)

resilient (233)
seasonal affective disorder (SAD) (219)
suicide attempt (247)
suicide prevention centers (254)
telephone hotlines (254)
unipolar depression (217)

SUMMARY

Features of Unipolar Depression

Mood, or *affective, disorders* are syndromes of depression or of a combination of depression and its opposite pole, *mania.* Unlike normal mood depression, which may last a few moments or hours following a negative event, *unipolar depression* involves persisting disturbances of negative mood and cognition as well as altered energy, motivation, behavior, and bodily functioning affecting sleep and appetite. Depressive symptoms, particularly if they persist, greatly impair a person's ability to function at work, in the home, and in relationships.

Major depressive disorder and *dysthymic disorder* are the most frequent forms of unipolar depression. Briefer or milder forms of depression may also be diagnosed. Subtypes include psychotic depression, melancholia, and *seasonal affective disorder (SAD).*

Depression is one of the most prevalent of all clinical syndromes, co-occurring frequently with other psychological and medical disorders. It affects women about twice as often as men. It occurs in all cultures, although it may be expressed somewhat differently in non-Western cultures than in the West. Increasingly, depression appears to be a disorder of young people. Depression is also recognized as a recurring disorder and, for some people, a chronic condition.

Causes of Unipolar Depression

Biological research suggests moderate heritability, given strong family patterns implicating both genes and family environment. Research has also focused on neurotransmitter functioning involving *monoamines* such as norepinephrine and serotonin. One model of depression emphasizes the dysregulation of neurotransmitter systems. The *hypothalamic-pituitary-adrenal*

(HPA) axis is a critical feature of the stress reaction process, producing *cortisol.* One theory holds that depression results from a maladaptive stress response — possibly genetically mediated or dysfunctional as a result of early traumatic experiences that alter brain reactivity to stress. Both the monoamine neurotransmitters and the HPA system are in turn affected by *circadian rhythms.* Both sleep disturbances (including reduced REM latency) and seasonal patterns in depression are suggestive of a disturbance of circadian rhythm functioning in recurrent depression. Female hormones account for postpartum blues and premenstrual dysphoric disorder, but are not clearly linked to other forms of depression.

Psychological factors — emphasized since Freud's time — are implicated in the loss of significant relationships or other experiences that sustain a person's sense of self-worth. Some people may be susceptible to depression because of negative thinking about the self, the world, and the future. These underlying negative beliefs are called *depressive schemas.* Vulnerability in the form of dysfunctional cognitions may cause depression if people experience a stressful event and their cognitive appraisal is that it diminishes their value or reflects some important defect that they are helpless to change. Dysfunctional parent-child relationships, especially those that create insecure attachment bonds by failing to provide consistent, supportive, and nurturant environments, may contribute to vulnerability in the sense of worth — and hence to depression. Parental depression often creates such negative environments.

Treatment of Unipolar Depression

Treatment of depression may involve *antidepressant medications,* such as tricyclic antidepressants, monoamine oxidase inhibitors (MAOIs), or serotonin reuptake blockers. These medications may be used for acute treatment, as well as for *continuation treatment* and *maintenance treatment*. For severe or drug-resistant depressions, electroconvulsive therapy (ECT) or combinations of medications might be tried. *Light therapy* may be effective for seasonal depressions, and patients treated with sleep deprivation tend to show short-term improvement. Various psychotherapies developed specifically for depression have also proven to be effective in acute treatment and somewhat helpful in preventing recurrences. These treatments focus on changing maladaptive behaviors and cognitions (as in cognitive-behavioral therapy) or on maladaptive interpersonal relationships (as in interpersonal therapy).

Features of Bipolar Disorder

Bipolar disorder involves both depression and *mania* or the milder *hypomania*. In turn, mania is characterized by euphoric or irritable mood, coupled with increased activity, grandiose beliefs, and excessive behaviors having a potential for harm or embarrassment. Bipolar disorder was previously known as manic-depression. Different people exhibit different patterns of mood cycles and different frequencies of episodes. Bipolar disorder, by definition, is recurrent and may be very impairing, although some people function relatively well between episodes.

Causes of Bipolar Disorder

Genetic studies using linkage and marker methods have strongly implicated genetic transmission, although different genes may be responsible for different versions of the disorder. Further exploration of the role of dopamine may confirm the hypothesis that this neurotransmitter plays a critical role in regulating type and level of activity and, hence, has relevance to bipolar disorders. Investigators are also pursuing the hypothesis that a desynchronization in the operation of circadian rhythms is affected by seasonal changes in light.

Psychological factors are not considered to be fundamental causes of bipolar disorder. Nevertheless, stressful conditions and personal traits may affect the course of episodes. One causal theory suggests that stressors may alter the brain over time, contributing to seemingly spontaneous episodes.

Treatment of Bipolar Disorder

Lithium carbonate is the recommended treatment for bipolar disorder. Continued over a lifetime, it is used to prevent severe recurrences of bipolar episodes. Lithium is helpful to some patients, but many who take it continue to experience episodes. Mood stabilizers, formerly used mainly as anticonvulsants — are also increasingly being administered because they seem to stabilize brain functioning. Psychotherapy may be a useful adjunct to medication to help people cope with this chronic and disruptive disorder, as well as to help prevent stressful conditions that may trigger recurrences of episodes.

Meaning and Context of Suicide

There are various motives for suicide, including escape and revenge. The goals underlying actual, rather than attempted, suicide may be different. The meaning of suicide and, hence, its rates vary greatly by culture, gender, and age. In the United States, older white males are the most common victims of suicide, whereas younger white females more often make *suicide attempts*. Increasing rates among adolescents and children are cause for alarm.

Causes of Suicide

The majority of suicides have been found to occur in the context of mental illness, chiefly affective disorders, alcoholism, and anxiety disorders. Hopelessness is a common theme among potential suicide victims; but because it is often linked to depressive thinking, it may not reflect an accurate appraisal of their circumstances. Other risk factors include social isolation, prior attempts, lethal methods, and communication of intent.

Treatment of Suicide Risk

Severe and immediate risk for suicide often requires hospitalization for the protection of the person. Treatments may also include psychotherapy, medication, or *crisis intervention* to resolve precipitating factors. As a recourse for the many people with suicidal wishes who do not seek therapy, *suicide prevention centers*, staffed by trained volunteers, offer an option to discuss personal pain and reconsider suicide. School-based prevention programs may also help to reach troubled youth — although their effectiveness is controversial.

Consider the following. . .

Suppose that for six months now, you have been depressed over the break-up of a long-time relationship. A friend of yours suggests you get some antidepressants to help you through this trying time. Under what conditions should antidepressants be used? What steps should you take to determine if this is the best step for you? Based on what you have learned in this chapter, you know that antidepressants are being widely used not only for depression but also for such things as eating disorders and even compulsive behavior. What are the advantages of the wide use of such drugs? What are the disadvantages?

Suppose that you are a state lawmaker on a committee charged with formulating guidelines under which doctors might assist people in taking their own lives. Try to set aside your religious and cultural beliefs about suicide. Instead, given what you have learned about depression and other conditions that influence suicide, is suicide a rational choice that ought to be granted? What conditions and guidelines do you think are necessary to protect individuals and to protect society?

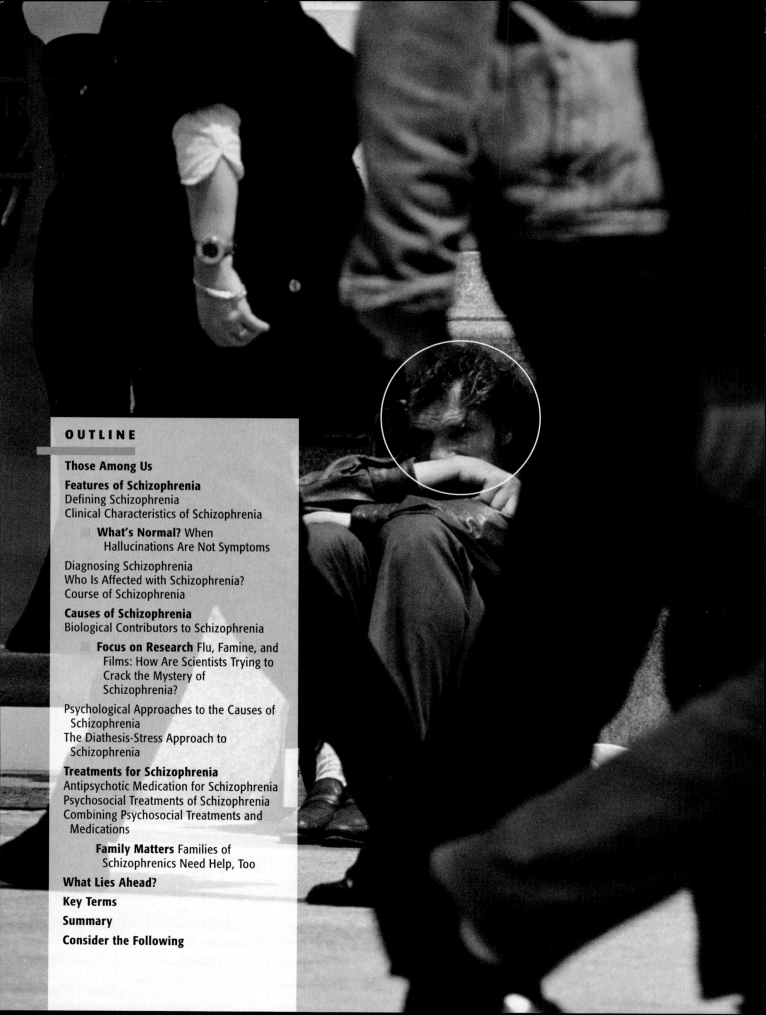

CHAPTER 9

Schizophrenia

Those among us . . .

■ Gerald is a guy you met in the dorm during your first year. He was smart and sociable, from a well-off and successful family. You are surprised to hear that he came to believe there was a plot against him, and that he had to be hospitalized.

■ Your cousin Marty has always been a little odd. In high school, he became more withdrawn and peculiar, staying in his bedroom, writing strange messages in a journal. Sometimes the family could hear him shouting and talking as if someone were in the room with him. That was ten years ago. Despite medication, he has been unable to go to school or keep a job, and spends all his time at home watching TV.

■ A homeless woman is often seen in your neighborhood. People complain about her behaviors, although they know she is not dangerous. Last week she rummaged in the trash cans in the alley and set up camp under a tree with her findings: bottles, ribbons and twine that she wrapped around the tree, and a broken chair. Regardless of the weather, she wears in layers all the clothing she possesses or finds.

■ Sally was an older, returning student in a large undergraduate class. She complained to the department chairperson that one of her professors was lecturing about her in an abnormal psychology course. She believed that everyone in the course was "in on it," and that her doctor had provided the professor with files about her.

Is schizophrenia a disease, like diabetes, or is it a mental "breakdown" due to some overwhelming stress that makes a person go "crazy"?

Can *anyone* develop this terrible condition? Are there degrees of madness?

Are schizophrenic people experiencing a "different" reality, one that we could understand if we knew the key?

Can schizophrenia be cured?

These individuals suffer the symptoms of schizophrenia, one of the most unusual and extreme forms of psychological disorder. Before treatment practices changed in the 1960s, an estimated two-thirds of all beds in mental hospitals and more than one-fourth of all available hospital beds in the United States were occupied by persons with schizophrenia. Today, an estimated 10 percent to 13 percent of homeless people are schizophrenic. The sheer numbers alone, however, do not convey the magnitude of the tragedy of lost lives to individuals and their families. Nor do they indicate the mysteries of this disorder in terms of its features and causes. In this chapter we discuss the perplexing symptoms of schizophrenia, research and speculation about its causes, and its treatment possibilities and problems.

FEATURES OF SCHIZOPHRENIA

Defining Schizophrenia

Is schizophrenia the same as insanity? The terms *madness, craziness, lunacy,* and *insanity* have all been applied to schizophrenia at one time or another. Insanity, however, is a legal — not a psychiatric — term, and the other words refer broadly to the general concept of psychosis. **Psychosis,** in turn, is a broad term that refers to all mental disorders characterized by major departures from reality. As we discuss in Chapter 8, a person can have a psychotic depression, and mania may sometimes involve psychotic states. There are also many types of brief psychosis, as well as psychotic conditions induced by drugs or brain disease.

Schizophrenia is a term for a specific type of psychosis marked by disturbances of thought, language, and behavior not due to a primary mood disorder or medical condition. Although researchers agree about some of the typical characteristics of this disorder, controversies exist about the most valid way to define the term. In fact, it might even be appropriate to refer to "the schizophrenias" because, like many major psychological disorders, this disorder may have different forms with somewhat different features and causes.

Schizophrenia gained its name only in this century. At the end of the nineteenth century Emil Kraepelin (1883) used the term *dementia praecox* to refer to various kinds of progressive, irreversible mental deterioration that begin early in life and involve thought disorders and departures from reality. Then, in 1911, the Swiss psychiatrist Eugen Bleuler, introduced the term *schizophrenia* to refer to disorders that he believed reflected a split (schism) of the mind (phrenos). This label should not be confused with split personality or multiple personality; it does *not* refer to people with "Dr. Jekyll–Mr.

German psychiatrist Emil Kraepelin, at the end of the 19th century, described many of the features of what we now call schizophrenia.

Hyde" personality switches. For Bleuler, schizophrenia was a splitting of psychic functions, such as cognition and emotion. Bleuler agreed with Kraepelin that the predominant and defining feature of this severe psychological abnormality was thought disorder and that it was a physical disease. But unlike Kraepelin, he did not believe that the disorder inevitably led to progressive mental deterioration. Some people, he observed, seemed to recover with only residual symptoms. Interestingly, more than eighty years later, researchers still debate about the course of this disorder.

Extensive efforts to further refine the definitions and understanding of schizophrenia have continued over the decades. Within just a few years, diagnostic criteria have changed substantially. People diagnosed as schizophrenic by some researchers in the 1950s might today be diagnosed with bipolar disorder, "schizophreniform" disorder, or some other form of mental disorder. The diagnostic criteria for schizophrenia have narrowed even further in the recent DSM-IV. And, indeed, research continues to illuminate features of the disorder that affect how it is defined.

Clinical Characteristics of Schizophrenia

From the standpoint of some people afflicted with schizophrenia, the experience is a terrifying jumble of perceptual alterations: a confusing mass of ideas, stimuli, and sensory messages. For other sufferers, the primary experience is one of withdrawal from social interactions into a private world of fantasy and personal preoccupation. People with schizophrenia usually do not "feel" crazy or recognize the unreality of their experiences. Communication with others is difficult for them because they have a unique frame of reference or peculiar logic or word usage. In addition, they may be emotionally flat — or depressed, anxious, scared, or angry — and experience profound disruptions in the sense of a coherent self.

Consider the following personal account, written by an individual diagnosed as schizophrenic, who has also learned self-awareness in her therapy.

> *I have never fought a fight harder than the fight my mind fights against itself.... When my brain is pulled together I feel "solid." I can literally feel my feet on the ground, and I can feel that my thinking is clear. This state occurs rarely. When I am crazy, the insane part takes over. I am a victim of delusions, unreal thoughts, and severe disorganization. I have some sorts of hallucinations and many visual and auditory distortions.... The state that is most unbearable and causes me the most pain is the state in between.... I am in this state almost all the time, and usually it feels like a vague confusion, a swirling mass of thoughts and images going on in my head and clouding my thinking and functioning. (Ruocchio, 1989)*

In this second description, a young woman relates her early experiences with disturbed thoughts and perceptions that began when she was about age fifteen, but she didn't admit to anyone what was happening to her until about age twenty-one.

> *I had major fantasies of suicide by decapitation and was reading up on the construction of guillotines.... I thought my inner being to be a deeply poisonous substance. The problem, as I saw it, was to kill myself, but then get rid of my essence in such a way that it did not harm creation. Also at the time I was very afraid. I had the feeling that I was dissolving and that pieces of me were going out into space.... I was also very ashamed and thought people were watching me. I was afraid of people to the extent that I wouldn't come out of my room when people were around. (Anonymous, 1992, p. 334)*

From the point of view of observers, schizophrenia is marked by fundamental disturbances in thought, speech, and perceptual processes, as well as by disturbances in behavior, mood, and interpersonal relationships. Clearly, the disorder disrupts a person's functioning in all areas that are essential to human adaptation. Table

---

Table 9.1   Symptoms and Experiences of Schizophrenia

Disturbances of thought and language
- Loose associations (personal meanings, intrusion of associations, incoherence)
- Conceptual difficulties (concrete thinking)
- Peculiar word usage (clang associations, neologisms, word salad)
- Poverty of speech (vague, overelaborated, overly abstract)
- Delusions (grandiose, paranoid, nihilistic)

Perceptual disturbances
- Increased intensity of sensations and perceptions
- Perceptions of changes in the environment
- Hallucinations

Affective disturbances
- Flat affect, apathy
- Inappropriate affect
- Lack of pleasure

Behavioral disturbances
- Peculiar mannerisms, posture, facial expressions
- Reduced spontaneous movement
- Social withdrawal or inappropriate social behavior
- Impairment in interpersonal relatedness
- Lack of motivation, lack of volition
- Lack of pleasure and motivation

These are the most characteristic symptoms of schizophrenia, although many of the same symptoms may also occur in other psychotic or cognitive impairment disorders. Schizophrenic patients differ from one another in terms of the number and pattern of symptoms exhibited.

9.1 summarizes the most characteristic symptoms of schizophrenia.

Disturbances of Thought and Language   People with schizophrenia commonly have idiosyncratic thoughts and associations that interfere with their ability to maintain a logical and consistent train of thought. They may change from one subject to another without any apparent connection between the topics. (In Table 9.1 this symptom is described as loose associations.) The train of thought is "derailed," as in the following example:

PSYCHOLOGIST: What have you been thinking about lately?

PATIENT: I gotta get out of here, the people are talking. They're talking about clocks, maps, and triangulating within the neighborhood. I can understand and see the dangers, I know how people operate, and there isn't any need to be upset.

PSYCHOLOGIST: Why are people talking about clocks and maps?

PATIENT: It's all a part of the family, you know, those who are in and the ones who never get to see the words. The deal has to be agreed to by one person, but it doesn't have to last a long time.

As this excerpt demonstrates, schizophrenic thought patterns are disorganized, and the resulting verbal behavior is incoherent. The spoken language may consist of real words and the grammar of the sentences may seem normal, but the associations fail to hold together in an understandable train of thought.

Schizophrenic speech may also include *clang associations*, or the use of words that are associated merely by the way they sound, not by their meaning. For instance, "The pen went to the hen, 'cause men said when," or "Sit you wit, no time to flit." Clang associations may also occur in other forms of psychosis such as mania. Schizophrenic speech can deteriorate to the point where it includes made-up words, called *neologisms*. For instance, one schizophrenic patient asked to sit at a desk said, "This thing is a cramstile" — perhaps referring to the desk as something that "cramps one's style." Another patient referred to someone wearing a hat as having an "easterhorned head." An attempt to communicate using predominately disorganized speech has been described as a *word salad*.

Poverty of speech may also occur in some patients with schizophrenia. This condition refers to speech that is adequate in form but conveys little information because it repeats simple phrases or is overly abstract and vague. Alternatively, speech may be overelaborate or digressive, as if the person loses a train of thought. *Concrete thinking*, which reflects a reduced ability to deal with abstractions, may be observed in patients' very literal interpretations. When asked to give the meaning of the proverb "When it rains, it pours," a person with schizophrenia replied, "It means nothing less than very wet weather."

Delusional Thinking People in general certainly hold different opinions and beliefs. These are variations in individual realities, and they are to be expected as an aspect of normality. However, there are larger realities that people everywhere would readily agree to, based on objective sensory data or shared principles of logic. Individuals who violate these larger, shared realities are considered to be disturbed. Consider the following beliefs: that buildings, such as the one in which your class meets, can float in the air; that barking dogs are communicating in a special language to representatives of a foreign

and corrupt power; or that radio transmissions of the news, if played backward, are signals to once-abandoned members of a race of people who came to earth thousands of years ago. Most people recognize that beliefs like these are not based in reality. Called **delusions**, these false beliefs have no basis in and are not influenced by reality.

Among the many types of delusions, several are common (and can occur in forms of psychosis other than schizophrenia). Persons with *delusions of grandeur* believe they have special powers or characteristics; they may think they are great inventors, reincarnated world leaders, or even God. Those with *delusions of persecution* believe that other people are plotting against and mistreating them. And individuals with *delusions of reference* believe that other people are making secret reference to them. The plot of a movie or television program, comments made in the media by political leaders, and the style and content of newspaper advertisements can all be sources of concern to such individuals. Relatedly, schizophrenic patients might believe that other people are capable of **thought insertion** (putting thoughts in their heads), controlling their behaviors, or stealing their thoughts. **Thought broadcasting** is another uniquely schizophrenic delusion, referring to the belief that one's thoughts are being broadcast out loud so that other people can hear them. Individuals with *nihilistic delusions* believe that they are dead, that nothing exists, or that people are only vapors and no longer meaningful physical entities.

Delusions can be simple or complex; they can be systematic, with an expanding web of information tied into the person's explanations; or they can be disorganized. They can also be tied into odd or disorganized behaviors. Consider the following actual examples of schizophrenic patients the authors have known:

> *Joel believed that women could control his erections with their cigarette lighters, which made him angry; he expected to find a better life on another planet and believed that aliens would come and take him there. Alice would walk through a room full of strangers and imagine that they were talking about her when she heard the words "slut" or "dog." Maria thought that she was dead; every day she would dress in black and lie on her bed all day, motionless, until it was time for dinner. Tommy believed that he could control the rain; the forces of nature were his to command.*

People with delusional thought processes do not respond to the facts in the environment. Despite objective evidence, people with delusions often do not recognize that their beliefs are not based in reality. This situation can be troubling to therapists and family members who try to convince delusional patients that their beliefs are incorrect. The lack of awareness of having a disorder or resistance to believing that one's experiences are due to mental illness is very common in schizophrenia.

There is considerable variety among the symptoms of thought disorder presented by people diagnosed with schizophrenia. Not all have constantly disorganized thoughts and speech, and not all are constantly troubled by delusional thinking. Many persons with schizophrenia can communicate fairly clearly some of the time.

Perceptual Disturbances   The alterations of perception linked to schizophrenia do not involve disturbances of the basic sensory functions — in other words, nothing is wrong with the person's ability to hear, see, feel, smell, and taste. Rather, the perceptual disorder involves the accuracy of perceptions and the cognitive operations involved in making sense of them. In the early stages of an episode, for example, the perceived intensity of sights and sounds often increases, causing confusion. One patient described his early experiences of schizophrenia that began when he was a student moving into his own lodgings:

> *I didn't sleep enough; I didn't eat regularly. After four months, I wanted to paint the large white wall in my room.... I started to paint a dark forest on the wall, with a reptile in the foreground. I have always been able to hear colors. They transmit vibrations. I can hear black, red, and deep brown. During the painting it was deathly quiet in the room.... In this silence, something frightening was slowly growing. Something threatening was coming up. I had the feeling I wasn't alone in the room any more. Then I heard a monotonous sound in my ears that didn't come from myself and which I couldn't explain. It was a bit like the squeaking you hear when your ears are closed.... It was like an emotion, but deeper. I had the feeling something was looking for me. (Anonymous, in Romme & Escher, 1989, p. 211)*

The perceptual disturbances most characteristic of schizophrenia are **hallucinations,** or reports of sensory stimulation when no such stimulation is present. The person reports hearing something, seeing something, or feeling something when there are no external stimuli to produce it.

Hallucinations can occur in any of the sensory modalities: seeing, hearing, tasting, touching, and smelling. Auditory and visual hallucinations are the most common. *Auditory hallucinations* can be voices that talk to or about the schizophrenic person, tell the person what to do, or analyze and criticize the person's actions. The exact quality of the voices is often difficult for patients to explain. Some report that the voices sound like their own, but many state that the voices are from other people. The voices are unwanted, often said to be interfering and confusing. *Visual hallucinations* are visions of persons or objects perceived to be present. *Tactile, taste,*

and *somatic hallucinations* have also been reported by persons with schizophrenia or other psychoses, as well as by patients undergoing detoxification from severe alcohol problems. Some schizophrenic patients report feeling (or seeing) tiny bugs crawling all over the skin or bodily fluids oozing from their pores. Others report feeling that their insides are rotting away or that they are empty inside.

WHAT'S NORMAL?
When Hallucinations Are Not Symptoms

Have you ever been so tired while driving at night that you thought the bright lights of an oncoming car had become a huge orange, rolling down the road? Or have you ever ingested a drug that caused you to "hear" colors or made you think that you could see inside people's heads? Or maybe in your place of worship you felt that God was speaking through you in a language that others couldn't understand? These perceptual experiences, and others like them, are not particularly rare; nor are they due to schizophrenia. But are they normal? Should having such sensory experiences be considered a warning that you are prone to schizophrenia?

An answer comes from studies by Loren and Jean Chapman, husband and wife researchers at the University of Wisconsin. As a way of investigating the measurement of early signs that might develop into schizophrenia or other psychotic states, the Chapmans created a self-report questionnaire of *perceptual aberration* as well as interview measures of unusual perceptual experiences and beliefs. The interview procedures obtained information on six forms of psychotic-like experiences: transmitting one's own thoughts, being controlled or influenced by outside forces, auditory hallucinations, removal of one's thoughts from one's head (thought withdrawal), other kinds of unusual beliefs, and unusual visual experiences.

In one study, the Chapmans and their colleague Bill Edell administered the interview to two groups: undergraduates who had scored high on the Perceptual Aberration Scale or on similar measures of unusual experiences, and a comparison group of undergraduates whose scores were in the normal range (Chapman, Edell & Chapman, 1980). Although the interview revealed that a few students were outrightly psychotic or likely to become psychotic, they also revealed that many kinds of unusual experiences occur in "normal" people. For instance, 15 percent of the subjects in the comparison group reported psychotic-like experiences involving auditory hallucinations. One subject heard his own voice give a running commentary on his behaviors. Another heard two voices, both his own, conversing with each other like a "good" and "bad" conscience. Several heard their

In some churches, individuals may have religious visions, "hear" the voice of God or Jesus, or speak in their own unintelligible languages believing that the Spirit is communicating through them. In the context of such religious practices, hallucinations or other unusual behaviors are not considered abnormal.

own voices giving them advice or speaking like their consciences, and several heard God's or Satan's voice. Six percent of the comparison students also reported thought-transmission experiences. One woman, for example, believed that she could transfer her thoughts directly to other people; and two students reported that their close friends sometimes received their thoughts.

As we note in Chapter 1, many otherwise normal, rational people believe in UFOs, spirits, ghosts, and alien abduction. Consider the findings from studies of recently bereaved persons: Widows not only reported frequently thinking about the lost loved one, but about one-half also said they had a sense that he was actually there, and many reported they could see him or hear him (reviewed in Bowlby, 1980).

These widows were not schizophrenic. Their experiences, and those of others, illustrate that unusual beliefs and perceptual experiences range from normal to highly psychotic and from rare to very common. Similarly, as the Chapmans' research revealed, having minor unusual experiences does not mean that one is a "little" schizophrenic or temporarily insane. Rather, such experiences simply demonstrate that under certain conditions — fatigue, stress, starvation, drug use, and religious fervor, among other examples — normal people may have psychotic-like experiences. Brief, isolated, and minor perceptual experiences are normal, albeit unusual. By contrast, schizophrenia involves much more extensive, enduring, and impairing difficulties in distinguishing reality, as we discuss in the following sections.

Affect Disturbances Disturbances of affect are common among schizophrenic patients. Those who show no facial expression and speak in a monotone voice are said to exhibit **flat affect,** or lack of emotionality. Interestingly, the inability to experience emotions such as those associated with depression may predict the severity and course of the disorder. Schizophrenics who display depression actually have a better prognosis than those with flat affect.

Affect disturbances may also take the form of difficulty in controlling emotions or inappropriate emotions. Patients may laugh in response to a sad situation or cry in response to a funny story. They may be inexplicably irritable, sensitive, and moody. Their emotional expressions may alter rapidly for no apparent reason. In general, they lack emotional rapport in interpersonal relations.

Behavioral and Psychomotor Dysfunction Persons with schizophrenia may exhibit peculiar mannerisms, gestures, and facial grimaces. Or they may show little spontaneity of movement or responsiveness to environmental changes. One patient in a hospital ward might sit for hours staring at the wall, while another might repeat a complex series of hand signals.

Impaired Interpersonal Relationships Schizophrenics are frequently unable to relate appropriately to others. Interpersonal impairment often takes the form of social withdrawal, in which the schizophrenic person retreats into a private world. Alternatively, schizophrenics may be socially unaware, or inappropriate — intruding on strangers, making unreasonable demands on others, and failing to accurately interpret other people's feelings and rights. Recall the homeless woman described at the beginning of the chapter.

Catatonic schizophrenia is marked by psychomotor disturbances. Often a person assumes a peculiar posture for long periods at a time.

> The homeless woman in your neighborhood — you think her name is Doris — stops strangers on the street and asks for cigarettes. She hangs around the bus stop and sits much too close to others waiting there, oblivious to their reactions. She shuffles down the street with her shopping cart and periodically shouts curses to no one in particular. Sometimes she appears to be having an argument with an unseen other; at other times she looks directly at passers-by and yells at them, much to their surprise and discomfort. Officials have tried to place her with relatives, but her only sister wants nothing to do with her since she's so weird to deal with — and Doris resists being confined in board and care facilities among other people.

Interpersonal impairment may also take the form of decreasing interest in relations that were once part of a person's life. The individual fails to contact friends, withdraws from participation in social activities, and expects that social events will prove conflictual and painful. The social events themselves become aversive, and the patient shows little interest or enjoyment in social relations generally.

Lack of Pleasure and Motivation   Lack of enjoyment of social relations may be accompanied by lack of pleasure in any activity, a condition often termed **anhedonia**. Anhedonia is also a symptom of other major disorders such as depression. In addition to loss of pleasure, schizophrenia commonly brings a lack of motivation, interest, or energy to the pursuit of meaningful tasks. Difficulties in self-initiated activity may greatly impair the person's ability to function at work or even in social or independent ventures.

Diagnosing Schizophrenia

To warrant a diagnosis of schizophrenia, a person must show at least two of the following behaviors or experiences for at least one month: delusions, hallucinations, disorganized speech, grossly disorganized or catatonic behavior, and negative symptoms such as flat affect and lack of motivation. Only one of these symptoms is required if bizarre delusions are present or if auditory hallucinations consist of a running commentary on the person's behavior or two voices conversing with each other. Finally, to be diagnosed with schizophrenia, the person must display major impairment in functioning.

Diagnostic Subtypes of Schizophrenia   Kraepelin originally proposed three subtypes of schizophrenia — *paranoid, catatonic,* and *hebephrenic (disorganized)* — and these subtypes have passed the test of time. Bleuler (1923) added the *undifferentiated* subtype. A fifth subtype, *residual,* is also recognized in DSM-IV. Figure 9.1 presents all five subtypes of schizophrenia and summarizes their features. These diagnostic subgroups are descriptive; they do not imply different origins and causal factors. In fact, a person's subtype diagnosis may change over time. Diagnoses of paranoid schizophrenia or disorganized schizophrenia tend to be fairly stable. Undifferentiated and residual subtypes, however, are diagnosed more commonly as a patient's schizophrenia progresses over time (McGlashan & Fenton, 1991).

Catatonic schizophrenia is marked by psychomotor disturbances ranging from rigid, stuporous inactivity to excited, excessive activity. Examples may include immobility along with *waxy flexibility,* in which, like a warm candle, the body posture can be molded; excessive motor activity that is apparently purposeless; and peculiar voluntary movements such as *posturing,* in which the catatonic person assumes a certain bizarre body posture, displays odd mannerisms or grimacing, or repeats what is said. Another motoric disturbance is extreme negativism — resistance to all instructions, maintenance of a rigid posture despite others' attempts to move the person, or refusal to speak. During periods of stuporous catatonia, patients may require assistance with feeding and self-care. Catatonics may even be unresponsive to threats of physical harm. The use of medications to

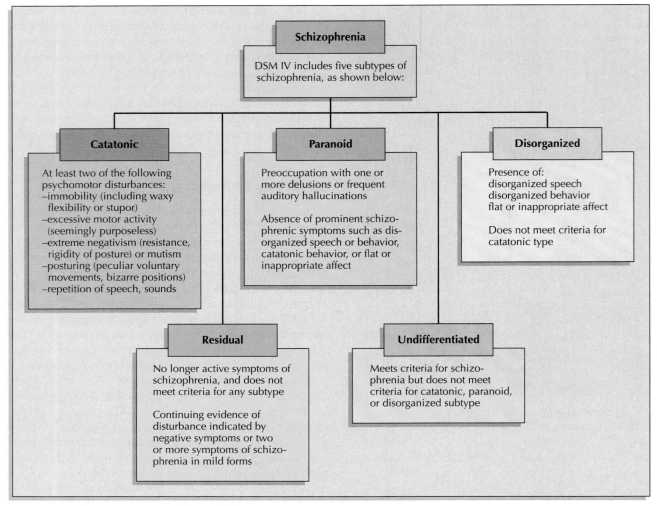

Figure 9.1   Subtypes of Schizophrenia
Five subtypes of schizophrenia are recognized in DSM-IV: catatonic, paranoid, disorganized, undifferentiated, and residual. These subgroups are descriptive in nature and do not imply different origins and causal factors.

control the most extreme symptoms has resulted in less frequent occurrence of catatonic schizophrenia. Consider the following example.

Todd is only sixteen, but his family had been noticing odd behaviors for some time. After starting tai chi lessons some months ago, he would assume karate-like positions for lengthy periods, seemingly oblivious to anything going on around him. When taken to a hospital, he would assume such postures; the psychiatrist could move his limbs, and Todd would remain "frozen" in that position for minutes at a time. He spoke rarely, and even when he answered his doctor's questions, little information was conveyed:

DOCTOR: Do you hear voices?

TODD: Do I hear voices? I hear voices. People talk. Do I hear voices? No … people talk. I hear voices. I hear voices when people talk.

DOCTOR: Are you sick?

TODD: Am I sick? No I'm not sick … these fidgeting habits, these fidgeting habits. I have habits. I have fidgeting habits. (Adapted from Spitzer, Skodol, Gibbon & Williams, 1983, p. 140).

The hallmark of **paranoid schizophrenia** is a preoccupation with delusions or hallucinations that have an organized theme. The delusional thinking may revolve around a plot that is believed to be of great importance such as invasion by aliens, takeover by a political underground, or a conspiracy of people "out to get me." Unlike other forms of schizophrenia, this type does not include disorganized behavior or thought, bizarre mannerisms, or inappropriate affect. Individuals with paranoid schizophrenia often seem relatively coherent and intact, except for their belief system. Research has generally found that compared with patients with other forms such as disorganized schizophrenia, those with paranoid schizophrenia have a later age of onset, better cognitive and social functioning, and more favorable outcome (McGlashan & Fenton, 1991).

The symptoms are nevertheless severe. Paranoid schizophrenics trust no one and are constantly suspicious of others. Consider the case of Bob, a very suspicious man who believed that the CIA was out to get him (McNeill, 1967). Notice how he incorporates peoples' attempts to reason with him into his paranoid thinking:

> *"Suppose for just a minute that I am right about what is going on," he suggested one day. "You know how the CIA operates. They gather a tiny bit here and a tiny bit there — most of it from easily available public sources — and they put it together like a giant anagram till, suddenly, it spells something meaningful." He continued, stating, "If what I know is going on is true, then it makes sense that everyone denies the truth of what I am saying. Sure, it looks like there is some other good explanation for everything that happens. That's the way they would arrange it if they are smart and they are.... I'm on to them and they don't know it yet. Everything looks innocent, sure. But that's the way they operate. You can't tell me that all the things that have happened are nothing but accidents. I know better."*

Disorganized schizophrenia is marked by severe disintegration of personality, involving incoherent and unintelligible speech, fragmentary delusions and hallucinations, extreme social impairment, disorganized behavior, and flat or inappropriate affect. Delusions and hallucinations can be slightly organized, as in the paranoid subtype, but in disorganized schizophrenia they usually lack a theme. The psychotic symptoms are fragmentary, and the behaviors are often childlike. This type of schizophrenia is said to have the earliest age of onset, an insidious development, and a chronic, deteriorating course. Here is one example (Zax & Stricker, 1963):

> *A 24-year-old man was being treated at a medical facility for a self-inflicted mutilation of his penis, which he explained as the result of trying to get his girlfriend pregnant from a long distance. He spoke about the special symbolism of words and numbers, and at times stopped to laugh inappropriately. He also stated that he was suffering because dwarfs had stuck him with green needles. Once in the mental hospital he was loud, threatening, and preoccupied with the sexual connotations of objects on the ward. He frequently indulged in open and prolonged masturbation. His speech was chatty, spontaneous, loud, and laced with delusional material.*

Undifferentiated schizophrenia includes symptoms that do not clearly fit into the other categories. Symptoms are mixed, possibly including features of several of the other subtypes. Often, patients who have been diagnosed as schizophrenic for many years are referred to as chronic and undifferentiated.

> *Joel got into trouble from an early age; he did poorly in school and ran around with other marginal and delinquent boys. After dropping out of high school, he held unskilled jobs for periods of time but never got along well with co-workers or bosses. In his late teens he was arrested for attempted rape. His attorney found out that Joel had been mad at the woman, whom he had picked up in a bar, because he thought she could control his erections with her cigarette lighter. There was no particular evidence that Joel had hallucinations, but he held several delusional beliefs; none of these, however, were systematic or paranoid.*

Residual schizophrenia describes persons who have had at least one episode of schizophrenia but currently are free of the psychotic symptoms. They commonly show flattened affect, social isolation, unusual thinking, and some eccentricities. Thus, although active psychotic symptoms are absent, there is continuing evidence of disorder. An example is Marty, described at the outset of the chapter, who spends all day watching television during periods when he is not actively delusional or experiencing hallucinations. Though free of psychotic symptoms, he is not "normal" during these periods, and he appears to show residual symptoms.

How common are the various subtypes of schizophrenia? One study of first-episode patients found 19 percent diagnosed as paranoid, 3 percent as disorganized, 1 percent as catatonic, and 54 percent as undifferentiated (Lieberman et al., 1992). Although the percentages might differ somewhat from population to population, these figures give an approximation of the subtypes' relative frequencies.

Positive- and Negative-Symptom Schizophrenia In addition to diagnostic subtypes based on descriptions of the symptoms, investigators have long searched for subcategories that provide meaningful distinctions in terms of causes and features of the disorder. The diverse patterns of schizophrenic behavior suggest that there may be different kinds of schizophrenia with different origins, courses, and recommended treatments.

At present, the most promising subtyping distinguishes between positive- and negative-symptom schizophrenia. The more bizarre symptoms, such as delusions, hallucinations, disorganized speech, and peculiar behaviors, have been called **positive symptoms** — not because they are desirable but because they are *present*. Conversely, the term **negative,** or **deficit, symptoms** refers to the deficiency or *absence* of behaviors. Negative symptoms include flat affect, lack of self-directed activity, lack of enjoyment or pleasure, apathy, absence of speech or minimal content, disturbances in social relatedness, and lack of motivation or poor persistence in work or activities. Recently, the category of positive symptoms has been further divided into *psychotic* symptoms (delusions and hallucinations) and *disorganized* symptoms (inappropriate affect, bizarre behavior, and thought disorder) (Andreasen et al., 1995). Some schizophrenic patients show primarily one type of symptoms or the other, although many present a mixture of both positive and negative symptoms.

Negative-symptom schizophrenia is generally viewed as the worse form of the disorder, associated with poorer personal, social, and academic adjustment before onset of schizophrenia; lower levels of educational, work, and social attainment; poorer cognitive performance, especially on tasks involving frontal lobe performance, and poorer outlook for improvement (Andreasen et al., 1990b; Buchanan et al., 1994; Mayerhoff et al., 1994). *Positive-symptom* schizophrenia, despite its bizarreness, is associated with better premorbid adjustment, less cognitive impairment, and better response to treatment.

In general, the type of symptoms displayed by an individual during any one episode predicts the type shown during future episodes. However, some studies suggest that, over time, individuals tend to show more of a mixture of the types of symptoms (e.g., Eaton et al., 1995). There also appears to be a relative decline in *positive*-symptom expression over time, as shown in Figure 9.2 (Arndt et al., 1995).

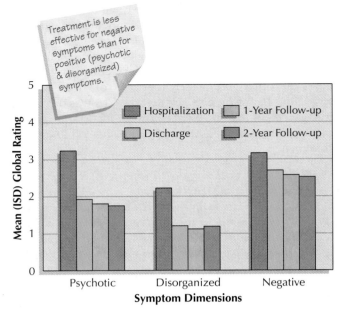

Figure 9.2   Changes in Positive-Symptom Expression Over Time

Across groups of new patients studied over a two-year period, *positive symptoms* (psychotic and disorganized) declined more sharply than did *negative symptoms,* but then remained relatively stable. Thus, treatment appears to have a more pronounced effect on the positive symptoms. In contrast to the view that schizophrenics might start off with positive symptoms and then develop negative symptoms over time, this study suggests that the negative ones are present from the beginning but remain relatively stable, whereas positive symptoms decline more markedly in response to treatment. *Source:* Adapted from Arndt et al. (1995, p. 357).

Comorbidity of Schizophrenia and Other Disorders

Schizophrenia is often complicated by the presence of additional mental health problems, some of which result from schizophrenic experiences. Depression and substance-use disorders, for instance, are especially common. In general, the ability to experience strong and appropriate emotional reactions, such as those associated with depression, may actually indicate a better prognosis for improvement than apathy and flat affect. In contrast, drug or alcohol abuse is very detrimental to the course of the disorder.

Rates of abuse of hallucinogenic and stimulant drugs are much higher among schizophrenic patients than in the general population (Mueser et al., 1990b; Turner & Tsuang, 1990). According to such studies, between 14 percent and 47 percent of treated schizophrenics are estimated to have alcohol-abuse disorders. Drug abuse may even hasten the age of onset — although drugs are unlikely to trigger a schizophrenic episode in someone not otherwise predisposed to the disorder. Also, drug abuse may precipitate relapses and subsequent hospitalizations (Turner & Tsuang, 1990). Alcohol-use disorders are associated with poor outcomes, including assaultiveness, housing instability, and psychotic symptoms (Drake et al., 1990). A further complication is that, because drug- and alcohol-addicted schizophrenics are difficult to manage or require special care, many facilities will not or cannot treat them. Drugs and alcohol may thus increase the likelihood that schizophrenic persons will be homeless and perceived as threats to their communities.

Who Is Affected with Schizophrenia?

Schizophrenia is the most common of the major mental illnesses. It occurs in every culture, in industrialized as well as nonindustrialized nations, and in every segment of the population. Indeed, as we note in Chapter 1, it has been recognized since the dawn of civilization in all parts of the world, although not all cultures view it in the same way. Despite differences in the way it is perceived and tolerated across different cultures (e.g., Kleinman,

Lionel Aldridge managed to have an All-Pro career for the Green Bay Packers, before developing schizophrenia at age 33.

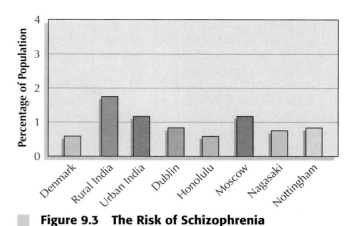

Figure 9.3   The Risk of Schizophrenia
This bar graph shows the estimated risk of schizophrenia among persons between the ages of fifteen and fifty-four in seven countries (eight sites). The study was sponsored by the World Health Organization, and collaborators used standardized diagnostic criteria. Although there are some regional variations, the rates are quite similar. *Source:* From Sartorius et al. (1986).

1988; Lin, 1991), its rates of occurrence are fairly consistent. Epidemiological surveys conducted in several cities in the United States have estimated that schizophrenia affects between 0.6 percent and 2 percent of the population of adults (Karno et al., 1987). Figure 9.3 presents data from a collaborative study sponsored by the World Health Organization, in which the risk of developing schizophrenia is compared across several countries. Despite regional variations, the rates of such risk are remarkably similar, averaging about 1 percent (Sartorius et al., 1986).

In the United States, schizophrenia appears to affect most cultural groups about equally. For example, epidemiological surveys have indicated essentially the same rates for African American and white groups, and slightly lower rates of schizophrenia among Hispanics (Karno et al., 1987). However, more African-Americans with the diagnosis of schizophrenia are found in public mental health facilities, probably reflecting differential access to public and private facilities (Snowden & Cheung, 1990).

In general, economically disadvantaged persons have more mental illness — a situation that certainly holds true for schizophrenia. Rates of schizophrenia are higher in groups with the lowest education and socioeconomic status (e.g., Robins et al., 1984). This pattern may in part reflect "downward drift"; in other words, schizophrenia itself may limit educational attainment, such that occupational and financial status suffers (e.g., Dohrenwend et al., 1992). In addition, genetic and environmental factors that contribute to schizophrenia may be more concentrated in lower socioeconomic conditions — an issue we discuss later.

What about *gender differences* in schizophrenia? Most epidemiological surveys have found that men and women are affected about equally. However, some community surveys suggest that rates may be slightly higher among women than men (Karno et al., 1987; Robins et al., 1984), whereas recent studies of first hospitalizations in North America and Europe suggest that schizophrenia may be more common, or at least more severe, among men (Iacono & Beiser, 1992).

Most of what was known about schizophrenia a decade or two ago was based mostly on studies of men, often conducted on veterans in VA hospitals. Recently, however, researchers have found important sex differences in the experience, course, and possible origins of the disorder. For example, the course of the disorder tends to be less severe among women than among men. According to one large ten-year study (Goldstein, 1988), female schizophrenics have fewer rehospitalizations and shorter hospital stays. They also exhibit better response to treatment overall (Szymanski et al., 1995). More male than female schizophrenic patients show a pattern of poor adjustment before diagnosis, as well as chronic symptoms, negative symptom patterns, and poor outcome. Men are also less likely than women to have graduated from high school, married or dated regularly, or worked steadily (reviewed in Lewine, 1991). Finally, women have a significantly later age of onset of schizophrenia than do men: For men the period of highest risk is the age range between fourteen and twenty-five years, whereas for women it is between twenty-four and thirty-five years (Lewine, 1991). Precise reasons for these gender differences are as yet unknown, but speculations point to superior social skills and support among women as well as to protective effects associated with the hormone *estrogen* (e.g., Szymanski et al., 1995).

Course of Schizophrenia

There is considerable variability in terms of how rapidly schizophrenia develops, how long an episode might last, the quality of functioning when the symptoms retreat, and the frequency of recurring symptoms or episodes. Some persons with schizophrenia have relatively good outcomes, whereas others live in and out of hospitals, unable to function independently.

Onset of Symptoms   As implied by Kraepelin's original term, *dementia praecox,* most cases of schizophrenia appear early in life — in late adolescence or early adulthood. Schizophrenia may appear to have a slow, *gradual onset* with increasing maladjustment over time before symptoms are evident. Or it may appear to have a rapid or *acute onset.*

Schizophrenia with a gradual onset is typified by poor functioning throughout childhood. Though not defined as schizophrenic symptoms, disruptive behavior (such as aggressiveness or poor classroom compliance), social withdrawal, and lack of good peer relations are common. Of course, not all preschizophrenic individuals display noticeable dysfunction; some may develop relatively normally.

Episodes and Outcomes   The course of schizophrenia varies greatly from person to person. One individual might have an acute onset followed by complete recovery, whereas another might have a gradual onset with continuing severe symptoms, no periods of normalcy, and a pattern of chronic symptoms. Manfred Bleuler (1978), son of the pioneering psychiatrist Eugen Bleuler, characterized several patterns of symptoms in his clinic sample. Common patterns included (1) acute onset with recovery and periodic episodes, varying in completeness of recovery over time; and (2) gradual onset with relatively sustained symptoms, with different levels of recovery over time. Rare patterns included (1) acute onset with continuing symptoms and no recovery, and (2) gradual onset with periodic episodes and good overall recovery. (See also Marengo, Harrow, Sands & Galloway, 1991.)

Unfortunately, for many individuals Kraepelin's original observations of schizophrenia as a lifelong disorder, with increasing deterioration and little chance of recovery, are accurate. Norman Watt and Christopher Saiz (1991) summarized the results of six international studies that followed patients an average of twenty-eight years after they were hospitalized for schizophrenia (see Figure 9.4). On average, recovery occurred in fewer than 30 percent of these cases. A more recent survey of nearly

A portion of the homeless population is comprised of individuals with schizophrenia. Perhaps both as a storage necessity and as an expression of the disorder, this person wears layer upon layer of clothing.

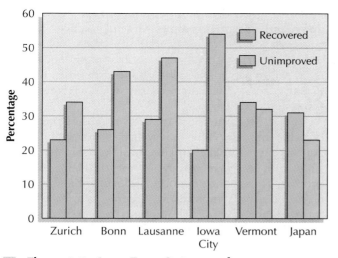

Figure 9.4 Long-Term Outcomes in Schizophrenia

Six international studies followed the status of patients with schizophrenia for periods of twenty-two to thirty-seven years. These studies showed that 30 to 50 percent of persons with schizophrenia do not get better. Alternatively, when the rates for those who recovered are added to the rates of those who improve (not shown), the figures suggested that 50 to 70 percent of schizophrenic patients at least improve over time. *Source:* From Watt & Saiz (1991).

a hundred years of studies between 1895 and 1992 concluded that only about 40 percent of patients were considered improved after follow-ups averaging about six years (Hegarty et al., 1994).

The majority of schizophrenic patients suffer relapses, often multiple ones. According to follow-up studies of persons hospitalized for the first time, about 60 percent relapse within two years after discharge (Ram et al., 1992). The same general finding has been corroborated by a study of schizophrenic patients in Maryland, Australia, Denmark, and England, the majority of whom relapsed within two to three years after discharge. This pattern is especially true for patients with a younger age of onset (Eaton et al., 1992b). About one-half of all schizophrenic patients function poorly or only moderately well over a period of years (Breier, Schreiber, Dyer & Pickar, 1991; Carone, Harrow & Westermeyer, 1991; Marengo, Harrow, Sands & Galloway, 1991).

Yet, poor functioning and deterioration are not inevitable. Long-term follow-up studies have indicated that many schizophrenic patients improve substantially; some even seem to become nonsymptomatic or mildly symptomatic in their later years. For example, Watt and Saiz (1991) found that whereas only 27 percent of the patients in their study had recovered, another 32 percent had improved. Even among chronic schizophrenic patients with a history of frequent episodes and multiple

hospitalizations, 14 percent to 20 percent were considered to have good outcomes (Breier, Schreiber, Dyer & Pickar, 1991; Carone, Harrow & Westermeyer, 1991). One of the longest follow-up studies, the Vermont Longitudinal Study, reported the best outcomes: After an average follow-up of thirty-two years, 62 percent of the patients had completely recovered or showed only mild impairment (Harding, Zubin & Strauss, 1987). However, as the patients in this study were older (mean age sixty-one years) at follow-up than those in most other studies, the unusually good outcomes might have had something to do with age. Other investigators have hypothesized that clinical improvement might correspond to a reduction in dopamine function in the brain that occurs as a normal result of aging (Breier, Schreiber, Dyer & Pickar, 1991; Harding, 1991). As we discuss, dopamine is a neurotransmitter that has been linked to schizophrenia.

With the availability of long-term follow-up studies of schizophrenia came the opportunity to characterize typical outcomes. Consider the attempt by Alan Breier and associates (Breier, Schreiber, Dyer & Pickar, 1991) to amend Kraepelin's overall dire predictions. These researchers speculated that the typical person with schizophrenia experiences a deteriorating phase lasting between five and ten years, followed by a lengthy period of stable symptoms. Specifically, a period of improvement occurs when the person reaches the late fifties or early sixties. Although this hypothesized pattern needs to be studied further, it certainly has implications for treatment — and for understanding the underlying causes of the disorder.

Recall the case of Sally, the older woman returning to college, who displayed delusions of reference that she was the target of lectures in abnormal psychology — and that everyone in the course was "in on it." After a reasonably normal development, she was schizophrenic since her late twenties, with periods of acute delusions and disorganization that seemed to clear up after a few months. She functioned fairly well between episodes, marrying, working part-time, and raising a couple of children. Her family, seeing early warning signs of impending episodes, helped take over child care when she needed treatment. As time passed, Sally needed fewer hospitalizations, and most of her episodes could be managed by medications and family support. She returned to college in an effort to finish a degree started long ago, and to stay involved in the world and with people. Unfortunately, the stresses of school exacerbated her psychotic symptoms, but she eventually reduced her course load and managed to cope without too much turmoil. As she gets older, her periods of symptoms are a bit shorter and less dramatic.

Predictors of the Course of Schizophrenia Three factors emerge from research as important predictors of the course of schizophrenia: quality of previous adjustment, supportive social relationships, and type of symptoms.

One of the best predictors of the course of schizophrenia and its outcome is **premorbid adjustment,** or the person's level of functioning before the apparent onset of the disorder. A schizophrenic patient with good premorbid adjustment has an early developmental history unmarked by defects, good overall physical health, established friendships and romantic relationships, and a record of adequate performance in school and at work. Typically, the beginning of the schizophrenic episode is acute, involving an identifiable precipitating stressful life event. Hallucinatory and delusional experiences (positive symptoms) are usually present. And a positive response to treatment is considered to be likely. Premorbid social competence has also been associated with better work adjustment and fewer psychiatric symptoms at a follow-up assessment two years after the initial hospitalization (Westermeyer & Harrow, 1986; see also Watt & Saiz, 1991).

In contrast, a schizophrenic patient with poor premorbid adjustment functions poorly, lacks basic problem-solving abilities, and displays inadequacies in work, social, and personal responsibilities. The person has often done poorly in school and has failed to achieve academic, work, and social skills. Social isolation and a lack of emotional responsiveness are evident before the actual episode. In cases of poor premorbid adjustment schizophrenia, there is typically no identifiable precipitating event or experience. Rather, the onset of the symptoms is insidious, gradually worsening until the psychotic symptoms become readily apparent.

The different outcomes for male and female schizophrenic patients probably relate to gender differences in prior social adjustment. Indeed, there is direct evidence of superior social competence among female schizophrenics. In one study, researchers observed men and women in-patients performing certain social tasks, which they systematically measured and rated in terms of skill of performance. Their results indicated that the female schizophrenics did better than the males overall, and the effects remained stable at a one-year follow-up (Mueser, Bellack, Morrison & Wade, 1990a). Perhaps it is a result of their greater social competence that women have a significantly later age of onset of schizophrenia than men.

In addition to social competence and prior adjustment, the experience of positive, supportive relationships plays an important role in the course of the disorder — an issue we discuss more fully in the section on family-related factors in schizophrenia. Another, related predictor of outcome is — not surprisingly — the negative-positive symptom distinction. People with predominantly negative symptoms tend to have chronic courses and inadequate overall adjustment, as well as poor premorbid social and occupational functioning (e.g., Andreasen et al., 1990b; Breier, Schreiber, Dyer & Pickar, 1991; Buchanan, Kirkpatrick, Henrichs & Carpenter, 1990).

What conclusions can we draw regarding predictors of schizophrenia? One possibility is that poor social adjustment before the apparent onset of schizophrenia is simply an early manifestation of the schizophrenia process. Thus, poor premorbid adjustment and its associated negative symptoms may represent a more severe form of the disorder, leading to a worse outcome. Another possibility is that people with poor premorbid adjustment and deficit symptoms do worse simply because they lack coping skills. Having failed to acquire these skills in childhood and adolescence, they lack stable work, family, and social conditions to return to after hospitalization. And as a result, they may break down again.

Why are the symptoms and outcomes of schizophrenia different in different people? This question of differences is a variation on the more general theme to which we turn now: What causes schizophrenia?

CAUSES OF SCHIZOPHRENIA

Research on the causes of schizophrenia has been a high priority for investigators for several decades. Even in ancient cultures, the bizarreness of schizophrenic behavior invited biological explanations — and, to a lesser extent, the suggestion that it is caused by massive psychological trauma. In the sections that follow, we attempt to capture a sense of the extraordinary attention paid to this disorder by considering both some historical issues and current research.

Biological Contributors to Schizophrenia

The extreme departures from reality and the strange thoughts and behaviors of some schizophrenic patients easily lead to the conclusion that something must be biologically wrong, especially in the brain. Indeed, some persons with known brain injuries or diseases display behaviors that resemble the symptoms of schizophrenia, such as apathy and withdrawal or hallucinations or delusions. It's therefore not surprising that much of the research on causes of schizophrenia has been conducted from a biological perspective. In earlier eras, investigators searched for unusual chemicals or malformations of the brain. As tools for discovery have become more sophisticated, however, theories have become more complex. Today the biological perspective takes the form of a search for defective genes or for abnormalities in brain structures, functions, or neurochemistry.

The Role of Genetics in Schizophrenia Schizophrenia runs in families, and probably more genetic research has been conducted on this psychiatric disorder than on any other. The general conclusion is that it is probably a genetically transmitted disease. However, there are still many unanswered questions about the mechanisms involved and the role of nongenetic factors.

As we describe in Chapter 5, the most direct way of seeking a genetic explanation for a disease uses linkage methods to explore specific patterns and locations of genes. One study of Icelandic and English families with high rates of schizophrenia seemed to pinpoint a schizophrenia gene on chromosome 5 (e.g., Sherrington, Brynjolfsson, Petursson & Potter, 1988). Several subsequent studies, however, have failed to replicate this finding in different family trees (e.g., Crowe et al., 1991). In a related area, a recent linkage study searched for a specific defect in the gene responsible for one of the *dopamine receptors,* hypothesized to account for some forms of schizophrenia, but found no evidence for its occurrence in families with schizophrenic members (Kalsi et al., 1996). Many investigators currently agree that a single dominant gene is unlikely to account for schizophrenia. Thus, linkage analyses searching for *the* schizophrenia gene may not be productive.

Nevertheless, other methods addressing the question of inherited patterns of schizophrenia have produced important evidence of some genetic influence. *Family* and *twin studies* are two such methods. For

example, a study of families in Ireland found that the risk of schizophrenia among close relatives of schizophrenic patients was thirteen times higher than that among relatives of nonschizophrenic controls (Kendler et al., 1993). Similarly, studies of children of schizophrenic parents indicate that they have a much higher risk for developing schizophrenia than do children of normal parents, as shown in Sarnoff Mednick's 25-year follow-up (Parnas et al., 1993) and Erlenmeyer-Kimling's 23-year follow-up (Erlenmeyer-Kimling et al., 1995). Figure 9.5 summarizes the results of various studies indicating that the closer the genetic relationship between two people, the higher the risk that if one person has schizophrenia the other will have it also.

Studying rates of **concordance** (similarity) for schizophrenia in *twin pairs* provides a powerful technique for examining the heritability of schizophrenia. Note in Figure 9.5 that, across various studies, the average rate of concordance between identical (monozygotic) twins is 48 percent, compared with 17 percent for fraternal (dizygotic) twins.

Because we expect twins to be exactly alike on all traits that are inherited, discordance for schizophrenia could mean either that genes are not involved or that genetic transmission has occurred but something other than genes is also involved — namely, an environmental or personal stressor that has activated the genes' effects. If the latter is true, some people (such as a discordant identical twin) may have inherited a tendency toward schizophrenia but do not display schizophrenia. In other words, the genotype is not expressed.

Until recently, there was little evidence that the unexpressed genotype actually existed. Then, in a study

Figure 9.5   Genetic Contribution to Schizophrenia

Various studies have shown that the closer the genetic relationship between two people, the higher the risk that if one person has schizophrenia the other will also. This pattern supports the idea of genetic contribution to the disorder. *Source:* Adapted from Gottesman (1991, p. 96).

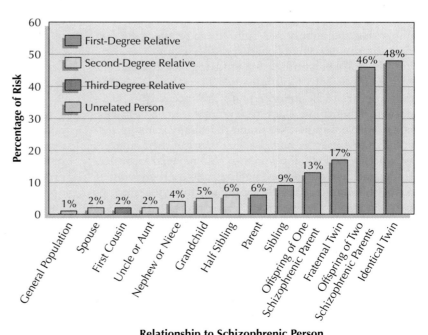

that spanned two continents, Irving Gottesman and Aksel Bertelsen (1989) used extensive Danish records to locate both identical and fraternal twin pairs in which at least one twin was hospitalized at some point for schizophrenia. They also located the children of these twins. The rates of schizophrenia in these offspring were consistent with the idea that an identical twin might carry the genes for schizophrenia — and transmit them to his children — even if he does not actually "express" the genes. Gottesman and Bertelsen speculated that some physical or psychological event must occur to release the ill effects of the genes for schizophrenia.

Adoption studies address the criticism that similarity between family members can be explained by psychological rather than genetic factors. In these studies, individuals born to schizophrenic parents but raised by nonschizophrenic individuals are compared with suitable controls. In general, the few such studies show that children of schizophrenic parents adopted into normal families have significantly higher rates of schizophrenia than do adopted children of normal parents (e.g., Kety et al., 1994).

Although these results have supported the existence of genetic contributions to schizophrenia, they do not rule out a role for psychological factors. A recent study conducted in Finland found that children of schizophrenic mothers who were adopted into families of nonschizophrenic parents were significantly more likely to become schizophrenic than were adopted children of normal mothers. Most of the seriously disturbed children were raised in adoptive families that had disturbed family relationships, however, while none of the children raised in normal, well-functioning families developed disturbances despite having a biological mother with schizophrenia (Tienari et al., 1987). These findings imply that the quality of family life may affect the outcome of an underlying genetic predisposition.

Yet another strategy for studying possible genetic contributions is to look for a genetic marker — a trait that appears to be inherited and that occurs in schizophrenic patients but is not itself related to schizophrenia. For example, suppose we found that many schizophrenics have an extra toe, and also that many of their relatives — who are not schizophrenic — also have an extra toe. Under such circumstances, having an extra toe would be a possible marker for schizophrenia, implying that the two conditions are genetically related. In other words, a person with an extra toe would appear to be genetically vulnerable for schizophrenia even if the disorder is not expressed in that person. Researchers could then look for people with an extra toe in an effort to identify possible gene carriers as well as to examine the mechanisms responsible for the emergence of schizophrenia.

Research has thus far uncovered two relatively well-established genetic markers that assist investigators searching for clues about schizophrenia. One of these involves eye movement dysfunction (EMD). Over the years, Philip Holzman and his colleagues have presented strong evidence for an EMD marker (Holzman, 1975; Holzman et al., 1988). They tested individuals on a task in which subjects visually follow a moving spot of light while the eye movements are recorded electronically. The pattern of eye movements in normal individuals differs from that often seen in schizophrenic patients. In fact, EMD occurs in about 4 to 5 percent of the normal population but much more commonly among schizophrenics and their relatives. Some studies indicate that EMD correlates with the presence of symptoms related to schizophrenia (schizoptypal symptoms) in relatives of patients (reviewed in Clementz & Sweeney, 1990). Other studies suggest that EMD may be related to cognitive functioning, specifically implicating deficits in the performance of tasks controlled by the frontal lobes of the brain (e.g., Katsanis & Iacono, 1991).

A second possible genetic marker concerns neurocognitive deficits, relatively mild or subtle decrements in the performance of various tasks. Faraone and associates (1995), for example, tested nonpsychotic relatives of schizophrenics and found that many showed mild forms of the same deficits exhibited by schizophrenic patients — specifically, difficulties in abstraction, verbal memory, and attention (see also Cannon et al., 1994; Park, Holzman & Goldman-Rakic, 1995). Studies of the children of schizophrenic parents have similarly demonstrated that, long before any psychotic symptoms have emerged, many such children display difficulties in various neurocognitive tests, including those measuring sustained attention (e.g., Nuechterlein & Dawson, 1984; Erlenmeyer-Kimling, Golden & Cornblatt, 1989). Thus, in some individuals there appears to be genetic transmission of a neurocognitive defect that, for as yet unknown reasons, develops into or is associated with schizophrenia.

In short, there is good evidence, from multiple sources, that schizophrenia is genetically transmitted. However, the very same evidence that supports heritability indicates that no single schizophrenia gene exists. Indeed, nongenetic factors must also be involved if we are to explain why some people who apparently have a genetic predisposition for schizophrenia do not develop the disorder. Another possibility is that different forms of schizophrenia are related to variations in the extent and nature of genetic contribution. We do not yet know precisely what is inherited, but one area of intense speculation concerns brain structure and function. To this topic we now turn.

Abnormalities of the Brain in Schizophrenia For decades, the search for abnormalities in the brains of schizophrenics relied on autopsy studies. Autopsies indicated that schizophrenics' brains were smaller in size, weight, and volume than normal persons' brains.

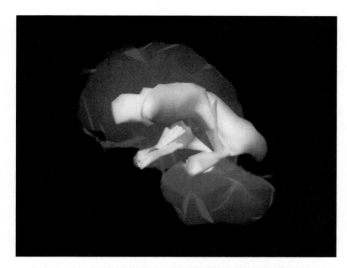

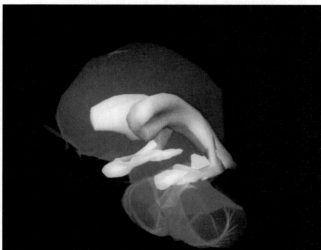

Figure 9.6   Evidence of Schizophrenia from Neuroimaging

Neuroimaging techniques such as magnetic resonance imaging (MRI) permit computer-constructed three-dimensional pictures of the brain. The upper panel shows a schizophrenic patient's brain, indicating a shrunken hippocampus (yellow) and enlarged ventricles (gray areas, fluid-filled space). Compare this to the brain of a normal person shown in the lower panel. Enlarged ventricles may imply that there is less tissue in the surrounding areas, perhaps due to injury, genetic defect, or faulty development in infancy or childhood when the brain is still forming. *Source:* Andreasen et al. (1992).

However, such studies were often crude in their measures, and they generally failed to control for age, medications, physical health, or other conditions that could affect the brain. Methods have since improved. Especially with the development of brain imaging techniques that permit views of the living brain and its functions well beyond the capability of older x-ray techniques, researchers can now more accurately explore the age-old

hypothesis that something is wrong with the brains of schizophrenics.

Evidence from neuroimaging studies (as we describe in Chapter 4) suggests the existence of two anatomical differences between the brains of schizophrenic patients and those of normal people. One difference concerns enlargement of the fluid-filled spaces in the brain, called *ventricles* — especially the lateral, or third, ventricle (e.g., Flaum et al., 1995). Figure 9.6 shows an MRI view of the ventricles of a schizophrenic patient compared to those of a normal person. Similar differences have even been found between unmedicated schizophrenic patients and normals, and between these two groups when age is controlled; hence, the differences are not by-products of treatment or age. Researchers have also wondered whether ventricular enlargements are the result of progressive deterioration in schizophrenia. Evidently they are not. Nancy Andreasen and her colleagues (1990c) found ventricular enlargement even in first-episode patients, and Sarnoff Mednick's high-risk study found ventricular enlargement in the offspring of schizophrenic mothers (Cannon et al., 1994). These results suggest that the abnormalities occurred before or concurrent with the onset of schizophrenia, rather than as a result of deterioration over the course of the disorder.

Note, however, that only *some* schizophrenic patients show enlarged ventricles (e.g., Andreasen et al., 1990c; Gur et al., 1991). Specifically, the enlargements are most commonly found in patients with cognitive impairments, severe symptoms, poor premorbid adjustment, and poor response to medications (e.g., Andreasen et al., 1990c; Raz & Raz, 1990). Some studies have also found an association between negative symptoms and ventricular enlargement (e.g., Andreasen et al., 1990a). The enlargements were once believed to occur mainly in male schizophrenics, but recent studies indicate that they are equally likely in males and females (e.g., Flaum et al., 1995).

What, then, do such structural abnormalities mean? First, we must emphasize that enlarged ventricles appear to be nonspecific abnormalities; that is, they may also occur in the brains of persons with other disorders, such as bipolar disorder and Parkinson's disease. Second, their presence suggests that something in the brain is disordered, but they do not indicate the source of the disorder. Third, according to the most common hypotheses, ventricular enlargements reflect either brain injury or damage (for example, birth injury, head injury, viral infection, genetic abnormality, or nutritional deficiency), or failure of the brain to mature and develop normally. We return later to a discussion of the causes of brain abnormality and their potential relationship to schizophrenia.

Another major factor revealed by neuroimaging techniques involves both structural and functional abnormalities of the cortical and subcortical areas of the brain. Figure 9.7 identifies several areas of the brain that might be implicated in schizophrenia. In particular, converging evidence points to the reduced size of areas in the prefrontal cortex, areas in the temporal lobe, and, possibly, subcortical regions in the limbic system such as the anterior hippocampus-amygdala (Breier et al., 1992; Flaum et al., 1995; Nopoulos et al., 1995).

Evidence of reduced prefrontal cortical matter is also consistent with findings that many schizophrenic people show **hypofrontality** — or reduced blood flow in the frontal regions, as measured by PET scans (see Figure 9.8). Reduced blood flow in an area of the brain suggests impaired or reduced functioning of that area. Hypofrontality has been observed even when possible confounding factors are controlled, as in patient medication histories; it has also been found in first-episode patients (Andreasen et al., 1992; Berman, Torrey, Daniel & Weinberger, 1992; Buchsbaum et al., 1992). In addition, hypofrontality is more common in patients with negative symptoms of schizophrenia (Andreasen et al., 1992; Wolkin et al., 1992).

One especially intriguing study of hypofrontality employed pairs of monozygotic twins. Karen Berman and her colleagues (1992) examined regional cerebral blood flow during performance of a cognitive task that involved functions of the frontal cortex, and the identical twins they tested were either concordant or discordant for schizophrenia. The investigators found that all of the schizophrenic twins showed hypofrontality of

functioning; indeed, among discordant twins, the schizophrenic twin demonstrated the hypofrontal pattern but the nonschizophrenic co-twin did not. Furthermore, the nonschizophrenic co-twins did not differ from the normal pairs of monozygotic twins. The investigators emphasized two conclusions: (1) Hypofrontality is associated specifically with schizophrenia; and (2) because it is discordant in identical twins, it must be due to nongenetic factors — a point to which we return shortly.

The cortical and subcortical areas of the brain are interconnected and therefore normally influence each other. The finding that these areas may be defective in some schizophrenic patients is important for two reasons. First, these areas of the brain are known to be associated with both emotional expression, on the one hand, and thinking and information processing, on the other — areas of major symptoms in schizophrenia. Second, the frontal area in particular is suspected to be a site of defective cognitive functioning — a subject that we next explore.

Abnormalities of Neurocognitive Functioning Studies of cognitive performance in schizophrenia — reflecting underlying brain functioning — have a long history in psychology. As we note in Chapter 4, modern neuropsychological testing involves administering performance tests that involve different parts of the brain. The profile of a person's scores, which shows their relative deficits and difficulties, may be used to infer

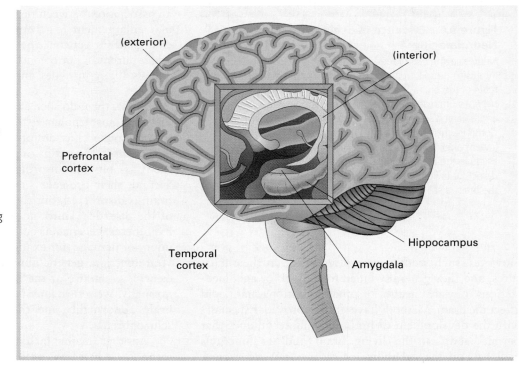

Figure 9.7 Areas of the Brain Suspected to Be Abnormal in Schizophrenia

Several areas of the brain might be implicated in schizophrenia. The reduced size of areas in the prefrontal cortex, areas in the temporal lobe, and subcortical regions in the limbic system, such as the anterior hippocampus-amygdala, are the most likely possibilities, reflecting atrophy, neurodevelopmental abnormality, or other damage that impairs their normal functioning.

(exterior)

(interior)

Prefrontal cortex

Temporal cortex

Hippocampus

Amygdala

Figure 9.8 PET Scans Showing Hypofrontality
These PET scans measure regional cerebral blood flow of patients and controls while they are performing cognitive tasks (2nd & 3rd panels) that involve activity in the frontal lobes. The patients and controls are identical twins who are discordant for schizophrenia. Notice that the schizophrenic twin's brain shows hypofrontality, or reduced activity in the frontal region. The results suggested that schizophrenia is associated with nongenetic factors; otherwise, the twins' brains would show identical patterns of blood flow. *Source:* From Berman, Torrey, Daniel & Weinberger (1992).

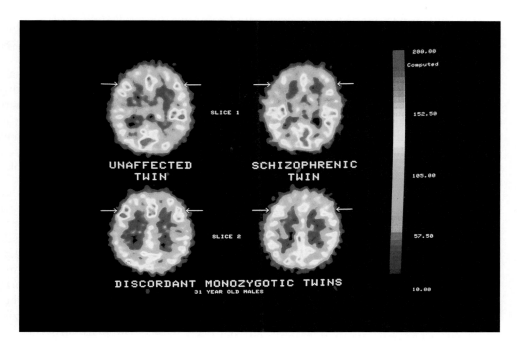

the location of possible brain lesions or structural impairments. Other kinds of experimental tasks have also been developed to assess specific functions, such as the ability to sustain focused attention or to hold information in short-term memory. Researchers compare the performance of schizophrenic and normal persons on these neuropsychological and cognitive tasks to determine whether deficits are associated with schizophrenia.

A vast amount of research has demonstrated deficits in neurocognitive test performance among most schizophrenics — including those who have never taken medication. Poor performances occur across most tests, indicating generalized deficits for most cognitive functions. But the greatest impairments appear in tasks related to memory and learning, which are functions that rely on the temporal-limbic (hippocampal) region of the brain (Saykin et al., 1991). Considerable evidence from tasks indicating attention deficits further suggests that many schizophrenic patients have dysfunction in frontal areas of the brain (e.g., Levin, Yurgelun-Todd & Craft, 1989).

As noted earlier, researchers also use neuropsychological and cognitive tasks to determine whether subtle cognitive deficits occur even in people who are not schizophrenic but are potentially vulnerable to the disorder, such as relatives of schizophrenics. In addition, they use these tasks to learn whether such deficits might predict further episodes in schizophrenic patients who are in remission from a previous schizophrenic episode.

Numerous studies have demonstrated that attention and information-processing deficits do occur in schizophrenics who are not in the acute phase of disorder (e.g., Nuechterlein et al., 1992), and even in nonschizophrenic relatives of schizophrenics or nonschizophrenics who have schizotypal traits — that is, in people who are not schizophrenic but who acknowledge unusual perceptual experiences and mild disturbances of thinking and language (e.g., Lenzenweger, Cornblatt & Putnick, 1991). Finally, as also noted earlier, neurocognitive dysfunctions have been observed in children at risk for schizophrenia due to parental disorder (e.g., Erlenmeyer-Kimling, Golden & Cornblatt, 1989).

What possible conclusions can be drawn from all this evidence of cognitive deficits in high-risk children? One speculation is that limitations in the ability to attend to and process complex information may impair the developing child's ability to process social and emotional information as well (Asarnow, Hornstein & Russell, 1991). In turn, the interaction among cognitive and social difficulties might lead to further stressful social maladjustment — creating pressures and circumstances that the high-risk child might be ill-equipped to cope with, and possibly contributing to schizophrenic symptoms. Another speculation, of course, is that the cognitive deficits are early warning signs of schizophrenia unfolding over time.

Neurodevelopmental Abnormalities In short, considerable evidence from high-risk studies has suggested that there are very early indicators of brain disorder, long before actual symptoms occur. Indeed, studies have found mild neurological impairments even in the *infants* born to schizophrenic patients (Fish et al., 1992; Marcus, Hans, Auerbach & Auerbach, 1993), as well as impaired verbal and linguistic skills in the adolescent offspring of schizophrenic parents (Harvey, 1991). This information is adding to a diverse array of findings from other studies to form the hypothesis of **neurodevelopmental abnormalities** as causes of schizophrenia. Let's take a look at the somewhat odd assortment of clues.

FOCUS ON RESEARCH

Flu, Famine, and Films: How Are Scientists Trying to Crack the Mystery of Schizophrenia?

Investigators have been trying to grapple with the observation that identical twins may be *discordant* for schizophrenia: If they are genetically identical, how can they be so different? Recent studies of discordant twins have found that their brains do indeed show differences — for example, in terms of frontal cortex activity or ventricular size (Berman et al., 1992; Suddath et al., 1990). If such differences are not due to genetic factors, then something must have happened prenatally, or in childhood, to affect brain development. This conclusion is supported by the Danish High-Risk Study, which found that, among children of schizophrenic mothers, those who showed CT scan brain abnormalities were significantly more likely to have experienced birth complications (Cannon et al., 1993). The implication is that a genetic predisposition may require the additional factor of pre- or postnatal injury to the developing brain or exposure to environmental toxins during gestation or in childhood, when the normal brain is growing and differentiating its functions. Consider the following interesting observations, which have added weight to the argument in support of neurodevelopmental origins for some forms of schizophrenia.

1. A disproportionate number of schizophrenic patients are born in winter months (Bradbury & Miller, 1985), lending support to speculations about exposure to some winter-related environmental stressor during gestation or shortly after birth. Investigations of elevated rates of schizophrenia in persons whose mothers were exposed to influenza virus while pregnant during known epidemics have provided indirect support for such speculations (e.g., Mednick, Machon, Huttunen & Bonett, 1988). Among the numerous studies of flu epi-

demics conducted thus far, many but not all support the idea that viral exposure during pregnancy, especially during the second trimester, may increase the risk of schizophrenia (e.g., Wright, Takei, Rifkin & Murray, 1995). However, there has been no evidence that schizophrenia is directly *caused* by a virus (e.g., Taller et al., 1996). Rather, it is speculated that viral exposure impairs normal development — especially among individuals who are genetically vulnerable.

2. If disruptive events impair brain development and thus contribute to risk for schizophrenia, then it may also be the case that nutritional deficiency during gestation increases the risk of schizophrenia. An example is provided by the Dutch Hunger Winter of 1944–1945, a famine that resulted when the Nazis cut off food supplies to many towns and cities in the Netherlands after the Dutch attempted to support the Allies. By analyzing community records of food supplies, Susser and associates (1996) were able to determine which individuals were conceived during the worst periods of this famine. They concluded that the rate of schizophrenia among those exposed to famine during gestation was twice the rate among those of similar birth years who were not exposed.

3. In line with the high-risk research that has begun to reveal subtle cognitive and neurological deficits in young children or infants of schizophrenic parents (e.g., Fish et al., 1992), Elaine Walker wondered if home movies of children who years later were diagnosed as schizophrenic held any clues. She found not only that judges could distinguish in the films between future schizophrenics and their normal siblings (Walker & Lewine, 1990) but also that experts could observe neuromotor abnormalities and less developed motor skills in the young preschizophrenic children compared to comparison groups (Walker, Savoie & Davis, 1994). Figure 9.9 indicates the presence of very early abnormalities among preschizophrenics that could suggest problems in brain development. These abnormalities were most common in a subgroup consisting of fewer than half of the future schizophrenic individuals. They were accompanied by numerous behavioral difficulties that also were present from an early age and that increased in severity as the children got older (Neumann, Grimes, Walker & Baum, 1995).

4. Evidence of yet another potential environmental stressor affecting brain development has recently emerged from the very personal experiences of one enterprising psychology graduate student. Meggin Hollister has a schizophrenic sister, whereas she and her brother are normal. Meggin and her brother are

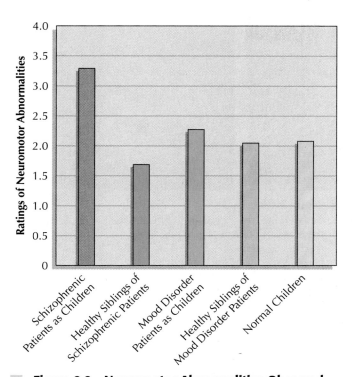

Figure 9.9   Neuromotor Abnormalities Observed in Home Movies Before Onset of Schizophrenia

It is extremely difficult and expensive to conduct longitudinal studies from birth to learn about the precursors of schizophrenia in adult life. Instead, Elaine Walker and her colleagues identified adult schizophrenic patients — and then went back to family home movies taken during infancy and childhood. Using the ratings of expert judges who knew nothing of the children's eventual diagnoses but who could detect the presence of neuromotor difficulties (such as peculiar posture or movements) in the movies, the researchers found that the preschizophrenic children showed significantly more abnormalities than all the comparison groups. Overall, these results are consistent with the neurodevelopmental hypothesis that some forms of schizophrenia arise from defective brain development that reveals itself in subtle ways early in life. *Source:* Walker, Savoie & Davis (1994).

ent projects. Their results indicated that the rate of schizophrenia was significantly higher among those with mother-infant Rh incompatibility. This study raises many intriguing questions for further research; certainly there is much more to be learned about possible mechanisms by which immunological reactions of the mother may impair brain development. One fascinating implication is that since the Rh factor is inherited, this characteristic, rather than a gene for schizophrenia, may contribute to genetic risk for the disorder.

Although the neurodevelopmental hypothesis requires further refinement, it has already stimulated a great deal of research. As the above examples demonstrate, the testing of this hypothesis provides a glimpse of the detective work in science that moves the field forward. The neurodevelopmental hypothesis also opens the door to the possibility that some cases of schizophrenia may actually be preventable at some future point.

In sum, advances in research from modern neuroimaging techniques and sophisticated neuropsychological testing procedures have converged to support the idea that at least some forms of schizophrenia — especially those marked by early onset and negative symptoms — involve damage to areas of the brain associated with emotional and cognitive functioning. But what mechanisms account for the forms of schizophrenia characterized by positive symptoms? One approach to this question, which we now consider, has focused primarily on brain neurochemicals.

also Rh-negative, like their mother, whereas the schizophrenic sister is Rh-positive and also experienced birth complications. It is well known that Rh incompatibility between mother and fetus is associated with adverse neurological complications in the fetus (due to maternal antibodies), and that such risk increases from one pregnancy to the next. Hollister and her colleagues Laing and Mednick (1996) wondered whether Rh incompatibility could be a cause of abnormal neurological developments leading to schizophrenia. They tested their hypothesis on a Danish sample of individuals born between 1959 and 1961 for whom data on pregnancy and blood types had originally been collected for differ-

Biochemical Abnormalities in Schizophrenia The search for chemical processes that might cause mental illness is not new. Over the years, there have been innumerable comparisons between the body fluids of schizophrenic patients and those of normals. But older studies were plagued by poor theory and inadequate controls for potential confounding variables. For example, schizophrenics residing in hospital wards and receiving medication were commonly compared with normal people who had very different diets and activity levels, were not taking medication, and differed in age, size, and gender — all factors that could affect biochemical analyses. Also, early studies lacked accurate tools and methods for measuring biological processes. Some of the methods were highly inventive. Consider the one illustrated in Figure 9.10, which tested whether schizophrenia is caused by a hallucinogenic substance in the brain. Researchers examined spiders' web-building processes to see if web patterns following administration of hallucinogenic drugs resembled those following admininistration of fluids from people with schizo-

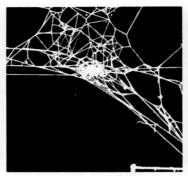

Figure 9.10   Web-Building of Spiders as a Test of Psychedelic Effects

In the 1950s researchers speculated about the similarity between psychedelic drug-induced states and psychosis. Some hypothesized that an abnormal metabolic pathway in psychotic patients might produce hallucinogenic substances responsible for their hallucinations. The search for such compounds led to many efforts to detect them. Peter Witt developed a procedure that was very sensitive — and novel. He determined that the web-building of spiders was disrupted by ingestion of different hallucinogenic drugs, as these photos illustrate. Having established web-building as a test of psychedelic effects, he and colleagues then attempted to determine if they could detect hallucinogenic substances in the urine of mental patients. After the urine of patients or controls was injected into the spiders, however, no differences were observed in the webs. *Source:* Witt (1963).

phrenia. Other methods were ethically suspect, as when prisoners were used as human guinea pigs to test the effects of biological substances extracted from schizophrenics.

Current biochemical research in schizophrenia focuses on neurotransmitters in the brain and their linkages to areas associated with emotional experience and information processing. In particular, the emphasis has been on the neurotransmitter **dopamine**. Figure 9.11 illustrates dopamine pathways in the brain and their importance to frontal lobe and limbic system (subcortical) functioning. Recall that neurotransmitters are released by the firing of one neuron and that they bind to receptors on a second, postsynaptic neuron, increasing the likelihood that the second neuron will itself fire.

In the early 1970s, biochemical theory held that schizophrenia resulted from *excess dopamine*. This theory was based largely on two sources of indirect data: (1) Phenothiazine drugs that reduce some symptoms of schizophrenia were observed to block receptors for dopamine and thereby reduce the activity of pathways in the brain that use dopamine as the neurotransmitter. And (2) some schizophrenic patients were found to exhibit higher levels of dopamine metabolites (chemical byproducts) in the brain than did normal controls.

Despite its promise, however, the excess-dopamine theory proved far too simple. Several findings in the past few years have necessitated a more complex theory. First, studies have shown that dopamine metabolite concentrations vary with type of symptoms (negative or positive) and, possibly, with regions of the brain (Davis, Kahn, Ko & Davidson, 1991; Heritch, 1990). Second, further studies of the effects of medication have indicated that not all schizophrenic patients respond to drugs that block dopamine receptors; and that the neuroleptic medications that appeared to work by binding to a specific subtype of dopamine receptors, the D2 receptors, commonly reduce the acute or positive symptoms, but have less effect on the negative symptoms or can even make them worse. Finally, scientists are learning that the dopaminergic systems have different subsystems, and that different types of dopamine receptors have varying characteristics. Overall, such complexity undermines any simple dopamine theory of causality. To date, we are unclear about the precise mechanisms by which dopamine activity regulates schizophrenic symptoms. We are even less clear about whether dysfunctional dopamine processes play a role in the *fundamental* cause of schizophrenia. (For instance, neurological damage may possibly underlie abnormalities of the dopamine system.) Despite such questions, however, we can be sure that dopamine processes, whether alone or in combination with other neurotransmitter systems, play an important role in the alleviation of some schizophrenic symptoms.

The tremendous variability in the nature, course, and presumed causes of schizophrenia also underscores the need to explore nonbiological factors that might shape the disorder. Thus, we turn to a consideration of possible psychological causes and contributors to schizophrenia.

Psychological Approaches to the Causes of Schizophrenia

Can stressors or psychological traumas cause schizophrenia? "I'm on the verge of a nervous breakdown," "He's driving me nuts," and "I think I'm going crazy" are common phrases suggesting that some people believe

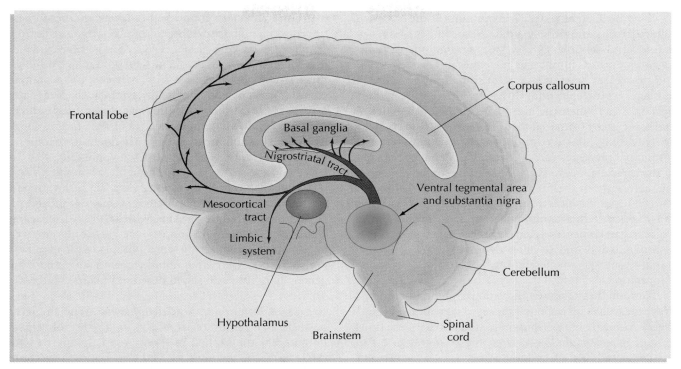

Figure 9.11   Dopamine Tracts in the Brain

This schematic drawing shows probable projections of dopamine tracts in the brain. The tracts serve the frontal and temporal areas of the cortex as well as the limbic (or subcortical) structures. The locations and interconnections between these areas of the brain and their relation to mental and emotional functioning suggest that the dopamine system may be relevant to schizophrenia. *Source:* Andreasen (1988).

psychological events can drive them into madness. In this section we consider theories and evidence suggesting that schizophrenia may be caused by psychological circumstances. Research has clearly failed to support the idea that a psychological event can be the sole origin of schizophrenia. Nevertheless, accumulating evidence indicates that stressors play an important role in the timing and course of episodes of schizophrenia — and may be significant in triggering the disorder in those individuals who are biologically predisposed.

Disturbed Family Interactions   Freud's intrapsychic theory of psychological abnormality viewed schizophrenia as a profound regression to a primitive stage of development stemming from internal conflict. His later followers, such as Frieda Fromm-Reichmann, Harry Stack Sullivan, and Silvano Arieti, emphasized the family context as a source of internal conflict. Fromm-Reichmann (1948) and Arieti (1955) focused on the **schizophrenogenic mother** (or schizophrenia-inducing mother), having speculated that mothers of adult schizophrenics behaved in ways that caused the schizophrenic breakdown. But controlled research to test this hypothesis was rare, and contradictory pictures emerged from clinical reports on mother-child relationships. Mothers of schizophrenics were variously reported to be overprotective or rejecting, overly hostile or subtly hostile, unduly restrictive or insufficiently restrictive, and neglectful of the child or overinvolved and intrusive. Moreover, these findings were often based on retrospective reports, having been gathered only after the child became schizophrenic. Finally, much of this research not only lacked a group of mothers of normal offspring for comparison purposes but also ignored information from the fathers.

Despite these limitations, valuable insights about disturbed family functioning emerged, leading to several theories about the origins of schizophrenia. One influential theory focused on disturbed role relationships within the family, suggesting, for example, that family members might form inappropriate alliances or show deviant patterns of dominance and control (Lidz, Fleck & Cornelison, 1965). But research stimulated by such views yielded conflicting results and little evidence that such patterns play a causal role in schizophrenia (Liem, 1980). Eventually, *family process theories* focused on communication between family members. These theories suggest that hidden messages, unclear or inconsistent communication, or peculiar language or logic directed toward a child will create problems in thinking, perceiving, and communicating that in turn lead to schizophrenia.

One problematic style of communication has been referred to as the double bind. According to Gregory Bateson and his colleagues (1956), *double-bind communication* creates conflicting messages involving verbal and nonverbal content. As an example, suppose that a mother says to her child, "Mommy loves you," while turning away when the child tries to kiss her. Bateson and associates postulated that preschizophrenic children are repeatedly subjected to incongruent, confusing, and conflictual messages such as these. They cannot respond to the messages reasonably without in some way denying themselves or their real experience; in short, they can neither leave the situation nor make sense of it. What can happen if this communication style persists? The children can come to selectively ignore aspects of human communication and develop defective ways of understanding interpersonal relationships and of processing information.

Despite the ingenuity of the double-bind hypothesis, little research evidence has supported its validity. Nevertheless, clinical observations of dysfunctional interactions in schizophrenic families have prompted investigators to persevere with better models and methods. One attempt uses the concept of **communication deviance (CD)**, which refers to problems in creating and maintaining a shared focus of attention. Noting that the parents of schizophrenic patients often express themselves in unclear, vague, fragmented ways, Margaret Singer and Lyman Wynne (1963) speculated that such styles disrupt meaningful sharing of information and expose the child to stress, faulty problem solving, and habits of unusual thinking that may increase the likelihood of schizophrenia. Singer and Wynne developed systematic measures of CD, which is marked by vague, indefinite communication; misperceptions and misinterpretations; odd or inappropriate word usage; and fragmented, disrupted, and poorly integrated communication. CD is measured either by individual administration of a projective task such as the Thematic Apperception Task, or TAT (described in Chapter 4) or by observation of actual interactions among family members. For example, David Miklowitz and his colleagues (1991) noted that during a TAT test a person described what was going on in a picture by saying, "They're trying to make a goal of their life." Researchers also observed interactions among this person's family members, which included the statements: "But the thing is as I said, there's got . . . you can't drive in the alley" and "It's gonna be up and downwards along the process all the while to go through something like this" (Miklowitz et al., 1991).

Several longitudinal studies have found that the families of high-risk children (those presumed to be at risk for developing schizophrenia) exhibited higher levels of communication deviance than did the families of low-risk youngsters (e.g., Jones et al., 1977). Other types of studies have also found higher levels of communication deviance in schizophrenic families than in normal families (reviewed by Liem, 1980). But is there evidence that CD plays a causal role in schizophrenia? Although these studies do suggest a link between CD in family communications and later schizophrenia, they have not established that faulty communication *caused* schizophrenia. Miklowitz and associates (1991) recently proposed that communication deviance might instead be an index of genetic liability to schizophrenia that is reflected as a mild version of thought or language disorder. They also reported evidence that CD is not specific to families with schizophrenic members; indeed, it occurs in families of patients with bipolar disorder as well. Thus, communication deviance in families may be unrelated to the onset of schizophrenia, or it may be a nonspecific stressor that interacts with an underlying genetic liability, resulting in disorder of some kind.

Expressed Emotion and Schizophrenia   The emphasis on disturbed family relationships as a cause of schizophrenia has diminished in recent years, owing to both the lack of supporting data and the increased focus on biological processes. However, some interesting developments have occurred in research examining the role of family interactions on the *course* of schizophrenia. Even if relationships do not cause schizophrenia, investigators have reasoned, they might still influence its course among individuals who are vulnerable to the disorder. In particular, researchers have asked whether certain family environments are more or less likely to be associated with *relapses* among schizophrenic patients when they return home from hospitalizations for episodes.

Current research addressing these questions has focused on **expressed emotion (EE)**, which concerns the degree to which family members either are critical of a recently hospitalized schizophrenic person or express overinvolved and overprotective attitudes toward the patient. To assess EE, researchers use a semistructured interview that lasts approximately one and a half hours. The interview focuses on the patient's most recent psychotic episode and the impact of that episode on the family during the last three months. The interview is tape-recorded and scored by trained judges to determine EE. Frequent comments that are critical, disliking, or resentful of the patient, or that express emotional overinvolvement, overprotectiveness, and self-sacrificing attitudes, contribute to high EE scores. An example of overinvolvement is the following statement made by a patient's relative: "I'd lay down my life for [this patient]. In fact, I've quit my job and gone into debt so I can be at home in case . . ." (Valone, Norton, Goldstein & Doane, 1983).

Do high EE scores in a patient's family indicate that the patient is likely to suffer a relapse? A wide range of studies have supported this link. In two studies, a high level of expressed emotion in a parent or spouse was found to be predictive of relapse at a nine-month follow-up after discharge (Brown, Birley & Wing, 1972) and at a two-year follow-up (Leff & Vaughn, 1981). According to a third study, patients from low-EE families exhibited a relapse rate of 15 percent during the observation period, compared to a relapse rate of 40 percent to 50 percent among patients from high-EE families (Mintz, Lieberman, Miklowitz & Mintz, 1987).

Expressed emotion is one of the first psychological constructs involving family functioning that has successfully predicted the future course of schizophrenia. But we need to ask, What is it about EE that causes relapse? High expressed emotion is generally viewed as creating a stressful environment that overwhelms the fragile schizophrenic patient's ability to cope, such that symptoms return. Initially, researchers in this field tended to view negative family attitudes and overinvolvement as resulting from traits of the caregiver, rather than from reactions to the patient's symptoms. For example, studies have found that measures of family EE predict relapse even among young patients after their first episodes, and even when such patients are carefully maintained on medication (Nuechterlein et al., 1992). However, negative attitudes in family members could also result from the schizophrenic person's dysfunctional behaviors. Several studies have suggested that relatives are especially critical or intrusive regarding the *negative* symptoms of schizophrenia. In other words, although relatives may view bizarre symptoms as uncontrollable expressions of a disease, negative symptoms such as apathy and withdrawal may be more likely to elicit negative attitudes because family members (erroneously) believe that the schizophrenic person can control them (e.g., Weisman, Lopez, Karno & Jenkins, 1993).

Even mildly symptomatic patients might provoke negative reactions from others. For example, when Rosenfarb, Goldstein, Mintz, and Nuechterlein (1995) observed families during an interaction task, they found that high-EE relatives were more likely to make a negative comment to a schizophrenic patient if the patient made an odd or disruptive statement. In turn, the relatives' negative comment increased the probability that the patient would make a further unusual verbalization. In contrast, patients from low-EE families displayed less unusual or disruptive behavior. Figure 9.12 shows the probability with which unusual, symptomatic thoughts are expressed by schizophrenic patients following negative reactions by relatives. Indeed, some families may become locked into highly stressful, tension-filled patterns that are associated with further breakdowns in the person with schizophrenia. As we discuss in the section on treatment, efforts to help families cope with schizophrenic patients and engage in more constructive

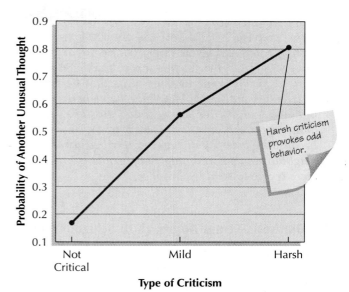

Figure 9.12   Expressed Emotion in the Families of Schizophrenic Patients

Patients and family members may have a mutual negative effect on each other's behavior in some situations. In families exhibiting high levels of expressed emotion, criticism in response to the patient's odd or disruptive behavior was highly likely to be followed by another unusual, symptomatic remark by the patient. Such stressful interactions may contribute to the patient's full symptomatic relapse. *Source:* Rosenfarb, Goldstein, Mintz & Nuechterlein (1995).

interactions seem to hold some promise of reducing relapse.

Your cousin Marty was first hospitalized for hearing voices about ten years ago, when he was a senior in high school. Although his medications now seem to prevent the worst of his bizarre beliefs and odd behaviors, he has never been able to work or stay in school. He lives at home with his mother, who is your Aunt Helen, and his younger brother. Helen tried to go back to work after her divorce, but found that she was too worried about Marty's well-being to tolerate the job. She was afraid that he'd wander out of the house and get into trouble, or that he'd accidentally set fire to the house, or that he'd just sit around all day and do nothing if she wasn't there to watch him. She quit her job, and spends much of her time looking after Marty. In fact, Marty, does sit around watching TV most of the day and late into the night, sometimes muttering to himself or laughing at odd moments. He hardly talks to anyone, shows little interest in people or activities, refuses to help with chores, and often exudes a pungent odor because he cares little about the basics of bathing and hygiene. Helen now nags him to get out of the house: "Why don't you go to the movies?" "You should try to get some exercise," "Did you call the rehab counselor yet?" "You'd feel better if you got a haircut." Marty mostly ignores her, saying very little. But you've noticed during some of your visits that he gets agitated when she tries to get him to take better care of himself. And last week you found out that he'd had another breakdown and needed to be hospitalized because he was found running terrified through the neighborhood, exclaiming that people on television were trying to steal his brain.

The Diathesis-Stress Approach to Schizophrenia

As we have seen, schizophrenia presents many faces. Its symptoms and its outcomes vary. What we call schizophrenia may even be different disorders with varying causes. The fact that identical twins with identical genes may be *discordant* for schizophrenia is a dramatic reminder that there is no simple genetic explanation for schizophrenia. Moreover, despite evidence that cognitive and information-processing deficits and brain anomalies might exist from birth, schizophrenia does not typically develop until late adolescence or young adulthood. These observations suggest that a combination of ingredients is necessary to produce schizophrenia, not just one causal factor. Accordingly, most investigators subscribe to the **diathesis-stress approach,** which holds that an interaction between biological and environmental factors determines the development of schizophrenia and the timing of its occurrence.

The *diathesis* part of the diathesis-stress equation refers to a kind of vulnerability (Zubin & Spring, 1977) to schizophrenia, possibly based on a genetically transmitted biological predisposition. We have reviewed various hypothesized types of biological dysfunction — structural alterations of the brain, deficits in the ability to attend to and organize complex information, and dysregulation in neurotransmitter systems. Such dysfunctions might reflect genetically based underlying vulnerabilities. However, in the view of most diathesis-stress models, a vulnerability is a necessary but not sufficient cause. In other words, a person does not inherit a disease or condition that inevitably leads to schizophrenia; instead, the person has a predisposition to schizophrenia that must interact with environmental and physical circumstances such as stressors.

The *stress* part of the diathesis-stress equation refers to some event or circumstance that shapes the developing organism or overtaxes the vulnerable individual's ability to cope. Speculations about possible stressors in the physical environment have pointed, for example, to injuries or viral infections that alter the developing brain. Stressors can also take the form of psychological adversity — negative life events and conditions. As discussed, stressful family interactions appear to play an important role in determining the course of the disorder. Recent research has further indicated that the timing of onset and relapses may be triggered by negative life events such as parental divorce, job difficulties, and loss of a relationship (Dohrenwend et al., 1986; Nuechterlein et al., 1992; Ventura, Neuchterlein, Lukoff & Hardesty, 1989). Stressors can also be inherent in the numerous difficulties faced by a child who is genetically vulnerable to schizophrenia, such as difficulties in processing social and emotional information, problems in mastering social skills, demoralizing failures at school and in interpersonal relationships, or subtle limitations in intelligence, perception, language, and reasoning (Watt & Saiz, 1991). Even low socioeconomic status can be a stressor — with both psychological and physical dimensions — inasmuch as it often results in poor prenatal care, birth complications, viral exposure, and family disruption.

An excellent example of research driven by a diathesis-stress model is the *high-risk* method employed by Sarnoff Mednick and his colleagues. These researchers extensively studied 207 children of severely schizophrenic mothers as well as 104 children from psychiatrically normal families who were similar in age, gender, and other demographic characteristics. Then, five, ten, and approximately twenty-five years after the original assessment, they reexamined the same children. As noted earlier, the children who were at genetic risk for schizophrenia and who actually developed schizophrenia were also more likely to have experienced birth complications (reported in Cannon et al., 1993). In addition, Mednick and associates (1988) proposed that viral exposure, such as influenza during the second trimester, might be particularly damaging to those already at genetic risk for schizophrenia. Cannon, Mednick, and Parnas (1989) further speculated, based on data from their high-risk sample, that genetic predisposition and birth complications may be especially predictive of negative-symptom schizophrenia with enlarged ventricles, whereas positive symptom schizophrenia may result from genetic predisposition plus severely disturbed and unstable early childhood experiences rather than obstetric complications and brain abnormalities.

Clearly, psychology must continue its search for ways to understand the complex relationships between genetic and environmental factors. Although we have not yet pinned down *the* origins of schizophrenia, the information gained from both the biological and psychosocial approaches to schizophrenia have contributed to important developments in the treatment of schizophrenia, as we now explore.

TREATMENTS FOR SCHIZOPHRENIA

In Chapter 1 we describe medieval views of madness that attributed its source to demon possession or witchcraft and therefore held the appropriate treatment to be exorcism (or burning at the stake). Even when schizophrenia was later viewed as an illness, the only treatment was confinement in an insane asylum. For the first half of this century, treatment in the United States usually involved confinement in a hospital with minimal direct treatment; images of padded cells, straitjackets, and shock therapies come from this era. The 1950s brought "milieu therapy," a somewhat more humane form of hospitalization based on the idea that the hospital would provide a safe haven in which mentally ill people could regain stability while practicing occupational and recreational therapy. Cynical critics might say that this treatment mostly involved keeping society separated from such people and freeing families from the tremendous burden of caring for them.

Hospitalization has had many undesirable effects on the adjustment and civil liberties of the mentally ill, leading to the movement toward deinstitutionalization that began in the 1960s. Today, brief hospitalization is often necessary to calm the acute phase of schizophrenia, but individuals are then usually returned to their communities as quickly as possible. Unfortunately, in the absence of halfway houses, board-and-care facilities, or day treatment hospitalization programs, many schizophrenic persons have become homeless (e.g., Koegel, Burnam & Farr, 1988). In this chapter we focus on the available treatments.

Antipsychotic Medication for Schizophrenia

In decades past, little could be done to control the demons of a person's madness and suffering. As we discuss in Chapter 3, mental health professionals sometimes resorted to somewhat extreme and questionable procedures such as shock therapies and psychosurgery — but with little evidence of significant positive changes in schizophrenia (although more recent ECT methods have been found useful for some depressive disorders). Continuing efforts to find ways to calm the agitation and psychotic experiences associated with schizophrenia led to experiments with chemicals called **phenothiazines,** which were thought to have tranquilizing properties. As a result, in 1952, the first drug to treat schizophrenia became available — chlorpromazine (brand name Thorazine). Originally considered a very strong tranquilizer, it was found to have *antipsychotic properties;* that is, it did not just sedate the person but also reduced

This man has been diagnosed with schizophrenia, and is chained to keep him in a mental hospital near Calcutta in 1997. Authorities at the hospital said that he is chained because there is no money for medications to calm such patients — a reminder of the care of mental patients in North America and Europe before psychotropic medications were available.

the intensity and frequency of hallucinations, delusions, and other psychotic behaviors.

A dozen or more antipsychotic, or **neuroleptic**, drugs similar to chlorpromazine, as well as others having somewhat different chemical structures, were soon developed and marketed. Some of the major neuroleptics and their brand names are listed in Table 9.2. In general, medications are the primary treatment for schizophrenics, with relatively good results in reducing the acute symptoms of schizophrenia and preventing relapse — especially if patients start taking the neuroleptics early in the course of their disorder (Wyatt, 1991).

Nevertheless, neuroleptics have three significant limitations. First, they require continuing use. About 53 percent of patients who discontinue them relapse within about nine months, with many relapses occurring as early as three months after discontinuation (Gilbert, Harris, McAdams & Jeste, 1995). Second, the medications have major side effects, including irreversible neurological symptoms. Third, a substantial minority of patients (10 percent to 20 percent) do not improve with use of the medications (Kane et al., 1988).

Effects of Neuroleptics   As we note in discussing the excess-dopamine theory of schizophrenia, neuroleptics appear to work by blocking the postsynaptic dopamine receptors. The chemical composition of many neuroleptics is such that they "fit" into the receptors (especially the D_2 receptors), preventing dopamine from having its effects. Neuroleptics appear to reduce acute psychotic thought processes such as disturbed thinking, delusions, and hallucinations, and to improve disordered information processing. They generally work most effectively when given early in the course of schizophrenia — because with progression of the disorder, there may be diminished effects (e.g., Szymanski et al., 1996). Still, many schizophrenic patients may have residual thinking deficits despite the medication.

Neuroleptics also work more effectively on the positive symptoms of schizophrenia (e.g., Szymanski et al., 1996) than on the negative symptoms, such as flat affect, apathy, anhedonia, social withdrawal, and lack of motivation; they may even intensify the latter behaviors. The following is an example of successful use of medication to control positive schizophrenic symptoms.

Gerald had his first psychotic episode during college, manifest as paranoid delusions that his mind was being controlled by "forces" that broadcast to him through radio waves, and that there was a plot to have him killed. He was hospitalized for a month, during which time his acute symptoms were reduced by use of the neuroleptic thiothixene (Navane). He had always seemed well-adjusted and successful,

Table 9.2	**Commonly Used Medications to Treat Schizophrenia**	
	Chemical Name	**Brand Name**
Phenothiazines	Chlorpromazine	Thorazine
	Thioridazine	Mellaril
	Trifluoperazine	Stelazine
	Fluphenazine	Prolixin
	Prochlorperazine	Compazine
Thioxanthenes	Chlorprothixene	Taractan
	Thiothixene	Navane
Others	Clozapine	Clozaril
	Haloperidol	Haldol
	Loxapine	Loxitane
	Risperdone	Risperdal

Neuroleptic drugs sedate the schizophrenic person and also reduce the intensity and frequency of hallucinations, delusions, and other psychotic behaviors. These are the chemical and brand names of the most commonly used neuroleptic medications.

and his family had no history of mental illness, although his parents did not know many of their relatives who had been killed in Europe in WWII. Eventually Gerald was able to return to school, and he hoped that the episode was behind him. He resisted continuing medication because it made him feel like a "mental patient," and he hated the dry mouth and spacey feeling the drug gave him. Also he felt that he was doing fine without it. He found that he was often preoccupied with suspicious beliefs, however, and thought that he heard words uttered by strangers that made him think they were talking about him, planning to harm him. To other people he appeared tense, jumpy, and guarded. During exam periods or when he had other pressures, some of the symptoms would intensify. Eventually, with his doctor's encouragement, he resumed his dosage of Navane at the minimum level that seemed to keep him in a comfortable state, although even with medication he sometimes experienced mild increases in fears and suspicions. He also knew that he had to work hard to keep his life stable, get sleep, reduce stress, and avoid believing in his paranoid thoughts. On the whole, he was unusually bright and insightful about his illness, and had a stable and supportive family and a few good friends. His prognosis for maintaining his recovery was good, but he recognized that the medication was likely to be crucial to his success.

Overall, there is no evidence that one antipsychotic drug is better than another, although some patients may respond more favorably to some drugs than to others (reviewed in Gitlin, 1996). In any case, because most schizophrenia is recurrent or chronic, doctors recommend that patients take their medication indefinitely. A recent controlled double-blind study found that maintenance medication (stable, ongoing treatment) results in fewer episodes than administration of medication only when the person begins to show early signs of relapse (Herz et al., 1991). This situation is unfortunate in that many patients are reluctant to comply with maintenance treatment — in part, because of its unwanted side effects.

Side Effects of Neuroleptic Medications The side effects of neuroleptics, which range from the bothersome to the dangerous, must be monitored carefully. There are several potential neurological side effects. In the initial stages of treatment, the person may experience tightening of the muscles, especially those of the neck and jaw. Symptoms similar to those of Parkinson's disease (described in Chapter 17) may also appear: Spontaneous movements decrease so that the person seems stiff or wooden. In addition, emotional spontaneity and motivation may be reduced, thus increasing the negative symptoms of schizophrenia. Side effects such as reduced spontaneous movements can be controlled by medications (for example, benztropine [Cogentin]). Another common neurological side effect is *akathisia*, characterized by motor restlessness in which the person shows fidgety movements, shifting constantly. The most severe and even fatal (though fortunately rare) side effect is called neuroleptic malignant syndrome, in which the patient develops fever, muscle rigidity, and rapid pulse, and must be treated immediately. Additional common side effects are similar to those associated with antidepressants: sedation, dry mouth, blurry vision, constipation, and weight gain, among others.

The most feared common side effect of antipsychotic medications is **tardive dyskinesia (TD)**. Though not life threatening, it is the only side effect that is irreversible even if medication is discontinued. The major manifestations of TD are involuntary facial movements such as grimacing, tongue thrusting, lip smacking, and eye blinking. There may even be involuntary motor behaviors involving the hands and feet, or respiratory movements that affect breathing patterns. An estimated 15 percent to 20 percent of patients on neuroleptics show some signs of tardive dyskinesia, generally after six months to a year of treatment. Rates are even higher among elderly patients (e.g., Jeste et al., 1995) and individuals taking high-level dosages (Chakos et al., 1996). TD is especially a problem for elderly women.

Obviously, long-term treatment with neuroleptics requires careful monitoring for TD symptoms, and may involve a difficult trade-off between side effects and schizophrenic symptoms. Schizophrenic patients, their families, and their doctors must weigh the risks of TD versus relapse. Researchers continue to try to determine whether some individuals may function relatively well without neuroleptics, while keeping in mind that younger patients with histories of recurrent episodes are at highest risk for further relapse without medication (e.g., Gilbert, Harris, McAdams & Jeste, 1995). There is also hope that new antipsychotic drugs that do not cause tardive dyskinesia will be developed.

Clozapine: New Wonder Drug? Clozapine (Clozaril) is among the several chemically new neuroleptics recently developed and released for use. First used in Europe in the 1970s, it is unique in having far fewer of the common side effects of neuroleptic medications. To date, there is no evidence that it causes tardive dyskinesia. Clozapine appears to work in part by blocking a different subtype of dopamine receptor (D_4) than the more traditional neuroleptics. More profoundly, as Figure 9.13 illustrates, it has been reported to reduce symptoms in patients who are unresponsive to standard treatments such as chlorpromazine (Kane et al., 1988; Pickar et al., 1992). It also reduces negative symptoms of schizophrenia. A dramatic consequence of its use is occasionally seen among formerly chronic, unresponsive schizophrenics who seem to suddenly awaken from years of psychosis to resume their lives. This has been labeled the "Rip Van Winkle effect."

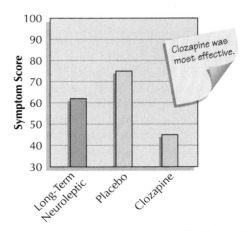

Figure 9.13 Treatment with Clozapine
Patients who were not helped by or could not tolerate typical neuroleptics were chosen for this study. Each patient had a trial of a neuroleptic drug (fluphenazine), followed by a placebo, followed by clozapine. Only the investigators — not the patients or the staff who gave the drugs — knew which drugs were given when. Patients did significantly better on clozapine than on fluphenazine or placebo. Clozapine (and similar newly emerging drugs) may also have fewer neurological side effects than other neuroleptics.

People with schizophrenia have often turned to art, poetry, and prose to express their experiences with the disorder. Anna-Marie Kuiper, the artist who created this wallhanging, entitled "Facing Delusions," offers this description of her work: "The wallhanging is constructed of fabric in all sorts of colors and textures that I cut, pieced, and sewed together. My art is an example of what goes on in my head. In this piece, hallucinations and delusions burst out of the top of my head and flow heavily down my troubled face. This psychotic feeling is very confusing, and there are no boundaries for reality. The chaos that I feel is uncontrollable and incredibly scary." Adolf Wolfli (1864–1930) was hospitalized in Switzerland for schizophrenia at age 31 and then spent the rest of his life in an asylum. He expressed his delusions in his drawings, in which he often represented himself as a supreme being, St. Adolf. This drawing, "Saint-Adolf-Grand-Grand-God-Father," was completed in 1915.

Although clozapine is certainly promising, it has two major drawbacks. First, because it is extremely expensive, its availability is severely limited. Often the public mental health agencies that need it most are the least able to fund its use. Second, in about 1 percent to 2 percent of patients, clozapine can cause a potentially fatal blood disease called agranulocytosis. Patients taking clozapine need to have their white blood cell counts monitored weekly, so that early signs of agranulocytosis can be discovered and treated. Because of the monitoring expenses involved, most state agencies responsible for care of treatment-resistant schizophrenic patients cannot afford to treat all patients who might profit from the drug.

The excitement about clozapine has been tempered of late. Having reviewed several studies, William T. Carpenter, one of the original enthusiasts of the drug, has recently concluded that — despite its utility for patients who do not respond to typical neuroleptics — it does not substantially reduce negative symptoms (Carpenter et al., 1995). Others disagree (e.g., Meltzer, 1995). Another atypical neuroleptic now on the market, *risperidone,* has been shown to have good effects and relatively few side effects (e.g., Peuskens, 1995). Similar new drugs will soon be available. It is hoped that they will work as well as clozapine, but without its serious drawbacks, and that they will prove effective with the deficit symptoms as well.

Gender and Ethnic Differences in the Use of Antipsychotic Medication Generally, antipsychotic medications have similar outcomes for men and women, as well as for different ethnic groups. However, research is beginning to reveal important exceptions. For example, a recent study has suggested that among first-episode schizophrenic patients, women respond better to neuroleptics than men do (Szymanski et al., 1995). And although analyses of the responses and side effects of neuroleptics taken by African American and white schizophrenics have not revealed significant differences (Levinson & Simpson, 1992; Van Putten, Marder & Mintz, 1992), controlled clinical trials indicate that

Asian schizophrenic patients require significantly lower dosages for effective treatment than white patients. Also, Asian schizophrenics show side effects at lower level dosages (Lin et al., 1989).

Antipsychotic medications have certainly changed the lives of countless schizophrenic patients. They have also permitted the end of institutionalization as the major or only available treatment option. But extensive use of medications to control symptoms has raised social and legal issues — as discussed more fully in Chapter 18. Moreover, medications alone may not be sufficient, given the role of psychological and environmental factors in the course of the disorder. Accordingly, we now turn to a discussion of psychologically based treatments.

Psychosocial Treatments of Schizophrenia

In years past, hospitalization and psychotherapy were the only treatments available for patients with schizophrenia. Recently, however, there has been a resurgence of interest in psychological interventions to supplement the effects of medication.

Psychotherapy for Schizophrenia Psychoanalytically oriented therapists such as Frieda Fromm-Reichmann (1954) and John Rosen (1947) argued that the delusions and thought disorder of schizophrenics could be understood as a defense against intrapsychic anxiety. Using traditional methods of psychoanalysis such as transference and interpretation, they attempted to comprehend the meaning of the seemingly irrational and confused utterances of schizophrenic patients, and then to confront and explore the symbolic significance of this material. Analysts reported successful work with some schizophrenic patients.

In the 1950s and 1960s humanistic therapies also made some attempts to treat schizophrenic individuals. Carl Rogers and his followers practiced nondirective therapy with such patients, but with limited evidence of success. The British psychiatrist Ronald D. Laing (1967) attracted attention for his view of schizophrenia as reflecting the person's attempts to regain selfhood, which had been lost due to the oppressive forces of society and overcontrolling or engulfing parents. Treatment thus consisted of providing a safe location and emotional support for the schizophrenic through a "journey," and encouraging total freedom of expression of symptoms, artistic inclinations, or any other methods of being the true self. Accounts of successful cases were reported, but no systematic evidence existed for the effectiveness of Laing's approach. Its attractiveness was apparently due to the antiestablishment sentiments of the 1960s.

Although humanistic and psychodynamic approaches are rarely used today, especially in the absence of med-ication, some schizophrenic patients may profit from supportive psychotherapy, as the following excerpt written by a 37-year-old woman suggests:

> *In the most recently published book I've read, a doctor writes that psychotherapy is useless with schizophrenics. How could he even suggest that without knowing me, the one over here in this corner, who finds a lot of support, understanding, and acceptance with my therapist? Marianne is not afraid to travel with me in my fearful times. She listens when I need to release some of the "poisons" in my mind. She offers advice when I'm having difficulty with just daily living. She sees me as a human being and not only a body to shovel pills into or a cerebral mass in some laboratory. Psychotherapy is important to me, and it does help. (McGrath, 1984, p. 639)*

Psychotherapy alone, however, is not considered to be the treatment of choice for schizophrenia.

Cognitive Rehabilitation and Cognitive Therapy Because cognitive deficits are central to schizophrenia during both its acute and residual phases, some investigators have argued for direct treatment of cognitive problems in sustaining attention, language use, abstraction, and the like. Michael Green (1996), for example, has shown that neurocognitive deficits are related to schizophrenic patients' social and vocational functioning. In particular, deficits in verbal memory and attention are associated with poor social and work functioning, suggesting that specific training to overcome or compensate for such decrements might facilitate better community adjustment. A few studies have provided preliminary support for the effectiveness of programs that teach such skills to schizophrenic patients (reviewed in Penn & Mueser, 1996; Kern, Green & Goldstein, 1995).

From a different perspective, Swiss psychiatrist Carlo Perris (1989) has modified Beck's cognitive-behavioral therapy procedures (described in Chapter 3) to apply to schizophrenic patients. Recall that cognitive therapy teaches patients to challenge their delusional beliefs — in favor of "reality-testing" and problem-solving processes. To date, little research has tested Perris's approach, but a few small studies suggest that it decreases psychotic thinking for some patients (e.g., Chadwick, Lowe, Horne & Higson, 1994; Tarrier et al., 1993).

Although cognitive-rehabilitation and cognitive therapy show some promise, we do not yet know whether their effects will generalize to real-life tasks and improved ability to function in social and work situations. Obviously, this controversial topic will continue to be the focus of research and debate.

Combining Psychosocial Treatments and Medications

As noted, neither medication nor individual psychotherapy alone is usually sufficient to improve the overall functioning of schizophrenic patients and to reduce the likelihood of relapse. Accordingly, three types of psychological intervention that are intended to be combined with medication have been developed and tested, with impressive results: token economies, social skills training programs, and family psychoeducation programs.

Token Economies   In previous decades, learning and conditioning principles were sometimes applied to understand the specific symptoms of schizophrenia, but there was no widespread adoption of this approach as a theory of the causes of the disorder. Nevertheless, investigators hypothesized that learning principles could be applied to reduce specific dysfunctional behaviors or increase adaptive behaviors. In the 1960s several projects were developed to expand operant conditioning techniques (see Chapter 3) to include token economies for treatment of schizophrenics in hospital wards. In such programs, desirable behaviors such as proper grooming, appropriate social interactions, and rational talk were reinforced by tokens that patients could exchange for privileges or candy and cigarettes. At a state hospital in Illinois, for example, Gordon Paul and his colleagues devised a program for chronically ill hospitalized schizophrenics based on social learning principles. Patients were assigned either to routine care or to social learning therapy. Staff members chosen to administer the therapy were carefully trained to teach and shape desired skills through verbal instructions, modeling, and reinforcements for positive behavior. Observers rated patients' behaviors on the wards as well as in after-care programs following discharge. Patients in the social learning program did significantly better than the comparison groups, mastering and displaying appropriate social behaviors and showing fewer symptoms (Paul & Lentz, 1977).

A somewhat different program was developed and tested by George Fairweather and his colleagues (1969) in California. Fairweather focused on social and vocational skills. He established a program in which the patients (male schizophrenics at a Veterans Administration hospital) had considerable responsibility for establishing and maintaining appropriate social skills among the members of their small work teams. Teams as well as individuals were rewarded for effective behaviors by being promoted to increasingly higher "steps" that brought more privileges as well as access to more passes and money. While in the hospital, patients in the social learning program did significantly better than comparison patients on traditional wards, in terms of social

interactions systematically recorded by raters. Even more important, after discharge they stayed out of the hospital longer and had better employment records. Indeed, the former patients helped establish a "lodge" that served as a residential center after discharge. At the lodge they maintained their program of rewards for healthy behavior and withdrawal of privileges for inappropriate behaviors. They even established their own employment agency to help place patients in jobs. Figure 9.14 shows that, compared with patients in traditional wards, those in Fairweather's program had significantly better employment records for the forty months of the study, and they maintained their gains even after the lodge closed. Other states adopted the procedure, with considerable success in programs as long as they were funded (Torrey, 1990).

As these examples suggest, token economy–based programs improve patients' functioning. But they require tremendous dedication by staff to implement the reinforcement contingencies. Nowadays, however, because of deinstitutionalization (described in Chapter 18), most schizophrenic patients are hospitalized only for brief periods. Residential programs, such as halfway houses and board-and-care facilities in communities, typically lack the staffing needed to implement behavior modification programs. Consequently, more recent efforts have been directed at out-patients and at family functioning.

Social Skills Training Programs   Behaviorally oriented interventions for schizophrenic in-patients and out-patients have specifically emphasized social skills and personal competence. For example, Robert Paul Liberman and his colleagues, Kim Mueser and Charles Wallace (1986) have developed an extensive cognitive-behavioral training program for medication-stabilized schizophrenics. It emphasizes cognitive skills such as focusing attention, correctly perceiving situations, understanding messages from others, and generating alternative solutions to problems. Basic behavioral skills such as conversational abilities, behaviors that assist in living independently, and vocational skills are also emphasized. For example, patients may be taught how to correctly identify someone else's emotions, how to maintain eye contact and speak at an appropriate volume, how to engage in a conversation with someone, and how to think through a problem and generate appropriate solutions. Methods of teaching include observing models, role playing, and practicing homework assignments.

In general, social skills training programs have succeeded in modifying various maladaptive behaviors (reviewed in Penn & Mueser, 1996). Though very effective for modifying specific behavioral skills, they appear to be only moderately effective in improving patients'

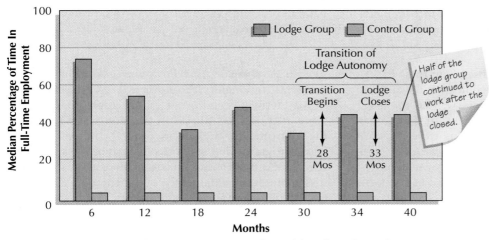

Figure 9.14   Social Learning Program for Schizophrenic Patients

Fairweather's hospital and lodge program for reducing symptoms and promoting appropriate skills and behaviors in schizophrenic patients was based on social learning principles, such as rewards and praise for appropriate behavior. As a result of the program, patients were much better able to maintain full-time employment than patients not in the program. The effects persisted for over three years. *Source:* Fairweather, Sanders, Maynard & Cressler (1969).

overall level of functioning and rate of relapse. Of course, social skills training programs are not a "cure" for schizophrenia because they do not eliminate the underlying defects, and many of the programs are too brief to have significant effects on patients' adjustment. However, they can be an important component of a treatment package that includes medication and possibly other services.

FAMILY   MATTERS

Families of Schizophrenics Need Help, Too

Families and patients alike have a difficult time with schizophrenia. Sometimes researchers and clinicians have paid so much attention to schizophrenic patients that they have ignored the concerns of family members.

I am sick to death of so-called mental health experts acting like I caused my son's schizophrenia! I have suffered from guilt and shame for years, worrying that something that I did or didn't do as a mother caused this wonderful boy to become so crazy. By now, if I act angry and impatient with him, it's because he has ruined our family's lives. We couldn't find any hospital that would keep him for long, and since he had no place to go he'd always come back home. His brother and sister were afraid to bring their friends over, and I long since gave up my own

social life. If we had anyone over to the house, we never knew if he'd come in with his pants down, or smell unwashed from three weeks without a bath — or would run up to our guests and say something really off the wall. Psychiatrists gave us no help at all.

We're at our wits' end. When she's at home with us, we have no privacy — she screams at her voices at all hours of the day and night, she took the lock off the door when we tried to find peace and quiet in the study. When we put her in the hospital, she's out in a few days. We tried to get her her own apartment, but she ends up on the streets poking through trash cans. My husband thinks she could control herself better if she really tried, and we have big fights about that. I believe she can't help it, but then again, there are times when I know she would do better if she took her medicines, but a lot of the time she refuses.

My brother caused living hell at home. He'd pick up a knife and chase one of us — or threaten to stab himself. A couple of times he ended up in jail because he'd run down the street naked, or attack someone because he thought his voices were warning him. My mother nearly had a breakdown herself, she was so worried and upset about him all the time, never knowing when we'd get a call from the police — or worse. There would be times when he was very reasonable and coherent — just like I remember him in high school, but just about the time we thought things would be okay, he'd flip out again. He's my own brother, and I love him and feel terribly sorry for him — but he robbed me of my family life.

These examples of families discussing their experiences with a schizophrenic relative come from the authors' files and from composites of letters written to "Dear Abby" (Group for the Advancement of Psychiatry, 1986). The common and overwhelming experiences of many families are years of anger and frustration compounded by blaming attitudes of ill-informed others, inadequate mental health care, and confusion about the disorder itself. And as we note in the discussion of research on expressed emotion, families that express their stress and frustration by being critical of patients may actually contribute to patients' increased risk for relapse when they come home from the hospital. What can alleviate this terrible vicious cycle?

Three strategies for assisting families and their schizophrenic members have become more visible in recent years. First, there has been increased lobbying and social activism by families to gain support for better public facilities, increase research funding, and improve the awareness of mental health professionals that patients are not merely helpless victims of bad mothering. Successful organizations (such as the National Alliance for the Mentally Ill) have grown into national networks and, as we note in Chapter 18, have been achieving some of their goals at both the national and community levels. Second, support groups that offer information, training in coping skills, and the opportunity to meet other families bearing similar burdens can be extremely helpful. Third, interventions are increasingly being developed and tested that specifically address communication and relations between family members and the schizophrenic

patients. Such interventions may be a crucial element of long-term treatment, as we discuss next.

Family Psychoeducation Programs With the onset of the deinstitutionalization movement and the reduction in long-term hospitalization of schizophrenic patients, more attention has turned to the family and its role in the adjustment of the patient. Several studies have evaluated programs that teach family members how to have realistic expectations of schizophrenic patients and how to communicate and interact with them more effectively. Such programs not only significantly reduce the likelihood of relapse in schizophrenic patients, but also improve the family environment (reviewed in Halford & Hayes, 1991).

In one study, for instance, Gerald Hogarty and his colleagues (1986) administered a family **psychoeducation** treatment (a combination of information about the disorder and psychological strategies for helping to deal with it), a social skills treatment, or a combination of both to a large number of schizophrenics treated with medication. They compared the outcomes for patients receiving these treatments with those for patients receiving only medication. The family psychoeducation treatment included such elements as a *survival skills workshop,* which provided information about schizophrenia, offered specific ideas for managing the patient's difficult behavior, and taught skills for improving communication. Families were also taught to increase their tolerance for mildly dysfunctional behaviors and, as noted, to have realistic expectations of the schizophrenic person. Thus, families received information, support, and encouragement to become allies in the treatment process. The results of this study indicated that, after

Figure 9.15 Family Psychoeducation Treatments
In this study, families of schizophrenic patients participated in psychoeducation treatments emphasizing effective coping and illness management. In the Multiple Family Group (MFG) treatment condition, groups of six families met regularly with counselors for two years; in the Single Family (SF) treatment condition, families met individually with a counselor for the same period. Patients whose families participated in the MFG treatment had fewer schizophrenic relapses, fewer symptoms, better employment records, and lower levels of medication. All patients were maintained on medication during the study, but staying on the medication improved outcomes very little beyond the effects of the family psychoeducation treatments. *Source:* Adapted from McFarlane et al. (1995, Table 2).

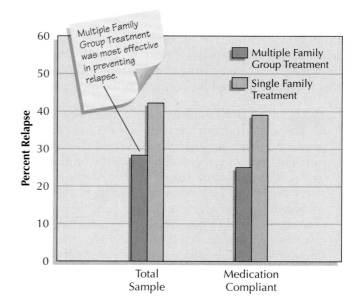

one year, 40 percent of the medication-only group had relapsed, compared to only 20 percent of the two psychological-treatment groups and *none* of those receiving the combined family psychoeducation–social skills treatment. At a two-year follow-up, the psychosocial treatments were still observed to be more effective than the medication-alone treatment (Hogarty et al., 1991). Recently McFarlane and associates (1995) used similar techniques to improve families' management of their relatives' illness, demonstrating that families who met together as a group had better patient outcomes than families who met individually with a counselor. As Figure 9.15 indicates, families appeared to derive additional support for themselves by meeting in groups, leading to improved relationships between themselves and the patients — and thus to better patient functioning.

Of course, not all schizophrenic patients have families to return to, or families who will support them. What happens to such patients? Unfortunately, as we explore in Chapter 18, community-based programs and assistance are in short supply, and greatly in need of increased funding and innovation.

What Lies Ahead?

Armed with new tools for brain imaging, genetic study, neuropsychological assessment, and increased knowledge of neurological functioning and development, research in the coming decade will doubtless move us closer to resolving some of the basic biological issues that have always been raised about schizophrenia. Other questions will also be addressed: Have the defining criteria for the disorder been established? Or is what we call schizophrenia in fact different disorders with different causes?

The years ahead will likely see the emergence of integrated diathesis-stress models of schizophrenia, including both biological and psychological factors. A clearer understanding of one set of factors can illuminate the other. For example, if we are able to understand exactly what role genetics and other neurobiological factors play, then we can evaluate more precisely the contributions of psychological factors such as family adversity and stressful events to both the origin and course of the disorder.

We can also look forward to exciting developments in the treatment of schizophrenia. In only the past few years, new antipsychotic medications with different modes of action, side effects, and outcomes have offered hope to many patients formerly unresponsive to traditional neuroleptics — and even newer drugs are on the way. Understanding the mechanisms of such drugs will in turn add to our knowledge of schizophrenia. In addition, there has been an upsurge in the systematic study of family and psychosocial treatments that improve the course of schizophrenia. We can look forward to the development of further options in this area, too. Ultimately, effective treatment of the massive public health problem of schizophrenia requires public commitment of funds and services — an important topic that we discuss more fully in Chapter 18.

KEY TERMS

anhedonia (265)
catatonic schizophrenia (265)
communication deviance (CD) (282)
concordance (273)
deficit symptoms (267)
delusions (262)
diathesis-stress approach (284)

disorganized schizophrenia (267)
dopamine (280)
expressed emotion (EE) (282)
flat affect (264)
hallucinations (263)
hypofrontality (276)
negative symptoms (267)
neurodevelopmental abnormalities (278)

neuroleptic (286)
paranoid schizophrenia (266)
phenothiazines (285)
positive symptoms (267)
premorbid adjustment (272)
psychoeducation (292)
psychosis (260)
residual schizophrenia (267)
schizophrenia (260)

schizophrenogenic mother (281)
tardive dyskinesia (TD) (287)
thought broadcasting (262)
thought insertion (262)
undifferentiated schizophrenia (267)

SUMMARY

Features of Schizophrenia

A specific type of *psychosis, schizophrenia* is a general term for disorders that involve major loss of contact with reality. Debate continues as to the defining features of schizophrenia because its characteristics can vary from one person to another. Indeed, there may be different forms of schizophrenia. Essential features include disorganization of thought and language as well as perceptual, affective, and behavioral disturbances. *Delusions* are a form of thought disorder involving beliefs that are not based on consensual reality. Their content may take the form of delusions of grandeur, persecution delusions, reference delusions, *thought insertion, thought broadcasting,* or nihilistic delusions. A schizophrenic person may also have perceptual distortions involving *hallucinations,* or sensory experiences that other people do not have. Auditory, visual, tactile, taste, and somatic hallucinations have been reported.

Schizophrenia commonly involves *flat affect* (lack of emotionality) or affect disturbance (in which the individual displays emotions that are inappropriate to the situation). Behaviors and movements may be bizarre and inappropriate. Many schizophrenics experience *anhedonia*, lack of motivation, lack of self-initiated behavior, and withdrawal from social contacts.

Diagnostic subtypes of schizophrenia include *catatonic schizophrenia* (bizarre movements, immobility), *paranoid schizophrenia* (delusions of persecution, ideas of reference), and *disorganized schizophrenia* (bizarre, disorganized, inappropriate affect). A patient whose schizophrenia shows characteristics of several subtypes has *undifferentiated schizophrenia*. And a patient who lacks hallucinations, delusions, or highly disorganized thoughts or behaviors but has some of the additional features of the disorder (such as lack of motivation, flat affect, or odd language) has *residual schizophrenia.*

Researchers make a distinction between the *positive symptoms* and the *negative,* or *deficit, symptoms* of schizophrenia. Positive-symptom schizophrenia involves bizarre and psychotic symptoms such as hallucinations and delusions, and grossly disorganized thought and affect. Negative-symptom schizophrenia refers to the absence of such behaviors, as well as to poverty of speech and lack of interest, motivation, initiative, and social interaction. These two forms of schizophrenia may be different in their origins and their outcomes; patients with negative-symptom schizophrenia display a worse course in terms of chronically impaired functioning.

Schizophrenia affects about 1 percent of the populations of most cultures. The course of the disorder varies from person to person. Some individuals may function relatively well between episodes, especially if their *premorbid adjustment* was good; but most individuals experience lifelong patterns of relapse and impaired functioning, especially if they had an onset in adolescence and generally poor premorbid adjustment before their schizophrenic symptoms first appeared. More women than men appear to have good outcomes and less severe courses of the disorder.

Causes of Schizophrenia

Linkage, family, twin, adoption, high-risk, and marker studies have supported the idea of genetic transmission. However, there is no evidence of a single major schizophrenia gene, and the lack of *concordance* between identical twins strongly suggests that nongenetic factors also are crucial to the development of schizophrenia. Thus, although some aspects of some forms of schizophrenia appear to be genetically transmitted, research has not established what is transmitted and whether genetic predisposition is a requisite for the development of schizophrenia.

Considerable evidence from neuropsychological studies, brain imaging, and autopsies has suggested the presence of defects in the brains of schizophrenics. Recent research has found enlarged ventricles and abnormalities in the frontal cortex (including *hypofrontality*) and subcortical areas of the limbic system in some schizophrenic patients. There is considerable speculation about what might cause such abnormalities. One hypothesis is that *neurodevelopmental abnormalities* caused by toxins, viral exposure, birth injury, or other environmental stressors prevent the brain from growing normally. The tendency for abnormal development may also be genetic.

Another biological arena of investigation concerns defects in the *dopamine* neurotransmitter system. The effectiveness of drugs that block certain dopamine receptors contributed to the belief that excess dopamine was a causal factor in schizophrenia. Although the original model of excess dopamine proved too simplistic, dopamine processes are thought to be involved in some forms of the disorder.

Most investigators have abandoned theories that implicate intrapsychic conflict, *schizophrenogenic mothers,* or family dysfunction as the origin of the disorder. Family process theories have effectively focused on communication patterns, however, and research has found evidence of *communication deviance (CD)* in the families of schizophrenics or preschizophrenics. Communication deviance appears to indicate mild, subclinical forms of psychosis in family members, suggesting a genetic rather than psychological cause of schizophrenia in the children. Family dysfunction has also been related to schizophrenia in studies of *expressed emotion (EE)*. In particular, critical attitudes and emotional overinvolvement by family members predict faster relapse of patients after hospital release. Few researchers argue that such attitudes originally caused schizophrenia, but studies suggest that stressful conditions in the family created by expressed emotion may make the prognosis worse. Other studies have confirmed that stressors have a negative impact on the course of schizophrenia.

Future models of schizophrenia will doubtless attempt to combine genetic-constitutional vulnerabilities with psychological and environmental stressors. The *diathesis-stress approach* to schizophrenia fits the existing data most clearly inasmuch as genetic contributions are seemingly insufficient to cause schizophrenia without the occurrence of additional factors.

Treatments for Schizophrenia

Medications for treating schizophrenia include *phenothiazines,* which have been available only since the middle of this century, and *neuroleptics* (antipsychotic drugs), which have revolutionized treatment and have contributed to the deinstitutionalization of the chronically mentally ill. Antipsychotic medications are particularly helpful in reducing acute, positive symptoms of schizophrenia, but have less impact on negative symptoms. Patients typically need to remain on medications to avoid relapses. Unfortunately, neuroleptics have major side effects including neurological problems such as irreversible *tardive dyskinesia (TD)*. New chemical compounds such as clozapine help schizophrenic patients who are unresponsive to traditional antipsychotics but do not appear to cause tardive dyskinesia.

Many argue that medications alone are not enough — especially for treating the residual or negative symptoms of schizophrenia. Behaviorally based programs in hospitals such as token economies have demonstrated that patients can be taught to improve their self-care and interpersonal behaviors and to acquire work skills, leading to better and longer functioning outside the hospital. Such programs also work to alter social skill deficits, and new cognitive interventions help patients become more realistic in their thinking and improve the skills involving attention, thinking, and learning that are impaired in schizophrenia.

Because family members play a prominent role in patient care after hospitalization, recently developed treatments involving family *psychoeducation* procedures help families cope with their highly stressful situations, learn realistic expectations about schizophrenia, and facilitate patients' improvement. They also improve communication between families and patients by reducing EE and teaching problem-solving skills. Controlled studies of family-based treatments show that they are more effective than medication alone in improving patient functioning and reducing relapses.

Consider the following. . .

Suppose that you are engaged to be married to someone who is the fraternal twin of a schizophrenic patient. Your fiancé does not have schizophrenia and seems to be quite well-adjusted. However, the two of you are wondering what the genetic implications might be in terms of whether your children might be at elevated risk for schizophrenia. Based on what you now know about schizophrenia, what is the magnitude of the genetic risk? What other factors might influence whether or not your children develop schizophrenia? What further scientific developments do you hope to see that would help you weigh the pros and cons of having children with this person if you are concerned about the risk for schizophrenia?

Suppose that you run a managed-care program for the seriously mentally ill, and the goal of this program is to provide the best possible service while containing costs. You are aware that medication for schizophrenia is relatively cheap, but what would you say are the drawbacks of just giving pills? Also, based on what you now know about reducing relapses and keeping people out of (costly) hospitals, what kinds of treatment programs would you try to develop?

CHAPTER 10

Psychophysiological Disorders and Behavioral Medicine

Those among us...

■ Louise, a college senior and a close friend of yours, has been reasonably successful in school. However, she changed her major last year and must now take four very challenging prerequisite courses that she had bypassed. A few days ago Louise's longtime boyfriend broke up with her. At present, she feels sick to her stomach. Earlier today, she broke a shoelace and started to cry.

■ Your friend's father, Mr. Siegel, was loud and sarcastic, and interrupted others when they spoke. He preached that "people are schemers, out to get all they can." He was said to be a "big-time" lawyer and was also involved in million-dollar real estate deals. Always working, he claimed to thrive on the competition of "the hunt" and "the deal," as he called them. At age fifty-three, Mr. Siegel died of a heart attack.

■ Three times a week your Aunt Evelyn receives chemotherapy for her cancer. Evelyn tells you she finds comfort in knowing that others are in a situation similar to hers. Nevertheless, she has been depressed, and psychologists, too, are working with her. Your uncle explains that their goal is not only to treat the cancer but also to foster her optimal adjustment to living with it.

■ Your brother David is happily married at age twenty-eight. A physically active, self-employed designer, he dislikes being "pushed" into creative productivity. He is able to afford a housekeeper and gardener, but his life seems hectic and demanding nevertheless. Several times a week, David has a painful, throbbing headache for which he takes an over-the-counter medicine. At such times he must also put his work aside to lie down for about an hour.

Can changes in a person's life — even those that might be considered only small hassles — contribute to illness?

Can an individual's personality and lifestyle put him or her at risk for a heart attack?

How might psychological programs affect individuals who are faced with a serious, life-threatening illness?

For those who experience frequent headaches, are there steps other than medication that they might take for relief?

As we think about the people just described, we might also ask whether they have psychological disorders or medical problems. In fact, the question is misleading. Today, medical problems are recognized as disturbances involving biological, psychological, and even social factors (Engel, 1977). Each of these individuals has a **psychophysiological disorder** — a medical condition that is influenced by psychological processes. Until recently, a select group of disorders were referred to as **psychosomatic,** suggesting that these specific bodily diseases had psychological origins. Although this term has been excluded from the current diagnostic system, there is growing acceptance of the broad role that psychological factors play in a wide range of physical illnesses.

Although psychological factors are involved in the physical distress and complaint associated with psychophysiological disorders, these illnesses are neither imaginary nor solely the result of emotional problems. In fact, psychophysiological disorders are conditions in which tissue damage has occurred and psychological factors are believed to play a role in the onset or exacerbation of this damage — as with coronary heart disease. In contrast, somatoform disorders (see Chapter 7) involve psychological factors that are presumed to cause a physical symptom or complaint in the absence of actual tissue damage.

Years ago, the DSM listed specific organs that could be affected by psychological problems. Now, DSM-IV recognizes that many, if not all, physical disorders can be influenced by psychological processes. How? In this chapter we consider basic models of the relationship between psychological processes and physical health. We also consider a concept central to the current understanding of psychophysiologic disorders — stress. Finally, we look at several specific diseases, including coronary heart disease, hypertension, and cancer. In particular, we examine how psychological processes can contribute to and exacerbate these illnesses and how psychological interventions can be used to help treat them.

MIND, BODY, AND STRESS

At the core of all approaches to psychophysiological disorders are notions about how the mind and body are related. Are they separate, distinct entities, or can the mind influence the body? In Chapter 1 we described some of the ways people have answered this question during different historical times and in different cultures. In the present section we focus on how Western medicine and psychology have described the relationship between the mind and body in health and illness during modern times.

Contemporary Psychophysiological Models

Modern Western medicine developed from the fundamental premise that the mind and body are separate. Yet even during the earliest years of modern medicine, many physicians had recognized the influence of the mind on the body. John Hunter (1729–1793), for example, was an important figure in early cardiology. He also apparently suffered from coronary heart disease and a bad temper. In commenting on the relationship between his

Astrological breakdown of body parts. Modern science has replaced astrological charts in describing the human body.

emotional responses and potentially life-threatening episodes of angina (chest pain from heart disease), he proclaimed, "My life is at the mercy of any rascal who chooses to put me in a passion." The observation turned out to be prophetic. After a heated argument at a faculty meeting at the Royal College of Physicians in Scotland, Hunter left and, according to cardiologist Sir William Osler, "in silent rage in the next room gave a deep groan and fell down dead" (cited in DeBakey & Gotto, 1977).

Much later, during the 1940s and 1950s, a psychoanalytic approach to psychosomatic illness gained in popularity. Franz Alexander (1950) and Florence Dunbar (1943) suggested that specific unconscious conflicts caused specific psychophysiological disorders (see Table 10.1). For example, they hypothesized that patients suffering from essential hypertension (high blood pressure) were suffering from repressed anger, which in turn resulted from an early neurotic conflict between the desire to display aggressive urges and intense anxiety about the consequences of doing so. As we see in our discussion of hypertension, there is a grain of truth to this assertion. But like many areas of abnormal psychology, the analysis of psychophysiological disorders has moved away from this early psychoanalytic model.

By the 1970s, medical and mental health professionals had recognized the importance of nonphysiological behavioral factors in health and illness, and behavioral medicine was born. **Behavioral medicine** is an interdisciplinary field concerned with the integration of behavioral and biomedical science relevant to health and illness, as well as with the application of this knowledge for prevention, diagnosis, and treatment (Carmody & Matarazzo, 1991; Schwartz & Weiss, 1978). A related field, **health psychology,** is the aggregate of specific contributions of psychology to the promotion and maintenance of health, the prevention and treatment of illness, and an understanding of the cause and correlates of health and behavior. Health psychology grew as researchers traced the relationship between illness and behaviors such as exercise and discovered how to help people alter risky behaviors. We examine these efforts further in a later section of the chapter.

Support for both behavioral medicine and health psychology came in two forms. First, there was growing evidence that certain behaviors alter a person's risk of becoming ill. If people smoke, drink alcohol to excess, fail to exercise, or neglect to eat balanced meals, they are increasing their risk of developing serious illness. For example, smoking and alcohol use increase the likelihood of ulcers (Whitehead & Schuster, 1985), and smoking has repeatedly been associated with lung cancer. Second, researchers have uncovered tantalizing links between how people think and feel and their physical well-being. One example was provided by Louise at the beginning of the chapter: Stress — a state that is influenced by thoughts and feelings — can increase the body's susceptibility to disease (Maier & Landenslager, 1985). The question is, *How* are these two domains — psychology and physiology — linked?

At the heart of much current research and theory on this question stands the **psychophysiologic model,** which is outlined in Figure 10.1. It holds that the first step toward illness is the combination of excessive levels of environmental challenges, threats, or demands — stimuli called **stressors** — and individual characteristics such as ways of perceiving stressors and psychological resources for coping with them. Particular combinations, such as high levels of environmental stressors and poor psychological resources, result in excessively high levels of physiological arousal. If these physiological changes occur over long periods of time, they can produce or exacerbate physical illness.

A more interactive approach to psychophysiological disorder applies a diathesis-stress model (see Figure 10.2). According to this model, the diathesis is a preexisting physical vulnerability to an illness, and the combination of stress and constitutional vulnerability is a primary mechanism of psychophysiologic disorders. For

Table 10.1 Sample Hypotheses from the History of Psychosomatic Disorders

Disorder	Unconscious Conflict
Asthma	The person with asthma has conflict over a dependent attachment; thus, the asthma may be a suppressed cry for the mother. The persons may also feel unloved or ignored and want to influence other individuals.
Hypertension	The person has repressed anger and feels threatened with being harmed by an ever present danger. There is a personal conflict about the expression of aggression, and, as a result, he or she feels the need to be on guard and prepared to meet outside threats.
Migraine	The person feels driven, as if something must be accomplished or some goal must be reached. The person can't relent until after the required effort has been exerted.

Source: Graham, Kabler & Graham (1962).

Researchers once thought that psychophysiological disorders were caused by unconscious conflicts. Here are examples of disorders that were believed to be caused by a personality characteristic.

Figure 10.1 The Psychophysiologic Model

The psychophysiologic model illustrates the interaction of environmental, psychological, and physical domains in the production of illness. When a person with poor psychological resources for coping with stress encounters excessive environmental challenges, threats, or demands, the likelihood of illness is increased.

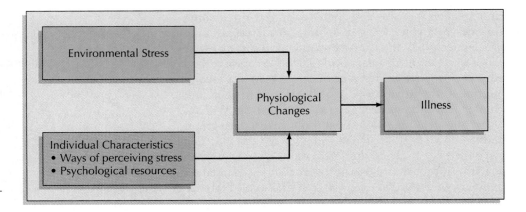

example, laboratory animals can be selectively bred to produce strains that are prone to develop hypertension, diabetes, or heart disease if exposed to stress. Indeed, vulnerable animals are less likely to develop the disease if they are not exposed to stress, and genetically invulnerable (or less vulnerable) strains do not show the same tendency to develop the psychophysiologic illness under conditions of stress.

What Is Stress?

Human beings suffer physically as a consequence of untoward stress. Indeed, stress is one of the central concepts in the psychology of physical illness. But what exactly is it?

In this text, consistent with psychologists in general, we use the word *stress* in at least three ways. First, stress can refer to an external event or situation that represents a demand or threat. According to this *stimulus definition,* a difficult midterm examination, a crowded dormitory room, and a daily commute congested with traffic are all common examples of stress. Second, according to the *response definition,* stress is an organism's reaction to the environmental threat or demand. Third, according to the *transactional definition,* stress lies neither in environmental stimuli nor in reactions to these stimuli but in a particular relationship between the individual and the situation (Lazarus & Folkman, 1984). Specifically, stress occurs in a person-situation interaction when an imbalance exists between situational demands and the individual's perceived ability to meet those demands — that is, when an important environmental demand is seen by the individual as taxing or exceeding his or her ability to meet the demand.

The environmental demand, or stressor, might take many forms, depending on the characteristics of the person. A small social gathering, which to most people would be an opportunity for pleasant interactions, can be an environmental demand for some young people.

Choosing a college major, selecting a mate, achieving a desired degree of success in a career path, or managing a home and family are other examples of environmental demands.

Notice that in the transactional view of stress, it is not the environment per se but the individual's appraisal that is central. A person first judges a situation's importance or threat ("What is at stake here?") and then assesses his ability to cope with the situation satisfactorily. For example, there is nothing inherently stressful about a final examination. Rather, stress exists when a person views the examination (1) as important and (2) as taxing or exceeding his ability to prepare for and complete the examination successfully. People who view an exam as unimportant are not likely to experience stress.

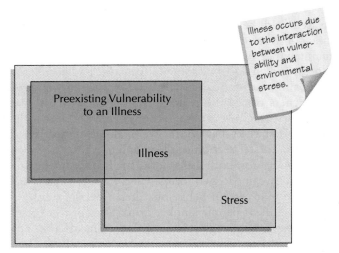

Illness occurs due to the interaction between vulnerability and environmental stress.

Figure 10.2 The Diathesis-Stress Model

The diathesis-stress model illustrates the interactiveness of preexisting physical and psychological domains in the production of illness. It represents the combination of stress and constitutional vulnerability that underlies psychophysiologic disorders.

As a result of the way a person appraises a stressor, that individual might take action to alter the situation or to change its effect. Alternatively, the person might just get angry or frustrated. Each of these **coping responses** — responses made to manage stress — has a different effect on the body's physiology and therefore on the person's health.

In sum, stress is a process that involves three components: (1) environmental events, or stressors; (2) appraisals of these events; and (3) coping responses. Each of these components may influence the body's health, and each is a potential target in efforts to prevent or treat psychophysiological disorders.

WHAT'S NORMAL?

Is Your Life Dangerously Stressful?

Psychologists have developed instruments to measure stress in people's lives. One of the best known is the Social Readjustment Rating Scale (SRRS), which measures the amount of "life change" an individual has experienced. Thomas Holmes and Richard Rahe (1967) developed this scale by asking people to examine a list of major **life changes** (such as getting married or divorced) and then asking them to rate each event in terms of how much stress or change it introduced into their lives. Each event on the SRRS is assigned a number of life change units (LCUs). LCUs indicate the magnitude of the event or the amount of adaptive effort it requires. A score consists of the total number of LCUs experienced in the preceding year, and, as Holmes and Rahe have reported, a high score is associated with a high likelihood of subsequent illness. Sample SRRS items and their stress values follow:

Death of a spouse	100
Jail term	63
Marriage	50
Pregnancy	40
Change in financial state	38
Change in living conditions	25
Trouble with boss	23
Change in schools	20
Change in social activities	18
Vacation	13

Notice that some of the events — such as marriage or vacation — are positive. We included them, however, because they are demanding of resources and require people to make adaptations and changes. Even positive experiences can produce stress.

Do the stressful events themselves promote unhealthy behaviors? Research has suggested that they do. For instance, negative life events lead to increased smoking among women and to increased smoking and alcohol use among men (Gottlieb & Green, 1984).

Over the years, the measurement of life events has been refined in numerous ways. For example, Horowitz and associates (1977) clarified the meaning of certain items on the original scale. Among other changes, the Horowitz Life Events Questionnaire (HLEQ) replaces "pregnancy" with "an unwanted pregnancy," and instead of specifying "the past year" it assigns different weights to events that occur at different times. In addition, the HLEQ associates more stress with events that occurred within the last month and less stress with events that happened between one and two years ago.

Because some items on the original scale were not relevant to special populations — for example, death of a spouse is unlikely in a college population — a specific scale was developed to study the role of life changes in the health status of university students (Crandall, Preisler & Aussprung, 1992). Preliminary reports suggest that the life events listed on this alternate scale are representative of the stressors facing college students. A few illustrative items follow: Have you experienced any of these events in the last week?

Went into an exam unprepared

Working while in school

Maintaining a long-distance relationship with a boyfriend or girlfriend

Parents getting a divorce

Had a class presentation

Recently, other researchers have focused directly on how the "little things" that go wrong, the accumulated **daily hassles,** can be the source of stress. In a "stress audit," the shoelace that breaks while you hurry to get dressed after oversleeping may indeed be important. Psychologists at the University of California at Berkeley (Delongis et al., 1982) constructed a scale to measure daily irritants such as unexpected company, traffic tickets, and being owed money. On a scale of 1 to 3, respondents rate the severity of each of the hassles. The score is the total of the ratings. For example, how many of the following hassles have you encountered in the past month, and how severe has each of those hassles been?

Too many responsibilities

Don't like current work duties

Friends or relatives too far away

Not enough money for clothing

Stress affects the body and the mind. Various experiences can be stressful, including a funeral, such as this service for victims of a disaster, and relocating one's home, such as this family on moving day. Under some circumstances, moving to a new house can have desirable qualities, but it is still a stressful experience. There is additional stress, of course, if the move was due to a financial setback or a change in employment that requires relocating to a new community.

Trouble making decisions

Unexpected company

Not getting enough sleep

Difficulties with friends

Like life events assessment, the measurement of daily hassles focuses on specific populations. College students, again, serve as an example. In a scale of daily hassles for college students (Kohn, Lafreniere & Gurevich, 1990), subjects respond by indicating how much the named experience "has been a part of your life over the past month." There are forty-nine items, each rated 1 to 4. Subjects whose scores are more than two standard deviations above the mean fall within the upper 2.5 percent of the population in terms of experienced daily hassles. This scale includes items such as the following:

Being taken for granted

Being disappointed by friends

Finding courses too demanding

Not enough leisure time

Ethnic or racial conflict

Lack of privacy

Clearly, there is both widespread interest in and a variety of assessments of a person's experience with events and hassles that can produce stress. A majority of studies provide support for a relationship between stress and physical health. However, the literature contains conflicting results with regard to whether life events or daily hassles are the better predictor of stress (e.g.,

Kanner, Coyne, Schaefer & Lazarus, 1981). In any event, both life changes and daily hassles are a part of normal existence. When kept to a minimum and met with adaptive coping, neither alone will cause serious illness.

Moreover, as the interactional approach emphasizes, the most important factor in understanding stress is understanding the process of cognitive appraisal: Not every event is stressful. Most events lead to normal responses unless they are misappraised in terms of the demanding nature of the environment, the availability of coping skills, or both.

Physiological Arousal and Stress

The body responds to a perceived stressor by preparing for action. More specifically, the area of the brain known as the hypothalamus stimulates the body's organs to increased levels of physiological arousal by sending signals along two pathways.

Along one pathway, the hypothalamus activates the part of the autonomic nervous system known as the *sympathetic nervous system*. The sympathetic nervous system is connected to a wide range of organs, and it stimulates these organs to produce what Cannon (1929) first described as the **fight-or-flight-response**. In particular, stimulation by the sympathetic nervous system affects the adrenal glands, resulting in the secretion of hormones that increase the heart rate as well as the force with which the heart contracts, so that a greater volume of blood is pumped each minute. Blood vessels in the skin and digestive organs constrict, whereas blood vessels in the major muscles may dilate. As a result of this increased and redirected blood flow, a higher level of oxygen is supplied to major muscles, thereby meeting the increased oxygen demand associated with physical action. Meanwhile, glucose is released from the liver, creating fuel to meet increased energy needs.

The sympathetic nervous system also stimulates the medulla (inner part) of the adrenal glands to secrete epinephrine (adrenaline) and norepinephrine (noradrenaline) into the bloodstream. These hormones have widespread effects. They enhance the responses produced by direct stimulation of the sympathetic system, such as increased heart rate, and they elicit preparatory responses in tissues not directly connected to sympathetic nervous system fibers (see Figure 10.3).

The second pathway involves the hypothalamic-pituitary-adrenocortical (HPA) axis, which we describe in Chapter 8. The hypothalamus stimulates the pituitary gland at the base of the brain to release corticotropin. In turn, corticotropin causes the cortex of the adrenal gland to release into the bloodstream another set of hormones — the corticosteroids (see Figure 10.4). These hormones have a variety of influences, including mobilization of energy. They also decrease the body's normal inflammation response to injury, probably because such inflammation would interfere with the mobility needed to "fight or flee."

The pituitary gland releases endorphins in addition to corticotropin (Asterita, 1985). Recall that endorphins

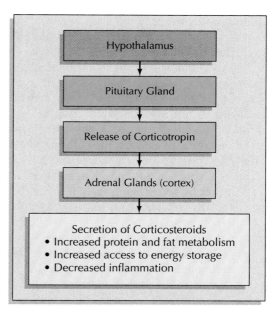

Figure 10.4   Physiology of the Fight-or-Flight Response: Involvement of the HPA Axis

When the body perceives stress, the hypothalamus stimulates not only the sympathetic nervous system but also the pituitary gland, which releases corticotropin to the adrenal glands. This process produces a variety of results that enable the body to fight or flee, including the mobilization of energy.

are morphine-like substances that have calming, analgesic effects. The adaptive value of analgesic effects during the fight-or-flight response is obvious; however, endorphins have also been implicated in some of the negative health effects of stress.

How could this marshaling of the body's forces to face the challenge of a stressor be harmful? Normally, it's not. As we discuss in Chapter 2, a second branch of the autonomic system, the *parasympathetic nervous system*, calms the arousal associated with the sympathetic system. According to Hans Selye (1956), the body undergoes three stages of physiological reactions in response to stress. These stages make up the **general adaptation syndrome (GAS)**.

The first stage of the GAS is the fight-or-flight response, which Selye called the *alarm reaction;* it rapidly prepares the body to meet a threat or demand. If the threatening stimulus persists, the organism enters the second phase — *resistance.* A different set of physiological changes serves to maintain and enhance the responses mobilized in the alarm phase. If the stressful stimulus persists further, the organism enters the third and final phase of *exhaustion.* In this phase the physiological resources used to contend with the environmental threat or demand are depleted, and the organism may show signs of physical deterioration or illness.

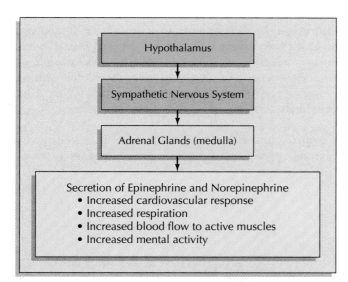

Figure 10.3   Physiology of the Fight-or-Flight Response: Involvement of the Sympathetic Nervous System

When the body perceives stress, the hypothalamus activates the sympathetic nervous system, which stimulates various organs associated with physical action — hence the term *fight-or-flight response.*

Another model for how the body reacts, the disregulation model, was proposed by Schwartz (1978, 1984). Based on the known presence of feedback systems within living organisms, and on the assumption that organisms behave in optimally self-regulated ways, the **disregulation model** holds that when proper feedback is disrupted and a corrective action to return to normal functioning does not occur, physical dysfunction may be the outcome. In essence, the culprit is the organism's failure to respond to a maladaptive physiological state. Thus, according to the disregulation model, stress is best met by recognizing the cues that the body provides naturally and reacting to them in a healthy way.

Stress certainly does affect the body as well as the mind. Likewise, bodily reactions and psychological forces can attenuate unwanted stress effects. In this context, it is interesting to note that different people display different reactions to what appears to be similar stress. Consider the following examples of employees who were laid off from their jobs.

Sara went home and sat by herself, angered by the abrupt treatment she had received. She began to drink alcohol, eventually isolating herself from her former co-workers and becoming despondent.

Sharon organized her co-workers and prepared a telephone chain. Then she contacted the employer and arranged a meeting. As job-related information became known, it could be conveyed through the communication system already in place.

Suzanne decided to get another job. Having reasoned that jobs would be increasingly rare as a result of the recent layoffs, she plotted how she could beat the others to the punch. Her scheme included a plan to interfere with the applications of her former co-workers.

Moderators of the Stress Response

Although psychologists can describe the general way in which the human body responds to stress, they are a very long way from being able to say exactly how any one individual will react to a particular stressor. Different kinds of stressors produce different responses, and different people interpret stressors in different ways at different times. Additionally, the magnitude, pattern, and effects of stress responses vary from person to person. In short, as Figure 10.5 shows, there are many moderators between the appearance of a stressor and the physiological response to it.

Coping Response One important influence on the physiological response to a stressor is the precise demands of the stressor itself. Some situations allow for **active coping,** whereby the individual is able to exert an effort to escape, avoid, or otherwise minimize exposure to the stressor (Obrist, 1981). In other situations, by contrast, only **passive coping** is possible: The individual, unable to minimize exposure to the stressor, simply tolerates it. In general, active coping produces greater cardiac arousal than passive coping (Contrada et al., 1982; Obrist, 1981). Thus, what the individual attempts to do when confronted with stressors is an important determinant of short-term physiological changes.

Another way of looking at the response to a stressor is to distinguish between problem-focused and response-focused coping. **Problem-focused coping** involves attempts to escape, avoid, or control the threatening event itself, whereas **response-focused coping** involves efforts to minimize the effects of the event. Studying for an exam is an example of problem-focused coping; exercising to reduce anticipatory anxiety is an example of response-focused coping. In either case, the coping behavior can be adaptive or maladaptive. Figure 10.6 provides additional examples of these responses.

Cognitive and Emotional Responses In actuality, the relation of coping to physiological responses is much

Figure 10.5 Moderators of the Stress Response

Responses to stress are not always the same. Different kinds of stressors produce different responses, and different people interpret stressors in different ways. Indeed, there are many possible moderators between the appearance of a stressor and the physiological response to it.

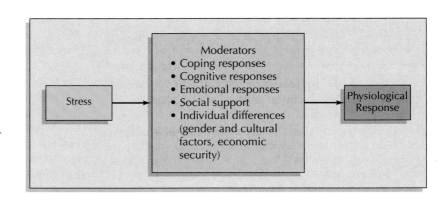

	Adaptive Response	Maladaptive Response
Problem-Focused Coping	Interpersonal Assertiveness	Avoidance or Procrastination
Response-Focused Coping	Meditation Aerobic Exercise	Excessive Drinking Smoking

(left axis label: Type of Coping)

Figure 10.6 Methods of Coping
Effective coping with the inevitable stresses of life is important. Coping behavior can focus either on the threatening event itself or on the effects of the event. Both kinds of coping behavior can be adaptive or maladaptive.

more complex than just active versus passive coping. Indeed, cognitive factors, such as appraisal, and emotional factors, such as emotion-focused coping, play an integral role (Lazarus & Folkman, 1984).

An individual's cognitive processing or appraisal of an event can influence its stressfulness. An event that is unexpected or unpredictable, for example, may be particularly stressful because the individual has no chance to cognitively prepare for it. Perceived control is another factor (Kanner & Feldman, 1991). A negative event that is controllable might be less stressful than one that is uncontrollable. Consider the example of a change in living arrangements. A relocation that results from personal choice is less stressful than one over which an individual has no control. Here, too, the person's cognitive processing plays an important role. If an uncontrollable event is mistakenly seen as something the person could have controlled, the event is likely to be much more stress-provoking.

Emotional reactions to a stressor also influence the body's response. In the case of **emotion-focused coping**, for example, effort is directed toward regulating the emotional consequences of the stressful event. Let's say an unfair situation at school or work makes you feel angry, and your coping is directed toward reducing the anger. When the anger is reduced, the body is calmed.

Social Support A person's social network appears to influence the effects of stressors as well. This interesting phenomenon has been observed literally at birth. Sosa and associates (1980) randomly assigned expectant mothers to undergo labor and delivery either with or without the presence of a supportive female companion. The expectant mothers did not previously know the companion. The role of the supportive companion was not to assist in the birth but simply to provide contact, reassurance, and comfort. As it turned out, mothers paired with a supportive companion experienced fewer

than one-half as many complications (such as Caesarian section, fetal distress, use of forceps) as mothers without support. Even when just the uncomplicated births in each group were examined, the researchers found a large difference in the length of time required for labor and delivery: slightly more than nineteen hours for unsupported women as compared to fewer than ten hours for women randomly assigned to a supportive companion. This provocative study has been replicated (Gjerdingen, Froberg & Fontaine, 1991), and a review of the literature has reached a consistent conclusion — that emotional, tangible, and informational support is positively related to mothers' mental and physical health around the time of childbirth (Gjerdingen, Froberg & Fontaine, 1991).

At the other end of the life span, the lack of close social ties is associated with an increased risk of early death (House, Landis & Umberson, 1988). Conversely, the presence of social support is related to avoidance of health-damaging behavior (Broman, 1993). Specifically, having a spouse or friend and being a member of an organization are related to healthy behavior (such as a lower likelihood of smoking or drinking heavily), whereas insufficient social contact (along with low

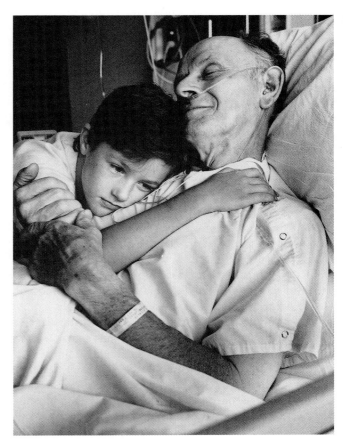

This man, in his hospital bed, receives a warm hug from a child. Stress, and its unwanted effects, can be reduced by the provision of social support.

income) is a strong predictor of death from heart disease (Williams et al., 1992). There is also some evidence that persons who believe they can draw on others during periods of stress are less likely to experience subsequent illness (Cohen & Wills, 1985). Finally, using a longitudinal design to study surgery patients, King and associates (1993) reported that when social support was provided consistently over the period from preoperation to one year after the operation, it was significantly related to positive emotional and functional outcomes. Thus, social support may provide a "buffer" or protection against the health-damaging effects of stress.

Is the determining factor the presence of a spouse or significant other — or the presence of an emotionally supportive person? (Kulik & Mahler, 1993). Indeed, the presence of an ornery and irascible spouse may well exacerbate existing problems and be an additional source of stress. The personality of the support provider thus influences whether the support itself is perceived and experienced as a source of stress. As truly supportive interpersonal relationships have a positive impact on health, we should not underestimate their healing value.

Individual Differences Are some people simply stress-prone (vulnerable) and others stress-resistant (invulnerable)? In fact, certain enduring characteristics of individuals determine how they interpret stressors and the nature and extent of their physiological reactions to them.

Gender is one such characteristic. In response to stressors such as reaction-time tasks or mental arithmetic problems, men show larger increases than women in blood pressure, various stress hormones, and blood lipids (fats) (Frankenhaeuser, Dunne & Lundberg, 1976; Stoney, Matthews, McDonald & Johnson, 1988). And in response to depressed mood, women are more likely to have a ruminative response style, which is associated with more severe and long-lasting periods of depression (Nolen-Hoeksema, Morrow & Fredrickson, 1993).

Furthermore, some individuals tend to be "blood pressure responders": Increases in blood pressure comprise their predominant autonomic stress responses. Others, in contrast, are "skin" or "stomach" responders. In short, individuals often display a pattern of physiological responses to stress that emphasizes a consistent autonomic reaction (Engel & Bickford, 1961). Many researchers in this area believe that characteristic autonomic responses, if pronounced, may represent a constitutional vulnerability or weakness, such that the individual is more likely to develop a psychophysiologic disorder in that particular organ system. In addition, there is evidence of genetic influences on human stress responses. For example, the magnitude of blood pressure responses to challenging mental tasks is more similar in monozygotic twins than in dizygotic twins

(Smith, Turner, Ford & Hunt, 1987). Why do some people develop ulcers in response to stress, whereas others develop hypertension and still others develop headaches? Accumulating evidence suggests a physical predisposition to certain types of psychophysiological disorders.

Procedures for Reducing Stress

Psychologists have discovered and developed many ways of helping people deal with and reduce stress. For example, regular aerobic exercise is associated with reductions in physiological responses to psychological stressors (Simon, 1991). Specific treatments, including outcome data, are described in more detail when we discuss individual psychophysiological disorders. For now, however, we provide an overview of interventions.

Relaxation training, meditation, and autogenic training are different names for similar approaches to reducing the physiological effects of stress. Through either progressive muscle relaxation (described in Chapter 6) or repetition of calming phrases while sitting quietly, individuals can learn to elicit a state of deep emotional and physical relaxation. Clearly, these methods reduce physiological arousal.

Another method of stress management is biofeedback, which detects changes in the biology of the person and, by means of visual and auditory signals, provides feedback to the person about those changes. Biofeedback has two main components. First, the person must learn to detect previously unfelt autonomic changes. Physiological responses are recorded with electronic monitors, and the level of physiological arousal is displayed through visual or auditory signals so that the individual learns to recognize changes in a particular physiological stress response (such as blood pressure and muscle tension). Second, the person learns to engage in activities that alter the response and reduce arousal.

Stress management may also employ the cognitive restructuring approach, which alters the way a person appraises threat. (Recall that the same technique is used to treat anxiety and depression.) Through visual imagery and other means, cognitive restructuring modifies the way events are perceived. It can also modify negative self-statements, thus providing a way of coping with and preventing the emotional and physiological impact of stress. Recent data suggest that cognitive training offers stress relief even to medical patients. African American adults with sickle cell disease who were taught cognitive coping strategies showed an increase in coping, a decrease in negative thinking, and an increase in pain endurance (Gil et al., 1996).

Finally, because stress is often associated with "taking on too much" or having "too hectic a schedule," stress management may include training in self-monitor-

"All work and no play" contributes to stress. Here, participants in a management training program play games to help prevent or reduce stress.

ing activities and scheduling as well as general procedures for time management. In practice, the majority of programs that teach stress management include more than one treatment strategy.

Deloris was driven and overwhelmed at work. She wanted to be a millionaire and believed that hard work was her path to success. Her desk was stacked with orders to fill, outstanding invoices, letters from customers, and a variety of memos and interoffice correspondence. Each morning she arrived at work early, thinking that "something had to be done" to beat out the other members of the sales staff. But rather than tending to the minor jobs that faced her, she saw the whole task as "too big," made coffee for the office staff, greeted other early-birds, and gossiped. She was not getting her work accomplished, and even considered quitting; but she needed the income and knew that she couldn't leave. She was also drinking more and more heavily, not getting enough sleep, and taking too many sick days from work. Her stress was overwhelming.

Treatment for Deloris included both relaxation training and cognitive restructuring. Her therapist used deep muscle relaxation during her sessions and prepared a take-home audiotape for her to listen to in the evenings. Having learned to relax, Deloris took the time to plan small steps that would get her back on track at work. She paid close attention to any requests for added responsibilities and declined to get involved in new enterprises. Equally important, Deloris knew she had to change the way she thought at work. No longer could she burden herself with overly competitive self-talk. In the past, when she saw

one of her associates on the phone, she assumed that this person was making a big sale and that the commission was "a whopper"; she also thought to herself that she was again falling behind. With her therapist's help, she realized that she had been misinterpreting the situation. In the end, she continued to strive for success, but not to the extreme that had plagued her previously. She adjusted the inordinate demands she had placed on herself and corrected her misperceptions of colleagues' activities.

Interventions designed to enhance problem-focused coping are also useful. For example, in cases where recurring interpersonal difficulties are a common source of stress, social skills or assertiveness training may be a useful addition to the overall stress-management treatment. But the question remains: If these techniques reduce stress, are they also effective in treating illnesses? We address this question in the following sections as we examine several specific illnesses.

CARDIOVASCULAR DISEASES

One hundred years ago, the major cause of death was infectious diseases. Today, cardiovascular disease is the leading cause of death in the United States, accounting for 40 percent of all deaths. Many of these deaths are considered premature, occurring well before the age of seventy-five. We discuss two cardiovascular diseases — coronary heart disease and essential hypertension.

Coronary Heart Disease

Each year, more than 500,000 Americans die from coronary heart disease, about one each minute. **Coronary heart disease (CHD)** is caused by decreased blood flow to the heart. The term encompasses three related conditions: angina pectoris, myocardial infarction, and sudden coronary death. Angina pectoris is severe chest pain caused by a temporary lack of oxygen to the heart. Myocardial infarction is the death of heart muscle due to sustained, severe lack of oxygen to the heart. The disease that causes CHD is **coronary atherosclerosis (CAD)**, in which the arteries carrying blood to the heart muscle are narrowed by fatty deposits in their walls. As a result, the supply of oxygen to heart muscle is reduced. Throughout the decades of young and middle adult life, CAD develops silently or asymptomatically. But late in the progression of the disease, blood flow to the heart is reduced enough to produce coronary heart disease.

Sudden coronary death is typically caused by a profound disturbance in the "beating" of the heart muscle. Rather than creating the smooth, wavelike contraction that effectively pumps blood, the heart muscle quivers chaotically. As a result, it is useless as a pump, and the life-sustaining circulation of oxygen in the blood ceases. Figure 10.7 shows the location of the coronary arteries, and Figure 10.8 illustrates the relationship between CAD and CHD.

CHD is most common among men, older age groups, and people with a history of the disease in their families. There are also ethnic differences: In the United States, Caucasians and blacks experience cardiovascular diseases at twice the frequency of Chinese Americans and Japanese Americans.

Smoking, high blood pressure, and the unwanted low-density lipoprotein (LDL) cholesterol are all risk factors for CHD, increasing an individual's chances of developing the disease. A growing body of evidence indicates that certain psychological factors can also be risk factors in that they influence the onset or course of CAD or affect the appearance of CHD after coronary atherosclerosis develops (Ader, Felton & Cohen, 1991; Manuck, Proietti, Rader & Polefrone, 1986). These psychological risk factors are widely accepted as important in CHD; even the most deleterious combinations of physical risk factors fail to account for more than 50 percent of new cases of CHD.

Stress and CHD   Some of the most compelling evidence concerning the role of psychological factors in CHD has come from research on stress among cynomolgus monkeys conducted by Kaplan and associates (1982, 1983) at Bowman Gray University. In captivity, as in the wild, these monkeys live in hierarchically arranged troops, each of which is typically headed by a large, dominant male. The investigators were able to determine any animal's place on the social ladder by observing patterns of aggressive and submissive behaviors.

To create a significantly stressful environment, the animals in the high-stress condition were periodically switched among troops. An average of once every two months, these animals faced a new set of group members, requiring the frequent establishment of dominance patterns. In contrast, animals in the low-stress condition remained in one troop during the twenty-one months of the experiment. According to the results, animals in the high-stress condition showed significantly greater thickening of the coronary artery wall than did those in the low-stress condition (Kaplan et al., 1983). In a similar experiment, the stress of unstable social conditions produced significantly higher levels of CAD only in dominant monkeys (Kaplan et al., 1982), perhaps because subordinate animals were relatively unaffected by the social stress.

Another study of animals suggested that stress can also produce the symptoms of CHD after CAD has

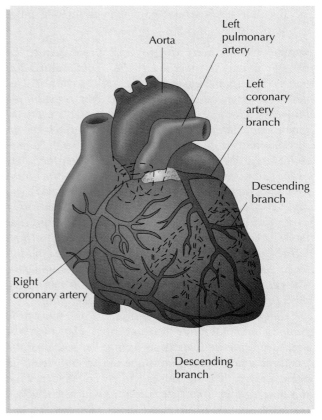

Figure 10.7   Coronary Circulation
The main coronary arteries descend from the aorta, then divide — like branches — into small distribution vessels. Stress influences human physiology, and increased likelihood and severity of heart disease are potential effects of stress.

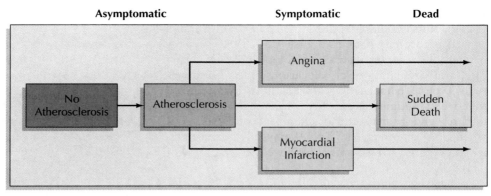

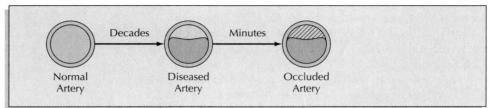

Figure 10.8 Coronary Artery Disease

Artery disease varies in terms of severity, symptoms, and potential risk of death. Psychological factors have been implicated in the process of coronary artery disease.

developed. The experimenters induced CAD in dogs by partially inflating a tiny "balloon" in a coronary artery; then they created an anger-like state. While the dog with CAD was eating, a second dog approached and threatened to compete for its food. Shortly after growling and baring their teeth, the dogs with CAD displayed a 35 percent reduction in blood flow to the heart muscle, and electrocardiogram (ECG) changes indicated ischemia — an insufficient supply of oxygen to the heart (Verrier, DeSilva & Lown, 1983).

In human beings, too, a relationship between stress and CHD has been demonstrated. For example, both increased occupational change and increased job responsibility are associated with the development of CHD (Karasek, Russell & Theorell, 1982; Theorell, Lind & Floderus, 1975). And in the year after the death of their spouses, widows and widowers are more likely to develop and die from CHD than are people who do not suffer such a loss (Parkers et al., 1969). Another study has indicated that psychological stress can trigger potentially dangerous changes in cardiac function among persons with CAD. When CAD patients engaged in a stressful discussion of their personal faults, the supply of oxygen to their hearts fell far short of the need for it — to about the same levels as when the patients performed physical exercise (Rozanski, Bairey, Krantz & Friedman, 1988).

Research ethics do not permit subjecting human beings to unhealthy levels of stress. Therefore, experimental research with animals plays an important role in the study of the causes of CAD. It is often through the study of animal responses to stress that we are able to learn about human psychophysiology. But the variety of

human personalities also influences the process, as research on the Type A personality has documented.

Personality and CHD: The Type A Pattern Perhaps the most famous stress-related CHD risk factor is the Type A behavior pattern. First proposed by Friedman and Rosenman (1959), the **Type A pattern** is characterized by hard-driving competitiveness, impatience, easily provoked hostility, overcommitment to work, and a loud, rapid speaking style. Type A persons may appear driven; they struggle to achieve more and more in less time and view themselves as competing with others. They lead overly scheduled and fast-paced lives, become bothered by others who are not as committed, and are often insensitive or intolerant of others. Mr. Siegel, the lawyer mentioned at the outset of this chapter, would qualify as a Type A. In contrast, the **Type B pattern** is characterized by the relative absence of these attributes. While stuck in morning rush-hour traffic on the way to work, for example, the Type A person is likely to grip the steering wheel, honk the horn, and angrily reflect on the intellectual shortcomings and family heritage of the drivers blocking the way. The Type B person, on the other hand, might sit back, relax, and select a station on the radio. Type A persons are twice as likely to develop CAD as their more relaxed counterparts. Although the number of studies is limited, current data suggest that Type A behavior is equally prevalent in African American and white populations (Sprafka et al., 1990).

Along with this difference in behavioral styles, Type A persons display greater *physiological reactivity* — a stronger or more frequent alarm (fight-or-flight) response — than Type B persons (Contrada et al., 1982).

Indeed, among children (Matthews & Jennings, 1984), young adults (Williams et al., 1992), and healthy adults as well as coronary patients (Corse et al., 1982), Type A persons show larger increases in blood pressure, heart rate, and circulating levels of various stress hormones than Type B persons. Researchers have hypothesized that over a lifetime this excessive physiological reactivity initiates and hastens the development of CAD. And when CAD is present, the Type A's physiological reactivity to potential stressors may produce the symptoms of CHD.

That such physiological differences could produce greater vulnerability to CHD is certainly plausible. In fact, by 1981, the American Heart Association was sufficiently impressed by the available evidence that it officially recognized Type A behavior as a risk factor for CHD (Cooper, Detre & Weiss, 1981). Type A individuals were believed to be about twice as likely to develop CHD as Type B persons. Since then, however, research has led to a more precise and complex portrayal of the relationship between Type A behavior and CHD (e.g., Ragland & Brand, 1988). Moreover, whereas the early research was conducted on men, contemporary research on women has suggested similar findings (Baker, Dearborn, Hastings & Hamberger, 1984; Powch & Houston, 1996).

Are all features of the Type A style equally likely to increase the risk of CHD? Although the overall evidence still supports the conclusion that Type A behavior is more likely to result in CHD than Type B behavior (Matthews, 1988), attention has shifted from the global Type A pattern to one of its specific components. For example, some scientific evidence has identified *hostility* (see Table 10.2) rather than competitiveness or job involvement as the most likely culprit (Siegman, 1994). When individual components of the Type A pattern were scored separately, ratings of hostility were reported to be the best individual predictor of subsequent CHD (Hecker, Chesney, Black & Frautschi, 1988). Indeed, among the several features of the Type A style, hostility has consistently emerged as the most strongly implicated risk factor for CHD (Dembroski & Costa, 1988; Miller et al., 1996). And like Type A behavior, hostility is associated with greater physiological reactivity, particularly in response to interpersonal stressors (Smith & Allred, 1989). For example, hostile individuals may contribute to a more stressful environment by creating more frequent, severe, and enduring difficulties in their relations with other people (Ravaja, Keltikangas-Jarvinen & Keskivaara, 1996).

Research on the association between Type A behavior and CHD has become more specific with regard to the nature of hostility, as well as more general in terms of the impact of a variety of negative emotional states. Research specific to hostility has suggested that cynical hostility is most associated with CHD. Cynical hostility

Table 10.2 The Cognitive Side of Hostility

The cognitive side of hostility consists of negative beliefs about and attitudes toward others, including cynicism, mistrust, and denigration.
Cynicism: the view that others are motivated by selfish concerns, and that one is in opposition to others.
Mistrust: the expectation that others will be provoking and harmful, and that they are likely sources of wrongdoing.
Denigration: devaluation of the worth and motives of others, and a desire to inflict harm or see others harmed.

Source: Smith (1994).

It may not seem surprising that hostility detracts from interpersonal relationships—but, apparently, going through life with a hostile mental attitude also diminishes one's own health. Consider what it is like to *think* in a hostile manner.

is characterized by resentment, suspiciousness, antagonism, frequent anger, and a distrust of others (Barefoot et al., 1989). Hostile cynics, according to Levine (1993), have a "mistrusting heart" and experience and express extreme levels of righteous indignation over others' incompetence. Moreover, among husbands involved in a discussion task with their wives, cynical hostility was associated with increased heart rate and, in some persons, higher systolic blood pressure (Smith & Brown, 1991).

Research has also become more specific with regard to gender. In several studies of the relationship between hostility and physiological response (e.g., Davidson & Hall, 1995; Powch & Houston, 1996), the results for men sometimes differed from those for women. For example, an index of hostility derived from a structured interview predicted resting blood pressure and hypertensive status in males and females, but in opposite directions (Davidson, Hall & MacGregor, 1996): Increased hostility predicted increased resting blood pressure in men, whereas increased hostility predicted decreased resting blood pressure in women. This research suggests that the nature of hostility varies across gender.

Acceptance of the hypothesis that CHD is caused by the Type A pattern, or hostility specifically, would be premature. Still a matter for research is the question of how extensively an underlying, perhaps genetic, predisposition contributes to Type A behavior. As part of their genetic makeup, Type A persons do have greater physiological reactivity and interact in the world with greater sympathetic and parasympathetic nervous system responsiveness. But the exact mechanism underlying the relationship between an individual's behavior and CHD remains uncertain. An important consideration for further research in this area is the role of negative emotional states — especially cynical hostility.

FAMILY MATTERS

Can Your Family Cause Type A Behavior?

Families can be both a source of interpersonal stress and a training ground for behavior — hence the question as to what role is played by family members in Type A behavior and coronary risk. Sparked by interest in this question, researchers have investigated "spouse effects," or the degree to which characteristics of the spouse influence Type A behavior. Because most Type A research has been conducted on men, studies of spouse effects have focused on the effects of wives on Type A men. Of course, Type A husbands might also contribute to coronary risk in Type A wives — an issue that future research needs to resolve. For now, however, we consider the former scenario.

One of the major studies in the Type A literature, the Western Collaborative Group Study (Rosenman et al.,

1975), was reexamined with an eye toward the role of the spouse (Carmelli, Swan & Rosenman, 1985). The findings indicated that the risk of CHD among Type A men was moderated by features of their wives. For example, Type A men married to women with thirteen or more years of education had a significantly greater risk of CHD than Type A men with less-educated wives. In addition, Type A men who were married to women who scored high on measures of activity level and interpersonal dominance were at significantly greater risk than Type A men married to less active and less dominant women. Perhaps, as Carmelli and associates suggested, highly educated, active, and dominant wives somehow threaten the self-esteem or sense of control needed by Type A husbands, with the result being chronic discordant marital interactions and pathological physical arousal.

In another study, researchers at the University of Utah (Sanders, Smith & Alexander, 1991) tested the role of wives' Type A status on the behavior of their husbands. Four types of couples were identified: (1) both Type A, (2) husband Type A/wife Type B, (3) husband Type B/wife Type A, and (4) both Type B. While at the research lab, each couple discussed both low-conflict and high-conflict themes. The researchers observed and recorded the couples' behavior, and coded it on two dimensions: (1) dominance versus submission and (2) hostility versus affection. Dominance behavior was char-

Mealtime can be a peaceful moment, with opportunities for family members to share their ideas or discuss experiences from their day. In contrast, some mealtimes are volatile. Hard-driving and impatient, the Type A person is easily provoked and often loud and forceful when speaking. Can family interaction patterns contribute to the development of the Type A behavior pattern?

acterized by assertiveness and attempts to control the interaction, whereas submissive behavior reflected conformity and compliance. Hostile speech communicated anger, sarcasm, or opposition, and affectionate statements communicated care, friendliness, and support.

Married couples in which both spouses showed Type A behavior displayed more hostile and dominant behavior during discussions than did the other types of couples — more than both Type B spouses, as expected, but also more than couples in which the husband was Type A and the wife Type B. In other words, the husband's Type A status alone was not sufficient: It took both Type A individuals to produce the heightened hostile dominance. In addition, when the couples were asked to interact around a high-conflict topic, there were marked increases in hostile dominance — but, again, only for those couples with two Type A spouses. Thus, the hostile and controlling marital interactions in couples in which both spouses are Type A apparently can contribute to the coronary risk associated with Type A behavior among the men. Interestingly, in a longitudinal study of newlyweds (Newton & Kiecolt-Glaser, 1995), it was hostility that predicted the erosion of the quality of the marriage. Hostile individuals are mistrustful and suspicious of others — characteristics that diminish marital satisfaction.

A related line of research concerns the relationship between parents' and children's Type A behavior. For example, Deborah and Donald Forgays (1991) of the University of Vermont studied 138 university students and their parents. Their results documented a cross-gender pattern: Type A behavior in fathers was related to Type A behavior in daughters, and Type A behavior in mothers was related to Type A behavior in sons. A particular strength of this study was that the researchers used multiple measures of Type A status for both the parents and their offspring. Nevertheless, there is reason for caution: Although several studies have shown a parent-to-child relationship in Type A behavior, there is limited consistency with regard to the cross-gender pattern.

Of course, there is also a possibility that the Type A behavior pattern is an expression of an inherited predisposition. As evidence of familial influences has been found, genetic factors cannot be dismissed.

Are You a Type A?   Many people describe themselves as Type A personalities, but not all of them qualify as Type A. Conversely, many genuine Type A personalities do not see themselves as such, or they see themselves as reformed. In short, self-appraisal is not a reliable method of determining Type A status.

In a conversation about Type A behavior during a commute on a crowded freeway, the driver of a speeding car — while honking, flashing his headlights, and tailgating the panicked driver in front of him, and in between fluttering comments about his fellow commuters — gave the following self-assessment: "Yeah, I used to be a Type A."

Several self-report questionnaires are available to measure the Type A personality. One such paper-and-pencil test might ask you to respond to questions like this: "Has your spouse or a friend ever told you that you eat too fast?" and "Would people you know well agree that you take your work too seriously?" One oft-used self-report measure is the Jenkins Activity Survey (Jenkins, Zyzanski & Rosenman, 1979). This questionnaire asks people about their typical responses in situations that are frustrating, difficult, and competitive. Two sample items follow:

1. Do you ever set deadlines or quotas for yourself at work or at home?

   _____ No

   _____ Yes, but only occasionally

   _____ Yes, once a week or more

2. When you listen to someone talking and this person takes too long to come to the point, how often do you feel like hurrying the person along?

   _____ Frequently

   _____ Occasionally

   _____ Never

Although questionnaires can help identify Type A behavior, the interview format has received greater endorsement. During an interview, it is not so much the content of a subject's answers that betrays Type A behavior as the style of the interaction between interviewer and interviewee. In the Type A Structured Interview, for example, a person's style of responding to the questions is more important than his or her answers. The interviewer purposely speaks slowly when asking a question and challenges the subject's answer to a particular question. How does the interviewee respond? Loud answers, responses given before the interviewer has finished asking the question, rapid speech, and signs of competitiveness or irritation with the interview are strong indicators of Type A behavior. In contrast, a quiet, slow, patient and cooperative style suggests a Type B — again, regardless of what the individual actually says in response to the question. Features of the structured interview are similar for men and women (Anderson & Meininger, 1993).

Self-report questionnaires and interviews do not always agree in their determinations of Type A behavior (Smith, 1994). However, because the interview format has been found to have a stronger association with the physiological changes that are associated with the development of CHD, it is considered the better method for assessing Type A behavior. Nevertheless, Thoresen and Powell (1992) have encouraged a broader perspective regarding measurement of Type A behavior, including consideration of the cultural factors that influence the development and maintenance of Type A behavior.

Reducing Risk for CHD: Modifying the Type A Pattern
Can CHD be treated by modifying Type A behavior? One answer was provided by the Recurrent Coronary Prevention Project (Friedman et al., 1986), which examined the effectiveness of modifying Type A behavior in patients who had already experienced a heart attack. More than eight hundred patients with CHD were randomly assigned to either cardiac counseling alone or a treatment that provided cardiac counseling plus attempts to reduce Type A behavior. The cardiac counseling consisted of patient education and instruction in ways to manage behavioral risk factors (such as smoking cessation, improved diet, and exercise), whereas the Type A intervention consisted of several cognitive and behavioral techniques to identify and alter overt Type A behaviors, beliefs that might support the pattern, and physiological responses to stress. Data compiled after four and a half years showed that the combined Type A and cardiac counseling treatment reduced Type A behavior significantly more than the cardiac counseling alone. More important, the combined treatment resulted in about 40 percent fewer fatal and nonfatal myocardial infarctions. In short, the psychological treatment was found to be successful in reducing physical maladies.

Another study supported the conclusion that interventions directed at reducing stress can help prevent recurrences of coronary events. In the Ischemic Heart Disease Life Stress Monitoring Program (Frasure-Smith & Prince, 1985), more than four hundred male myocardial infarction patients were randomly assigned to either a stress-management program or a standard-care control group. Patients in the stress-management program were contacted monthly for one year, and at each contact their stress levels were assessed. A patient whose stress score rose above a critical level received stress-related interventions including social support, cognitive restructuring, and a wide variety of other approaches tailored to meet the patient's needs. Compared to the control group, the intervention group reported significantly less stress and experienced half as many coronary deaths during the year. Specifically, the rate of such deaths was 8.9 percent in the control group versus 4.4 percent in the treatment group (see also Frasure-Smith, 1991).

A related study conducted in Great Britain (Bennett, Wallace, Carroll & Smith, 1991) found similar results: A

cognitive-behavioral stress-management intervention reduced Type A behavior, and the psychological gains were associated with physiological changes. An eight-session hostility-reduction treatment was also found to meaningfully reduce the likelihood of CHD (Gidron & Davidson, 1996).

Although the results of such studies have demonstrated the general modifiability of Type A behavior patterns, some Type A individuals are very resistant to change. Resistance is evident in the following quote from a treatment participant (Friedman & Ulmer, 1984, p. 203):

> *I do not believe that I have excess hostility; this is due in part to the fact that my intellectual, physical, cultural, and hereditary attributes surpass those of 98 percent of the bastards I have to deal with. Furthermore, those dome-head, fitness-freak, goody-goody types that make up the alleged 2 percent are no doubt faggots anyway, whom I would beat out in a second if I weren't so damn busy fighting every minute to keep that 98 percent from trying to walk over me.*

Many Type A persons who do not want to change their behavior are quick to point out that not all persons with Type A behavior develop CHD — and each tends to believe that he or she is one of those who will be unaffected and unharmed. Other resistant persons point to the rewards provided by Western culture for certain Type A behaviors: "How can I change when, in my world, I am encouraged to be consumed by work, competitive, time-driven, and goal directed?" For such individuals, the costs of reducing Type A behavior must be weighed against the health benefits that accrue.

For the majority of patients, however, stress-management programs that combine behavior skills training and cognitive restructuring have shown considerable promise in modifying Type A behavior. In turn, the changes in behavior have had a favorable impact on the course of CHD. Do these findings suggest that psychological treatment can replace medical care? Certainly not. But research on the modification of Type A behavior has documented that psychological factors are linked to the disease and that changes in these factors have a favorable effect on health. Unfortunately, evidence regarding the effects of intervention among women and ethnic minorities is not currently available (Thoresen & Powell, 1992).

Essential Hypertension

Left untreated, high blood pressure, or hypertension, can lead to heart disease or stroke. *Blood pressure* refers to the force with which blood presses against the artery walls. It is influenced by cardiac output, which is the amount of blood the heart pumps each minute, and by peripheral resistance, the resistance to blood flow in the small arteries of the body. Increases in the heart rate, in the force of the heart's contractions, or in the total volume of blood returning to the heart lead to increased cardiac output and thus may cause blood pressure to rise. Forcing a greater flow through the arteries also raises the pressure exerted against the artery wall. In other words, constriction of small arteries and capillaries increases peripheral resistance to blood flow and therefore raises blood pressure.

Estimates have suggested that 35 million Americans have hypertension and that another 25 million have borderline hypertension. Within the black population, the prevalence of hypertension is greater among women than men, whereas in the white population it is about equal among women and men (Anastos et al., 1991). Ten to 15 percent of these cases are attributed to some form of disease. Specifically, when a disease is present, water and salt may be abnormally retained by the kidneys, leading to hypertension. In a small minority of patients, high blood pressure is caused by a specific condition, such as a blocked artery in the kidney. In the 10 to 15 percent of cases where a physiological cause is found, *secondary hypertension* is the term used to describe the condition. The remaining 85 to 90 percent of the cases are of unknown origin and are referred to as **essential hypertension**. Because of this majority of cases in which there is no obvious biological cause, research has examined psychological sources of high blood pressure.

Predisposing Factors in Hypertension Even when a clear-cut biological cause has not been identified, biological or other predisposing forces may be present. Although human studies of a potential genetic influence cannot eliminate possible environmental forces, animal studies have suggested a modest genetic component. For example, animals that are genetically prone to hypertension are also particularly susceptible to develop hypertension when exposed to stressful stimuli (Lawler, Cox, Sanders & Mitchell, 1988).

Psychological Factors in Hypertension A variety of stressful stimuli — such as social crowding and frequent electric shocks — can produce hypertension in laboratory animals (Campbell & Henry, 1983). And among human beings, social and occupational stress can contribute to hypertension. One study, for example, compared air traffic controllers in either very busy or less busy control towers. Among controllers older than forty, hypertension was twice as common in the high-stress group, consisting of those working in very busy control towers (Cobb & Rose, 1973).

Another approach to hypertension has examined not environmental stimuli but behavior patterns. Early

psychosomatic theories speculated that essential hypertension was related to suppressed anger, and considerable evidence now supports this assertion. For example, in a study of 10,000 Israeli men, those who reported that they brooded, restrained themselves, and avoided discussing conflict when angry were more than twice as likely to develop hypertension as those who expressed their anger (Kahn et al., 1972). Other studies (Dimsdale, Pierce, Schoenfeld & Brown, 1986; Gentry et al., 1982) have consistently supported the hypothesis that a habitual style of suppressing anger is linked to elevated blood pressure. Anger was also found to be a predictor of hypertension in a three-year prospective study of women (Markovitz et al., 1991). We should note, however, that high blood pressure is more likely caused by the physiological consequences of suppressed anger than by the suppressed anger itself. Possible mechanisms for this process are discussed in a later section of the chapter.

Links Between Stress and Hypertension Because the sympathetic nervous system stimulates cardiac output, it is not surprising that a great variety of stressors and anger produce increases in blood pressure (Krantz & Manuck, 1984). These changes are short-lived, however, because homeostatic mechanisms quickly return blood pressure to normal levels. If stress contributes to essential hypertension, it must produce more permanent changes in the physiological factors controlling blood pressure.

How does this permanent alteration occur? Changes in peripheral resistance might be one way. Paul Obrist (1981) has argued that in the early stages of hypertension, exaggerated increases in cardiac output during stress give many tissues an excessive supply of oxygen. In response, the small arterioles and capillaries constrict, reducing blood flow and oxygenation. If this constriction is repeated frequently, the muscles controlling the small vessels could become permanently constricted, eventually leading to permanently increased peripheral resistance and thus high blood pressure. Several research findings are consistent with this explanation (Jorgensen & Houston, 1981; Manuck, Proietti, Rader & Polefrone, 1985; Sherwood, Allen, Obrist & Langer, 1986). For example, young patients with mild hypertension are often characterized by high cardiac output and normal peripheral resistance, whereas older patients with established hypertension typically exhibit normal cardiac output and increased peripheral resistance (Obrist, 1981).

There are other ways in which stress could produce lasting changes in the physiological factors that control blood pressure. For example, among young men at risk for hypertension, stress apparently inhibits the kidney's secretion of salt and water in the urine (Light, Koepke, Obrist & Willis, 1983). If such changes in kidney function become more permanent, a greater volume of blood

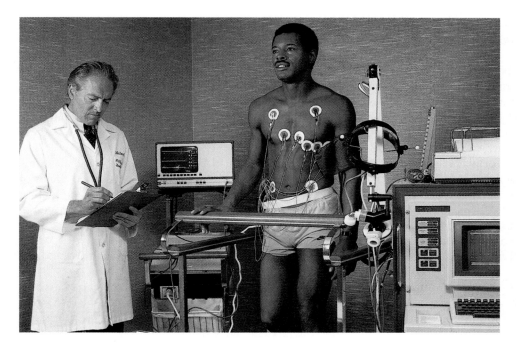

This man is having his blood pressure, and other psychophysiological responses, monitored during a physical examination. Because there are no symptoms, it is especially important that hypertension be assessed. Because there is a higher incidence of essential hypertension among African Americans, it is important that these individuals have their blood pressure checked routinely.

must be pumped by the heart, and hypertension is a likely result. Another study suggests that persons at risk for hypertension may have a deficiency in the ability to suppress the sympathetic nervous system (McCubbin, Surwitt & Williams, 1985). Thus, although the scientific evidence is not definitive, there are several plausible connections between reactions to stress and essential hypertension.

Are There Racial Differences in Essential Hypertension?

Norman Anderson and his colleagues at Duke University (Anderson, McNeilly & Myers, 1991; Anderson, Myers, Pickering & Jackson, 1989) reviewed the literature on hypertension in blacks. They opened their 1989 report with the following observation:

> "The higher prevalence of essential hypertension in black than in white populations in Westernized societies is a consistent finding in the epidemiological literature." (p. 161)

What might contribute to or account for this finding? One method or one study devoted to answering that question would not be enough. Let's consider some of the various data concerning biological, behavioral, and social forces that contribute to the reported racial difference in rates of hypertension.

Biology. Keep in mind that essential hypertension is not biologically caused. Therefore, a simple genetic explanation of the difference in rates is inadequate. Nevertheless, the cause of this disease may include disturbances in physiological functioning. For example, we note earlier that the processing of salt and water in the renal system (kidneys) contributes to the maintenance of long-term high blood pressure. Do blacks take in more sodium than whites? Research has failed to indicate differences in the routine sodium intake of blacks and whites. However, what about differences in processing sodium? To examine this question, researchers intentionally gave blacks and whites a hefty loading of sodium. The results showed that the blacks excreted significantly less sodium in their urine. This sodium-loading procedure helped the researchers determine that, after high intakes of sodium, blacks experienced significantly higher blood pressure than whites. The implication is that blacks are more susceptible to the negative effects of sodium.

Behavior. As we discuss earlier, the dominant psychological factor in theories of the cause of essential hypertension is suppressed hostility. But do these theories hold for blacks and whites alike? The answer lies in research on "John Henryism," named for the African American steel-driving folk hero who conquered a mechanical steam drill but then supposedly died from exhaustion. John Henryism has been defined as an individual's self-perception that he can meet the demands of his environment through hard work and determination (James, Hartnett & Kalsbeek, 1983). This research suggests that blacks who display such a behavior pattern — but lack the resources needed for coping — are at greater risk for hypertension.

Gathering data from rural black North Carolinians, James and associates (1983) found that those men with fewer than eleven years of formal education and above-average scores on a measure of John Henryism had the highest mean blood pressure. Later research (James, LaCroix, Kleinbaum & Strogatz, 1984) also documented that a higher percentage of blacks scoring high on a measure of John Henryism and low on socioeconomic status had hypertension — yet no such relationship existed among white subjects. It was important that whites were included in this research. Without a comparison of the two groups, it would not have been possible to ascertain that the John Henryism hypothesis holds for blacks only. Indeed, it is the specificity to blacks that is intriguing. In short, although more research is needed (Wiist & Flack, 1992), it is likely that behavioral factors contribute to and interact with other forces in essential hypertension.

Social Forces. One social force is socioeconomic status. Although socioeconomic status has been found to be associated with hypertension among blacks, not all blacks of lower socioeconomic status develop hypertension. Perhaps the social stressors or inadequate nutrition that are associated with low socioeconomic status interact with other etiologic forces.

Another social force — environmental stress — was found to independently influence the blood pressure levels of men living in Detroit (Harburg et al., 1973). To study environmental stress, researchers classified neighborhoods as high- versus low-stress on the basis of crowding and income levels as well as rates of crime and divorce. Blood pressure was also measured. According to the results, high blood pressure was most common among blacks in high-stress neighborhoods; whites and blacks in low-stress areas exhibited equal, lower blood pressure levels. Other research suggests that suppressed hostility interacts with environmental stress. In one study, suppressing anger was found to be particularly unhealthy for blacks living in chronically stressful situations (Gentry et al., 1982). Because psychologists cannot directly manipulate the stressful nature of an environment, correlational research strategies are useful in this area of study. Among blacks reporting high levels of interracial hostility, job stress, or family strain, and among those living in high-stress neighborhoods, there is a strong relationship between anger suppression and high blood pressure. At lower levels of stress, there is little or no such relationship.

Environmental stress has also been studied by comparing the prevalence of hypertension among urban and rural blacks. Studies conducted in South Africa (Sever, Gordon, Peart & Beighton, 1980), Kenya (Poulter et al.,

1984), and Senegal (Beiser, Collomb, Ravel & Nafziger, 1976) have reported that hypertension is higher in urban than in rural regions, and that hypertension increases more steeply with age among the urban dwellers. In another study, Seedat, Seedat, and Hackland (1982) assessed hypertension among urban and rural South African Zulus. The prevalence of hypertension in the urban group was 25 percent compared with 16 percent in the rural group.

Taken together, these data document racial differences in the prevalence of hypertension and the effects of psychological forces. They also reflect an interaction between environmental stress and race, thus providing yet another instance of the applicability of the diathesis-stress model.

Treating Hypertension Hypertension can be controlled by low-sodium diets, but these diets are controversial because they have unwanted effects on the nervous system. Weight loss and exercise are also recommended to reduce blood pressure. Nevertheless, a common treatment is pharmacologic, as when diuretics are used to reduce blood volume by promoting the excretion of sodium. However, although diuretics and other medications have shown some success, they are associated with a high degree of noncompliance as well as adverse physical side effects. For instance, both diuretics and adrenergic inhibitors can actually irritate the sympathetic nervous system. Of special concern is the fact that although these medications have the desired short-term effect — reduced blood pressure — they do not have the desired long-term effect. In short, they do not prevent coronary artery disease.

Many behavioral and cognitive-behavioral programs are also used in treating essential hypertension. A variety of stress-management approaches have been employed successfully as well (Wadden, Luborsky, Greer & Crits-Cristoff, 1984). Relaxation procedures are not as effective as medication in controlling hypertension and therefore cannot be considered as an alternative to traditional medical treatment. Nonetheless, these techniques can produce reductions in blood pressure beyond those obtained with medication. Most of the interventions used today combine a basic stress-management skill such as progressive relaxation with cognitive modification techniques and practice in applying the new skills in the presence of stressors (Meichenbaum, 1985). Dubbert's (1995) review of the literature further emphasizes that lifestyle changes (weight loss, restricting salt and alcohol, increased activities) can prevent and reduce hypertension.

One interesting feature of stress-management interventions for hypertension concerns their ability to lower blood pressure levels during the workday. Among persons with hypertension, blood pressure levels recorded at work are more closely correlated with a serious medical complication of hypertension — enlargement of the left coronary ventricle — than are blood pressure levels recorded at home (Devereux et al., 1983). Recall that the left ventricle is the main pumping part of the heart, pushing blood through the circulatory system. The added resistance caused by high blood pressure causes the left ventricle to increase in size, much as any muscle gets larger with added exercise. Unfortunately, an enlarged heart is also more vulnerable to ischemia — the reduced oxygenation that contributes to CHD. Thus, blood pressure levels during the regularly recurring stresses of work may be associated with one of the serious medical consequences of hypertension. Several studies have indicated that stress-management procedures can be useful in reducing blood pressure levels on the job (e.g., Taylor, Kraemer & Southam, Agras et al., 1987; Charlesworth, Williams & Baer, 1984).

A novel approach to the treatment of hypertension involves marital communication. Ewart and associates (1984) established that teaching hypertensive patients and their spouses to engage in effective, noninflammatory discussion of their problems resulted in lower levels of the patients' blood pressure during such discussions — a good example of the potential benefits of training in problem-focused coping skills.

In a related study, Florida Bosley and Thomas Allen (1989) examined the effects of stress-management training among mild to moderately hypertensive black men. Subjects were randomly assigned to either stress-management or control conditions. The stress-management program employed cognitive and behavior procedures. For example, subjects were trained to monitor their behavior in stressful situations and to become aware of their bodies' reactions and the negative self-talk that occurred in such situations. They were also given the opportunity to experience the relationship between cognitive processing and emotional arousal, and taught to change their thinking as a way of reducing their response to stress. The results indicated that subjects receiving the stress-management training reported significant increases in the use of cognitive coping strategies, significant decreases in anxiety and systolic blood pressure, and some reduction in diastolic blood pressure as well.

Like medications, however, stress-management programs are associated with certain problems. One is noncompliance: Participants sometimes drift away from their healthy regimen and fail to maintain gains. In addition, although stress-management programs reduce blood pressure, data concerning their effects on coronary artery disease are limited. Perhaps because hypertension is symptomless — indeed, many people erroneously believe that they can tell when their blood pressure is high — there is little in the way of daily reminders for patients to take their medications or engage in stress management.

STRESS AND THE IMMUNE SYSTEM: CANCER AND THE COMMON COLD

Once final examinations are over, college students often develop colds or flu symptoms, just in time to ruin a long-awaited vacation. Why? One possibility is that the stress of exams increases the body's susceptibility to infection by reducing the effectiveness of the immune system. The **immune system** is the body's defense against the microscopic invaders that produce infections (Male, Champion, Cooke & Owen, 1991). The study of psychological influences on the immune system is the topic of an exciting new field called **psychoneuroimmunology**. Researchers have long suspected that stress can lower the body's resistance to infection, and recent research has provided evidence of just such a relationship. Cohen, Tyrrell, and Smith (1991) prospectively studied the relationship between stress and susceptibility to colds by exposing volunteers either to one of five different cold viruses or to a placebo. They reported that as psychological stress increased, so did rates of both respiratory infection and clinical colds. For example, infection occurred at a rate of 74 percent among those who received the lowest psychological stress scores, compared to a rate of 90 percent among those with the highest stress scores. Moreover, the same relationship held across all five of the viruses. This well-controlled study demonstrated increased infection with increased stress. Is the body's immune system involved?

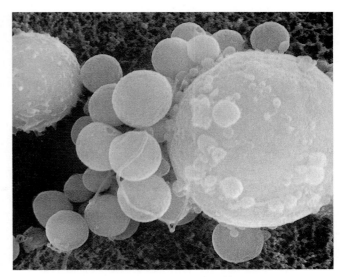

Helper T-cells. A large T-cell (right) detaches blisters from its surface to form a barrier against attack of small lymphocyte killer cells (left).

An Overview of the Immune System

The body is equipped with an exquisite defense against the germs and other microorganisms responsible for infectious disease. Foreign organisms or substances — *antigens* — face a variety of external barriers. Skin, mucous membranes, and stomach acid, for example, all prevent foreign bodies from entering our own. If these systems are breached, however, the immune system attacks the invaders (Kaplan, Sallis & Patterson, 1993).

The immune system is composed largely of white blood cells, or *lymphocytes.* Several types of lymphocytes are found in the blood, spleen, thymus, and lymph nodes. For example, *macrophages* are large lymphocytes that trap invading antigens. The macrophage alerts a T-cell, which in turn multiplies into several kinds of T-cells, which, in turn, "presents" the antigen to another lymphocyte. *Helper T-cells* "turn on" the system by stimulating the proliferation of several other types of lymphocytes, including the following:

- *B-lymphocytes,* which produce antibodies — immunoglobulins (Ig) — that circulate in the blood and attack antigens

- *Cytotoxic T-lymphocytes,* which destroy antigens, principally those in lymph nodes

- *Natural killer cells,* which directly attack foreign cells, especially virally infected cells and tumor cells

- *Suppressor T-cells,* which "turn off" the system

Communication between all of these different cells is accomplished through *interleukin* and *interferon,* which are products of the helper T-cells (see Figure 10.9). The body's immune functions are related to the levels of these T cells; when an individual has sufficient strength to fight off pathogens, the body is said to be immunocompetent. Through the administration of vaccines, the immune system can be stimulated to recognize and be prepared to kill specific viruses such as polio. The immune system can also be "trained," as when individuals are injected with small doses of a substance to which they are allergic and develop a tolerance for the substance.

But the immune system can make mistakes (Kaplan, Sallis & Patterson, 1993). For example, it can respond too much or too little. A limited response might lead to infections. In other cases, such as rheumatoid arthritis, the immune system is confused and attacks normal cells as if they were invaders.

The vital importance of the immune system is tragically illustrated by the consequences of acquired

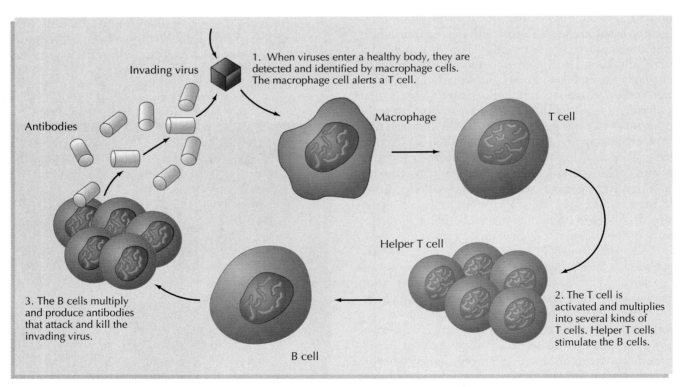

Figure 10.9 Activities of the Immune System

When a virus enters the body, it is detected by large macrophage cells that alert T-cells. The T-cells then multiply and, through the helper T-cells, stimulate B-cells. The B-cells then multiply and produce antibodies that attack and kill the invading virus.

immune deficiency syndrome (AIDS). The human immunodeficiency virus (HIV) infects and destroys helper T-cells — the cells that activate the immune system. This destruction profoundly impairs T-cell–mediated immunity. The resulting multiplication of various bacteria and cancer cells, which would otherwise easily be held in check, is lethal. People die because the immune system becomes incapable of fighting off infectious agents.

The Effects of Stress on Immune Function

The effectiveness of an individual's immune system can be influenced by a variety of factors, including stressors (Kiecolt-Glaser & Glaser, 1992). Stress affects people of both genders and of all ages and ethnic backgrounds. Moreover, the stressors themselves range from seemingly minor to profound, as shown by the following examples:

- Among dental students, levels of salivary IgA (a B-cell product that prevents viral and bacterial growth in mucous membranes, thereby reducing the likelihood of colds) were significantly lower during three examination periods than during low-stress periods (Jemmott et al., 1983).

- The stress of examinations reduced natural killer cell activity in medical students. Indeed, the cold that follows final exams — the "vacation cold" — may be the result of examination stress and its impact on immune functioning (Kiecolt-Glaser et al., 1984).

- Recent unemployment and marital disruption have also been found to impair immune function (Arnetz, Wasserman, Petrini & Brenner, 1987; Kiecolt-Glaser, Fisher, Ogrocki & Stout, 1987). Among married persons, lower marital satisfaction is associated with impaired immune responses, as is greater attachment to ex-spouses among recently divorced persons.

- Highly stressed elderly women, compared to non-stressed counterparts, exhibited a less activated immune system and a reduced ability to respond to foreign invaders (McNaughton, Smith, Patterson & Grant, 1990).

- Bereavement (for example, loss of a spouse) has been shown to produce impaired immune functioning (Bartrop et al., 1977; Schleifer et al., 1983).

Recall our earlier discussion of the relationship between life stress (both major life events and daily hassles) and subsequent illness. The changes in immune function that are found with increased stress offer a potential explanation for the association between major life events and subsequent illness: Stress reduces immune function and increases risk for illness.

But how does this link occur? At present, there are several possible explanations. For example, as we note in the earlier discussion of the HPA axis, the psychological energy needed to adjust to stressful events involves activation of parts of the brain and the secretion of hormones, processes that could eventually affect immune function. Moreover, data have supported other hormones' influence on immune competence as well as on the receptivity of neurotransmitter substances. Although no one single explanation has been proven, stress can clearly influence immunocompetence in several ways.

If stressful events can suppress immune functioning, can stress reduction enhance it? Several studies have suggested that it can. In one study of older adults, relaxation training not only increased natural killer cell activity but enhanced other areas of immune function as well (Kiecolt-Glaser et al., 1985). In another study, James Pennebaker and his colleagues (1988) at Southern Methodist University showed that individuals who wrote about past stressful events had improved cellular immunity when compared to subjects who wrote about superficial topics. The investigators suggested that actively inhibiting expression of one's thoughts and feelings about traumatic events might arouse sympathetic nervous system activity, with associated reductions in immunocompetence. The "unburdening" process, in contrast, was stress reducing. This provocative finding has interesting implications for the potential health benefits of psychotherapy.

Although psychological interventions can influence immune function, it is erroneous to assume that changes in immune function automatically translate into improved health (Kiecolt-Glaser & Glaser, 1992). The changes in immune function may be short-lived or small relative to the changes needed to reduce disease. In addition, we are uninformed about gender and racial variations and the possibility of genetic predispositions to reduced immune system function. The number of psychoneuroimmunology studies is limited, but the results thus far are promising. Clearly, more research is needed.

Stress and Cancer

The term *cancer* actually refers to more than one hundred diseases that have a feature in common: All **cancers** involve a dysfunction of the controls for growth and reproduction within the cells. Unlike normal cells, cancerous cells do not provide benefit to the body, yet they reproduce and drain the system. Cancer cells proliferate and can spread throughout the body. For reasons not yet understood, these cells are not controlled by the normal bodily processes that inhibit cell growth.

Beyond fighting infectious illnesses, the immune system can help protect against cancer by destroying carcinogens (cancer-causing substances) and controlling cancerous tissues. In particular, natural killer cells suppress the rate of tumor growth (Herberman & Ortaldo, 1981) and apparently help detect and control malignancies. Therefore, by impairing the functioning of these cells, stress may also influence the development or progression of cancer.

Certain factors — cigarette smoking, ultraviolet light, and specific foods and drink — contribute to the onset of cancer by affecting the chemistry and physiology of the body. It is also the case, however, that stress influences risk behaviors such as cigarette smoking: Even a cursory look at the data from the American Cancer Society (1991) presented in Figure 10.10 reveals a dramatic increase in lung cancer deaths since 1930. It has also been estimated that 85 percent of lung cancers are attributable to cigarette smoking. And smoking as well as alcohol consumption rise under stress conditions. In both direct and indirect ways, then, cancer is touched by psychological factors.

Women who die from cancer are likely to die from breast cancer. In any one year, an estimated 150,000 new cases of breast cancer will be identified in the United States. But breast cancer is treatable (the five-year survival rate for localized cancer is 90 percent), and known

risk factors can be altered. Not all of these risk factors are well understood, but one in particular — a family history of breast cancer — clearly promotes early assessment (self-examination, mammography) among women who have a relative with breast cancer. Diet also plays a role; for example, obese persons with a high-fat diet are at greater risk for cancer. But diet, too, can be modified. Lung cancer is becoming a leading cause of cancer death among women, which corresponds to the increased smoking rate among women.

It is extremely difficult to study psychosocial influences on the initial development of cancer. Animal research has documented that stress can facilitate the progression of malignancies (Laudeslager et al., 1983; Sklar & Anisman, 1979; Visintainer, Volpicelli & Seligman, 1982), but results of research on human beings are inconsistent. Still, there is some evidence that psychological stress affects the progression of cancer (Cooper, 1984). For example, loss of close relationships from death or divorce and other major stressful events have been implicated as potential contributors to the progression of cancer.

Stress has been implicated in the impairment of yet another bodily defense against cancer: DNA repair (Glaser, 1985). Through DNA repair, the body mini-

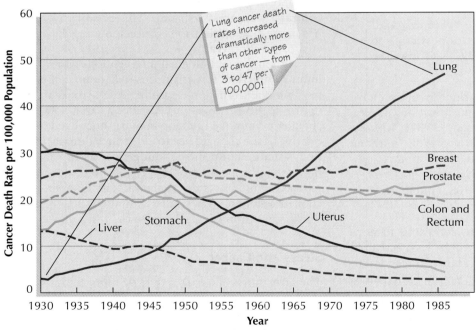

Figure 10.10 Changes in Cancer Death, 1930–1986
These data illustrate the changes that occurred in the cancer death rate per 100,000 persons between 1930 and 1986. The most dramatic change was the increase in the frequency of lung cancer deaths. Given the relationships between stress and cigarette smoking and between smoking and lung cancer, it is reasonable to suggest that stress reduction and smoking cessation programs can help reduce the incidence of lung cancer.

Note: Population rates have been standardized for age on the basis of the 1970 U.S. population. These rates apply to both sexes combined, except in the categories of breast and uterus cancer (female population only) and prostate cancer (male population only). *Source:* Data from National Center for Health Statistics and Bureau of the Census, United States. American Cancer Society, 1991. Reprinted with permission.

Emotional support can be powerfully expressed by actions as well as words. The boys shown in this photograph, who referred to themselves as the "Bald Eagles," shaved their heads so that their classmate who lost his own hair during chemotherapy for cancer would not feel alone.

mizes the impact of dangerous exposure to carcinogens. Altered, cancer-causing DNA can be restored, unless something — such as stress — interferes with the repair process.

Psychological Interventions for Cancer Patients

Cancer is not only physically challenging but also psychologically distressing. For example, some individuals blame themselves for causing their cancer, and there is some evidence that doing so can play an adverse role in the adjustment to the diagnosis of cancer (Malcarne, Compas, Epping-Jordan & Howell, 1995). Fortunately, psychological intervention can help in a variety of ways. It can alter risk behaviors in at-risk subjects, it can reduce the distress associated with learning about a cancer diagnosis, and it can aid adjustment during extended medical treatment (Andersen, 1992). In general, such programs involve learning about cancer, facing the disease with a positive cognitive perspective, using behavioral strategies to reduce stress and pain, and promoting social support (Fawzy, Fawzy, Arndt & Pasnau, 1995).

Psychological interventions for patients with cancer are largely intended to enhance their quality of life (Andersen, 1992) and improve their living with cancer (Fawzy, Fawzy, Arnett & Pasnau, 1995), whereas medical interventions are usually directed to the prolongation of life or remediation of the cancer. It was surprising, therefore, when David Spiegel and his associates at Stanford Medical School (Spiegel, Bloom, Kraemer & Gottheil, 1989) reported impressive findings concerning not just adjustment to cancer but survival. These researchers conducted a ten-year follow-up of patients with metastatic breast cancer. Some of the

patients had received a one-year psychotherapy intervention that took place during routine oncological care; the others were designated as the control group. The psychotherapy consisted of weekly, ninety-minute support group meetings in which coping with cancer was the main theme and subjects openly expressed their feelings about their illness and its effects on their lives. The group participation countered their social isolation. Physical problems — such as side effects from chemotherapy — were also discussed, and self-hypnosis was taught as a pain control strategy. In the intervention group, the duration of survival was 36.6 months; in the control group, only 18.9 months. Interestingly, assessments of the patients' characteristics at pretreatment did not predict survival, nor did differences in survival emerge until eight months after the year-long treatment had ended. Only then did the researchers associate the psychological intervention with an average of nearly eighteen months of extended survival.

OTHER STRESS-RELATED DISORDERS

Stress contributes to a variety of disorders other than those already discussed. Two such disorders are ulcers and headaches.

Ulcers

Paul was a husband, a father of four children, and a financially successful stockbro-

ker who earned commissions. He was somewhat overweight and inactive. At parties he seemed calm; as a father he was considered patient. But his life was a mixture of activities producing severe stress.

Each workday morning his alarm sounded at 5:45 A.M. Paul was shaved, showered, suited, and on the road before 6:30 A.M. He raced to beat the rush hour, but usually faced bottlenecks, accidents, and early traffic. By 7:45 A.M. he arrived at his desk. From then until 5:00 or 5:15 in the evening, he was on the phone with clients, taking only very brief breaks.

Arriving home at 7:00 P.M., Paul was met with dinner, a cocktail, and a seemingly endless series of family issues to discuss, wants and needs to satisfy, and requests for his time. His impulsive, volatile wife yelled at the children and at Paul whenever anything was less than perfect. On three nights out of five, he awoke, went to the bathroom to vomit, and returned to bed.

When Paul died at fifty-four, his death was attributed to several physical factors, of which the leading one was internal bleeding related to severe stomach ulcers.

Peptic ulcers are disruptions of the lining of the stomach or duodenum (the point where the stomach and small intestine meet). Excessive acid and pepsin, a digestive enzyme, break down the lining, producing pain and in some cases internal bleeding, which can become dangerous. The physiological mechanism for the development of peptic ulcers is believed to involve an increase in gastric acid secretion, deficient secretion of the mucus that coats and protects the stomach, or both. Most ulcers are duodenal rather than gastric (stomach-related). About 10 percent of the U.S. population will develop peptic ulcers at some point in their lives.

Causal Influences on Ulcers What causes ulcers? Although psychological factors have been implicated, recent findings indicate that some patients with ulcers respond to antibiotic treatment, suggesting that what has been considered psychogenic is really a bacterial process. Presumably that process is affected by stress, but as yet we don't know for certain.

A look at who is affected by ulcers does strongly suggest that stress plays a role in development of the disease. For instance, ulcers are more common in wartime than in peacetime, and in urban rather than rural areas (Pflanz, 1971). A study of air traffic controllers has shown that controllers at busier towers were more likely to have ulcers than those at less busy towers (Cobb & Rose, 1973). And other research has found that, at least in the case of duodenal ulcers, an increase in stressful life changes is likely to precede development of the ulcers (Shapiro & Cross, 1982).

Tom, an ulcer patient, was fitted with an opening in his stomach to facilitate drainage of stomach acids. This procedure allowed researchers to observe changes in acid secretion and the mucus of the stomach lining. In this classic study, Wolf and Wolff (1947) reported observing that when Tom was sad or withdrawn, the mucosa became pale and acid secretion was reduced, and that when Tom was angry, the mucosa became engorged with blood and acid secretion increased. As the authors suggested, intense emotions produced intense physiological reactions, including hemorrhaging.

How does stress cause ulcers? One possibility is that stress, and the intense emotional states associated with it, may lead to oversecretion of stomach acid, and the excessive digestive acids end up digesting some of the stomach wall. Ulcers tend to develop between the ages of twenty and forty; they are found in both men and women and in people of all cultural and ethnic backgrounds. But, obviously, not everyone who experiences stress develops ulcers. Early psychosomatic theorists suspected that ulcers are caused by long-standing, unconscious conflicts that grow out of exaggerated interpersonal dependency. However, a famous experiment with monkeys suggested another explanation that received quick acceptance.

John Brady (1958) examined the effects of electric shock on the development of ulcers in monkeys. Teamed in pairs, the monkeys were constrained in an apparatus that delivered electric shocks several times each minute for several hours. One member of each pair — the "executive" monkey — could turn off the shocks by pressing a nearby switch. The other animal could do nothing; its schedule of shocks depended on what the first member of the pair, the executive, did. At the end of the experiment, the executive monkeys had developed more ulcers than the passive, yoked animals.

Brady's study was widely reported to show that people who had control over events, like the executive monkeys, were prone to develop ulcers. But several other studies failed to replicate Brady's findings. A closer look at how the monkeys were assigned to the executive versus yoked roles suggests one explanation: Animals that exhibited a higher rate of switch-pressing *before the experiment began* were given the job of executive, whereas those who showed a slower rate became the yoked, passive partners. This preexisting difference in response rate, not the difference between the executive and passive roles, may account for Brady's results.

In another experiment, Weiss (1971) randomly assigned rats to executive versus yoked, passive roles. Before each shock, a warning signal was delivered. If the executive rat turned a wheel, the shock was prevented. Yoked animals received the same shocks that the executive animals did, but turning the wheels in their cages had no effect on the shock. In this case, the executive animals developed fewer ulcers than did the yoked, passive animals. The implication is that the uncontrollability of stressors contributed to the ulcers. Furthermore, during trials in which a flashing light informed the executive animals that their response was going to be successful in preventing shock, even fewer ulcers developed. Thus, this study also suggested that unpredictable stressors are more likely to lead to ulcers. The types of ulcers seen in animals differ from those in human beings, and the findings may have other possible explanations, but this line of research with animals does imply that stress can cause ulcers and that control and predictability over stressors can provide at least partial protection against ulceration.

Genetics also plays a role in the development of ulcers. For example, some individuals are born with predispositions, in terms of both behavioral style and physiological constitution, that contribute to the development of ulcers. Indeed, contemporary biomedical research has highlighted the importance of genetic makeup in affecting conditions that once were thought to be primarily psychogenic. The diathesis-stress model has some application as well, in that the interaction of an inherited biological vulnerability with personal and environmental stressors can apparently help answer the question, "Why do some people respond to stress by developing ulcers, others develop hypertension, and others develop headaches?"

Treatment for Ulcers   Ulcers can be treated in a variety of medical and psychological ways. Psychological treatment is typically directed toward reducing stress (Whitehead, 1992). For example, Brooks and Richardson (1980) compared the effectiveness of a stress-management intervention that combined relaxation and assertiveness training with the effectiveness of supportive therapy. Their results indicated that the stress-management intervention not only reduced anxiety and increased assertiveness but also had a positive effect on duodenal ulcers. In fact, during the two months after treatment, those who received the stress-management intervention, compared to those who received the supportive therapy, reported fewer days with ulcer pain and less consumption of antacid medication. Over a 3 1/2-year follow-up, the intervention was also associated with fewer severe recurrences of the disease. Stress-management programs, alone or in conjunction with coordinated medical treatments, are thus useful in the reduction of duodenal ulcers.

Headaches

Recurrent headaches are one of the most common reasons people seek medical treatment for pain. Almost everyone has experienced a headache at some point, yet only some people are disabled by them. It has been estimated that each year there are two million new cases of disabling headache in the United States (Goldstein & Chen, 1982).

Causal Influences on Headaches   Although some headaches are caused by serious medical conditions (such as a brain tumor), most do not reflect the presence of life-threatening illness. Chronic headaches are classified as either tension headaches or migraines. The typical **tension headache** involves an ache or sensation of tightness or pressure that begins in the neck or back of the head. The sensation worsens and spreads until it is a dull, steady pain on both sides of the head, like a "band" around the head. In contrast, **migraine headaches** involve a "throbbing" or "pulsating" headache pain that is typically experienced on one side of the head and is often associated with nausea or even vomiting. Migraine headaches begin with a constriction of the blood vessels in the brain, which reduces the flow of blood, and a subsequent dilation of the blood vessels, which allows the blood to flow rapidly. This process has been said to underlie the throbbing sensation described by patients. Some sufferers report a warning sensation before the migraine begins; others report being overly sensitive to light during the migraine. Migraines tend to run in families.

Do these two types of headaches have distinct physiologies? According to a popular view, tension headaches reflect sustained, stress-induced muscle tension in the head and neck, whereas migraines are believed to be caused by a two-phase vascular process. Research, however, does not provide strong support for this description of differences between the sources of tension and migraine headaches (Blanchard & Andrasik, 1982). According to the data, both types of headaches are often associated with similar muscular and vascular stress responses. On the other hand, this failure to confirm differences between the types of headaches may reflect the fact that the stressors administered in these studies are not as long or severe as the stressors that precipitate real-life headaches.

Several other studies have suggested that both migraine and tension headaches are influenced by emotional stress (Bakal, 1979). Prolonged muscle tension, for example, is considered a maladaptive response to stress. Rather than engaging in relaxation and coping with stressful situations, the patient responds with prolonged muscle tension that eventually results in headache. Recall our earlier description of the wide array of sources of stress: All of these stressors can contribute to headache. Indeed, recurrent headache sufferers report a greater number of daily life stressors than matched headache-free controls (Holroyd & French, 1994), and they are more likely than controls to report

Three Balkan presidents and then-U.S. Secretary of State Warren Christopher at a treaty-signing ceremony. Stress-related disorders, such as headaches or ulcers, can result from intense pressure surrounding high-stakes situations.

use of potentially ineffective strategies for coping with stress (Edhe & Holm, 1992). What we do not yet fully understand, however, is why some people report headaches as a consequence of stress while others report different psychophysiological problems.

An emerging body of research, such as the work of Ken Holroyd and his colleagues at Ohio University, underscores the role that cognitive factors can play in the onset and treatment of headaches. For example, expectancies have been implicated. That is, some headache sufferers believe that headaches are controlled by external and chance factors and expect that efforts to influence headaches will be futile (Holroyd, France, Nash & Hursey, 1993). Cognitive influences are also seen in the way that headache sufferers interpret stress; compared to headache-free controls, they typically interpret the events they experience as more stressful. As one study demonstrated, when the impact of a stress was ambiguous, recurrent headache sufferers appraised the event more negatively and perceived themselves as having less control over the situation than did controls (Holm, Holroyd, Hursey & Pensien, 1986).

Treatments for Headaches A number of drugs, both preventive and in response to symptoms, are used to treat headaches. At the mention of a headache, the average person immediately thinks of aspirin. But is aspirin the only cure? Given the role of stress and mistaken thinking in headaches, psychological interventions may also be effective.

In 1982, a review of the literature on the treatment of headache concluded that two forms of psychological treatment were relatively well established: relaxation training and biofeedback (Blanchard & Andrasik, 1982). Ten years later, these forms of treatment were again acknowledged to be well accepted, and a growing body of literature supported the addition of cognitive therapy (Blanchard, 1992). Let's take a closer look at each of these three interventions.

Various types of relaxation training, such as progressive muscle relaxation, have yielded a 50 percent reduction in tension headaches and a 37 percent reduction in migraine headaches, based on daily records of participants' headaches (Holroyd & French, 1994). Because of the success of relaxation-training procedures, they are often included in comprehensive programs for the treatment of headache.

Biofeedback, which is described earlier in this chapter, has also been used to treat tension headaches. Given that tension headaches are linked to excessive and extended contraction of muscles in the head and neck, biofeedback is directed toward muscle relaxation and control. In the application of biofeedback for headache (Blanchard & Andrasik, 1985), patients are taught to relax and to reduce the level of muscle activity in the forehead, especially the frontalis muscle, through feedback of that muscle's activity. This activity is monitored, through electromyography (EMG), and fed back to the patient. Holroyd and French's (1994) summary indicated, on average, a 46 percent reduction in headaches by means of EMG biofeedback.

The rationale for the use of cognitive therapy in the treatment of headache derives from studies of how headache sufferers deal with stress and with the headache episodes themselves. For example, they illustrate that cognitive-behavioral interventions can be linked to assessment data reflecting overly negative self-statements during periods of stress. Cognitive therapy teaches headache sufferers to identify stressful circumstances early on, to employ coping strategies before headache onset, to better manage their distress once a headache has occurred, and to prevent "catastrophizing" when a headache occurs.

How do the psychological treatments stand up against medication? Holroyd and associates (1991) compared the preferred pharmacologic agent (amitriptyline) to cognitive-behavioral treatment (relaxation plus cognitive therapy) for patients with chronic tension headaches. Both therapies yielded significant improvements, but changes resulting from the cognitive-behavioral treatment were much greater than those resulting from the medication: When gains were assessed using patients' daily recordings, there were reductions of 56 percent and 27 percent, respectively. And when a neurologist's ratings of improvement were used as a basis for assessment, 94 percent and 69 percent of patients, respectively, were rated as at least moderately improved.

Effective psychological treatments for tension headaches include muscle tension biofeedback, relaxation therapy, cognitive-behavioral therapy, and combinations of these techniques, whereas for migraine headaches, relaxation therapies are effective, but the usefulness of various other forms of treatment is less clear. As Blanchard (1992) concluded, "These [psychological] treatments . . . have gained widespread acceptance in the medical world specializing in headaches. The effects hold up over long-term follow-up, the side effects tend to be positive (reduced anxiety and depression), and the treatments can be readily adapted to more cost-effective formats" (p. 548).

TARGETING HEALTH-RELATED BEHAVIOR

The theories and research we discuss in this chapter reflect the achievements of the related fields of behavioral medicine and health psychology. Together, these fields have already greatly influenced not only the ways in which health is assessed and treated but also the public's understanding of the significance of lifestyle choices.

Moreover, as health policy issues continue to be considered, work in these fields is likely to have a major impact on medical practice in the future.

Targets for Assessment

Unlike the other disorders covered in this text, the illnesses discussed in the present chapter — cardiovascular disease, cancer, ulcers, and headache — are not psychological abnormalities and are not listed as disorders within DSM-IV. Rather, these specific illnesses are seen as influenced by psychological forces and relevant to the understanding and management of the patient. Accordingly, they are included on DSM-IV's Axis III, which is reserved for the reporting of general medical conditions.

The DSM is also concerned with identifying whether psychological factors are believed to play a role in the onset or course of an illness. Specifically, Axis IV is reserved for the recording of psychosocial or environmental problems that may affect the diagnosis, treatment, or prognosis of mental disorders. With this system, biological and psychological influences on the client's problems are considered jointly and a great range of medical problems are seen as potentially influenced by psychological processes.

A complete understanding of an individual's health requires not only a complete physical examination but also an assessment of a variety of psychological factors. In short, the psychologist involved in health care must

Figure 10.11   Health Practices and Mortality
Are healthy behaviors linked to longevity? At different ages (from younger than forty-five to older than eighty-five) the total number of healthy practices shows a relationship with longevity. Stated differently, the fewer the healthful practices, the higher the mortality rate at a given age. This pattern holds true for both men and women. Examples of healthy practices include not smoking, maintaining one's weight in relation to desirable standards for height, drinking little if any alcohol, getting adequate sleep, eating regularly, and exercising. *Source:* Carmody & Matarrazzo (1991).

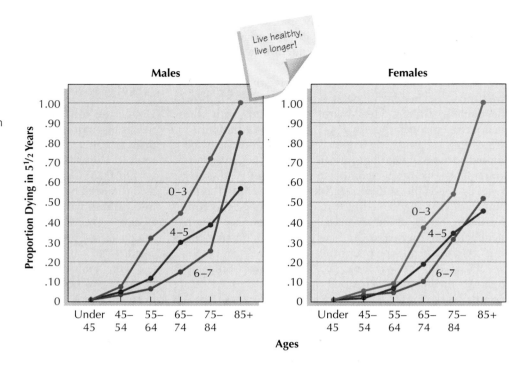

perform a "biopsychosocial audit," which assesses psychological and social assets and liabilities related to physical health. In particular, a biopsychosocial audit identifies potential stressors such as recent life changes and daily hassles. Maladaptive cognitive appraisals of threat can contribute to stress responses, as can low expectations regarding one's ability to cope with the stressor or its impact. Does the individual misperceive the environment as containing an excessive number of demands, or misperceive small requests as demands? Does the individual distort appraisals of personal abilities and think that he or she does not have the ability to meet routine challenges? Both overestimating threat and underestimating one's abilities contribute to stress.

Asking individuals how they have tried to cope with stress is also instructive because coping responses are important influences on stress responses. The Ways of Coping Checklist is an inventory for measuring what people do in response to a stressor (Folkman & Lazarus, 1980; Vitaliano et al., 1985). Moderator variables, such as the individual's level of social support and any biological vulnerabilities, should be assessed as well.

A complete assessment requires a behavioral risk profile. Smoking, lack of exercise, and an unhealthy diet contribute to illness, whereas positive changes in such behaviors reduce risk for illness. These facts are important because the total number of health practices (such as daily exercise and quitting smoking) is linked to illness and mortality. Figure 10.11 shows how the total number of health practices among men and women is associated with mortality.

Health-Behavior Relationships

Cognitive factors influence the health-behavior relationship. Knowing the extent to which people believe that their physical health or illness is under their own control (an internal locus of control) or is something that happens *to* them (an external locus of control) facilitates intervention. Altering health behavior is more difficult if the individual believes that health is a matter of fate rather than related to good habits.

Another cognitive approach to health behavior suggests that the practice of health behaviors is determined by two cognitive factors: (1) the perception that a personal health risk exists, and (2) the perception that a particular behavior will reduce the risk. Figure 10.12 illustrates this **health-beliefs model** (Rosenstock, 1974). It predicts, on the one hand, that health-protective behaviors will occur when the individual recognizes a health risk and believes that the specific behavior will reduce the risk; and, on the other hand, that if the individual either fails to recognize the risk or does not believe that the behavior change is useful, health practices will suffer (e.g., Schafer, Keith & Schafer, 1995).

The health-beliefs model intimates that treatment interventions should address both the subject's acknowledgment of a health threat and his or her belief that particular behaviors can reduce the threat. It also points to the usefulness of preventive interventions that provide early education about how to identify and influence health threats. Of course, motivation is an important component; even the most avid supporter of the health-

Figure 10.12   The Health-Beliefs Model

According to the health-beliefs model, the likelihood that a person will engage in a healthy behavior can be determined by the degree to which the person perceives (1) that a personal health risk exists and (2) that a particular behavior will reduce the health risk. Interventions therefore address both the person's acceptance of the health threat and his or her belief in the efficacy of health-enhancing behavior.

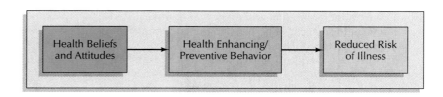

beliefs model must maintain the motivation needed to change health-related behavior.

What Lies Ahead?

Not long ago, the clear majority of studies in the field of psychophysiological disorders concerned health problems in men — cardiovascular disease, hypertension, and ulcers. Currently, women's health issues are receiving equal time (Rodin & Ickovics, 1990); studies of psychological factors in cardiovascular disease and health among women (Wenger, Speroff & Packard, 1993) and of mammography (Lerman et al., 1993) epitomize this trend. In the future we are likely to see a continued focus on the psychology of women's health, as well as a greater focus on health behaviors within ethnic and cultural groups.

Meanwhile, both health professionals and the public have taken notice of AIDS, which has been the challenge of the 1990s and will remain a challenge into the next century. Given that the immune system is involved, and that certain behaviors can cause the transmission of AIDS, psychological factors have taken on a central role. How and at what level should psychological interventions be utilized to fight the AIDS epidemic? This question is another focus of continuing research.

Finally, data emerging from contemporary research document the important roles of stress, social support, and individual appraisals of situations in both psychological distress and physical illness. We now know that numerous medical conditions are exacerbated, if not causally influenced, by psychological forces. As a result, the practice of medicine, as it incorporates these modern findings, will change. Indeed, the future is likely to witness a greater interface of the mind and body in the care of psychological and medical health.

KEY TERMS

active coping (304)
behavioral medicine (299)
cancers (319)
coping responses (301)
coronary atherosclerosis (CAD) (308)
coronary heart disease (CHD) (308)
daily hassles (301)
disregulation model (304)

emotion-focused coping (305)
essential hypertension (314)
fight-or-flight response (302)
general adaptation syndrome (GAS) (303)
health-beliefs model (326)
health psychology (299)
immune system (317)

life changes (301)
migraine headache (323)
passive coping (304)
peptic ulcers (322)
problem-focused coping (304)
psychoneuroimmunology (317)
psychophysiological disorder (298)

psychophysiologic model (299)
psychosomatic (298)
response-focused coping (304)
stressor (299)
tension headaches (323)
Type A pattern (309)
Type B pattern (309)

SUMMARY

In the past, the term *psychosomatic* was used to suggest that specific bodily diseases had psychological origins. Today, *psychophysiological disorders* is the preferred label for conditions in which actual tissue damage has occurred and psychological factors are believed to play a role in the conditions' onset or exacerbation.

Mind, Body, and Stress

Notions of the relationships among the mind, body, and stress have evolved into behavioral medicine and health psychology. *Behavioral medicine* is concerned with the integration of behavioral and biomedical science, and with the application of this knowledge for prevention, diagnosis, and treatment. *Health psychology* is the aggregate of specific contributions of psychology to the promotion and maintenance of health, the prevention and treatment of illness, and the understanding of causes and correlates of health and illness.

The *psychophysiologic model* holds that the first step toward illness occurs when excessive levels of environmental challenges, threats, or demands — called *stressors* — combine with individual characteristics; that is, when faced with high levels of environmental stress and poor psychological resources, a person suffers excessively high levels of physiological arousal. In the diathesis-stress model the diathesis is a preexisting physical vulnerability to an illness, and the combination of stress and constitutional vulnerability results in psychophysiologic disorders.

Stress has several meanings. According to the stimulus definition, stress is a stimulus that represents an environmental demand; according to the response definition, it refers to the organism's response to that demand; and according to the transactional definition, it lies in the relationship between person and situation. Stress occurs in a person-situation interaction when an environmental demand is seen by the individual as taxing or exceeding his or her ability to meet the demand. And a *coping response* occurs when the person takes action to alter the demanding situation or to change its effect. Stress assessments have been examined in terms of (1) *life changes* or major life events weighted according to the amount of adaptive effort they require, and (2) *daily hassles,* or the "little things" that go wrong and cause distress.

The body responds to stress with sympathetic nervous system arousal and activation of the HPA axis. Organs are stimulated to produce the *fight-or-flight response*. The *general adaptation syndrome (GAS)* refers to the three stages that the body undergoes in its response to stress: alarm reaction, resistance, and exhaustion. According to the *disregulation model,* when feedback is disrupted and a corrective action to return to normal functioning does not occur, physical dysfunction results. Psychologically, the effects of stress can be moderated by factors such as the person's manner of coping, cognitive and emotional processing, individual differences, and social and economic factors. Psychological interventions to reduce stress often involve relaxation training, biofeedback, or cognitive therapy. Combinations of these strategies occur in stress-management programs.

Cardiovascular Diseases

In cases of *coronary atherosclerosis (CAD)* the arteries carrying blood to the heart muscle are narrowed by fatty deposits in their walls. *Coronary heart disease (CHD)* involves severe chest pain caused by a temporary lack of oxygen supply to the heart and the death of heart muscle because of sustained, severe lack of oxygen.

Personality is related to CHD. The *Type A pattern* is characterized by hard-driving competitiveness, easily pro-

voked hostility, and a loud, rapid speaking style. In contrast, the *Type B pattern* is characterized by the relative absence of these attributes. Type A persons appear driven and view themselves in competition with others. Type A persons also display greater physiological reactivity — a stronger or more frequent alarm (fight-or-flight) response — than do Type B persons.

Blood pressure is the force with which the blood presses against the artery walls; *essential hypertension* is elevated blood pressure that is not due to a known biological cause. There are ethnic differences in the prevalence of essential hypertension; it occurs more frequently among blacks than among whites.

Unhealthy behavior patterns (such as the Type A pattern) and other risk factors have been found to be treatable using psychological interventions.

Stress and the Immune System: Cancer and the Common Cold

The *immune system* is the body's defense against infections. The study of psychological influences on the immune system is called *psychoneuroimmunology*. Stress can disarm the immune system in several ways.

Cancers involve a dysfunction of the controls for growth and reproduction within the cells of the body. Behaviors such as cigarette smoking increase the risk of cancer, and psychological interventions are designed to reduce this risk by modifying risk behavior. Other interventions are designed to improve the quality of life for persons dying from cancer.

Other Stress-Related Disorders

Ulcers and headaches are two additional stress-related disorders. *Peptic ulcers* involve disruptions of the lining of the stomach, and both *tension* and *migraine headaches* have been studied. Successful psychological treatments for stress-related disorders include relaxation, biofeedback, and cognitive therapy.

Targeting Health-Related Behavior

An understanding of an individual's health requires not only a complete physical examination but also an assessment of various psychological factors. A contemporary paradigm known as the *health-beliefs model* predicts that health-protective behaviors occur when the individual recognizes a health risk and believes that a specific behavior will reduce the risk. Risk-reduction efforts are successful to the extent that patients believe that they can have an effect.

Consider the following. . .

Suppose that you had surgery for colon cancer several weeks ago, and you are now preparing to attend your first meeting of a cancer support group in your community. Given what you have learned in this chapter, what do you expect and hope to learn from this group? What might you contribute to it?

Suppose that you are asked to design a prevention program for your school district that is aimed at getting children and young adults to behave in ways that will prevent coronary heart disease in the future. You have the support of local health organizations, government, businesses, and parent groups. It seems that money is no object. However, several of the businesses are fast-food restaurants, and they have expressed some concern about how you intend to go about your task. Detail the possible strategies that you would include in your proposal.

CHAPTER 11

Substance-Related Disorders

Those among us...

■ Sheila is an intelligent young woman with a funky look that invites conversation. But she's drinking more and more these days, and you are worried for her because she boasts, "I'm really into booze." Sheila's older brother has had alcohol problems, and her father is an alcoholic.

■ You hear your parents reminiscing about John, a television and movie star, who was such an entertaining comedian and who seemed to have everything going for him . . . until he died from a drug overdose.

■ After taking several classes together, you and Karen have become fairly good college friends. Although Karen's father died a slow, painful death from lung cancer, Karen continues to smoke cigarettes, but you can see that she feels a great deal of conflict about doing so.

■ At forty-five, your uncle Brian has already put in twenty-four years on the loading dock. In the worker's union he has seniority, but at the treatment clinic he is the new member of the group. As he tells his story to his new "friends," his speech slows and his eyes tear. "Sure, I drink a few beers, and maybe a cocktail or two at night. I've also used speed. But I never thought it would come to this. My boss says I'm going to lose my job if I don't shape up, and my family says they don't want me around anymore if I'm drinking."

How do alcohol problems develop? Are there familial causes? Do people inherit them from their parents? Is alcoholism a disease?

Does drug use always end in addiction and sometimes death? What is so beguiling about drugs that adults and even young people continue to use and abuse them in the face of such risks?

Individuals with addictions often have to stop working, stop drinking, and/or stop their drug habit—all at the same time. For most, it seems an impossible task. Is it?

Psychoactive substances — substances that affect thoughts, behavior, and emotions — are used worldwide. For most people, drinking small doses of alcohol as a "social lubricant," using the caffeine in coffee or tea as a morning stimulant, or taking analgesics to relieve pain involves either acceptable levels of health risk or none at all. For some people, however, substances such as alcohol, cocaine, and sedatives create problems ranging from mild abuse to serious addiction. Psychoactive substance-use disorders are among the most common of all psychological disorders requiring treatment.

Of all the psychological disorders, the addictions are most likely to have implications not only for psychological well-being but also for physical health. Most psychoactive substances have acceptable levels of health risk when used sparingly, but in excess even the most benign compound can cause sickness or even death. Substance users experience health problems at rates far exceeding national averages. Many of the nation's medical centers' beds are filled by patients whose admitting illness was caused or exacerbated by substance use. Many psychological disorders are exacerbated by or traced to excessive use of alcohol or other drugs.

To understand the seriousness of the substance-use problem, consider the following facts (Rice, Kelman, Miller & Dunmeyer, 1990): In the United States, in 1988 alone, alcohol abuse was estimated to have cost the nation $85.8 billion, including $4.3 billion for related crime expenditures and $2.6 billion for motor vehicle accidents in which alcoholism was a factor. For those incarcerated in prisons, the cost was $2.7 billion. To care for infants born with fetal alcohol syndrome, the cost was $1.6 billion.

In 1995, costs of substance abuse were estimated to be $177 billion annually (Dorgan, 1995). In only one year (1985), $2.1 billion was spent for the care of addicted persons in short-stay hospitals. In 1992, over 18,000 deaths were associated with alcohol abuse (Gall & Lucas, 1996).

Researchers have estimated, based on surveys, that 21.5 million persons in the United States have alcohol-abuse problems and 5.2 million persons, or 3.6 percent of the population, have drug-abuse problems. Based on a recent survey, researchers estimate that one-fourth of the population aged fifteen to fifty-four has a history of substance-use disorder (Kessler et al., 1994).

In this chapter we consider the definition of addiction and examine the addictive agents. Next, we discuss the physical and psychological effects of the agents and the processes involved in the development of an addiction. Finally, we examine the various interventions designed to prevent, curb, or end addictive substance use.

DEFINING THE PROBLEM OF ADDICTION

Where is the line between pathologic and nonpathologic substance use, or between substance use and abuse? What about the cultural and situational factors that contribute to use and abuse? Although the problems and costs are massive and long-standing, the concept of addiction is relatively new. An **addiction** involves behavioral and physical processes: Behaviorally, there is a subjective compulsion to use a drug and progressive compromise of activities that are not drug related. Physical processes, such as tolerance and withdrawal, are discussed next.

Physical Processes of Addiction

Physical dependence involves the twin signs of tolerance and withdrawal. **Tolerance** is the body's decreased response to repeated administrations of a drug, so a person must use more of the drug to obtain the same effect. Tolerance may occur after long use of the substance, or it may occur by the end of just one episode of drug use. When the frequency or amount of the substance is decreased, the person suffers withdrawal. **Withdrawal** results when the prolonged use of a substance has altered the body to such an extent that it is affected when the substance is not taken. In general, withdrawal effects reverse the drug effects that precede them. Thus, the withdrawal syndrome that follows sustained use of a tranquilizing agent tends to be characterized by agitation; withdrawal from a euphoriant drug typically includes depression.

Behavioral and Psychological Aspects of Addiction

A major hazard of drug use is the development of a psychological dependence. A person who is psychologically dependent on a drug will continue to take it, often despite adverse social and medical consequences, and behave as if the effects are needed for continued well-being (Jaffe, 1990). Consistent with the approach to the addictions taken by DSM-IV (see Table 11.1), diagnoses of substance dependence are based on a psychological concept of dependency. Three of seven criteria in Table 11.1 are necessary: Criteria 1 and 2 may or may not be

Table 11.1 Diagnostic Criteria for Substance Dependence

1. Tolerance, as defined by either (a) need for markedly increased amounts of the substance to achieve intoxication or desired effect or (b) markedly diminished effect with continued use of the same amount of the substance.

2. Withdrawal, as manifested by either (a) the characteristic withdrawal syndrome for the substance or (b) the same (or closely related) substance is taken to relieve or avoid withdrawal symptoms.

3. The substance is often taken in larger amounts or over a longer period than was intended.

4. A persistent desire or unsuccessful efforts to cut down or control substance use.

5. A great deal of time is spent in activities necessary to obtain the substance (e.g., driving long distances), use the substance (e.g., chain smoking), or recover from its effects.

6. Important social, occupational, or recreational activities given up or reduced because of substance use.

7. Continued substance use despite knowledge of having had a persistent or recurrent physical or psychological problem that was likely to have been caused or exacerbated by the substance (e.g., continued drinking despite recognition that an ulcer was made worse by alcohol consumption).

Source: DSM-IV. Reprinted with permission from *The Diagnostic and Statistical Manual of Mental Disorders*, Fourth Edition. Copyright © 1994 American Psychiatric Association.

Substance dependence, according to DSM-IV, is defined as a maladaptive pattern of substance use, leading to clinically significant impairment or distress, as manifested by three or more diagnostic criteria occurring at any time in the same twelve-month period. The diagnosis then specifies one of the following: with physiological dependence (evidence of tolerance or withdrawal; either item 1 or 2 is present) or without physiological dependence (neither item 1 nor 2 is present).

present, so substance dependence can be either with or without physiological dependence. Signs of tolerance or withdrawal, which are terms a physiologist would use to describe drug dependence, are no longer thought of as necessary components of psychoactive substance-dependence disorders. This shift is not without controversy: some researchers argue in favor of a physiological definition of dependence; others adhere to the psychological (social) aspect of dependence. Whatever the outcome of the controversy, one result of this shift to psychological definitions of dependence may be increased estimates of the prevalence of psychoactive substance-use disorders.

WHAT'S NORMAL?
Consider Cultural Context

In the domain of alcohol and other drug use, what's normal is a highly individual matter. What passes as normal use is based on the individual, family, peer group, and cultural background that is peculiar to each one of us. To complicate matters, what's normal in the domain of alcohol and other drug use is not necessarily the same as what's healthy or what's legal. Most substance-use patterns are a combination of the normal and abnormal, healthy and unhealthy, and legal and illegal.

Consider the implications of this "relative" definition of normal use. For example, in some of the wine-growing regions of France, it is normal and legal, but unhealthy, to drink large quantities of wine each day. It is even normal and legal, but unhealthy, for children to do this. In fact, it is "normal" (accepted) in these areas to be physically addicted to alcohol, to experience withdrawal when abstaining. Although children develop early warning signs of cirrhosis at a young age and expect a shortened lifespan because of subsequent liver disease, drinking alcohol is accepted as normal.

Not long ago it was normal and legal, but unhealthy, for adults to be severely addicted to nicotine. Only within the past few years has society begun to understand nicotine addiction as a drug-dependence problem. In Jamaica it is normal (most do it), but unhealthy and illegal, for Rastafarians to smoke large quantities of marijuana; in the former Soviet Union it is normal and legal, but unhealthy, to drink a fifth-gallon of vodka per week; and in the United States it is abnormal and unhealthy, but legal, to drink to such a degree, though during Prohibition (sixty years ago) it was abnormal, unhealthy, and illegal (see MacCoun, 1993, for a discussion of drugs and the law). Table 11.2 explains how to calculate blood alcohol levels.

In the Bolivian highlands it is normal, yet illegal, to chew coca leaf; in the Sonoran desert it is normal, sometimes legal, and usually unhealthy to chew peyote; and in some Asian American communities at the turn of this century it was normal, unhealthy, but legal to be addicted to opium (although it became illegal in 1922 with the passage of the Jones-Miller Act). The truth is that it is normal in almost every culture and at every point in history to use intoxicating substances. Usually, it's legal. Occasionally, it's healthy. Rarely, when in excess, is it wise.

What's normal in regard to the use of alcohol and other drugs is so unique to the individual, family, social,

Cultural factors contribute to how we view substance use and how substance abuse is defined. Here, farmers and workers in France consume wine with their lunch. In many other cultures, consumption of alcohol "on the job" is wholly forbidden.

and cultural context of the questioner that the question loses its meaning. It is wiser to ask, "What's legal?" and wiser still to ask, "What's healthy?"

The Role of Expectancies in Substance Use

The relationship between the pharmacologic effects of a drug and its psychological and behavioral effects is not simple. A drug's effects are mediated by the user's beliefs and expectations about the drug's effects (Siegel, 1989; Wilson, 1977). An individual's beliefs or **expectancies** can sometimes exert greater control over psychological and behavioral functioning than the pharmacological effects of the drugs themselves. This finding has been demonstrated in a number of laboratory studies (Marlatt, Demming & Reid, 1973) during the past two decades.

Most impressive of the experimental methods used to test the notion of expectancy effects is the so-called balanced placebo design used by Marlatt, Demming, and Reid (1973) of the University of Washington (see Figure 11.1). In the **balanced placebo design,** four groups are used. In one group, the subjects are told that they will receive an experimental dose of a drug (alcohol) and are then given it; in this group, both expectancies and pharmacological drug effects can be presumed active. In a second group, the subjects are told that they will receive a placebo beverage and are then given it; in this group, neither expectancies nor pharmacological drug effects are active. In a third group, the subjects are

Table 11.2   Calculating Blood Alcohol Level

Body Weight (lb)	1	2	3	4	5
100	.038	.075	.113	.150	.188
120	.031	.063	.094	.125	.156
140	.027	.054	.080	.107	.134
160	.023	.047	.070	.094	.117
180	.021	.042	.063	.083	.104
200	.019	.038	.056	.075	.094
220	.017	.034	.051	.068	.085

Note: one drink = 1.5 ounces of 80 proof distilled spirits = 5 ounces of 12% wine = 12 ounces of 5% beer

This table can be used to estimate blood alcohol levels (BALs) according to body weight and the number of alcoholic drinks taken. Because alcohol in the blood decreases over time, subtract .015% for each hour that has passed since the first drink. BALs are also affected by rate of consumption, whether the stomach is empty or full, and the percent of body fat. Blood alcohol level of more than .050% is possible intoxication, more than .100% is probable intoxication, and more than .150% is intoxication. In the United States, the legal definition of intoxication varies from state to state.

	Given Alcohol	Given a Placebo
Expecting Alcohol	Participants expect and receive alcohol	Participants expect alcohol but receive a placebo
Not Expecting Alcohol	Participants expect a placebo but receive alcohol	Participants both expect and receive a placebo

Figure 11.1   The Balanced Placebo Design

The balanced placebo design is used to study the separate and combined effects of (1) actual alcohol and (2) expectations about alcohol. A large group of participants is divided into four smaller groups. Some participants expect to receive alcohol but are given a placebo instead. Their reactions, compared with other participants, is the result of their expectations about alcohol. Other participants are given real alcoholic beverages but believe they were given a placebo; their reactions are the result of the actual alcohol.

told that they will receive a dose of alcohol but are deceptively given a placebo; in this group, only expectancy effects will be active because the placebo has no pharmacological effects. In the fourth and last group, the subjects are told that they will receive a placebo but are deceptively given a dose of alcohol; in this group, only the pharmacological effects of alcohol can be presumed active because the subjects can have no expectations about the behavioral and psychological effects of a placebo. Using this balanced placebo design enables experimenters to study the pharmacological effects of a drug on psychology and behavior, the role of expectancies, the effects of both combined, and the results obtained from a control group in which neither pharmacology nor expectancy plays a role.

The balanced placebo design was used in an experiment to test whether alcohol enhances sexuality and sexual interest. Wilson and Lawson (1976) tested this question using four groups of college-aged male social drinkers. Subjects were given sexually explicit films to watch after having consumed beverages. Each man's level of sexual arousal during the films was monitored physiologically. The effects were striking. When subjects expected alcohol and received alcohol (the experimental condition), sexual arousal was indeed elicited, in conformance with the subjects' beliefs about drinking. But sexual arousal was nearly as intense in some of the other conditions. Specifically, subjects showed arousal in the condition in which they expected alcohol but actually received a placebo. In those who expected a placebo but received alcohol — the condition in which there is no expectation for the effects of alcohol and only the purely pharmacological effects of alcohol play a role — sexual arousal was markedly lower than that experienced by subjects in either of the placebo conditions. These men

received alcohol, but because they expected to receive a placebo, their arousal was lessened!

Such experiments and recent additional studies (Darkes & Goldman, 1993) have provided strong evidence that beliefs about the effects of alcohol, as well as the effects themselves, exert powerful control over what people experience while intoxicated. Put most simply, it's not only what you drink but also what you think that influences the role of alcohol in our lives.

THE ADDICTIVE AGENTS AND THEIR EFFECTS

Numerous agents can be addictive, and many are discussed in this chapter. Information about the use of these agents comes from several epidemiologic studies. The National Comorbidity Study interviewed over 8,000 15- to 54-year-olds in the United States (Kessler et al., 1994). The National Institute on Drug Abuse has compiled some data bearing on substance use among U.S. teenagers, college students, and young adults between 1975 and 1993 (Johnston, O'Malley & Bachman, 1987, 1994). Three U.S. government publications — *Health, United States, 1991, Statistical Abstract of the United States, 1992,* and *Alcohol and Health, 1993* — provide current estimates of substance use. Portions of the following discussions of prevalence are based, often without further attribution, on these studies of national patterns of alcohol and other drug use.

The discussion will focus on the use of addictive agents among young people for several reasons: (1) There is currently a considerable amount of misinformation about drug use among youths, (2) active use of most agents is concentrated among the young, and (3) as a group youths show the most promise for prevention and early intervention.

Alcohol

By his twenty-fifth birthday he led into battle the mightiest army ever to tread the earth. By his thirtieth birthday he had conquered all the known world, and he was pressing ever forward to reach and claim new territories. By his thirty-third birthday, he was dead, a victim of his own drinking and, finally, of a large quantity of wine he consumed while celebrating the conquest of Babylon. His name was Alexander of Macedon — Alexander "The Great."

Beverage **alcohol,** or ethanol, is one of the most ubiquitous of drugs, occurring as beer, wine, fortified wines,

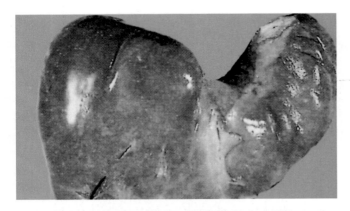

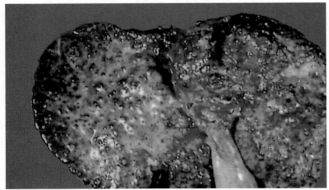

Gradual disease processes result from alcohol intake. For example, liver disease is frequent. There are dramatic and visible differences in the healthiness of a nondiseased and diseased (cirrhotic) liver.

and stronger distilled liquors. Except for the rarest instances, alcohol is ingested by drinking. Once ingested, alcohol takes a direct route into body systems. It travels to the stomach and small intestine and is then absorbed into the bloodstream and distributed throughout the body. Absorption is rapid, especially on an empty stomach.

Properly classified as a *sedative-hypnotic agent*, alcohol exercises a temporary and nonspecific depressant effect on the central nervous system similar to that of the barbiturates ("downers") and benzodiazepines (minor tranquilizers). Some individuals find the fact that alcohol is a depressant to be contrary to their personal experience — "But it makes me wild and excited," they say. Alcohol depresses the central nervous system, but at low doses, the inhibitory centers of the brain are depressed first. Thus, there is an initial perception of disinhibition when low doses of alcohol are consumed. Later, alcohol depresses the arousal centers. Importantly, note that at high doses, alcohol's depressant effects can interfere with hand-eye coordination, walking, and verbal and sensory functioning and can lead to unconsciousness, serious problems in respiration, and even death.

Patterns of alcohol use are highly variable; in most cases alcohol use is thoroughly integrated into the user's lifestyle. To address the heterogeneity among alcohol users, researchers have divided the group into subgroups (subtypes of alcoholics). Proposals for *alcoholic subtypes* are common, but they rarely hold up under close scrutiny. Nevertheless, some useful broad generalizations about problematic use patterns may be recognized. These include chronic daily use of large quantities; chronic regular use of large quantities restricted to weekends, holidays, and other leisure intervals; and binge or spree use, in which long periods of abstinence are punctuated by quite intense drinking binges. Alcohol frequently is used in conjunction with all other classes of psychoactive substances.

Unwanted Effects of Alcohol Alcohol is chief among substances that often lead to medical crises. A consequence of alcohol use may be trauma: injuries in fights or, more usually, in accidents on the road, at work, or at home. Interestingly, one of the most informative questions you can ask a possible alcohol abuser is, "Have you experienced a serious accident in the past year?" This question underlies the close relationship between alcohol consumption and accidental injury or death.

Alcohol consumption by an expectant mother can influence the health of her unborn child. In pregnant women, beverage alcohol readily crosses the placenta, exposing the developing fetus to a wide range of harmful effects. For each 10,000 births, 4 to 12 infants are born with permanent damage caused by the mother's drinking during pregnancy. This damage is called **fetal alcohol syndrome (FAS)**. Pregnant women who are heavy drinkers, compared with those who are light drinkers or nondrinkers, give birth to a greater number of infants compromised by abnormal growth and development. Newborns of heavy-drinking mothers were lighter in weight and smaller in size, with some facial and limb irregularities (see Table 11.3). Mental and motor retardation often accompany abnormal development. Of interest, research with both animals and human beings has documented the serious unwanted effects of alcohol consumption during pregnancy (Secretary's Report, 1993). Initial government publications warned against drinking more than one ounce of alcohol per day; more recent recommendations suggest that pregnant women should abstain from using alcohol. Fortunately, data have indicated that at least some pregnant adolescents voluntarily and substantially reduce their substance use during pregnancy (Gilchrist, Gillmore & Lohr, 1990).

Many serious gradual disease processes result from high alcohol intake as well. Most frequently encountered are diseases of the hepatic system or liver. Chief among these are alcoholic hepatitis and pancreati-

Table 11.3 Fetal Alcohol Syndrome

1. Prenatal or postnatal growth retardation (or both)

2. Symptoms of neurological, developmental, or intellectual impairment (profound intellectual impairment is common; see Chapter 16)

3. Odd facial structure of the following types:
   a. Small head size
   b. Tiny apparent eye size
   c. Flattening of the facial profile, with a small space between the nose and upper lip

Effects characteristic of FAS are listed (Jones & Smith, 1973, 1975). The actual amounts of maternal drinking necessary to produce FAS in the developing child are not well understood at this time, but increasingly, concerned and health-conscious pregnant women are discontinuing alcohol consumption during pregnancy.

tis, which are resolvable in most cases, and cirrhosis (extensive scarring of the liver that interferes with the organ's function), which is manageable in most cases but fatal in some.

Alcohol problems often co-occur with other psychological disorders: In one report, 82.4 percent of persons with an alcohol abuse diagnosis also qualified for at least one other diagnosis (Secretary's Report, 1993). Varying degrees of depression frequently are linked to heavy alcohol intake. Other psychological effects of long-term heavy drinking include anxiety and even paranoia, which may result from the isolation and lack of human contact that accompany drinking episodes. Acts of violence, with subsequent serious detrimental effects on spouses, children, and even the extended family, have been associated with acute intoxication (see Lau, Pihl & Peterson, 1995). Alcohol has been implicated in explosive disorder, in which violence may occur unexpectedly at high dose levels. A central effect of alcohol is damage to the brain itself. In severe cases, permanent or at least abiding brain damage may occur, involving the profound loss of memory and information-processing ability known as *Wernicke-Korsakoff's syndrome.*

Compared with some other drugs, tolerance of alcohol is usually not marked. With sustained use, tolerance of up to only about 200 percent of an initially tolerable dose of alcohol usually develops, although persons vary considerably in their capacity to develop tolerance. Withdrawal typically lasts only a few days and rarely longer than five to seven days. It is normally characterized by autonomic hyperactivity, physical complaints such as headache and nausea, mood disorder such as anxiety or depression, and occasionally more serious symptoms including convulsions, alcohol withdrawal delirium tremens (DTs), and alcoholic hallucinosis, which require medical intervention because withdrawal can be fatal if not adequately treated. The DTs are marked by trembling, sweating, fever, and impaired thinking.

Epidemiology of Alcohol Use   Alcohol tends to have one of the highest *continuation rates* (the percentage of first-time users who persist in use of a drug) of any substance. Alcohol is the most widely used of all psychoactive substances worldwide. In terms of per capita consumption, the United States ranks about fifteenth (behind Russia of the former USSR, France, Italy, Spain, and the former West Germany). Korea, Canada, and Taiwan have major problems with alcohol (Helzer et al., 1990).

In the United States, about 35 percent of adults now abstain from alcohol entirely. Abstinence appears to have risen among both males and females (Secretary's Report, 1993). About 55 percent of U.S. adults drink fewer than three drink equivalents per week, and about 10 percent consume more.

With *perestroika,* the Soviet Union began to acknowledge a societal problem with alcohol — they had the highest concentration of alcohol problems of any country in the world. A few authors have published estimates of the scope of Soviet alcohol problems, working primarily from indirect sources but occasionally from data bearing directly on alcoholism and its effects on the Soviet population. Their results were astounding. For instance, Treml (1982) found that the average Soviet citizen fifteen years of age and older consumed about 523 ounces of absolute alcohol per year: about fifty-one "fifths" of 80-proof vodka per year or about a fifth per week, more than eight times the average U.S. consumption.

Among young people in the United States, alcohol is by far the most widely used substance (see Figure 11.2). About 91 percent of high school students reported alcohol use at some point. College students tend to use alcohol at a rate substantially above their non-college–age peers. The percentage of people who use alcohol over their lifetime is also quite high.

Males have a much larger problem with alcohol than females (see Figure 11.3). For instance, Kessler et al. (1994) examined national survey data and reported that 20.1 percent of males (ages fifteen to fifty-four), but only 8.2 percent of females had a lifetime prevalence of alcohol dependence. Across genders, by far the greatest number of problems with alcohol emerge between the ages of twenty-one and thirty-four. Women generally begin to drink pathologically at a later age than men; men gradually become alcoholic, whereas women are

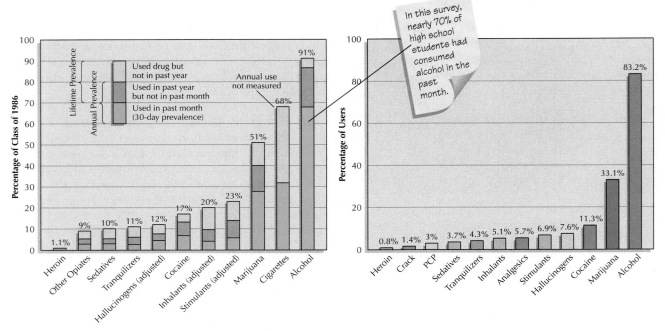

Figure 11.2 Prevalence of Substance Use

The left graph represents the percentage of high school students using each of eleven different types of substances. Alcohol, cigarettes, and marijuana received the highest reported use (more than 50 percent), with heroin at the low end of the continuum (1.1 percent). The right graph represents the 1990 lifetime percentage of users of twelve different substances. Alcohol (83.2 percent) and marijuana (33.1 percent) top the list. Although used by a lesser percentage of people, cocaine and several other drugs also present real problems for society.

Source: Data based on the National Institute of Drug Abuse (1991).

much more likely to follow a traumatic event with a rapid onset of alcoholism.

According to the recent National Household Survey on Drug Abuse (National Institute on Drug Abuse, 1992), the percentages of African Americans, Hispanics, and whites (ages eighteen to twenty-five) engaging in alcohol use at least once a week did not show meaningful differences — all three groups were approximately 25 percent. With regard to heavy consumption of alcohol among different ethnic groups, however, some studies have reported meaningful differences (e.g., Welte & Barnes, 1987). As shown in Figure 11.4, Native American and white adolescents have a higher percentage of heavy drinkers than Asian, African American, and Hispanic groups. Note, however, that there is a wide range of alcohol use across Native American tribes (see also Thurman, Swaim & Plested, 1995; Young, 1988).

Cannabis

Bob described himself as follows: "I was an average student in school, and I played sports and went to dances and things. I had friends, but I wasn't the best friend of anybody. When I started smoking marijuana, it was a little here and a little there, with different groups of friends. Then I'd smoke by myself before I went out. I really liked the mellow feeling, and the way music became so intense. People who weren't high seemed out of it. I'd say that I was getting high, but as I think back, it was just a way to dull my feelings. Instead of feeling left out, I thought I was cool. I still smoke several times a day." Bob has been called names by today's youth — they call him a "hippy leftover."

Cannabis products include marijuana, hashish, cannabis resin, and the pure form of their psychoactive ingredient, delta-9-tetrahydrocannabinol or THC. Cannabis is usually classified as a hallucinogenic agent, although hallucinogenic dose levels are uncommon. Cannabis has a broad and varied effect on the user's arousal states and perceptual faculties.

Cannabis is usually smoked (as marijuana or hashish), although it is sometimes added to foods and beverages. When smoked, marijuana is quickly absorbed into the lungs, and the THC in the smoke is transported to the brain. At this point, the mechanism of action is poorly understood (Jaffe, 1990). Patterns of use are variable: daily, occasional, and mild spree use are all encountered frequently. Typically users take a variety of other agents concurrently, particularly alcohol. Marijuana smokers who also abuse other substances have been found to have more psychological distress

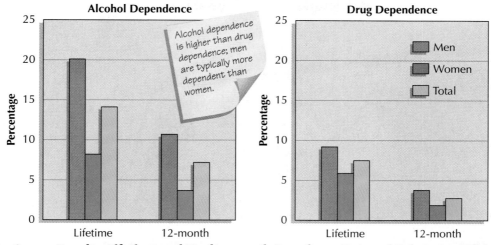

Figure 11.3   Survey Results: Lifetime and Twelve-month Prevalence Rates of Substance-Related Disorders

Shown here are reported prevalence rates from a national sample of fifteen- to fifty-four-year-old noninstitutionalized people. Data are presented as percentages, with lifetime prevalence equal to the proportion of the sample that *ever* experienced the disorder and twelve-month prevalence equal to the proportion that experienced the disorder within the year before the interview.

than smokers who do not (Stephens, Roffman & Simpson, 1993).

Unwanted Effects of Cannabis   The tars associated with the cannabis resin and the mode of smoking cannabis — inhaling deeply and holding the smoke in the lungs — make lung diseases a notable health risk for heavy users. Cannabis has been implicated in a number of psychological complaints associated with long-term use. One such condition, *cannabis amotivational syndrome,* comprises elements of lethargy, an inability to derive pleasure from activities, and unpleasant mood. Other symptoms include impaired judgment and loss of interest in personal appearance and the pursuit of conventional goals. Cannabis also has deleterious effects on attentional and memory functions and can be implicated, in rare cases, in severe mood disturbance and persecutory ideation.

Investigators believe that tolerance of cannabis, at least in some of its effects, does develop and may contribute to its sustained use. However, tolerance more often is manifested by increasing frequency of use than by increasing the dose. Withdrawal symptoms are rare.

Epidemiology of Cannabis Use   With a history of use almost as long as that of alcohol, cannabis is also a substance used worldwide. In some societies that prohibit alcohol use such as Muslim cultures, cannabis is the preferred and sanctioned recreational drug. In the United States, cannabis appears to be the most widely used substance other than alcohol and has one of the highest continuation rates. Its use peaked in the late 1970s, when almost 11 percent of high school seniors smoked marijuana daily. By 1986, only about 4 percent of both high school seniors and college students reported daily use,

and this pattern has remained level through 1993. However, among twelve- to seventeen-year-olds, monthly marijuana use has increased dramatically— jumping 105 percent since 1992 (Jones, 1996). Four percent of the adult population of the United States report having experienced substantial health and motivational problems as a result of using cannabis.

As with most other substances, the use of cannabis is concentrated in some population subgroups. Again, males are heavier users of cannabis, with a rate of daily

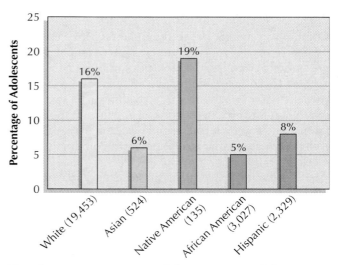

Figure 11.4   Heavy Drinkers among Adolescents by Ethnic Group

Although the percentage of heavy drinkers is less than 20 percent for all ethnic groups of adolescents, the percentage of Asians, African Americans, and Hispanics is considerably lower than that of whites and Native Americans.

Source: Data from Welte & Barnes (1987).

Question: What do these famous performers — Jim Morrison, Janis Joplin, John Belushi, and River Phoenix — have in common? Answer: Overuse and abuse of drugs and alcohol. There is something else they have in common: they are all dead as a consequence of their substance abuse.

use at some point in their lives about $1\frac{1}{2}$ times that observed among females. Males typically begin using cannabis at an earlier age than females and continue using cannabis for a longer time. In 1985, approximately 13 percent of white and black young adults reported use within the past month, whereas only 8 percent of Hispanics did so. Similar percentages were evident in 1992. Marijuana has limited medicinal use, such as for the control of glaucoma or in the reduction of pain.

Amphetamines or Similarly Acting Drugs

Commonly available as stimulants (for example, "speed") or as appetite suppressants, **amphetamines** are among the large class of stimulant-euphoriant agents. These agents mimic the stimulation of the sympathetic nervous system and have a powerful excitatory effect. Typical effects of these drugs include decreased fatigue, increased alertness, and occasionally heightened feelings of esteem and sexual potency (commonly called a "rush").

Usually taken orally, these drugs, particularly methamphetamine in its pure crystalline form, can be injected intravenously or taken by nasal inhalation. Patterns of use range from chronic daily use, which is relatively rare, to binge use, which is more common.

Unwanted Effects of Amphetamines Health risks are associated with the vasoconstrictive effect of the amphetamines. They cause a very rapid elevation in blood pressure and an extreme increase in pulse rate during the "rush" that constitutes the pleasurable effect. Such cardiac stimulation can cause improper functioning of the heart's pumping action, and a number

of deaths have been associated with the use of amphetamines.

Amphetamines are sometimes implicated in cases of delirium — a profound disturbance of sensation and mental state — and in delusional disorders, particularly episodes of intense agitation and paranoid thought. Less severe consequences from even short-term use are more common: These include depression in particular, irritability, anger, anxiety, sexual dysfunction, and loss of concentration and memory.

Tolerance of this type of drug has been observed, but little is known about its development. Withdrawal is characterized by depression, frequent paranoid or suicidal ideation, irritability, fatigue, and sleep disorder. Most symptoms persist for only a few days, although depression and irritability may persist for several months.

Epidemiology of Amphetamine Use The use of amphetamines is relatively common. Despite the fact that these drugs are synthetic compounds, they do have medical and other uses, they have sometimes been prescribed for obesity, and they have been given to soldiers, sailors, and pilots in wartime to help maintain alertness. Obsessive users ("speed freaks") are not uncommon, but the amphetamines typically do not have a high continuation rate. Technically not a part of this drug class is the large group of over-the-counter stimulant and diet pills, the national consumption of which, unlike that of true amphetamines, has increased markedly in recent years.

About 2 percent of the U.S. adult population have experienced a diagnosable amphetamine disorder at some time in their past. Among youths, amphetamines are the second most widely used illicit drug, after cannabis. Annual prevalence had fallen from over 15 percent in high school seniors and college students (that is, from 21 percent to 4 percent) from 1982 to 1992. However, there has been a recent increase in amphetamine use among high school seniors.

The amphetamines constitute one of only two drug classes (the other is nicotine) in which increased use is concentrated in females rather than in males (Johnston & O'Malley, 1986). However, this appears to be a phenomenon of instrumental, not social or recreational use. As is true of the sedative-hypnotic and opioid users, a sizable proportion of amphetamine users initially began use under physicians' orders as part of a medically supervised weight-loss program. Although in decline, a number of dieters and members of some occupational classes who require prolonged alertness (such as long-distance truckers) steadily use amphetamines.

Cocaine

Cocaine is available in several forms, including the coca leaf and its crude extract, coca paste; cocaine hydrochloride powder ("snow"); and the smokable cocaine alkaloid forms known as "freebase" or "crack." These substances are classified as stimulant-euphoriant agents, producing a temporary and powerful excitatory effect on the central nervous system. Pharmacologically, the euphoric effect is produced by blocking of the reuptake of neurotransmitter substances such as dopamine and norepinephrine (Jaffe, 1990). These substances are active in the experience of reward and emotion and, when they are present in excessive amounts, are associated with the subjective report of excitement, arousal, energy, and sometimes euphoria. For instance, the brain chemical dopamine, under certain circumstances, helps trigger good feelings, but it is usually reabsorbed after it has had its effect. Cocaine somehow blocks the reabsorption. The nerves can become overexcited, and the euphoria intensifies. One theory of the biochemistry of cocaine suggests that the drug prevents the brain from calming itself. In the end, however, the drug effects are exhausted, and the user experiences a profound depression.

Cocaine may be taken in a number of forms. Its crude forms are chewed, but in North America and Europe it is usually inhaled nasally, smoked, or administered intravenously. Use patterns are variable: Those who use the drug daily or almost daily are also involved in activities such as trafficking to defray costs. Individuals who use cocaine "when it is available" illustrate episodic abuse.

Typically, cocaine is used concurrently with other drugs, particularly alcohol or other sedative-hypnotics, which are used to mitigate the unpleasant effects of the "crash" that usually follows the use of cocaine. In some subcultures, cocaine is mixed with and injected simultaneously with heroin, a substance admixture known colloquially as "speedball."

Unwanted Effects of Cocaine As the following case illustrates, there can be tragic effects from cocaine use.

> *John, who was mentioned in the chapter opener, played football as a teenager and was even elected Homecoming King, but his talent, his love, was always for comedy. It came very easy to him, and the money came even easier. "Cocaine is nature's way of telling you that you're making too much money," he said, but his appetites ran in other directions, too — toward food, heroin, liquor, and always toward more and more success. On March 5, 1982, he was found dead in a Los Angeles hotel room. The pathologist found both cocaine and heroin metabolites in his blood and urine and injection marks on his left arm, evidence of a huge "speedball" binge that he'd been on for days, months, or perhaps years before his death. On March 9, 1982, he was buried in Abel's Hill Cemetery on Martha's Vineyard, where he'd bought a mansion with some of the movie money that he hadn't spent on cocaine and heroin. He was from Chicago, the Blues City, and thought of himself as the original Blues Brother. He starred in the original Saturday Night Live. He was thirty-three years old at the time of his death. His name was John Belushi.*

Like the amphetamines, cocaine causes a very rapid elevation in blood pressure and an extreme increase in pulse rate, which in some persons cause improper pumping of the heart. A number of deaths have been associated with the use of even small quantities of cocaine. Cocaine is sometimes implicated in delirium and delusional disorders, particularly episodes of intense agitation and paranoid thought. Even short-term use can lead to depression, irritability, anger, anxiety, sexual dysfunction, and loss of concentration and memory.

The development of tolerance to cocaine has been established but is not well understood. Withdrawal symptoms include brief symptoms such as fatigue, sleep disorder, and agitation; longer-lasting symptoms such as depression; and occasional states with paranoid, homicidal, and suicidal elements that clear gradually over the course of weeks and even months.

Epidemiology of Cocaine Use For several years cocaine use has been the most newsworthy drug problem in the United States and Europe. It has a fairly high continuation rate, in the general range of that for cannabis and nicotine. Like these two agents, cocaine appears to be most dangerous in its smokable form (crack), which produces a brief but intense intoxication within just a few seconds of administration.

Cocaine is one of the very few drugs for which active use climbs after high school. This situation in the 1980s may have been because of the costliness of cocaine and the higher disposable incomes of adults. Because cheap, smokable cocaine has become readily available, active use is now concentrated among youths. Presently, by their late twenties, about 40 percent of Americans report some experience with cocaine in their lifetimes. In general, though, only a small percentage of adults have experienced diagnosable problems with this agent during their lives. Male cocaine abusers were found to be more likely to be employed, to hold higher-status jobs, and to be self-supporting than female cocaine abusers, who were more likely to be diagnosed as depressed and not employed or self-supporting (Griffin, Weiss, Mirin & Lange, 1989).

Among young people, cocaine use appears to have peaked in the mid-1980s, with the drug now in decline in most communities. However, annual prevalence among college students and other young adults is much higher, and researchers also have observed an important shift in route of administration from nasal inhalation to smoking. Among high school students, crack users exhibit the lowest level of psychological functioning of any other drug-using group (Kandel & Davies, 1996).

Ethnic group differences vary for cocaine and crack. Data from the National Institute of Drug Abuse (1992) indicated minor group differences: Between 2 and 3.5 percent of the whites, Hispanics, and blacks used cocaine within the last month. For crack, however, the differences were slightly greater, with more use by African Americans than either whites or Hispanics. In 1991, across ages, blacks (4.3 percent) reported the highest rate of use (whites, 1.5 percent; Hispanics, 2.1 percent).

In general, data have suggested a trend away from cocaine use, but problems with cocaine are in the process of becoming concentrated. The drug is used almost twice as frequently among urbanites as among suburban or rural Americans (Warner & Kessler, 1995). Cocaine, especially in the relatively inexpensive and smokable form of crack, appears to be developing into an entrenched drug problem of inner-city underclass youth.

Hallucinogens

Hallucinogens are both natural and synthetic. Naturally occurring agents include peyote, its derivative mescaline, and psilocybin. Synthetics include lysergic acid diethylamide (LSD). Hallucinogenic agents produce varied and sometimes very powerful perceptual alterations and excitation of the central nervous system, from the cortex to the spinal cord. The experienced effect of a hallucinogen is a sensory distortion: Persons who have consumed a hallucinogen might see and hear things that are altered, deformed, or not in reality. Perceptions that do not have a basis in reality are referred to as *hallucinations*.

Typically taken orally and in an episodic fashion, hallucinogens produce powerful and sometimes unpredictable effects. Daily or near-daily use and spree use are quite rare. Hallucinogens frequently are used by people who take other drugs, especially cannabis and alcohol.

Unwanted Effects of Hallucinogens Because hallucinogenic agents are relatively rare, physical dependence is virtually not an issue. Use is almost always too infrequent for physiological habituation leading to withdrawal in abstinence to develop. Similarly, tolerance among experienced users of some hallucinogenic agents is rare. Still, serious physiological and neuropsychological complications sometimes accompany use of these drugs.

Hallucinogens can be involved in delusional thinking and severe mood disorders. Hallucinogens are associated with panic attacks, especially in persons not comfortable with the altered awareness produced during the intoxicated state. Severe dangers are associated with driving while taking a hallucinogen, and work and social relationships also can suffer greatly. Further, some researchers have suggested that among individuals who are susceptible, prolonged hallucinogen use can lead to psychotic disorder. Flashbacks — or the reappearance of effects resembling the earlier hallucinogenic condition — can occur months and sometimes years after the drug was ingested initially. Although what causes flashbacks or why they occur in some individuals and not in others is not clear, they are troublesome and unwanted.

Epidemiology of Hallucinogen Use The use of hallucinogens peaked in the mid-1970s and until quite recently has become less common in the United States and abroad. Researchers have estimated that less than 1 percent of the adult population has experienced a diagnosable problem with hallucinogens at some time in their lives. Among youths, in 1993, 6.8 percent of graduating high school seniors had used a hallucinogen in the past year.

Hallucinogen use shows variability across ethnic groups (*Statistical Abstract of the United States, 1992*). For young adults (eighteen to twenty-five), only 7.5 percent of Hispanics and 5.4 percent of blacks had ever used hallucinogens, whereas 15.8 percent of whites reported having used a hallucinogen. Males are about 40 percent more likely to use hallucinogens than females, and young people are more likely users than adults. Use is concentrated among non-college–bound young people and is about 50 percent more prevalent in urban than in rural areas.

Nicotine

Nicotine is widely available in tobacco products (cigarettes, cigars, pipe tobacco, snuff, and chewing tobacco). Classified as a stimulant-euphoriant, nicotine is an extremely fast-acting drug that increases arousal. For the skeptical reader, it bears emphasizing that many people consider nicotine to be a very powerful psychoactive drug (Henningfield, Miyasato & Jasinski, 1985) that alters behavior, mood, and physical sensation. When tobacco leaves are burned, nicotine vapors are produced; when tobacco is smoked, these vapors are absorbed into the lungs and then into the bloodstream. Once in the bloodstream, nicotine is carried to the heart and to the brain. One effect on the brain is stimulation of the area controlling respiration, which increases breathing rate. In addition, nicotine affects the peripheral nervous system, leading to increased heart rate and blood pressure. Of late, there is increased acceptance of the classification of nicotine as a drug.

As tobacco, nicotine is usually smoked, but it also may be taken as snuff through nasal inhalation. It also may be taken orally. Nicotine often has been called the most addictive of all drugs; 70 percent of first-time users ultimately develop dependence on nicotine, a far higher proportion than that for any other substance. As such, nicotine typically is used in a chronic daily fashion. The pack-a-day smoker takes about 200 doses of nicotine daily, or 75,000 doses each year. Because of the ease with which the most common form of the drug (a cigarette) is used, most users are able to exercise extremely fine control over their dose levels.

Recall Karen, whose father died of lung cancer. You and her other friends have provided social support, but have also tried to encourage her to quit smoking. At the same time, Karen's work office has become a "no smoking" zone, and her new boyfriend is a nonsmoker. Her conflict was reduced when she announced that "now is the time to quit." Six months later, now living alone, Karen considers herself an ex-smoker — though she has on a few occasions unlocked her office window so that she could "sneak a smoke" behind her closed door. Her cigarette habit has gone from more than a pack a day to two or three cigarettes a month.

Unwanted Effects of Nicotine Nicotine has complex and potentially fatal effects on health. Because nicotine is a vasoconstrictor, it causes blood pathways to narrow temporarily and contributes to high blood pressure and coronary artery disease. Other unhealthy effects are related to the carcinogenic effects of either nicotine itself or the tars that co-occur in the tobacco leaf, including lung cancer and emphysema in smokers and a variety of oral and gastric cancers in smokers and users of smokeless tobacco.

Both tolerance and withdrawal have been documented for nicotine. Withdrawal symptoms begin soon after the last dose, often within one to two hours, and can include irritability, loss of concentration, decreased metabolic rate, and cravings (urges). Hunger, restlessness, and anxiety (Hughes, 1992) and weight gain (Perkins, 1993) also have been reported. Symptoms peak during the first few days but may persist for weeks and even months.

Among those trying to quit, the urge to smoke has been described as powerful. What emotions are associated with such urges? Recent research on the emotions related to the urge to smoke revealed interesting differences between those who continue to smoke versus those who are withdrawing from smoking: For those who were trying to quit, the urge to smoke was associated with negative feelings. In contrast, the urges of continuing smokers were related to positive affect — urges were linked to the pleasurable anticipation or aftereffects of smoking (Zinser, Baker, Sherman & Cannon, 1992).

Epidemiology of Nicotine Use Perhaps as a result of media campaigns and large-scale prevention programs, the prevalence of nicotine use in the United States has been declining since the 1960s. This trend is not evident in other parts of the world, however. Cigarette use is still widespread and has even increased in some subgroups. In general, more people are dependent on nicotine than are dependent on any other legal or illegal drug. Its continuation rate of 83 percent is among the highest.

Two lungs—one from a smoker and one from a nonsmoker. Pathologists can easily and readily identify the diseased lung—the effects of nicotine are obvious once a person has died and the lungs can be examined in this manner.

Nicotine has been implicated in about 300,000 U.S. deaths each year. This figure represents more Americans than were lost in all the battles of World War II, and it dwarfs the mortality figures associated with any other drug. Currently, researchers estimate that about 53 million Americans, or more than 25 percent of the population, are regular, addicted users of nicotine. Nicotine is one of the few drugs in which use is not concentrated among males. In two studies of peer group association and tobacco use among both male and female adolescents, use of both cigarettes and smokeless tobacco was greatest among problem-prone youth (Mosbach & Leventhal, 1988; Sussman et al., 1990).

Opioids

Opiates can be natural, such as opium, morphine, heroin, and codeine, and synthetic, such as methadone and hydromorphone (Dilaudid). Opiate agents produce a profound generalized and abiding sedative, anesthetic, and euphoriant effect on the central nervous system. The body contains opiate receptors, such as those in the pain centers of the brain. Synthetic opiates, like natural opiates, bind to these opiate receptors and block the experience of emotional and physical pain. In certain circumstances, the body naturally produces opioids (beta-endorphins) to deaden the sensation of pain. Those who abuse opioids are perhaps seeking to create a state of blunted physical and emotional pain.

Overdose is a major risk with opiate use. Opiate users frequently know little about the potency of the drugs they purchase, and accidental overdoses can and do occur. Although "overdose" death is a major public health problem, its mechanisms are unclear (Siegel, 1989). Infections such as hepatitis and acquired immune

deficiency syndrome (AIDS) can be passed from person to person through shared drug needles. The psychological effects of prolonged use of opiates include depression, which is quite common, and anxiety, particularly if the user begins to involuntarily withdraw.

The opiate withdrawal syndrome is brief but usually so very uncomfortable that once a person is habituated to the drug, opiates must be used daily to avoid the onset of withdrawal. The opiates usually are used in combination with a variety of other agents, including alcohol and other sedative-hypnotics, cocaine, and marijuana.

Tolerance of the opiates develops rapidly and can become quite pronounced (Zacny, 1995); experienced users of the drug can tolerate up to 5,000 percent of the dose level tolerable by a naive and inexperienced user. Withdrawal is also well documented, commencing within six to eight hours of the last dose, peaking typically within two days, and remitting within a week. Symptoms include intense physical discomfort, diarrhea, tearing, irritability, and craving for the drug. The user experiences chills, and goose bumps appear on the skin, giving the appearance of a plucked turkey (McKim, 1986). These signs are the source of the phrase "going cold turkey." Later in the withdrawal, after a period of sleep, there may be twitching of the extremities, such as kicking of the legs — the source of the phrase "kicking the habit." The severity of the withdrawal depends on the daily dose of the addict.

In general, opiates such as heroin are among the rarest of drugs used illicitly. Nevertheless, the addiction is powerful and so leads to regular use among addicts, who are often willing to go to any length to acquire the drug or money and so avoid the onset of withdrawal. A very small percentage of first-time users ultimately develops dependence, and the continuation rate for opiates is among the lowest. Because the opioids are administered intravenously and users may unwisely share needles, they risk contracting the AIDS virus.

Among U.S. adults, less than 1 percent report having experienced a problem with the opiates in their lifetimes. However, a high percentage of military personnel serving in the field during the Vietnam War initiated opiate use and continued to use opiates regularly; an overall prevalence among U.S. troops in Vietnam of 25 percent is frequently cited. A measure of the relatively low addictive potential of the opiates is that very few of these persons continued use on returning to the United States. Use of opiates among young people is quite rare.

Sedatives, Hypnotics, and Anxiolytics

Leslie told us, "I would take two and sometimes three sedatives a day. I didn't tell my friends or my husband: I worked hard to maintain the image of the wonder woman. I had tried to do it all: be successful at my work, keep the house clean, get the kids to their activities — you know, all the routine stuff that can drive you crazy. I wanted it all to be just right, and I'd be tense and worried almost all the time."

"One day it hit me — at forty-six, with two children, a law degree, and a successful businessman for a husband, it only seemed that I had it all. I had a lot of things — a live-in housekeeper, a vacation home, and a closet full of the best clothes — but I also had a serious drug problem. At first, simply admitting that I had a problem caused conflict . . . people didn't want it to be true. They accepted my problem, but only after several emotional outbreaks. It was with the help of my husband and family that I eventually discontinued my three separate prescriptions for sedatives and sought help for my drug problem."

Sedative-hypnotic-anxiolytic agents include the broad classes of barbiturates ("downers"), the benzodiazepines or minor tranquilizers (such as Valium, Librium, and Xanax), and some analgesics such as chloral hydrate or methaqualone (Quaaludes, or "ludes"). They produce a temporary and nonspecific depressant effect, not unlike that of alcohol, on the central nervous system. Barbiturates (low dose) result in a sense of relaxation and light-headedness. Higher doses produce poor coordination, slurred speech, and sleep. The effects are the opposite of the stimulants — there is no excitatory high or energetic arousal.

Use of sedative-hypnotics can produce fatal overdoses. The drugs are particularly dangerous when used with alcohol because co-use can multiply each drug's sedative effect, leading to respiratory suppression or failure and to death.

The sedative-hypnotics tend to promote a severe and abiding withdrawal syndrome when their use is terminated. Tolerance of these agents develops rapidly, and experienced users are capable of tolerating doses of more than 1,000 percent the dose level tolerable by inexperienced users. Withdrawal, too, is well documented; it is characterized by autonomic hyperactivity, sleep disturbance, and anxiety and other signs of irritability. Seizures and delirium are common, and patients with marked dependence must have close medical supervision.

The sedative-hypnotics other than alcohol occupy a middle ground in terms of problem prevalence. They have a continuation rate in the midrange of psychoactive substances. Among U.S. adults, only slightly more than 1 percent report a history of problems with these agents, but a larger number of users take the drug "legitimately" (by prescription). Among youths, annual prevalence for most sedative-hypnotics has declined steadily since the mid-1970s. At that time, about 11 percent of high school seniors reported some use of barbiturates or benzodiazepines; this figure have declined currently to 3.5 percent.

ADDICTIVE PROCESSES

Each of us likely knows or has known someone with a substance-abuse problem: a friend, a relative, or even a member of the immediate family. Perhaps the cause of the problem was attributed to economic hard times, peer pressure, moral weakness, or an inherited illness. Besides attempting to explain a single instance of substance abuse, have you considered the physiological and social processes involved in the development of these disorders?

Some of the first efforts were by writers who were psychodynamically oriented. Originally their focus was on drinking disorders, sometimes called *dipsomania* ("drinking madness"). They highlighted the pleasurable, consummatory, and oral aspects of drinking (for example, Abraham, 1908/1960; Freud, 1905/1955) and viewed problem drinkers as immature, regressed personalities to whom the bottle is symbolic of the mother's breast and for whom intoxication recapitulates the drowsy dependency of infancy. More recently, psychodynamic authors have explored the role of the family and of relationships to significant others during childhood, although research evaluations continue to be nonexistent.

In general, explanations for substance-use disorders include genetic factors, environmental forces, family factors, and peer influences. We can learn a great deal about the development of substance-abuse disorders by taking a closer look at the proposed explanations for and the research data on the causes of a major substance-abuse disorder — alcoholism. Although a high percentage of Americans think alcoholism is a disease, there is no universally accepted "single cause" for alcoholism (or any of the substance-use disorders) among scholars and scientists.

Alcoholism as a Disease

In 1814, Dr. Benjamin Rush hypothesized the existence of a progressive addictive illness, *intemperance,* that had a well-defined causal agent (liquor), characteristic symptoms (compulsive drinking), a predictable course (progressive deterioration), a common outcome (insanity or death), and an effective cure (total abstinence) (Rush, 1947). Rush believed that alcohol, through its destruction of the "moral centers" of the brain, led to loss of control over drinking, then to deviance and violence, and ultimately to poverty and crime. He held that there was only one solution — temperance or abstinence.

A more modern perspective is the **unitary disease model** of addiction. This model holds that alcoholics differ from normal persons in terms of psychological predisposition and "allergic" sensitivity to alcohol (Pollock, 1992); it maintains that these differences cause alcoholics during their drinking careers to experience psychological or physiological changes (or both) that are progressive and irreversible and that lead to (1) craving and (2) loss of control regarding alcohol. According to the model, alcoholism and other drug-use disorders can be remedied only by lifelong abstinence. This notion is widely used in the field and was perhaps best expressed in an influential book, *The Disease Concept of Alcoholism* (Jellinek, 1960).

Working from survey data gathered from active members of Alcoholics Anonymous, Jellinek formulated the idea that in most persons alcoholism is initially engendered by personality or social causes that promote heavy drinking but that it is later sustained by a physiological factor that causes a disease condition outwardly manifested by craving for and loss of control over drinking. He described a sequential stage theory of the development of alcoholism: in a *stage theory,* the person develops alcoholism after going through a series of mutually exclusive invariant phases. Jellinek's (1952) stages included (1) the prealcoholic symptomatic phase, in which social drinking becomes habitual and highly desirable because of the tension-relieving effects of liquor; (2) the prodromal phase, in which guilt, denial, secretiveness, and occasional blackouts begin to occur; (3) the crucial phase, in which loss of control and the beginnings of social damage occur; and (4) the chronic phase, during which drinking becomes wholly obsessive and sustained and considerable deterioration occurs ("hitting bottom"), leading frequently to "insanity or death."

Is the unitary disease model of any worth? By providing a palatable explanation of addiction, the model improved public awareness of the problem and cultivated optimism about its treatability. For example, it was during Jellinek's heyday that alcoholism was recognized as a medical condition open to treatment. Further, clinicians could argue that alcoholism is a disease because there is a fairly uniform and predictable set of features, course, prognosis, and treatment.

The disease model of alcoholism has been criticized on many grounds, however (e.g., Caddy, 1978; Fingarette, 1988; Mello, 1975; Pattison, 1976). First, there are limited scientific foundations for many of the predicates of the disease model, such as the idea that alcohol or other drug problems are progressive diseases (developing from the presymptomatic to the prodromal, the crucial, and the chronic phases). Second, the model reduces the addict's accountability for the damage he or she causes and could subvert the addict's autonomy and will to change. Third, some of the postulates of the model (such as that one drink leads inevitably to a full-blown relapse) function as self-fulfilling prophesies (if you believe that one drink will lead to a full relapse, then, after one drink, the prediction of a relapse is likely to be fulfilled). These beliefs, which focus so exclusively on a disease process, suppress attention to the psychological and contextual features of problematic alcohol and other drug use. Critics further argue that the concept of addiction communicated to the public may prevent many drinkers and drug users who do not fit this stereotype from identifying their use patterns as problematic and thereby entering treatment. Finally, the disease model is inconsistent with the data that have suggested that controlled use is a viable goal for the treatment of some alcohol and drug users and that some addicts "recover" by natural processes or after minimal intervention.

What, then, is the status of the unitary disease model? It is prudent to acknowledge that a group of patients with alcohol- and other drug-use disorders can be described by the unitary disease model. Similarly, although abstinence is clearly not a treatment goal for all patients, it is indicated sometimes and can be recommended for some persons. However, it is important to note that alcohol- and other drug-use disorders constitute a heterogeneous class of problems in living for which the unitary disease model is perhaps metaphorical: Although not literally a disease, substance-use disorders do have serious negative physical effects.

Heredity and Alcoholism

In classical Greece, Plutarch's saying *"Ebrii gignunt ebrios"* ("Drunkards beget drunkards") was recognized as true and has been, in fits and starts, endorsed by some scientists throughout history. During the 1970s and 1980s, several independent research teams reported data that supported the idea that alcoholism is, in some instances, genetically transmitted. Sheila, who we read about at the beginning of this chapter, might be a case in point. In an adoption study, D. Goodwin (1971, 1976, 1979) and his colleagues (Goodwin et al., 1973, 1974) followed four groups of subjects in Denmark, a country that keeps excellent lifetime adoption and medical records. All subjects were the offspring of alcoholic parents. The first group consisted of young men who were surrendered for adoption at birth and then raised by nonalcoholic adoptive parents. The second group consisted of young men who had remained in their homes to be raised by their alcoholic parents. A third group consisted of young women, daughters of alcoholics, who were surrendered for adoption at birth and raised by nonalcoholic adoptive parents. The fourth group consisted of similar young women who had remained with their alcoholic parents. Paired with each group was a control group — sons or daughters of nonalcoholics — some of whom had been placed for adoption in nonalcoholic foster homes. All subjects were interviewed about their drinking practices by Danish psychiatrists who sought to diagnose alcoholism in the subjects but who were otherwise "blind" to the genetic background of the subjects.

Although only about 10 percent of the male control subjects (sons of nonalcoholics) were diagnosed as alcoholic themselves, 40 percent of the sons of alcoholics had developed alcoholism, and this was true whether they had been raised by their alcoholic parents or had been adopted into nonalcoholic families. The sons of alcoholics were found in the Goodwin studies to be at increased risk for alcoholism, and this risk did not appear to be reduced by the palliative effects of being raised in a nonalcoholic home. The results concerning the daughters of alcoholics were different: Between 4 and 5 percent of these women were alcoholic, but so were a similar percentage of the adopted control subjects (that is, the daughters of nonalcoholics).

Similar findings concerning the high risk for alcoholism among the children of alcoholic parents have been reported by others. However, the role of genetic factors seems to vary with the type of alcoholism. For example, Cloninger, Bohman and Sigvardsson (1981) studied a sample of 2,000 adoptees in Sweden, paying particular attention to the drinking practices and lifestyles of the biological parents. Cloninger and his colleagues reported that the type of alcoholism found in the parents seemed to affect the development of alcoholism in the adopted biological sons. In what was termed **type 1 alcoholism,** which was the most common type, the parents had begun drinking by early adulthood but tended not to have developed problems with their drinking until middle age. At that stage in their lives, they had frequent health effects (such as liver problems) and were often hospitalized, but they showed very few, if any,

compromises of their social, family, or occupational standing. Their adopted biological sons were about twice as likely to develop alcoholism as the adopted biological sons of nonalcoholic parents.

In what was termed **type 2 alcoholism,** the alcoholic parents had few, if any, medical problems but did experience severe disruption of their marital, family, social, and occupational lives — divorce, job loss, and disruption of social activities. Their adopted biological sons were nine times as likely to develop alcoholism as the biological sons of nonalcoholic parents. Later in life, 90 percent of sons of type 2 alcoholic parents developed alcoholism themselves (see also Cloninger, 1987). Although other researchers have used alternate subtypings to examine the genetic contribution (e.g., Cadoret et al., 1995), the research findings (such as those of Pickens et al., 1991) do support differential genetic contributions to alcoholism.

As noted, males and females have been found to differ with regard to their genetic risk for alcoholism (see also Pollock, Schneider, Gabrielli & Goodwin, 1986). The recent data reported by McGue, Pickens, and Svikis (1992) add to our understanding. These investigators found that genetic factors played a greater role in alcoholism for males than for females and that the genetic influence in males was greater for early-onset as compared with late-onset alcoholism. More specifically, although the findings for all subjects indicated a modest genetic influence, the authors reported that the genetic influence in the cause of alcoholism was substantial for males with early-onset alcoholism.

Although most investigators would agree that alcoholism is not solely a genetically transmitted disease, many would argue that genetic factors influence the risk for alcoholism. Do offspring of alcoholics inherit a physiological system that leaves them at greater risk for developing alcoholism? Two groups of nonalcoholic men were compared in a study conducted by Peter Finn, Nathalie Zeitouni, and Robert Pihl (1990). The two groups were similar in age and education and in their pattern of alcohol consumption; they differed, however, in their family history of alcoholism. One group had a multigeneration family history of alcoholism, the other group had no such history. The groups showed different patterns of physiological reactivity (for example, skin conductance and heart rate) and sensitivity to alcohol: As compared with the men with no family history of alcoholism, those with a family history of alcoholism were more physiologically reactive to stimulation and showed larger reductions in reactivity after consuming alcohol.

Despite the acceptance of genetic contributions to risk, investigators have raised questions about the methodology of some of the earlier studies (Searles, 1988). For instance, when examining the quality of the studies that have been reported, the diagnostic criteria used to determine alcoholism have been questioned:

Have studies used too broad and inclusive a definition and thereby increased the estimation of the role of genetics? Researchers also have raised the question of the presence of other psychological disorders: Have studies failed to take into account the presence of other psychological abnormalities in the homes of the foster parents? Moreover, the precise manner of transmission is not well understood: What particular characteristic of the offspring of alcoholics might make them susceptible to the development of alcoholism? The pathways for the genetic transmission of risk for alcoholism are now the objects of intense scrutiny by scientists (see Cadoret et al., 1995).

Personality Factors and Substance Abuse

Theories of personality, such as the psychodynamic model of personality development, propose that a certain type of person is likely to develop into an alcoholic or a substance abuser. Early writings (Fenichel, 1945) suggested that alcoholics had regressed to the oral stage of psychosexual development. This *oral-dependent personality* described an individual whose need for oral gratification was not satisfied by parents early in life. As an outcome, the individual has a passive and dependent interpersonal style and strives to secure oral satisfaction through substance use such as drinking, smoking, or both.

The regression explanation and the oral-needs description received little empirical support, leading researchers to turn to other personality factors that might be related to substance abuse. Some researchers selected samples of alcoholics or drug abusers and tried to identify characteristics of a "substance-abuse personality" by comparing these individuals with nonabusers. Results suggested that men who developed substance-abuse (alcohol) problems were more antisocial, impulsive, and depressive than other people (e.g., Labouvie & McGee, 1986). Substance abusers showed less persistence than nonabusers (Quinn, Brandon & Copeland, 1996), and college women who consumed a large amount of alcohol showed a high concern for anxiety symptoms (Stewart, Peterson, & Pihl, 1995).

This approach, while occasionally documenting differences in the personalities of abusers and nonabusers, has a methodological weakness: whether the reported personality differences were the cause of the abuse or the result of abuse was not clear. Other research suggested that children and adolescents who did not value conventional mores and were impulsive and aggressive (an antisocial behavior pattern) were more likely than others to engage in substance abuse in adulthood (Zucker & Gomberg, 1986), whereas others theorized that alcohol and drug use was a cover for underlying depression. To properly test these and other theories, a longitudinal design is needed (e.g., Kwapil, 1996).

In a longitudinal inquiry conducted at the University of California at Berkeley, Jonathan Shedler and Jack Block (1990) studied 101 eighteen-year-olds who originally had been recruited into their study at the age of three and who had been assessed psychologically on numerous occasions (at ages three, five, seven, eleven, and eighteen). In this sample, subjects were divided into three groups according to their usage pattern: frequent drug users, experimenters, and abstainers. Frequent users reported using marijuana once a week or more and had tried at least one drug in addition to marijuana. Experimenters had used marijuana on occasion but had tried no more than one other drug. Abstainers had never tried marijuana or any other drug.

Adolescents who used drugs frequently were found to be different from abstainers: They showed a personality that was marked by poor impulse control, interpersonal alienation, and emotional distress. By looking back to the data gathered when these subjects were younger, Shedler and Block were able to address the question of cause or effect. At the time when they were aged seven and eleven, those subjects who at eighteen were frequent drug users had been judged by the experimenters to have been insecure, unable to form healthy relationships, and emotionally distressed. Based on this study, a personality characterized by difficulties with interpersonal relationships, weak impulse control, and subjective distress appears to be associated with frequent drug use at age eighteen. Certainly, data support that psychopathy (see Chapter 14) is strongly associated with alcohol and other drug abuse (e.g., Smith & Newman, 1990), that impulsive nonconforming and psychosis-prone persons are at risk for substance use disorders (Kwapil, 1996), and that cigarette, alcohol, and other drug use is highly correlated among adolescents (e.g., Farrell, Danish & Howard, 1992).

Critics of the earlier research have pointed out that having sought to find the one personality trait that was linked to substance abuse, one must be disappointed by the wide range of personality factors found. In contrast, when one sees the potential interrelatedness of the several personality descriptors, it may be that there are multiple personality traits that, in combination, are associated with substance abuse.

Alcoholism as Learned Behavior

An early and important learning explanation for the development of alcoholism was Conger's (1956) tension reduction hypothesis. By applying principles of learning and experimental findings with nonhuman subjects to an analysis of human alcohol problems (Conger, 1951; Masserman & Yum, 1946), John Conger advanced the theory that alcoholic drinking is a product of escape learning. That is, alcoholics learn to drink because drinking is followed in most cases by a reduction in the state of a drive (fear) or aversive emotional state (such as anxiety or conflict). Examples of this situation include individuals who fear social disapproval yet feel a sense of approval when drinking, fear the withdrawal symptoms that emerge when alcohol consumption is discontinued, and are tense about social interaction yet feel socially lubricated when drinking. Put simply, this **tension reduction hypothesis** holds that people learn to use alcohol and other drugs because such use relieves the sensation of tension, which can be variously described as anxiety, depression, fear, or social avoidance.

During the 1960s and 1970s, the tension reduction hypothesis received considerable attention in the laboratory. For example, in one study laboratory rats were first trained to eat in a specific location. Later, they were subjected to electric shock as they approached their food. These animals displayed signs of tension around eating: They showed definite signs of conflict and distress as they neared their food. Half these conflicted animals were then given alcohol, and half were not. For the animals given alcohol, approach behavior and eating were conducted with less distress. Contemporary theorists have suggested that it is only partially complete because it relies exclusively on principles of operant conditioning and pays little notice to cognitive, biological, and social influences.

One cognitive factor, attention allocation, has been investigated. Researchers know that alcohol impairs performance on tasks requiring attention and that stress requires attention. Perhaps because alcohol undermines attention, it serves to reduce tension. When one's capacity to pay attention is reduced by alcohol, and one has a task to perform that requires attention, then one has less attention to allocate to stressful thoughts, and anxiety is reduced. Indeed, studies have supported the idea that as the attentional demands of a distracting activity increased, so did alcohol's reduction of anxiety. Without the distracting task, subjects showed an increase in anxiety (e.g., Josephs & Steele, 1990).

Another cognitive factor, expectations, has been found to be important in understanding tension reduction. Among people in general, stressful life situations contribute to increased alcohol consumption. Persons exposed to trauma (such as disasters, assault, or combat), for instance, show significant increases in alcohol abuse (Stewart, 1996). Stress was a more powerful influence among a subset of individuals, however: Those men who typically coped with stress by avoidance and who expected positive effects from alcohol were quite likely to use alcohol. In contrast, for men who did not cope by avoidance and who had low expectations for alcohol, stressful events were not positively related to alcohol use. Similarly for women, regardless of their expectations or coping style, life events were not a positive pre-

dictor of alcohol use (Cooper et al., 1992). As Cooper and associates noted, these results suggest that a general tension reduction theory is overly broad and that individual expectations and coping styles must be considered to understand the stress-related effects on alcohol use and abuse.

Social Learning Processes and Substance Abuse

More current learning models, such as cognitive social learning models, pay special attention to the "payoff" from the use of alcohol and other drugs and to the role of observational learning. Certain drugs are powerful reinforcers, and animals given access will self-administer these drugs in patterns similar to those exhibited by human users (Jaffe, 1990). In combination, reinforcement and modeling may contribute to the ultimately destructive patterns of substance use. Genetic predisposition can be accommodated by social learning models, although the disease model is typically discounted.

Human beings learn a great deal from observing others — how to dress, where to shop, and so forth; there is substantial evidence that this vicarious learning or modeling also influences drinking and other drug use (Bandura, 1969, 1985). In a large body of literature (e.g., Caudill & Marlatt, 1975; Collins & Marlatt, 1981; Hendricks, Sobell & Cooper, 1978; Lied & Marlatt, 1979), researchers have shown that male heavy drinkers will rather reliably adjust their own drinking style (its rate and the total quantity consumed) to the style they observe in their drinking companions. Sometimes studied as the "bottle gang" phenomenon of chronic drinkers, youths also appear especially sensitive to the alcohol- and other drug-related modeling influences of their peer group (Jessor & Jessor, 1975).

The influence of one's friends — *peer pressure* — is frequently cited as a cause of alcohol and other drug use, particularly among adolescents (e.g., Biglan, Duncan, Ary & Smolkowski, 1995). It is true that most psychoactive substance use does commence during a "developmental window" beginning at puberty and extending into the mid-twenties, and it is during this window of human development that peer groups have a broad influence on members' behavior, values, and norms for conduct. Vaz (1967) argued that peer groups function by each member's maintaining group cohesion and that group interactions take place where adult supervision is minimized or absent. Within the interacting and cohesive group, subtle competitions are conducted when undertaking new forms of behavior such as driving, dating, and drug-taking. Based on these competitions, status and prestige are distributed to members, and group leaders emerge. Under these conditions, values and conduct norms emerge that govern licit and illicit substance use.

A "street party," not unlike Mardi Gras, with people consuming alcohol. If not kept in check, the pleasantries of the social process can contribute to the acquisition of the addictive habit.

Cognitive Influences and Alcoholism

A **cognitive expectancy theory** (Marlatt, 1978) has been invoked to explain some of the developmental features of alcoholic drinking. According to this notion, people learn from family, friends, the media, and other models to expect that drinking will have positive consequences for them, that it will be socially stimulating, and when necessary, that it will help them "forget" aversive events or unpleasant memories.

For example, Brown, Goldman, Inn, and Anderson (1980) found that drinkers subscribe to six separate positive expectations about drinking: (1) Alcohol is expected to help the drinker construe events in a positive, pleasurable way, (2) alcohol is expected to increase social and physical pleasure, (3) alcohol is expected to enhance sexual experience, (4) alcohol is expected to increase feelings of personal dominance, (5) alcohol is expected to increase assertiveness in social situations, and (6) alcohol is expected to relieve subjective tension. These results are similar to other findings among alcoholics (e.g., Holloway, 1969; Wanberg, 1969). These expectations develop at a very early age, well before personal experience with actual drinking commences (Dunn & Goldman, 1996). In a survey of U.S. teenagers aged twelve to nineteen years, twelve-year-olds who had not yet begun to experiment with alcohol endorsed these expectations (Christiansen & Goldman, 1983). Moreover, teenagers who believed that alcohol increases social pleasure tended to report frequent social drinking, whereas those who expected alcohol to reduce tension tended to drink for relief of this symptom and to be on the way to developing problem drinking. In a two-year longitudinal study it was found that the adolescents who

endorsed greater expectations for social facilitation from alcohol were those with the greater subsequent drinking (Smith, Goldman, Greenbaum & Christiansen, 1995). Similar results emerged from research on the expectations of the effects of marijuana and cocaine (Schafer & Brown, 1991). Use and nonuse patterns of both drugs were associated with expectations: Nonuse was associated with expectations for stronger negative drug consequences, and to a lesser degree, the most frequent use was associated with expectations of positive drug effects.

According to **perceived effects theory** (Smith, 1980), alcohol (and other drugs) are used excessively because of their perceived effects — effects that are positively valued by the user and that are marshaled by the user to repair defects of character or to achieve subjective sensations that the user values. The perceived benefits of substance use — relaxation, heightened sexual pleasure, and the fruits of close friendships with like-minded, drug-using peers — outweigh the perceived costs or negative consequences of drug use, which typically are delayed. These positively valued, perceived beneficial effects "seduce" the user into continuing alcohol use even after the cost-benefit ratio changes substantially.

Cognitive influences are suggested as part of the stress-reducing effects of alcohol. The stress that is typically experienced as anxiousness, autonomic hyperactivity, and fear often can be suppressed by a dose of alcohol. Drinking, then, can function as part of an individual's pattern of adaptation — as a tranquilizer that preserves equanimity and spares the nerves of the user, even in highly stressful circumstances.

Paradoxically, the cognitive processing of the user may see alcohol as adaptive because of its detrimental effects on performance. According to self-handicapping theory (Jones & Berglas, 1978), the anticipation not of improved performance but rather of poor performance explains the problem drinker's attraction to the bottle. Jones and Berglas suggested that when individuals who lack confidence in themselves (a common characteristic in alcoholics) approach a stressful situation or encounter, they may capitalize on alcohol's performance-impairing effects by drinking in advance of the encounter. In this way, the drinker provides a self-handicap. When the feared encounter then goes awry, the attribution for failure is to the effects of the drinking, not to any abiding inadequacy of character. Simply, "It was the booze that did it!" Tension is resolved, and the drinker has survived a situation with self-esteem intact.

Physiologically, alcohol has effects, and evidence has suggested that individuals are genetically predisposed toward problems with alcohol. Nevertheless, what is thought about alcohol exerts a powerful influence — what an individual expects from drinking alcohol contributes to problem drinking.

FAMILY MATTERS

Are There Alcoholic Families?

The family can play a part in the genesis of alcohol and other drug problems by placing a burden on the shoulders of the alcohol or drug user. A traumatic family loss, a premature and overwhelming death, separation, or immigration is often implicated in the development of alcohol and other drug problems in a family. Some years ago, Vaillant (1966) published the interesting finding that among the youths of New York City, the children of recent immigrants (families that had sustained a traumatic loss of their native culture, language, and many extended family ties) were at significant risk of developing drug problems. He noted that these families tended to depend excessively on these first-generation children for support, as though the children could make up for the enormous cultural losses sustained by the parents in their immigration.

Not all family influences on the genesis of substance-use disorders are indirect or malign (or both). Many family influences are very direct, such as modeling. Longitudinal data showed that adolescents with alcoholic fathers had more substance abuse over time than adolescents without alcoholic fathers (Chassin, Curran, Hussong & Colder, 1996). Other direct influences include hostile and conflictual interactions and a restriction in granting of autonomy (Humes & Humphrey, 1994).

Ethnic influences — of which the family is a primary bearer — have a major role in determining personal attitudes and norms concerning alcohol and other drug use (Schaefer, 1982). Also, the family system frequently models the use of and attitudes toward a variety of addictive agents. For example, parental influences are almost as potent as peer influences in initiating alcohol use by adolescents (Kandel, Kessler & Margulies, 1978). Similarly, James McCord (1988) studied the effects of both alcoholic and nonalcoholic families on the development of alcoholism in their offspring. Among the sons of nonalcoholic families, the main predictor of later alcohol problems appeared to be a lack of parental control during early adolescence. Among the sons of alcoholic families, however, the best predictor of later alcoholism was the high esteem in which some of the alcoholic fathers were held by their wives. Boyhood imitation of this esteemed, masculine, but alcoholic role apparently set the stage for the later onset of alcoholism.

Vulnerability: Synthesizing Genetic and Environmental Factors

Because there is evidence of environmental influence, as well as a genetic predisposition, the most promising etiological models of alcohol- and other drug-use disorders include both genetics and learning (Pihl & Peterson, 1992). Often, these integrative explanations involve vulnerability to the disorder.

Vulnerability refers to how likely a person is to respond maladaptively to a situation. Vulnerability is increased, for example, in persons who have a particular type of heredity. In general, a person is vulnerable when at risk, and "at risk" factors are those which are associated with (though not necessarily causal) conditions of substance abuse. With reference to alcoholism, we have already seen that gender is a risk factor: Alcoholism occurs predominantly in males. The presence of other mental health problems is also a risk factor, with increased risk in persons with disorders such as depression and antisocial personality. There are also biological risk factors (Schuckit, 1987), such as the lower reaction to modest doses of alcohol for sons of alcoholics. The lower response to alcohol would then require heavier than normal drinking for a normal effect.

An example of a **vulnerability model** is that described by Kumpfer (1987). Kumpfer argued that it is not whether these disorders are genetically transmitted or whether they are learned that makes for meaningful questions. Rather, the data show complex patterns of vulnerability to addictive behaviors — potentials for addiction that stem from a variety of sources and may or may not be actualized. For example, the presence of stressful events contributes to an individual's vulnerability (Stewart, 1996). Witnessing a violent crime, being the victim of unfair practices, surviving a family member's death, and any of the large number of situations that cause stressful disruption to life all contribute to vulnerability. In a study of Caucasian and Hispanic youth,

Manuel Barrera and his colleagues at Arizona State University (Barrera, Li & Chassin, 1993) reported that Caucasian adolescents were more vulnerable to the effects of life stress and parental alcoholism than were Hispanics (see also Chassin et al., 1993). In a study of male and female Caucasian and African American adolescents, measures of risk predicted substance abuse comparably for all groups (Gottfredson & Koper, 1996).

A system that predicts adolescent alcohol and other drug use and relies on the sheer number of risks involved is called a **multiple-risk-factor model** (Bry, McKeon & Pandina, 1982). Many factors put an individual at risk for substance use, and the presence of an increased number of these risks was hypothesized to be predictive of an increased likelihood of substance use. Bry and associates (1982) correlated the influence of six different risk factors, both separately and combined. The list of potential risk factors included (1) grades in school, (2) church affiliation, (3) age at first drug use, (4) the presence of psychological distress, (5) the adolescent's self-esteem, and (6) the adolescent's perception of parental love. To what extent do these risk factors inform us about the extent of drug use?

To examine the question, Bry and associates studied nearly 2,000 New Jersey high school students. Although the authors did not find that any one risk factor or any specific combination of factors predicted the extent of drug use, there was a linear relationship between extent of drug use and the sheer number of risk factors (see Figure 11.5). The more risk factors present, the more substances were used — a similar finding, based on a study of Native American youths, was reported by Moncher, Holden, and Trimble (1990). Bry and associates concluded that "drug abuse is a general instead of a specific coping mechanism, that its likelihood is dependent on how much rather than exactly what there is to cope with, . . . that there are "multiple pathways" to drug abuse and that the number of factors an individual must cope with is more important than exactly what those factors are" (pp. 274–277). In other words, it is not only poor school grades, low self-esteem, or any other single factor that "causes" substance abuse. Rather, the presence of a combination of risk factors is associated with an increased likelihood of abuse. These data are informative not only about the onset of substance-use disorders but also about the need for early intervention for those persons who are at risk.

THE COURSE OF DISORDER

Substance-use disorders do not emerge full-blown, nor do they disappear at the first suggestion of treatment. Quite the contrary is true. For most, the course of

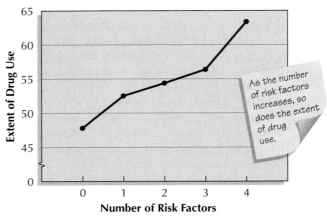

Figure 11.5   Multiple Risk Factors in Substance Use

To what extent do risk factors contribute to drug use? As the multiple risk model suggests, there is no single cause of drug use. Vulnerability to and predictions of drug use can be based on the presence of multiple risk factors.

Source: From Bry, McKeon & Pandina (1982).

substance-use disorders includes forward progress and frustrating errors. Important concepts in the course of the substance-use disorders include remission, relapse, and recovery.

Remission

Remission is a term used to describe a state of health in which a previously active disorder or illness has receded or disappeared entirely. Remission is a common occurrence in the addictive disorders. For example, authorities have estimated that among those who have been at some time labeled "alcoholic," only about one-third are actually drinking today. The remainder are in the process of recovery, are abstaining ("on the wagon") for a brief period, are beginning to migrate or mature out of alcoholism, or simply do not feel like drinking today and may or may not feel like it tomorrow. The same is true of most other drug users. Interestingly, rates for all alcohol and other drug disorders decline with age, not solely because of mortality (although this is a factor) but more frequently because addictive patterns are given up, through either active treatment or natural remission.

In 1975, Smart conducted a review of the available research and found that a large proportion of alcoholics' drinking problems remit without treatment and without the help of peer-support groups. The true proportion is difficult to determine because these are people who by definition are rarely, if ever, observed by scientists or clinicians.

In a follow-up study of ninety-four alcoholics who had abstained from drinking for three months or more, Ludwig (1972) found that temporary remission of drinking was associated with a variety of factors. Nearly one-fourth of the drinkers claimed to have experienced a simple loss of desire, and an additional 19 percent cited a fear of consequences as the primary reason. Smaller percentages of the drinkers attributed their remissions to such factors as family influence, achieving insight into their problems, and "no special reason." As is typical of such studies, relatively few of the subjects attributed their improvement to treatment or peer-support factors.

F O C U S   O N   R E S E A R C H

Can You Kick the Cigarette Habit?

This question can be addressed in two ways: Can you kick the habit on your own? And can you kick the habit with professional help?

How effective are individuals — by themselves and without professional contact — at kicking the cigarette habit? This phenomenon about which so little is known — the spontaneous remission of smoking (and other drug-use disorders) — has excited intense debate. In a provocative early study, Stanley Schachter (1982) reported that 63 percent of people who had attempted to quit smoking did so on their own. Although this figure may be encouraging to those who want to quit, it has been questioned because it is much higher than the success rate reported by smoking-cessation programs (that is, 15 percent). A careful look at Schachter's methods reveals that the study examined a series of retrospective self-reports by members of his psychology department at Columbia University and residents of a nearby suburban town. Are these samples representative? The subjects were not selected randomly, and the validity of their self-reports was not determined. Might there also be systematic biases in self-reports of accomplishments given to friends? Because of these methodological concerns, one can certainly question whether these data are of any use in assessing whether self-quitting is the way to go.

Five years later, Randy Rzewnicki and Donald Forgays (1987) reported the results of their retrospective interviews of members of their psychology department at the University of Vermont. Reporting results similar to those published by Schachter, the authors stated that 58 percent of their subjects reported success as self-quitters. The data appeared consistent across the two studies, but the methodology was again questioned, and the findings were not necessarily accepted by a large group of researchers in the smoking-cessation field.

For instance, Sheldon Cohen, of Carnegie Mellon University, and sixteen co-authors from across the United States (1989) combined their data and examined a collection of studies that included more than 5,000 persons. When these authors studied smokers' first attempts to quit, the success rate was no better than that reported for completers of treatment programs, namely, 15 percent. In addition, light smokers (less than a pack a day) were 2.2 times more likely to self-quit than heavy smokers, and 87 percent of the subjects reported previously unsuccessful attempts to quit.

What might explain these observed differences in self-quitting? Again, a closer look at the methods used in the research is revealing. First, the subjects studied by means of retrospective interviews may not be entirely accurate in their reports. They may self-proclaim that they quit on their own, but other factors may have been active but not identified. A second explanation concerns the nature of the samples studied. People in smoking-cessation programs may be hard-core smokers. People who self-quit, obviously, do not join smoking-cessation programs, and those who self-select and volunteer for smoking-cessation programs are probably those who have not had success with self-change. More methodologically rigorous studies have revealed a rate for unaided quitting at one-year follow-up to be in the 10 to 20 percent range, with continuous quitting in the 3 to 5 percent range (Lichtenstein & Glasgow, 1992).

Other factors also may help explain the observed differences. People who try to quit may be at different stages of the process of change — some just beginning to think about quitting and others having thought it through and being committed to change (Prochaska, DiClemente & Norcross, 1992). Other differences among people may be predictive. For example, a higher likelihood of quitting was associated with being female, attaining some college education, and perceiving smoking as dangerous to your health (Rose, Chassin, Presson & Sherman, 1996). Surprisingly, although 70 percent of pregnant women smokers knew of the health risks, they did not report a greater intent to quit than nonpregnant smokers (Hutchison, Stevens, & Collins, 1996). Men were found to be more likely than women to quit smoking initially, but relapse rates are the same for both genders (Nides et al., 1995). Although the process of change also was found to be similar for both genders, women, more than men, were found to have concerns regarding weight gain after quitting (O'Connor, Carbonari & DiClemente, 1996; see also Frederick et al., 1996).

Despite the success of some smokers in quitting smoking of their own will and effort, there is still a need for the development and evaluation of treatments for the majority who find their habit to be intractable. The number of studies of smoking cessation has increased markedly (Shiffman, 1993), and treatment methods used (such as nicotine chewing gum; Cepeda-Benito, 1993) have broadened. Examples of recent evaluations of programs for smoking cessation include a culturally sensitive program for Hispanics (Nevid, Javier & Moulton, 1996), behavior therapy for smokeless tobacco users (Hatsukami et al., 1996), behavior

Smokers gather outside their workplace. Because of the widespread acceptance of the unhealthy effects and addictive features of smoking, smoking is no longer permitted in most office buildings. Gathered in the shadows, these smokers shown here do not appear to be enjoying themselves. In contrast, the smiling women on the opposite page (p. 355) celebrate completion of a recovery program. Despite their varied backgrounds, they have retrieved their lives from drugs.

therapy plus the nicotine patch for smokers (Cinciripini et al., 1996), and an adolescent-targeted school-based program with an emphasis on the physical consequences of smoking (Dent et al., 1995). One study (Ossip-Klein et al., 1991) indicated that a "smokers' hotline," with taped messages and access to paraprofessional counselors, significantly improved the self-help quit rates. Moreover, greater amounts of phone counseling were increasingly effective (Zhu et al., 1996) for participants who were seeking to quit. Somewhat different results were obtained when nonvolunteers were studied: Telephone counseling increased smoking cessation initially, but the effects did not hold at 21-month follow-up (Curry et al., 1995).

Appropriately, studies of the effects of smoking-cessation programs use the experimental method with representative samples and follow-up measurement: There is random assignment of subjects to conditions, and the assessments of outcome are gathered at several points in time. For example, Gruder and associates (1993), at the University of Illinois at Chicago, recruited subjects through promotion of a free televised smoking-cessation program. Thousands of men and women of minority and nonminority backgrounds expressed an interest, and of those allotted to this particular study, 235 were assigned randomly to a no-contact control condition, 271 to the social support condition, and 287 to the discussion condition. All subjects were given a self-help manual and told to watch the quit-smoking television program. The no-contact subjects received the manual and instructions to watch the television program but no other intervention. The subjects in the social support condition were taught how to get help from others and to neutralize people who were unhelpful. They also

were taught how to avoid and cope with slips or lapses. The discussion condition provided subjects with discussions of the content of the manual and telephone calls to provide support and encouragement. Nurses and health educators ran the groups at sites in the community, and project staff made unannounced visits to monitor the treatments that were being provided.

Telephone interviews were used to assess outcomes: The first was immediately after treatment, and the follow-ups were six, twelve, and twenty-four months after treatment. A subject was considered to be abstinent at follow-up if he or she had not smoked a cigarette for seven days. Gruder and associates (1993) reported that the social support condition most enhanced the initial cessation rates of the televised self-help program — increased personal contact provided additional beneficial effects over the self-help program alone (49.0 versus 17.4 percent). Unfortunately, the social support condition did not enhance the maintenance of abstinence (25.6 versus 18.2 percent).

The methodology allowed for considerable confidence in the findings. For example, the three conditions did not differ significantly on subject characteristics or smoking history, and monitoring of the treatments documented that they were provided properly. However, telephone reports may not be valid indicators of true abstinence. It would be interesting, for at least a subset of participants, to ensure the validity of the telephoned reports by checking the data against physiological evidence or the reports provided by clients' co-workers or significant others.

Nevertheless, with the general finding that less than 25 percent of participants are nicotine-free after experimental studies with one-year follow-up, permanently

kicking the nicotine habit appears more difficult than suggested by some of the initial nonrepresentative reports of self-quitting.

Relapse

When a substance-abuse disorder, formerly in remission, has become exacerbated and has again blossomed symptomatically, the condition is known as **relapse.** Relapse is observed frequently in alcohol- and other drug-use disorders. According to Alan Marlatt and Judith Gordon of the University of Washington (1985), during periods of remission or recovery, an individual experiences perceived control over the substance-use problem, which is reinforced by the duration of abstinence or nonproblem use. Periodically, however, the individual encounters *high-risk situations* that, as cues, may prompt a drinking or drug-taking response. The individual at this point is at "a fork in the road, with one path returning to the former problem level . . . and the other continuing in the direction of positive change" (p. 33).

A study by Cummings and associates (Cummings, Gordon & Marlatt, 1980) sampled 311 relapse episodes reported by users of nicotine, alcohol, and heroin and by persons with problems of compulsive overeating or gambling. In about three-quarters of cases, the high-risk situations to which the relapses were attributed fell into three categories. In the largest number of relapses (35 percent), the individual had encountered a negative emotional state (such as boredom, anger, depression, anxiety, or disappointment). Somewhat less frequent (20 percent) were instances of social pressure (for example,

the presence of other people who encouraged or simply modeled the addictive behavior). Finally, in about 16 percent of cases, interpersonal conflict such as arguments, fights, and distressing confrontations with family, friends, and employers was the high-risk situation. With regard to first lapses to smoking, negative mood and smoking cues were seen as high-risk situations (Shiffman et al., 1996).

Marlatt and Gordon (1985) argued that when the individual has suitable coping skills to survive high-risk situations, the feeling of perceived control is enhanced, and relapse is less likely to occur. When coping is not sufficient, however, a sequence of events begins to unfold. First, the individual's sense of perceived control is diminished. The individual attends not to past negative experiences with the substance but only to the lure of the immediate prospect — feeling more relaxed, happy, confident, and so on. As a result, the drug is then used. A person's reaction to an initial lapse has been called the *abstinence violation effect (AVE)* (Marlatt, 1978). When abstinence is violated, feelings of conflict and guilt arise as the individual blames himself or herself for the relapse. Because in many cases these kinds of feelings (conflict and guilt) drove the active addictive pattern in the first place, the individual moves from a single relapse to another pattern of sustained use to relieve these unpleasant feelings. A negative spiral of unpleasant feelings and increased drug use occurs. A single lapse has turned into a pattern of relapse.

Relapse is an important concept within substance abuse, and mood and cognition have increasingly become central research topics. Regarding mood, for example, depression is linked to relapse, and researchers have found that enhancing positive mood was a factor associated with reduced relapse among cocaine abusers

(Hall, Havassy & Wasserman, 1991). A study of eighty opiate addicts at the time of their admission to a hospital in Great Britain reported that addicts' attributions were predictive of abstinence and relapse (Bradley et al., 1992). At six-month follow-up the researchers found that addicts who attributed to themselves greater responsibility for negative outcomes and who attributed relapse to personally controllable factors were more likely to be either completely abstinent or to have contained the effects of temporary lapses.

An important advantage of the Marlatt and Gordon model, and a focus on relapse in general, is the ability to point to ways to intervene in the relapse process. Later we consider relapse-prevention training.

Recovery

A sizable proportion of addicts achieve **recovery** — a stable separation from the substance. The precise proportion of the total who achieve a stable recovery is not known and can only be inferred, but it certainly includes a majority of alcohol and drug users, if we include in the total those who experience transient problems in their youth before "maturing out." Ludwig (1985) conducted extensive interviews with twenty-nine alcoholic men and women who had been abstinent or nearly so for an average of more than six years without treatment or peer support.

More than half of these people reported initiating recovery after having reached a personal bottom. As one of Ludwig's subjects explained, "I was arrested, put in jail for three weeks . . . I realized what had gotten me there was nothing but drinking. . . . There was no way to go except to a grave . . . and I wasn't about to go to the grave" (p. 54). About one-fifth of the subjects reported that their recovery began when they developed serious illnesses as a result of their drinking. Finally, about 10 percent stated that their recoveries began when they (1) developed an aversion to alcohol, (2) decided to make a serious change in their lifestyle, or (3) underwent a spiritual experience, a change of heart that led them away from drinking and toward the more difficult but in the end more beneficial prospect of sobriety.

As their recovery progressed, these individuals relied on an assortment of strategies to maintain their gains. More than half stated that they had from time to time exercised sheer will power, and most reported that they had to remind themselves of the damage alcohol had done in their lives; that is, they had to talk to themselves and restate the negative connotations of drinking. More than a third of the sample, as recovery progressed, gradually experienced a loss of the desire to drink. Not everyone with an alcohol or drug problem can recover without assistance, however.

GETTING CLEAN AND SOBER: TREATING THE ADDICTIONS

In the end, the task of getting clean and sober must be faced by all substance abusers. A fairly consistent finding across studies is that although formal treatment for alcohol problems (and other abuse disorders) is often effective, the different approaches do not produce strikingly different outcomes. For example, reports (Armor, Polich & Stambul, 1978; Polich, Armor & Braiker, 1981) from the Rand Corporation's study of approximately 14,000 persons treated for alcoholism were consistent with the notion that although treatments are effective, the type of treatment did not influence outcome.

Practitioners and researchers have suggested "participant" factors that might influence treatment outcomes. For example, Nathan and Skinstad (1987) noted that a cognitive-behavioral program that focuses on the self-control of drinking (e.g., Miller, Hedrick & Taylor, 1983) might be more effective for an educated, youthful, and motivated client who has an early-stage alcohol-abuse problem. When the client is enmeshed in an alcohol-involved family, then family therapy may be preferred. Research is needed to examine the differential effectiveness of treatment programs for different types of alcohol abusers.

Brian, from the chapter opener, admitted having been drunk before and having lost his temper several times — and this certainly wasn't the first time he was mumbling and incoherent, and stumbling and uncoordinated. But, for his family, this had to be the last time. "I'm tired of this @+*#. I don't have to live like this," said his wife. Brian's older daughter often cried in her room when her father was drunk; his younger daughter clung to her mother and, when she spoke, would simply say, "Tell him to stop."

An ambulance took Brian to the hospital. In the detox unit (detoxification, or drying out, is often the first step in treatment), Brian was a noncompliant patient. When heavy drinking is stopped or when alcoholics reduce their consumption, they experience withdrawal symptoms. Brian was no exception. He experienced increased blood pressure, physical agitation, and sweating. He was confused and at times delirious. He shook with tremors and sometimes spoke incoherently. Two days later, the withdrawal symptoms subsided — but Brian didn't sleep well, appeared anxious and agitated, and said he felt depressed. "I'm not gonna make it, I'm no good. Why do I have to be in this place anyway? I won't make it." Although his language wasn't always clear, the message was understandable to those who knew him: Brian lacked confidence that he could live without alcohol.

Brian underwent a cognitive-behavioral treatment that also involved his family. As part of the treatment, for example, Brian had to admit that drinking was causing him problems, and he had to disclose and examine the situations that were most likely to result in his drinking. The therapist helped him identify risky situations and make alternate plans that reduced the risk of relapse. Several sessions included his spouse and daughters, and they, too, participated in the planning of how best to reduce risky situations. Brian, among other influences, was empowered to see that he could make choices that were more likely to keep him sober and less likely to result in relapse.

Six months after treatment and an equal amount of time free from alcohol, Brian stated that he could recall very little of his behavior during his drunken binges. "I don't know what I did, and I didn't hear what people were saying. Didn't hear my wife either. I wasn't really there, I mean, beyond physically. My girls grew up, and I missed it. I can't go back either." Brian had completed detoxification, a stay in the hospital, and an outpatient program. He continues in treatment today, working to learn alternate ways to cope with work-related stress and to overcome his occasional sense of depression.

One peculiar difficulty with the treatment of addictions is the relative rarity of addicts who volunteer for treatment. The addictions often are characterized as problems in which the primary symptom is the denial that there are any symptoms. Most candidates for alcohol and other drug treatment never receive treatment, primarily because of their own resistance to recognizing that a problem exists. Only approximately 15 percent of people with a chemical dependency seek treatment, and involvement varies by race (see Figure 11.6).

Society's agents for dealing with criminal offenses, civil disputes such as divorce, the protection of minor children, and other issues are becoming sensitive to the large role played by alcohol and other drugs in matters that come before them. Large numbers of litigants are now being referred for professional assessment of and sometimes intervention for the substance-use problems that precipitated the legal action. In some instances, individuals are referred as *coerced clients*, required by the courts to receive evaluation and treatment. Typically, these coercive programs are guided by the logic that some criminal and civil issues (such as drunk driving, adolescent vandalism, and child endangerment) are best viewed not as offenses to be handled by the justice sys-

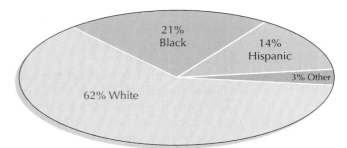

Figure 11.6   People Seeking Treatment for Chemical Dependency, by Race
Of those with a chemical dependency who seek treatment, 62 percent are white, 21 percent are black, and 14 percent are Hispanic. Clearly, approaches to treatment need to be sensitive to cultural and ethnic differences. Also, these data suggest that a lower percentage of minorities with a chemical dependency are in treatment and support further that an outreach effort may be worthwhile.
Source: USA Today (1993).

tem but rather as symptoms of alcohol or drug addiction, which are best resolved by the mental health system. For example, intoxicated driver education programs are becoming commonplace in the United States and abroad.

A different approach was used by William Miller, Gayle Benefield, and Scott Tonigan (1993) at the University of New Mexico. These researchers used the offer of a free "drinker's checkup" to recruit participants for a study of treatment outcome. An advertisement solicited drinkers who wanted to learn if alcohol was harming them in any way. Then information about each participant was gathered using a set of measures sensitive to early alcohol-related risk, and later the information was given to participants in individual feedback meetings. Drinkers at risk were then given treatments that were found to produce an overall 57 percent reduction in drinking.

The wide variety of treatments that are provided for persons with problems with alcohol ranges from simple medications to complex group therapy situations and from brief counseling to lengthy stays in hospitals or halfway houses. Psychodynamic and humanistic approaches to treatment have taken a back seat to the more action-oriented treatments, such as the behavioral, cognitive-behavioral, and family approaches. The following sections illustrate the diversity of treatments used for alcohol- and drug-use problems.

Goals of Addiction Treatments

What exactly is a favorable outcome of treatment — reduced drinking behavior (or drug use) or a more comprehensive set of criteria including changes in drinking behavior, emotional and physical health, and improvements in family and social functioning (Emrick & Hansen, 1983)? What about reductions in automobile driving after alcohol consumption (Yates & Dowrick, 1991) and even reductions in predatory illegal acts and overall criminal behavior (French, Zarkin & Hubbard, 1993)? Debates about the different costs for different programs also have entered the arena. Perhaps the biggest debate in the substance-abuse literature, however, surrounds alcohol and the issue of **abstinence versus controlled drinking**. Should persons who abuse alcohol be taught (1) that the goal of treatment is the achievement of moderate, controlled consumption or (2) that abstinence is the target goal?

Early research showed that it was possible for an alcoholic to engage in controlled drinking. That is, some individuals who had at one time abused alcohol were able to drink on a controlled basis. The studies that documented this finding, reported in 1973 and 1976, were conducted by Mark and Linda Sobell. At the time, researchers suggested that controlled drinking was an acceptable treatment goal for one-time alcoholics. Another study was conducted by the Rand Corporation and reported by Polich, Armor, and Braiker (1981). More than 900 subjects were studied, and four years after treatment in one of several alcohol treatment centers, almost half were either abstinent or able to drink in a controlled manner. For those subjects who were younger than forty at the start of their treatment program and who had lower levels of dependence, controlled drinking was associated with fewer relapses. For those older than forty and with greater dependence, abstinence was more likely to be associated with fewer relapses. Because controlled drinking is possible and sometimes associated with fewer relapses, should it be the goal of choice?

Who among alcoholics and problem drinkers will be able to achieve controlled drinking? In 1981, Heather and Robertson reported that based on a review of nine studies, lower severity of drinking symptoms, younger age, regular employment, and less contact with Alcoholics Anonymous (AA) were predictors of controlled drinking. More recently, Harold Rosenberg (1993) addressed this question by reviewing current research that had examined factors as potential predictors of controlled drinking. The following factors were considered: severity of dependence, client attitudes and beliefs about controlled drinking, previous treatment, pretreatment drinking style, psychological and social stability, demographic characteristics, family history of drinking, and pretreatment adjustment. Although no single personal characteristic was found to be a consistent predictor, a low severity of dependence and a persuasion that controlled drinking is possible were associated with controlled drinking after treatment.

Practitioners who work with alcoholics have emphasized that controlled drinking is an option only for some individuals. Their position is that it is more functional on a day-to-day basis for the majority of alcoholics to strive for and maintain abstinence. As one practitioner put it, "OK, so maybe some of these guys can possibly be controlled drinkers. But the large majority can't . . . and to even tell them of the option would be at best to tease them and at worst a prompt to relapse." In addition, few studies of controlled drinking have yielded outcomes superior to those with abstinence as a goal (Nathan & McCrady, 1987). Both practical issues and research evaluations have contributed to the widespread belief that abstinence is the goal for the treatment of alcoholism.

Formats and Settings for Treating Substance Use

The treatment of substance-abuse disorders has employed individual therapy, treatment in a group of similarly addicted individuals, and efforts to treat the person within the context of the family. In the United States, there are now several thousand outpatient treatment providers, representing the fastest-growing sector of the alcohol- and other drug-treatment community. In outpatient treatment, the patient remains in the community, at home, on the job, or in school, where social and interpersonal events bearing on recovery can be brought to treatment and discussed. Treatments are provided while the patient stays in his or her living situation.

Hospitals are often involved in the treatment of substance-abuse problems. Programs include inpatient and outpatient services, partial hospitalization, and detoxification. Inpatient rehabilitation units typically offer a wide variety of individual, group, and family therapies combined with extensive educational and motivational components. Partial hospitalization combines the daily therapeutic work, group therapy, and close supervision of an inpatient treatment unit with the low cost and in-community–integration properties of outpatient care. These programs typically see their patients daily or nearly so for up to eight hours each day and for a total of three to six weeks. Individual, group, and marital or family therapies along with some medication schedules are commonplace. For some, partial hospitalization may represent a "wave of the future" in alcohol- and drug-treatment services.

With reference to the data on inpatient and outpatient hospitalization, and aside from the differences in cost, there is little difference in terms of outcome. According to several reviewers (e.g., Cox, 1987), a residential program does not appear to have a meaningful advantage over a nonresidential one.

Many patients with substance-use disorders require **detoxification** (see also Reilly et al., 1995). The goal of detoxification is to permit the patient's body to become free of all intoxicating agents, typically including completion of episodes of withdrawal. Treatment on a hospital "detox" unit is typically brief (three to five days) but is fully residential; it is designed to provide physical safety and medication management during withdrawal of alcohol and other drugs. Beyond providing the most rudimentary advice, therapy on a detox unit is rare.

Finally, halfway houses, also known as *long-term residential treatments* or *group homes,* combine several forms of treatment. Patients commonly stay between six and eighteen months, and most residents progress through a schedule of gradually diminishing levels of treatment and control. For instance, a patient might progress from a thirty-day, fully residential quarantine, to having passes home or to work as in a partial residence, to "graduate status" and frequent visits to the unit as in a partial hospital, to less frequent follow-up visits as in outpatient care. Medication treatment is very rare; marital or family therapy is also rare because most residents of halfway houses have few intact social bonds, typically having destroyed them all due to their abuse of substances. Individual and especially group therapies are the primary treatment vehicles.

A Cognitive-Behavioral Approach to Treatment

The goal of treatments for substance abusers is the discontinuation of drug use. Although this goal is sometimes reached in the short term, there are many instances of relapse — alcoholics, for example, evidence a high relapse rate. It is important to note, therefore, that a treatment that exposes alcoholics to the cues for drinking (such as open beverages) and teaches coping skills (such as imagining negative consequences of drinking and encouraging self-talk) during the exposure has been reported to significantly reduce drinking three to six months after treatment (Monti et al., 1993).

Unlike the disease model, in which relapse may be seen as out of the person's control, a cognitive-behavioral view suggests that relapse represents a failure at a choice point. Treatment, therefore, requires therapy to increase understanding of important "risky" choice points to prevent relapse.

Relapse prevention training (Marlatt & Gordon, 1985) is a combination of cognitive and behavioral skills taught to clients who are trying to gain self-control over their drinking. The program is based on the idea that drinking to excess represents a sacrifice of long-term goals for the immediate satisfaction of near-term gratifications. Such choices, often made under conditions of stress, can become habitual. Marlatt and Gordon proposed that in contrast to the other treatment models that typically teach all-or-none thinking (if you have a drink, you are again a drunk), individuals need to be able to

distinguish between a minor lapse and a major relapse. A minor lapse should not be seen as proof that alcohol cannot be mastered nor as evidence that self-control efforts should be abandoned. Rather, a lapse should be seen as a temporary setback that can be overcome. Relapse prevention provides skills in the interpretation of lapses and the mastery of the stressful experiences that have led to the excessive consumption of alcohol.

The specifics of the relapse prevention model include teaching clients to identify the high-risk situations that predispose them to lapses, helping clients identify and develop alternative activities that reduce risky situations, and providing decision-making skills to facilitate choices of short-term versus long-term gratifications. According to the model, once the individual is in a high-risk situation, there are two possible outcomes: coping and a reduction in the likelihood of relapse or failing to cope and triggering a chain of responses that is more likely to lead to relapse.

The theoretical model of relapse prevention is presented in Figure 11.7. A real illustration of the model involved Bill, a 28-year-old roofer. Bill reported that he would typically stop for a beer after a hard day at work. He didn't go home to have a beer with his dinner but instead stopped at a pub with some of his co-workers. Once at the pub, after his first and second beers, he was again en route to an inebriated evening. Bill was in his high-risk situation at the point that he decided to go with his co-workers. Having identified this high-risk choice point, the therapy focused on the generation of alternative activities that would be acceptable to Bill but much less risky in terms of relapse. Inviting one friend to his home to share a meal would allow some camaraderie and build friendships but would avoid the pub setting and the social pressure to stay and consume excessive alcohol.

How an individual perceives a lapse is important within the relapse prevention model. As noted earlier, a common reaction to an initial lapse has been termed the *abstinence violation effect (AVE).* That is, once an individual has a lapse, the meaning of this "violation" becomes important — how the person explains the lapse to himself or herself and to what the lapse is attributed. If the person attributes the lapse to an internal, global, and stable characteristic that he or she thinks is uncontrollable (for example, lack of willpower or having the "disease" of alcoholism), then there is likely to be continued drinking: "See there, I'm an alcoholic, and I can't control my drinking."

One aspect of the relapse prevention plan is somewhat controversial — the idea that if one needs to learn to cope with lapses, then the treatment could include "planned lapses" that set the stage for the client to practice the relapse prevention skills. The controversy pertains to the intentional quality of the planned lapses. The

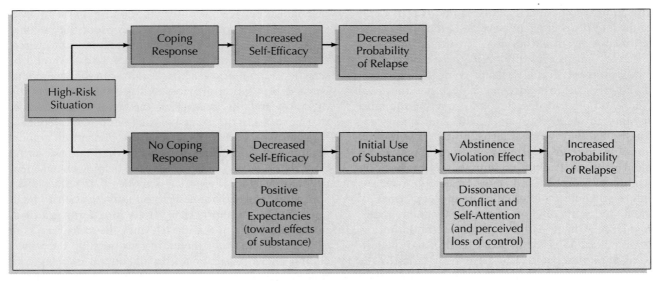

Figure 11.7 **The Cognitive-Behavioral Model of the Relapse Process**

An important choice takes place when the person is in a high-risk situation. If a coping response is made, the person feels increased self-efficacy, and there is a decreased probability of relapse. In the absence of coping, there is decreased self-efficacy and an initial use of the substance, which is followed by the abstinence violation effect and eventual increased probability of relapse.

Source: After Marlatt and Gordon (1980) and reprinted from Curry and Marlatt (1987).

therapist is very cautious to avoid allowing a lapse to turn into full-blown relapse, but this feature of the program is in need of further research evaluation before it is given widespread application.

Family Approaches to Treating Addictions

Marital and family systems exert a strong influence over addictive behaviors and over the outcomes of their treatment (Moos & Finney, 1983), and therapies that focus on marital and family relationships are becoming more commonplace in alcohol and other drug treatment regimes. Recent work has shown that marital violence (O'Farrell & Murphy, 1995) and child behavior problems (Nye, Zucker & Fitzgerald, 1995) are reduced following successful treatment for alcohol problems.

In practice, substance abusers often receive a variety of versions of family therapy. Unfortunately, there are few empirical evaluations of such treatments. The work of Stanton and Todd (1982) stands as a welcome, though rare, example of research evaluation of action-oriented family treatment for substance abuse. The family treatment was *structural-strategic family therapy,* which included both strategic (Haley, 1976) and structural interventions (Minuchin, 1974). In strategic family therapy, the therapist actively defines the problem for the family, initiating specific interactions among family members and designing and recommending specific strategies for solving problems. In structural family therapy, the emphasis is on actively changing the relationships among individual pairs within the family.

The subjects treated by Stanton and Todd were opiate addicts who had previously tried to kick their habit. Subjects were assigned randomly to several versions of treatment, including both paid and unpaid family therapy and an individual counseling approach that also provided methadone. (In the paid family therapy condition, subjects were given $5 per member for attending, and clean urine was required at each session.) Both family therapies decreased family conflict, and the paid family therapy was associated with more meaningful changes in drug use than the individual counseling–methadone treatment. The treatments did not have beneficial effects on measures of work or school adjustment. Yet the overall findings are encouraging, since the family treatment did have desirable effects on the participants. Because of the nature of the individual treatment that was provided, however, it would be premature to conclude that the family approach is better than an individual therapy for substance abuse. Development of action-oriented individual treatments with subsequent comparisons with family treatments is much needed. Recalling the serious unwanted physical and psychological effects linked to the substance-use disorders and the fact that these disorders are so widespread, it is easy to see that additional research, especially when high-risk groups are treated with culturally sensitive programs (e.g., VanHasselt, Hersen & Null, 1993), would be welcomed.

The Need for Culture-Specific Treatment Programs

That different cultures are exposed to different risk factors (e.g., Catalano et al., 1993) and use alcohol differently is not controversial: Southern Mediterranean cultures are said to use wine like food, whereas northern Europeans are heavier consumers of grain liquors (Room, 1968). In the United States, alcohol abuse has been described as the most frequent medical and social problem among Native Americans, and evaluations of treatment programs for these groups often point to disappointingly low rates of success. It is often the Anglo cultural bias that is deplored, while the need for greater integration of the Native Americans' traditional healing practices is encouraged.

In the majority culture in the United States, individuals respond verbally to questions and often maintain eye contact. For some Native Americans, eye contact is considered disrespectful, and words are to be used only when necessary. To these individuals, it would be insulting if they were to look you in the eye to answer your questions, and it is troubling that the Anglo culture is full of people who talk far too much, wasting words and saying little. Knowledge that Native Americans can be biased by this guiding philosophy will influence the design of an ideal psychological treatment.

Culture-specific treatments also must integrate the interventions that are valued by the subject's culture (Thurman, Swaim & Plested, 1995). For Native Americans, this may require cooperation with tribal healers. Although foreign to most conventional treatments, the tribal healer's suggested prayers, rituals, or herbs may be especially potent for individuals from certain cultures. Treatment modifications are also necessary to be respectful of the culture of African American men (Pena & Koss-Chioino, 1992). Outcomes may be improved now that the Indian Health Service has increased its involvement in addressing the alcohol problems of Native Americans.

Addressing the question of how best to deal effectively with cultural heterogeneity is often troublesome for alcohol treatment programs. This dilemma holds true even within the Native American group. As Weibel-Orlando (1987) noted, "The middle-aged, full-blood, Navajo-speaking man who had lived (and drunk) most of his life on the reservation or in one of the border towns that cater to native Americans may not understand or respond to conventional alcoholism treatment modalities. He may truly believe his cirrhosis of the liver

is due to witchcraft practiced on behalf of a vengeful enemy" (p. 275). Conventional treatments may be effective with another Navajo who holds no such belief system and who has been socialized differently. When cultures are held together by spiritual, social, and family views that are divergent from the culture that has developed the intervention, roadblocks in the path to sobriety are not surprising.

Treating Addictions with Medication

Medications are widely available to promote specific goals in the treatment of alcohol and other drug problems (Jaffe & Ciraulo, 1985). For example, such goals include the management of acute drug intoxication states and withdrawal states. In many instances, specific medications have been found to be helpful in the relief of the chronic mental symptoms and disorders that are comorbid with alcoholism (O'Brien, 1996).

Other agents are used to deter the consumption of alcohol itself. One such drug, disulfiram (or Antabuse), is inert in the systems of persons who remain alcohol or drug free. When alcohol is introduced, however, Antabuse promotes an array of extremely unpleasant effects such as nausea, tachycardia, dizziness, cold sweats, and blurred vision. Antabuse is particularly useful in the treatment of impulsive drinkers because it can remain in the system for days after the last dose, and it presents a powerful incentive for the drinker to reevaluate the desire to drink before taking action. Antabuse is self-administered, however, and it is therefore successful only when the individual is motivated to quit drinking and, relatedly, to take the "preventive" medication. Because substance abusers are not known for their self-motivation to quit, a medication such as Antabuse may be most effective when it is used in combination with other psychosocial interventions that can engender motivation and empower the person to adhere to the necessary treatment.

Other medications are available for the treatment of opiate dependence. One of the most widely used treatments for opiate addiction is **methadone** — an orally administered synthetic drug whose action is similar to that of the opioids but lasts much longer (two to four days compared with six to twelve hours). When administered and taken regularly, methadone does not produce the intense euphoria that is associated with opioids (for example, heroin). At high doses of methadone, heroin no longer produces a euphoric high. That methadone curtails the craving for heroin is an important beneficial effect. Methadone is usually administered as part of an outpatient treatment program.

Supporters of the use of medications for the treatment of substance-abuse disorders point to their relatively low cost and effectiveness. Dissenters, however, are quick to point out that the person is not relieved of drug dependency but merely shifted from an illegal drug to one that is legal. In Britain, an effort was made to control heroin abuse by providing, through a series of legal clinics, a maintenance dose of the drug. Here again, however, controversy over the government's provision of drugs prevents detailed and careful study and replication of this approach. In practice, when medications are used, they are often given in combination with other forms of treatment.

"Anonymous" Peer-Support Programs

Colloquially called "the program," peer-support systems in the United States and around the globe encompass **Alcoholics Anonymous (AA)**, Narcotics Anonymous, Cocaine Anonymous, and other sister organizations for compulsive gamblers, overeaters, and other individuals.

"Alcoholics Anonymous is a fellowship of men and women who share their experience, strengths, and hopes with each other, that they may solve their common problem and help others to recover from alcoholism. The only requirement for membership is a desire to stop drinking" (from the *AA Grapevine*). This self-help organization adheres to the twelve steps listed in Table 11.4. Although there are testimonials to its effectiveness, AA

Alcoholics Anonymous (AA) is a self-help peer-support program that helps people overcome their addiction. An offshoot program for teenagers, AlaTeen, also provides peer support during the process of getting clean and sober.

remains resistant to a rigorous scientific examination of its outcomes.

Since its founding in the 1930s in Akron, Ohio, after a conversation between a local surgeon and a visiting New York businessman, Alcoholics Anonymous has blossomed. Aside from the Democratic and Republican political parties in the United States, AA is the single largest organization in the world. AA offers services in 114 countries. Based on a twelve-step program of recovery rooted in the individual experiences of participating, recovering alcoholics, and now generalized to the problems of other drug users, Alcoholics Anonymous and its related programs, through their function of exchange and mutual peer support, are by several orders of magnitude the largest "treatment source" for alcohol and other drug users anywhere. (Treatment is in quotations here because AA steadfastly refuses to describe itself as a treatment.) The principles of AA are reflected in its twelve steps (see Table 11.4). Much of AA's philosophy is very simply captured in its Serenity Prayer:

> God grant me the serenity to accept the things I cannot change, courage to change the things I can, and wisdom to know the difference.

There are two types of AA meetings: open meetings, which are open to family, friends, and the alcoholics themselves, and closed meetings, which are restricted to men and women who want to stop drinking. Here is how one person described a meeting:

> The meeting lasts about an hour, and it's a good thing. I get too fidgety to stay longer. We meet in the community room at the hospital. We do the usual reading of the prayer, then some of us get up in front and tell our story. You know, how we used to drink it up pretty good. How we'd end up in trouble, be hungover, lose jobs, and stuff. My first time I didn't say much. . . . it was hard enough just to go up front and say my name.
>
> . . . I've led a few meetin's myself. I couldn't at first, but after a while I needed to get up there, tell my story, and maybe help somebody else. And besides, the younger guys expected it, and I guess I owed 'em at least that much. Now, it's going to the meetings that keeps me sober. It took me years to figure it, but I need the meetin' more than it needs me.

There are currently more men in AA than women (69 to 31 percent), but the percentage of women has risen. More than half of AA members (51 percent) are between the ages of thirty-one and fifty; 15 percent are aged thirty and younger.

Some individuals are religious adherents to the AA model, and others are conscientious in their questioning of the effectiveness of AA. AA does not open itself to sci-

Table 11.4 The Principles of Alcoholics Anonymous (AA)

1. We admitted we were powerless over alcohol—that our lives had become unmanageable.

2. Came to believe that a Power greater than ourselves could restore us to sanity.

3. Made a decision to turn our will and our lives over to the care of God, as we understood Him.

4. Made a searching and fearless moral inventory of ourselves.

5. Admitted to God, to ourselves, and to another human being the exact nature of our wrongs.

6. Were entirely ready to have God remove all these defects of character.

7. Humbly asked him to remove our shortcomings.

8. Made a list of all persons we had harmed, and became willing to make amends to them all.

9. Made direct amends to such people whenever possible, except when to do so would injure them or others.

10. Continued to take personal inventory, and when we were wrong promptly admitted it.

11. Sought through prayer and meditation to improve our conscious contact with God as we understood Him, praying only for knowledge of His will for us and the power to carry that out.

12. Having had a spiritual awakening as the result of these steps, we tried to carry this message to alcoholics and to practice these principles in all our affairs.

Source: AA World Services, Inc. The Twelve Steps are reprinted with permission of Alcoholics Anonymous World Services, Inc. Permission to reprint this material does not mean that AA has reviewed or approved the contents of this publication or that AA agrees with the views expressed herein. AA is a program of recovery from alcoholism only. Use of the Twelve Steps in connection with programs and activities that are patterned after AA but that address other problems does not imply otherwise.

entific evaluation, and the absence of hard data renders the claims somewhat limp. One study, though limited by its target group, did report on the results of AA for a largely male sample of factory workers (Walsh et al., 1991). The alcohol-abusing workers were assigned randomly to compulsory inpatient hospitalization, compulsory attendance at AA meetings, and a choice of options. All three groups improved on measures of job perfor-

mance, but the hospitalization group fared the best on measures of drinking and drug use. AA may serve best in the maintenance of gains: the authors found "hospitalization with AA follow-up addressed drinking problems significantly more effectively than did compulsory AA alone" (p. 780). Independent of one's views about the AA association, many people find that the AA Serenity Prayer offers a healthy perspective on life in general.

Prevention Programs

We know that excessive consumption of alcohol and other substance abuse have unwanted physical and psychological outcomes. We also know that the dissemination of important preventive information is needed during the early years — before youths develop misinformed expectations about substance use. In addition, we understand some of the factors that place an individual at risk for a substance-use disorder. Guided by this information and the results of prevention efforts already reported (Gorman, 1992), can we coordinate efforts and create and implement programs that will prevent substance-abuse problems before they begin?

Interventions to prevent the development of alcohol and other drug problems are important. The idea behind **prevention** is simple: Spend the time and money on programs during early adolescence and prevent or reduce the later substance-abuse problems. Often, the prevention programs are based on studies of adolescent predictors of later substance use (e.g., Newcomb & Bentler, 1988b; Oetting & Beauvais, 1990; Windle, 1990). Two examples of successful prevention programs document the need for their continued support.

Gilbert Botvin and his colleagues at Cornell University (Botvin et al., 1990) worked in fifty-six schools (with more than 4,400 subjects) and provided a cognitive-behavioral intervention that included training in life skills (general) and substance-specific information. The life-skills component taught youths how to cope with social situations that involve pressure to smoke, drink, or use drugs. Using demonstrations, opportunities to role play and practice, rewards, and homework assignments, young people built self-esteem and learned how to communicate effectively. They also learned to resist advertising and to assert their own rights. The substance-specific information did not emphasize the long-term detrimental effects of substance abuse, which is seen as less relevant to adolescents, but instead emphasized the immediate negative consequences of substance use (such as decreased social acceptance). The prevention program was taught in class units that covered fifteen class periods.

The desired outcome of a prevention program is the reduction in substance use and abuse for those receiving the intervention as compared with those in a control

With regard to smoking, there is a changing social climate in the United States and to a lesser degree in other countries. The message is becoming clearer and stronger — smoking is detrimental to one's health.

condition. Botvin and associates (1990) reported that prevention effects were found for immoderate alcohol use, cigarette smoking, and marijuana use. Because this preventive program was implemented in a manner that resembles "real-world conditions," the authors suggested that the program has transportability; that is, it can be taken and used elsewhere. One possible limitation to this conclusion, however, is that the study involved predominately white middle-class urban and rural subjects, and we do not yet know if the effects would be comparable with youths of a lower socioeconomic status or with members of minority ethnic or cultural groups (see Friedman & Utada, 1992).

Ethnic diversity was better represented in the sample of youths who participated in the prevention program conducted and reported by C. Anderson Johnson and his colleagues at the University of Southern California (Johnson et al., 1990). Their sample included approximately 25 percent minorities (predominately African Americans and Hispanics). The prevention program was provided from 1984 to 1987. The components of the program included the school, the parents, the community, and the mass media. In the school program (grades six and seven), the youths were taught "resistance" skills and were given opportunities to practice how to resist drug use. The parent program taught parents how to engage in positive parent-child interactions and how to communicate better with their children. Parents also were involved in reviewing the school's drug policies. Community leaders were included in drug-free task forces, and mass media gave the entire effort needed publicity. The results of this multicomponent prevention program indicated that for marijuana and tobacco use, the program had desired effects. Importantly, the effects held for a variety of persons — it was able to reduce tobacco and marijuana use for junior high school children who were at both high and low risk for substance abuse. There was no significant effect, however, for alcohol use. The authors reported that, as expected, although the rate of use for these substances increased over time, the rate of increase was significantly less (at ninth and tenth grades) for those in the prevention program than for those in control schools.

It is hoped that through widespread distribution of factual and useful information about substance use, a healthier generation will follow. It is pleasing to see bulletin boards and television ads and to hear sports stars and radio commercials speak directly to the problems of substance abuse. Although substance abuse remains a central problem in many countries, there is some evidence of positive progress toward a safer and saner society.

What Lies Ahead?

Drugs and alcohol are available and used worldwide, and substance-use disorders continue to be a problem for societies as diverse as the world itself. No cultural, ethnic, or religious group is entirely immune. The continued presence of drugs and alcohol foretells a future with individuals who continue to suffer from substance-use disorders.

On the positive side, the increased recognition of the deleterious effects of substance use has led to a corresponding increase in efforts to prevent them. In the United States, for example, funds have been available for early interventions designed to prevent youths from the unwanted physical and psychological effects of drugs and alcohol. Some results have been promising, but the problem is large and much additional work is required.

Cultural adjustments seem to be having positive effects on substance abuse. For example, less than a decade ago, cigarette smoking was allowed and prevalent in restaurants, theaters, and public buildings and on public transportation. Today, this is not the case. In fact, many communities have enacted laws to ensure access to clean air for the nonsmoking members of society.

The widespread nature of substance-abuse disorders requires added research and professional notice. On the research front, efforts are increasing to study and understand the biochemical actions that underlie addiction and the cognitive and social learning factors that influence substance abuse. The components of treatment that are needed to rectify abuse patterns and the treatment strategies that are most effective in reaching the goal are receiving research evaluation. We are learning more about the factors that place an individual at risk for substance abuse, and the outcomes of these studies of vulnerability will no doubt inform future treatment and prevention programs.

On the professional side, substance abuse is a major concern facing practicing psychologists. Not only do the individuals who seek help for substance-abuse disorders need and require treatment, but also the many patients who are receiving treatment for any of the other various disorders in this book may have complications from substance abuse as well. The co-morbidity of substance abuse and other psychological disorders is high, rendering the problem among those most in need of continued attention.

KEY TERMS

abstinence versus controlled drinking (358)
addiction (332)
alcohol (335)
Alcoholics Anonymous (AA) (362)
amphetamines (340)
balanced placebo design (334)
cannabis (338)
cocaine (341)

cognitive expectancy theory (350)
detoxification (358)
expectancies (334)
fetal alcohol syndrome (FAS) (336)
hallucinogens (342)
methadone (361)
multiple-risk-factor model (352)
nicotine (343)

opiates (344)
perceived effects theory (350)
physical dependence (332)
prevention (363)
recovery (356)
relapse (355)
relapse prevention training (359)
remission (352)

sedative-hypnotic-anxiolytic agents (345)
tension reduction hypothesis (349)
tolerance (332)
type 1 alcoholism (347)
type 2 alcoholism (347)
unitary disease model (346)
vulnerability model (351)
withdrawal (332)

SUMMARY

Defining the Problem of Addiction

Psychoactive substance-use disorders are widespread, detrimental to the user, and very costly to society. Substance abusers can develop an *addiction*, have *physical dependence*, and complications linked to *tolerance* and *withdrawal*. What an individual thinks are likely to be the effects of alcohol (*expectancies*) influence how that individual will react, as research, such as studies using the *balanced placebo design*, has shown. Although the substance-abuse puzzle is not solved, it is clear that the pieces include both physical and psychological components.

The Addictive Agents and Their Effects

Alcohol typically ranks the highest in terms of the percentage of people who use it. Unwanted effects of alcohol include *fetal alcohol syndrome (FAS)* as well as diseases such as hepatitis, pancreatitis, and cirrhosis. Alcohol has a high continuation rate.

Large numbers of people also have experienced the unwanted effects of *cannabis, amphetamines, cocaine, hallucinogens, nicotine, opiates,* and *sedatives-hypnotic-anxiolytic agents.* The biological processes that are affected by these substances typically involve neurotransmitter substances and brain activity that either add to one's excitation or reduce arousal. Alcohol abuse, and substance abuse in general, is often co-morbid with other psychological disorders and requires intervention.

Addictive Processes

Explanations for the substance-use disorders include genetic inclinations, environmental forces, cognitive processes, family factors, and peer influences. A traditional yet controversial concept refers to alcoholism as a disease. A modern version of this notion, the *unitary disease model,* documents the physical aspects of the disorder but may be best viewed as a metaphor.

Studies of the genetic contribution to alcoholism have suggested that the risk of alcoholism is greater, for example, among offspring of alcoholics than among offspring of nonalcoholic parents.

Although no single personality is linked directly to substance abuse, at least one longitudinal study has suggested a cluster of personality characteristics (difficulties with interpersonal relationships, weak impulse control, and the report of subjective distress) that are associated with frequent substance use among eighteen-year-olds.

Alcohol has tension-reducing qualities. A more comprehensive account based on learning includes social and cognitive influences. Social processes, such as peer pressure, affect both the initial exposure to substance use and the extent of substance use. Notions of the role of the family as a model for attitudes and behavior regarding substance use and as a source of support to reduce risk factors are relatively accepted. What an individual expects from substance use determines, in part, his or her use pattern — as suggested by *cognitive expectancy theory* and *perceived effects theory*. In the end, one's vulnerability to substance abuse is influenced by both heredity and environmental forces.

Contemporary theorizing about the various processes involved in the addictions takes an integrative posture in the *multiple-risk-factor model*. There are multiple risk factors that contribute to the disorder, and an understanding requires a synthesis of the genetic and environmental factors that make an individual vulnerable to substance abuse.

The Course of Disorder

Descriptions of the course of substance-use disorders include the important concepts of *remission, relapse,* and *recovery.* Remission refers to the return to a state of health after a disorder. Remission can be the result of treatment or may emerge from natural "self-determined" change. The success of self-change is a controversial topic. Relapse refers to the reappearance of the substance abuse following a period of remission, and it is typical for relapse to be observed during the treatment of substance-abuse disorders. Recovery, the return to and maintenance of a healthy state following relapse, can be prompted by treatment programs, the maturation process, "hitting bottom," or an individual's developing a serious physical illness related to substance abuse.

Getting Clean and Sober: Treating the Addictions

Substance abusers do not always volunteer for treatment. Indeed, many receiving treatment can be considered coerced clients — sent by judges to receive treatment. The goal of treatment is the elimination of the substance-abuse pattern, but more comprehensive goals include improving emotional and physical health and remedying familial and social relationships. Within the treatment of alcoholism, for instance, there is a controversy between the treatment goal of *abstinence versus controlled drinking*.

Hospitals provide both inpatient and outpatient programs. Hospitals are essential to the *detoxification* of alcoholics and, occasionally, are a part of the long-term residential treatment of patients with severe disorders.

Psychosocial therapy for substance abuse has used individual, group, and family treatment approaches. Behavioral, cognitive-behavioral, and family systems theories have guided the majority of treatments. *Relapse prevention training,* a cognitive-behavioral strategy, teaches clients to identify high-risk situations that predispose them to relapse and to make healthier choices early in the chain of responses that lead to relapse. Treatment efforts involving the abuser's family, or *structural-strategic family therapy,* strive to change the nature of the interactions among family members and provide recommendations for identifying and solving problems. In general, although the various treatments do not evidence striking differences in results, treatments for substance abuse are considered to be effective.

Medications continue to be used as a part of a comprehensive program for substance abuse (for example, *methadone*). Unfortunately, however, there are no medications that cure alcoholism or other substance abuse. Most medications are used for co-morbid conditions.

Alcoholics Anonymous (AA), a peer-support system for alcoholics, is guided by the goal of abstinence and uses a twelve-step program. AA believes that regular attendance at meetings is the basis for the abuser's recovery.

Interventions that focus on the *prevention* of substance abuse have been developed and evaluated. Data have suggested that early intervention can accurately inform youths about alcohol and drugs and that, when compared with control conditions, those receiving the prevention programs show a lessened rate of abusive substance use. With changing societal beliefs about substance use, the impact of preventive efforts may be increasingly effective.

Consider the following. . .

Suppose that you are a lawyer who has been asked to represent (1) a group of lung cancer patients in a lawsuit against the major cigarette companies or (2) a major cigarette corporation against all those smokers who are now suing them because they are dying of cancer. Given what you have learned in this chapter, how might you go about presenting your case? Some considerations include: Do you believe nicotine is a drug? Are cigarettes addicting, and are they dangerous to our health? Do you think the government should restrict children's access to cigarettes? Should the government enact stricter regulations in terms of cigarette smoking, even for adults?

Should tobacco companies have to pay restitution to those individuals who have lung cancer because of their smoking? Or should smokers who get cancer just accept the fact that they made informed choices about their health risks and that, in this case, they made a poor choice? How do the positions you take relate to matters of freedom, responsibility, and choice — touchstones of our democratic society?

Suppose that you have a relative who is an alcoholic. How might you apply some of the things you have learned in this chapter to better understand your rela-tive's situation or perhaps to try to help? For example, consider the thinking that alcoholism is a disease. What are the implications if that is the case? Must alcoholics discontinue all alcohol consumption to have a successful outcome? What about the data that suggest that con-trolled drinking is an option? How might these findings be interpreted in light of the practical advice of many professionals who recommend abstinence? Does the dis-ease model apply for some but not for others? Must the new thinking on controlled drinking always clash with the disease model, or are there practical ways in which they can coexist?

CHAPTER 12

Sexual Dysfunctions and Disorders

Those among us...

- Your best friend, Nancy, shyly confided to you that she wanted to discuss sex. Then she related her confusion: She enjoys lovemaking with her boyfriend, and greatly treasures touching and being held, but has never experienced an orgasm. She wonders if something is wrong with her.

- Bobby, a weird guy from your neighborhood, was sent to prison for exposing his genitals in front of several teenage girls in town. Now he's out of jail and back home, and the neighborhood is really worried and angry.

- You've noticed Martin several times in the drugstore. The first time, he looked like a tall woman with long painted fingernails; but up close you could see slight beard growth and a muscular masculine face. Recently, the same face is softer and hairless, and he seems to be "evolving" into a feminine woman.

- You've read in the newspapers about the death of Dr. Edgar B., a successful doctor and community leader, good husband, and father of three grown kids. You've heard through the grapevine that he died of a heart attack — at his girlfriend's house. There, police discovered whips, ropes, and handcuffs that were apparently used in sexual activities.

Given the huge variety of sexual activities that people seem to enjoy, what's "normal"?

What about sex crimes: Can the people who commit them be treated and changed?

What goes wrong when people are born one gender but feel like they are of the opposite sex?

How do people develop preferences for peculiar sex, like bondage or exposing themselves?

Sexuality: a subject of poets' verses and everyone's fantasies, a motive of kings and conquerors, a frequent inspiration and theme of novelists. How can something so powerful, so basic, and so natural and wonderful be linked to so many problems? And cause problems it surely does. The road to "normal" patterns of sexual behavior is full of potholes. People sometimes cannot enjoy or perform sex easily or cannot integrate sexuality within their adult relationships; they may have powerful preferences that push beyond the bounds of social norms.

There are two very different kinds of problems in sexual functioning: *sexual dysfunctions,* which are difficulties in normal sexual activity related to arousal and performance; and *paraphilias,* which are atypical forms of sexual behavior or desire. Some paraphilias can be indulged in privacy either alone or with another consenting adult, but other atypical sexual activities such as rape, incest, and pedophilia victimize people and are therefore illegal. In this chapter we explore the nature, possible causes, and treatments for sexual dysfunctions and paraphilias. We see that research on these topics is strikingly scarce. Finally, we discuss *gender identity disorder,* which involves identification with and desire to be the gender different from one's biological sex.

NORMAL SEXUAL FUNCTIONING

Sexual functioning is the result of complex interactions between the brain and the sex organs, mediated by two ingredients that affect much of human behavior: cognitions and hormones. First we discuss the mechanisms of the process of sexual functioning. Then we present the elements of the sexual response cycle in men and women. We also consider what is meant by normal sexual behavior — including the topic of same-sex preferences.

Mental and Biological Processes in Sexual Functioning

Both mind and body contribute to the experience and expression of sexuality, as we briefly review.

Mental Processes in Sexual Functioning   As a Woody Allen character once said, the most important sex organ is the brain. Unlike the sexual behaviors of lower species, which are controlled largely by hormones, human sexuality is greatly affected, for better or worse, by mental processes.

In a complex feedback system involving different aspects of biological functioning, stimuli interpreted by the cerebral cortex as sexual, because of their acquired meaning, trigger hormonal reactions that in turn stimulate physical responses. External stimuli include sights, scents, touch, and any other sensations to which the person attaches sexual significance. Internal stimuli such as emotions, fantasies, memories, and images generated in the mind (cerebral cortex) may also play an important role in triggering or inhibiting sexual responses. Not all sexual stimuli operate through conscious mental mechanisms; some sensations and scents, for instance, may elicit sexual reactions reflexively. Human beings, however, are highly influenced by their thoughts and conscious perceptions.

Sexual cognitions — the recognition and interpretation of stimuli as sexual — are strongly influenced by learning. Attitudes, beliefs, emotions, and personal

Sex has always been used by advertisers to sell products, and changing sexual norms are reflected in ads over the decades. In recent ads, slightly "kinky" images hint that such practices are okay, even valued.

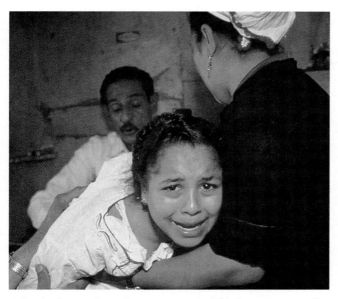

Cultural values and practices exert a powerful influence on sexuality. Many cultures still practice removal of the clitoris of young girls, as this child is experiencing. One goal is to prevent women's sexual pleasure as a way of reducing infidelity.

experiences play an enormous role in sexual responding. Cultural and historical trends in attitudes toward sexuality, toward our experiences of our bodies, and toward men's and women's sexual and nonsexual roles have a powerful impact on the biological ability to function sexually because they influence the ways that people interpret potentially erotic stimuli. Moreover, the meaning of sexual activities is greatly influenced by the nature of the relationship between partners, which is itself affected not only by the actual current relationship but also by one's history of relationships, including those with the family. Thus, the ability to enjoy and function in sexual relationships is subject to many variations. Not surprisingly, when something is amiss in sexual functioning, we often look to the mental aspects of the process that interact with the biological aspects. In this chapter we provide many examples of dysfunctional learning and cognition that affect sexual behavior.

Hormonal Factors and Sexual Desire Prompted by messages from the central nervous system, hormones are secreted by the hypothalamus that stimulate the anterior pituitary gland to secrete hormones that affect the gonads (ovaries and testes). They produce sex steroid hormones such as **estrogen** and **androgens**, which affect sexual and reproductive characteristics. In males, androgens — hormones such as testosterone — are related to sexual desire and motivation. In females, the link between sexual desire and androgens is far more uncertain: Women's level of androgens peaks at mid-menstrual cycle, but many studies have not shown accompanying increases in sexual desire and motivation

(e.g., Andersen & Cyranowski, 1995). Variations in other hormones such as estrogen and progesterone, along with changes in mood and energy level, may also contribute to variable female sexual desire throughout the menstrual cycle. Bancroft (1989) speculated that women's sexual desire may be more susceptible to social learning effects than is men's sexual desire.

Sexual Response Cycle

Human sexual response occurs in stages. The clinical observations of Helen Singer Kaplan (1979) and the pioneering laboratory research of William Masters and Virginia Johnson (1966) have identified several stages that occur in sequence: desire, arousal (excitement), plateau, orgasm, and resolution. The human response cycle involves the same stages and sequences in same-sex as in opposite-sex interactions and among adults of all ages and cultures.

Figure 12.1 depicts the physiological changes that occur in the genitals of both men and women during stages of the sexual response cycle. **Desire** is usually the beginning stage (although sometimes couples engage in sex before they experience desire). Desire is a state of interest in or motivation for sexual activity. The **arousal,** or **excitement,** phase includes vasocongestion (swelling) of various areas of the body including the sexual organs, resulting in erections in men and vaginal lubrication in women. Both sexes also experience nipple erection and increases in muscle tension, heart rate, and blood pressure. The excitement phase is followed by a **plateau** during which sexual tension mounts to a peak leading to orgasm. The **orgasm** phase includes involuntary muscle spasms involving uterine contraction in women and ejaculation in men. Some women experience orgasms from direct clitoral stimulation as stronger, sharper, and more localized, whereas orgasms from coital stimulation may feel diffused throughout the body (Masters & Johnson, 1966). Women thus may have a preference for one kind of stimulation or the other.

The final **resolution** phase involves a return to the normal physical state, varying in time for women and men and also as a function of extent and duration of the arousal. Although most people experience pleasurable relaxation during this state, individuals differ in the extent to which they want touching, continued sexual activity, or solitude. Men, but not women, experience a refractory period during which no amount of stimulation will result in orgasm. Its duration depends on a variety of factors such as age, sexual activity, and emotional characteristics. Figure 12.2 illustrates male and female sexual response cycles in terms of intensity of sexual excitement and progression over time. Masters and Johnson (1966) observed that women's patterns are more variable than men's. As shown in the figure, there may be distinctly different types: In pattern B the woman remains at the plateau stage without orgasm, pattern C

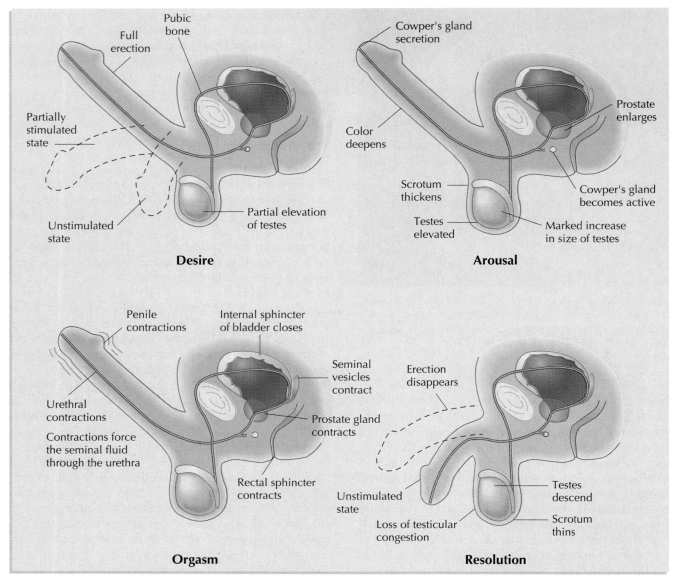

Figure 12.1 Genital Changes Associated with Stages of the Human Sexual Response Cycle

All normal adults experience the physiological changes and sequence illustrated in this figure. (Male genitals are depicted on this page; female genitals, on the opposite page.) These patterns

Source: Crooks & Baur (1990).

were first described by clinician Helen Singer Kaplan and researchers Masters and Johnson.

Note: The plateau phase is not included in this figure.

shows the experience of a very rapid rise in excitement followed by an intense orgasm and rapid resolution, and pattern A is similar to that of the male. Other patterns not shown may occur as well, according to the clinical studies of Masters and Johnson. Men also report subjective experiences of differences in their sexual responses, but these mostly reflect variability in duration rather than in intensity or sequence (Masters & Johnson, 1966).

In light of the differences between men and women, and given individual variability in the sexual response cycle, it is easy to understand that communication is an

essential ingredient in sexual experiences and that a lack of communication can create or exacerbate problems in such experiences. Couples who lack information or assume that there is only one right way to experience sexual pleasure are especially likely to have difficulties if they cannot discuss their needs and preferences, and listen to each other, in nonjudgmental ways.

Normal Sexual Behaviors and Variations

Entire courses and textbooks are devoted to the topic of human sexuality, indicating its scope and variety. For a

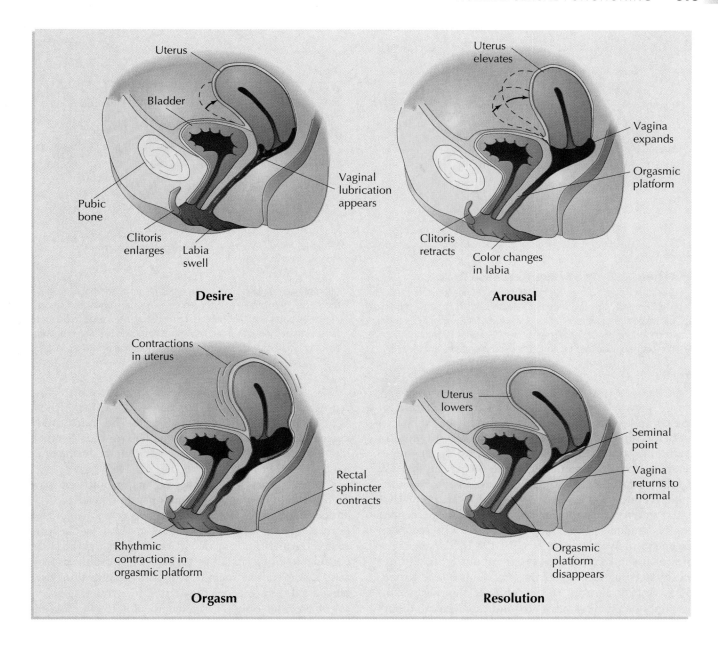

Uterus
Bladder
Pubic bone
Clitoris enlarges
Labia swell
Vaginal lubrication appears

Desire

Uterus elevates
Vagina expands
Orgasmic platform
Clitoris retracts
Color changes in labia

Arousal

Contractions in uterus
Rectal sphincter contracts
Rhythmic contractions in orgasmic platform

Orgasm

Uterus lowers
Seminal point
Vagina returns to normal
Orgasmic platform disappears

Resolution

course in abnormal psychology, however, we are interested in what is not normal. One of the intriguing truths about sexuality is that what is now considered normal was formerly considered deviant.

Normality Changes Over Time

At one time it was believed that masturbation not only was immoral but also caused mental illness, or at least revealed immature sexual preferences. Yet, surveys of adults have indicated that the vast majority of males masturbate, and that female masturbation has greatly increased. The landmark Kinsey studies of the 1940s and 1950s found that 25 to 30 percent of young women masturbated (Kinsey, Pomeroy & Martin, 1948; Kinsey, Pomeroy, Martin & Gebhard, 1953; Kinsey data reanalyzed by Gebhard & Johnson, 1979); by 1974 the same age group was reporting a rate of 60 percent (Hunt, 1974); and according to a recent survey of students, 75 percent of women reported that they masturbate (Leiblum et el., 1993).

Premarital intercourse was certainly considered deviant throughout most of the early part of the twentieth century. How dramatically this has changed! In the

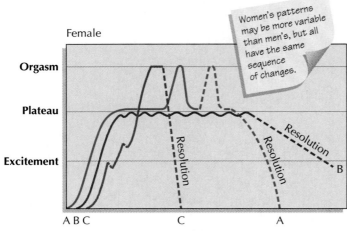

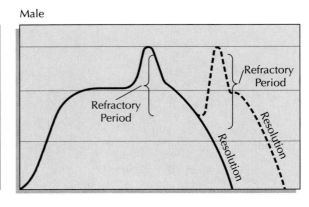

Figure 12.2   The Sexual Response Cycle

Based on direct observation and physical measurements, William Masters and Virginia Johnson characterized the overall physiological response cycle for men and women. Men experience a period of mounting sexual excitement up to a point of leveling off, called the plateau, followed by an intense, brief orgasm, and then a resolution phase in which physical changes return to the baseline state. The sexual response cycle for women may be similar to men (as shown by pattern A), although patterns for women tend to be more variable than men's; B and C represent common reactions, but others may occur as well. *Source:* Masters & Johnson (1966, p. 5).

Kinsey surveys of several decades ago, 20 percent of women and 45 percent of men reported that they had sex before marriage. Among young women surveyed in a national sample, rates of premarital sex by age nineteen rose from 46 percent in 1971 to 69 percent in 1979 (Zelnik & Kantner, 1980). And in a survey of women students conducted between 1988 and 1992, premarital sexual activity was reported by more than 80 percent of the respondents (Leiblum et al., 1993; see also Feigenbaum, Weinstein & Rosen, 1995). For men, the rates of premarital intercourse are about 80 to 90 percent by age nineteen (Feigenbaum, Weinstein & Rosen, 1995; Mott & Haurin, 1988; Zelnik & Kantner, 1980). Two national surveys have also indicated ethnic differences in the occurrence of premarital sex: African American teenagers exhibit higher rates of premarital sex than do whites, and Hispanic males exhibit higher rates than whites; among Hispanic women, however, rates of premarital sex are lower than among white and African American women (Mott & Haurin, 1988; Zelnik & Kantner, 1980).

What about homosexual experiences? Although the majority of adults do not have same-sex sexual contact, such behaviors are common during childhood and adolescence. Sorenson (1973) surveyed thirteen- to nineteen-year-olds and found that 6 percent of females and 11 percent of males had experienced same-sex contact during adolescence. Moreover, a large interview study of homosexual and heterosexual men and women found that, among the heterosexual men, 20 percent reported being aroused by males in adolescence and 36 percent

reported some physical contact with a male (Bell, Weinberg & Hammersmith, 1981). The same study determined that 42 percent of the heterosexual women had reported some form of same-sex contact during adolescence.

Recent years have witnessed major shifts in how homosexuality is viewed. From a psychological and scientific standpoint, homosexuality is now considered a normal variation in sexual behavior. Until 1973, however, the American Psychiatric Association and the DSM considered homosexuality to be a diagnosable psychiatric disorder. The members of this organization were persuaded to reconsider the matter. In a stunning reversal of previous opinion, the members voted homosexuality out of the DSM.

What led to their changed opinion and to the conclusion that homosexuality is simply a variation of sexual preference? First, a volume of research demonstrated that the personalities of homosexual men and women did not differ from those of heterosexuals, and there was no evidence of greater psychiatric impairment in homosexuals than in heterosexuals. Gay people experience psychological challenges related to homophobia, but otherwise they have the same life problems as do heterosexuals (Garnets & Kimmel, 1991). Moreover, research investigating the parental functioning and children of gay couples has found that the children of such couples do not differ in terms of adjustment from those of heterosexual families (e.g., Flaks, Ficher, Masterpasqua & Joseph, 1995). Second, the growing emphasis on human rights and social justice — the same spirit that

CLINTON'S COATTAILS: CAN HE WIN BACK CONGRESS?

Newsweek

We're Having a Baby

Can Gay Families Gain Acceptance?
What It's Like for the Kids

Singer Melissa Etheridge and her pregnant partner, Julie Cypher

More and more adults are "coming out" and openly acknowledging preferences for sex and intimacy with same-sex partners. Psychologists view homosexuality as a variation of human sexuality — not deviance or disorder. In many communities, gays and lesbians seek the same rights and family lifestyles as heterosexuals.

was also profoundly increasing awareness of women's and minorities' rights — encouraged psychiatrists to consider homosexuals simply as people expressing a different sexual preference and subject to the same psychological concerns and issues as anyone else. Probably most psychiatrists also recognized that among their colleagues, family members, friends, and associates in other walks of life were homosexuals who were functioning effectively in their work, their families, and their communities.

Homosexuality Homosexuality refers not only to sexual contact between persons of the same sex but also to individuals whose psychological, emotional, and social preferences pertain to members of the same sex. Homosexuality is thus far more than just sexual behavior. It is not to be confused with gender identity difficulties; indeed, gay men and women experience themselves as persons of their biological sex and typically have no desire to be otherwise.

Sexual orientation is not simply an either-or proposition. The Kinsey survey of U.S. sexual behaviors conducted in the 1940s was one of the first to indicate a possible continuum of sexual orientation, with exclusive heterosexuals on one end, exclusive homosexuals on the other, and the middle ranges reflecting degree of preference for one or the other. Many people described themselves in this survey (Kinsey, Pomeroy & Martin, 1948) as having intermediate levels of attraction to and sexual experience with members of the same or opposite sex. Other studies have estimated that 4 percent of the male population (less for women) have relatively frequent homosexual experiences (Fay, Turner, Klasser & Gagnon, 1989). Because of secrecy or reluctance to admit such behavior, exact figures are difficult to obtain, but recent estimates have ranged from about 3.3 to 6.2 percent for men, including those who are currently or formerly married (Fay, Turner, Klassen & Gagnon, 1989).

Discussing the *causes* of homosexuality presents a dilemma. Because homosexuality is a normal variant of behavior according to the mental health profession, its causes need no more explaining than do the causes of heterosexuality. On the other hand, an explanation of the issue might be worthwhile because many people have misconceptions that are potentially destructive.

In an extensive interview study of several hundred gay men and women, investigators found no support for certain common myths. They found that homosexuality is not caused by dominant mothers and passive fathers, it does not typically originate with a seduction by an older man or woman, and it is not due to a hormonal imbalance (Bell, Weinberg & Hammersmith, 1981). On the contrary, it is probably most accurate to say that any sexual orientation, gay or straight, reflects the interaction of multiple factors, including biological factors that determine prenatal development, cultural and experiential factors, and socialization history (Garnets & Kimmel, 1991; Money, 1988).

One of the strongest predictors of adult homosexuality is **gender nonconformity**, or the rejection of traditional masculine or feminine roles, during childhood and adolescence. As boys, many future gay men did not enjoy sports, did not have super-masculine traits, and expressed preferences for artistic activities. As girls, future lesbians rejected doll-playing, quiet activities, and frilly dresses. As reviewed by Bailey and Zucker (1995), prospective studies of highly feminine boys and retrospective studies of gay men and lesbians support the association between childhood gender nonconformity and homosexuality. However, many later homosexuals do not show gender nonconformity, and the majority of boys and girls who reject traditional sex roles do not grow up as homosexuals. Based on data from several studies, Bailey and Zucker (1995) estimated that only about 51 percent of boys and 6 percent of girls who display cross-gender behavior in childhood will become homosexual.

Thus, gender nonconformity by itself does not explain the development of sexual preferences for the same sex. Many theorists believe that biological factors may also be critical. One leading hypothesis is that prenatal or perinatal exposure to abnormal levels of sex hormones (perhaps as the result of maternal stress, administration of steroidal medications to pregnant women, or other medical causes) leads to the masculinization or feminization of neural structures, affecting sex-typed behaviors or sexual orientation, or both (Meyer-Bahlburg et al., 1995). Excess steroidal hormones may masculinize or defeminize the developing brain, and deficiencies may feminize or demasculinize it. In normal human beings, development progresses along feminine lines until males are masculinized by androgens secreted by fetal gonads. The male and female brains then begin to differ somewhat in structure and function as a result of these hormonal processes. For instance, an area of the hypothalamus suspected to influence sexual preference is significantly larger in the normal male brain than in the female brain. Numerous animal studies as well as medical studies of humans have provided suggestive evidence in support of this hypothesis. For instance, Meyer-Bahlburg and his colleagues (1995) demonstrated that women exposed prenatally to diethylstilbestrol (DES), a synthetic estrogen that was once used to treat high-risk pregnancies, exhibited a higher incidence of bisexual or homosexual preferences in adulthood.

The hypothalamus is considered a likely candidate as a source of sexual orientation that might be influenced by prenatal neuroendocrine abnormalities. Recently, Simon LeVay (1991) examined a tiny area of the hypothalamus called the INAH3 region, about the size of a grain of sand, and found that it was significantly larger in heterosexual men than in gay men. LeVay speculated that this anatomic difference might be a contributor to different sexual preferences, although about one-third of heterosexual men scored in the low-size range whereas some of the gay men scored in the high-size range).

Three recent genetic studies also support the hypothesis of a biological factor in homosexuality. Michael Bailey and his colleagues recruited gay men and lesbians from advertisements in gay publications, seeking subjects who had twins or nonbiologically related adoptive siblings (Bailey & Pillard, 1991; Bailey, Pillard, Neale & Agyei, 1993). After determining the sexual orientation of the siblings, they found much higher rates of concordance for homosexuality among the monozygotic (identical) twins (52 percent for gay men and 48 percent for lesbians) compared with dizygotic (fraternal) twins (22 percent for gay men and 16 percent for lesbians). A genetic linkage study also determined that a DNA marker on the X-chromosome is highly correlated with the occurrence of homosexuality among families in which male homosexual siblings are present (Hamer et al., 1993; see also Pattatucci & Hamer, 1995).

In short, neuroendocrine and genetic findings have strongly contested the commonly held belief that homosexuality results from a person's conscious, deliberate choice to pursue relationships with someone of the same sex. These results suggest that at least some forms of homosexuality reflect biological variation.

Sex and Normal Aging   Community surveys and studies of volunteer participants have generally indicated declines in sexual activity among older persons in U.S. and European cultures (Gebhard & Johnson, 1979, reporting from the Kinsey surveys; see also research review in Rinehart & Schiff, 1985). For instance, a survey of 4,246 persons conducted in the early 1980s found that the proportion of sexually active women was 93 percent in their fifties, declining to 65 percent among those older than age seventy; and for sexually active men, 98 percent in their fifties and 79 percent among those older than age seventy. These figures reflect rates of masturbation and nonmarital sex as well as marital sex (Breecher, 1983). Other studies have shown even greater declines in sexual activity (Rinehart & Schiff, 1985).

What might account for these declines? In older adults, alterations in hormonal activity — beginning gradually after about age fifty in men and rapidly after menopause in women — cause physiological changes that may result in reduced speed and intensity of responses to sexual stimulation. In men, androgen levels begin to decline slowly and progressively from about age fifty (Vermeulen, Rubes & Verdonck, 1972), and decreased testosterone level is correlated with reduced sexual desire and activity among older men (Davidson et al., 1983). However, the decline in interest is by no means inevitable, and hormonal decreases account for only a small portion of the reduced motivation. These physiological changes typically result in slower time to erection. Some men experience greater difficulty achieving and maintaining an erection. Nevertheless, a study of men between the ages of forty-five and seventy-four found that, despite decreased sexual arousal and activity, a man's enjoyment of marital sex and satisfaction with his own sexual performance does not change with age (Schiavi et al., 1990).

In older women, reduced vaginal lubrication and thinning of the vaginal wall because of reduced estrogen may create discomfort. As Masters and Johnson (1966) observed in their studies, however, older women with regular sexual activity have fewer problems than women with little sexual activity.

Romance and sexual enjoyment do not end at middle-age. Older adults can — and do — experience sexual pleasure if they care to.

Most sex researchers and clinicians have noted that physiological changes accompanying aging are less of an obstacle to sexual enjoyment than are *negative attitudes*. Many people in our culture consider sex between older adults to be improper, if not a sure sign of "senility." Such attitudes may in part be prompted by religious prohibitions about nonreproductive sexual activity. And older individuals themselves may be discouraged by the belief that bodily changes resulting in slower sexual responding mean that they are no longer capable of sexual performance. Unfortunately, many normal and healthy individuals who are capable of sexual enjoyment may prefer to give up sexual contact rather than modify their practices as needed.

Cross-cultural studies of sexual practices in traditional, nonindustrial societies have indicated that sexual activity in old age is common. Investigators searching through anthropological records have determined that these societies showed evidence of continued sexual functioning in 70 percent of old men and 84 percent of old women (Winn & Newton, 1982). Although some of the societies disapproved of sexuality in the elderly or revealed negative attitudes toward older adults as sexual partners, relatively few censured sex in old age. Thus, it seems that attitudes, rather than biological changes as such, may underlie cultural expectations of decreased sexual pleasure in older age.

Sex and the Young In light of increasing rates of sexual activity among teens, no account of normal sexuality would be complete without a mention of the risk that sexual behaviors may turn deadly if they lead to exposure to the human immunodeficiency virus (HIV).

What Predicts Safer Sex Among Youth at Risk for AIDS?

Anyone who exchanges sexual fluids or shares syringes with a partner who might be infected with HIV is at risk for contracting AIDS. The risk is distressingly high among gay and bisexual adolescent males, as well as among Hispanic and African American youth because of low rates of condom use in some situations, high rates of injecting drugs, and high rates of oral and anal sex (reviewed in Rotheram-Borus, Rosario, Reid & Koopman, 1995). Accordingly, Mary Jane Rotheram-Borus and her colleagues undertook a study to learn if they could reduce high-risk behaviors (sex acts unprotected by condoms) among primarily Hispanic and African American gay or bisexual teenage males. They also wanted to learn what factors would help predict increased use of condoms. Among the factors they uncovered were knowledge about AIDS, self-control, friend or partner support of condom use, stress, self-esteem, anxiety and depression, and substance use.

The participants in this study were young men between the ages of fourteen and nineteen who visited an agency in New York City offering recreational and social services to gay and bisexual youth. The 119 young men who joined the study were able to provide follow-up information about their sexual behavior over a one-year period. The investigators provided a twenty-session "risk reduction" intervention program that met two or three times a week in groups of about ten each. The program included increasing knowledge about

AIDS, learning how to cope with risky sexual situations, increasing access to health care and other social services, encouraging positive experiences about being gay, dealing with prejudice against homosexuality, and identifying and addressing personal issues and cognitions that might interfere with AIDS safety practices.

Certain predictive factors, such as measures of attitudes about condom use and the psychological issues such as self-esteem noted above, were assessed prior to the intervention; then, every three months the youth were interviewed about their sexual practices. Figure 12.3 summarizes the outcomes reported over twelve months. According to the results, about seventy-five percent of the youth showed either substantially improved or fully protected anal sex, and about fifty percent showed substantially improved or fully protected oral sex.

To test the importance of the predictive factors in this study, the researchers compared protected, improved, variable, relapse, and unprotected groups on each of the variables. The most significant predictors — the ones that best distinguished between youth who improved in terms of safer anal sex and youth who

relapsed into unprotected sex — were self-esteem, anxiety, depression, and alcohol use. Those who improved had scored in a more positive direction on such factors, but they did not differ with respect to the other attitude and knowledge factors.

This study showed that some youth were already practicing safer sex and that about one-third further increased condom use over the year. Unfortunately, it also indicated that the majority were not consistently protecting themselves, and that the most depressed and emotionally disordered youth were the ones least likely to change their sexual practices. Indeed, for many of them, current life stresses and emotional turmoil took precedence over practicing safer sex. Some indicated that, when depressed, they didn't bother with condoms because they felt hopeless about preventing AIDS. Therefore, as the authors argued, AIDS prevention efforts directed at high-risk youth should include more comprehensive mental health care (Rotheram-Borus, Rosario, Reid & Koopman, 1995). As many studies of therapy outcomes have revealed, those who need treatment the most often benefit the least.

With this understanding of the variations of normal sexual behavior and the human sexual response cycle, we turn now to a consideration of problems in sexual functioning and their treatments.

SEXUAL DYSFUNCTION

Sexual dysfunction is a general term referring to problems in sexual interest or performance that cause distress to individuals or difficulties in their relationships. Temporary disruptions of sexual performance due to physical factors such as drugs, alcohol, and illnesses, as well as to psychological factors such as stress, fatigue, and emotional upset, are quite common. To be considered a clinically diagnosable problem, sexual dysfunctions must be persistent or recurrent and disturbing to the individual or relationship. (Rates of occurrence are noted in later sections.) Sexual dysfunctions are categorized in DSM-IV according to the phase of the sexual response cycle in which they occur. An additional category refers to sexual pain disorders.

Sexual Desire Disorders

The concept of a distinct disorder of inhibited sexual desire is relatively new, having entered the DSM in 1980. Currently termed **hypoactive sexual desire**, this disorder is characterized by low or absent desire for sexual activities (or even lack of sexual fantasies). Although some individuals who are disinterested in sex can nonetheless

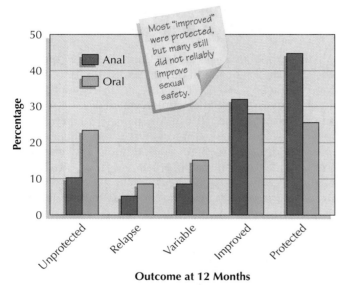

Figure 12.3 Reduced Risk for AIDS Through Increased Condom Use

This AIDS prevention study of high-risk (gay and bisexual) youth measured changes in condom use for oral and anal sex over a one-year period following a twenty-session intervention designed to increase safer sex practices. Participants were grouped according to changes in their patterns. For example, those in the "improved" category exhibited at least a 15 percent increase in condom use compared to their pretreatment behavior; those designated "variable" varied 15 percent or more across different assessments; and those who were "protected" used condoms 88 percent or more of the time.

Source: Rotheram-Borus, Rosario, Reid & Koopman (1995).

"Phone-sex on Line Four, Mr. Davis."

become aroused and experience orgasm and enjoyment, others cannot. *Lack of sexual arousal,* a different kind of sexual dysfunction, is discussed later. Hypoactive sexual desire can be lifelong, with some people apparently engaging in little sexual activity or fantasy as children or adults. Others develop it at a specific time in their lives, such as with a particular partner.

Features of Sexual Desire Disorders Some couples experience an imbalance between the two partners' desired frequency of sexual contact; others are content with quite low levels of sexual activity. To warrant a clinical diagnosis of sexual desire disorder, however, an individual must display little or no sexual interest at all — a condition that creates personal distress and relationship difficulties.

One of the most common complaints of couples seeking treatment of sexual problems is lack of interest by one or both partners (e.g., Beck, 1995). This problem is estimated to affect 15 percent of men and 35 percent of women (Nathan, 1986), and its frequency appears to have increased in recent years (reviewed in Rosen & Leiblum, 1995). Individuals with low desire commonly report that they are uninterested in sex, lack sexual urges, have few or no fantasies, and view themselves as asexual (Andersen & Cyranowski, 1995).

Sexual aversion disorder is a more severe form of sexual desire disorder, involving extreme aversion to sexual contact and total avoidance of sexual activity. Although the prevalence of this disorder is unknown, researchers believe that it is relatively rare and occurs mostly in women. Kaplan and Klein (1987) used the terms *sexual phobia* or *sexual panic states* to characterize the discomfort a person with the disorder may experience upon sexual contact. Unlike a person with hypoactive sexual desire, who may be able to enjoy sex-

ual contact once it has been initiated, people with sexual aversion disorder experience marked distress, fear, or revulsion. Some people with this disorder may be able to endure sexual contact by detaching themselves or focusing on the pleasure given the partner, but others are so uncomfortable that they cannot tolerate the experience and may actually feel panic or nausea.

Causes of Sexual Desire Disorders Most accounts suggest that there are multiple contributors to sexual desire disorders: personal issues, cognitions, biological factors, and couple issues (e.g., Beck, 1995). Kaplan (1985) speculated that most cases of hypoactive sexual desire are associated with major relationship and psychological problems, especially those causing intrapsychic anxiety or anger. For example, some individuals may have experienced family and cultural prohibitions against sexual enjoyment, to the extent that they feel guilty and distressed if they experience pleasure. As a result, their sexual desire may be suppressed. Other individuals may have deep-seated difficulties with permitting psychosexual closeness and vulnerability. Still others may have sexual preferences that are psychologically unacceptable to them, leading to suppression of desire. Stress may also reduce sexual desire. That is, important negative events may dramatically affect desire to participate in sexual activity — operating not only biologically by reducing hormonal activity, but also psychologically by creating preoccupation, depression, and fatigue. Certainly anxiety, threat, and other negative emotional states can interfere with the processing of erotic stimuli and cause a person to experience inhibited sexual feelings.

Research confirms that for many couples, sexual desire problems stem from or are intensified by relationship conflicts that cause anger and distrust (Beck, 1995). None of us could easily have thoughts or fantasies of pleasurable sex with a partner we are angry at. Relationship difficulties may also include poor communication and sexual technique; for instance, a partner may be unenthusiastic or unskilled or physically unappealing. Individuals who are turned off anticipate little enjoyment and therefore lose interest in initiating or participating in sexual contact. Women may lose sexual interest in partners for whom sexual release, but not affection, is the goal; men may lose interest in partners they feel are demanding too much.

In addition to psychological and marital factors, biological and medical issues may play an important causal role in low sexual desire. As noted earlier, normal aging — after about age fifty — may cause changes in hormones that reduce sexual drive in men, and physiological changes associated with aging may alter sexual *performance* in both men and women. Although the effects of testosterone on sexual desire are better established for men than women, their relative contribution to clinical hypoactive sexual desire disorders is still unclear (e.g., Beck, 1995). Clinical states of depression commonly include reduced sexual interest and may therefore be an underlying factor. And many medical illnesses alter sexual desire either directly through biological changes or indirectly through their effects on pain, energy, emotional distress, and disability (Schiavi, 1985). Certain medications such as some hypertensive drugs, psychoactive medications, and antihistamines may also reduce sexual drive. And, of course, abuse of alcohol, narcotics, and sedative drugs inhibits sexual desire. In short, many biological factors impair sexual performance.

The causes of sexual aversion disorders are undoubtedly psychological, rooted in dysfunctional learning or trauma. The same factors that contribute to milder sexual desire disorders, such as personal conflicts, family values and practices, and relationship issues, are relevant to sexual aversion disorders. For example, childhood or adult experiences that have colored sexual contact with revulsion or fear can set the stage for phobic anxiety and avoidance, unless the person is endowed with skills and compensatory resources such as a good relationship that can help overcome such attitudes. In addition, as we note in Chapter 14 when we discuss the effects of violence, sexual assault and molestation may be traumatic causes of sexual aversion (e.g., Browne & Finkelhor, 1986).

Sexual Arousal Disorders

Features of Sexual Arousal Disorders Difficulties that occur in the excitement (arousal) phase of the sexual response cycle are female sexual arousal disorder and male erectile disorder. As Figure 12.2 illustrates, this phase is normally associated with increased blood flow and other changes in the genital region. **Female arousal**

disorder refers to difficulties in attaining or maintaining physical features of arousal such as lubrication and genital swelling. Lubrication difficulties are fairly common in women, as reported by 19 percent of the respondents in a national survey (Laumann, Gagnon, Michael & Michaels, 1994). However, the diagnosis of arousal disorder in women is rarely seen separately from orgasm disorders. Similar causal factors contribute to both, so these factors are discussed in the section on female orgasm disorders.

Note that a defining diagnostic factor in female arousal disorder is deficiency of lubrication/swelling reactions — in parallel to lack of erection in men. However, women's subjective perception of lack of arousal is also important; in many cases, there is an actual discrepancy between physiological arousal and perceived arousal. Since women lack an observable physical reaction such as men have, some may fail to notice or accurately label their bodily reactions (Palace, 1995). In a recent study of sexually dysfunctional women, Palace (1995) reasoned that increasing autonomic arousal (heart rate, respiration) in women, and also giving false feedback to the women that they were aroused, might facilitate arousal. Figure 12.4 shows that autonomic arousal induced by watching a film about a dangerous situation did lead to greater genital arousal when the women subsequently viewed an erotic film. Moreover, women given feedback that they were more aroused than they actually (physically) were subsequently experienced greater genital arousal than did women who received no feedback. Palace (1995) concluded that *anxiety* as such does not inhibit arousal — and, indeed, that both cognitive experiences (expectations) and physical experiences (exercise, laughter, strong emotions) can facilitate sexual arousal in women. Her results suggest that sexually dysfunctional women might profit from having more positive expectations of arousal and from learning to label nonsexual physical cues as contributing to their arousal.

Arousal disorders in men, collectively called **male erectile disorder**, involve difficulties in attaining or sustaining adequate erection until completion of sexual activity. The term *erectile disorder* is preferable to the older term *impotence*, which implied that a man without an erection has no power and no value as a lover. This problem is the most frequent disorder of men seeking help in sex therapy clinics; it is also relatively common in the general population. Nine percent of the adult male population report difficulty maintaining an erection, 7 percent report difficulty achieving an erection (Mohr & Beutler, 1990), and 52 percent of men between forty and seventy years of age report some degree of erectile difficulties (Feldman et al., 1994). Erectile dysfunction may be lifelong, but most men with the disorder were previously able to sustain erections. Because a majority of men experience occasional erectile inhibition as a result of stress, fatigue, or

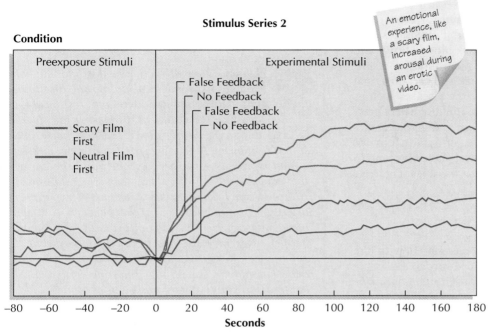

Figure 12.4 Modifications of Dysfunctional Sexual Response

Eileen Palace speculated that because their sexual arousal is less visible than men's arousal, some women may not perceive or accurately label their sexual reactions — or, more problematically, they may believe that they are not aroused when they really are. She tested sexually dysfunctional women in a special laboratory where their genital arousal could be measured under different conditions. When the women were shown erotic tapes following viewing a frightening nonsexual tape, they displayed greater sexual arousal. Also, when the women were given false feedback that they were more sexually aroused than they actually (physically) were, they subsequently displayed more arousal than women who received no feedback.

Source: Palace (1995).

other psychological discomfort, it is difficult to say how frequently the disorder must occur to be a diagnosable problem. According to DSM-IV, such diagnosis is warranted when distress and relationship difficulties are present.

Causes of Sexual Arousal Disorders Psychological factors discussed earlier in the context of sexual desire disorders may also be relevant to erectile disorders. Examples include personal conflicts that inhibit free expression of sexuality stemming from learning histories and family experiences, as well as issues pertaining to relationship quality and communication. An additional psychological ingredient, first labeled by Masters and Johnson (1970), is **performance anxiety** exacerbated by the *spectator role*. This formulation emphasizes the importance of cognitive factors in the vicious cycle of erectile difficulties: Once erectile failure has occurred, the man subsequently becomes so focused on how he's doing (performance anxiety) that his role as critical spectator gets in the way of his being an aroused participant. In short, the spectator role increases distraction and self-evaluation, thus exacerbating whatever difficulty is already present. This problematic cycle may be compounded by the partner's reactions, which in turn add to

the man's guilt, worry, or even anger — all emotions that may interfere with arousal. Other psychological factors in erectile difficulties may include depression, acute emotional states such as stress and anxiety, and relationship issues (reviewed in Ackerman & Carey, 1995).

In addition, researchers have estimated that 50 percent of erectile problems are caused primarily by physiological problems, and that another 25 percent may be mostly psychological but with contributory physical problems (Melman & Tiefer, 1992). Of course, cognitive and relationship factors may play an important role even when physical factors predominate. In any case, it is important to determine whether a physical problem is the source of the difficulty. One commonly used procedure measures nocturnal penile tumescence (NPT). Because erections during sleep occur in normal men, evidence of NPT in a man with erectile dysfunction suggests that psychological rather than organic factors are operating. NPT can be measured in sleep laboratories, and devices have recently been developed to allow testing at home and in clinical settings as well (Ackerman & Carey, 1995).

As noted, erectile problems often affect older men. Slowly declining testosterone levels may not only diminish interest but also cause physiological changes that might make erection more difficult — as when more intense or direct stimulation is required for erection to occur. Many medical illnesses inhibit erections; for example, vascular disorders affect blood flow and changes in circulation in the pelvic area. Illnesses resulting in nerve damage, such as diabetes and certain spinal cord injuries, as well as other systemic diseases such as kidney, thyroid, and liver problems, can also affect erectile functioning. Psychotropic drugs and hypertensive medications can interfere with erections (Mohr & Beutler, 1990). And, of course, alcohol and drugs tend to diminish performance capabilities, as does cigarette smoking (Ackerman & Carey, 1995).

Orgasm Disorders

The two most common disorders associated with the orgasm phase are female orgasmic disorder and male premature ejaculation. A third disorder, *male orgasmic disorder* (inhibited male orgasm), is rare and likely due to psychological causes similar to those we describe for female orgasmic disorder.

Female Orgasmic Disorder Female orgasmic disorder refers to a woman's inability to sustain arousal or achieve orgasm. This disorder was formerly known as "frigidity," a highly pejorative term implying total unresponsiveness or coldness. Some therapists use the term *anorgasmia* instead. Surveys and studies of sexual functioning have suggested that global, lifelong lack of orgasms is fairly common in women, affecting as many as 10 to 15 percent of the total female population. Another 10 to 15 percent experience orgasm only occasionally. Does this mean that all such women have diagnosable orgasm disorders? No, because many women who do not achieve orgasm are nonetheless able to enjoy sexual activity. The diagnosis of female orgasm disorder is applied only to women whose failure to achieve orgasm is a source of great distress and feeling of failure or causes interpersonal difficulties. Female anorgasmia is the most frequent reason that women seek treatment for sexual dysfunction (Rosen & Leiblum, 1995).

The diagnosis of this disorder makes no distinction about how orgasm is achieved. Following Freud's pronouncement that female orgasms that do not result from intercourse (penetration) are "immature and neurotic," many women as well as clinicians considered that orgasms achieved by manual or oral stimulation were problematic. However, Masters and Johnson's (1966) laboratory studies determined that all orgasms are physically the same whatever their source, as illustrated in Figure 12.2. Thus, a woman who rarely achieves "vaginal" orgasms during intercourse but who does attain orgasm through manual or oral stimulation is not considered to have a sexual dysfunction disorder. Indeed, only perhaps 50 percent of women achieve orgasm in intercourse at least fairly often (LoPiccolo & Stock, 1987). Consider the following case example of Nancy, who was first mentioned in the chapter opening.

Nancy is an attractive young woman who had been raised in a loving but disciplined family that valued achievement and responsibility. She worked hard as a student, preparing for a career — and did some dating along the way, with occasional romances. A year ago she fell in love with Jeff, a man who was very special to her, and she enjoyed the development of their sexual relationship. Although she became aroused, she never experienced orgasm; for the most part, she believed that with increasing experience and comfort with Jeff, it would happen. Recently she has begun to worry that the experience of orgasm should have happened by now, and that maybe something is wrong with her. She confesses to you that her family was extremely hidden about sexual matters, and she always got the idea somehow that women weren't supposed to want or enjoy sex. She is concerned that maybe she has acquired a "resistance" to really allowing herself full enjoyment. She is also concerned that Jeff might be upset or disappointed. You urge Nancy to talk more openly with Jeff about their sexual experiences. You also wisely suggest that she talk to one of the health counselors at the college, who in fact reassures her that she and Jeff might try methods of achieving orgasm besides intercourse, because not all women find that's the best way for them. The counselor tells Nancy that as long as she is enjoying sex with Jeff, she shouldn't think of herself as having a "problem."

Women with orgasmic dysfunction often report low levels of sexual desire or excitement. Subtypes of the disorder may therefore exist, involving combinations of absent orgasm and low arousal that require treatment strategies somewhat different from those applied to absent orgasm and satisfactory arousal (Andersen & Cyranowski, 1995).

Premature Ejaculation Premature ejaculation occurs when a man reaches orgasm so quickly that his own enjoyment or that of his partner (or both) is reduced. If neither person considers it to be a problem, then it is not diagnosed as such. This form of male orgasmic disorder is relatively common, affecting about 40 percent of men (Spector & Carey, 1990).

Whereas erectile difficulties are more frequent among older men, premature ejaculation is more likely among younger men. Many young men having their first sexual encounters are likely to ejaculate quickly; but with increased experience, they learn to delay. Attitudes may play an important role in premature ejaculation. During the Kinsey era of the 1940s and 1950s, rapid ejaculation was the norm — especially among less-educated, working-class men (Kinsey, Pomeroy, Martin & Gebhard, 1953). Over the years, however, the norm has favored more prolonged intercourse with an emphasis on mutual enjoyment, thus putting more pressure on men to delay ejaculation.

Causes of Orgasm Disorders Anorgasmia in women is rarely caused by physical factors, although medical conditions such as diabetes, disorders affecting circulation, some medications, and age-related changes that alter the vagina may be involved in some patients. More commonly, psychological factors are implicated. For example, relationship factors are vitally important, inasmuch as positive qualities that heighten the woman's attraction to her partner and relationship satisfaction are associated with orgasm attainment (Heiman, Gladue, Roberts & LoPiccolo, 1986). In particular, the couple's ability to communicate preferences for certain kinds of touching and stimulation enhance the likelihood of orgasm, whereas poor sexual techniques and the inability to discuss such obstacles doubtless inhibit that likelihood. Personal qualities such as positive attitudes about sex, and a healthy willingness to "let go," are also important. Indeed, a woman who is inhibited about experiencing her own preferences and expressing them to a partner might have difficulties in helping her partner improve technique.

Premature ejaculation is also typically psychological rather than physical in origin (Bancroft, 1989). One of the most likely causes has to do with learning and conditioning history. Perhaps in earlier sexual experiences a man attempted to achieve orgasm rapidly — for example, while experimenting in illicit situations where he risked detection. Or maybe he believed that rapid ejaculation is a sign of sexual prowess, a belief sometimes promoted among adolescent males. In such cases, the man may learn that the sooner orgasm is over, the sooner his anxiety about performance is relieved.

Indeed, performance anxiety may exacerbate the problem. Watching and judging one's sexual actions is likely to hasten orgasm because anxiety stimulates the sympathetic nervous system, which controls ejaculation (Bancroft, 1989). In addition, men who have infrequent sex may ejaculate prematurely because lower frequency and recency of orgasm increases sensitivity of the penis (Bancroft, 1989).

Learning experiences can also affect a man's ability to detect the signals of impending orgasm. By learning to discriminate the point before ejaculatory inevitability, the man can reduce stimulation and allow arousal to subside, thus prolonging lovemaking. But failure to detect such signals or to learn to control sexual activity may result in premature ejaculation.

Sexual Pain Disorders

Two sexual disorders are marked by painful sensations in the genital area. **Dyspareunia** refers to genital pain during or after intercourse in either men or women, whereas **vaginismus** involves involuntary muscular spasms of the outer portion of the vagina, interfering with entry of the penis. The frequency of these problems in the general population is unknown (Spector & Carey, 1990), but research indicates that they are less commonly seen in sexual dysfunction clinics than are problems with sexual desire or orgasm. One clinic study in Philadelphia found dyspareunia in 6 percent and vaginismus in 2 percent of women seeking treatment (Lief, 1985). And a clinic in Edinburgh reported that 11 percent sought treatment for dyspareunia whereas 13 percent sought treatment for vaginismus (Bancroft, 1989). Sexual pain disorders are rare in men.

Causes of Sexual Pain Disorders Vaginismus is caused not by physiological disorders per se but by muscular spasms that result from a conditioned fear response to vaginal penetration. Conditioned fear responses may result from unpleasant or even traumatic experiences, including sexual victimization or painful penetration by an insensitive or impatient lover. Such fears may also result from negative attitudes about sex that have been learned, thus creating anxiety, tension, and physical "resistance" in anticipation of pain or emotional discomfort (Rosen & Leiblum, 1995).

Dyspareunia, by contrast, commonly has a physical cause such as inadequate lubrication, vaginal infections, allergies, or irritations resulting from lotions, soaps, or other chemicals and manufactured fibers. Also, damage to the pelvic region during childbirth is a common cause of painful intercourse. In cases involving inadequate lubrication, the problem may be lack of arousal.

Treatment of Sexual Dysfunction

Treatment specifically for sexual dysfunction is a relatively modern development. In Freud's time and during the period of dominant influence by psychodynamic therapies, sexual problems were viewed as manifestations of deeper, underlying intrapsychic conflicts that required intensive insight-oriented therapy focusing on early childhood experiences. In the 1950s and 1960s, behavior therapies were sometimes applied to sexual problems, and successful applications of systematic desensitization for sexual difficulties stemming from anxiety were reported in case studies. But the greatest advance was provided by the publication in 1970 of *Human Sexual Inadequacy* by William Masters and Virginia Johnson. They introduced several fundamental principles and techniques that came to be known as **sex therapy** — brief, behaviorally oriented therapy aimed specifically at sexual problems, typically treated in the context of a couple relationship. The authors reported high success rates with two weeks of intensive treatment, as well as good results over long-term follow-ups. However, their research lacked the scientific standards usually required of therapy outcome studies. Nonetheless, the new sex therapy provided striking support for the role of brief, behavioral approaches to treatment.

Nowadays sex therapies are *multimodal:* They use a variety of techniques and commonly include extensive assessment, communication skills training, and cognitive-behavioral and behavioral components — as well as medical interventions where useful (e.g., LoPiccolo, 1990). When necessary, therapists may also include marital therapy, insight-oriented individual psychotherapy, and recommendations for medical treatments. Although many clinical reports attest to the success of multimodal sex therapies, only a limited amount of controlled outcome research has tested their efficacy.

We first describe some of the common ingredients of sex therapies, and then discuss specific techniques that may be added to treat particular sexual dysfunctions.

Shared Components of Sex Therapies   When possible, sex therapy involves treatment for both members of a couple. Even though just one partner may have the symptoms, the problem is defined as a shared one, and the treatment is viewed as the responsibility of both partners. A second common ingredient is education: Sex therapists typically provide explicit information about sexual functioning and about the biological and psychological components of a particular problem. All too often, persons have misconceptions or inadequate information that may contribute to their difficulties.

A third ingredient concerns identifying and correcting maladaptive cognitions about sexual functioning. Rigid or erroneous beliefs acquired in childhood from parents and religious figures ("sex is nasty," "good girls don't") may need to be countered. Sex-role myths about male and female behavior, including sexuality, are often another potent source of discomfort ("men only want one thing," "men must be in charge of sexual activity," "women should have multiple orgasms"), and they need to be identified and challenged. And traumatic experiences may have left legacies of dread, fear, and mistrust that require cognitive techniques — a process that may be supplemented by supportive, insight-oriented psychotherapy.

A fourth ingredient involves learning more about one's body and sexual sensations, and then communicating sexual information to the partner. Frequently an individual's knowledge or acceptance of his or her body and sexual anatomy is shrouded by embarrassment, guilt, or negative judgment. Indeed, discomfort with one's own body often results in limited knowledge of one's needs and preferences. Sex therapists may thus suggest exercises for individuals — particularly women — to explore their own bodies in private, and to experiment in very directed ways with masturbation as a means of identifying particular sensual preferences. Learning to communicate one's sexual preferences is another skill strongly emphasized in sex therapy. Individuals learn not only what to tell partners but also how and when to tell them. To improve sexual practices, partners need to communicate their desires and teach each other exactly what they enjoy or do not enjoy.

Sensate focus is a technique intended to improve both exploration and communication. Developed by Masters and Johnson (1970), the procedure also helps couples who have been troubled by sexual difficulties to reestablish pleasure and sensuality in their intimate contact. An additional goal of sensate focus is to provide an environment for sexual experience that is nondemanding and not oriented toward performance.

Sensate focus is a homework (or "homeplay") procedure that couples do in the privacy and security of their own homes. In a series of exercises, couples explore touching to experience pleasure, communicating preferences, and refraining from intercourse as a way to reduce performance pressures. Then, during therapy sessions, they discuss their sensate focus experiences and clarify concerns and dysfunctional thoughts. Eventually they proceed to intercourse, often incorporating specific techniques for particular sexual dysfunctions.

For example, treatment of *erectile dysfunction* includes a component in which genital stimulation is stopped when the man achieves erection. The couple is paradoxically told to get rid of the erection, with the goal of helping them learn that erections can come and go as a result of stimulation. Gradually, the couple implements intercourse — typically with the woman in the female-superior position, permitting her to control vaginal entry. Couples practice brief periods of entry, gradually increasing duration. To reduce performance anxiety, they are encouraged to achieve the woman's orgasm through manual or oral stimulation (LoPiccolo, 1977; Masters & Johnson, 1970). These techniques are supplemented by marital and communication therapy as well as cognitive restructuring.

According to outcome studies of psychological treatments of erectile dysfunction, many of which use the multimodal sex therapy described, the overall success rate of such treatments is fairly high though variable; moreover, about two-thirds of men achieve satisfactory results that continue during follow-up evaluations six weeks to six years later (Mohr & Beutler, 1990; Rosen & Leiblum, 1995).

Treatment of *premature ejaculation* also commonly applies the techniques of Masters and Johnson (1970), integrating sensate focus with a procedure called "pause-and-squeeze." During manual stimulation of the man's genitals, he is instructed to tell his partner to stop just before reaching the point of orgasmic inevitability. This process is repeated many times over days or weeks. Eventually, as increased delay of ejaculation is achieved, the couple switches to vaginal stimulation — with brief periods of entry followed by stopping until greater delay is achieved. If mere stopping is not sufficient, the woman is instructed to squeeze the penis slightly to inhibit ejaculation, a procedure known as the "squeeze technique" (Masters & Johnson, 1970). Initial reports concerning this procedure indicated high rates of success; more recent studies reflect lower success rates (e.g., Rosen & Leiblum, 1995). As we discuss later, medical interventions are also increasingly being employed.

Treatment of *female arousal and orgasmic disorders* focuses initially on the woman's exploration of her own body and directed masturbation experiences (Heiman & LoPiccolo, 1988). The goal is increased knowledge and pleasurable sensations, as well as reduced performance anxiety and sexual inhibitions. After a certain level of comfort and experience has been achieved, sensate focus exercises with the partner are included to build communication and identify pleasurable sexual procedures. Julia Heiman and Joseph LoPiccolo (1988) reported that more than 90 percent of women who receive this treatment learn to have orgasms through masturbation, about 80 percent learn to have orgasms through partner stimulation, and 30 percent learn to have them during intercourse. Success rates for the treatment are moderately good overall, particularly for women with lifelong anorgasmia in which emotional or relationship issues are less problematic (Rosen & Leiblum, 1995).

Treating *hypoactive sexual desire* or *sexual aversion disorder* is typically considered to be more challenging than treating other sexual dysfunctions because sexual anxiety may be deeply rooted in the individual's psychological conflicts. Kaplan and Klein (1987) have recommended psychodynamically oriented sex therapy, which combines behavioral procedures such as sensate focus or other prescribed exercises and insight-oriented therapy for underlying conflicts, guilt, and marital problems. Other specialists have recommended cognitive-behavioral approaches to confront traumatic fears and overcome sexual inhibitions (e.g., LoPiccolo & Friedman, 1988).

Only a small number of controlled outcome studies on treatments of hypoactive sexual desire have been conducted. Interestingly, most of these treatments do not focus specifically on desire but instead emphasize arousal or orgasmic attainment. Most are also multifaceted, combining basic sex therapy with marital therapy or testosterone treatment with sex therapy (reviewed in Beck, 1995). As Beck and others have argued, considerably more research is needed on hypoactive sexual desire disorders, with interventions aimed more specifically at increasing desire.

Vaginismus, a sexual pain disorder, can be treated effectively by teaching the woman to voluntarily contract and expand the pubococcygeal muscle surrounding the vagina. The woman is also instructed to insert dilators of graduated sizes into the vagina, essentially desensitizing herself to the sensations of penetration. As she becomes more comfortable, the partner is included in the exercises, participating in insertion of the dilators and, eventually, of the penis. This treatment is apparently quite effective; more than 90 percent of women who receive it are subsequently able to have intercourse without pain (LoPiccolo, 1990).

The following vignette illustrates some of the elements of sex therapy. It also shows how a basically sound marital relationship can facilitate the therapy and, conversely, how the therapy can further improve the relationship.

Ned and Katy are in their thirties and have been married nearly ten years. They have a six-year-old son. Katy had lost nearly all sexual desire over the years, and has had sex with Ned as little as possible. She was never consistently orgasmic with him, and he sometimes had a problem with premature ejaculation; then, as the marital problems grew, she lost interest altogether. He, thinking she didn't care, made few attempts to please her; she silently resented what she thought was his insensitivity; and he in turn silently resented what he thought was her rejection of him. Eventually they drifted apart emotionally, remaining together only for the sake of their son. Suddenly Katy found herself involved with a neighbor who was much younger than herself, and experienced intense sexual pleasure with him. She stopped the affair after a short time, however, because of her guilt. Ned soon discovered what had happened, and moved out in a fit of anger and betrayal. Over a period of several days of cooling off, Katy and Ned discovered that they weren't ready to abandon their marriage. They acknowledged that sexual problems were foremost in their dissatisfaction with each other, and sought treatment with a therapist specializing in sex dysfunctions.

The therapist assessed the situation and concluded that Ned and Katy were good candidates for sex therapy, noting that the initial problem of low sexual desire was related to earlier orgasmic difficulties that probably occurred in the context of a somewhat repressed couple who communicated poorly about their feelings and needs. Following educational discussions and exploration of sexual attitudes, the first step involved masturbation exercises for Katy. With great embarrassment and reluctance she followed the prescribed exercises for several weeks; but to her surprise she began to enjoy the experiences and feel more comfortable with sexual sensations. Next, sensate focus exercises involving both partners helped improve their pleasure in each other's bodies and taught them both not only about Katy's preferred areas of touch and stimulation but also about techniques to delay premature ejaculation. On their own, but with encouragement from the therapist, Ned and Katy began to plan romantic outings to increase their ability to focus on each other and get away from daily distractions, as well as to set the stage for sexual activities. They increasingly enjoyed intercourse and varied erotic stimulation, and over a period of time Katy experienced more and more consistent orgasms. Yet they both enjoyed the entire erotic experience, focusing less on orgasm as such. The new trust and appreciation for each other that they discovered carried over into many other areas of their marriage.

Medical Treatments for Sexual Dysfunctions   Recent years have seen the widespread "medicalization" of treatments for sexual dysfunctions, especially among men. For instance, physical treatments for erectile dysfunction are now well established. These treatments include surgical implantation of **penile prostheses** (artificial means of achieving erections, involving either an inflatable or noninflatable device) or other devices that cause engorgement of the penis such as vacuum pumps. A relatively recent development is the injection of drugs that stimulate erection — such as prostaglandin E_1 — into the penis. Men can self-administer these fast-acting drugs, producing normal-appearing erections in many cases (Ackerman & Carey, 1995). Recently, oral medications have also been used to stimulate erections; these

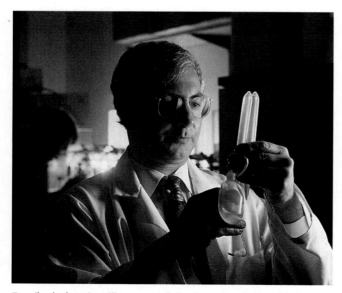

Erectile dysfunction ("impotence") is often a medical problem, and for many men treatment may include implantable devices that can be inflated to achieve erection. Here a physician demonstrates the procedure for pumping up a penile implant.

may hold considerable promise for improving sexual functioning (reviewed in Rosen & Leiblum, 1995). Serotonergic antidepressant medications are sometimes prescribed for premature ejaculation, although the mechanism of action is still unknown (Rosen & Leiblum, 1995). And, finally, hormone replacement or enhancement may be helpful in cases where reduced hormones play a role in sexual dysfunctions. For example, estrogen is given to women to increase postmenopausal vaginal lubrication, and testosterone is used to treat men who have endocrine or genetic conditions resulting in low levels of the hormone.

In summary, sexual dysfunctions are defined in highly relative terms as variations in the human response cycle that create distress for the individual or couple. Many of these disorders have emotional or psychological causes originating in learned maladaptive beliefs or behaviors. As such, they can often be reversed through new learning experiences. In the next section we discuss additional variations — this time, among preferred sexual behaviors.

PARAPHILIAS AND SEX CRIMES

In some cases of sexual disorder, the person's sexual response cycle is normal, but the object of sexual preference makes the act abnormal or, at times, illegal — as when the individual's pursuit violates the rights of others.

Features of Paraphilias and Sex Crimes

Paraphilia literally means "beyond usual love." According to the DSM it refers to recurrent, intense, sexual urges and fantasies about an atypical choice that may be acted on or cause marked distress for at least six months. There are many forms of paraphilias. Making obscene telephone calls (*telephone scatalogia*), having sex with corpses (*necrophilia*) or animals (*bestiality*), preferring sex with amputees or with elderly persons, and rubbing up against strangers (*frotteurism*) are all examples of sexual paraphilias. The sexual urges associated with this disorder usually involve (1) nonhuman objects, (2) suffering or humiliation of oneself or one's partner, or (3) children or other nonconsenting persons. The implication of these criteria is that a person who has fantasies but is not troubled by them and does not act them out would not be considered to have the disorder. Thus, mild, nonclinical sexual fantasies and urges fall within the normal range.

Some persons depend solely on paraphilias for sexual gratification; others may have conventional sexual experiences apart from paraphilic urges and acts. For some, the behaviors and urges are chronic and lifelong;

Jeffrey Dahmer confessed to the torture and mutilation of 17 young men and was found guilty of multiple counts of first-degree murder. His ritualized and sadistic sexual activities indicate sexual paraphilia of the most extreme sort commonly found in serial lust murders.

for others, they may be episodic, occurring only in periods of unusual stress. In milder cases of paraphilia the individual may be able to share the experiences with consenting adult partners. In more extreme cases potential partners are not available or reject the activity, so it is acted out in isolation or perpetrated against a nonconsenting person. Thus, many persons with marked paraphilias lack intimate relationships. Those who act out their sexual urges with nonconsenting adults, with children, or in public places commit sex crimes. Diagnosed individuals commonly have more than one paraphilia, and additional psychiatric problems (such as personality disorders or substance-use disorders) are common, especially in persons whose paraphilias lead to treatment seeking or prison. These coexisting conditions can affect the extent to which the person acts out, rather than controls or finds acceptable expressions of, the paraphilia.

Who is affected? The true incidence of paraphilias is unknown because only the most severe cases receive attention through the legal system or treatment-seeking channels. As some investigators have noted, the market for sexual paraphilic pornography is large, suggesting that paraphilias or paraphilic fantasies may be somewhat common (e.g., Abel & Osborn, 1992). In terms of demographic characteristics, paraphilias occur overwhelmingly more often in men than in women.

Cultural and ethnic differences in the expression of sexuality have been the topic of extensive anthropological investigations. Researchers have firmly established that many non-Western cultures tolerate variations in expressions of sexuality, although each culture has extensive rules and traditions that constrain sexual and relationship experiences. The concept of paraphilias is therefore highly relative. There is little specific informa-

tion about the existence of Western-defined paraphilias in non-Western cultures, except as noted below.

Some Common Paraphilias

The following sections describe common types of paraphilias, as categorized by DSM-IV. Table 12.1 presents an organizing framework that reflects the hypothesized motivations behind some of these paraphilias. The framework itself was developed by noted sex researcher John Money (1988) of Johns Hopkins University, but its separate categories might be misleading given that — at least within clinic-referred or sex offender populations — men with one paraphilia are likely to have others as well (Abel & Osborn, 1992; Bradford, Boulet & Pawlak, 1992).

Exhibitionism and Voyeurism   Money (1988) hypothesized that, for some men, gratification is derived from the "preliminaries" to sexual activity. In such cases, looking at genitals, displaying genitals, and perhaps talking about sex — normally preludes to intercourse — become the end goal. Among the common paraphilias in this category are exhibitionism and voyeurism.

Exhibitionism is the display of genitals to an involuntary observer. It usually involves a man displaying himself to an unsuspecting woman or child. The man may derive satisfaction from the observer's shock or interest, or he may fantasize that the other person will become sexually aroused by him. The exhibitionist does not typically seek further sexual contact with the observer. He may achieve orgasm from the exposure itself, later use fantasies of the exposure while masturbating, or, less commonly, masturbate during the exposure. Although victims are rarely in danger of being harmed or raped by an exhibitionist, they often fear that they will be and they suffer as a result of both the unwanted sexual intrusion and the fear that it may engender.

Most of what we know about exhibitionists is based on information related by those arrested for "indecent exposure," who may represent a biased sample. Typically the problem starts in adolescence. It occurs most frequently among young men in their twenties and thirties. About 50 percent of exhibitionists are (or were) married; often they are characterized as shy, unassertive, and insecure (Maletzky & Price, 1984). Many were raised in sexually repressive households and have little sexual experience with women. Through their exhibitionism they seek female attention and affirmation of their masculinity, while avoiding rejection. The goal of eliciting an extreme emotional reaction suggests that an important element of exhibitionism is the experience of power and control over women. Interestingly, researchers have noted that exhibitionism rarely occurs outside of Western Europe and the United States and is

Table 12.1 Paraphilic Types According to John Money

Paraphilic Type	Paraphilia
Solicitation/allure: Substitution of sexual preliminaries for normal intercourse	Exhibitionism Voyeurism
Fetishistic/talismanic: Substitution for normal intercourse	Fetishism Transvestic fetishism
Sacrifice/expiation: Atonement for sinful lust by penance or sacrifice	Lust murder Sexual sadism Sexual masochism
Marauding/predatory: Partner must be stolen, abducted, or coerced	Paraphilic rape
Mercantile/venal: Lust must be traded or purchased and paid for	Commercial sex/ blackmail (not necessarily paraphilia)
Stigmatic/eligibilic: Partner must be disparate in age, race, appearance of the body, etc.	Pedophilia Acrotomophilia (amputee partners)

Source: Money (1988).

John Money, a noted researcher in gender identity and sexual object choice, observed that although more than forty different paraphilias have been identified, they can be categorized according to six types. These he calls "six grand paraphilic stratagems," or essential motives that the paraphilia serves.

---

especially uncommon in African countries (Rooth, 1973).

Consider the following case of Bobby, the "weird" neighbor (mentioned in the chapter opening) who was recently released after doing prison time:

A teenager new to the neighborhood did her regular early-morning jogging through an affluent neighborhood of tree-lined streets and expensive homes. One house on a curve in the road has a picture window that she couldn't avoid looking into, and she often saw a youngish man in a bathrobe inside. Several times when she came into view running down the street, he got up from the sofa, went to the window, and opened his bathrobe, revealing his unappealing nakedness underneath. She complained to her mother, who talked to others and found out that Bobby was a strange loner living with his elderly mother. Soon after, Bobby was arrested, because it turned out that he had been going over to the junior high school and exhibiting himself to young girls walking home from school. He seemed to get excited by their fear and upset, and would go home and masturbate to the fantasy that they too had been excited by the sight of him. Now that he is home again, the neighbors are up in arms, concerned that he might act on his urges again.

Voyeurism is another example of engaging in a "preliminary" act that serves as an end in itself without any attempt at further sexual contact. The so-called Peeping Tom attempts to watch unsuspecting people, usually strangers, who are nude, undressing, or engaging in sexual activity. Masturbation may accompany the watching, or it may occur later when the viewing is replayed in fantasy. Voyeurism is thought to begin before age fifteen. It usually has a chronic course in which the person prefers the activity to sexual intercourse and also derives a measure of thrill from the forbidden or risky act itself. Voyeurs, like exhibitionists, are insecure and have poorly developed social skills. They may experience enormous curiosity about sexual matters, yet feel very insecure or anxious about direct sexual activity. Thus, peeping is a vicarious form of sexual gratification, and the individuals who engage in it may derive additional feelings of power over those they secretly observe (Bancroft, 1989).

Fetishes In Money's (1988) typology, fetishistic or talismanic paraphilias are substitutes for a lover. Two relatively common forms observed in clinical practice are fetishism and transvestic fetishism. The key feature of **fetishism** is an intense sexual urge involving a nonsexual item — commonly an inanimate extension of the body such as clothing (women's undergarments, shoes,

Transvestic fetishism typically involves cross-dressing to enhance sexual pleasure. Often the man will wear women's undergarments or nightgowns. More rarely, transvestites enjoy dressing fully in women's clothing for periods of time, and appearing in public. Transvestism as a sexual fetish is not the same as being a "drag queen" or a transsexual.

purses) or a material of a particular texture, often leather or rubber. The fetish might also be a part of the body — for example, feet (Bancroft, 1989). The person holds, rubs, or wears the fetish while masturbating or asks his sexual partner to wear it. The person may be unable to experience sexual arousal without the fetish. The degree of compulsiveness varies: Some men collect the fetish, whereas others even steal it (Gosselin & Wilson, 1980).

Transvestism, also termed **transvestic fetishism**, is a fetish involving a man's wearing of women's clothing. The man believes himself to be male and typically lives as a man, but he cross-dresses for sexual purposes. Transvestic fetishism is distinguished from cross-dressing that is done primarily for fun and does not cause sexual arousal; from wearing the clothing of the opposite gender due to an identification as that gender, as in gender identity disorder (Schott, 1995); and from female impersonation, in which male performers dress as women and impersonate female stars but do not derive sexual arousal from the cross-dressing and do not experience frustration if the cross-dressing is blocked.

In general, transvestites have relatively normal personalities. According to a classic study of transvestites based on questionnaires from more than five hundred men subscribing to the magazine *Transvestia*, 89 percent were heterosexual, and the majority were married and had children (Prince & Bentler, 1972). More than one-half reported that their cross-dressing started before age ten (see also Schott, 1995). The wives of 80 percent of the men knew about their preferences; about one-half of the wives were accepting of these preferences, whereas one-half had difficulty with them.

Sexual Sadism and Masochism   According to Money (1988), a key strategy in the disorder known as sacrifice/expiation paraphilia is atonement or sacrifice for lustful feelings. Whether or not this description accurately reflects the underlying motives involved, the central element is the experience or infliction of pain. Sexual **masochism** involves recurrent, intense, sexually arousing fantasies and urges involving being humiliated, beaten, bound, or otherwise made to suffer. A person — male or female — may act on the fantasies alone (for example, by sticking oneself with pins or other self-mutilation) or with a partner (for example, using physical bondage, spanking, whipping, or verbal or physical humiliation). Sexual **sadism** is characterized by sexually arousing urges and fantasies involving acts that inflict physical or psychological suffering on another person. The person may employ the fantasies during sexual activity or actually perform the acts with a consenting partner (who may have sexual masochism). The sadistic acts and fantasies involve having complete control over the other person.

"Honestly, Arthur, I said 'cross-train, it's the secret of success!,' not 'cross-dress.'"

Remember Dr. Edgar B. from the beginning of the chapter? A pillar of your community, he died in shocking circumstances — revealing a hidden side of himself that no one had suspected. By day he exerted considerable power and authority in his work and family, but by night — when he visited his mistress — it was a different matter. He longed to be tied up and have her humiliate, kick, insult, and whip him. Naked, on his knees, and bound with leather, he begged her to forgive him. The ritual would last an hour or two, involving some physical and emotional pain but also a great deal of excitement for him. There was usually no intercourse, but sometimes he would masturbate afterward, and feel relieved and relaxed. His mistress was good at playacting, deriving little satisfaction herself, but understanding that pain and pleasure had been linked in his mind since childhood when he'd been whipped for peeking at his beloved mother having a sexual fling with his uncle. He'd been horribly frightened and guilty — but also aroused — so that sexual pleasure became, for him, indelibly tied to suffering and humiliation. He never had the courage to reveal his needs to his wife, whose rather cold and critical nature was consistent with her lack of interest in sexual experiences.

The amount of pain inflicted by sadistic and masochistic sexual behavior and its actual dangerousness appear to vary considerably. On the less extreme side, mutually consenting adults act out elaborate rituals of domination or submission, involving costumes and fetishistic objects such as boots or leather, with the understanding that physically damaging activity will be minimal. Thus, sadistic and masochistic rituals may be relatively playful and not necessarily malignant. If they do not cause distress or involve dangerous activity, they are not clinically relevant. Clubs have formed for the purpose of permitting consenting adults to meet each other to practice sadomasochistic activities harmlessly. According to research reviewed and summarized by Gosselin and Wilson (1984), male members of such clubs included both heterosexual and homosexual men, and most kept their activities secret from their families. Research has also shown that when the wives knew about the sadomasochistic behaviors, they generally tolerated such practices. Only a minority of the club members were exclusively masochistic or sadistic in their sexual activities. Also, society members varied considerably in terms of how dependent they were on the sadomasochistic behaviors for sexual satisfaction. Many required at least some sadistic or masochistic fantasy or behavior to achieve sexual gratification. Consider the following case:

Although the majority of sadistic and masochistic acts are harmless rituals, severe and dangerous forms of sexual masochism and sadism do exist. For example, a very dangerous form of sexual masochism is **hypoxyphilia**, or autoerotic asphyxia, which involves sexual arousal by oxygen deprivation. The person attempts to achieve sexual orgasm during semi-asphyxiation with a noose, plastic bag, or other devices or with chemicals such as amyl nitrate that reduce oxygen to the brain. The semi-asphyxiation is often accompanied by fantasies involving asphyxiation of the self or others. Most individuals involved in this activity allow themselves the opportunity to escape before losing consciousness, but errors and death have occurred (Uva, 1995).

Severe and dangerous forms of sexual sadism involve rape, assault, or murder. Researchers have estimated that approximately 10 percent of rapes occur as the result of sexual sadism in which the amount of force far exceeds what is needed for compliance and the suffering of the victim appears to be sexually arousing. When severe sexual sadism is accompanied by antisocial personality disorder in which the person lacks self-control, conscience, or empathy for other people, the potential for serious injury and death to victims is great. An example is *lust murders*, an extreme form of sexual paraphilia. Money (1986) hypothesized that the perpetrator of lust murders is attempting to atone for sinful lust by doing penance or by making sacrifices.

Lust murders are often serial murders involving mutilation. Researchers have long been baffled by this seemingly senseless form of crime. Robert Prentky and his colleagues (1989) compared twenty-five serial lust killers with seventeen men who had murdered only a single person. Unlike the murderers of a single person, the serial lust murderers had extensive fantasies involving intentional infliction of harm in a sadistic or sexually violent way; in fact, 86 percent of them had violent fantasies that were reported in their crime records. In contrast to killers of a single person, they also exhibited higher rates of paraphilias of all kinds, but especially fetishism and transvestism. The investigators emphasized that paraphilias in general involve the use of fantasies, which the perpetrators eventually attempt to act out. This may also be the case with serial lust murderers, who rehearse and then keep on practicing their sexually violent fantasies. What makes individuals go from fantasizing to acting out violent behavior is not presently known, however.

Pedophilia Yet another type of sexual victimization occurs in cases of **pedophilia**, which involves recurrent intense sexual urges and fantasies about sexual activity with a child (usually age thirteen or younger) by persons at least sixteen years old and at least five years older than the child. *Child molestation* is the *legal* concept describing sexual activities perpetrated by an older person on a child. Figure 12.5 portrays the relationship between legal concepts and psychological diagnoses. While molestation is always a sex crime, the motives underlying it do not always reflect pedophilic urges. The perpetrator may be a stranger, acquaintance, or relative. **Incest** is a form of sexual molestation involving sexual contact between family members. Incest may be a form of pedophilia, but, as we discuss later, most incest is probably not primarily motivated by pedophilic urges.

Both homosexual and heterosexual pedophilia occur. The great majority of instances are perpetrated by males, and attraction to girls is estimated to be about twice as common as attraction to boys. The molester may gently fondle the child, masturbate in the child's presence, or use force to achieve sexual contact of some kind. Commonly the molester rationalizes his activity, believing that it is "educational" or pleasurable for the child, or even that the child is sexually provocative and has caused the sexual activity. Such beliefs are clearly distortions of reality. As illustrated in Figure 12.6, sexual arousal to children is likely the predominant motive of pedophiles, and children's expressions of distress do not appear to invoke empathic reactions in them (Chaplin, Rice & Harris, 1995).

Pedophiles differ considerably in terms of how actively they pursue opportunities to molest. Some enter professions such as teaching or scouting that give them

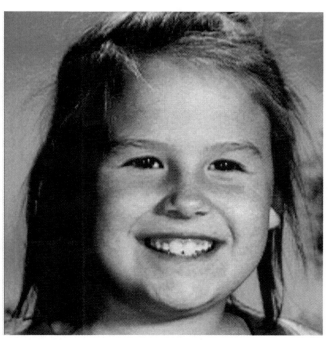

Megan Kanka was murdered by a man who was released to her community after serving time in prison for sexual crimes against children. Unfortunately, prison typically does not rehabilitate those arrested for sex crimes, and many will continue to act out their sexual paraphilias against innocent victims. Because of the outcry surrounding Megan's death, many states have now passed versions of "Megan's Law," which permits police to notify communities when a sex offender is released from prison and moves into a neighborhood.

considerable access to children. Others kidnap children. Still others do not specifically seek out children but take advantage of opportunities as they arise. Although the course of pedophilia tends to be chronic, among some individuals sexual desire for children might be precipitated when a preferred adult partner is unavailable. In such instances, sexual activity with a child may then be substituted. Events that cause severe stress in the adult's life might reduce the controls or exacerbate the needs and urges involved, leading to opportunistic rather than chronic pedophilia.

Research on the characteristics of pedophiles (and other sex offenders) is limited. But one study, conducted by Leonard Bard and his colleagues (1987), suggests that — compared to rapists — child molesters are less socially active and competent, more passive and less aggressive, less likely to have conduct problems in school, and of lower intelligence. Both groups, however, tend to come from lower socioeconomic groups and from highly dysfunctional families with a history of marital breakups, parental mental illness, substance abuse, or criminality. Both groups also experienced high rates

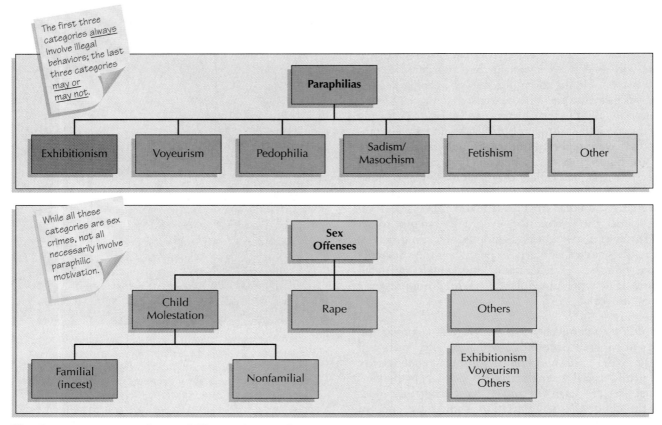

Figure 12.5 Sexual Paraphilias and Sex Crimes

Not all paraphilias are sex offenses, and not all sex offenses are paraphilias. Paraphilias are defined by the person's persistent sexual arousal to unusual or inappropriate stimuli; sex offenses are acts that the community defines as illegal because they infringe on the rights of others.

of physical abuse and neglect. Interestingly, 57 percent of the child molesters observed in this study had been victims of sexual assault themselves, compared with 23 percent of the rapists. Another study has confirmed a high incidence of childhood sexual abuse in adolescent male sex offenders. As it turns out, this effect was gender related; the investigators found that 75 percent of boys who assaulted other boys had been sexually victimized as children, but only 25 percent of those who assaulted females had been victimized themselves (Worling, 1995).

What about child molesters who commit incestuous acts with their own children?

FAMILY MATTERS

Incest

Pedophilia refers to ongoing sexual preoccupation with children, whereas incest is a broader concept involving sexual activities between relatives. Incestuous activity may result from pedophilic urges, but it may also refer to *transient* sexual behaviors with a relative. It often involves situations in which a person is taking advantage of a situation — as when a father who has a sexually disinterested wife, or a stepfather who lacks biological ties to a daughter, turns to the daughter for sexual gratification.

The frequency of incest is perhaps surprising, given that nearly every culture prohibits most forms of sexual relationships between close relatives. A significant proportion (23 percent) of all sexual molestation of children occurs in the family (Siegel et al., 1987). Although incest is most commonly committed by biological fathers, rates of incest by stepfathers are disproportionately high relative to the percentage of stepfathers in the general population (reviewed in Faust, Runyon & Kenny, 1995). Males are also the victims of incest, although they experience any kind of childhood sexual victimization at a rate much lower than that for females. Specifically, only about 4 percent of molestations involve males. In terms of potential harm to families — and certainly in terms of

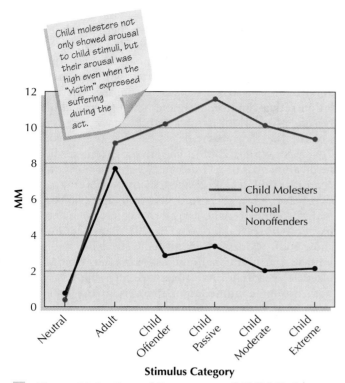

Figure 12.6 Sexual Responses of Child Molesters
Measures of penile erection during audiotapes of sexual situations were used to examine the reactions of men who had been charged with sexual contact with girls fourteen years of age or younger, as compared to the reactions of normal men. The investigators used tape-recorded *simulations* of sex with girls or with women to test preferences for sexual encounters with girls and deterrence of arousal by the girls' expression of traumatic reaction and suffering. As shown in the graph, normal men exhibited little arousal in response to the child stimuli, whereas child molesters showed high levels of arousal to sexual situations involving molestation of children and minimal decrease in arousal when the children expressed distress. The investigators concluded that treatment of child molesters needs to alter their preference for sexual activity with children and increase their empathy for children's feelings. *Note:* All of the men were measured while listening to a set of tapes depicting different situations: neutral (nonsexual situation); adult (heterosexual activity between consenting adults); child offender (child molestation described from the sex offender's point of view, emphasizing his enjoyment); child passive (child molestation described from a passive victim's point of view); and child moderate and child extreme (child molestation described from the point of view of a victim of moderate or extreme coercion). *Source:* Chaplin, Rice & Harris (1995).

legal consequences — father-child incest is considered very serious. Father-daughter incest is estimated to occur in about 1.5 percent of families (Finkelhor, 1980).

Children who are sexually victimized may experience severe, lifelong consequences, depending on the severity and duration of the activities. As we note earlier in this chapter, sexual molestation frequently leads to adult sexual problems. We also indicate in Chapter 7 that childhood sexual abuse may lead to a blocking out of awareness, leading to dissociative experiences; and in Chapter 14 we further discuss the psychological consequences of abuse. Many investigators have agreed that incestuous family experiences are particularly disruptive to healthy development because they distort normal relationship bonds, violate trust, and show disregard for a child's needs separate from those of the parent.

Most research on the topic of incest has focused on the victimization of daughters by fathers (or stepfathers). How do these situations come about, and what are such men like? Sometimes the sexual activity begins harmlessly with playful touching and tickling, such that the child is initially unaware that anything is wrong. Over time, however, it may progress to genital touching and eventually to intercourse. The father commonly takes advantage of the child's trust and even enjoyment of the special attention she receives. He is likely to reassure her that the touching is harmless, or even that he is giving her some important "experience." As she becomes more aware that something is wrong about the sexual activity, the child may feel mixtures of pleasure and guilt; in addition, the father may threaten her in an effort to prevent her from revealing the "secret" or may even tell her that it is her fault. The child may be tormented by her fear or guilt but believe that she has no recourse.

Incest occurs in families at all socioeconomic levels. It often arises in the context of a poor marital relationship; for example, the wife may be rejecting the husband's sexual advances. Some clinicians have suspected that the mother often knows about the sexual activity with the child but for various reasons tolerates it. The father may have alcoholism or some other mental illness, and often the family is highly stressed by economic hardship and unemployment (Faust, Runyon & Kenny, 1995; Rosenberg, 1988). On the other hand, studies have found that about one-fourth to one-third of the fathers are normal in the sense of having no diagnosable condition (e.g., Williams & Finkelhor, 1990). Incestuous fathers may be very different from each other, but they often (though not invariably) share certain common characteristics: They have difficulties in empathy and expression of nurturance, they lack social skills and are frequently socially isolated, and they report frequent histories of childhood sexual or especially physical abuse or rejection by their own parents (Williams & Finkelhor, 1990).

The fathers' immaturity and social ineptness may also be accompanied by faulty beliefs. Researchers have found that many incestuous fathers believe that their children actually "want" the sexual contact (the rationale being that if they do not resist, they desire it), that child-adult sex is a good way for the children to learn about sex, or that their sexual activity enhances their relationship (Abel, Becker & Cunningham-Rather, 1984).

The consequences of incest itself may be accentuated by the general family circumstances. Many mothers of victims are young, depressed, divorced, or isolated (Faust, Runyon & Kenny, 1995). A child who experiences her mother as unavailable or unsupportive may perceive that she cannot disclose the sexual events that her perceptions tell her are "bad" or sinful. Or if the marital relationship is already strained, the child may experience herself as being responsible for holding things together (or for causing its disintegration if she tells). If she does disclose the events, she may be disbelieved or even accused of harming the family. In short, maternal support is an important predictor of the child's adjustment.

Rape As noted, a minority of rapes (about 10 percent) involve sexual sadism. Such rapes are therefore examples of a paraphilia, and they commonly involve extreme violence. The violence is often focused on erogenous areas of the body, suggesting ritualized activity intended to stimulate sexual pleasure for the perpetrator by inflicting suffering and humiliation on the victim (Prentky & Knight, 1991). Although rape and other forms of sexual violence are always sexual offenses in the legal sense and are certainly deviations of sexual expression, as Figure 12.5 indicates, most rapes are not sex disorders in the clinical diagnostic sense. We fully discuss rape and its causes in Chapter 14, which focuses on violence.

Causes of Sexual Paraphilias and Sexual Violence

Sex is a basic biological urge, but in human beings its expression is extensively shaped by cultural norms and learned values. Not surprisingly, therefore, few theories of the causes of sexual deviance emphasize only the biological or only the psychological aspects. To date, however, no theory has adequately integrated the two themes into a comprehensive model.

Biological Approaches In this field, genetic studies are rare and inconclusive because of small sample sizes. The fact that some forms of sexual misconduct such as child molestation run in families is likely due to psychological factors rather than to heritability as such. Another approach has been to investigate whether something related to biological masculinity gives rise to sexual paraphilias. Thus, for instance, researchers have speculated that chromosomal anomalies underlie certain types of sexual disorders. In fact, some persons are born with

extra chromosomes. In males, two of the abnormal patterns are XYY, often considered a hypermasculine form, and XXY, perhaps a more "feminized" form; both differ from the normal XY pattern. One of the best studies of deviant sexual behavior associated with chromosomal abnormalities was based on men from the general population rather than on a sample taken from a clinical or prison population, which would have been biased toward the most extreme cases (Schiavi, Theilgaard, Owen & White, 1988). The investigators studied the medical records of a large sample of men born during a certain period in Copenhagen, identifying a final sample of twelve XYY men and fourteen XXY men, with matched controls, who agreed to participate in extensive psychological evaluation. The XYY men did indeed show more evidence of unusual sexual behaviors and fantasies, including paraphilias, than did the more feminized XXY and normal subjects. Interestingly, however, both groups exhibited similar levels of the male hormone *testosterone*: Although the extra "male" chromosome was correlated with some sexual behavioral anomalies, it was not associated with excess male hormone. Thus, the underlying mechanism of deviant sexual behaviors is unclear.

Researchers have conducted other studies of male hormones in an attempt to understand the connections among testosterone, sexual interest, and arousability that we discuss earlier. Many such studies have tried to link sexual aggression and testosterone, but reviews of these studies indicate little clear or conclusive evidence of hormonal abnormality (Hucker & Bain, 1990). On the other hand, some paraphilias have been found to be associated with high levels of male hormones; and other paraphilias, with lower-than-normal levels of male hormones. However, even when high levels of the hormones have been shown to be correlated with violent sexual crimes, the question of whether testosterone specifically predicts sexual aggression, or aggression in general, is unresolved (Hall, 1990).

One interesting and recurring finding links epilepsy and certain fetishistic behaviors. A certain minority of men with temporal lobe epilepsy display sexually anomalous behavior, especially fetishism (Langevin, 1992). Minor brain malfunctions, especially in the temporal lobe area (possibly present at birth or arising from early childhood injuries), have been found in the histories of many individuals with paraphilic behaviors. In fact, clinical cases of paraphilias often contain descriptions of men performing their sexual acts during states resembling petit mal seizures, adding to the interest in pursuing a link between certain types of subtle brain dysfunction and sexual compulsions.

Despite the evident biological aspects of sexual expression, few scholars would argue that biological factors are sufficient explanations for sexual paraphilias. Accordingly, we turn to psychological perspectives for additional information on causal factors.

Psychological Approaches Psychoanalytic explanations of sexual disorders point to the symbolic meaning of the fetishistic object or ritualized behavior as an expression of unresolved conflicts. For instance, fetishism is viewed as a consequence of a severe castration complex in which the fetish represents a penis to protect against castration (reported in Bancroft, 1989). These psychodynamic theories are largely untestable, however.

Most modern approaches to variant sexual preference emphasize the role of *learning experiences*. People can learn attitudes and preferences, as well as actual behaviors, through classical and operant conditioning and observational learning. For example, classically conditioned erections to unusual objects have been demonstrated in the laboratory (Rachman & Hodgson, 1968). Researchers have speculated that fetishes and paraphilias develop in similar ways. Thus, a child who experiences sexual arousal while playing with "forbidden objects" such as his mother's clothing or with a particular substance such as rubber might develop a conditioned reaction, reinforced by masturbation and orgasm. For males, the observable presence of erection may promote the cognition that a particular situation or object is sexually stimulating (Bancroft, 1989). Sadomasochism may involve a learned association between dominance or submission and sexual pleasure, or be related to the arousing effects of pain under certain circumstances (Bancroft, 1989). The finding of sexual victimization in the backgrounds of adolescent sex offenders is certainly compatible with this kind of learning and conditioning model (e.g., Worling, 1995). Similarly, many transvestites and transsexuals report that their mothers or female relatives dressed them in girls' clothing and reinforced feminine appearance (Schott, 1995). And hypoxyphilia (autoerotic asphyxia) has been linked in some case studies to child abuse that involved choking (drowning, strangulation), which in turn became linked with sexual arousal (Friedrich & Gerber, 1994).

Other kinds of learning might also play a role. Adams and McAnulty (1993) have speculated that experimentation with inappropriate sexual outlets may result from a lack of accepted outlets, possibly due to lack of skills, physical unattractiveness, or sexually repressive upbringing. For example, a timid and fearful boy whose sexual overtures have been rejected by girls his own age might be more accepted by younger girls. Indeed, deficient or inappropriate social skills may reduce the chances of sexual gratification in a relationship with a peer, thus promoting the alternative of solitary, fantasy-based experiences or of sexual encounters with inappropriate partners. By the same token, maladaptive cognitions may be learned that cause individuals to misinterpret cues as sexual when they are not, or alter their perceptions of what is sexually appropriate and desirable.

Family backgrounds and early childhood environments, too, undoubtedly contribute to the nature of sexual learning experiences. Families need to provide children with opportunities to acquire accurate information and healthy attitudes regarding sexuality, and parents need to serve as models for children to learn how affection and sexuality can be integrated. Retrospective studies of the family lives of sex offenders and diagnosed paraphiliacs have repeatedly indicated excessive rates of family disruption, conflict, parental disorder, and substance abuse, as well as abuse, neglect, and even sexual deviance on the part of a parent (e.g., Bard et al., 1987; Williams & Finkelhor, 1990). Unfortunately, conditioning and learning models do not explain why males acquire paraphilias whereas females, for the most part, do not.

What is the nature of the evidence we have that deviant sexuality is learned in one way or another? Although considerable correlational evidence of maladaptive learning and family experiences exists, the research itself is limited by the shortcomings associated with retrospective, correlational accounts. Also, most such research is based on incarcerated or clinical populations who might represent only the most severe and antisocial cases. Finally, few studies have separated and compared different groups of paraphilic individuals to determine specific rather than general predictors and the course of sexual disorder (Furby, Weinrott & Blackshaw, 1989). For example, the question still remains as to why a particular individual might develop pedophilia rather than exhibitionism.

Treatment of Sex Disorders

Most of the available information regarding treatment of paraphilias is based on men convicted of sex crimes. Consider the built-in obstacles to working with such a group. These men probably have the most severe disorders (given that persons with milder disorders are not as likely to be detected or incarcerated, especially if they were committing a first offense). They may be receiving treatment involuntarily (that is, they may be required to receive treatment), in which case their motivation may be limited and they might drop out. And, finally, many are likely to have antisocial personality disorders or substance abuse disorders. In light of these limitations, it is hardly surprising that studies of treatment outcomes report mixed results.

An additional challenge facing sex disorder treatments is conceptual. The Freudian approaches to such therapy were developed largely to treat anxiety-based neuroses, requiring resolution of underlying conflicts through insight and interpretation (as discussed in Chapter 3). But these traditional insight-oriented techniques and their underlying premises have proven to be woefully inadequate in treating the difficult problems of sex disorders. The early behavioral techniques were equally inadequate because they assumed that the offending sexual behavior arose only from deviant sexual desire, probably acquired through conditioning. Numerous well-controlled studies attempted to extinguish such sexual preferences, but their results indicated that simply reducing deviant sexual arousal did little to alter the behavior and adjustment of men with sex disorders (Marshall & Barbaree, 1990b).

Recent reviews of sex offender outcomes have underscored the challenge of finding effective treatments and rehabilitation programs. The typical measure of a treatment's effectiveness is relapse — or, in the case of sex offenders, *recidivism,* the likelihood that after release from prison the man is later convicted of another sex crime. A review of recidivism rates for sex offenders both with and without treatment found considerable recurrence of criminal activity across forty-two studies and varying populations. The rates of recurrence ranged between about 5 and 60 percent (Furby, Weinrott & Blackshaw, 1989).

These and other results suggest that rehabilitative efforts are not particularly effective. For example, lack of treatment success was also reported in an investigation of a six-year follow-up of fifty child molesters (non-familial) who had been treated in a maximum security psychiatric institution compared with those not treated (Rice, Quinsey & Harris, 1991). The researchers found that, of the total sample, 58 percent were arrested for some crime, 31 percent were convicted of a new sex offense, and 43 percent committed a sexual or violent crime. The rates for those treated were the same as for those not treated.

Cognitive-Behavioral Treatments of Sex Disorders In reaction to the failures of traditional psychodynamic techniques, simplistic behavioral therapies, and rehabilitative efforts, researchers have developed cognitive-behavioral treatment programs that include several components considered essential: altering sexual preferences through aversive conditioning and retraining, modifying social incompetence through skill-building and problem-solving, and changing distorted cognitions (such as those fostering evasion of responsibility or the belief that victims enjoy the experience). Although the specific techniques may vary from program to program, these basic components are now widely included in both institutionalized and outpatient settings (Marshall & Barbaree, 1990; Perkins, 1993).

How well do the cognitive-behavioral treatments work? Encouraging results were reported in a review by Marshall and associates (1991), who concluded that these treatments produced relatively good results among child molesters (heterosexual and homosexual pedophiles as well as committers of incest) and exhibitionists but worked less well among rapists. For example, a program in Canada that included broad-based cognitive-behavioral techniques tailored to individual needs followed sex offenders for up to four years after release from prison. The reconviction rates for treated subjects increased to 25 percent by four years, but the corresponding rates for untreated sex offenders was 64 percent (Marshall, Laws & Barbaree, 1990). In terms of reducing recidivism, this program achieved the greatest success among child molesters (including committers of incest) and the least success among exhibitionists. Rapists were not included in the study (Marshall & Barbaree, 1990b). Thus, cognitive-behavioral treatments may be promising for certain types of sexual disorders (although communities have sound reasons for being concerned about releasing offenders).

Figure 12.7 reports a summary of outcome studies published between 1985 and 1995, using the method of meta-analysis (described in Chapter 5). This summary also suggests that cognitive-behavioral treatments are associated with relatively good outcomes — compared with behavioral treatments — and that sex offenders treated in outpatient settings do better than those incarcerated in institutions.

Physical Treatments of Sex Disorders In past years, and especially in European countries, somewhat radical treatments for sex offenders were conducted that involved either psychosurgery (typically ablation of the hypothalamus or destruction of the ventromedial nucleus of the hypothalamus) or castration. Evidence of the effectiveness of such methods never materialized, however, and the side effects were certainly extreme; thus, on both medical and ethical grounds, surgical treatments such as these have been abandoned.

Also controversial, but at least reversible, is the current use of antiandrogen medications such as medroxyprogesterone acetate, or MPA [trade name Depo-Provera]. This hormonal suppression of testosterone (chemical castration) appears to be useful in reducing sexual drive as well as compulsive fantasies and actions, but psychotherapy is often needed as well to help the individual develop more appropriate sexual goals and social and interpersonal behaviors (Marshall et al., 1991; Money, 1986). Although preliminary studies have indicated some promising results from hormonal treatments (Hall, 1995), these results are not as dramatic as advocates had hoped in several respects. First, many men refuse the treatment, discontinue the use of the

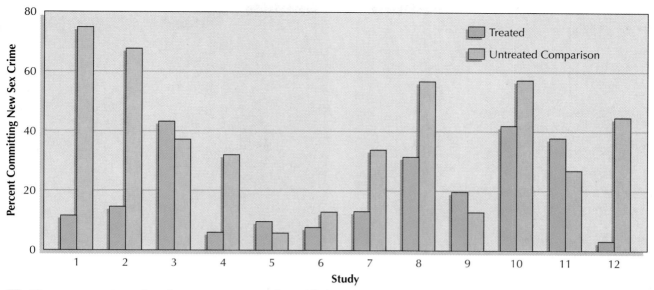

Figure 12.7   Sex Disorder Treatments and Recidivism
Here, the results of twelve studies of treatment of sex offenders are plotted according to the percentage of *recidivists* — those who committed repeat sex crimes after their release from prison. Overall, 19 percent of the treated men committed additional sex crimes, but this number is smaller than the 27 percent of untreated men who committed new sex crimes. The hormonal and cognitive-behavioral therapies, which were equally effective, did better than the behavioral-only treatments.

Source: Hall (1995).

drugs, or drop out of treatment (Marshall et al., 1991). Second, antiandrogens work best for patients with the least severe disorders — for example, those who do not have antisocial personality disorder, who are nonviolent, and who have relatively focused and consistent preferences. Third, the use of antiandrogens is based on the assumption that testosterone level determines atypical sexual behaviors, but once sexual arousal is established it may be independent of testosterone level. Despite these limitations, further research on the combined use of antiandrogens and psychotherapy for treatment of the most severe sex offenders is certainly called for.

GENDER IDENTITY DISORDER

Because one's identification as male or female is a fundamental aspect of the sense of self and a major determinant of behavior, a disturbance in gender identity can be profoundly problematic. Although a number of biological intersex conditions are caused by hormonal or chromosomal anomalies, gender identity disorder is a psychological condition not caused by mixed biological gender. In the following pages we discuss the features of this syndrome and its possible causes and treatments.

Features of Gender Identity Disorder

According to DSM-IV, **gender identity disorder** is a condition in which a person persistently experiences discomfort with his or her biological sex and expresses profound identification with the other gender. Adults with the most severe form of this disorder are sometimes called **transsexuals;** such persons have an intense desire to be transformed through hormonal and surgical means into the opposite sex, and they identify with the feelings and experiences of the other gender. They may be convinced that they were born into the wrong gender, and attempt to deny or reverse their anatomical sex — experiencing their genitals and secondary sex characteristics as disgusting or alien. Many transsexuals live as the opposite sex through dress, behavior, sexual preference, and attitudes. Their actual sexual anatomy and hormonal functioning are normal, however.

The term **gender dysphoria** is used to characterize feelings of dissatisfaction with one's biological identity. If we think of gender dysphoria as a scale with different degrees of distress, transsexualism (gender identity disorder) is at the extreme end whereas other conditions may involve milder feelings of gender dissatisfaction. Transsexualism differs from transvestic fetishism in that transsexuals do not obtain sexual gratification by dressing in garments of the opposite sex. They feel that such

Dr. Richard Raskin was an ophthalmologist, skilled tennis player — and a transsexual. After undergoing sex reassignment surgery, she became the female she had always believed herself to truly be, named Renee Richards. Renee Richards had to win a court battle to play in the women's singles division of the U.S. Open tournament in 1977.

garments are appropriate to their own preferred gender and do not use them as sources of sexual arousal. Most transsexuals consider themselves heterosexual and wish to relate to men as women, or as women to men. Such individuals are also distinguished from effeminate homosexuals or masculine lesbians who may adopt the dress and some of the behaviors or mannerisms of the opposite sex, but who do not experience a profound rejection of their biological gender or anatomy. Finally, transsexuals differ from male homosexual transvestites who cross-dress but not out of a serious desire to impersonate or be women (Bancroft, 1989). The following is a case of transsexualism:

> *Martin, first mentioned in the chapter opening, was a pretty child; his mother proudly showed him off, carefully curled his hair, and dressed him in outfits too cute to play in. He was a happy little boy, but grew increasingly anxious about having to play with other boys who were rougher and meaner than he; Martin preferred to play with dolls and doll houses along with his sister and her friends. As he grew older he told his mother he wanted to be a girl, and privately he was convinced that he really was a girl but that some horrible joke had been played on him, leaving him with the wrong body. In early adolescence he became morose and withdrawn as increasing evidence of his masculinity developed in the form of body hair, larger genitals, and deeper voice. In secret he would dress up in his sister's prom dress and high heels, and imagine himself being swept away by Prince Charming. As he grew older he acquired feminine mannerisms but learned that he had to play act "like a man" in public or people would scorn him and call him names. Looking in the mirror was painful because he hated his outward appearance of maleness; he consoled himself with dreams of sex with handsome men where he was the beautiful and sexy woman. It was hard to go to school or work steadily in a job because he felt like an imposter, unable to really be himself. Finally he moved to a distant city and was determined to start his life over as Martina, a tall attractive woman with make-up carefully applied to hide facial hair, long fingernails, and sexy dresses. He sought treatment at the local university known for its surgical sex reassignment program: If they accepted him he had hope that he would be happy; if they didn't accept him for treatment, he resolved to end his life. They did accept him, and presently he is going through the "real life" phase of treatment, adjusting to "being" Martina, before the sex surgery is performed to alter his genitalia.*

Course of Gender Identity Disorder For many, gender identity disorder begins in childhood. *Childhood gender identity disorder* may be expressed by the child's insisting that he or she is really a girl or boy, rejecting activities and dress typical of his or her sex, preferring cross-sex dressing and play, and experiencing disgust at having genitals of the "wrong" sex. Gender identity disorder in childhood may be difficult to distinguish from gender nonconformity in which the child rejects the typical features of his or her gender role, seemingly more comfortable with opposite-sex peers and playthings. Gender-atypical behaviors are fairly common in childhood, according to a community survey concerning six-to ten-year-olds completed by parents: About 23 percent of the boys and 39 percent of the girls engaged at least occasionally in multiple gender-atypical behaviors (Sandberg, Meyer-Bahlburg, Ehrhardt & Yager, 1993). But gender identity disorder does not involve merely "tomboy" girls or "sissy boys" who sometimes prefer non-sex-role stereotyped activities: The children actually want to *be* the opposite sex, and feel that they really are the other gender even though the anatomy of their sex organs is "wrong."

Among children with gender identity disorder it is common to find evidence of cross-dressing and preference for the other gender as young as four or five. Young boys who reject rough-and-tumble play with other boys and who prefer feminine toys and playing with girls may receive considerable abuse for their "sissy" behavior (Bancroft, 1989; Pauly, 1985). But girls who prefer active sports and reject frilly dresses rarely raise concern from others unless their behavior is extreme. Consequently, more boys than girls are *diagnosed* as having gender identity disorder.

Researchers are not clear as to how many children who display gender identity disorder become transsexuals in later life, or are simply gender nonconformists who adapt to heterosexual roles. Many adult transsexuals report that they felt convinced that they were the opposite sex from the time of their earliest memories. One researcher, Richard Green (1979, 1985), studied young boys brought to treatment for gender disorders and periodically evaluated their status. According to his most recent report, about 40 percent of the boys developed homosexual preferences by adulthood. Whether homosexuality is an adjustment that accommodates underlying gender identity problems for some people, or is simply a common outcome of gender nonconformity, remains to be seen.

Although childhood gender identity disorder may result in adult transsexualism, it is not inevitable. Also, some persons develop gender identity difficulties later in life. For instance, a study of adult male transsexuals seeking sex reassignment surgery found that 50 percent reported normal male self-concept during childhood (Green, 1974). Others may express transsexual experiences in adulthood after unsuccessfully trying to make a homosexual or transvestite adjustment to underlying gender dissatisfaction.

An additional feature of gender identity disorder is noteworthy in that it illustrates the influence of society's rules and values. Specifically, most studies and clinical reports have found that female-to-male transsexuals are better adjusted than are male-to-female transsexuals. For example, female transsexuals often have better and more stable relationships, less personality disturbance, and less exaggerated cross-gender role behavior (Bancroft, 1989; Pauly, 1985). This finding is consistent with the fact that Western culture is particularly insistent on masculine traits in males and greatly values maleness, possibly providing males with harsher and narrower standards for suitable behavior and greater rejection for nonconformity. Because male-identified women may experience greater tolerance if not encouragement for their masculine behaviors, they may be able to adjust more readily and fit in more naturally.

Epidemiology of Gender Identity Disorder How common is transsexualism? Epidemiological data are unavailable, but most estimates are based on the frequency with which individuals seek gender reassignment treatments. Obviously, such statistics encompass only those most desperate, or those who are knowledgeable about the possibility of treatment procedures. Several studies estimate the rate at more than 1 transsexual in 50,000 people older than age fifteen (e.g., Pauly, 1985). A recent study conducted in the Netherlands suggests that the disorder is even more prevalent, though still rare — and points out that the Dutch culture is a more benevolent climate for treatment of the problem, possibly resulting in more accurate data (Bakker, Van Kesteren, Gooren & Bezemer, 1993). Other studies suggest that the rate of gender identity disorder among men is three to five times higher than that among women (Bakker, Van Kesteren, Gooren & Bezemer, 1993; Pauly, 1985).

Causes of Gender Identity Disorder

There is no empirically validated theory of gender identity difficulties, but most models include both biological and psychological factors. Physiologically, transsexuals are normal in terms of their sex and reproductive organs, and their chromosomes are normal for their biological gender. However, some researchers have speculated that prenatal brain development may have proceeded abnormally and, as we discuss earlier, that gender identity disorder might be an extreme version of gender nonconformity. If abnormal sexual differentiation occurs, the resulting features of the brain may therefore be inconsistent with anatomical gender. To date there is no direct evidence of defects in prenatal development among transsexuals, but, as also noted, there is growing evidence of the role of prenatal hormonal influence on homosexuality. Endocrinological hypotheses of transsexualism remain mostly theories at this point.

Psychological factors include social and cultural influences. Freud and his followers would have argued that male transsexualism results from faulty resolution of the oedipal stage of psychosexual development, in which the young boy normally comes to identify with his father and with male traits and behaviors. More contemporary approaches emphasize the extent to which the child acquires the preferences and behaviors of the opposite sex through cognitive social learning processes. A boy whose mother encourages dressing up in her clothing and discourages rough-and-tumble play, or a girl whose beloved father inspires her to be just like him, might internalize these behaviors and beliefs to form a gender identity.

Richard Green's (1979) study of feminine boys, compared with normal boys, provided some evidence supporting reinforcement as a mechanism in gender identity disorder. Green found that about 10 percent of the mothers of these boys had wanted a girl so badly that they tended to see their baby sons as girls, and about 15 percent of the mothers dressed their boys in feminine clothing. About one-third of the boys were pretty children, possibly influencing adults to treat them in a feminine manner. About one-third of the boys had no father in the home from an early age, and even those with a father present tended to be closer to their mothers, who in turn were protective and prohibited rough-and-tumble play. Finally, about one-third of the boys lacked opportunities for male playmates during their early years. These results suggest that many of the boys were rewarded for feminine activities and may have had limited occasions to interact with males or learn male-appropriate behaviors. Green emphasized that nearly all of the families failed to discourage feminine behavior in the boys for lengthy periods of time — possibly during a phase crucial to gender identity development. Alternatively, the findings do not exclude the possibility that the boys were "feminine" from birth and elicited different behaviors from adults than if they had been more classically masculine.

Does this mean that parents should be excessively careful to ensure that their sons are rewarded for only masculine behavior and aggressive play, and shamed and punished for quieter preferences and dislike of sports? Definitely not. Rigidity and extreme adherence to either pole of masculinity or femininity are regarded by child psychologists as detrimental to children's development. For example, boys raised to show no feelings or to overemphasize aggressive means of resolving disputes would be disadvantaged, as would girls who believe that they always need to be taken care of by others.

Green and his colleagues (1982) have also begun a longitudinal study of tomboy girls. Interestingly, despite the girls' characteristic masculine behaviors, researchers have observed no differences between the tomboys' families and those of the comparison group. Thus, the origins of female gender identity problems in family upbringing remain to be clarified; indeed, relatively little research exists on this general topic.

At the cultural level, societal values may also play a role in the origins of transsexualism. One investigator, for instance, has argued that transsexualism is more common in nations that are more rigidly rejecting of male homosexuality. A gender-nonconforming man who also has sexual preferences for men would be enormously devalued in such countries. And anxiety about his gender identity and sexual preferences might lead to adoption of transsexual beliefs as a solution (Ross et al., 1981).

Overall, the existing data on causal factors in gender identity disorder are skimpy and inconclusive. Many investigators have suspected that both social-psychological and biological factors are important, but much more research is needed (Bancroft, 1989; Money, 1989; Pauly, 1985).

Treating Gender Identity Disorders

Because of transsexuals' deep-seated and long-standing conviction that they were born with the wrong sex anatomy, psychotherapy has not proven effective in helping resolve their gender conflict; in other words, attempts to change the mind to match the body are generally unsuccessful. Efforts to change the body to match the mind have been somewhat more successful, however. Medical treatments using surgery and hormonal alterations are available to alter sexual anatomy and sex characteristics. These procedures do not literally change a man into a woman, or the reverse, because the person is still chromosomally his or her original gender; and a male-to-female transsexual cannot bear children, nor can a female-to-male transsexual impregnate women. Nevertheless, anatomical and hormonal changes can help the person function more fully as the gender he or she prefers.

Sex reassignment treatment typically consists of several stages, and clinics that perform this treatment are insistent on meeting certain standards since the procedures involved are largely irreversible (Petersen & Dickey, 1995). Initially, counseling and psychological evaluation establish whether the person is an acceptable candidate for the treatment, which is lengthy, costly, and emotionally arduous. Then, if the candidate seems reasonably stable and knowledgeable, and has realistic expectations and prospects of suitable adjustment, the next stage is usually hormonal treatment. For example, a male who believes he is female might be given testosterone-inhibiting hormones to reduce male characteristics and estrogen to enhance feminine characteristics. There may be some breast growth, reduction of facial and body hair, softening of the body shape, and reduction of muscle mass. For women desiring to become men, the opposite kinds of changes are induced by hormone treatment. Usually, sex reassignment programs insist that individuals take the hormone treatments for at least one or two years, while also living the life of the desired gender. This "real-life test" is required to determine how successfully the person can adapt to and integrate the life of a person of the opposite sex. Only after this period is the more drastic step of surgery undertaken.

The surgery for male-to-female transformation involves removal of the penis and scrotum and the construction of a vagina from pelvic tissue, relocating sensitive tissue so that sexual pleasure, and sometimes orgasm, are possible. Generally, male-to-female surgery works better than female-to-male surgery because the latter involves construction of a penis that is not capable of natural erections (Pauly, 1985).

Several studies have suggested that, following such surgery, people are happy with their changes. One study found that nine of ten transsexuals were satisfied with the results (Lundstrom, Pauly & Walinder, 1984). According to another, 94 percent of the transsexuals said they would have the surgery again if they had it to do over (Blanchard, Steiner & Clemmensen, 1985). A third evaluation indicated that the social adjustment of those who had undergone the surgery was much better than those who did not (Kockott & Fahrner, 1987). The great majority of reputable medical centers that provide sex reassignment procedures carefully screen out people who are unlikely to benefit from them. The ultimate suc-cess of these procedures most likely depends on the extent to which the individuals can make a satisfactory adjustment to the life of the gender they choose, and the extent to which their friends and family support the change.

What Lies Ahead?

The sexual revolution of the 1960s ushered in an era not only of liberalized sexual experiences but also of increased expectations about sexual enjoyment, resulting pressures on performance, and perhaps increased fears, conflicts, and responsibilities. At the same time, open interest in sexual matters stimulated new research on understanding sexual functioning and on recognizing and treating sexual dysfunctions.

In asking what lies ahead, we find that the horizon is dominated by the specter of AIDS, a disease transmitted largely through sexual contact. In what has become one of the worst epidemics in human history, millions are affected and may infect others. AIDS has had an enormous impact on sexual behavior, since all sexually active men and women are at risk. Its legacy may yield increased knowledge about sexual behaviors, as the disease certainly affects attitudes, communication between individuals in relationships, and sexual practices.

Sexual openness has also apparently contributed to increased information about sexual victimization. In the past decade we have witnessed major changes in our

Most communities now accept that teens are sexually active. To protect them against the unwanted outcomes of sex — like pregnancy, AIDS, and other sexually-transmitted diseases — they must be taught condom use and other matters that require open and honest communication. Despite ever-changing sexual awareness, the goal of responsible, enjoyable, and healthy sexual experience is not always easy to attain.

awareness of — and intolerance for — sexual victimization, especially of women and children. Behaviors formerly kept hidden in families, neighborhoods, schools, and offices — including sexual harassment, rape, and severe child molestation — have been brought to light and their negative consequences taken seriously. Scientists continue to study the origins of such abhorrent practices and attempt to develop effective means of treating, if not preventing, their occurrence.

KEY TERMS

androgens (371)
arousal (371)
desire (371)
dyspareunia (383)
estrogen (371)
excitement (371)
exhibitionism (387)
female arousal disorder (380)
female orgasmic disorder (382)

fetishism (388)
gender dysphoria (398)
gender identity disorder (397)
gender nonconformity (375)
hypoactive sexual desire (378)
hypoxyphilia (391)
incest (392)
male erectile disorder (380)
masochism (390)

orgasm (371)
paraphilia (386)
pedophilia (392)
penile prostheses (386)
performance anxiety (381)
plateau (371)
premature ejaculation (382)
resolution (371)
sadism (390)
sensate focus (384)

sex reassignment treatment (401)
sex therapy (383)
sexual aversion disorder (379)
sexual dysfunction (378)
transsexuals (397)
transvestic fetishism (390)
vaginismus (383)
voyeurism (388)

SUMMARY

Normal Sexual Functioning

The brain plays a critical role in sexual experiences, both in terms of thoughts and interpretations of erotic and environmental stimuli, and in terms of regulation of hormones that serve vital functions in biological responses and reproductive functions. Human sexual responding has been characterized as occurring in phases: *desire, arousal (excitement), plateau, orgasm,* and *resolution.* Each phase has different physiological features. These features may alter as a result of hormonal changes associated with aging, but the capability for sexual enjoyment continues.

Enormous changes have occurred in recent years regarding acceptance of sexual behaviors and experiences once considered unacceptable, including premarital sex, masturbation, and homosexuality. Research suggests that homosexuality can be predicted, though incompletely, by childhood *gender nonconformity,* and that biological variations in the brain, or unknown genetically transmitted factors, may also play a role.

Sexual Dysfunction

The DSM defines various *sexual dysfunctions* associated with phases of the sexual response cycle. *Hypoactive sexual desire* is a relatively common complaint reflecting lack of interest that may be lifelong or specific to one relationship. *Sexual aversion disorder* is characterized by fear and extreme discomfort with sexual activity. Arousal phase disorders include *female arousal disorder* and *male erectile disorder.* Male erectile problems are relatively common. Two disorders of the orgasm phase are *female orgasmic disorder* and *premature ejaculation.* Finally, sexual pain disorders include *dyspareunia* (genital pain) and *vaginismus* in women.

The causes of these disorders are varied, usually involving dysfunctional learning experiences and maladaptive cognitions, communication and relationship difficulties, and, in some cases, sexual traumas. Several of the disorders, such as erectile dysfunction, may have contributory medical causes.

Treatment of sexual disorders, or *sex therapy,* generally involves multimodal approaches including cognitive, behavioral, and relationship focuses, often using specific assignments and behavioral techniques pioneered by Masters and Johnson. Sex therapy has been relatively successful for most sexual dysfunctions, but research in this field is scarce. Some medically based problems are successfully treated; for example, devices such as *penile prostheses* exist for attaining erections in men with erectile dysfunctions. More severe psychologically based problems may require additional therapy.

Paraphilias and Sex Crimes

Paraphilia refers to unusual sexual preferences. Those not practiced in private or involving nonconsenting adults may lead to criminal convictions. Examples include *exhibitionism, voyeurism, fetishism* (including *transvestic fetishism*), sexual *masochism* (the most severe form is *hypoxyphilia*), sexual *sadism* (the most severe forms include sadistic rape and lust murders), and *pedophilia.* Child molestation, a legal term for improper sexual contact with children, may include pedophilia and *incest* (which is not necessarily caused by paraphilic urges). Individuals vary in their reliance on such activities for sexual satisfaction and in the extent to which they participate in normal relationship-based sex.

Social learning factors probably contribute to the origins of sexual disorders, although evidence is indirect and systematic research is scarce. Biological causal factors are unclear. Treatment using various cognitive-behavioral techniques shows promise in reducing rates of recidivism in sex offender populations, although most treatments overall are not very effective in preventing recurrence. Controversial medical treatments of sex offenders include hormonal suppression of testosterone by means of antiandrogen medications.

Gender Identity Disorder

People whose biological features are normal but who identify with the opposite sex have *gender identity disorder.* Sometimes people with this disorder are called *transsexuals.* Transsexualism occurs in both men and women, although women tend to seek treatment less often. Varying degrees of distress characterize *gender dysphoria.* For many, the disorder begins with childhood gender identity disorder and involves early experiences of wishing to be (or believing they truly are) the opposite sex; but some cases develop later in life, perhaps after unsuccessful efforts to adjust.

Little research has been done to establish causal factors of gender identity disorder. Social learning experiences, such as parental approval of cross-sex characteristics, may contribute, but abnormal hormone-based gender differentiation in utero may also play a role. *Sex reassignment treatment* is a radical therapy typically implemented only after careful psychological screening and hormonal treatment, but it works well for those capable of psychological adjustment to the life of the opposite sex.

Consider the Following. . .

Suppose that, as a member of city council, you are voting on business licenses for stores selling sex aids, films, and pornography. As you consider this scenario, keep in mind that our culture is deeply ambivalent about sexual matters, espousing both permissive attitudes on the one hand and restrictive ones on the other. Given what you have learned in this chapter, what are some of the possible advantages about openness and permissiveness? What are some of the disadvantages of such attitudes? Would you argue for or against "sex shops" in terms of the good of the community? Is there a place for such businesses—or do they only contribute to further maladaptive attitudes and behaviors?

Suppose that your daughter knows a boy from her nursery school who loves to play with her and often comes to your home for "play dates." He is very feminine in appearance and seems to enjoy playing dolls as much as T-ball and other activities in the back yard. When other children are around, you've heard them call him "sissy boy," and your daughter has asked you what that means. Based on what you have read in this chapter, describe what might be going on with this child. What further information might you want to know? What would you want to do for this boy to ensure that he is happy and well adjusted? What might you want to tell your daughter, and how would you want her to behave toward him?

CHAPTER 13

Personality Disorders

Those among us . . .

■ Edith used to be a checker in your supermarket. While all the other checkers were friendly and talkative, Edith seemed painfully shy and had a hard time even looking at people. When you'd try to converse with her, she'd blush and seemed tongue-tied, and didn't know what to say. She was very efficient as a worker but didn't stay in that job very long.

■ Your brother-in-law, Arnold, is a workaholic who never takes vacations and seems to get uptight if he's not doing something "useful." He makes a good salary as a lawyer but is always tense and perfectionistic. Despite being successful, he's always behind in paying his bills, and for such a bright guy, he never seems to be able to get to appointments on time.

■ Halley is in your dorm. She has a stunning figure but usually wears really trashy outfits with extremely short skirts and low-cut tops. She's dating a 42-year-old man. Although she's bright, she seems very childlike in her demands to be the center of attention, and you are amazed that she doesn't see that her behavior, while attractive to some men, alienates most other men and women.

■ There is a rumor about Randall, a local businessman who also has been a political figure in your community. The rumor is that he masturbated in front of his secretary, telling her how fortunate she was that she turned him on, that most women find him irresistible, but that he himself is choosy.

Are these people "normal"? What's the line between odd or obnoxious and abnormal? How should we think about their problems?

These people don't seem like they would ever seek help for psychological problems. What happens to people like this?

How do personality styles and traits originate? How do they become problems?

We call the problems displayed by these individuals *personality disorders.* Each personality disorder is described by a group of personality traits and behaviors. Of course, everyone has **traits,** which are characteristic attitudes, beliefs, behaviors, reactions, and ways of thinking about oneself and the world. But when traits are extreme, are applied indiscriminately or inappropriately, or cause problems in cognition or interpersonal relationships, then the traits may be linked to psychological disorder.

Consider the trait of self-confidence. A certain amount is necessary and healthy, and people normally display self-confidence in situations where they reasonably expect to succeed. When people are excessively confidant and openly boastful and arrogant, when they talk incessantly of their great capabilities, or when they have modest talents or attributes but seem unaware of the gap between their views of themselves and how they really are, then the trait has become rigid and maladaptive. In this extreme form the trait is likely to interfere with personal relationships and work and may be part of a pattern of traits that forms a personality disorder. Of course, many people have traits that make them different — eccentric, obnoxious, intriguing — but merely being different is not a disorder. As we will see, the diagnosis of personality disorder is made only in the context of significant interpersonal, occupational, or other personal impairments.

In this chapter we first consider how DSM-IV defines personality disorders in general and specific personality disorders in particular. Then we consider the objections to this classification, research on the causes of personality disorders, and how they are treated. Because one of the personality disorders, called *antisocial personality disorder,* is often associated with criminality and sometimes with violence, we discuss it in more detail in Chapter 14.

FEATURES OF PERSONALITY DISORDERS

Depending on one's professional point of view, personality disorders are

- True disorders, distinct from each other, with clear boundaries and causes and effective treatments.
- A conceptually and clinically useful supplement or alternative to the DSM-IV Axis I diagnoses.
- Among the most interesting and pervasive psychological disorders of our time.
- An arbitrary hodge-podge of disorders that do not clearly distinguish between normal and abnormal character structures.
- A set of largely pejorative labels for individuals that mental health professions find difficult, obnoxious, or unfamiliar and cannot treat very effectively.
- A set of diagnoses for people whose problems cannot be characterized easily in other terms.

As we will see, there is probably some truth in all these points of view.

Defining Personality Disorders

The object of all this controversy is ten specific constellations of personality traits that are diagnosed on Axis II of DSM-IV. Table 13.1 presents the personality disorder diagnoses. As we discuss in Chapter 4, Axis I contains the current, often temporary, symptoms and disorders, and Axis II diagnoses capture inflexible and maladaptive traits and styles that either markedly impair a person's

Table 13.1 Personality Disorders Defined on Axis II

Cluster A: Eccentric/odd
  Paranoid
  Schizoid
  Schizotypal

Cluster B: Dramatic/erratic
  Histrionic
  Borderline
  Narcissistic
  Antisocial

Cluster C: Anxious/fearful
  Obsessive-compulsive
  Avoidant
  Dependent

Source: DSM-IV. Reprinted with permission from *The Diagnostics and Statistical Manual of Mental Disorders,* Fourth Edition. Copyright © 1994 American Psychiatric Association.

Ten personality disorders are currently defined on Axis II of the DSM. Previous DSM editions included others, which subsequently were found not to be sufficiently valid or clinically useful and were dropped. Other proposed personality disorders are being studied for possible inclusion in future editions.

This photo illustrates one of the problems of defining disorder, especially personality disorder: when is a behavior symptomatic of pervasive and maladaptive excesses (such as masochistic or antisocial or borderline or histrionic characteristics) *or* just a fashion statement?

functioning or create subjective distress. These traits and styles may exist along with certain disorders defined on Axis I, or they may themselves be the problem requiring treatment. Thus, a person may receive both Axis I and Axis II diagnoses or only a diagnosis on Axis I or Axis II.

In short, a **personality disorder** is a continuing pattern of perceiving and relating to the world that is maladaptive across a variety of contexts and results in notable impairment or distress. The patterns usually appear in later childhood and adolescence, are relatively stable and chronic, and occur in a variety of situations. They are nonpsychotic conditions. These disorders were added to the DSM because they may have implications for treatment and for understanding the course of the disorders in the person's life. As we will see later, presence of a personality disorder usually implies poorer prognosis for adjustment, treatment, and recovery.

A common theme in the personality disorders is some dysfunction involving relations with other people. Different personality disorders involve different types of dysfunction, as we see, but all involve basic problems in attitudes and actions toward others. In fact, while many of those with personality disorders suffer greatly, some people with such disorders are not so much personally *disturbed* as *disturbing to others*. They are likely to be a source of irritation, worry, consternation, fury, or fear to others. Unfortunately, one common characteristic of people who display a personality disorder is that they do not have much personal understanding of their own contribution to the problem. A person who is depressed or anxious is likely to be very aware of real or exaggerated shortcomings that are creating problems. In contrast, people with personality disorders are not likely to go to a therapist and report, "I'm self-centered" (or shallow, manipulative, weird, or cruel). They are likely to blame others or blame their situations for their problems rather than recognize their own contributions to their difficulties.

Some of the personality disorders are among the least well-defined and agreed-upon of the disorders covered in DSM-IV because empirical information on them is limited. Later in this chapter we examine the problems with the current description and classification of personality disorders. For now, however, we focus on how they are currently handled by DSM-IV. Much of what we present is descriptive because research for some of the personality disorders has not progressed beyond simply defining and describing them.

By convention, the ten personality disorders are grouped into three broad clusters called A, B, and C, which sometimes have been termed the *eccentric/odd, dramatic/erratic,* and *anxious/fearful.* In the following sections we look at the characteristics of the disorders in each of these groups.

Cluster A: The Eccentric/Odd Personality Disorders

The paranoid, schizoid, and schizotypal personality disorders make up Cluster A.

Paranoid Personality Disorder   Individuals with **paranoid personality disorder** are pervasively suspicious of others and distrust their motives. They may believe that others are deliberately demeaning or threatening. They constantly expect to be harmed or exploited. They doubt the loyalty or faithfulness of friends and lovers. These individuals are guarded in revealing information about themselves for fear that it will be used against them, and they tend to read hidden meanings into remarks or events. They are very sensitive to perceived slights, respond angrily, and hold grudges. The motto of a person with this disorder might be, "Don't forgive, get even." Paranoid persons are often seen as hostile, stubborn, needing to control situations, and preoccupied with power — their own need for it, jealousy of those who have it, and avoidance of anything that makes them look or feel weak. Delusions, hallucinations, or thought disorders are absent, however, in contrast to psychotic conditions such as paranoid schizophrenia. The following case captures many of these features.

> Sharon always seemed to have a chip on her shoulder, frequently complaining about ill treatment by her boss, co-workers, teachers, father, and boyfriend. At work she was vigilant about who talked with whom and who was out to get whom. When asked a question, she'd act suspicious and seemed to wonder what the person was up to by asking. She annoyed people with her righteousness, seemed to believe that her motives and values were superior to those of others, and was stubbornly argumentative about her political and social views. Her family members found her very prickly and irritable; she'd feel insulted even when they didn't intend to hurt her or be annoyed at them if she thought they were being weak or emotional. She was ambitious and capable, but people generally tried to give her a wide berth; they were afraid to get on her bad side because she was known to hold grudges and find ways of retaliating if she thought someone was against her. In a previous job, some of her co-workers had received anonymous poison pen letters or obscene phone calls, and she had been suspected of these acts, although no one could ever prove it.

Schizoid Personality Disorder Aloofness from relationships is the chief mark of **schizoid personality disorder**. Schizoid personalities are the classical "loners." They seem not to value contacts with others. They may appear preoccupied with hobbies or interests and spend a lot of time in solitary pursuit of these activities. This does not seem to be due to fear of other people but rather to disinterest in others. They are also emotionally constricted, cold, aloof, and unresponsive to others; they don't seem to experience pleasure. Consider the case of Nick.

> At first Nick just seemed to his fellow students to be absentminded and nerdish because he would walk by them without noticing them, usually hurrying back to his room after classes. He stayed in his room most of the time and appeared completely uninterested in socializing with anyone in the dorm. Eventually, it became clear that he wasn't just shy or awkward with social skills. He just didn't have any interest in people.

Schizotypal Personality Disorder *Schizotypal* refers to peculiarities of thought and behavior, and **schizotypal personality disorder** is marked by difficulties in interpersonal relationships as well as by abnormalities of thought, behavior, and appearance — abnormalities that are somewhat similar to, but not severe enough to be considered, schizophrenia. The interpersonal difficulties may involve extreme social anxiety, lack of close friends, and inappropriate affect in social situations (silly, aloof). The abnormalities can involve excessively vague or abstract speech, unusual beliefs, strange perceptual experiences, and eccentricities of mannerisms or appearance. Consider the example of a man seeking treatment.

> Greg was a young man who appeared at the Adult Outpatient Services with vague complaints, including stuttering, feeling alienated from himself, and "wanting to study the stars." He elaborately described himself as suffering from a combination of neurotic and narcissistic problems. The interview was difficult because Greg did not provide direct answers to questions; it included peculiar and odd language and perceptual experiences. For instance, he stated that he had problems with his parents and that they "live in a triangle of denial," which he described as his parents' "inability to think about thinking." He stated that he could see things others couldn't, such as being able to tell if the devil is in someone's eyes. During the interview, his emotional expression was occasionally inappropriate; he often giggled at unexpected times and stared too intently at the interviewer. Despite his oddness, he held a steady job as an electronics assembler. He had no close friends and said that he didn't really want any. There was no evidence of clear hallucinations or delusions.

Loren and Jean Chapman and their colleagues have developed scales for assessing odd perceptual experiences such as body-image distortion (see Chapter 9). Table 13.2 shows some items from the Perceptual Aberration Scale. College students who scored high on the Perceptual Aberration Scale often reported unusual experiences and beliefs (e.g., Chapman, Edell & Chapman, 1980). Ten years later, many of the high scorers had schizotypal symptoms (Chapman et al., 1994). A study of hospitalized patients found that schizotypal personality disorder was strongly associated with high scores on the measure of Perceptual Aberration (Lenzenweger & Loranger, 1989).

In terms of long-term adjustment, people with schizoid and schizotypal disorders show chronic, unchanging features. Studies of such patients indicate that they remain isolated and function relatively poorly (e.g., Stone, 1993).

Cluster B: The Dramatic/Erratic Personality Disorders

Four personality disorders are included in the dramatic/erratic cluster: histrionic, borderline, narcissistic,

Table 13.2 Items from Perceptual Aberration Scale

1. Sometimes I have had the feeling that I am united with an object near me.	T	F
2. I have sometimes felt that some part of my body no longer belongs to me.	T	F
3. I have sometimes had the feeling that my body is decaying inside.	T	F
4. My hands or feet seem far away.	T	F
5. Occasionally it has seemed as if my body had taken on the appearance of another person's body.	T	F

Source: Chapman, Chapman & Raulin (1978).

The Perceptual Aberration Scale assesses odd perceptual experiences, such as body-image distortions. In examining this scale, be careful not to self-diagnose. These are the kinds of unusual experiences likely to be endorsed by persons with this form of personality disorder, but answering "True" to one or more sample questions does not necessarily indicate schizotypal disorder.

One characteristic of the histrionic personality disorder might be attention-attracting manner of dress (although not all such displays are, of course, about personality disorder).

and antisocial. Although they share the feature of the exhibition of dramatic behaviors, they differ enormously in the form of behaviors, the presumed origin and clinical meaning of the symptoms, the frequency of the disorder, and the actual research data available.

Histrionic Personality Disorder Overemotional, attention-seeking behaviors characterize **histrionic personality disorder.** The attention seeking often takes the form of seductiveness, excessive concern with physical attractiveness, or flamboyant patterns of dress and emotional expression. The person seems excitable, overreactive, and highly suggestible. The histrionic individual appears emotionally shallow, changeable, and self-centered. Feelings are expressed in an exaggerated, theatrical way, and conversation is vague and impressionistic, as if the person is unable to focus on detail or lacks analytic skills. In the pre-DSM-III era (that is, before 1980), this category was often termed *hysterical personality* or *hys-*

terical neurosis and played an important role in the development of Freud's theory.

This personality disorder is found in many social environments, as the following case illustrates.

Halley is an attractive young woman with a dazzling smile. She easily attracts the attention of men, especially by wearing tight clothes. At first her friends in the dorm were happy to have her in the group because she was cute, enthusiastic, and friendly. But increasingly, as the women got to know her, they found her gushy and insincere, emotionally shallow, and remarkably gullible — believing improbable stories that men told her. Her habit of trying constantly to be the center of attention was annoying to others, and she was very moody and seemed to overdramatize every minor problem she experienced. Recently, she's been dating a much older, rich man suspected by Halley's friends to be connected with drugs, and they are concerned about what might happen to her.

Borderline Personality Disorder At various times, *borderline* has been used to refer to the border between neurotic and schizophrenic, the border of psychotic but not necessarily schizophrenic, or the border of affective illnesses. Only in recent years have the boundaries of this condition been sharpened into their present form (not really on any border, but a profound disturbance of emotional reactions and identity). The topic has attracted considerable theoretical and research interest, as we discuss further in sections on causes and treatments.

The characteristic features of **borderline personality disorder** are pervasive instability of mood, relationships, and self-image. Mood disturbances commonly include rapid, intense shifts into negative emotions such as depression, anxiety, and anger. The person may suffer intense emotional distress. Anger may be especially frequent, marked by its inappropriateness, intensity, or persistence. There is a universal tendency to have intense but unstable personal relationships, often alternating between idealizing and devaluing the other person. The individual is often fearful of being alone and will frantically attempt to avoid abandonment. In terms of self-image, there may be a subjective sense of emptiness and a display of uncertainty about basic issues of self-definition: occupational or career choice, long-term goals, sexual orientation, preferred values, and the like. There is also characteristic impulsivity that is potentially self-destructive, such as overspending, excessive sexual activity, reckless driving, shoplifting, drug use, and binge eating. Sometimes there are impulsive suicidal threats, gestures, actions, or self-mutilating behaviors, including cutting oneself with a razor blade or burning the flesh with cigarettes. Among violent and nonviolent criminals, borderline traits were found to predict more extreme levels of violence (Raine, 1993).

Persons with borderline personality disorder may sometimes display temporary but severe psychotic-like dissociative reactions or paranoid ideation when they are under stress. Consider the following case of borderline personality disorder.

> Jack was living in his car at the time we first met. He'd been thrown out of his father's house because of his temper and undependability, and he worked irregularly in auto repair shops to support himself. He was intermittently extremely depressed, sometimes to the point of suicidal feelings. Once he telephoned me and told me that he had a gun in front of him at that moment. When depressed, he complained of a desperate loneliness and a self-loathing that sometimes felt so bad to him that he would slice himself with a knife or drive as fast as he could on the freeway, hoping that fate would take over and he'd crash. He reported that once, when he was extremely upset, he looked in the mirror and his reflection was

Actress Glenn Close played the borderline personality disorder character in *Fatal Attraction,* capturing the character's instability and many other features of the diagnosis.

> gone (a dissociative reaction). He was often angry at me for not doing enough to help him, at his bosses, and at his family. He was unsure what to do with his life and where he "belonged"; he often joined cultlike groups to find an identity, only to leave because of personal problems with other members. He seemed really committed to only one goal: More than anything else he wanted to meet a woman he could settle down with, although from his descriptions of past relationships with girlfriends, it was hard to imagine that there would be the peace and tranquillity he longed for.

Several longitudinal follow-up studies of persons with borderline personality disorder have documented the severe impairment of functioning that occurs, particularly in the younger-adult years (including a 3 to 10 percent suicide rate). However, outcomes are highly variable, and some studies have suggested that with increasing age there may be a "mellowing" that permits as many as two-thirds to function fairly well (Stone, 1989, 1993).

Narcissistic Personality Disorder The defining characteristic of the **narcissistic personality disorder** is grandiosity — an inflated sense of self-importance, accompanied by the expectation of being treated as special and being entitled to favorable treatment or exemption from the rules others must follow. Because of this self-centeredness, the individual may exploit others. The person may be strikingly lacking in empathy or understanding of how others feel. Such patterns are very damaging to the person's interpersonal relationships. The narcissistic person wants constant attention and admiration, often revealing acute sensitivity to criticism. The person is preoccupied with fantasies of unlimited success, power, brilliance, or whatever is the goal and is chronically envious of the success of others or imagines that they envy him or her. Curiously, the narcissistic person also may have low self-esteem and feel uniquely unworthy, paradoxically, like "the most important little piece of nothing in the universe." Such persons frequently lack the level of talent or accomplishment to which they aspire but may magnify their accomplishments and expect others to treat them accordingly. Even if they are extremely successful, they appear to derive little genuine satisfaction from their activities. The following case illustrates the features of narcissistic personality disorder.

Randall is a politician of outward charm and good looks who has done well in local elections. He sought out the services of the most well-known therapist in his community, who has written books and has a media following, and approached him with the attitude that "we are two special people, and you're special enough to understand me." Randall expected that the therapist would be delighted to work with such an important person and expressed some consternation that the therapist couldn't immediately fit him into his busy schedule. When they finally did meet, Randall's chief complaint was his frustration with his wife. He wondered whether he should divorce her; he feared it might harm his public image. He claimed that he had "care-

fully chosen her because she could play the right kind of role to help get me into the White House." He was angry when she resisted playing the "first lady" role, and he was confused. "Why wouldn't she want to help me get elected President?" He was utterly sure that he was destined for high places but was finding it hard to win the support of senior party officials, who found him arrogant and unimpressive. His wife, meanwhile, was indeed resentful of his attempts to use her for his own gains, and she was disillusioned by her discovery that his talents were far more modest than he claimed. Also, he was being sued for sexual harrassment by his former secretary.

There is a great range of opinion about the validity and frequency of narcissistic personality disorder. It is included in the DSM because clinicians believe that it really does occur. However, its occurrence is only about 4 per thousand (Weissman, 1993). Some clinicians have suggested that more people with narcissistic personality disorders are in treatment now than ever before. Others have argued that recent theorizing about the disorder has led therapists to "find" it more often in their patients. Social critic Christopher Lasch (1979) took yet another view and argued that ours is "a culture of narcissism," although he was referring to personality traits and not necessarily to the diagnostic category of narcissistic personality disorder. He indicted the U.S. population for living for the moment, self-indulgently preoccupied with appearance, wealth, power, and fame rather than true accomplishment and respect.

Antisocial Personality Disorder Antisocial personality disorder is defined as a pervasive pattern of disregard for the rights of others and lack of conformity to social norms and legal standards. To be diagnosed, there must be evidence of **conduct disorder** (a childhood or adolescent version of antisocial disorder we discuss in Chapter

14) before age fifteen and evidence during adulthood of major irresponsibility. For example, the person may violate the law repeatedly or get into physical fights because of aggressiveness or irritability. The person is deceitful, using lies or conning others to get what he or she wants. Antisocial individuals are irresponsible in their work, family, or financial obligations — often unable to hold a steady job. They are impulsive and oriented toward immediate gratification rather than planning ahead and show reckless disregard for safety. When confronted with evidence of illegal or irresponsible behavior, they lack remorse — often rationalizing their behavior as the fault of someone else or of circumstances. Here is a short example of antisocial personality disorder.

> *Andy's eyes are blank, and he smiles scornfully at the fallen figure of the man he has just knocked out with a beer bottle. Andy believed that the man insulted him in the bar, so he figured the guy had it coming when he pounced on him from a side street. Some of his earliest memories are of beating up other kids if they bothered him, quick to anger and always unmoved by their fear and pleading. Long years of running away from home, getting kicked out of school for truancy and fighting, and having no real friendships had taught Andy how to take care of himself with his hands if needed. He did what he wanted, when he wanted it—and enjoyed the fear he saw in the eyes of others.*

Because antisocial personality disorder oftens involves conduct that breaks the rules or laws of society, it is found in relatively high concentrations in prison populations. This personality style has such a major impact on society that it is discussed extensively in Chapter 14, on antisocial conduct.

Cluster C: The Anxious/Fearful Personality Disorders

The three current diagnostic subtypes of the anxious/fearful cluster are obsessive-compulsive, avoidant, and dependent personality disorders. These disorders are probably the least well studied, partly because they are relatively new additions to the DSM. Individuals with these disorders are usually anxious, and their symptomatic behaviors may be ways to try to cope with or avoid their anxieties.

Obsessive-Compulsive Personality Disorder   Obsessive-compulsive personality disorder is distinguished from the Axis I obsessive-compulsive *disorder* (OCD). The two may coexist, or they may occur independently. The major difference is that true obsessions or compulsions must be present for the diagnosis of OCD but not obsessive-compulsive personality disorder, whereas certain personality traits predominate in obsessive-compulsive personality disorder.

Obsessive-compulsive personality disorder is marked by preoccupation with perfectionism, orderliness, and control over the self and others — to the point of rigidity and inefficiency. There is a focus on details, rules, form, organization, and schedules so that the person seems to have lost the forest for the trees, getting sidetracked by minute matters and paying more attention to the letter of the law than to its intent. Relatedly, the person may be moralistic and judgmental. Also, the individual's high standards and attentiveness to detail often prevent tasks from being completed or decisions made. They often miss deadlines, even though they are preoccupied with work and productivity. The emphasis on productivity leads to the exclusion of spontaneity and neglect of leisure time and relationships. Obsessive-compulsive individuals may be rigid and stubborn and tend to believe that their way of doing things is the right way; they may therefore insist that people submit to their way of doing things (or have a hard time allowing others to do things). Many such individuals are seen as miserly and stingy. They hate to discard anything, however used or worthless, if they think it could come in handy some day. They are not generous in giving money and gifts, believing that they need to hoard their funds for future catastrophes. The case of Arnold is distilled from several actual examples of people with obsessive-compulsive personality disorder.

> *Arnold is a lawyer who has a good reputation among clients for being extremely conscientious and careful. Because he works very long hours and brings in lots of money to the firm, his partners are willing to overlook the fact that he is humorless and takes lots of time at staff meetings on procedural details and arguments about organizational matters. He is particularly adept at highly technical details of taxes and finances. Occasionally clients complain that he takes forever to complete the work, however, and only Arnold knows that it is because he often goes off on tangents in his overattention to irrelevant detail. His secretary must constantly remind him of legal deadlines. If it were not for her efforts, he would probably appear to be far less successful. Fortunately, she is good natured, whereas he is often critical and tense. She keeps telling him he needs a vacation, but it's now been four years since he last took more than two days off from work. He is married and spends time with his wife and parents but has virtually no recreational life. What really drives his secretary crazy, however, is that he never throws away anything; he keeps broken rub-*

ber bands ("you can tie them and use them"), memos ("it's good to have a record of everything"), old calendars ("sometimes I wrote down client meetings, and I should keep a record . . . just in case"), and duplicate copies of documents ("it'll be a waste if we have to copy that one again in the future, so let's just keep it in case we need it"). Since childhood Arnold has been very particular and "adult" (he used to play "school" with collections of pens and paperclips, notebooks, and record-keeping).

Obsessive-compulsive personality disorder demonstrates the difficulty raised by a lack of guidelines for separating normal from nonnormal traits. For instance, a certain degree of perfectionism, attention to detail, task orientation, and conscientiousness is adaptive and even desirable for some roles. We all want our dentists and accountants to have these qualities, and workers in technical specialties need to have such characteristics to succeed. When these traits become too rigid and extreme, however, they may interfere both with work and with personal relationships.

Avoidant Personality Disorder The major feature of **avoidant personality disorder** is social discomfort — timidity and fear of negative social evaluation. Unlike the schizoid personality disorder, in which the individual avoids social contact because of little interest, the avoidant person wants to enjoy the presence of others but is afraid of their reactions. Fearful of criticism or disapproval, the avoidant individual may avoid jobs and activities that involve major interpersonal interactions and is reluctant to risk any behaviors that might prove embarrassing. In social situations, the avoidant person is inhibited for fear of seeming foolish, worries constantly about others' negative reactions, and believes that he or she is inept and inferior.

Edith's father got her a job as a checker in the supermarket, but she quickly quit because she was terrified at having to interact with the other employees and customers for fear they'd think she was dumb and awkward. She is now much more comfortable working night shift on an assembly line, where she can avoid all but minimal contact. The other women don't try to befriend her because they can see how nervous she is around others. She worries that they will disapprove of her and, while working, broods a lot about how stupid she'd felt when the supervisor asked her questions about her work. Off duty, she spends a lot of time alone but socializes with her family members and occasionally with a group at the church she has attended since childhood. She enjoys herself on those occasions because she can stop worrying about whether she is liked, seems foolish, or

is acceptable. Last week her church group asked her to organize the charity rummage sale, but she declined, fearing that she lacked the intelligence and energy to do it right.

Dependent Personality Disorder Marked by pervasive patterns of dependent and submissive behavior, individuals with **dependent personality disorder** seem unable to make even everyday decisions for themselves. They require enormous amounts of reassurance from others and allow others to make decisions for them, to the point of playing a very passive role in their own lives. Because of an excessive feeling of helplessness, the person feels so dependent on others that she or he may go to great lengths to try to retain or win their approval — including agreeing with them even when they are wrong, volunteering to do unpleasant tasks, or putting up with mistreatment. They worry about being abandoned, hate being alone, and in fact are desperate to be in or to maintain close relationships because they fear that they cannot take care of themselves. An example of such dependency is Roberta.

Since childhood Roberta has lacked self-confidence, relying on her mother to help her decide what to wear, what friends to have, and what classes to take. She always seemed most comfortable when her mother was around and often made excuses to avoid going away to summer camp or staying with girlfriends at slumber parties. She lived at home when she went to college. She met a man in English class who seemed to enjoy her devotion, and he liked helping her make decisions about her life. They got married, and both seem content with the arrangement: He decided where they would live, whether she should work, when they would start having a family, and with whom they would socialize. Roberta functions well but is chronically nervous; she worries about her mother's and husband's health and wonders where her husband is when he is late from work and whether he is pleased with her. Fortunately, he is a mild man. Her boss, on the other hand, takes advantage of her submissiveness and gets her to do even demeaning tasks such as taking his laundry to the cleaners. She has been afraid to tell her husband or superiors that her boss has made improper physical advances several times.

Who Is Affected with Personality Disorders?

Rates of personality disorders in the general population are difficult to estimate. Earlier survey studies conducted before the development of the DSM criteria for personality disorders used nonstandard measures. Recent epidemiological interview studies based on diagnostic

Figure 13.1 Rates for Diagnosable Personality Disorders

The data from epidemiological assessment in large samples of the population are tentative but still suggestive. Here the bars represent the estimated rates of different personality disorders (in percentage of the total adult populations); the pink portions of the bars represent the range of results reported by various studies.

Source: Weissman (1993).

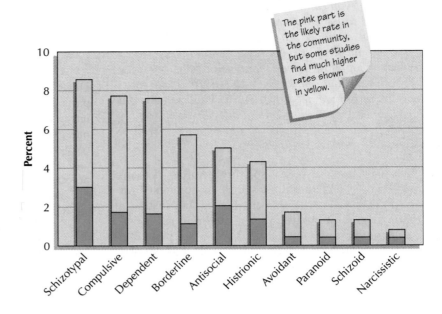

The pink part is the likely rate in the community, but some studies find much higher rates shown in yellow.

criteria have not included personality disorders except for antisocial personality disorder. Nevertheless, several interview or questionnaire studies in the United States and other countries using standard criteria have now been conducted. Summarizing the findings from these studies, Weissman (1993) estimates that between 10 and 13 percent of the adult population have a diagnosable personality disorder. Rates for each disorder are presented in Figure 13.1.

These studies generally found higher rates among urban populations than among rural groups, as well as among those of lower socioeconomic status. Both community surveys and studies of patient populations have suggested that schizoid and schizotypal disorders in Cluster A are more common in men, whereas Cluster C (anxious/fearful) disorders are more common in women (except obsessive-compulsive personality disorder). Cluster B (dramatic/erratic) includes antisocial personality disorder, which is strongly more prevalent in men, as well as histrionic and borderline disorders, which are generally more common in women. Males are more likely to be diagnosed with narcissistic personality disorder (Golomb, Fava, Abraham & Rosenbaum, 1995; Loranger, 1996; Merikangas & Weissman, 1986). Aside from antisocial personality disorder, which is discussed in Chapter 14, relatively little information exists on ethnic and cultural group differences in expression of personality disorders.

One of the most striking features of the prevalence of personality disorders is their frequency among treated populations. Figure 13.2 presents results from various

studies of inpatients and outpatients compiled by Widiger and Rogers (1989). Even when individuals seek treatment for Axis I disorders, there is considerable likelihood that they also have a personality disorder. The figures indicate that more than one-third of patients seen in outpatient and inpatient settings have borderline personality disorder.

The elevated rates of personality disorders in inpatients and outpatients reflect two challenging issues we discuss in more detail later: the co-occurrence of Axis II disorders with Axis I disorders and the reduced treatment success in the presence of Axis II disorders.

Problems with Classification of Personality Disorders

Several issues to be discussed in this section raise significant questions about the reliability and validity of the personality disorder diagnoses as they are presently conceived, as well as about the most effective ways to construe and measure them.

Selection and Definition of Axis II Disorders A problem with the disorders included in DSM-IV is that there is no rational or theoretical basis for choosing which groups of maladaptive traits ought to be included. Clinicians currently look for and diagnose ten types; other types have been recommended for consideration for future editions of the DSM. Yet there are thousands of personality traits and probably hundreds of clusters of related traits. Thus, the choice of ten pathological

Figure 13.2 Prevalence of Personality Disorders in Patient Samples

These figures are averaged across four studies of inpatients and outpatients. They represent the relative prevalence of personality disorders in treatment populations. They are considerably higher rates than in the general population and demonstrate that the borderline personality disorder is most common, followed by histrionic, with schizoid and obsessive-compulsive personality disorders seen relatively rarely.

Source: Widiger and Rogers (1989).

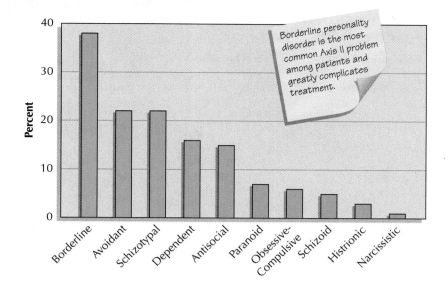

Borderline personality disorder is the most common Axis II problem among patients and greatly complicates treatment.

manifestations of personality is somewhat arbitrary. This number seems to be a compromise between having too few and therefore oversimplifying and including too many, which might provide precision at the cost of overcomplexity.

Some disorders in earlier diagnostic manuals have been retained in the current DSM; others have been dropped. Some of the current categories originated largely from psychoanalytic theory and practice (such as the compulsive, narcissistic, and histrionic types). Others were developed from frequent clinical observations, such as the borderline and antisocial personality disorders. As Table 13.3 indicates, there are other prospects for personality disorders that are not currently included in the DSM because they lack empirical and clinical verification at this point.

Another difficulty in selecting personality disorder categories for inclusion in the DSM is the potential for *sex or cultural bias.* Consider some of the characteristics of the histrionic personality disorder, such as excessive emotionality, overconcern with physical appearance, and seductiveness. Or consider some of the elements of the dependent personality disorder, such as dependency, submissiveness, and allowing one's life to be directed by others (such as spouses or bosses). These traits in fact reflect conformity to sex-role stereotypes traditionally urged for women. The following pointedly but humorously offers a fictitious disorder that could be reflective of the *male* sex-role stereotype (Pantony & Caplan, 1991):

The following are characteristic of the individual's current and long-term functioning, are not limited to episodes of illness, and cause either significant impairment in social functioning or subjective distress:

A. Puts work (career) above relationships with loved ones (as evidenced by traveling a lot on business, working late at night and on weekends).

B. Is reluctant to take into account the other's needs when making decisions, especially concerning the individual's career or leisure time (e.g., expects spouse and children to relocate to another city because of the individual's career plans).

C. Passively allows others to assume responsibility for major areas of social life because of inability to express necessary emotion (e.g., lets spouse assume most child-care responsibilities).

The point is that sex-role stereotypes — or cultural differences — may play a role in what types of behavior come to be viewed as disorders of personality. As critics have pointed out, however, the diagnostic categories do not represent men and women equally — that is, there is no classification for "independent personality disorder" to parallel the dependent personality disorder (e.g., Tavris, 1992).

Clinicians who diagnose also may be biased. As we note in Chapter 1, experimental research has indicated that clinicians seem to be reluctant to label women as antisocial or to view men as histrionic (reviewed in Widiger & Spitzer, 1991). What is bias in clinician judgments or in the actual diagnostic criteria, however, and what are the actual differences in the prevalence of disorders in men and women? As Widiger and Spitzer (1991) pointed out, ultimately the issue must be resolved by establishing the validity and accuracy of the diagnostic systems through further research.

Table 13.3 Alternative Personality Disorder Types

Personality Type	Characteristics
Type A personality	Impatient, hostile, sense of time urgency (see Chapter 10)
Addictive personality	Becomes easily "addicted" to behavioral excesses such as eating, substances, smoking, gambling; no actual evidence exists for this type (Nathan, 1988), but it persists in everyday language
Depressive personality	Gloomy, dysphoric, difficulty enjoying self; proposed by some (Akiskal, 1981; Klein & Miller, 1993)
Self-defeating personality	"Masochistic" traits; proposed and reviewed for DSM (Spitzer, Williams, Kass & Davies, 1989)
Passive-aggressive personality	Resistant, indirectly hostile and obstructive; formerly in DSM-III but lacked sufficient validation

Are the ten current personality disorders the only possible ones? Definitely not. Other constellations of traits might have defined "disorders" in the past; still other constellations of traits are being considered for future diagnostic systems.

Diagnostic Overlap and Comorbidity A further criticism is that the DSM method of characterizing the disorders of personality is based on the assumption of separate, distinct categories. Yet categories in general can be gross oversimplifications. In reality, classifying people's personalities successfully into just one category is difficult. In fact, about two-thirds of patients who receive one diagnosis of a personality disorder will meet criteria for at least one more (e.g., Clarkin et al., 1983; Pilkonis et al., 1995). This comorbidity may extend not just to conditions within the same cluster but also between clusters. For instance, one Scandanavian study found that only 52 percent of people with personality disorder had the disorder limited to one cluster (Ekselius et al., 1994). According to Weissman's (1993) review, borderline, avoidant, paranoid, and schizotypal personality disorders are especially highly likely to coexist with one or more other disorders — but schizoid and depen-

dent personality disorders commonly occur in isolation. Such high levels of overlap call into question the validity of separate diagnostic categories. Also, co-occurrence makes the task of identifying "pure" diagnostic groups for research on the disorders and their causes, as well as on treatment outcome studies, extremely difficult.

The co-occurrence of Axis II disorders may result either from the presence of shared risk and causal factors or from the indistinct boundaries and overlapping features of the disorders. Indeed, many critics have suggested that a major reason for Axis II comorbidity is the considerable overlap of symptoms. For example, because of the unusual perceptual experiences and interpersonal difficulties, borderline personality disorder has a significant overlap with schizotypal personality disorder, although recent studies have confirmed the validity of keeping them separate because each also has unique features that are not shared (Rosenberger & Miller, 1989; Widiger, Frances, Warner & Bluhm, 1986). Borderline personality disorder also co-occurs commonly with histrionic and antisocial personality disorders, probably because the symptoms of emotional instability and impulsive behaviors are similar.

In addition to co-occurrence of multiple personality disorder diagnoses for many people with an Axis II diagnosis, there is also considerable co-occurrence with Axis I disorders. Table 13.4 presents results of a recent study indicating common kinds of overlap between Axis I and Axis II disorders. Co-occurrence of Axis I and Axis II diagnoses may arise from several sources, including shared causal factors (for example, severe childhood deprivation might lead both to depression and to personality disorders). An additional source of comorbidity is that one disorder is the cause of the other (for example, underlying personality disorders might cause vulnerability to certain Axis I disorders). Depressive disorders, for example, are quite common among people with personality disorders. We might speculate that dependent people may become depressed when they experience a loss or separation, or avoidant individuals may be depressed as a result of their low self-esteem and loneliness (Widiger & Rogers, 1989).

Another source of comorbidity is conceptually more problematic: Axis I and Axis II disorders may overlap because of imprecise or arbitrary diagnostic boundaries. Three categories illustrate this problem (Widiger & Shea, 1991): depression and borderline conditions, schizophrenia and schizotypal disorder, and social phobia and avoidant personality disorder.

The diagnoses of depression and borderline personality disorders overlap considerably (e.g., Farmer & Nelson-Gray, 1990). Because of the frequent comorbidity, it was once believed that borderline personality disorder was a subtype of depression, but different genetic and clinical patterns of the two disorders have failed to

Table 13.4 Co-occurrence of Axis I and Axis II Disorders

Axis I Disorder	Personality Disorders
Mood disorders	Avoidant Dependent (Borderline)
Anxiety disorders	Borderline Avoidant Dependent
Psychotic disorders	Schizotypal Borderline Avoidant Dependent
Substance-use disorders	Borderline Histrionic
Eating disorders	Schizotypal Borderline Avoidant

Source: Oldham et al. (1995).

The co-occurrence of different Axis I and Axis II disorders was evaluated in a study of 200 patients. These combinations represent the patterns that were statistically significant. For instance, mood disorders commonly were accompanied by avoidant and dependent personality disorders, but borderline symptoms also were likely (though not statistically significant). Many other symptoms of different personality disorders also might accompany each Axis I disorder, but these are the most common combinations in this particular sample.

support this claim (e.g., Pepper et al., 1995). Borderline personality disorder may share causal features with depressive disorders, but co-occurrence of the two disorders also might simply reflect shared symptoms such as negative emotions and poor self-image.

The overlap between schizotypal personality disorder and schizophrenia is also noteworthy (see Table 13.4). The co-occurrence may reflect both genetic and phenomenological similarities, as discussed in the section on causes of personality disorders. The diagnostic distinction between Axis I and Axis II disorders is especially difficult for generalized social phobia (an anxiety disorder) and avoidant personality disorder. Several investigators have found considerable coexistence of these diagnoses, raising the possibility that they are simply forms of the same disorder. Careful studies of the characteristics of Axis I social phobics with and without avoidant personality disorder, however, have suggested that whereas they overlap, they are not entirely redun-

dant diagnoses (for example, generalized social phobia often emerges at older ages and may fluctuate in severity according to situations more than does avoidant personality disorder). More than likely they differ mainly in severity (e.g., see Holt, Hamburg & Hope, 1992; Turner, Boatel & Townsley, 1992).

Overall, despite considerable comorbidity of Axis I and Axis II disorders, drawing the distinctions between the acute Axis I condition and the underlying, pervasive Axis II disorder is often useful and valid. The information of Axis II clarifies the nature and extent of longstanding patterns, and presence of Axis II disorders helps in treatment planning because longer and sometimes more intensive treatment is needed than with Axis I disorders alone. As Widiger and Shea (1991) pointed out, however, dividing personality disorders into distinct categories is "at times problematic and perhaps even illusory."

Categories versus Dimensions   Researchers have proposed several solutions to resolve the problems of personality disorder selection and categorization. Perhaps the most persistent suggestion is to characterize personality disorders not as specific entities but as personality dimensions, traits that can be measured on a continuum from low or none to extreme (e.g., Livesley, Schroeder, Jackson & Jang, 1994). In other words, patients could be described not by the presence of a specific diagnostic category but by the degree to which they display specific characteristics. Investigators have offered two versions of this proposal. One approach rates patients on the degree to which they show symptoms associated with the personality disorders. Procedures using this method report excellent agreement between raters, superior to methods using categorical decisions (e.g., Pilkonis et al., 1995). The alternative approach is to rate everyone according to certain specific traits.

Consider, for example, borderline personality disorder. As we note earlier, it overlaps considerably with other Axis I and Axis II disorders. A possible explanation is that it is not a separate entity but rather represents a nonspecific dimension of impulsivity and instability that cuts across diagnostic categories (Fyer et al., 1988). And indeed, this is the conclusion reached by Timothy Trull, Thomas Widiger, and Pamela Guthrie (1990). They analyzed the distribution of DSM borderline personality disorder symptoms in 409 adult patients and, based on statistical patterns, concluded that the disorder is better viewed as a dimension rather than as a category. They proposed that borderline personality disorder should be viewed as a dimensional variable with patients differing in the extent to which they show borderline psychopathology, rather than categorizing people as borderline or not borderline.

Pursuing the issue of dimensionality, Widiger and associates (1987) evaluated all the symptoms shown by a sample of people diagnosed as having a personality disorder of some kind. By using sophisticated statistical techniques, they found that the symptoms actually seemed to fall into three groups. That is, most of the symptoms formed three distinct dimensions: social involvement (similar to introversion-extraversion), assertion-dominance, and anxious rumination versus behavioral acting out.

A somewhat different approach opens up the possibility of defining personality disorders as differing only in degree from normal traits.

Using the Dimensions of Normal Personality to Define Personality Disorders

Personality theorists have a long tradition of trying to distill the essence of human traits into a few basic dimensions by which everyone can be characterized (Digman, 1990). Aided by modern computer techniques that facilitate the use of complex statistical analyses of associations between variables, in the past decade we have witnessed considerable convergence of views about the basic structure of personality. Many investigators and theoreticians have proposed that underlying the hundreds of human traits there are five key dimensions that keep turning up regardless of the specific methods or scales that are analyzed. Called the "Big Five," these trait dimensions are

1. Extroversion/introversion: dominance, sociability, liveliness, and cheerfulness (contrasting with aloofness, introversion)

2. Friendliness/hostility (or agreeableness): trust, warmth, altruism, and nurturance (contrasting with cynical, cold-hearted, self-centered antagonism)

3. Conscientiousness (or will): disciplined striving after goals and strict adherence to principles

4. Neuroticism/emotional stability: experiencing psychological distress in the form of anxiety, depression, anger, and other negative affects

5. Intellect (or openness to experience): esthetic sensitivity, intellectual curiosity, need for variety and nondogmatic attitudes (Costa & McCrae, 1990; Digman, 1990)

If these are basic traits, can they be used to define personality disorders? Several studies have tested the hypothesis that current DSM formulations of personality disorders can be characterized as extreme or inflexible manifestations of some or all of these dimensions. For example, Jerry Wiggins and Aaron Pincus (1989)

had several hundred college students complete both a self-report checklist based on DSM personality disorder diagnoses and a questionnaire assessing the Big Five dimensions. As illustrated in Figure 13.3, using just *two* of the Big Five dimensions thought to characterize *interpersonal* functioning (dominance or extroversion and friendliness or warmth), many of the ten personality disorder types could be described by their relative scores on these two items. Other analyses not shown here but using all five of the dimensions describe the entire set of disorders. Similar results were obtained on samples of community adults (e.g., Costa & McCrae, 1990). These investigators noted that further research is needed in clinical populations: Self-reported personality disorder symptoms in a normal population are not the same as actual diagnoses because they do not indicate impairment of functioning. The authors suggested, however, that the five-factor personality model offers the promise of integrating research on normal personality functioning with psychiatric terminology (see also Widiger & Costa, 1994).

Researchers who have attempted to map dimensional models of personality onto diagnosed clinical populations have found the task to be complicated. John Livesley and his colleagues (1992) suggested that as many as fifteen dimensions may be needed to characterize existing personality traits; moreover, the fifteen factors showed only a moderate relationship to DSM categories.

At the University of Miami, Theodore Millon (1983) has developed a multiple dimension assessment procedure aimed specifically at characterizing the cur-

Figure 13.3 Personality Disorders Mapped on Two Dimensions of the Big Five Personality Traits
College students completed personality disorder self-rating scales as well as two Big Five scales that permitted assessment of *dominance* (extroversion) and *friendliness* (agreeableness). The results indicated that a broad range of the personality disorder types could be captured by placement on the two normal personality dimensions.

Source: Wiggins & Pincus (1989).

rent personality disorders. Containing scales for each disorder, individuals can be characterized by scores on all the dimensions, yielding a profile similar to that of the Minnesota Multiphasic Personality Inventory, as described in Chapter 4. Systems including ten to fifteen dimensions, however, raise practical problems for clinical use because they are considerably more complex to interpret than simpler models.

As opposition to the categorical system of diagnosing Axis II disorders grows, researchers look to dimensional systems. Investigators must still agree on which dimensions will be useful and then establish their validity in characterizing clinical conditions. If they do, Axis II classification — characterizing enduring and pervasive dispositions — may eventually be accomplished by relying on what we know about normal personality structure.

In sum, the diagnoses of personality disorders may help focus attention on stable aspects of the dysfunctional individual that must be treated and taken into account in the treatment of symptomatic disorders. However, the personality disorders appear to raise numerous unresolved questions about validity and method of assessment. In the absence of a unifying theoretical base for defining and measuring them, the personality disorders of DSM seem to represent the triumph of clinical habit and diagnostic politics over science. Alternatively, it is clear that if personality disorders were not available as diagnoses, we might have to invent them because they represent impairments occurring relatively frequently in the population and challenge our understanding of psychopathology and therapy.

CAUSES OF PERSONALITY DISORDERS

Three factors contribute to the inconclusive state of research on the origins of personality disorders: We are not sure of the exact rates of the disorders; if they exist, we are not sure about the validity of our assessment of them; and some of the types are only recently defined, so research has not yet been done. Nevertheless, researchers are exploring several promising leads.

Biological Perspectives on Personality Disorders

Genetic patterns and neurotransmitter processes have been the major focus of biological research on personality disorders. Genetic studies have followed two strategies, one exploring specific disorders and the other

examining personality traits or dimensions of potential relevance to personality disorders.

With respect to disorders, the clearest genetic pattern is the link between schizotypal personality disorder and schizophrenia, with less clear association of schizophrenia with paranoid and schizoid disorder (Battaglia et al., 1995; Kendler, McGuire, Gruenberg & Walsh, 1995; Kendler & Walsh, 1995; Nigg & Goldsmith, 1994). Thus, schizotypal disorder is on the "schizophrenia spectrum" and appears to have an inherited component. Also like schizophrenia, male patients with schizotypal personality disorder show greater enlargement of lateral ventricles in the brain than do patients with other personality disorders (e.g., Siever et al., 1995).

Other disorders are less clearly genetically linked. Some studies have found that certain disorders may run in families (e.g., avoidant personality disorder and borderline personality disorder; Johnson et al., 1995). Riso and associates (1996) have found that patients with early-onset dysthymic disorder commonly have personality disorders (especially Cluster B) and that their relatives also show these disorders; these authors speculate that both disorders may share a common etiology that may in part be genetic. Borderline personality disorder and depressive disorders were once thought to be genetically linked, but more recent evidence suggests that in general they are separate disorders, although there may be a subtype of borderline disorder that is genetically related to depression (Nigg & Goldsmith, 1994).

Recent biological research has suggested the value of exploring the origins of these disorders by working with *dimensions of personality* instead of diagnostic categories. For example, instead of looking directly for biological contributions to specific disorders, researchers might examine whether biological factors explain traits such as impulsive aggressiveness, which is a dimension of various personality disorders such as antisocial personality disorder or borderline conditions. Several studies have suggested biological mechanisms responsible for such traits. For instance, high rates of impulsive aggressive behavior toward oneself or others have been linked to abnormalities in the level and functioning of the neurotransmitter serotonin, as we discuss in Chapter 14.

Several other investigators have proposed that some of the major dimensions of maladaptive personality functioning may be related to complex neurotransmitter processes in the brain. Robert Cloninger (1987; Cloninger, Svarkic & Przybeck, 1993) has theorized that most personality disorders can be characterized not only by characteristic traits and behaviors but also by brain systems and neurotransmitters specific to different types of traits. He argues that a behavioral inhibition–harm avoidance system of the brain, served largely by the

Some personality traits have a genetic basis. Jim Springer (left) and Jim Lewis (right) were separated four weeks after their birth and lived in different communities. As participants in the University of Minnesota Study of Twins Reared Apart, they discovered that they were incredibly similar: both chain-smoked Salems, both drove the same model blue Chevrolet, both chewed their fingernails, and both had dogs named Toy. They responded almost identically when tested for personality traits such as sociability and self-control. This twin pair shared many similarities, but not all pairs do. Clearly, not all traits and behavioral preferences have a genetic basis, but heredity does play some role.

serotonergic system, for example, would be responsible for behaviors and traits such as those of the anxious/fearful cluster of personality disorders, reflecting avoidance and sensitivity to signals of potential harm. A somewhat different model has been proposed by Larry Siever and Kenneth Davis (1991), who suggest that Axis II personality disorders are related to four dimensions: cognitive/perceptual organization, impulsivity/aggression, emotion instability, and anxiety/inhibition. Each of these, in turn, is hypothesized to be associated with different biological processes, traits, and coping or defense mechanisms.

These biological-based models remain largely speculative at this time. However, preliminary research by Richard Depue and his colleagues (1994) has supported the basic assumption of the approaches: that core personality dimensions are related to biological (neurotransmitter) mechanisms. These investigators found evidence that the trait dimension of "positive emotionality" (friendliness in the Big Five) is related to indicators of dopaminergic function in the brain. Although the research is correlational and therefore does not address whether personality disorder is a result or a cause of neurochemical dysfunction, this intriguing research offers considerable promise for integrating biological and psychological perspectives on normal and potentially abnormal personality.

Additional information contributes to the importance of a biological perspective on certain personality characteristics. First, evidence is accumulating that some traits have a genetic basis. For example, characteristics such as outgoingness and sociability (sometimes measured on scales of introversion/extraversion) are considered to be substantially hereditary (Carey & DiLalla, 1994). And the Minnesota Study of Twins Reared Apart reported that monozygotic (identical) twins raised apart since infancy were just as similar on personality scales as were twins raised together (Bouchard et al., 1990). The correlations between the twins for the nineteen scales of the California Personality Inventory were quite high, suggesting that considerable similarity of personalities is transmitted genetically rather than as a result of shared environments.

Second, numerous studies in child development have shown that even in the earliest months of life infants have different **temperaments** or dispositions (e.g., Thomas & Chess, 1977, 1984). Some infants are calm and easily soothed, whereas others are irritable and hard to calm; some are outgoing and fearless, whereas others seem shy and inhibited. Shy babies, for example, are likely to withdraw from novel objects or strangers and seek comfort from a familiar person. These differences in temperament show up at such an early age that they appear to reflect biological and perhaps genetic influences.

Does an infant's temperament persist into adulthood, and do certain temperaments and traits represent risk factors for the development of personality disorders? Definitive answers to these questions could lead to a clear framework for examining the origins of personality disorders. As the following feature illustrates, the work of Jerome Kagan on the influence of infant temperament on later personality is especially intriguing.

Do Infant Traits Portend Personality Disorders?

Jerome Kagan and his colleagues have been especially interested in the possibility that certain children, from a very early age, are shy, timid, and inhibited and that these traits may be biologically based and persist throughout the person's lifetime. Such patterns might be forerunners of avoidant or dependent personality disorders.

To determine whether inhibition is a persisting, general trait, Kagan studied children at various ages as young as twenty-one months and in different settings. How do you determine whether youngsters are "inhib-

ited"? Kagan and associates asked volunteer mothers to describe how shy or outgoing their babies seemed. Those children who were described as shy, quiet, and timid (inhibited) or as sociable, talkative, and spontaneous (uninhibited) were then brought to the laboratory. There, the children and their mothers were videotaped while the child was exposed to novel rooms, people, and objects (such as an unfamiliar female examiner dressed in unusual costume, toys, a talking robot). Raters then coded the videotapes for specific behavioral signs of inhibition, such as prolonged clinging to the mothers or reluctance to approach a stranger (Kagan, Reznick & Gibbons, 1989; Reznick et al., 1986). In other samples children also were observed with unfamiliar children of the same age in the laboratory, home, or school settings (Kagan, Reznick & Snidman, 1987). The children were tested several times up through age $7^{1}/_{2}$, and the tasks were varied somewhat for different ages; older children, for example, were exposed to mildly risky tasks such as a balance beam.

On the basis of these methods, the researchers identified consistently inhibited and consistently uninhibited children. For example, inhibited children waited much longer before playing with another child or speaking to the female examiner and also spent longer periods close to the mothers (e.g., Kagan, Reznick & Snidman, 1987, 1988). The inhibited children generally were quiet and socially avoidant with unfamiliar people, and the uninhibited youngsters were talkative and interactive. Moreover, Kagan and associates found that children in the two extremes of restraint tended to display stability over testings. Although not all the children remained

Dr. Jerome Kagan of Harvard University interacts with a shy and inhibited young boy in his studies of children with strong patterns of behavioral inhibition or lack of inhibition. Such patterns appear from the earliest ages and are fairly stable and consistent.

restrained or uninhibited over time, most did. About three-fourths of the children who were uninhibited by two years of age were likely to be uninhibited at age seven, and the same was true of the inhibited children (Kagan, Reznick & Snidman, 1988). Kagan described a typical scene in which several children were brought together for a play session: A group of three or four children would be playing close together and talking, and one or two children would be standing apart or playing alone. Those isolated, quiet children were the same ones who had been inhibited five years earlier (see Kagan, Reznick & Snidman, 1988; Kagan, Reznick, Snidman, Gibbons & Johnson, 1988).

Is there a biological aspect underlying these differences? Kagan addressed this question by examining whether differences in physiological reactivity correlated with the differences in behavioral inhibition. Specifically, Kagan and associates examined whether the physiological reactions to novelty or change were greater among inhibited than uninhibited children (see Kagan, Reznick & Snidman, 1987). They looked at several physiological indicators of reactivity: heart rate and autonomic activity; norepinephrine and its metabolites, and cortisol.

The researchers obtained the psychophysiological measures during testing sessions, and they obtained samples of norepinephrine and its derivatives from urine and measured levels of cortisol from the children's saliva. Figure 13.4 illustrates heart rates for a sample of the children, measured at several times during their lives, and shows that rates are especially high among children who were consistently behaviorally inhibited at different testings (and low for the consistently uninhibited children; Kagan, Reznick & Snidman, 1988).

Further, the testing of norepinephrine and cortisol also indicated that the inhibited children were relatively more aroused or had lower thresholds for response to unexpected change or challenge. Figure 13.5 reports cortisol levels for inhibited and uninhibited children obtained in different settings. The inhibited children showed the greatest mean level of physiological arousal, as indicated by cortisol levels, in all settings, but especially just before engaging in unfamiliar tasks in the laboratory (Kagan, Reznick & Snidman, 1987).

Overall, Kagan and associates concluded that for the majority of children who exhibit extremes of inhibition or lack of inhibition, these behavioral styles show significant, although not perfect, stability over time. They speculated that the inhibited children belong to a qualitatively distinct group of infants who were born with a greater tendency to react to unexpected changes or novelty or with a tendency to react to lower levels of change. They speculated that these tendencies are the result of lower thresholds of arousal to stressors, mediated by brain processes — but likely influenced by the extent to which children also experience stress in their

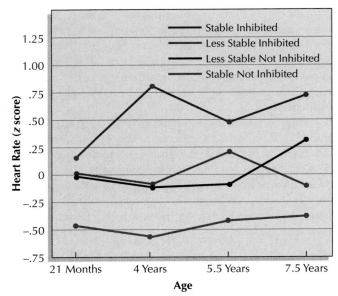

Figure 13.4 Mean Heart Rates Assessed at Different Ages for Children Initially Classified as Inhibited or Uninhibited

Children were classified at age twenty-one months as inhibited or uninhibited. Note that the children who remained behaviorally inhibited or uninhibited as evidenced by their behaviors in laboratory situations at testing later in childhood showed stable high or low heart rates. Kagan and colleagues speculated that the inhibited children are fearful and autonomically hypersensitive, presumably contributing to their inhibited and timid behavior.

Source: Reprinted with permission from Kagan, Reznick & Snidman (1988), Biological bases of childhood shyness, from *Science, 240,* 167–171. Copyright © 1988 American Association for the Advancement of Science.

environments, such as family disruption. Recently, this research group also has found evidence of the heritability of inhibition by comparing levels of observed behavioral inhibition in infant twin pairs (e.g., DiLalla, Kagan & Reznick, 1994; Robinson, Kagan, Reznick & Corley, 1992).

Do we know for sure that inhibited children will go on to have personality disorders of the anxious/fearful kind? Assessment of psychopathology in the inhibited sample that was studied through age 7½ determined that those who were stably inhibited had higher rates of anxiety disorders than children who were not consistently inhibited at multiple testings (Hirshfeld et al., 1992). Meanwhile, Rosenbaum and associates have applied Kagan's measures of behavioral inhibition to children of parents with anxiety disorders, including panic disorder or agoraphobia. They found that compared with children of normal or control parents, children of parents with anxiety disorder were significantly more likely to display behavioral inhibition in response to an unfamiliar situation set up in the observation lab-

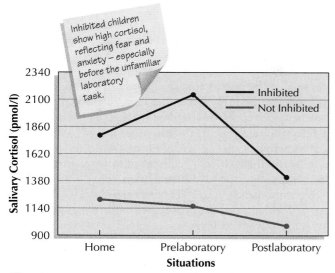

Figure 13.5   Mean Salivary Cortisol Level of Inhibited and Uninhibited Children

Recall from Chapter 8 that cortisol is a hormone involved in the hypothalamic-pituitary-adrenal (HPA) axis that regulates reactions to stressful situations. Note that children identified as inhibited at twenty-one months of age have consistently elevated cortisol levels across various situations, but with greatest arousal in anticipation of novel laboratory tasks.

Source: Kagan, Reznick & Snidman (1987).

oratory (Rosenbaum et al., 1988, 1993). When followed up over 3 years, the inhibited children of parents with anxiety disorders tended to develop new or additional disorders, including both anxiety disorders and avoidant disorder (Biederman et al., 1993). Overall, it appears that marked and stable behavioral inhibition seen in the youngsters might reflect a biological, genetically transmitted risk factor for later anxiety disorder — and, we might speculate, forms of anxious/fearful personality disorder.

These studies of extreme temperament, or behavioral style, also have suggested the need for further study of psychological and environmental processes that might be relevant to the development of maladaptive processes given underlying physiological vulnerability. To pursue psychological issues further, we turn to theories and research about psychological contributions to the development of personality disorders.

Psychological Contributors to Personality Disorders

As with biological perspectives, relatively little research has focused specifically on the causes of personality dis-

order diagnoses. In general, psychodynamic and cognitive-behavioral theories have been most influential in characterizing the psychological origins of Axis II disorders. These divergent perspectives agree that *early childhood experiences* are critical in understanding the origins of these long-standing and pervasive disorders.

Research in personality disorders is constrained by methodological problems. *Retrospective reports* of patients about their families have been a major source of information for testing psychological explanations of personality disorders. As we note earlier, however, such information may be biased not only by forgetting but also by individuals' constructions of what they believe happened in their early years. Retrospective information is also limited to what people are able to report, potentially omitting important but nonconscious processes. Also, many retrospective studies lacked appropriate comparison groups.

Prospective or longitudinal studies, such as those which identify children at risk and then follow their development, are badly needed to avoid overreliance on subjective reports. Recently, two longitudinal studies have shown that disruptive disorders (for example, conduct, oppositional, and attention-deficit disorders, as we describe in Chapter 15) in childhood or adolescence may portend later personality disorders in all three clusters; by contrast, emotional disorders such as depression and anxiety were significantly less predictive of personality disorders later on (Bernstein et al., 1996; Rey et al., 1995). Thus, further studies of children at potential risk for personality disorders due to childhood or adolescent disruptive behaviors may facilitate further understanding of the origins of Axis II disorders.

Psychodynamic Explanations According to classical Freudian theory, personality disorders reflect fixation at particular stages of psychosexual development and the use of maladaptive defense mechanisms. For example, obsessive-compulsive personality disorder is seen as reflecting fixation at the anal stage of psychosexual development with defense mechanisms of reaction formation and undoing; paranoia is viewed as involving projection of unacceptable libidinal impulses. (For a review of these Freudian concepts, see Chapter 2.) Little empirical work has substantiated formulations like these, and virtually no controlled research is testing them today.

In contrast, applications of contemporary psychodynamic theory are attracting considerable attention. Of particular interest is the interpretation of borderline personality disorder as the product of disturbed **object relations** — or disturbances in the processes of attachment of the infant with the mother and becoming an individual separate from the mother (Kernberg, 1975, 1984; Masterson, 1976). When these processes are disturbed, the individual fails to develop an adequate sense of self; the person does not form a cohesive personality structure and manifests primitive defense mechanisms. Failure to develop a coherent sense of self and positive relations with others from an early age contributes to borderline or narcissistic psychological disorder, according to various object relations or self-psychology theorists (e.g., Kernberg, 1975, 1984; Kohut, 1977; Masterson, 1976; Winnicott, 1951) — and as discussed in more detail below.

Retrospective research has begun to document the disturbed family relations of borderline patients (e.g., Gunderson & Zanarini, 1989; Norden et al., 1995). Moreover, investigators have commonly obtained reports of traumatic experiences such as sexual and physical abuse from borderline patients (Norden et al., 1995; Ogata, Silk & Goodrich, 1990; Rose, Abramson, Hodulik, Halberstadt & Leff, 1994). The link between borderline pathology and sexual abuse may be particularly likely for severe, ongoing abuse by a parent (e.g., Silk, Lee, Hill & Lohr, 1995). Can object relations theory hypotheses about inner experiences in borderline disorder be tested? Consider the following research program.

FAMILY MATTERS

Borderline Personality Disorder and Malevolent Object Relations

While behaviorists and social learning theorists have been particularly focused on overt behaviors, psychodynamically oriented theorists have emphasized the role of unconscious processes — and these are extremely difficult to study. However, Drew Westen and his colleagues have attempted to study such internal mechanisms in their pursuit of understanding the origins of borderline personality disorder.

Using projective techniques (as we describe in Chapter 4), the investigators have attempted to shed light on how people with borderline personality disorder think about themselves and their world. Object relations models of psychodynamic theory propose that borderline and other personality disorders reflect fundamental disturbances in the object world — a term referring to how people construe and feel about the self and others. Specifically, researchers have theorized that the extreme lack of stable self-definition and emotional instability of borderline personality disorder reflects malevolent object representations — views of others as hurtful, dangerous, uncaring, and untrustworthy. They further assume that these beliefs are acquired in early family experiences because of poor parenting. The theory spec-

ulates that a child treated badly by parents fails to acquire a positive sense of the self and acquires as well distorted views of the reliability and benevolence of others.

Westen and associates attempted to test some of these ideas by postulating that borderline patients would tell stories about the Thematic Apperception Test (TAT) cards whose content would be marked by malevolent or neglectful relationships with other people (and other characteristics also were hypothesized). As predicted, the borderline patients, compared with normal people and with psychiatric patients with different disorders, were significantly more likely to report stories of people as malevolent and also displayed negative expectations of relationships, poorer understanding of other people, and grossly illogical explanations of behavior (Westen et al., 1990).

The investigators also employed an interview aimed at eliciting earliest memories to learn if the memories — like projective tests — included negative representations of others. As predicted, patients with borderline personality disorder were significantly more likely than comparison groups of depressed and normal people to report injurious and malevolent themes and to indicate that they viewed others as unhelpful in times of need (Nigg et al., 1992). For example, a borderline person might report that her earliest memory is of her mother slapping her because she spilled her milk, whereas a nonborderline person might recall getting a tricycle for her birthday.

These results are consistent with accumulating evidence of sexual and physical abuse in the childhoods of patients with borderline personality disorder, as we note earlier. In a further analysis, therefore, Westen's group specifically examined whether *abused* borderline patients are adversely affected because they internalize the abuse experiences in the form of malevolent representations of others — presumably leading to distorted negative views of the self and of relationships. In this study, borderline and depressed patients and normal people were asked to report their earliest memories. The memories of patients who were abused sexually (but not physically) contained significantly more malevolent experiences compared with those who were not abused (Nigg et al., 1991).

The investigators argued that these studies indicated that early childhood experiences marked by maladaptive interactions — even sexual abuse — may become incorporated in the person's tendencies to expect malevolence from others and to believe that others will be ineffective in helping them. According to the object relations perspective, such experiences contribute in later life to anxiety, rage, and depression in relationships — and to maladaptive behaviors aimed at bolstering an inadequate sense of the self.

"*Eat your carrots!*"

These studies have limitations, of course. They do not directly prove the link between early family experiences and borderline personality disorder, nor do they fully clarify how a person develops borderline characteristics rather than some other form of disorder. Also, the same studies also could support cognitive-behavioral formulations of how children acquire negative schemas in family relationships, as we discuss in the next section, so that object relations assumptions may not be needed to explain the findings. Nevertheless, the studies represent an important step in the difficult process of studying internal processes and clarifying the mechanisms by which maladaptive family experiences predispose a person to later maladjustment.

Cognitive-Behavioral Explanations Another intriguing way to explain personality disorders focuses on schemas. As we discuss in earlier chapters, cognitive theorists define *schemas* as assumptions, beliefs, and attitudes that guide the selection and interpretation of information. Because people tend to notice and seek information that confirms their schemas and to distort or ignore information that does not fit them, schemas are self-perpetuating and difficult to change. The cognitive approach suggests that personality disorders arise as a result of maladaptive schemas that produce behaviors that cause or perpetuate distress and other difficulties.

For example, the core schema that characterizes the paranoid personality might be suspicion, the belief that one could be harmed intentionally by others: "A suspicious person is a person who has something on his mind. He looks at the world with fixed and preoccupying expectation, and he searches repetitively, and only, for confirmation of it" (Shapiro, 1965, p. 56). The paranoid person has an intense, acute, and continuous focus of attention on the search for information to confirm the suspicion schema.

In contrast, for the obsessive-compulsive personality, the core schema seems to be the belief that certainty is essential. It is as if the person says, "I must be absolutely certain in everything I do (so that I won't make any mistakes)." This need for certainty manifests itself in a concern with perfection and an associated preoccupation with detail, as well as in an attempt to live by a set of rules (Shapiro, 1981). For borderline personality disorder, one common schema might be, "It is terrifying to be alone and yet others cannot be trusted and will hurt or abandon me."

From the cognitive perspective, the major characteristic distinguishing personality disorders from Axis I disorders is that the maladaptive schemas are acquired in the earliest years. As a result, these schemas exert a pervasive influence and may exist without — or even prevent — the development of compensatory positive schemas. A child who acquires the belief that he is helpless and totally dependent on others, for example, may never actually learn ways of calming or soothing himself in challenging situations, relying instead on the reassurances of others.

As an example of how maladaptive schemas may arise, develop, and produce personality disorder, consider the avoidant personality. According to Christine Padesky (1987), individuals with this disorder usually have a past history of very critical or shaming parents or family members. In response, they develop "explanations" such as "I must be a bad person to be treated so badly" and "If my parents don't like me, no one could." In other words, they develop a schema of negative beliefs about themselves. Later, out of this core schema, negative thoughts about specific situations arise automatically. In a social situation, the avoidant person might have thoughts such as "I'm unattractive," "I don't have anything interesting to say," and "What's the use of going any place, since I'll end up alone anyway." These beliefs produce both social and cognitive avoidance. In other words, the person not only stays away from social interactions but also tries to keep negative thoughts and feelings at bay. Perhaps the person watches television endlessly or uses food and alcohol to excess and tries to avoid any risk of emotional or physical discomfort. Thus, cognitions, behaviors, and their outcomes create a self-perpetuating, self-defeating cycle.

Cognitive-behavioral formulations also may incorporate the behavioral emphasis on failure to acquire adaptive skills (or learning dysfunctional behaviors). An avoidant person, for example, is viewed as someone who not only acquired maladaptive beliefs about the self but also failed to learn how to interact comfortably with others — such as how to initiate conversations, ask questions, or make assertive requests. Or a histrionic person might be viewed as someone who learned to be dramatic and attention seeking as a result of modeling a parent with those traits. Not all personality disorders appear to lend themselves to specifically behavioral formulations, however, and relatively little research has explored behavioral formulations.

Notice that in cognitive-behavioral models, as in object relations theory, understanding the family environment is essential to understanding the cause of personality disorder. Certainly, enormous quantities of research have indicated that disturbed parent-child relationships or conflicts between parents are associated with various diagnoses in children, as we discuss in Chapter 15. Qualities of the family environment that interfere with the development of basic social skills, coping and problem-solving capacities, and a positive view of the self and the world seem likely to lead to lifelong difficulties of the sort we currently call personality disorders. Although relatively little empirical research substantiates these perspectives for personality disorders, investigators generally think that such approaches are on the right track.

Toward Integrative Models of Causality   As we note earlier, several models of etiology have focused specifically on personality traits and their biological underpinnings. All these models embrace the necessity of including psychological processes to characterize how the combination of biological vulnerabilty and learning experiences creates personality disorders. Theodore Millon (1983), for example, articulated a biosocial approach that starts with the proposition that constitutional differences and neuropsychological maturation stages in the child set the stage for later learning. Subsequently, caretakers and others respond to the child's characteristics and further accentuate the dispositions, creating rewards and punishments that further shape the behaviors. For instance, a highly active and responsive child and a very passive child will relate differently to the environment, evoke different responses from it, and encounter different emotional experiences.

Millon proposed that several dimensions of constitutional and experiential differences underlie personality patterns: activity-passivity, focus on the self versus others, and orientation toward pleasure or avoidance of pain. Although not all of Millon's classification subtypes exactly resemble those of the DSM, they provide a unifying theoretical framework. On the other hand, so far no empirical research supports Millon's hypotheses about the causes of the personality disorders.

Research on causes of personality disorders is at an early phase, and it promises to shed light not only on clinical conditions but on normal personality development as well. We turn next to the challenge of treating these pervasive and entrenched patterns.

TREATMENT OF PERSONALITY DISORDERS

Three issues are important in discussing the treatment of personality disorders: Clinicians have found that these problems are very difficult to treat, relatively little research has been conducted on treatment effectiveness (compounded by problems in reliability and validity of diagnosis), and this is a very hot topic stimulating important theoretical and research initiatives.

Obstacles to Successful Treatment

The personality disorders are notoriously difficult to treat successfully for a variety of practical and theoretical reasons. The problems are lifelong for many people, and the patterns are therefore entrenched and pervasive. Unlike treatment of a marital crisis, a major depression, or a panic disorder, there is no relatively healthier baseline condition to which to return. Often, because the styles of thinking and behaving are so much a part of the person's daily life, taking responsibility for having a problem is difficult, and he or she often blames the distress and upheaval on others or on circumstances. Thus, the motivation and acceptance of responsibility — qualities essential to therapeutic success — are limited.

Additionally, the person may have massive problems in living and few supportive resources to draw on; therapy may be sidetracked constantly by crises and realistic difficulties to overcome. Personality disorders, as we have seen, are often viewed as major deficiencies in the sense of self and of healthy ego functioning. As a result, such patients may lack some of the basic ingredients essential for therapy: the ability to work collaboratively and cooperatively, the capacity to retain a sense of continuity of the self and of the therapeutic relationship between therapy sessions, and the ability for objective appraisal of reality. Stemming from such deficiencies, the relationship between the patient and therapist may be marked by excessive dependency or mistrust or resistance. Thus, the working, collaborative relationship that normally facilitates therapy may become conflict ridden or an arena for playing out many of the patient's ineffective or "primitive" defenses. Not only is therapy potentially arduous, therefore, but it is also considered to be slower and to require a much longer duration than typical treatments for most Axis I disorders.

Two outcomes follow from such difficulties. One is that therapists often have thrown up their hands in futility, refusing to accept patients for treatment. Psychoanalysts considered most personality disorders as "unanalyzable," and behaviorists and cognitive-behaviorists did not include them in their models of treatment. There is thus little research on treatments targeted specifically for persons with such disorders.

The other outcome is that personality disorders interfere with treatment effectiveness of programs targeted at Axis I disorders. Therapy outcome research for problems such as depression, anxiety disorders, and alcoholism consistently demonstrates that individuals with both Axis I and personality disorders do significantly worse in treatment than do patients with Axis I disorders but no personality disorders (e.g., Hardy et al., 1995; Johnson & Lydiard, 1995; Reich & Green, 1991).

Thus, personality disorders traditionally have discouraged therapeutic efforts, or they actually dilute the success of treatments for other psychological disorders. This seems to be a bleak picture indeed, but fortunately, a new trend is apparent.

New Therapies and Research on Treatments for Personality Disorders

The increasing recognition of the frequency of personality disorders in clinical populations has helped stimulate extensive efforts by both psychodynamically oriented and cognitive-behavioral theorists to develop effective treatments. As we note in Chapter 3, contemporary versions of psychodynamic approaches focus on self-development and "object relations" and view many of the personality disorders as defects in these fundamental processes. Despite a few successful studies, as noted later, we know little about the effectiveness of psychotherapies for personality disorders (Shea, 1993).

Object Relations Approaches Borderline, narcissistic, and schizoid disorders (although generally more broadly defined than in the DSM-IV) have attracted particular interest by theoreticians and clinicians (e.g., Kernberg, 1976; Kohut, 1977; Masterson, 1976; Winnicott, 1971). The therapy aims at repairing the fundamental defects of the self that resulted from maladaptive formative experiences in early childhood. Such efforts require the therapist to confront the patient's maladaptive defenses and distortions by providing a supportive environment, exploring the affect and meaning of the patient's emotional experiences, interpreting the link between actual events and the patient's experiences, and using the "transference" relationship as a vehicle for these activities. Many different theoretical subgroups emphasize different therapeutic operations and methods. The following case describes one self-psychology perspective that has served as the basis for a controlled research study on treating borderline patients.

> *The goal of this therapy is to help the patient discover and elaborate a mature personal reality. By providing empathy the therapist facilitates exploration, but inevitably, being human, the empathy "fails," and the patient's typically pathological reactions to the therapist's imperfections need to be explored and evaluated more realistically — contributing to a more adaptive experience of the self and others.*
>
> *The authors describe a man who spent much of his early life in an orphanage but could remember nothing before age ten. He began a session reporting that his girlfriend was pregnant, but it was no problem because she would get an abortion. Later in the session he noted that his memory of early childhood was possibly returning because he had had "images" of himself as a terrified child being dragged from under a bed, presumably to be taken to the orphanage. The therapist then remarked that the forthcoming abortion seemed to have triggered feelings relating to his being "gotten rid of" by his own mother. The patient said, "Good point," in a rather pompous voice. He then went on to tell about several unrelated incidents of being physically attacked, humiliated, and enraged. The therapist noted that reporting these events pulled the man away from talking about his internal states and represented an escalation from agitation to rage. The therapist also observed that this all happened after his interpretation about the abortion — and concluded that the patient experienced his interpretation as a failure of empathy that intruded on his own internal experiencing of his memories. The therapist recognized he had made a mistake and proceeded to try to help the patient explore his feelings about the intrusion. (Adapted from Stevenson & Meares, 1992, p. 359.)*

This case reveals the painstaking, moment-to-moment effort to reconstruct a damaged self and to repair dysfunctional and unrealistic views of the self and others. In one of only a few controlled outcome studies of the effectiveness of such psychodynamic treatments, thirty borderline patients were seen twice per week for a year and then followed up one year later (Stevenson & Meares, 1992). Measuring changes from one year before therapy to the end of the follow-up, the treated patients showed significant improvements in borderline symptoms, as well as reductions in hospital admissions, violent episodes, self-harm, time away from work, and overall social functioning. Fully 30 percent of the treated patients no longer met DSM criteria for borderline personality disorder.

Methods of object relations/self-psychology treatment for severe personality disorders are being studied in many locations. These exciting developments offer new hope for people formerly rejected or treated unsuccessfully, as well as new avenues for theoretical and scientific development.

Cognitive-Behavioral and Behavioral Approaches

Cognitive-behavioral theorists have been equally active in recent years in developing approaches to treatment of personality disorders. The therapy seeks to identify fundamental maladaptive schemas and underlying beliefs that contribute to patients' dysfunctional relationships and adjustment (for example, a dependent person might believe that "I am incapable of doing anything for myself," or an obsessive-compulsive person might believe that "I have to be certain and perfect and in control of everything"). Once core themes are identified, they can be challenged by cognitive restructuring techniques and systematic behavioral assignments. Additionally, the deficient problem-solving skills and gaps in effective, self-reliant behavior are addressed by instruction, role-playing, practice, and behavioral assignments (see Beck et al., 1990; Freeman & Leaf, 1989). In recognition of the difficulties of working with such patients, cognitive therapists view the therapies as longer-term than "traditional" brief cognitive therapy and make extensive use of the relationship between therapist and patient as an arena for awareness and behavior change.

The following is an imaginary case illustrating cognitive-behavioral techniques. It draws on some of the features described by Marsha Linehan and her colleagues at the University of Washington (1991, 1993) in their treatment of chronically parasuicidal borderline patients (those with intentional self-destructive behaviors including both self-mutilation and suicide attempts).

Pamela reported that last night after she returned home from being with a friend she felt so lonely and anxious about being by herself that she couldn't stand it and made cuts on her arm with a razor blade because she preferred physical pain to emotional pain. Her therapist explored with her what led up to her upset that evening and what were the thoughts that went through her mind. They discovered some familiar schema-based beliefs: Pamela is terrified that being alone means that she'll always be alone and abandoned and that when she feels upset there is nothing she can do to console herself. They also discovered that during the evening with her friend, the friend had been critical of something about Pamela that made her feel rejected and led to deeper beliefs that she is worthless.

Together, Pamela and the therapist attempted to challenge some of these maladaptive beliefs and explore some different alternatives for Pamela. For instance, when she feels lonely late at night, she can remind herself that the following day she can spend time with others, that there is no evidence that she will always be alone, and that being alone at night is appropriate and it is healthy to tolerate periods of being alone. They explored what Pamela might do when she gets upset instead of cutting herself: Try relaxation exercises, listen to music or watch television, call a friend if necessary, or call her therapist. The therapist also encouraged Pamela to think of other ways to deal with her friend's criticism: If justified, accept it as an area for improvement; if unjustified, respond assertively. Together the therapist and Pamela helped Pam plan at least one evening alone before their next session, during which she could practice tolerating her negative feelings and actually plan something pleasurable but solitary for herself to do.

Linehan and associates (1991) compared female borderline patients randomly assigned to treatment in year-long weekly individual and group therapy or "treatment as usual" in the community. After one year of treatment the women were compared, and the cognitive-behavioral patients proved to have significantly fewer and less serious parasuicidal incidents and less time hospitalized than the control patients. The two groups did not differ, however, on measures of depression or hopelessness — although both groups improved over time. Similar results were obtained in a second group of female borderline patients, and the study further demonstrated that the positive effects of treatment persisted at six-month and one-year follow-ups and positively altered their interpersonal adjustment (Linehan, Heard & Armstrong, 1993; Linehan, Tutek, Heard & Armstrong, 1994). The Linehan studies showed promising results for cognitive-behavioral treatment and have reported one of the only randomized clinical trials for borderline patients. Additional controlled studies using cognitive-behavioral approaches are under way, and recent reports suggest that structured, problem-focused cognitive-behavioral applications to borderline *inpatients* also may be useful (e.g., Silk et al., 1994; Springer, Lohr, Buchtel & Silk, 1995).

Behavioral techniques or programs combining behavioral and cognitive methods have been applied to people with avoidant personality disorder with some success. For example, programs that include social skills training and desensitization of social anxiety reduced symptoms after a relatively few sessions (e.g., Alden, 1989; Rennenberg, Goldstein, Phillips & Chambless,

1990; Stravinski, Marks & Yule, 1982; Stravinski, Lesage, Marcouiller & Elie, 1989). These authors have observed that the actual mechanism of change is unclear, however, and that the addition of behavioral social skills training to the programs does not appear to enhance their effectiveness beyond other ingredients such as gradual exposure to social situations. In addition, the persistence and significance of changes in short-term treatments need to be evaluated. Alden (1989) noted that even after treatment improvements, most of the patients with avoidant disorder were still functioning below normal levels of social comfort.

Medications   Psychotropic medications are also used increasingly to treat personality disorders (e.g., Kutcher, Papatheodorou, Reiter & Gardner, 1995; Stein et al., 1995). To date, no drug has been specifically proven to be effective for a disorder, and psychiatrists generally treat specific symptoms — for example, "psychotic-like" symptoms in borderline conditions are often treated with neuroleptic (antipsychotic) medications at low dosages, and they appear to help improve functioning of borderline patients and to reduce impulsive, hostile, and schizotypal traits (Soloff, 1989). Others use mood stabilizers or antidepressants to control mood symptoms or compulsive behaviors. Such uses are largely experimental.

Medications are not typically recommended as the sole treatment, however, and may serve as adjuncts to psychotherapy. Some of the biopsychosocial models of personality disorders suggest that specific neurotransmitter abnormalities may be treated, but to date this approach has not been pursued.

Overall, systematic treatment of personality disorders is in its infancy. The research is complicated by potential problems in defining patient groups — not only because of extensive co-occurrence of disorders but also because different theorists may employ different diagnostic definitions. Although there is great hope that new efforts to develop treatments will be successful, so far the field is overly reliant on case studies and unsystematic clinical reports.

What Lies Ahead?

The personality disorders represent a topic of enormous theoretical and practical interest. The challenge of defining and characterizing them not only stimulates considerable research on the diagnostic system itself but also promises to align the study of psychological abnormality more closely with the study of normal personality and functioning. The scientific challenge is to establish the validity of formulations of characterological impairment that are free from the biases of traditional theoretical leanings and cultural and gender stereotypes. Many investigations are under way to measure and characterize dimensions of personality pathology and the best ways to evaluate personality disorder.

The future holds considerable promise for intense research activity not only because of the theoretical issues but also because of the practical necessities. Lifelong, pervasive, disruptive personality disorders are extremely resistant to most methods of treatment, and they interfere with the effectiveness of established methods. As methods of empirically validated treatments for Axis I disorders have met with widespread adoption, many investigators are now developing and testing treatments for Axis II disorders. Research on clinical features and causal factors is also benefiting from the increased effort to conceptualize, measure, and treat these problems. The future promises new developments, including the continuing resurgence of modern psychodynamic methods, a focus on familial influences, and fuller understanding of genetic and temperament influences on personality. To date, there is relatively little research on personality pathology in children, although such research usually follows when advances in adult disorders have blazed a pathway.

KEY TERMS

antisocial personality disorder (411)

avoidant personality disorder (413)

borderline personality disorder (410)

conduct disorder (411)

dependent personality disorder (413)

histrionic personality disorder (409)

narcissistic personality disorder (410)

object relations (423)

obsessive-compulsive personality disorder (412)

paranoid personality disorder (407)

personality disorders (407)

schizoid personality disorder (408)

schizotypal personality disorder (408)

temperaments (420)

traits (406)

SUMMARY

Features of Personality Disorders

When personality traits are extreme or cause problems in cognition and interpersonal relationships, the *traits* may be linked to psychological disorder. *Personality disorders* are diagnosed on Axis II of the DSM and refer to a pervasive, chronic maladaptive pattern of perceiving the world and behaving, usually present since childhood or adolescence. The personality disorders are the person's "style" of behaving, and their problems typically affect their relations with people as well as adjustment in other areas. A person may have an Axis II personality disorder in addition to an Axis I disorder or an Axis II disorder alone.

Currently, there are ten personality disorder diagnoses. Three refer to odd/eccentric but not psychotic behaviors: *paranoid, schizoid,* and *schizotypal personality disorders.* Four refer to dramatic/erratic behaviors: *histrionic, borderline, narcissistic,* and *antisocial personality disorders.* The antisocial diagnosis requires the presence of childhood conduct disorder and is one of the most common, but it is also one that poses threats to society. It is discussed in a separate chapter. The final group contains three types associated with anxiety/fearfulness: *obsessive-compulsive, avoidant,* and *dependent personality disorders.*

Researchers have estimated that 10 percent or more of the population manifests a personality disorder, and personality disorders are particularly represented among individuals in treatment.

The personality disorders are controversial in several ways. The selection of ten is somewhat arbitrary given the enormous range of personality traits and clusters. Some have argued that they overrepresent characteristics that depart from the norm of masculine mental health. A particular problem is that they co-occur frequently with each other and with Axis I conditions — suggesting that some of them may not be distinct categories separate from Axis I conditions. Some have proposed that instead of using a categorical classification system — that someone does or does not have a personality disorder — we might define abnormality on dimensions of normal personality or as degrees of personality disorder characteristics.

Causes of Personality Disorders

Relatively little research addresses etiological matters, largely because of the controversies about how to define personality disorders. Biological models have been proposed, suggesting biological mechanisms such as neurotransmitter systems, genetic transmission, and constitutional or *temperament* factors as important elements in vulnerability.

Psychological factors have been emphasized by both contemporary object relations and cognitive-behavioral theorists. Both camps agree that early negative childhood experiences produce personality disorders. *Object relations* models have particularly focused on borderline and narcissistic personality disorders and emphasize the acquisition of unconscious attitudes and expectations about the lack of benevolence and trustworthiness of significant others. Indirect support comes from frequent reports of abusive relationships, especially sexual, with parents. Cognitive-behavioral approaches also emphasize learning experiences that create maladaptive schemas or core beliefs about the self and others and failure to acquire appropriate skills.

Treatment of Personality Disorders

Formerly, patients with severe and long-standing personality disorders were considered untreatable. Because of the high frequency of such patients in help-seeking populations, however, theorists have actively searched for new treatments suitable for such patients. Scant but promising results from controlled studies of object relations, cognitive-behavioral, and behavioral methods are emerging. Medications are also being tried. Because of the practical necessity of addressing this group of patients, further developments are expected in time.

Consider the Following. . .

Suppose that you've been dating someone you first met at a social gathering. From the beginning, he (she) has been energetic, outgoing, and always the life of the party. He (she) cracks jokes, talks a lot, and seems to be unfailingly cheerful and entertaining. You find this person charming and great fun to be with and have started having serious feelings for him (her). Your roommate has noticed your feelings and has gently suggested that this person might be charming and entertaining but also might be shallow and self-centered. Given what you now know about personality disorders, how can you distinguish between normality and "disorder"? What would you want to find out in order to make sure that this attractive person is someone you can really be with for a long time in a stable and happy relationship? What are the hallmarks of (any) personality disorder, and how would you go about determining whether this person is someone to really commit yourself to?

Suppose that your sister's four-year-old child is very shy. He almost literally clings to her skirts when someone comes for a visit and hangs back when other kids are playing. He cries easily when he has bumps or scrapes or when someone teases him. Your sister says, "Oh, he'll grow out of it" and generally babies and protects him when he shows fears. Do you think this is just a phase he's going through that he will outgrow? What might be other possible explanations, and what information might you want to know in order to predict whether he will change? What are the advantages of being very gentle and protective of him? What are the disadvantages? Do you have some suggestions about how to treat and interact with him that might help him develop healthy attitudes and skills?

CHAPTER 14

Antisocial Personality and Violent Conduct

Those among us . . .

■ The high school you went to is no longer recognizable: There is a chain-link fence around it, with guards at the entrances checking your belongings for weapons and drugs. Just last week a student was killed on campus; when he got into a fight, someone pulled a hidden knife and stabbed him. Your younger brother, who is now attending this school, is sometimes scared that someone will jump him as he's walking home and rob or beat him up.

■ Your neighbor's daughter, Erin, ran away from home at fifteen, got into drugs and sex, became pregnant, and had a baby at seventeen. She can't seem to hold a job, and she's on probation for writing bad checks. Just recently, her baby was removed from her care because bruises were discovered all over his body. Physical abuse is suspected.

■ Your roommate, Miki, recently came home from a date looking shaken. When you asked her what was wrong, she burst into tears and told you that her date had raped her. She is only now trying to deal with the anger and shame, and is very fearful of a future sexual relationship.

■ At an after-school program for children where you volunteer your time, there is one eight-year-old who really concerns you. Mark is so aggressive that he has to be watched constantly so that he doesn't hit, push, or bite another child.

There seems to be a rising tide of crime and violence in our society, especially among young people: What can be done about it? Can we ever reverse this trend? Are crime and violence preventable?

What makes children — or loving parents or caring friends — behave in brutal ways that physically or mentally maim or even kill the ones they love?

Are violent people mentally ill? Can a normal person suddenly "snap"? What is the difference between mental disorder and violent behavior?

Are some people just born evil, or does society make them that way? We hear that violent people usually had been abused as children; what is the process by which violent behavior is transmitted from parents to children?

Every day the news is filled with tales of crime, despicable antisocial acts, and the horror of violence. Violent and antisocial behaviors are often linked in the public's mind with mental illness. A course on abnormal psychology appropriately explores the causes of violent and antisocial behavior and the extent to which they are related to mental illness. And because violent and antisocial behaviors affect other people — victims, witnesses, families, and friends — the aftermath of these behaviors is also related to mental health.

In this chapter we explore the complex relationships among mental illness, antisocial behavior, and violence. We discuss various forms of violence, with a particular emphasis on domestic violence and sexual violence. And we consider the causes and consequences of these behaviors and possible treatment options.

FEATURES OF ANTISOCIAL PERSONALITY DISORDER

Several concepts with overlapping meaning are discussed in this chapter: antisocial personality disorder, psychopathy, violence, and criminality.

Defining Antisocial Personality Disorder

Antisocial personality disorder (APD) is a sustained pattern of behaviors and traits reflecting disregard of social conventions and the rights of others. It is a DSM-IV category that is diagnosed on Axis II, according to the criteria listed in Table 14.1. The case of Erin, first mentioned at the beginning of the chapter, illustrates some of the essential features of a diagnosis of APD:

Erin's troubled behavior began at an early age. Her mother, a single woman supporting three children alone, found her hard to control and aggressive with her siblings. Her nursery school

Table 14.1 DSM-IV Criteria for Antisocial Personality Disorder (APD)

A. Current age at least eighteen years

B. Evidence of conduct disorder (see Chapter 15) with onset before age fifteen

C. A pervasive pattern of disregard for and violation of the rights of others occurring since age fifteen, as indicated by at least *three* of the following:
1. Failure to conform to social norms with respect to lawful behaviors, as indicated by repeated performance of acts that are grounds for arrest.
2. Irritability and aggressiveness, as indicated by repeated physical fights or assaults
3. Consistent irresponsibility, as indicated by repeated failure to sustain consistent work behavior or to honor financial obligations
4. Impulsivity or failure to plan ahead
5. Deceitfulness, as indicated by repeated lying, use of aliases, or conning others for personal profit or pleasure
6. Reckless disregard for the safety of self or others
7. Lack of remorse, as indicated by indifference to or rationalization of having hurt, mistreated, or stolen from another

D. Occurrence of antisocial behavior not exclusively during the course of schizophrenia or a manic episode

Source: DSM-IV. Reprinted with permission from *The Diagnostic and Statistical Manual of Mental Disorders,* Fourth Edition. Copyright © 1994 American Psychiatric Association.

The current criteria for APD, which were simplified somewhat from DSM-III-R, tend to emphasize overt behaviors, especially unlawful acts, rather than underlying traits as in psychopathy.

teachers complained that she was uncooperative, broke rules, rarely completed assignments, and generally stirred up trouble on the playground. As a preadolescent she hung out with older kids who were dropouts and got into trouble regularly; they introduced her to alcohol and drugs. By age 14, she had been suspended from school several times for misconduct and truancy, and was suspected of vandalism and shoplifting. She and her mother were constantly in conflict over her poor school performance, staying out late, disobedience, and drug use. She was regularly grounded, but sneaked out at night anyway. At age 15 she ran away from home, staying with friends. She got pregnant several times but decided not to terminate the pregnancy that occurred when she was 17, thinking that keeping the baby would be fun. With financial help from her mother and public assistance, she gave birth and tried to raise the child while working part-time at menial jobs requiring little education. She usually quit or got fired after a few weeks because she wouldn't keep regular hours. When broke, she'd appeal to her mother for funds, always promising that she'd go back to school and make something of herself. She was a poor parent — occasionally loving, but impatient and neglecting at other times. A day-care worker found bruises on the baby and reported Erin for suspected child abuse. The baby, now a toddler, is in foster care, and Erin at age twenty has gone off to another town with a new boyfriend. Her mother is emotionally drained, and her siblings bitterly resent the upheaval she has caused in the family.

A major feature of antisocial personality disorder is that it involves an enduring pattern of irresponsible and antisocial behaviors that is recognizable by adolescence or earlier. In fact, to warrant a diagnosis of APD, an individual has to meet criteria for childhood *conduct disorder,* which encompasses a variety of antisocial, aggressive, destructive, or truant behaviors (see Chapter 15). People with APD display personally and socially irresponsible behaviors, such as unstable work history, aggressive or assaultive behaviors toward others (including spouses or children), financial and parental irresponsibility, inability to sustain monogamous relationships, and unsafe or reckless behaviors. They also lie when it is advantageous to do so, have little regard for the welfare of others, and rarely express remorse for hurtful acts. Characteristically, however, such people are stunningly likely to deny their negative traits and instead describe themselves as "friendly, considerate, dependable, and capable" (Sutker, DeSanto & Allain, 1985).

The current diagnostic criteria for APD thus include both unlawful or antisocial behaviors and underlying traits that indicate callousness and lack of remorse. These underlying traits were long considered the identifying features of the related concept of *psychopathy,* similar to the earlier term *sociopathy,* from which the diagnosis of antisocial personality disorder evolved.

Psychopathy **Psychopathy** refers to a type of personality in which the prominent traits are selfishness, deceitfulness, and callousness. These traits can be — but are not always — reflected in illegal acts.

In a classic book called *The Mask of Sanity,* Cleckley (1941) described psychopathic persons as violators of norms and the rights of others, but also noted that because they are often intelligent and likeable, they can present a good front. They may seem poised, articulate, and calm; but, in fact, they are insincere and lie with ease to manipulate others and to serve their own needs. These qualities enable them to exploit others who are conned by their smoothness or taken in by their glib promises.

Antisocial personality disorder is marked by callous disregard for the rights of others and often involves commission of illegal acts. Amy Fisher, shown here leaving the Nassau County Courthouse, made headlines in 1992 as an 18-year-old, when she tried to murder the wife of her 36-year-old lover. The world was astonished at her seeming lack of concern about the seriousness of her actions.

Their social skills are developed far more than their consciences. They are enormously egocentric, unable to empathize with others, and feel no guilt or remorse over their callous or injurious behaviors toward others. Lack of foresight and an inability to inhibit impulses often contribute to their irresponsible, reckless behaviors. These traits, together with an inability to form deep attachments, make such individuals difficult spouses, poor parents, and untrustworthy business associates.

Some researchers have argued that the DSM diagnostic criteria of APD should be altered to include more of the traits of psychopathy. For example, Robert Hare, Stephen Hart, and Timothy Harpur (1991) pointed out that previous DSM criteria largely omitted such characteristics as selfishness, egocentricity, manipulativeness, and lack of empathy. The criteria they proposed for their concept of psychopathy, called *psychopathic personality disorder,* are shown in Table 14.2, which lists not only personality traits but also some of the behavioral indicators — as in the DSM — of irresponsible behavior. These characteristics were used in various DSM-IV field trials

No segment of society is immune from violence and antisocial personality disorder. Lyle and Erik Menendez were two sons of a wealthy Beverly Hills couple and raised with all the advantages of wealth. Yet they killed their parents with multiple shotgun blasts and then went to the movies. Later they staged an elaborate but apparently deceitful defense claiming child abuse and were eventually convicted of first-degree murder.

Table 14.2 Proposed Criteria for Psychopathic Personality Disorder

1. Glib and superficial
2. Inflated and arrogant self-appraisal
3. Lacks remorse
4. Lacks empathy
5. Deceitful and manipulative
6. Early behavior problems
7. Adult antisocial behavior
8. Impulsive
9. Poor behavioral controls
10. Irresponsible

Source: Hare, Hart & Harpur (1991).

These characteristics were used in DSM-IV field trials aimed at improving the criteria for antisocial personality disorder. They are based on the revised Psychopathy Checklist (Hare, 1990; Hare et al., 1990), an interview procedure that also draws on information from any other available source, such as criminal or case records. The first five characteristics pertain to a subscale referring to selfish, callous, and remorseless use of others, and the other five pertain to a chronically unstable and antisocial lifestyle (Hare, Hart & Harpur, 1991; Harpur, Hakstian & Hare, 1988).

aimed at improving the criteria for antisocial personality disorder (Widiger et al., 1996). As a result of the findings, psychopathy items were *not* added to the diagnostic criteria, in part because they are difficult to define reliably. Nevertheless, psychopathic personality traits are of interest to researchers because they help predict outcomes within prison populations, as we discuss further.

APD, Psychopathy, and Criminality **Criminality** is a legal rather than a mental health concept, referring to violations of the law owing to *any* cause — which can include social and political as well as psychological contributors. Because the criteria for diagnosing antisocial personality disorder emphasize overt violations of social rules, it is not surprising that APD and criminality considerably overlap. In fact, antisocial personality disorder is commonly found in criminal populations — at least among those who are caught, convicted, and serve time in penal institutions. Canadian researcher Robert Hare (1983) reported that 40 to 50 percent of prisoners met DSM criteria for antisocial personality disorder, and that in some Canadian prison populations the rate is as high as 75 percent (e.g., see Hare, Hart & Harpur, 1991).

Yet, despite the frequency of APD in prison populations, most people with APD are not criminals. As Table 14.3 shows, the most common symptoms observed in persons meeting criteria for antisocial personality disorder involve not serious legal violations but aggression, job problems, and promiscuity (Robins, 1986).

In addition, most criminals are not psychopaths, and most psychopaths are not criminals. As measured by the Psychopathy Checklist, psychopathy is thought to define a much narrower range of criminals in prison — perhaps 25 to 30 percent — than does APD (Hare, Hart & Harpur, 1991; Widiger et al., 1996). However, psychopathy may contribute to worse outcomes among those who do have criminal careers, reflecting their irresponsibility, impulsivity, and poor planning. Research has shown that among whites and African Americans, psychopathic prisoners spent more time in jail and, once released, stayed out of prison less successfully than did nonpsychopathic prisoners (Hare, Kropp & Hare, 1988; Hare, McPherson & Forth, 1988; Kosson, Smith & Newman, 1990).

The Relationship of Violence to APD and Psychopathy **Violence** — a term that refers to both lawful and unlawful acts of destruction — overlaps somewhat with the clinical concepts of antisocial personality disorder and psychopathy. As we see later in this chapter, much violence arises not from mental illness or psychological abnormality as such but, rather, from situational factors such as stress, conflict, or diminished self-control. And, indeed, in probing the various causes of violence we

Table 14.3 Twelve Common Symptoms of Antisocial Personality Disorder

	Persons Meeting DSM Antisocial Personality Criteria	Persons Not Diagnosed with Antisocial Personality
Fighting (more than once)	78%	10%
More than three jobs in five years	70%	22%
More than ten sex partners in one year	61%	7%
More than four moving traffic offenses	56%	14%
Deserted spouse if married	45%	10%
Infidelity: three or more partners	45%	9%
Arrested more than once	44%	2%
Late or absent from work three times per month	44%	7%
Illegal earnings	43%	2%
Quit job three or more times	40%	5%
Vagrant	36%	2%
Fought with weapon	33%	3%

Source: Robins (1986).

Based on epidemiological data collected in a multisite ECA study (Robins, 1986), these are the most common symptoms associated with antisocial personality disorder — compared with the frequency of the same behaviors in the normal population. These behaviors characterize the pattern of irresponsible conduct, even in situations in which the behaviors are not illegal.

have to face the possibility that, in contemporary society, violence is arguably normal.

WHAT'S NORMAL?

Violence in U.S. Society

Despite public statements abhorring violence, U.S. culture tolerates, glorifies, and otherwise legitimizes violence to the degree that it has become a "normal" part of our society. Compared with other industrialized countries, the United States has a higher rate of violent crime and a greater proportion of people in jail. There were 1,281 murders in all of Japan in 1995, but that many occurred in New York City alone. People in the United States have and use more guns. And our films and television programs, which we export globally, feature a degree of violence that shocks people in other parts of the world.

Particularly among young people in the United States, violence is an everyday experience. Exposure to media violence, participating in violence as a means to resolve conflicts, witnessing violence, or being the victim of violence — even violent death — are among the ways that American youths can be exposed to violence. Led by homicide rates that are between 4 and 73 times higher than in any other industrialized nation in the world (Fingerhut & Kleinman, 1990), young American men die from violent causes such as homicide, motor vehicle accident, and suicide at the rate of more than 70 per

100,000 (Rockett & Smith, 1989). African Americans have higher rates of homicide death, and whites have higher rates of accidents and suicide. Among young people with histories of delinquency possibly reflecting conduct disorder or antisocial personality disorder, violent deaths are especially high and apparently on the rise. A seven-year follow-up of incarcerated delinquent youth found that many had died by homicide, drug overdose, suicide, or motor vehicle accidents: They exhibited 76 times the national rate of violent death for fifteen- to twenty-four-year-olds (Yeager & Lewis, 1990).

For certain youth, exposure to violence as a victim or witness is also common. A broad national survey of youngsters aged ten to sixteen found that more than one-third had been victims of assault (Boney-McCoy & Finkelhor, 1995). And children in inner-city neighborhoods are highly likely to witness murder and serious assault (reviewed in Osofsky, 1995). Daily exposure to violence in films and on television is another way that children of all backgrounds experience violence; later in the chapter we discuss the impact of this form of exposure to violence.

There is ample evidence that violence is a "normal" method of dealing with interpersonal conflict in the United States. Figure 14.1, which summarizes the frequency of physical fights among high school students, indicates that one in eight males and one in twenty-five females (especially African American and Hispanic youth) had been in a fight within the previous thirty days. Obviously, physical fights not only cause injuries

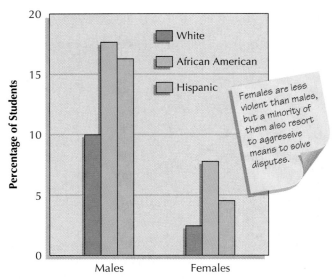

Figure 14.1 Incidence of Physical Fighting Among High School Students

A survey of nearly 12,000 representative students in all fifty states of the United States in grades nine through twelve asked whether *in the last thirty days* students had been in a physical fight in which they or the other person was injured and had to be treated by a doctor or nurse. These figures indicate that a substantial proportion of the youth, especially non-white males, resorted to violent means of resolving disputes, suggesting that violence is an accepted part of everyday life for many people.

Source: Centers for Disease Control (1992).

but can even lead to death, especially given the increasing number of firearms at schools across the United States. Although such fighting occurs only among a minority of students, its frequency is nonetheless remarkable.

Figure 14.1 suggests a high degree of acceptance of solving interpersonal disputes by violent means. And such behavior patterns are not limited to youth. Research analyses have suggested that some segments of the population are more likely than others to condone the use of violence in resolving interpersonal conflicts. Social psychologist Richard Nisbett (1993) provided data to support the hypothesis that, due to regional differences in values in the United States, southerners (and westerners in states initially settled by southerners such as Arizona) condone violence more than northerners do. Specifically using analyses based only on white males, Nesbitt found higher rates of argument-related homicides in the South, particularly in rural and small-city areas. Further, although southern men do not endorse violence in surveys when asked in general terms, they are significantly more likely than nonsoutherners to endorse violence in situations involving protection of self, family, and property; in response to insults; and as a child-discipline technique. Nisbett also demonstrated in a labora-

tory experiment with college students at a midwestern university that white males from southern states showed more anger in a staged "insult" situation than did students from nonsouthern states. Nisbett argued that the attitudes of some southern males are consistent with a long-standing regional emphasis on male honor and masculine courage. Certainly these points of view are shared by many in the United States and are hardly limited to those of southern backgrounds.

Overall, these research findings indicate not only extensive exposure to violence but also permissive attitudes toward the use of violence that may normalize it, thereby creating a powerful social context contributing to the further experience of violence.

Mental Illness, Violence, and Criminality As we have noted, a sizable proportion of prisoners meet diagnostic criteria for APD or psychopathy. But what about other forms of disorder? In the recent past, bolstered both by research and the desire to avoid further stigmatizing sufferers of mental illness, the assertion was often made that these concepts are separate: that the mentally ill are not particularly violent or apt to commit crimes, and that crime and violence are not related to mental illness. Recent research, however, supports a different point of view that brings these concepts closer together.

Several studies have shown that people diagnosed with major mental disorders commit more crimes — and more violent acts — than those without such diagnoses. For example, a study of Swedish citizens who were followed from birth to age thirty found that men with a major mental disorder (primarily schizophrenia or mood disorder) were two and a half times more likely to have been convicted of a criminal offense than men without disorders. Among women, the risk was five times higher for those with a major mental disorder. With respect to *violent* offenses, the rates were four times higher for men and twenty-seven times higher for women with major disorders (Hodgins, 1992). Moreover, when researchers in Denmark studied the records of people who had been hospitalized for treatment of mental disorder (Hodgins et al., 1996), they found that among those with major mental disorders the rate of committing at least one crime was three to four times higher than that among those with no mental disorder. The rates of violent crimes were even higher among those with major mental disorders.

Other research has examined the diagnoses of people convicted of crimes. For example, a study in Finland found that rates of schizophrenia and antisocial personality disorder were substantially higher among homicide offenders than in the general population (Eronen, Hakola, & Tiihonen, 1996). And in a related study, Eronen (1995) determined that rates of schizophrenia or personality disorder were ten times higher among female murderers than in the general population. It might be

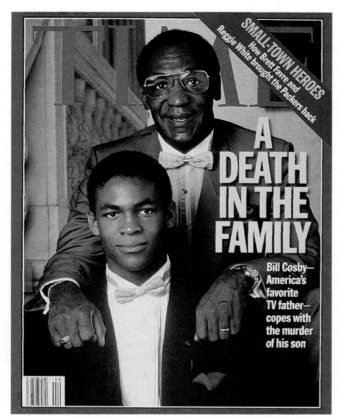

Violence is part of the American way. Our country exceeds all other industrialized nations in number of murders and other acts of violence perpetrated by firearms. No family is immune, and no segment of society is unaffected by violence. Recently, TV personality Bill Cosby and his wife experienced the death of their son—who was gunned down in an apparent random robbery when he stopped on the side of the freeway at night to change a flat tire.

noted that this and other studies also found that the highest rates of criminality and violent conduct were associated with alcohol and drug use disorders (Eronen, 1995; Hodgins et al., 1966). U.S. studies, too, have shown that people in prison have high rates of diagnoses for mental disorders, especially substance use disorders but including psychoses, depressive disorders, and post-traumatic stress disorders as well (e.g., Teplin, Abram & McClelland, 1996; Jordan, Schlenger, Fairbank & Caddell, 1996).

It is important that correct conclusions be drawn from these studies. The majority of persons with mental disorders do not commit crimes or violent acts. Mental illness is only a small contributor to the total causes of crime and violence. And it is probably more of a factor in homogeneous, relatively affluent Scandanavian countries than in the United States, where living conditions are extremely diverse and crime statistics are highly influenced by drug and gang activity. Nevertheless, the studies showing links among crime,

violence, and mental illness remind us, at the very least, that effective treatment of mental disorders might play an important role in reducing the costs of disorder not just to the individual but to society as a whole.

Who Is Affected with Antisocial Personality Disorder?

Antisocial personality disorder is among the most frequent of the personality disorders, affecting about 3.5 percent of the population (Kessler et al., 1994). It is primarily a disorder of young, low-income, poorly educated males.

Gender Differences in APD Virtually every survey of antisocial personality disorder has found it to be considerably more frequent in men than in women — as much as five or six times more so (Kessler et al., 1994; Robins et al., 1984). Deviant behaviors also apparently begin earlier in males than in females. Even at the preschool level, boys engage in disruptive behaviors that predict antisocial behaviors years later (e.g., Tremblay, Pihl, Vitaro & Dobkin, 1994). In contrast, girls who later develop adult antisocial personality disorder are often not seen as having problems until adolescence.

There also appear to be gender differences in patterns of symptoms. Robins (1986) found that among women the most common antisocial symptoms are marital desertion, spouse hitting, and employment difficulties, whereas among men the most common antisocial symptoms are numerous traffic citations (moving violations), more than one arrest, sexual promiscuity, and illegal occupations.

These gender differences in rates of antisocial personality disorder might in part reflect the bias inherent in cultural stereotypes that discourage thinking of women as antisocial, destructive, or insensitive to others. Recall from Chapter 1 our description of a study in which clinicians rating descriptive vignettes were biased against diagnosing antisocial personality disorder among women (Ford & Widiger, 1989). In short, the diagnosis of APD in women possibly does not reflect its actual frequency. As we discuss later, however, various biological and environmental factors contribute substantially to actual gender patterns of APD occurrence.

Cultural and Ethnic Differences in APD Cross-cultural comparisons of APD are difficult because of a lack of comparable diagnostic criteria. However, as noted earlier, by most measures the United States is one of the most violent nations on earth and has a higher proportion of people in prison than any other industrialized country. Even within the United States there are great sociocultural variations in the incidence of both APD and criminal conduct — ranging from a rate of virtually zero in the rural religious communities to relatively high rates in urban, inner-city areas.

Crime, violence, and APD are all highly correlated with poverty (e.g., Robins et al., 1984; Hill, Soriano, Chen & LaFromboise, 1994). High rates of criminality and violence have been reported among African American and Hispanic males, and these patterns are strongly correlated with economic and social disadvantage. With respect to diagnoses, however, the rates of APD in groups with similar socioeconomic backgrounds were about the same among African Americans and whites (Kessler et al., 1994), and somewhat higher among Hispanics than among non-Hispanic whites (Karno et al., 1987; Kessler et al., 1994).

As also noted earlier, recent dramatic increases in violence among young people, including homicide, suicide, and assault, have drawn considerable publicity. Homicide rates have sky-rocketed among African American males in particular (e.g., Rockett & Smith, 1989), and nonwhite teenagers, especially males, exhibit high rates of physical fighting (as shown in Figure 14.1). Therefore, we need to ask ourselves what specific factors are promoting increased antisocial conduct and violent behavior in certain segments of our society. Although we consider the broad question of causality later in the chapter, Table 14.4 can be consulted now for some statistics that show a link between violence and the availability of guns.

The Development and Course of Antisocial Personality Disorder

Adult antisocial personality disorder begins in childhood. While not all childhood misconduct leads invariably to adult APD, many antisocial children go on to show stable patterns of deviant behavior. Accordingly, the DSM diagnosis of antisocial personality disorder is reserved for those with evidence of childhood conduct disorder. Chapter 15 provides detailed information on conduct disorder, a pattern of behavior problems reflecting disregard for social rules and lack of respect for the rights of others. It also provides information essential to understanding the childhood development of APD.

The Course of Childhood Deviance Problems that start in childhood tend to continue. A case in point is early antisocial and aggressive behavior, which is found to be associated with continuing conduct problems (Loeber, 1990). Beginning in the preschool years, children (especially boys) who show behavior problems tend to "diversify" their antisocial conduct and to be at increasing risk for delinquent and aggressive behavior. The longer the pattern persists, the less likely these youngsters are to "outgrow" their deviant behaviors. A typical pattern might start with truancy, school failure,

and lying; continue with stealing and discipline problems; and later include drinking problems followed by arrests, expulsion from school, and drug use (Robins, 1986). A study of young boys aged seven to twelve who were diagnosed with conduct disorder found that 88 percent met criteria for the disorder at least once over the next four years (Lahey et al., 1995).

Which children with conduct problems are likely to develop antisocial personality disorder? By definition, all individuals with adult APD had preceding childhood conduct disorder. But among children with conduct disorder, only about 40 percent of males and 24 percent of females will be diagnosed with adult antisocial personality disorder (Robins, 1986). Only about one-half of children with conduct problems become adolescent delinquents, and approximately 50 to 75 percent of adolescent delinquents go on to be adult offenders (reviewed in Patterson, DeBaryshe & Ramsey, 1989). What factors separate those who have good outcomes from those who continue deviant patterns? Several follow-up studies have indicated that children end up better adjusted if they come from higher socioeconomic status, have parents who are not themselves disturbed, have higher intellectual abilities, and are less aggressive (Lahey et al., 1995; Loeber, 1990; Robins, 1966).

Recent research also suggests that poor impulse control and childhood hyperactivity contribute to an elevated risk for adult antisocial behaviors (e.g., Tremblay, Pihl, Vitaro & Dobkin, 1994). **Poor impulse control** refers to difficulty in delaying or suppressing an immediate urge or response when a careful or controlled response might produce more desirable or appropriate results. When conduct disorder and attention deficit hyperactivity disorder (discussed in Chapter 15) co-occur in childhood, there is increased risk for criminal behavior in adulthood (Lilienfeld & Waldman, 1990; Mannuzza, Klein, Konig & Giampino, 1989, 1993; Mannuzza et al., 1993). One explanation is that because children with attention deficit hyperactivity disorder have difficulty sustaining attention and inhibiting their disruptiveness, they also have school and peer problems. As a result, their frustration increases and their opportunities to learn positive, adaptive behaviors diminish.

The Stability of Aggression Childhood aggressiveness is a strong predictor of adolescent and adult aggressiveness and antisocial conduct. Aggressive behavior patterns rarely emerge for the first time in late childhood or adolescence. Summarizing the research on the relation between violent conduct and childhood aggressiveness, Loeber (1990) concluded that 70 percent to 90 percent of violent offenders had been highly aggressive when young, and that boys who display early childhood patterns of aggressiveness, poor academic ability, and poor social skills and peer relationships have particularly negative futures.

Table 14.4   Some Facts About Guns and Violence

1. **Firearms are highly associated with homicides and suicides.** In the United States the death rate from firearms is about 60 percent of the total, and among teenagers the rate is even higher (O'Donnell, 1995). There has been a huge increase in homicide deaths (for example, firearm homicides increased 61 percent between 1979 and 1989 for persons aged 15 to 19), and African American male teens have had the highest rates and increases (Fingerhut, Ingram & Feldmen, 1992).

2. **There is a statistical association between gun availability and death.**
   - Analyses of seventeen nations show that a higher rate of gun ownership is associated with more *accidental* firearm deaths (Lester, 1993).
   - In studies of fourteen countries, frequency of gun ownership is related to higher rates of *suicide* and *homicide* (Killias, 1993; Lester, 1993).
   - Since statistical associations do not prove that one causes the other, additional research studies have attempted to determine the direction of the causality. For example, Carrington and Moyer (1994) showed that both gun-related and total suicides decreased in Ontario, Canada, after passage of gun-control laws.
   - When Kellerman and associates (1993) studied homicide deaths *occurring in homes,* they found that such deaths were nearly three times more likely if a gun was kept in the home; the victims' homes also were more likely to contain drug users and histories of physical fights. The authors concluded that in such "high-risk" households, guns were associated not with protection but with increased likelihood of being killed by a family member or intimate associate.

3. **Kids have guns.**
   - Half of all U.S. households have guns, and youngsters report that they have no trouble getting one if they want one.
   - A national survey of high school students found that 4.1 percent of all students and 21.4 percent of African American male students had carried a gun in the past month (Centers for Disease Control, 1991).
   - A survey of junior high kids in New York City (predominately Hispanic youth) found that 21 percent of the total — especially older boys — reported carrying guns or weapons (Vaughan et al., 1996).
   - Access to guns is not limited to inner-city kids. High rates of gun possession have also been found among suburban youth. Although these juveniles often reported that they carried guns for "protection," the variables most linked to gun ownership were involvement in drug and illegal activities, and being male (Sheley & Brewer, 1995; Sheley & Wright, 1993; see also Webster, Gainer & Champion, 1993).

4. **Availability of a firearm increases the risk that guns will be used impulsively under high-risk conditions.** Psychologists speculate that while the vast majority of gun owners are careful and law-abiding citizens, high-risk conditions include alcohol and drug use, anger and intense emotion, poor impulse control, need to impress others, poor reasoning and planning — conditions that may be especially pronounced among male juveniles (e.g., Kellerman et al., 1993; Saltzman, Mercy, O'Carroll, Rosenberg & Rhodes, 1992).

A study by Rowell Huesmann and his colleagues (1984) provided a unique glimpse into the stability of aggression over a 22-year period. Nearly 900 third-graders were evaluated and then retested when they were about thirty years old, using ratings of aggressiveness by peers, parent interviews, and, later, self- and spouse-reports and records of criminal offenses. The researchers found significant correlations between aggression at age eight and aggression in adulthood — particularly among the males. Those most aggressive as boys were likely to have more criminal convictions and drunk driving and traffic violations, and to be more punitive toward their own children. A Swedish study of aggressiveness in 1,000 ten-year-olds drew similar conclusions when their criminal records were reviewed at age twenty-six (Stattin & Magnusson, 1989). Half of all

Ted Bundy in the 1980s was described as a classic psychopath—cunning, charming, callous, and in his case, deadly. He was convicted of multiple murders of young women. Lawrence Singleton, in 1997, was a different kind of killer—not charming but brutal and

sadistic. After serving in prison for chopping off the arms of a teenage hitchhiker he had raped (crimes he always denied), he viciously stabbed to death a woman who apparently had tried to befriend him.

the "high-aggressive" boys went on to commit *serious* crimes, including most of the violent crimes committed by the entire group. A similar pattern occurred among the most aggressive girls, but their rates of crime were considerably lower than those for the males.

Adult Patterns of APD   The highest rates of antisocial personality disorder are diagnosed in the adult years between ages twenty-five and forty-four. Then, around middle age, improvement appears to occur, as if the individual has "mellowed." A well-controlled follow-up study of criminal psychopaths by Hare, McPherson, and Forth (1988) found that the rate of conviction declined sharply after age forty, although the majority still had criminal careers. In a comparison group of criminals who were not psychopaths, the rates of conviction were relatively stable over their lifetimes. Hare and associates speculated that the psychopathic criminals might have finally learned the skills needed to remain out of prison, or finally decided that their lives needed to change.

Despite this positive trend, however, some people with antisocial personality disorder do not live long enough to "mellow." Among those with APD and conduct disorder, there is a high rate of early death from sui-cide, homicide, accidents, and complications associated with drug and alcohol use.

CAUSES OF ANTISOCIAL PERSONALITY AND VIOLENT CONDUCT

A discussion of the research on causes of antisocial personality disorder is complicated by the variety of definitions that investigators have used to characterize study samples; such definitions include factors as diverse as criminal records, antisocial behaviors, violent offenses, and histories of serious or less serious crimes. Since violence and criminality refer to an enormous range of behaviors, efforts have also been made to study traits that might underlie acts, involving impulsiveness, aggression, lack of inhibition, and similar traits. Relatively little of the research on causal factors has focused on those who meet DSM criteria for antisocial personality disorder as such. Bear in mind, therefore, that few of the studies in this area are about exactly the same groups.

Biological Perspectives

Over the centuries there has been a pronounced interest in the "criminal mind" or other biological causes of heinous behavior. In modern times, the pendulum has swung in the direction of the search for social and environmental causes — and as we shall see, there is ample evidence of the influence of family dysfunction and adverse social conditions. However, in just the past few years a renewed interest in biological factors has emerged — with both provocative and controversial consequences. In the sections that follow, we review several themes: genetics, neurochemical abnormalities, neuropsychological dysfunction, and psychophysiological arousal.

Genetics: Is There a Bad Seed?   Research on twins has suggested a higher similarity of antisocial traits and criminal behaviors between male monozygotic (identical) twins (average 51.5 percent) than between dizygotic (fraternal) twins (23.1 percent) (reviewed in Gottesman & Goldsmith, 1994). In addition, a recent large-scale twin study of men found greater evidence of heritability for antisocial traits during adulthood than for antisocial traits during adolescence — a period that is heavily influenced by family and environmental factors as well as by genetic factors (Lyons et al., 1995). Among the twin pairs at either age, however, genetic influences were less important predictors of antisocial conduct than were environmental factors outside the family (such as friends and life events and circumstances).

Because of the obvious confounding of nature and nurture in twin research, researchers often turn to adoption studies as an informative method for separating possible genetic and environmental influences. Large-scale Danish and Swedish adoption studies (Bohman, Cloninger, Sigvardsson & von Knorring, 1982; Mednick, Gabrielli, & Hutchings, 1984) found support for genetic influences, in that rates of criminality among adoptees were more similar to those of the biological parents than to those of the adoptive parents. Moreover, a recent adoption study conducted in Iowa specifically examined the combined influence of biology and environment, testing the hypothesis that the combination of adverse home environment (such as marital discord or adoptive parent substance abuse) and having a biological parent with antisocial personality disorder or substance abuse would predict higher rates of adoptee aggressivity and conduct disorder (Cadoret et al., 1995). As expected, there was a significant interaction between the two factors, suggesting that adverse family conditions are associated with antisocial traits and behaviors only when the adoptee had a genetic vulnerability due to biological parents' antisocial personality. Together, the

twin and adoption studies support the hypothesis that there is modest genetic contribution to predisposition for some forms of antisocial conduct. Yet these studies make clear that environmental factors are extremely important as well.

Geneticists have also been intrigued by the discovery of large families with high rates of violent behavior and borderline mental retardation among male members in several generations. The patterns of occurrence of these problems might reflect psychological factors, but another hypothesis suggests possible genetic transmission on the X-chromosome. A team of investigators from the Netherlands (Brunner et al., 1993) recently studied one such family with excessive incidence of male violence — including rape, arson, and other forms of impulsive aggressiveness. They identified a genetic defect. Their results may help provide the link that has been missing in efforts to determine what kind of genetic problem may be transmitted, as we discuss in the following section.

Neurochemical Abnormalities and APD   A growing body of research shows an association between monoamine neurotransmitter functioning — especially *serotonin* — and impulsive, aggressive behavior. Research from a variety of sources has begun to converge on at least one biological feature of violence.

FOCUS ON RESEARCH

Is a Brain Chemical Responsible for Violence?

Methodological improvements over the last twenty years have facilitated the study of associations between neurotransmitters and psychological disorders in both human beings and animals, as we indicate in several chapters. Typically, this initial research was not guided by hypotheses based on specific models — simply because so little was known about the role of neurotransmitters in the control of normal behavior. Nevertheless, interesting patterns sometimes emerged from various descriptive, exploratory studies.

Such was the case in a study on behavior characterized as impulsive and aggressive. In 1976 investigators published their observation of a significant association between violent suicide attempts in unipolar patients and low levels of serotonin (Asberg, Traskman & Thoren, 1976; see also Coccaro et al., 1989; Roy, De Jong & Linnoila, 1989). Serotonin is measured by the level of its metabolite, 5-hydroxyindoleacetic acid (5-HIAA), in cerebrospinal fluid. Attempting to determine whether outward-directed aggression (as well as self-directed aggression, as in suicide attempts) was also related to low serotonin activity, researchers found that low serotonin indicators predicted later discharge of certain Marines as unfit because of excessive violence and antisocial behavior (Brown et al., 1982). Moreover, a series of studies on violent offenders, conducted in Finland by Matti Virkkunen and his colleagues, has consistently shown that those who committed impulsive violence (sudden, unpremeditated actions directed toward a relative stranger with no economic motivation) had significantly lower levels of serotonin activity than violent criminals whose behaviors were planned and calculated (Virkkunen, Nuutila, Goodwin & Linnoila, 1987; Virkkunen et al., 1994). The investigators further reasoned that if impulsiveness is particularly associated with low serotonin, then those with lowest levels of serotonin would be most likely to get into trouble again after being released from prison. In two samples they did find that recidivism — repeat offending — was significantly higher in those who originally tested low on serotonin metabolite level (Virkkunen et al., 1989; Virkkunen, Eggert, Rawlings & Linnoila, 1996). In the latter study, higher rates of new violent crimes occurred in the group characterized by both low 5-HIAA and paternal absence during childhood due to divorce. It should be noted that the majority of the Finnish criminals studied by Virkkunen were alcoholics, and that virtually all of the

Researchers have found that nonhuman primates offer an opportunity to learn about some aspects of human behavior. This researcher is collecting data on behavioral patterns in monkeys living in a natural habitat—methods used by Higley and his colleagues in studying aggression.

repeat violent offenders were under the influence of alcohol when committing their crimes — a factor that possibly exacerbated problems with controlling their impulses.

A further research question is whether such low serotonin patterns might generalize to nonprison samples. Child and adolescent inpatients in treatment for various *disruptive behavior disorders* (behavioral excesses and poorly controlled behaviors that are bothersome to others, as described in Chapter 15) were tested for serotonin metabolite level and other physiological markers. All the patients showed impulsive and aggressive behaviors. The outcomes of the youngsters during a two-year follow-up indicated that low serotonin significantly predicted later severity of physical aggression (Kruesi et al., 1992).

One limitation of all the serotonin research on human beings was neglect of psychological factors that might play a role in aggression. Among such variables are socioeconomic status, race, and IQ scores. Another limitation of the research was that it focused on quite heterogeneous groups in terms of antisocial behaviors and traits. Accordingly, investigators at the National Institutes of Health turned to naturalistic investigations of rhesus monkeys, nonhuman primates who show similarities to human beings in certain aspects of neurotransmitter functioning (Higley et al., 1992). Although the obvious disadvantage of primate research is its limited generalizability to human beings, the advantages are that the animals are presumed to be homogeneous in their environmental experiences and that they have some of the same complex social systems and motivations that human beings do. Also, they can be closely observed in their natural habitats.

Wild monkeys being raised in a monkey colony where they roamed freely were observed for evidence of extreme aggressive behaviors or avoidance of aggressive behaviors. Samples of highly aggressive, nonaggressive, and "normal" comparison monkeys were captured, examined, and tested for several neurochemical levels. The investigators also made aggressiveness ratings of each animal based on observations in the wild as well as on patterns of scars and wounds on the animal's body. The results indicated that aggressiveness ratings correlated significantly with low serotonin metabolite level — just as with human beings (Higley et al., 1992). In a later observation study of adolescent male monkeys, low serotonin measured three months earlier was found to be associated with two behaviors: violent forms of aggression toward other monkeys, and loss of impulse control as indicated by highly risky long leaps through the trees (Mehlman et al., 1994). Over a four-year period, the rate of death was significantly higher among those juvenile monkeys who had earlier tested with low serotonin metabolite levels (Higley et al., 1996), as indicated in Figure 14.2. The investigators suggested that these monkeys died prematurely because of excessive

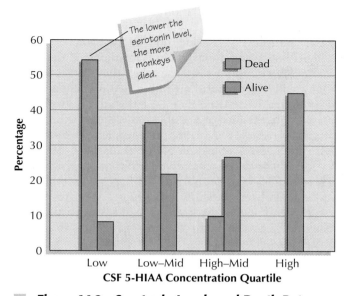

Figure 14.2   Serotonin Levels and Death Rates

Rates of death among juvenile male rhesus monkeys due to fighting or risk-taking over a four-year period were significantly higher for those who had tested with low serotonin.

Source: Higley et al. (1996).

aggression and/or risk-taking behaviors. Perhaps future studies of monkeys will be able to test specific theories about interactions between biological predisposition to aggression or risk-taking and social-environmental conditions. (Is it possible, for instance, that "high-risk" monkeys raised with highly nurturant mothers may be less aggressive than those raised with less nurturant mothers?) Obviously, such manipulations are not ethically possible with human beings, but in animal studies they are invaluable scientific methods for testing causal hypotheses.

Finally, genetic abnormalities concerning serotonin may be linked to some forms of violence. The Brunner group (1993) in the Netherlands, who studied the family with violent males mentioned earlier, determined through an intricate series of lab studies that all the affected males had a genetic defect that causes complete deficiency of an enzyme known as monoamine oxidase-A. Because serotonin is a monoamine, low concentrations of the serotonin metabolite 5-HIAA may suggest that the predictor of impulsive aggressiveness is deficient metabolism of serotonin.

Why deficient serotonin is associated with impulsive aggressiveness remains unknown. We might presume that it is related to functioning of the frontal cortex of the brain, which affects self-control and judgment, as well as other areas of the brain relevant to the integration of emotional and behavioral information. Nevertheless, this important piece of the puzzle is missing.

The exploration of serotonin's role continues. Studies testing the serotonin hypothesis are examples of

research with social implications so powerful that we run the risk of thinking we know more than we actually do. Defective serotonin functioning is obviously far too simplistic an explanation for certain antisocial aggression. The major question, therefore, is what do all these biological results mean? Do they imply that impulsive violence is basically due to faulty biology? Do they reflect a cause, merely a marker of proneness to violence, or something else? And if they do reflect such a marker, what psychological and social factors affect the way this vulnerability is expressed? We cannot ignore the extensive evidence of social and psychological factors associated with aggressive, violent antisocial conduct. Careful research — and reasoned interpretation — must continue.

Among other neurochemical abnormalities, animal studies indicate a clear link between aggressiveness and the male hormone **testosterone** in males of the species. Human studies have proven to be somewhat inconsistent, with results depending on when testosterone is measured, what samples are studied, and what kinds of behaviors it is used to predict (reviewed in DiLalla & Gottesman, 1991). Nevertheless, when aggression is measured behaviorally, as in the context of violent criminal conduct, the results consistently show that higher testosterone is found in more violent or violent-impulsive men (Raine, 1993; Virkkunnen et al., 1994).

Deficiencies in Emotional Arousal   Investigators have speculated that normal people inhibit dangerous or unlawful behavior out of fear of getting into trouble or of evoking negative reactions from others. It may follow, therefore, that persons with APD and conduct disorder do not experience the same emotional states that inhibit negative behavior. Perhaps they have underlying **deficient emotional arousal,** characterized by low levels or an absence of physical reactions to fearful or aversive conditions.

Having examined psychophysiological arousal such as heart rate, electrodermal (sweat gland) activity, and respiration rate, early researchers concluded that psychopaths are less physiologically reactive to negative stimuli or anticipation of aversive stimlui and show much slower rates of conditioning than normal people (reviewed in Harpur & Hare, 1990). Not all investigations were consistent in their findings, however. Also, some of the earlier studies were limited by exclusive use of institutionalized prisoners, lack of appropriate control groups, and absence of controls for the effects of stress on psychophysiological arousal.

In view of these limitations, a study by Adrian Raine, Peter Venables, and Mark Williams (1990) is of interest. They took recordings of heart rate, skin conductance, and electroencephalographic activity in 101 male fifteen-year-olds in England. Nine years later they searched criminal records for all of these subjects. As it turned out, seventeen of the young men had become involved in criminal activity. Comparing their earlier physiological scores with those of subjects who did not have criminal records, the researchers found that the men with adult criminal records had significantly lower arousal on all of the measures. More recently, Raine, Venables, and Williams (1995) compared these seventeen adult criminals with seventeen from the same sample who had early histories of antisocial behavior (according to teacher- and self-reports) but did not develop criminal histories. They found that those who "desisted" from a criminal path had significantly higher arousal levels than those who went on to develop adult criminal careers. In addition, Raine (1993) has argued that psychophysiological activity may be mediated by serotonin and other neurotransmitters, thus possibly providing a link between findings of low serotonin activity and low physiological arousal reported in studies of antisocial conduct.

Other researchers have speculated that the link between underarousal and antisocial behaviors might instead be related to **sensation-seeking,** the desire for exciting, stimulating, or even dangerous experiences. Given their state of underarousal, psychopaths may actually seek excitement, engage in impulsive acts, and show intolerance for routine and boredom (see Hare, 1968; Quay, 1965). Experiments have demonstrated that psychopaths and normal persons do differ in their responses to monotonous tasks, tests of preferences for novelty, and the like. Furthermore, studies have shown that high scores on a scale of preference for sensation-seeking behaviors (Zuckerman, 1972, 1978) are associated with various kinds of antisocial conduct. Whether such tendencies have a constitutional basis, however, is unknown.

Learning and Neurocognitive Deficits In trying to account for the apparent failure of psychopaths to learn from experience (avoid punishment), psychologists have studied not only reduced physiological arousal but also learning patterns. A classic study by Lykken (1957) showed that, although psychopaths performed as well as controls in a laboratory task when the correct answers were rewarded, they had difficulty learning a laboratory task when the wrong answers were punished with electric shock. In short, they exhibited **deficient avoidance learning,** impaired learning when wrong answers were punished. Consistent with the theory of deficient emotional arousal, Lykken's interpretation was that psychopaths are not anxious and, therefore, do not respond to fear-arousing learning situations.

A series of subsequent investigations has qualified and clarified this idea of deficient avoidance learning,

with the further speculation that the failure of psychopaths to inhibit unlawful behavior or to learn to avoid punishment is due not to emotional arousal deficits but to cognitive deficits. One theory is that normal people inhibit a response when they detect signals that it will lead to punishment, but that psychopaths are *disinhibited* — that is, they lack this ability to inhibit response in the face of possible punishment. Numerous laboratory studies involving prisoners as well as people with high levels of psychopathic traits have explored various aspects of cognitive information-processing. These studies lend support to the hypothesis that such individuals have difficulty inhibiting certain responses even when they are incorrect or lead to negative consequences (e.g., Newman & Kosson, 1986; Newman, Patterson & Kosson, 1987; Howland, Kosson, Patterson & Newman, 1993).

As experimental paradigms increasingly move away from motivational or emotional explanations for psychopathic behaviors, and toward cognitive models emphasizing deficiencies in information processing, they overlap with models that emphasize **neurocognitive dysfunction,** or impaired brain functioning that causes cognitive deficits. Unfortunately, there are many sources of potential damage to the brains of developing fetuses and infants: poor maternal prenatal care, exposure to alcohol or drugs, neurotoxic substances such as the metal lead, not to mention injuries and genetic factors. Antisocial conduct and violent behavior would appear to involve inability to plan, reason, evaluate consequences, show good judgment, and inhibit or restrain inappropriate impulses — all considered "executive" functions of the brain, particularly the frontal cortex. As noted, many studies have found an association between low intellectual performance (IQ) and antisocial behavior (e.g., Moffitt, 1993). A more recent example is provided by a Canadian study of aggressive boys that found further support for the association of antisocial activities and deficient neurocognitive functioning (Seguin et al., 1995). The investigators studied boys over time from ages six to twelve, identifying those who were stably aggressive at various evaluation points and comparing their functioning on neurocognitive tests of executive processes to those of boys who were not aggressive or were only sometimes aggressive. As predicted, the stably aggressive boys exhibited significant deficits in tests of executive (frontal lobe) functioning compared to the other groups, even when the effects of socioeconomic status and parental education were controlled. The authors speculated that boys with a combination of aggressive patterns and deficits in executive cognitive functioning are at great risk for continuing antisocial behavior (see also Moffitt, Lynam & Silva, 1994).

Adrian Raine and his colleagues have made a strong case for the influence of nonspecific neurological problems — namely, such critical problems as birth defects and pregnancy complications. In a large sample of Danish eighteen-year-olds, they found that the combination of birth complications and maternal rejection (as when the pregnancy was unwanted or the mother gave the child up for adoption or care by others) strongly predicted violent criminality (Raine, Brennan & Mednick, 1994). Subsequently, Raine and associates (1995) reviewed neurological and obstetric data, collected at birth and after one year, on a random subsample of the original group. According to their results, those subjects who had *both* neuromotor deficits in infancy and poverty/family instability accounted for 70 percent of all the crimes committed by the total group; those with only one of the risk factors (neuromotor or social) exhibited significantly less criminal conduct. The authors drew a conclusion that is very appropriate for this entire review of biological factors: The combination or interaction of biological and psychological factors — that is, a *biosocial model* — is probably the best model for understanding antisocial conduct and violent behavior. We turn now to a discussion of the psychological factors considered to be important contributors.

Cognitive Social Learning Perspectives on Antisocial Personality Disorder and Violence

Early Freudian theorists believed that aggression is a universal drive in human beings, requiring suppression and regulation through the mechanisms of ego and superego. Defects in the superego, for example, were alleged to account for poor control of aggression and failure to conform to social rules. Instead of focusing on aggressive instincts and ego controls, most modern psychological theorists emphasize the role of learning and cognition in understanding antisocial behavior and aggression. Also unlike adherents of Freud's approach, modern theorists heavily emphasize the importance of the *external* environment. As recent studies have shown, poverty, stress, and other forms of social adversity greatly increase the likelihood of antisocial conduct and violence (e.g., Guerra et al., 1995).

More specifically, *social learning theorists* argue that children acquire both behavioral tendencies and cognitive schemas through experience — that is, through learning. These tendencies and schemas may be either appropriate or inappropriate. Cultural, familial, and environmental experiences provide models and reinforcement contingencies for learning. For example, a child learns to be aggressive to the extent that the environment provides aggressive role models, reinforces aggressive conduct, and instigates aggression through frustration and provocation. Most social learning theorists believe that the origins of antisocial conduct and aggressiveness are multidetermined, stemming from a host of both biological and psychological factors. A more complete description of the origins of childhood conduct disorder and aggressiveness is presented in Chapter 15. For now, however, we briefly review evidence of the impact of family, cognitive, and role modeling experiences.

The Family Environment One of the most extensively studied areas of risk for antisocial conduct concerns the family environment. From a social learning perspective, this is the primary milieu in which learned attitudes and behavior patterns are acquired. As we review in Chapter 15 in relation to the origins of conduct disorder, research has shown that deviance or mental illness in parents, rejecting attitudes, coercive parenting style, the difficulties faced by single mothers who are overwhelmed and unable to provide supervision, marital distress, and child abuse are all patterns that occur frequently. And, indeed, a family environment characterized by considerable conflict, negativity, criticism, and inconsistent (explosive) anger may be particularly predictive of antisocial conduct in children (e.g., Reiss et al., 1995). Observed even as early as infancy, maladaptive patterns of relating to others may be associated with later aggressiveness. These patterns are likely due to deficiencies in the parents' ability to maintain a responsive, warm, and consistently nurturing bond (Lyons-Ruth, 1996). It is hardly surprising that, under such conditions, young people grow into adults with patterns of poorly controlled anger and aggressiveness, poor problem-solving skills, and negative expectations of others that contribute to the symptoms of antisocial personality disorder, aggressive conduct, or both.

Unfortunately, the factors that place children at risk for antisocial conduct often co-occur. (As noted, examples include marital instability, poor parenting, parental mental illness, substance abuse, poverty, and exposure to high rates of stress.) One follow-up study in England that reported on children after thirty years found that 60 percent of those with multiple "deprivation" experiences had criminal records in adulthood — a much higher rate than that among individuals without deprivation experiences (Kolvin, Miller, Fleeting & Kolvin, 1988). Interestingly, another family factor associated with antisocial personality disorder is the extent to which adults with APD tend to have children with conduct disorder. Studies have shown that perhaps one-half of such offspring have conduct problems (Robins, 1966; Rutter & Quinton, 1984). The situation is compounded by the tendency of persons with APD to marry each other — a pattern called *assortative mating*. Women with APD, for example, are especially likely to marry men with APD or drug and alcohol problems. Such marriages increase children's risk for disorder, not only because of genetic factors but also because of the high rates of marital discord, economic adversity, family violence, and deviant parenting that such relationships entail.

How can children survive the ill effects of multiple environmental and family adversities? Several studies now indicate that children at risk may nonetheless remain free of antisocial conduct to the extent that they have higher IQs (e.g., Moffitt, 1993), possibly leading to an interest in succeeding in school and the ability to do so (e.g., O'Donnell, Hawkins & Abbott, 1995). Also, problem-solving and social competence skills appear to predict better adjustment among aggressive children (O'Donnell, Hawkins & Abbott, 1995), possibly because such skills contribute to good judgment and planning ahead, as well as to avoidance of peer rejection that can otherwise lead to membership in deviant, marginal groups that encourage antisocial conduct.

Distorted Cognitions

Dysfunctional thoughts, beliefs, and attitudes may also contribute to the social learning of antisocial traits and conduct. These cognitions may shape a person's ability or willingness to conform behaviors to social norms. One intriguing example comes from research on **hostile attributional biases,** or the tendency to believe that negative events are caused by other people intending harm.

Kenneth Dodge argued that the belief that others are "out to get you" is an important determinant of responding aggressively — at least among children and adolescents. Dodge and his colleagues tested this cognitive model in a group of severely aggressive adolescents who were in a maximum security prison for juvenile offenders (Dodge, Price, Bachorowski & Newman, 1990). The researchers presented videotaped vignettes in which the actor does something that causes a negative outcome for another person — and the vignettes were varied according to whether the event was accidental or whether the actor's intentions were positive, hostile, or ambiguous. As predicted, the extent to which the young men believed that the intentions of the actor in the films were hostile (even in ambiguous or accidental situations) was significantly correlated with their history of violent interpersonal crimes — but not nonviolent crimes. Also, the more extensive the juvenile offenders' history of reactive aggression (bad temper, easily angered, fighting in response to anger), the more likely they were to perceive hostile intent.

A recent study conducted by Dodge, Pettit, Bates, and Valente (1995) shed light on how hostile attributional biases may be acquired. The researchers found that children who had been physically abused early in their lives were four times more likely to be aggressive by the time they reached third or fourth grade. Most notably, they observed that the abused children were sig-nificantly more likely to interpret hostile attributions in videotapes and cartoons, as well as more likely to view aggression positively. In addition, the more cognitive biases toward aggression they showed prior to kindergarten, the more severe their aggressive conduct was several years later.

Exposure to Violent Models

Beyond the role of child-rearing by antisocial or otherwise deviant parents, social learning theory emphasizes **observational learning** (the acquisition of behaviors and attitudes from watching others) as a contributor to antisocial and aggressive conduct. Observational learning takes place on three levels: through exposure to culture-wide attitudes (recall our earlier discussion of the societal tolerance of violence), exposure to abusive parents (which we discuss in detail in the later section on specific forms of violence), and exposure to violence on television, in films, and in music lyrics.

Does exposure to television violence cause aggression in children? Considerable research has been conducted on this controversial topic. Researchers have hypothesized that since children are highly susceptible to influence, when they witness violence in the media, they not only observe the condoned and modeled use of aggression to solve problems but also learn attitudes that permit and justify, if not glorify, the use of force. The general conclusion — though not shared by everyone — is that modest but significant associations exist between viewing violence on television and behaving aggressively.

Methods of studying television's effects have included laboratory studies with carefully controlled but perhaps unrealistic conditions, as well as naturalistic studies of the link between viewing habits and actual behavior. Evidence from both kinds of research supports the conclusion of a negative impact of viewing violence on subsequent aggressive behavior (reviewed by Heath, Bresolin & Rinaldi, 1989). For example, a ten-year follow-up of more than two hundred American children found that the amount of violent television watched at age nine was the best single predictor of juvenile delinquency offenses related to aggression at age nineteen (Lefkowitz, Eron, Walder & Huesmann, 1972). More recently, Rowell Huesmann and Leonard Eron (1986) reported on children studied over a three-year period, exploring causal relations between television viewing and aggressiveness. Their results indicated that, among both boys and girls as young as seven or eight, there was a significant association between viewing violence on television and aggressive behaviors reported by peers and parents. The effect was bidirectional, however: Not only did the children who watched aggressive television become more aggressive over time, but also the more aggressive children watched increasing amounts of violent television over time.

Violence as entertainment is increasingly recognized as a contributor to actual violence. In TV, movies, songs, cartoons, and computer video games, kids learn violent methods of solving problems; they learn values that condone aggression. As a result of seeing so many acts of brutality in living color, they also can become insensitive to the effects of real violence on real people.

The association between television violence viewing and aggressiveness in children has been found in other countries as well. Results of a cross-national study, reported by Huesmann and Eron (1986), found that in three of the five countries sampled — that is, in the United States, Finland, and Israel, but not in Australia or Poland) — either boys or girls (or both) showed statistically significant modest associations between the amount of time they spent viewing violent television programs and ratings of their aggressive behavior.

In general, investigators have speculated that the unwanted effects of television violence are in part a result of the way children think about and make sense of the violence they see. Children who view violent behavior as a realistic means of resolving problems are more likely to "use" what they have learned than children who do not consider such behavior to be a realistic means of resolving disputes.

Other issues related to television violence concern its effects on attitudes toward victims as well as increased callousness toward violence and increased perceptions of the world as a violent place. Exposure to aggression in television leads to **emotional desensitization,** a tendency to be numb, unresponsive, or even callous (e.g., Widom, 1989a). It may also lead to distortions in perceptions of real-life violence. After seeing countless guns fired, punches thrown, and cars crashed, viewers are no longer affected by the violence of these acts.

Multiple Roots of Risk for Antisocial Conduct and Violence By way of summarizing the complex and interacting psychological determinants of risk for deviance, we present Figure 14.3, which suggests a range of factors from broad cultural values all the way down to the biological characteristics and neurocognitive abilities of the individual child. Those critics who decry the loss of "family values" are correct in their observation, but the problem is far more complex than that. Indeed, Ervin Staub (1996) describes many other social changes of recent years (some of which are reflected in the figure) that have contributed to the apparent increase in youth violence. Unlike many problems in the area of abnormal psychology about which the causes are not fully understood, in this topic we know very well what the causal factors are (though not necessarily their relative importance in an individual case). Instead, our greatest challenge is treatment and prevention, to which we now turn.

TREATMENT AND PREVENTION OF ANTISOCIAL CONDUCT

As much as we might dream of a society free of antisocial attitudes and behavior, effective treatment of APD and conduct disorder is difficult. One problem is that the individuals who need the treatment typically lack the personal insight to seek treatment. They are unwilling to assume personal responsibility because they tend to blame others or circumstances for their behaviors — a situation that creates little motivation for self-exploration. Another problem is that, given their deficiencies in conscience and emotional development, and their difficulties in inhibiting impulses, insight-oriented psychotherapy is a generally ineffective process for antisocial persons.

Figure 14.3 Multiple Factors Promoting Antisocial Conduct and Violence

There are multiple levels at which risk for antisocial conduct occurs, ranging from attitudes held by society down to the biological characteristics of the individual.

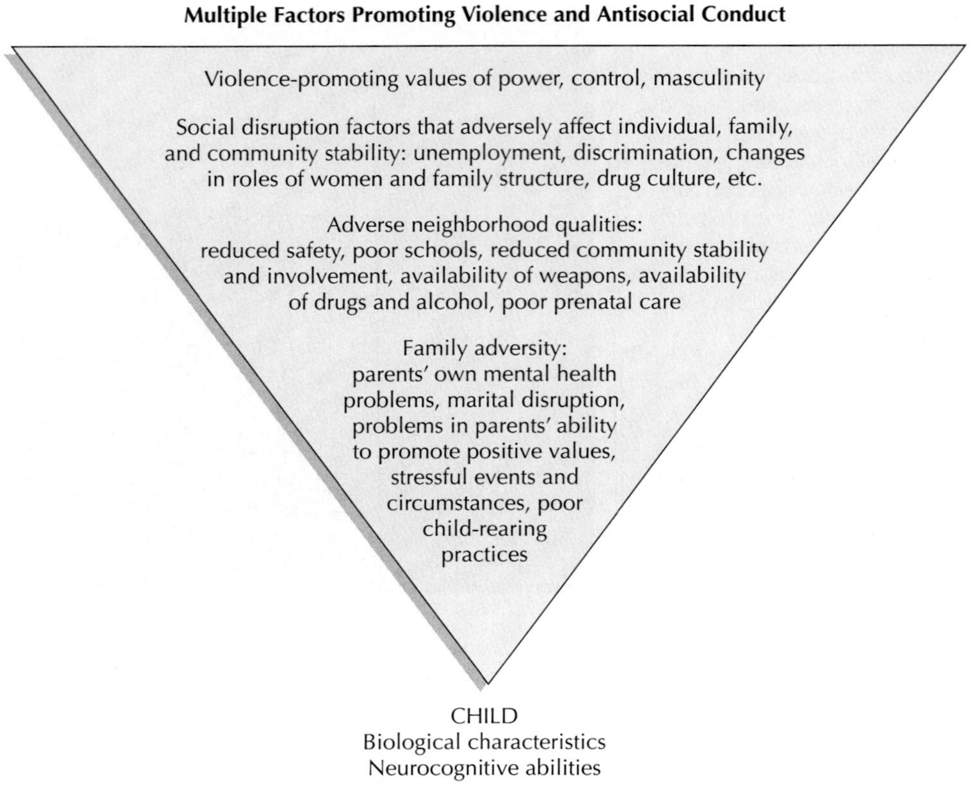

Multiple Factors Promoting Violence and Antisocial Conduct

Violence-promoting values of power, control, masculinity

Social disruption factors that adversely affect individual, family, and community stability: unemployment, discrimination, changes in roles of women and family structure, drug culture, etc.

Adverse neighborhood qualities: reduced safety, poor schools, reduced community stability and involvement, availability of weapons, availability of drugs and alcohol, poor prenatal care

Family adversity: parents' own mental health problems, marital disruption, problems in parents' ability to promote positive values, stressful events and circumstances, poor child-rearing practices

CHILD
Biological characteristics
Neurocognitive abilities

More often than not, then, intervention takes the form of *incarceration,* or imprisonment as punishment for a crime. As noted earlier, probably more than one-half of prisoners meet the criteria for APD. Incarceration, however, is notoriously unsuccessful at "rehabilitation" for the majority of such individuals, and repeat offending is very common, particularly among those with psychopathic traits. Treatment, when it does exist, is often involuntary — required by courts, juvenile justice systems, or other public agencies either as an alternative to incarceration or as part of a prison or detention program. Even when treatment is voluntary, individuals may enter into it as a way of manipulating a more favorable outcome of legal proceedings.

There is generally little evidence that court-required treatments are effective. Specific programs with particular goals, however, have provided limited evidence of effectiveness. For example, as we note in Chapter 12, interventions directed at child molesters or exhibitionists may help reduce recurrence of sex offending. (What has not been clearly defined is the extent to which APD or psychopathy may alter the effectiveness of such interventions.) Similarly, because there is often a high overlap between antisocial personality disorder and substance abuse, programs aimed at substance-abuse treatment may sometimes prove useful, as we discuss in Chapter 11.

In view of the difficulties involved in treating or modifying adult antisocial personality disorder and conduct disorder, investigators have focused more directly on *prevention* of APD, largely by treating children's antisocial behavior symptoms early in life before they become severe or chronic. The juvenile justice system in the United States is built on the premise of rehabilitation and prevention of future crime. *Juvenile diversion programs,* for example, represent the efforts of public agencies to provide counseling and community and school programs as an alternative to incarceration. Most of the time, however, these programs do little to help youth acquire the skills and attitudes necessary to change the course of their deviant lives. Moreover, the recent upsurge in severely violent crimes committed by youth has pushed many states to press for adult punishment.

In the absence of evidence that intervention programs can succeed with violent or deviant youngsters, there is likely to be further pressure to incarcerate juveniles under adult statutes. And, unfortunately, the evidence for prevention is relatively sparse thus far; although some programs for violent juveniles have successfully focused on problem-solving and cognitive skills, their outcomes in preventing further crimes are not encouraging (Tate, Reppucci & Mulvey, 1995). One difficulty with many of these programs is that they did not attack the multiple causes of antisocial behavior, often dealing with only one aspect such as social problem-solving or parent-training. Recent efforts that target both individual and environmental factors appear to be promising, however. For example, Borduin and associates (1995) offered *multisystemic treatment* (MST) to severe juvenile offenders ages twelve to seven-

Prevention may be our best hope of curbing antisocial conduct and violence. Many community efforts have been mounted to give young people positive rewards for prosocial behaviors. Ex-gang member Lefty Gordon started a midnight basketball league for youngsters in the Fillmore district of San Francisco, where participation in the league requires attending workshops on employment preparation, AIDS education, and other essentials. Of the 60 young men who completed the program, he placed 12 in jobs, 14 enrolled in a high school equivalency program, and three started college.

teen. This treatment, which included cognitive, school, family, and peer focuses, was compared to standard supportive individual psychotherapy. According to the results, compiled during a four-year follow-up, the multisystemic treatment group had significantly fewer arrests overall and committed fewer violent crimes.

Psychologists are also making increasing efforts to prevent the development of childhood conduct disorders — specifically, by identifying high-risk conditions and offering interventions to correct the difficulties *before* childhood misconduct occurs. Examples include programs for abused children, programs for persons who witness violence, and parent training for disadvantaged families. For instance, Tremblay and associates (1995) in Canada included both home-based parent training and school-based social skills components in a program aimed at disruptive kindergarten boys. Follow-up analyses conducted when the boys were ten through fifteen years of age revealed that those in the treatment program did better than nontreated comparisons in terms of school adjustment; they also committed fewer delinquent acts. Certainly early prevention remains an important research and social goal.

VIOLENCE: CHARACTERISTICS, PREDICTORS, AND CONSEQUENCES

Each year about 3 percent of all Americans are victims of violent crime. Despite the incidence of antisocial per-

sonality disorder and psychopathy among perpetrators of crime and violence, much violent activity is not a product of such disorders. **Domestic violence,** which is violence that occurs in the home between intimates, is considered to be the most common form of violence, affecting millions of people yearly (Widom, 1989a). And many — perhaps most — instances of domestic violence do *not* involve APD, psychopathy, or mental illness. Thus, a complete discussion of the topic of violence must consider the characteristics and causes of domestic violence, as well as its psychological impact on victims. In the sections that follow, we explore three of the most common forms of domestic violence: physical abuse of children, marital violence, and sexual assault.

Physical Abuse of Children

Physical abuse is the infliction of damage to another person; it can lead to severe injury and even death. Physical abuse of children can sometimes occur within the context of what parents consider discipline, a matter that was once thought to be completely private because parents "owned" their children. History reveals centuries of maltreatment of children in different eras and cultures — infanticide of female children, painful binding of girls' feet, forced genital mutilation, exploitation of children as laborers, and many other examples. In most industrialized nations today, the welfare of children is subject to public and legal scrutiny.

Attitudes about what constitutes appropriate discipline have also changed. At one time, parents and teachers in the West believed that "spare the rod and spoil the child" was the appropriate guideline, and corporal punishment was the rule rather than the exception. Now, however, parents and teachers who use physical punishment run the risk of crossing a line between discipline and abuse. The following case describes what we mean by physical abuse.

> *Eight-year-old Mark is the boy we described at the beginning of the chapter as being highly aggressive toward other kids. Recently his teacher noticed big bruises on his arms and sent him to the school nurse, who discovered other marks and scars that could not have been caused by "falling down," as Mark claimed. A child abuse report was filed. Investigators discovered that Mark's father, who was sporadically employed as a delivery truck driver, punished the boy severely when he didn't do his homework fast enough, when he had the television turned on too loud, or when he violated any of the father's rigid standards. The physical punishment — usually Mark's father socked him with a fist or shoved him to the ground — was most severe when the father was upset and angry about something in his own life. For instance, he was recently fired, and he believed that Mark's mother was being unfaithful because she was often absent from the house. The father had always had a bad temper, but he had gotten into trouble with the law only once, in an episode involving drunk driving. In his own boyhood he had been taught that children should be beaten if they misbehaved. Mark is now an angry and aggressive boy. He's also a sad and lonely child usually shunned by his peers.*

More than two million official reports of child physical abuse are filed each year in the United States, and we suspect that the true incidence of abuse is far higher. For that matter, the extent of child abuse and neglect appears to be *increasing* (Eckenrode et al., 1988; Wolfe & Wekerle, 1993). **Neglect** refers to the failure to provide proper care for children or to meet their nutritional, emotional, medical, and physical needs.

Consequences to the Abused Child To study the effects of abuse on children, researchers have used retrospective reports by adults who were abused as children, comparisons of abused and nonabused children, and the rare longitudinal follow-up study of maltreated children. All of the results have suggested that, compared with nonabused or neglected children, abused children are more aggressive and show more behavioral conduct problems (e.g., Dodge, Pettit, Bates & Valenti, 1995). Abused children exhibit a higher incidence of depression and emotional problems, as well as lower intellectual functioning (reviewed in Emery, 1989; Boney-McCoy & Finkelhor, 1995). And according to some but not all studies, abused children are less compliant and less socially competent. Overall, significant disruption in behavioral and socioemotional adjustment is also evident among children who were neglected (Wolfe & Wekerle, 1993).

However, no single pattern of behavioral or emotional reactions characterizes all abused children (Emery, 1989). The impact of abuse appears to vary according to severity, duration, and overall social context — a function of parental attitude, parental conflict, stress, socioeconomic status, and many other factors. For example, a child with a supportive, attentive mother who severely beats him as a disciplinary tactic may suffer less psychological harm than a child whose mother not only rejects him but is also abusive.

Does Violence Beget Violence? We have seen that abused children are often more aggressive than nonabused children (e.g., Dodge, Pettit, Bates & Valente, 1995). Do physically abused children themselves become violent adults?

Case histories of violent criminal offenders do often reveal abuse in their backgrounds, and evidence from many kinds of investigations generally confirms that childhood abuse perpetuates the cycle of violence in adulthood (Malinoksy-Rummell & Hansen, 1993). In a methodologically careful follow-up study of abused and neglected children, Cathy Widom (1989b) found that 26 percent of them went on to commit juvenile offenses and 11 percent were arrested for a violent crime — rates significantly higher than those exhibited by a comparison group. In addition, the relationship between abuse and later criminality was stronger for men than for women, and for African Americans than for whites. Luntz and Widom (1994) also found that the abused group eventually exhibited a significantly higher rate of antisocial personality disorder than did the comparison group, especially among males. Earlier, Widom (1989b) had speculated that the consequences of childhood abuse for women are probably more subtle than for men, and that they involve depression and psychiatric problems rather than violence, crime, and APD. She also emphasized that the majority of abused youngsters did not turn to crime and violence.

FAMILY MATTERS

Intergenerational Transmission of Abuse

Does abuse by parents increase the chances that the child will grow up to be an abusive parent? Unfortunately, the answer seems to be *yes*. Although a great deal of research on abuse has emphasized the possible contributions of factors outside the individual, such as poverty, stress, and ignorance of appropriate parenting skills, intrafamilial factors must also be considered.

Research from various sources has documented that families tend to transmit abuse from one generation to

MANKOFF

"Dad, can I borrow the gun tonight?"

the next. Some of these data come from clinical case studies. The infamous Juke family in nineteenth-century New York, for example, produced 1,200 individuals over six generations stemming from five ancestral sisters. According to the historian Dugdale (1877), 300 of the 1,200 children died young from neglect, disease, physical abuse, and criminality. More recent clinical case studies as well as contemporary surveys and prospective studies have also generally documented intergenerational transmission of abuse. For example, studies conducted in England and the United States have found relatively high rates of cases of abused children whose parents were also abused (e.g., Egeland, Jacobvitz & Sroufe, 1988; Oliver, 1988), with an average across many of these studies reported at 30 percent (Kaufman & Zigler, 1989).

Accurate data on familial patterns are difficult to obtain solely through interviews. According to British researcher J. E. Oliver (1993), many abusive parents deny that they themselves were abused. Often such individuals present idealized accounts of their own parents, distorting and denying the reality of information that might even be a matter of public records. Oliver argued that this situation is far more than merely a methodological problem inasmuch as the denials of these parents may actually increase the risk of abuse to their own children. By contrast, individuals who recognize and accept their own maltreatment as children may be far better equipped to try different methods of childrearing than they themselves experienced, or to seek help when they recognize problems in their own childrearing practices.

Why do some families show high rates of repeated abusive discipline of their children? In attempting to

answer this question, most researchers have emphasized the role of learning experiences. Not only do children learn to use violence as a solution to interpersonal problems (as their parents did), but at a profound and pervasive level they may have acquired *maladaptive interpersonal schemas* (negative beliefs and expectations about other people's values, trustworthiness, and caring) that limit their abilities to relate effectively to others, including their own children. As we note in Chapter 8, attachment theory (Bowlby, 1979) holds that the quality of the parent-infant bond guides fundamental aspects of the child's social, intellectual, and self-esteem development by shaping the ways in which the child views the self and other people. Thus, for instance, a parent with maladaptive attachment caused by abuse is likely to relate to his or her child in maladaptive ways, resulting in damaged attachment in yet another generation. Considerable research on parent-child attachment quality in abused children documents maladaptive attachment compared to nonabused children (e.g., Lyons-Ruth, 1996). In short, the mechanism of intergenerational transmission of abuse is likely to include early-acquired attitudes and characteristics, creating a vulnerability for abuse if they are activated by stressful conditions of childrearing.

Are Abusive Parents Mentally Ill? Some abusive parents are mentally ill, and some have personality disorders including antisocial personality disorder. The majority of abusing parents do not have diagnosable disorders, however, and there is no evidence of an "abusive personality" (Emery, 1989; Wolfe, 1985). But abusive parents do tend to share a few characteristics. They have been found to be deficient in their ability to cope with stress (Gaines, Sandgrund, Green & Power, 1978), in social competence, in relationship and parenting skills (Dietrich, Starr & Kaplan, 1980); and in their ability to control angry impulses (Rohrbeck & Twentyman, 1986). In addition, they are often socially isolated from family and friends and have marital problems, rigid and domineering interpersonal styles, and alcohol or drug abuse problems (reviewed in Wolfe & Wekerle, 1993).

Abusive parents also have distorted cognitions and inappropriate expectations. Maltreating mothers may describe their babies as very difficult to care for, even though there is no objective evidence of such, and they commonly have unrealistic beliefs about what babies should be like (for example, quiet, well-controlled, happy). Studies have indicated that parents with a history of abusing children misinterpret their children's behavior. And they are more likely than other parents to interpret misbehavior as intentional. For example, Bauer and Twentyman (1985) found that abusive mothers, more than either neglectful or normal mothers, described their children as deliberately acting to annoy them. Thus, an abusive mother who is asked, "Why does your twelve-month-old child mess his diaper?" is likely to say, "He does it just to get me mad." This response is typical of the *hostile attributional biases* shown by Dodge and colleagues (e.g., Dodge, Price, Bachorowski & Newman, 1990) as possibly leading to aggressive behaviors.

Abuse is also linked to an interrelated set of situational factors, including marital distress, background stress such as unemployment, and values that tolerate the use of violence (Emery, 1989). Further, characteristics of the child, such as being "difficult," may influence whether parents resort to physical abuse. All of these conditions — parent qualities, situational factors, and child characteristics — contribute to situations in which a parent may fail to inhibit aggression.

Marital Violence

The incidence of marital violence is alarmingly high. Nearly one-third of marriages, at some point or another, involve physical aggression of one spouse against the other (Straus & Gelles, 1986). This rate reflects not only minor acts such as shoving, grabbing, and throwing something at the partner but also more serious health-endangering acts. Three of every one hundred women each year are *severely* assaulted by their male partners — punched, kicked, beaten, choked, threatened, or actually injured with a knife or gun (Browne, 1993). A study of women's emergency room visits in one Rocky Mountain city found that 12 percent were due to domestic violence (Abbott, Johnson, Koziol-McLain & Lowenstein, 1995).

Women themselves also resort to violence, but the consequences are quite different for the two sexes. Nearly 1,700 women die each year in the United States as a direct result of spousal abuse (Strube, 1988). Women's aggression invokes less fear in the partner and inflicts less physical harm than does men's aggression. In addition, researchers have argued that women's aggression toward men is often committed in self-defense (Browne, 1987; Walker, 1989).

Children are also victims of spousal abuse. According to one estimate, three million U.S. children annually observe spousal abuse, and hundreds may witness the rape or murder of their mothers (Eth & Pynoos, 1985). Emotional and behavioral problems increase

This woman and her daughter are victims of domestic violence, a woeful combination of two words that should never go together. Unfortunately, however, spouse and child abuse are quite common—and their psychological consequences may be lifelong or even transmitted to the next generation.

among children who have witnessed spousal violence, even when they themselves are not abused, and such witnessing might be as harmful as actual abuse (reviewed in Emery, 1989; Widom, 1989a).

Causes of Spousal Abuse   Spousal abuse occurs at all levels of society, but more often in younger populations (O'Leary et al., 1989) and in lower socioeconomic groups. One way to predict the incidence of abuse is to examine whether aggression occurred in the relationship before marriage. Individuals who do not use aggression early in a relationship generally do not develop such patterns later on; those who do resort to aggression are very likely to continue to do so (O'Leary et al., 1989). Once physical violence has begun, it tends to continue and escalate. In turn, physical aggressiveness can be predicted by psychological aggressiveness, which involves insulting the partner, stomping out of the house, deliberately doing something to spite the partner, and so on (Murphy & O'Leary, 1989). Psychological aggressiveness usually includes control and coercion as well. For example, a husband may attempt to limit his wife's activities and social contacts, and even try to define her reality (e.g., Cascardi, O'Leary, Lawrence & Schlee, 1995).

Clinical analyses have suggested that spousal violence, like child abuse, is not associated with DSM diagnosis of a disorder, although one subgroup of batterers is generally violent and antisocial outside the family as well (Holtzworth-Munroe & Stuart, 1994). Spousal violence has been tied to certain emotional characteristics — in particular, to underlying hostility and an inability to control it (e.g., Margolin, John & Gleberman, 1988). Moreover, many abusive spouses may have an unstable self-concept, impulsivity, and a fear of abandonment (Dutton, 1995). Excessive use of alcohol is also frequently involved in spousal violence (O'Leary, 1988). Hostility combined with the lowering of inhibitions and controls by alcohol likely sets the stage for violent acts against the marital partner. Finally, cultures vary in terms of their acceptance of a man's right to beat his wife, and these norms are highly predictive of wife assaults (e.g., Kantor, Jasinski & Aldarondo, 1994).

Responses to Spousal Abuse   Certainly no discussion of domestic violence is complete without considering the role of the spousal victim, typically the wife. Based on interviews and clinical analyses, researchers have speculated that a spouse's apparent tolerance of violence, unwillingness to file criminal complaints, and efforts to cope with rather than escape the violence might contribute to its perpetuation. In effect, tolerance may reinforce the violence (reviewed in Follingstad, Neckerman & Vormbrock, 1988).

Why do women stay in abusive relationships? One explanation is that **battered women** (women who have been physically beaten by their domestic partners), like other victims of violent events, display psychological characteristics that interfere with their ability to make appropriate decisions. They are typically very fearful of their husbands and of the consequences of leaving (e.g., Cascardi, O'Leary, Lawrence & Schlee, 1995). They may experience flashbacks, numbing, withdrawal, and other symptoms of posttraumatic stress disorder (Astin, Ogland-Hand, Coleman & Foy, 1995; Browne, 1993). Further, battered women may experience themselves as unable to control the events in their lives, and this *learned helplessness* may prevent them from taking action to get out of the situation even when escape is possible (Strube, 1988; Walker, 1989). Battered women commonly report that they have no place to turn or that they cannot support themselves economically (reviewed in Strube, 1988) — and, indeed, for many such women, these are accurate interpretations of their situations. In addition, the partners of these women often isolate them from friends and family, not only contributing to the women's perceptions that they are alone, with no resources to turn to, but also likely increasing their fear of the consequences of escaping.

Battered women also cognitively distort abuse situations. For instance, they often "misinterpret" the event: They deny that violence has occurred, believe that it was an isolated case, or think that they can "help" the spouse get over his problems by enduring his wrath (e.g., Follingstad, Neckerman & Vormbrock, 1988). Studies have indicated that their decision to stay with abusive spouses is related not just to a lack of economic means but to commitment to the relationship, love for the partner, and a belief that the violence is caused by some factor that is temporary (Holtzworth-Munroe, 1988; Strube, 1988). Obviously, these cognitions might lead them to remain in the marriage, expecting that the circumstances will change and that the abuse will not recur.

Sexual Assault

Miki was excited about her first date with Jon as she got dressed in her dorm room. She'd met him in a class and thought he was good-looking. He took her to a nice restaurant, and they had wine — which she wasn't accustomed to. Feeling a little tipsy, she initially enjoyed kissing when he stopped the car on a deserted road. But then he started to go further. She told him to stop, but he told her to shut up as he ripped off her underwear, held her down, and forcefully engaged in sexual intercourse with her. He dropped her off at the dorm, crying and disheveled, and she sneaked back to her room, ashamed and terrified, not wanting to be seen. Fortunately, her roommate was home early and comforted her, and convinced her to report the incident to campus police.

Many women in our culture are not safe from sexual violence outside or even inside the home. Incidents involving both childhood and adult sexual assault — directed primarily but by no means exclusively at women — are frequent and devastating in their consequences.

Different research projects have defined **sexual assault** in varying ways. Typically, however, it refers to the use of psychological pressure or physical force to engage in sexual contact that involves genital touching or intercourse. Sexual assault that involves sexual penetration with physical coercion or threat of harm is called **rape.** Designations of childhood sexual assault usually specify that the assailant is at least several years older than the child. In this section we discuss both sexual victimization of adults and children, as well as sexual assault by family, acquaintances, and strangers.

Frequency and Characteristics of Sexual Assault

National surveys, limited by victims' unwillingness to disclose such events, have estimated that from one in seven to as many as one in four women has been raped at some time in her life (Koss, 1993). Most rapes occur during adolescence and young adulthood. Rape is less frequent among Hispanic women than among white women (Sorenson & Siegel, 1992), but the rates among African American and white women are similar (Wyatt, Guthrie & Notgrass, 1992). The best way to estimate actual occurrence is to gather information from randomly selected residents of representative communities. Police records are inadequate because the vast majority of rapes are not reported, and most officially reported rapes do not lead to conviction. According to the Los Angeles Epidemiological Catchment Area study, some form of assault occurred after age sixteen among 13.5 percent of women and 7.2 percent of men (Sorenson, Stein, Siegel, Golding & Burnam, 1987). About one-half of these incidents involved forced intercourse.

Childhood sexual victimization is also alarmingly frequent. Among randomly selected adults in Los Angeles, 5.3 percent had experienced sexual assault during childhood (Siegel et al., 1987). The rate for men was 3.8 percent. Most assaults occurred for the first time when the victims were around age ten, and more than one-half of the victims reported more than one assault. Although a significant proportion of **sexual molestation** (usually defined as sexual contact with a minor child by someone at least several years older) occurs in the family (23 percent), acquaintances are involved more often (56 percent) and strangers are involved less often (22 percent) (Siegel et al., 1987). Virtually all studies have found that both male and female victims are molested by predominantly male perpetrators. As with rape, sexual molestation occurs at a higher rate among whites and African Americans than among Hispanics (see Sorenson & Siegel, 1992).

Who are the victims of rape? According to surveys, the individuals at greatest risk are young women, especially those of college age — and with education beyond high school (e.g., Winfield, George, Swartz & Blazer, 1990). This finding is probably related to the fact that educated women are more willing to recognize and label an act as rape. Victims of rape are also somewhat more likely than others to have experienced sexual victimization as children (see Koss & Dinero, 1989). Apart from these characteristics, however, comparisons of psychological, social, and situational characteristics indicate that women who have been raped are not different from nonvictims. The unfortunate conclusion to be drawn is that rape can happen to virtually anyone. At least one-half of rapes are committed by acquaintances or friends, compared to about 21 percent by strangers. And perhaps surprisingly, 26 percent of the acts are committed by spouses (11 percent) or lovers (15 percent)(Sorenson et al., 1987).

Koss, Gidycz, and Wisniewski (1987) have provided further information on sexual assault from a nationwide random sample of college students. They found that a considerable proportion of women and some men have experienced psychological pressure and coercion in their sexual contacts. Most notably, nearly 5 percent of the men in this study admitted attempting to rape someone, and more than 3 percent admitted actually committing rape. Other studies of college men have found even higher rates at which men admitted that they had coerced a woman to have intercourse against her will (e.g., Craig, 1990).

Consequences of Sexual Assault

Clinical studies of sexually abused children have generally found immediately observable problems such as behavioral difficulties, learning problems, depressed mood, guilt, and sleep disturbances, as well as symptoms of posttraumatic stress disorder, or PTSD (e.g., Boney-McCoy & Finkelhor, 1995). In addition, abused girls often exhibit heightened sexual preoccupation and evidence of having learned inappropriate sexual responding and sexually precocious behaviors (Goldston, Turnquist & Knutson, 1989; see also Einbender & Friedrich, 1989). Children may experience some aspects of a sexual assault situation as representing increased affection and attention, although fear and guilt often arise as well.

The long-term consequences of childhood sexual assault may be quite negative and enduring. The effects of sexual victimization can be delayed; they may also last for years (Koss, 1993). Numerous studies have found sexual abuse in the early histories of many psychiatric patients with depression, anxiety disorders, alcohol and substance abuse, suicidal and self-mutilation behaviors, and personality disorders such as borderline personality disorder (e.g., Briere & Zaidi, 1989; Brown & Anderson, 1991). It was once thought that the eating disorder *bulimia* was related to childhood abuse, but recent studies, including a multinational study do not suggest that the link is specific to sexual abuse (Pope et al., 1994; Rorty, Yager & Rossotto, 1994). Surveys of the general population have found elevated rates of depression, anxiety disorders, and substance abuse in those who were abused as children (Burnam et al., 1988). Long-term consequences also include mistrust of others and difficulties in intimate relationships, including abusive marriages (e.g., Astin, Ogland-Hand, Coleman & Foy, 1995).

There is considerable variability in the ways that individuals respond to childhood and adult sexual assault. Why do some people show great distress and others much less? In general, outcomes appear to be worse when the abuse is repeated, as in childhood molestation; when the perpetrator has a close relationship to the victim; and when the childhood background of the person is characterized by disruption, conflict, and stressful conditions (Wyatt & Newcomb, 1990; Ussher & Dewberry, 1995).

Among adults, sexual assault causes a variety of immediate reactions such as fear, shame, depression, social withdrawal, and sexual functioning difficulties, as well as symptoms of posttraumatic stress disorder (e.g., Briere & Runtz, 1988). Indeed, the vast majority of rape victims experience PTSD, and many continue to experience such symptoms even months later (Koss, 1993). Interestingly, a study of adult female victims of crime in South Carolina determined that rape was a strong predictor of PTSD — stronger than any other type of crime, including injury and threat to life (Kilpatrick et al., 1989). A random community sample in North Carolina similarly found rates of several disorders that were significantly higher among women who reported previous sexual assault than among nonassaulted women: major depression, alcohol and substance abuse, panic disorder, and PTSD (Winfield, George, Swartz & Blazer, 1990). The Los Angeles epidemiological survey found that men and women victims were equally likely to have long-term psychiatric problems (Burnam et al., 1988).

Causes and Predictors of Sexual Assault In Chapter 12 we discuss the causes of sexual molestation of children, including incest and pedophilia. In this chapter we focus mainly on the causes of adult sexual assault, particularly rape.

It has become almost a cliché to say that rape is not a sexual act but an act of aggression. This claim makes an important point by emphasizing the violence involved in rape, but it is also an oversimplification. Equally flawed is the theory that rape reflects a sexual preference for force and violence (Barbaree & Marshall, 1991). Most rapes are not sexual paraphilias; perhaps only 10 percent of rapes involve the motivation of inflicting suffering and humiliation on the victim for purposes of sexual pleasure. There are simply too many kinds of rape for a single theory to cover all of them.

Rape includes acts as varied as assaults against women in dating situations, single impulsive rapes, and multiple, vicious, premeditated, and sadistic rapes. But all forms of rape have at least one thing in common: sexual aggression.

Sexual violence probably involves some combination of both biological factors and learning deficits (Ellis, 1991). Recall from Chapter 12 our discussion of possible contributors to abnormal sexual behaviors. In general, the evidence of any link between sexual aggressiveness and abnormalities in hormones such as testosterone is unclear (reviewed by Hucker & Bain, 1990), although biological factors may be related to some forms of impulsive aggressiveness, as we note earlier in the present chapter. Physiological *arousal* in response to rape situations may be a biological instigating factor for some rapists. However, many men — not just rapists — are sexually aroused by sexually aggressive stimuli (see Malamuth & Check, 1983). Physical arousal alone does not determine actual behavior; rather, normal individuals learn to control the expression of their sexual urges and limit them to appropriate, mutually decided circumstances.

Whatever the physical basis for sexual violence, learned attitudes are paramount. In part, these attitudes reflect the influence of culture. For example, not all cultures recognize the experience of rape or even the concept of coercive sex. According to one anthropological analysis of 156 societies (Sanday, 1981), 47 percent were rape-free and 18 percent were rape-prone (the rest were unclassified). The rape-free cultures promoted sexual equality, valued women and female qualities, and exhibited low levels of interpersonal violence. The rape-prone cultures promoted male-female antagonism and an ideology of male toughness, and displayed high rates of interpersonal violence and low levels of female decision making.

Sexual violence is most likely determined by multiple factors. For example, Lisak and Roth (1988) found that sexually aggressive men, compared to nonsexually aggressive men, more often have negative relationships with women, are more impulsive, see themselves as more likely to lose control under the influence of alcohol, and have less respect for society's rules. Also, men whose friends highly value sexual prowess are more likely to use coercive methods than are men without such friends (reviewed in Craig, 1990). Neil Malamuth (1986, 1991; Malamuth, Sockloskie, Koss & Tanaka, 1991) found evidence supporting several factors that determine sexual violence: (1) physiological arousal to aggressive stimuli, (2) motivation for dominance in sexual acts, (3) negative attitudes toward women such as hostility, and (4) personal preferences shaped by childhood role models and sexual experiences.

After reviewing evidence for various models of rape, Barbaree and Marshall (1991) concluded that different models are needed to account for different types of

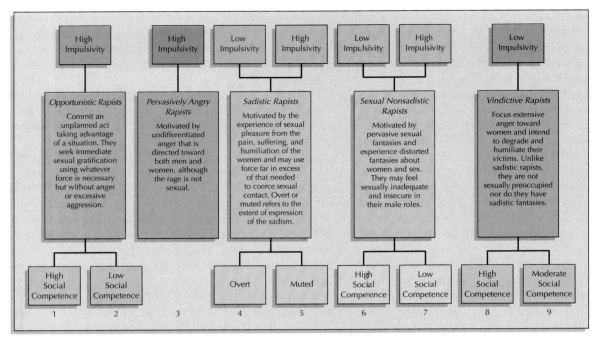

Figure 14.4 Proposed Typology of Rapists

Robert Prentky and Raymond Knight (1991) developed one of the most complete categorizations of rapists. Their system identifies several types of rapists based on the primary motivation for the rape, the degree of impulsivity in the rapist's lifestyle, and his level of social competence. Thus, rape is the common outcome of a variety of motives, interpersonal skills, and levels of ability to regulate the self when gratification is desired. These various combinations yield different types of rapes that might have different causes and implications for prevention or treatment.

Source: Adapted from Prentky & Knight (1991) and Knight & Prentky (1990).

rapists, and that each might have specific implications for treatment. For example, *repeat rapists* tend to have long histories of antisocial conduct and law violation, to be aggressive and impulsive, and to frequently abuse substances that probably reduce their control over aggressiveness (Bard et al., 1987). *Date rapists,* on the other hand, rarely want to dominate women; they are primarily sexually motivated (Ellis, 1991). They may first try deception and persuasion, resorting to force or threat if the initial methods don't work. Often they believe that women really "want" to be raped and will become aroused if force is used.

Based on existing typologies, case records, empirical evidence, and theory, investigators Raymond Knight and Robert Prentky (1990; Prentky & Knight, 1991) proposed that there are nine types of rapists, arising from five primary motives for rape — opportunistic, pervasively angry, sadistic, nonsadistic sexual, and vindictive (see Figure 14.4). They further proposed that impulsivity and level of social competence involving interpersonal and heterosexual skills are factors that modify the expression of the primary motive, creating the different subtypes. Rapists with high levels of impulsivity tend to display lifelong patterns of inability to defer gratification, taking action without concern for consequences,

and disregard for the rights and feelings of others. The five primary motives for rape are more fully described as follows:

- *Opportunistic rapists* commit an unplanned act taking advantage of a situation. They seek immediate sexual gratification using whatever force is necessary but without anger or excessive aggression.

- *Pervasively angry rapists* are motivated by undifferentiated anger that is directed toward both men and women, although the rage is not sexual.

- *Sadistic rapists* are motivated by the experience of sexual pleasure from the pain, suffering, and humiliation of women and may use force far in excess of that needed to coerce sexual contact.

- *Sexual nonsadistic rapists* are motivated by pervasive sexual fantasies and experience distorted fantasies about women and sex. They may feel sexually inadequate and insecure in their male roles.

- *Vindictive rapists* focus extensive anger toward women and intend to degrade and humiliate their victims. Unlike sadistic rapists, they are not sexually preoccupied nor do they have sadistic fantasies.

TREATING VICTIMS AND PREVENTING VIOLENCE

Two themes stand out in the context of treatment for the victims of violence. One is that services are overwhelmed and ill-equipped to deal with the sheer numbers of people who need help. The other — related to the size of the need plus the unwillingness of many victims to seek help — is the necessity for preventing the problem in the first place. In this section we briefly review both treatment and prevention approaches.

Treating and Preventing Child Abuse

Treating Child Abuse The U.S. Advisory Board on Child Abuse and Neglect has proclaimed a child abuse and neglect national emergency. Yet communities are so swamped by the sheer magnitude of cases that they often do little more than count cases and remove children from unsafe homes. Treatment programs have largely developed along three lines: child-focused interventions, parent-focused treatments, and multiservice programs (Wolfe & Wekerle, 1993). Most of the child-oriented programs that have been evaluated empirically involve day-treatment interventions focused on appropriate play and peer interactions. Some of these have demonstrated improved social functioning in maltreated children, but they typically do not conduct follow-ups over time to determine whether the gains are stable (Fantuzzo et al., 1988).

More frequently studied are the behavioral and cognitive-behavioral programs aimed at changing parents' dysfunctional child management and anger control, as well as unreasonable expectations for their children's behaviors. Many of these programs also attempt to teach parents to cope more effectively with the stresses in their lives. David Wolfe and Christine Wekerle (1993) reviewed nearly a dozen such interventions, noting that many are effective in modifying parent skills relevant to abuse and that some have demonstrated reduced rates of repeat abuse compared with untreated control groups. Nevertheless, such programs do not change long-standing personality deficits or eliminate the crushing stressors that many families face. Thus, more multiservice programs are needed — programs that provide parental skills training and improve coping but that also provide comprehensive services to the entire family, often in the home, such as crisis management and medical, educational, and other social service assistance to stabilize dysfunctional situations.

Preventing Child Abuse Perhaps the greatest hope for improving the lives of abused children is to prevent the abuse in the first place. A number of studies have been designed to identify high-risk situations and then to intervene with programs to enhance parental competency. As young, low-income mothers with small children exhibit disproportionately high rates of child abuse, they have been targeted for preventive treatments focused on enhancing their parental competence. Other studies have targeted teenage parents, or first-time parents, especially those who are socially disadvantaged. These programs use a variety of techniques, including home visits and group educational sessions on parenting. Overall, they have been shown to be effective in changing both parenting skills and attitudes, and many have even resulted in modest gains in children's intellectual functioning (Wekerle & Wolfe, 1993). The programs have also reduced the number of child injuries, emergency room visits, and reports to child protective

Prevention is one of the best hopes of reducing violence in society. Sometimes the most important step is to teach people that violent solutions to problems are not acceptable. As this billboard suggests, the message is that women should not tolerate physical mistreatment at home, and that they can get help if needed.

agencies — although many did not study child maltreatment as such. An unfortunate limitation of such programs is that virtually all involve mothers only. Their failure to include fathers and male partners — who play a major role in physical and sexual abuse — represents an important gap in prevention efforts.

Treating Spousal Violence

Many communities are uncertain about whether to treat spousal abuse as a legal or psychological matter. Many cities and grass-roots organizations offer temporary, usually secret, shelters for abused women and families; a few provide extensive treatment and rehabilitation services to help women overcome dependency on abusive men or to help families learn effective ways to resolve problems. Nevertheless, psychological services to battered women — and to their children who have witnessed domestic violence — are limited and only rarely evaluated systematically for their effectiveness (Browne, 1993). A recent controlled investigation illustrates the need for a focus on multiple issues: Behavioral marital therapy for couples in physically abusive relationship demonstrated that reductions in marital violence occurred only when the alcoholic husbands also controlled their drinking (O'Farrell & Murphy, 1995).

Many communities are also experimenting with legal reforms, addressing such questions as whether it is best (in terms of dangerousness and repeat offending) to arrest violent spouses even if the victim does not bring charges, which is commonly the case. One study of a community that requires arrest and prosecution evaluated the extent of repeat battering during an eighteen-month period after the initial incident. It concluded that arrest had a significant deterrent effect on subsequent domestic violence (Tolman & Weisz, 1995). More and more communities are adopting this strategy and taking the decision to prosecute out of the woman's hands.

There is also a good case to be made for prevention. Amy Holtzworth-Munroe and her colleagues (1995), having noted that early signs of domestic violence predict continued or even escalating battery, proposed that treatments be developed for such couples early in their relationship. This "behavioral-cognitive" prevention program is currently being tested for its effectiveness in reducing future marital violence.

Treating Sexual Assault

Unfortunately, most victims of sexual assault do not seek treatment. For example, researchers have estimated that only 5 percent of college rape victims use campus crisis center programs (Koss, 1985). Individuals are often reluctant to disclose the event to others because they fear that their credibility will be questioned ("you must have caused it" or "you could have prevented it"), and they may refuse treatment simply because they wish

Rape is potentially preventable; the great majority of rapes occur in situations where the victim and rapist know each other, and the man may erroneously believe that the woman "wants" it. No means no, and this important message for both men and women may help to prevent rape.

to deny the impact of the event. Over the years many crisis-oriented counseling centers have sprung up, and many forms of therapy have aimed at reducing distress and improving emotional and sexual functioning. A number of experts advocate group treatment with other rape survivors. Few programs have been systematically evaluated, but those shown to be effective share certain features in common. These include avoiding victim blame, providing a nonstigmatizing view of rape, establishing an environment that encourages overcoming social avoidance and withdrawal, and giving information about trauma reactions and conveying a positive expectation of overcoming them (reviewed in Koss, 1993). A key goal of one recent program for victims of abuse was to prevent the development of PTSD and depression symptoms. When evaluated six months later, this four-session cognitive-behavioral program, which focused on dealing with recent trauma, was shown to be successful in reaching that goal (Foa, Hearst-Ikeda &

Perry, 1995). Figure 14.5 illustrates the significant reduction in PTSD symptoms following treatment.

Many communities and campuses now offer rape prevention programs aimed at eliminating myths about rape ("women really want to be raped"), helping young men and women communicate clearly about sexual matters, and educating people about the meaning and consequences of sexual assault.

Treating Childhood Sexual Abuse   Treatment of childhood sexual abuse is also vital to the well-being of the victim. Well-validated programs for children are not widely available, although most communities provide some services. A recent review of treatment studies found that the majority were not methodologically sound (Finkelhor & Berliner, 1995). Those judged to be adequately designed, however, demonstrated significant improvement in children's symptoms and maladaptive behaviors. More generally, they revealed that aggressiveness and sexualized behaviors are resistant to change.

Currently, there is also considerable current interest in treatment for adult survivors of childhood sexual abuse, along with few well-designed studies (e.g., Alexander et al., 1989). Unfortunately, in the absence of empirical evidence for effective methods, overzealous therapists have sometimes claimed that virtually all adult psychological abnormality stems from "repressed" childhood abuse, and some offer "memory restoration" methods of dubious validity. To date, there are no data to support such claims. Real incidents of repression and denial definitely occur, as we discuss in Chapter 7, but there is little research available to indicate how common these experiences are, how specific they are to sexual abuse, the best methods for retrieving the experiences from memory, and the most effective means of repairing psychological damage caused by sexual abuse.

Preventing Child Molestation   It seems reasonable that if children could learn how to resist or avoid abusive situations, less abuse would occur. Accordingly, numerous agencies have developed prevention programs — including lectures, films, and workbooks — to teach children what physical contact is appropriate and how they should respond to inappropriate contact. Other programs for teachers and child-care workers aim to improve their abilities to instruct children in useful concepts and methods.

Do these programs work? According to one view, most such programs have not been effectively evaluated (Kolko, 1988; Miller-Perrin & Wurtele, 1988). Other experts have argued that there is relatively little evidence that prevention programs work, that these programs may be based on questionable assumptions, and that they might even be harmful (Reppucci & Haugaard, 1989). For example, certain children may not be able to recognize sexual abuse or to form a plan for resisting it, and attempts to teach them about abuse may cause con-

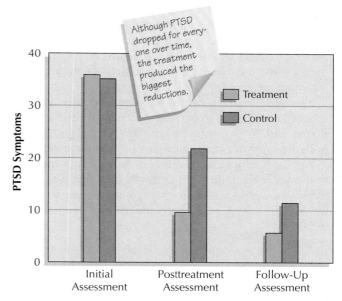

Figure 14.5   Reduction of Posttraumatic Stress Disorder Symptoms Following Assault
Recently assaulted women were assigned either to a brief cognitive-behavioral treatment group or to a no-treatment group (assessment only). They were evaluated for PTSD symptoms three times: two weeks after the assault; two months later, after the treatment (or assessment); and then approximately six months after the assault. The results indicated significant decreases in trauma-related symptoms of PTSD among those women who received the treatment.
Source: Foa, Hearst-Ikeda & Perry (1995).

fusion or inappropriate applications of what they are taught. Indeed, although increased public awareness of child sexual victimization has undoubtedly proven useful for many youngsters, it has also contributed to numerous reports of unsubstantiated child abuse (e.g., Eckenrode et al., 1988). Overall, we seem to be on the right track by promoting greater awareness and alertness, but more work is needed to demonstrate the effectiveness of child abuse prevention efforts.

What Lies Ahead?

By nearly every measure we could employ, antisocial conduct and violence are on the rise, with no signs of leveling off in the foreseeable future. As more citizens are affected by violence in their daily lives — or witness its effects on others — public concern continues to mount. In the next few years, efforts to define, understand, and control these problems will increase. This is a topic of enormous controversy because it tends to polarize firmly held political, religious, and philosophical viewpoints. Researchers who look to explanations and cures at the societal level in terms of economic justice and equality of opportunity are disputed by those who emphasize intraindividual or intrafamilial contributions to the problems. By the same token, those who focus on the biological and psychological factors are accused of ignoring the enormous importance of the social context in which people live. Thus, the years ahead will be filled with contention and demands for answers, reflecting the urgency and complexity of the problems of violence and antisocial conduct.

Invariably much of the focus of scientists and citizens alike will be on the family — the institution that has the potential not only to create our best selves but also to be a source of danger and violence to an extent rarely recognized before the past few decades. The forms and functions of the family are radically different from those of previous generations. As we shine our scientific lights into the dark corners of family life, we will acquire much fuller understanding of the shaping of normal — as well as dysfunctional — personality and adjustment.

Increasingly, communities are being asked to bear the burden of the failures of family life to socialize, monitor, and protect children. What are the best, and most affordable, methods? Certainly the need for effective and widely available treatments has become evident. In the future, psychologists and other professionals will feel increasing pressure for scientific understanding of violence and practical solutions to the problems it causes. While we recognize the enormous advantage of preventive services, future research holds the key to determining whether such methods work well enough to justify their considerable cost.

KEY TERMS

antisocial personality disorder (APD) (434)
battered women (455)
criminality (436)
deficient avoidance learning (446)

deficient emotional arousal (445)
domestic violence (451)
emotional desensitization (449)
hostile attributional bias (448)

neglect (452)
neurocognitive dysfunction (446)
observational learning (448)
physical abuse (451)
poor impulse control (440)

psychopathy (435)
rape (456)
sensation-seeking (446)
sexual assault (456)
sexual molestation (456)
testosterone (445)

SUMMARY

Features of Antisocial Personality Disorder

There is considerable overlap in the DSM-IV between *antisocial personality disorder (APD)* and *psychopathy,* a set of traits reflecting callousness and disregard for others' rights. These mental health terms also overlap with *criminality* and violence. Only some criminals meet criteria for APD and even fewer for psychopathy. There is an elevated risk of crime and violence among the mentally ill, but most such people are law-abiding. Far more men than women meet APD criteria, and, by definition, APD requires childhood onset of antisocial patterns. Not all children with conduct disorder go on to have adult APD; but, once established, aggressive patterns tend to be highly stable.

Causes of Antisocial Personality and Violent Conduct

Among the biological explanations of APD, psychopathy, and aggressive conduct, genetic and neurotransmitter abnormalities are currently emphasized. Serotonin metabolite levels appear to be lower in persons with impulsive aggressiveness. One explanation for these low levels is a genetic defect leading to lack of an enzyme for metabolizing serotonin. *Testosterone,* the male hormone, has also been implicated in aggressiveness. Other biological approaches concern the roles of *deficient emotional arousal, sensation-seeking, deficient avoidance learning,* and *neurocognitive dysfunction.*

Social learning theories of antisocial and aggressive conduct emphasize rewards for deviant behavior. The family is typically the source of learned adaptive and maladaptive behaviors, and research finds strong correlations between conduct disorder and poverty, family disruption, divorce, mentally ill parents, poor parenting, and abuse in the family. Dysfunctional cognitions, such as *hostile attributional bias,* are often found in aggressive subjects, suggesting that their aggressiveness may result from interpreting other people's behaviors as intentionally hostile. Social learning theory also emphasizes *observational learning* from role models, including violent television programs. Indeed, watching violent models on television is consistently associated with aggressiveness in children, as well as with *emotional desensitization* toward violence.

Treatment and Prevention of Antisocial Conduct

Treating persons with APD or psychopathy is notoriously difficult because they lack both motivation and a sense of personal responsibility. Incarceration is the major method of changing antisocial behaviors, although it does not accomplish that goal very often. More promising are programs aimed at preventing the development of antisocial and aggressive behaviors; most such programs are directed toward high-risk youth.

Violence: Characteristics, Predictors, and Consequences

Domestic violence is the most common form of violence, including not only murder but also *neglect* of children and *physical abuse* of children and spouses. Physical abuse of children results in various outcomes, including considerable psychological distress and aggressive behavior. Some abusive parents may have diagnosable conditions (usually substance abuse), but many are better characterized as stressed, overwhelmed, socially isolated, personally immature, and ignorant of child-rearing skills or appropriate expectations of children. There is considerable evidence that violence begets violence; a sizable proportion of abused children commit antisocial and aggressive acts as adults, and become abusive parents themselves.

Abuse also affects spouses, and rates of spousal violence are extremely high. *Battered women* often experience symptoms of posttraumatic stress disorder, which makes them less able to leave or accurately perceive their situations.

Sexual assault includes *rape*, childhood sexual assault, and *sexual molestation*. Most acts of both adult and childhood assault are committed by family or acquaintances. Psychological reactions to severe, repeated acts — and those committed by persons known to the victim — appear to be more pronounced. Such reactions may be immediate or delayed, and sexual victimization can have long-term consequences including depression, difficulties in sexual functioning, and PTSD.

Causes of rape cannot be easily characterized because there are many different kinds of, and motives for, rape. However, common to many forms of rape are such themes as motivation for sexual dominance, negative attitudes toward women, and features of personal history that promote use of force.

Treating Victims and Preventing Violence

Most private and public agencies are overwhelmed with the need for supportive services for child and adult victims of violence. Although such services can be very helpful, most people who need them either cannot get them or might not even come forward to seek help. Accordingly, prevention and early intervention are thought to be more useful approaches. Numerous programs have been developed to prevent physical and sexual abuse. For instance, preventing child abuse might involve targeting high-risk groups such as teenage mothers, and providing information on child rearing and help with problem solving. Such programs are generally effective in the short run, but long-term studies have not been conducted.

Consider the Following. . .

Suppose that it is an election year, and you have been listening to the candidates present their views on various issues. A key theme of this election is community violence — everyone agrees that it is a serious problem and that something ought to be done. In past years many people wanted to build more prisons to solve the problem, but some questioned what this would accomplish, and whether it represents the best use of public money. This year candidates are talking about *prevention*. One candidate gives ringing speeches about the need for a "return to family values" to stop the moral depravity underlying violence, while the other candidate stirringly focuses on economic issues such as higher minimum wages and bringing industry back to the inner cities. Given what you now know about crime, violence, and antisocial personality disorder, what makes sense to you? What are the specific ways in which *poverty* — both directly and indirectly — affects risk for antisocial behavior? Would greater prosperity make a difference?

Are "family values" enough to turn the tide? What kinds of conditions support families in their efforts to raise healthy, well-functioning children?

Suppose that one of your best friends has been married for a couple of years and now has a baby. When you ran into her at a store yesterday, you saw that she had a big bruise on her face. She said she'd run into something in the dark while getting up for the 2 A.M. feeding. While she was dating her husband, she once confided in you that he hit her during a fight but later apologized and said it would never happen again. You are starting to worry that she is a victim of spousal violence. Given what you've learned in this chapter, what should you do? If you find out that he has in fact been hitting her, what future do you foresee — both for her and for her child(ren)? What do you think she would say if you confronted her on this issue? What kind of assistance might be helpful to her?

CHAPTER 15

Behavioral and Emotional Disorders of Childhood and Adolescence

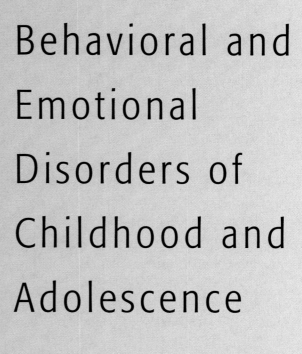

Those among us . . .

- A fire alarm sounds, and your concern mounts as the fire trucks arrive at a house just two doors from where you live. Joe, a tough and troublesome twelve-year-old, lives with his mother in house that is burning. You know that Joe has been in trouble for excessive fighting, temper outbursts, and vandalism. You wonder, might Joe have set the fire?

- Dorothy, a colleague at work, has complained for years about her conflicted marriage. Today, her divorce is complete. She hopes the fighting will end, and she is especially hopeful that things will be better for her children.

- You volunteer at a mental health center, answering the phone. A voice speaks haltingly, "Uh, can I like talk to somebody who knows about being crazy." You reply, "Can I help you?" The caller stumbles, "I need to talk to somebody because . . . well, because I don't think straight. But I really do. Nobody understands. I don't know, I just don't fit." The caller — a lonely and depressed adolescent who is seeking relief from the psychological pain of feeling useless, alone, and unloved — is sixteen years old.

> ■ The loud music and dancing contribute to a lively party. As the hour gets late, the partiers get hungry, and pizzas are ordered and delivered. They are wolfed down by everyone, especially Sandra. Soon after eating, you notice Sandra, who doesn't want to gain weight, in the bathroom making herself vomit.

Do children act out their psychological problems? Does divorce typically reduce the distress of a troubled marriage? Will it help the children?

Can children become depressed? How do they handle feelings of sadness? Unlike adults, children and adolescents typically do not seek psychological help for themselves.

Can someone really lose weight by vomiting after eating? Is it healthy?

Children and adolescents differ from adults in the problems that bring them into treatment, in their response to therapies, and in the course of their disorders. Thus, the psychological difficulties of childhood and adolescence require special study to be understood and treated. Addressing these difficulties is very important to the individual and to society. If left untreated, children do not outgrow serious problems but instead can develop into adults with psychological disorders. Also, a grave psychological disorder in a child is likely to have serious consequences — often more serious than in an adult — because the disorder may interrupt the child's learning and development. A psychologically impaired child may fail to master key tasks such as developing self-esteem, establishing relationships with peers, resolving conflict, and acquiring academic skills. These inadequacies may in turn lead to increased frustration and rejection.

The early formative years are important to later adjustment: Difficulties during these years are the precursors of later maladjustment. For example, as we discuss in Chapter 14, once children learn to be aggressive, they tend to remain aggressive. Left untreated, aggression is stable. In fact, the level of antisocial behavior in childhood predicts the level of antisocial behavior in adulthood (Robins, 1966; Robins & Price, 1991).

Our discussion of the psychological problems of youth is divided into two chapters. In this chapter we examine the behavioral and emotional disorders, such as attention-deficit hyperactivity disorder, conduct disorder, anxiety, and depression. In the next chapter we examine the disorders associated with intellectual, developmental, and physical conditions.

UNDERSTANDING THE DISORDERS OF YOUTH

Researchers have estimated that 15 to 22 percent of the children and adolescents in the United States have problems severe enough to need treatment (Costello, Burns, Angold & Leaf, 1993), but fewer than 20 percent of youngsters with current problems actually receive services (Tuma, 1989). And, as was found in a twenty-year follow-up of children in London (Champion, Goodall & Rutter, 1995), many of these children go on to become adults with psychological disorders. As we note in Chapter 1, in several disorders, the median age of onset is between thirteen and twenty-five; other disorders are identified before age seven.

Developmental Psychopathology

The human organism completes many changes over the life span — cognitive, social, sexual, and biological changes, to name a few. Developmental psychology studies these and other changes as a part of normal human development.

Emerging from the study of normal child development and its interface with child maladjustment (Cicchetti, 1993), **developmental psychopathology** views psychological maladjustment in relation to the major changes that occur across the life cycle. No one theory of psychopathology is followed, but emphasis is greatest on the rapid development that occurs between birth and maturity (Achenbach, 1990).

Developmental psychopathology recognizes the importance of the interaction between the child and the context. There are different behavioral styles as well as different beliefs about acceptable behavior, and if the "fit" between the person and the context is not good (e.g., an energetic child in a setting that is intolerant of even normal amounts of activity), maladjustment may result (Lerner, Hess & Nitz, 1990). The person-context interaction of developmental psychopathology is embodied in the child's adjustment to the challenges of normal development (Sroufe & Rutter, 1984). For instance, during ages three to five, children face the developmental challenges of self-control, self-reliance, and peer contacts. Ages six to twelve involve challenges of social understanding, whereas the challenges of adolescence address flexible thinking, emancipation, and identity. Success or failure in facing issues at one point in development are seen as laying the groundwork for the issues that will need to be addressed later in life.

An important feature of developmental psychopathology is that it places child disorders against the backdrop of what is normal for a given age (Campbell,

Dressing alike is common among youth, as evident in this photo of teenage girls. Only under more menacing circumstances would people in similiar clothes, such as gang colors, be a concern for society.

1986). For example, is it a disorder when a four-year-old reports a specific fear such as fear of the dark? Normative data indicate that nearly 90 percent of children between the ages of two and fourteen reported at least one specific fear, and it is hardly fair to call it abnormal when it appears instead to be a part of the challenges of normal development. Seeing fears as abnormal depends more on the disruption in daily functioning such fears might cause.

Assessing Childhood and Adolescent Disorders

As we discuss in Chapter 4, psychological disorders are assessed by using methods such as self-report inventories, observations, structured interviews, and performance on laboratory tasks. With children and adolescents, similar assessment procedures are used, but there are important differences because young people may be inarticulate or uncooperative or lack insight into their emotions or actions. For example, the psychological assessment of children includes ratings of the child's behavior by parents and teachers, structured interviews of children and their parents, and increased use of structured behavioral observations. The Child Behavior Checklist (Achenbach, 1991; Achenbach & Edelbrock, 1983), the Diagnostic Interview for Children and Adolescents (Herjanic & Reich, 1982), and the Response Class Matrix (Mash, Terdal & Anderson, 1973) illustrate these approaches to assessment.

The *Child Behavior Checklist* (CBCL; Achenbach, 1991) is a rigorously developed and standardized rating scale, available for both parents and teachers, for assessing the most common dimensions of psychological dis-

order in childhood (for example, social problems, aggressive behavior, anxiety or depression). It includes 113 questions that assess behavior problems and 20 that measure social competence. The scores of each child are judged against a distribution of scores obtained by a normative sample of children with backgrounds representing the range of social and economic status. The normative data provide the backdrop for the profile of scores received by the target child; Figure 15.1 gives an example.

There has been considerable effort over the past several years to improve structured interviewing procedures for use with children and adolescents (Edelbrock & Costello, 1988). The face-to-face interview can help establish rapport with children and families and permits asking questions that are geared to reaching diagnostic decisions. Most of the structured diagnostic interviews for use with youths follow an established diagnostic system (such as the DSM) and include the full range of childhood disorders. For example, the *Diagnostic Interview for Children and Adolescents* (DICA; Herjanic & Reich, 1982) assesses 185 symptoms and can be conducted in forty to forty-five minutes with parents or children six years of age and older. As is true for structured interviews in general, the DICA has specific questions and scoring procedures that use a branching system to lead to diagnoses. Favorable reliability and validity data are available to support the use of structured diagnostic interviews (Edelbrock & Costello, 1988).

The *Response Class Matrix* is a method for observing and assessing parent-child interactions (Mash, Terdal, & Anderson, 1973). Trained observers record an

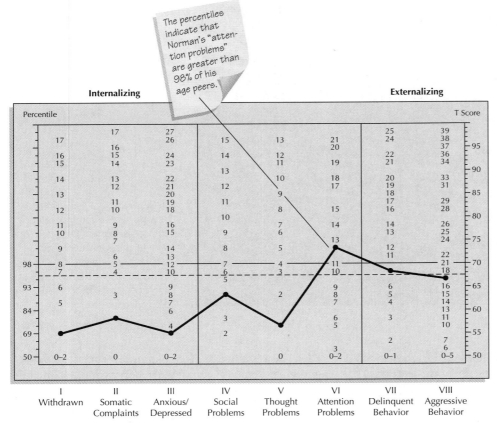

Figure 15.1 Child Behavior Checklist (CBCL) Profile

This CBCL profile belongs to Norman G., a ten-year-old boy with what his mother referred to variously as "an active motor" and "ants in his pants." Both his teachers and parents noticed that he switched in the middle of activities and was unable to sit still and focus for even a modest amount of time. In conversations, Norman kept talking, without care for whether the other person was listening. The CBCL shows normal-range scores on the internalizing side of the profile (if scores less than 70 are considered within normative levels). His ratings of attention problems are well above the normal range. His delinquent and aggressive behavior scores also were elevated. He was diagnosed as having an attention-deficit hyperactivity disorder. T scores are standardized scores, allowing the scores different children receive on different scales to be compared with one another. The mean T score (50) and two standard deviations above and below the mean constitute one definition of the normal range. T scores over 70 are indicative of clinical extremes on the scale.

observation every ten seconds. They record both parent and child behaviors by placing a single checkmark in one of the cells of a matrix. The rows of the matrix are different child behaviors (such as play and negative behavior), and the columns are different parent reactions (such as praise and commands). Thus, the matrix for one session might show that each negative child behavior was tied to a parental command and that desired child behaviors received no praise from the parent. By providing data about the pattern of interactions, the Response Class Matrix is helpful in identifying specific patterns that the therapist can target for change.

Information from direct observational methods such as the Response Class Matrix has the advantage of being representative of actual behavior in the real world (e.g., Tuteur, Ewigman, Peterson & Hosokawa, 1995). However, normative information about the behaviors is often lacking. That is, we do not yet know exactly what

constitutes the healthy patterns of "good" parents and "well-adjusted" children. As a result, although observations are helpful to identify target behaviors for treatment, they may not be as valuable as structured interviews or checklists for making a diagnosis. Observations, checklists, and structured interviews play vital roles in the battery of assessments used in the measurement of childhood psychological disorders.

Classifying Childhood and Adolescent Disorders

The most widely used classification system for disorders of youth is the DSM system. In the original DSM (1952), children were diagnosed in the adult categories because there were no categories specifically for childhood disorders. Over the years, as we discuss in Chapter 4, the classification scheme has become increasingly data-based and responsive to input from researchers. DSM-

Table 15.1   DSM Disorders Usually First Diagnosed in Infancy, Childhood, or Adolescence

Disorder	Description
Mental retardation	Substantial limitations in present functioning, characterized by significantly subaverage intellectual functioning and limitations in adaptive living skills (e.g., self-care)
Learning disorders	Achievement substantially below that expected given age, intelligence, and education (examples of these learning disorders are reading, mathematics, writing)
Motor skills disorder	Coordination substantially below expected level, given the person's age and intelligence
Pervasive developmental disorders	Impairment in communication and social interaction, together with restricted and stereotyped patterns of behavior (a common example is autism)
Disruptive behavior and attention-deficit disorders	These disorders are associated with acting-out, such as annoying, destructive, and dangerous behavior (conduct disorder) and extreme inattentiveness and restlessness [attention-deficit hyperactivity disorder (ADHD)]
Feeding and eating disorders	Disorders associated with self-feeding; for example, pica, the persistent eating of nonnutritive substances that is inappropriate to developmental level (anorexia is another example)
Tic disorders	Sudden repetitive motor movements or utterances; for example, Tourette's disorder, which involves both motor and verbal tics that occur many times a day
Communication disorders	Disruption in the normal fluency and time patterning of speech; for example, stuttering
Elimination disorders	Encopresis, the repeated passage of feces into inappropriate places, and enuresis, the repeated voiding of urine into bed or clothes
Other disorders of infancy, childhood, or adolescence	These disorders include separation anxiety disorder, selective mutism, and reactive attachment disorder

IV has a separate section for disorders usually first diagnosed in infancy, childhood, or adolescence; youths also can receive other diagnoses (such as depression or generalized anxiety disorder). For example, an adolescent who displays symptoms of depression would be diagnosed and classified within the system as having a mood disorder. Table 15.1 provides an overview of the DSM classification of the disorders specific to youths.

A related but different approach for childhood disorders comes with an imposing title—*multivariate statistical taxometric system* — but the basic idea behind the system is straightforward: to classify disorders by using statistical procedures to determine what symptoms occur together with what other symptoms. Using correlations between pairs of symptoms or pairs of behavior ratings, the researcher then examines these relationships to look for patterns of co-occurring characteristics (Achenbach, 1982).

This method has led researchers to describe childhood disorders as falling into two broad categories: (1) internalizing disorders and (2) externalizing disorders (Achenbach & Edelbrock, 1978). **Internalizing disorders** are psychological difficulties that are considered inner-directed; core symptoms are associated with overcontrolled behaviors (Reynolds, 1992). Internalizing disorders include such psychological disorders as anxiety, depression, social withdrawal and isolation, and the eating disorders. **Externalizing disorders** are maladaptive behavior patterns in children, across several situations, that create problems for others. In these undercontrolled disorders, which are also called *behavioral disorders*, the child's behavioral problems result in conflicts between the child and the social context. Conduct disorder, discussed later, is an example.

Studies of adolescents, including studies of African American youth (Resnicow, Ross-Grady & Vaughan, 1995), suggest a gender distinction; more females report internalizing disorders, whereas more males are identified with externalizing difficulties. By a ratio of 2:1 or 3:1, boys show more problems linked to externalizing than girls (Quay, 1986).

Critics point out that many externally disordered children also have very tormented inner lives — if not because of their own internal personal turmoil, then perhaps because of the punishment, ridicule, or unwanted attention that their behavior generates. This concern is not adequately addressed by the taxometric distinction. In response, advocates have suggested that youths with externalizing disorders display their problems outwardly but may still experience some inner distress. In externalizing problems, for example, the child suffers less internally relative to the problems that are discharged onto the environment.

Treating Disorders of Youth

As we note earlier, children and adolescents typically come to the attention of the mental health system when parents, teachers, or officials of some type decide that the youths need professional assistance. The fact that children are sent for treatment, whereas adults may seek it, is an important distinction.

A number of theories and types of therapy are applied to children and adolescents (Kazdin, 1994b; Kratochwill & Morris, 1993). For example, young persons may be treated individually using a cognitive-behavioral (Kendall et al., 1997) or psychodynamic (Target & Fonagy, 1994) approach, or the family may be treated using a behavioral approach. Recent reviews of research on the effectiveness of therapy with children have suggested that interventions based on a behavioral or cognitive-behavioral perspective tend to be the most effective (Weiss & Weisz, 1995; Weisz, Weiss, Han & Granger, 1995), although there does not appear to be one treatment that is consistently more effective than others. This is to be expected, however. It is unlikely that one method of treatment would be effective for all childhood behavior disorders (Shirk & Russell, 1996).

There are three important differences between adult and child therapy: (1) the role of parents, (2) the use of play in therapy, and (3) the use of medications. Parents play a central role in children's lives, and the degree to which parents and other family members are involved in treatment requires consideration. Instead of working one-to-one with the child, therapists may choose to spend time teaching the parents to work with the child. Such parent training is often used with younger children. In other instances, the family may be seen together in family therapy (Fauber & Long, 1991).

Play is used by a variety of therapists as a means to involve children in the tasks of treatment. However, a specific form of play therapy is psychodynamic and uses play as the central means for the child to express thoughts and emotions. The method remains somewhat popular despite a lack of data to support its use.

Biomedical treatments, specifically medications, also have been used for childhood and adolescent disorders. Many people think that children's disorders can be treated with the same medications used for adults. With the exception of Ritalin, which is used to treat childhood attention-deficit hyperactivity disorder (see the next section), however, there are far fewer controlled studies on the effectiveness of psychotropic medications for children than there are for adults (Biederman, 1992), and the studies that have been done sometimes paint a less than optimistic picture of the effects of the medications. For instance, several medications that are effective in the treatment of adult depression are not effective with depressed youths (Gadow, 1992; Sommers-Flanagan & Sommers-Flanagan, 1996), and medications for adult anxiety disorders have not been evaluated in children. Also, the use of neuroleptics in children may result in high levels of neurological symptom side effects that are different from those of adults (Richardson, Haugland & Craig, 1991).

BEHAVIOR DISORDERS

The majority of difficulties brought to professional attention have to do with externalizing, undercontrolled behavior problems. Our focus will be on attention-deficit hyperactivity disorder (ADHD) and conduct disorder.

Attention-Deficit Hyperactivity Disorder

Even at age six, Zach was "unpredictable," according to his parents. His mother, a real estate agent, reported that "he's always on the go, but I'm not always sure where he is going. He's into so many things." Zach's father, an attorney for a large firm, described Zach as "rash and impetuous" and "having his engine running constantly." Both parents were distressed when Zach's school performance suffered because of his impulsivity and poor attention: He was determined to be a bright child, but his ADHD was interfering.

DENNIS THE MENACE

"BY THE TIME I THINK ABOUT WHAT I'M GONNA DO...I ALREADY **DID** IT!"

Hyperactivity is the popular term for this psychological problem of childhood. Other terms professionals have used include *hyperkinetic reaction, minimal brain dysfunction,* and *attention-deficit disorder.* Today it is formally called **attention-deficit hyperactivity disorder (ADHD),** a disorder that has three essential features: developmentally inappropriate levels of inattention, impulsivity, and hyperactivity, with onset before age seven (Barkley, 1997; Bauermeister et al., 1995; Iaboni, Douglas & Baker, 1995). Comparable features were identified in nine- to seventeen-year-old Puerto Rican children.

Few disorders have received such widespread attention from professionals, teachers, and parents. During the last decade, for example, ADHD has been one of those widely studied childhood disorders, and DSM-IV provides criteria for different types of ADHD: ADHD predominantly inattentive type, ADHD predominantly hyperactive type, and ADHD combined type. The possibility that these are separate disorders requires additional research.

What constitutes an attentional or hyperactive problem? Is it a diagnosable problem, and if so, can it be treated? Should the 3 to 5 percent of children who receive this diagnosis be medicated? Discussions of these and other questions have made "hyperactivity" a topic of considerable controversy.

Clinical Characteristics of ADHD Over the years, researchers have come to recognize that the problem is not simply excessive levels of motor activity (hyperactivity). Difficulties in the three essential features of inattention, impulsivity, and hyperactivity are seen across situations — at school, at home, and in social contexts.

Inattention is observed in behaviors such as seeming not to listen and failing to complete tasks. More specifically, a short attention span is seen in rapid shifts from one activity to another before the first activity is completed (Alessandri, 1992). The child goes from one toy to another without focused play with either toy; in the classroom, the child is easily distracted and fails to pay attention to directions. Is the problem tied to an inability to pay attention or to difficulty in sustaining attention? The exact nature of the attentional problems seen in ADHD children is still a subject of debate, requiring further research.

Impulsivity is acting without thinking. Although many children can be impulsive, ADHD children routinely interrupt others, blurt out responses to questions, and fail to wait their turn. They have problems organizing schoolwork and a general need for greater supervision. When joining a game of soccer, the impulsive child runs onto the field and chases the ball, eager to kick it — without knowing the team he or she is on or which goal to shoot toward. In the classroom, the impulsive child tries to answer a question before the question is completely stated.

Inordinate **overactivity** is often reported by parents and teachers, who cannot keep up with these children. The children are fidgety, restless, and unable to sit still. Using direct observations and mechanical recordings, researchers have found an excess of activity among diagnosed hyperactive children (Milich, Loney & Landau, 1982). They are "on the go," unable to play quietly, and inept at shifting from free to structured activities such as from recess to a classroom activity.

Investigators increasingly see peer relationship difficulties as central to ADHD, with rule violations and aggression often linked to ADHD children's being viewed negatively by their peers. Moreover, the social rejection appears to develop after only brief periods of interaction (Bickett & Milich, 1990). Drew Erhardt and Stephen Hinshaw (1994) asked students what factors contributed most to the peer status of ADHD youths. They found that physical attractiveness, athletic skill, intelligence, and academic achievement, for example, were not the main concerns. Aggression and noncompliance were two specific social behaviors that contributed to initial peer impressions of previously unfamiliar ADHD children (Erhardt & Hinshaw, 1994). In a different line of research that focuses on family relationships, ADHD children showed less compliance and more opposition to their parents than non-ADHD children. Interactions between ADHD children and their parents are marked by greater than normal levels of parental commands, reprimands, and punishment (Barkley, 1988).

ADHD does not exist alone: There is a high degree of comorbidity among ADHD children. According to one source, up to 44 percent have at least one other disorder (Szatmari, Offord & Boyle, 1989). For example, researchers have estimated that 20 to 25 percent of ADHD children also have learning disabilities (Barkley, 1990). In both the United States and England (McArdle, O'Brien & Kolvin, 1995), ADHD youths also have been found to have problems with aggression (such as conduct disorder). As we mention earlier, the possibility of subtypes of ADHD is gaining attention, and there seem to be important differences between ADHD youths with and without comorbid conduct disorder (Hinshaw, 1987).

Who Is Affected with ADHD?

ADHD has been identified in both boys and girls, but gender differences are regularly identified. A male-to-female ratio of between 4:1 and 8:1 is typical (Barkley, 1996). Gender differences also have been reported in the expression of ADHD. Among clinic-referred children, girls with ADHD have fewer behavior and conduct problems (less aggression) and more social withdrawal and anxiety and depression than boys with ADHD.

ADHD has been identified in a variety of ethnic groups and across cultures, with some cross-cultural differences emerging. For example, there is a lower prevalence of ADHD in Great Britain (Taylor, 1994) and a high rate of hyperactivity in China (Luk & Leung, 1989). Because of inconsistent diagnostic practices, however, interpretations of these rates must be made with caution (Mann et al., 1992).

Although ADHD children come from urban and rural as well as rich and poor families, socioeconomic status differences also have been reported: There is a somewhat greater frequency of ADHD among lower social classes. Three possible explanations have been suggested. Lower socioeconomic class mothers are likely to have poor nutrition and care during their pregnancies, as well as a high incidence of complications, perhaps affecting the developing brain of the as-yet unborn child. Second, the troubled environment of low socioeconomic status families might account for higher rates of family instability, divorce, and parental psychological disorders (Biederman et al., 1995). Last, the high incidence of ADHD among low socioeconomic status children may be due to a predisposition on the part of teachers and others to expect ADHD behavior among them. How the ADHD child is treated, even if not specific to the onset of disorder, certainly influences the course of the disorder.

The Course of ADHD

Don't all children show difficulties in attention, impulsivity, and excessive activity? Isn't it a part of normal development for children to run about and play spontaneously? Importantly, diagnoses of ADHD should be made in terms of **developmental appropriateness**: Only those children whose attention and activity problems are judged to be excessive relative to what is appropriate for the child's level of development should receive the label ADHD. Certainly, children's ability to exercise selective attention improves with age (Hagen & Hagen, 1973); a four-year-old is not expected to have the attentional focusing skills of a twelve-year-old. The impulsivity of a first-grader may be evident in fast and inaccurate responding to assigned math problems, whereas an impulsive adolescent is more likely to display impulsiveness in an increase in automobile accidents (Barkley et al., 1993). The developmental inappropriateness of the behaviors is essential in determining the presence of ADHD.

It was once thought that hyperactive children did not need treatment — that they would "outgrow" their problems. Some parents therefore refrained from seeking help and waited for a natural change to occur at puberty. In fact, some ADHD children do show a decrease in excessive motor activity at puberty, but the other ADHD problems do not seem to go away (Cantwell, 1987; Weiss & Hechtman, 1986). In approximately one-half of the patients, and some suggest in as many as three-fourths, the problems of attentional focus and related academic and social difficulties persist into adolescence (Fisher, Barkley, Edelbrock & Smallish, 1990; Gittelman, Mannuzza, Shenker & Bonagura, 1985) and potentially into adulthood.

FOCUS ON RESEARCH

Are There ADHD Adolescents? Adults?

The diagnosis of ADHD typically is made at about age six, when a child begins formal schooling. Do ADHD children become ADHD adolescents and then grow to be ADHD adults? To determine the adolescent and adult outcomes of ADHD youths, longitudinal research is required. But even this desirable research strategy has potential problems.

Russell Barkley and his colleagues at the University of Massachusetts Medical Center (see Barkley, Fisher, Edelbrock & Smallish, 1991) studied 100 ADHD and 60 non-ADHD children eight years after their initial diagnosis. Ratings of behavior problems and family conflicts, as well as direct observations of mother-child interactions, were taken in childhood and again at adolescence. The hyperactive children were rated by their mothers as having more numerous and intense family conflicts than the non-ADHD children, although the adolescents themselves did not differ in their own ratings of family conflict. Observations of mother-adolescent interactions revealed more controlling and negative behaviors and less positive and facilitating behaviors among the hyperactive dyads than among the controls. Interestingly, the presence of conduct-disordered behavior was associated with the persistence of the conflicted family situation — a finding that suggested that at least part of the persistence of ADHD can be explained by the comorbid existence of other behavior problems.

Despite the value of prospective longitudinal research, whenever researchers try to measure the same psychological dimension at two different points in time, certain problems emerge. For example, observations of mother-child interactions are different at age six and age fourteen. At age six mother-child interactions are observed within a free play situation; at fourteen, however, mother-child interactions are observed while the participants engage in neutral and conflicted verbal discussions. Different behavioral observation coding systems are needed for these two different interaction situations. The Barkley study used age-appropriate interaction situations, and the findings nevertheless evidenced meaningful consistencies. Children who were noncompliant as youngsters (in the free play situation) continued to be difficult with their parents at adolescence (in the discussion situation).

Barkley and associates could have chosen to use the same assessment situation at both points in time (parent-child interactions in free play), but such a choice, while creating equivalence of measurement at different ages, would have reduced the meaningfulness and relevance of the second assessment. Reviewers would have criticized the work for having used a developmentally inappropriate context for assessing mother-adolescent interaction. As it turned out, use of the developmentally appropriate situation provided the opportunity to observe and record behaviors that permitted reasonable tests of the authors' hypotheses. It also permitted reasonable confidence in the conclusion that the mother-child interaction conflicts continue to be significantly greater in ADHD than non-ADHD children at eight-year follow-up.

The likelihood that ADHD will persist into adolescence depends in part on several factors. First, how were the children with ADHD first identified? When ADHD is first seen in clinic-referred children, 50 to 80 percent may continue to have the disorder into adolescence (Barkley, 1996). This estimate is lower when the ADHD children are first identified via a school screening procedure. Also, the persistence of ADHD problems into adolescence is associated with other features of ADHD children at the time of the initial identification: the presence of conduct problems, the presence of oppositionality, and poor family relations.

The likelihood that ADHD persists into adulthood cannot be answered with confidence at this time. Only one study (Mannuzza & Klein, 1992) provides substantive data on the topic, and there are features of the study that may restrict the estimation of adult prevalence. That is, children with conduct problems — those most likely to have persistent ADHD — were excluded from the initial sample of ADHD children who were later assessed in adulthood. Thus, the 30 to 50 percent estimate of adult ADHD is likely to be lower than other estimates based on the full range of ADHD children at the initial identification. Although the exact adult prevalence awaits further research, the distractibility, inattentiveness, and difficulties with goal-directed persistence remain a serious concern for those adults with chronic ADHD (Biederman et al., 1993; Mannuzza et al., 1991; Spencer, Biederman, Wilens & Faraone, 1994; Weiss, Hechtman, Milroy & Perlman, 1985).

Assessing and Diagnosing ADHD   Identifying ADHD in children should involve several separate assessments:

- *Ratings of the child's behavior by parents and teachers.* The CBCL (Child Behavior Checklist), for example, can be used to place the level of the child's problem in comparison with other children (recall Figure 15.1).

- *Interviews with the child, parents, and teachers.* Details that may be lost on rating scales can be gathered through interviews. Interviews with parents and teachers can be especially helpful in assessing whether the child's behavior is consistent in different situations and what conditions exacerbate or reduce problematic behaviors.

- *Direct observation of behavior and task performance.* Observing the child also can provide valuable information in assessing ADHD. For example, trained observers can reliably distinguish hyperactive from nonhyperactive children by observing and recording behavior — such as out-of-seat behavior and disruptiveness (e.g., Milich, Loney & Roberts, 1986). As an example of a performance task, consider Figure 15.2, which shows an item from the Matching Familiar Figures Test (MFFT; Kagan, 1966). The MFFT is a measure of cognitive impulsivity, and impulsivity is an oft-noted feature of ADHD. In one study, performance on this task (one of more than twenty-five tests given) was found to be useful in identifying hyperactive children (Homatidis & Konstantereas, 1981).

Most assessments of ADHD employ a combination of data-gathering techniques and strive to determine a

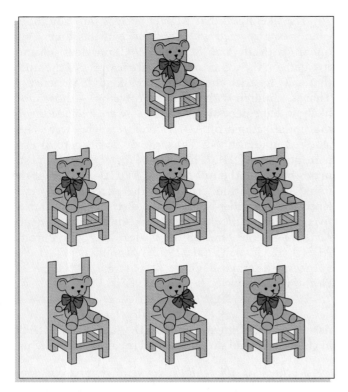

Figure 15.2 Sample Item from the Matching Familiar Figures Test

The child is asked to examine the pictures and to select from six variations the one that matches exactly the standard picture at the top. Fast and inaccurate performance (short response latencies and a high error rate) reflect impulsivity. Although impulsivity is not the same as ADHD, it is one of the central features of the disorder.

Source: From Kagan (1966).

diagnosis. Structured diagnostic interviews, for example, are used to gauge the child against the diagnostic criteria (see Table 15.2).

Causes of ADHD   Many factors contribute to the onset of ADHD. Genetically determined predispositions, brain damage and dysfunction, diet and toxic substances, and environmental forces have all been implicated.

Some evidence has suggested that genetic factors play a role in the disorder. For starters, it is widely accepted that genetic transmission influences individual differences in general activity level. But do genetics contribute to the disorder? Some data have suggested that the answer is yes — an individual may genetically acquire a predisposition to develop ADHD in response to environmental events. For monozygotic twins, the concordance rate was 81 percent, whereas it was only 29 percent for dizygotic twins (Gilger, Pennington & DeFries, 1992), and ADHD occurs more often in first-degree biological relatives of those with the disorder

than would be expected in the general population. Approximately 25 percent of the natural parents of ADHD children, compared with 4 percent of adoptive parents, had histories (gathered retrospectively) of ADHD (Deutsch, 1987). Interestingly, there is also a higher incidence of other disorders (such as mood disorder) among the natural parents and extended relatives of children with ADHD (Biederman et al., 1987).

Siblings of a person with ADHD are at greater risk for ADHD, especially when parents have a history of ADHD, and monozygotic twins are more likely to be concordant than dizygotic twins (McMahon, 1980). The data also suggest that the more serious the symptom picture, the greater is the genetic contribution to the disorder. A specific mechanism for genetic transmission of ADHD, however, has not been identified.

Researchers have studied the possible role of brain damage, brain dysfunction, and neurological immaturity in ADHD. Decades ago, "minimal brain damage" was a label used for the behaviors seen in ADHD. Not surprisingly, researchers sought to document a brain damage–ADHD causal link. In studies of identified ADHD patients, only 5 to 10 percent were found to have histories suggestive of brain damage, and most children with well-documented brain damage did not develop ADHD (Rutter, 1977). The use of computerized axial tomography (CT) scans also failed to reveal anatomical brain differences (Shaywitz et al., 1983) and brain metabolism differences (Zametkin et al., 1993) between ADHD children and controls. These results led to the conclusion that brain damage is clearly not the sole cause of ADHD and may not even be a correlate of ADHD.

Studies have suggested that brain function may be impaired: ADHD children show performance deficits on tasks sensitive to brain function, and they perform less well on measures requiring vigilance and impulse control (Homatidis & Konstantareas, 1981). Specific parts of the brain, such as the frontal and frontal-limbic areas, have been implicated. The so-called neurological immaturity of ADHD children refers to their being chronically delayed relative to same-aged peers. The attention span, social behavior, and even electroencephalographic (EEG) patterns of ADHD children suggest immature brain activity. Although research results are consistent with the hypothesis that brain function is involved in ADHD, poor task performance and delayed functioning could be due to other influences.

Another hypothesis holds that hyperactivity is related to diet. For example, sugar as a cause of ADHD is considered a myth. Also, eating foods with artificial dyes and preservatives has been suggested as a cause. After claims were published that a change in diet could reduce hyperactivity (Feingold, 1975), parents rushed to implement the diet program, while scientists undertook more rigorous tests of the diet hypothesis. Overall, the

Table 15.2 Diagnostic Criteria for ADHD

I. Inattention, as seen in at least six of the following:

Often fails to give close attention to details or makes careless mistakes in school, work, or other activities

Often has difficulty sustaining attention in tasks or play activites

Often does not seem to listen to what is being said to him or her

Often does not follow through on instructions and fails to finish schoolwork or chores

Often has difficulties organizing tasks and activities

Often avoids or strongly dislikes tasks that require sustained mental effort

Often loses things necessary for tasks

Is often easily distracted by extraneous stimuli

Is often forgetful in daily activities

2. Hyperactivity/impulsivity, as seen in at least six of the following:

Hyperactivity

Often fidgets with hands or feet or squirms in seat

Often leaves seat in situations when remaining seated is expected

Often runs about or climbs excessively in situations when it is inappropriate

Often has difficulty playing or engaging in leisure activities

Impulsivity

Often blurts out answers to questions before the questions have been completed

Often has difficulty awaiting turn

Often interrupts or intrudes on others

For a diagnosis of ADHD, the onset can be no later than seven years of age, symptoms must be present in two or more situations and for a duration of at least six months, and the symptoms must produce clear evidence of clinically relevant distress.

Source: Adapted from DSM-IV. Reprinted with permission from *The Diagnostic and Statistical Manual of Mental Disorders,* Fourth Edition. Copyright © 1994 American Psychiatric Association.

data were equivocal but generally failed to support the hypothesis (Conners, 1980). After reviewing several studies, James Swanson and Marcel Kinsbourne (1980) noted that the more rigorous the investigation, the less support it provided for the diet hypothesis.

Some have hypothesized social and environmental causes for ADHD, particularly the child's failure to learn adequate cognitive and behavioral skills. Perhaps, like socially appropriate behavior, ADHD behaviors are shaped by the social environment (O'Leary, 1980). Lack of a structured learning environment, observing inappropriate behavior by others, receiving rewards for fast guessing, not being taught cognitive strategies for modulating attention, and disruption and disorganization in the home can contribute to a child's failure to acquire sufficient self-control. For example, Wahler and Dumas (1989) viewed a variety of childhood problems as the result of dysfunctional parent-child interactions. Overall, however, few studies have examined the social environmental factors suggested as causal in ADHD. Data have suggested that parents of ADHD children provide more direct commands and supervision than others, but these actions seem the result rather than the cause of the ADHD behavior. Also, following effective use of stimulant medication, mothers show a diminished

pattern of control (Barkley, Karlsson, Pollard & Murphy, 1985). As Braswell and Bloomquist (1991) noted, environmental factors seem to play a more important role in the course and ultimate outcome of ADHD than in its initial cause.

A final note about the possible causes of ADHD: It is not caused by the soft x-rays emitted from fluorescent lighting. Although one study (Mayron, Ott, Nations & Mayron, 1974) reported that children exposed to full-spectrum lighting systems showed greater reduction in hyperactivity than did children who were exposed to standard cool-white fluorescent lamps, the study had several flaws. The observational period was quite brief, and the authors did not specifically control for the level of illumination produced by the two lighting systems. Another study (O'Leary, Rosenbaum & Hughes, 1978) alternated broad-spectrum and standard cool-white fluorescent systems at the end of each week of an eight-week period. This research team took care to ensure equivalent illumination and brightness across the weeks of the study. Their findings were clear: Lighting conditions had no effect on hyperactive behavior.

The accepted explanation of ADHD invokes a multiple pathways model, not unlike the diathesis-stress model described earlier in this book. The growing consensus is that persons with ADHD have a biological predisposition and that the disorder can be exacerbated by environmental forces. Despite our less than full understanding of the cause of ADHD, several approaches to treatment have been developed and evaluated.

Treatments for ADHD: Medications and Psychosocial Programs The major current treatments for ADHD are medications and behavioral and cognitive-behavioral strategies. Both pharmacological and psychological treatments for ADHD have received considerable application and study. In many instances, the approaches are combined, and the efforts of parents, professionals, and schools are included and integrated.

Medications for ADHD typically involve stimulants that, in proper dosage, have a "focusing" effect. Because the effects wear off within hours, they are commonly given two or three times a day. A review of over 150 studies (Spencer et al., 1996) concluded that use of the *psychostimulant medications* [typically methylphenidate (Ritalin) but also pemoline (Cylert) and dextroamphetamine (Dexedrine)] by children with ADHD can increase their ability to sustain attention, decrease impulsiveness, and improve performance on fine motor tasks. The positive response rate is approximately 70 percent. Also, numerous investigations have indicated that children's performances on a wide variety of cognitive tasks improve while on stimulants (Klorman et al., 1994; Rapport & Kelly, 1991), and a recent study (Spencer et al., 1995) reported that ADHD adults benefited from methylphenidate. Stimulants probably have a positive effect on attentional symptoms, which leads to a decrease in physical hyperactivity. However, the attentional focusing does not always translate into increased academic performance. Although there has been reservation about the use of medications for ADHD children who have tics (involuntary rapid stereotyped motor movements), recent data suggest that medications did not alter tic frequency (Gadow et al., 1995).

That stimulant medications have a quieting effect on ADHD children may seem "paradoxical." Indeed, for some years investigators thought a *paradoxical effect* occurred when a child was quieted by a stimulant. Moreover, the quieting effect was thought to be evidence of the presence of attentional hyperactive problems. This belief is false. Stimulant medications have a quieting and focusing effect on all children, both ADHD and non-ADHD (Rapoport et al., 1978; Weingartner et al., 1980).

Despite some positive effects linked to stimulant medications, there are shortcomings. Researchers have estimated that 70 percent of children with ADHD show a positive response to stimulants (Spencer et al., 1996), but stimulants also have potential, unwanted side effects — including anxiety, insomnia, irritability, weight loss, increased blood pressure and heart rate, and occasional motor tics (Barkley, McMurray, Edelbrock & Robbins, 1990). Also, not all children can be given these medications, nor do all who take them improve (Whalen & Henker, 1991). In the majority who improve, the effects are short-lived, persisting only as long as the drugs are taken.

The number of children given the diagnosis of ADHD is rising rapidly. Correspondingly, increasing numbers of youths are being placed on medications (e.g., Ritalin). In the United States alone, some 750,000 children take Ritalin (Rapport & Kelly, 1991). Based on biannual surveys conducted in Baltimore since 1971 (Safer & Krager, 1988), the prevalence of medication treatment for ADHD has doubled every four years, with approximately 6 percent receiving such treatment in 1987. The trend is said to have continued, resulting in widespread use of medications for inattention and hyperactivity.

Questions have been raised about the reasons for the increase in diagnoses and use of medications. Some researchers suggest that 30 to 50 percent of those taking Ritalin may not even have ADHD (Bocella, 1995). Misidentification of ADHD is on the rise. For example, government regulations now provide special education services for children with ADHD, so there is an incentive for some parents to seek and receive an ADHD diagnosis for their child. A related problem: Because of the heightened sense of well-being produced by the drug, there are increased reports of children selling their medicine, with some youths breaking the pills and snorting the drug.

Psychological approaches to treating ADHD emphasize teaching children the skills necessary to pay attention, engage in self-control, and reduce excessive motor activity. Following the statement of Dan O'Leary in 1980 that hyperactive children need skills, not just pills, these methods aim to modify the environment and provide structured opportunities for children to learn self-control skills that they can take into new situations. Psychological treatments characteristically teach behavioral management and may feature parent training, structured classroom programs, and training in cognitive skills.

Comprehensive parent training programs typically provide parents with some basic education about ADHD and teach them behavior management skills. As Barkley (1990) argued, many of the interpersonal difficulties associated with hyperactivity come from the child's noncompliance and lack of self-control. Accordingly, parents are taught skills to reduce noncompliance (e.g., Forehand & McMahon, 1981) and to help the child develop self-control (e.g., see Braswell & Bloomquist, 1991; Kendall & Braswell, 1993). Parents learn to reward appropriate behavior, shape desired responses, reduce and eliminate inappropriate behaviors, and use additional rewards to maintain behavior gains. Use of a brief "time out" from desired activities, for instance, can be an effective punishment for misbehavior. Parents can be taught how to ignore unwanted actions, provide nonabrasive commands, and pay attention to positive behavior. Based on the positive outcomes of a comparison between parent training and a wait-list condition, researchers have stated that parent training increased parents' self-esteem, reduced their stress, and produced overall improvements in their children's ADHD symptoms (Anastopoulos, Shelton, DuPaul & Gouvremont, 1993). Not all skills that are evident during parent training, however, are maintained after the program is completed.

Classroom management programs are designed to develop the child's ability to benefit from classroom instruction, decrease activity levels, and increase focused attention. For example, in one ten-week program, teachers first determined academic and behavioral goals and reinforcers for each child (O'Leary, Pelham, Rosenbaum & Price, 1976). The teachers completed a daily checklist rating the child's behavior in the classroom, and the child could receive reinforcers according to the results of the checklist at the end of the day and at the end of each week. Compared with untreated children, the children who completed this program were rated as being less hyperactive and as showing improved behavior. Like parent training, classroom skill training is effective while the program is operating but diminishes in effectiveness after the program is discontinued.

Overcoming this backsliding — by shaping and encouraging the child to internalize and take to other situations the skills learned in behavioral management programs — is one goal of cognitive-behavioral treatments. Thus, cognitive-behavioral treatments combine behavioral management training with direct efforts to teach both self-control skills, such as self-evaluation and self-reward, and attention-focusing skills. The treatment strives to instill problem-solving skills that the child can apply in the classroom and with parents and peers, but the goal of generalization outside and after the program has not always been met; some research reports have shown generalization of one aspect of ADHD (impulsivity), but others have been disappointing.

In a comparative study (Abikoff & Gittelman, 1985), the authors reported greater effectiveness for medications over parent and teacher contingency management in reducing ADHD behavior. Separate applications of behavioral therapy and medications produced relatively comparable effects on classroom behavior in one study (Carlson, Pelham, Milich & Dixon, 1992), whereas medications were superior to behavior modification in another study, although both treatments were effective (Pelham et al., 1993).

Recognizing the central role of anger management for ADHD youths, Stephen Hinshaw, Barbara Henker, and Carol Whalen (1984) compared a cognitive-behavioral anger control program and Ritalin. Relative to their behavior before treatment, children in all conditions displayed less fidgeting and verbal aggression. The children receiving the cognitive-behavioral treatment were rated as having higher degrees of self-control and displaying more appropriate coping behaviors than the children receiving just medication. Although medications did not alter the content of the child's response, they did produce changes in the intensity of the child's behavior. Unfortunately, no follow-up studies were done to determine if these beneficial gains were lasting.

The findings that stimulant medications and behavioral programs can have desirable effects on ADHD have sparked a growing belief that the combination of medication and behavior therapy may offer the most promising comprehensive treatment for these children. A series of research studies as well is questioning the potential utility of treatment combinations. What are the outcomes of programs that employ both medications and behavioral or cognitive-behavioral training?

Although research on combined treatments has been described as having major methodological barriers (Whalen & Henker, 1991), investigators have reached some tentative conclusions. In an examination of combined medication and cognitive therapy, the combined treatment was compared with cognitive therapy alone and medication alone (Abikoff et al., 1988). In this study, the cognitive therapy focused on academic work. All three conditions demonstrated comparable levels of improvement, suggesting not only that each approach is useful but also that the academically focused cognitive components did not add meaningfully to the effects achieved by medications.

Conduct Disorders

Josh was twelve years old when he was brought home at 12:30 A.M. by the police. He had run away from home the day before, slept in a parked car that he had broken into, and was identified as the perpetrator of a theft at a neighborhood convenience store. He also had been sought by school officials because, on more than one occasion, he had been in fights and had skipped school for several consecutive days. Josh's mother claims that she can't control him, and his teachers report that he is defiant and uncooperative in class and cruel to some of the other children. Josh did not report feeling emotional distress, but those around him suffered from his lack of socially appropriate behavior.

Clinical Characteristics and Diagnosis of Conduct Disorder The essential features of **conduct disorder** (according to DSM-IV) are a repetitive and persistent pattern of behavior that involves violation of the basic

Two youths fighting. Sometimes, youth resort to physical aggression. This situation can arise when youth misinterpret the actions of others or when they have a low level of tolerance for social demands.

rights of others and of the major age-appropriate social norms. The conduct problems are evident at school, in the home, within the community, and with peers. A common feature of conduct disorder is physical aggression, taking the form of cruelty, damage to the property of others, or fire-setting. For example, Joe, in the chapter opening, was a suspect in setting the fire. Stealing, lying, and cheating are also common among children diagnosed with conduct disorder. To warrant a diagnosis of conduct disorder, the behavior must last at least six months, during which three of the problems listed in Table 15.3 are present.

In many ways, conduct disorder resembles **oppositional defiant disorder**, which is another type of disruptive behavior disorder. Whereas conduct disorders are essentially concerned with serious violations of the basic rights of others, oppositional defiant disorder involves a pattern of negativistic, hostile, and defiant behavior that has lasted a minimum of six months. Diagnosis of oppositional defiant disorder requires the presence (often) of four of the following behaviors: loses temper, argues with adults, defies rules, intentionally annoys others, blames others for mistakes, is easily annoyed, is angry and resentful, is spiteful and vindictive, and is easily annoyed by others. When conduct disorder is present, the behaviors associated with oppositional defiant disorder also likely will be present. Therefore, a diagnosis of conduct disorder preempts a diagnosis of oppositional defiant disorder.

Diagnostically, conduct disorders are a heterogeneous grouping. There are cases with and without significant aggression, with and without illegal activities, with and without family psychopathology, and with and without comorbid diagnoses such as ADHD or learning disabilities. These youths are often impulsive, have a high need for stimulation, are low in empathy and moral development, and have troubled interpersonal relationships (Martin & Hoffman, 1990). Substance abuse is also a concern.

In an effort to better understand conduct problems, Loeber and associates (1993) studied about 500 boys aged three to sixteen years over a three-year period and identified three developmental pathways or trajectories that lead to disruptive behavior problems. According to

According to DSM-IV, conduct disorder is diagnosed when there is a repetitive and persistent pattern of behavior in which either the basic rights of others or major age-appropriate societal norms or rules are violated. Three (or more) of the following criteria are present in the last twelve months, with at least one present in the last six months.

Table 15.3 Criteria for Diagnosing Conduct Disorder

Often bullies, threatens, or intimidates others

Often initiates physical fights

Has used a weapon that can cause serious physical harm to others

Has been physically cruel to people

Has been physically cruel to animals

Has stolen with confrontation of a victim

Has forced someone into sexual activity

Has deliberately engaged in fire-setting with the intention of causing serious damage

Has deliberately destroyed others' property

Has broken into someone else's house, building, or car

Often lies or breaks promises to obtain goods or favors or to avoid obligations

Has stolen items of nontrivial value without confrontation with the victim either within the home or outside the home

Often stays out at night despite parental prohibitions, beginning before thirteen years of age

Has run away from home overnight at least twice while living in parental or parental surrogate home

Often truant from school, beginning before age thirteen

Perhaps homeless or on the road without supervision, two teens with a sign expressing their need. Although they may be asking to be used as workers, there is the risk that they might be misunderstood by others and mistaken as prostitutes to be used and exploited sexually.

Loeber and associates, the overt behavior pathway consists of those antisocial actions which are confrontive, such as fighting, arguing, and temper tantrums, whereas the covert behavior pathway consists of concealed actions, such as stealing, truancy, and lying. A third pathway — early authority conflict (e.g., stubborn, defiant) — also was identified. The lowest rates of offending were seen in boys in the overt and authority conflict pathways, whereas those youths with the highest delinquency and most violent offenses showed escalation over the years on scores on all three pathways. Researchers may come to further identify different etiological pictures, and eventually, distinctions such as these may produce subgroups of children who are differentially responsive to interventions.

Who Is Affected with Conduct Disorder?

According to several estimates, 4 to 10 percent of children meet criteria for conduct disorder (Martin & Hoffman, 1990). Moreover, when teenagers are asked to self-report their experience with the specific behaviors that comprise conduct disorder, they report an alarmingly high rate: More than 50 percent admit to theft, and 45 percent admit to property destruction. Based on a review of prevalence studies conducted with clinic-referred children, Karen Wells and Rex Forehand (1985), of the University of Georgia, noted that 33 to 75 percent of the referrals were for conduct-disordered behaviors.

Gender differences in conduct disorder are evident. The precise gender ratio in the prevalence of the disorder is difficult to determine because of the varying types of assessments that have been used: Estimates that vary from 3:1 to 7:1 (males to females) are common (Earls, 1994), with biological and psychosocial theories offered to explain the observed difference (Eme & Kavanaugh, 1995). Gender differences are apparent in the age of onset of conduct disorder (Kazdin, 1990). Whereas most boys had an onset before age ten, the onset of conduct disorder in girls was concentrated in the early teens (ages thirteen to sixteen). Gender differences are evident in symptoms as well: Theft is more common among males, and sexual misbehavior is more common among females.

What can be said about the meaning of these gender differences? Clearly, one cannot determine the causes of the observed differences without further investigation. One speculative explanation is that the socialization process, in both families and schools, shapes boys and girls in different directions. For example, aggressiveness is tolerated more in boys than in girls, and boys are expected to discharge their tensions in more physical ways. Others have speculated that there are biological differences and biological predispositions toward different types of behavior problems.

Conduct disorders are found around the globe (e.g., Rutter et al., 1976). In a sample of youths in New Zealand, 9 percent of boys and 4.6 percent of girls were found to have chronic antisocial behavior patterns (McGee, Silva & Williams, 1984). Conduct problems are more prevalent among those of low socioeconomic status and among those from urban (8 percent) rather than rural (4 percent) settings (e.g., Barclay & Hoffman, 1990), although an urban-rural difference was not found in one study (Offord, Boyle & Racine, 1991).

The Course of Conduct Disorder

A large number of young people engage in single behaviors that resemble conduct problems, but this number decreases with age.

Of those who continue and who show wider ranges of conduct problems, there is an increased likelihood of antisocial behavior in adulthood. As we discuss in Chapter 14, there is transgenerational consistency in antisocial and aggressive behavior patterns. Indeed, perhaps the most troublesome feature of conduct disorder is its stability over time (Lahey et al., 1995). Early evidence of conduct disorder is related to later aggression, antisocial behavior, and other adult difficulties. As argued by Leonard Eron and Rowell Huesmann (1990), aggressive behavior, if untreated, has been shown to be stable over a thirty-year period of time.

What accounts for the onset of conduct disorder? A number of influences have been identified — cognitive factors, biological forces, and the role of the family.

Cognitive Factors in Conduct Disorder   The factors most often associated with the risk of conduct disorder include features of the individual child, the child's parents, and the interaction patterns between child and parent. Investigators have found that academic and intellectual difficulties, for example, predict conduct disorder (West, 1982), although many children with limited academic abilities do not display antisocial actions. Other aspects of the child that are possible risk factors include cognitive and biological characteristics.

Aggressive young people often show cognitive deficiencies (e.g., Sequin et al., 1995). They lack problem-solving skills (Spivack & Shure, 1982), scoring low on measures of the ability to generate multiple solutions to problems. Also, conduct-disordered children seem more likely than nondisordered children to think of solutions that others would rate as aggressive and less likely to think of socially appropriate solutions to interpersonal problems.

Aggressive children also display cognitive distortions when thinking about social interactions. Kenneth Dodge (1985) and other researchers have documented this tendency in a series of studies. For example, Dodge et al. (1995) presented children with videotaped vignettes that showed one child doing something that caused a negative outcome for another child. In some of the tapes the intention of the actor was ambiguous. The children were asked to choose an explanation for the actor's behavior. The studies consistently showed that relatively aggressive children were more likely than nonaggressive children to believe that the actors in the ambiguous tapes had hostile intentions. In contrast, nonaggressive children were likely to see ambiguous actions as accidental. For example, suppose that you have a new Walkman radio. You loan it briefly to a friend, and when it is returned, the headset no longer works. Why did this happen? A greater percentage of aggressive than nonaggressive children will say that the damage was done on purpose, "to get me mad" or "because he was jealous."

In short, aggressive children seem to have a **hostile attributional bias**: When a situation is ambiguous, they tend to attribute negative motivations to others. This distortion may then prompt the aggressive child to retaliate, and a vicious cycle can result.

Genetic Factors   At present, there are no twin studies reporting on conduct disorder as currently conceptualized (Earls, 1994). A recent study of adoptees (Cadoret et al., 1995), however, sheds some light on the issue. These researchers studied the male and female offspring, separated at birth, of parents with known antisocial behavior. The results indicated that a biological background for antisocial behavior predicted adolescent aggression and conduct disorder. Importantly, however, the study also examined the adoptive home environments: Adverse environments independently predicted later conduct problems. As the authors concluded, an adverse adoptive home environment and biological background of antisocial behavior interact in producing increased aggression and conduct disorder.

The many labels used to describe externalizing problems — *conduct disorder, aggression, antisocial behavior* — have clouded the picture. Among twin studies that specifically examine aggression, no consistent pattern of genetic influence on aggressiveness has been reported (Plomin, Nitz & Rowe, 1990). Still, genetic contributions to antisocial behavior clearly exist and have been found in lesser amounts for adolescent delinquency as well (DiLalla & Gottesman, 1989; Wicks-Nelson & Israel, 1991). Based on the studies to date, there may be a genetic component to conduct disorder as well.

The Role of the Family   Many research findings have supported the idea that the family is a major factor in the cause of conduct disorders (e.g., Jouriles, Bourg & Farris, 1991). Four alternative patterns are common in the families of youngsters with conduct disorder: parental deviance, parental rejection and coerciveness, lack of discipline or supervision of children, and marital conflict and divorce (Hetherington & Martin, 1979).

Overt marital conflict can contribute to oppositional behavior in children (Mann & MacKenzie, 1996). Furthermore, many parents of children with conduct disorder are themselves deviant, displaying maladjustment, anger, and sometimes criminal behavior. Indeed, many children with conduct disorder have a parent with antisocial personality disorder (Rutter & Quinton, 1984). Criminal behavior and alcoholism, particularly in the father, put the child at high risk for conduct disorder (Robins, 1966; West, 1982). Separation from an antisocial father does not seem to protect the child from this risk, perhaps because with the father absent, discipline may weaken.

Parents of conduct-disordered children tend to respond coercively and often negatively to their children. Although measuring parental practices is difficult, there seems to be a strong association between negative parent-child relations and antisocial conduct in youngsters (e.g., Loeber, 1990). An extreme form of parental negativism is physical abuse. In a study of 584 Caucasian and African American youths (grades one to four), those who had been abused physically had significantly more conduct problems than those not abused (Dodge, Pettit, Bates & Valente, 1995). Although such a correlation does not permit a causal statement, it can be suggested that the experience of abuse fashions these childrens' view of the world as a dangerous place in which aggression is a reasonable way to solve problems. In a study of Danish sons of alcoholic fathers, a past history of severe physical abuse by the father was a significant predictor of antisocial traits in the son (Pollock et al., 1992).

A close look at specific patterns of parent-child interactions that are related to antisocial activity comes from the work of Gerald Patterson (1982). He observed parents and their conduct-disordered children and found that parents had difficulties appropriately disciplining their offspring. According to Patterson's analysis, the parents of children with conduct disorder tended to reward positive and negative behaviors inconsistently. In particular, the parents often reinforced — by attention or laughter — coercive child behaviors, such as demanding, defying, yelling, and arguing. Thus, the child learns to use coercive behaviors. Over time, the child learns to be even more coercive, possibly hitting and attacking. Meanwhile, positive behaviors by the child often were ignored or responded to inappropriately. In effect, the youngster was rewarded for displaying antisocial acts and failed to learn adaptive behavior. Thus, according to Patterson, families with children with conduct disorder are characterized by coercive interactions. Poor parent-ing skills, he argued, produce and promote antisocial behavior.

Such a parenting style was studied in 708 families, some of which had monozygotic (93) and dizygotic (99) twins (Reiss et al., 1995). These authors reported that almost 60 percent of the variance in adolescent antisocial behavior could be accounted for by conflictual and negative parenting behavior directed toward the adolescent.

Finally, high rates of divorce have been associated with conduct disorders (Rutter & Quinton, 1984), but the divorce itself may not contribute significantly to the problem. Instead, there is some evidence that divorce is frequent among parents and families with certain characteristics and that those characteristics — not divorce itself — contribute to the onset of conduct disorder.

Treatments for Conduct Disorder From several vantage points the conclusions appear consistent: Family conflict and poor parenting skills characterize the family relations of children with conduct disorder, and the children themselves display cognitive as well as behavioral difficulties. These characteristics suggest several possible approaches to treating these children, and recent reviews have suggested that treatments for young children with emerging conduct disorder can be beneficial. Many of the more effective methods involve systemwide programs in schools or behaviorally oriented parent training.

Can programs implemented at a schoolwide level catch the problem early and prevent the emergence of conduct disorder? In a school-based program, Roger Weissberg and his colleagues (Caplan et al., 1992) taught broad-based problem-solving skills and included specific applications of problem solving to problems facing sixth- and seventh-grade inner-city youths. After the program, the youths were rated as improved in handling personal problems, impulse control, and popularity.

Parents participate in a parent training meeting. Children do not come with "owner's manuals." As a result, there are many things that can be learned from involvement in parent training. Here, parents are involved in a role-playing activity where they gain experience with various ways to handle child problems and manage the stress of parenting.

Excessive alcohol use also was reduced. Long-term follow-up studies and rigorous research designs are needed, including measurement of delinquent and criminal acts, but prevention is a first step in dealing with aggressive and antisocial behavior problems.

Parent training is another approach to treatment. It is suggested by the association between conduct disorder and ineffective, punitive, and inconsistent parenting. In **action-oriented family therapy** (briefly described in Chapter 3), parents are taught skills for managing their children (e.g., Alexander, Holtzworth-Munroe & Jameson, 1994). These treatments are aimed toward undermining the coercive family interactions associated with antisocial behavior. The family and the therapist set goals in terms of changes in target behaviors. Through written manuals, practice with the therapist, and homework assignments, parents learn to identify problem behavior, to observe and record the frequency of the behavior, to reward proper behavior effectively, and to stop rewarding unwanted behavior.

Numerous studies have indicated that action-oriented family therapy can lead to improvements in children's functioning, reductions in antisocial behaviors, and continuing improvements for at least brief follow-up periods. For example, in one study, Patterson (1974) documented that after treatment the frequency of a target behavior dropped to a level within the range found in nondeviant families. In another study (Patterson, Chamberlain & Reid, 1982), the changes in parental discipline were accompanied by reductions in children's antisocial behaviors, whereas there was no change in antisocial behavior in families whose discipline practices did not change. Home-based programs sometimes have been associated with improved behavior in the classroom and even with reductions in siblings' deviant behavior.

Despite some promising results, much more research is needed to identify the specific types of antisocial conduct and specific groups of children and families that benefit from parent training programs (Dumas, 1989). Studies of the effectiveness of these programs are often marred because some families drop out before completing the therapy. Treatment success is greater when the problem children are identified early and is probably also better for families that are less stressed and relatively better off socioeconomically. Data are supportive, but these programs tend to be relatively brief, and antisocial conduct problems may represent a long-term problem requiring long-term treatment.

Another approach to treatment focuses on cognitive processing; therapy targets the deficient and distorted thinking tied to conduct disorders. Cognitive-behavioral treatments aim to teach children to stop, think, and engage in reflective problem solving. They often teach problem-solving skills and provide experiences to rectify misperceptions such as the hostile attribution bias. For

example, in one program that aims to train children to cope with their anger, the therapist teaches the children the process of problem solving and models how to manage arousal without getting upset (Lochman, White & Wayland, 1991; Nelson & Finch, 1995). The therapist also gives homework assignments, provides the children with opportunities to practice their new skills in provocative situations, and gives rewards for improvement.

Studies of cognitive-behavioral treatments have examined various measures of success, such as ratings by parents and teachers, number of behavior problems, progress in school, participation in social activities, and amount of cooperative play. These studies and follow-up reports of the effects of booster sessions (e.g., Lochman, 1992) testify to the value of teaching children cognitive and behavioral skills for solving interpersonal dilemmas. For example, cognitive-behavioral treatments have shown some success in decreasing aggressive behavior and increasing prosocial behavior (Kazdin, Esveldt-Dawson, French & Unis, 1987) (see Figure 15.3). In one study, twenty sessions of a program that taught impulse control and problem-solving skills produced significant improvements in social behavior (Kendall et al., 1990), but some youths continued to display conduct-disordered behavior even when their prosocial interactions increase. Additional research is needed to fine-tune the

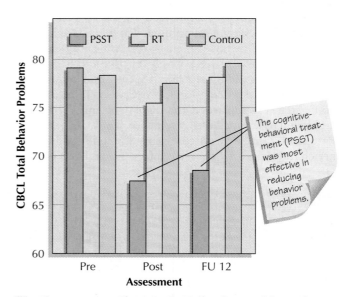

Figure 15.3 Changes in Behavior Problems from Pretreatment Through Follow-Up for Conduct-Disordered Youth

Psychological treatments have shown some success in decreasing aggressive behavior and increasing prosocial behavior in conduct-disordered youths. Compared with relationship therapy (RT) and the control condition, a cognitive-behavioral therapy called problem-solving skills training (PSST) was more effective at reducing behavior problems.
Source: From Kazdin, Siegel & Bass (1992).

interventions for children of different ages and to ensure the maintenance of any gains from the treatment.

Promising leads for future treatment of youths with conduct disorder come from programs that improve either parents' behavior-management skills or the child's cognitive processing. In addition, we have learned that preventive efforts are best directed toward younger children who have not yet become immersed in delinquent or antisocial behavior patterns. A prime example is the work of Tremblay and associates in Montreal, Canada (Tremblay et al., 1990): A two-year program was provided to oppositional and aggressive kindergarten boys from low-income families. The intervention included parent training and child social skills development. At three-year follow-up, the program, compared with control conditions, resulted in less fighting and delinquent behavior, as well as less frequent grade retention. Early intervention is important because once the problematic behavior patterns become entrenched, they are resistant to treatment.

EMOTIONAL DISORDERS

Emotional development is a challenge for all human beings. Over the course of less than a decade, children move from a state of limited emotional understanding to become complex emotional individuals. With age, the number and complexity of emotional experiences, as well as the demands for modulating emotional expression, all increase. It is not surprising that some children are overwhelmed by these challenges and experience emotional disorders.

When children are asked to answer a question in the classroom or to perform in front of relatives, they may become anxious. When a pet dies, a close friend moves to another state, or a favorite toy or book is damaged, children are likely to feel sad. These reactions are normal. The anxiety disorders of childhood and adolescence and the depressive disorders with onset in childhood or adolescence are characterized by more extreme and persistent emotional reactions. It is the severe manifestations of emotional behaviors that require intervention. Emotional disorders are discussed in Chapters 6 and 8, but we are concerned here with the anxious and depressive disorders that occur in infants, children, and adolescents.

WHAT'S NORMAL?
Facing Emotional Challenges

As we embark on a discussion of emotional disorders of childhood, let's begin by asking ourselves a question: Have we ever felt extreme emotional upset? The answer

is most probably yes. Everyone has, and alone it is not sufficient to warrant a judgment of abnormality or a negative reflection on one's character. Similarly, children experience fears and anxieties — normal emotional challenges — but these fears and anxieties signal psychological disorder only when they are intense and prolonged.

Consistently, research findings over the past fifty years indicate that fears and anxieties in childhood are numerous and common (Jersild & Holmes, 1935; McFarlane, Allen & Honzik, 1954; Lapouse & Monk, 1958; Ollendick & King, 1991). Miller, Barrett, and Hampe (1974) assessed 249 children ages seven to twelve. The study showed that 25 to 45 percent showed no fear, 50 to 60 percent showed normal fear, and 4 to 6 percent showed excessive fear. It should not be surprising that the vast majority of children (86 percent of the 568 studied) exposed in 1992 to Hurricane Andrew reported at least mild disaster-related symptoms

Challenges often require skills and courage, and normal development is full of challenging situations. Here, a teen meets the challenge of a high ropes course. Although some anxiety may be associated initially with the task, mastering the task builds confidence for future challenges.

(Vernberg, LaGreca, Silverman & Prinstein, 1996). Regarding gender, studies are relatively consistent in finding that girls report more fears than boys (Ollendick & King, 1991), although both genders report fears associated with the same stimuli (such as getting lost in a strange place or a burglar's breaking into the house).

There are different fears for different years. Children aged eight months to two years fear separation from the caregiver, although this diminishes between the ages of one and two. Between the ages of two and four the tight attachment weakens and new fears appear — such as fears of animals and the dark. Between the ages of four and six the child's imagination develops and creates visions of ghosts, half-human/half-animal monsters, and unexplained sounds in the night. After age six children are more likely to have fears of injury, death, or natural catastrophes. Both Caucasian and African American youth reported similar fears (Neal & Knisley, 1995), centering around harm befalling self or others. As adolescence approaches, the child may fear not being an accepted member of the peer group.

At different points along the life span, the social environment presents different challenges that require the development of new skills, beliefs, or feelings. Fears and anxieties represent such challenges during childhood. Through learning to cope with anxious and fearful situations in childhood, children learn ways to cope with the fears and anxieties of later life. For instance, recognizing a fear, addressing the fear, coping with the fear, and eventually no longer experiencing the fear constitutes a developmental sequence that can bolster the individual's ability to cope with anxiety in the future.

Fears and anxieties are normal developmental challenges facing the maturing individual. During adolescence, autonomy and independence become major developmental challenges. The adolescent must establish a difficult balance between complying with rules and expressing independent competency. Again, it is normal to be involved in the conflicts of emerging independence, but the challenge posed by autonomy can trigger or exacerbate interpersonal problems. Child behaviors that may or may not be signs of psychological disorder must consider the culture (Lambert et al., 1992) and be judged against the frequency of the same behaviors among nontroubled children. The relative intensity, frequency, and duration of the behaviors must be evaluated, and their role in the course of normal development must be considered.

Anxiety Disorders

Like adults, children and adolescents are diagnosed with the anxiety disorders discussed in Chapter 6, including generalized anxiety disorder (GAD) and social phobia. In general, the symptoms associated with anxiety in

THE FAR SIDE By GARY LARSON

"I've got it again, Larry . . . an eerie feeling like there's something on top of the bed."

youth resemble those found in adults, including physiological, behavioral, and cognitive manifestations. Although the symptoms of anxiety disorders in young people may be seen in expressions such as stomach aches, headaches, muscle tension, sweating, jittery behavior, or feelings of suffocation or choking, not all young people recognize these bodily reactions as related to anxiety. Cognitively, anxious youths worry, often based on misperceptions of the demands in the environment and underestimates of their abilities to cope.

One anxiety disorder, separation anxiety disorder, is specific to children and remains a distinct category in DSM-IV. **Separation anxiety disorder (SAD)** is manifested by obvious distress from and excessive concern about being separated from those to whom the child is attached. Refusing to sleep away from home, staying excessively close to a parent while at home, and separation problems occurring when the child is about to begin school are relatively common. What distinguishes the disorder from normal behavior is the persistent and unrealistic concern — the child is overly worried about the harm that might befall major attachment figures. The diagnostic criteria appear in Table 15.4. When such symptoms are present and cause clinically significant

Table 15.4   Diagnostic Criteria for Separation Anxiety Disorder

Recurrent excessive distress when separation from home or major attachment figures occurs or is anticipated
Persistent and excessive worry that an untoward event will lead to separation from a major attachment figure
Persistent reluctance or refusal to go to school or elsewhere because of fear of separation
Persistent and excessively fearful or reluctant to be alone or without major attachment figures at home or without significant adults in other settings
Persistent reluctance or refusal to go to sleep without being near a major attachment figure or to sleep away from home
Repeated nightmares involving the theme of separation
Repeated complaints of physical symptoms when separation from major attachment figures occurs or is anticipated
Persistent and excessive worry about losing, or possible harm befalling, major attachment figures

Separation anxiety disorder (SAD) is developmentally inappropriate and excessive anxiety concerning separation from home or from those to whom the child is attached. A diagnosis of SAD requires that the disorder appears before age eighteen, lasts at least four weeks, and includes at least three of the following criteria.

distress or impairment in social, academic, or other important areas of functioning, a SAD diagnosis is appropriate.

> *Unlike her twelve-year-old peers, Marsha doesn't go to school with friends, choosing instead to walk alongside her mother. On many days Marsha refuses to go to school because she does not want to be separated from her mother. Following a discussion, the clinician learned that Marsha preferred not to have friends over because she feared that she might be away from her mom. The clinician also learned that Marsha worried excessively every night, often crawling into bed with her parents for security.*

Separation anxiety provides a clear illustration of the contrast between normal and abnormal forms of anxiety depending on age. Anxiety about separation involves a child being distressed in anticipation of or subsequent to being apart from an attachment figure (caregiver). New parents customarily note that around the ages of six to eight months their child seems extremely "clingy." The child's demands for being in the same room as the adult, being able to see the adult, and being held by the adult are heightened during this time, and the presence of strangers produces more noted discomfort. It can be argued, therefore, that at this period in development attachment and separation are major issues for the challenge of growth and competence. Infant-adult attachment (Bowlby, 1969) plays an important role in development, and its disruption can have unwanted effects. In early childhood, separation anxiety appears and recedes naturally as part of normal development. In contrast, when separation anxiety occurs in a twelve-year-old, it signals anxiety that is beyond the normal developmental timetable, evidences attachment problems, and can reflect maladaptive adjustment (Jones, 1996). Some data from England hint that SAD is a precursor of adult panic disorder–agoraphobia (Silove et al., 1995).

School phobia, a specific phobia seen in children, is a fear and avoidance that is relatively well circumscribed to the school environment. Whereas the separation anxious child will avoid a variety of situations that are related to separation, the school phobic child will be fearful and avoid school alone. Separation anxious children often stay in the presence of the attachment figure (or at home), whereas a child with a school phobia can be equally comfortable in any setting other than the school environment (Last, 1992).

Who Is Affected with Anxiety Disorders?   As noted, when community samples are studied, fears and worries are found to be quite common. In terms of meeting diagnostic criteria, much less is known, with estimates of 5 to 8 percent (slightly higher in mid-adolescence) (Kashani & Orvaschel, 1988). It is difficult to reach conclusions on the prevalence of anxiety in youth because of methodological and diagnostic variations across the studies.

In terms of meeting diagnostic criteria, boys and girls are comparable in the prevalence of anxiety disorders in childhood, but the ratio changes in adolescence to 1:3. Some recent research has examined the fears and anxieties of minority group children. In two studies, African American and white youths showed similarity in the situations that were feared (Neal, Lilly & Zakis, 1993) and clinical features of anxiety disorder (Last & Perrin, 1993), although rates of diagnoses were higher for African American than for white youths (Kashani & Orvaschel, 1988).

Causal Forces and Treatment Approaches in Anxiety Disorders

As we explain in Chapter 6, emotional development is influenced by a variety of factors, including genetic predispositions, parental psychological disorder, early trauma, the child's cognitive and behavioral learning history, and peer and familial interrelationships. These explanations of anxiety disorders in adults apply to child anxiety disorders as well.

The psychosocial treatment of anxiety disorders in youth often combines skill in the management of unwanted arousal with exposure to the feared situation. That is, children are first taught about their emotional, cognitive, and behavioral fear reactions, and then they are taught strategies to manage the arousal. Once the children learn the skills, they practice them in the once-feared context. Investigators found that a sixteen-session version of this approach was an effective means of treating youths diagnosed with anxiety disorders (Kendall, 1994).

A diagnosis of school phobia is appropriate in the presence of severe difficulty in attending school that results in prolonged absence from school, severe emotional upset, staying home from school with the parent's knowledge, and the absence of antisocial or conduct problems (Ollendick & Mayer, 1984). Nigel Blagg and William Yule (1984), in Great Britain, conducted a comparison of (1) behavioral treatment, (2) hospitalization, and (3) psychotherapy with home tutoring for school phobic children. In the behavioral treatment, coping strategies were taught, behavior consequences were put into effect, and the child was placed in school directly. Members of the hospital group discussed issues of separation, were encouraged to be independent, and received exercises to build self-concept and self-esteem. Tranquilizers were sometimes prescribed. Members of the home-tutoring group were allowed to remain at home while receiving individual therapy at a community clinic and educational tutoring in the home. Using regular school attendance and improved psychological adjustment as the criteria for success, the behavioral group's success rate of 93.3 percent was significantly superior to the 37.5 percent for the hospital group and the 10 percent for the home treatment group. The study provided a clear indication that certain kinds of treatment can be effective.

Antidepressant medications (such as clomipramine) have been used to treat obsessive-compulsive disorders in children (e.g., see Leonard et al., 1989) and to a lesser extent school-phobic children. Because of tolerance and withdrawal effects, however, their use is limited.

Studies of the optimal treatment of children and adolescents who are diagnosed as suffering from an anxiety disorder are just beginning to appear (Barrett, Dadds & Rapee, 1996; Kendall et al., 1992; Piacentini et al., 1994). Until recently, the anxiety disorders of childhood have taken a back seat to the study of the more disruptive behavior problems. The added attention being given to emotional problems will likely produce noted improvements in our knowledge of the causes and our application of treatments for anxiety disorders of youth.

Depression: Does It Exist in Children and Adolescents?

Until fairly recently, experts believed that children did not experience clinical depression. Depression might have been overlooked simply because no one asked the child about his or her feelings and moods. Children who were brought to clinics for behavior problems also might have suffered from depression, but clinicians did not notice. Children who were quiet and withdrawn often were ignored. When researchers began to ask children directly about depressive symptoms, they learned that children can in fact have clinical depression (Harrington, 1994).

> *José was thirteen when he was first seen in therapy. His parents made an appointment with a clinical child psychologist at the recommendation of a psychiatrist who had been unable to get José to talk. His parents reported that he stayed in his room, did not play with other kids, and often awoke during the night. School was uninteresting, sports were out of the question, and even music was unfavored. After several sessions during which the psychologist was very calm and patient, José began to talk. Weeks later, he expressed hatred toward his hypercritical parents, an absence of closeness with any of his siblings, and disappointment with himself. His emotional state was one of depression.*

Adult criteria for depression can be applied to children, although there are some differences in how the disorder is expressed. For instance, younger children might complain of physical symptoms more than adults and might be irritable; older children might have more subjective symptoms than younger children, such as helplessness and pessimism. In general, however, most experts believe that depression generally presents a similar picture regardless of the person's age.

We know a lot less about childhood and adolescent depression than about adult depression, but several facts are clear. One is that depressive syndromes are relatively

A depressed teen. Although not all youth with sad facial expressions meet criteria for clinical depression, those who do might report low mood, irritability, feeling unloved, difficulty concentrating, withdrawal, and sleep problems.

rare in early childhood but become more common with increasing age. About 1 percent of preschool children, especially those older than ages two or three, are estimated to have clinically diagnosable depression (Kashani & Carlson, 1987). In middle childhood (ages six to twelve), the estimate rises to 2 percent, based on large New Zealand and U.S. samples (Anderson, Williams, McGee & Silva, 1987; Costello et al., 1988). By the time the child reaches adolescence, the rates jump enormously, up to about the same rates as adults — between 4 and 8 percent if both major depression and dysthymia are combined (Cooper & Goodyear, 1993; Roberts, Lewinsohn & Seeley, 1991). Comorbidity adds to the number of youths who are depressed: Children who meet criteria for other disorders, such as an anxiety disorder or ADHD, also may meet criteria for a secondary diagnosis of depression.

A second feature of depression in youth is the pattern of gender differences. A 1:1 (male-to-female) ratio in childhood changes to 1:2 in adolescence. One study reported rates of major depression to be 4.5 percent for girls and 2.9 percent for boys (Whitaker et al., 1990).

Third, depression in youth may be increasing. Although we do not have high-quality surveys from pre-

vious generations for comparisons, there is some evidence that those born in more recent decades are more likely to meet criteria for major depression than are their older counterparts (Klerman & Weissman, 1989).

Assessing Depression in Youth   Measuring depression in youth has proven more complex than once thought. There are structured interviews, self-report questionnaires, peer nomination methods, and parent and teacher rating forms, yet the data produced by these various sources show limited agreement. Depression as assessed by one method is relatively unrelated to assessments of children's depression gathered in other ways (e.g., Kazdin, Esveldt-Dawson, Unis & Rancurello, 1983; Saylor et al., 1984; Wolfe et al., 1987). For instance, peer and staff ratings of depression are not meaningfully related to children's own reports about their level of depression. Self-reports of anxiety are often more highly correlated with depression than are self-reports and teacher ratings of depression (Wolfe et al., 1987).

Further research is needed to unravel the overlap between anxiety and depression and to better understand the differences between self-reports and the reports of others. Still, the child's self-report is an essential part of the assessment of emotional distress. Indeed, when we need to assess clinical depression in children, researchers recommend that children and their parents be interviewed separately because parents often simply do not know what their children's private experiences might be.

Do Depressed Children Become Depressed Adults? Because we do not yet have sufficient longitudinal studies that follow depressed children into adulthood, we can only speculate about the relationship between depressed children and depressed adults. The likely answer is yes, however: Some depressed youths will have problems with depression in adulthood (Garber, Kriss, Koch & Lindholm, 1988). Marika Kovacs and her colleagues found that 72 percent of the depressed children they studied had a relapse within five years (Kovacs et al., 1984a, 1984b). Researchers in England recontacted former child patients and found that 60 percent of those treated for depression in childhood an average of eighteen years earlier had experienced at least one recurrence of major depression during adulthood (Harrington et al., 1990). Certainly not all children who are clinically depressed will continue to have depressive episodes, but episodes of depression in childhood seem to predict future depression (Lewinsohn et al., 1994).

What Causes Depression in Youth?   Probably the best model for understanding depression is the diathesis-stress approach. In this instance, biological and genetic predispositions interact with family distress.

As we discuss in Chapter 8, depression tends to run in families. Thus, it is possible that the early childhood onset of depression represents a genetically transmitted tendency (Strober, 1992). However, family disruption is also common. Several sources of evidence link negative quality of relationships between parents and children with depression. One is based on depressed adults' reports of their own childhoods. They report a variety of problems such as rejection by parents, neglect or lack of interest, hostility, or overcontrolling behaviors by the parents (Hammen, 1991). One would be skeptical of the accuracy of these results if they were the only information available because depressed people might be biased to report only the negative memories of their childhoods. However, evidence from studies of depressed children and from studies of children of depressed parents also has indicated hostility, arguments, and generally negative quality of interactions (see Hammen, 1991). Having a poor relationship with one's parents may set the stage for many different kinds of childhood problems, not just depression. We might speculate that depression is especially likely to occur when the child feels bad about himself or herself because of feeling unloved, unwanted, or insecure (for example, as a result of a poor early mother-child bond) (Cummings & Cicchetti, 1990).

FAMILY MATTERS
The Effects of Divorce

Divorce is common in the United States. Half the marriage contracts do not last. Approximately 40 percent of children grow up in a divorced family. How do children adjust to the changes associated with divorce? Children are not homogeneous on this issue. Their response depends in part on their age and gender.

Most preschool children experience a two- to three-year period of readjustment following divorce; they may show aggression, depression, noncompliance, acting-out, and problems in peer relationships (Hetherington, Stanley-Hagen & Anderson, 1989; Wallerstein, Corbin & Lewis, 1988; Weiss, 1979). After the initial distress, however, young children's adjustment appears to improve. Interviews with preschool and older children ten years after their parents' divorce have indicated that the younger children exhibited fewer problems than children who were older (Wallerstein & Blakeslee, 1989).

The postdivorce adjustment of preschoolers varies according to gender. For boys, the problems are more intense and enduring. Perhaps boys tend to find the breakup more distressing, perhaps they are less adept at coping with divorce, or perhaps they tend to show their distress more overtly than girls. Another possibility is that girls fare better after divorce because mothers have custody in most single-parent homes. There is some evidence that children who are in the custody of a parent of the same gender show healthier emotional adjustment after divorce (Camara & Resnick, 1988; Furstenberg, 1988; Santrock & Warshak, 1986; Zill, 1988). Other data have suggested that the child's style of processing information contributes to postdivorce adjustment: Children who catastrophized and overgeneralized showed more symptoms, whereas children who perceived high personal control and were optimistic about the future showed fewer symptoms (Mazur, Wolchik & Sandler, 1992).

Among early adolescents, the initial postdivorce response is characterized by acting-out and difficulties in school and by early withdrawal and disconnection from the family (Hetherington, 1987; Wallerstein, Corbin & Lewis, 1988). This disengagement can have beneficial effects if the activities outside the family involve positive interactions with supportive caregivers. However, early disengagement by boys from single-parent homes may expose them to higher rates of problem behavior and increase their susceptibility to antisocial peer pressure (Dornbusch et al., 1985; Steinberg, 1987).

The responses of adolescents who are thirteen to eighteen years old at the time of their parents' divorce vary greatly. One longitudinal study found that middle-adolescent youths, like younger children, expressed anger, depressive symptoms, and some acting-out behavior immediately after divorce (Wallerstein & Blakeslee, 1989; Wallerstein & Kelly, 1974, 1980). Additionally, these adolescents reported a sense of loss, betrayal, and concern about future financial resources and relationship stability. Middle-adolescent youths also tended to distance themselves from their families. Generally, adjustment improved with time, but one-third of older children continued to express feelings of sadness and anger regarding the divorce five to ten years after it had happened.

Why do children whose parents divorce show behavioral and emotional difficulties? It could be that the divorce is a trauma, that the family unit is forever disturbed, or that the parenting practices of the divorcing adults are severely disrupted. It also could be that the children are, before the divorce, doing less well than other children. Andrew Cherlin and his colleagues (1991) reported on the outcomes of two longitudinal studies, one conducted in Great Britain and the other conducted in the United States. The results indicated that, for boys, the effect of separation or divorce on behavior and achievement was sharply reduced when one took into account the behavior problems, achievement levels, and family difficulties that were present earlier. The reduction in the apparent effect of divorce occurred for girls as well, but to a slightly lesser extent. Thus, conditions before the separation predicted much of the effect of divorce.

Treating Depression in Youth   Interestingly, one of the major treatments for adult depression, antidepressant medication, has not been found to be effective with children (Sommers-Flanagan & Sommers-Flanagan, 1996). A number of other treatment approaches are used in clinics, but outcome evaluations have not yet appeared. Cognitive-behavioral therapy, which has been used successfully in adults, is now being applied and evaluated in children and adolescents. Although there are few controlled studies, the gains are promising.

In one of the rare outcome evaluations, Kevin Stark, William Reynolds, and Nadine Kaslow (1987) compared a self-control training program, a problem-solving therapy, and a wait-list control condition. The treatments, each focusing in different ways on the teaching of self-management skills, self-monitoring, and social problem solving, were found to produce meaningful gains in both child self-report and interview measures of depression. Participating youths learned to plan and schedule potentially pleasant activities, to be less critical in their self-evaluation, and to view social dilemmas as problems to be solved. The positive gains from such treatment remained evident at an eight-week follow-up.

A study with depressed adolescents reported encouraging outcomes. Peter Lewinsohn and his colleagues (Lewinsohn, Clarke, Hops & Andrews, 1990) provided and evaluated a treatment that involved a cognitive-behavioral group that taught skills for increasing pleasant activities, controlling depressive thoughts, improving social interactions, and resolving conflict. In a research design that allowed for examination of the effects of parental involvement, parents of some of the depressed adolescents were told of the program given to their teens and were encouraged to be supportive and reinforcing, especially when the adolescent used the coping skills to address family problems. A look at the overall effects, in terms of self-reported depression and the percentage of patients meeting diagnostic criteria (see Figure 15.4), shows the improvements that were achieved. Indeed, the significant reduction in symptoms and diagnoses held up at a two-year follow-up evaluation. Given the likelihood of persistent depression if left untreated in adolescence and the likelihood for cognitive-behavioral treatment–produced gains (Clarizio, 1994), we can easily recommend that depressed young people seek and receive psychological intervention.

EATING DISORDERS

Because eating disorders are first identified during the preadult years, they are sometimes considered psychological problems of youth. When the problems persist, however, they are troublesome for adults as well. Eating disorders often have emotional and behavioral qualities as well as physical consequences. Indeed, although not all persons with eating disorders have other problems, of those who do, they are comorbid with a wide variety of other disorders. The two major disturbances in eating

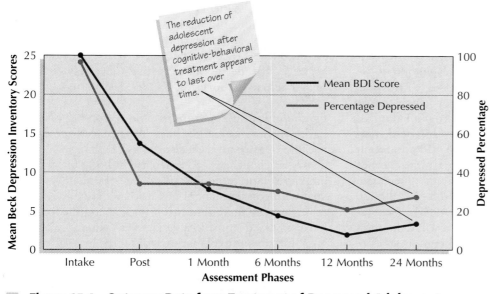

Figure 15.4   Outcome Data from Treatment of Depressed Adolescents
A study of depressed adolescents provided and evaluated a cognitive-behavioral group treatment (teaching skills to increase pleasant activities, control depressive thoughts, improve social interactions, and resolve conflict). Beneficial changes were evidenced in self-reported depressive symptoms (measured by the Beck Depression Inventory, BDI) and in participants' diagnostic status. Major changes took place between initial intake and posttreatment, but effects were maintained through two years after treatment. *Source:* From Lewinsohn, Clarke, Hops & Andrews (1990, p. 396), Cognitive behavioral treatment for depressed adolescents, *Behavior Therapy, 21,* 385–401. Copyright © 1990 by the Association of Behavior Therapy. Reprinted by permission of the publisher.

behavior that we discuss are anorexia nervosa and bulimia.

Anorexia Nervosa

The phrase *anorexia nervosa* means "nervous loss of appetite." It was originally applied because investigators believed that anorexic patients did not experience pangs of hunger. As it turns out, they do experience hunger pangs, often intensely, so the phrase may be a misnomer. Nevertheless, **anorexia nervosa** is an eating disorder characterized by an intense fear of becoming obese, a distorted self-perception of body image, refusal to maintain minimal normal body weight (significant weight loss), and in females, the cessation of menstruation.

Individuals with anorexia are persistent in the desire for additional weight loss. They believe that they are fat when others would evaluate them as thin or even emaciated. They have a distorted self-perception of body size; they fail to recognize successful weight loss and their need to control their body by weight loss. It is safe to say that the average dieter does not share these characteristics, although certain groups (such as ballet dancers and female athletes) may be considered at risk.

The risk for onset of anorexia is high at ages fourteen and eighteen (Foreyt & McGavin, 1988). The estimates of prevalence vary greatly, depending on the manner used to identify patients with anorexia, but there is one consistency: The disorder is eight to eleven times more common in females than in males (Steinhausen, 1994), but men and women with eating disorders are quite similar (Olivardia & Pope, 1995). Some data (Pope, Hudson & Yurgelun-Todd, 1984) have suggested that 1 in every 200 school-aged girls qualifies as anorexic, whereas more conservative estimates have placed the prevalence at 1 in 200,000.

Anorexia nervosa has been identified worldwide. Incidence rates in North America vary (Jones, Fox, Babigian & Hutton, 1980; Lucas, Beard, O'Fallon & Kurland, 1991), but it is generally accepted that anorexia affects less than 1 percent of the adolescent population. Anorexia is quite rare in China (Lee & Chiu, 1989) but quite common in Japan (Suematsu, Kuboki & Itoh, 1985). An incidence of 6.3 per 100,000 was reported in a Dutch study (Hoek, 1991). Whereas anorexia is rare among blacks in the United States (Dolan, 1991), Africa, and the United Kingdom, it does exist (Nwaefuna, 1981). There are more reported cases of anorexia nervosa now than there were a few years ago. Researchers believe that these increases reflect increases in the number of young women in the population and increased awareness of the disorder, however, and not true changes in frequency (Williams & King, 1987).

Unlike many psychological problems, anorexia can lead to serious physical illness and even to death.

Estimates vary, but a typical estimate holds that two-thirds of patients are treated successfully and one-third are chronically ill. Less than 5 percent of patients are said to die from the disorder (Steinhausen, 1994). Extreme weight loss can be severe, as is evident in the following case.

At fifteen Alma had been healthy and well developed, had menstruated at age twelve, was five feet six inches tall, and weighed 172 pounds. At that time her mother urged her to change to a school with higher academic standing, a change she resisted. Her father suggested that she should watch her weight, an idea that she took up with great eagerness, and she began a rigid diet. She lost weight rapidly, and her menses ceased. Being thin gave her a sense of pride, power, and accomplishment. She also began a frenetic exercise program, swimming for miles, playing tennis for hours, or doing calisthenics to the point of exhaustion. Whatever low point her weight reached, Alma feared that she might become "too fat" if she regained as little as an ounce. Most of the time her weight was less than 70 pounds, and when she yielded to others' efforts to make her gain weight, she lost it immediately. There was also a marked change in her character and behavior. Formerly sweet, obedient, and considerate, she became more and more demanding, obstinate, irritable, and arrogant. There was constant arguing, not only about what she should eat but about all other activities as well. (Adapted from Bruch, 1978.)

Anorectic patients have been described as obsessional, neurotic, and having a heightened need for personal control, and they have been found to have low estrogen levels (Leon & Phelan, 1985). They hold more negative attitudes about sexuality and rarely engage in sexual activity (Coovert & Kinder, 1989).

Psychological Explanations for Anorexia Nervosa

Eating disorders are most likely to appear in adolescence because of the convergence of physical changes and psychosocial challenges. The increase in body fat, which is most dramatic in adolescent girls, is frequently associated with concerns about increased weight and the need to do something about it. Researchers and theoreticians have amassed considerable data about anorexia nervosa, but no one explanation is accepted by all the workers in this field.

Current psychodynamic theorizing (e.g., Bruch, 1973, 1978) argues that because of disturbed mother-child interactions, anorectic children failed to develop a body identity and a sense of owning their own bodies. They are overpowered by the body's needs; not eating can provide a false sense of control. The sense of control derived from not eating also appears in explanations based on other theoretical points of view.

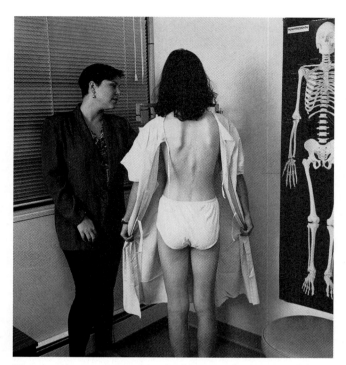

Woman with anorexia nervosa. Physician examinations reveal that she is well below a healthy body weight, but part of the psychology of anorexia is that the woman in the photo reports thinking that she is "too fat to be photographed."

Have personality traits been linked to anorexia? Although limited by retrospective reporting that is typical in clinical history taking, a pattern of compliance, perfectionism, and dependence, as well as the absence of school or educational problems, has been described (Steinhausen, 1994). Obsessive-compulsive tendencies and early eating and digestive problems may be present (Manchi & Cohen, 1990).

In Chapter 2 we describe a variation of the psychodynamic approach developed by Salvador Minuchin and his colleagues (Minuchin, Roseman & Baker, 1978). Minuchin views the family as a system and argues that the symptoms of anorexia cannot be understood outside the system. The family of an anorectic child, in his view, is marked by enmeshment. In an enmeshed family, each member lacks a distinct identity. A child in such a family can feel protected by the group but also fails to develop a personal sense of autonomy or independence. The anorectic individual challenges the family system and wants to break out; failure to eat is the rebellion.

Rigidity and a failure to resolve conflicts also mark the families of anorectic children in Minuchin's view. Family conflicts are inevitable. According to Minuchin, the symptoms of the anorectic child regulate the family by keeping parental conflict from getting out of control. The symptoms thus protect the stability of the family. Although these ideas have not received rigorous research evaluations, data are consistent with the view that the

families of anorectics have increased parental conflict (Kalucy, Crisp & Harding, 1977).

Anorexia also has been described as an avoidance response, where excessive anxiety is associated with the avoidance of food. The food avoidance is then reinforced by the attention that it brings to the individual (Leitenberg, Agras & Thomson, 1968). The anorectic, therefore, is seen as having learned that not eating is a successful way to get attention.

Other learning explanations emphasize the social pressures on young women to be thin. It is easy to imagine how one might learn the expected body size: Evidence of the pressure for thinness is in the photographs and articles in newspapers and magazines and in the ads and scripts of television programs and movies. It is often a part of the developing self-concept of teenage girls.

Cultural forces are operative in the eating disorders. In the United States the cultural ideal for female beauty has increasingly become a lean woman, and the influence of this ideal is spreading to other cultures. Using a bust-to-waist ratio calculated on female figures in popular magazines, researchers have documented that the cultural ideal of beauty has become increasingly leaner (Williamson, Kahn, Remington & Anda, 1990). However, the discrepancy between ideal and real has created a widespread desire for "magical" programs that make women healthier, slimmer, and more aesthetically appealing (Brownell, 1991). There are mass-marketed diet aids and stimulant drugs that curb hunger. The pressure is on women, and it seems to be internalized in adolescence (Wadden, Brown, Foster & Linowitz, 1991).

Follow-up reports from former anorectics suggested another explanation to David Garner and Kelly Bemis-Vitousek (1985). They saw a persistent pattern of distorted thinking among anorectic individuals and built the beginnings of a cognitive model. They noted that the behavior of anorectic individuals reflects their conviction that they "must" be thin — not just a desire or wish to be thin, but a controlling and demanding must. The striving to lose weight may be a route to alleviate the dysphoria, isolation, low sense of self-worth, and sense of inadequacy often felt by young adolescents. Anorectics also make inaccurate cognitive evaluations, for example, "I must lose more weight since I am not yet thin" and "I must continue to lose weight so I can continue to be in control of my body." While losing weight at alarming and dangerous rates, the anorectic processes the weight loss as success, as evidence of power and control. More is better, so the weight loss continues as the sense of power continues. This aberrant thinking leads to self-destructive behavior.

Biological Factors in Anorexia Nervosa   A few years ago the hypothalamus was considered to be the brain area likely to control eating. Possible biological factors in anorexia, therefore, included malfunctioning of the hypothalamus. For example, researchers found that animals will stop eating and can literally starve to death when they are given lesions in one portion of the hypothalamus or when stimulation is applied to other areas of the hypothalamus. Currently, the hypothalamus is considered important in controlling a variety of motivated behaviors (eating, drinking, temperature, sex).

Studies have shown correlations between anorectic behavior and changes in norepinephrine and serotonin (Fava et al., 1989), but the direction of influence is not clear. The extended starvation might cause physiological malfunctioning, just as it is possible that the physiological dysfunction produces the eating symptoms (Weiner, 1985).

Genetic factors may predispose some people to the onset of the disorder. A review of twin studies noted that monozygotic twins had a concordance rate that was higher than that for dizygotic twins (Scott, 1986). In one study (Holland, Sicotte & Treasure, 1988), 56 percent of monozygotic twin pairs were concordant for anorexia nervosa, and only 5 percent were concordant among dizygotic twins. Some genetic explanations of anorexia link it to family patterns of depression, but this view is not universally accepted (e.g., Strober & Katz, 1987).

Given the evidence to date, a diathesis-stress model for anorexia nervosa has merit (Bemis-Vitousek & Orimoto, 1993). Indeed, as is true for other disorders described in this book, it is the interaction between a biological predisposition and adverse environmental forces that affects the individual.

Bulimia

Bulimia (also called *bulimia nervosa*) is characterized by binge eating, the rapid consumption of a large quantity of food in a discrete period of time, and the feeling of a lack of control over the eating. Bulimia is also characterized by self-induced vomiting, use of diuretics, fasting, vigorous exercise to prevent weight gain, and a persistent overconcern with body weight and shape. A diagnosis of bulimia requires a minimum of two binges per week for at least a three-month period. Bulimia has been referred to as the **binge-purge syndrome** because massive quantities of food are eaten and then actions are taken to rid the body of potentially fat-producing calories — recall Sandra from the chapter opening. Fairburn and Beglin (1990) concluded that the prevalence among adolescents is about 1 percent. Although epidemiological data are often based on questionnaires, a number of studies (e.g., Timmerman, Wells & Chen, 1990) have documented the existence of bulimia in a number of countries. The majority of studies have focused on North American subjects, but there are data on binge eating among various racial groups in Zimbabwe (Hooper & Garner, 1986). Given the worldwide occur-

Bulimia is characterized by the rapid consumption of a large quantity of food in a discrete period of time, and by self-induced vomiting, diuretics, fasting, or vigorous exercise to avoid weight gain. Princess Diana wrote, among other disclosures, about her struggles with and success over bulimia.

rence of binge eating, a cultural explanation is not likely to be entirely satisfactory.

Dieting was a common practice for Jenny, with small portions of food at meals and exercise in both the morning and evening being a regular part of every day. Often on weekends when she was home alone, however, Jenny would make eggs, bacon, and pancakes with whipped cream and syrup and eat massive quantities of these breakfast foods at one sitting. Soon after the feast and the kitchen cleanup, she would go to the bathroom and self-induce vomiting. For years she told no one of her habit. In therapy, however, as her therapist asked the proper questions and her comfort level was sufficient, she disclosed the binge-purge habit.

Bulimia, like anorexia, occurs much more often in females. Although the age of onset of bulimia is typically in late adolescence (18.4 years; Fairburn & Cooper, 1984), as opposed to early adolescence for anorexia, bulimia often has been linked to anorexia. In fact, roughly 50 percent of anorectic clients show some evidence of bulimia. Apparently, a sizable number of anorectic people use binge eating and purging as part of their effort to be remarkably thin. This practice has unwanted effects, with potentially serious health ramifications such as the acids from vomiting damaging the enamel on your teeth and chemical imbalances in the body — and the practice is not even all that effective in getting rid of the calories!

The etiological models that have been advanced for anorexia are often applied to bulimia. For example, Humphrey, Apple, and Kirschenbaum (1986) studied the interpersonal behaviors of families with a normal adolescent female and others with an anorectic-bulimic female. The families interacted around the topic of the daughter's separation from the family, and trained observers recorded the frequencies of specific target behaviors. The frequencies of "helping" and "trusting" behaviors on the positive side and "ignoring" and "walling off" behaviors on the negative side differentiated the families. Families with an anorectic-bulimic daughter displayed more of these negative and fewer of these positive interactions. Although these observed differences may possibly be the result of having a family member with an eating disorder, problematic family interactions are one proposed causal factor.

Regarding the role of cognitive factors in bulimia, an interesting series of studies was reported by Polivy and Herman (1985). Normal eating is generally under the control of appetite; when people feel full, they stop eating. According to Polivy and Herman, however, people who watch their weight (restrict their eating) use cognitive strategies to control their eating. That is, they eat when they believe they "should" eat and ignore biological signals of hunger and fullness. Unfortunately, this pattern sets them up for binge eating. Polivy and Herman located groups of normal eaters and restrained eaters (those usually dieting) and had them participate in what they believed were studies of taste preference. The participants consumed high-caloric milkshakes and then were led to a room with unrestricted access to snacks — they could eat whenever they wanted — while they awaited the next part of the study. Normal eaters did not eat much; they were already full. But the restrained eaters ate a lot. It seems that once they decided that their diets were broken by the milkshake, they figured they might as well eat what they wanted. Because they do not detect the physical cues of satiation, they do not know when to stop. Polivy and Herman (1985, 1987) speculated that the line between this eating pattern in typical dieters and clinical bulimia may be only a matter of degree.

Treating Eating Disorders

Treatments for anorexia nervosa include psychodynamic, behavioral, cognitive, and family systems approaches. Hospitalization, diet modification, medications, and force feeding also have been tried.

Psychodynamic treatments of anorexia have reported gains (Bruch, 1973), but rigorous evaluations are lacking. Minuchin and associates (Minuchin, Roseman

& Baker, 1978) reported a successful family systems treatment, claiming that 86 percent of the fifty-three patients recovered from the anorexia. These results are encouraging, although the evaluation was lacking in methodological rigor. In Chapter 3 (pages 81–82) we describe one treatment session with the family of an anorectic child. Minuchin used a family lunch to engage the family members and watch the family interaction while they were eating. As conflicts emerged, the therapist's task was to see the disordered interactions and transform them into functional and adaptive interactions.

Well-controlled outcome evaluations have looked primarily at behavioral or cognitive-behavioral treatments for anorexia (Vitousek & Orimoto, 1993). These programs aim to modify eating patterns, offer specific rewards for eating larger amounts of food, help the client identify faulty beliefs or expectations, and introduce doubt about the beliefs to diminish them.

One study compared cognitive-behavioral therapy, interpersonal psychotherapy, and behavioral therapy for bulimia nervosa (Fairburn et al., 1995). The outcomes (see Figure 15.5) show that cognitive-behavioral therapy and interpersonal psychotherapy produced comparable effects. The behavioral treatment was less effective than the other two. Over 5.5 years later, Fairburn and associates followed up 90 percent of the treated patients and reported that over 50 percent of those receiving cognitive-behavioral or interpersonal therapy no longer qualified as having an eating disorder. The behavior therapy condition produced half the positive results of the other treatments. These results indicate that bulimia can be treated successfully.

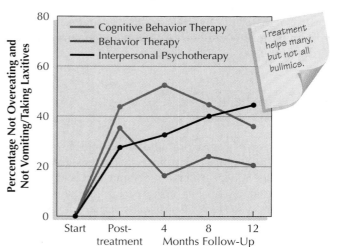

Figure 15.5   Percentage of Bulimic Patients Not Overeating and Not Vomiting or Taking Laxatives after Three Forms of Therapy

In this study of treatments for bulimic patients, the initial post-treatment effects were greatest for cognitive-behavioral therapy. At 12-month follow-up, cognitive-behavioral therapy and interpersonal therapy were comparable and more effective than behavior therapy.

Table 15.5 Normal Body Weights

Height	Age 19 to 34	Age 35 and older	Height	Age 19 to 34	Age 35 and older
5′0″	97–128	108–138	5′10″	132–174	146–188
5′1″	101–132	111–143	5′11″	136–179	151–194
5′2″	104–137	115–148	6′0″	140–184	155–199
5′3″	107–141	119–152	6′1″	144–189	159–205
5′4″	111–146	122–157	6′2″	148–195	164–210
5′5″	114–150	126–162	6′3″	152–200	168–216
5′6″	118–155	130–167	6′4″	156–205	173–222
5′7″	121–160	134–172	6′5″	160–211	177–228
5′8″	125–164	138–178	6′6″	164–216	182–234
5′9″	129–169	142–183			

Source: New York Times, September 26, 1992, p. 32. Data from the Department of Agriculture and Department of Health and Human Services.

Many social pressures push individuals to be "thin." Using your height without shoes and your age, determine the healthy range of your weight (in pounds). The lower weight for each height generally apples to women; the higher weight to men. To help you think about a *healthy* weight, rather than some ideal and often unattainable weight, think of a friend or family member, of the same age and body frame, whose weight looks normal to you. Then, find out what this person actually weighs. The person may weigh more than you think!

Medications also have been used to treat bulimia (Craighead & Agras, 1991; Wilfley et al., 1993). Medications such as antidepressants are sometimes used in combination with therapy; they have been found to reduce binge eating-purging, but no long-term follow-up studies have been reported.

Considering the pressure placed on women in most cultures (Cohen, Brownell & Felix, 1990), it is not surprising that many hold a strong desire to be thin. In excess, however, this desire is abnormal (see Table 15.5 for normal ranges of weight). Present approaches to treating and understanding anorexia implicate family systems, the need for behavior modification, and the relevance of distorted cognitive processing that is in need of reformulation. Multifaceted treatments seem to be the order of the day.

OTHER DISORDERS

Our coverage of behavioral and emotional disorders of childhood and adolescence closes with consideration of tic disorders and disorders associated with elimination (enuresis and encopresis). Some children with tic or elimination disorders also display other diagnosable conditions, whereas some cases occur in otherwise normal children.

Tic Disorders

Tics are involuntary, rapid, recurrent, and stereotyped motor movements or vocalizations. Tics are sudden and nonrhythmic. Usually of brief duration, individual tics rarely last more than a second, but many tics tend to occur in bouts with a brief intertic interval (Leckman &

Cohen, 1994). The tics occur many times a day, nearly every day or intermittently. In DSM-IV, both motor and verbal tics may be classified as either chronic or transient, depending on the duration. Chronic tics have a history of lasting for a period of more than one year, whereas the transient tic has been seen for less than twelve consecutive months. Transient tic disorders, which are almost invariably a disorder of childhood, wax and wane over periods of weeks or months (Leckman & Cohen, 1994).

Some common motor tics include neck jerking and facial grimacing, and common verbal tics include grunting and throat-clearing. Some tics are more complex, such as self-biting, smelling objects, and repeating sounds made by others. Tic behaviors may be exacerbated by stress, diminished during absorbing activities (such as reading), and reduced during sleep.

Of the several tic disorders, Tourette's is perhaps the most complex. In 1885, Gilles de la Tourette described nine cases of tic disorder characterized by motor incoordinations or tics and inarticulate shouts. Known today as **Tourette's disorder,** this tic disorder involves both multiple motor and one or more verbal tics. The tics can be simultaneous or occur at different times; they may occur daily or intermittently; and the location, frequency, and intensity of the tics may change over time. The tics usually involve the head, although complex tics involving other parts of the body are often present. **Coprolalia,** in which the individual utters, calls, or screams obscenities, is apparent in only about one-third of all patients with Tourette's disorder. Simple swearing when angry is not coprolalia.

The average age of the first appearance of Tourette's disorder is approximately seven years (Friedhoff & Chase, 1982). Often the initial symptoms are rapid eye-blinking, facial grimacing, and throat-clearing (Comings & Comings, 1985). Although Tourette's tics are markedly reduced during the sleep of children and adolescents, they do not disappear completely (Janovic & Rohaidy, 1987). Many young children are oblivious to their tics and experience them as entirely involuntary. By the age of ten, most children with tics are aware of any signals or urges that come before the tic (Leckman, Walker & Cohen, 1993).

Children with Tourette's disorder have difficulty maintaining age-appropriate social skills (Stokes et al., 1991). As is the case for several other childhood difficulties, one of the recurring themes in interviewing the families of persons with Tourette's disorder is the presence of discipline problems (Comings & Comings, 1985). Parents reported that the discipline problems were greater than routine and more severe than for non-affected siblings. "Overreactive," "explosive," and "unpredictable" were typical descriptions used by parents. Of the behavioral and emotional problems that frequently complicate Tourette's, impulsive, disinhibited, and immature behavior and compulsive touching and sniffing are common. At present, there are no clear dividing lines between these disruptive behaviors and complex tics on the one hand and comorbid conditions of ADHD and obsessive-compulsive disorder (OCD) on the other (Leckman & Cohen, 1994).

Because there is an increased incidence of Tourette's disorder in the first-degree relatives of people with the disorder, a genetic factor has been implicated in the etiology. Some researchers believe that it is an inherited disorder (e.g., Comings, Comings, Devor & Cloninger, 1984), and others have noted an increased frequency among Jewish people (Shapiro, Shapiro, Brunn & Sweet, 1978). However, the high frequency of Jews reported in earlier studies may simply reflect the high percentage of Jews in the community (New York) where the research was carried out (Nee, Caine & Polinsky, 1980). A more recent study (Pauls, Raymond, Stevenson & Leckman, 1991) found that first-degree relatives of patients with Tourette's disorder were at substantially higher risk for developing Tourette's disorder, chronic motor tic disorder, and obsessive-compulsive disorder than were unrelated individuals. Interestingly, risk was gender related: The risk to male first-degree relatives for any tic disorder was 50 percent (18 percent for Tourette's disorder, 31 percent for chronic motor tics, and 7 percent for OCD) and only 31 percent for females (5 percent for Tourette's disorder, 9 percent for chronic motor tics, and 7 percent for OCD).

Medications such as haloperidol are often prescribed for Tourette's disorder, and 70 to 80 percent of patients show some benefit. Because of unwanted side effects, only 20 to 30 percent take the drug for extended periods. In lower doses, however, patients may experience a remission of symptoms and few adverse reactions (Leckman & Cohen, 1994).

Paul Bliss (1980) provided a rare self-description of the experience of Tourette's disorder. He reported on his 35-year attention to events that preceded, accompanied, and followed his motor and verbal tics. According to Bliss, the tics are actions taken to satisfy unfulfilled sensations and urges. By paying close attention, he claimed to be able to identify when his sensations would be overwhelming and when he needed to substitute a socially appropriate action. Bliss's self-description is not a scientific study, and some researchers have argued that this disorder is not under voluntary control. Bliss did provide a glimpse into the experiential qualities of Tourette's disorder, however, and his report suggested that behavioral management programs and training in self-awareness skills may help some Tourette's patients.

Enuresis and Encopresis

Enuresis, the occurrence of wetting in the absence of a urologic or neurologic pathology, can be a source of concern to parents whose child is three to five years of age or older. Some sources estimate that as many as 20 percent of all five-year-olds wet their beds a sufficient number of times to qualify as enuretic (Doleys, 1983). Fortunately, the problem is much less frequent among older children; it occurs in less than 2 percent of twelve- to fourteen-year-olds. There are some gender differences: Bed-wetting is equally common for boys and girls until age five, but by age eleven boys are twice as likely to be wet as girls (Shaffer, 1994). **Encopresis,** the fecal parallel to enuresis, is reported in approximately 2 to 3 percent of three- to five-year-olds with a 3:1 male-to-female ratio (Hersov, 1994). By ages ten to twelve, 1 percent or fewer children are encopretic.

Research on these disorders has focused on enuresis; encopresis has not been studied extensively. Potential explanations of enuresis include genetic inheritance, a response to arousal during sleep, the expression of underlying emotional conflicts, smaller bladder capacity, and the failure to learn an adaptive response to the sensation of a full bladder. The research evidence is nonexistent for some of these explanations and equivocal in others. It appears that there are multiple causes for the problem.

Although the cause of the problem remains a puzzle, there are well-studied, effective methods for bladder control training. The clear majority of the programs that have been demonstrated to be effective apply behavioral procedures. Medications such as imipramine (the same medication used to treat depression in adults) increase bladder control in a reported 85 percent of patients (Shaffer, 1977), although total continence is achieved in only 30 percent of the patients: Up to 95 percent relapse after the medication is withdrawn (Doleys, 1983). Based on a meta-analytic review of the research, the customary psychological treatment was reported to be superior to medications (Houts, Berman & Abramson, 1994).

Perhaps the most often used treatment is the urine alarm system sometimes called the "*bell and pad*." The bell and pad system is based on classical conditioning. A urine-sensing device rests between the child and the mattress during sleep hours. Urine that passes onto the device triggers an alarm. Once awake, the child urinates in the toilet and can then return to bed. Summarizing results over fifteen years, Dan Doleys (1977) concluded that 75 percent of the more than six hundred patients treated with the urine alarm showed remission. The average length of treatment with the urine alarm is five to twelve weeks. Relapse remains a problem, however, since 41 percent of the patients were unable to maintain the dry state after treatment discontinued.

Two modifications to the urine alarm approach help reduce the relapse rate (Doleys, 1983; Finley, Wansley & Blenkarn, 1977; Jehu, Morgan, Turner & Jones, 1977). First, because responses are more persistent under conditions of partial reinforcement, the alarm is set to go off 50 to 75 percent of the time that the pad is wet. Second, the child sometimes consumes liquids before bed and after dryness days have been achieved. Thus, the child learns bladder control when the bladder is full as well as when it is not as full.

Dry-bed training combines other behavioral procedures with the urine alarm (Azrin, Sneed & Fox, 1974). This program includes opportunities for positive practice, nighttime awakening, practice in retention control, and full cleanliness training. In research reported by Fincham and Spettell (1984), parents who were actually involved in the treatment of enuretic children viewed the urine alarm as more acceptable than the dry-bed training.

What Lies Ahead?

The issues of troubled youths have been brought to our attention by media exposure of children who are involved in crime, victims of violence, abandoned by their parents, and suffering from poverty and hunger. Research suggesting that problems of youth do not go away and that early intervention may be the most efficient and effective approach alerts us to the need for action. Owing to society's increased awareness of child and adolescent adjustment, there has been and is likely to continue to be a broadening of the research scope and a flourishing of the research literature that addresses the causes and treatments for child and adolescent psychological disorders. The challenges that face young people as a part of normal development will continue to play important roles in our understanding.

That childhood experiences influence adult behavior patterns is a principal theme in several theories of psychopathology. For example, both cognitive and learning approaches accent acquired patterns. The outlook witnesses greater specificity in theory and treatment regarding the precise nature of the cognitive processing style and behavioral pattern of youths with specific behavioral and emotional disorders.

Research on topics within family psychology has come of age. No longer are family approaches burdened by sole reliance on nonempirical theories: The increased experimental focus on parent-child interactions, parenting styles, and parent and family interventions combines to promote an evolving and expanding knowledge base about the contribution of family forces in adjustment and maladjustment. The present decade is witness to this emerging focus.

KEY TERMS

action-oriented family therapy (482)
anorexia nervosa (490)
attention-deficit hyperactivity disorder (ADHD) (471)
binge-purge syndrome (492)
bulimia (492)
conduct disorder (477)

coprolalia (494)
developmental appropriateness (472)
developmental psychopathology (466)
encopresis (495)
enuresis (495)
externalizing disorders (469)

hostile attributional bias (480)
impulsivity (471)
inattention (471)
internalizing disorders (469)
oppositional defiant disorder (478)

overactivity (471)
school phobia (485)
separation anxiety disorder (SAD) (484)
tics (494)
Tourette's disorder (494)

SUMMARY

Understanding the Disorders of Youth

One model for understanding psychological disorders in children and adolescents is *developmental psychopathology,* in which maladjustment is seen in relation to the major changes that occur across the life span. This approach has led to classifying the psychological problems of youth as either *internalizing* or *externalizing disorders.* Using assessments often similar to those used with adults, those specific to children such as the Child Behavior Checklist (CBCL), the Response Class Matrix, and the Diagnostic Interview for Children and Adolescents (DICA), and parent and teacher ratings of child behavior, behavior and emotional problems are classified into categories that can guide treatment. Child and adolescent problems can be treated individually, in school- or clinic-based programs, in families, or using medications.

Behavior Disorders

Attention-deficit hyperactivity disorder (ADHD) is characterized by *inattention, impulsivity,* and *overactivity.* The *developmental appropriateness* of behavior influences a diagnosis of ADHD: only when the problems are excessive relative to what is appropriate for the child's age is the diagnosis accurate. Affecting more boys than girls, the symptoms of ADHD affect academic and social arenas and may persist into adolescence and sometimes adulthood. Multiple causal pathways are implicated in the onset of ADHD, and there have been some positive results from treating ADHD with psychostimulant medications as well as with behavioral approaches.

Conduct disorder involves behavior that violates the basic rights of others and of the age-appropriate social norms. Aggression, property damage, stealing, and cheating are common among conduct-disordered youth. *Oppositional defiant behavior* is another type of disruptive behavior disorder, involving temper outbursts, arguments, rule violations, vindictiveness, and a general negativistic and hostile behavior pattern toward adults. More common among boys and evident worldwide, conduct-disordered youth evidence a *hostile attributional bias* by which they tend to attribute negative motivations to others. Family distress and ineffective parenting, for example, are implicated in the cause of conduct disorder. Although treatments such as *action-oriented family therapy,* school-based prevention, and cognitive-behavioral therapy have produced beneficial outcomes, the effects are greater for younger patients.

Emotional Disorders

Fears are a normal part of development, but extreme fears can be a part of an anxiety disorder of childhood (for example, *separation anxiety disorder*). *School phobia* is a fear and avoidance that is relatively circumscribed to the school environment. Children and adolescents also can suffer depression, and these same youths are at risk for depression in their later years. Family influences, learning histories, cognitive processing distortions, and biological predispositions all contribute to the onset of emotional disorders in youth. Although the number of studies is limited, cognitive-behavioral procedures have been found to alleviate anxiety and depression.

Eating Disorders

Anorexia nervosa is characterized by an intense fear of becoming obese, a distorted self-perception of body image, refusal to maintain minimal body weight, and in females, a cessation of menses. By far more common among females, anorexia, if unchecked, can lead to death. Family influences have been implicated in anorexia: In an enmeshed family, each family member lacks a distinct identity, and the child fails to develop a personal sense of autonomy and independence. Family treatment and cognitive-behavioral treatments, as well as medications, have been applied with anorectic patients.

Bulimia is characterized by the rapid consumption of a large quantity of food in a discrete period of time while feeling out of control over the eating. It is also characterized by self-induced vomiting, use of diuretics, fasting, vigorous exercise, and overconcern with body weight. *Bulimia* has been referred to as the binge-purge syndrome.

Other Disorders

Tics are involuntary, rapid, recurrent, and stereotyped movements or verbalizations. Tics may be motor or verbal, simple or complex, and transient or chronic. *Tourette's disorder* involves both multiple motor and one or more verbal tics. *Coprolalia* occurs when an individual utters, calls, or screams obscenities.

Enuresis, wetting in the absence of urologic or neurologic disorder, is common among three- to five-year-olds but becomes a source of concern as age progresses. Treatment with the bell and pad has been reported to be quite successful. *Encopresis,* the fecal parallel to enuresis, occurs less frequently and is much less studied.

Consider the Following. . .

Suppose that your six-year-old son, Ron, is described by his teacher as wiggly and full of excess energy. You know there are times when Ron can be very difficult to manage, but you didn't expect his teacher to suggest that he has ADHD. You and your spouse have to consider whether or not to have Ron tested and, if he is diagnosed, whether or not to use medications. Given what you have learned in this chapter, can you anticipate the issues to weigh? What data sources would you want the diagnostician to consider?

Suppose that your younger sister, who is quite athletic and healthy, begins to complain about her weight and to follow a strict diet. No one else thinks she is heavy, but somehow she got the idea in her head and has convinced herself that she is fat. Our society praises thinness, so much so that industries have developed around the process of weight loss. Advertisements clearly promote a certain "look." Is it acceptable for advertisers to use inordinately thin (if not "sickly") figures in sexually explicit modeling situations? What are the effects on the developing young teen? Should advertisers be asked or required to use "healthy" models?

CHAPTER 16

Mental Retardation and Developmental Disorders

Those among us...

■ You've been babysitting for Dorie today, something you've done since she was an infant. Now in preschool, she was late to walk and is slow to learn, but she's a real charmer all in all. Soon, her mother returns from a meeting with Dorie's teacher; you find her visibly shaken. The teacher told her that Dorie is unable to understand lessons and to organize and plan her projects; she has recommended that Dorie be formally evaluated. Later, psychological testing indicates that Dorie's IQ score is 62.

■ Your best friend's brother Chip never seemed to hear or respond to other people. He wasn't "cuddly" as an infant, didn't enjoy playing with other children, and hadn't developed normal communication. Although his parents once thought he was deaf, he was recently identified as having a pervasive developmental disorder called autism.

■ You remember Ramey, a boy who lived down the block. All sharp objects, especially pins, paper clips, and needles, had to be kept away from Ramey — not to protect others from harm but to prevent Ramey from sticking himself. On one occasion, inch-long pins were found in his thumb. On another, a needle had entered a vein, requiring that he be taken to the emergency room.

What kind of adjustment can children with low IQs attain as they grow older?

What is autism, and what causes it?

To what lengths must a caregiver go to prevent a child from hurting himself?

This chapter covers those disorders of infancy, childhood, and adolescence that have predominant intellectual and developmental features. Specifically, we examine mental retardation, learning disorders, and pervasive developmental disorders such as autism. Although these disorders have commonalities — cognitive deficits are present in all — they vary in terms of the type and magnitude of the cognitive deficits.

MENTAL RETARDATION

According to the American Association on Mental Retardation (AAMR, 1994), **mental retardation** is defined as significantly subaverage general intellectual functioning that exists concurrently with deficits in adaptive behavior. **Adaptive behavior** involves the self-care skills (such as the ability to appropriately dress and groom oneself and to hold a simple job) needed to live independently. A person diagnosed with mental retardation is significantly subaverage in intellectual functioning and is sometimes incapable of self-care or independent living. The disorder must be identified before the eighteenth birthday. Persons older than eighteen years of age who, for the first time, display subaverage intellectual functioning and fail to adapt independently are not diagnosed as mentally retarded.

Keep in mind that, to warrant a diagnosis of mental retardation, a person must exhibit impairment in both intellectual and adaptive functioning. No single test can identify who is mentally retarded; instead, criteria are combined to make this judgment. For example, mental retardation is not simply a low IQ score: In fact, some psychologists assess IQ levels only after deficits in adaptive behavior have been identified.

To assess adaptive behaviors, psychologists use inventories such as the Adaptive Behavior Scale, which aims to measure independent functioning, language development, and responsibility, as well as economic, domestic, and physical activity. Examples of the areas of competence that are assessed can be found in Table 16.1. To assess intellectual ability, psychologists use standardized tests such as revised forms of the Wechsler Intelligence Scale for Children (WISC-III) or the Stanford Binet. (These tests are described in Chapter 4.)

Who Is Affected with Mental Retardation?

Several studies have been conducted to determine the prevalence of mental retardation. Early estimates varied from 1 percent to 13 percent. However, a review of studies conducted around the world suggests that a range between 1 and 3 percent is a more reasonable prevalence estimate (Scott, 1994). Other reviews of studies have suggested that, when IQ score is the criterion used to assess mental retardation, prevalence rates of 3 percent are typical, whereas when adaptive behavior is the criterion, prevalence rates drop to 1 percent (McLaren & Bryson, 1987) — a considerable difference. Assessments that use only IQ seem to leave many more people with a limiting label, though in daily life it doesn't really matter so much what your IQ is; more important is whether you demonstrate adaptive behavior.

WHAT'S NORMAL?

Are IQ Test Scores "Fair"?

One of the criteria for mental retardation is an IQ score equal to or greater than two standard deviations below

Determinations of the presence of mental retardation include assessments of the person's adaptive functioning. As you scan these lists you will see that adaptive functioning is a broad concept, including both competent and maladaptive behaviors.

Table 16.1 Sample Areas Assessed by the Adaptive Behavior Scale	
Areas of Competence	**Areas of Maladaptive Behavior**
Independent functioning	Violent and destructive
Physical development	Antisocial behavior
Economic activity	Rebellious behavior
Language development	Untrustworthy
Numbers and time	Withdrawal
Domestic activity	Stereotyped behavior
Vocational ability	Unacceptable vocal habits
Self-direction	Self-abusive behavior
Responsibility	Sexually aberrant behavior
Socialization	Psychological disturbances

the mean. On the WISC-III, for example, the average score is 100, with a standard deviation of 15; thus, a person with a score of 70 or less would meet the above criterion for a diagnosis of mental retardation. Keep in mind that a change in this criterion — say, one or one and a half standard deviations — would have a dramatic effect on the identification of mental retardation. Thus, what is normal, in terms of IQ scores, is based solely on a chosen criterion and the distribution of scores.

Figure 16.1 shows the theoretical (normal) distribution of IQ scores, whereas Table 16.2 lists both the theoretical and actual percentages of persons achieving varying IQ scores. As is evident, the distribution of actual scores closely resembles the normal curve. Because only about 2 percent of the scores in this distribution are lower than 70, we can conclude that approximately 2 percent of the population—about 7.5 million people in the United States — meet this criterion. But not all persons who score in the retarded range on IQ tests lack adaptive behavior, and vice versa.

One source of controversy regarding tests of intelligence has to do with the "fairness" or "unfairness" of such tests for disadvantaged individuals. To address the issue, we must know who the disadvantaged are. But this conceptualization tends to be relative: The disadvantaged are those who, compared to others, are hindered in leading productive lives in their society. This group may include low-income families, ethnic minorities, very rural families, and, in some cases, members of bilingual families. If these disadvantaged groups score lower on IQ tests, are the tests unfair?

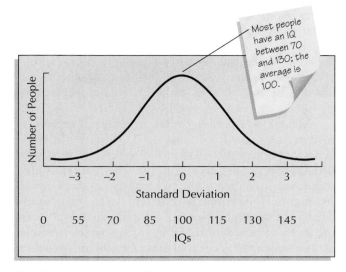

Figure 16.1   Distribution of IQ Scores
This theoretical (normal) distribution illustrates the relative frequencies of IQ scores within standard deviations from the mean.

Contemporary IQ tests (as we discuss in Chapter 4) use standardized samples, which include representatives from all types of backgrounds. By so doing, these tests strive to remain fair to all groups. Similarly, the content of the tests — the test questions — strive to be free from cultural bias. The way that test results are interpreted by human beings, however, may still be open to unfairness. For example, someone could, in error, make a statement about a person's ethnic group based on the test perfor-

Table 16.2   Descriptive Distribution of WISC-III IQ Scores

IQ Score	Classification	Theoretical Normal Curve	Actual Sample[a]
		Percent Included	
130 and above	Very superior	2.2	2.1
120–129	Superior	6.7	8.3
110–119	High average	16.1	16.1
90–109	Average	50.0	50.3
80–89	Low average	16.1	14.8
70–79	Borderline	6.7	6.5
69 and below	Intellectually deficient[b]	2.2	1.9

[a]The percentages shown are for the full-scale IQ and are based on the total standardization sample (N = 2,200). The percentages obtained for the verbal IQ and performance IQ are very similar.

[b]In place of the term *mentally retarded* used in the WISC-R, the WISC-III uses the term *intellectually deficient*. This practice avoids the implication that a very low IQ score is sufficient evidence for the classification of "mental retardation." The term *intellectually deficient* is descriptive and refers only to low intellectual functioning.

Source: Wechsler Intelligence Scale for Children — Third Edition (1989). Copyright ©1991, 1974, 1971 by The Psychological Corporation. Reproduced by permission.

The table includes both the theoretical distribution and the actual distribution of IQ scores using data from the Wechsler Intelligence Scale for Children–Third Edition.

mance of only one individual from the group — an interpretation as biased as saying that all tall people are unintelligent because one tall person performed poorly. Here, the user of the test results would be the one who is unfair, not necessarily the test itself.

Mental retardation occurs in varying degrees of severity, as shown in Table 16.3. Whereas adaptive behavior and intellectual functioning serve as criteria for determining the presence of mental retardation, IQ test scores are often used to differentiate the levels of mental retardation. Nevertheless, different levels of adaptive behavior can also be expected for individuals with varying levels of retardation. Table 16.3 provides examples of the variations in potential outcomes for individuals at different ages. Among the total number of people with mental retardation, approximately 89 percent are mildly retarded, 7 percent moderately retarded, 3 percent severely retarded, and 1 percent profoundly retarded (Madle, 1990).

The prevalence of mental retardation is affected by factors such as gender, socioeconomic status, and race. Most of the variation occurs within the category of mildly retarded persons; severe levels of retardation are more evenly distributed across these factors. Somewhat higher prevalence estimates are found among males than among females (the ratio is approximately 2:1), and among blacks than among whites, although the ethnic variation is likely due to cultural and socioeconomic status factors. Social class is also regularly linked to variations in the prevalence of mental retardation, with

Table 16.3   Levels of Mental Retardation and Adaptive Behavior Across the Lifespan

Level	Preschool Age 0–5	School Age 6–21	Adult 21+
Mild	These preschoolers can develop social and communication skills, with minimal retardation in sensorimotor areas. Until later age, these children are rarely distinguished from normal.	These school-aged youth can learn academic skills to approximately 6th-grade level by their late teens. Typically they cannot learn general high school subjects and need special education, particularly at secondary school age levels.	These adults are capable of social and vocational adequacy with proper education and training. They frequently need supervision and guidance when under serious social or economic stress.
Moderate	These preschoolers can talk or learn to communicate but show poor social awareness and only fair motor development. They can be managed with moderate supervision.	These youngsters can learn functional academic skills to approximately 4th-grade level by late teens; special education is necessary.	These adults are capable of self-maintenance in unskilled or semi-skilled occupations, but they need supervision and guidance when under mild social or economic stress.
Severe	These preschoolers show poor motor development, and speech is minimal. Generally they are unable to profit from training in self-help, and they show little or no communication skills.	These school-aged youth can talk or learn to communicate, and can be trained in elemental health habits. They cannot learn functional academic skills, but they do profit from systematic habit training.	These adults can contribute partially to self-support under complete supervision, and they can develop self-protection skills to a minimal useful level in a controlled environment.
Profound	Gross retardation; minimal capacity for functioning in sensorimotor areas. These youth need nursing care.	Some motor development is present in these youth, but they cannot profit from training in self-help. They need total care.	These adults show only some motor and speech development. They are totally incapable of self-maintenance and need complete care and supervision.

Differentiations within mental retardation are based on severity of impairment. Although adaptive behavior plays a role, IQ scores are sometimes used to distinguish levels of mental retardation: *mild mental retardation* (IQ level 50–55 to approximately 70), *moderate retardation* (IQ level 35–40 to 50–55), *severe mental retardation* (IQ level 20–25 to 35–40), *profound mental retardation* (IQ level less than 20 or 25), and *mental retardation, severity unspecified* (strong presumption of mental retardation, but the person is untestable by standard intelligence tests). Different levels of retardation are associated with different levels of adaptive functioning that can be achieved. With increasing age, too, adaptive functioning changes.

Two boys reading in a classroom. Children with disabilities, like regular classroom youth, can develop important friendships based on shared learning experiences.

groups of low socioeconomic status accounting for a disproportionate number of cases, especially in the category of mild retardation (Crnic, 1988; Scott, 1994).

Individuals with mental retardation sometimes have other difficulties as well. Ambulatory problems, fine motor problems, and speech, hearing, and visual impairments are likely to coexist with mental retardation. In addition, some patients have comorbid epilepsy or cerebral palsy.

Psychological problems have also been identified (Einfeld & Aman, 1995; Johnson, Lubetsky & Sacco, 1995). Data gathered in Great Britain suggest that 22 percent of young adults with mental retardation have problems with anxiety and that 20 percent exhibit conduct disorder or antisocial behavior (Richardson et al., 1979). Self-injurious behaviors have been reported among people with mental retardation (Scott, 1994), as have depression (Matson & Barrett, 1982) and schizophrenia (Romanczyk & Kistner, 1982). According to one study, psychiatric disorders are three to four times more common in children and adults with mental retardation than in the general population (Scott, 1994). Further, a relationship has been found between the presence of psychiatric disorder and the level of intellectual functioning: The rates of disorder increase with more severe retardation. One hypothesis is that low intellectual functioning reduces the ability to cope with stress, restricts the environment, and contributes to distress in the family, and that these factors, in turn, contribute to psychiatric disorder. Alternatively, it might be that the presence of disorder not only limits a person's intellec-

tual development but also influences *others* to place limitations on that person's intellectual development.

Causes of Mental Retardation

The influence of genetics on normal as well as abnormal intelligence has been the subject of enormous controversy and a great many studies. Generally, research shows that as the degree of genetic relatedness between two people increases, so does the correlation between their IQ scores (Neisser et al., 1996). For example, the IQ scores of monozygotic (identical) twins are more alike than the scores of dizygotic (fraternal) twins (Plomin, 1989). Similarly, there are larger correlations between adoptees' IQ scores and those of their biological families than between adoptees' scores and those of their adoptive families (Plomin & DeFries, 1980; Scarr & Weinberg, 1976). An individual's IQ score, then, is not determined solely by genes; it is influenced by environmental factors as well (Neisser et al., 1996).

Indeed, mental retardation itself is a disorder whose cause is generally considered to be multifaceted, with both genetic and environmental factors contributing. However, some instances of retardation *can* be attributed to genetics. In the following sections, we consider biological, prenatal, and social environmental factors that have been found to be influential.

Biological Factors in Mental Retardation Certain biological factors are implicated in mental retardation. For example, chromosomal aberrations are associated with a specific syndrome of mental retardation first described in 1866 by the British physician Langdon Down. **Down syndrome** is a form of mental retardation caused by the presence of an extra twenty-first chromosome (Vandenberg & Crowe, 1989). As Figure 16.2 shows, chromosome 21 emerges as a set of three instead of two — unlike all of the other chromosomes. The physical characteristics of the Down syndrome child are usually quite apparent: The neck is short and broad, there is loose skin on the sides and back of the neck, height is below average, the head is small and the back of the head is flat, the eyes slant upward and have folds in the corners, muscle tone is poor (floppy), and the hands are often short and square with short fingers. Brain anomalies in persons with Down syndrome include low brain weight, reduced number of cells, and short dendrites (Coyle, Oster-Granite & Gearhart, 1986). Individuals with this chromosomal abnormality regularly score in the subaverage range on measures of intellectual ability, although there is considerable variability in terms of intelligence scores and adaptive behavior.

The age of the mother at the time of the child's birth has been found to be related to the incidence of Down syndrome (Hook, 1987; Hook, Cross & Regal, 1990). Risk increases with age. For mothers of age twenty, the incidence of Down syndrome is 1 in 2,000 births. At

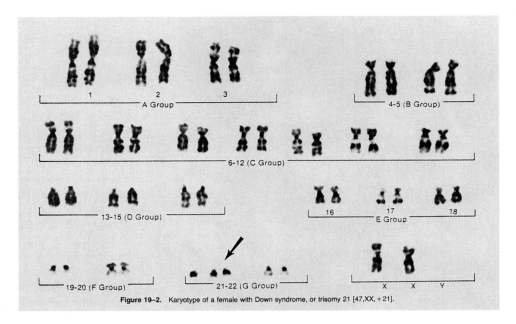

Figure 16.2 Chromosomal Abnormality in Down Syndrome

Shown here are the chromosomes of a person with Down syndrome. Notice that the twenty-first pair is a set of three rather than two. This chromosomal aberration is consistently linked to Down syndrome, a form of mental retardation associated with specific physical characteristics.

Figure 19–2. Karyotype of a female with Down syndrome, or trisomy 21 [47,XX, + 21].

maternal age thirty-five, it is 1 in 500 births. And at maternal age forty-five, the incidence rises to 1 in 20 (Evans & Hammerton, 1985). Some data suggest that the rate of Down syndrome is also related to the father's age, but this conclusion is not widely accepted (Hook, Cross & Regal, 1990; Steen & Steen, 1989).

> *Lee has the physical characteristics of most Down syndrome children: His nose is flat, his square-shaped ears and his mouth are small, his tongue protrudes, and his neck is short and broad. Unfortunately, these characteristics, as well as his mental retardation, were the target of teasing by several youths in his neighborhood. Although he rarely voiced complaints, Lee did feel the rejection.*
>
> *Lee is now in his middle teens. Earlier, at the age of seven, he was enrolled in a special placement class and made friends with several other Down syndrome children in his school. His teacher described him as very likeable, responsive to directions and instructions, and popular among the youngsters in his group. One of Lee's major accomplishments was his designation as the student responsible for his classroom's fish tank — for feeding the fish and cleaning the tank. A few prompts were required, but Lee was nevertheless very proud of "his tank."*

Although it was once thought that adults with Down syndrome would show a rapid age-related decline in functioning, follow-up studies in the United States (e.g., Burt et al., 1995) and the United Kingdom (e.g., Shepperdson, 1995) have reported minimal changes with age. Similarly, Lee's abilities as an adult are best predicted by his initial IQ and not likely to show any more decline with age than would be seen in other adults.

In addition to Down syndrome, other forms of mental retardation are associated with chromosomal abnormalities. For example, **fragile X syndrome,** named for a constricted region at the end of the X chromosome, is associated with specific physical features as well as intellectual deficiencies. The physical features include short stature, prominent forehead, prominent mandible, and large ears, hands, and feet. This disorder is more commonly seen among males than among females. One study (Dykens, Hodapp, Ort & Leckman, 1993) found that males with fragile X syndrome made positive gains in adaptive behavior over a two-year period. The older subjects, in particular, showed strengths in daily living skills. In a later study (Dykens et al., 1996), further changes with development were examined using both longitudinal and cross-sectional approaches, with data coming from six centers. The researchers reported that boys with fragile X showed significant gains in adaptive behavior from ages one to ten, but that their adaptive behavior plateaued and remained stable from ages eleven to twenty.

Another disorder, **phenylketonuria (PKU),** is organic and genetically determined. Specifically, it involves a hereditary error of metabolism resulting from an inactive liver enzyme. Infants with PKU appear normal at birth but, if untreated, will develop mental retardation during the first year of life. If placed on a special diet soon after birth, they develop normally.

Carriers of PKU pass on a recessive gene to their children. If these children marry a person who also carries the recessive gene, their offspring may be affected (Vandenberg & Crowe, 1989). PKU is rare, occurring at a rate of approximately 1 in 14,000 births (Rubenstein, Lotspeich & Ciaranello, 1990), and it is associated with moderate to profound retardation. This form of retar-

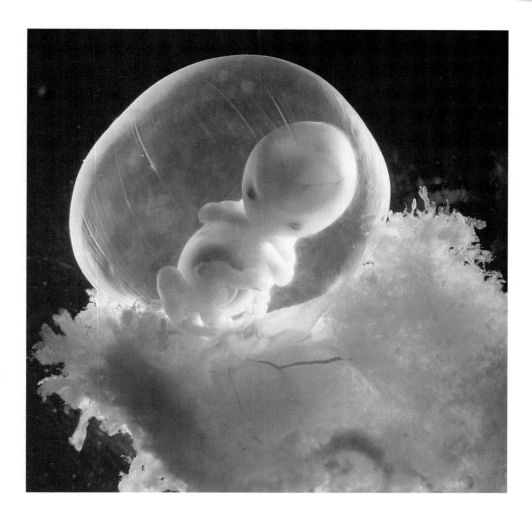

The human fetus in utero, at seven weeks, is approximately an inch long and weighs about two grams. Genetic and environmental forces are operating: the genetic contribution is unfolding as the fetus grows — the mother is providing the prenatal environment. Both factors, as well as many other forces that impinge on the organism after birth, can contribute to mental retardation.

dation is no more prevalent in family members of the affected individual than in the general population, and it occurs equally across all social classes. Unlike many other forces that cause mental retardation, the intellectual deficit associated with PKU can be prevented through early detection and dietary modification. In North America, for example, the law requires postnatal blood testing to promote prevention.

Other organic forces, such as infections, poisons, and malnutrition, are factors in retardation, as are cranial anomalies and head injuries. Clearly, malformed or dysfunctional portions of the brain, as well as injuries to regions of the brain, can have serious detrimental effects on mental functioning.

Prenatal Environment and Mental Retardation
Prenatal environmental influences can also damage intellectual ability. Indeed, health problems in the mother may have significant effects on the fetus. Maternal conditions such as nutrition, tobacco smoking, alcohol consumption, infections, drugs, radiation, and a lack of oxygen can all contribute to subnormal intelligence in the child. Nevertheless, these maternal health behaviors can be monitored and improved, thus

mitigating the damage to the fetus (Streissguth et al., 1989).

Consider the serious and unwanted effects of alcohol. In the pregnant woman, alcohol readily crosses the placenta, exposing the developing fetus to a wide range of harmful effects. Because even small amounts of alcohol may not be safe (Jones, 1988), researchers *uniformly* recommend that pregnant women not consume alcohol during pregnancy. In the most extreme cases, involving 4 to 12 infants per 10,000 births, the mother's drinking during pregnancy causes permanent physical damage to the infant — a condition known as fetal alcohol syndrome (Clarren & Smith, 1978; Jones & Smith, 1973). Fetal alcohol effects include retardation of physical growth as well as of neurological and intellectual development (Neisser et al., 1996). The exact amount of maternal alcohol consumption necessary to produce fetal alcohol syndrome is not yet known, but concerned, health-conscious women are increasingly discontinuing their alcohol consumption during pregnancy.

Social Environment and Mental Retardation
Environmental factors, such as extreme psychological and social deprivation, have also been implicated as

Pregnant women who consume alcohol add to the health risk of their unborn child. Beverage alcohol crosses the placenta, and excessive drinking during pregnancy can result in damage called fetal alcohol syndrome (FAS). The FAS child suffers growth retardation, intellectual impairment, and changes in facial structure.

causes of mental retardation. For example, animal studies have shown that animals reared in deprived environments exhibit behavioral deficits as well as lighter brains, with less cortical depth and fewer synapses (e.g., Rosenzweig, Bennett & Diamond, 1972). And among humans, intellectual development is impeded by lack of contact with others of normal intelligence, limited access to books and verbal stimulation, and an absence of educational opportunities. It is not difficult to imagine that individuals raised in a **culturally deprived environment** — one that lacks learning opportunities — would likely show lower IQ scores. Poverty, too, hampers intellectual development. **Economically disadvantaged** youth are at risk for intellectually deprived lives. Other factors include large family size, poor nutrition, lack of organization in the home, and low expectations for academic achievement. Consider the following example described by Repp and Deitz (1983).

> *Steve came from a family of migrant workers, so he has moved numerous times. His mother went back to work shortly after he was born, and an older sister took care of him. His sister wanted him to be quiet and nondemanding, and she yelled at him for most behaviors other than sitting quietly. When his parents came home from work, they were tired and wanted to be left alone. He was again urged to keep quiet and out of trouble. The family's living quarters were always sparsely furnished, and Steve had only a few toys, of which he had tired long ago.*
>
> *When Steve enrolled in school, his language level was very low for his age. In addition, he did not possess the academic readiness skills that his peers exhibited. Steve was referred for evaluation; after being given a battery of standardized tests, he was labeled as retarded and placed in a classroom for the retarded.*

Placement, Treatment, and Education in Mental Retardation

Rita Wicks-Nelson and Allen Israel (1991) described three types of interventions for mental retardation: placement, treatment, and education. **Placement** refers to the living arrangements that must be organized for the person. At one time, most patients with mental retardation were placed in large public institutions that provided nothing more than custodial care. Since the 1960s, however, this practice has declined in the United States — in part, because of criticisms directed at the institutions themselves. Specifically, they were described as being cold and lacking in human interaction, having a shortage of services, and being poorly staffed. Current arrangements, such as community centers, provide a more homelike atmosphere and a greater opportunity for the person with mental retardation to interact with people and the local environment. A trend that is on the rise involves not seeking an outside-the-home placement but, rather, allowing the retarded child to stay at home with the family. Although parents need assistance with care and a break from the demands of continuous supervision, an increasing number of mentally retarded youth are remaining with their families throughout childhood.

Treatment for individuals with mental retardation typically involves interventions aimed at remediation of the associated emotional and behavioral problems. Research findings have indicated that a substantial number of mentally retarded persons also suffer from psychological disorders (Matson & Barrett, 1982). For example, a survey of more than 8,000 mentally retarded persons (infants to adolescents) conducted in New York revealed that 9.8 percent had significant mental health needs (Jacobson, 1982a, 1982b). Among the problems they faced were cognitive disorders (hallucinations), emotional disorders (depression), and behavioral disorders (aggression and self-injury). Across various levels of intellectual functioning, an average of one-half of the patients were found to have behavior problems. Not surprisingly, those with dual diagnoses were more likely to have behavior problems.

The treatments of emotional and behavior problems in persons with mental retardation resemble those used with the general population, but with adjustments tailored to the clients' level of conceptual ability. These treatments tend to follow the behavioral orientation (Baer, Wolf & Risley, 1968; Birnbauer, 1976). For example, some behavioral training programs focus on teaching clients specific skills for more adaptive functioning. They also emphasize the contingent application of rewards, which take many forms. Social reinforcers (such as smiles, verbal praise, or a pat on the back) work particularly well with retarded persons. Behavioral methods have been successfully used to reduce disruptive behavior (Zimmerman, Zimmerman & Russell, 1969), control aggressive behavior (Mace, Kratochwill

The founder of Vita-Living, a tile-making business exclusively employing those with mental retardation, works here with one of her employees. People with mental retardation can hold circumscribed jobs and experience the pleasure of a job well done.

& Fiello, 1983), improve toileting (Giles & Wolf, 1966), and control public masturbation (Barmann & Murray, 1981).

Increasingly, family members are involved in treatments for children with mental retardation (Baker, Landen & Kashima, 1991; Crnic, Friedrich & Greenberg, 1983; Crnic & Reid, 1989). Maintaining a behavioral orientation, these treatments focus not only on specific child problems that require change but also on the goals and feelings of the family and the family's learning and use of behavior modification procedures to rear their special-needs child. Indeed, when family members are taught behavioral procedures, the result is an increase in the opportunities for application of these procedures (both in the home and elsewhere) as well as a corresponding increase in the potential for beneficial effects. Of course, treatments for retardation do not cure the disorder. But they do produce desired gains in the targeted behaviors — and these gains contribute to a better life for the recipients.

Achievement of a better life is also contingent on education. In the United States, considerable litigation eventually produced laws aimed at guaranteeing education for persons with mental retardation (Katz-Garris, 1978). In particular, the Education for All Handicapped Children Act of 1975 (Public Law 94-142) requires that all handicapped children receive a free public education designed to meet their specific needs, that the rights of the handicapped be protected, and that the effectiveness of their educational programs be assessed and evaluated. It also stipulates that the education be provided in the **least restrictive environment,** which means that retarded children should be placed in classrooms with nonretarded children whenever possible.

Educational interventions for mentally retarded individuals include both specific teaching strategies to facilitate their learning and programmed learning environments at school and at home to meet their needs. Although these teaching strategies resemble those used in regular classes, adjustments are made in keeping with the pace and level of individual learners.

Regarding the learning environment at school, concerns about class size and teacher-student ratios have been addressed in special education classrooms. In the ideal scenario, these classes would have fewer students and a higher teacher-student ratio than regular classes. But special education settings have been criticized for isolating retarded children and limiting their contact with normal children. The movement away from segregated classes and toward the integration of special-needs children with regular students has been called *mainstreaming.* Preliminary research suggested that the integrated classroom may offer moderate benefits (Haywood, Meyers & Switzky, 1982). Moreover, communities have been reported to hold mildly positive attitudes toward mainstreaming (Eiserman, Shisler & Healey, 1995), and recommendations for facilitating mainstreaming have been offered (Mortimer, 1995). However, reviews of the research suggest that mainstreaming has not enhanced social development in special-needs children, and there is little convincing evidence that they perform any better academically as a result of being mainstreamed (MacMillan, Keogh & Jones, 1986).

Other programs have been designed to enhance the learning environments of children whose homes lack adequate resources for development. Head Start is one example of a preventive intervention designed to increase cognitive and social stimulation for youth who are at risk because of economic and cultural deprivation.

Use of Medications with Mentally Retarded Persons

Drug therapy does not cure retardation or improve intellectual abilities. As with other disorders, it is aimed at reducing psychopathological conditions. Examples of the conditions likely to improve with medication are disruptive behavior, psychotic symptoms, and attentional problems. Surveys of institutionalized persons with mental retardation have indicated that 40 to 50 percent are receiving psychotropic medications (Aman & Singh, 1983). Those most likely to be medicated are older individuals with more severe behavior problems. The overall medication rate is lower for noninstitutionalized individuals, perhaps because of their distance from mental health services.

Anticonvulsant medications, routinely prescribed for the suppression of seizures, are widely used among persons with mental retardation — although evidence of seizure disorder is not always present. Researchers have suggested that this practice may be a result of the unsupported belief that anticonvulsants reduce behavior problems (Crnic & Reid, 1989). In addition, stimulant medications are used with mentally retarded children who evidence attentional problems. Although data support the effectiveness of these medications for children who have attention-deficit hyperactivity disorder (ADHD), their effectiveness for youth with mental retardation has yet to be clearly demonstrated. Preliminary data have suggested a relationship between effectiveness and severity: Stimulants are not useful for children with severe retardation (Gadow, 1992), but they can be safe and effective for some hyperactive children with mild to moderate retardation (Henden et al., 1990).

Despite the widespread use of medications with mentally retarded individuals, outcome studies have been scarce. And of the few that have been conducted, the absence of appropriate control groups and the failure to include a measure of learning are two major weaknesses (Crnic & Reid, 1989). Truly determining the effects of medications is not possible until these methodological problems are corrected.

LEARNING DISABILITIES

Ethan — an attractive and athletic twelve-year-old — was not mentally retarded, but his mathematical ability was severely restricted. Despite the results of intelligence tests indicating that his IQ score was in the normal range, his performance in math was well below his age and grade level. As a sixth grader, and despite his parents' *efforts to help, Ethan was alone in his struggles with basic subtraction and multiplication. When shopping, for example, Ethan could not determine the total costs of his purchases or calculate correct change.*

Identifying Learning Disabilities

Use of the phrase *learning disability* has become widespread, and the number of children identified as learning disabled has increased markedly, with estimates ranging from 5 to 15 percent (Taylor, 1989). Males are more frequently identified than females, in a ratio that ranges between 2:1 and 5:1 (Taylor, 1989).

The variations in these estimates result from inconsistencies in the definitions used to identify children with a learning disability. One method defines learning disability as a discrepancy between performance on tests of intellectual functioning and performance on tests of educational achievement — as when a student with a normal IQ score displays below-average achievement in a particular academic topic. Individuals evaluated according to this criterion have been described as "failing in one or more basic achievement skill areas despite normal intelligence" (Kistner & Torgesen, 1987, p. 289).

An alternate definition of learning disability points to below-expected age- and grade-level performance. Recall Ethan, whose mathematics learning disability was based on below-expected grade-level performance. Use of age or grade level as a cutoff creates problems, however: How extensive must the discrepancy be? One year? Two years? Although a one- or two-year discrepancy is often specified, the impact of a grade-level discrepancy changes with increasing age. For example, being two years behind is more troublesome for a fourth grader than for a seventh grader.

In sum, determinations of learning disabilities are not without methodological limitations. Based on a review of the literature, Morris (1988) offered a critical conclusion: "The most commonly used classification systems and definitions of learning disabled children do not meet basic empirical criteria for reliability and validity" (p. 793).

DSM-IV defines **learning disorders** (also called academic skills disorders or learning disabilities) using a combination of the IQ score–achievement discrepancy approach and the below age- and grade-level approach. DSM-IV diagnoses include **reading disorder, mathematics disorder,** and **disorder of written expression** (see Table 16.4), as well as learning disorder not otherwise specified. In each disorder, specific academic achievement, as measured by an individually administered standardized test, is considered below that expected given the person's chronological age, measured intelligence, and age-appropriate education. In addition, the condition must interfere with academic achievement or activities of daily living.

To what extent does the environment offer opportunities for knowledge and stimulate the desire for learning? Consider the differences in these environments in terms of the opportunities for creativity, interpersonal exchange, and learning: two children in a room with only a television versus young children engaged in play with a variety of toys available.

What about exclusionary criteria? Should a learning disability be independent of emotional or behavioral problems? Research often finds emotional and behavioral complications in children with learning disability (e.g., Lahey, Green & Forehand, 1980). For instance, ADHD (discussed in Chapter 15) is associated with learning difficulties. In a sample from the United States, approximately 75 percent of ADHD boys were underachieving, and about 33 percent were performing at least one grade below their expected level (Cantwell, 1986). Estimates of the percentage of ADHD children who have learning disabilities vary widely — from 9 to 92 percent (Wicks-Nelson & Israel, 1991). Learning disabled youth are also less socially competent than their peers (Toro, Weissberg, Guare & Liebenstein, 1990), more likely to have internalizing disorders (Thompson & Kronenberger, 1990), and more likely to be involved in delinquency (Brier, 1989). Not all learning-disordered youth have these or other emotional or behavior problems, but the extent of comorbidity is sufficient to rule out the idea that a learning disorder must be independent of an emotional or behavioral problem.

Possible Causes of Learning Disabilities

The exact causes of learning disabilities are, at present, unknown. Genetic factors, difficulties in brain function, and cognitive and motivational influences have all been examined as possible links to learning disorders. We are not yet certain, for example, whether learning disabilities result from deficits in cognitive processing or deficits in motivation or achievement.

Research into genetic causes has been reviewed by Smith, Pennington, Kimberling, and Ing (1990). Data suggest that children of parents with reading difficulties have a greater chance of reading problems than children of parents who read normally, but this finding could be viewed as supporting either a genetic or a family environment explanation, or both. Moreover, improvements have been observed. For example, a four-year follow-up study of Latin American children found that 17 percent of those with reading disabilities eventually became average readers (Bravo-Valdivieso, 1995).

Brain dysfunction may also play a role in learning disorders. According to Taylor (1989), children who have experienced head injury, central nervous system infection, neurological problems, or epilepsy are at

Table 16.4	DSM-IV Categories and Terms Used for Learning Disabilities	
Developmental Learning Disorder	**Term**	**Description**
Mathematics disorder	Dyscalculia	An inability to perform the operations of arithmetic
Reading disorder	Dyslexia	An inability to read, or related difficulties in reading skills
Disorder of written expression	Aphasia[a]	Children's expressive-language disorder

[a]The term *aphasia*, referring to loss of language, may not be exactly correct for children. *Dysphasia* is sometimes used, referring to language abilities that never developed.

higher risk for learning problems than are other children. Not all children with a history of these conditions develop a learning disability, however, and the same conditions can contribute to other emotional and behavioral problems.

Finally, psychological theories have tended to emphasize either motivational or cognitive explanations of learning disability. According to the motivational approach, learning-disabled children may experience an initial degree of failure, come to doubt their abilities, and fail to put forth effort on future tasks. Their expectations for success would thus be lower. As one study found, learning-disabled youth are less likely than nondisabled youth to attribute success to their ability, yet more likely to attribute failure to a lack of ability (Tarnowsky & Nay, 1989).

On the other hand, several writers, based on reviews of the literature, have suggested that there is empirical support for differentiating learning-disabled from nondisabled children on the basis of information-processing characteristics (Keogh & Margolis, 1976; Kistner & Torgeson, 1987; Torgeson, 1986; Wong, 1985). The difficulties in cognitive processing that have been promoted as influential in learning disability include limited attentional focusing and failure to use effective learning strategies. For example, when learning a list of words, nondisabled readers use memory strategies such as rehearsal, clustering, and elaboration to enhance recall. Reading-disabled youth, by contrast, are less likely to use memory strategies.

Treatments for Learning Disabilities

Treatments for learning-disabled children are often consistent with the view that these children have difficulties with cognitive-processing strategies. For example, one group of learning-disabled children showed improvements in reading comprehension after they were taught to monitor their performance by asking themselves questions while they read (Wong & Jones, 1982). Interestingly, when the same strategy was taught to students who were not learning disabled, their performance was not as enhanced. Perhaps self-questioning helped the learning-disabled children, but not the nondisabled group, because the learning-disabled group initially lacked self-questioning and self-monitoring.

Torgeson (1979) also documented the effectiveness of strategy training. Pictures of objects from four different categories were shown to good and poor readers in the fourth grade. The children were instructed that they would be asked to recall the pictures and that they could do anything they wanted to help them remember the pictures. The children's behavior was observed through a one-way mirror. Compared with the good readers, the poor readers were less likely to organize the pictures into categories, spent more time off-task, and recalled fewer pictures. However, when the same poor readers were taught to use a categorical clustering strategy, they were able to recall as well as the good readers. Moreover, the time they spent off-task fell to a level that was comparable to that of the good readers. Apparently, various cognitive strategy training approaches have had some beneficial effects with children identified as learning disabled (Hallahan, Kneedler & Lloyd, 1983; Wong, Harris & Graham, 1991).

PERVASIVE DEVELOPMENTAL DISORDERS: AUTISM

Nadia, at age six, made the drawing of the rooster shown in Figure 16.3. The drawing is intricate, complex, and accurate. Nadia possessed genuine artistic talent, but she did not speak. She preferred to be alone, in a room that she kept in rigid order, where she would sit unresponsive to the presence of others. Nadia was diagnosed as autistic. A pervasive developmental problem, autistic disorder involves a lack of responsiveness to people and severely delayed language development. The problems begin before the child is thirty-six months old. It is interesting, if not sad, to note that when therapy was effective in promoting Nadia's communication with other people, her artistic talents declined.

Pervasive developmental disorders, a phrase currently used to refer to severe psychological problems emerging in infancy, involve severe upset in children's cognitive, social, behavioral, and emotional growth that produces widespread complication of the developmental process (Lord & Rutter, 1994; Rutter & Schopler, 1987). DSM-IV lists several pervasive developmental disorders, although one, autism, is clearly considered the dominant pervasive developmental disorder in both the research and clinical realms. **Autism** affects basic human qualities: interpersonal socialization and complex communication. Youth with autism demonstrate severe impairments in social interaction and relationships, interpersonal play, and communication.

Historically, there were believed to be two pervasive developmental disorders: autism and childhood schizophrenia. However, because childhood schizophrenia is essentially the same as the adult disorder with differences only in age of onset and extent of hallucinations and delusions, descriptions of the adult disorder and the diagnostic procedures for adult schizophrenia apply also to children. Specifically, childhood schizophrenia resembles the adult disorder in terms of the presence of severe withdrawal and an inability to relate to others, but delusions and hallucinations are less common in children. The age of onset is important, however, in differentiating childhood schizophrenia from autism:

Figure 16.3 Nadia's Drawing of a Rooster

Nadia, an autistic child, showed remarkable artistic ability. When she was six years old, she rendered this drawing based on a model in a children's picture book.

Source: Reprinted with permission from *Nadia: A Case of Extraordinary Drawing Ability in an Autistic Child,* by Lorna Selfe. Copyright by Academic Press Inc. (London) Ltd. 1977.

Children with schizophrenia have a period of relatively normal adjustment followed by onset of the severe symptoms of schizophrenia, whereas autism is evident very early in life.

Characteristics of Autistic Disorder

Leo Kanner (1943) was the first to describe autism. (We discuss his study of autistic children in Chapter 5.) According to Kanner, its outstanding, fundamental feature is "the children's inability to relate themselves in the ordinary way to people and situations from the beginning of life" (p. 242). The severity of the disorder is exemplified by Chip, who, as described in the chapter opener, had many of the characteristic features of autism:

> *Chip was an attractive four-year-old of average height and weight, but he never seemed to hear or respond to other people. His parents had once thought that he was deaf or severely hearing impaired. Adults could come and go from the room, and there would be no indication that Chip was aware of their movement. When someone called him by name, there was no answer. Usually, adults had to tap his shoulder before he'd show any signs of acknowledgment. Yet when a chair was moved to add a place at the kitchen table, Chip had a temper outburst. Rearranging living room furniture or adding a new bookcase to a room distressed Chip. He was unlikely to initiate any form of communication. Even in play there was something odd about his behavior. He showed an extreme intensity while playing alone. In one instance, Chip played with a broken light switch for more than thirty minutes.*

Christopher Borden and Thomas Ollendick (1992) have outlined some of the early symptoms of autistic disorder. In the newborn, the baby seems different from other babies, seems not to need the mother, is indifferent to being held, has flaccid muscle tone, and cries infrequently but may be intensely irritable. In the first six months, the baby fails to notice the mother; is undemanding; has delayed or absent smiling, babbling, or anticipatory responses; and lacks interest in toys. In the second six months, the child shows no interest in social games, is unaffectionate, demonstrates an absence of verbal and nonverbal communication, and is underreactive or overreactive to stimulation.

Indeed, parents of autistic children consistently report that the children are unresponsive socially. The severely autistic child's imperviousness to the social and physical environment does not lie on a continuum with normal behavior (Wenar, Ruttenberg, Kalish-Weiss & Wolf, 1986). According to Charles Wenar (1982), the autistic child approaches the world as intrinsically noxious. Descriptions of autistic children often include their lack of cuddling in the early months of life, an obsessive desire for sameness in the environment, self-stimulatory behaviors (such as rocking, spinning, and arm flapping), self-destructive behaviors (such as head banging, arm banging, and self-biting), lack of eye contact with other people, and fascination with inanimate objects. In a recent study, autistic children were found to engage in more ritualized behavior and to initiate interactions with peers much less frequently than retarded youth (Hauck, Fein, Waterhouse & Feinstein, 1995). Lack of responsiveness to people is a characteristic of autistic youth that can contribute to frustration among parents when faced with the challenge of caregiving.

From this wide array of unusual behaviors, DSM-IV identifies four key features of autism: (1) qualitative impairment in social interaction, (2) qualitative impairments in communication, (3) restricted, repetitive, and stereotyped patterns of behavior, interests, and activities; and (4) onset before age 3. According to Volkmar (1996), this definition is consistent with the International Classification of Diseases (WHO, 1992). More detailed criteria are presented in Table 16.5.

One striking example of the communication difficulties typical of autistic children is **echolalia,** the repetition or echoing back of speech, as in this example:

THERAPIST: Can you point to Chip's shoe?

CHIP: Can you point to Chip's shoe?

THERAPIST: Use this finger (*touches finger*) and point like this to your shoe (*directs finger pointing*).

CHIP: Point like this to your shoe.

Because communication problems like this occur very early in life, they probably reflect an inherent cognitive defect (Rutter, 1978).

What could this deficit be? Much recent research has focused on perceptual and cognitive difficulties that might underlie echolalia and other symptoms of autism (Donnelan, 1985; Litrownik & McInnis, 1986; Prior, 1984). For example, autistic children display **stimulus overselectivity,** responding to only select aspects of stimulus materials (e.g., Lovaas, Koegel & Schreibman, 1979). Suppose that a therapist trying to teach language skills shows a picture of a shoe, says the word, and emphasizes the movements of the mouth to make the sounds. Autistic children might attend to the picture, but fail to attend to the sounds. These children seem unable to pay attention to more than one cue at a time. In addition, they may pay attention to idiosyncratic and often irrelevant stimuli. This tendency can hinder their ability to communicate and interact with the social and physical environment.

Autistic children also have difficulty processing and integrating information. For example, they do not use the meaning of words to assist in the recall of information, nor do they reorganize incoming information to reduce redundancy (Hermelin, 1976). In addition, they have difficulty transforming or manipulating information in their minds (Shulman, Yirmiya & Greenbaum, 1995).

Table 16.5 DSM-IV Criteria for Autistic Disorder

1. *Qualitative impairment in social interaction*

   Marked impairment in the use of multiple nonverbal behaviors such as eye-to-eye gaze, facial expression, body posture, and gestures to regulate social interaction

   Failure to develop peer relationships appropriate to developmental level

   Lack of spontaneous seeking to share enjoyment, interests, or achievements with other people

   Lack of social or emotional reciprocity

2. *Qualitative impairments in communication*

   Delay in, or total lack of, the development of spoken language in individuals with adequate speech

   In individuals with adequate speech, marked impairment in the ability to initiate or sustain a conversation with others

   Stereotyped and repetitive use of language or idiosyncratic language

   Lack of varied spontaneous make-believe play or social imitative play appropriate to developmental level

3. *Restricted repetitive and stereotyped patterns of behavior, interests, and activities*

   Encompassing preoccupation with one or more stereotyped and restricted patterns of interest that is abnormal either in intensity or focus

   Apparently compulsive adherence to specific, nonfunctional routines or rituals

   Stereotypes and repetitive motor mannerisms (e.g., hand- or finger-flapping or twisting, or complex whole body movements)

   Persistent preoccupation with parts of objects

4. *Onset before age three*

Source: DSM-IV. Reprinted with permission from *The Diagnostic and Statistical Manual of Mental Disorders,* Fourth Edition. Copyright ©1994 American Psychiatric Association.

To meet diagnostic criteria for autistic disorder, a child must evidence a total of at least six items from the four categories shown in this table, with at least two from category 1 and one from each of categories 2 and 3.

Some autistic children achieve IQ scores in the normal range, whereas others (5 to 10 percent of all autistic persons) display remarkable abilities (O'Connor & Hermelin, 1988). However, the majority of persons with autism show some intellectual deficits that fall into the retarded range (Bristol et al., 1996; Rutter & Schopler, 1987). Because lower IQ scores are related both to more severe communication problems and to a poorer prognosis, researchers have suggested that children with autistic disorder be divided into high- and low-functioning groups. High-functioning autistic children typically have a better prognosis, but not all studies find meaningful differences between high- and low-functioning cases (Myles, Simpson & Johnson, 1995).

With regard to the rare but quite interesting "remarkable special skills" seen in some autistic persons, recall the character portrayed by Dustin Hoffman in the movie *Rain Man*. This character, whose pattern was that of someone with an autistic disorder, could perform remarkable calendar calculations, determining the day of the week on which a date several years in the future would occur. Equally impressive, if not equally puzzling, Nadia's drawing of a rooster at the beginning of this section illustrates remarkable special talents in some autistic youth.

Who Is Affected with Autistic Disorder?

Autistic disorder is relatively rare, occurring in only 5 to 10 births per 10,000 (Bristol et al., 1996; Lord & Rutter, 1994). Autism is seen in both genders, at a frequency three to four times higher among boys than among girls (Bryson, 1996). A recent study of gender differences among higher-functioning persons with autistic disorder reported that males were rated to be more severely autistic than females in terms of early social development but not stereotypic behaviors (McLennan, Lord & Schopler, 1993).

Autism has been found in families throughout the world and in all social classes (Gilberg, 1990). However, recent data have identified different prevalence rates in certain countries. In China, for instance, Kuo-Tai (1987) reported only 5 cases of autism among 1,190 childhood psychiatric clients over a 26-year period. What about the rate of autism relative to all births? Only 2 cases of autism came from the entire population of Nanjing, a city in China whose population Kuo-Tai set at 4.5 million. At the other end of the distribution is Japan, where the prevalence rates for autism have been estimated to be higher than elsewhere in the world. One study found a prevalence of .16 percent (Tanoue, Oda, Asano & Kawashima, 1988). Another, which examined 12,263 Japanese children, reported a minimum prevalence of .13 percent (Sugiyama & Abe, 1989).

At present there is no definitive explanation for these different prevalence rates — although one specula-

Persons with autism have severe impairments in social interactions and communication. Dustin Hoffman portrayed a character with autism in the movie *Rainman*.

tion is that failure to identify *all* cases of autism in China, owing to various reasons, may account for the very low frequency in that country. Some researchers are also considering methodological dissimilarities (for example, studies of population-based samples versus clinic samples) and diagnostic differences (such as use of different diagnostic criteria). Others, accepting the differences as real, are beginning to test hypotheses to help explain them. For example, are birthing practices, nutritional variations, or genetic factors contributing to the different prevalence rates?

Course of Autistic Disorder

Although some individuals with autistic disorder show improvements, most continue into adulthood severely handicapped and unable to take full care of themselves. What factors predict who will and who will not improve? Language skills and IQ scores are the best prognostic indicators: Early language development and high IQ score suggest a better prognosis (Lord & Rutter, 1994).

Only about 50 percent of autistic persons develop useful speech. During adolescence, behavior and emotional problems emerge: The aggression, oppositional behavior, and tantrums that may occur are quite distressing to parents. Estimates have suggested that approximately 75 percent of autistic children fall in the moderate range of mental retardation and that 25 percent develop seizure disorders by adulthood (Crnic & Reid, 1989).

Possible Causes of Autism

What could cause this extremely serious problem called autism? A theory proposed by Bruno Bettelheim (1967) was influential for well over a decade. During the 1950s and 1960s, the psychoanalytic approach was prevalent, and Bettelheim's notions were in this tradition. He argued that when a child faces an unresponsive world that is frustrating and destructive, the child withdraws from it and from people. Thus, Bettelheim's theory blamed autism on the actions of the caregiver: on the cold and unloving "refrigerator" parent. But this theory has not maintained its prominence; increased interest in behavioral and biological theories, as well as a lack of scientific evidence needed to support the theory, contributed to its being largely abandoned.

A contrasting explanation, proposed by Charles Ferster (1961), attempted to untangle autistic behavior using an analysis of individual children's reinforcement history. This behavioral theory, too, failed to receive empirical support (Schreibman, 1988), although the behavioral approach overall has had a favorable impact on the treatment of autistic disorder.

Apparently, autistic disorder is not caused by parents who are cold, disinterested, or in some other way pathological. Autistic children are not the product of being reared by unemotional and ineffectual parents, and they do not seem to have experienced any undue stress in the early years of their lives. Indeed, studies of the parents of autistic children have generally failed to find any characteristic pattern of maladjustment (McAdoo & DeMeyer, 1978).

Alternatively, do these children suffer from a genetically transmitted abnormality? Studies have been conducted and literature reviews published, but disagreements exist. In a thorough review of the research data available at the time, David Hansen and Irving Gottesman (1976) concluded that no strong evidence implicated genetics in the development of autism: Few siblings are affected, and cases of autism do not predict greater incidence among family members. Other researchers have argued, however, that the very rarity of autism and the fact that adult autistic persons are unlikely to have offspring may account for the low rate among relatives (Folstein & Rutter, 1977).

Data that do suggest a genetic factor have come from a study of twenty-one pairs of same-sex twins in which one twin of each pair met stringent criteria for autism (Folstein & Rutter, 1978). Of the identical twins, 36 percent were concordant for autism, as compared to none of the fraternal twins. Moreover, when the criteria for autism were loosened, and concordance was sought in cognitive and linguistic problems, not just in the diagnostic criteria for autistic disorder, 82 percent of the identical twins and only 10 percent of the fraternal twins were found to be concordant. Rubenstein and associates (1990) argued that these data — the higher concordance for monozygotic twins than for dizygotic twins and a higher than normal incidence among siblings of children with autism — suggested a genetic contribution (see also Bailey, 1993; Bailey et al., 1995). Other data (see Smalley, 1991; Smalley & Collins, 1996) are not as clear-cut, and many researchers have concluded that autism is still not known to be an entirely genetic disorder.

Newer research, using a wide range of recent technologies, has identified a biological component to autism, however. In one study, autistic subjects exhibited reduced brain activity (Dawson et al., 1995); in another, the brains of persons with autism were found to be slightly larger and heavier than those of normal people, and the neurons themselves were described as developmentally immature (Minshew, 1996). These anatomical differences are consistent with the hypothesis that a developmental curtailment takes place in autistic individuals at some point earlier than thirty weeks of gestation — that is, before birth (Denckla, 1996; cited in Bristol et al., 1996). Although certain features of brain function are unaffected by autism, the disorder nevertheless involves widespread brain dysfunction consistent with a biological explanation.

A small proportion of autistic cases have been said to arise from diseases as diverse as congenital rubella, tuberous sclerosis, and neurofibromatosis. For example, children with **congenital rubella** (measles existing at birth) are affected with the rubella virus early in prenatal development. As a result of this infection, the children are born with a variety of malformations, deafness, blindness, central nervous system abnormalities, seizures, and retardation. Two decades ago, studies reported that 8 percent to 13 percent of children with rubella were autistic (e.g., Chess, 1977). Today, however, researchers believe that diseases account for only a tiny minority of cases. According to Rutter and Schopler (1987), the vast majority of cases of autism have no identifiable medical cause.

The possibility remains that prenatal damage or disrupted development contributes to the cause of autism. In earlier research, autistic persons were found to evidence central nervous system disorder and neurological abnormalities (e.g., Gubbay, Lobascher & Kingerlee, 1970). And more recently, Geri Dawson and associates observed reduced activity in the left hemisphere — the area important for communication — among individuals with autistic disorder (Dawson, Warrenburg & Fuller, 1983).

Yet to the present day, there is no compelling evidence to fully explain why autistic children behave in their very unusual ways. The consensus among experts is that autism is largely a cognitive and social disorder, and that it has multiple biological causes occurring sometime between conception and birth. Autistic children enter the world biologically different. Environmental factors, however, do affect the development of the disorder and the prognosis for later adjustment. For example, although autistic children themselves contribute to the production of an interpersonal environment that is suboptimal, specially designed educational settings and supportive homes can improve their chances of acquiring some self-help skills.

Programs for Autistic Persons

Without treatment, the long-term prognosis for persons with autistic disorder is guarded; generally, these persons do not form strong interpersonal relationships, nor do they develop the ability to interact socially in ways that are considered "normal." Levels of functioning vary among persons with autistic disorder, however. For example, children who, early in life, have at least some language ability and score near the normal range on nonverbal tests of intelligence have a much better long term prognosis than children who do not show either of these qualities. Nevertheless, even optimistic estimates suggest that at least two-thirds of autistic children remain severely handicapped into adulthood. Only a small proportion of autistic individuals live somewhat independent lives without any signs of the disorder.

Despite these prognostications, the care of the autistic child can include intervention programs at home or in an institution designed to improve communication, reduce disruptive behavior, and enhance socialization.

In fact, a wide variety of treatments for autism have been employed over the years. During the period that the psychoanalytic explanation of autism was dominant, the treatment followed from the theory. That is, on the assumption that the disorder resulted from faulty or failed parenting, autistic children were taken from their parents and placed in an environment where the therapeutic milieu would presumably allow them to return to more normal development. However, reviews of evaluations of such treatment programs found them to be ineffective with autistic youth (Levitt, 1963; Rimland, 1974).

More recently, the use of medications has received some attention, although the results have not provided unbridled encouragement (Campbell, 1988; Conners & Wherry, 1979). Stimulants, antidepressants, and antipsychotic medications have been tried, with little or no evidence of beneficial gains. One study (Quintana et al., 1995) found that stimulants improved the hyperactivity of autistic children but did not alter the autistic symptoms, and another (Gordon et al., 1993) reported that clomipramine reduced compulsive ritualized behaviors in autistic youth. The use of vitamins has also been studied, but methodological shortcomings in the research have prevented solid conclusions (Pfeiffer, Norton, Nelson & Shott, 1995).

Today, psychological programs for autism based on research evaluations emphasize the application of behavior modification procedures and parent training. This raises the question, "If autism is a cognitive and

Intensive and extensive interventions, involving many hours of one-to-one treatment each week, typically take place in living environments, such as the group home shown here. Persons with autism require therapists with a great deal of patience. Long periods of time and many interactions may be needed to achieve even a basic socially appropriate response. The prognosis for persons with autism remains guarded.

social disorder produced by biological causes, why is the treatment a behavioral program?" As one of many possible answers, consider the case of Helen Keller (after Rimland, 1974). Blind and deaf from birth, she learned to speak and write, not through treatments for blindness and deafness, but as a result of training like that used in behavioral programs. In short, the cause of a problem need not be behavioral for a behavioral treatment to be useful.

Educational opportunities for autistic youth are a source of debate: Should autistic children be mainstreamed to receive **full inclusion**? In other words, should they be educated in the same settings as their normally developing peers? Or are special education classrooms or specialized schools more appropriate? (Zigmond & Baker, 1995). As Mesibov and Shea (1996) pointed out, advocates of full inclusion mention increased expectations by teachers, modeling of normal development by peers, increased learning, and potentially improved self-esteem as supportive reasons. However, Mesibov and Shea themselves, having reviewed the literature, concluded that autistic youth benefit from small, highly structured environments — environments more likely in the specialized schools designed specifically for them.

FOCUS ON RESEARCH

What Can Be Done About Self-Injury?

Severely handicapped children sometimes engage in **self-injurious behavior,** such as head-banging, hair-pulling, self-biting, and eating nonedible substances. At times, the self-injurious behavior is so extreme that it threatens the life of the child. Recall, from the chapter opening, the pin-sticking engaged in by Ramey. And forceful head-banging, for example, can result in extreme brain damage. What should be done when a disabled child engages in uncompromising self-injurious actions?

To some, the use of physical restraints is the preferred approach: Put the self-injurious child in a restraint and prevent actions that are harmful. Others see medications, or chemical restraints, as desirable (Hammock, Schroeder & Levine, 1995). Unfortunately, both physical and chemical restraints, though options in some cases, prevent the individual from participating in other therapeutic, social, and educational programs. Let us now consider some treatments that, through proper research, have been found effective. In the process, we discuss a related controversy surrounding the use of certain procedures.

In a monograph on the treatment of self-injurious behavior prepared by a special task force, Judy Favell and her colleagues (1982) noted that such behavior is repetitious and chronic, and that its incidence and severity are greatest among retarded and autistic patients with severe disabilities. The task force consisted of fourteen preeminent clinicians and researchers who reviewed the research literature and provided recommendations.

Regarding treatment, Favell and associates (1982) recommended that whatever intervention is used should be evaluated in terms of its ability to reduce the self-injurious behavior by a clinically significant amount — that is, reduce its frequency and intensity to the extent that the individual refrains from self-injury and is capable of participation in therapeutic activities. Although the need for evaluation may seem obvious, evaluation of treatments for self-injurious behavior is especially important

This child opts to be isolated and engages in repetitive rocking and occasional headbanging. These behaviors may be a part of a pervasive developmental disorder called autism.

because of the controversy that exists among practitioners and parents about the use of aversive procedures.

Single-subject designs (see Chapter 5) are the most appropriate methods for evaluating the clinical significance of treatments for self-injurious behavior — primarily because other methods are problematic. For example, group comparison studies would require that large numbers of self-injurious clients be available, and this is not typically the case. Alternatively, the assignment of self-injurious clients to a no-treatment control group would present researchers with a thorny ethical dilemma because those clients miss out on treatments that may work. Hence the preference for single-subject designs, including careful measurement of the baseline frequency of self-injurious behavior before treatment and ongoing recording of the frequency of the self-injury during treatment, as a way of judging the effectiveness of treatments.

Behavioral procedures, such as removing reinforcement for self-injury, punishing self-injury, and reinforcing more desirable behavior, have been evaluated as methods to produce clinically significant changes in self-injurious behavior (Baumeister & Rollings, 1976; Favell & Green, 1981; Russo, Carr & Lovaas, 1980). One behavioral procedure, **differential reinforcement of other behavior (DRO)**, involves providing reinforcement after periods of time during which no self-injury occurs. The use of DRO may result in an increase in self-injurious behavior at first, but this is generally followed by a meaningful reduction. Another procedure, *extinction*, involves withholding previously given reinforcement after episodes of self-injury. And *time-out* consists of taking the self-injuring child away from the opportunity to receive reinforcement for self-injury. Each of these procedures has been used singly and in combination with other approaches in an effort to reduce self-injury. There are documented cases in which the procedures were successful, but also cases in which the reinforcements were difficult to identify or manipulate, and still other cases in which the procedures were less than fully effective.

What about the use of aversive procedures — such as mild electric shock? What does the research tell us, and what can we do with the information? According to the Favell task force report, "Aversive electrical stimulation (informally termed shock) is the most widely researched and, within the parameters of shock employed in the research literature, the most generally effective method of initially suppressing self-injury" (1982, p. 540). Though effective, it is considered appropriate only in extreme cases — and, even then, only when applied in carefully controlled situations by experienced and trained professionals. In such treatments, a physically harmless but subjectively noxious electrical stimulus is applied for a brief duration immediately after each occurrence of self-injury. Yet despite documented demonstrations of effectiveness — clinically significant

reductions in self-injury — controversy over the use of shock continues (Mudford, 1995). Ultimately, it appears, not just methodologically sound research but also politics and personal beliefs must be factored into decisions about which treatments to employ.

More typically, behavioral programs seek to treat behavioral deficits or excesses by applying reinforcements on a contingent basis. Because autistic children are not as social as normal children, they do not respond in the same way to smiles, verbal praise, or peer social events. Accordingly, more concrete and sensory rewards are employed. The case of Dicky illustrates this approach (Wolf, Risley & Mees, 1964).

Dicky received a behaviorally based treatment beginning at age three. First, to overcome his refusal to wear eyeglasses, the therapist used a shaping procedure. Dicky was rewarded for touching and holding his glass frames, for trying them on, and, eventually, for wearing them. Second, to control his tantrum behaviors, the therapist removed him from the pleasant environment he was in whenever a tantrum occurred and placed him in "time out." Similarly, his food plate was taken away whenever he ate with his fingers, and he was physically removed for throwing food or taking the food of others. Finally, the therapist addressed his lack of communication through a consistent program of showing Dicky a picture, labeling the object, prompting Dicky to repeat the label, and eventually rewarding him (for example, with applesauce) for identifying the object in the picture without the therapist's prompting.

Many behavioral programs focus on language development. The shaping process is evident in the sequence of the training. Initially, the child is rewarded for any verbalizations at all. Then, a reward is pro-vided only when the verbalization follows a prompt by the therapist. Next, a reward is given only when the child makes closer and closer approximations to the verbalization supplied by the therapist. Once the child has acquired the actual word, the therapist provides a reward only when the child follows the correct prompt, in spite of the therapist's introduction of other sounds. Through this shaping sequence, using modeling and rewards, the child gradually learns language skills. The improvements are noteworthy when judged against initial levels, but the process is painstaking and the end result is not "normal" communication. A great deal of time and effort is required for autistic children to respond verbally and to generate sentences.

An example of both an intensive and extensive intervention was provided by O. Ivar Lovaas (1987) at the University of California in Los Angeles. Lovaas initiated an **intensive behavior modification** program involving full-time treatment of children diagnosed as autistic. All of the participants were younger than 3 years and 10 months of age, and all evidenced a minimal level of mental ability. Three groups of children were compared: 19 children received intensive training, 19 received minimal training, and 21 children served as controls. The intensive training lasted two or more years and involved more than forty hours of one-to-one treatment per week. The minimal training, though similar, involved ten hours of one-to-one treatment per week.

The treatment itself focused on several goals. In the first year, the therapists sought to achieve compliance to verbal commands, imitation, and appropriate play. To reduce self-stimulation or aggression, they ignored these undesirable behaviors. As a last resort, they also used a loud "no" or a slap on the thigh. Language growth was emphasized in the second year, and preacademic skills and emotional expression were goals in the third year. An overarching goal was placement of the children into regular school settings.

According to Lovaas (1987), the children in the intensive training achieved significantly higher educational placements than the other two groups of children. For example, 47 percent of those in the intensive training condition completed regular first grade, as compared to 0 percent and 5 percent of those in the other groups. A further study of the intensively treated youth at age thirteen reported that, in terms of clinical interviews and measures of adaptive behavior, eight of the original nineteen were "indistinguishable" from an age-matched control group of normal children (Lovaas, Smith & McEachin, 1989, p. 166).

These results are very encouraging, but they should be viewed with some caution. Other treatments, though less intense, have not had as great a success rate — so the required replication has not been achieved. Moreover, given that a minimum mental age was required for inclusion in the study, the eight autistic children who so dramatically improved were probably from the high-functioning end of the continuum, thus limiting generalization to all autistic youth.

The dramatic effect reported by Lovaas (1987) caused others to take notice. But Schopler, Short, and Mesibov (1989) offered a more conservative conclusion: Due to methodological problems (such as the apparent absence of random assignment to treatment and control groups), it is not possible to determine the true effects of Lovaas's intervention. Nevertheless, his study adds evidence of the benefits of behavior programs for autistic children, while also suggesting that intensive and extensive treatments may be necessary to have a meaningful affect on such a pervasive disorder as autism.

A summary of the many applications of behavior modification to autistic youth would provide evidence of measurable progress over the years, but such progress has been slow. Not all interventions with autistic children produce dramatic success, and, indeed, the prognosis for most autistic children is not optimistic. The highest levels of success are achieved through very intensive intervention (forty hours per week) with very young, select patients. However, according to at least one study, when parents are trained in the behavioral program and take over as therapists, the results remain stable and the program-produced gains are maintained (see Lovaas, Koegel, Simmons & Long, 1973). We consider this treatment option next.

FAMILY MATTERS

Training Parents of Autistic Children

Originally, training for parents of autistic children focused on the disruptive and sometimes dangerous behaviors that were evident in the home. More recently, to facilitate generalization to settings outside of treatment, parents have become involved in language training as well. Given that parents may suffer emotional problems linked to parenting an autistic child, these, too, can become targets for parent training interventions.

As is true for parent training in general, treatments include a variety of procedures, such as lectures and readings, demonstrations and role-playing, and home visits and telephone contacts. The main focus is training in elementary behavior modification principles — shaping, reinforcement, ignoring unacceptable behavior, and generalization. At the same time, parent groups provide opportunities for discussion of difficulties as well as social support.

With regard to the shaping of communication skills, a parent would be taught to reward eye contact as a first step toward increased communicativeness. For example, a parent would be told, "When Joanne makes eye contact with you, immediately provide a reward, no matter how busy you might be at the time." Later on, parents can become involved in teaching specific words — saying the word "shoe" when pointing to Joanne's shoe — as well as concepts of ownership — pointing to Joanne when saying "your shoe" and pointing to oneself when saying "my shoe."

The work of Robert Koegel, Laura Schreibman, and their colleagues (Koegel et al., 1982) illustrates some of the benefits of parent training. Their project compared twenty-five to fifty hours of parent training in behavior modification procedures with out-patient clinic treatment (four to five hours a week for a year). Both the training and the treatment improved the social behavior, play, and speech and decreased tantrums and echolalia. However, the clinic-treated youth did not show generalization of their improvements during an assessment in the home, whereas the parent-training condition resulted in observable gains in the home environment. According to a more recent report, parent training procedures resulted in improved parent-child interactions: The children were happier, and the parents were more interested and less stressed (Koegel, Bimbela & Schreibman, 1996).

A program in Great Britain also produced some illuminating findings related to home-based parent training (Howlin, 1981; Howlin & Rutter, 1987). Sixteen families, each with a high-functioning autistic boy (average age six years), received treatment over an eighteen-month period. Comparison groups received out-patient treatment. Mothers were individually trained to use behavioral procedures and to teach language and manage behavior problems. Psychologists visited the parents in their home for two to three hours weekly or biweekly for six months and monthly for the last twelve months. There were also instances of counseling regarding other matters and the occasional inclusion of additional services.

The outcomes were favorable, yet mixed. For example, the autistic boys whose parents received training showed significantly more social responsiveness to their parents, but not more interactive play with peers. Among the same boys there were fewer tantrums and instances of aggression, but no changes in stereotypic behavior or hyperactivity. And based on an examination of audiotapes, the children with trained parents showed improved quantity and communicativeness of speech but no significant differences in IQ scores. In short, differences were not always observed — but when they were, they favored the parent-training approach. As Howlin and Rutter (1987) concluded, the results were sufficiently positive to be encouraging, but not so overwhelming as to preclude the need for more intensive intervention. Indeed, their recommendation is for a more comprehensive parent-training intervention (see also Agosta & Melda, 1996).

Parents of autistic children have their own concerns. Living with a child with a pervasive developmental disorder involves problems in addition to those related to interacting with the child. Not the least of these problems is simply facing the lifelong task of managing a severely handicapped child. Accordingly, Sandra Harris (1983) provided a set of recommendations that include pragmatic issues (dealing with a community that may not have resources), emotional issues (personal distress), and interpersonal problems (withdrawal of the extended family). Parents, while addressing their responsibilities toward the autistic child, must recognize their *own* work and recreational needs as well. And siblings must face the challenge of being responsible members of the helping family while also maintaining an independent existence. In families in which these issues are met with insufficient adjustment, depression, guilt, anger, and a sense of inadequacy can become a source for serious concern. Thus, treatments for parents — even if they do not directly affect the behavior of the autistic child — are nevertheless valued because they improve the home and general family environment and can prevent parental burnout and distress.

Autistic children may also receive treatment while in a residential setting. However, the trend for autistic children has shifted from institutionalization to the provision of appropriate treatment in home and public school settings (Schopler & Hennike, 1990). The trend for autistic adults, on the other hand, has shifted toward group homes in the community, thus helping adolescents and adults move toward independence from their families (Van Bourgondien & Schopler, 1990).

Other Pervasive Developmental Disorders

There are other pervasive developmental disorders, but they are less common than autism. Rett's disorder, Asperger's disorder, and childhood disintegrative disorder are included in DSM-IV among the pervasive developmental disorders. We review these briefly here.

Rett's disorder is characterized by multiple specific deficits, but the deficits appear after a period of normal motor development (for example, after the first five months of life). Head size is normal at birth, but head growth decelerates between five months and four years of age. Noteworthy, too, is the loss of previously purposeful hand movements between five months and two and a half years of life. Among children with Rett's disorder, interest in social activities diminishes, language development is impaired, and there is the appearance of poorly coordinated gait or trunk movements. The disorder has been reported in females only. It is usually accompanied by severe mental retardation. Rett's disorder is progressive and the communicative and behavioral deficits persist throughout life.

The essential features of **Asperger's disorder** are severe and sustained impairment in social interaction and the development of repetitive patterns of behavior and activities. These features cause clinically meaningful impairment in functioning, yet there are no clinically meaningful delays in cognitive development of age-appropriate self-help skills. Though similar to autism, Asperger's disorder less frequently involves deviance in language and communication. It is more common among males, and in the majority of cases the disorder is lifelong.

A child who exhibits two years of normal development in communication, social relationships, play, and adaptive behavior, followed by a clinically meaningful loss of previously acquired skills before age ten, may have **childhood disintegrative disorder.** The essential feature of this very rare disorder is marked deterioration of functioning following at least two years of apparently normal development. The social and communicative deficits seen in autism and severe retardation are also seen in childhood disintegrative disorder. Somewhat more common in males, this disorder is relatively constant throughout life.

Since the initial recognition of autism, much work has been completed, and the disorder is now better understood and treated. With like efforts directed at the other pervasive developmental disorders, the future will bring a clearer understanding of and treatment for them as well.

What Lies Ahead?

A trend in the treatment of childhood disorders in general, and in mental retardation and pervasive developmental disorders specifically, is increased involvement of the family. In particular, the trend is away from custodial care, especially for retarded children, with a corresponding increase in community centers and family programs. Advances in the treatment of behavior problems in individuals with mental retardation and autism have been significant, and these advances are now being coordinated with interventions for the family. For example, there is widespread recognition that the family of a retarded or autistic child is a part of the system that influences the child's behavior and adjustment (Baker, 1984).

As also discussed, advances in genetic research methods will have application to the study of the causes of autism. Some forms of retardation, too, have an underlying genetic cause, and advances in genetic research methods can and will be applied. Meanwhile, the lack of any meaningful breakthrough in the use of medications suggests that the focus of treatment for autism will continue to employ the behavioral interventions that have proven effective. As previously noted, these are likely to be increasingly adapted to include family members along with the identified child.

Early identification of yet-to-be-born children with Down syndrome or autism unearths a potential predicament. On the one hand, it is clear that there are sizable benefits to be gained by early identification; in cases of PKU, for example, early identification leads to treatment that prevents the disorder. On the other hand, both personal and professional ethics must be weighed. How will the parents of these offspring address prebirth decisions? And what role will the attending physician play in these decisions? As we have seen, advances in science can stimulate social debates, provoke personal challenges, and create new dilemmas as yet unknown to future parents. Nevertheless, the real and potential gains associated with early identification merit continued investigation.

KEY TERMS

adaptive behavior (500)
Asperger's disorder (519)
autism (510)
childhood disintegrative disorder (519)
congenital rubella (514)
culturally deprived environment (506)
differential reinforcement of other behavior (DRO) (517)

disorder of written expression (508)
Down syndrome (503)
echolalia (512)
economically disadvantaged (506)
educational interventions (507)
fragile X syndrome (504)
full inclusion (516)

intensive behavior modification (517)
learning disorders (508)
least restrictive environment (507)
mathematics disorder (508)
mental retardation (500)
pervasive developmental disorders (510)
phenylketonuria (PKU) (504)

placement (506)
reading disorder (508)
Rett's disorder (519)
self-injurious behavior (516)
stimulus overselectivity (513)
treatment of mental retardation (506)

SUMMARY

Mental Retardation

Mental retardation involves significantly subaverage general intellectual functioning that exists concurrently with deficits in adaptive behavior. Indeed, *adaptive behavior* (self-care skills, appropriate dress and grooming, and the ability to hold a simple job and live independently) is an important component of the determination of mental retardation. In terms of intellectual functioning, IQ scores that are equal to or greater than two standard deviations below the mean are indicative of retardation.

Estimates have suggested that mental retardation affects about 2 percent of the overall population, and that among the total number of people with retardation approximately 89 percent fall within the mildly retarded range. The prevalence rate is affected by gender, race, and socioeconomic factors. Within the mildly retarded range, for example, there is a higher prevalence of males, blacks, and members of the low socioeconomic classes. The causes of mental retardation include biological as well as environmental forces.

Interventions for individuals with mental retardation — *placement, treatment,* and *education* — strive not to cure the problem but to teach adaptive skills and maximize individual potential.

Learning Disabilities

One definition used to identify children with learning disabilities relies on a discrepancy between intellectual ability and achievement. An alternate definition refers to below-expected age- and grade-level performance. DSM-IV defines *learning disorders* (academic skills disorders) using a combination of the IQ-achievement discrepancy approach and the below age-

and grade-level approach. Both biological and environmental factors are said to contribute to learning disorders, but the exact causes are unknown.

Pervasive Developmental Disorders: Autism

Pervasive developmental disorders involve severe upset in children's cognitive, social, behavioral, and emotional growth, producing widespread distortion of the developmental process. One such disorder, *autism,* affects basic human qualities: interpersonal socialization and complex communication. Though relatively rare, autism occurs worldwide and with no pattern linked to social class or educational background. It is not thought to be caused by the actions of the caregiver, nor can it be explained in terms of behavioral learning principles. Emerging data have suggested a potential genetic component.

Programs for autistic persons do not expect to cure the disorder; rather, they are designed to maximize personal adjustment. Neither psychodynamic programs nor medications have provided effective leads. Specific problem behaviors, such as *self-injurious behavior,* are often the target of treatment. Intensive behavior modification interventions have shown promising results. Increasingly, such interventions focus on the family, providing parent training to address child problems and parent counseling to address the difficulties associated with rearing autistic children.

Consider the following...

Suppose that your neighbor Sam has mental retardation. He lives with his parents, but every day he goes to a sheltered workshop. You hear that he has met a young woman, Mary, who also has mental retardation, and that they have fallen in love and want to get married. Sam's parents are happy for him, but they are concerned as well. They believe that Sam and Mary will always need some sort of special care, and they worry about the possibility that Sam and Mary may want to have a baby — something Sam's parents do not think he is capable of handling. Given what you have learned in this chapter, what options might you recommend for Sam and Mary? Who is to say whether or not a retarded couple should marry and reproduce? Should the couple be given sex education? To what extent should they be counseled about the risks and rewards associated with their particular reproduction situation? Should society impose rules and regulations to govern reproduction among mentally retarded persons? And, if so, what should be the criterion for determining who can and cannot reproduce? Who should decide?

Suppose that your daughter is a very bright third-grade student who has come home complaining that she is bored in her classes because the teacher spends so much of her time repeating things for some of the slower learners. As you consider this scenario, ask yourself the following: Should the bright students be separated and given more advanced work? Is it optimal to mainstream the slower learners or developmentally delayed children into the regular classroom, or should they be selected out for special education opportunities? Do you see benefits in having a variety of educational levels represented in one class? Are there benefits to classrooms that are stratified by ability levels? Would the benefits of such an arrangement outweigh the related problems?

CHAPTER 17

Cognitive and Neuropsychiatric Disorders

Those among us . . .

- Great-aunt Sheila looks like her same old self, in her late seventies but physically healthy. But instead of the sweet and patient person she has always been, she's now verbally abusive, suspicious, and forgetful.

- You read about Justin in the paper; he was injured in a freak accident when a rock on a hillside came crashing into his car through the sunroof. He had a head injury but then seemed to make a complete recovery — but did he? His family thinks his whole personality has changed.

- Your grandfather, Henry, has been diagnosed with dementia caused by small strokes; it's sad and amazing to watch the decline of such an intelligent and successful man.

- Arlene is a friend from high school; you recently heard that she was shot as an innocent bystander in a robbery. She's physically fine now but has almost no ability to recall recent events.

What is the link between the mind and the body?

If we live long enough, is loss of mental abilities inevitable?

How can a head injury cause a change in personality?

What is the treatment for people who have brain disorders?

These examples illustrate a fact we have seen repeatedly: Not all psychological symptoms arise from psychological causes. When psychological problems occur unexpectedly or persist, a good medical evaluation is needed. In Chapter 11 we discuss medical conditions that are caused or worsened by psychological disorders. In this chapter we consider the reverse: psychological disorders that are caused by medical conditions.

Of course, psychological symptoms might result from people's perceptions of their injuries and illnesses or from the challenges that these medical conditions create. After all, people who have experienced a reduction of cognitive capabilities have a great deal to be upset about. In many patients, however, a medical condition *directly* causes psychological disorders, and these are the disorders we discuss here. Head injuries, diseases of the brain, endocrinological disorders, and exposure to toxins are among the many medical problems that can cause mental impairment, depression, anxiety, delusions, hallucinations, aggressiveness, and a variety of other psychological symptoms and syndromes.

We begin by considering some of the problems in defining and diagnosing disorders created by damaging changes to the brain. Next, we describe the problems in mental functioning that DSM-IV calls cognitive disorders. We then consider the medical conditions that can cause these and other psychological disorders. Finally, we look at how the disorders can be treated.

ASSESSING AND CLASSIFYING DYSFUNCTIONS OF THE BRAIN

Before DSM-IV, conditions that were known or suspected to be due to a medical problem were classified as **organic mental disorders.** This classification implied that the psychological problems categorized as "organic" were directly caused by physical (organic) factors, whereas other disorders were psychological in origin. However, this terminology has two major problems: It suggests, first, that mind and body are separate entities and, second, that many disorders are "nonorganic." In fact, as we show throughout this book, advances in understanding biological factors have suggested that many or even most disorders probably reflect a mix of biological and psychological factors (Spitzer et al., 1992). Because of these problems, DSM-IV replaced the section on organic mental disorders.

Today's diagnostic system deals with disorders brought on by medical conditions in two ways. First, DSM-IV has a section on **cognitive disorders,** which includes three types of cognitive deficits: delirium, dementia, and amnestic disorders (see Figure 17.1). Second, a diagnosis depends on its essential features, but if a medical cause is known to be responsible, the diagnosis may include such information. Thus, if a medical, substance-use, or neuropsychiatric condition produces any other psychological disorder — such as depression or anxiety — that disorder is diagnosed according to the customary criteria, but its relation to the originating problem is noted (for example, substance-induced mood disorder).

Diagnosing Brain Dysfunctions

The disorders covered in this chapter all result from damaging changes in brain structure and function. Studies of the human brain have indicated that different functions are served not only by different lobes and structures but also by different hemispheres. In nearly all right-handed and most left-handed people, for example, the left hemisphere controls language and speech functions. Depending on where brain damage occurs (in

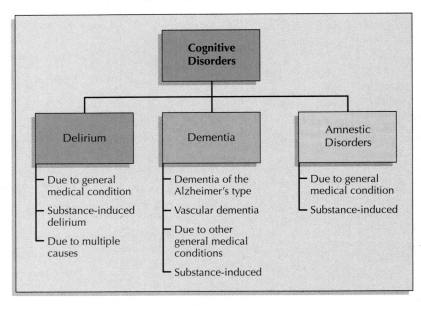

Figure 17.1 Overview of DSM-IV Diagnostic Categories of Cognitive Disorders
Cognitive disorders include deficits in mental functioning known to be caused by physical factors. In addition to a cognitive disorder diagnosis, psychological disorders that are known or suspected to be caused by physical conditions may also be characterized as a disorder due to a general medical condition or as substance-induced disorder. For example, delusions induced by pesticide poisoning might be diagnosed as psychotic disorder (with delusions) due to a general medical condition. A depression due to cocaine abuse might be diagnosed as cocaine mood (depression) disorder in the section on mood disorders.

frontal or temporal areas, for example), the person may experience trouble understanding language or producing it. However, important conceptual aspects of speech are controlled by the right hemisphere — including production and interpretation of emotional aspects of communication, intonation, and possibly some aspects of humor. The parietal and temporal lobes are important in perception and integration of sensory input from somatic, visual, and auditory regions. Further complicating the precise localization of functions is the extensive intercommunication among the regions of the brain, resulting in complex patterns of reception, integration, and production of information. Figure 17.2 indicates the locations of these brain regions. The extent and permanence of the changes depend on the severity of the damage to brain tissue, as well as on the personality and coping capabilities of the person. Once destroyed, brain tissue does not regenerate, and the capacity of injured parts of the brain to take over the functions of the damaged areas is limited.

The ability to assess brain damage and brain functioning has improved considerably in recent years, largely because of two types of tools we describe in Chapter 4. First, neuroimaging techniques such as positron emission tomography (PET) scans, magnetic resonance imaging (MRI), and computerized axial tomography (CT) scans provide ways of viewing the living brain to observe changes or abnormalities of function. Second, neuropsychological testing has made it increasingly possible to use particular patterns of performance to locate lesions in the brain.

Table 17.1 illustrates a very simple but widely used test for overall cognitive functioning, with items from the Mini-Mental State Exam (Folstein, Folstein, & McHugh, 1975). The test includes basic items concerning the person's awareness of where he or she is, use of language, ability to perform simple mental tasks, and memory.

Even if we know that cognitive impairment exists, locating its source may be difficult. As we noted, the

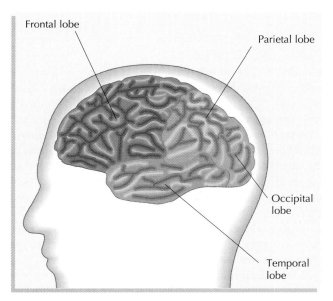

Figure 17.2 Cortical Areas of the Brain
Any accident, injury, or disease that affects the brain has the potential to cause intellectual and psychological changes. To some degree, we can predict the kinds of intellectual and physical changes that will accompany damage in particular regions of the brain, as noted in the text.

Table 17.1	Sample Items from the Mini Mental State Exam (MMSE)

Orientation

Ask the person for today's date. Ask specifically for parts omitted (e.g., Can you also tell me what season it is?). Score 1 point each for correct year, season, day of month, month, and day of week.

Registration

Say the names of three unrelated objects (e.g., chair, ball, rabbit), and then ask the person to repeat the three items. Score 1 point for each correct response on the first try; repeat them until the person can get all three correct. Note how many trials it takes up to a maximum of six.

Attention and Calculation

Ask the person to begin with 100 and count backwards by 7; stop after 5 subtractions. Score the total number of correct answers.

Recall

Ask the person to recall the three words you previously asked him or her to remember; score 1 point for each correct response.

Language

Show the person a wristwatch and ask him or her what it is; do the same for a pencil. Score 1 point for each correct label.

Follow a three-stage command: Give the person a blank sheet of paper and say, "Take the paper in your right hand, fold it in half, and put it on the floor." Score 1 point for each step correctly executed.

Draw a design on a blank piece of paper (intersecting pentagons). Ask the person to copy it exactly as it is. Score 1 point if the person correctly copies all ten angles and the figures intersect.

Source: Folstein, Folstein & McHugh (1975).

The MMSE can be used to quickly screen for gross cognitive impairment, such as in an emergency room. Most people without cognitive impairment score high on all eleven items. For greater precision in defining the nature and location of cognitive dysfunctions, vastly more sophisticated techniques are available.

While the brain and body change with aging, intellectual deterioration is by no means inevitable. Staying physically and mentally active ("use it or lose it") — and, of course, engaging in pleasurable pastimes — is the best prescription for cognitive and physical health.

brain's interconnections are enormously complex. Also, many illnesses or injuries of the brain are widespread, not localized. Even something relatively simple like a blow to one side of the head is likely to cause damage on the other side when the brain mass hits the bony substance inside the skull. A gunshot in one specific area may cause generalized swelling that causes damage in another area. Degenerative disease might affect scattered areas of the brain.

An additional complication in diagnosing neuropsychiatric disorders is that the human brain differs somewhat from person to person. These individual differences include those due to gender and, especially, age. Indeed, brain changes associated with aging present a particular challenge to neuropsychological evaluation in distinguishing normal and abnormal patterns.

Assessing the Aged

Not so long ago the public used the words *senile* and *senility* to refer to mental difficulties occurring in elderly individuals. The words suggested that only old people showed mental deterioration and may even have hinted that old age invariably means becoming senile. However, a decline in mental functioning is by no means inevitable in aging people, nor is it limited to them. Nowadays, the diagnostic system uses the term *dementia* instead of *senility* to describe an abnormal pattern of mental deterioration that involves deficits of memory, of information processing, and of judgment, planning, and other higher functions. Dementia is not limited to any age group, although it does occur more often in older adults because the risk for certain diseases that cause dementia increases with age.

Misunderstandings about older adults are very common; take the quiz in Table 17.2 to test your knowledge. Assessing the aged who have hearing problems or experience depression or medical illnesses that impair energy presents challenges; without taking such factors into account, clinicians and others may draw erroneous conclusions about mental abilities. Psychological adjustment and mental health in older age appear to be related

Table 17.2 Quiz on Aging

T	F	1.	The majority of people past age 65 are senile (i.e., defective memory, disoriented, or demented).
T	F	2.	All five senses tend to decline in old age.
T	F	3.	Most old people have no interest in or capacity for sexual relations.
T	F	4.	Lung capacity tends to decline in old age.
T	F	5.	The majority of old people feel miserable most of the time.
T	F	6.	Physical strength tends to decline in old age.
T	F	7.	At least one-tenth of the aged are living in long-stay institutions (i.e., nursing homes, mental hospitals, homes for the aged).
T	F	8.	Aged drivers have fewer accidents per person than drivers younger than age sixty-five.
T	F	9.	Most older workers cannot work as effectively as younger workers.
T	F	10.	About 80 percent of the aged are healthy enough to carry out their normal activities.
T	F	11.	Most old people are set in their ways and unable to change.
T	F	12.	Old people usually take longer to learn something new.
T	F	13.	Most old people find it almost impossible to learn something new.
T	F	14.	The reaction time of most old people tends to be slower than reaction time of young people.
T	F	15.	In general, most old people are pretty much alike.
T	F	16.	The majority of old people are seldom bored.
T	F	17.	The majority of old people are socially isolated and lonely.
T	F	18.	Older workers have fewer accidents than younger workers.
T	F	19.	More than 15 percent of the U.S. population are now age sixty-five or older.
T	F	20.	Most medical practitioners tend to give low priority to the aged.
T	F	21.	About 3 percent *less* of the aged have incomes below the official poverty level than the rest of the population.
T	F	22.	The majority of old people are working or would like to have some kind of work to do (including housework and volunteer work).
T	F	23.	Older people tend to become more religious as they age.
T	F	24.	The majority of old people are seldom irritated or angry.
T	F	25.	The health and socioeconomic status of older people (compared with younger people) in the year 2000 will be about the same as now.

Source: Palmore (1977).

Answers: All odd-numbered items are false; all even-numbered items are true.

This is a quiz to see how much you know about normal aging. See the footnote for correct answers, which are based on research data.

not to changes with age as such but to earlier health and adjustment. George and Caroline Vaillant (1990) followed the same group of men from age twenty to age sixty-five to examine the predictors of mental health and physical health. They found that individuals who were well adjusted earlier in life are the ones most likely to stay healthy and well adjusted.

WHAT'S NORMAL?

Aging and Intellectual Functions

People often worry that when they are older they will be unable to learn new information or skills ("You can't teach an old dog new tricks"), and many people get anxious about signs of memory difficulties ("I misplaced my checkbook — is that an early warning sign?"). In fact, intellectual abilities do not invariably decline with age, and it is not true that everyone who lives long enough will become demented. But some capabilities do change. So what *is* normal? Here are three things that appear to be true about normal aging.

First, the people who worry the most about memory problems may not be the ones who really have something to worry about. A study in England screened more than 2,600 persons seventy-five years old for evidence of cognitive impairment and then selected groups of demented, normal, and depressed individuals for intensive study of their memory (O'Connor et al., 1990). The normal elderly complained little and had good memory functioning. Otherwise, there was a poor relationship between what people thought about their memory functioning and their actual level of memory functioning. For example, the depressed elderly were the ones most likely to *complain* that they had memory problems, but they showed only mild actual deficits. The mildly demented subjects reported that they had few memory problems, when in fact their memory functioning was significantly impaired.

Second, the brain changes and physically ages, but this does not necessarily reflect reduced cognitive capabilities. For example, the brain's cellular volume shrinks with age (*cortical atrophy*), and 30 percent of elderly people experience lesions in the area of the brain called the *deep white matter*. However, even the presence of such lesions does not necessarily indicate impaired cognitive functioning or progressive deterioration (e.g., Fein et al., 1990).

Third, tests of mental performance by older adults do indicate certain changes in cognitive function but not general deterioration. For instance, mental activity may slow somewhat in terms of performance on tests that are timed, and certain memory-related and other functions may not be as efficient as those of 35-year-olds. Unfortunately, people who worry and ruminate a lot about supposed changes in mental efficiency may actually increase the problem through poor concentration and distractibility. It is important to emphasize that normal changes associated with aging are different from those associated with Alzheimer's dementia. For instance, a normal person may forget details of an event, but the person with Alzheimer's might forget the event altogether.

In most people, long-term memory and the ability to reason and to draw from experience do not decline with age (e.g., Benedict & Nacoste, 1990). These cognitive activities provide the basis for active engagement in the world. Indeed, staying active and involved in enjoyable pursuits is probably an excellent antidote to mental decline and demoralization. Also, improvements in diet, exercise, and health care may contribute to improved mental functioning later in life.

COGNITIVE IMPAIRMENT DISORDERS

Diseases and injuries of the brain cause impairment of mental function ranging from profound changes in consciousness to more specific and localized oddities such as the ability to sing words that one is unable to say. The nature and degree of cognitive impairment depend on the extent and location of the brain damage. In this section we focus specifically on three syndromes of cogni-

tive disorders that are defined in DSM-IV: *delirium*, *amnesia*, and *dementia*. The essential feature of these disorders is abnormality of behavior or mental function that is known to be caused by brain dysfunction. These disorders are heterogeneous as to characteristics and causes, but each is defined by the impairment of at least a particular feature such as consciousness, memory, or quality of intellectual functioning.

Delirium

Delirium refers to reduced level of consciousness or ability to focus, sustain, and shift attention. It is accompanied by cognitive changes that could include memory or language deficit, disorientation, or perceptual disturbances such as hallucinations. It usually has a rapid onset over hours or days and tends to fluctuate in intensity over the course of the day. In general, delirium is considered to be a temporary, reversible state signaling a serious medical condition, although in some patients delirium progresses to coma and death.

Delirium has numerous causes. Several kinds of patients have a particularly high risk for delirium associated with usually temporary changes in brain activity: medically frail elderly patients, burn victims, heart surgery patients, patients with preexisting brain damage (strokes, dementia), drug-dependent patients experienc-

Muhammad Ali, one of the great heavyweight boxing champs of all time, suffers from Parkinson's disease caused by repeated blows to the head during his career.

ing withdrawal (from alcohol or benzodiazepines), and patients with acquired immune deficiency syndrome (AIDS)(Wise & Brandt, 1992).

Numerous medications (overdoses or toxic combinations), toxic substances, infectious diseases, and head injuries also may cause delirium. For example, a person experiencing severe drug or alcohol withdrawal may be distractible, incoherent, and disoriented, possibly misperceiving stimuli (for example, spots are seen as spiders); the person may go in and out of lucidity and, after a period of hours or days, then return to normal consciousness.

Amnestic Disorders

Your high school friend Arlene, mentioned at the beginning of the chapter, suffered a non-fatal gunshot wound as an innocent bystander during a robbery. Even after physical recovery, not only did she have no recollection of events in the few weeks before her accident, but she also had enormous difficulty recalling simple things that occurred during the day. Although she recognized and conversed relatively normally with family members, she did not recall that they had visited, even if earlier the same day. It became clear that she could not resume her job as a cashier; although she could joke and talk with customers, each day she had to be shown again how to work the cash register and make change. Her distant memory for her school days was good, but she recalled any new information for only a short time.

The second type of cognitive disorder we discuss is amnesia due to a medical condition. **Amnesia** refers to impairment of short- or long-term memory. Memory disorders that are linked to the psychological condition of dissociation (see Chapter 7), sometimes called *psychogenic amnesia*, have attracted widespread public interest, but they are not the topic of this chapter. Instead, we focus here on medical conditions or injuries to the head that primarily affect the *hippocampus, amygdala,* and related medial temporal structures of the brain. Such injuries may produce severe memory impairment but leave language, judgment, or personality unchanged.

The memory impairment may be displayed as difficulty in learning new information (*anterograde amnesia*) or inability to recall previously learned information (*retrograde amnesia*). Individuals who have had accidents or injuries may, for example, be unable to recall events surrounding the trauma. Only when such memory loss persists and causes notable impairment in the person's work or social life would an amnestic disorder be diagnosed. Such impairment typically involves problems in memory for new information. Amnestic disorders are not diagnosed if they occur only during delirium or dementia.

Dementia

Dementia refers to general, multiple cognitive deficits reflecting a decline in previously higher levels of functioning. Dementia is an acquired (in contrast to something one is born with, such as mental retardation) impairment of mental functioning. To be diagnosed, the person must show at least one of four cognitive deficits, shown in Table 17.3, along with memory impairment.

A person with dementia may be very forgetful and disoriented and have trouble performing tasks involving abstraction and integration of spatial and verbal infor-

Table 17.3 Types of Cognitive Deficits in Dementia

Aphasia

A language disturbance of speech, writing (agraphia), or reading (alexia). There are many kinds of aphasia. For example, a person may be able to understand speech but have difficulty speaking (known as expressive, or nonfluent aphasia). Or the person may be able to speak fluently but be unable to comprehend spoken or written words or phrases (also called receptive or fluent aphasia). Another kind (anomic aphasia) refers to the inability to find the right word to name an object, although comprehension and speaking are unimpaired.

Apraxia

The inability to carry out motor activities despite intact motor functions. A person may be asked to demonstrate the use of a hammer; despite verbal knowledge of what a hammer does, he or she cannot make the proper movement even though nothing is wrong with the arm or hand. Or, if asked to pantomime performing a task, the person may not be able to produce the actions in the correct sequence.

Agnosia

The failure to identify or recognize an object even though sensory abilities are intact. The person may have agnosia only in one sensory modality. For example, visual agnosia means the person can be shown a comb but not know what it is, yet if they touch it and explore it, they might not have difficulty. Agnosias might be specific to recognition of sounds or of faces of friends and relatives.

Disturbance of Executive Functions

Describes the impairment of abilities such as planning, organizing, sequencing, and abstracting that might occur in dementia. These high-level capabilities underlie the ability to use good judgment, plan and execute complex sequences leading to goal attainment, and display good reasoning abilities.

Dementia refers to generalized decline in cognitive functioning; to be diagnosed, at least one of these four areas of cognitive impairment must be present.

mation. For example, the person might be able to see and to talk but be unable to correctly name an object or understand or perform its function. Language might be affected, and an individual might show reduced spontaneous speech or reduced comprehension about the meaning of abstract concepts. The person might *perseverate*, or repeat ideas, come back to the same theme, or have difficulty switching topics appropriately. Commonly, judgment is impaired so that the person cannot function independently. The demented person makes poor decisions or cannot plan ahead or cannot carry out complex sequences of action. Personality changes usually occur. Although dementia has some features in common with schizophrenia, it is quite different in that language and thought disturbances are related to defective cognitive processes (such as memory and reasoning) rather than to unusual content.

Who Is Affected with Dementia?   Although dementia is not just a disorder of old age, it is more frequent among older people. It affects perhaps 2 to 4 percent of persons aged sixty-five or younger and appears to increase dramatically with age. About 30 percent of individuals eighty or older have dementia of varying degrees of severity. Figure 17.3 shows that this pattern is true not only for the United States, but may represent other populations as well.

The average lifespan of the U.S. population is increasing. According to a U.S. Census Bureau report, today one in one hundred Americans is eighty-five or older; but by 2050, 5 percent of the population will be eighty-five or older — expanding from 3 million now to about 15 million in 2050. If we project how many of these will likely be demented, the care required for this staggering number of individuals far exceeds the current capacities of institutions. This situation is a public health and public policy crisis in the making.

Racial and Gender Differences in Dementia   In general, dementia cuts across the boundaries of race and ethnicity (e.g., Mak et al., 1996). With respect to gender, there appears to be a greater prevalence of women at the most advanced ages, due mainly to greater longevity (e.g., Lobo et al., 1995). However, both gender and race may affect the rates of particular forms of dementia. For example, fairly consistent evidence from large-scale surveys has indicated higher rates of dementia among the African American elderly (Robins et al., 1984). Why might this be the case? One study attempted to shed light on this issue by intensive study of a representative sample of elderly white and African Americans in North Carolina (Heyman et al., 1991). The groups were carefully selected to avoid sampling biases (such as differential rates of placing demented persons into institutions). The researchers verified that indeed African Americans had significantly higher rates of dementia than whites — 16 versus 3 percent. Whereas rates of white men and women did not differ, African American women had a rate of nearly 20 percent, compared with about 9 percent for black men. The factor that seemed to be most

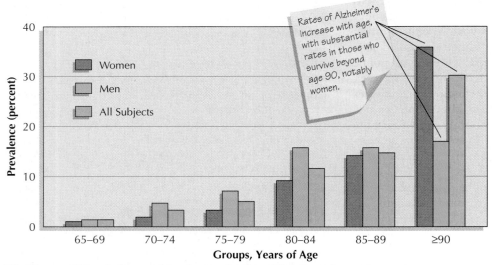

Figure 17.3   Aging and Increases in Cognitive Impairment

In Zaragosa, Spain, more than 1,000 persons aged sixty-five and over were initially screened with the Mini-Mental State Examination and other screens for cognitive impairment. Those with suspected cognitive deficits were later given more extensive tests. These rates of dementia indicate two patterns that are typically observed worldwide: dramatically increasing rates by age and highest rates among the oldest women (mostly due to their greater longevity). Alzheimer's dementia was the most common, followed by multi-infarct dementia.

Source: Lobo et al. (1995).

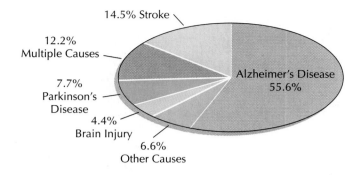

14.5% Stroke

12.2% Multiple Causes

7.7% Parkinson's Disease

4.4% Brain Injury

6.6% Other Causes

Alzheimer's Disease 55.6%

Numbers do not add up to 100 percent because of rounding off.

Figure 17.4 Causes of Dementia
The most common cause of dementia is Alzheimer's disease. The category of "other causes" may include medications, vitamin B$_1$ deficiency, chronic alcoholism, tumors or infections of the brain, and metabolic imbalances including those resulting from thyroid, kidney, or liver disorders.

Source: From D. Selkoe (1992), Aging brain, aging mind, *Scientific American* (September), 138. Copyright ©1992 by Scientific American. All rights reserved.

strongly associated with dementia was the presence of medical problems. Compared with whites, African Americans, especially women, had significantly higher rates of high blood pressure; their medical histories were more likely to include strokes, diabetes, and heart attacks as well. The investigators speculated that such chronic health problems contributed to the overall rate of cognitive disorders among elderly African Americans.

Causes of Dementia Many different medical conditions may cause dementia. We understand the causes of some dementias but not others. Some are the primary manifestation of a progressive brain disease such as Alzheimer's disease, but degenerative brain diseases do not always produce dementia. Figure 17.4 indicates the contributions of several causes to overall dementia rates.

Dementia is potentially reversible in perhaps 10 to 20 percent of patients (Benedict & Nacoste, 1990), such as those with certain cardiovascular or endocrine disorders, medication-induced dementia, infections, or operable tumors. Dementia in most patients, however, is irreversible and progressive, including those with Alzheimer's or Huntington's disease. We describe these and other brain dysfunctions in the sections that follow.

SOME DEGENERATIVE BRAIN DISEASES

Many forms of brain disease grow progressively worse with time. Some primarily affect motor behaviors (such as Parkinson's disease or multiple sclerosis), and others

affect primarily mental functions, such as Alzheimer's or Huntington's disease. The causes for some are known; for others the cause is unknown. In this section we discuss three diseases that illustrate some of the clinical and research challenges of degenerative brain diseases.

Alzheimer's Dementia

Aunt Sheila was age 60 when her husband died, and some of the disturbing changes in her behavior (forgetfulness, a decline in personal hygiene, apathy) were attributed by her family and friends to grief and depression. Her daughter, Ellen, began to suspect something more serious, however, when old family friends told Ellen told they didn't want to play cards with Sheila any more because she was losing too much money. Always a sharp card player, for years Sheila had enjoyed playing for money, and now it seemed that she couldn't count her points accurately or play a hand skillfully. Gradually, other changes appeared: Sheila became too forgetful to manage her own cooking, shopping, and bill paying, and keeping paid attendants was difficult because she was irritable and abusive to them at times. In time, she could not be left alone because she wandered away from home and got lost, or she forgot to put out lighted cigarettes, causing a grave fire danger in her house. When her children and grandchildren came to visit, she often looked at them blankly, clearly not recognizing them. Or she would forget that they had just visited an hour ago and complain that they never came to see her. She seemed to be irritable some of the time and apathetic at other times. Eventually, the family made fewer phone calls and visits. Fortunately for them, they could afford full-time care for their mother's physical needs, but the mother with the strong, witty personality was long since gone. Eventually she was bedridden with various physical ailments; she died of pneumonia when she was only 69. She represents a fairly typical case of Alzheimer's dementia.

In 1906 a German neurologist, Alois Alzheimer, observed severe memory loss and disorientation in a woman who was only fifty-one years of age. On the woman's death at fifty-five, Alzheimer characterized neurofibrillary tangles in her brain tissue during autopsy. For many years this type of damage to brain tissue was considered a sign of a rare "presenile dementia." By the 1960s, however, "presenile dementia of the Alzheimer's type" was found to be neither rare nor different from dementia found in much older patients.

Characteristics of Alzheimer's Disease Alzheimer's **dementia (AD)** is a disease, not just brain degeneration from aging. The damage to the brain is especially pronounced in the cortex and hippocampus — regions of the brain that are critical for cognitive and memory functions. As Figure 17.5 shows, the damage consists of **plaques** (which are extracellular protein deposits with a core consisting of fibers of beta-amyloid, a protein material) and **neurofibrillary tangles** (which are nerve cell malformations). The extent of plaques and tangles appears to be correlated with loss of cholinergic neurons that originate in the basal forebrain.

The cognitive impairments described in Table 17.3 are used to diagnose Alzheimer's dementia. In addition to intellectual changes, pronounced personality changes also affect virtually all AD patients. Sometimes the personality changes are the earliest signs of the disorder. The person typically shows many deficit symptoms, such as apathy, disengagement, passivity, and loss of energy, interest, enthusiasm, and affection. Some individuals may be self-centered, insensitive, and disinhibited (Cummings, 1992). Many patients wander away from their residences and get lost. Many have angry outbursts and even assault their caretakers.

Hallucinations affect only a minority of AD patients, but delusions occur in 30 to 50 percent (Cummings, Miller, Hill & Neshkes, 1987), most com-

Two-term U.S. president, California governor, and actor, Ronald Reagan was charming, handsome, and extremely popular with the public for nearly two decades. Sadly, Alzheimer's dementia has altered his life, necessitating full-time care and preventing the public appearances that ex-presidents normally enjoy.

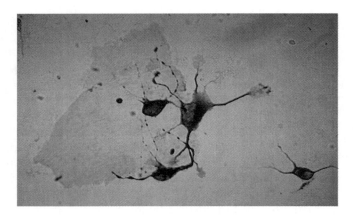

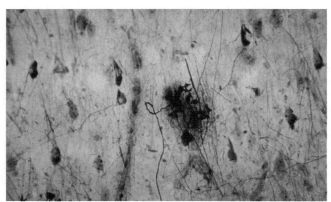

Figure 17.5 Plaques and Neurofibrillary Tangles
Alzheimer's dementia is characterized by damaged neurons associated with beta-amyloid protein substances forming dense plaques and tangles. Researchers are actively pursuing the causes of such damage.

monly paranoid delusions involving themes of persecution, infidelity of the spouse, being robbed, and the like (Wragg & Jeste, 1989). Depressive symptoms may occur in 30 to 40 percent of Alzheimer's patients, with diagnosable mood disorders in about 20 percent (Wragg & Jeste, 1989). Interestingly, depression may even be a predictor of later development of AD; one longitudinal study found that depressed mood symptoms increased the risk of development of AD over the next several years compared with those who were not depressed (Devanand et al., 1996). It is unclear whether depression is an early clinical sign of AD or affects the process of its development.

Diagnosing Alzheimer's Dementia Distinguishing patients with Alzheimer's dementia from those suffering from depression is especially important. Depression in an older person might involve difficulties in concentration and memory, disorientation, distractibility, physical complaints, apathy or anxiety and irritability, psychomotor slowing or agitation, and expressions of pessimism and helplessness — all symptoms that are difficult to distinguish from dementia (Benedict & Nacoste, 1990). The price of misdiagnosis might be enormous if a person with treatable depression is regarded as having an untreatable dementia. Thus, in addition to careful evaluation of symptoms, a clinician might wish to determine whether the person has had a previous history of depression and whether the current depression had an acute onset related to events or circumstances that might help characterize it as psychological.

A *definitive* diagnosis of Alzheimer's can be made only postmortem, when an examination of the brain tissue confirms the characteristic damage first observed by Alzheimer. In most patients, *probable* AD is diagnosed by the presence of the characteristic dementia symptoms we describe earlier. In addition, making a diagnosis of AD requires ruling out any other factor that could be the cause of the dementia, such as another medical condition or psychiatric problem or even overmedication for other disorders. Alzheimer's disease is diagnosed only when the dementia has no other apparent explanation. Investigators are actively pursuing methods of neuroimaging or neurochemical assessment of AD in living persons, but to date there is no reliable test.

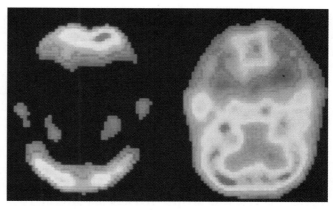

Although there is no neuroimaging technique available to definitively diagnose Alzheimer's dementia, this PET scan shows evidence of reduced activity — presumably because of degeneration — in the brain.

Course of Alzheimer's Disease   The case of Sheila presented earlier illustrates a typical course of Alzheimer's dementia. Dementia of the Alzheimer's type is a progressive disease that lasts for an average of ten years from diagnosis to death. It typically begins after age fifty-five. Symptoms progress over time, beginning with forgetfulness and mild personality changes, followed by problems in intellectual functioning and eventually confusion, disorientation, and sometimes dramatic personality changes. According to a study of the typical progression of symptoms in patients followed over three years, "instrumental" activities of daily life such as recalling recent events and handling money were lost before "basic" activities such as dressing ability and toileting and hygiene (Galasko et al., 1995). In the typical patient, the dementia symptoms are marked, at least in the middle and later stages, but motor and sensory functioning are relatively unaffected. The symptoms are irreversible, progressing to nearly total loss of intellectual functioning and loss of many bodily functions. Death is usually the result of disorders associated with the physical decline or independent, age-related diseases, such as pneumonia and heart disease.

Whether Alzheimer's is a single disease or has different subtypes is unclear. DSM-IV distinguishes between earlier-onset and later-onset Alzheimer's. Patients with the more rare earlier-onset Alzheimer's (that is, younger than age sixty-five) appear to progress more rapidly, with greater deterioration in a shorter time; the early-onset type accounts for about 25 percent of cases. A distinction is also made between familial and sporadic forms of the disease. *Familial* refers to a pattern of apparent heritability, and *sporadic* means no apparent family pattern of transmission. The familial type is less common.

As noted in Figure 17.4, at least 55 percent of persons with dementia probably have Alzheimer's disease. Men and women are equally affected, although, because women live longer, more women have AD. How prevalent is the disease? Based on preliminary screening for cognitive impairment of all those aged sixty-five and over in East Boston, followed by extensive testing of those with some cognitive impairment, Denis Evans and his colleagues (1989) estimated that 10 to 15 percent of adults older than age sixty-five in the United States are afflicted with Alzheimer's disease. Although there is no evidence that Alzheimer's is inevitable, advanced age is associated with the development of this disorder (e.g., Fichter, Meller, Schroppel, & Steinkirchner, 1995).

Causes of Alzheimer's Disease   The changes in the brain that characterize Alzheimer's disease have been attributed to various causes: Genetic mechanisms, viral infection, and environmental pollutants such as exposure to toxic metals are just a few. Researchers have pursued numerous lines of investigation in the quest for causes. Aluminum toxicity, for example, was once considered a promising suspect because the brains of AD patients sometimes contained excessive amounts of the element aluminum. But this theory has been discredited, in part because regions with high aluminum concentration in the water do not have elevated rates of AD. Also, research on the effects of aluminum injections on the brain cells of animals proved to be contradictory. A recent study in England found no association between aluminum exposure and early onset of Alzheimer's disease (Forster, Newens, Kay, & Edwardson, 1995).

Other hypotheses include the possibility that a slowly developing or incubating virus, the effects of head trauma, and many aspects of neuroendocrine abnormalities might bring on Alzheimer's disease. The slow-virus hypothesis was boosted by the finding that a different degenerative neurological disorder (Creutzfeldt-Jakob disease) was caused by a virus, but to date no consistent evidence of viral material has been found in the brains of AD patients.

Currently researchers are most intensively focused on two factors: genes and the beta-amyloid protein substance that forms the characteristic Alzheimer plaques in brain cells. Family studies clearly indicate that family history of the disease is a risk factor for developing it (e.g., Li et al., 1995; Forster, Newens, Kay & Edwardson, 1995). However, AD is a heterogeneous disorder in that different genetic patterns have been found. Using linkage analyses and gene sequencing methods, researchers have identified three forms of early-onset AD associated with autosomal dominant gene transmission, accounting for only about 2 percent of all Alzheimer's cases (Roses, 1996). One suspected location is chromosome 21, and there appears to be a defect in the gene for producing the precursor to the beta-amyloid protein. Beta-amyloid protein is a major component of the senile plaques observed in the brains of persons with AD. There is another group of early-onset patients with AD apparently associated with an unidentified gene on chromosome 14, and yet other forms of early-onset familial AD are not associated with any known location (e.g., Roses, 1996).

FOCUS ON RESEARCH

Have We Found the Genetic Predisposition for Common Alzheimer's Disease?

In early 1993 investigators reported the discovery of genes that were associated with the more common forms

of late-onset Alzheimer's disease (e.g., Corder et al., 1993; Strittmatter et al., 1993). Located on chromosome 19, the apolipoprotein E type ε4 allele, which occurs naturally in about 14 percent of the population, is associated with an increased risk of developing Alzheimer's disease; individuals who have two copies of the apoE ε4 allele have an even greater likelihood of developing Alzheimer's than those who have only one or no copies. In the past few years there has been an explosion of research on apoE ε4, and the basic findings have now been replicated in many laboratories worldwide using samples of known patients or examining brain tissue of deceased patients to confirm Alzheimer's. The association has been verified in many cultures and ethnic groups (e.g., Mak et al., 1996; Oyama, Shimada, Oyama & Ihara, 1995; Saunders et al., 1996; Tang et al., 1996). Individuals with one apoE ε4 gene are about three times overrepresented, and those with two of the alleles are about 15 times overrepresented among those with Alzheimer's. Figure 17.6 shows results of a study showing this association (Henderson et al., 1995). Similarly, the apoE ε4 alleles were more frequent in people who reported memory problems even before the onset of probable Alzheimer's, suggesting that they may signal a risk for developing the disorder (e.g., Blesa et al., 1996).

Do these findings mean that these genes *cause* Alzheimer's disease? Initially, scientists seemed to believe that they did, noting that apoE ε4 binds to beta-amyloid peptides, increasing senile plaques and neurofibrillary tangles that constitute Alzheimer's pathol-

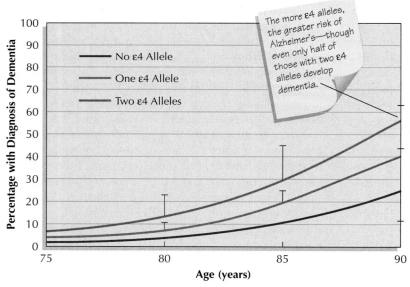

Figure 17.6   ApoE ε4 Alleles and Risk of Developing Dementia
The figure shows that the chances of having a diagnosis of dementia (mostly Alzheimer's) projected by age increased with presence of the apoE ε4 alleles. However, the data also show that presence of the suspect apoE ε4 genes was not sufficient to cause Alzheimer's disease, since many people with the apoE ε4 alleles reached old age without cognitive impairment. *Source:* Henderson et al. (1995).

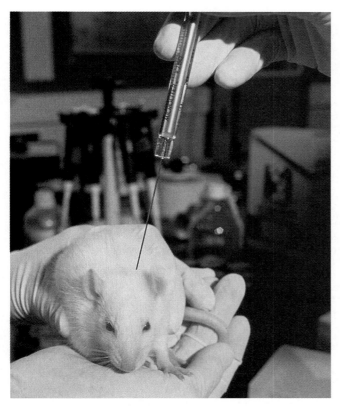

Researchers inject the brain of a laboratory rat in an effort to learn more about the processes that result in neurofibrillary plaques and tangles in the neurons of those afflicted with Alzheimer's dementia.

ogy (e.g., Gomez-Isla et al., 1996; Olichney et al., 1996). However, others caution that they may not *cause* Alzheimer's disease, because only about 50 percent or fewer of individuals who have both apoE ε4 alleles develop Alzheimer's in old age (e.g., Myers et al., 1996; see also Henderson et al., 1995; Hyman et al., 1996). Even family studies of siblings and identical twins suggest that these genes may be a predisposing factor but do not *cause* Alzheimer's (e.g., Bennett et al., 1995; Breitner et al., 1995), since the heritability patterns indicate that something more than just possession of the genes is required for Alzheimer's to be present. Some suggest, for instance, that the genes do not cause the disease as such but rather affect the rate of progression of the disorder (faster) or its age of onset (earlier) (e.g., Bennett et al., 1995; Corder et al., 1993; Sobel et al., 1995).

Despite a lack of understanding of the mechanisms that link the apoE ε4 genes to Alzheimer's disease, the discovery gives scientists tools to work with. Identifying samples that differ on the presence of the apoE ε4 alleles will help to characterize more fully how they differ in terms of intracellular functioning, as well as disease progression. Moreover, the fact that most people who do carry the suspect genes do not develop the disorder strongly suggests that other biological and environmental factors need to be studied to clarify their role in the

expression of the disorder. The rapid developments of just the past few years suggest that important discoveries that may influence treatment or even prevention are at hand.

Molecular biologists are leading the way to understand the processes that *cause* Alzheimer's disease. Since beta-amyloid deposits characterized the diseased brain tissue, there has been considerable focus on their formation. However, the question of cause and effect is still unanswered. Whether the beta-amyloid deposits are merely the result of neuronal degeneration or are a cause of the damage is a topic of considerable research — particularly because the functions of the apoE ε4 alleles of chromosome 19 are critical to the transport of cholesterol and other lipids between cells. A defective interaction between beta-amyloid peptides and apolipoprotein E might be implicated (e.g., Mahley, Nathan, & Pitas, 1996).

Parkinson's Disease

Tremor, muscle rigidity, and difficulty initiating movement are the primary symptoms of **Parkinson's disease.** Symptoms are most likely to appear between the ages of fifty and sixty-nine and generally progress to severe impairment and death over a period of years if untreated. The course varies in severity, with older age of onset often predicting a more rapid and deteriorating progression (Hely et al., 1995). Some persons with Parkinson's disease also show cognitive impairments in memory, judgment, and reasoning, but many display only subtle or no cognitive disturbance (Poewe & Wenning, 1996; Whitehouse, Friedland & Strauss, 1992). About 30 percent of Parkinson's patients show evidence of dementia, which is most likely to occur in the advanced stages of the disorder (e.g., Marder, Tang, Cote & Stern, 1995).

Other psychological symptoms often occur as well (Rao, Huber & Bornstein, 1992; Stein, Henser, Junoos & Uhde, 1990). Some patients with Parkinson's disease have psychotic symptoms, but depression is the most common concern. Major depression or dysthymia occurs in about 40 percent of patients with Parkinson's disease.

The prevalence of Parkinson's is thought to be about 60 to 170 per 100,000 (Knight, Godfrey & Shelton, 1988). Some researchers have concluded that there are few gender or racial differences (review by Knight, Godfrey & Shelton, 1988). Others have found that men are at greater risk than women, however; that three to four times as many deaths can be attributed to Parkinson's disease in whites as in African Americans; that the rates for Asian Americans are equal to those for whites; and that there is a strong geographic pattern to the incidence of Parkinson's disease (Kurtzke & Goldberg, 1988). Specifically, in northern states, rates are significantly higher than in the south, and these differences also occurred within racial groups. These results suggest that some (unknown) environmental factor may contribute to the disorder. What could this environmental factor be? Interest is considerable in the possibility that environmental toxins such as pesticides, polluted well water, and industrial use of heavy metals are etiological factors for at least some forms of Parkinson's disease (Malaspina, Quitkin & Kaufman, 1992; Rybicki, Johnson, Uman, & Gorell, 1993).

Other causal factors also have been implicated, depending on the type of Parkinson's disease. The causes of Parkinson's symptoms can be characterized as drug-induced, postencephalitic (following inflammation of the brain caused by numerous conditions), or idiopathic. *Idiopathic* means that the cause is unknown, and this is typically the case in Parkinson's disease. Although the cause of the disease is unknown, the mechanism of the disorder is well understood. The cells of a brain nucleus, the *substantia nigra*, which produce dopamine, die — because of a viral infection or an unknown cause. These cells project to the basal ganglia, causing dysfunction of motor control. In drug-induced parkinsonism, the activity of the dopaminergic cells of the substantia nigra is temporarily blocked by the administration of neuroleptic medications and other dopamine-blocking agents. Schizophrenic patients undergoing phenothiazine treatment therefore may display some of the motor abnormalities of Parkinson's disease.

Because the loss of dopaminergic cells in certain areas of the brain appears to underlie the motor abnormalities, the administration of levodopa (L-dopa), a dopamine-enhancing drug, can help control the motor dysfunctions, usually temporarily, in at least some affected persons — and appears to reduce mortality from Parkinson's (Poewe & Wenning, 1996).

Huntington's Disease

Another degenerative brain disease of motor functioning is **Huntington's disease (HD)**, which causes severe dementia and personality change as well as *chorea* — irregular jerks, grimaces, and twitches. HD is relatively rare: Estimates of prevalence range between 7 and 19 per 100,000. It has an onset between the ages of twenty-five and fifty.

Often the first signs of Huntington's are psychological — problems with memory and concentration and commonly depression, irritability, or erratic behavior. Depression, for example, may precede cognitive impairment by years. As the disease progresses, intellectual deficits become more pronounced. Death ensues ten to twenty years after the first symptoms appear. The case of Samuel P. illustrates some of the typical features of the course of HD.

Samuel P. was referred for evaluation of depression. He reported that he had been increasingly depressed over the past two years, since he retired at age forty-eight, left his law practice, and moved from his midwestern town to California. He said that he was unhappy with the move, with not working, and with increasingly severe marital problems. He further complained of difficulty concentrating, and had actually left his law practice because he was having some difficulties with concentration and memory and felt he couldn't handle it. Also, his professional partners and his wife felt that he was depressed and oversensitive, sometimes blowing up at minor events. The irritability was one of the reasons for the increasing marital difficulties. His wife revealed that he had had a neurological examination before moving to California because of some of his complaints and that there was strong suspicion that Samuel's mother — who had died in an automobile accident in middle age — may have begun to develop symptoms of Huntington's disease before she died. A referral to a local neurologist specializing in HD confirmed the presence of subtle, jerky movements consistent with HD pathology. During the period of his psychological and medical evaluations, Samuel's judgment and cognitive functioning worsened markedly — for example, he "lost" a large sum of cash. Although the diagnosis of Huntington's disease could not be established definitively in the absence of clear family history information, it is very likely that Samuel has the disease — plus a wife who is increasingly estranged. And perhaps most tragically of all, they have two young children to whom the disorder may have been passed.

Huntington's disease always runs in families. It is transmitted by a dominant gene, conferring a 50 percent chance of developing the disorder if one of the parents was affected. Tragically, HD still appears in the population because its onset occurs after the peak period of reproduction; an affected person can pass the gene before being aware that he or she has it. The gene defect responsible for HD was generally located a decade ago through linkage studies on the short arm of chromosome 4, but the precise gene responsible was found only in 1993 (Gusella, MacDonald, Ambrose & Duyao, 1993). Genetic testing for the children of HD patients is now available, provided that suspected carriers wish to know their status.

Despite knowledge of the specific mutant gene that causes HD, the mechanism of its action — and therefore a clue to a cure — is unclear. HD is a disease of the basal ganglia, and many neurotransmitter changes occur in HD, but the hope of determining a selective deficit and therefore of having a specific mechanism for corrective treatment has yet to be realized (Purdon et al., 1994).

Woody Guthrie was a popular and successful folk singer in the pre-World War II United States. In middle age he was diagnosed with Huntington's disease, leading to severe mental and physical deterioration that finally claimed his life. His son, Arlo, lived for many years with the knowledge that he had a 50 percent chance of developing the disease also. With the passage of time without showing symptoms, it seems that he has been spared — and enjoys his own career as a singer.

OTHER SOURCES OF BRAIN DAMAGE

In addition to cognitive impairment disorders and degenerative brain diseases, a variety of illnesses and injuries can cause neuropsychological disorders.

Traumatic Brain Injury

Some head injuries are preventable, and we hope that this section will make you take care of your head: Wear seatbelts and use protective headgear! Head injuries take many forms and are the most common neurological problem with the exception of headaches. Some are *penetrating injuries* such as gunshot wounds, and others are *closed head injuries* such as falls, motor vehicle accidents, and getting hit with objects. There are more people with permanent or transient **traumatic brain injuries** than there are people with schizophrenia, panic disorder, or bipolar disorder. Figure 17.7 indicates the major causes of head injury.

Head injuries are considered a major public health problem. The U.S. government has estimated that the total economic cost of brain injury is $25 billion per year in the United States alone. Most victims are relatively young, and they may require prolonged care and reha-

bilitation. The disruption in human terms is astounding. Victims of traumatic brain injury may never fully recover their ability to function at work, in school, or in relationships (Silver, Hales & Yudofsky, 1992). They also may create a severe psychological burden for family members and caretakers. Even mild injuries resulting in brief or no loss of consciousness (such as a concussion) can be associated with problems in attention, memory, and concentration for up to a year or more later.

Both intellectual and personality changes are typical after head injuries (Stuss, Gau & Hetherington, 1992). Cognitive changes may be relatively subtle but can occur even in fairly mild injuries; common difficulties include problems in memory, concentration, language, and higher functioning such as reasoning, planning, and abstraction. The extent of intellectual deficits depends in part on the preexisting personality characteristics and educational level: Better previous adjustment and good coping resources predict better functioning. The consequences of trauma also depend on its severity and location.

Certain symptoms such as apathy, *mood lability* (rapid changes in emotion), and slowed thinking that occur with traumatic head injuries may sometimes suggest depression. The patient must be evaluated carefully to determine whether diagnosable depression is present or whether the apathy and withdrawal are a result of the injury itself. Rates of diagnosed depression in persons

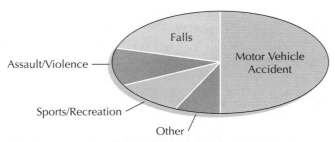

Figure 17.7   Major Causes of Traumatic Brain Injury

Children are particularly vulnerable to head injuries, sustaining five million per year. Bicycle accidents alone may cause 50,000 head injuries in children, and infant and child abuse also account for high rates of serious head injury.

Source: Department of Health and Human Services (1989).

with traumatic brain injury appear to be fairly high (Fann, Katon, Uomoto & Esselman, 1995). Even brief episodes of mania have been observed to occur in some brain-injured patients, although less commonly than depression. Also, delusions and hallucinations have been observed to occur in some patients with traumatic brain injury.

Closed head injuries (particularly motor vehicle accidents) mostly cause damage to the frontal and temporal regions. **Frontal lobe injuries** typically produce the kinds of deficits summarized in Table 17.4 — although the specific problems may depend on location in the frontal areas and whether the injury is to one or both sides.

Interestingly, brain-injured individuals often deny that there are changes in their abilities and potential — a neurologically based reaction called *anosognosia* rather than a psychological defense. The person's social competence and appropriateness of behavior and judgment typically decline. Injured individuals may seem shallow and unconcerned about the consequences of their behaviors.

The following case is adapted from a news article describing some of the consequences of a frontal lobe injury.

Justin's story concerns the freak accident that severely injured him and his comeback from that incident. He had been hit in the head by a boulder that crashed through his car sunroof during a storm, and he was unconscious for two weeks. Now, some six months later, the reporter interviewed him on his remarkable recovery. He boasted of regaining all his skills and being about to return to his demanding job as a business executive. Unlike his former, somewhat quiet and cautious self, he was loud and outgoing. He noted that his neurologist had cautioned that he might not be able to perform the same job as before, but he insisted, "I'll beat this problem. I feel fine, and nothing is wrong anymore."

Unfortunately, his optimism was unwarranted. Although physically recovered, he was forgetful, distractible, and unable to plan ahead or perform simple calculations accurately. His loved ones could not penetrate his denial of difficulties. Besides, this boastful, outgoing, and sometimes socially inappropriate Justin was not the same personality that he was before the accident.

In sum, head injuries, ranging from concussions with only brief or no loss of consciousness to severe head injuries, may alter both the intellectual and personality functioning of the victim. Mild cases, involving **postconcussion syndrome** (usually mild symptoms following a blow to the head causing little or no loss of conscious-

Table 17.4   Common Symptoms of Frontal Lobe Injuries

Social and Behavioral Changes

Exacerbation of preexisting behavioral traits such as disorderliness, suspiciousness, argumentativeness, disruptiveness, and anxiousness

Apathy, loss of interest in social interactions, and global lack of concern for consequences of behavior

Uncharacteristic lewdness with loss of social graces and inattention to personal appearance and hygiene

Intrusiveness, boisterousness, increased volume of speech, and pervasive, characteristic profanity

Increased risk taking, unrestrained drinking of alcoholic beverages, and indiscriminate selection of foods and gluttony.

Affective Changes

Apathy, indifference, and shallowness

Lability of affect, irritability, and manic states

Inability to control rage and violent behavior

Intellectual Changes

Reduced capacity to use language, symbols, and logic

Reduced ability to use mathematics, to calculate, to process abstract information, and to reason

Diminished ability to focus, to concentrate, and to be oriented in time or place

Source: Silver, Hales & Yudofsky (1992).

These are some of the commonly observed results of frontal lobe damage. The type of symptoms depends on the location of the injury to the frontal lobes [e.g., near the eyes (orbitofrontal) or upper, side (dorsolateral)], and also depends on whether the injury is unilateral or bilateral. For example, injury to the forehead (orbitofrontal areas) is more associated with emotional lability, irritability, and socially inappropriate behavior, whereas damage to the dorsolateral areas is associated with apathy, problems in sustaining or initiating behaviors, and attentional deficits.

Thousands of children (not to mention adults) annually are the victims of traumatic brain injury from falls, baseballs, and other accidents. Such injuries, if not fatal, may result in challenged lives due to irreversible brain damage. All are potentially preventable: wear your helmets!

ness), may almost completely clear up over time, although moderate and severe injuries have lifelong consequences. Both the cognitive and personality changes may contribute to ongoing difficulties in social adjustment, suffered both by the injured person and by his or her family and friends. A person's injury may heal, but he or she may never again "be themselves."

Cerebral Vascular Disorders

Whereas traumatic head injuries are most likely to occur to young people (children and young adults), cerebral vascular disorders are more likely to affect older people. **Cerebral vascular disorders** occur when hemorrhaging occurs in the brain or when the blood supply to an area of the brain is cut off, damaging that area. Sudden and localized damage from the blockage or hemorrhage of blood is commonly called a *stroke*. Most often, cerebrovascular disorders are the outcome of high blood pressure and accumulated fatty deposits in the arteries, which possibly also cause coronary heart disease, but the disorders also may result from fibromuscular diseases, inflammatory diseases, or head injuries.

Cerebrovascular diseases create obvious neurological changes that affect movement, behavior, and cognition — depending on the location and extent of the lesion. For instance, strokes occurring in the frontal areas may cause some of the cognitive and behavioral symptoms described in Table 17.4. Also, numerous psychological symptoms have been found associated with cerebrovascular disease, including depression and, more rarely, anxiety, hallucinosis, paranoia, and mania. Inappropriate emotional reactivity occurs with some patients, which may take the form of difficulties in expressing or interpreting emotions. For example, some patients display indifference — denial of illness or lack of concern, similar to that displayed after frontal lobe injuries. In time, some recovery of function may occur when other areas of the brain take over lost functions — depending on the extent of the damage.

Vascular Dementia   There are many kinds of strokes. A massive stroke can be fatal or can leave the person with major paralysis, but even a small stroke kills an area of the brain. If over time a person suffers an accumulation of small strokes, they may destroy large areas of the brain and produce **vascular dementia,** also called *multi-infarct dementia,* the second most common form of dementia after Alzheimer's disease. It is diagnosed with the same criteria as any other dementia but requires medical evidence of cerebrovascular disease.

Vascular dementia results from cerebrovascular disease that causes interruptions and blockages of blood circulation in the brain. It most commonly affects men older than the age of fifty. It may have an abrupt onset with progressive worsening, or it may be very gradual with accumulating damage.

The extent of intellectual, motor, and personality changes depends on the extent of tissue damage. The individual is likely to have symptoms in all these areas. Diagnosis of the disorder may be based on laboratory tests that indicate cerebrovascular disease, neuroimaging studies that reveal areas of tissue damage, and clinical evidence of progression of damage. Vascular dementia may involve psychological symptoms. Depressive symptoms are common; delusions and psychotic features may be present in as many as 50 percent of patients. The following case illustrates typical features of vascular dementia.

> *Henry is your grandfather. He is retired from his career as a successful doctor and, like many of his age, is overweight, a smoker, and suffers from high blood pressure. He and your grandmother used to take great pleasure in entertaining their children and grandchildren. Increasingly, however, the grandchildren have noticed Grandpa's forgetfulness. He forgets that he has food cooking on the stove, for-*

gets that he told the same story an hour ago, forgets where he left his car keys. When his children telephone, he sometimes seems confused about to whom he is talking. Over time your grandmother has become more concerned because your grandfather has begun dressing sloppily and spilling food on himself. She became especially alarmed when she realized that he was writing checks to people she did not know. She finally learned that he was giving away large sums of money to strangers he met in the park. Eventually, she got him to agree to medical evaluations, where the presence of essential hypertension and evidence of small strokes led to a diagnosis of multi-infarct dementia. Medication to control his blood pressure may slow the rate of deterioration, but his death from a major stroke or progressive cerebrovascular disease is likely within a few years.

Poststroke Depression   One of the most common psychological syndromes associated with stroke is **poststroke depression,** affecting between 30 and 50 percent of patients after acute stroke (Robinson et al., 1983). The quality of the depressions does not differ from those of depressed persons who do not have strokes or medical problems. Patients generally recover from their depressions, but recovery may take one to two years (Robinson, Bolduc & Price, 1987) and may depend on the location of the lesion in the brain.

Are some types of strokes more likely to be followed by depression than others? Studies that control for relevant variables such as the person's age and time since the stroke have suggested that poststroke depression may be more common when the stroke occurs on the left side of the brain, especially toward the frontal region (Starkstein & Robinson, 1992). Strokes on the right side also may be associated with depressive disorders, especially if they occur in the posterior areas of the right side of the brain. However, other investigators have suggested that simple formulations of frontal or nonfrontal or left or right "depression regions" following stroke may be premature because such effects also depend on whether the lesions are in upper or lower areas (Stern & Bachman, 1991).

Brain Tumors

Clinicians in training are often told a standard cautionary tale about a man who had been in psychoanalysis for six years only to die of a brain tumor that had caused his psychological symptoms in the first place. Brain tumors, like many other neurological disorders, can cause numerous psychological symptoms that seem identical to many psychological disorders found in DSM-IV, including anxiety disorders, psychoses, personality disorders, and nearly any other diagnosable condition. Autopsy studies of mental patients have suggested that 1 to 2 percent of patients who are given a mental health

diagnosis actually may have a brain tumor that is responsible for their condition (Price, Goetz & Lovell, 1992).

Tumors may be fast or slow growing, benign or malignant, invasive or encapsulated, and metastasized from another primary tumor site (such as lung or breast cancer) or not. They typically affect not only the functions of the locations where they grow, but they also create damage and disturbance from intracranial pressure. Symptoms commonly include headache and vomiting and — depending on the affected areas — personality, cognitive, and motor or perceptual changes. Consider the case of Arnie, a middle-aged man.

Arnie appeared to be in good health, but over a period of several weeks his mood shifts were increasingly erratic. He would be in an uncharacteristically high mood for no apparent reason, only to become irritable and enraged over little annoyances. He was agitated and became messy and disorganized in his appearance; his ability to plan ahead and make reasonable business decisions seemed impaired. Colleagues were worried because the behaviors were atypical for him. When they tried to talk to him about their concern, he accused them of plotting against him and trying to control his mind. One day he had a seizure, and they took him to the hospital. CT scans revealed the presence of a fast-growing glioblastoma of the right frontal area, and neuropsychological testing confirmed considerable cognitive impairment.

The location of the tumors affects the nature of cognitive and personality changes, as we note elsewhere. Slow-growing tumors, compared with fast-growing tumors, are more likely to produce subtle personality changes that are sometimes misinterpreted as psychological rather than medical in origin.

Unfortunately, treating brain tumors is problematic. Even when brain tumors are benign, they may cause damage and pressure requiring treatment. Surgery to remove both benign and malignant tumors unavoidably causes damage to brain tissue, sometimes resulting in permanent changes in cognitive or motor abilities. Some tumors that are very invasive or deep in the brain cannot be removed surgically because of the risk for significant injury. Radiation treatment may prove helpful for some kinds of tumors, but chemotherapy is so far unsuccessful in part because of failure of the chemicals to cross the *blood-brain barrier,* the structure of blood vessels that allows only certain chemicals to leave the blood and interact with brain tissue.

Endocrinological Disorders

Numerous medical disorders disrupt the delicate balance of hormones and other chemicals needed to maintain healthy functioning. Examples of endocrine disorders include an insufficiency or excess of thyroid, calcium, parathyroid, and insulin. Many endocrine disorders cause anxiety and mood disorders and even psychotic symptoms, as well as major observable medical symptoms. Severe or acute cases also can cause profound alterations in consciousness such as coma or delirium, sometimes associated with hallucinations and other psychotic experiences, as well as dementia. For instance, dementia may result from insufficiencies of cortisol and parathyroid hormones, as well as from hyperinsulinism.

Consider, for example, **hypothyroidism** (too little thyroid), which is typically caused by thyroid gland disease, autoimmune disorders, or certain drugs (such as lithium). Short-term cognitive effects include problems in memory and concentration. Thyroid deficiencies also may cause anxiety and depression.

Severe — and especially long-standing — thyroid deficiencies may cause psychosis, delirium, and dementia. In adults, the symptoms largely may be reversible by correcting the thyroid insufficiency. Infants born with congenital hypothyroidism, however, may be severely and irreversibly retarded unless treated early.

Thyroid deficiencies are seen commonly in patients with mood disorders and also may result from lithium treatment. Accordingly, effective treatment of such psychiatric conditions may require monitoring, and even administering, thyroid hormones.

Infectious Diseases

Numerous infectious diseases can cause temporary or permanent brain injury and mental dysfunction — including viral, bacterial, and fungal infections. We mention two that have particular contemporary or historical importance: AIDS and syphilis.

AIDS   The human immunodeficiency virus that causes acquired immune deficiency syndrome (AIDS) damages the immune system, leaving the body vulnerable to a wide variety of both mild and fatal diseases whose impact would ordinarily be blocked by normal immune defenses. The AIDS virus is thought to enter the brain in the early stage of infection. With the increasing dysfunction of the immune system over time, the virus proliferates and causes diffuse and variable damage mostly to subcortical, rather than cortical, areas of the brain (in addition to its effects on numerous other organs and systems of the body). In many affected individuals, cognitive impairment may not be observable until later stages of the disease. Increasing evidence has suggested, however, that at least mild cognitive symptoms may develop long before full AIDS-related symptoms occur, even in individuals who are only HIV positive and have not yet developed AIDS (Lunn et al., 1991; Perry, 1990). Yaakov Stern and his colleagues (1991) at Columbia University in New York, for example, found mild but significant impaired performance on neuropsychological tests involving verbal memory, abstract reasoning, attention, and planning in HIV-positive men who had no medical symptoms of AIDS compared with HIV-negative men.

Individuals with HIV infection may report a subjective sense of apathy and depression, mental slowing, concentration problems, and memory impairment (e.g., Lipton & Gendelman, 1995). Eventually, in the later stages of AIDS, psychosis, amnesia, and "subcortical dementia" may occur. In general — but not inevitably — once central nervous system disease is obvious, survival time is decreased.

Ted's once large and muscular body is now wasted and weak as he nears the end of the terrible progression of AIDS. The burden of lifting,

AIDS, like many other infectious diseases, often results in brain degeneration and cognitive impairment.

moving, and caring for him has been a heavy one for his life partner, Jake, but increasingly the hardest part is to deal with Ted's dementia. Ted's memory is poor, and he worries about legal and financial matters they are trying to sort out. He called his insurance company to complain that they had cut him off; he forgot that only yesterday Jake told him that everything had been resolved satisfactorily. Some of the time he doesn't know where he is or what day it is. Occasionally, he is delusional and has hallucinations. Increasingly, Ted grows more confused and apathetic, remaining in bed as his mental and physical functions diminish.

Syphilis The disease of *general paresis* was well-known in the developing world of several centuries ago, as we note in Chapter 2. One of the most severe mental illnesses of the time, if untreated, it produces memory problems and poor intellectual functioning, bad judgment, dementia, personality changes, and delusions — with a deteriorating course leading to death. Eventually, doctors and scientists in the nineteenth century concluded that general paresis was linked to **syphilis,** an infectious, often sexually transmitted disease that led to

Exposure to toxic chemicals, such as some pesticides used in crop dusting, poses a risk for illness including brain damage.

a kind of skin disorder (the great pox). It became increasingly clear that in its later stages, syphilis would sometimes affect the central nervous system. In the early twentieth century, researchers discovered that the spirochete *Treponema pallidum* was the cause of syphilis, and in 1906 von Wassermann discovered a blood test to check for its presence. Presently, syphilis blood tests are required by some states before marriage certificates can be issued, in the hope of preventing the spread of the disease.

Syphilis in its early stages can be treated with penicillin. It remains a threatening disease, however, because 5 to 10 percent of those with untreated syphilis go on to develop general paresis years later.

Poisons, Toxins, and Drugs

Numerous naturally occurring metals can cause mild to severe medical and mental symptoms if absorbed in quantity. In addition, since the industrial revolution, exposure to toxic substances through pollution, consumer use, and industrial contact has increased greatly. Table 17.5 indicates the neurological consequences of exposure to several metals.

The heavy metal *lead*, for example, may cause delirium, dementia, psychosis, irritability, depression, and seizures, as well as headache, nausea, and other medical problems. Tragically, children absorb lead more readily than do adults, and they may suffer exposure through paint (especially if they eat paint chips), as well as through contaminated water, air, food, and dust (or unfired pottery or gasoline sniffing). Research has indicated that lead ingestion in children is associated with increased impulsivity, hyperactivity, low tolerance for frustration, and other behavioral problems (Loeber, 1990). Among factory workers exposed to even low levels of lead, neurological testing commonly reveals deficits in intellectual performance (Eskenazi & Maizlish, 1988). Unfortunately, lead and certain other metals cannot be removed from the body.

Another example among numerous toxic substances is exposure to *organic solvents*. Sniffing solvent-containing substances such as paint thinner, printing and photograph-processing chemicals, glues, spot remover, or even marking pens, may cause euphoria in the short run, but exposure over long periods or in acute concentrations can cause intellectual performance deterioration and problems in memory, concentration, and motor abnormalities (Eskenazi & Maizlish, 1988). The effects may be reversible at least in part if exposure is discontinued, but residual effects may remain after long-term exposure. Similarly, exposure to organophosphate pesticides may contribute to severe, even fatal effects.

Drugs and Alcohol Substances such as drugs and alcohol not only cause intoxication but also may be responsible for cognitive impairment disorders — delirium,

Table 17.5   Selected Metals That Cause Major Neurological Problems

Metal	Delirium	Dementia	Mood Changes	Psychosis	Personality Changes	Seizures	Peripheral Neuropathy
Aluminum		X			X	X	
Arsenic	X	X	X	X	X	X	X
Lead	X	X	X	X	X	X	X
Lithium	X					X	X
Manganese	X	X	X	X	X		
Mercury	X	X	X		X	X	X
Thallium	X	X	X	X		X	X

Source: Gross & Nagy (1992).

Many metals, in addition to the metals shown here, are toxic. Sufficient exposure may cause death, but for many metals, the cumulative effects may take years to recognize.

amnesia, and dementia—as well as a variety of psychological disturbances such as psychosis, depression, and anxiety. Prolonged and heavy use of substances eventually may cause irreversible damage to the brain and therefore severe amnesia disorders or dementia. For example, **Korsakoff's syndrome** is usually caused by vitamin B$_1$ (thiamine) deficiency stemming from nutritional neglect during prolonged alcohol abuse. Called *alcohol amnestic disorder* in the DSM, its key feature is severe retrograde and anterograde amnesia. Korsakoff's syndrome sometimes may follow an acute episode of Wernicke's disease, a thiamine-deficiency syndrome often caused by severe alcohol abuse characterized by confusion, loss of coordination, and other neurological signs. If treated early with large doses of thiamine, Wernicke's disease may not develop into alcohol amnestic syndrome. Once established, however, alcohol amnestic syndrome is generally irreversible. *Alcohol dementia* is also associated with extensive alcohol abuse; it is diagnosed when the multiple cognitive symptoms of dementia occur in patients with a history of alcohol use and when no other causes of dementia are present. Chapter 11 presents a fuller discussion of the effects of alcohol and drug intoxication and withdrawal.

TREATMENT OF COGNITIVE IMPAIRMENT DISORDERS

When the medical condition underlying a cognitive or secondary psychological disorder can be treated, mental functioning also may improve. For instance, "drying out" from alcohol or drug intoxication may eliminate delirium and reverse problems in concentration and intellectual performance. Administering thyroid hormones to adult hypothyroid patients normally reverses dementia symptoms. Such medical treatments are generally beyond the scope of this book. However, we note two recent developments that promise future hope for sufferers of Alzheimer's and Parkinson's diseases. Investigations of *tacrine (Cognex)* suggest that it may improve the intellectual functioning of some people with Alzheimer's dementia by repairing the cholinergic deficiency that results from cell damage. It appears to improve cognitive functioning and even to reduce the need for placement in nursing homes (e.g., Foster, Petersen, Gracon, & Lewis, 1996; Holford & Peace, 1994; Knopman et al., 1996). A recent study indicated that it is significantly more effective for individuals with Alzheimer's who do not have the apoE ε4 allele compared with those who do (Farlow, Lhiri, Poirier, Davignon, & Hui, 1996). Huntington's disease does not have a known treatment, but investigators have begun to experiment with the use of agents to reverse the process believed to account for neuronal death (e.g., Peyser et al., 1995).

Meanwhile, a few controlled investigations have shown promising results in improving motor functioning in patients with Parkinson's disease by brain implantation of fetal tissue. Tissue containing dopamine-producing brain cells is transplanted into the midbrain areas of Parkinson's patients where the dopamine-producing cells have died. The tissue appears to generate new cells, leading to improved functioning (Freed et al., 1992; Spencer et al., 1992). Limited research has been conducted to date, so the potential of these transplantation techniques has not yet been evaluated.

Psychotropic Medications

Often, psychotropic medications can help by reducing accompanying symptoms of depression or psychosis. Because insight-oriented therapy is useless for many persons afflicted with cognitive disorders, antidepressant

Studies have suggested that pets are good medicine. Programs that give the elderly and those with dementia a chance to interact with dogs and cats report that they have a soothing effect on patients.

medications are frequently the main treatment for mood symptoms. Considerable success has been reported for the use of antidepressants by persons with Parkinson's disease (Cummings, 1992). Results of antidepressant medication for depression in persons with Alzheimer's dementia also seem promising to reduce not only depression but also agitation and hostility, although well-controlled clinical trials are still needed (Teri & Wagner, 1992). Neuroleptic medications may reduce psychotic symptoms such as hallucinations and delusions among patients with dementias from injuries or degenerative disorders. Caution is needed in using medications with the elderly, however, since dosages appropriate for younger persons may not be suitable, as well as problems with side effects accentuating medical problems (e.g., hypotensive effects of some antidepressants). Due to health problems, some older adults may be exposed to multiple drugs that have unknown interaction effects with each other that can cause adverse reactions.

Behavioral Change Programs

In many patients with brain disease or injury, the damage to the brain is irreversible, and its effects cannot be overcome. The majority of degenerative dementias, for example, presently cannot be treated directly. For these patients, the main goals of treatment are to reduce psychological distress and to assist the patient and family in coping with the limitations created by the disorder. In some patients with brain injury, rehabilitation may involve retraining areas of the brain to take over functions of the damaged area.

To cope with the problem behaviors that often accompany dementia, such as aggressiveness, wandering, and incontinence, behavior modification programs can be very helpful. Simple procedures based on learning principles that alter the environment sometimes reduce these problems (Jorm, 1994). For example, poor hygiene might be improved by providing a large comb and toothbrush with enlarged handles in an easily accessible area without distracting furniture or television. Also, the person might be rewarded with food or praise for self-care. Several studies (reviewed by Fisher & Carstensen, 1990; Woods, 1994) have indicated that wandering can be reduced by rewarding the person for following colored arrows to return to his or her room and that incontinence can be reduced by prompting the person to go to the bathroom regularly. Even if these gains are only temporary, they might improve the quality of life for patients, families, and other caregivers.

The progressive symptoms of dementia ultimately may overwhelm family members' abilities or willingness to provide care at home; as a result, many demented individuals spend their waning days in institutions such as convalescent homes and hospitals. The burden of caring for a family member with a progressive neurological disease is enormous and often causes great distress.

FAMILY MATTERS

Caregivers Have Their Own Problems

Imagine having to change your mother's diapers or her looking at you as if you were a total stranger and angrily

Grandpa Fred has suffered from Alzheimer's for many years, and his full-time care has fallen on his wife, Fran. She works a second shift job at a factory to maintain her health insurance benefits for his medical care. She also tries to provide as full a life for him as she can, including sharing time with the grandchildren. Caretakers like Fran often experience tremendous strain and even psychological disorders as a result of their nonstop efforts and worries.

accusing you of stealing her purse. Imagine that your once-handsome and smart husband of many years cannot be taken out in public because he drools, smells bad, and masturbates in front of people, and at home it takes all your strength to bathe him and change his clothes. Picture your elderly father sitting in his chair crying, pacing and wringing his hands, unwilling to eat but unable to express what's on his mind because he's lost much of his mental functioning. Or picture your younger brother in the throes of AIDS dementia, hallucinating and terrified as you try unsuccessfully to comfort him. These are not isolated horror stories; they are the realities that thousands of people face every day as caregivers of relatives with dementia.

So demanding, unrelenting, and unnerving are the careers of caregivers that professionals began to take note of the tremendous cost to their mental health. Several studies have found that more than 50 percent of caregivers met criteria for diagnosable depression (e.g., Teri & Wagner, 1992). Those who previously had problems with depression and anxiety are especially at risk for developing new episodes when they become responsible for the care of an Alzheimer's patient (Russo, Vitaliano, Brewer, Katon, & Becker, 1995). Caregivers report many experiences of stress and psychiatric symptoms and often seek tranquilizers and other psychotropic medications for themselves (Pruchno & Potashnik, 1989). Several of these studies have suggested that the effects are especially severe when the caregiver is a spouse — particularly a wife. Not only the mental health but also the physical health of caregivers may decline (Pruchno et al., 1990).

What is it that is so distressing to caregivers? Surprisingly, it does not seem to be the cognitive impairment, such as the forgetfulness or the thinking difficul-

ties. Research has indicated two main sources of distress to caregivers: depression, withdrawal, and apathy in the person with Alzheimer's (Teri & Wagner, 1992) and the person's disruptive behaviors — the assaultiveness, swearing, and lack of cooperation and social withdrawal (Deimling & Bass, 1986). It may be that caregivers understand that the cognitive impairment is due to uncontrollable causes but believe that the disruptive behaviors are controllable — hence their heightened anger and frustration.

Although most people find it stressful to care for a relative with Alzheimer's disease, a recent study reminds us that there are considerable cultural variations in family members' reactions. Haley and associates (1996) at the University of Alabama at Birmingham, for instance, found that African Americans reported less depression and less stressfulness associated with caregiving than did white caregivers. The investigators speculate that African Americans are more likely to tolerate disturbance in family members and to perceive taking care of an elder as expected rather than as an unexpected disruption to plans for retirement. The African American culture also may accord more respect to elders, particularly older women.

Many communities have now recognized the great needs of family members for support and relief and offer support groups and self-help organizations. These activities encourage caregivers to share their burdens with others going through the same process. In the future, however, fewer people may be willing to subject themselves to the great burden of caregiving. Demanding — and paying for — good quality care for elders is likely to be a major public policy issue in the early decades of the twenty-first century.

Cognitive Rehabilitation

A relatively new field in neuropsychology is **cognitive rehabilitation.** Its goals are to retrain the individual or provide compensatory skills to counteract the effects of brain damage, just as physical rehabilitation attempts to do after limbs are damaged. Much of this work has used behavioral techniques, usually for individuals with closed head injuries. Some individuals may profit from techniques to improve attention and memory. For instance, computer video games and tasks have been used to train brain-injured patients to improve attention. Using either commercially available games that reward focused attention or by developing computer-administered tasks, patients can practice and be rewarded by performance feedback (possibly supplemented by verbal praise or tokens). Various methods have now been employed and evaluated, with results that promise useful options for patients with various neurocognitive disorders (e.g., Prigitano, Glisky, & Konoff, 1996).

Other cognitive rehabilitation efforts have focused on patients' self-regulation skills. Because impulsiveness and outbursts of anger are common in some head-injured patients, cognitive techniques may help them generate self-talk that is incompatible with outbursts. Similarly, patients may be trained to perform computer tasks that require suppression of impulsive responding to get the correct moves. They can be taught to generate problem-solving strategies that enhance correct answers and reduce immediate, impulsive responses (reviewed in Benedict, 1989; Corrigan & Yudofsky, 1996). Cognitive rehabilitation is an area of active research and new developments, and its overall utility remains to be clarified.

What Lies Ahead?

Knowledge about the brain and its functions is growing enormously. Developments in both basic knowledge and techniques for exploring brain function promise to reveal more and more about this most mysterious of organs. By the end of this decade, we expect that there will be important advances in what we know about memory, thinking, learning, and emotion — and the effects of injury, disease, and stress on these processes. All these advances will further our understanding of both normal and abnormal behavior.

The next decade is also likely to be marked by rapid advances in our understanding of the dementias, especially Alzheimer's disease. With growing recognition that ours is an aging society and one in which people live longer and physically healthier lives, scientists are responding to the challenge of understanding the causes of this disorder. At the same time, researchers are seeking treatments, cures, and possible prevention of degenerative brain disorders. Will there be pills to improve memory and learning? Transplants to regenerate destroyed tissue? Genetic testing to identify those at high risk for certain diseases? Improved behavioral techniques for retraining and rehabilitation of brain-injured persons? We think the answer is yes.

KEY TERMS

Alzheimer's dementia (AD) (531)
amnesia (529)
cerebral vascular disorders (539)
cognitive disorders (524)
cognitive rehabilitation (546)

delirium (528)
dementia (529)
frontal lobe injuries (538)
Huntington's disease (HD) (536)
hypothyroidism (541)
Korsakoff's syndrome (543)

neurofibrillary tangles (532)
organic mental disorders (524)
Parkinson's disease (535)
plaques (532)
postconcussion syndrome (538)

poststroke depression (540)
syphilis (542)
traumatic brain injuries (537)
vascular dementia (539)

SUMMARY

Assessing and Classifying Dysfunctions of the Brain

Formerly called *organic mental disorders, cognitive disorder* diagnoses include dementia, delirium, and amnesia. Other psychiatric disorders, such as depression, may be due to a medical disorder or substance abuse, when their cause is known to be physical. Improved neuropsychological testing and imaging techniques have greatly aided the assessment of cognitive impairment disorders.

Cognitive Impairment Disorders

Delirium refers to changes in level of consciousness that may be accompanied by other cognitive changes; it may be temporary or progressive. *Amnesia* is a memory disorder that has a physical cause, and it is different from psychogenic amnesia, a psychological condition not involving damage to areas of the brain. *Dementia* — often called senility in the past — refers to a pattern of mental deterioration that is caused by disease. There are multiple areas of mental dysfunction, including problems with memory and learning new information, impaired intellectual functioning such as reasoning and planning, and poor judgment — and personality deterioration is usually also present. Although some forms of dementia may be reversible, the majority are not.

Some Degenerative Brain Diseases

Alzheimer's dementia (AD) is the most common form of progressive dementia and is characterized by distinctive changes in brain tissue called *plaques* and *neurofibrillary tangles.* It more commonly strikes elderly individuals but sometimes may begin in persons in their forties. Genetic abnormalities account for several rare forms of the disorder, and recently, a variant of a gene associated with transporting cholesterol (apolipoprotein E ε4 alleles) in the brain has been shown to be a risk factor for developing the disease.

Parkinson's disease impairs movement through destruction of dopaminergic tracts in the brain and also can include depression and dementia. Most causes of this disorder are unknown. *Huntington's disease (HD)* is a rare but severe form of degenerative disorder causing dementia and other neurological symptoms and death. It is caused by a defective gene, and tests for its presence are now available.

Other Sources of Brain Damage

Traumatic brain injuries are a leading cause of cognitive impairment, ranging from mild and relatively temporary to severe. *Frontal lobe injuries* may cause impaired memory, concentration, reasoning, and learning, as well as personality changes. Disinhibition, aggression, and impairment of higher mental processes such as judgment are common; apathy and withdrawal also may occur frequently. Even mild head injuries with brief or no loss of consciousness can induce *postconcussion syndrome,* problems of concentration, memory, and personality changes.

Cerebral vascular disorders may cause brain-damaging strokes, as well as small strokes that cause progressive neurological problems called *vascular dementia.* The nature of cognitive and psychological impairment is determined by location of the lesions, and some strokes appear to cause *poststroke depression.*

Mental impairment and personality changes also can be caused by brain tumors and endocrinological disorders. Severe *hypothyroidism,* for example, causes dementia symptoms over time that often may be reversed with thyroid treatment. Infectious diseases also can affect the central nervous system (an example is general paresis, a severe syndrome of mental disorder caused by *syphilis*). Exposure to poisons and toxic substances, including drugs and alcohol, also can cause cognitive impairment. Alcohol abuse can cause *Korsakoff's syndrome,* or alcohol amnestic disorder, as a result of severe thiamine deficiency.

Treatment of Cognitive Impairment Disorders

When it is possible to treat the underlying disease process (such as vascular dementia due to cerebrovascular disease), such treatment may reverse or stop the progression of cognitive impairment. However, many cognitive impairment conditions do not have a known or treatable cause. Psychotropic medications may be used to treat symptoms — such as depression or psychosis — but do not affect the underlying disorder. Behavioral programs and *cognitive rehabilitation* are sometimes used to modify unwanted behaviors or retrain particular skills. In the absence of widely effective techniques, however, much of the care of brain-injured and demented patients falls on family members who are greatly stressed by the experience or on scarce and largely inadequate community resources.

Consider the Following. . .

Suppose that you are a researcher employed by a biotechnology firm pushing for marketing tests for apoE type ε4 alleles on chromosome 19, arguing that people can now find out their susceptibility for developing Alzheimer's disease in their sixties or seventies. Consider this development from two perspectives, the scientific and the psychological. Scientifically, what would the gene test for the apoE ε4 alleles tell you, and what would it not tell you? What would a person need to know in order for this test to be really useful? Psychologically, what do you consider to be the advantages and disadvantages of discovering your own genetic predisposition? Under what conditions might this be useful or harmful?

Suppose that you have a friend who loves to ride a motorcycle but who feels that part of the thrill is lost when he is forced by law to wear a helmet. He argues with you that he has a right to do whatever he wants — it's his head, and he'll risk it if he chooses. What is your argument for why the helmet law makes sense? Is there justification for overriding individual "freedom?"

CHAPTER 18

Legal, Ethical, and Social Issues in Mental Health

Those among us...

■ You read in the newspaper that John Smith killed two people during a robbery because he thought they could testify against him if he was caught. John Jones killed two people who came to his door selling brushes because voices told him that they were aliens who had come to take him to another planet.

■ There are two measures on your local ballot, one for more schools and one for more prisons. The community cannot afford both, so you wonder which is best for the community.

■ Your friend Su-Yan is depressed and worried about personal matters. You urge her to see a therapist at your college, but she looks at you as if that's the last thing on earth she would consider.

■ Your mother is a great fan of talk shows on TV and radio and often quotes from "Dr. So-and-So" about psychological problems and personal matters. You're not so sure that this is the kind of help that people really profit from.

Do we apply the same standards of legal responsibility when John Smith and John Jones come to trial?

How should we think about long-term solutions to mental health problems?

Is therapy for everyone with problems? Are some segments of our population more likely to use therapy, and profit from it, than others?

What is the value of radio "therapists" and self-help books? Do they really help people?

Throughout this book we present scientific information concerning mental disorders and their treatment. We make every effort to present conclusions based on systematic observation, data, and logic, and we emphasize the latest applications of scientific methods. There is a limit, however, to what science can tell us. Abnormal psychology raises important legal, ethical, and social issues, and these are matters of values, beliefs, and judgment.

We conclude this book with an examination of these issues. In this chapter we discuss matters that affect all of us, as consumers and citizens trying to define the kind of community and society we want for ourselves and our children. Our goal is to acquaint you with the principles and practices that help to clarify these decisions. We examine the legal standards for determining when a person is mentally competent to be held responsible for a crime and the conditions under which a person can be treated against her or his will. These laws are made and implemented by citizens. We also discuss consumer issues pertaining to treatment: when to seek treatment, where to go, and what ethical standards to expect from a therapist. We discuss some of the barriers to effective treatment and why it is unrealistic to expect psychotherapy and medications to solve all the problems of mental illness. Finally, we review alternatives to traditional treatments and the possibility of preventing psychological problems.

THE LAW AND MENTAL ILLNESS

Every society struggles to find the right balance between protecting the community and protecting the rights of individuals. This section focuses on laws in the United States, although the same issues arise in most nations. In some eras of U.S. history, the balance has tipped in the direction of protecting the community; at other times, in the direction of individual liberties. This ever-changing process of defining liberties is clearly evident in laws concerning the mentally ill. For example, in some periods, emphasis on the general community interest has eased the path for incarcerating the mentally ill against their will. The present era generally tips the balance toward protection of individual freedom. The laws are somewhat different state by state and between federal and state jurisdictions, and issues concerning individual rights versus community needs are particularly controversial in several of the topics to be discussed. Laws continue to change, however, and you will undoubtedly be called on to participate in this process as voters.

Legal Protection for the Mentally Ill in Criminal Cases

For centuries it has been a fundamental principle of English law that a person cannot be held morally and criminally responsible, and hence punished, unless he or she *intended* to commit a crime. The person must have *mens rea* — a guilty mind. Intention to commit a crime requires that the person know right from wrong and have the free will to act as he or she chooses. A three-year-old who points a loaded gun at a playmate and pulls the trigger is assumed to lack criminal responsibility because it is thought that the child does not understand the nature and consequences of the act or have free will in the action. By the same token, for nearly 500 years English law has held that persons who commit crimes but have "unsound" minds cannot be held criminally responsible for the crimes. Moreover, a person cannot be brought to trial unless he or she is able to understand and participate in the proceedings. The law thus provides two protections for those with mental illness or disability. People cannot be tried unless they are mentally competent, and they cannot be held criminally responsible unless they are sane.

One of the heirs to the Dupont fortune, John E. Dupont, supported a training center for U.S. Olympic wrestlers. He is shown here with wrestler Dave Schultz, whom he shot to death in 1996. He was found "guilty but mentally ill" by a jury who learned that he suffered from paranoid schizophrenia. He was sentenced to serve time in a prison facility that will provide treatment for his illness.

Competence to Stand Trial   If a person is **mentally incompetent to stand trial** — not sufficiently rational to understand and assist in his or her own defense — there can be no trial or legal process. Court proceedings cannot go forward without the accused. Mentally incompetent defendants are confined in a prison hospital until they are deemed competent to stand trial. As a result, they may be held for a considerable time before being brought to trial. Fortunately, however, in most jurisdictions they cannot be held longer that the maximum length of incarceration had they been found guilty of the crime, but it still amounts to confinement without being found guilty.

Each year many thousands of individuals are evaluated for competency; this process typically involves expert testimony by mental health professionals presented to a judge. Some have argued that because of these numbers, the determination of competency is the most significant mental health issue pursued in the criminal justice system. We would like to think that such competency decisions are based on determinations of the person's coherence and rationality. For the most part, research has shown that the characteristics most strongly associated with incompetency were psychotic diagnoses, symptoms of severe psychological disorder, and poor performance on psychological tests specifically aimed at testing functional ability relevant to legal issues (Nicholson & Kugler, 1991).

The Insanity Defense   The **insanity defense plea,** or the legal plea of not guilty by reason of insanity (NGRI) at the time of the crime, results in the defendant being sent to a treatment facility instead of prison. *Insanity* is a legal term, not a psychological term, and it has been defined in several ways, which we describe in this section. A diagnosis of a disorder is not the same as insanity. Nor does insanity refer only to psychotic experiences. During a trial, both defense and prosecution expert witnesses might agree, for instance, that the defendant is a paranoid schizophrenic — but disagree on whether the defendant was legally insane. Ultimately, the jury has to use its common sense in applying expert testimony to the legal definitions of insanity.

Consider the following actual cases; each illustrates the difference between having a diagnosable condition and insanity. Also, in each instance, different legal definitions may lead to different decisions.

Linda P., age twenty-three, lived with her mother and stepfather, but they did not know that she was pregnant. She gave birth in private, wrapped the infant in a towel, and placed him in a dresser drawer in her bedroom. Her mother discovered the body eleven days later. Six years earlier, she had similarly concealed a birth, but the baby was discovered and placed for adoption, and Linda was put on probation for child endangerment. Psychiatrists who have evaluated her suggest that her personality fragments under stress and that she probably did not have conscious awareness of her acts — in other words, she displayed extreme dissociation and denial. Linda certainly understands that murdering babies is wrong but believes that the baby was stillborn. Commentary: *Although Linda was not delusional and generally functioned relatively normally, did she have a dissociative condition that literally kept her from "knowing" what was going on? Would a jury believe that she was mentally disabled and consider her not guilty, given that a similar event had happened in the past?*

Gilbert M. carefully built an elaborate bunker in his backyard and stocked it with more than one hundred guns — allegedly to protect himself and his family from what he believed to be the impending end of the world, when the forces of good and evil would do battle. He financed his preparations for Armageddon by robbing banks, and he had committed a string of nine robberies before he was caught. His wife and four children said that he was a reasonable and rational man who wouldn't hurt a fly, and allegedly they knew nothing of his robberies. Commentary: *Were Gilbert's beliefs delusional, and if so, did they prevent him from "understanding" that what he did to finance his actions was wrong? Would a jury believe that his extreme beliefs were delusional or that such an elaborately planned scheme was the product of insanity?*

Stephen D. is a 25-year-old man who lived with his parents. His brother found blood in their home and called the police, who discovered the parents' bodies buried in a shallow grave. Stephen has been charged with the murder. Police were told that he had been treated for bipolar disorder but resisted taking medication for his condition because he felt that he didn't need it. Apparently, two days before the murders, his mother had taken him to the Veterans Administration (VA) hospital, but he slipped out without being treated. Commentary: *By attempting to conceal the murder, Stephen seemed to indicate that he knew what he did was wrong. But did he "know" at the time of the killing, and if he did know, was he able to control himself? How would a jury react to the fact that he refused to take his medication for a treatable condition?*

Each of these cases illustrates the complexity of the insanity defense. What mental health professionals may diagnose does not necessarily meet legal requirements for insanity. And sometimes mental health concepts do not conform to jury members' common sense ideas about a person's ability to understand and control behaviors.

When is a person legally insane? Several formulations of the legal definition of insanity have been developed over the years in an attempt to improve clarity and fairness. Essentially, these definitions all include some statement as to the defendant's *cognitive ability*, the mental capacity to know right from wrong; some definitions also include statements about the person's *control*, or ability to exercise free will. Here are five of the major legal definitions:

1. *The M'Naghten Rule.* The modern formulation of the insanity defense stems from the statement of the House of Lords in 1843 in the case of Daniel M'Naghten, who killed the assistant to Robert Peel, the prime minister of England. M'Naghten suffered from delusions of persecution that led to his attempt on the life of the prime minister, which killed his assistant instead. The jury rendered a decision of not guilty by reason of insanity. In the wake of the public controversy afterward, the House of Lords formulated legal rules to apply to such cases. The **M'Naghten Rule** states:

> To establish a defense on the ground of insanity, it must be clearly proved that, at the time of the committing of the act, the party accused was labouring under such a defect of reason, from disease of the mind, as not to know the nature and quality of the act he was doing; or if he did know it, that he did not know he was doing what was wrong.

This formulation raises several questions. What do we mean by "know" — is it rational knowing? Is it the same as emotional understanding, or is it the ability to appreciate the difference between right and wrong? How do we prove the condition of the person's mind at the time of the crime? Is rational understanding the only thing that counts?

2. *Irresistible impulse.* Unlike the rational definition of insanity in the M'Naghten Rule, the **irresistible impulse** doctrine emphasizes control. By this formulation, even if the person knew the difference between right and wrong, the insanity defense could be argued if the person could not control his or her behavior. Similarly, some jurisdictions hold that an individual cannot be found guilty of an intentional act if it was caused by **diminished capacity** — mental or physical factors that impaired the person's ability to understand the nature of the act or to control it. For example, in 1979 in San Francisco, Dan White successfully argued that because of stress and the consumption of high quantities of sugar-laden junk food, he was unable to understand and control his acts when he assassinated Mayor Moscone and City Councilman Harvey Milk. White's argument, which became known as the "Twinkie

defense," led to his being found guilty of manslaughter, a lesser crime than first-degree murder. Today, most U.S. jurisdictions do not accept these formulations because the public came to believe that they were unjust.

3. *The Durham Rule.* In an effort to bring scientific judgment into insanity determinations, Judge David Bazelon introduced the doctrine of "product of mental illness" as the insanity standard for the federal courts of the District of Columbia in 1954 in the case of *Durham v. the United States* (1954). The **Durham Rule** stated that individuals are not criminally responsible if their "unlawful act was the product of mental disease or mental defect." It continued through 1972 but was heavily criticized because it was overly inclusive, suggesting that anyone with a diagnosis of mental disorder could be found not guilty of a crime.

4. *The American Law Institute's Model Penal Code.* In the 1960s and 1970s, many jurisdictions used a definition of insanity proposed by the American Law Institute (ALI). The **ALI Model Penal Code** states:

> A person is not responsible for criminal conduct if at the time of such conduct as a result of mental disease or defect he lacks substantial capacity either to appreciate the criminality (wrongfulness) of his conduct or to conform his conduct to the requirements of law.

This doctrine combines aspects of the M'Naghten, Durham, and irresistible impulse standards, incorporating both the rational and the control criteria for insanity. In place of M'Naghten's cognitive understanding, it substitutes an "appreciation" of criminality, thus broadening the definition to include a more emotional aspect of understanding. It also does not require total lack of understanding of right and wrong, but only "lack of substantial capacity."

5. *American Psychiatric Association definition.* In 1982 the American Psychiatric Association argued that there is probably a stronger scientific basis for determining a defendant's understanding of the wrongfulness of his or her acts (cognitive criterion of insanity) than for judging whether he or she had the ability to control behavior (volitional criterion). It therefore proposed a standard for judging insanity that resembles the first part of the ALI doctrine but omits the portion concerning substantial ability to conform conduct to the requirements of the law:

> A person charged with a criminal offense should be found not guilty by reason of insanity if it is shown that as a result of mental disease or mental retardation he was unable to appreciate the wrongfulness of his conduct at the time of the offense.

Congress adopted this **APA insanity standard** for *federal* cases in 1984, after the attempted assassination of then President Reagan by John Hinckley and his subsequent acquittal under the ALI insanity defense. Congress hoped that this return to a narrower, cognitive definition of insanity would diminish the public's concerns that the insanity defense was being abused. Stimulated by the federal changes, within a few years, thirty-four states had altered their insanity defense laws, including changes in the test of insanity, in the burden and standard of proof, and in commitment and release procedures. Today, most U.S. jurisdictions use mainly cognitive rules to define insanity. A few states abolished the insanity plea altogether and enacted the alternative "guilty but mentally ill" laws (discussed later in this section) in an attempt to avert problems with the insanity defense.

Does the definition of insanity matter? Is the outcome of cases affected by the application of different definitions? Research studies have suggested that refinements in the laws make some but not a great deal of difference. One study, for example, found high agreement using various cognitive definitions of not guilty by reason of insanity, although a certain percentage met only the control criteria but not the cognitive definitions (Wettstein, Mulvey, & Rogers, 1991). Thus, refinements in the law may mean that judges and juries can interpret them differently, but most defendants who meet criteria for NGRI under one also will meet the criteria under other definitions.

Do people use the insanity defense to get away with murder? Public opinion surveys indicate that a prevalent concern is that the insanity defense is used as a loophole to escape punishment (Silver, Cirincione & Steadman, 1994). However, in the United States, the insanity plea is used in less than 1 percent of felony cases. The people who plead not guilty by reason of insanity are generally not clever schemers. The great majority of those who are acquitted as NGRI are diagnosed as schizophrenic or as psychotic (typically unipolar and bipolar psychosis). Moreover, studies of actual use of the plea show that the public greatly overestimates how frequently and how successfully it is used (Silver, Cirincione & Steadman, 1994). One reason that insanity defenses are not widely abused is that people who are judged NGRI are not simply set free. Typically, they are confined to mental or prison hospitals, often for a lengthy time. Data from felony indictments indicate that overall, those found not guilty by reason of insanity are generally less likely to be released than those found guilty, and the lengths of their confinements were strongly associated with the seriousness of their crimes (Silver, 1995).

Some argue that those mentally ill people who commit crimes simply should be found guilty (**guilty but mentally ill**), and if they are mentally ill, they should receive treatment while in prison. This solution, however, has at least two problems. First, the state has to be willing to actually provide treatment. Second, the guilty-but-mentally-ill alternative moves away from fundamental principles of holding only for those of sound mind criminally responsible. Do we really want to give up or weaken the principle that people can be punished only if they are morally responsible?

For this as for other questions about the disposition of mentally ill criminals, answers cannot come solely from scientific analyses; they depend on judgments by citizens about the kinds of communities they wish to build. We have seen that reforms in the standards used to judge insanity probably have not altered use of the insanity plea significantly. And although there may be occasional cases that outrage the public, there is no evidence that the system is abused or that people get away with crimes that they should be punished for. In the final analysis, the most-needed reforms probably involve the *treatments* that are made available and their efficacy in preventing future crimes.

Civil Commitment: Involuntary Hospitalization

Criminal commitment occurs when a person is confined after being found not guilty by reason of insanity. Mentally ill persons also can be confined involuntarily for treatment through civil commitment. In **civil commitment**, individuals initially may be held for a short period (such as three days); longer-term involuntary hospitalization requires further judicial procedure and review by legal and mental health experts.

Laws governing civil commitment reflect changing trends in the balance between protecting individual and public welfare. If we commit a few people who do not really need to be held, there is the benefit of added safety to society but at a cost to these individuals' personal lives. If we do not hold people, thinking that they are safe when in fact they are not safe, then society is at risk. When a "protect society" theme rules the day, more people are held against their will who might be harmless. When a "personal freedom" viewpoint rules, there is increased risk to society.

In the United States before 1969 — and currently in certain Western industrialized nations such as Great Britain — people could be hospitalized involuntarily if they *needed* treatment and were unable to consent to voluntary treatment because they were not mentally competent. The concept of **need for treatment** is broad and typically leaves the decision of hospitalization to a physician. In the United States, however, since 1969, virtually every state has passed laws restricting the grounds for civil commitment in an effort to protect individuals' civil liberties. In most states, civil commitment may occur only when persons display **imminent danger** *to themselves or others* or are *gravely disabled* and incapable of caring for themselves. Can health professionals judge who is dangerous and who is not? Several studies have shown that health professionals (typically psychiatrists and physicians) can apply the specific legal criteria for dangerousness fairly consistently in establishing those who are dangerous to themselves or others at that moment (e.g., Lidz, Mulvey, Appelbaum & Cleveland, 1989). Whether such individuals would in fact harm themselves or others in the *future*, however, is not known. Research has generally shown that clinicians are accurate in predicting future violence among mentally disordered people less than one-third of the time, and even the most recent and sophisticated studies have not improved on this figure (e.g., Menzies & Webster, 1995).

Another concern about using the dangerousness standard for civil commitment is that many people who desperately need treatment cannot be committed and helped because they do not meet legal requirements of dangerousness. If these people cannot be "talked into" voluntary hospitalization, they do not receive treatment.

Finally, the dangerousness standard may bring into the hospitals many people who do not respond very well to treatment. Britain uses *need-for-treatment* standards, and elderly women account for the largest proportion of first admissions to public psychiatric facilities (Segal, 1989). The United States uses *dangerousness criteria* for civil commitment, and young adult males make up the largest proportion of admittees — probably the most violent and impulsive segment of the community. Researchers have argued that young adult aggressive males are not particularly responsive to psychiatric or psychological treatment.

Legal Rights of Patients

During much of the twentieth century, we have witnessed enormous infringements on the rights of patients — loss of liberty, lengthy or even indefinite confinement, poor standards of care or minimal treatment, and potentially harmful treatments. Patients might have been held in restraints or overmedicated. Standards of care and humane treatment of patients have been resolved largely through legal means, not from scientific advances. Table 18.1 summarizes some of the major principles that have emerged in the last twenty to thirty years.

The **right to treatment, least restrictive alternative,** and **right to refuse treatment** are now considered essential elements of humane care for severely mentally ill patients. There also have been important developments in standards of ethical care for people in psychotherapy who may not be as seriously ill; some of these principles are further explored in the section on consumers' rights, but here we also discuss *confidentiality*, a principle that applies to all patients receiving mental health care.

The ability of a therapist to conduct appropriate treatment depends on the patient's trust and willingness to expose and explore his or her most personal experiences and thoughts. **Confidentiality**, the protection from disclosure of all personal information, is a fundamental necessity. Information about whether a person is in treatment and information about that treatment can be revealed only when the person or his or her legal representative signs a document consenting to release such information.

Exceptions to confidentiality exist, however, such as the need to inform others if the patient is a threat to himself or herself or others. In recent years, laws also have limited confidentiality when child or elder abuse is suspected and when clients threaten violence against another specific person. In many jurisdictions, for example, therapists (and certain other professionals such as teachers and school officials) are *required* to report suspected child abuse to authorities; failure to report is punishable by law. It is assumed that the price of breaking confidentiality is outweighed by the potential protection of children.

Many states also limit confidentiality when a client threatens harm to another person. The precedent for this limitation was set by decisions of the California courts in the case of *Tarasoff* v. *Regents of the University of California* (1974). The case was brought by the family of Tatiana Tarasoff, a student at the University of California in Berkeley, who was murdered by a graduate student who felt romantically rejected by her. At the campus counseling service he had told his therapist that he planned to kill Tatiana when she returned from a vacation. The therapist and his supervisors thought that the student should be hospitalized, and they contacted campus police for that purpose. The campus police detained him briefly. But when the student promised to stay away from Tarasoff, they let him go. He did not return to therapy, and two months later he murdered Tarasoff. In 1974 the California court initially held that the therapist had a **"duty to warn"** the intended victim. Subsequently, in 1976 the California Supreme Court ruled that psychotherapists who determine that their patients are likely to be dangerous to another identifiable person or persons have a duty to take whatever steps are reasonably necessary to protect potential victims (*duty to protect*). Warning the victims is one possible course of action, but the therapist might take other steps such as notifying law enforcement agencies or hospitalizing the patient (Appelbaum & Rosenbaum, 1989). Different states may have somewhat different duty to protect requirements.

The *Tarasoff* ruling has been criticized by many therapists because it undermines the concept of absolute confidentiality. It also presents another important problem for therapists: It requires them, in effect, to be able to predict dangerousness. Unfortunately, scientific studies have found that future dangerousness is very difficult to predict accurately, but the essence of the law is to

Table 18.1   Legal Rights of Mental Patients

Right to Treatment

Two landmark cases defined contemporary standards of care for hospitalized patients in the United States, *Wyatt v. Stickney* (1972) and *O'Connor v. Donaldson* (1975). Together these cases upheld the principles that patients cannot be confined without receiving active treatment in humane environments (they cannot simply be sheltered); persons cannot be confined who are not dangerous to themselves or others or who are capable of surviving on their own or with the help of willing friends or family.

Right to Least Restrictive Alternative

Several court cases have established the principle that involuntarily committed patients should be confined in environments that are the least restrictive alternative (an environment that permits the greatest freedom consistent with their condition in terms of personal security and the safety of others). Thus, some individuals might be able to live in group homes or board-and-care facilities in the community, where they have supervision but also some freedom, whereas only patients who would be considered to be a threat to themselves or others would be confined in more restrictive facilities such as mental hospitals. Within hospitals, some patients might require locked wards or restraints only when necessary to reduce harm to themselves or others.

Right to Refuse Treatment

Many states now require that patients (or their legal guardians) be fully informed of the treatment they will receive and sign *informed consent* statements that outline the nature of the treatments intended, the side effects, expected benefits, and the alternative treatments available. Patients also can *refuse* treatment, which typically refers to physical treatment such as medication. This might seem paradoxical, but U.S. courts have established that the right to obtain treatment does not require a person to accept treatment. However, if the person is judged to be legally incompetent to make a judgment or to pose a threat to himself or herself or others, the refusal may be overridden when reviewed by court-mandated procedures. Not surprisingly, studies have shown that when patients refuse treatment, it is usually due to the illness itself — denial of having a problem, delusions, grandiosity, or hostility (e.g., Hoge et al., 1990). Nevertheless, this is an important safeguard against some of the worst treatment excesses of the past.

make sure that clinicians at least make all reasonable efforts to collect relevant information about dangerousness and make as good an effort as possible to take suitable precautions (Monahan, 1993). In any case, the *Tarasoff* and related legal decisions appear to impose some limits on what can remain private in psychotherapy, and they require therapists to take some measure of responsibility for the safety of nonpatients.

CONSUMERS' RIGHTS AND THERAPISTS' RESPONSIBILITIES

For any product or service, the more you know, the more you can understand what you can reasonably expect from it and what you should buy. For therapy, the basic ingredients of good service are not difficult to describe in

principle: The therapy adheres to the standards of appropriate treatment based on current scientific knowledge, is administered by a properly trained and licensed person, and is conducted in a manner that maintains the welfare of the client. With psychotherapy, however, the process is usually private and unfamiliar to people, and there is a confusing array of therapies and therapists. The average person has little access to the information needed to judge whether the essential ingredients are present. In this section, we discuss what the public should know about selecting a therapist, as well as the standards of ethical conduct that might help judge whether clients' interests are being served.

When to Go for Therapy

People often wonder, "When do I know if I need help, or if someone close to me does?" If one is seriously mentally ill and out of touch with reality or is suffering greatly, he or she should seek help. But treatment also may be appropriate in three additional situations:

1. *The experience of persisting or recurring distress.* Distress that lasts for a long time or keeps recurring is a good indication that a person should consider assistance. If excessive worries, fears, depression, low self-esteem, and the like continue, they undermine satisfaction and personal peace and likely impair functioning.

2. *The impairment of the ability to carry out important roles* (such as student, employee, friend, romantic partner, or parent). If emotional distress or behaviors impede effective functioning, this is a strong clue to seek help.

3. *Uncertainty about goals, the presence of vague dissatisfaction, feelings that something is missing, or the experience of a traumatic event.* Sometimes people just want to become more self-aware, to grow, or to make sense of their experiences. Now more than ever before, there is greater acceptance of psychotherapy not only for those who need it but also as a tool for self-understanding and personal improvement. Or people may experience a very difficult or traumatic event and find therapy helpful for understanding and integrating the event and its meaning.

Another question that people sometimes ask is, "Why go to therapy when I can just talk to my friends?"

WHAT'S NORMAL?

Social Support and Therapy: Same or Different?

"Friendships are good medicine" was a slogan used in some schools to encourage children's social participation and to acknowledge the value of friendships. And indeed, turning to friends (and family) during difficulties is not only normal but helpful as well. Indeed, there are common-sense alternatives to psychotherapy, and their importance and effectiveness should not be ignored. People commonly and effectively cope with adversity by seeking comfort, support, and advice from friends and family members; this is called **social support**. Typically, the sense of being understood, encouraged, and cared about bolsters our strength and resolve to get through difficult times.

Considerable research confirms several common-sense notions: Supportive relationships with other people help reduce psychological symptoms and even physical symptoms in the face of stressors, and the absence of supportive or confiding relationships with other people may increase symptoms when stress is encountered (Brown & Harris, 1978; Cohen & Wills, 1985). Social support also can help prevent relapse among people who have recovered from depression (Sherbourne, Hays, & Wells, 1995). Furthermore, the absence of, or loss of, close relationships with others actually may constitute a stressor and lead to symptoms of distress. Or, as James Coyne and Geraldine Downey

Sixteen students and five adult chaperones from Montoursville, Pennsylvania, were on a field trip to France when their TWA Flight 800 exploded. Whether grieving for classmates — or facing other tribulations — support from friends provides comfort and assurance. Ultimately, we all get by — with a little help from our friends.

Figure 18.1   Use of Friends and Family as a Treatment Resource by Diagnostic Category

Multisite epidemiological survey data were obtained on the extent to which adults sought different kinds of services to deal with psychological symptoms, substance abuse, or emotional distress. Of all those who reported some kind of help, use of friends or family ranged from about 10 percent for those with schizophrenia to nearly 30 percent for those with unipolar depression or alcohol-use disorder.

Source: Regier et al. (1993).

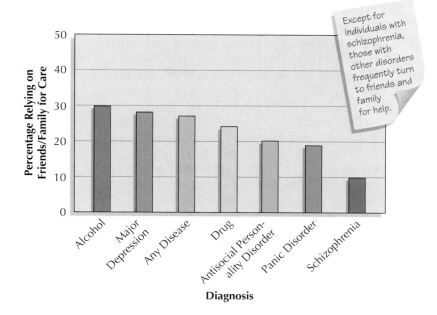

Except for individuals with schizophrenia, those with other disorders frequently turn to friends and family for help.

(1991) have argued, being married to a spouse with whom one cannot talk during periods of turmoil actually may contribute to psychological symptoms.

The perception that talking to one's friends is useful was demonstrated in a study by British researcher Vicky Rippere (1977a, 1977b). She asked normal volunteers, "What does common sense say is the thing to do when you're feeling depressed?" The open-ended replies were tallied. The most frequently mentioned response was, "See people, a friend." Respondents also provided other antidepressive suggestions, such as keeping active and doing something enjoyable.

To what extent do people with psychological disorders report seeking help with their problems from their family and friends? A survey asked people if they turned to various services specifically for help with mental or addictive symptoms or emotional distress. Results indicated that 3.5 percent of the adult U.S. population said that they sought such help from friends or family in a one-year period (Regier et al., 1993). Figure 18.1 shows the rates of use of friends and family among those with different disorders who reported this or any form of treatment.

Thus, friends and family may provide help for those suffering from diagnosable disorders, substance abuse, and various problems in living. However, does this mean that friendship and professional treatment are equally effective? How are friendships and psychotherapeutic relationships different? The first question is difficult to answer because systematic studies have not been done in which patients are randomly assigned to treatment or to their friends. (Although "no-treatment" control groups may in fact resort to their support networks, such controls rarely improve at the same rate as actively treated patients.) We can probably safely say, however, that mild problems — especially those experienced by otherwise normal and well-functioning people — can be greatly helped by supportive relations with other people. Severe and chronic problems, however, may actually prove to be a great burden to the social supports, as we discuss in chapters on schizophrenia, mood disorders, and cognitive impairment, and may even contribute to stressful circumstances that trigger relapses.

The distinction between mild and severe problems highlights one of the most obvious differences between talking to friends or family and to psychotherapists, despite some obvious parallels. A therapist has special training in how to deal with severe problems, including the ability to maintain a professional neutrality that helps encourage personal responsibility by the patient while keeping the therapist from being overwhelmed by the patient's problems. Moreover, therapists are expected to be unconditionally accepting of the person and able to be relatively objective about the patient and his or her circumstances. Family and friends may be loving but are rarely totally uncritical, and they are usually unwilling or unable to view the patient objectively and free from the influence of their own needs, circumstances, and biases. Nor are they able to act in the best interests of the patients at all times, even if they knew what those interests are. Thus, therapy is a very special kind of relationship, sharing some of the caring, supportive, and good-advice aspects of a friendship but able to offer special expertise and professionalism that friend and family relationships cannot provide.

Choosing a Therapist

Consumers are not expected to be up to date on the latest scientific information about what treatment works and what does not, but their therapists are supposed to know this information. Consumers should ask questions about the types of procedures a therapist intends to use and what criteria will be used for determining the method's effectiveness.

In most states, individuals are not supposed to call themselves therapists or conduct psychotherapy or charge fees for service unless they are licensed to practice in the specialty for which they have received training. Sadly, however, there are numerous violations of the rules, and some states grant considerable freedom for people to consider themselves therapists and charge fees. *Licensure* is a potential protection for consumers and requires completion of a special course of training in an approved institution, completion of a certain number of hours of delivery of service under the supervision of licensed professionals, and completion of examinations. (In Chapter 1, Table 1.3 summarizes several of the major kinds of professional degrees associated with treatment of mental disorders and the education and characteristics of each.)

If choice is available, how does someone select the right therapist for herself, himself, or a family member? For most people, financial considerations are a major factor. To reduce costs, one may seek help in a public facility such as a community mental health agency or a university-based clinic. At these facilities the client may not have many choices because the staff is assigned according to availability. For those with financial resources or insurance coverage, the choices may include therapists in private practice. If the question arises as to the need for medication, a psychiatrist is likely to be consulted. Many therapists collaborate with psychiatrists when both psychotropic medication and psychotherapy are indicated. If psychotherapy is the primary goal, various practitioners are available, with varying fees, training, experience, and orientation. Certainly, some theoretical orientations have a much better empirical track record than others, and a prospective client would do well to ask if there is evidence that the proposed therapy works for his or her problem.

What about personal characteristics of a therapist? Because the effectiveness of therapy depends on the client's trusting and cooperating with the therapist — and therapy is more effective when the quality of the relationship is positive (e.g., Blatt, Zuroff, Quinlan, & Pilkonis, 1996) — it is important to consider personal characteristics. Would a person's comfort be increased by working with a male or female therapist, one who is ethnically similar or different, or one who has other characteristics (for example, older, feminist, gay or lesbian, physically challenged)? Today we recognize that similarity of gender and also ethnicity are among the factors that might increase client comfort and possibly facilitate the process of successful treatment. At the very least, someone who is trained and sensitive to gender and cultural issues might be more effective (e.g., Yutrzenka, 1995).

Maintaining the Client's Welfare: Ethical Conduct

It is not enough for a therapist to be well trained and skilled; in addition, the therapist must meet the **ethical standards** of the profession, the written principles of appropriate professional values and behaviors. Determining these standards becomes ever more complex in a rapidly changing world.

Some Basic Ethical Standards   Therapists must know and adhere to many ethical standards. Each professional group sets its own guidelines. Here are several standards adopted by the American Psychological Association:

1. *Confidentiality.* Therapists must maintain the client's privacy except in certain instances specified by law, as we discuss earlier. This means making certain that information about the person's identity and what is disclosed in therapy are kept secret. Only with the specific consent of the client can information be given to insurance companies, schools, employers, and the like. For example, a therapist cannot reveal that someone is a client, discuss a client in a social conversation, leave files around where the janitor can read them, or write an article about a case that would reveal the identity of the client. Confidentiality also means that a family member cannot get information about a client's treatment from the therapist: A wife cannot find out what a husband is doing, and the parent of a college student cannot find out what the child is talking about in treatment (only when the child is a minor does the parent have a right to such information). In these and countless other ways, the therapist must provide a secure and private place for disclosure.

2. *Informed consent.* Individuals should be fully informed about procedures before they agree to them. In psychotherapy, this means that the therapist ought to tell a prospective client what to expect in the intended therapy, how long it will take, possible risks, and alternative methods.

3. *Competence.* Therapists cannot perform services beyond the boundaries of their competence (ability to perform effectively), based on training, education, supervision, or experience. A person trained, for example, in pastoral counseling cannot do psychotherapy, nor can a hypnotherapist perform psychotherapy. Relatedly, therapists may not misrepresent themselves or what they do. Also, therapists are supposed to maintain their expertise by staying aware of and properly trained in new developments in the field.

Deborah saw an ad for a correspondence course in hypnotherapy and eagerly enrolled to fulfill her quest to find a career to supplement the family income. Within weeks, she began to advertise in the local paper, claiming that hypnotherapy could help people control their weight, improve self-esteem, and relax. When people consulted her, she had no training in careful evaluation of their problems, nor the ability to determine whether they might need some other kind of treatment. She applied hypnotherapy no matter what, and as a result of news articles she read, she expanded her work to include "memory recovery" for people with possible past histories of incest. Within no time she had several clients convinced that they could now recall childhood sexual abuse through hypnotic techniques. Her claims are at best a potential misuse of clients' money but at worst might cause grave damage to individuals and their families.

Sarah was about thirty years old and recently divorced when she first started therapy with Dr. Jones. She was depressed, lonely, and discouraged, and as she poured out her sadness, fears, and self-recriminations, Dr. Jones consoled her. Over a period of weeks, his comforting took the form of holding her hand when she wept or putting his arm around her and extending the therapy beyond its normal time limit. Eventually, he suggested that they meet for coffee afterward "so he could get to know her even better," and he began to tell her that she needed the comfort of a man and that her self-esteem would improve if she had a sexual relationship with him. Because she was vulnerable, she welcomed his attention and even the sexual contact. Only later, when she realized that the relationship was mainly serving his needs and not hers, did she end it. She felt bitter but also guilty, and now she has even more trouble trusting men and believing that she could be desirable to someone for herself as a person.

4. *Multiple relationships.* Therapists may not have any other relationships with clients outside the therapeutic relationship (multiple or **dual relationships**). This professional standard attempts to guard against exploitation of the client, to protect clients' welfare, and to encourage the therapist's objectivity. Thus, a therapist should not engage in business or other professional relationships, friendships, or social activities with clients. Such relationships are assumed to be inherently harmful to clients by causing conflicts of interest or by blurring the lines between therapeutic and nontherapeutic encounters. For instance, a therapist cannot serve as a psychotherapist for a nephew, on the assumption that being a family member pulls certain kinds of behaviors or values from the therapist that may be in conflict with the needs of the client. Similarly, a therapist cannot work on a screenplay with a client because the goals in one role might conflict with the needs of the client. In some communities it may be difficult for therapists to avoid running into clients at social or business events, but it is nonetheless essential to attempt to limit such contacts.

Certainly one of the most extreme and unacceptable forms of dual relationships is sex between the therapist and client; we discuss sexual contact in more detail because of the sensitivity of the issue.

Sexual Intimacy Between Therapist and Client

Because therapy occurs in privacy and secrecy, and because clients often come to see the therapist as wonderful, understanding, and accepting, the intimacy of therapy is unique and powerful. Sometimes clients wish to extend this intimacy into a romantic relationship, or the therapist takes advantage of the client's feelings. As a consequence, sexual intimacy may result.

Sexual contact between therapist and client is now explicitly prohibited by professional therapy organizations, and it is a felony crime in many states. Therapists' seducing or responding to the seductions of a client — both during therapy and after termination of treatment — is *always* wrong. It is assumed that such relationships are inherently exploitative because the client, by definition, is in a help-seeking role lacking equal power and status and may be unduly influenced by a therapist to act in ways not in her or his best interests. The revised *1993 Ethical Standards of Psychologists* suggests that therapists should never even be involved with former clients but indicates that a minimum two-year time limit should pass after termination of treatment before it is proper to consider a romantic relationship. That is, someone who develops a romantic interest in a client should terminate the treatment and not pursue the relationship — or at least avoid contact with the individual until a notable period of time has passed. Some have argued that there should *never* be a relationship due to the difference in "power," regardless of how much time has passed.

Obtaining accurate data about the extent and effects of sexual contact is difficult. In several national surveys of practicing therapists who are members of professional societies, between 1 and 12 percent of therapists (responding anonymously) reported that they had had sexual involvement (not necessarily intercourse) with client at some point in their career. A recent study clinical social workers found that 3.6 percent of m and 0.5 percent of female therapists had sex with a cl (Bernsen, Tabachnick, & Pope, 1994). This study reviewed eight national studies of therapists ove past ten years and generally found two sign trends: higher rates for male therapists and abo percent annual decrease in rates of offenses sinc

Fortunately, rates appear to be declining, possibly because of increased information and publicity, huge malpractice suits, and criminalization of the act (Pope, 1990).

If someone ever has reason to question the conduct of a psychotherapist, what should the person do? Most counties or states have professional organizations that can give information on ethical standards. All states have regulatory agencies controlling licensure that may investigate complaints, and all professional disciplines have national associations that receive and process complaints against members.

BARRIERS TO TREATMENT

The road to delivering mental health services to those in need is filled with obstacles. As we have seen throughout this book, there are many disorders that can be treated with methods proven to be effective, yet there is a constant effort and need to expand and improve our methods. In this section we discuss other treatment difficulties: barriers to mental health services in the form of financing and access to services, poor services for the severely mentally ill including deinstitutionalized patients and the mentally ill homeless, and services for minority groups.

Mental Health Financing and Access to Services

One of the greatest problems faced by the United States and most other nations is the gap between the number of people who need psychological treatment and the resources available to provide it. Although the public is more aware of mental health issues than ever before, only 28.5 percent of people with a disorder actually get help (Regier et al., 1993) (see Figure 18.2 for a display of the proportion of major disorders that receive treatment). This figure includes both professional *and* nonprofessional help such as friends, family, clergy, and self-help groups. Only about 25 percent had contact with any professional — including general medical doctors — for help with psychological or addictive disorders.

These figures show overall limited use of services. Perhaps even more dramatic is the evidence that the *most severely impaired people* — adults and children suffering from chronic psychological disorders and disorders that greatly interfere with daily living — are not receiving enough services. The National Advisory Mental Health Council (1993) estimated that 2.8 percent of the adult U.S. population (5 million persons) experience severe mental disorders in any given year. The cost of treating them is estimated to be $20 billion a year, and the social costs (lost productivity, burdens on families, costs to social service and the criminal justice systems) are an additional $74 billion per year. An additional 3.2 percent of the child and adolescent population is impaired with similar disorders. Yet only 62 percent of the *severely* mentally ill adults and a far smaller percentage of children received services (National Advisory Mental Health Council, 1993).

Why — despite relatively helpful treatments and staggering social costs — are people not getting help for even major disorders? The primary problem is money. Public funding is woefully inadequate, and private inpatient facilities increasingly turn away chronic patients

Figure 18.2 Proportion of Individuals with Specific Mental or Addictive Disorders Treated in a One-Year Period

Data taken from the multisite epidemiological study have indicated that only a fraction of people who have certain disorders receive treatment within a one-year period. Treatment is defined as specifically seeking help for psychological or addiction problems at clinics or hospitals, general medical visits, contact with human service professionals (clergy, counselors, therapists) or support networks (friends, family, self-help groups). Those who received treatment averaged fourteen visits per year. Even some of the more severe disorders such as schizophrenia and bipolar disorder had large percentages of people who did not seek (or receive) treatment.

Source: Regier et al. (1993, adapted from Table 3); also Narrow et al. (1993).

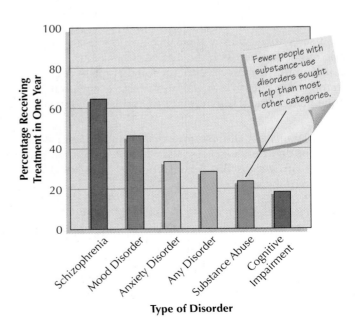

because of lack of insurance coverage. Mental health coverage by insurance is limited, and often, those who cannot afford insurance at all have the most need for mental health coverage (Norquist & Wells, 1991).

Even for those fortunate enough to have insurance, there have been dramatic changes in insurance coverage in recent years pressured by companies' desire to cut costs. One barrier to treatment stems from **managed care**, the process of limiting treatment by pre-review and authorization of a designated amount of treatment. Figure 18.3 shows the results of a study of inpatient treatment in managed care, demonstrating the significant tendency for insurance carriers to fund fewer treatment days than clinicians request (Wickizer, Lessler, & Travis, 1996). Another consequence of changes in insurance coverage for mental health services is that many individuals join *health maintenance organizations* or managed care providers that charge *copayments* for outpatient visits. One study of the effects of copayments demonstrated that the institution of a $20 fee for outpatient psychotherapy visits resulted in a 16 percent decrease in use of services (Simon et al., 1996). In effect, the fee reduced access to treatment, even among those who had insurance. Moreover, it affected people with all levels of severity of disorder; even those in severe need were unable to get access due to the increased financial cost.

Together, the shrinking services available are particularly a problem for the poor and disadvantaged and those with chronic mental illnesses. Other groups whose needs have not been met adequately are children and adolescents, the elderly, and those living in rural areas. Fortunately, during the past decade, federal and local legislation has attempted to increase services for these groups (DeLeon et al., 1989; Newman, Griffin, Black, & Page, 1989; Smyer, 1989). In the sections to follow we discuss the specific problem of deinstitutionalization and two underserved populations with special needs who have begun to attract increased attention: the mentally ill homeless and members of minority groups.

Deinstitutionalization

As we note earlier, there has been a massive movement throughout the United States toward **deinstitutionalization** of the mentally ill, or the movement of people out of large mental hospitals and back into their communities. From a peak in the 1950s, when state mental hospitals held more than half a million people, less than 130,000 were housed in such facilities by the late 1980s (see Figure 18.4). Extensive loss of freedom, often inadequate treatment, poor conditions, and the detrimental effects of long-term institutionalization were all among the reasons for eliminating many state hospitals. This trend was pushed on by landmark court decisions that identified and addressed violations of patients' rights (as noted in Table 18.1) and by 1963 federal legislation, the Mental Retardation Facilities and Community Mental Health Center Construction Act. As an alternative to

Figure 18.3 Requests and Approvals for Initial Inpatient Stays

The records of a large insurance company representing nearly one million people in forty-seven states were examined for requests for authorization of psychiatric inpatient services. The investigators determined that while nearly all requests were approved, on average, only about one-third of the days that clinicians wanted for the treatment of their patients were approved. These patterns also appear to be true of *outpatient* services, and therapists often complain bitterly that individual patient needs are seemingly disregarded in favor of limiting insurance coverage.

Source: Wickizer, Lessler & Travis (1996).

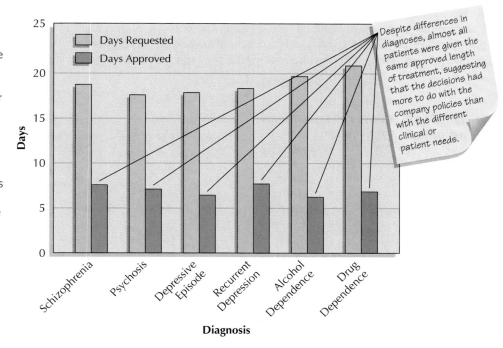

Despite differences in diagnoses, almost all patients were given the same approved length of treatment, suggesting that the decisions had more to do with the company policies than with the different clinical or patient needs.

Deinstitutionalization attempted to eliminate many of the ills of mental hospitalization, such as warehousing, poor treatment, and loss of dignity and rights. Unfortunately, however, the alternative services for the severely mentally ill have not been able to meet the tremendous needs of this population, sometimes resulting in homelessness and undue burdens on families.

long-term hospitalization, the federal legislation provided for treatment centers to be built in local communities where patients could receive care (including brief hospitalization if necessary) and be reintegrated into their own familiar environments.

Unfortunately, despite success in achieving deinstitutionalization, the *outcome* for the mentally ill has been bleak. Many communities failed to provide services sufficient to provide for care of the mentally ill after deinstitutionalization, or they later curtailed services. Moreover, most communities do not provide the array of outpatient services needed by those who are not presently severely ill but require crisis interventions or short-term counseling. The decline in support for large

custodial hospitals was supposed to be replaced by services in communities such as residential care, halfway houses, day treatment, crisis intervention, outpatient services, occupational rehabilitation, and case management. *Case management* refers to coordination of total care sufficient to provide for housing, supervision, and vocational and self-management skills to help patients live comfortable and useful lives. Unfortunately, despite successful efforts in some regions, most communities have not been able to fulfill such needs for the chronically mentally ill.

Changes in the funding of psychiatric facilities have compounded the problems of deinstitutionalization. One problem has been that government entities try to

Figure 18.4   Census of State Mental Institutions, 1950–1988

ates of institutionalization for mental health blems have declined markedly in the since community mental health reform re passed. Although less dramatic, ionalization has also progressed for d in hospitals for mental

k (1992).

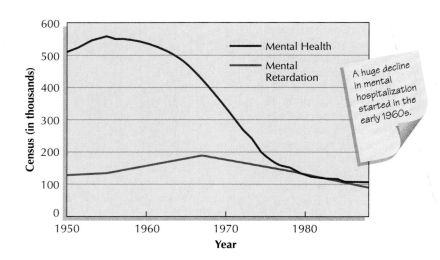

A huge decline in mental hospitalization started in the early 1960s.

shift the costs to each other — for example, from local to state or state to federal — resulting in inadequate resources. Another funding difficulty has been a widespread shift throughout medicine toward "**privatization**" of health care — or the movement away from public funding and nonprofit facilities toward for-profit ownership of hospitals and emphasis on the business aspects of health care. Twenty years ago, 95 percent of psychiatric hospital beds were in the public sector; currently, less than 50 percent are government owned (Dorwart et al., 1991). Why does this matter? Compared with private hospitals, public hospitals are significantly more likely to take and treat schizophrenic patients; privately owned hospitals treat more patients with depression (Dorwart et al., 1991). These figures suggest that private facilities are specializing in disorders that usually respond to short-term treatment, leaving the more chronic cases to public facilities. Moreover, because of the sheer numbers of chronically ill patients and inadequate funding, public psychiatric facilities have far fewer professional staff members per patient. In addition, the for-profit facilities are less likely to engage in unprofitable community-oriented activities such as crisis telephone lines or emergency services, further burdening public resources. Thus, despite positive intentions, the reality of deinstitutionalization has been far from satisfactory.

Mentally Ill Homeless

Researchers have estimated that about one-half to three-fourths of the homeless in the United States suffer from alcohol or drug abuse or mental illness, and many suffer from various combinations of problems (Fischer & Breakey, 1991). For instance, rates of alcohol problems are estimated to be six or seven times greater among the homeless than in the general population (Fischer & Breakey, 1991). Severe mental illness is common; several studies have found that 10 to 13 percent of the homeless are schizophrenic, 21 to 29 percent have mood disorders, and 14 to 20 percent have antisocial personality disorders (Fischer & Breakey, 1991; Koegel, Burnam & Farr, 1988). Somewhat similar patterns were observed in Melbourne, Australia, where 21 percent were found to have psychotic disorders, 49 percent had substance-use disorders, and 25 percent had mood disorders (some people had multiple diagnoses)(Herrman et al., 1989).

Deinstitutionalization of mental health services has doubtless contributed to the numbers of **mentally ill homeless**. Many of these people might have been institutionalized for long periods in the past, but currently there are fewer provisions for their shelter and care. Researchers have estimated that the majority of the chronically mentally ill live in inadequate housing or are

homeless. Many are poor, and because of their debilities, they cannot compete for jobs; without active rehabilitation, they may lack the skills and supports needed for successful community living (Carling, 1990). Their overburdened families may be unable to support them financially, or their mental problems may lead to discrimination by landlords who would prefer to rent to non-ill persons. Also, affordable housing has greatly diminished in the past few decades. For all these reasons, the mentally ill may end up without housing.

Nevertheless, deinstitutionalization cannot be blamed for all the problems of the mentally ill homeless. For one thing, most mentally ill persons do not become homeless. What factors predict or contribute to homelessness in the mentally ill? Several studies have now suggested that disrupted early family lives, foster care placement, and domestic violence predict homelessness (Shinn, Knickman, & Weitzman, 1991; Susser, Lin, Conover, & Struening, 1991; Wood, Valdez, Hayashi, & Shen, 1990). When coupled with severe economic hardship and lack of affordable housing, a failure to live successfully with others — or an absence of supportive family members — may contribute to risk for homelessness.

One group at great risk for mental health problems is children of homeless mothers — especially those of mothers with mental disorders.

FAMILY MATTERS
Children of Homeless Mentally Ill Mothers

A generation ago most homeless people were male, but nowadays families with children make up a large segment of the homeless population and in some cities account for more than half the homeless population. Many of these families are single women with children — perhaps abandoned or even forgotten by the fathers of the children. A large proportion of homeless mothers suffer from mental disorders. A recent study of 110 homeless mothers living in shelters found that more than half of them reported high levels of psychological distress; 21 percent were estimated to have suffered from a severe mental illness (major depression or psychosis), and 25 percent suffered from substance abuse. Overall, 72 percent had either significant current distress or a lifetime diagnosis of major disorder (Zima, Wells, Benjamin & Duan, 1996). Not only are many homeless women psychologically impaired, but also they themselves are frequently exposed to domestic violence in their own relationships and as children and came from homes where their parents abused drugs or alcohol (Wood et al., 1990). Unsurprisingly, these women often

Women with children have increasingly entered the ranks of the homeless. Many are fleeing domestic abuse or facing mental illness or substance use disorders. The children of homeless mentally ill parents may face a double challenge of disrupted lives and inadequate parenting.

had their first children in adolescence, were young and poorly educated (e.g., Zima, Wells, Benjamin & Duan, 1996). They desperately may have wanted better lives for their children but are without resources to provide them.

Consider the impact of these conditions on the children's adjustment. Youngsters are exposed to the serious stress of having no home and unstable living conditions, poor access to schools and health services, and mothers who themselves may be mentally ill and have histories of their own exposure to poor parenting and few social resources. Thus, it is tragic but not surprising to learn that when these children are studied, they reveal significant problems. In the study by Zima, Wells, Benjamin, and Duan (1996), of 157 children who were examined, more than one-third displayed depression, and substantial proportions also had externalizing behavior problems. Children who had more severe symptoms were more likely to have mothers with disorders (depression, alcohol abuse, or schizophrenia) than children whose mothers did not have a disorder. Academic measures of children's reading and vocabulary showed that 40 percent or more were below the tenth percentile for their age — although such deficiencies occurred among the

children regardless of their mothers' mental health. Similar results were seen in a study of homeless mothers and their children in Minnesota (Masten, 1990) — homeless children had significantly elevated emotional and behavioral problem scores, considerably higher than those of poor but not homeless children. In addition, Masten found that mothers' own symptoms were significantly related to their children having higher symptom levels.

Unfortunately, few homeless mothers and their children receive mental health services. Zima and associates (1996) found that only 15 percent of the homeless mothers received mental health care despite their high rates of disorder. There is little information on children's use of mental health services. Clearly, the children of homeless mothers suffer from enormous exposure to situations that we have shown throughout the book to be risks for maladjustment. These include not only parental disorder but also family disruption, severe stressors including abuse, and low educational attainment. Without massive intervention, the outcomes for these children — and for their families down the line — are not difficult to predict.

Currently, the challenges of offering effective help to the mentally ill homeless are being faced in a variety of projects designed to experiment with different methods of delivering service and follow-up (Levine & Rog, 1990). Federal action generally has been limited compared with the magnitude of the problem, but efforts are underway to evaluate pilot projects to determine effective methods of addressing the problem of the homeless mentally ill.

Minority Status and Mental Health Treatment

As we discuss throughout the book, the meaning of psychological problems and their treatments varies from one segment of the society to another. Gender, age, and culture influence the expression of disorders, views of mental illness, and appropriate treatment. For example, as we discuss in Chapter 1, Asian Americans may be more likely than whites to believe that mental problems are caused by physical imbalances and that mental health is associated with will power, discipline, and positive attitudes. Accordingly, treatment seeking might suggest personal weakness and therefore be avoided.

Su-Yan, mentioned in the chapter opening, is a good friend of yours, a talented young Chinese American woman seeking an advanced degree in social work. She hopes to work in an Asian Pacific mental health center serving the vast immigrant population of her region. Ironically, however,

The United States, like most Western nations, is home to many cultural groups with different customs and values. Psychotherapy practices were originally developed by and for whites of European ancestry. It is a challenge to modify such practices, for example, for the needs of Alaskan Native Americans and Salvadoran immigrants and to help diverse groups feel comfortable in recognizing psychological problems and being willing to seek help for them.

despite her extensive coursework in psychological services and her personal belief that psychotherapy is worthwhile, she is unwilling to seek treatment herself. Her father died recently, her marriage has some difficulties, and she is upset and depressed — but she believes that she must be strong and overcome her emotional problems on her own. She also fears the disapproval of her family and friends if she sought help and revealed personal matters.

Different ethnic groups also may emphasize different values and standards of conduct. Thus, mental health services that do not recognize and respond appropriately to different attitudes and beliefs may present a barrier to effective treatment. In the following sections we explore the evidence for this barrier, and then we discuss some of the proposed solutions.

Use of Services   Studies of the use of community mental health services such as outpatient treatment are fairly consistent in showing differential rates by ethnic groups. For example, according to a review by Sue, Chun, and Gee (1995), Mexican Americans are significantly less likely than whites to use *outpatient* mental health services (that is, compared with actual rates of disorder, they use services proportionately less); Asian Americans also significantly **underutilize** services. African Americans appear to use outpatient mental health services at higher rates than whites. With respect to *inpatient* treatment for the most severe disorders, Figures

18.5 and 18.6 summarize the results of a large-scale national survey of hospitalization (Snowden & Cheung, 1990). The patterns are generally consistent with results from other surveys showing that African Americans and Native Americans are overrepresented and Hispanic and Asian American groups are underrepresented.

Examination of the different diagnoses by racial group has suggested several possible explanations (though no actual research to determine their accuracy). Groups may differ in their accepting attitudes toward treatment for specific disorders, thus affecting help seeking; individuals' and families' tolerance for different conditions might alter the rates of treatment seeking. Also, the ability and willingness of families to maintain a mentally ill relative in the community and knowledge of and access to different services also may affect rates of treatment of different disorders (Snowden & Cheung, 1990).

Responsiveness to Treatment   Whatever the rates of treatment for different groups, do ethnic groups differ in their rates of completing treatment or their rates of improvement? Some studies have found that ethnic minority patients tend to **drop out** of, or prematurely leave, treatment before it can be effective. In a large-scale survey of use and outcomes of mental health services in the multiethnic Los Angeles area, the percentage of African Americans who dropped out after only one visit was 19.4 percent; Mexican Americans, 14.6 percent; and Asian Americans, 10.7 percent — compared

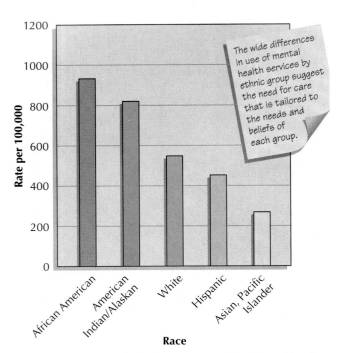

Figure 18.5 Admissions to Inpatient Psychiatric Services by Race

There are enormous differences in proportions by race of individuals treated as psychiatric inpatients. These differences reflect not only access to inpatient services by race, but also the tendencies of different groups to define a mental health problem as one requiring psychological treatment and their willingness to seek assistance for it.

Source: From Snowden & Cheung (1990).

with whites, 15.3 percent. Similarly, African Americans were likely to have fewer overall sessions and to improve less compared with other groups (Sue et al., 1991).

The rates of termination and success of treatment among different ethnic groups in the Los Angeles survey were significantly influenced by whether those providing mental health services are themselves members of ethnic minorities (Sue et al., 1991; Sue, Chun & Gee, 1995). Based on existing records of ethnically diverse patients and therapists (rather than a random assignment of clients to therapists of different kinds), the investigators examined the influence of matching of ethnic minority therapist and the effect of matching of language and gender. In general, results indicated that **ethnic matching,** pairing clients and therapists of the same ethnicity, was associated with lower dropout rates and higher numbers of treatment sessions for Asian American and Mexican American clients. Language match, for those whose primary language was not English, was additionally a positive predictor of treatment outcome. Ethnic match was not, however, associated with numbers of sessions and outcomes for African American clients.

Overall, the real need, as Stanley Sue (1992) pointed out, is for *cultural sensitivity* on the part of therapists whatever their own ethnicity and cultural background — that is, an awareness of different cultural values and customs that affect individuals' behaviors and expectations. One step toward promoting such understanding is increased training of minority therapists or training non-minority therapists how to work with minority clients (Sue, Chun & Gee, 1995; Yutrzenka, 1995).

Another needed step is to tailor services to the needs of certain groups. Accordingly, many communities are attempting to provide services that display cultural sen-

Figure 18.6 Percentages of Diagnoses in State and County Mental Hospitals by Race, 1980

Often serving the low-income residents of a community, state and county mental hospitals tended to admit mostly patients with schizophrenia and alcohol-use disorders. Despite similarities in the most frequently diagnosed disorders in these facilities, the racial groups differed considerably in proportions of patients with specific diagnoses.

Source: Snowden & Cheung (1990).

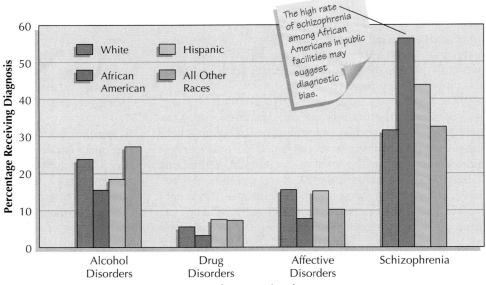

sitivity — including ethnic staff members or those trained to be aware of cultural values and beliefs and reaching out to particular communities. Such programs, for example, have been shown to be effective in reaching severely mentally ill Asian American patients in San Francisco (Lee, 1985), African Americans, African Caribbeans, Cubans and Puerto Ricans in Miami (Bestman, 1986), and Southeast Asian refugees in the San Francisco Bay area (Gong-Guy, Cravens, & Patterson, 1991). Sometimes called *parallel* programs, these ethnic-specific services may work even better than mainstream programs. For example, a recent survey of outcomes of Asian American children who were treated in either ethnic-specific agencies and programs compared with standard community agencies serving mostly white populations found that Asian American youngsters were less likely to drop out and had better outcomes at discharge than those treated in mainstream programs (Yeh, Takeuchi, & Sue, 1994).

Finally, a critical need is for evaluation of ethnic group differences in treatment outcome programs. Unfortunately, minorities have been severely underrepresented in psychotherapy studies, so our appraisal of the effectiveness of those programs truly can be generalized only to white subjects. Accordingly, the National Institutes of Health recently mandated that all research funded by that agency must include minority and female populations in the research (e.g., Hohmann & Parron, 1996). Research in health services, both medical and mental health, must be designed in such a way as to clarify what services and treatments provide benefit to members of different ethnic and gender groups. Eventually, therefore, we may come closer to our goal of determining whether certain types of psychological treatments work better with different groups.

ALTERNATIVES TO TRADITIONAL MENTAL HEALTH TREATMENTS

As we note throughout this text, talk-based and medication treatments have several important limitations: They are inappropriate to or unwanted by segments of the population, they are limited in availability and effectiveness, and they are costly. We also consider two broad alternative approaches: One is to try to prevent the development of problems in the first place — a strategy we discuss in the next section. The other approach is to try to build on people's natural coping strategies to deal with psychological problems.

As we mention earlier, friends and family provide a natural support system for many individuals suffering from behavioral or emotional problems. We might add

that talking to one's clergy, teachers, or others in counseling or authority positions may provide additional social support. Perhaps the next step beyond getting support from friends is getting support from self-help groups and from nonprofessionals. In this section we consider these two alternatives to traditional mental health treatment, plus the issues of mental health marketing.

Self-Help Groups and Self-Care Programs

One of the most dramatic recent developments in alternative treatments is the proliferation of **self-help groups**, or groups of individuals who are united by common experience and meet to receive mutual aid and to share information and strategies for coping (Jacobs & Goodman, 1989). These groups are free of charge (or have nominal fees) and member-governed, typically without professional leadership.

The growing importance of self-help groups is indicated by their inclusion in a recent analysis of all mental health service utilization in the United States. Darrel Regier and his colleagues at the National Institute of Mental Health (1993) reported that in a one-year period

more than one million people used self-help groups for mental or addictive disorders. Analyzing the data from the point of view of the diagnoses of people who sought different treatments, 5.2 percent of people with any diagnosable disorder or addiction went to self-help groups (Narrow et al., 1993).

Self-help groups cover an extraordinarily broad range of problems, and hundreds of different groups exist, from **twelve-step programs** based on practicing twelve central tenets for change, such as Alcoholics Anonymous (AA) and those based on the AA model, to those dealing with rare problems. They reach out to people with all serious medical problems and who have experienced many severe stressful events such as parents of deceased children (e.g., Reif, Patton, & Gold, 1995), survivors of the Holocaust, caregivers for Alzheimer's patients, or incest survivors. Support groups exist for persons dealing with lifestyle issues and gender, race, or sexual orientation (for example, Parents and Friends of Lesbians and Gays and groups for widows, the divorced, and single mothers).

The twelve-step programs, based on incorporating a series of principles for healthy living into daily life, have proliferated well beyond their initial development in Alcoholics Anonymous, founded in 1935. Originally most were alcohol-related, such as Al-Anon for family members of alcoholics. Now, however, they include not only various drug habits (nicotine, cocaine) but also overeating, gambling, workaholics, sexaholics, and those raised in dysfunctional families. A recent representative national survey determined that 13.3 percent of all U.S. adults at one time had attended a twelve-step program (5.3 percent in the past year)(Room & Greenfield, 1993). The popularity of these groups may stem in part from the inadequacy of traditional mental health services. However, many members view their group not as an affordable alternative to psychotherapy but as the treatment of choice. Despite vast differences in philosophy, twelve-step programs may share important behavior change principles with cognitive-behavioral interventions (e.g., McCrady, 1994).

Janet could probably afford individual psychotherapy if she wanted to, but she actually prefers the advice and support that she gains from attending weekly meetings of Al-Anon, a twelve-step program that includes but is not limited to relatives of alcoholics. She recognizes that the men in her life, including her current husband, have been irresponsible and abusive — and that she felt she had to put up with it. By listening to other people "share" their experiences and what they have learned about their own ineffective as well as constructive efforts to cope, she feels better able to evaluate her relationship issues realistically and put some of her own needs first instead of automatically deferring to the needs of her husband. Going to the group regularly helps her avoid slipping back into habitual patterns that usually leave her feeling miserable and angry.

Are self-help groups effective in reducing psychological impairment or improving adaptive coping? In general, the few reviews of existing studies suggest that they are indeed helpful in terms of reducing distress or improving functioning (Christensen & Jacobson, 1994; Lieberman, 1986; Levine, Toro & Perkins, 1993). Thus, self-help groups offer a great deal to individuals who might not profit from traditional treatment or who might never seek treatment. They represent a welcome addition to resources for improving psychological adjustment under adverse conditions. They are not a complete alternative to professional interventions, however, because they have limitations. People with major psychological problems may not receive sufficient help, and the groups might work best for those already functioning relatively well.

Self-directed treatments also have been explored as an inexpensive alternative to therapy (Christensen & Jacobson, 1994). For example, numerous studies have shown that self-directed smoking cessation treatments can be helpful, especially if supplemented with occasional telephone counseling sessions or support groups (e.g., Jason et al., 1995; Zhu et al., 1996). One study demonstrated that a treatment for the eating disorder bulimia that included self-care manuals for eight weeks followed by cognitive-behavioral treatment with a therapist did as well as standard cognitive-behavioral therapy (Treasure, Schmidt, Troop, & Todd, 1996). Media-delivered treatments may also prove helpful; one study showed that regular television programs concerning weight loss were as helpful to those trying to lose weight as actual live-contact groups (e.g., Meyers, Graves, Whelan, & Barclay, 1996). Thus, manuals and media may provide useful and cost-effective interventions for some kinds of behavior change programs, although their use with more severe mental health problems has not been demonstrated.

Nonprofessionals and Paraprofessionals

Yet another alternative in natural social supports are those people who share our circumstances or who are somewhat like us but who may have some formal training in dealing with psychological problems. Underserved ethnic populations, for instance, might be reached by specially trained, ethnically similar community residents with whom they might feel more comfortable talking. Recently widowed women might join a group led by a trained nonprofessional who herself was widowed, and high-school students at risk for dropout might be counseled by a student from their neighborhood. Not all nonprofessionals, or **paraprofessionals** as they are sometimes called, are similar to their constituents, however. College student and housewife volunteers, for example, frequently have been trained to serve as crisis counselors or telephone hot-line counselors.

A common ingredient in these kinds of contacts is that the nonprofessionals are similar enough in status or demographic features to those in need that they can provide an understanding and availability that might not be present with highly trained middle-class professionals. The nonprofessional might be perceived as an understanding friend or mentor who provides support and practical advice rather than psychotherapy. Their training is focused on the specific needs of their intended clientele and is limited to very specific goals.

Do nonprofessionals actually help? Reviews of studies comparing the two groups of therapists generally have concluded that paraprofessionals are at least as effective — and sometimes more so — than professionals (e.g., Christensen & Jacobson, 1994; Weisz et al., 1995). Whether — and how much — training is important remains a matter of controversy. On the whole, however, it seems that for many applications, well-trained and experienced nonprofessionals can provide effective help and at considerable savings.

The Marketing of Mental Health

No section on alternatives to psychotherapy would be complete without noting the proliferation of commercial activities aimed at improving mental health. It is hard to turn on the television in the daytime or the radio in a big city without encountering "Dr. So and So," whose soothing voice and pointed comments sound like what you might imagine psychotherapy to be like. You hear strangers reveal intimate details of their lives and feelings, and you hear the host dispense psychological interpretations and advice. Is this therapy?

No, it's not really therapy; it's entertainment. In one or two minutes it is impossible to establish a personal relationship and gather sufficient information to make informed professional judgments or to follow through on them. Viewers and listeners are not eavesdropping on something like therapy. Callers and participants are not forming a personal relationship with the talk show host, and what is offered is not a substitute for treatment.

Perhaps you will learn something helpful by listening. Perhaps it is useful to find out that other people have issues similar to the ones that bother you. These kinds of programs have many potential benefits if they raise public awareness of psychological issues and demystify the help-seeking process. Nevertheless, probably only the best and most carefully produced of the shows inform callers of the limits of this type of intervention and make appropriate referrals of individuals if they seem to truly need professional help.

The risk of such talk shows is that they trivialize people's problems and the process of exploring them, condensing life's more painful conflicts and dilemmas into catchy phrases and pungent one-liners. In effect, they may exploit people's vulnerability and need for help in the name of entertainment. The dangers of such programs need to be spelled out: People are not getting professional advice or therapy, the talk show host's goal is not to understand them or even to help them as much as it is to provide entertainment, and callers might get poor or harmful advice, given the unknown complexities of their unique circumstances, and listeners might end up believing that life's difficulties are simpler than they are. Finally, a few individuals might have such a negative experience with the program that it adversely affects their attitudes toward psychotherapy so that they might not seek professional help if they need it. Or, after attempting to follow the advice and finding that it does not work, the person might become more discouraged and worse off than before.

Many of the same advantages and disadvantages also apply to the burgeoning field of self-help tapes, books, and seminars. On the one extreme, some products were designed by people with no training whatever in psychotherapy or psychology, whose sole interest was marketability, without a shred of interest in the usefulness of the materials. On the other extreme, many self-help books and manuals were written by prominent clinical psychologists and psychiatrists based on methods that, when applied by therapists, were shown to be effective in controlled studies.

These materials may provide information, and relevant information is often the foundation of effective coping. Sometimes the materials may provide useful techniques that, if implemented and practiced appropriately, can help reduce distress. Most of the marketed materials are intended for people with relatively mild problems, who can apply the techniques to their own lives without the aid of a therapist. Even if the writer intends such materials to be used by mildly disordered people, however, he or she has no control over who actually buys and attempts to use them. The additional disadvantages of these materials are the same we mention for talk show therapy, plus two additional ones: expense (costs of the products) and the possibility of indoctrination if consumers are induced to follow particular practices or adopt certain beliefs without evidence of their effectiveness in dealing with their problems.

No laws restrict publishers, producers, and seminar organizers beyond general consumer protection guidelines. The public may be ripped off by products that do not work, and trusting and unwary consumers may spend millions of dollars. Licensed mental health professionals are constrained by ethical and professional standards against offering or advertising services that make inappropriate claims. Yet even the best cases — such as

These youths are involved with Food from the Hood, a hands-on program that teaches at-risk kids about gardening and business. Participants produce, market, and sell their salad dressing. Not only do such positive, prevention-oriented programs help kids achieve useful business skills, but they also pay dividends in self-esteem and sense of purpose. Community efforts toward preventing youth problems can take many forms.

books based on methods that are effective when applied by a therapist — do not offer any reassurance that the product is effective when applied by the individual without the help of a therapist (Rosen, 1987).

Let the buyer beware.

PREVENTING PSYCHOLOGICAL DISORDERS

The numbers of people who need treatment — or children who are at risk for developing serious problems needing future treatment — are staggering. Researchers have estimated that 15 to 22 percent of the nation's 63 million children and adolescents have problems severe enough to need treatment (Costello, 1990; National Advisory Mental Health Council, 1990). But fewer than 20 percent of youngsters with current problems actually receive services (Tuma, 1989). Let's express the problem another way: Growing numbers of youth are engaging in severely risky behaviors that threaten their current and future well-being: drug abuse, teen pregnancy, exposure to AIDS, school drop out, and delinquency. Researchers have estimated that one-fourth of the 28 million ten- to seventeen-year-olds are at high risk for such behaviors, and another one-fourth are at moderate risk. Can you picture 7 to 14 million youngsters sitting down with counselors to discuss these problems and finding solutions?

The magnitude of these problems represents nothing less than a national emergency. There are not enough counselors and therapists, not enough money to pay them, not enough evidence that therapy would even work, and certainly not enough access to care for those who might need it the most.

What can be done? Some have proposed that *prevention* is the best hope. In this section we consider what is meant by prevention and what elements that contribute to disorders could serve as targets of preventive efforts. Finally, a few examples of preventive interventions are noted.

Defining Prevention

Traditionally, prevention of mental health problems has been defined by community psychologists in terms of levels, such as primary, secondary, and tertiary (e.g., Caplan, 1964). **Primary prevention** is eliminating or altering the conditions that give rise to problems or changing conditions so that the person will be able to resist the negative effects of risk conditions; it is the only true prevention in the sense of preventing the development of psychological difficulties. **Secondary prevention** is aimed at early detection and limiting the negative consequences once a problem has manifested itself, and **tertiary prevention** refers to controlling the long-term consequences of a chronic problem.

With respect to mental health, early detection (secondary prevention) is important to the extent that it leads to early intervention and therefore keeps difficulties from accumulating. For instance, if signs of early attention-deficit hyperactivity disorder (ADHD) or schizophrenia in young people could be detected before onset of the full-blown disorder, early treatment might prevent the academic and social impairments that contribute to a negative course. However, early detection requires both scientific information about the disorder and an educated public. For example, because many disorders are first manifested in childhood, parents and teachers need to be taught what to look for. And for early detection to be helpful, services must be available. Thus, although early detection is a worthwhile goal, its contributions are limited by the extent of knowledge, awareness, and services.

Primary prevention is even more limited. Two general approaches are possible. One is to ensure that the institutions of society contribute to healthy adjustment. Generally, we consider stable and effective families, good education, access to jobs, and safe and supportive neighborhood systems to have positive effects on development and maintenance of mental health. Thus, we might say that our politicians are in the business of primary prevention by supporting prosperity, peace and lawfulness, healthy environments, and stable communities. A second approach to primary prevention is to eliminate the conditions that put people at risk for developing disorders or to provide skills and resources to neutralize the risk and its impact. We turn to a brief discussion of high-risk conditions.

Targets for Prevention: Contributors to Psychological Disorders

Some of the fundamental roots of mental illness are in the social conditions of our communities. In particular, poverty and social adversity and family disruption can contribute both directly and indirectly to many preventable mental health problems because they are stressful and because they reduce the person's resources for coping with adverse conditions. This book emphasizes many intraindividual factors such as biological or psychological variables — presumed to cause psychological problems. The context of peoples' lives, however, provides an important determinant of the development of disorders among those at presumed risk.

Poverty, Social Adversity, and Mental Health   Epidemiological surveys have consistently found that people in lower socioeconomic status groups have higher rates of mental illness (e.g., Kessler et al., 1994; see also Dohrenwend et al., 1992). Considerable research into the origins of psychological abnormality also has identified **risk factors** (conditions that are significantly associated with the disorder and presumed to have causal significance) that are more frequent among the poor. Table 18.2 lists risk factors that investigators from diverse perspectives studying various psychological problems have identified as "generic" — that is, they are associated with many disorders and conditions of psychological impairment. Notice that many of these are directly associated with poverty or are compounded by poverty.

Table 18.3 presents data from a study on the *development* of disorders among the poor. Why are poverty and social disadvantage associated with greater risk for some psychological disorders? Clearly, it is not the lack of material things as such, because there is no evidence that poor nutrition or poor housing or lack of a car or a color television causes mental illness. Rather, the effect is apparently due to the stressfulness of the disadvantaged person's life. In other chapters we discuss evidence of an association between stressful life events and certain disorders such as depression, anxiety, and the timing of schizophrenic episodes. Poverty increases risk of exposure to stressors — for example, worrying about not having adequate housing and food, increased risk of crime, increased risk of physical illness because of less medical care and poor physical conditions, and increased likelihood of marital difficulties and separation because of strain. Individuals are also stressed by the greater difficulties that befall their family members and friends and may be additionally burdened by the needs of those others for material and emotional support. Similarly, racial discrimination exacerbates exposure to stress, both by being a source of stress and by contributing to poverty that increases stressors. Poverty not only increases exposure to such stressors but also reduces the individual's resources such as money, education, psychological strength, and stable friends and family — all factors that are helpful in coping with adversity.

Families and Mental Health   Another major contributor to mental illness is family dysfunction (again, refer to Table 18.2, and notice how many risk factors are associated directly or indirectly with quality of family functioning). This does not mean that a child has to have a mother and a father who are married to each other to have a chance at healthy psychological adjustment. The major ingredients are probably stable and healthy adult role models providing loving, supportive, consistent, and supervised care.

Numerous times in the book we discuss evidence that children exposed to stressful family conditions and to parental abuse, neglect, or rejection are at greater risk for psychological disorders than children from stable, loving, and effective families. This includes "crack" babies and those born with fetal alcohol syndrome, children of mentally ill mothers, homeless children, sexually

Table 18.2 Generic Risk Factors for Psychological Maladjustment

Family Circumstances	Skill Development Delays	Emotional Difficulties
Low social class	Subnormal intelligence	Child abuse
Family conflict	Social incompetence	Apathy or emotional blunting
Mental illness in the family	Attentional deficits	Emotional immaturity
Large family size	Reading disabilities	Stressful life events
Poor bonding to parents	Poor work skills and habits	Low self-esteem
Family disorganization		Emotional dyscontrol
Communication deviance	**Ecological Context**	
	Neighborhood disorganization	**Interpersonal Problems**
Constitutional Handicaps	Racial injustice	Peer rejection
Perinatal complications	Unemployment	Alienation and isolation
Sensory disabilities	Extreme poverty	
Organic handicaps		**School Problems**
Neurochemical imbalance		Academic failure
		Scholastic demoralization

Source: From Coie et al. (1993).

These conditions have been repeatedly identified by researchers as predictors of maladjustment. They are called generic risk factors because each may contribute to various kinds of disorders rather than to only one kind of problem. Moreover, multiple risk factors increase the likelihood of disorder. Notice that most factors are linked with poverty, either directly (unemployment, stressful life events, low social class) or indirectly (perinatal complications, family disorganization). That is, poverty is a direct cause or greatly exacerbates the effects of risk factors.

and physically abused youngsters, children from disrupted or high-conflict families, children of teenage mothers — and many more.

A Sampling of Preventive Efforts

Although there are many legitimate targets for preventive efforts, children represent a major focus because they are exceedingly vulnerable and because early difficulties usually pile up and affect the child's entire life. Here are some examples of different types of prevention.

One prevention example is early childhood education of a high-risk population. Especially when combined with parent involvement, it has long been viewed as a way to reduce educational and social disruption in high-risk youngsters. This is the premise of Head Start,

An epidemiological survey collected information on income and mental illness at two points in time six months apart. People below the poverty line but who were well at the first assessment were significantly more likely to have developed a disorder six months later (the risk ratio is the likelihood that someone below the poverty line developed a disorder during the follow-up compared with someone above the poverty line). Poverty was certainly not the only factor associated with disorder, but it was associated with a significant proportion of the new cases that were detected at the follow-up.

Table 18.3 Poverty and Increased Risk of Mental Illness

Disorder	Risk Ratio	Proportion of New Episodes Among Poor
Any Axis I disorder	1.82	6.0
Alcohol abuse or dependence	2.10	9.7
Bipolar disorder	2.15	11.3
Drug abuse or dependence	1.52	14.5
Major depression	2.06	10.4
Panic disorder	1.27	1.7
Schizophrenia	79.84	<1

Source: Adapted from Bruce, Takeuchi & Leaf (1991).

a program initiated by the federal government in the 1960s, targeted at preschool children of disadvantaged families. A major goal is to prepare these children and their parents for the child's entry into school by teaching basic school-readiness skills and attitudes. Numerous studies have shown that when these programs use well-trained teachers and developmentally appropriate curricula and also involve the parents, high-quality preschool programs bring long-term benefits. For instance, compared with children who do not participate in such programs, children in these programs are less likely to be retained in grades or to require special education; they are more likely to graduate from high school, have lower arrest rates and higher employment rates, and less use of welfare assistance (Weissberg, Caplan & Harwood, 1991). Lower-quality programs, however, do not succeed nearly so well.

Another example of prevention that is *selective* for a defined population focuses on those at risk for disorder because they have already begun to show "early warning signs." In a Canadian city, kindergarten teachers rated boys on *disruptiveness*, and disruptive boys were considered to be at risk for later antisocial conduct. A prevention treatment program consisted of home-based training for the parents that taught principles of positive reinforcement for desirable behavior and effective discipline procedures and a school-based social-skills component for the boys that focused on effective problem solving, conflict resolution, and self-control (Tremblay et al., 1995). The program lasted for two years, and then the boys were followed up to age fifteen. Compared with the untreated control boys, the youngsters in the prevention program displayed significantly less delinquent behavior, and therefore, the program appeared to be successful in its mission.

Another example of early intervention prevention is a program to reduce depressive symptoms in children.

Can We Prevent Depression in Children?

As we have seen, depression is a major public health issue, and there is ample evidence that it is becoming more of a problem among young people. Investigators have been eager to learn if depression can be prevented by programs aimed at reducing maladaptive skills and cognitions that are thought to create risk for developing depression. One of the largest programs was developed by Martin Seligman and his colleagues, called the Penn Prevention Program (Gillham, Reivich, Jaycox, & Seligman, 1995; Jaycox, Reivich, Gillham, & Seligman, 1994). It was aimed at ten- to thirteen-year-olds who were at risk because they had either depressive symptoms or exposure to marital or family conflict.

Prevention may be our best hope for dealing with many of the psychological and behavioral problems of children and adolescents. Prevention efforts may range from relatively simple efforts to alter attitudes by increasing knowledge and awareness, like this antidrug message, to very elaborate treatment programs to prevent the emergence of problems in children considered to be at risk.

Children at high and low risk were chosen from screening questionnaires given at schools. The final sample included sixty-nine in the treatment group and seventy-four in the control group, which received no treatment. The groups included both boys and girls and white and African American youngsters. The treatment included two components, cognitive restructuring and social problem solving. Children in the prevention treatment met in small groups at school once a week for an hour and a half for twelve sessions. The cognitive treatments included identifying negative thinking, challenging the accuracy of pessimistic thoughts, and looking for realistic solutions. The problem-solving sessions included learning to set goals, generating solutions, decision making, and seeking social support.

At the end of the prevention treatment, six months later, and two years later, children's depression symptoms and other indicators of adjustment were measured. The results indicated that at the end of treatment, children in the prevention group had significantly lower depression scores and lower conduct problem scores, and these results continued at the six-month follow-up (Jaycox, Reivich & Seligman, 1994). Figure 18.7 shows the results up through two years, in terms of the number of children who scored high on the Children's Depression Inventory. The prevention program appeared to reduce the number of children who displayed clinically significant levels of depressive symptoms compared with the no-treatment group. Thus, the program appeared to achieve its goal of truly reducing depression. Clearly,

**Figure 18.7
Preventing Depression
in Young People**

When outcomes were measured in terms of percentage of youngsters who had high levels of depression suggesting clinically significant symptoms, it was clear that the Penn Prevention Program's work on dysfunctional cognitions and poor problem solving led to gains that lasted for most youngsters for the two-year period — although there was some increase in depression after one year. These results are impressive, given that the prevention program did not include direct work with parents or other factors that might have contributed to the children's problems.
Source: Gillham, Reivich, Jaycox & Seligman (1995).

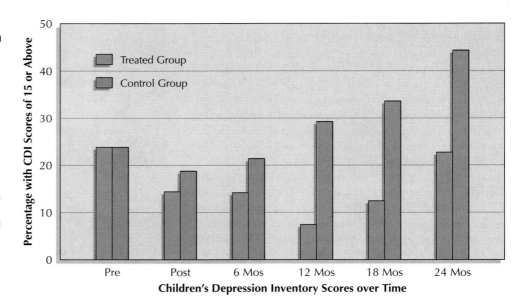

however, the gains eroded over time, but the results encourage us to continue to find methods to help children cope with stresses and think less pessimistically.

Some prevention programs are also aimed much more broadly, considered *universal* rather than selective. For instance, a media-based program aimed at reducing conflict and aggression among youngsters in New York City was called "Choose to De-Fuse" (Zimmerman, 1996). Televised public service announcements presented youths engaging in nonviolent solutions to conflict. Similar kinds of universal programs also target resistance to drug use, safe sex for avoiding sexually transmitted diseases and AIDS, and other issues. Often we do not know how well they work, however, since many such programs are not evaluated systematically.

For adults, most prevention efforts are aimed at keeping severe stresses and emotional reactions from doing major psychological harm. For instance, rape crisis groups and telephone hotlines are aimed at helping people deal with immediate crises, as we discuss in previous chapters. Many communities have disaster teams that can work with the victims and survivors of natural disasters or accidents to help them explore their reactions and find ways to cope with the aftermath. In addition, community psychologists have developed pilot programs of many kinds to keep adults from developing psychological difficulties in the face of extremely stress-

ful conditions. However, there are very few widely disseminated programs, little public funding to support such efforts, and often little data on exactly how effective they may be.

Recent immigrants make up one high-risk group. Around the world, populations have shifted enormously even in the last decade, with millions of political and economic refugees seeking residence in industrialized nations. Many of these people have experienced great stress — from the atrocities or adversities they have fled, from the process of leaving, and from the difficulty of adapting to a new country. As a result, many exhibit high rates of mental disorders, including posttraumatic stress disorders (Gong-Guy, Cravens & Patterson, 1991; Williams & Berry, 1991).

Secondary prevention efforts — aimed at identifying problems and facilitating treatment — might be appropriate for these people. Traditional mental health services, however, are typically inappropriate for recent immigrants. Southeast Asian refugees, for instance, associate mental health problems with severe stigma and would therefore rarely seek help, and they might attribute moderate emotional and psychological problems to physical causes (Gong-Guy, Cravens & Patterson, 1991). One program in California for Southeast Asians addressed these problems by training a refugee staff to present discussions of psychological problems and facilitate referrals to treatment. Treatment programs themselves incorporated traditional services such as acupuncture. One clinic employed a Buddhist monk trained as a social worker (Gong-Guy, Cravers & Patterson, 1991).

In conclusion, prevention efforts hold promise for reducing the development of adjustment difficulties or for making them more manageable if they do surface. However, prevention requires long-range goals in a society that usually emphasizes short-term solutions. It means spending money, sometimes very large sums, that may not reap gains for years. Also, prevention programs may be handicapped by lack of knowledge about what really works or whom to target.

Finally, if research produces effective methods of prevention, some of these could bring risks to individual liberties. Suppose that it becomes possible to use behavioral and biological indicators to identify, by ages nine or ten, the 5 percent of the population that is likely to be violent. Then these children and their families might be given special training and other help. Sounds good, but consider the potential costs: A child might be stigmatized by being labeled as high risk, some children would be incorrectly labeled as high risk who are not (false positives), or a child who was aggressive but who might otherwise have gone on to channel the aggressiveness into constructive means (a leader in business or government, a soldier, an athlete) might be altered for life. Thus, preventive efforts are likely to have drawbacks that must be weighed against their potential benefits. Despite these obstacles, however, it is undoubtedly true that an ounce of prevention is worth a pound of cure, and efforts continue to identify and address the principal factors that contribute to mental disorders.

What Lies Ahead?

Increasing our knowledge about psychological disorders is an admirable achievement, but it creates increasingly complex issues for citizens to resolve. Knowing more about the biological aspects of many forms of disorder does not resolve the dilemma of human responsibility and accountability for illicit and dangerous behaviors. Thus, the laws governing protection for the mentally disabled will continue to change as we try to grapple with such issues. Similarly, the increasing complexity of the modern world creates ongoing struggles to define and uphold ethical conduct among mental health professionals and to find the right balance between protecting individuals and protecting the community.

Increased knowledge of psychological disorders and their treatments also has created the dilemma that we know more and do less. Behavioral scientists have greater understanding of what to do to treat, if not prevent, such problems while also facing the reality that we are not delivering the services to all who need them. A major obstacle is cost, and yet cost-consciousness may be a blessing in disguise for the future. We cannot retreat from the knowledge that early detection and prevention efforts may be essential for avoiding the staggering personal and social costs of chronic, disabling psychological disorders. The mental health goals of industrialized nations generally have given prevention little support, but the future holds the possibility that such priorities may change if only because of the enormous cost of failing to deal with them early or to prevent them.

KEY TERMS

ALI Model Penal Code (552)
APA insanity standard (552)
civil commitment (553)
confidentiality (554)
criminal commitment (553)
deinstitutionalization (561)
diminished capacity (552)
drop out (565)
dual relationships (559)
Durham Rule (552)

duty to warn (554)
ethical standards (558)
ethnic matching (566)
guilty but mentally ill (553)
imminent danger (553)
insanity defense plea (551)
irresistible impulse (552)
least restrictive alternative (554)
managed care (561)

mentally ill homeless (563)
mentally incompetent to stand trial (551)
M'Naghten Rule (552)
need for treatment (553)
paraprofessionals (568)
primary prevention (570)
privatization (563)
right to refuse treatment (554)

right to treatment (554)
risk factors (571)
secondary prevention (570)
self-help groups (567)
social support (556)
tertiary prevention (570)
twelve-step programs (568)
underutilize (565)

SUMMARY

The Law and Mental Illness

Western law insists that if a person is *mentally incompetent to stand trial*, there can be no trial or legal process. The *insanity defense plea* upholds another basic principle of Western law: People must be capable of intending to commit a crime. Various legal standards decide whether a mentally ill person is

not guilty by reason of insanity. These standards differ in their emphasis on cognitive ability, or understanding of right and wrong, and the ability to control behavior. Five of the major standards are the *M'Naghten Rule, irresistible impulse doctrine, diminished capacity, the Durham Rule, the ALI Model Penal Code, and the APA insanity standard.* Very few crimes use this defense because even if successful, many individuals are confined for considerable periods of time. Jurisdictions have changed the laws to reduce possible misuse, a few even adopting a *guilty but mentally ill* standard.

Individuals also may be subject to *civil, or involuntary, commitment* if certain legal standards are met in the judgment of their mental illness. *Need for treatment* is not acceptable in the United States as a reason for involuntary commitment, and instead, we judge whether there is *imminent danger* to the self or others or grave disability.

Mentally hospitalized patients have extensive rights based on numerous court decisions: *right to treatment* (not just confinement), *least restrictive alternative*, *right to refuse treatment*, and informed consent concerning treatment. They also have the right to *confidentiality*; this right may be overridden by the therapist's *duty to warn* and protect specific others who are threatened with harm by a patient.

Consumers' Rights and Therapists' Responsibilities

There are many reasons for seeking treatment — distress, impaired functioning, and self-exploration. Although *social support* is an important source of help with psychological difficulties for many people, it is not always a sufficient or positive option, and seeking professional help may be warranted. It is important to make sure that a therapist has proper licensure, indicating supervised training, knowledge, and dedication to uphold *ethical standards*. Sexual misconduct by therapists is an extreme and especially damaging form of *dual relationship*.

Barriers to Treatment

Financial limitations are a serious barrier to treatment; those who need help most are often least able to afford it, and *managed care* has limited coverage for those who have insurance. Also, *privatization* of mental hospitals has reduced access to treatment among those who require public facilities. *Deinstitutionalization* was effective in eliminating many of the "side effects" of long-term hospital care, but failure to provide community services has been a contributor to the problem of the *mentally ill homeless*.

An additional barrier to treatment is that many services are not responsive to the unique needs of minority groups that may have different beliefs and values concerning psychological disorders and needed care. Some groups, for example, *underutilize* community services or *drop out* of treatment prematurely if they do seek help. Increased *ethnic matching*, where possible, and cultural sensitivity through training may help lower barriers to treatment.

Alternatives to Traditional Mental Health Treatments

Self-help groups, including *twelve-step programs* modeled on Alcoholics Anonymous, are a growing and useful service to individuals who will not or cannot seek traditional services. Programs staffed by trained nonprofessionals or *paraprofessionals* may provide limited but useful services at far less cost and sometimes greater acceptance. Individuals also increasingly have access to media that provide potentially useful information: talk shows, books, tapes, and seminars. However, these products — and indeed many of the alternatives noted — may be helpful mostly to those who are already relatively well functioning.

Preventing Psychological Disorders

Primary, secondary, and tertiary prevention aim to prevent the development of the problem or limit its consequences. True primary prevention at its most fundamental level would eliminate poverty because poverty and social disadvantage are *risk factors* for many forms of mental disorder. Early interventions targeted at high-risk groups may be the best solution to some problems that have lifelong consequences and affect the lives of others. Children are an obvious target for prevention programs, but preventive interventions can be used in many ways to help adults deal with traumas to avoid long-term psychological disorders. Prevention research is urgently needed to resolve questions of effectiveness relative to cost, but it is likely that our society can ill afford to ignore preventive interventions.

Consider the Following. . .

Suppose that constant media attention to dramatic criminal acts causes you to be exposed to many legal issues, and now you have been selected to be on a jury. The case is a woman who shot her husband while he was sleeping. The prosecutor calls it first-degree (premeditated) murder, while the defense calls it temporary insanity due to years of violent abuse leading to severe injury and threats of death. The defense says that the defendant suffers from posttraumatic stress disorder causing impaired thinking and "re-experiencing" to the point that she believed herself to be in danger of being killed. What are the key issues for deciding on her criminal responsibility? What information would you need in order to evaluate the role of her psychological disorder on her criminal act?

Suppose that you won a lottery and through investments transformed your winnings into a huge fortune, and you wished to help your community with $10 million. You are persuaded that prevention efforts directed toward the physical and psychological health of children would be the best way to help. The following groups advocate for their causes: runaway teenagers, physically abused children, children of teenage mothers, schools trying to prevent drop-out, a group wanting to promote conflict resolution training in schools to prevent violence. What are the merits and disadvantages of each? Who do you select, and why?

GLOSSARY

A-B-A-B design A research design used to assess the effects of an intervention by demonstrating that the problem behavior changes systematically with the provision and removal of treatment.

abstinence versus controlled drinking The debate over whether treatment for alcoholism should be total cessation of drinking alcohol or moderately controlled drinking.

abstinence violation effect (AVE) A person's reaction to an initial relapse into drug use, usually resulting in increased consumption.

accurate empathy According to the principles of person-centered therapy, a characteristic of therapists whereby they come to see and understand the world the way the client experiences it.

action-oriented family therapy A treatment applied to families with children who show psychological disorders, in which parents are taught skills for better managing their children with the aim of undermining detrimental family interactions.

active coping Responding to stress by exerting an effort to minimize exposure to the stressor.

acute stress disorder A disorder that occurs when reactions similar to posttraumatic stress disorder (PTSD) persist for at least two days but less than four weeks.

adaptive behavior Self-care skills (such as the ability to appropriately dress and groom oneself and hold a simple job) that are needed to live independently. These skills are the criteria used to determine the presence of mental retardation.

addiction Use of a psychoactive substance characterized, first, behaviorally by a subjective compulsion to use the drug and progressive compromise of activities that are not drug related and, second, physically by tolerance and withdrawal.

adoption studies Research method for separating the influences of nature versus nurture that compares the rates of disorder among adopted children whose biological parents had a diagnosable disorder with the rates among adopted children whose biological parents did not have disorders.

affective disorder Another term for *mood disorder.*

agoraphobia A marked fear of being alone or of being in public places where escape is difficult or help is not readily available; formerly defined as the pathological fear of open or public places.

akathisia Motor restlessness in which the person shows fidgety movements, shifting constantly; a neurological side effect of antipsychotic medications.

alarm reaction The first stage of the general adaptation syndrome (GAS); another term for *fight-or-flight response.*

alcohol A central nervous system depressant that interferes with coordination and sensory functioning.

Alcoholics Anonymous A self-help organization founded and run by alcoholics to rehabilitate alcoholics.

ALI's Model Penal Code A definition of legal insanity proposed by the American Law Institute that incorporates both rational and volitional criteria for determining insanity.

Alzheimer's dementia (AD) A progressive disease, usually occurring in older ages, involving cognitive impairment due to brain changes especially in the cortex and hippocampus.

amnesia Impairment of short- or long-term memory.

amphetamines Central nervous system stimulants that cause excitation, agitation, and increased energy and, in large doses, nervousness, sleeplessness, and delusions.

analogue A scaled-down facsimile of reality that contains certain basic characteristics of the real thing in a simplified and controlled manner; the basis of some research designs.

androgens Male hormones such as testosterone that are related to sexual desire and motivation.

anhedonia Lack of pleasure in any activity.

anorexia nervosa An eating disorder characterized by intense fear of becoming obese, distorted self-perception of body image, refusal to maintain normal body weight, and, in females, cessation of menstruation.

antianxiety drugs Psychotropic medications that reduce muscular tension and have a calming and soothing effect on the emotions but can cause drowsiness and lethargy.

anticonvulsants Psychotropic medications that have been used to reduce acute manic symptoms.

antidepressant medications Psychotropic medications that elevate mood and increase activity.

antipsychotics Psychotropic medications that reduce the intensity and frequency of hallucinations, delusions, and other aspects of psychotic thinking.

antisocial personality disorder (APD) A personality disorder characterized by a history of callousness, disregard for social conventions and others' rights and feelings, and illegal conduct.

anxiety A feeling of apprehension over an anticipated situation or object that typically would not produce discomfort in rational individuals.

anxiety disorders Psychological disorders associated with pervasive and persistent symptoms of anxiety and avoidance behavior that cause clinically significant distress or impairment of functioning in social and work situations.

anxiety hierarchy A list of situations rank-ordered according to the amount of anxiety they evoke.

anxiety sensitivity The belief that anxiety experiences have negative implications; suggested by some psychologists as a component of a model to explain the development of agoraphobia.

anxious apprehension   Chronic, persistent anxiety, characteristic of generalized anxiety disorder (GAD).

APA insanity standard   A definition of legal insanity proposed by the American Psychiatric Association that uses a cognitive approach in which the accused must be judged as "unable to appreciate the wrongfulness of his conduct at the time of the offense."

aphonia   A conversion disorder in which the patient, though physically capable, is unable to speak above a whisper.

arousal   Another term for *sexual excitement.*

Asperger's disorder   A pervasive developmental disorder with severe and sustained impairment in social interaction and the development of repetitive patterns of behavior and activities. Akin to autism.

assessment   The measurement and interpretation of information about people's characteristics and behaviors that help to describe and understand behavior, classify psychological problems, predict future behavior, and plan and evaluate treatments for problem behavior.

assortative mating   Marriage between persons with similar psychological disorders or who both have some psychological disorder.

asylums   Old-fashioned term for mental hospitals.

attachment   The quality of the early parent-child relationship; said to be crucial to the formation of a positive view of the self.

attachment theory   A theory maintaining that the quality of the parent-infant bond guides fundamental aspects of the child's social, intellectual, and self-esteem development by shaping how the child views the self and other people.

attention-deficit hyperactivity disorder (ADHD)   A disruptive behavior disorder of children that has three essential features with onset before age seven: developmentally inappropriate levels of inattention, impulsivity, and hyperactivity.

auditory hallucinations   The experience whereby individuals hear voices talking to or about them when no such voices exist (the most common form of hallucinations).

autism   When associated with schizophrenia, autism involves social withdrawal, whereby the person retreats into a private fantasy world. As a pervasive developmental disorder — infantile autism — its symptoms appear early in life. Infantile autism has three features: qualitative impairment in social interaction, severe impairments in communication, and restricted, repetitive, and stereotyped patterns of behavior.

automatic negative thoughts   Self-critical, pessimistic, or exaggerated negative statements that clients make to themselves without testing their accuracy.

autonomic nervous system   A part of the nervous system that regulates the motivational and emotional states of the body and monitors its basic physiology.

avoidance learning   Following initial escape responses (to stop a negative condition) as a strategy to alleviate discomfort, the individual gradually uses avoidance responses (to prevent a negative condition) even when the response is not necessary.

avoidant personality disorder   A personality disorder characterized by social discomfort — timidity and fear of negative evaluation.

balanced placebo design   A research strategy in which four groups are used in an effort to separate the pharmacological from the expectancy effects of drugs.

baseline   The naturally occurring frequency of a target behavior.

battered women   Women who have been physically beaten by their domestic partners.

behavioral marital therapy (BMT)   An action-oriented therapeutic approach used with couples. Often, specific skills such as communication skills are taught.

behavioral medicine   An interdisciplinary field concerned with the integration of behavioral and biomedical science relevant to health and illness and the application of this knowledge for prevention, diagnosis, and treatment.

behavioral model   A model that holds that abnormal behavior, like normal behavior, is the result of learning. Observable behavior and environmental factors are emphasized.

behavioral sensitization   The exhibition of progressively more rapid and extreme behaviors in response to stimuli as a result of repeated administrations of the stimuli.

behavior therapy   A therapeutic approach in which it is assumed that human action is acquired through the learning process. Treatment emphasizes the acquisition and practice of appropriate behaviors in the relevant situation.

bell and pad   A urine-sensing device that rests between the child and the mattress during sleeping hours and that sounds an alarm if the child urinates in bed; used to treat enuresis.

beta-amyloid protein   A major component of the plaques observed in the brains of persons with Alzheimer's dementia.

binge-purge syndrome   See *bulimia.*

biomedical model   Approach(es) to abnormal psychology suggesting that the symptoms of psychological disorders are caused by biological factors.

bipolar disorder   A mood disorder that includes both depression and mania or hypomania.

blood pressure The force with which the blood presses against artery walls; includes systolic and diastolic blood pressure.

borderline personality disorder A personality disorder characterized by pervasive instability of mood, chaotic relationships, and uncertain self-definition.

bulimia An eating disorder characterized by binge eating (the rapid consumption of a large quantity of food in a discrete period of time), the feeling of a lack of control over eating, and inappropriate behaviors to prevent weight gain (such as self-induced vomiting or use of laxatives).

cancers Any of more than one hundred diseases caused by a dysfunction of the controls for growth and reproduction within cells.

cannabis A hallucinogenic agent that has a varied effect on arousal and perception.

cannabis amotivational syndrome A set of behaviors including lethargy, an inability to derive pleasure, unpleasant mood, impaired judgment, lack of interest in conventional goals, and perhaps some deterioration of attention and memory, which may result from long-term use of cannabis.

case study A detailed examination and description of an individual's current feelings, thoughts, and behaviors.

catatonic schizophrenia A subtype marked by psychomotor disturbances ranging from rigid posture or stuporous inactivity to excited, excessive activity.

cerebral vascular disorders Problems in the circulatory system feeding the brain, which may cause brain-damaging strokes.

Child Behavior Checklist (CBCL) A standardized rating scale completed by parents (and teachers) to assess the most common dimensions of psychological disorders in children.

childhood disintegrative disorder A pervasive developmental disorder that follows two years of normal development in communication, social relationships, and adaptive behavior.

childhood gender identity disorder Early experiences of wishing to be (or believing that one truly is) the opposite sex.

cingulotomy Surgical interruption of the cingulate bundles of the brain performed by passing current through precisely placed electrodes.

circadian rhythms Regular daily cycles of changes in such functions as sleep-wake cycles, neuroendocrine activity, and body temperature.

civil commitment A period of involuntary confinement for treatment in a hospital when a person is judged by professionals to be dangerous to the self or others; can be required of persons found to be unable to care for themselves due to mental illness.

clang associations The use of words that are associated merely because of the way they sound, not by their meaning — as in schizophrenia.

classical conditioning A form of learning in which once-neutral stimuli, after repeated pairings over time, come to evoke involuntary responses.

classification variables Specified criteria used to identify two groups of experimental subjects — those who are classified a certain way and those who are not; applied in research comparisons.

claustrophobia The intense and irrational fear of closed spaces.

clinical significance Used (in addition to statistical significance) to evaluate the efficacy of a treatment method — as when treated individuals are compared to normals in a normative comparison.

clopazine A neuroleptic drug that appears to have fewer side effects than other neuroleptics and may be helpful for patients who did not respond to other drugs.

cluster suicides Suicides committed in imitation of a publicized suicide.

cocaine Central nervous system stimulant, from the coca plant, that produces increased mental energy, euphoria, and responsiveness to environmental stimuli. In large doses causes paranoia and hallucinations.

cognitive ability The mental capacity to know right from wrong; a component of the legal standard for "not guilty by reason of insanity."

cognitive appraisals Ways of thinking about or interpreting stressors, which may be linked to emotional distress.

cognitive-behavioral model A psychological view that emphasizes the learning process and the influences of the environment while underscoring the importance of cognitive-mediating and information-processing factors in the development and treatment of psychological disorders.

cognitive-behavioral therapy A therapeutic approach that combines behavioral performance-based interventions with strategies that address the client's thinking.

cognitive content The actual information that is stored in memory.

cognitive deficiencies The absence of thinking, as when an individual's responses and emotional states do not benefit from careful thinking or planning.

cognitive disorders The DSM-IV term for medically caused delirium, dementia, or amnesia.

cognitive distortions Thought processes that are dysfunctional, such as active misperceptions and misconstruals of the environment.

cognitive expectancy theory The view that people learn from models to expect that behaviors (e.g., drinking) will have positive consequences for them (e.g., that such behaviors will be socially stimulating and help them forget events or unpleasant memories).

cognitive model An explanation of psychopathology emphasizing that an individual's cognitive functioning contributes to emotional or behavioral distress.

cognitive processes The operation or manner of operation by which the individual system inputs, stores, transforms, and governs the output of information.

cognitive products The results of an individual's manipulation of the information within the cognitive system.

cognitive rehabilitation A field of neuropsychology, the goals of which are to retrain the individual or provide compensatory skills to counteract the effects of brain damage.

cognitive structures The internal organization of information that influences how new experiences are perceived and understood.

cognitive therapy for depression A therapeutic approach that modifies depressive emotional states by altering the client's cognitive and behavioral functioning.

cognitive triad According to Beck, a person's views of the self, the world, and the future, which, if negative, cause a person to be susceptible to depression.

collaborative empiricism A therapeutic process based on cognitive-behavioral theory by which the client participates actively in suggesting ideas, trying out new behaviors, and reporting back to the therapist.

collective unconscious According to Jung, a collection of primitive ideas and images that are inherited and shared across the human race.

communication deviance (CD) Problems in creating and maintaining a shared focus of attention; a pattern observed in some families with schizophrenic offspring.

community mental health centers Public facilities in many communities that provide out-patient services and, sometimes, short-term in-patient care.

comorbidity The co-occurrence of different types of disorders within one person.

competence to stand trial An accused person's ability to understand and participate in the proceedings of a trial.

compulsions Ritualistic and repetitive behavioral patterns that are not ends in themselves but involve avoidance of other actions.

computerized axial tomography A neuroimaging technique involving passage of a radioactive ray through bone and brain tissue to show structures of the brain.

concordance The principle used in genetic studies with twin pairs, whereby the diagnostic similarity between those with identical genes (monozygotic twins) is compared to the diagnostic similarity between those with less shared genetic make-up (dizygotic twins).

concrete thinking The reduced ability to understand abstractions observed in some people with schizophrenia.

concurrent validity Agreement between a measure of a variable and some criterion that is obtained at about the same time.

conditioned response The type of response an organism makes to a conditioned stimulus as a result of learning.

conduct disorder A childhood or adolescent problem characterized by a repetitive and persistent pattern of behavior that involves violation of the basic rights of others and of major age-appropriate social norms.

confidentiality In psychotherapy, the principle that anything about a patient may not be disclosed by a therapist to anyone without the patient's written consent. In testing and in research, the principle that participants' responses to psychological tests or tasks are not open to the public.

congenital rubella Measles present in an infant at birth.

conjoint family therapy A therapeutic approach that requires all family members to be seen together as a single group with the goal of changing their dysfunctional patterns of communication.

construct validity A method of establishing the validity of a measure of a hypothetical construct, by showing that the measure is related in consistent ways to other characteristics as specified by the theory about the construct.

content validity The degree to which the items of an assessment device represent examples of what the test is targeting.

continuation rates The percentage of first-time users who persist in using a drug.

continuation treatment Administration of antidepressant medication after the initial symptoms of depression have diminished for a period of at least sixteen to twenty weeks, involving the prescribed dosage followed by a gradual reduction.

continuity theory A view stating that psychological dysfunctions and normal behavior form one continuum ranging from normal behavior to mild disturbance to moderate disturbance to severe disturbance.

control group A group of participants exposed to all features of an experiment with the exception of the independent variable.

conversion disorder Disorders, psychological in origin, that involve one or more symptoms or deficits affecting voluntary functioning that cannot be explained by a neurological or general medical condition.

coping model A therapeutic approach in which a therapist (model) initially demonstrates difficulties similar to the observer's, then models strategies to overcome the difficulties, and eventually models the desirable behavior.

coping responses Responses made to manage stress.

coprolalia Seen in approximately one-third of persons with Tourette's disorder, the individual utters, calls, or screams obscenities.

coronary atherosclerosis (CAD) The disease causing coronary heart disease (CHD), in which the arteries carrying blood to the heart muscle are narrowed by fatty deposits on their walls.

coronary heart disease (CHD) A disease caused by decreased blood flow to the heart and associated with angina pectoris (chest pain), myocardial infarction (death of the heart muscle from lack of oxygen), and sudden coronary death (death caused by interruption in the heart's blood-pumping).

correlational studies Approaches to research questions that focus on the relationship (covariation) among variables.

correlation coefficient A measure, ranging from +1.0 to −1.0, used to express the direction and magnitude of the relationship between variables.

cortisol The hormone produced in the adrenal glands that physiologically prepares the body for response to stress.

counterbalancing Presenting research events to subjects in different orders, so as to control unwanted sequence effects.

counterconditioning A process, as in systematic desensitization, in which the client is gradually taught to replace an undesirable response — the anxiety response — with a response that is incompatible with the undesirable response — the relaxation response.

countertransference The therapist's feelings about the client.

couples therapy A therapeutic approach in which the therapist works with two persons who share a long-term relationship; also called marital therapy.

criminal commitment The type of confinement to a mental or prison hospital used for people found "not guilty by reason of insanity."

criminality A legal rather than a mental health concept, referring to violations of the law owing to any cause.

crisis intervention Brief therapies, conducted either as in-patient or out-patient treatment, that attempt to identify and quickly resolve the immediate crisis by drawing on the person's own resources, including the support of friends and family.

criterion-related validity The degree to which a measure agrees with an external standard, or criterion.

cross-fostering studies Research that examines the children of parents with known psychological problems or no problems who have been adopted and raised by either normal or disordered parents — as when a "normal" child raised by disordered parents is compared with other children as a way to clarify the influences of nature versus nurture.

cross-sectional studies Research that examines the same characteristics in different individuals at one point in time.

culturally deprived environment A social and familial milieu that lacks learning opportunities.

cultural sensitivity An awareness by a therapist of different cultural values and customs that affect individuals' behaviors and expectations.

cyclothymic disorder A bipolar disorder characterized by mild and frequent mood swings.

daily hassles In the context of measuring stress, the little things in life that can go wrong and cause distress.

debrief To provide participants in a study with a clear statement of the rationale and methods of the study when their participation is completed.

decay theory An explanation for memory loss suggesting that it results from disuse and the passage of time.

defense mechanisms According to Freudian (psychodynamic) theory, unconscious processes that try to protect the ego from anxiety provoked by unwanted or unacceptable impulses.

deficient avoidance learning Difficulty learning a task when wrong answers are punished.

deficit symptoms Another term for *negative symptoms* of schizophrenia.

deinstitutionalization The movement to replace the huge mental hospitals that often served an entire state with community out-patient and aftercare facilities providing short-term care that enable patients to be more fully integrated into their own communities.

delirium Changes in level of consciousness that may be accompanied by cognitive changes; may be temporary or progressive.

delusions Beliefs held by individuals with psychotic disorders that have no basis in reality and are not influenced by facts.

delusions of grandeur Beliefs that one has special powers or characteristics.

delusions of reference Unwarranted beliefs that others are making secret reference to oneself; sometimes called ideas of reference.

dementia General, multiple cognitive deficits reflecting a decline in previously higher levels of functioning. These deficits are acquired rather than present at birth, as in mental retardation.

demonology The study of the supposed influences of demons in causing disturbed behavior.

dependence The craving for continued doses of a substance. Physical dependence involves tolerance and withdrawal; psychological dependence involves continued use despite adverse consequences and the belief that the substance is needed for continued well-being.

dependent personality disorder A personality disorder characterized by pervasive patterns of dependent and submissive behavior, leaving the affected persons seemingly unable to make even everyday decisions for themselves.

dependent variable The variable used to measure the effects, if any, of the manipulated independent variable in an experiment.

depressive schemas According to Beck's theory of depression, underlying negative beliefs that distort information, as when people select interpretations that fit their beliefs while ignoring or reinterpreting information that does not fit those beliefs.

descriptive approaches General procedures used to summarize and organize samples of data; two forms are case studies and surveys.

desire The first stage of the sexual response cycle; a state of interest in or motivation for sexual activity.

detoxification Treatment directed toward ridding the body of alcohol or other drugs.

developmental appropriateness The suitableness of a child's behavior to his or her stage of development. In the context of ADHD, the suitableness of attention, impulsivity, and level of activity.

developmental psychopathology The study of maladjustment and its interface with normal development, whereby maladjustment is viewed in relation to the major changes that occur throughout the life cycle.

dexamethasone A synthetic cortisol that temporarily suppresses the release of cortisol in the body; some depressed people show abnormal cortisol reactions if given dexamethasone.

diagnosis Determination of symptoms and how they fit the classification system for mental disorders.

Diagnostic and Statistical Manual, 4th Edition (DSM-IV) A widely accepted system in the United States and around the world for classifying psychological problems and disorders.

diatheses Predisposing factors, including biological determinants and characteristic manners of responding, that interact with stress to contribute to psychological disorders.

diathesis-stress approach A view that explains psychological abnormalities in terms of an active interaction between genetic and other biological dispositions and stressful environmental influences.

differential reinforcement of other behavior (DRO) A behavioral procedure that involves providing rein-forcement after periods of time in which an undesirable response does not take place. Used in treating self-injurious behavior.

diminished capacity A definition of legal insanity — now prohibited in most jurisdictions — that allows the insanity defense if the accused can point to mental or physical factors that temporarily impaired his or her ability to understand the nature of the act or to control it.

directionality The question of which of two correlated variables caused the other.

discontinuity theory A view stating that mild and severe psychological dysfunction are distinct from each other and from normality, and that they stem from different causes and follow different courses.

disinhibited Describing a person who lacks the ability to inhibit responses, as when facing possible punishment.

disorder of written expression A type of learning disorder described by DSM-IV.

disorganized schizophrenia A subtype marked by severe disintegration of personality, involving incoherent and unintelligible speech, fragmentary delusions and hallucinations, extreme social impairment, disorganized behavior, and flat or inappropriate affect.

disregulation model A view of stress stating that when proper feedback is disrupted and a corrective action to return to normal functioning does not occur, physical dysfunction may result.

disruptive behavior disorders Behavioral excesses or poorly controlled behaviors that are bothersome to others.

dissociation A process of awareness said to exist when a person displays two different indicators that suggest that one component of the mind is aware while another component is not aware.

dissociative disorder Disorders characterized by severe disruption or alteration of a person's identity, memory, or consciousness; three types are dissociative amnesia, dissociative fugue, and dissociative identity disorder (multiple personality disorder).

dissociative identity disorder (DID) A dissociative disorder that involves alteration in one's sense of identity, memory, or consciousness, which may include loss of a sense of identity or assumption of a new identity (formerly called multiple personality disorder, or MPD).

dissociative (psychogenic) fugue A dissociative disorder in which a person suddenly and unexpectedly travels away from his or her home or place of work and is unable to recall the past; often associated with the assumption of a new identity.

dizygotic twins Fraternal twins, who, like any siblings, share 50 percent of genetic make-up. See also *monozygotic twins*.

domestic violence Violence that occurs in the home between intimates.

dopamine A type of neurotransmitter.

double-blind control A preferred design for experiments measuring the effectiveness of a psychotropic medication, in which both the investigator and the patient are unaware of whether a placebo or an active drug is being administered.

double depression A pattern of chronic low-grade depression involving periodic major depression.

Down syndrome A form of mental retardation caused by the presence of an extra set of genes in the twenty-first chromosome.

drop out Discontinue treatment prematurely.

DSM-IV. See *Diagnostic and Statistical Manual, 4th Edition.*

dual relationship A relationship with a patient outside the therapeutic relationship, such as a sexual or business association, which is unethical for a therapist to form or maintain.

Durham rule A definition of legal insanity specifying that individuals could not be criminally responsible if their "unlawful act was the product of mental disease or mental defect."

duty to protect The principle that a therapist who knows of a patient's intention to harm another person has the responsibility to take whatever steps are reasonably necessary to protect the other person.

duty to warn The principle that a therapist who knows of a patient's intention to harm another person has the responsibility to notify that person.

dyspareunia Genital pain during or after intercourse in either males or females.

dysthymic disorder Mild, prolonged depression; a category of unipolar depression.

echolalia The repetition or echoing back of speech sometimes seen in autistic children.

eclecticism The use of different treatments for clients with different disorders or of a rational combination of various treatments for the same client; a dominant force in the provision of psychological treatments.

economically disadvantaged Suffering the reduced opportunities associated with poverty.

educational interventions Regarding retarded persons, approaches to treating mental retardation that include specific teaching strategies to facilitate learning.

effect size A measure of the difference between mean (average) scores of the various conditions under investigation.

ego The hypothesized mental structure that mediates the wishes of the id, the demands of reality, and the strictures of the superego.

ego psychologists Psychologists who are more concerned with functions of the ego than with those of the superego or the id.

electroconvulsive therapy (ECT) A method of inducing convulsions by applying electricity to the brain, with the aim of resolving depression.

emotional desensitization A tendency to be numb, unresponsive, or even callous to observed violence to others.

emotion-focused coping Responding to stress by directing efforts toward regulating the emotional consequences of the stressful event.

encopresis Inappropriate elimination of feces in the absence of a physical disorder; the fecal parallel to enuresis.

enmeshment A family situation in which no member can have a separate identity.

enuresis Inappropriate urination in the absence of a urologic or neurologic disorder.

epidemiological surveys Surveys in which researchers, using standard, consistent methods of interviewing, interview large numbers of randomly selected people who represent all segments of the population — different sexes, ages, races, and socioeconomic status.

epidemiology The study of the incidence and prevalence of disorders in a specific population.

essential hypertension High blood pressure that is not due to a known biological cause.

estrogen A female sex hormone, the levels of which affect the development and maintenance of secondary sex characteristics in women.

ethical standards The written principles of appropriate professional values and behaviors to which psychologists (researchers and therapists) must adhere.

ethnic matching Providing therapy to someone of the same ethnicity; may enhance treatment effectiveness.

excitement A stage of the sexual response cycle during which various areas of the body, including sexual organs, experience vasocongestion (swelling) and muscle tension, heart rate, and blood pressure increase.

exhaustion The third stage of the general adaptation syndrome (GAS), in which the organism's physiological resources to contend with stress are depleted, and the organism may show signs of physical deterioration or illness.

exhibitionism A sexual paraphilia involving the display of genitals to an involuntary observer.

existential therapy A therapeutic philosophy, rather than a set of approaches, strategies, or techniques, concerning the treatment of psychological disorders.

expectancies Beliefs about what an individual anticipates will occur; anticipated consequences.

experiment   A preferred research method in which a researcher directly influences or manipulates one or more independent variables and assesses their effects on dependent variables.

exposure   In behavioral and cognitive-behavioral models, an approach whereby patients confront once-feared objects or situations. Exposure is considered an active component of several treatments for various anxiety disorders.

expressed emotion (EE)   The degree to which family members either are critical of a recently hospitalized schizophrenic person or express overinvolved and overprotective attitudes toward the patient; high levels of EE are thought to predict relapse.

externalizing disorders   Maladaptive behavior patterns in children, across several situations, that create problems for others.

external validity   The degree to which research findings can be generalized to situations, persons, or locations beyond those employed in the study.

face validity   The degree to which items on a test appear to measure what the test purports to measure.

factitious disorders   Somatic disorders in which the patient intentionally produces physical or psychological signs or symptoms, motivated by the desire to assume a "sick role."

familial   Referring to a pattern of disorder among family members; possibly heritable and possibly environmentally influenced.

family studies   Research that addresses the question of whether the frequency of a particular disorder is higher among family members than in the general population.

family therapy   A therapeutic approach whose underlying assumption is that disturbances in relationships or the social context influence individual adjustment, and that when one member of a couple or family develops a problem, the others are involved in the problem and should be involved in the treatment as well.

fear   A reasonable and rational reaction to a genuinely alarming situation.

female arousal disorder   A disorder of females characterized by difficulties in attaining or maintaining sexual arousal.

female orgasmic disorder   A disorder of females characterized by inability to sustain sexual arousal or achieve orgasm.

fetal alcohol syndrome (FAS)   A collection of symptoms — including low weight and small size at birth, some facial and limb irregularities, and mental and motor retardation — exhibited by some children born of women who drank excessive alcohol while pregnant.

fetishism   Intense sexual urges involving nonsexual items or a part of the body.

field trials   Research projects specifically aimed at testing particular diagnostic questions by examining relevant populations.

fight-or-flight response   Bodily reactions to a stressful situation, controlled by the sympathetic system, involving increased heart rate, greater blood flow and increased oxygen supply to the major muscles, and release of glucose and hormones into the bloodstream.

fixation   According to Freud, a stoppage or arrest at some point in the person's psychosexual development.

flat affect   A form of affect disturbance in schizophrenia characterized by lack of emotionality.

flooding   Exposure to many cues or features of a fearful or phobic situation in which the client experiences maximum anxiety.

folk healers   Though not a part of modern mental health systems, folk healers were observers of psychological disorders in traditional societies. They used healing rituals and exorcism as well as herbal medicines to try to alleviate distress.

follow-back studies   Research that identifies adult patients and examines their earlier records at schools or treatment agencies.

follow-up studies   Research that identifies patients at a particular point (e.g., when they are first diagnosed) and studies them again at a later time — as when subjects are reassessed at some point in time after the completion of an intervention.

fragile X syndrome   A form of mental retardation named for a constricted region at the end of the X-chromosome that is more common in males than in females.

free association   A technique of psychoanalysis in which a client expresses thoughts and feelings as they come to mind and without fear of censure; believed to reveal unconscious conflicts.

frontal lobe injuries   Damage to the anterior part of the brain that can result in impaired memory, concentration, reasoning, learning, and possible personality changes.

fundamental attribution error   The tendency of people, when explaining the behavior of others, to generally underestimate the influence of situations and overestimate the influence of personality traits.

galvanic skin response (GSR)   A measure of the conductance of the skin, which is influenced by sweat, to determine a subject's emotional reactions.

gender dysphoria Feelings of dissatisfaction with one's biological identity.

gender identity disorder A condition in which a person persistently experiences discomfort with his or her biological sex and expresses profound identification with the other sex.

gender nonconformity The rejection of traditional masculine or feminine roles.

gender socialization The process of learning expected feminine and masculine behaviors and attitudes.

general adaptation syndrome (GAS) A three-stage set of physiological reactions to stress.

generalized anxiety disorder (GAD) An anxiety disorder marked by unrealistic or excessive anxiety and worry that do not appear to be linked to specific situations or external stressors.

generalized dissociative amnesia A dissociative disorder in which a person forgets his or her entire life history.

general paresis A severe mental disorder caused by syphilis involving memory problems, poor intellectual functioning, bad judgment, dementia, personality changes, and delusions on a deteriorating course leading to death.

genes Codes for the potential expression of characteristics; found in chromosomes.

genuineness A characteristic of therapists, as described in person-centered therapy, whereby they allow their true inner feelings and thoughts to emerge honestly and openly.

glove anesthesia A conversion disorder in which the patient is unable to feel anything with one hand (whereby sensation ends in a straight line at the wrist, reminiscent of a "glove"), despite apparently normal neuroanatomy.

group therapy A therapeutic approach in which a therapist brings together previously unacquainted individuals to interact in ways that will help to resolve personal problems.

guilty but mentally ill A relatively new standard adopted in some jurisdictions that abandons the "not guilty by reason of insanity" plea, allowing a legal judgment that the accused, though suffering from a psychological disorder, committed the crime, leading to confinement and treatment.

hallucinations Reports of sensory perceptions in the absence of actual stimuli.

hallucinogens Drugs or chemicals that induce hallucinations (sensory perceptions with no external stimuli) and excitation of the central nervous system.

health-beliefs model A cognitive approach to health behaviors suggesting that the practice of such behaviors is determined by the degree to which the individual perceives a personal health threat and the perception that a particular behavior will reduce that threat.

health psychology The aggregate of the specific contributions of psychology to promotion and maintenance of health, prevention and treatment of illness, and understanding of the causes and correlates of health and related behaviors.

healthy thinking A pattern of thinking that is associated with a 2:1 ratio of positive thinking to negative thinking.

help-seeking Entering treatment for a disorder.

hierarchy of human needs A view of human motivations as multileveled, ranging from basic human needs for food, drink, and sex at the bottom to the need for self-actualization at the top.

high-risk situations Circumstances that may lead a former substance abuser to begin drinking or taking drugs again.

high-risk studies Research that looks at children who are exposed to conditions thought to contribute to disorder.

histrionic personality disorder A personality disorder characterized by traits such as excessive emotionality, flamboyance, and attention seeking.

hopelessness An outlook of profound pessimism about resolving difficulties and a belief that matters will never change for the better; studied by cognitive-behavioral theorists and considered to be a factor in suicide.

hopelessness theory A view of depression that builds on learned helplessness theory by including additional environmental and cognitive features, and that applies only to a subgroup of depressed persons.

hostile attributional bias The tendency to believe erroneously that negative events are caused by other people who intend harm.

humanistic therapy A therapeutic approach emphasizing that each person has an inherent tendency toward growth and self-actualization.

humanistic view A psychological model that emphasizes each individual's values, free choices, and personal sense of purpose, with central roles given to the notion of the self and the nature of human needs and personal growth experiences.

humoral theory A view of health originated by Hippocrates in which the body is seen as being composed of four fluids produced by various organs — blood, phlegm, yellow bile, and black bile — and disease or disorder is seen as developing due to excesses or imbalance of these substances from internal or external causes.

Huntington's disease (HD) A genetically caused degenerative brain disease of motor functioning characterized by severe dementia and personality change as well as chorea (irregular jerks, grimaces, and twitches).

hypoactive sexual desire Low or absent desire for sexual activities; lack of sexual fantasies.

hypochrondriasis A somatic disorder in which the sufferer is preoccupied with concerns and fears about having a disease.

hypofrontality Reduced blood flow in the frontal regions of the brain, suggesting damage; a characteristic of many people with schizophrenia.

hypomania A mild version of mania.

hypothalamic-pituitary-adrenal (HPA) axis A neuroendocrine system that is highly important to the body's mobilization in the face of stress and may be involved in depression.

hypothalamus A region of the forebrain that regulates hunger, thirst, sex drive, and body temperature.

hypothyroidism Diminished production of thyroid hormone, which can impair cognitive abilities and cause other psychological disorders.

hypoxyphilia A form of sexual masochism that involves sexual arousal by oxygen deprivation.

id The hypothesized mental structure that is said to represent the reservoir of forbidden wishes and passions of our basic sexual and aggressive drives. The id strives for immediate gratification, bypassing the demands of reality, order, and logic.

imaginal exposure A method for treating anxiety disorders in which the client is exposed through images to the feared situation.

imminent danger The principle that people can be held in civil commitment only if they are dangerous to themselves or others and show signs of harming self or others in the near term.

immune system The body's defenses against infections.

impaired functioning Difficulty in performing appropriate and expected roles.

impulsivity The tendency to take action suddenly, without considering the consequences; a characteristic of attention-deficit hyperactivity disorder (ADHD).

inattention A child's seeming inability to pay sustained attention and failure to complete tasks; a characteristic of attention-deficit hyperactivity disorder (ADHD).

incest A form of sexual molestation involving sexual contact between family members.

incidence The number of new cases of a disorder reported during a specified period of time.

independent variable The variable that a researcher manipulates in an experiment to investigate its effects on dependent variables.

individual therapy A therapeutic approach in which the client is seen alone. As with other therapies, the goal is to remedy personal adjustment problems and to enable the client to function autonomously.

inferential statistics Methods for determining the probability that the effects of an experiment are explained not by chance but by the variable being investigated.

informed consent The principle that participants in a study must be told about the study and give their permission to be involved before they participate.

inhibited A descriptive term referring to a person who is shy, quiet, and timid.

insane asylums An old-fashioned term for mental hospitals.

insanity An old-fashioned term for *psychosis*. Also, a legal rather than psychological term referring to severe mental illness that affects a person's reason and self-control.

insanity defense plea The legal statement by the accused that he or she is not guilty because of insanity at the time of the crime.

insight A person's ability to understand the basis of his or her thinking, behavior, emotions, and perceptions.

insulin shock therapy Treatment involving administration of an overdose of insulin to deprive the brain of glucose, inducing a coma, with the aim of resolving depression; used in the early part of the twentieth century.

intelligence (IQ) tests Tests of intellectual functioning, most widely used to place children in academic settings or to screen adults for occupational placement.

intensive behavior modification A program of treatment for autism that lasts two years or longer and involves more than forty hours of one-on-one treatment per week.

interactional perspective A view of anxiety, and other disorders, holding that individual dispositions and situational influences interact in a causal way in the development and maintenance of psychological disorders.

interference theory An explanation for memory loss suggesting that a person's memory has a limited capacity, and that when its capacity is reached the person is susceptible to confusion and forgetting.

internal consistency A form of psychometric reliability, referring to a correspondence between test items intended to measure the same concepts.

internalizing disorders Psychological difficulties that are considered inner-directed; core symptoms are associated with overcontrolled behaviors.

internal validity The extent to which the methodology of a study allows for strong conclusions to be drawn.

interpersonal schemas Beliefs and expectations about other persons' availability, trustworthiness, and caring. They can be positive or negative and can influence one's interpersonal interactions.

interpersonal therapy   A therapeutic approach in which the therapist's essential task is to disrupt the client's vicious cycle of self-defeating interpersonal interactions.

interpretations   Statements made by a therapist (typically a psychodynamic therapist) that identify features of something the client has said or done, of which the client had not been fully aware.

interrater reliability   Consistency among separate scorers or observers rating the same characteristic.

intervention   Efforts or programs, such as therapy and prevention, designed to remediate or prevent psychological disorders.

intrapsychic conflict   Conflict among the ego, id, and superego, that, according to psychodynamic theory, contributes to thoughts, attitudes, and behaviors.

in vivo practice   A method for treating anxiety disorders in which the client practices coping while exposed to stimuli in the real environment.

irrational beliefs   Misguided and inaccurate assumptions that influence one's perceptions and can lead to maladaptive behavior.

irresistible impulse doctrine   A definition of legal insanity that emphasizes volition by allowing the insanity defense if the accused — even if capable of knowing the difference between right and wrong — could not control his or her actions.

juvenile diversion programs   Efforts of public agencies to provide counseling and community and school programs as alternatives to incarceration for youths found guilty of criminal or antisocial behavior.

kindling   An electrophysiological process whereby repeated low-level electrical stimulation of the amygdala area of the brain produces seizures, which eventually occur spontaneously when the stimulation has been sufficiently repeated.

Korsakoff's syndrome   A condition caused by vitamin B1 deficiency that produces severe retrograde and anterograde amnesia; also called alcohol amnesic disorder.

la belle indifference   A nonchalant and matter-of-fact attitude of patients, seemingly reflecting a lack of concern about their suffering and disability, that in the past was thought to be a requirement of conversion disorder.

latent content   Repressed conflictual material in a dream, interpreted by the therapist in relation to the client's personality, daily activities, and symbolic meaning given to events and objects in the dream.

learned helplessness   A cognitive model of depression suggesting that persons are susceptible to depression if they have an erroneous expectation that they can-

not control important outcomes, and that unchanging and pervasive negative qualities of the self are the causes of negative events.

learning disorders   A condition in which academic achievement is below that expected given a person's chronological age, measured intelligence, and age-appropriate education, as measured by an individually administered standardized test.

least restrictive alternative   A term used to characterize the environment to which involuntarily committed persons should be confined; it should permit the greatest freedom consistent with their own personal security and the safety of others.

least restrictive environment   A term referring to the idea that children with disabilities should be placed in classrooms with nondisabled children whenever possible.

life changes   Major life events weighted according to the amount of adaptive effort they require.

light therapy   Exposure to bright full-spectrum light for a prescribed period during the day; a treatment for seasonal affective disorder (SAD).

limbic system   The area of the brain that includes parts of the cortex, the thalamus, and the hypothalamus; it provides homeostasis, or constancy of the internal environment, by regulating the activity of endocrine glands and the autonomic nervous system.

linkage studies   Research that combines molecular genetics and statistical methods to determine patterns of genetic transmission of disorders.

lithium carbonate   A naturally occurring salt that has antimanic properties, used in preventing bipolar episodes.

lobotomy   A surgical procedure in which nerve fibers that connect to the frontal cortex are severed; used as treatment for extremely disturbed patients, but rarely practiced today.

longitudinal designs   Research that studies changes and stability over time by repeatedly measuring the same subjects at select intervals.

loose associations   A common speech characteristic of people with schizophrenia, involving unusual and idiosyncratic meanings of words or movement from one idea to another in ways that are hard to understand.

mainstreaming   The policy of placing once-separated children with disabilities in classrooms with nondisabled students.

maintenance treatment   Continuing use of psychotropic drugs at a level sufficient to prevent recurrence of episodes or symptoms.

major depressive disorder   A form of unipolar depression characterized by a distinct period of at least two weeks of moderate-to-severe symptoms.

male erectile disorder A disorder of males characterized by difficulties in attaining or sustaining adequate erection until completion of sexual activity.

male orgasmic disorder A disorder of males characterized by inhibited orgasm.

malingering The faking of physical symptoms for reasons having to do with external incentives such as achieving economic gain or avoiding work or legal responsibility.

managed care The process of limiting medical and psychiatric care by prereview and curbs on type and duration of treatment.

mania A phase of bipolar disorder characterized by grandiose or irritable mood; increased energy, activity, and distractibility; and excessive engagement in pleasurable behaviors that might lead to painful consequences.

manic-depression A term previously used to refer to *bipolar disorder*.

manifest dream The content of a dream as it is recalled by the dreamer.

mastery model A therapeutic approach in which the therapist demonstrates successful adjustment and nondisturbed behavior. See also *coping model*.

matching A method of ensuring that the subjects in all conditions in an experiment are comparable — first, by defining the important ways that subjects could differ from one another and, then, by putting an equal number of subjects of each type in each group.

mathematics disorder A type of learning disorder involving numeric calculations, defined by DSM-IV.

melancholia A distinct quality of severe depressive experience involving loss of pleasure in almost all activities or lack of responsiveness even when something good happens; specific physical symptoms may also be present.

mental illness A term sometimes used interchangeably with *psychological abnormality*.

mentally ill homeless People who in the past were institutionalized but now live on the streets because of a lack of care facilities.

mentally incompetent to stand trial A phrase applied to an accused person who is not sufficiently rational to understand and assist in his or her own defense.

mental retardation Significantly subaverage general intellectual functioning that exists concurrently with deficits in adaptive behavior. To warrant a diagnosis of mental retardation, a person must display these deficits before his or her eighteenth birthday.

meta-analysis A correlational technique for comparing the sizes of the effects found in different studies and for examining the relationship between certain variables and the outcomes of different studies.

methadone A synthetic drug administered orally, the actions of which are similar to those of the opioids; used in some programs to treat opiate dependence.

migraine headaches Headaches in which the pain is typically experienced on one side of the head, is described as "throbbing" or "pulsing," and is often associated with nausea and even vomiting.

Minnesota Multiphasic Personality Inventory (MMPI) One of the most widely used objective measures for assessing personality and psychopathology; now revised and known as MMPI-2.

M'Naghten rule A cognitive definition of legal insanity of British origin, based on the principle that the accused did not know what he or she was doing or did not know that the action was wrong.

model A guiding framework (paradigm) that helps conceptualize and organize available information.

modeling The process of learning behavior as a result of observing others.

molestation The legal definition of sexual activity perpetrated by an older person on a child.

monoamine oxidase inhibitors (MAOIs) A class of drugs used to treat depression by blocking the effects of substances that break down the monoamine transmitters.

monoamines Neurotransmitters (primarily norephinephrine, dopamine, and serotonin) known to be important in the limbic system of the brain and widely distributed into other areas that affect and integrate emotional, psychomotor, and biological functions.

monozygotic twins Identical twins, who share 100 percent of genetic make-up. See also *dizygotic twins*.

mood disorders A condition defined by intense emotional states as well as related behavioral, cognitive, and physical symptoms.

moral anxiety According to Freud, anxiety in which the superego is the source of the individual's sense of threat and worry about being punished for doing or thinking something that violates an accepted standard of behavior.

moral treatment A treatment method for the hospitalized mentally ill that emerged in the early nineteenth century and included treating patients kindly and respectfully, offering guidance and support, and encouraging fresh air and activity.

multiaxial Referring to a feature of the DSM designed to provide a comprehensive picture of the characteristics and functioning of a person by providing an evaluation on five different scales, or axes, each representing different aspects of the person's adjustment and life.

multimodal A term applied to therapies that use a variety of techniques and commonly include extensive assessment, communication skills training, and cognitive-behavioral and behavioral components.

multiple baseline design A research method used with single (or few) cases in which two or more baselines are recorded simultaneously and an intervention is applied for only one of the baselines.

multiple personality disorder A rare but famous dissociative identity disorder in which a person displays more than one identity, each of which acts and thinks in a different way.

multiple-risk-factor model A system that predicts adolescent alcohol and other drug use by assessing the sheer number of risks involved.

multivariate statistical taxometric system A plan for classifying disorders by using statistical procedures to determine which symptoms co-occur with which other symptoms.

narcissistic personality disorder A personality disorder characterized by grandiosity, which involves an inflated sense of self-importance, accompanied by the expectation of being treated as special and being entitled to favorable treatment or exemption from the rules that others must follow.

need for treatment The principle that people can be involuntarily hospitalized if they need treatment but are unable to consent to voluntary treatment because they are not mentally competent; no longer used in the United States as a basis for civil commitment.

negative distortions Perceptions that distort reality in unnecessarily fatalistic ways.

negative reinforcement A type of reinforcement in which the likelihood of a behavior increases by the removal of an unpleasant stimulus or situation.

negative symptoms Schizophrenic symptoms characterized by a predominance of behavioral and emotional deficits, such as lack of motivation, enjoyment, emotional responsiveness, and self-initiated behavior.

neglect A legally defined concept of failure to provide proper care for children or meet their nutritional, emotional, medical, and physical needs.

neologism A made-up word, characteristic of the speech of some people with schizophrenia.

neurocognitive dysfunction Abnormality of mental functioning due to brain disease or injury.

neurodevelopmental abnormalities Patterns of abnormal mental or motor functioning arising during pre- or postnatal brain development.

neuroendocrine system Complex interconnections among the brain, certain hormones, and various organs, two of which (HPA and HPT) may play a role in depression.

neurofibrillary tangles Nerve cell malformations in the brain; one kind of damage brought on by Alzheimer's dementia.

neuroimaging techniques Methods of measuring the brain based on computerized synthesis of highly sensitive detection methods.

neuroleptic Another term for medication with antipsychotic properties.

neuropsychological assessment An approach to cognitive assessment that tests numerous types of cognitive functioning to identify the nature and extent of possible brain impairment.

neurotic anxiety As defined by Freud, the threat that engenders this unpleasant emotional state is a sense of being overwhelmed by an uncontrollable urge to engage in some thought or behavior that might prove harmful or socially unacceptable.

neurotransmitters Chemicals used to transmit electrical impulses from one neuron to another.

nicotine A mild stimulant found in tobacco that narrows blood pathways.

nihilistic delusions A psychotic experience often associated with depression, involving beliefs that one is dead, that nothing exists, that people are only vapors rather than meaningful physical entities, or other delusions about nonexistence or destruction.

noncompliance A patient's tendency to refuse medication or to fail to take it regularly in the prescribed amounts; a major problem for patients with psychological disorders. Noncompliance is also a symptom of child behavior problems, involving refusal to follow the rules of conduct.

norepinephrine A neurotransmitter substance that is thought to be related to certain psychological disorders such as depression.

normative comparisons The principle that, for a treatment to be clinically significant, clients after treatment must be indistinguishable from a representative nondisturbed group.

nuclear magnetic resonance imaging (NMR or MRI) An advanced neuroimaging technique for evaluating brain structures that produces sharp images and does not require radioactive substances.

objective anxiety According to Freud, unpleasant emotions whose sources are in the outside world.

object relations therapy Treatment based on a psychodynamic theory of psychotherapy that deemphasizes impersonal forces and counterforces and focuses on the influences of interpersonal relations stemming from the early mother-child relationship.

observational learning Acquisition of behavior and attitudes from watching others.

observational techniques Assessments achieved by actually watching and recording (coding) what a person does in a particular setting.

obsessions Persistent thoughts, ideas, or images that a person does not want, does not intentionally produce, and perceives as invading his or her thinking.

obsessive-compulsive disorder (OCD)   A psychological disorder in which persistent thoughts or ritualized behavior hampers a person's ability to manage daily living.

obsessive-compulsive personality disorder   A personality disorder marked by preoccupation with perfectionism, orderliness, and control over the self and others to the point of rigidity and inefficiency; not the same as obsessive-compulsive disorder.

operant conditioning procedures   A therapeutic approach that seeks to alter problem behaviors by applying positive and negative reinforcements and shaping by successive approximations.

operant learning   The process by which a response becomes more or less probable when it is followed by reward or punishment, respectively.

opiates   Drugs derived from opium that produce a sedative, anaesthetic and euphoric effect.

oppositional defiant disorder   A condition characterized by a pattern of negativistic, hostile, and defiant behavior that has lasted a minimum of six months.

oral-dependent personality   A term used in psychodynamic theories to describe individuals who are prone to alcoholism because their need for oral gratification was not satisfied early in life.

organic medical disorders   The pre-DSM-IV term for psychological conditions known or suspected to be caused by a medical problem.

orgasm   A stage of the sexual response cycle characterized by involuntary muscle spasms and the release of tension.

overactivity   A characteristic of attention-deficit hyperactivity disorder (ADHD) in which children, relative to peers and development level, are fidgety, restless, and unable to sit still.

overcontrolled behavior   Psychological abnormalities such as inhibition, anxiety, and fearfulness.

panic attacks   Discrete periods of intense fear, ocurring unpredictably and without apparent provocation.

panic disorder   An anxiety disorder characterized by vulnerability to and the experience of frequent panic attacks.

paradigm   Another word for *model*.

paradoxical effect   The calming and focusing effect of stimulant medications on ADHD children's behavior was once thought to be paradoxical. In fact, the effect is similar for ADHD and non-ADHD youth and is not paradoxical.

paradoxical intervention   A treatment strategy in which clients with an anxiety disorder are instructed and encouraged to do or wish for exactly what is feared.

paranoid personality disorder   A personality disorder marked by pervasive suspicion of others and distrust of their motives.

paranoid schizophrenia   A subtype of schizophrenia characterized by preoccupation with delusions or hallucinations that have an organized theme of persecution.

paraphilia   A pattern of recurrent, intense sexual urges and fantasies about an atypical sexual choice that may be acted on or cause marked distress for at least six months.

paraprofessional   Another term for *nonprofessional*.

parasympathetic system   The part of the autonomic nervous system that works to conserve the body's resources and restore homeostasis by slowing the heart rate, reducing blood pressure, and preparing the body for rest.

Parkinson's disease   A degenerative brain disease that causes tremor, muscle rigidity, and difficulty initiating movement. It may also involve cognitive impairment.

partial reinforcement   Reinforcement that occurs only with some rather than all instances of desired behavior. Partially reinforced behavior is often more persistent than continually reinforced behavior.

passive coping   Responding to stress by tolerating it.

pedigree analysis   A research method that attempts to assess the pattern of distribution of disorder in an extended family to evaluate the possibility of genetic transmission.

pedophilia   A pattern of recurrent intense sexual urges and fantasies about sexual activity with a child by persons at least sixteen years old and at least five years older than the child.

peer pressure   The influence of one's friends.

penile prostheses   Surgically implanted artificial means of achieving erections.

peptic ulcers   Disruptions of the lining of the stomach or duodenum (the point where the stomach and small intestine meet).

perceived effects theory   Regarding alcohol and other drugs, the view that such substances are used excessively because the user perceives that they will have positive effects and that those effects are desired to repair defects of character or to achieve subjective sensations.

performance anxiety   Increased worry about personal sexual performance by a male who has experienced erectile disorder in the past; often paired with the spectator role.

performance tests   Psychological measures that involve the completion of tasks believed to indicate cognitive abilities, that include manipulation of objects and mental tasks, or that reveal personality characteristics through clients' stories about or perceptions of ambiguous stimuli.

personal authenticity   Living in a way that reflects awareness and care of one's self and others, which includes being spontaneous, open to new experiences, self-directed, and accepting of personal responsibility.

personality disorder   A continuing pattern of perceiving and relating to the world, usually present since childhood or adolescence, that is maladaptive across a variety of contexts and results in notable impairment or distress.

personality inventories   Questionnaires with numerous items scored on multiple scales that, via self-report, attempt to derive complex pictures of a person's overall personality.

person-centered therapy   A humanistic approach to therapy, developed by Carl Rogers, that emphasizes the therapist's understanding of the client's personal experiences.

pervasive developmental disorders   Severe upsets in a child's cognitive, social, behavioral, and emotional growth that produce widespread distortion of the developmental process — as in childhood autism, for example.

phenothiazines   A class of psychotropic medications initially thought to have tranquilizing properties and later found to have antipsychotic properties and thus used to treat schizophrenia and other psychotic disorders.

phenylketonuria (PKU)   A hereditary error of metabolism resulting from an inactive liver enzyme, which, if untreated in the first year of life, can produce mental retardation.

phobias   Intense, recurrent, and irrational fears that are disproportionate to the actual situation.

physical abuse   The infliction of damage sufficient to cause injury and even death, as well as psychological scars. The term is usually applied to children as victims.

physical dependence   Physiological need for a drug, characterized by tolerance and withdrawal.

physiological reactivity   The stronger or more frequent fight-or-flight response exhibited by people with the type A pattern of personality.

placebo   In an experimental setting, an inert pill or treatment given in such a way that the person believes that the medication or therapy is active.

placebo effect   An effect that results from factors other than the active medication or therapy administered in an experimental setting.

placement   With regard to a mentally retarded person, the living arrangements that must be organized.

plaques   Extracellular protein deposits that damage the brain, as an aspect of Alzheimer's dementia (AD).

plateau   A stage of the sexual response cycle during which sexual tension mounts to a peak, usually leading to orgasm.

poor impulse control   Difficulty in delaying or suppressing an immediate urge or response when a careful or controlled response might produce more desirable or appropriate results.

positive symptoms   Schizophrenic symptoms characterized primarily by the presence of bizarre behaviors and symptoms such as delusions, hallucinations, and thought disorder.

positron emission tomography (PET)   Biological assessment that shows actual brain activity.

postconcussion syndrome   Problems of concentration, memory, and personality changes, usually mild, that follow a blow to the head involving little or no loss of consciousness.

postpartum blues   A pattern of relatively brief spells of crying, sadness, anxiety, and upset experienced by a majority of women after giving birth.

postpartum depression   A depressive episode occurring after a woman gives birth that is more severe than postpartum blues.

poststroke depression   A depressive episode associated with damage to certain areas of the cortex associated with stroke.

posttraumatic stress disorder (PTSD)   A cluster of psychological symptoms that follow a psychologically distressing event.

poverty of speech   Conversation that is adequate in form but conveys little information because it is stereotyped, abstract, characteristic, or vague, occurring among some people with schizophrenia.

predictive validity   Validity based on agreement between an assessment measure and a criterion — that is, a future indicator of a behavior.

premature ejaculation   Ejaculation that occurs so quickly that a male's own enjoyment or that of his partner is reduced.

premenstrual dysphoric disorder   A type of depressive disorder, not otherwise specified, that is marked by impaired functioning in women and associated with mood and depressive syndrome changes limited to the late portion of the menstrual cycle.

premorbid adjustment   A person's level of functioning before the apparent onset of a disorder, usually in reference to schizophrenia.

prevalence   The overall frequency of a disorder in a specified population.

prevention   A collective term referring to interventions, often with at-risk subjects, to reduce the likelihood of future pathology (e.g., suicide or substance abuse).

preventive treatment   The targeting and treating of clients at risk for later development of disorders.

primary prevention   Elimination or alteration of conditions that give rise to mental health problems so that a person will be able to resist the negative effects of these conditions.

privatization   The movement away from public funding and nonprofit facilities toward for-profit ownership of hospitals and emphasis on the business aspects of health care.

problem-focused coping   Responding to stress by escaping, avoiding, or controlling the threatening event itself.

problem-solving therapists   Practitioners whose aim is to help clients overcome deficiencies in thinking by teaching the process (steps) useful in solving problems.

projective test   A performance test that seeks to reveal a person's underlying personality by measuring how he or she responds to an ambiguous task.

prospective hypothesis-testing   A technique of cognitive-behavioral therapy in which clients are guided by therapists to formulate and test specific predictions related to their dysfunctional beliefs.

psychoanalysis   A talking-based psychodynamic treatment based on Freud's theories of personality, the unconscious, and the mental structure of the id, ego, and superego.

psychodynamic model   A model that emphasizes the role of internal mental processes and early childhood experiences in later psychopathology.

psychodynamic therapy   A therapeutic approach that addresses internal conflicts that are said to have been established in childhood and influence adult adjustment.

psychoeducation   A method of treatment that combines information about a disorder and the teaching of psychological strategies to help deal with it, as in work with schizophrenic patients and their families.

psychogenic   Originating from psychological factors.

psychogenic amnesia   A memory disorder linked to the psychological condition of dissociation.

psychological abnormality   Impaired functioning with respect to expected performance suitable for the person in a relevant context, which includes consideration of the situation in which the behaviors occur as well as gender, age, cultural values, and historical perspective.

psychological autopsy   A process of interviewing relatives and friends of a person who committed suicide about the person's thoughts and behaviors preceding the fatal act.

psychological disorder   A term used interchangeably with *psychological abnormality.*

psychoneuroimmunology   The study of psychological influences on the immune system.

psychopathology   The scientific study of psychological disorders.

psychopathy   A personality type characterized by selfishness, deceitfulness, and callousness that can be reflected — though not necessarily demonstrated — in various illegal ways.

psychopharmacology   A term referring to the use and study of psychotropic drugs.

psychophysiological arousal   Bodily signs of awareness such as heart and respiration rate and electrodermal activity.

psychophysiological disorders   Physical conditions in which tissue damage has occurred and psychological factors are believed to play a role in the onset or exacerbation of the physical conditions.

psychophysiological techniques   Assessment instruments based on the assumption that emotional states involve changes in the autonomic nervous system.

psychophysiologic model   A view of the link between mental states and physical health maintaining that the first step toward illness involves a combination of excessive levels of environmental challenges, threats, or demands, on the one hand, and individual characteristics such as ways of perceiving these stressors and psychological resources for coping with them, on the other.

psychosis   One of several mental disorders characterized by major departures from reality, such as delusions and hallucinations.

psychosomatic   Referring to psychological origins of physical symptoms.

psychostimulant medications   Medicines administered to children with ADHD to increase their ability to sustain attention, decrease their impulsiveness, and improve their performance on tasks.

psychosurgery   An operation on the brain intended to alter the symptoms of severe psychological disorder.

psychotic depression   A type of major depressive disorder that may include severe symptoms plus departures from reality such as delusions or hallucinations with a depressive content.

psychotropic drugs   Medicines used to control symptoms of mental disorder and to reduce distress associated with psychological problems.

quasi-experiments   Research designs in which the conditions of a true experiment are only approximated — as when subjects are not randomly assigned to an experimental condition.

questionnaire   A written set of questions to which a person provides written replies.

randomization   The assignment of subjects to one or another condition in an experiment purely by chance.

random sampling   A method of selecting participants in a sample such that, regardless of the sample's size, every member of the population being studied has an equal chance of being included.

rape   Sexual assault that involves sexual penetration in the context of physical coercion or the threat of harm.

rational-emotive therapy (RET) A therapeutic approach that seeks to teach clients to identify and change the irrational notions that underlie their distressing symptoms.

reactivity The degree to which those being observed may behave atypically because they know that they are being watched.

reading disorder A type of learning disorder defined by DSM-IV.

reality monitoring Distinguishing real from imagined events; thought by some psychologists to be deficient among individuals who are compulsive.

rebound effects The behaviors observed after a medication is stopped, when anxiety symptoms appear to be worse.

recidivism The likelihood that, after release from prison, an offender is later convicted of another crime.

recovery The return to and maintenance of a healthy state following relapse.

"refrigerator" parent A term related to the dated and discarded notion that a cold and unloving parent causes a child to withdraw into autism.

regression Reversion to an earlier, and therefore more immature, form of behavior; said to be the result of external stress or internal conflict.

relapse Reappearance of substance abuse or other disorders following a period of remission.

relapse prevention training A combination of cognitive and behavioral skills taught to clients who are trying to gain self-control.

relaxation-induced anxiety A phenomenon among patients with generalized anxiety disorder (GAD) whereby the process of inducing relaxation paradoxically produces anxiety and tension.

reliability The consistency or repeatability of results of a measurement.

remission A state of health in which a previously active disorder or illness has receded or disappeared entirely.

representativeness The degree to which important characteristics of the sample of persons studied match these characteristics in the population.

repression The unconscious but purposeful exclusion of painful thoughts or unacceptable desires or impulses from consciousness.

residual schizophrenia A subtype defining persons who have had at least one episode of schizophrenia and continuing evidence of the disorder but are currently free of the psychotic symptoms.

resilient Showing no ill effects despite negative circumstances.

resistance The unwillingness of a client in therapy to express true feelings, divulge actual thoughts, or accept the therapist's interpretations; also, the second stage of the general adaptation syndrome (GAS), in which the organism maintains and enhances the bodily responses mobilized during the first phase.

resolution The final stage of the sexual response cycle, consisting of a return to the normal physical state after orgasm.

response biases The tendencies of clients to represent themselves in a particular but not accurate way, as by acknowledging only socially desirable responses or saying "yes" to any symptoms.

response class matrix A method for observing and recording the behavior of both the parent and the child during parent-child interactions.

response definition of stress Defining stress in terms of an organism's reaction to an environmental threat or demand.

response-focused coping Responding to stress by dealing with the causes and consequences of the negative event.

response prevention A treatment for a disorder in which the client is deflected from making a dysfunctional avoidance response.

Rett's disorder Seen only in girls, this pervasive developmental disorder appears after a period of normal motor development. There is a loss of purposeful hand movements, interest in social activities diminishes, and language is impaired.

right to refuse treatment The patient's right to turn down physical procedures such as medication; subject to review by professionals who may override the patient's wishes if such action is medically justified.

right to treatment The principle that jurisdictions cannot commit individuals to institutions without providing minimal standards of care, including active efforts to reduce symptoms and provision of humane conditions to support their treatment.

risk factors Conditions that are significantly associated with a disorder and presumed to play a causal role.

Rorschach inkblot test The best-known projective test, in which subjects are presented with a series of ten inkblots and asked to describe what they "see"; intended to reveal the underlying personality and its dynamics.

sampling The process of selecting groups of people from populations for study.

scatterplots Graphs used to display data from correlational studies, in which values of one variable are shown on the horizontal axis and values of the other variable are shown on the vertical axis.

schizoid personality disorder A personality disorder marked by aloofness from relationships and emotional coldness.

schizophrenia A type of psychosis marked by disturbances of thought, language, and behavior not due to a primary mood disorder or medical condition.

schizophrenogenic mother   The concept of a schizophrenia-inducing mother was proposed by earlier models of the disorder but is no longer considered valid.

schizotypal personality disorder   A personality disorder marked by difficulties in interpersonal relationships as well as by abnormalities of thought, behavior, and appearance that are similar to the symptoms of schizophrenia but not severe enough to be diagnosed as such.

school-based competency training   Prevention programs aimed at all children, not just those thought to be at risk, that attempt to incorporate into the curriculum certain attitudes, values, and skills that support health-enhancing behaviors.

school-based prevention programs   Programs integrated into the curriculum that teach teens about various problems (such as suicide), including information about warning signs and about resources for helping with the problems.

school phobia   A specific phobia, seen in children, characterized by fear and avoidance that is focused on the school environment.

seasonal affective disorder (SAD)   A depressive disorder in which a person becomes depressed on a recurring basis in one season of the year (usually winter) and improves in the following season.

secondary prevention   Early detection of people with a mental health problem and actions to limit the negative consequences once the problem has manifested itself.

sedative hypnotic agent   Drugs, including alcohol, that exert temporary and nonspecific depressant effects on the central nervous system.

sedative-hypnotic-anxiolytic agents   Central nervous system depressants, chronic use of which can cause deterioration in coordination, speech, and sleep.

selective association   As suggested by some psychologists, the tendency of human beings and many animals to learn certain fears as a result of natural selection.

selective dissociative amnesia   A dissociative disorder in which a person forgets some but not all of what happened during a certain period of time.

self-actualization   Ongoing fulfillment of personal potentials and missions, a fuller acceptance of one's intrinsic nature, and a willingness to be oneself yet share fully with others.

self-efficacy   Expectations of success in a given situation and confidence in one's ability to cope with difficulties.

self-help groups   Collections of individuals united by common challenges and difficulties who meet to receive mutual aid and to share information and strategies for coping.

self-injurious behavior   Personally harmful actions such as head-banging, hair-pulling, self-biting, and eating nonedible substances, which some severely handicapped children may engage in.

self-monitoring   A behavioral observation procedure in which an individual records for herself or himself the frequency of behavior or thoughts in certain contexts.

sensate focus   A technique used in sex therapy to improve both physical exploration and communication, in which partners progress through various types of touching to learn more about what gives pleasure to each other.

sensation-seeking   Desire for exciting, stimulating, or even dangerous experiences, hypothesized to be related to antisocial behavior.

separation anxiety disorder   A childhood condition manifested by obvious distress from and excessive concern about being separated from those to whom the child is attached.

serotonin   A neurotransmitter thought to be associated with various disorders, including impulsive aggressiveness.

sex reassignment treatment   A course of treatment that includes careful psychological screening and counseling, administration of hormones, and sex-change surgery, all aimed at enabling an individual to alter lifestyle and physical characteristics to match gender identity.

sex therapy   Brief, behaviorally oriented treatments involving techniques aimed specifically at sexual problems and typically provided in the context of a couple relationship.

sexual assault   The use of psychological pressure or physical force to engage in unwanted sexual contact that involves genital touching or intercourse.

sexual aversion disorder   A more severe and infrequent form of sexual desire disorder, involving extreme aversion to sexual contact and total avoidance of sexual activity.

sexual dysfunction   The general term for problems involving sexual interest or performance that cause distress to individuals or difficulties in their relationships.

sexual masochism   Recurrent, intense, sexually arousing fantasies and urges involving being humiliated, beaten, bound, or otherwise made to suffer.

sexual molestation   Another term for *childhood sexual assault.*

sexual sadism   Sexually arousing urges and fantasies involving acts that cause physical or psychological suffering to another person.

shaping   The process of rewarding successive approximations of desired behavior, which does not require the learner to produce an entire new response pattern to receive the reinforcement.

side effects Unwanted effects associated with certain treatments (e.g., psychopharmacology).

simple phobia The former term used to refer to *specific phobia.*

single-subject designs Research designs in which the effects of an intervention can be evaluated using a single case.

sleep deprivation An experimental treatment for depression in which patients are kept awake during part of the night.

social learning theory A psychological model that explains behavior as the product of both external stimulus events and internal cognitive processes.

social phobias Phobias characterized by a persistent fear of being in a social situation in which one is exposed to scrutiny by others and by a related fear of acting in a way that will be humiliating or embarrassing.

social support The network of individuals with whom a person has social or personal contact within a certain time period. Social support refers especially to the support related to emotional well-being, the absence of which is thought to be a factor in many stress disorders.

somatization disorder A disorder in which a person has a long-standing history of physical complaints that result in treatment for impaired social and occupational functioning.

somatoform disorders Physical symptoms that have no organic basis, that are associated with psychological conflicts and stress, and that are not produced voluntarily. Three types of somatoform disorders are somatization disorder, hypochondriasis, and conversion disorder.

somatosensory amplification As posited by some researchers, the tendency of hypochondriacal patients to report more fears and beliefs about disease and to attend more to bodily sensations.

specificity The idea that some models of psychopathology are specific to a single disorder.

specific (simple) phobias Phobias characterized by pathological (excessive and unrealistic) fears of specific animals, objects, or situations.

spectator role In sexual dysfunctions, adoption of a role as critical observer of oneself rather than as participant. The spectator role grows out of performance anxiety and can impair sexual functioning, as in erectile disorder.

sporadic Referring to the form of Alzheimer's dementia in which no family pattern of transmission is apparent.

stage theory A theory suggesting that a person develops alcoholism after going through a series of mutually exclusive, invariant phases.

states Characteristics of emotion, behavior, or cognition that are temporary conditions.

statistical risk factor models Attempts to compile lists of demographic and personal characteristics most frequently associated with problems in the general population.

statistical significance A correlation or covariation between variables that would not occur as a result of chance alone.

stimulus definition of stress Defining stress in terms of an external event or situation that represents a demand or threat.

stimulus overselectivity Responding to only select aspects of stimulus materials, as is typical of autistic children.

stress The feeling of unease that occurs when an important environmental demand is seen by the individual as taxing or exceeding his or her ability to meet that demand.

stressor An environmental challenge, threat, or demand.

structural-strategic family therapy A therapy for clients and their families that includes designing specific strategies that the families can use to solve problems and changing the relationships among individual pairs within the family.

structured interviews Interviews that follow a specific format.

suicide attempt A nonfatal act of self-destruction.

suicide prevention centers Organizations providing services to suicidal people, usually involving telephone help lines.

superego A hypothesized mental structure representing the storehouse of moral and ethical standards taught by parents and culture (what we generally think of as "conscience").

survey A method of research that provides information about the nature and scope of mental health problems across large populations or regions.

sympathetic system The part of the autonomic nervous system that mediates the body's response to stress, speeding up the heart rate, increasing blood pressure, and generally preparing for action.

syndrome The entire set of defining symptoms of a condition.

syphilis An infectious, often sexually transmitted disease that causes general paresis.

systematic desensitization A behavioral therapy based on classical conditioning, in which fear responses are paired with relaxation. Specifically, images of fearful situations are presented while the person relaxes.

tardive dyskinesia (TD) An irreversible, undesirable neurological side effect of antipsychotic medications marked by involuntary facial movements and motor activity in the hands and feet.

telephone hotlines   Services for dealing with psychological crises, such as suicidal urges, staffed by trained volunteers.

temperament   Behavior tendencies believed to be biologically based and present from birth; another term for disposition.

tension headaches   Headaches in which discomfort begins as an ache or sensation of tightness in the neck or back of the head and worsens and spreads until it is a dull, steady pain on both sides of the head.

tension reduction hypothesis   According to learning theory, the view that people learn to use alcohol and other drugs because such use relieves tension, whether from anxiety, depression, fear, or social avoidance.

tertiary prevention   Controlling the long-term consequences of a chronic mental health problem.

testosterone   A hormone associated with male characteristics, which has been studied in regard to a possible role in aggressiveness and sexual behaviors; also associated with sex drive in men.

test-retest reliability   The consistency of a test's results over time.

thalamus   An area of the forebrain that is important in the processing and relaying of information between other regions of the central nervous system and the cerebral cortex.

therapeutic alliance   The extent to which a patient believes that he or she and the therapist are working together constructively on important issues.

therapy   An attempt by a mental health professional to assist a client to adjust to or overcome dysfunctions. Various approaches may be used, but all are designed to be corrective and helpful, all involve an interpersonal relationship between therapist and client, and all have the goal of increasing the client's adaptive and autonomous functioning.

third variable   An unknown variable that may be responsible for the changes in two other variables, even when those variables are highly correlated.

thought broadcasting   The delusional belief that one's thoughts are being broadcast aloud so that others may hear them; may occur in psychotic disorders such as schizophrenia.

thought insertion   The delusional belief that others may put thoughts in one's head; may occur in psychotic disorders such as schizophrenia.

tics   Involuntary, rapid, recurrent, and stereotyped motor movements or vocalizations.

token economy   A therapeutic approach based on learning principles in which patients earn tokens as rewards for accomplishing specific desirable behaviors; the tokens may be exchanged for privileges and items of value to the patient. Sometimes used in institutional settings for severely impaired patients.

tolerance   The need for increased dosages of psychotropic medications to experience the same effects; also relevant to drug and alcohol use.

Tourette's disorder   A tic disorder characterized by multiple motor tics (usually involving the head) and one or more verbal tics.

trait   A characteristic attitude, belief, behavior, reaction, or way of thinking about oneself and the world that is enduring and unchanging.

transactional definition   Defining stress not in terms of environmental stimuli or the organism's response but in terms of the particular relationship that exists between the individual and the situation.

transference   A process by which a client reexperiences toward the therapist the thoughts and feelings that were experienced in childhood when relating to an authority figure such as a parent.

transsexuals   Another term for persons with gender identity disorder.

transvestic fetishism   A fetish in men involving the wearing of women's clothing as a means of increasing sexual pleasure.

traumatic brain injuries   Damage to the brain, caused either by penetrating injuries (as by gunshot) or closed head injuries (as by blow to the head).

treatment   Interventions aimed at the remediation of emotional, cognitive, and behavioral problems. See also *therapy*.

treatment-etiology fallacy   An error of logic in which the treatment mode is assumed to imply the mechanism of the original cause of a disorder.

tricyclic antidepressants   A class of medications used to treat depression.

twelve-step programs   Self-help groups that focus on helping members practice twelve central tenets believed to be essential for healthy functioning.

twin studies   Research that attempts to test genetic hypotheses by determining the extent to which co-twins of twins with a disorder also experience the disorder.

Type A pattern   A pattern of behavior characterized by hard-driving competitiveness, impatience, easily provoked hostility, overcommitment to work, and a loud, rapid speaking style.

Type B pattern   A pattern of behavior characterized by a more relaxed and easygoing attitude than that associated with the Type A pattern. Type B individuals are also less competitive and less driven than Type A individuals.

type 1 alcoholism   A class of alcoholism typified by individuals who begin to drink in early adulthood and show health effects in middle age.

type 2 alcoholism   A class of alcoholism typified by individuals who have few medical problems but experience severe disruptions of life; the sons of such individuals are far more likely than the sons of normal parents to become alcoholic.

unconditional positive regard A characteristic of therapists in person-centered therapy involving active acceptance of the client as a valued person, regardless of the client's own motivation and ability to improve.

unconscious Mental activity outside a person's awareness.

undercontrolled behavior Psychological abnormalities such as aggression, impulsivity, and distractibility.

underutilize To seek therapy services disproportionately less frequently than a disorder occurs.

undifferentiated schizophrenia A subtype in which symptoms do not clearly fit the other categories of schizophrenia.

uninhibited A descriptive term referring to a person who is sociable, talkative, and outgoing.

unipolar depression A disorder characterized by persisting disturbances of negative mood and cognition and altered energy, motivation, behavior, and bodily functioning that affects sleep and appetite but is not accompanied by shifts to the extreme positive mood known as mania.

unitary disease model A model of addiction suggesting that alcoholics differ from normal persons in terms of psychological predisposition and "allergic" sensitivity to alcohol, which lead to a craving for alcohol and loss of control regarding alcohol.

utility The degree to which an assessment procedure is useful and provides information not otherwise available or obtained more cheaply.

vaginismus Involuntary muscle spasms of the outer portion of the vagina that interfere with entry of the penis.

validating Acknowledging that one has heard what another person has just said.

validity The degree to which a measuring procedure (e.g., an assessment or test) measures what it purports to measure.

variables Any aspects of a person, group, or setting that are measured for the purpose of a study.

vascular dementia A form of dementia caused by the accumulated effect of many small strokes.

ventricles Fluid-filled spaces in the brain that are enlarged in some people with mental disorders such as schizophrenia, suggesting brain damage or dysfunction.

visual hallucinations Visions of persons or objects perceived to be present but, in fact, are not.

volition The ability to exercise free will; one aspect of certain legal criteria for determining a "not guilty by reason of insanity" verdict.

voyeurism A paraphilia characterized by the desire to watch unsuspecting people, usually strangers, who are nude, undressing, or engaging in sexual activity.

vulnerability The likelihood that a person will respond maladaptively to a situation.

vulnerability model Factors that stem from a variety of sources and that render an individual susceptible to addiction.

withdrawal A set of symptoms, usually opposite in nature to the effects of the drug itself, that result when prolonged use of a substance has altered the body to such an extent that it is affected when the substance is not taken.

working through The process in psychodynamic therapy by which a client in therapy comes to accept formerly unconscious experiences, eventually relating to the therapist and, by extension, to the parent in a positive way.

yin and yang In Chinese belief, the two forces within the universe — good and bad, male and female, dark and light, positive and negative — that must be maintained in balance, achieved by following the prescribed ways of nature and society and by adhering to moderation of thought and deed, to achieve normal and healthy functioning.

REFERENCES

Abbott, J., Johnson, R., Koziol-McLain, J., & Lowenstein, S. R. (1995). Domestic violence against women: Incidence and prevalence in an emergency department population. *Journal of the American Medical Association, 273,* 1763–1767.

Abel, G., Becker, J., & Cunningham-Rather, J. (1984). Complications, consent, and cognitions in sex between children and adults. *International Journal of Law and Psychiatry, 7,* 89–103.

Abel, G., & Osborn, C. (1992). The paraphilias: The extent and nature of sexually deviant and criminal behavior. *Psychiatric Clinics of North America, 15,* 675–687.

Abelson, J. L., & Curtis, G. C. (1993). Discontinuation of alprazolam after successful treatment of panic disorder: A naturalistic follow-up study. *Journal of Anxiety Disorders, 7,* 107–117.

Abikoff, H., Ganeles, D., Reiter, G., Blum, C., Foley, C., & Klein, R. G. (1988). Cognitive training in academically deficient ADHD boys receiving psychostimulant medication. *Journal of Abnormal Child Psychology, 16,* 411–432.

Abikoff, H., & Gittelman, R. (1985). Hyperactive children treated with stimulants: Is cognitive training a useful adjunct? *Archives of General Psychiatry, 42,* 953–965.

Abraham, K. (1908/1960). *Selected papers on psychoanalysis.* New York: Basic Books.

Abrahamson, D. J., Barlow, D. H., & Abrahamson, L. S. (1989). Differential effects of performance demand and distraction on sexually functional and dysfunctional males. *Journal of Abnormal Psychology, 98,* 241–247.

Abramowitz, I. A., & Coursey, R. D. (1989). Impact of an educational support group on family participants who take care of their schizophrenic relatives. *Journal of Consulting and Clinical Psychology, 57,* 232–236.

Abramson, L. Y., Alloy, L. B., & Metalsky, G. I. (1988). The cognitive diathesis-stress theories of depression: Toward an adequate evaluation of the theories' validities. In L. B. Alloy (Ed.), *Cognitive processes in depression* (pp. 3–30). New York: Guilford Press.

Abramson, L. Y., Seligman, M. E. P., & Teasdale, J. D. (1978). Learned helplessness in humans: Critique and reformulation. *Journal of Abnormal Psychology, 87,* 49–74.

Achenbach, T. M. (1982). Assessment and taxonomy of children's behavior disorders. In B. B. Lahey & A. E. Kazdin (Eds.), *Advances in clinical child psychology* (Vol. 5). New York: Plenum.

Achenbach, T. M. (1990). Conceptualization of developmental psychopathology. In M. Lewis & S. M. Miller (Eds.), *Handbook of developmental psychopathology.* New York: Plenum Press.

Achenbach, T. M. (1991). *Manual for the child behavior checklist/4–18 and 1991 profile.* Burlington, VT: University of Vermont, Department of Psychiatry.

Achenbach, T. M., & Edelbrock, C. (1978). The classification of child psychopathology: A review and analysis of empirical efforts. *Psychological Bulletin, 85,* 1275–1301.

Achenbach, T. M., & Edelbrock, C. (1983). *Manual for the child behavior checklist and revised child behavior profile.* Burlington, VT: Psychiatry Associates, University of Vermont.

Ackerman, M. D., & Carey, M. P. (1995). Psychology's role in the assessment of erectile dysfunction: Historical precedents, current knowledge, and methods. *Journal of Consulting and Clinical Psychology, 63,* 862–876.

Adams, H. E., & McAnulty, R. (1993). Sexual disorders: The paraphilias. P. Sutker & H. Adams (Eds.), *Comprehensive handbook of psychopathology* (2nd ed; pp. 563–579). New York: Plenum.

Adams, H. E., Wright, L. W., & Lohr, B. A. (1996). Is homophobia associated with homosexual arousal? *Journal of Abnormal Psychology, 105,* 440–445.

Ader, R., Felton, D. L., & Cohen, N. (Eds.). (1991). *Psychoneuroimmunology.* San Diego: Academic Press.

Agosta, J., Melda, K. (1996). Supporting families who provide care at home for children with disabilities. *Exceptional Children, 62,* 271–282.

Akhtar, S., Wig, N., Verma, V., Pershad, D., & Verma, S. (1975). A phenomenological analysis of symptoms of obsessive-compulsive neurosis. *British Journal of Psychiatry, 127,* 342–348.

Akiskal, H. S., Maser, J. D., Zeller, P. J., Endicott, J., Coryell, W., Keller, M., Warshaw, M., Clayton, P., & Goodwin, F. (1995). Switching from 'unipolar' to bipolar II: An 11-year prospective study of clinical and temperamental predictors in 559 patients. *Archives of General Psychiatry, 52,* 114–123.

Alden, L. (1989). Short-term structured treatment for avoidant personality disorder. *Journal of Consulting and Clinical Psychology, 57,* 756–764.

Aldridge-Morris, R. (1995). Commentary on a skeptical reflection on the diagnosis of multiple personality disorder. *Irish Journal of Psychological Medicine, 12,* 81–82.

Alessandri, S. M. (1992). Attention, play, and social behavior in ADHD preschoolers. *Journal of Abnormal Child Psychology, 20,* 289–302.

Alexander, F. (1950). *Psychosomatic medicine: Its principles and applications.* New York: Norton.

Alexander, J. F. (1973). Defensive and supportive communications in normal and deviant families. *Journal of Consulting and Clinical Psychology, 40,* 223–231.

Alexander, J. F., Holtzworth-Munroe, A., & Jameson, P. (1994). The process and outcome of marital and family therapy: Research review and evaluation. In S. Garfield & A. Bergin (Eds.), *Handbook of psychotherapy and behavior change* (4th ed.). New York: Wiley.

Alexander, P. C., Neimeyer, R. A., Follette, V. M., Moore, M. K., & Harter, S. (1989). A comparison of group treatments of women sexually abused as children. *Journal of Consulting and Clinical Psychology, 57,* 479–483.

Alford, B. A., & Norcross, J. C. (1991). Cognitive therapy as integrative therapy. *Journal of Psychotherapy Integration, 1,* 175–190.

Alloy, L. B., Lipman, A. J., & Abramson, L. Y. (1992). Attributional style as a vulnerability factor for depression. *Cognitive Therapy and Research, 16,* 391–407.

Altshuler, L. L., Curran, J. G., Hauser, P., Mintz, J., Denicoff, K., & Post, R. (1995). T2 Hyperintensities in bipolar disorder: Magnetic resonance imaging comparison and a literature meta-analysis. *American Journal of Psychiatry, 152,* 1139–1144.

Aman, M. G., & Singh, N. N. (1983). Pharmacological intervention. In L. Matson & F. Andrasik (Eds.), *Treatment issues and innovations in mental retardation.* New York: Plenum Press.

American Association on Mental Retardation (1994). *Mental retardation: Definition, classification, and systems of support* (9th ed.). Washington, DC: AAMR Publications.

American Psychiatric Association (1983). American Psychiatric Association statement on the insanity defense. *American Journal of Psychiatry, 140,* 681–688.

American Psychiatric Association (1993). Practice guideline for major depressive disorder in adults. *Supplement to the American Journal of Psychiatry, 150(4),* 1–26.

American Psychological Association, Committee for the Protection of Human Participants in Research. (1982). *Ethical principles in the conduct of research with human participants.* Washington, DC: Author.

American Psychological Association, Committee for the Protection of Human Participants in Research. (1990). Ethical principles of psychologists. *American Psychologist, 45,* 390–395.

Ammerman, R. T., & Hersen, M. (Eds.). (1995). *Handbook of child behavior therapy in the psychiatric setting.* New York: Wiley.

Anastopoulos, A. D., Shelton, T., DuPaul, G. J., & Gouvremont, D. C. (1993). Parent training for Attention-Deficit Hyperactivity

Disorder: Its impact on parent functioning. *Journal of Abnormal Child Psychology, 21,* 581–596.

Anchin, J., & Kiesler, D. J. (1982). *Handbook of interpersonal psychotherapy.* New York: Pergamon Press.

Andersen, B. L. (1992). Psychological interventions for cancer patients to enhance the quality of life. *Journal of Consulting and Clinical Psychology, 60,* 552–568.

Andersen, B. L., & Cyranowski, J. M. (1995). Women's sexuality: Behaviors, responses, and individual differences. *Journal of Consulting and Clinical Psychology, 63,* 891–906.

Anderson, J. C., Williams, S., McGee, R., & Silva, P. A. (1987). DSM-III disorders in preadolescent children: prevalence in a large sample from the general population. *Archives of General Psychiatry, 44,* 69–76.

Anderson, J. R., & Meininger, J. C. (1993). Components analysis of the structured interview for assessment of Type A behavior in employed women. *Journal of Behavioral Assessment, 16,* 371–385.

Anderson, N. B., McNeilly, M., & Myers, H. (1991). Autonomic reactivity and hypertension in blacks: A review and proposed model. *Ethnicity and Disease, 1,* 154–170.

Andreasen, N. C. (1988). Brain imaging: Applications in psychiatry. *Science, 239,* 1381–1388.

Andreasen, N. C., Arndt, S., Alliger, R., Miller, D., & Flaum, M. (1995). Symptoms of schizophrenia: Methods, meanings, and mechanisms. *Archives of General Psychiatry, 52,* 341–351.

Andreasen, N. C., Ehrhardt, J. C., Swayze, V. W., Allinger, R. J., Yuh, W. T. C., Cohen, G., & Ziebell, S. (1990a). Magnetic resonance imaging of the brain in schizophrenia: The pathophysiologic significance of structural abnormalities. *Archives of General Psychiatry, 47,* 35–44.

Andreasen, N. C., Flaum, M., Swayze, V. W., Tyrrell, G., & Arndt, S. (1990b). Positive and negative symptoms in schizophrenia: A critical reappraisal. *Archives of General Psychiatry, 47,* 615–621.

Andreasen, N. C., Rezai, K., Alliger, R., Swayze II, V. W., Flaum, M., Kirchner, P., Cohen, G., & O'Leary, D. S. (1992). Hypofrontality in neuroleptic-naive patients and in patients with chronic schizophrenia: Assessment with Xenon 133 single-photon emission computed tomography and the Tower of London. *Archives of General Psychiatry, 49,* 943–958.

Andreasen, N. C., Swayze, V. W., Flaum, M., Yates, W. R., Arndt, S., & McChesney, C. (1990c). Ventricular enlargement in schizophrenia evaluated with computed tomographic scanning: Effects of gender, age, and stage of illness. *Archives of General Psychiatry, 47,* 1008–1015.

Angold, A., & Rutter, M. (1992). Effects of age and pubertal status on depression in a large clinical sample. *Development and Psychopathology, 4,* 5–28.

Angst, J., Baastrup, P. C., Grof, P., Hippius, H., Poeldinger, W., & Weiss, P. (1973). The course of monopolar depression and bipolar psychoses. *Psychiatrie, Neurologie et Neurochirurgie, 76,* 246–254.

Anonymous. (1976). *Alcoholics Anonymous.* New York: Alcoholics Anonymous World Services.

Anonymous. (1992). First person account: Portrait of a schizophrenic. *Schizophrenia Bulletin, 18,* 333.

Aponte, H., & Hoffman, L. (1973). The open door: A structural approach to a family with an anorectic child. *Family Process, 12,* 1–44.

Aponte, J. F., Rivers, R. Y., & Wohl, J. (1995). *Psychological interventions and cultural diversity.* Boston, MA: Allyn and Bacon.

Appelbaum, P. S., & Greer, A. (1994). Who's on trial? Multiple personalities and the insanity defense. *Hospital and Community Psychiatry, 45,* 965–966.

Appelbaum, P. S., & Rosenbaum, A. (1989). Tarasoff and the researcher: Does the duty to protect apply in the research setting? *American Psychologist, 44,* 885–894.

Applebaum, K. A., Blanchard, E. B., Nicholson, N. L., Radnitz, C., Kirsch, C., Michultka, D., Attanasio, V., Andrasik, F., & Dettinger, M. P. (1990). Controlled evaluation of the addition of cognitive strategies to a home-based relaxation protocol for tension headache. *Behavior Therapy, 21,* 293–304.

Arieti, S. (1955). *Interpretation of schizophrenia.* New York: Basic.

Armor, D., Polich, J., & Stambul, H. (1978). *Alcoholism and treatment.* New York: Wiley.

Arndt, S., Andreasen, N. C., Flaum, M., Miller, D., & Nopoulos, P. (1995). A longitudinal study of symptom dimensions in schizophrenia: Predictions and patterns of change. *Archives of General Psychiatry, 52,* 352–360.

Arnetz, B. B., Wasserman, J., Petrini, B., & Brenner, S. O. (1987). Immune function in unemployed women. *Psychosomatic Medicine, 49,* 3–12.

Arnkoff, D. B., & Glass, C. R. (1982). Clinical cognitive constructs: Examination, evaluation, elaboration. In P. C. Kendall (Ed.), *Advances in cognitive-behavioral research and therapy.* Vol. 1. New York: Academic Press.

Arrindell, W. A., & Emmelkamp, P. M. (1986). Marital adjustment, intimacy, and needs in female agoraphobics and their partners: A controlled study. *British Journal of Psychiatry, 149,* 592–602.

Asarnow, R. F., Hornstein, N., & Russell, A. (1991). Childhood-onset schizophrenia: Developmental perspectives on schizophrenic disorders. In E. F. Walker (Ed.), *Schizophrenia: A life-course developmental perspective.* San Diego: Academic Press.

Asberg, M., Traskman, L., & Thoren, P. (1976). 5-HIAA in the cerebrospinal fluid: A suicide predictor? *Archives of General Psychiatry, 33,* 1193–1197.

Asterita, M. F. (1985). *The physiology of stress.* New York: Human Science Press.

Astin, M. C., Ogland-Hand, S. M., Coleman, E. M., & Foy, D. W. (1995). Posttraumatic stress disorder and childhood abuse in battered women: Comparisons with maritally distressed women. *Journal of Consulting and Clinical Psychology, 63,* 308–312.

Athanasiou, R., Shaver, P., & Tavris, C. (1970). Sex. *Psychology Today* (July), pp. 39–52.

Atthowe, J. M., & Krasner, L. (1968). Preliminary report on the application of contingent reinforcement procedures (token economy) on a "chronic" psychiatric ward. *Journal of Abnormal Psychology, 73,* 37–43.

Azrin, N. H., Sheed, T. J., & Foxx, R. M. (1974). Dry bed: rapid elimination of childhood enuresis. *Behaviour Research and Therapy, 12,* 147–156.

Bailey, A. J. (1993). The biology of autism. *Psychological Medicine, 23,* 7–11.

Bailey, A., Le Couter, A., Gottesman, L., Bolton, P., Simonoff, E., Yuzda, E., & Rutter, M. (1995). Autism as a strongly genetic disorder: Evidence from a British twin study. *Psychological Medicine, 25,* 63–77.

Baer, D., Wolf, M., & Risley, T. (1968). Some current dimensions of applied behavior analysis. *Journal of Applied Behavior Analysis, 1,* 91–97.

Bailey, J. M., Bobrow, D., Wolfe, M., & Mikach, S. (1995). Sexual orientation of adult sons of gay fathers. *Developmental Psychology, 31,* 124–129.

Bailey, J. M., & Pillard, R. C. (1991). A genetic study of male sexual orientation. *Archives of General Psychiatry, 48,* 1089–1096.

Bailey, J. M., Pillard, R. C., Neale, M. C., & Agyei, Y. (1993). Heritable factors influence sexual orientation in women. *Archives of General Psychiatry, 50,* 217–223.

Bailey, J. M., & Zucker, K. J. (1995). Childhood sex-typed behavior and sexual orientation: A conceptual analysis and quantitative review. *Developmental Psychology, 31,* 43–55.

Bakal, D. A. (1979). *Psychology and medicine: Psychological dimensions of health and illness.* New York: Springer.

Baker, B. L. (1984). Interventions with families with young severely handicapped children. In J. Blacker (Ed.), *Severely handicapped young children and their families*. New York: Academic.

Baker, B. L., Landen, S. J., & Kashima, K. J. (1991). Effects of parent training on families of children with mental retardation: Increased burden or generalized benefit? *American Journal on Mental Retardation, 96*, 127–136.

Baker, F. M. (1990). Black youth suicide: Literature review with a focus on prevention. *Journal of the National Medical Association, 82*, 495–507.

Baker, L. J., Dearborn, M., Hastings, J. E., & Hamberger, K. (1984). Type A behavior in women: A review. *Health Psychology, 3*, 477–497.

Bakker, A., Van Kesteren, P. J., Gooren, L. J., & Bezemer, P. D. (1993). The prevalence of transsexualism in the Netherlands. *Acta Psychiatrica Scandinavica, 87*, 237–238.

Ballenger, J. C., Burrows, G. D., & Dupont, R. L. (1988). Alprazolam in panic disorder and agoraphobia: Results from a multicenter trial: Efficacy in short-term treatment. *Archives of General Psychiatry, 45*, 413–422.

Bancroft, J. (1989). *Human sexuality and its problems* (2nd ed.). Edinburgh: Churchill Livingstone.

Bandura, A. (1969). *Principles of behavior modification*. New York: Holt, Rinehart, & Winston.

Bandura, A. (1973). *Aggression: A social learning analysis*. Englewood Cliffs, NJ: Prentice-Hall.

Bandura, A. (1977). Self-efficacy: Toward a unifying theory of behavioral changes. *Psychological Review, 84*, 191–215.

Bandura, A. (1985). *Social foundations of thought and action*. Englewood Cliffs, NJ: Prentice-Hall.

Bandura, A. (1986). *Social learning theory*. Englewood Cliffs, NJ: Prentice-Hall.

Bandura, A., Adams, N. E., & Beyer, J. (1977). Cognitive processes mediating behavioral change. *Journal of Personality and Social Psychology, 35*, 125–139.

Bandura, A., Grusec, J., & Menlove, F. (1967). Vicarious extinction of avoidance behavior. *Journal of Personality and Social Psychology, 5*, 16–23.

Barbaree, H. E., & Marshall, W. L. (1991). The role of male sexual arousal in rape: Six models. *Journal of Consulting and Clinical Psychology, 59*, 621–630.

Barbarin, O., & Soler, R. (1993). Behavioral, emotional, and academic adjustment in a national probability sample of African American children: Effects of age, gender, and family structure. *Journal of Black Psychology, 19*, 423–446.

Barclay, M., & Hoffman, J. A. (1990). Conduct disorders. In M. Lewis & S. Miller (Eds.), *Handbook of developmental psychopathology*. New York: Plenum Press.

Bard, L. A., Carter, D. L., Cerce, D. D., Knight, R. A., Rosenberg, R., & Schneider, B. (1987). A descriptive study of rapists and child molesters: Developmental, clinical, and criminal characteristics. *Behavioral Sciences and the Law, 5*, 203–220.

Barefoot, J. C., Dodge, K. A., Peterson, B. L., Dahlstrom, W. G., & Williams, R. B. (1989). The Cook-Medley hostility scale: Item content and ability to predict survival. *Psychosomatic Medicine, 51*, 46–57.

Barkley, R. A. (1988). The assessment of attention deficit-hyperactivity disorder. In E. J. Mash and L. G. Terdal (Eds.), *Behavioral assessment*. New York: Guilford.

Barkley, R. A. (1990). *Attention deficit hyperactivity disorder: A handbook for diagnosis and treatment*. New York: Guilford Press.

Barkley, R. A. (1996). Attention-deficit/hyperactivity disorder. In E. J. Mash & R. A. Barkley (Eds.), *Child psychopathology*. New York: Guilford Press.

Barkley, R. A. (1997). Behavioral inhibition, sustained attention, and executive functions: constructing a unifying theory of ADHD. *Psychological Bulletin, 121*, 65–94.

Barkley, R. A., Fischer, M., Edelbrock, C., & Smallish, L. (1991). The adolescent outcome of hyperactive children diagnosed by research criteria—III. Mother-child interactions, family conflicts and maternal psychopathology. *Journal of Child Psychology and Psychiatry, 32*, 233–255.

Barkley, R. A., Guevremont, D. C., Anastopoulos, A. D., DuPaul, G. J., & Shelton, T. L. (1993). Driving-related risks and outcomes of attention-deficit hyperactivity disorder in adolescents and young adults: A 3- to 5-year follow-up survey. *Pediatrics, 92*, 212–218.

Barkley, R. A., Karlsson, J., Pollard, S., & Murphy, J. U. (1985). Developmental changes in the mother-child interactions of hyperactive boys: Effects of two dose levels of Ritalin. *Journal of Child Psychology and Psychiatry, 26*, 705–715.

Barkley, R. A., McMurray, M. B., Edelbrock, C., & Robbins, K. (1990). Side effects of methylphenidate in children with attention-deficit hyperactivity disorder: A systematic, placebo-controlled evaluation. *Pediatrics, 86*, 184–192.

Barlow, D. H. (1988). *Anxiety and its disorders*. New York: Guilford.

Barlow, D. H. (1989). Treatment outcome evaluation methodology with anxiety disorders: Strengths and key issues. *Advanced Behavior Research Therapy, 11*, 121–132.

Barlow, D. H., Brown, T. A., & Craske, M. G. (1994). Definitions of panic attacks and panic disorder in the DSM-IV: Implications for research. *Journal of Abnormal Psychology, 103*, 553–564.

Barmann, B. C., & Murray, W. J. (1981). Suppression of inappropriate sexual behavior by facial screening. *Behavior Therapy, 12*, 730–735.

Barnett, P. A., & Gotlib, I. H. (1988). Psychosocial functioning and depression: Distinguishing among antecedents, concomitants, and consequences. *Psychological Bulletin, 104*, 97–126.

Baron, M., Risch, N., Hamburger, R., Mandel, B., Kushner, S., Newman, M., Drumer, D., Belmaker, R. H. (1987). Genetic linkage between X-chromosome markers and bipolar affective illness. *Nature, 326*, 289–292.

Barrera, M., Li, S. A., & Chassin, L. (1993). Ethnic and group differences in vulnerability to parental alcoholism and life stress: A study of Hispanic and non-Hispanic caucasian adolescents. *American Journal of Community Psychology, 21*, 15–35.

Barrett, P. M., Dadds, M., & Rapee, R. M. (1996). Family treatment of childhood anxiety: A controlled trial. *Journal of Consulting and Clinical Psychology, 64*, 333–342.

Barsky, A. J., Cleary, P., Sarnie, M., & Klerman, G. (1993). The course of transient hypochondriasis. *American Journal of Psychiatry, 150*, 484–488.

Barsky, A. J., Wyshak, G., & Klerman, G. L. (1992). Psychiatric comorbidity in DSM-III-R hypochondriasis. *Archives of General Psychiatry, 49*, 101–108.

Bartrop, R. W., Luckhurst, E., Lazarus, L., Kiloh, L. G., & Penny, R. (1977). Depressed lymphocyte function after bereavement. *Lancet, 1*, 834–836.

Bass, E., & Davis, L. (1988). *The courage to heal*. New York: Harper & Row.

Bateson, G., Jackson, D. D., Haley, J., & Weakland, J. (1956). Toward a history of schizophrenia. *Behavioral Science, 1*, 251–264.

Battaglia, M., Bernardeschi, L., Franchini, L., Bellodi, L., & Smeraldi, E. (1995). A family study of schizotypal disorder. *Schizophrenia Bulletin, 21*, 33–45.

Baucom, D., & Epstein, N. (1989). *Cognitive-behavioral marital therapy*. New York: Brunner/Mazel.

Baucom, D., & Lester, G. (1986). The usefulness of cognitive restructuring as an adjunct to behavioral marital therapy. *Behavior Therapy, 17*, 385–403.

Bauer, W. D., & Twentyman, C. T. (1985). Abusing, neglectful, and comparison mothers' reactions to child-related and non-child-related stressors. *Journal of Consulting and Clinical Psychology, 53*, 335–343.

Bauermeister, J. J., Bird, H. R., Canino, G., Rubio-Stipec, M., Bravo, M., & Alegria, M. (1995). Dimensions of attention deficit hyperactivity disorder: Findings from teacher and parent reports in a community sample. *Journal of Consulting and Clinical Psychology, 24,* 264–271.

Baumeister, A. A., & Rollings, J. P. (1976). Self-injurious behavior. In N. R. Ellis (Ed.), *International review of research in mental retardation* (Vol. 8). New York: Academic.

Baxter, L. R., Schwartz, J. M., Mazziotta, J. C., et al. (1989). Cerebral glucose metabolic rates in non-depressed obsessive-compulsives. *American Journal of Psychiatry, 145,* 1560–1563.

Beahrs, J. O. (1994). Dissociative identity disorder: Adaptive deception of self and others. *Bulletin of the American Academy of Psychiatry and the Law, 22,* 223–237.

Beardsley, R. S., Gardocki, G. J., Larson, D. B., & Hidalgo, J. (1988). Prescribing of psychotropic medication by primary care physicians and psychiatrists. *Archives of General Psychiatry, 45,* 1117–1119.

Beck, A. T. (1963). Thinking and depression. *Archives of General Psychiatry, 9,* 324–333.

Beck, A. T. (1967). *Depression: Clinical, experimental, and theoretical aspects.* New York: Harper & Row.

Beck, A. T. (1976). *Cognitive theory and the emotional disorders.* New York: International Universities Press.

Beck, A. T. (1987). Cognitive models of depression. *Journal of Cognitive Psychotherapy, 1,* 5–38.

Beck, A. T., Brown, G., Berchick, R. J., Stewart, B. L., & Steer, R. A. (1990). Relationship between hopelessness and ultimate suicide: A replication with psychiatric outpatients. *American Journal of Psychiatry, 147,* 190–195.

Beck, A. T., & Emery, G. (1985). *Anxiety disorders and phobias: A cognitive perspective.* New York: Basic Books.

Beck, A. T., Freeman, A., Pretzer, J., Davis, D. D., Fleming, B., Ottaviani, R., Beck, J., Simon, K. M., Padesky, C., Meyer, J., & Trexler, L. (1990). *Cognitive therapy of personality disorders.* New York: Guilford Press.

Beck, A. T., Rush, A. J., Shaw, B. F., & Emery, G. (1979). *Cognitive therapy of depression.* New York: Guilford Press.

Beck, A. T., Ward, C. H., Mendelson, N., Mock, J., & Erbaugh, J. (1961). An inventory for measuring depression. *Archives of General Psychiatry, 4,* 53–63.

Beck, J. G. (1995). Hypoactive sexual desire disorder: An overview. *Journal of Consulting and Clinical Psychology, 63,* 919–927.

Beck, J. S. (1995). *Cognitive therapy: Basics and beyond.* New York: Guilford Press.

Beiser, M., Collomb, H., Ravel, J., & Nafziger, C. (1976). Systemic blood pressure studies among the Serer of Senegal. *Journal of Chronic Diseases, 29,* 371–380.

Bell, A. P., Weinberg, M. S., & Hammersmith, S. K. (1981). *Sexual preference: Its development in men and women.* Bloomington, IN: Indiana University Press.

Bemis-Vitousek, K., & Orimoto, L. (1993). Cognitive-behavioral models of anorexia nervosa, bulimia nervosa, and obesity. In K. S. Dobson & P. C. Kendall (Eds.), *Psychopathology and cognition.* San Diego: Academic Press.

Benca, R. M., Obermeyer, W. H., Thisted, R. A., & Gillin, J. C. (1992). Sleep and psychiatric disorders: A metaanalysis. *Archives of General Psychiatry, 49,* 651–668.

Benedict, K. B., & Nacoste, D. B. (1990). Dementia and depression in the elderly: A framework for addressing difficulties in differential diagnosis. *Clinical Psychology Review, 10,* 513–537.

Benedict, R. H. B. (1989). The effectiveness of cognitive remediation strategies for victims of traumatic head-injury: A review of the literature. *Clinical Psychology Review, 9,* 605–626.

Bennett, C., Crawford, F., Osborne, A., Diaz, P., Hoyne, J., Lopez, R., Roques, P., Duara, R., Rossor, M., & Mullan, M. (1995). Evidence that the APOE locus influences rate of disease progression in late onset familial Alzheimer's disease but is not causative. *American Journal of Medical Genetics, 60,* 1–6.

Bennett, L., Janca, A., Grant, B., & Sartorius, N. (1993). Boundaries between normal and pathological drinking. *Alcohol Health and Research World, 17,* 190–195.

Bennett, P., Wallace, L., Carroll, D., & Smith, N. (1991). Treating Type A behaviors and mild hypertension in middle-aged men. *Journal of Psychosomatic Research, 35,* 209–223.

Berman, A. L., & Jobes, D. A. (1991). *Adolescent suicide: Assessment and intervention.* Washington, DC: American Psychological Association.

Berman, K. F., Torrey, E. F., Daniel, D. G., & Weinberger, D. R. (1992). Regional cerebral blood flow in monozygotic twins discordant and concordant for schizophrenia. *Archives of General Psychiatry, 49,* 927–934.

Berman, R. J. (1979). Psychogenic visual disorders in an abused child: A case report. *American Journal of Optometry and Psychological Optics, 5,* 735–738.

Bernard, M. E., & DiGiuseppe, R. (Eds.). (1989). *Inside rational-emotive therapy. A critical appraisal of the theory and therapy of Albert Ellis.* San Diego: Academic Press.

Bernsen, A., Tabachnick, B. G., & Pope, K. S. (1994). National survey of social workers' sexual attraction to their clients: Results, implications, and comparison to psychologists. *Ethics and Behavior, 4,* 369–388.

Berstein, D. P., Cohen, P., Skodol, A., Bezirganian, S., & Brook, J. S. (1996). Childhood antecedents of adolescent personality disorders. *American Journal of Psychiatry, 153,* 907–913.

Bestman, E. W. (1986). Cross-cultural approaches to service delivery to ethnic minorities: The Miami model. In M. R. Miranda & H. H. Kitano (Eds.), *Mental health research and practice in minority communities: Development of culturally sensitive training programs.* Washington, DC: U.S. Government Printing Office.

Bettelheim, B. (1967). *The empty fortress.* New York: Free Press.

Betz, N. E., & Fitzgerald, L. F. (1993). Individuality and diversity: Theory and research in counseling psychology. *Annual Review of Psychology, 44,* 343–381.

Beutler, L. E., Clarkin, J. F., Crago, M., & Bergan, J. (1991). Client-therapist matching. In C. R. Snyder & D. R. Forsyth (Eds.), *The handbook of social and clinical psychology: The health perspective.* New York: Pergamon Press.

Beutler, L. E., Machado, M., & Neufeldt, K. (1994). Therapist variables. In A. E. Bergin & S. L. Garfield (Eds.), *Handbook of psychotherapy and behavior change* (4th ed.). New York: Wiley.

Beutler, L. E., Scogin, F., Kirkish, P., Schretlen, D., Corbishley, A., Hamblin, D., Meredith, K., Potter, R., Bamford, C. R., & Levenson, A. I. (1987). Group cognitive therapy and alprazolam in the treatment of depression in older adults. *Journal of Consulting and Clinical Psychology, 55,* 550–556.

Bickett, L., & Milich, R. (1990). First impressions formed of boys with learning disabilities and attention deficit disorder. *Journal of Learning Disabilities, 23,* 253–259.

Biederman, J. (1992). New developments in pediatric psychopharmacology. *Journal of the American Academy of Child and Adolescent Psychiatry, 31,* 14–15.

Biederman, J., Faraone, S. V., Spencer, T., Wilens, T., Norman, D., Lapey, K., Mick, E., & Krifcher-Lehman, B. (1993). Patterns of psychiatric comorbidity, cognition and psychosocial functioning in adults with attention deficit hyperactivity disorder. *American Journal of Psychiatry, 150,* 1792–1798.

Biederman, J., Milberger, S., Faraone, S. V., Kiely, K., Guite J., Mick, E., Ablon, S., Warburton, R., & Reed, E. (1995). Family-environment risk factors for attention-deficit hyperactivity disorder. *Archives of General Psychiatry, 52,* 464–470.

Biederman, J., Munir, K., Knee, D., Armentano, M., Autor, S., Waternaux, C., & Tsuang, M. (1987). High rate of affective disorders in probands with attention deficit disorder and in their relatives: A controlled family study. *American Journal of Psychiatry,* *144,* 330–333.

Biederman, J., Rosenbaum, J. F., Bolduc-Murphy, E. A., Faraone, S. V., Chaloff, J., Hirshfeld, D. R., & Kagan, J. (1993). A 3-year follow-up of children with and without behavioral inhibition. *Journal of American Academy of Child and Adolescent Psychiatry, 32,* 814–821.

Biederman, J., Rosenbaum, J. F., Hirshfeld, D. R., Faraone, S. V., Bolduc, E. A., Gersten, M., Meminger, S. R., Kagan, J., Snidman, N., & Reznick, S. (1990). Psychiatric correlates of behavioral inhibition in young children of parents with and without psychiatric disorders. *Archives of General Psychiatry, 47,* 21–26.

Biglan, A., Duncan, T. E., Ary, D. V., & Smolkowski, K. (1995). Peer and parental influence on adolescent tobacco use. *Journal of Behavioral Medicine, 18,* 315–329.

Birnbauer, J. S. (1976). Mental retardation. In H. Leitenberg (Ed.), *Handbook of behavior modification and behavior therapy.* Englewood Cliffs, NJ: Prentice-Hall.

Bjorkly, S. (1995). Prediction of aggression in psychiatric patients: A review of prospective prediction studies. *Clinical Psychology Review, 15,* 475–502.

Blagg, N. R., & Yule, W. (1984). The behavioural treatment of school refusal—a comparative study. *Behaviour Research and Therapy, 22,* 119–127.

Blanchard, E. (1992). Psychological treatment of benign headache disorders. *Journal of Consulting and Clinical Psychology, 60,* 537–551.

Blanchard, E., & Andrasik, F. (1982). Psychological assessment and treatment of headache: Recent developments and emerging issues. *Journal of Consulting and Clinical Psychology, 50,* 859–879.

Blanchard, E., & Andrasik, F. (1985). *Management of chronic headaches: A psychological approach.* New York: Pergamon Press.

Blanchard, R., Steiner, B., & Clemmensen, L. (1985). Gender dysphoria, gender reorientation, and the clinical management of transsexualism. *Journal of Consulting and Clinical Psychology, 53,* 295–304.

Blatt, S. J., & Zuroff, D. (1992). Interpersonal relatedness and self-definition: Two prototypes for depression. *Clinical Psychological Review, 12,* 527–562.

Blatt, S. J., Zuroff, D. C., Quinlan, D. M., & Pilkonis, P. (1996). Interpersonal factors in brief treatment of depression: Further analyses of the National Institute of Mental Health treatment of depression collaborative research program. *Journal of Consulting and Clinical Psychology, 64,* 162–171.

Blazer, D. G., Kessler, R. C., McGonagle, K. A., & Swartz, M. S. (1994). The prevalence and distribution of major depression in a national community sample: The national comorbidity survey. *American Journal of Psychiatry, 151,* 979–986.

Blehar, M. C., Weissman, M. M., Gershon, E. S., & Hirschfeld, R. M. A. (1988). Family and genetic studies of affective disorders. *Archives of General Psychiatry, 45,* 289–292.

Blesa, R., Adroer, R., Santacruz, P., Ascaso, C., Tolosa, E., & Oliva, R. (1996). High apolipoprotein E epsilon 4 allele frequency in age-related memory decline. *Annals of Neurology, 39,* 548–551.

Bleuler, E. (1911). *Dementia Praecox or the group of schizophrenias.* (Translated 1950 by J. Zinkin.) New York: International Universities Press.

Bleuler, E. (1923). *Lehrbuch der psychiatrie* (4th ed.). Berlin: Springer.

Bleuler, M. N. (1978). *The schizophrenic disorders: Long-term patient and family studies.* New Haven, CT: Yale University Press.

Bliss, J. (1980). Sensory experiences of Gilles de la Tourette syndrome. *Archives of General Psychiatry, 37,* 1343–1347.

Bocella, K. (1995). Use of Ritalin for children is on the rise. *Philadelphia Inquirer,* Sept. 24, 1995, pp. B1–B4.

Bohman, M., Cloninger, C. R., Sigvardsson, S., & von Knorring, A. (1982). Predisposition to petty criminality in Swedish adoptees, I: Genetic and environmental heterogeneity. *Archives of General Psychiatry, 39,* 1233–1241.

Boney-McCoy, S., & Finkelhor, D. (1995). Psychosocial sequelae of violent victimization in a national youth sample. *Journal of Consulting and Clinical Psychology, 63,* 726–736.

Boon, S., & Draijer, N. (1993). Multiple personality disorder in the Netherlands: A clinical investigation of 71 patients. *American Journal of Psychiatry, 150,* 489–494.

Borden, M. C., & Ollendick, T. H. (1992). The development and differentiation of social subtypes in autism. In B. Lahey & A. E. Kazdin (Eds.), *Advances in clinical child psychology* (Vol. 14). New York: Plenum Press.

Bordouin, C. M., Mann, B. J., Cone, L. T., Henggeler, S. W., Fucci, B. R., Blaske, D. M., & Williams, R. A. (1995). Multisystemic treatment of serious juvenile offenders: Long-term prevention of child and adolescent antisocial behavior. *Journal of Consulting and Clinical Psychology, 63,* 569–578.

Borkovec, T. D. (1982). Facilitation and inhibition of functional CS exposure in the treatment of phobias. In J. Boulougouris (Ed.), *Learning approaches to psychiatry* (pp. 95–102). New York: Wiley.

Borkovec, T. D. (1985). Worry: A potentially valuable concept. *Behaviour Research and Therapy, 4,* 481–482.

Borkovec, T. D., & Costello, E. (1993). Efficacy of applied relaxation and cognitive-behavioral therapy in the treatment of generalized anxiety disorder. *Journal of Consulting and Clinical Psychology, 61,* 611–619.

Borkovec, T. D., & Mathews, A. M. (1988). Treatment of nonphobic anxiety disorders: A comparison of nondirective, cognitive, and coping desensitization therapy. *Journal of Consulting and Clinical Psychology, 56,* 877–884.

Borkovec, T. D., Wilkinson, L., Folensbee, K., & Lerman, C. (1983). Stimulus control applications to the treatment of worry. *Behaviour Research and Therapy, 21,* 247–251.

Borys, D. S., & Pope, K. S. (1989). Duel relationships between therapist and client: A national study of psychologists, psychiatrists, and social workers. *Professional Psychology, 14,* 185–196.

Boscarino, J. A. (1996). Posttraumatic stress disorder, exposure to combat, and lower plasma cortisol among Vietnam veterans: Findings and clinical implications. *Journal of Consulting and Clinical Psychology, 64,* 191–201.

Bosley, F., & Allen, T. (1989). Stress management training for hypertensives: Cognitive and physiological effects. *Journal of Behavioral Medicine, 12,* 77–90.

Botvin, G. J., Baker, E., Dusenbury, L., Tortu, S., & Botvin, E. (1990). Preventing adolescent drug abuse through multimodal cognitive-behavioral approach: Results of a 3-year study. *Journal of Consulting and Clinical Psychology, 58,* 437–446.

Bouchard, T. J., Lykken, D. T., McGue, M., Segal, N. L., & Tellegen, A. (1990). Sources of human psychological differences: The Minnesota study of twins reared apart. *Science, 250,* 223–250.

Bowen, M. (1978). *Family therapy in clinical practice.* New York: Jason Aronson.

Bowlby, J. (1961). Childhood mourning and its applications to psychiatry. *American Journal of Psychiatry, 118,* 481–498.

Bowlby, J. (1969). *Attachment and loss: Attachment.* New York: Basic Books.

Bowlby, J. (1979). *The making and breaking of emotional bonds.* London: Tavistock.

Bowlby, J. (1980). *Loss: Sadness and depression.* New York: Basic.

Braddock, D. (1992). Community mental health and mental retardation services in the United States: A comparative study of resource allocation. *American Journal of Psychiatry, 149,* 175–183.

Bradford, J. M. W., Boulet, J., & Pawlak, A. (1992). The paraphilias: A multiplicity of deviant behaviours. *Canadian Journal of Psychiatry, 37,* 104–108.

Bradley, B., Mogg, K., Millar, N., & White, J. (1995). Selective processing of negative information: Effects of clinical anxiety, concurrent depression, and awareness. *Journal of Abnormal Psychology, 104,* 532–536.

Bradley, B. P., Gossop, M., Brewin, C. R., Phillips, G., & Green, L. (1992). Attributions and relapse in opiate addicts. *Journal of Consulting and Clinical Psychology, 60,* 470–472.

Brady, E. U., & Kendall, P. C. (1992). Comorbidity of anxiety and depression in children and adolescents. *Psychological Bulletin, 111,* 244–255.

Brady, J. V. (1958). Ulcers in "executive" monkeys. *Scientific American, 199,* 95–100.

Braswell, L., & Bloomquist, M. L. (1991). *Cognitive-behavioral therapy with ADHD children: Child, family and school interventions.* New York: Guilford Press.

Bravo-Valdivieso, L. (1995). A four year follow-up study of low socioeconomic status Latin American children with reading difficulties. *International Journal of Disability, Development and Education, 42,* 189–202.

Breecher, E. M. (1983). *Love, sex, and aging: A consumers' union report.* Boston: Little, Brown.

Breier, A., Buchanan, R. W., Elkashef, A., Munson, R. C., Kirkpatrick, B., & Gellad, F. (1992). Brain morphology and schizophrenia: A magnetic resonance imaging study of limbic, prefrontal cortex, and caudate structures. *Archives of General Psychiatry, 49,* 921–926.

Breier, A., Schreiber, J. L., Dyer, J., & Pickar, D. (1991). National Institute of Mental Health longitudinal study of chronic schizophrenia: Prognosis and predictors of outcome. *Archives of General Psychiatry, 48,* 239–246.

Breitner, J. C., Welsh, K. A., Gau, B. A., McDonald, W. M., Steffens, D. C., Saunders, A. M., Magruder, K. M., Helms, M. J., Plassman, B. L., Folstein, M. F., Brandt, J., Robinette, D., & Page, W. F. (1995). Alzheimer's disease in the National Academy of Sciences–National Research Council Registry of Aging Twin Veterans: III. Detection of cases, longitudinal results, and observations on twin concordance. *Archives of Neurology, 52,* 763–771.

Brennan, C. (1955). *An elementary textbook of psychoanalysis.* New York: International Universities Press.

Brent, D. A., Perper, J. A., Goldstein, C. E., Kolko, D. J., Allan, M. J., Allman, C. J., & Zelenak, J. P. (1988). Risk factors for adolescent suicide: A comparison of adolescent suicide victims with suicidal inpatients. *Archives of General Psychiatry, 45,* 581–588.

Brier, N. (1989). The relationship between learning disability and delinquency: A review and reappraisal. *Journal of Learning Disabilities, 22,* 546–553.

Briere, J., & Runtz, M. (1988). Post-sexual abuse trauma. In G. E. Wyatt & G. J. Powell (Eds.), *The lasting effects of child sexual abuse* (pp. 85–99). Newbury Park, CA: Sage Publications.

Briere, J., & Zaidi, L. Y. (1989). Sexual abuse histories and sequelae in female psychiatric emergency room patients. *American Journal of Psychiatry, 146,* 1602–1606.

Bristol, M. M., Cohen, D. J., Costello, E. J., Denckla, M., Eckberg, T. J., Kallen, R., Kraemer, H. C., Lord, C., Maurer, R., McIlvane, W. J., Minshew, N., Sigman, M., Spence, M. A. (1996). State of the science in autism: Report to the national institutes of health. *Journal of Autism and Developmental Disorders, 26,* 121–153.

Broadhead, W. E., Blazer, D. G., George, L. K., & Tse, C. K. (1990). Depression, disability days, and days lost from work in a prospective epidemiologic survey. *Journal of the American Medical Association, 264,* 2524–2528.

Broman, C. L. (1993). Social relationships and health-related behavior. *Journal of Behavioral Medicine, 16,* 335–350.

Brown, D. R., Ahmed, F., Gary, L. E., & Milburn, N. G. (1995). Major depression in a community sample of African Americans. *American Journal of Psychiatry, 152,* 373–378.

Brown, F. W., Golding, J. M., & Smith, G. R. (1990). Psychiatric comorbidity in primary care somatization disorder. *Psychosomatic Medicine, 52,* 445–451.

Brown, G. L., Ebert, M. H., Goyer, P. F., Jimerson, D. C., Klein, W. J., Bunney, W. E., & Goodwin, F. K. (1982). Aggression, suicide, and serotonin: Relationships to CSF amine metabolites. *American Journal of Psychiatry, 139,* 741–746.

Brown, G. R., & Anderson, B. (1991). Psychiatric morbidity in adult inpatients with childhood histories of sexual and physical abuse. *American Journal of Psychiatry, 148,* 55–61.

Brown, G. W., Birley, J. L. T., & Wing, J. D. (1972). Influence of family life on the course of schizophrenic disorders: A replication. *British Journal of Psychiatry, 121,* 241–258.

Brown, G. W., & Harris, T. D. (1978). *Social origins of depression: A study of psychiatric disorder in women.* New York: Free Press.

Brown, G. W., & Harris, T. O. (1989). Depression. In G. W. Harris and T. O. Harris (Eds.), *Life events and illness* (pp. 49–93). New York: Guilford Press.

Brown, G. W., & Harris, T. O. (1993). Aetiology of anxiety and depressive disorders in an inner-city population. 1. Early adversity. *Psychological Medicine, 23,* 143–154.

Brown, H. D., Kosslyn, S. M., Breiter, H. C., Baer, L., & Jenike, M. A. (1994). Can patients with obsessive-compulsive disorder discriminate between percepts and mental images? A signal detection analysis. *Journal of Abnormal Psychology, 103,* 445–454.

Brown, L., & Ballou, M. (Eds.). (1992). *Personality and psychopathology: Feminist reappraisals.* New York: Guilford Press.

Brown, S. A. (1985). Expectancies versus background in the prediction of college drinking patterns. *Journal of Consulting and Clinical Psychology, 53,* 123–130.

Brown, S. A., Goldman, M. S., Inn, A., & Anderson, L. R. (1980). Expectations of reinforcement from alcohol: Their domain and relation to drinking patterns. *Journal of Consulting and Clinical Psychology, 48,* 418–425.

Brown, T. A., & Barlow, D. H. (1995). Long-term outcome in cognitive-behavioral treatment of panic disorder: Clinical predictors and alternative strategies for assessment. *Journal of Consulting and Clinical Psychology, 63,* 754–765.

Brown, T. A., Marten, P. A., & Barlow, D. (1995). Discriminant validity of the symptoms constituting the DSM-III-R and DSM-IV associated symptom criterion of generalized anxiety disorder. *Journal of Anxiety Disorder, 9,* 317–328.

Browne, A. (1987). *When battered women kill.* New York: Free Press.

Browne, A. (1993). Violence against women by male partners: Prevalence, outcomes, and policy implications. *American Psychologist, 10,* 1077–1087.

Brownell, K. D. (1991). Dieting and the search for the perfect body: Where physiology and culture collide. *Behavior Therapy, 22,* 1–12.

Bruce, M. L., Takeuchi, D. T., & Leaf, P. J. (1991). Poverty and psychiatric status: Longitudinal evidence from the New Haven Epidemiologic Catchment Area Study. *Archives of General Psychiatry, 48,* 470–474.

Bruch, H. (1973). *Eating disorders: Obesity, anorexia nervosa, and the person within.* New York: Basic Books.

Bruch, H. (1978). *The golden cage: The enigma of anorexia nervosa.* Cambridge: Harvard University Press.

Brunner, H. G., Nelen, M., Breakefield, X. O., Ropers, H. H., & van Oost, B. A. (1993). Abnormal behavior associated with a point mutation in the structural gene for monoamine oxidase A. *Science, 262,* 578–580.

Bry, B. H., McKeon, P., & Pandina, R. J. (1982). Extent of drug use as a function of number of risk factors. *Journal of Abnormal Psychology, 91,* 273–279.

Bryant, R. A. (1995). Autobiographical memory across personalities in dissociative identity disorder: A case report. *Journal of Abnormal Psychology, 104,* 625–631.

Bryant, R. A., & Harvey, A. G. (1995). Processing threatening information in posttraumatic stress disorder. *Journal of Abnormal Psychology, 104,* 537–541.

Bryant, R. A., & McConkey, K. M. (1989). Visual conversion disorder: A case analysis of the influence of visual information. *Journal of Abnormal Psychology, 98,* 326–329.

Bryson, S. E. (1996). Brief report: Epidemiology of autism. *Journal of Autism and Developmental Disorders, 26,* 165–167.

Buchanan, R. W., Kirkpatrick, B., Heinrichs, D. W., Carpenter, W. T. (1990). Clinical correlates of the deficit syndrome of schizophrenia. *American Journal of Psychiatry, 147,* 290–294.

Buchanan, R. W., Strauss, M. E., Kirkpatrick, B., Holstein, C., Breier, A., & Carpenter, W. T., Jr. (1994). Neuropsychological impairments in deficit vs. nondeficit forms of schizophrenia. *Archives of General Psychiatry, 51,* 804–811.

Burge, D., & Hammen, C. (1991). Maternal communication: Predictors of outcome at follow-up in a sample of children at high and low risk for depression. *Journal of Abnormal Psychology, 100,* 174–180.

Burke, K. C., Burke, J. D., Regier, D. A., & Rae, D. S. (1990). Age at onset of selected mental disorders in five community populations. *Archives of General Psychiatry, 47,* 511–518.

Burnam, M. A., Stein, J. A., Golding, J. M., Siegel, J. M., Sorenson, S. B., Forsythe, A. B., & Telles, C. A. (1988). Sexual assault and mental disorders in a community population. *Journal of Consulting and Clinical Psychology, 56,* 843–850.

Buros, O. K. (1988). *The supplement to the Mental Measurements Yearbook* (9th ed.). Lincoln, NE: The Buros Institute of Mental Measurements.

Burt, D. B., Loveland, K., Chen, Y., Chuang, A., et al. (1995). Aging in adults with Down syndrome: Report from a longitudinal study. *American Journal on Mental Retardation, 100,* 262–270.

Butcher, J. N., Dahlstrom, W. G., Graham, J. R., Tellegen, A., & Kaemmer, B. (1989). *Minnesota Multiphasic Personality Inventory-2: Manual for administration and scoring.* Minneapolis, MN: University of Minnesota Press.

Butcher, J. N., Graham, J. R., & Ben-Porath, Y. S. (1995). Methodological problems and issues in MMPI, MMPI-2, and MMPI-A research (Special issue: Methodological issues in psychological assessment research). *Psychological Assessment, 7,* 320–329.

Butcher, J. N., & Spielberger, C. D. (Eds.). (1995). *Advances in personality assessment* (Vol. 10). Hillsdale, NJ: Lawrence Erlbaum.

Butler, S., & Strupp, H. H. (1991). Psychodynamic psychotherapy. In M. Hersen, A. E. Kazdin & A. Bellack (Eds.), *The clinical psychology handbook* (2nd ed.). (pp. 519–533). New York: Pergamon.

Caddy, G. R. (1978). Toward a multivariate analysis of alcohol abuse. In P. E. Nathan, G. A. Marlatt & T. Loberg (Eds.), *Alcoholism: New directions in behavioral research and treatment.* New York: Plenum Press.

Cadoret, R. J., Yates, W. R., Troughton, E., Woodworth, G., & Stewart, M. A. (1995). Adoption study demonstrating two genetic pathways to drug abuse. *Archives of General Psychiatry, 52,* 42–52.

Cadoret, R. J., Yates, W. R., Troughton, E., Woodworth, G., & Stewart, M. A. (1995). Genetic-environmental interaction in the genesis of aggressivity and conduct disorders. *Archives of General Psychiatry, 52,* 916–924.

Calabrese, J. R., & Woyshville, M. J. (1995). Lithium therapy: Limitations and alternatives in the treatment of bipolar disorders. *Annals of Clinical Psychiatry, 7,* 103–112.

Camara, K. A., & Resnick, G. (1988). Interparental conflict and cooperation: Factors moderating children's post-divorce adjustment. In E. M. Hetherington & J. D. Arasteh (Eds.), *Impact of divorce, single parenting, and stepparenting on children* (pp. 169–195). Hillsdale, NJ: Erlbaum.

Cameron, R. (1978). The clinical implementation of behavior change techniques: A cognitively oriented conceptualization of therapeutic "compliance" and "resistance." In J. P. Foreyt & D. P. Rathjen (Eds.), *Cognitive behavior therapy: Research and application.* New York: Plenum Press.

Campbell, D. T., & Stanley, J. C. (1963). *Experimental and quasiexperimental designs for research.* Chicago: Rand McNally.

Campbell, M. (1988). Annotation. Fenfluramine treatment of autism. *Journal of Child Psychology and Psychiatry, 29,* 1–10.

Campbell, S. M. (1986). Developmental issues. In R. Gittelman (Ed.), *Anxiety disorders of childhood.* New York: Guilford Press.

Cannon, T. D., Mednick, S. A., & Parnas, J. (1989). Genetic and perinatal determinants of structural brain deficits in schizophrenia. *Archives of General Psychiatry, 46,* 883–889.

Cannon, T. D., Mednick, S. A., Parnas, J., Schulsinger, F., Praestholm, J., & Vestergaard, A. (1993). Developmental brain abnormalities in the offspring of schizophrenic mothers: Contributions of genetic and perinatal factors. *Archives of General Psychiatry, 50,* 551–564.

Cannon, T. D., Mednick, S. A., Parnas, J., Schulsinger, F., Praestholm, J., & Vestergaard, A. (1994a). Developmental brain abnormalities in the offspring of schizophrenic mothers: Structural brain characteristics of schizophrenia and schizotypal personality disorder. *Archives of General Psychiatry, 51,* 955–962.

Cannon, T. D., Zorrilla, L. E., Shtasel, D., Gur, R. E., Gur, R. C., Marco, E. J., Moberg, P., & Price, R. A. (1994b). Neuropsychological functioning in siblings discordant for schizophrenia and healthy volunteers. *Archives of General Psychiatry, 51,* 651–661.

Cannon, W. B. (1929). *Bodily changes in pain, hunger, fear and rage* (2nd ed.). New York: Appleton.

Cantwell, D. P. (1986). Attention deficit and associated childhood disorders. In T. Mellon & G. L. Klerman (Eds.), *Contemporary directions in psychopathology: Toward DSM IV.* New York: Guilford Press.

Cantwell, D. P. (1987). *Presentation at the conference on attention-deficit hyperactivity disorders: Assessment and intervention.* Minneapolis, MN: June, 1987.

Caplan, G. (1964). *Principles of preventive psychiatry.* New York: Basic Books.

Caplan, M., Weissberg, R. P., Grober, J. S., Sivo, P. J., Grady, K., & Jacoby, C. (1992). Social competence promotion with inner-city and suburban young adolescents: Effects on social adjustment and alcohol use. *Journal of Consulting and Clinical Psychology, 60,* 56–63.

Carey, G., & DiLalla, D. (1994). Personality and psychopathology: Genetic perspectives. *Journal of Abnormal Psychology, 103,* 32–43.

Carey, G., & Gottesman, I. (1981). Twin and family studies of anxiety, phobic, and obsessive disorders. In D. Klein & J. Rabkin (Eds.), *Anxiety: New research and changing concepts.* New York: Raven Press.

Carling, P. J. (1990). Major mental illness, housing, and supports: The promise of community integration. *American Psychologist, 45,* 969–976.

Carlson, C. L., Pelham, W., Milich, R., & Dixon, J. (1992). Single and combined effects of methylphenidate and behavior therapy on the classroom performance of children with attention-deficit hyperactivity disorder. *Journal of Abnormal Child Psychology, 20,* 213–232.

Carmelli, D., Swan, G., & Rosenman, R. H. (1985). The relationship between wives' social and psychological status and their husbands' coronary heart disease. *American Journal of Epidemiology, 122,* 90–100.

Carmody, T. P., & Matarrazzo, J. D. (1991). Health psychology. In M. Hersen, A. Kazdin & A. Bellack (Eds.), *The clinical psychology handbook* (2nd ed.). New York: Pergamon Press.

Carone, B. J., Harrow, M., & Westermeyer, J. F. (1991). Posthospital course and outcome in schizophrenia. *Archives of General Psychiatry, 48,* 247–253.

Carpenter, W. T., Jr., Conley, R. R., Buchanan, R. W., Breier, A., & Tamminga, C. A. (1995). Patient response and resource management: Another view of Clozapine treatment of schizophrenia. *American Journal of Psychiatry, 152,* 827–832.

Carrington, P., & Moyer, S. (1994). Gun control and suicide in Ontario. *American Journal of Psychiatry, 151,* 606–608.

Carter, M. M., Hollon, S. D., Carson, R., & Shelton, R. C. (1995). Effects of a safe person on induced distress following a biological challenge in panic disorder with agoraphobia. *Journal of Abnormal Psychology, 104,* 156–163.

Cascardi, M., O'Leary, D., Lawrence, E. E., & Schlee, K. A. (1995). Characteristics of women physically abused by their spouses and who seek treatment regarding marital conflict. *Journal of Consulting and Clinical Psychology, 63,* 616–623.

Cashdan, S. (1988). *Object relations therapy: Using the relationship.* New York: Norton.

Catalano, R. F., Hawkins, J. D., Krenz, C., Gillmore, M., Morrison, D., Wells, E., & Abbott, R. (1993). Using research to guide culturally appropriate drug abuse prevention. *Journal of Consulting and Clinical Psychology, 61,* 804–811.

Cattell, R. B. (1965). *The scientific analysis of personality.* Baltimore: Penguin.

Caudill, B. D., & Marlatt, G. A. (1975). Modeling influences on social drinking: An experimental analogue. *Journal of Consulting and Clinical Psychology, 43,* 405–415.

Centers for Disease Control. (1991). Attempted suicide among high school students: United States 1990. *Morbidity and Mortality Weekly Report, 40,* 633–635. (Reprinted from *Journal of the American Medical Association, 266,* 1911–1912.)

Centers for Disease Control. (1992). Physical fighting among high school students: United States, 1990. *Morbidity and Mortality Weekly Report, 41,* 91–94. (Reported in *Journal of American Medical Association, 267,* 3009–3010, 1992.)

Centers for Disease Control and Prevention. (1991). Weapon-carrying among high school students—United States, 1990. In R. A. Goodman (Ed.), *Chronic disease and health promotion: 1990–1991 youth risk behavior surveillance system* (pp. 17–19). Atlanta: Centers for Disease Control and Prevention.

Cepeda-Benito, A. (1993). Meta-analytical review of the efficacy of nicotine chewing gum in smoking treatment programs. *Journal of Consulting and Clinical Psychology, 61,* 822–833.

Chadwick, P. D. J., Lowe, C. F., Horne, P. J., & Higson, P. J. (1994). Modifying delusions: The role of empirical testing. *Behavior Therapy, 25,* 35–49.

Chakos, M. H., Alvir, J. M. J., Woerner, M. G., Koreen, A., Geisler, S., Mayerhoff, D., Sobel, S., Kane, J. M., Borenstein, M., & Lieberman, J. A. (1996). Incidence and correlates of tardive dyskinesia in first episode of schizophrenia. *Archives of General Psychiatry, 53,* 313–319.

Chambless, D., & Hollon, S. (1998). Defining empirically supported therapies. *Journal of Consulting and Clinical Psychology, 66.*

Champion, L. A., Goodall, G., & Rutter, M. (1995). Behavior problems in childhood and stressors in early adult life. A 20 year follow-up of London school children. *Psychological Medicine, 25,* 231–246.

Chaplin, T. C., Rice, M. E., & Harris, G. T. (1995). Salient victim suffering and the sexual responses of child molesters. *Journal of Consulting and Clinical Psychology, 63,* 249–255.

Chapman, L. J., & Chapman, J. P. (1967). Genesis of popular but erroneous psycho-diagnostic observations. *Journal of Abnormal Psychology, 72,* 193–204.

Chapman, L. J., & Chapman, J. P. (1969). Illusory correlation as an obstacle to the use of valid psychodiagnostic signs. *Journal of Abnormal Psychology, 74,* 271–280.

Chapman, L. J., Chapman, J. P., & Raulin, M. L. (1978). Body-image aberration in schizophrenia. *Journal of Abnormal Psychology, 87,* 399–407.

Chapman, L. J., Chapman, J. P., Kwapil, T. R., Eckblad, M., & Zinser, M. C. (1994). Putatively psychosis-prone subjects 10 years later. *Journal of Abnormal Psychology, 103,* 171–183.

Chapman, L. J., Edell, W. S., & Chapman, J. P. (1980). Physical anhedonia, perceptual aberration, and psychosis proneness. *Schizophrenia Bulletin, 6,* 639–653.

Charlesworth, E. A., Williams, B. J., & Baer, P. E. (1984). Stress management at the worksite for hypertension-related variables. *Psychosomatic Medicine, 46,* 387–397.

Charney, D. S., Deutch, A. Y., Krystal, J. H., Southwick, S. M., & Davis, M. (1992). Psychobiologic mechanisms of posttraumatic stress disorder. *Archives of General Psychiatry, 50,* 294–305.

Chassin, L., Curran, P. J., Hussong, A. M., & Colder, C. R. (1996). The relation of parent alcoholism to adolescent substance use: A longitudinal follow-up study. *Journal of Abnormal Psychology, 105,* 70–80.

Chassin, L., Pillow, D., Curran, P., Molina, B. S., & Barrera, M. (1993). Relation of parental alcoholism to early adolescent substance use: A test of three mediating mechanisms. *Journal of Abnormal Psychology, 102,* 3–19.

Cherlin, A. J., Furstenberg, F. F., Chase-Lansdale, P. L., Kiernan, K., Robins, P., Morrison, D., & Teitler, J. (1991). Longitudinal studies of effects of divorce on children in Great Britain and the United States. *Science, 252,* 1368–1389.

Chess, S. (1977). Report on autism in congenital rubella. *Journal of Autism and Childhood Schizophrenia, 7,* 68–81.

Chodorow, N. (1978). *The reproduction of mothering: Psychoanalysis and the sociology of gender.* Berkeley: University of California Press.

Chrisler, J. C. (1993). Feminist perspectives on weight loss therapy. *Journal of Training and Practice in Professional Psychology, 7,* 35–48.

Christensen, A., & Jacobson, N. S. (1994). Who (or what) can do psychotherapy: The status and challenge of nonprofessional therapies. *Psychological Science, 5,* 8–14.

Christiansen, B. A., & Goldman, M. S. (1983). Alcohol-related expectancies versus demographic/background variables in the prediction of adolescent drinking. *Journal of Consulting and Clinical Psychology, 51,* 249–257.

Cicchetti, D. (1993). Developmental psychopathology: Reactions, reflections, projections. Special Issue: Setting a path for the coming decade: Some goals and challenges. *Developmental Review, 13,* 471–502.

Cinciripini, P. M., Cinciripini, L. G., Wallfisch, A., Waheedul, H., & Van Vunakis, H. (1996). Behavior therapy and the transdermal nicotine patch: Effects of cessation outcome, affect and coping. *Journal of Consulting and Clinical Psychology, 64,* 314–323.

Clarizio, H. F. (1994). *Assessment and treatment of depression in children and adolescents.* Brandon, VT: Clinical Psychology.

Clark, D. A., & de Silva P. (1985). The nature of depressive and anxious intrusive thoughts: Distinct or uniform phenomena. *Behavior Research and Therapy, 23,* 383–393.

Clark, D. C., & Fawcett, J. (1992). Review of empirical risk factors for evaluation of the suicidal patient. In B. Bongar (Ed.), *Suicide: Guidelines for assessment, management, and treatment.* New York: Oxford University Press.

Clark, D. M. (1986). A cognitive approach to panic. *Behaviour Research and Therapy, 24,* 461–470.

Clark, D. M. (1989). Anxiety states: Panic and generalized anxiety. In K. Hawton, P. Salkovskis, J. Kirk & D. M. Clark (Eds.),

Cognitive behaviour therapy for psychiatric problems: A practical guide. Oxford, Engl.: Oxford University Press.

Clark, D. M. (1991). *Cognitive therapy for panic disorder.* Paper presented at the NIH Consensus Development Conference on the treatment of panic disorder, September 23–25, Bethesda, MD.

Clark, D. M., & Beck, A. T. (1988). Cognitive approaches. In C. G. Last & M. Hersen (Eds.), *Handbook of anxiety disorder.* New York: Pergamon Press.

Clark, D. M., Salkovskis, P. M., & Chalkley, A. J. (1985). Respiratory control as a treatment for panic attacks. *Journal of Behavior Therapy and Experimental Psychiatry, 16,* 23–30.

Clark, L. A. & Watson, D. (1991). Tripartite model of anxiety and depression: Psychometric evidence and taxonomic implications. *Journal of Abnormal Psychology, 100,* 316–336.

Clarkin, J. F., Pilkonis, P. A., & Magruder, K. M. (1996). Psychotherapy of depression: Implications for reform of the health care system. *Archives of General Psychiatry, 53,* 717–723.

Clarkin, J. F., Widiger, T., Frances, A., Hurt, S., & Gilmore, M. (1983). Prototypic typology and the borderline personality disorder. *Journal of Abnormal Psychology, 92,* 263–275.

Clarren, S., & Smith, D. W. (1978). The fetal alcohol syndrome. *The New England Journal of Medicine, 298,* 1063–1068.

Cleckley, H. (1941). *The mask of sanity* (5th ed.). St. Louis, MO: Mosby. (Revised in 1976).

Clementz, B. A., & Sweeney, J. A. (1990). Is eye movement dysfunction a biological marker for schizophrenia? A methodological review. *Psychological Bulletin, 108,* 77–92.

Cloninger, C. R., (1987). A systemic method for clinical description and classification of personality variants. *Archives of General Psychiatry, 44,* 573–588.

Cloninger, C. R. (1987). Neurogenic adaptive mechanisms in alcoholism. *Science, 236,* 410–416.

Cloninger, C. R., Bohman, M., & Sigvardsson, S. (1981). Inheritance of alcohol abuse: Cross-fostering analysis of adopted men. *Archives of General Psychiatry, 38,* 861–868.

Cloninger, C. R., Martin, R., Clayton, P., & Guze, S. (1981). A blind follow-up and family study of anxiety neurosis: Preliminary analysis of the St. Louis 500. In D. F. Klein and J. Rabkin (Eds.), *Anxiety: New research and changing concepts.* New York: Raven.

Cloninger, C. R., Svarkic, D. M., & Przybeck, T. R. (1993). A psychobiological model of temperament and character. *Archives of General Psychiatry, 50,* 975–990.

Clum, G. A., & Knowles, S. L. (1991). Why do some people with panic disorders become avoidant: A review. *Clinical Psychology Review, 11,* 295–313.

Cobb, S., & Rose, R. M. (1973). Hypertension, peptic ulcer, and diabetes in air traffic controllers. *Journal of the American Medical Association, 224,* 489–492.

Coccaro, E. F., Siever, L. J., Klar, H. M., Maurer, G., Cochrane, K., Cooper, T. B., Mohs, R. C., & Davis, K. L. (1989). Serotonergic studies in patients with affective and personality disorders: Correlates with suicidal and impulsive aggressive behavior. *Archives of General Psychiatry, 46,* 587–599.

Coffey, C. E., Weiner, K., Djang, W., Figiel, G., Soady, S., Patterson, L. J., Holt, P. D., Spritzer, C. E., & Wilkinson, W. E. (1991). Brain anatomic effects of electroconvulsive therapy: A prospective magnetic resonance imaging study. *Archives of General Psychiatry, 48,* 1013–1021.

Cohen, R. Y., Brownell, K., & Felix, M. R. J. (1990). Age and sex differences in health habits and beliefs of school children. *Health Psychology, 9,* 208–224.

Cohen, S., Lichtenstein, E., Prochaska, J. D., Rossi, J., Gritz, E. R., Carr, C. R., Orleans, C. T., Schoenbach, V. J., Biener, L., Abrams, D., DiClemente, C., Curry, S., Marlatt, G. A., Cummings, K., Emont, S., Giovino, G., & Ossip-Klein, D. (1989). Debunking myths about self-quitting: Evidence from 10 prospective studies of persons who attempted to quit smoking by themselves. *American Psychologist, 44,* 1355–1365.

Cohen, S., Tyrrell, D., & Smith, A. P. (1991). Psychological stress in humans and susceptibility to the common cold. *New England Journal of Medicine, 325,* 606–612.

Cohen, S., & Wills, T. A. (1985). Stress, social support, and the buffering hypothesis. *Psychological Bulletin, 98,* 310–357.

Cohn, J. F., Campbell, S. B., Matias, R., & Hopkins, J. (1990). Face-to-face interactions of postpartum depressed and nondepressed mother-infant pairs at 2 months. *Developmental Psychology, 26,* 15–23.

Coie, J. D., Watt, N. F., West, S. G., Hawkins, J. D., Asarnow, J. R., Markman, H. J., Ramey, S. L., Shure, M. B., & Long, B. (1993). The science of prevention: A conceptual framework and some directions for a national research program. *American Psychologist, 48,* 1013–1022.

Collins, R. L., & Marlatt, G. A. (1981). Social modeling as a determinant of drinking behavior: Implications for prevention and treatment. *Addictive Behaviors, 6,* 233–240.

Comings, D. E., & Comings, B. G. (1985). Tourette syndrome: Clinical and psychological aspects of 250 cases. *American Journal of Human Genetics, 37,* 435–450.

Comings, D. E., Comings, B. G., Devor, E. J., & Cloninger, C. R. (1984). Detection of a major gene for Giles de la Tourette syndrome. *American Journal of Human Genetics, 36,* 586–600.

Conger, J. J. (1951). The effects of alcohol on conflict and avoidance behavior. *Quarterly Journal of Studies on Alcohol, 12,* 1–29.

Conger, J. J. (1956). Reinforcement theory and the dynamics of alcoholism. *Quarterly Journal of Studies on Alcohol, 17,* 296–305.

Conners, C. K. (1980). Artificial colors in the diet and disruptive behavior. In R. M. Knights & D. J. Bakker (Eds.), *Treatment of hyperactive and learning disabled children.* Baltimore, MD: University Park Press.

Conners, C. K., & Wherry, J. S. (1979). Pharmacotherapy. In H. C. Quay & J. S. Wherry (Eds.), *Psychopathological disorders of childhood.* New York: Wiley.

Conrad, M., & Hammen, C. L. (1989). Role of maternal depression in perceptions of child maladjustment. *Journal of Consulting and Clinical Psychology, 57,* 663–667.

Conrad, M., & Hammen, C. (1993). Protective and resilience factors in high and low risk children: A comparison of unipolar, bipolar, medically ill and normal mothers. *Development and Psychopathology, 5,* 593–607.

Consumer Reports (1995). Does therapy help? (November, pp. 734–739).

Contrada, R. J., Glass, D. C., Krakoff, L. R., Krantz, D. S., Kehoe, K., Iseke, W., Collins, C., & Elting, E. (1982). Effects of control over aversive stimulation and Type A behavior on cardiovascular and plasma catecholamine responses. *Psychophysiology, 19,* 408–419.

Cook, M., & Mineka, S. (1989). Observational conditioning of fear to fear-relevant versus fear-irrelevant stimuli in rhesus monkeys. *Journal of Abnormal Psychology, 98,* 448–459.

Cook, P. J. (1991). The technology of personal violence. In M. Tonry (Ed.), *Crime and justice: A review of research* (pp. 67–91). Chicago: University of Chicago Press.

Cooper, C. L. (1984). *Psychosocial stress and cancer.* Chichester, Eng.: John Wiley.

Cooper, M. L., Russell, M., Skinner, J., Frone, M., & Mudar, P. (1992). Stress and alcohol use: Moderating effects of gender, coping, and alcohol expectancies. *Journal of Abnormal Psychology, 101,* 139–152.

Cooper, P. J., & Goodyer, I. (1993). A community study of depression in adolescent girls: Estimates of symptom and syndrome prevalence. *British Journal of Psychiatry, 163,* 369–374.

Cooper, T., Detre, T., & Weiss, S. M. (1981). Coronary prone behavior and coronary heart disease: a critical review. *Circulation, 63,* 1199–1215.

Coovert, D. L., & Kinder, B. (1989). The psychosexual aspects of anorexia nervosa and bulimia nervosa: A review of the literature. *Clinical Psychology Review, 9,* 169–180.

Corder, E. H., Saunders, A. M., Strittmatter, W. J., Schmechel, D. E., Gaskell, P. C., Small, F. W., Roses, A. D., Haines, J. L., & Pericak-Vance. (1993). Gene dose of apolipoprotein E Type 4 in late onset families. *Science, 261,* 921–924.

Corder, E. H., Saunders, A. M., Strittmatter, W. J., Schmechel, D. E., Gaskell, P. C., Small, G. W., Roses, A. D., Haines, J. L., & Pericak-Vance, M. A. (1993). Gene dose of apolipoprotein E type 4 allele and the risk of Alzheimer's disease in late onset families. *Science, 261,* 921–923.

Corrigan, P., & Yudofsky, S. (Eds.). (1996). *Cognitive rehabilitation for neuropsychiatric disorders.* Washington, D.C.: American Psychiatric Press.

Corse, C. D., Manuck, S. B., Cantwell, J. D., Giorani, B., & Matthews, K. A. (1982) Coronary-prone behavior pattern and cardiovascular response in persons with and without coronary heart disease. *Psychosomatic Medicine, 44,* 449–459.

Coryell, W., Akiskal, H., Leon, A., Winokur, G., Maser, J., Mueller, T., & Keller, M. (1994). The time course of nonchronic major depressive disorder: Uniformity across episodes and samples. *Archives of General Psychiatry, 51,* 405–410.

Coryell, W., Endicott, J., Maser, J. D., Keller, M. B., Leon, A. C., & Akiskal, H. S. (1995a). Long-term stability of polarity distinctions in the affective disorders. *American Journal of Psychiatry, 152,* 385–390.

Coryell, W., Endicott, J., Winokur, G., Akiskal, H., Solomon, D., Leon, A., Mueller, T., & Shea, T. (1995b). Characteristics and significance of untreated major depressive disorder. *American Journal of Psychiatry, 152,* 1124–1129.

Coryell, W., Scheftner, W., Keller, M., Endicott, J., Maser, J., & Klerman, G. L. (1993). The enduring psychosocial consequences of mania and depression. *American Journal of Psychiatry, 150,* 720–727.

Costa, P. T., & McCrae, R. R. (1990). Personality disorders and the five-factor model of personality. *Journal of Personality Disorders, 4(4),* 362–371.

Costello, E. J., Burns, B., Angold, A., & Leaf, P. (1993). How can epidemiology improve mental health services of children and adolescents? *Journal of the American Academy of Child and Adolescent Psychiatry, 32,* 1106–1117.

Costello, E. J. (1990). Child psychiatric epidemiology: Implications for clinical research and practice. In B. B. Lahey & A. E. Kazdin (Eds.), *Advances in clinical child psychology* (Vol. 13). New York: Plenum Press.

Costello, E. J., Costello, A. J., Edelbrock, C., Burns, B. J., Dulcan, M. K., Brent, D., & Janiszewski, S. (1988). Psychiatric disorders in pediatric primary care: Prevalence and risk factors. *Archives of General Psychiatry, 45,* 1107–1116.

Costello, E. J., Edelbrock, C. A., & Costello, A. J. (1985). Validity of the NIMH Diagnostic Interview Schedule for Children: A comparison between psychiatric and pediatric referrals. *Journal of Abnormal Child Psychology, 13,* 579–595.

Cox, B. J., Wessel, I., Norton, G. R., Swinson, R. P., & Direnfeld, D. M. (1995). Publication trends in anxiety disorders research: 1990–1992. *Journal of Anxiety Disorders, 9,* 531–538.

Cox, W. M. (Ed.) (1987). *Treatment and prevention of alcohol problems: A resource manual.* New York: Academic Press.

Coyle, J. T., Oster-Granite, D., & Gearhart, L. (1986). The neurobiological consequences of Down's syndrome. *Brain Research Bulletin, 16,* 773–787.

Coyne, J. C. (1982). A critique of cognitions as causal entities with particular reference to depression. *Cognitive Therapy and Research, 6,* 3–13.

Coyne, J. C., & Downey, G. (1991). Social factors and psychopathology: Stress, social support, and coping processes. *Annual Review of Psychology, 42,* 401–425.

Coyne, J. C., Kessler, R. C., Tal, M., Turnbull, J., Wortman, C. B., & Greden, J. F. (1987). Living with a depressed person. *Journal of Consulting and Clinical Psychology, 55,* 347–352.

Craig, M. E. (1990). Coercive sexuality in dating relationships: A situational model. *Clinical Psychology Review, 10,* 395–423.

Craighead, L., & Agras, S. (1991). Mechanism of action in cognitive-behavioral and pharmacological interventions for obesity and bulimia nervosa. *Journal of Consulting and Clinical Psychology, 59,* 115–125.

Craighead, W. E., Kimball, W. H., & Rehak, P. J. (1979). Mood changes, physiological responses, and self-statements during social rejection imagery. *Journal of Consulting and Clinical Psychology, 47,* 385–396.

Crandall, C. S., Preisler, J. J., & Aussprung, J. (1992). Measuring life event stress in the lives of college students. *Journal of Behavioral Medicine, 15,* 627–662.

Craske, M. G. (1991). Models and treatment of panic: Behavioral therapy of panic. *Journal of Cognitive Psychotherapy, 5,* 199–214.

Craske, M. G., & Barlow, D. H. (1988). A review of the relationship between panic and avoidance. *Clinical Psychology Review, 8,* 667–685.

Craske, M. G., Glover, D., & DeCola, J. (1995). Predicted versus unpredicted panic attacks: Acute versus general distress. *Journal of Abnormal Psychology, 104,* 214–223.

Craske, M. G., & Krueger, M. T. (1990). Prevalence of nocturnal panic in a college population. *Journal of Anxiety Disorders, 4,* 125–139.

Crawford, J. R., Gray, C. D., & Allan, K. M. (1995). The WAIS-R(UK): Basic psychometric properties in an adult UK sample. *British Journal of Clinical Psychology, 34,* 237–250.

Crino, R. D., & Andrews, G. (1996). Obsessive-compulsive disorder and axis I comorbidity. *Journal of Anxiety Disorders, 10,* 37–46.

Crnic, K. A. (1988). Mental retardation. In E. J. Mash & L. Terdal (Eds.), *Behavioral assessment of childhood disorders* (2nd ed.). New York: Guilford Press.

Crnic, K. A., Friedrich, W. N., & Greenberg, M. T. (1983). Adaptation of families with mentally retarded children: A model of stress, coping, and family ecology. *American Journal of Mental Deficiency, 88,* 125–138.

Crnic, K. A., & Reid, M. (1989). Mental retardation. In E. Mash & R. Barkley (Eds.), *Treatment of childhood disorders.* New York: Guilford Press.

Crooks, R., & Baur, K. (1990). *Our sexuality* (4th ed.). Redwood City, CA: Benjamin Cummings.

Cross-National Collaborative Group (1992). The changing rate of major depression: Cross-national comparisons. *Journal of the American Medical Association, 268,* 3098–3105.

Crow, R. R., Noyes, R., Pauls, D. L., & Slymen, D. J. (1983). A family study of panic disorder. *Archives of General Psychiatry, 40,* 1065–1069.

Crow, T. J. (1980). Molecular pathology of schizophrenia: More than one disease process? *British Medical Journal, 280,* 1–9.

Crowe, R. R., Black, D. W., Wesner, R., Andreasen, N. C., Cookman, A., & Roby, J. (1991). Lack of linkage to chromosome 5q11-q13 markers in six schizophrenia pedigrees. *Archives of General Psychiatry, 48,* 357–361.

Cummings, C., Gordon, J., & Marlatt, G. A. (1980). Relapse: Strategies of prevention and prediction. In W. R. Miller (Ed.), *The addictive behaviors.* Oxford, UK: Pergamon Press.

Cummings, E. M., & Cicchetti, D. (1990). Attachment, depression, and the transmission of depression. In M. T. Greenberg, D.

Cicchetti & E. M. Cummings (Eds.), *Attachment during the preschool years*. Chicago: University of Chicago Press.

Cummings, J. L. (1992). Depression and Parkinson's disease: A review. *American Journal of Psychiatry, 149,* 443–454.

Cummings, J. L., Miller, B., Hill, M. A., & Neshkes, R. (1987). Neuropsychiatric aspects of multiinfarct dementia and dementia of the Alzheimer type. *Archives of Neurology, 44,* 389–393.

Curry, S. G., & Marlatt, G. A. (1987). Building self-confidence, self-efficacy, and self-control. In W. M. Cox (Ed.), *Treatment and prevention of alcohol problems: A resource manual*. New York: Academic Press.

Curry, S. J., McBride, C., Grothaus, L. C., Louie, D., & Wagner, E. H. (1995). A randomized trial of self-help materials, personalized feedback, and telephone counseling with nonvolunteer smokers. *Journal of Consulting and Clinical Psychology, 63,* 1005–1014.

D'Zurilla, T. (1986). Problem-solving therapy. *A social competence approach to clinical intervention*. New York: Springer.

Dager, S. R., Cowley, D. S., & Dunner, D. L. (1987). Biological markers in panic states: Lactate-induced panic and mitral valve prolapse. *Biological Psychiatry, 22,* 339–359.

Dalgleish, T., & Watts, F. N. (1990). Biases of attention and memory in disorders of anxiety and depression. *Clinical Psychology Review, 10,* 589–604.

Darkes, J., & Goldman, M. S. (1993). Expectancy challenge and drinking reduction: Experimental evidence for a mediational process. *Journal of Consulting and Clinical Psychology, 61,* 344–353.

Darves-Bornoz, J. M., Degiovanni, A., & Gaillard, P. (1995). Why is dissociative identity disorder infrequent in France? *American Journal of Psychiatry, 152,* 1530–1531.

Davidson, J. M., Chen, J. J., Crapo, L., Gray, G. D., Greenleaf, W. J., & Catania, J. A. (1983). Hormonal changes and sexual function in aging men. *Journal of Endocrinal Metabolism, 57,* 71.

Davidson, J., Kudler, H., Smith, R., Mahorney, S., et al. (1990). Treatment of posttraumatic stress disorder with amitriptyline and placebo. *Archives of General Psychiatry, 47,* 259–266.

Davidson, J., Schwartz, M., Storck, M., Krishnan, R., & Hammett, E. (1985). A diagnostic and family study of posttraumatic stress disorder. *American Journal of Psychiatry, 142,* 90–93.

Davidson, K., & Hall, P. (1995). What does potential for hostility measure? Gender differences in the expression of hostility. *Journal of Behavioral Medicine, 18,* 233–247.

Davidson, K., Hall, P., & MacGregor, M. (1996). Gender differences in the relation between interview-derived hostility scores and resting blood pressure. *Journal of Behavioral Medicine, 19,* 185–201.

Davidson, S. (1990). Management. In G. MacLean (Ed.), *Suicide in children and adolescents* (pp. 89–127). Ontario: Hogrefe & Huber.

Davis, K. L., Kahn, R. S., Ko, G., & Davidson, M. (1991). Dopamine in schizophrenia: A review and reconceptualization. *American Journal of Psychiatry, 148,* 1474–1486.

Davis, K., Thal, L., Gamzu, E., et al., (1992). Tacrine in patients with Alzheimer's disease: A double-blind, placebo-controlled, multicenter study. *New England Journal of Medicine, 327,* 1253–1259.

Davison, G. C. (1968). Systematic desensitization as a counter-conditioning process. *Journal of Abnormal Psychology, 73,* 91–99.

Dawson, G., Klinger, L. G., Parragioticles, H., Lewy, A., et al. (1995). Subgroups of autistic children based on social behavior display distinct patterns of brain activity. *Journal of Abnormal Child Psychology, 23,* 569–583.

Dawson, G., Warrenburg, S., & Fuller, P. (1983). Hemispheric functioning and motor imitation in autistic persons. *Brain and Cognition, 2,* 346–354.

Deahrs, J. O. (1994). Dissociative identity disorder: Adaptive deception of self and others. *Bulletin of the American Academy of Psychiatry and the Law, 22,* 223–237.

DeBakey, M., & Gotto, A. (1977). *The living heart*. New York: Charter Books.

de Jong, P., Merckelbach, H., & Arntz, A. (1995). Covariation bias in phobic women: The relationship between a priori expectancy, on-line expectancy, autonomic responding, and a posteriori contingency judgement. *Journal of Abnormal Psychology, 104,* 55–62.

de Silva, P., & Rachman, S. (1992). *Obsessive-compulsive disorder: The facts*. Oxford, Engl.: Oxford University Press.

de Wilde, E. J., Kienhorst, C. W. M., Diekstra, R. F. W., & Wolters, W. H. G. (1992). The relationship between adolescent suicidal behavior and life events in childhood and adolescence. *American Journal of Psychiatry, 149,* 45–51.

Deffenbacher, J., Zwemer, W., Whisman, M., Hill, R., & Sloan, R. (1986). Irrational beliefs and anxiety. *Cognitive Therapy and Research, 10,* 281–292.

Deimling, G. T., & Bass, D. M. (1986). Symptoms of mental impairment among elderly adults and their effects on family caregivers. *Journal of Gerontology, 41,* 778–784.

DeLeon, P. H., Wakefield, M., Schultz, A. J., Williams, J., et. al. (1989). Rural America: Unique opportunities for health care delivery and health services research. *American Psychologist, 44,* 1298–1307.

DeLongis, A., Coyne, J. C., Dakof, G., Folkman, S., & Lazarus, R. S. (1982). Relationship of daily hassles, uplifts, and major life events to health status. *Health Psychology, 1,* 119–136.

Dembroski, T. M., & Costa, P. T. (1988). Assessment of coronary prone behavior: A current overview. *Annals of Behavioral Medicine, 10,* 60–63.

Dent, C. W., Sussman, S., Stacy, A. W., Craig, S., Burton, D., & Flay, B. R. (1995). Two-year behavior outcomes of project towards no tobacco use. *Journal of Consulting and Clinical Psychology, 63,* 676–677.

Department of Health and Human Services. (1989). *Interagency Head Injury Task Force Report*. Washington, DC: U.S. GPO.

Depue, R. A., & Iacono, W. G. (1989). Neurobehavioral aspects of affective disorders. *Annual Review of Psychology, 40,* 457–492.

Depue, R. A., Luciana, M., Arbisi, P., Collins, P., & Leon, A. (1994). Dopamine and the structure of personality: Relation of agonist-induced dopamine activity to positive emotionality. *Journal of Personality and Social Psychology, 67,* 485–498.

Depue, R. A., & Monroe, S. M. (1986). Conceptualization and measurement of human disorder and life stress research: The problem of chronic disturbance. *Psychological Bulletin, 99,* 36–51.

DeRicco, D. A., & Niemann, J. E. (1980). In vivo effects of peer modeling on drinking rate. *Journal of Applied Behavior Analysis, 13,* 149–152.

Deutsch, K. (1987). Genetic factors in Attention Deficit Disorders: Paper presented at symposium on Disorders of Brain and Development and Cognition, Boston, MA. As cited in Anastopoulos, A. D., & Barkley, R. A. (1988). Biological factors in attention-deficit hyperactivity disorder. *The Behavior Therapist, 11,* 47–53.

Devanand, D. P., Dwork, A. J., Hutchinson, E. R., Bolwig, T. G., & Sackeim, H. A. (1994). Does ECT alter brain structure? *American Journal of Psychiatry, 151,* 957–970.

Devanand, D. P., Sano, M., Tang, M. X., Taylor, S., Gurland, B. J., Wilder, D., Stern, Y., & Mayeux, R. (1996). Depressed mood and the incidence of Alzheimer's disease in the elderly living in the community. *Archives of General Psychiatry, 53,* 175–182.

DeVeaugh-Geiss, J., Landau, P., & Katz, R. (1989). Treatment of obsessive compulsive disorder with clomipramine. *Psychiatric Annals, 19,* 97–101.

Devereux, R. B., Pickering, T. G., Harshfield, G. A., Kleinert, H. D., Denby, L., Clark, L., Pregibon, D., Jason, M., Kleiner, B., Porer, J. S., & Laragh, J. (1983). Left ventricular hyptertrophy in patients with hypertension: importance of blood pressure response to regularly recurring stress. *Circulation, 68,* 470–476.

Diener, E., & Diener, C. (1996). Most people are happy. *Psychological Science, 7,* 181–185.

Dietrich, K. N., Starr, R. H., & Kaplan, M. G. (1980). Maternal stimulation and care of abused infants. In T. M. Field, S. Goldberg, D. Stern & A. M. Sostek (Eds.), *High-risk infants and children: Adult and peer interactions.* New York: Academic Press.

Digman, J. M. (1990). Personality structure: Emergence of the five-factor model. *Annual Review of Psychology, 41,* 417–440.

DiLalla, L. F., & Gottesman, I. I. (1989). Heterogeneity of causes for delinquency and criminality: Lifespan perspectives. *Development and Psychopathology, 1,* 339–349.

DiLalla, L. F., & Gottesman, I. I. (1991). Biological and genetic contributors to violence: Widom's untold tale. *Psychological Bulletin, 109,* 125–129.

DiLalla, L. F., Kagan, J., & Reznick, J. S. (1994). Genetic etiology of behavioral inhibition among 2-year-old children. *Infant Behavior and Development, 17,* 405–412.

Dimsdale, J. E., Pierce, C., Schoenfeld, D., & Brown, A. (1986). Suppressed anger and blood pressure: The effects of race, sex, social class, obesity, and age. *Psychosomatic Medicine, 48,* 430–436.

DiNardo, P., & Barlow, D. H. (1990). Syndrome and symptom co-occurrence in the anxiety disorders. In J. Maser & C. Cloninger (Eds.), *Comorbidity of mood and anxiety disorders.* Washington, DC: American Psychiatric Press.

Dinges, N., & Cherry, D. (1995). Symptom expression and the use of mental health services among American ethnic minorities. In J. Aponte, R. Rivers, & J. Wohl (Eds.), *Psychological interventions and cultural diversity* (pp. 40–56). Boston: Allyn & Bacon.

Dobson, K. S. (1989). A meta-analysis of the efficacy of cognitive therapy for depression. *Journal of Consulting and Clinical Psychology, 57,* 414–419.

Dodge, K. A. (1985). Attributional bias in aggressive children. In P. C. Kendall (Ed.), *Advances in cognitive-behavioral research and therapy* (Vol. 4). New York: Academic Press.

Dodge, K. A., Bates, J. E., & Pettit, G. S. (1990). Mechanisms in the cycle of violence. *Science, 250,* 1678–1683.

Dodge, K. A., Pettit, G. S., Bates, J. E., & Valente, E. (1995). Social information-processing patterns partially mediate the effect of early physical abuse on later conduct problems. *Journal of Abnormal Psychology, 104,* 632–643.

Dodge, K. A., Price, J. M., Bachorowski, J., & Newman, J. P. (1990). Hostile attributional biases in severely aggressive adolescents. *Journal of Abnormal Psychology, 99,* 385–392.

Dohrenwend, B. P., & Dohrenwend, B. S. (1967). Field studies of social factors in relation to three types of psychological disorders. *Journal of Abnormal and Social Psychology, 70,* 369–378.

Dohrenwend, B. P., Levav, I., Shrout, P. E., Schwartz, S., Naveh, G., Link, B. G., Skodol, A. E., & Stueve, A. (1992). Socioeconomic status and psychiatric disorders: The causation-selection issue. *Science, 255,* 946–952.

Dohrenwend, B. P., Shrout, P. E., Link, B. G., Martin, J. L., & Skodol, A. E. (1986). Overview and initial results from a risk-factor study of depression and schizophrenia. In J. E. Barrett (Ed.), *Mental disorder in the community: Progress and challenges* (pp. 184–215). New York: Guilford Press.

Dolan, B. (1991). Cross-cultural aspects of anorexia nervosa and bulimia: A review. *International Journal of Eating Disorders, 10,* 67–79.

Doleys, D. M. (1977). Behavioral treatments for nocturnal enuresis in children: A review of the recent literature. *Psychological Bulletin, 84,* 30–54.

Doleys, D. M. (1983). Enuresis and encopresis. In T. H. Ollendick & M. Hersen (Eds.), *Handbook of child psychopathology.* New York: Plenum Press.

Donnellan, A. M. (Ed.). (1985). *Classic readings in autism.* New York: Teachers College Press.

Dorgan, C. A. (1995). (Ed.). *Statistical record of health and medicine.* Detroit: Gale Research.

Dornbusch, S. M., Carlsmith, J. M., Bushwall, S. J., Ritter, P. L., Leiderman, H., Hastorf, A. H., & Gross, R. T. (1985). Single parents, extended households, and the control of adolescents. *Child Development, 56,* 326–341.

Dorwart, R. A., Schlesinger, M., Davidson, H., Epstein, S., & Hoover, C. (1991). A national study of psychiatric hospital care. *American Journal of Psychiatry, 148,* 204–210.

Downey, G., & Coyne, J. C. (1990). Children of depressed parents: An integrative review. *Psychological Bulletin, 108,* 50–76.

Drake, R. E., Osher, F. C., Noordsy, D. L., Hurlbut, S. C., Teague, G. B., & Beaudett, M. S. (1990). Diagnosis of alcohol use disorders in schizophrenia. *Schizophrenia Bulletin, 16,* 57–68.

Dubbert, P. M. (1995). Behavioral (life-style) modification in the prevention and treatment of hypertension. *Clinical Psychology Review, 15,* 187–216.

Ducey, C., & Simon, B. (1975). Ancient Greece and Rome. In J. G. Howells (Ed.), *World history of psychiatry.* New York: Brunner/Mazel.

Dugdale, R. L. (1877). *The Jukes: A study in crime, pauperism, disease, and heredity.* R. C. Wade (Ed.). New York: Arno Press.

Dumas, J. E. (1989). Treating antisocial behavior in children: Child and family approaches. *Clinical Psychology Review, 9,* 197–222.

Dunant, Y., & Israel, M. (1985). The release of acetylcholine. *Scientific American, 252,* 58–83.

Dunbar, F. (1943). *Psychosomatic diagnosis.* New York: Harper & Row.

Dunn, M. E., & Goldman, M. S. (1996). Empirical modeling of an alcohol expectancy memory network in elementary school children as a function of grade. *Experimental and Clinical Psychopharmacology, 4,* 209–217.

Dupont, R. M., Jernigan, T., Heindel, W., Butters, N., Shafer, K., Wilson, T., Hesselink, J., & Gillin, J. C. (1995). Magnetic resonance imaging and mood disorders: Localization of white matter and other subcortical abnormalities. *Archives of General Psychiatry, 52,* 747–755.

Durkheim, E. (1897/1951). *Le suicide.* Paris: Librarie. J. A. Spaulding & G. Simpson (Trans.), *Suicide.* Glencoe, IL: Free Press.

Dutton, D. G. (1995). Male abusiveness in intimate relationships. *Clinical Psychology Review, 15,* 567–581.

Dwairy, M., & Van Sickle, T. (1996). Western psychotherapy in traditional Arabic societies. *Clinical Psychology Review, 16,* 231–249.

Dykens, E., Ort, S., Cohen, I., Spiridigliozzi, G., Lachiewicz, A., Reiss, A., Freund, L., Hagerman, R., & O'Connor, R. (1996). Trajectories and profiles of adaptive behavior in males with fragile X syndrome: Multicenter studies. *Journal of Autism and Developmental Disorders, 26,* 287–301.

Dykens, E., Hodapp, R. M., Ort, S., & Leckman, J. F. (1993). Trajectory of adaptive behavior in males with fragile X syndrome. *Journal of Autism and Developmental Disorders, 23,* 135–146.

Earls, F. (1994). Oppositional-defiant and conduct disorders. In M. Rutter, E. Taylor & L. Hersov (Eds.), *Child and adolescent psychiatry.* Oxford: Blackwell Scientific Publications.

Eaton, W. W., Dryman, A., & Weissman, M. M. (1991). Panic and phobia. In L. N. Robins & D. A. Reiger (Eds.), *Psychiatric disorders in America.* New York: The Free Press.

Eaton, W. W., Thara, R., Federman, B., Melton, B., & Liang, K.-Y. (1995). Structure and course of positive and negative symptoms in schizophrenia. *Archives of General Psychiatry, 52,* 127–134.

Echeburua, E., Corral, P. D., Sarasua, B., & Zubizarreta, I. (1996). Treatment of acute posttraumatic stress disorder in rape victims: An experimental study. *Journal of Anxiety Disorders, 10,* 185–199.

Eckenrode, J., Powers, J., Doris, J., Munsch, J., & Bolger, N. (1988). Substantiation of child abuse and neglect reports. *Journal of Consulting and Clinical Psychology, 56,* 9–16.

Edelbrock, C., & Costello, A. J. (1988). Structured psychiatric interviews for children. In M. Rutter, A. H. Tuma & I. S. Lann (Eds.), *Assessment and diagnosis in child psychopathology*. New York: Guilford Press.

Edelmann, R. J. (1992). *Anxiety: Theory, research, and intervention in clinical and health psychology*. Chichester, Engl.: Wiley.

Edhe, D., & Holm, J. E. (1992). Stress and headache: Comparisons of migraine, tension, and headache-free subjects. *Headache Quarterly, Current Treatment and Research, 3*, 54–60.

Edman, S. O., Cole, D. A., & Howard, G. S. (1990). Convergent and discriminant validity of FACES-III: Family adaptability and cohesion. *Family Process, 29*, 95–103.

Efran, J. S., & Caputo, G. C. (1984). Paradox in psychotherapy: A cybernetic perspective. *Journal of Behavior Therapy and Experimental Psychiatry, 15*, 235–240.

Egeland, B., Jacobvitz, D., & Sroufe, L. A. (1988). Breaking the cycle of abuse. *Child Development, 59*, 1080–1088.

Egeland, J. A., Gerhard, D. S., Pauls, D. L., Sussex, J. N., Kidd, K. K., Allen, C. R., Hostetter, A. M., & Housman, D. E. (1987). Bipolar affective disorders linked to DNA markers on chromosome 11. *Nature, 325*, 783–787.

Ehlers, A. (1995). A 1-year prospective study of panic attacks: Clinical course and factors associated with maintenance. *Journal of Abnormal Psychology, 104*, 164–172.

Ehlers, A., & Breuer, P. (1995). Selective attention to physical threat in subjects with panic attacks and specific phobias. *Journal of Anxiety Disorders, 9*, 11–31.

Einfeld, S. L., & Aman, M. (1995). Issues in the taxonomy of psychopathology in mental retardation. *Journal of Autism and Developmental Disorders, 25*, 143–167.

Eiserman, W. D., Shisler, L., & Healey, S. (1995). A community assessment of preschool providers' attitudes toward inclusion. *Journal of Early Intervention, 19*, 149–167.

Ekselius, L., Lindstrom, E., von Knorring, L., Bodlund, O., & Kullgren, G. (1994). Comorbidity among the personality disorders in DSM-III-R. *Personality and Individual Differences, 17*, 155–160.

Elkin, I., Gibbons, R. D., Shea, M. T., Sotsky, S. M., Watkins, J. T., & Pilkonis, P. A. (1995). Initial severity and differential treatment outcome in the national institute of mental health treatment of depression collaborative research program. *Journal of Consulting and Clinical Psychology, 63*, 841–847.

Elkin, I., Shea, M. T., Watkins, J. T., Imber, S. D., Sotsky, S. M., Collins, J. F., Glass, D. R., Pilkonis, P. A., Leber, W. R., Docherty, J. P., Fiester, S. J., & Parloff, M. B. (1989). National Institute of Mental Health Treatment of Depression Collaborative Research Program: General effectiveness of treatment. *Archives of General Psychiatry, 46*, 971–982.

Elkin, I., Shea, T., Watkins, J. T., Imber, S. D., Sotsky, S. M., Collins, J. F., Glass, D. R., Pilkonis, P. A., Leber, W. R., Docherty, J. P., Fiester, S. J., & Parloff, M. B. (1989). National Institute of Mental Health Treatment of Depression Collaborative Research Program: General effectiveness of treatments. *Archives of General Psychiatry, 46*, 971–982.

Ellenberger, H. F. (1972). The story of "Anna O.:" A critical review with new data. *Journal of the History of the Behavioral Sciences, 8*, 267–279.

Ellicott, A., Hammen, C., Gitlin, M., Brown, G., & Jamison, K. (1990). Life events and the course of bipolar disorder. *American Journal of Psychiatry, 147*, 1194–1198.

Ellis, A. (1962). *Reason and emotion in psychotherapy*. New York: Stuart.

Ellis, A. (1971). *Growth through reason*. Hollywood: Wilshire.

Ellis, A. (1977). The basic clinical theory of rational emotive therapy. In A. Ellis & G. Grieger (Eds.), *Handbook of rational-emotive therapy*. New York: Springer.

Ellis, A. (1989). Comments on my critics. In M. E. Bernard & R. DiGiuseppe (Eds.), *Inside rational-emotive therapy: A critical appraisal of the theory and therapy of Albert Ellis*. New York: Academic Press.

Ellis, A. (1996). *Better, deeper, and more enduring brief therapy: The rational-emotive behavior therapy approach*. New York: Brunner/Mazel.

Ellis, A., & Harper R. (1961). *A guide to rational living*. North Hollywood, CA: Wilshire Books.

Ellis, L. (1991). A synthesized (biosocial) theory of rape. *Journal of Consulting and Clinical Psychology, 59*, 631–642.

Eme, R. F., & Kavanaugh, L. (1995). Sex differences in conduct disorder. *Journal of Consulting and Clinical Psychology, 24*, 406–426.

Emery, R. E. (1989). Family violence. *American Psychologist, 44*, 321–328.

Emmelkamp, P. M. G. (1990). Obsessive-compulsive disorder in adulthood. In M. Hersen & C. Last (Eds.), *Handbook of child and adult psychopathology: A longitudinal perspective* (pp. 221–234). New York: Pergamon Press.

Emmelkamp, P. M. G. (1994). Behavior therapy with adults. In S. Garfield & A. Bergin (Eds.), *Handbook of psychotherapy and behavior change*. (4th ed.). New York: Wiley.

Emmelkamp, P. M. G. (1995). Behavior therapy with adults. In A. Bergin & S. Garfield (Eds.), *Handbook of psychotherapy and behavior change* (4th ed.). New York: Wiley.

Emmelkamp, P. M. G., Visser, S., & Hoekstra, R. J. (1988). Cognitive therapy vs. exposure in vivo in the treatment of obsessive-compulsives. *Cognitive Therapy and Research, 12*, 103–114.

Emrick, C. D., & Hansen, J. (1983). Assertions regarding effectiveness of treatment for alcoholism. *American Psychologist, 38*, 1078–1088.

Endicott, J., & Spitzer, R. L. (1978). A diagnostic interview: The Schedule for Affective Disorders and Schizophrenia. *Archives of General Psychiatry, 35*, 837–844.

Engel, B. T. & Bickford, A. F. (1961). Response-specificity: Stimulus-responses and individual-response specificity in essential hypertensives. *Archives of General Psychiatry, 5*, 478–489.

Engel, G. L. (1977). The need for a new medical model: Challenge for biomedicine. *Science, 196*, 129–136.

Epstein, N., & Baucom, D. H. (1993). Cognitive factors in marital disturbance. In K. S. Dobson & P. C. Kendall (Eds.), *Psychopathology and cognition*. San Diego, CA: Academic Press.

Erdberg, P., & Exner, J. E. (1984). Personality assessment: Rorschach assessment. In G. Goldstein & M. Hersen (Eds.), *Handbook of psychological assessment* (pp. 332–347). New York: Pergamon Press.

Erdelyi, M. H. (1985). *Psychoanalysis: Freud's cognitive psychology*. New York: Freeman.

Erhardt, D., & Hinshaw, S. P. (1994). Initial sociometric impressions of ADHD and comparison boys: Predictions from social behaviors and from nonbehavioral variables. *Journal of Consulting and Clinical Psychology, 62*, 833–842.

Erlenmeyer-Kimling, L., Squires-Wheeler, E., Adamo, U., Bassett, A., Cornblatt, B., Kestenbaum, C., Rock, D., Roberts, S., & Gottesman, I. (1995). The New York High Risk Project: Psychoses and Cluster A personality disorders in offspring of schizophrenic parents at 23 years of follow-up. *Archives of General Psychiatry, 52*, 856–865.

Erlenmeyer-Kimling, L., Golden, R. R., & Cornblatt, B. A. (1989). A taxometric analysis of cognitive and neuromotor variables in children at risk for schizophrenia. *Journal of Abnormal Psychology, 98*, 203–208.

Eron, L. D., & Huesmann, L. R. (1990). The stability of aggressive behavior—even unto the third generation. In M. Lewis & S. M.

Miller (Eds.), *Handbook of developmental psychopathology*. New York: Plenum Press.

Eronen, M. (1995). Mental disorders and homicidal behavior in female subjects. *American Journal of Psychiatry, 152*, 1216–1218.

Eronen, M., Hakola, P., & Tiihonen, J. (1996). Mental disorders and homicidal behavior in Finland. *Archives of General Psychiatry, 53*, 497–501.

Eskenazi, B., & Maizlish, N. A. (1988). Effects of occupational exposure to chemicals on neurobehavioral functioning. In R. E. Tarter, D. H. Van Thiel & K. L. Edwards (Eds.), *Medical neuropsychology: The impact of disease on behavior* (pp. 223–264). New York: Plenum Press.

Eth, S., & Pynoos, R. S. (Eds.). (1985). Post-traumatic stress disorder in children. Washington, DC: *American Psychiatric Press*.

Evans, D. A., Funkerstein, H., Albert, M. S., Scherr, P. A., Cook, N. R., Chown, M. J., Hebert, L. E., Hennekens, C. H., & Taylor, J. O. (1989). Prevalence of Alzheimer's disease in a community population of older persons. *Journal of the American Medical Association, 262*, 2551–2556.

Evans, D. L., Folds, J. D., Petitto, J. M., Golden, R. N., Pedersen, C. A., Corrigan, M., Gilmore, J. H., Silva, S. G., Quade, D., & Ozer, H. (1992). Circulating natural killer cell phenotypes in men and women with major depression: Relation to cytotoxic activity and severity of depression. *Archives of General Psychiatry, 49*, 388–395.

Evans, J. A., & Hammerton, J. L. (1985). Chromosomal anomalies. In A. M. Clarke, A. D. Clark & J. M. Berg (Eds.), *Mental deficiency: The changing outlook*. New York: Free Press.

Evans, M. D., Hollon, S. D., DeRubeis, R. J., Piasecki, J. M., Grove, W. M., Garvey, M. J., & Tuason, V. B. (1992). Differential relapse following cognitive therapy and pharmacotherapy for depression. *Archives of General Psychiatry, 49*, 802–808.

Everaerd, W., & Dekker, J. (1982). Treatment of secondary orgasmic dysfunction: A comparison of systematic desensitization and sex therapy. *Behaviour Research and Therapy, 20*, 269–274.

Ewart, C. K., Taylor, C. B., Kraemer, H. C., & Agras, W. S. (1984). Reducing blood pressure reactivity during interpersonal conflict: Effects of marital communication training. *Behavior Therapy, 15*, 473–484.

Exner, J. (1990). *A Rorschach Workbook for the Comprehensive System*. Rorschach Workshops: Ashville, NC.

Faedda, G. L., Tondo, L., Teicher, M. H., Baldessarini, R. J., Gelbard, H. A., & Floris, G. F. (1993). Seasonal mood disorders: Patterns of seasonal recurrence in mania and depression. *Archives of General Psychiatry, 50*, 17–23.

Fairbank, J. A., McCaffrey, R. J., & Keane, T. M. (1985). Psychometric detection of fabricated symptoms of posttraumatic stress disorder. *American Journal of Psychiatry, 142*, 501–503.

Fairburn, C. G., & Beglin, S. J. (1990). Studies of the epidemiology of bulimia nervosa. *American Journal of Psychiatry, 147*, 401–408.

Fairburn, C. G., & Cooper, P. J. (1984). The clinical features of bulimia nervosa. *British Journal of Psychiatry, 144*, 238–246.

Fairburn, C. G., Norman, P. A., Welch, S. L., O'Connor, M. E., Doll, H. A., & Peveler, R. C. (1995). A prospective study of outcome in bulimia nervosa and the long-term effects of three psychological treatments. *Archives of General Psychiatry, 52*, 304–312.

Fairweather, G. W., Sanders, D. H., Maynard, H., & Cressler, D. L. (1969). *Community life for the mentally ill: An alternative to institutional care*. Chicago: Aldine.

Fann, J. R., Katon, W. J., Uomoto, J. M., & Esselman, P. C. (1995). Psychiatric disorders and functional disability in outpatients with traumatic brain injuries. *American Journal of Psychiatry, 152*, 1493–1499.

Faraone, S. V., Seidman, L. J., Kremen, W. S., Pepple, J. R., Lyons, M. J., & Tsuang, M. T. (1995). Neuropsychological functioning among the nonpsychotic relatives of schizophrenic patients: A diagnostic efficiency analysis. *Journal of Abnormal Psychology, 104*, 286–304.

Farlow, M., Lahiri, Poirier, J., Davignon, J., & Hui, S. (1996). Apolipoprotein E genotype and gender influence response to tacrine therapy. *Annals of the New York Academy of Sciences, 802*, 101–110.

Farmer, R., & Nelson-Gray, R. O. (1990). Personality disorders and depression: Hypothetical relations, empirical findings, and methodological considerations. *Clinical Psychology Review, 10*, 453–476.

Farrell, A. D., Danish, S. J., & Howard, C. W. (1992). Relationship between drug use and other problem behaviors in urban adolescents. *Journal of Consulting and Clinical Psychology, 60*, 705–712.

Farrington, D. P., Loeber, R., & van Hammen, W. B. (1993). Long-term criminal outcomes of hyperactivity-impulsivity-attention deficit and conduct problems in children. In L. N. Robins & M. R. Rutter (Eds.), *Straight and devious pathways to adulthood*. New York: Cambridge University Press.

Fauber, R. L., & Long, N. (1991). Children in context: The role of the family in child psychotherapy. *Journal of Consulting and Clinical Psychology, 59*, 813–820.

Faust, J., Runyon, M. K., & Kenny, M. C. (1995). Family variables associated with the onset and impact of intrafamilial childhood sexual abuse. *Clinical Psychology Review, 15*, 443–456.

Fava, M. et al. (1989). Neurochemical abnormalities of anorexia nervosa and bulimia nervosa. *American Journal of Psychiatry, 146*, 963–971.

Fava, M., & Kaji, J. (1994). Continuation and maintenance treatments of major depressive disorder. *Psychiatric Annals, 24*, 281–290.

Favell, J. E., Azrin, N. H., Baumeister, A. A., Carr, E. G., Dorsey, M. F., Forehand, R., Foxx, R. M., Lovaas, O. I., Rincover, A., Risley, T. R., Romanczyk, R. G., Russo, D. C., Schroeder, S. R., & Solnick, J. V. (1982). The treatment of self-injurious behavior. *Behavior Therapy, 13*, 529–554.

Favell, J. E., & Green, J. W. (1981). *How to treat self-injurious behavior*. Lawrence, KS: H & H Enterprises.

Fawcett, J., Sheftner, W. A., Clark, D. C., Hedeker, D., Gibbons, R. D., & Coryell, W. (1987). Clinical predictors of suicide in patients with major affective disorders: A controlled prospective study. *American Journal of Psychiatry, 144*, 35–40.

Fawzy, F. I., Fawzy, N. W., Arndt, L. A., & Pasnau, R. O. (1995). Critical review of psychosocial interventions in cancer care. *Archives of General Psychiatry, 52*, 100–112.

Fay, R. E., Turner, C. F., Klassen, A. D., & Gagnon, J. H. (1989). Prevalence and patterns of same-gender sexual contact among men. *Science, 243*, 338–348.

Feigenbaum, R., Weinstein, E., & Rosen, E. (1995). College students' sexual attitudes and behaviors: Implications for sexuality education. *Journal of American College Health, 44*, 112–118.

Fein, G., Van Dyke, C., Davenport, L., Turetsky, B., Brant-Zawadzki, M., Zatz, L., Dillon, W., & Valk, P. (1990). Preservation of normal cognitive functioning in elderly subjects with extensive white-matter lesions of long duration. *Archives of General Psychiatry, 47*, 220–223.

Feingold, B. F. (1975). *Why your child is hyperactive*. New York: Random House.

Feldman, H. A., Goldstein, I., Hatzichristou, G., Krane, R. J., & McKinlay, J. B. (1994). Impotence and its medical and psychosocial correlates: Results of the Massachusetts male aging study. *Journal of Urology, 151*, 54–61.

Fenichel, O. (1945). *The psychoanalytic theory of neuroses*. New York: Norton.

Ferster, C. B. (1961). Positive reinforcement and behavioral deficits in autistic children. *Child Development, 32*, 437–456.

Fichter, M. M., Meller, I., Schroppel, H., & Steinkirchner, R. (1995). Dementia and cognitive impairment in the oldest old in the community: Prevalence and comorbidity. *British Journal of Psychiatry, 166,* 621–629.

Fincham, F., & Spettell, C. (1984). The acceptability of dry bed training and urine alarm training as treatments of nocturnal enuresis. *Behavior Therapy, 15,* 388–394.

Fingarette, H. (1988). Alcoholism: The mythical disease. *The Public Interest, 91,* 3–22.

Fingerhut, L. A., & Kleinman, J. C. (1990). International and interstate comparisons of homicide among young males. *Journal of American Medical Association, 263,* 3292–3295.

Fingerhut, L. A., Ingram, D. D., & Feldman, J. J. (1992). Firearm and nonfirearm homicide among persons 15 through 19 years of age: Differences by level of urbanization, United States, 1979 through 1989. *Journal of the American Medical Association, 267,* 3048–3053.

Finkelhor, D. (1980). Sex among siblings: A survey on prevalence, variety, and effects. *Archives of Sexual Behavior, 9,* 171–194.

Finkelhor, D., & Berliner, L. (1995). Research on the treatment of sexually abused children: A review and recommendations. *Journal of the American Academy of Child and Adolescent Psychiatry, 34,* 1408–1423.

Finkelhor, D., & Dziuba-Leatherman, J. (1994). Victimization of children. *American Psychologist, 49,* 173–183.

Finley, W. W., Wansley, R. A., & Blenkarn, M. M. (1977). Conditioning treatment of enuresis using a 70% intermittent reinforcement schedule. *Behaviour Research and Therapy, 15,* 419–427.

Finn, P. R., Zeitouni, N., & Pihl, R. O. (1990). Effects of alcohol on psychophysiological hyperreactivity to nonaversive and aversive stimuli in men at high risk for alcoholism. *Journal of Abnormal Psychology, 99,* 79–85.

Fischer, C. (1991). Phenomenological-existential psychotherapy. In M. Hersen, A. E. Kazdin & A. Bellack (Eds.), *The clinical psychology handbook* (2nd ed.). New York: Pergamon Press.

Fischer, M., Barkley, R. A., Edelbrock, C. S., & Smallish, L. (1990). The adolescent outcome of hyperactive children diagnosed by research criteria: Academic, attentional, and neuropsychological status. *Journal of Consulting and Clinical Psychology, 58,* 580–588.

Fischer, P. J., & Breakey, W. R. (1991). The epidemiology of alcohol, drug, and mental disorders among homeless persons. *American Psychologist, 46,* 1115–1128.

Fish, B., Marcus, J., Hans, S. L., Auerbach, J. G., & Perdue, S. (1992). Infants at risk for schizophrenia: Sequelae of a genetic neurointegrative defect: A review and replication analysis of Pandymaturation in the Jerusalem Infant Development Study. *Archives of General Psychiatry, 49,* 221–235.

Fishbain, D. A., & Goldberg, M. (1991). The misdiagnosis of conversion disorder in a psychiatric emergency service. *General Hospital Psychiatry, 13,* 177–181.

Fisher, J. E., & Carstensen, L. L. (1990). Behavior management of the dementias. *Clinical Psychology Review, 10,* 611–629.

Flaks, D., Ficher, I., Masterpasqua, F., & Joseph, G. (1995). Lesbians choosing motherhood: A comparative study of lesbian and heterosexual parents and their children. *Developmental Psychology, 31,* 105–114.

Flaum, M., Swayze, V. W., O'Leary, D. S., Yuh, W. T. C., Ehrhardt, J. C., Arndt, S. V., & Andreasen, N. C. (1995). Effects of diagnosis, laterality, and gender on brain morphology in schizophrenia. *American Journal of Psychiatry, 152,* 704–714.

Foa, E. , & Kozak, M. J. (1995). DSM-IV field trial: Obsessive-compulsive disorder. *American Journal of Psychiatry, 152,* 90–96.

Foa, E. , Hearst-Ikeda, D., & Perry, K. J. (1995). Evaluation of a brief cognitive-behavioral program for the prevention of chronic PTSD in recent assault victims. *Journal of Consulting and Clinical Psychology, 63,* 948–955.

Foa, E., Rothbaum, B. O., Riggs, D. S., & Murdock, T. B. (1991). Treatment of posttraumatic stress disorder in rape victims: A comparison between cognitive-behavioral procedures and counseling. *Journal of Consulting and Clinical Psychology, 59,* 715–723.

Foa, E., & Steketee, G. (1984). Behavioral treatment of obsessive-compulsive ritualizers. In T. Insel (Ed.), *New findings in obsessive-compulsive disorder.* Washington, DC: American Psychiatric Press.

Folkman, S., & Lazarus, R. (1980). An analysis of coping in a middle-aged community sample. *Journal of Health and Social Behavior, 21,* 219–239.

Follingstad, D. R., Neckerman, A. P., & Vormbrock, J. (1988). Reactions to victimization and coping strategies of battered women: The ties that bind. *Clinical Psychology Review, 8,* 373–390.

Folstein, M., Folstein, S., & McHugh, P. (1975). Mini-mental State: A practical method for grading the cognitive state of patients for the clinician. *Journal of Psychiatric Research, 12,* 189–198.

Folstein, S., & Rutter, M. (1977). Autism: Familial aggregation and genetic implications. *Journal of Autism and Developmental Disorders, 18,* 3–30.

Folstein, S., & Rutter, M. (1978). A twin study of individuals with infantile autism. In M. Rutter & E. Schopler (Eds.), *Autism: A reappraisal of concepts and treatment.* New York: Plenum Press.

Fombonne, E. (1994). The Chartres study: I. Prevalence of psychiatric disorders among French school-aged children. *British Journal of Psychiatry, 164,* 69–79.

Ford, M. R., & Widiger, T. A. (1989). Sex bias in the diagnosis of histrionic and antisocial personality disorders. *Journal of Consulting and Clinical Psychology, 57,* 301–305.

Forehand, R., & McMahon, R. J. (1981). *Helping the noncompliant child: A clinician's guide to parent training.* New York: Guilford.

Forehand, R., Sturgis, E., McMahon, R. J., Aguar, D., Green, K., Wells, K., & Breiner, J. (1979). Parent behavioral training to modify child noncompliance: Treatment generalization across time and from home to school. *Behavior Modification, 3,* 3–25.

Foreyt, J. P., & McGavin, J. K. (1988). Anorexia nervosa and bulimia. In E. J. Mash & L. G. Terdal (Eds.), *Behavioral assessment of childhood disorders* (2nd ed.). New York: Guilford Press.

Forgays, D. K., & Forgays, D. G. (1991). Type A behavior within families: Parents and older adolescent children. *Journal of Behavioral Medicine, 14,* 325–339.

Forster, D. P., Newens, A. J., Kay, D. W. K., & Edwardson, J. A. (1995). Risk factors in clinically diagnosed presenile dementia of the Alzheimer type: A case-control study in Northern England. *Journal of Epidemiology and Community Health, 49,* 253–258.

Forward, S., & Buck, C. (1988). *Betrayal of innocence: Incest and its devastation.* New York: Penguin Books.

Foster, N., Petersen, R., Gracon, S., & Lewis, K. (1996). An enriched-population, double-blind, placebo-controlled, crossover study of tacrine and lecithin in Alzheimer's disease. The Tacrine 970-6 Study Group. *Dementia, 7,* 260–266.

Foy, D., Donahoe, C., Carroll, E., Gallers, J., & Reno, R. (1987). Posttraumatic stress disorder. In L. Michelson & M. Ascher (Eds.), *Anxiety and stress disorders: Cognitive behavioral assessment and treatment.* New York: Guilford Press.

Foy, D., Sipprelle, R., Rueger, D., & Carroll, E. (1984). Etiology of posttraumatic stress disorder in Vietnam veterans: Analysis of premilitary, military, and combat exposure influences. *Journal of Consulting and Clinical Psychology, 52,* 79–87.

Frank, E., Kupfer, D. J., & Perel, J. M. (1989). Early recurrence in unipolar depression. *Archives of General Psychiatry, 46,* 397–400.

Frankenhaeuser, M., Dunne, E., & Lundberg, U. (1976). Sex differences in sympthetic-adrenal medullary reactions induced by different stressors. *Psychopharmacology, 47,* 1–5.

Frankl, V. E. (1960). Paradoxical intention: A logotherapeutic technique. *American Journal of Psychotherapy, 14,* 520–535.

Frasure-Smith, N. (1991). In-hospital symptoms of psychological stress as predictors of long-term outcome after acute myocardial infarction in men. *The American Journal of Cardiology*, January 15, 121–127.

Frasure-Smith, N., & Prince, R. (1985). The Ischemic Heart Disease Life Stress Monitoring Program: Impact on mortality. *Psychosomatic Medicine, 47*, 431–445.

Frederick, S. L., Hall, S. M., Humfleet, G. L., & Munoz, R. F. (1996). Sex differences in the relation of mood to weight gain after quitting smoking. *Experimental and Clinical Psychopharmacology, 4*, 178–185.

Freed, C. R., Breeze, R. E., Rosenberg, N. L., Schneck, S. A., Kriek, E., Qi, J., Lone, T., Zhang, Y., Snyder, J. A., Wells, T. H., Ramig, L. O., Thompson, L., Mazziotta, J. C., Huang, S. C., Grafton, S. T., Brooks, D., Sawle, G., Schroter, G., & Ansari, A. A. (1992). Survival of implanted fetal dopamine cells and neurologic improvement 12 to 46 months after transplantation for Parkinson's Disease. *New England Journal of Medicine, 327*, 1549–1555.

Freeman, A., & Leaf, R. C. (1989). Cognitive therapy applied to personality disorders. In A. Freeman, K. M. Simon, L. E. Beutler & H. Arkowitz (Eds.), *Comprehensive handbook of cognitive therapy*. New York: Plenum Press.

French, M. T., Zarkin, G., & Hubbard, R. (1993). The effects of time in drug abuse treatment and employment on posttreatment drug use and criminal activity. *American Journal of Drug and Alcohol Abuse, 19*, 19–33.

Freud, S. (1905/1955). Three essays on the theory of sexuality. In *The standard edition of the complete psychological works of Sigmund Freud*. London: Hogarth Press.

Freud, S. (1913). *The interpretation of dreams.* (A. A. Brill, Trans.). London: Allen & Unwin.

Freud, S. (1914). *Psychopathology of everyday life.* London: Fischer Unwin.

Freud, S. (1917). *A general introduction to psychoanalysis.* Garden City, NY: Garden City. (1943 version of 1917 German text).

Freud, S. (1936). *The ego and mechanisms of defense.* (Rev. ed., 1967). New York: International Universities Press.

Friedhoff, A. J., & Chase, T. N. (Eds.) (1982). *Gilles de la Tourette syndrome.* New York: Raven Press.

Friedman, A. S., & Utada, A. T. (1992). Effects of two group interaction models on substance-abusing adjudicated adolescent males. *Journal of Community Psychology, 19*, 106–117.

Friedman, M. Thoresen, C., Gill, J. Ulmer, D., Powell, L. H., et al. (1986). Alterations of type A behavior and its effects on cardiac recurrence in post myocardial infarction patients: Summary results of the coronary prevention recurrence project. *American Heart Journal, 112*, 653–665.

Friedman, M., & Rosenman, R. (1959). Association of specific overt behavior pattern with blood and cardiovascular findings. *Journal of the American Medical Association, 169*, 1286–1296.

Friedman, S., & Paradis, C. (1991). African-American patients with panic disorder and agoraphobia. *Journal of Anxiety Disorders, 5*, 35–41.

Friedman, S. L., & Haywood, H. C. (Eds.). (1994). *Developmental follow-up: Concepts, domains, and methods.* San Diego: Academic Press.

Friedrich, W. N., & Gerber, P. N. (1994). Autoerotic asphyxia: The development of a paraphilia. *Journal of the American Academy of Child and Adolescent Psychiatry, 33*, 970–974.

Fromm-Reichmann, F. (1948). Notes on the development of treatment of schizophrenia by psychoanalytic psychotherapy. *Psychiatry, 11*, 263–273.

Fromm-Reichmann, F. (1954). Psychotherapy of schizophrenia. *American Journal of Psychiatry, 15*, 711–721.

Fruzzetti, A., & Jacobson, N. (1991). Marital and family therapy. In M. Hersen, A. Kazdin & A. Bellack (Eds.), *The clinical psychology handbook* (2nd ed.). New York: Pergamon Press.

Furby, L., Weinrott, M. R., & Blackshaw, L. (1989). Sex offender recidivism: A review. *Psychological Bulletin, 105*, 3–30.

Furnham, A., & Baguma, P. (1994). Cross-cultural differences in the evaluation of male and female body shapes. *International Journal of Eating Disorders, 15*, 81–89.

Furstenberg, F. F. (1988). Child care after divorce and remarriage. In E. M. Hetherington & J. D. Arasteh (Eds.), *Impact of divorce, single parenting, and stepparenting on children.* Hillsdale, NJ: Erlbaum.

Fyer, A. J., Mannuzza, S., Chapman, T. F., Liebowitz, M. R., & Klein, D. F. (1993). A direct-interview family study of social phobia. *Archives of General Psychiatry, 50*, 286–293.

Fyer, A. J., Mannuzza, S., Chapman, T. F., Martin, L. Y., & Klein, D. F. (1995). Specificity in familial aggregation of phobic disorders. *Archives of General Psychiatry, 52*, 564–573.

Fyer, A. J., Mannuzza, S., Gallops, M. S., Martin, L. Y., Aaronson, C., Gorman, J. M., Liebowitz, M. R., & Klein, D. F. (1990). Familial transmission of simple phobias and fears. *Archives of General Psychiatry, 47*, 252–256.

Fyer, M. R., Frances, A. J., Sullivan, T., Hurt, S. W., & Clarkin, J. (1988). Comorbidity of borderline personality disorder. *Archives of General Psychiatry, 45*, 348–352.

Gadow, K. D. (1992). Pediatric psychopharmacology: A review of recent research. *Journal of Child Psychology and Psychiatry, 33*, 153–195.

Gadow, K. D., Sverd, J., Sprafkin, J., Nolan, E. E., & Ezor, S. N. (1995). Efficacy of methylphenidate for attention-deficit hyperactivity disorder in children with tic disorder. *Archives of General Psychiatry, 52*, 444–455.

Gaines, R., Sandgrund, A., Green, A. H., & Power, E. (1978). Etiological factors in child maltreatment: A multivariate study of abusing, neglecting, and normal mothers. *Journal of Abnormal Psychology, 87*, 531–540.

Galasko, D., Edland, S. D., Morris, J. C., Clark, C., Mohs, R., & Koss, E. (1995). The consortium to establish a registry for Alzheimer's disease (CERAD): XI. Clinical milestones in patients with Alzheimer's disease followed over 3 years. *Neurology, 45*, 1451–1455.

Gall, T. L., & Lucas, D. M. (1996). (Eds.). *Statistics on alcohol, drug and tobacco use.* Detroit: Gale Research.

Garber, J., Kriss, M. R., Koch, M., & Lindholm, L. (1988). Recurrent depression in adolescents: A follow-up study. *Journal of the American Academy of Child and Adolescent Psychiatry, 27*, 49–54.

Garcia, J., & Koelling, R. A. (1966). Relation of cue to consequence in avoidance learning. *Psychonomic Science, 4*, 123–124.

Garfield, S. L. (1980). *Psychotherapy: An eclectic approach.* New York: Wiley.

Garfield, S. L. (1986). Research on client variables in psychotherapy. In S. L. Garfield & A. E. Bergin (Eds.), *Handbook of psychotherapy and behavior change.* New York: Wiley.

Garfield, S. L. (1995). *Psychotherapy: An eclectic-integrative approach* (2nd ed.). New York: Wiley.

Garfield, S. L., & Bergin, A. E. (1994). Introduction and historical overview. In S. Garfield & A. Bergin (Eds.), *Handbook of psychotherapy and behavior change* (4th ed.). New York: Wiley.

Garnets, L., & Kimmel, D. (1991). Lesbian and gay male dimensions in the psychological study of human diversity. In J. Goodchilds (Ed.), *Psychological perspectives on human diversity in America.* Washington, DC: American Psychological Association.

Gebhard, P., Cagnon, J., Pomeroy, N., & Christenson, C. (1965). *Sex offenders.* New York: Harper & Row.

Gebhard, P. M., & Johnson, A. B. (1979). Marginal tabulations of the 1938–1963 interviews conducted by the Institute for Sex Research. *The Kinsey Data*. Philadelphia: Saunders.

Gentry, W. D., Chesney, A. P., Gary, H. E., Hall, R. P., & Harburg, E. (1982). Habitual anger-coping styles: I. Effect on mean blood pressure and risk for essential hypertension. *Psychosomatic Medicine, 44*, 195–202.

Gerlsma, C., Emmelkamp, P. M. G., & Arrindell, W. A. (1990). Anxiety, depression, and perception of early parenting: A meta-analysis. *Clinical Psychology Review, 10*, 251–277.

Gershon, E. S. (1990). Genetics. In F. K. Goodwin & K. R. Jamison (Eds.), *Manic-depressive illness*. New York: Oxford University.

Gewirtz, J. L., & Pelaez-Nogueras, M. (1992). B. F. Skinner's legacy to human infant behavior and development. *American Psychologist, 47*, 1411–1422.

Gidron, Y., & Davidson, K. (1996). Development and preliminary testing of a brief intervention for modifying CHD-predictive hostility components. *Journal of Behavioral Medicine, 19*, 203–220.

Gil, K. M., Wilson, J. J., Edens, J. L., Webster, D. A., Abrams, M. A., Grant, M., Orringer, E., Clark, W. C., & Janal, M. N. (1996). Effects of cognitive coping skills training on coping strategies and experimental pain sensitivity in African American adults with sickle cell disease. *American Psychological Association, 15*, 3–10.

Gilberg, C. (1990). Autism and pervasive developmental disorders. *Journal of Child Psychology and Psychiatry, 31*, 99–119.

Gilbert, P. L., Harris, M. J., McAdams, L. A., & Jeste, D. V. (1995). Neuroleptic withdrawal in schizophrenic patients: A review of the literature. *Archives of General Psychiatry, 52*, 173–188.

Gilchrist, L., Gillmore, M., & Lohr, M. (1990). Drug use among pregnant adolescents. *Journal of Consulting and Clinical Psychology, 58*, 402–407.

Giles, D. K., & Wolf, M. W. (1966). Toilet training institutionalized, severe retardates: An application of operant behavior modification techniques. *American Journal of Mental Deficiency, 70*, 766–780.

Gilger, J. W., Pennington, B. F., & DeFries, J. C. (1992). A twin study of the etiology of comorbidity: Attention-deficit hyperactivity disorder and dyslexia. *Journal of the American Academy of Child and Adolescent Psychiatry, 31*, 343–348.

Gillham, J. E., Reivich, K. J., Jaycox, L. H., & Seligman, M. E. P. (1995). Prevention of depressive symptoms in schoolchildren: Two-year follow-up. *Psychological Science, 6*, 343–351.

Ginther, L., & Roberts, M. (1982). A test of mastery versus coping modeling in the reduction of children's dental fears. *Child and Family Behavior Therapy, 4*, 41–51.

Gitlin, M. J. (1996). *The psychotherapist's guide to psychopharmacology*, 2nd ed. New York: Free Press.

Gitlin, M. J., & Pasnau, R. O. (1989). Psychiatric syndromes linked to reproductive function in women: A review of current knowledge. *American Journal of Psychiatry, 146*, 1413–1422.

Gitlin, M. J., Swendsen, J., Heller, T., & Hammen, C. (1995). Relapse and impairment in bipolar disorders: A longitudinal study. *American Journal of Psychiatry, 152*, 1635–1640.

Gittelman, R. (1985). Anxiety disorders in children. In B. B. Lahey & A. E. Kazdin (Eds.), *Advances in clinical child psychology* (Vol. 8). New York: Plenum Press.

Gittelman, R. (1986). *Anxiety disorders of childhood*. New York: Guilford Press.

Gittelman, R., Mannuzza, S., Shenker, R., & Bonagura, N. (1985). Hyperactive boys almost grown up. *Archives of General Psychiatry, 42*, 937–947.

Gjerdingen, D. K., Froberg, D. G., & Fontaine, P. (1991). The effects of social support on women's health during pregnancy, labor and delivery, and the postpartum period. *Family Medicine, 23*, 369–375.

Glanz, L., Haas, G., & Sweeney, J. (1995). Assessment of hopelessness in suicidal patients. *Clinical Psychology Review, 15*, 49–64.

Glaser, R. (1985). Effects of stress on methyltransferase synthesis: An important DNA repair enzyme. *Health Psychology, 4*, 403–412.

Gleaves, D. H. (1996). The sociocognitive model of dissociative identity disorder: A reexamination of the evidence. *Psychological Bulletin, 120*, 42–59.

Gold, P. W., Goodwin, F. K., & Chrousos, G. P. (1988a). Clinical and biochemical manifestations of depression: Relation to the neurobiology of stress, Part I. *The New England Journal of Medicine, 319*, 348–413.

Gold, P. W., Goodwin, F. K., & Chrousos, G. P. (1988b). Clinical and biochemical manifestations of depression: Relation to the neurobiology of stress, Part II. *The New England Journal of Medicine, 319*, 413–420.

Goldberg, J. F., Harrow, M., & Grossman, L. S. (1995). Course and outcome in bipolar affective disorder: A longitudinal follow-up study. *American Journal of Psychiatry, 152*, 379–384.

Goldfried, M. R. (1980). Toward the delineation of therapeutic change principles. *American Psychologist, 35*, 991–999.

Goldfried, M. R. (1988). Application of rational restructuring to anxiety disorders. *The Counseling Psychologist, 16*, 50–68.

Goldfried, M. R. (1995). Toward a common language for case formulation. *Journal of Psychotherapy Integration, 5*, 221–224.

Goldfried, M. R., Decenteceo, E. T., & Weinberg, L. (1974). Systematic rational restructuring as a self-control technique. *Behavior Therapy, 5*, 247–254.

Goldfried, M. R., & Sobocinski, D. (1975). Effect of irrational beliefs on emotional arousal. *Journal of Consulting and Clinical Psychology, 43*, 504–510.

Goldin, L. R., & Gershon, E. S. (1988). The genetic epidemiology of major depressive illness. In A. J. Frances & R. E. Hale (Eds.), *Review of Psychiatry*. Washington, DC: American Psychiatric Press.

Golding, J. M., Smith, G. R., & Kashner, T. M. (1991). Does somatization disorder occur in men? *Archives of General Psychiatry, 48*, 231–235.

Goldman, M. S., & Rather, B. C. (1993). Substance use disorders: Cognitive models and architecture. In K. S. Dobson & P. C. Kendall (Eds.), *Psychopathology and cognition*. San Diego: Academic Press.

Goldstein, M. J., (1988). Gender differences in the course of schizophrenia. *American Journal of Psychiatry, 145*, 684–689.

Goldstein, M., & Chen, T. C. (1982). Epidemiology of disabling headache. In M. Critchley, A. Friedman, S. Goring & F. Sicuter (Eds.), *Advances in neurology*. New York: Raven Press.

Golomb, M., Fava, M., Abraham, M., & Rosenbaum, J. F. (1995). Gender differences in personality disorders. *American Journal of Psychiatry, 152*, 579–582.

Golombok, S., & Tasker, F. (1996). Do parents influence the sexual orientation of their children? Findings for a longitudinal study of lesbian parents. *Developmental Psychology, 32*, 3–11.

Gomez-Beneyto, M., Bonet, A., Catala, M., Puche, E., et al. (1994). Prevalence of mental disorders among children in Valencia, Spain. *Acta Psychiatrica Scandinavica, 89*, 352–357.

Gomez-Isla, T., West, H. L., Rebeck, G. W., Harr, S. D., Growdon, J. H., Locascio, J. J., Perls, T. T., Lipsitz, L. A., & Hyman, B. T. (1996). Clinical and pathological correlates of apolipoprotein E epsilon 4 in Alzheimer's disease. *Annals of Neurology, 39*, 62–70.

Gong-Guy, E., Cravens, R. B., & Patterson, T. E. (1991). Clinical issues in mental health service delivery to refugees. *American Psychologist, 46*, 642–648.

Goodwin, D. W. (1971). Is alcoholism hereditary? A review and critique. *Archives of General Psychiatry, 25*, 545–549.

Goodwin, D. W. (1976). *Is alcoholism hereditary?* New York: Oxford University Press.

Goodwin, D. W. (1979). Alcoholism and heredity. *Archives of General Psychiatry, 36*, 57–61.

Goodwin, D. W. (1985). Genetic determinants of alcoholism. In J. H. Mendelson & N. K. Mello (Eds.), *The diagnosis and treatment of alcoholism* (2nd ed.). New York: McGraw-Hill.

Goodwin, D. W., Schulsinger, F., Hermansen, L., Guze, S. B., & Winokur, G. (1973). Alcohol problems in adoptees raised apart from alcoholic biological parents. *Archives of General Psychiatry, 28,* 238–243.

Goodwin, D. W., Schulsinger, F., Moller, N., Hermansen, L., Winokur, G., & Guze, S. B. (1974). Drinking problems in adopted and nonadopted sons of alcoholics. *Archives of General Psychiatry, 31,* 164–169.

Goodwin, F. K., & Jamison, K. R. (Eds.). (1990). *Manic-depressive illness.* New York: Oxford University Press.

Gordon, C. T., State, R. C., Nelson, J. E., Hamburger, S. D., & Rapoport, J. L. (1993). A double-blind comparison of clomipramine, desipramine, and placebo in the treatment of autistic disorder. *Archives of General Psychiatry, 50,* 441–447.

Gorman, D. M. (1992). Using theory and basic research to target primary prevention programs: Recent developments and future prospects. *Alcohol and Alcoholism, 27,* 583–594.

Gorman, J. M., Liebowitz, M. R., Fyer, A. J., & Stein, J. (1989). A neuroanatomical hypothesis for panic disorder. *American Journal of Psychiatry, 146,* 148–161.

Gosselin, C. C., & Wilson, G. D. (1980). *Sexual variations.* London: Faber & Faber.

Gosselin, C. C., & Wilson, G. D. (1984). Fetishism, sadomasochism and related behaviours. In K. Howells (Ed.), *The psychology of sexual diversity* (pp. 89–110). Oxford: Basil Blackwell.

Gotlib, I. H., & Colby, C. (1987). *Treatment of depression: An interpersonal systems approach.* New York: Pergamon Press.

Gotlib, I. H., & Hammen, C. L. (1992). *Psychological aspects of depression: Toward a cognitive-interpersonal integration.* Chichester, Eng.: Wiley.

Gotlib, I. H., & Lee, C. M. (1989). The social functioning of depressed patients: A longitudinal assessment. *Journal of Social and Clinical Psychology, 8,* 223–237.

Gotlib, I. H., & Lee, C. M. (1990). Children of depressed parents: A review and directions for future research. In C. D. McCann & N. S. Endler (Eds.), *Depression: New directions in research, theory and practice.* Toronto: Wall & Thompson.

Gottesman, I. I. (1991). *Schizophrenia genesis.* New York: Freeman.

Gottesman, I. I., & Bertelsen, A. (1989). Confirming unexpressed genotypes for schizophrenia: Risks in the offspring of Fischer's Danish identical and fraternal discordant twins. *Archives of General Psychiatry, 46,* 867–872.

Gottesman, I. I., & Goldsmith, H. H. (1994). Developmental psychopathology of antisocial behavior: Inserting genes into its ontogenesis and epigenesis. In C. A. Nelson (Ed.), *Threats to optimal development: Integrating biological, psychological, and social risk factors* (pp. 69–104). Hillsdale, NJ: Erlbaum.

Gottesman, I. I., & Shields, J. (1972). *Schizophrenia and genetics: A twin study vantage point.* New York: Academic Press.

Gottesman, I. I., McGuffin, P., & Farmer, A. E. (1987). Clinical genetics as clues to the "real" genetics of schizophrenia. *Schizophrenia Bulletin, 13,* 23–47.

Gottfredson, D. C., & Koper, C. S. (1996). Race and sex differences in the prediction of drug use. *Journal of Consulting and Clinical Psychology, 64,* 305–313.

Gottlieb, N. H., & Green, L. W. (1984). Life events, social network, life-style, and health: An analysis of the 1979 national survey on personal health practices and consequences. *Health Education Quarterly, 11,* 91–105.

Gould, M., Wallenstein, S., Kleinman, M., O'Carroll, P., & Mercy, J. (1990). Suicide clusters: An examination of age-specific effects. *American Journal of Public Health, 80,* 211–214.

Govind, C. K., & Pearce, J. (1986). Differential reflex activity determines claw and closer muscle asymmetry in developing lobsters. *Science, 233,* 354–357.

Graham, D. T., Kabler, J. D., & Graham, F. K. (1962). Physiological response to the suggestion of attitudes specific for hives and hypertension. *Psychosomatic Medicine, 24,* 159–169.

Green, M. F. (1996). What are the functional consequences of neurocognitive deficits in schizophrenia? *American Journal of Psychiatry, 153,* 321–330.

Green, R. (1974). *Sexual identity conflict in children and adults.* London: Duckworth.

Green, R. (1979). Childhood cross-gender behavior and subsequent sexual preference. *Journal of Psychiatry, 136,* 106–108.

Green, R. (1985). Gender identity in childhood and later sexual orientation: Follow-up of 78 males. *American Journal of Psychiatry, 142,* 339–341.

Green, R. (1987). *The "Sissy Boy" syndrome and the development of homosexuality.* New Haven, CT: Yale University Press.

Green, R., Williams, K., & Goodman, M. (1982). Ninety-nine "tom-boys" and "non-tomboys": Behavioural contrasts and demographic similarities. *Archives of Sexual Behavior, 11,* 247–266.

Greist, J. H., Chouinard, G., DuBoff, E., Halaris, A., Kim, S. W., Koran, L., Liebowitz, M., Lydiard, R. B., Rasmussen, S., White, K., & Sikes, C. (1995b). Double-blind parallel comparison of three dosages of sertraline and placebo in outpatients with obsessive-compulsive disorder. *Archives of General Psychiatry, 52,* 289–295.

Greist, J. H., Jefferson, J. W., Kobak, K. A., Katzelnick, D. J., & Serlin, R. C. (1995a). Efficacy and tolerability of serotonin transport inhibitors in obsessive-compulsive disorder. *Archives of General Psychiatry, 52,* 53–60.

Grenyer, B. F. S., & Luborsky, L. (1996). Dynamic change in psychotherapy: Mastery of interpersonal conflicts. *Journal of Consulting and Clinical Psychology, 64,* 411–416.

Griffin, M., Weiss, R., Mirin, S., & Lange, U. (1989). A comparison of male and female cocaine abusers. *Archives of General Psychiatry, 46,* 122–126.

Gross, A. M., & Isaac, L. (1982). Forced arm exercise and DRO in the treatment of bruxism in cerebral palsied children. *Child and Family Behavior Therapy, 4,* 175–181.

Group for the Advancement of Psychiatry. (1986). *A family affair: Helping families cope with mental illness: A guide for the professions.* New York: Brunner/Mazel.

Group for the Advancement of Psychiatry. (1989). *Suicide and ethnicity in the United States.* New York: Brunner/Mazel.

Grove, W. M., Lebow, B. S., Clementz, B. A., Cerri, A., Medus, C., & Iacono, W. G. (1991). Familial prevalence and coaggregation of schizotypy indicators: A multitrait family study. *Journal of Abnormal Psychology, 100,* 115–121.

Gruder, C. L., Mermelstein, R. J., Kirkendol, S., Hedeker, D., Wong, S., Schreckengost, J., Warnecke, R. B., Burzette, R., & Miller, T. Q. (1993). Effects of social support and relapse prevention training as adjuncts to a televised smoking-cessation intervention. *Journal of Consulting and Clinical Psychology, 61,* 113–120.

Guarnaccia, P. J., Good, B. J., & Kleinman, A. (1990). A critical review of epidemiological studies of Puerto Rican mental health. *American Journal of Psychiatry, 147,* 1449–1456.

Gubbay, S. S., Lobascher, M., & Kingerlee, P. (1970). A neurological appraisal of autistic children: Results of a Western Australian survey. *Developmental Medicine and Child Neurology, 12,* 424–429.

Guerra, N. G., Huesmann, L. R., Tolan, P. H., Van Acker, R., & Eron, L. D. (1995). Stressful events and individual beliefs as correlates of economic disadvantage and aggression among urban children. *Journal of Consulting and Clinical Psychology, 63,* 518–528.

Gunderson, J. G., & Zanarini, M. C. (1989). Pathogenesis of borderline personality. In A. Tasman, R. E. Hales & A. J. Frances (Eds.),

Review of Psychiatry. Washington, DC: American Psychiatric Press.

Gusella, J., MacDonald, M., Ambrose, C., & Duyao, M. (1993). Molecular genetics of Huntington's Disease. *Archives of Neurology, 50,* 1157–1163.

Guze, S. B., Cloninger, C. R., Martin, R. L., & Clayton, P. (1986). A follow-up and family study of Briquet's syndrome. *British Journal of Psychiatry, 149,* 17–23.

Haber, R. N., & Erdelyi, M. H. (1967). Emergence and recovery of initially unavailable perceptual material. *Journal of Verbal Learning and Verbal Behavior, 6,* 618–628.

Hagen, J. W., & Hale, G. H. (1973). The development of attention in children. In A. Pick (Ed.), *Minnesota Symposium on Child Psychology* (Vol. 7). Minneapolis: University of Minnesota Press.

Haley, J. (1976). *Problem solving therapy.* San Francisco: Jossey-Bass.

Haley, W. E., Roth, D. L., Coleton, M. I., Ford, G. R., West, C. A. C., Collins, R. P., & Isobe, T. L. (1996). Appraisal, coping, and social support as mediators of well-being in black and white family caregivers of patients with Alzheimer's disease. *Journal of Consulting and Clinical Psychology, 64,* 121–129.

Halford, W. K., & Hayes, R. (1991). Psychological rehabilitation of chronic schizophrenic patients: Recent findings on social skills training and family psychoeducation. *Clinical Psychology Review, 11,* 23–44.

Hall, G. C. N. (1990). Prediction of sexual aggression. *Clinical Psychology Review, 10,* 229–245.

Hall, G. C. N. (1995). Sexual offender recidivism revisited: A meta-analysis of recent treatment studies. *Journal of Consulting and Clinical Psychology, 63,* 802–809.

Hall, S. M., Havassy, B., & Wasserman, D. A. (1991). Effects of commitment to abstinence, positive moods, stress, and coping on relapse to cocaine use. *Journal of Consulting and Clinical Psychology, 59,* 526–532.

Hallahan, D. P., Kneedler, R. D., & Lloyd, J. W. (1983). Cognitive behavior modification techniques for learning disabled children. In J. D. McKinney & L. Feagans (Eds.), *Current topics in learning disabilities* (Vol. 1). New York: Ablex.

Hamer, D. H., Hu, S., Magnuson, V. L., Hu, N., & Pattatucci, A. M. (1993). A linkage between DNA markers on the X chromosome and male sexual orientation. *Science, 261,* 321–327.

Hammen, C. (1991). *Depression runs in families: The social context of risk and resilience in children of depressed mothers.* New York: Springer-Verlag.

Hammen, C. (1996). *Depression.* London: Lawrence Erlbaum.

Hammen, C., Burge, D., & Adrian, C. (1991). Timing of mother and child depression in a longitudinal study of children at risk. *Journal of Consulting and Clinical Psychology, 59,* 341–345.

Hammen, C. L., & Compas, B. E. (1994). Unmasking unmasked depression in children and adolescents: The problem of comorbidity. *Clinical Psychology Review, 14,* 585–603.

Hammen, C., & Gitlin, M. (1997). *American Journal of Psychiatry, 154,* 856–857.

Hammen, C., Marks, T., deMayo, R., & Mayol, A. (1985). Self-schemas and risk for depression: A prospective study. *Journal of Personality and Social Psychology, 49,* 1147–1159.

Hammen, C., & Peters, S. (1977). Differential responses to male and female depressive reactions. *Journal of Consulting and Clinical Psychology, 45,* 994–1001.

Hammock, R. G., Schroeder, S. R., & Levine, W. R. (1995). The effect of clozapine on self-injurious behavior. *Journal of Autism and Developmental Disorders, 25,* 611–626.

Hansen, D. R., & Gottesman, I. I. (1976). The genetics, if any, of infantile autism and childhood schizophrenia. *Journal of Autism and Childhood Schizophrenia, 6,* 209–234.

Harburg, E., Erfort, J. C., Havenstein, L. S., Chape, C., Schull, W. J., & Schork, M. A. (1973). Socio-ecological stress, suppressed hostil-ity, skin color, and black-white male blood pressure: Detroit. *Psychosomatic Medicine, 35,* 276–296.

Harding, C. M. (1991). Aging and schizophrenia: Plasticity, reversibility, and/or compensation. In E. F. Walker (Ed.), *Schizophrenia: A life-course developmental perspective* (pp. 257–268). San Diego: Academic Press.

Harding, C. M., Zubin, J., & Strauss, J. S. (1987). Chronicity in schizophrenia: Fact, partial fact, or artifact? *Hospital and Community Psychiatry, 38,* 477–486.

Hardy, G. E., Barkham, M., Shapiro, D. A., Stiles, W. B., Rees, A., & Reynolds, S. (1995). Impact of Cluster C personality disorders on outcomes of contrasting brief psychotherapies for depression. *Journal of Consulting and Clinical Psychology, 63,* 997–1004.

Hare, R. D. (1968). Psychopathy, autonomic functioning and the orienting response. *Journal of Abnormal Psychology, 73(2),* 1–24.

Hare, R. D. (1983). Diagnosis of antisocial personality disorder in criminals. *American Journal of Psychiatry, 140,* 887–890.

Hare, R. D., Hart, S. D., & Harpur, T. J. (1991). Psychopathy and the DSM-IV criteria for antisocial personality disorder. *Journal of Abnormal Psychology, 100,* 391–398.

Hare, R. D., McPherson, L. M., & Forth, A. E. (1988). Male psychopaths and their criminal careers. *Journal of Consulting and Clinical Psychology, 56,* 710–714.

Harpur, T. J., & Hare, R. D. (1990). Psychopathy and attention. In J. T. Enns (Ed.), *The development of attention: Research and theory.* North Holland: Elsevier Science.

Harrington, R. (1994). Affective disorders. In M. Rutter, E. Taylor & L. Hersov (Eds.), *Child and adolescent psychiatry.* Oxford: Blackwell Scientific Publications.

Harrington, R. C., Fudge, H., Rutter, M., Pickles, A., & Hill, J. (1990). Adult outcomes of childhood and adolescent depression: I. Psychiatric status. *Archives of General Psychiatry, 47,* 465–473.

Harris, S. L. (1983). *Families of the developmentally disabled: A guide to behavioral intervention.* New York: Pergamon Press.

Hart, S. D., Kropp, P. R., & Hare, R. D. (1988). Performance of male psychopaths following conditional release from prison. *Journal of Consulting and Clinical Psychology, 56,* 227–232.

Harvey, P. D. (1991). Cognitive and linguistic functions of adolescent children at risk for schizophrenia. In E. F. Walker (Ed.), *Schizophrenia: A life-course developmental perspective* (pp. 140–154). San Diego: Academic Press.

Haskey, J. (1994). Estimated numbers of one-parent families and their prevalence in Great Britain in 1991. *Population Trends, 78,* 5–19.

Hathaway, S., & McKinley, C. (1948). *The Minnesota Multiphasic Personality Inventory.* New York: Psychological Corporation.

Hatsukami, D., Jensen, J., Allen, S., Grillo, M., & Bliss, R. (1996). Effects of behavioral and pharmacological treatment on smokeless tobacco users. *Journal of Consulting and Clinical Psychology, 64,* 153–161.

Hauck, M., Fein, D., Waterhouse, L., & Feinstein, C. (1995). Social initiations by autistic children to adults and other children. *Journal of Autism and Developmental Disorders, 25,* 579–595.

Hayes, J. A., & Mitchell, J. C. (1994). Mental health professionals' skepticism about multiple personality disorder. *Professional Psychology Research and Practice, 25,* 410–415.

Hays, R. D., Wells, K. B., Sherbourne, C. D., Rogers, W., & Spritzer, K. (1995). Functioning and well-being outcomes of patients with depression compared with chronic general medical illness. *Archives of General Psychiatry, 52,* 11–19.

Haywood, H. C., Meyers, C. E., & Switzky, H. N. (1982). Mental retardation. In M. R. Rosenzweig & L. W. Porter (Eds.), *Annual review of psychology.* Palo Alto, CA: Annual Reviews Inc.

Headley, L. A. (Ed.). (1983). *Suicide in Asia and the Near East.* Berkeley, CA: University of California Press.

Heath, L., Bresolin, L. B., & Rinaldi, R. C. (1989). Effects of media violence on children. *Archives of General Psychiatry, 46,* 376–379.

Heather, N., & Robertson, I. (1981). *Controlled drinking*. New York: Methuen.

Hecker, M. H., Chesney, M. A., Black, G. W., & Frautschi, N. (1988). Coronary-prone behaviors in the western collaborative group study. *Psychosomatic Medicine, 50,* 153–164.

Hegarty, J. D., Baldessarini, R. J., Tohen, M., Waternaux, C., & Oepen, G. (1994). One hundred years of schizophrenia: A meta-analysis of the outcome literature. *American Journal of Psychiatry, 151,* 1409–1416.

Heide, F., & Borkovec, T. D. (1984). Relaxation-induced anxiety: Mechanisms and theoretical implications. *Behaviour Research and Therapy, 22,* 1–12.

Heiman, J. R., & LoPiccolo, J. (1988). *Becoming orgasmic: A personal sexual growth program for women.* New York: Prentice-Hall.

Heiman, J. R., Gladue, B. A., Roberts, C. W., & LoPiccolo, J. (1986). Historical and current factors discriminating sexually functional from sexually dysfunctional married couples. *Journal of Marital Family Therapy, 12(2),* 163–174.

Heimberg, R. G. (1989). Social phobia: No longer neglected. *Clinical Psychology Review, 9,* 1–3.

Heimberg, R. G., Liebowitz, H., Hope, D., & Schneier, A. (Eds.). (1995). *Social phobia: Diagnosis, assessment and treatment.* New York: Guilford Press.

Hellerstein, D. J., Yanowitch, P., Rosenthal, J., Samstag, L. W., Maurer, M., Kasch, K., Burrows, L., Poster, M., Cantillon, M., & Winston, A. (1993). A randomized double-blind study of fluoxetine versus placebo in the treatment of dysthymia. *American Journal of Psychiatry, 150,* 1169–1175.

Hely, M., Morris, J., Reid, W., O'Sullivan, D., Williamson, P., Broe, G., & Adena, M. (1995). Age at onset: The major determinant of outcome in Parkinson's disease. *Acta Neurologica Scandinavica, 92,* 455–463.

Helzer, J. E., Canino, G. J., Yeh, E., Bland, R. C., Lee, C. K., Hwu, H., & Newman, S. (1990). Alcoholism: North America and Asia—A comparison of population surveys with the Diagnostic Interview Schedule. *Archives of General Psychiatry, 47,* 313–319.

Henden, B., Breaux, A., Gosling, A., Ploof, D., & Feldman, M. (1990). Efficacy of methylphenidate among mentally retarded children with attention-deficit hyperactivity disorder. *Pediatrics, 86,* 922–930.

Henderson, A. S., Easteal, S., Jorm, A. F., Mackinnon, A. J., Korten, A. E., Christensen, H., Croft, L., & Jacomb, P. A. (1995). Apolipoprotein E allele epsilon 4, dementia, and cognitive decline in a population sample. *Lancet, 346,* 1387–1390.

Hendricks, R. D., Sobell, M. B., & Cooper, A. M. (1978). Social influences on human ethanol consumption in an analogue situation. *Addictive Behaviors, 3,* 253–259.

Henningfield, J. E., Miyasato, K., & Jasinski, D. R. (1985). Abuse liability and pharmacodynamic characteristics of intravenous and inhaled nicotine. *Journal of Pharmacology and Experimental Therapy, 234,* 1–12.

Henriques, J., & Davidson, R. (1990). Regional brain electrical asymmetries discriminate between previously depressed and healthy control subjects. *Journal of Abnormal Psychology, 99,* 22–31.

Henry, W. P., Strupp, H. H., Schacht, T. E., & Gaston, L. (1994). Psychodynamic approaches. S. Garfield & A. Bergin (Eds.), *Handbook of psychotherapy and behavior change* (4th ed.). New York: Wiley.

Herberman, R. B., & Ortaldo, J. R. (1981). Natural killer cells: Their role in defenses against disease. *Science, 214,* 24–30.

Heritch, A. J. (1990). Evidence for reduced and dysregulated turnover of dopamine in schizophrenia. *Schizophrenia Bulletin, 16,* 605–615.

Herjanic, B., & Reich, W. (1982). Development of a structured psychiatric interview for children: Agreement between child and parent on individual symptoms. *Journal of Abnormal Child Psychology, 10,* 307–324.

Hermelin, B. (1976). Coding and the sense modalities. In L. Wing (Ed.), *Early childhood autism* (2nd ed.). Oxford, Engl.: Pergamon.

Herrman, H., McGorry, P., Bennett, P., van Riel, R., McKenzie, D., & Singh, B. (1989). Prevalence of severe mental disorders in disaffiliated and homeless people in inner Melbourne. *American Journal of Psychiatry, 146,* 1179–1184.

Hersen, M., & Barlow, D. (1989). *Single-subject research designs.* (2nd ed.). New York: Pergamon Press.

Hersov, L. (1994). Faecal soiling. In M. Rutter, E. Taylor & L. Hersov (Eds.), *Child and adolescent psychiatry.* Oxford: Blackwell Scientific Publications.

Hetherington, E. M. (1987). Family relations six years after divorce. In K. Pasley & M. Ihinger-Tallman (Eds.), *Remarriage and step-parenting: Current research and theory.* New York: Guilford Press.

Hetherington, E. M., & Martin, B. (1979). Family interaction. In H. C. Quay & J. Werry (Eds.), *Psychopathological disorders of childhood* (2nd ed.). New York: Wiley.

Hetherington, E. M., Stanley-Hagan, M., & Anderson, E. R. (1989). Marital transitions: A child's perspective. *American Psychologist, 44,* 303–312.

Heyman, A., Fillenbaum, G., Prosnitz, B., Raiford, K., Burchett, B., & Clark, C. (1991). Estimated prevalence of dementia among elderly black and white community residents. *Archives of Neurology, 48,* 594–598.

Higley, J. D., Mehlman, P. T., Higley, S. B., Fernald, B., Vickers, J., Lindell, S. G., Taub, D. M., Suomi, S. J., & Linnoila, M. (1996). Excessive mortality in young free-ranging male nonhuman primates with low cerebrospinal fluid 5-Hydroxyindoleacetic acid concentrations. *Archives of General Psychiatry, 53,* 537–543.

Higley, J. D., Mehlman, P. T., Taub, D. M., Higley, S. B., Suomi, S. J., Linnoila, M., & Vickers, J. H. (1992). Cerebrospinal fluid monoamine and adrenal correlates of aggression in free-ranging rhesus monkeys. *Archives of General Psychiatry, 49,* 436–441.

Hill, H., Soriano, F. I., Chen, A., & LaFromboise, T. D. (1994). Socio-cultural factors in the etiology and prevention of violence among ethnic minority youth. In L. D. Eron, J. H. Gentry, & P. Schlegel (Eds.), *Reason to hope: A psychological perspective on violence and youth* (pp. 59–97). Washington, DC: American Psychological Association.

Hinshaw, S. P. (1987). On the distinction between attentional deficits/hyperactivity and conduct problems/aggression in child psychopathology. *Psychological Bulletin, 101,* 443–463.

Hinshaw, S. P. Henker, B., & Whalen, C. (1984). Self-control in hyperactive boys in anger-inducing situations: Effects of cognitive-behavioral training and of methylphenidate. *Journal of Abnormal Child Psychology, 12,* 55–77.

Hirschfeld, R. M. A. (1994). Guidelines for the long-term treatment of depression. *Journal of Clinical Psychiatry, 55,* 61–69.

Hirshfeld, D. R., Rosenbaum, J. F., Biederman, J., Bolduc, E. A., Faraone, S. V., Snidman, N., Reznick, J. S., & Kagan, J. (1992). Stable behavioral inhibition and its association with anxiety disorder. *Journal of the American Academy of Child and Adolescent Psychiatry, 31,* 103–111.

Hitchcock, P. B., & Mathews, A. (1992). Interpretation of bodily symptoms in hypochondriasis. *Behaviour Research and Therapy, 30,* 223–234.

Hoaker, P., & Schurr, R. (1980). Genetic factors in obsessive compulsive neurosis. *Canadian Journal of Psychiatry, 25,* 167–172.

Hodgins, S. (1992). Mental disorder, intellectual deficiency, and crime: A birth cohort. *Archives of General Psychiatry, 49,* 476–483.

Hodgins, S., Mednick, S. A., Brennan, P. A., Schulsinger, F., & Engberg, M. (1996). Mental disorder and crime: Evidence from a Danish birth cohort. *Archives of General Psychiatry, 53,* 489–496.

Hodgkinson, S., Sherrington, R., Gurling H., Marchbanks, R., Redders, S., Mallet, J., McInnis, M., Petursson, H., & Brynjolfsson, J. (1987). Molecular genetic evidence for heterogeneity in manic depression. *Nature, 325,* 805–806.

Hoek, H. (1993). Review of the epidemiological studies of eating disorders. *International Review of Psychiatry, 5,* 61–74.

Hoek, H. W. (1991). The incidence and prevalence of anorexia nervosa and bulimia nervosa in primary care. *Psychological Medicine, 21,* 455–460.

Hogarty, G. E., Anderson, C. M., Reiss, D. J., Kornblith, S. J., Greenwald, D. P., Javna, C. D., & Madonia, M. J. (1986). Family psychoeducation, social skills training, and maintenance chemotherapy in the aftercare treatment of schizophrenia. I: One year effects of a controlled study on relapse and expressed emotion. *Archives of General Psychiatry, 43,* 633–642.

Hogarty, G. E., Anderson, C. M., Reiss, D. J., Kornblith, S. J., Greenwald, D. P., Ulrich, R. F., Carter, M., & The Environmental-Personal Indicators in the Course of Schizophrenia (EPICS) Research Group. (1991). Family psychoeducation, social skills training, and maintenance chemotherapy in the aftercare treatment of schizophrenia: II. Two-year effects of a controlled study on relapse and adjustment. *Archives of General Psychiatry, 48,* 340–347.

Hoge, S. K., Appelbaum, P. S., Lawlor, T., Beck, J. C., Litman, R., Greer, A., Gutheil, T. G., & Kaplan, E. (1990). A prospective, multicenter study of patients' refusal of antipsychotic medication. *Archives of General Psychiatry, 47,* 949–956.

Hohmann, A. A., & Parron, D. L. (1996). How the new NIH guidelines on inclusion of women and minorities apply: Efficacy trials, effectiveness trials, and validity. *Journal of Consulting and Clinical Psychology, 64,* 851–855.

Hokanson, J. E., Rupert, M. P., Welker, R. A., Hollander, G. R., & Hedeen, C. (1989). Interpersonal concomitants and antecedents of depression among college students. *Journal of Abnormal Psychology, 98,* 209–217.

Holford, N., & Peace, K. (1994). The effect of tacrine and lecithin in Alzheimer's disease: A population pharmacodynamic analysis of five clinical trials. *European Journal of Clinical Pharmacology, 47,* 17–23.

Holland, A. J., Sicotte, N., & Treasure, J. (1988). Anorexia nervosa—evidence for a genetic basis. *Journal of Psychosomatic Research, 32,* 561–572.

Hollister, J. M., Laing, P., & Mednick, S. A. (1996). Rhesus incompatibility as a risk factor for schizophrenia in male adults. *Archives of General Psychiatry, 53,* 19–24.

Hollon, S. D., & Beck, A. T. (1979). Cognitive therapy of depression. In P. C. Kendall & S. Hollon (Eds.), *Cognitive-behavioral interventions: Theory, research, and procedures.* New York: Academic.

Hollon, S. D., & Beck, A. T. (1994). Cognitive and cognitive-behavioral therapies. In S. Garfield & A. Bergin (Eds.), *Handbook of psychotherapy and behavior change* (4th ed.). New York: Wiley.

Hollon, S. D., DeRubeis, R. J., & Evans, M. (1987). Causal mediation of change in treatment for depression: Discriminating between nonspecificity and noncausality. *Psychological Bulletin, 102,* 139–149.

Hollon, S. D., DeRubeis, R. J., Evans, M. D., Wiemer, M. J., Garvey, M. J., Grove, W. M., & Tuason, V. B. (1992). Cognitive therapy and pharmacotherapy for depression: Singly and in combination. *Archives of General Psychiatry, 49,* 774–781.

Hollon, S. D., Shelton, R. C., & Davis, D. D. (1993). Cognitive therapy for depression: Conceptual issues and clinical efficacy. *Journal of Consulting and Clinical Psychology, 61,* 270–275.

Holloway, I. (1969). *Some psychological concomitants of addiction.* Unpublished doctoral dissertation, University of Adelaide.

Holm, J., Holroyd, K. A., Hursey, K., & Pensien, D. (1986). The role of stress in recurrent tension headache. *Headache, 26,* 160–167.

Holmes, T., & Rahe, R. (1967). The Social Readjustment Rating Scale. *Journal of Psychosomatic Research, 11,* 213–218.

Holroyd, K. A., France, J. L., Nash, J., & Hursey, K. (1993). Pain state as artifact in the psychological assessment of recurrent headache sufferers. *Pain, 53,* 229–235.

Holroyd, K. A., & French, D. J. (1994). Recent developments in the psychological assessment and management of recurrent headache disorders. In A. J. Goreczny (Ed.), *Handbook of health and rehabilitation psychology.* New York: Plenum Press.

Holroyd, K. A., Nash, J. M., Pingel, J., Cordingly, G., & Jerome, A. (1991). A comparison of pharmacological (amitriptyline HCL) and nonpharmacological (cognitive-behavioral) therapies for chronic tension headaches. *Journal of Consulting and Clinical Psychology, 59,* 387–393.

Holt, C. S., Heimberg, R. G., & Hope, D. A. (1992). Avoidant personality disorder and the generalized subtype of social phobia. *Journal of Abnormal Psychology, 101(2),* 318–325.

Holtzworth-Munroe, A., & Stuart, G. L. (1994). Typologies of male batterers: Three subtypes and the differences among them. *Psychological Bulletin, 116,* 476–497.

Holtzworth-Munroe, A., Markman, H., O'Leary, K. D., & Neidig, P. (1995). The need for marital violence prevention efforts: A behavioral-cognitive secondary prevention program for engaged and newly married couples. *Applied and Preventive Psychology, 4,* 77–88.

Holtzworth-Munroe, A. (1988). Causal attributions in marital violence: Theoretical and methodological issues. *Clinical Psychology Review, 8,* 331–344.

Holtzworth-Munroe, A., & Hutchinson, G. (1993). Attributing negative intent to wife behavior: The attributions of maritally violent versus nonviolent men. *Journal of Abnormal Psychology, 102,* 206–211.

Holzman, P. S. (1970). *Psychoanalysis and psychopathology.* New York: McGraw-Hill.

Holzman, P. S. (1975). Smooth-pursuit eye movements in schizophrenia: Recent findings. In D. X. Freedman (Ed.), *Biology of the major psychoses.* New York: Raven Press.

Holzman, P. S., Kringlen, E., Matthysse, S., Flanagan, S. D., Lipton, R. B., Cramer, G., Levin, S., Lange, K., & Levy, D. L. (1988). A single dominant gene can account for eye tracking dysfunctions and schizophrenia in offspring of discordant twins. *Archives of General Psychiatry, 45,* 641–647.

Homatidis, S., & Konstantareas, M. M. (1981). Assessment of hyperactivity: Isolating measures of high discriminant validity. *Journal of Consulting and Clinical Psychology, 49,* 533–541.

Hook, E. B. (1987). Issues in analysis of data on paternal age and 47, =21: Implications for genetic counseling for Down's syndrome. *Human Genetics, 77,* 303–306.

Hook, E. B., Cross, P. K., & Regal, R. R. (1990). Factual, statistical and logical issues in the search for a paternal age effect for Down syndrome. *Human Genetics, 85,* 387–388.

Hope, D., Gansler, D. A., & Heimberg, R. G. (1989). Attentional focus and causal attributions in social phobia: Implications from social psychology. *Clinical Psychology Review, 9,* 49–60.

Horowitz, M. (1983). Posttraumatic stress disorders. *Behavioral Sciences and the Law, 1,* 9–23.

Horowitz, M. J. (1986). *Stress-response syndromes* (2nd ed.). New Jersey: Jason Aronson.

Horowitz, M., Schaefer, C., Hiroto, D., Wilner, N., & Levin, B. (1977). Life event questionnaires for measuring presumptive stress. *Psychosomatic Medicine, 39,* 413–431.

Horwath, E., Johnson, J., & Hornig, C. D. (1993). Epidemiology of panic disorder in African-Americans. *American Journal of Psychiatry, 150,* 465–469.

Horwath, E., Johnson, J., Klerman, G. L., & Weissman, M. M. (1992). Depressive symptoms as relative and attributable risk factors for first-onset major depression. *Archives of General Psychiatry, 49,* 817–823.

Houts, A. C., Berman, J. S., & Abramson, H. (1994). The effectiveness of psychological and pharmacologic treatments for nocturnal enuresis. *Journal of Consulting and Clinical Psychology,* in press.

Howells, J. G., & Osborn, M. L. (1975). Great Britain. In J. G. Howells (Ed.), *World history of psychiatry*. New York: Brunner/Mazel.

Howland, E. W., Kosson, D. S., Patterson, M., & Newman, J. P. (1993). Altering a dominant response: Performance of psychopaths and low-socialization college students on a cued reaction time task. *Journal of Abnormal Psychology, 102,* 379–387.

Howlin, P. A. (1981). The effectiveness of operant language training with autistic children. *Journal of Autism and Developmental Disorders, 11,* 89–105.

Howlin, P. A., & Rutter, M. (1987). *Treatment of autistic children.* New York: Wiley.

Hucker, S., & Bain, J. (1990). Androgenic hormones and sexual assault. In W. Marshall, D. Laws & H. Barbaree (Eds.), *Handbook of sexual assault: Issues, theories, and treatment of the offender.* New York: Plenum Press.

Huesmann, L. R., & Eron, L. D. (1986). The development of aggression in children of different cultures: Psychological processes and exposure to violence. In L. R. Huesmann & L. D. Eron (Eds.), *Television and the aggressive child: A cross-national comparison.* New Jersey: Lawrence Erlbaum.

Huesmann, L. R., Eron, L. D., Lefkowitz, M., & Walder, L. (1984). Stability of aggression over time and generation. *Developmental Psychology, 20,* 1120–1134.

Hughes, J. R. (1992). Tobacco withdrawal in self-quitters. *Journal of Consulting and Clinical Psychology, 60,* 689–697.

Humes, D. L., & Humphrey, L. L. (1994). A multimethod analysis of families with a polydrug-dependent or normal adolescent daughter. *Journal of Abnormal Psychology, 103,* 676–685.

Humphrey, L. L., Apple, R. F., & Kirschenbaum, D. S. (1986). Differentiating bulimic-anorexic from normal families using interpersonal and behavioral observational systems. *Journal of Consulting and Clinical Psychology, 54,* 190–195.

Hunsley, J. (1988). Conceptions and misconceptions about the context of paradoxical therapy. *Professional Psychology: Research and Practice, 19,* 553–559.

Hunt, M. (1974). *Sexual behavior in the 1970s.* Chicago: Playboy.

Hunt, N., Bruce-Jones, W., & Silverstone, T. (1992). Life events and relapse in bipolar affective disorder. *Journal of Affective Disorders, 25,* 13–20.

Hutchison, K. E., Stevens, V. M., & Collins, F. L. (1996). Cigarette smoking and the intention to quit among pregnant smokers. *Journal of Behavioral Medicine, 19,* 307–316.

Hutt, M. L. (1969). *The Hutt adaptation of the Bender-gestalt test.* Second Edition. New York: Grune & Stratton.

Hyman, B. T., Gomez-Isla, T., Briggs, M., Chung, H., Nichols, S., Kohout, F., & Wallace, R. (1996). Apolipoprotein E and cognitive change in an elderly population. *Annals of Neurology, 40,* 55–66.

Iaboni, F., Douglas, V. I., & Baker, A. G. (1995). Effects of reward and response costs on inhibition in ADHD children. *Journal of Abnormal Psychology, 104,* 232–240.

Iacono, W. G., & Beiser, M. (1992). Where are the women in first-episode studies of schizophrenia? *Schizophrenia Bulletin, 18,* 471–480.

Ingram, R. E. (1984). Toward an information processing analysis of depression. *Cognitive Therapy and Research, 8,* 443–478.

Ingram, R. E. (Ed.). (1986). *Information processing approaches to clinical psychology.* New York: Academic Press.

Ingram, R. E., & Kendall, P. C. (1986). Cognitive clinical psychology: Implications of an information processing perspective. In R. E. Ingram (Ed.), *Information processing approaches to clinical psychology.* New York: Academic Press.

Insel, T., Gillen, J., Moore, A., Mendelson, W., Loewenstein, R., & Murphy, D. (1982). The sleep of patients with obsessive-compulsive disorder. *Archives of General Psychiatry, 39,* 1372–1377.

Insel, T., Murphy, D., Cohen, R., Alterman, I., Kilts, C., & Linnoila, M. (1983). Obsessive compulsive disorder: A double blind trial of clomipramine and clorgyline. *Archives of General Psychiatry, 40,* 605–612.

Jacobs, M. K., & Goodman, G. (1989). Psychology and self-help groups: Predictions on a partnership. *American Psychologist, 44,* 536–545.

Jacobson, J. W. (1982a). Problem behavior and psychiatric impairment within a developmentally disabled population: I. Behavior frequency. *Applied Research in Mental Retardation, 3,* 121–139.

Jacobson, J. W. (1982b). Problem behavior and psychiatric impairment within a developmentally disabled population: I. Behavior severity. *Applied Research in Mental Retardation, 3,* 369–381.

Jacobson, N. (1988). Defining clinically significant change: An introduction. *Behavioral Assessment, 10,* 131–132.

Jacobson, N., Dobson, K., Fruzzetti, A., Schmaling, K., & Salusky, S. (1991). Marital therapy as a treatment for depression. *Journal of Consulting and Clinical Psychology, 59,* 547–557.

Jacobson, N. S., Dobson, K. S., Truax, P. A., Addis, M. E., Koerner, K., Gollan, J. K., Gortner, E., & Prince, S. E. (1996). A component analysis of cognitive behavioral treatment for depression. *Journal of Consulting and Clinical Psychology, 64,* 295–304.

Jacobson, N. S., & Hollon, S. D. (1996). Cognitive behavior therapy vs. pharmacotherapy: Now that the jury's returned its verdict, it's time to present the rest of the evidence. *Journal of Consulting and Clinical Psychology, 64,* 74–80.

Jacobson, N. S., & Margolin, G. (1979). *Marital therapy: Strategies based on social learning and behavior exchange principles.* New York: Brunner/Mazel.

Jaenicke, C., Hammen, C., Zupan, B., Hiroto, D., Gordon, D., Adrian, C., & Burge, D. (1987). Cognitive vulnerability in children at risk for depression. *Journal of Abnormal Child Psychology, 15,* 559–572.

Jaffe, J. H. (1990). Drug addiction and drug use. In A. Gitman, T. Rall, A. Nies & P. Taylor (Eds.), *The pharmacological basis of therapeutics* (8th ed.). New York: Pergamon Press.

Jaffe, J. H., & Ciraulo, D. A. (1985). Drugs used in the treatment of alcoholism. In J. H. Mendelson & N. K. Mello (Eds.), *The diagnosis and treatment of alcoholism* (2nd ed.). New York: McGraw-Hill.

Jahoda, M. (1953). The meaning of psychological health. *Social Casework, 34,* 349–354.

Jahoda, M. (1958). *Current concepts of positive mental health.* New York: Basic Books.

James, S., Hartnett, S. A., & Kalsbeek, W. D. (1983). John Henryism and blood pressure differences among black men. *Journal of Behavioral Medicine, 6,* 259–278.

James, S., LaCroix, A., Kleinbaum, D., & Strogatz, D. (1984). John Henryism and blood pressure differences among black men. II. The role of occupational stressors. *Journal of Behavioral Medicine, 7,* 259–275.

Jamison, K. R. (1989). Mood disorders and seasonal patterns in British writers and artists. *Psychiatry, 52,* 125–134.

Jamison, K. R., Gerner, R. H., & Goodwin, F. K. (1979). Patient and physician attitudes toward lithium: Relationship to compliance. *Archives of General Psychiatry, 38,* 866–869.

Janca, A., Isaac, M., Bennett, L. A., & Tacchini, O. (1995). Somatoform disorders in different cultures: A mail questionnaire survey. *Social Psychiatry and Psychiatric Epidemiology, 30,* 44–48.

Janovic, J., & Rohaidy, H. (1987). Motor, behavioral, and pharmacologic findings in Tourette's syndrome. *Canadian Journal of Neurological Science, 14,* 541–546.

Jason, L. A., McMahon, S. D., Salina, D., Hedeker, D., Stockton, M., Dunson, K., & Kimball, P. (1995). Assessing a smoking cessation intervention involving groups, incentives, and self-help manuals. *Behavior Therapy, 26,* 393–408.

Jaycox, L. H., Reivich, J. G., & Seligman, M. E. P. (1994). Prevention of depressive symptoms in school children. *Behavior and Research Therapy, 32,* 801–816.

Jehu, D., Morgan, R. T. T., Turner, R. K., & Jones, A. (1977). A controlled trial of the treatment of nocturnal enuresis in residential homes for children. *Behavior Research and Therapy, 15,* 1–16.

Jellinek, E. M. (1952). Current notes: Phases of alcohol addiction. *Quarterly Journal of Studies on Alcohol, 13,* 673–684.

Jellinek, E. M. (1960). *The disease concept of alcoholism.* New Brunswick, NJ: Hillhouse Press.

Jemmott, J. B., Borysenko, J., Borysenko, M., McClelland, D. C., Chapman, R., Meyer, D., & Benson, H. (1983). Academic stress power motivation and decrease in secretion rate of salivary secretory immunoglobin A. *Lancet, 1,* 1400–1402.

Jenike, M. A., Baer, L., Ballantine, T., Martuza, R. L., Tynes, S., Giriuna, I., Buttolph, M. L., & Cassem, N. (1991). Cingulotomy for refractory obsessive-compulsive disorder: A long-term follow-up of 33 patients. *Archives of General Psychiatry, 48,* 548–555.

Jenkins, C. D., Zyzanski, S. J., & Rosenman, R. H. (1979). *Jenkins Activity Survey.* Cleveland, OH: Psychological Corporation.

Jenkins, J., & Ramsey, G. (1991). Minorities. In M. Hersen, A. E. Kazdin & A. Bellack (Eds.), *The clinical psychology handbook* (2nd ed.). New York: Pergamon Press.

Jensen, P., Roper, M., Fisher, P., Piacentini, J., Canino, G., Richters, J., Rubio-Stipec, M., Dulcan, M., Goodman, S., Davies, M., Rae, D., Shaffer, D., Bird, H., Lahey, B., & Schwab-Stone, M. (1995). Test-retest reliability of the diagnostic interview schedule for children (Disc. 2.1): Parent, child, and combined algorithms. *Archives of General Psychiatry, 52,* 61–71.

Jersild, A. T., & Holmes, F. B. (1935). *Children's fears.* New York: Teachers College, Columbia University.

Jessor, R., & Jessor, S. L. (1975). Adolescent development and the onset of drinking. *Journal of Studies on Alcohol, 36,* 27–31.

Jeste, D. V., Caligiuri, M. P., Paulsen, J. S., Heaton, R. K., Lacro, J. P., Harris, M. J., Bailey, A., Fell, R. L., & McAdams, L. A. (1995). Risk of tardive dyskinesia in older patients: A prospective longitudinal study of 266 outpatients. *Archives of General Psychiatry, 52,* 756–765.

Joffe, R. T., & Offord, D. R. (1990). Epidemiology. In G. MacLean (Ed.), *Suicide in children and adolescents.* Toronto: Hogrefe & Huber.

Johnson, B. A., Brent, D. A., Connolly, J., Bridge, J., Matta, J., Constantine, D., Rather, C., & White, T. (1995). Familial aggregation of adolescent personality disorders. *Journal of the American Academy of Child and Adolescent Psychiatry, 34,* 798–804.

Johnson, C. A., Pentz, M. A., Weber, M. D., Dwyer, J., Baer, N., MacKinnon, D., Hansen, W., & Flay, B. (1990). Relative effectiveness of comprehensive community programming for drug abuse prevention with high-risk and low-risk adolescents. *Journal of Consulting and Clinical Psychology, 58,* 447–456.

Johnson, C. R., Lubetsky, M. J., & Sacco, K. A. (1995). Psychiatric and behavioral disorders in hospitalized preschoolers with developmental disabilities. *Journal of Autism and Developmental Disorders, 25,* 169–182.

Johnson, J., Weissman, M. M., & Klerman, G. (1992). Service utilization and social morbidity associated with depressive symptoms in the community. *Journal of the American Medical Association, 267,* 1478–1483.

Johnson, M. K. (1985). The origin of memories. In P. C. Kendall (Ed.), *Advances in cognitive-behavioral research and therapy* (Vol. 4). New York: Academic Press.

Johnson, M. R., & Lydiard, R. B. (1995). Personality disorders in social phobia. *Psychiatric Annals, 25,* 554–563.

Johnston, L. D., & O'Malley, P. M. (1986). Why do the nation's students use drugs and alcohol? Self-reported reasons from nine national surveys. *Journal of Drug Issues, 16,* 29–66.

Johnston, L. D., O'Malley, P. M., & Bachman, J. G. (1987). *National trends in drug use and related factors among American high school students and young adults, 1975–1986.* National Institute on Drug Abuse. DHHS (ADM) 87–1535. Washington, DC: U.S. Government Printing Office.

Johnston, L. D., O'Mally, P. M., & Bachman, J. E. (1994). *National survey results on drug use from the monitoring the future study, 1975–1993,* Vol. II: *College students and young adults.* Washington, D.C.: National Institute on Drug Abuse.

Jones, D. J., Fox, M. M., Babigian, H., & Hutton, H. (1980). Epidemiology of anorexia nervosa in Monroe County, New York: 1960–1976. *Psychosomatic Medicine, 42,* 551–558.

Jones, E. (1996). Special section on attachment and psychopathology, part 1. *Journal of Consulting and Clinical Psychology, 64,* 5–7.

Jones, E., Krupnik, J. L., & Kerig, P. K. (1987). Some gender effects in brief psychotherapy. *Psychotherapy, 24,* 336–352.

Jones, E. E., & Berglas, S. (1978). Control of attributions about the self through self-handicapping strategies: The appeal of alcohol and the role of underachievement. *Personality and Social Psychology Bulletin, 4,* 200–206.

Jones, K. L. (1988). *Smith's recognizable patterns of human malformation* (4th ed.). Philadelphia: Saunders.

Jones, K. L., & Smith, B. W. (1973). Recognition of the fetal alcohol syndrome in early infancy. *Lancet, 2,* 999–1001.

Jones, K. L., & Smith, B. W. (1975). The fetal alcohol syndrome. *Teratology, 12,* 1–10.

Jones, R. L. (1996). Sharp rise reported in teenagers' drug use. *Philadelphia Inquirer,* August 21, 1996, A1–A15.

Jordan, B. K., Schlenger, W. E., Fairbank, J. A., & Caddell, J. M. (1996). Prevalence of psychiatric disorders among incarcerated women: Convicted felons entering prison. *Archives of General Psychiatry, 53,* 513–519.

Jorgensen, R. S., & Houston, B. K. (1981). The type A behavior pattern, sex differences, and cardiovascular response to and recovery from stress. *Motivation and Emotion, 5,* 201–214.

Jorm, A. F. (1994). Disability in dementia: Assessment, prevention, and rehabilitation. *Disability and Rehabilitation, 16,* 98–109.

Josephs, R. A., & Steele, C. M. (1990). The two faces of alcohol myopia: Attentional mediation of psychological stress. *Journal of Abnormal Psychology, 99,* 115–126.

Jouriles, E. N., Bourg, W. J., & Farris, A. M. (1991). Marital adjustment and child conduct problems: A comparison of the correlation across subsamples. *Journal of Consulting and Clinical Psychology, 59,* 354–357.

Kagan, J. (1966). Reflection-impulsivity: The generality and dynamics of conceptual tempo. *Journal of Abnormal Psychology, 71,* 17–24.

Kagan, J., Reznick, J. S., & Gibbons, J. (1989). Inhibited and uninhibited types of children. *Child Development, 60,* 838–845.

Kagan, J., Reznick, J. S., & Snidman, N. (1987). The physiology and psychology of behavioral inhibition in young children. *Child Development, 58,* 1459–1473.

Kagan, J., Reznick, J. S., & Snidman, N. (1988). Biological bases of childhood shyness. *Science, 240,* 167–171.

Kagan, J., Reznick, J. S., Snidman, N., Gibbons, J., & Johnson, M. (1988). Childhood derivatives of inhibition and lack of inhibition to the unfamiliar. *Child Development, 59,* 1580–1589.

Kalat, J. W. (1995). *Biological psychology* (5th ed.). Pacific Grove, CA: Brooks/Cole.

Kalsi, G., Sherrington, R., Mankoo, B. S., Brynjolfsson, J., Sigmundsson, T., Curtis, D., Read, T., Murphy, P., Butler, R., Petursson, H., & Gurling, H. M. D. (1996). Linkage study of the D^5 dopamine receptor gene (DRD5) in multiplex Icelandic and English schizophrenia pedigrees. *American Journal of Psychiatry, 153,* 107–109.

Kalucy, R. S., Crisp, A. H., & Harding, B. (1977). A study of 56 families with anorexia nervosa. *British Journal of Medical Psychology, 50,* 381–395.

Kandel, D. B., & Davies, M. (1996). High school students who use crack and other drugs. *Archives of General Psychiatry, 53,* 71–80.

Kandel, D. B., Kessler, R. C., & Margulies, R. Z. (1978). Antecedents of adolescent initiation into stages of drug use: A developmental analysis. In D. B. Kandel (Ed.), *Longitudinal research on drug use: Empirical findings and methodological issues.* Washington, DC: Hemisphere Publishing.

Kane, J., Honigfeld, G., Singer, J., Meltzer, H., & the Clozaril Collaborative Study Group. (1988). Clozapine for the treatment-resistant schizophrenic: A double-blind comparison with chlorpromazine. *Archives of General Psychiatry, 45,* 789–796.

Kanner, A. D., Coyne, J. C., Schaefer, C., & Lazarus, R. S. (1981). Comparison of two modes of stress measurement: Daily hassles and uplifts versus major life events. *Journal of Behavioral Medicine, 4,* 1–39.

Kanner, A. D., & Feldman, S. S. (1991). Control over uplifts and hassles and its relationship to adaptational outcomes. *Journal of Behavioral Medicine, 14,* 187–202.

Kanner, L. (1943). Autistic disturbances of affective contact. *Nervous Child, 21,* 217–250.

Kanner, L. (1971). Follow-up study of eleven autistic children originally reported in 1943. *Journal of Autism and Childhood Schizophrenia, 1,* 119–145.

Kantor, G. F., Jasinski, J. L., & Aldarondo, E. (1994). Sociocultural and incidence of marital violence in Hispanic families. *Violence and Victims, 9,* 207–222.

Kao, J. J. (1979). *Three millennia of Chinese psychiatry.* Brooklyn: Institute for Advanced Research in Asian Science & Medicine.

Kaplan, H. S. (1974). *The new sex therapy: Active treatment of sexual dysfunction.* New York: Brunner/Mazel.

Kaplan, H. S., & Klein, D. F. (1987). *Sexual aversion, sexual phobias, and panic disorder.* New York: Brunner/Mazel.

Kaplan, J., Manuck, S., Clarkson, T., Lusso, F., Taub, D. (1982). Social status, environment, and arterosclerosis cynomolgus monkeys. *Arteriosclerosis, 2,* 359.

Kaplan, J., Manuck, S. B., Clarkson, T. B., Lusso, F. M., Taub, D. M., & Miller, E. W. (1983). Social stress and atherosclerosis in normocholesterolemic monkeys. *Science, 220,* 733–735.

Kaplan, R. M., Sallis J. F., & Patterson, T. L. (1993). *Health and human behavior.* New York: McGraw Hill.

Karasek, R. A., Russell, R. S., Theorell, T. (1982). Physiology of stress and regeneration in job-related cardiovascular illness. *Journal of Human Stress, 8,* 29–42.

Karno, M., & Golding, J. M. (1991). Obsessive compulsive disorder. In L. N. Robins & D. Regier (Eds.), *Psychiatric disorders in America.* New York: The Free Press.

Karno, M., Hough, R. L., Burnam, M. A., Escobar, J. I., Timbers, D. M., Santana, F., & Boyd, J. H. (1987). Lifetime prevalence of specific psychiatric disorders among Mexican Americans and non-Hispanic whites in Los Angeles. *Archives of General Psychiatry, 44,* 695–701.

Kashani, J. H., & Orvaschel, H. (1988). Anxiety disorders in mid-adolescence: A community sample. *American Journal of Psychiatry, 145,* 960–964.

Kashani, J. H., & Carlson, G. A. (1987). Seriously depressed preschoolers. *American Journal of Psychiatry, 144,* 348–350.

Kashner, T. M., Rost, K., Cohen, B., & Anderson, M. (1995). Enhancing the health of somatization disorder patients: Effectiveness of short-term group therapy. *Psychosomatics, 36,* 462–470.

Kasper, S., Wehr, T. A., Bartko, J. J., Gaist, P. A., & Rosenthal, N. E. (1989). Epidemiological findings of seasonal changes in mood and behavior: A telephone survey of Montgomery County, Maryland. *Archives of General Psychiatry, 46,* 823–833.

Katerndahl, D. A., & Realini, J. P. (1993). Lifetime prevalence of panic states. *American Journal of Psychiatry, 150,* 246–249.

Katsanis, J., & Iacono, W. G. (1991). Clinical neuropsychological and brain structural correlates of smooth-pursuit eye tracking performance in chronic schizophrenia. *Journal of Abnormal Psychology, 100,* 526–534.

Katz-Garris, L. (1978). The right to education. In J. Wortis (Ed.), *Mental retardation and developmental disabilities* (Vol. 10). New York: Brunner/Mazel.

Kaufman, J., & Zigler, E. (1989). The intergenerational transmission of child abuse. In D. Cicchetti & V. K. Carlson (Eds.), *Child maltreatment: Theory and research on the causes and consequences of child abuse and neglect.* New York: Cambridge.

Kazdin, A. E. (1974). Comparative effects of some variations in covert modeling. *Journal of Behavior Therapy and Experimental Psychiatry, 5,* 225–231.

Kazdin, A. E. (1982). Single-case experimental designs. In P. C. Kendall & J. N. Butcher (Eds.), *Handbook of research methods in clinical psychology.* New York: Wiley.

Kazdin, A. E. (1990). Conduct disorder in childhood. In M. Hersen & C. Last (Eds.), *Handbook of adult and child psychopathology: A longitudinal perspective.* New York: Pergamon Press.

Kazdin, A. E. (1992). *Research design in clinical psychology.* New York: Macmillan.

Kazdin, A. E. (1994). *Behavior modification in applied settings* (5th ed.). Pacific Groves, CA: Brooks/Cole Publishing.

Kazdin, A. E. (1994). Methodology, design and evaluation in psychotherapy research. In A. Bergin & S. Garfield (Eds.), *Handbook of psychotherapy and behavior change* (4th ed.). New York: Wiley.

Kazdin, A. E. (1994). Psychotherapy for children and adolescents. In S. Garfield & A. Bergin (Eds.), *Handbook of psychotherapy and behavior change* (4th ed.). New York: Wiley.

Kazdin, A. E., Esveldt-Dawson, K., French, N. H., & Unis, A. S. (1987). Problem solving skills training and relationship therapy in the treatment of antisocial child behavior. *Journal of Consulting and Clinical Psychology, 55,* 76–85.

Kazdin, A. E., Esveldt-Dawson, K., Unis, A. S., & Rancurello, M. D. (1983). Child and parent evaluations of depression and aggression in psychiatric inpatient children. *Journal of Abnormal Child Psychology, 11,* 401–413.

Kazdin, A. E., Siegel, T. C., & Bass, D. (1992). Cognitive-problem-solving skills training and parent management training in the treatment of antisocial behavior in children. *Journal of Consulting and Clinical Psychology, 60,* 733–747.

Kazdin, A. E., & Wilcoxon, L. (1976). Systematic desensitization and nonspecific treatment effects: A methodological evaluation. *Psychological Bulletin, 83,* 729–758.

Keane, T. M., Fairbank, J. A., Caddell, J. M., Zimering, R. T., & Bender, M. (1985). A behavioral approach to assessing and treating posttraumatic stress disorder in Vietnam veterans. In C. R. Figley (Ed.), *Trauma and its wake: The study and treatment of post-traumatic stress disorder.* New York: Brunner/Mazel.

Keane, T. M., & Kaloupek, D. G. (1982). Imaginal flooding in the treatment of posttraumatic stress disorder. *Journal of Consulting and Clinical Psychology, 50,* 138–140.

Keitner, G. I., Ryan, C. E., Miller, I. W., Kohn, R., Bishop, D. S., & Epstein, N. B. (1995). Role of the family in recovery and major depression. *American Journal of Psychiatry, 152,* 1002–1008.

Keller, M. B. (1988). Diagnostic issues and clinical course of unipolar illness. In A. J. Frances & R. E. Hales (Eds.), *Review of Psychiatry.* Washington, DC: American Psychiatric Press.

Keller, M. B., Klein, D. N., Hirschfeld, R. M. A., Kocsis, J. H., McCullough, J. P., Miller, I., First, M. B., Holzer, C. P., Keitner, G. I., Marin, D. B., & Shea, T. (1995). Results of the DSM-IV mood disorders field trial. *American Journal of Psychiatry, 152,* 843–849.

Keller, M. B., Lavori, P. W., Coryell, W., Endicott, J., & Mueller, T. I. (1993). Bipolar I: A five-year prospective follow-up. *Journal of Nervous and Mental Disease, 181,* 238–245.

Kellerman, A., Rivara, F., Rushforth, N., Banton, J., Reay, D., Francisco, J., Locci, A., Prodzinski, J., Hackman, B., & Somes, G. (1993). Gun ownership as a risk factor for homicide in the home. *New England Journal of Medicine, 329,* 1084–1091.

Kellner, R. (1985). Functional somatic symptoms and hypochondriasis. *Archives of General Psychiatry, 42,* 821–833.

Kelsoe, J. R., Ginns, E. I., Egeland, J. A., Gerhard, D. S., Goldstein, A. M., Bale, S. J., Pauls, D. J., Long, R. T., Kidd, K. K., Conte, G., Housman, D. E., & Paul, S. M. (1989). Re-evaluation of the linkage relationship between chromosome 11p loci and the gene for bipolar affective disorder in the Old Order Amish. *Nature, 342,* 238–243.

Kendall, P. C. (1978). Anxiety: States, traits—situations? *Journal of Consulting and Clinical Psychology, 46,* 280–287.

Kendall, P. C. (1993). Cognitive-behavioral therapies with youth: Guiding theory, current status, and emerging developments. *Journal of Consulting and Clinical Psychology, 61,* 235–247.

Kendall, P. C. (1994). Treating anxiety disorders in youth: Results of a randomized clinical trial. *Journal of Consulting and Clinical Psychology, 62,* 100–110.

Kendall, P. C., & Braswell, L. (1993). *Cognitive-behavioral therapy for impulsive children* (2nd ed.). New York: Guilford Press.

Kendall, P. C., Chansky, T. E., Kane, M. T., Kim, R., Kortlander, E., Ronan, K. R., Sessa, F. M., & Siqueland, L. (1992). *Anxiety disorders in youth: Cognitive-behavioral interventions.* Needham, MA: Allyn & Bacon.

Kendall, P. C., & Grove, W. M. (1988). Normative comparisons in therapy outcome research. *Behavioral Assessment, 10,* 147–158.

Kendall, P. C., & Hollon, S. D. (Eds.). (1979). *Cognitive-behavioral interventions: Theory, research and procedures.* New York: Academic Press.

Kendall, P. C., & Hollon, S. D. (1981). *Assessment strategies for cognitive-behavioral interventions.* New York: Academic Press.

Kendall, P. C., Howard, B. L., & Hays, R. C. (1989). Self-referent speech and psychopathology: The balance of positive and negative thinking. *Cognitive Therapy and Research, 13,* 583–598.

Kendall, P. C., & Ingram, R. E. (1989). Cognitive-behavioral perspectives: Theory and research on depression and anxiety. In P. C. Kendall & D. Watson (Eds.), *Anxiety and depression: Distinctive and overlapping features.* New York: Academic Press.

Kendall, P. C., Panichelli-Mindel, S., Sugarman, A., & Callahan, S. A. (1997). Exposure to child anxiety: Theory, research, and practice. *Clinical Psychology: Science and Practice, 4,* 1–11.

Kendall, P. C., Reber, M., McLeer, S., Epps, J., & Ronan, K. R. (1990). Cognitive-behavioral treatment of conduct-disordered children. *Cognitive Therapy and Research, 14,* 279–297.

Kendall, P. C., & Watson, D. (Eds.). (1989). *Anxiety and depression: Distinctive and overlapping features.* New York: Academic Press.

Kendler, K. S. (1996). Parenting: A genetic-epidemiologic perspective. *American Journal of Psychiatry, 153,* 11–20.

Kendler, K. S., Heath, A. C., Martin, N. G., & Eaves, L. J. (1986). Symptoms of anxiety and depression in a volunteer twin population. *Archives of General Psychiatry, 43,* 213–221.

Kendler, K. S., Kessler, R. C., Walters, E. E., MacLean, C., Neale, M. C., Heath, A. C., & Eaves, L. J. (1995). Stressful life events, genetic liability, and onset of an episode of major depression in women. *American Journal of Psychiatry, 152,* 833–842.

Kendler, K. S., McGuire, M., Gruenberg, A. M., O'Hare, A., Spellman, M., & Walsh, D. (1993). The Roscommon family study: Methods, diagnosis of probands, and risk of schizophrenia in relatives. *Archives of General Psychiatry, 50,* 527–540.

Kendler, K. S., McGuire, M., Gruenberg, A. M., & Walsh, D. (1995). Schizotypal symptoms and signs in the Roscommon family study: Their factor structure and familial relationship with psy-

chotic and affective disorders. *Archives of General Psychiatry, 52,* 296–303.

Kendler, K. S., Neale, M. C., Kessler, R. C., Heath, A. C., & Eaves, L. J. (1992). A population-based twin study of major depression in women: The impact of varying definitions of illness. *Archives of General Psychiatry, 49,* 257–266.

Kendler, K. S., Neale, M. C., Kessler, R. C., Heath, A. C., & Eaves, L. J. (1992a). Generalized anxiety disorder in women: A population-based twin study. *Archives of General Psychiatry, 49,* 267–272.

Kendler, K. S., Neale, M. C., Kessler, R. C., Heath, A. C., & Eaves, L. J. (1992b). The genetic epidemiology of phobias in women: The interrelationship of agoraphobia, social phobia, situational phobia, and simple phobia. *Archives of General Psychiatry, 49,* 273–281.

Kendler, K. S., & Walsh, D. (1995). Schizotypal personality disorder in parents and the risk for schizophrenia in siblings. *Schizophrenia Bulletin, 21,* 47–52.

Kendler, K. S., Walters, E. E., Neale, M. C., Kessler, R. C., Heath, A. C., & Eaves, L. J. (1995). The structure of the genetic and environmental risk factors for six major psychiatric disorders in women. *Archives of General Psychiatry, 52,* 374–383.

Kendrick, M. J., Craig, K., Lawson, D., & Davidson, P. O. (1982). Cognitive and behavioral therapy for musical-performance anxiety. *Journal of Consulting and Clinical Psychology, 50,* 353–362.

Kent, D. A., Tomasson, K., & Coryell, W. (1995). Course and outcome of conversion and somatization disorders: A four-year follow-up. *Psychosomatics, 36,* 103–112.

Keogh, B. K., & Margolis, J. (1976). Learn to labor and to wait: Attentional problems of children with learning disorders. *Journal of Learning Disabilities, 9,* 276–286.

Kern, R. S., Green, M. F., & Goldstein, M. J. (1995). Modification of performance on the span of apprehension, a putative marker of vulnerability to schizophrenia. *Journal of Abnormal Psychology, 104,* 385–389.

Kernberg, O. F. (1975). *Borderline conditions and pathological narcissism.* New York: Jason Aronson.

Kernberg, O. F. (1976). *Object relations theory and clinical psychoanalysis.* New York: Jason Aronson.

Kernberg, O. F. (1986). *Severe personality disorders: Psychotherapeutic strategies.* New Haven: Yale University Press.

Kessler, R. C., McGonagle, K. A., Zhao, S., Nelson, C. B., Hughes, M., Eshleman, S., Wittchen, H. U., & Kendler, K. S. (1994). Lifetime and 12-month prevalence of DSM-III-R psychiatric disorders in the United States. *Archives of General Psychiatry, 51,* 8–19.

Kessler, R. C., Sonnega, A., Bromet, E., Hughes, M., & Nelson, C. B. (1995). Posttraumatic stress disorder in the national comorbidity survey. *Archives of General Psychiatry, 52,* 1048–1060.

Kety, S. S., Wender, P. H., Jacobsen, B., Ingraham, L. J., Jansson, L., Faber, B., & Kinney, D. K. (1994). Mental illness in the biological and adoptive relatives of schizophrenic adoptees. *Archives of General Psychiatry, 51,* 442–455.

Keyes, D. (1981). *The minds of Billy Milligan.* New York: Random.

Kiecolt-Glaser, J. K., Fisher, L. D., Ogrocki, P., & Stout, J. C. (1987). Marital quality, marital disruption, and immune function. *Psychosomatic Medicine, 49,* 13–34.

Kiecolt-Glaser, J. K., Garner, W., Speicher, C., Penn, G. M., Holliday, J., & Glaser, R. (1984). Psychosocial modifiers of immunocompetence in medical students. *Psychosomatic Medicine, 46,* 7–14.

Kiecolt-Glaser, J. K., & Glaser, R. (1992). Psychoneuro-immunology: Can psychological interventions modulate immunity? *Journal of Consulting and Clinical Psychology, 60,* 569–575.

Kiecolt-Glaser, J. K., Stephens, R., Lipetz, P., Speicher, C., & Glaser, R. (1985). Distress and DNA repair in human lymphocytes. *Journal of Behavioral Medicine, 8,* 311–320.

Kiesler, D. J. (1991). Interpersonal methods of assessment and diagnosis. In C. R. Snyder & D. R. Forsyth (Eds.), *Handbook of social and clinical psychology.* New York: Pergamon Press.

Kiesler, D. J. (1996). *Contemporary interpersonal theory and research: Personality, psychopathology, and psychotherapy.* New York: Wiley.

Kihlstrom, J. F. (1987). The cognitive unconscious. *Science, 237,* 1445–1452.

Kihlstrom, J. F., Glisky, M. L., & Angiulo, M. J. (1994). Dissociative tendencies and dissociative disorders. *Journal of Abnormal Psychology, 103,* 117–124.

Killias, M. (1993). International correlations between gun ownership and rates of homicide and suicide. *Canadian Medical Association Journal, 148,* 1721–1725.

Kilpatrick, D. G., Saunders, B. E., Amick-McMullan, A., Best, C. L., Veronen, L. J., & Resnick, H. S. (1989). Victim and crime factors associated with the development of crime-related post-traumatic stress disorder. *Behavior Therapy, 20,* 199–214.

King, B., Reis, H., Porter, L., & Norsen, L. (1993). Social support and long-term recovery from coronary artery surgery: Effects on patients and spouses. *Health Psychology, 12,* 56–63.

King, D. W., King, L. A., Gudanowski, D. M., & Vreven, D. L. (1995). Alternative representations of war zone stressors: Relationships to posttraumatic stress disorder in male and female Vietnam veterans. *Journal of Abnormal Psychology, 104,* 184–196.

Kinsey, A., Pomeroy, W., & Martin, C. (1948). *Sexual behavior in the human male.* Philadelphia: Saunders.

Kinsey, A., Pomeroy, W., Martin, C., & Gebhard, P. (1953). *Sexual behavior in the human female.* Philadelphia: Saunders.

Kistner, J. A., & Torgeson, J. K. (1987). Motivational and cognitive aspects of learning disabilities. In B. Lahey & A. E. Kazdin (Eds.), *Advances in clinical child psychology* (Vol. 10). New York: Plenum.

Klein, D. N., & Miller, G. A. (1993). Depressive personality in non-clinical subjects. *American Journal of Psychiatry, 150,* 1718–1724.

Kleinman, A. (1988). *Rethinking psychiatry.* New York: Free Press.

Kleinman, A. (1991, April). *Culture and DSM-IV: Recommendations for the introduction and for the overall structure.* Paper presented at the National Institute of Mental Health-sponsored Conference on Culture and Diagnosis, Pittsburgh, PA.

Kleinmuntz, B., & Szucko, J. J. (1984). On the fallibility of lie detection. *Law and Society, 17,* 85–104.

Klerman, G. L., & Weissman, M. M. (1989). Increasing rates of depression. *Journal of the American Medical Association, 261,* 2229–2235.

Klerman, G. L., Weissman, M. M., Markowitz, J. C., Glick, I., Wilner, P., Mason, B., & Shear, M. K. (1994). Medication and psychotherapy. In S. Garfield & A. Bergin (Eds.), *Handbook of psychotherapy and behavior change* (4th ed.). New York: Wiley.

Klerman, G. L., Weissman, M., Rounsaville, B., & Chevron, E. (1984). *Interpersonal psychotherapy of depression.* New York: Basic Books.

Klorman, R., Brumaghim, J. T., Fitzpatrick, P. A., Borgstedt, A. D., & Strauss, J. (1994). Clinical and cognitive effects of methylphenidate on children with attention deficit disorder as a function of aggression/oppositionality and age. *Journal of Abnormal Psychology, 103,* 206–221.

Knight, R. A., & Prentky, R. A. (1990). Classifying sexual offenders: The development and corroboration of taxonomic models. In W. L. Marshall, D. R. Laws & H. E. Barbaree (Eds.), *Handbook of sexual assault: Issues, theories, and treatment of taxonomic models* (pp. 23–52). New York: Plenum Press.

Knight, R. G., Godfrey, H. P. D., & Shelton, E. J. (1988). The psychological deficits associated with Parkinson's disease. *Clinical Psychology Review, 8,* 391–410.

Knopman, D., Schneider, L., Davis, K., Talwalker, S., Smith, F., Hoover, T., & Gracon, S. (1996). Long-term tacrine (Cognex) treatment: Effects on nursing home placement and mortality. The Tacrine Study Group. *Neurology, 47,* 166–177.

Kockott, G., & Fahrner, E. (1987). Transsexuals who have not undergone surgery: A follow-up study. *Archives of Sexual Behavior, 16,* 511–522.

Koegel, P., & Burnam, M. (1988). Alcoholism among homeless adults in the inner city of Los Angeles. *Archives of General Psychiatry, 45,* 1011–1018.

Koegel, P., Burnam, A., & Farr, R. K. (1988). The prevalence of specific psychiatric disorders among homeless individuals in the inner city of Los Angeles. *Archives of General Psychiatry, 45,* 1085–1092.

Koegel, R. L., Bimbela, A., & Schreibman, L. (1996). Collateral effects of parent training on family interactions. *Journal of Autism and Developmental Disorders, 26,* 347–359.

Koegel, R. L., Schreibman, L., Britten, K. R., Burke, J., & O'Neill, R. E. (1982). A comparison of parent training to direct child treatment. In R. L. Koegel, A. Rincover & A. L. Egel (Eds.), *Educating and understanding autistic children.* San Diego: College Hill Press.

Kohn, P. M., Lafreniere, K., & Gurevich, M. (1990). The inventory of college students' recent life experiences: A decontaminated hassles scale for a special population. *Journal of Behavioral Medicine, 13,* 619–630.

Kohut, H. (1977). *The restoration of the self.* New York: International Universities Press.

Kolb, B., & Whishaw, I. (1985). *Fundamentals of human neuropsychology,* 2nd ed. New York: Freeman.

Kolko, D. J. (1988). Educational programs to promote awareness and prevention of child sexual victimization: A review and methodological critique. *Clinical Psychology Review, 8,* 195–209.

Kolvin, I., Miller, F. J. W., Fleeting, M., & Kolvin, P. A. (1988). Social and parenting factors affecting criminal-offence rates: Findings from the Newcastle Thousand Family Study (1947–1980). *British Journal of Psychiatry, 152,* 80–90.

Koss, M. P. (1993). Rape: Scope, impact, interventions, and public policy responses. *American Psychologist, 10,* 1062–1079.

Koss, M. P., & Dinero, T. E. (1989). Discriminant analysis of risk factors for sexual victimization among a national sample of college women. *Journal of Consulting and Clinical Psychology, 57,* 242–250.

Koss-Chioino, J. (1995). Traditional and folk approaches among ethnic minorities. In J. Aponte, R. Rivers, and J. Wohl (Eds.), *Psychological interventions and cultural diversity* (pp. 145–163). Boston: Allyn and Bacon.

Kosson, D. S., Smith, S. S., & Newman, J. P. (1990). Evaluating the construct validity of psychopathy in black and white male inmates: Three preliminary studies. *Journal of Abnormal Psychology, 99,* 250–259.

Kovacs, M., & Beck, A. T. (1977). An empirical clinical approach toward a definition of childhood depression. In J. G. Schulterbrandt (Ed.), *Depression in childhood: Diagnosis, treatment and conceptual models.* New York: Raven Press.

Kovacs, M., Feinberg, T. L., Crouse-Novak, M. A., Paulauskas, S. L., & Finkelstein, R. (1984a). Depressive disorders in childhood. I. A longitudinal prospective study of characteristics and recovery. *Archives of General Psychiatry, 41,* 229–237.

Kovacs, M., Feinberg, T. L., Crouse-Novak, M. A., Paulauskas, S. L., Pollock, M., & Finkelstein, R. (1984b). Depressive disorders in childhood. II. A longitudinal study of the risk for a subsequent major depression. *Archives of General Psychiatry, 41,* 643–649.

Kraepelin, E. (1883). *Lehrbuch der psychiatrie* (1883; 8th ed., 1915). Clinical psychiatry. Translated from the 7th German edition by A. R. Diefendorf. Delmar, NY: Scholars' Facsimiles and Reprints.

Krantz, D. S., & Manuck, S. B. (1984). Acute psychophysiologic reactivity and risk of cardiovascular disease: A review and methodological critique. *Psychological Bulletin, 96,* 435–464.

Kratochwill, T. R., & Morris, R. J. (Eds.) (1993). *Handbook of psychotherapy with children and adolescents*. Boston, MA: Allyn & Bacon.

Kruesi, M. J. P., Hibbs, E. D., Zahn, T. P., Keysor, C. S., Hamburger, S. D., Bartko, J. J., & Rapoport, J. L. (1992). A 2-year prospective follow-up study of children and adolescents with disruptive behavior disorders. *Archives of General Psychology, 49*, 429–435.

Kulik, J. A., & Mahler, H. I. (1993). Emotional support as a moderator of adjustment and compliance after coronary artery bypass surgery longitudinal study. *Journal of Behavioral Medicine, 16*, 45–64.

Kumpfer, K. L. (1987). Special populations: Etiology and prevention of vulnerability to chemical dependency in children of substance abusers. In B. S. Brown & A. R. Mills (Eds.), *Youth at high risk for substance abuse*. National Institute on Drug Abuse. DHHS Publication No. (ADM) 87–1537. Washington DC: U.S. Government Printing Office.

Kuo-Tai, T. (1987). Infantile autism in China. *Journal of Autism and Developmental Disorders, 17*, 289–296.

Kupfer, D. J., & Reynolds, C. F. (1992). Sleep and affective disorders. In E. S. Paykel (Ed.), *Handbook of affective disorders* (2nd ed.). New York: Guilford Press.

Kupfer, D. J., Frank, E., Perel, J. M., Cornes, C., Mallinger, A. G., Thase, M. E., McEachran, A. B., & Grochocinski, V. J. (1992). Five-year outcome for maintenance therapies in recurrent depression. *Archives of General Psychiatry, 49*, 769–773.

Kurtzke, J. F., & Goldberg, I. D. (1988). Parkinsonism death rates by race, sex and geography. *Neurology, 38*, 1558–1561.

Kutcher, S., Papatheodorou, G., Reiter, S., & Gardner, D. (1995). The successful pharmacological treatment of adolescents and young adults with borderline personality disorder: A preliminary open trial of flupenthixol. *Journal of Psychiatry and Neuroscience, 20*, 113–118.

Kwapil, T. R. (1996). A longitudinal study of drug and alcohol use by psychosis-prone and impulsive-nonconforming individuals. *Journal of Abnormal Psychology, 105*, 114–123.

Labott, S. M., Preisman, R. C., Popovich, J., & Iannuzzi, M. C. (1995). Health care utilization of somatizing patients in a pulmonary subspecialty clinic. *Psychosomatics, 36*, 122–128.

Labouvie, E. W., & McGee, C. R. (1986). Relation of personality to alcohol and drug use in adolescence. *Journal of Consulting and Clinical Psychology, 54*, 289–293.

Lahey, B. B., Green, K., & Forehand, R. (1980). On the independence of ratings of hyperactivity, conduct problems, and attentional deficits in children: A multiple regression analysis. *Journal of Consulting and Clinical Psychology, 48*, 566–574.

Lahey, B. B., Loeber, R., Hart, E., Frick, P. J., Applegate, B., Zhang, Q., Green, S. M., & Russo, M. F. (1995). Four-year longitudinal study of conduct disorder in boys: Patterns and predictors of persistence. *Journal of Abnormal Psychology, 104*, 83–93.

Laing, R. D. (1967). *The politics of experience*. New York: Ballantine.

Lambert, M. C., Weisz, J. R., Knight, F., Desrosiers, M., Overly, K., & Thesiger, C. (1992). Jamaican and American adult perspectives on child psychopathology: Further exploration of the threshold model. *Journal of Consulting and Clinical Psychology, 60*, 146–149.

Lambo, T. A. (1975). Mid and West Africa. In J. G. Howells (Ed.), *World history of psychiatry*. New York: Brunner/-Mazel.

Landau, R. J. (1980). The role of semantic schemata in phobic word interpretation. *Cognitive Therapy and Research, 4*, 427–434.

Langevin, R. (1992). Biological factors contributing to paraphilic behavior. *Psychiatric Annals, 22*, 307–314.

Lapouse, R., & Monk, M. A. (1958). An epidemiologic study of behavior characteristics in children. *American Journal of Public Health, 48*, 1134–1144.

Lasch, C. (1979). *The culture of narcissism: American life in an age of diminishing expectations*. New York: Norton.

Last, C. G., Hersen, M., Kazdin, A., Orvaschel, H., & Perrin, S. (1991). Anxiety disorders in children and their families. *Archives of General Psychiatry, 48*, 928–934.

Last, C. G. (1992). Anxiety disorders in childhood and adolescence. In W. M. Reynolds (Ed.), *Internalizing disorders in children and adolescents* (pp. 61–106). New York: Wiley.

Last, C. G., & Perrin, S. (1993). Anxiety disorders in African-American and white children. *Journal of Abnormal Child Psychology, 21*, 153–164.

Lau, M. A., Pihl, R. O., & Peterson, J. B. (1995). Provo-cation, acute alcohol intoxication, cognitive performance, and aggression. *Journal of Abnormal Psychology, 104*, 150–155.

Laudenslager, M. L., Ryan, S. M., Drugan, R. C., Hyson, R. L., & Maier, S. F. (1983). Coping and immunosuppression: Inescapable but not escapable shock suppresses lymphocyte proliferation. *Science, 221*, 568–570.

Laumann, E. O., Gagnon, J. H., Michael, R. T., & Michaels, S. (1994). *The social organization of sexuality*. Chicago: University of Chicago Press.

Lawler, J. E., Cox, R. H., Sanders, B. J., & Mitchell, V. P. (1988). The borderline hypertensive rat: A model for studying the mechanisms of environmental induced hypertension. *Health Psychology, 7*, 137–147.

Lazarus, R. S., & Folkman, S. (1984). *Stress, appraisal, and coping*. New York: Springer.

Leckman, J. F., & Cohen, D. J. (1994). Tic disorders. In M. Rutter, E. Taylor & L. Hersov (Eds.), *Child and adolescent psychiatry*. Oxford: Blackwell Scientific Publications.

Leckman, J. F., Walker, D. E., & Cohen, D. J. (1993). Premonitory urges in Tourette's syndrome. *American Journal of Psychiatry, 150*, 98–102.

Lee, E. (1985). Inpatient psychiatric services for Southeast Asian refugees. In T. C. Owan (Ed.), *Southeast Asian mental health: Treatment, prevention, services, training, and research*. Washington, DC: U.S. Government Printing Office.

Lee, S., & Chiu, H. F. (1989). Anorexia nervosa in Hong Kong— why not more in Chinese? *British Journal of Psychiatry, 154*, 683–688.

Leenaars, A. A. (1992). Suicide notes, communication, and ideation. In R. Maris, A. L. Berman, J. T. Maltsberger & R. I. Yufit (Eds.), *Assessment and prediction of suicide*. New York: Guilford.

Leff, J., & Vaughn, C. (1981). The role of maintenance therapy and relatives' expressed emotion in relapse of schizophrenia: A two-year follow up. *British Journal of Psychiatry, 138*, 102–104.

Lefkowitz, M. M., Eron, L. D., Walder, L. O., & Huesmann, L. R. (1972). Television violence and child aggression: A follow-up study. In G. A. Comstock & E. A. Rubinstein (Eds.), *Television and social behavior* (Vol. 3). Washington, DC: U.S. GPO.

Leibenluft, E. (1996). Women with bipolar illness: Clinical and research issues. *American Journal of Psychiatry, 153*, 163–173.

Leibenluft, E., & Wehr, T. A. (1992). Is sleep deprivation useful in the treatment of depression? *American Journal of Psychiatry, 149*, 159–168.

Leiblum, S., Rosen, R., Platt, M., Cross, R., & Black, C. (1993). Sexual attitudes and behavior of a cross-sectional sample of United States medical students: Effects of gender, age, and year of study. *Journal of Sex Education and Therapy, 19*, 235–245.

Leitenberg, H., Agras, W. S., & Thomson, L. E. (1968). A sequential analysis of the effect of selective positive reinforcement in modifying anorexia nervosa. *Behaviour Research and Therapy, 6*, 211–218.

Lenzenweger, M. F., & Loranger, A. W. (1989). Psychosis proneness and clinical psychopathology: Examination of the correlates of schizotypy. *Journal of Abnormal Psychology, 98*, 3–8.

Leon, G. R., & Phelan, P. W. (1985). Anorexia nervosa. In B. Lahey & A. E. Kazdin (Eds.), *Advances in clinical child psychology* (Vol. 8). New York: Plenum Press.

Leonard, H., & Rapoport, J. (1989). Pharmacotherapy of childhood obsessive-compulsive disorder. *Psychiatric Clinics of North America, 12,* 963–970.

Leonard, H., Swedo, S., Rapoport, J., Koby, E., Lenane, M., Cheslow, D., & Hamburger, S. (1989). Treatment of obsessive-compulsive disorder with clomipramine and desipramine in children and adolescents: A double-blind crossover comparison. *Archives of General Psychiatry, 46,* 1088–1092.

Lerman, C., Daly, M., Sands, C., Balshem, A., Lustbader, E., Heggan, T., Goldstein, L., James, J., & Engstrom, P. (1993) Mammography adherence and psychological distress among women at risk for breast cancer. *Journal of the National Cancer Institute, 85,* 1074–1080.

Lerner, R. M. (1984). *On the nature of human plasticity.* New York: Cambridge University Press.

Lerner, R. M., Hess, L. E., & Nitz, K. (1990). A developmental perspective on psychopathology. In M. Hersen & C. Last (Eds.), *Handbook of child and adult psychopathology: A longitudinal perspective.* New York: Pergamon Press.

Lester, D. (1993). Firearm availability and accidental deaths from firearms. *Journal of Safety Research, 24,* 167–169.

Lester, D. (1993). Firearm deaths in the United States and gun availability [letter]. *American Journal of Public Health, 83,* 1642.

LeVay, S. (1991). A difference in hypothalamic structure between heterosexual and homosexual men. *Science, 253,* 1034–1037.

Levin, S., Yurgelun-Todd, D., & Craft, S. (1989). Contri-butions of clinical neuropsychology to the study of schizophrenia. *Journal of Abnormal Psychology, 98,* 341–356.

Levine, I. S., & Rog, D. J. (1990). Mental health services for homeless mentally ill persons: Federal initiatives and current service trends. *American Psychologist, 45,* 969–975.

Levine, M. (1993). The quest for a trusting heart: Identifying the links between hostility and coronary heart disease. *Kenyon College Alumni Bulletin,* 24–28.

Levine, M., Toro, P. A., & Perkins, D. V. (1993). Social and community interventions. *Annual Review of Psychology, 44,* 525–558.

Levinson, D. F., & Simpson, G. M. (1992). Blacks, schizophrenia, and neuroleptic treatment: In reply. *Archives of General Psychiatry, 49,* 165.

Levitt, E. E. (1963). Psychotherapy with children: A further evaluation. *Behaviour Research and Therapy, 21,* 326–329.

Lewin, T. (1992, October 5). Rise in single parenthood is reshaping U.S. *New York Times,* pp. B1, B5.

Lewinsohn, P. M., Biglan, A., & Zeiss, A. M. (1976). Behavioral treatment of depression. In P. O. Davidson (Ed.), *The behavioral management of anxiety, depression, and pain.* New York: Brunner/Mazel.

Lewinsohn, P. M., Clarke, G. N., Hops, H., & Andrews, J. (1990). Cognitive-behavioral treatment for depressed adolescents. *Behavior Therapy, 21,* 385–401.

Lewinsohn, P. M., Roberts, R. E., Seeley, J. R., Rohde, P., Gotlib, I. H., & Hops, H. (1994). Adolescent psychopathology: II. Psychosocial risk factors for depression. *Journal of Abnormal Psychology, 103,* 302–315.

Lewinsohn, P. M., Rohde, P., & Seeley, J. R. (1995). Adolescent psychopathology: III. The clinical consequences of comorbidity. *Journal of the American Academy of Child and Adolescent Psychiatry, 34,* 510–519.

Lewinsohn, P. M., Rohde, P., Seeley, J. R., & Fischer, S. A. (1993). Age-cohort changes in the lifetime occurrence of depression and other mental disorders. *Journal of Abnormal Psychology, 102,* 110–120.

Lewis, M., & Miller, S. M. (Eds.) (1990). *Handbook of developmental psychopathology.* New York: Plenum Press.

Lewis-Fernandez, R., & Kleinman, A. (1994). Culture, personality, and psychopathology. *Journal of Abnormal Psychology, 103,* 67–71.

Ley, R. (1985). Agoraphobia, the panic attack, and the hyperventilation syndrome. *Behavior Research and Therapy, 23,* 79–81.

Ley, R. (1986). Panic disorder: A hyperventilation interpretation. In L. Michelson & M. Ascher (Eds.), *Anxiety and stress disorders: Cognitive behavioral assessment and treatment.* New York: Guilford Press.

Ley, R. (1987). Panic disorder and agoraphobia: Fear of fear or fear of the symptoms produced by hyperventilation? *Journal of Behavior Therapy and Experimental Psychiatry, 18,* 305–316.

Li, G., Silverman, J. M., Smith, C. J., Zaccario, M. L., Schmeidler, J., Mohs, R. C., & Davis, K. L. (1995). Age at onset and familial risk in Alzheimer's disease. *American Journal of Psychiatry, 152,* 424–430.

Liberman, R. P., Mueser, K. T., & Wallace, C. J. (1986). Social skills training for schizophrenic individuals at risk for relapse. *American Journal of Psychiatry, 143,* 523–526.

Liberman, R. P., Mueser, K. T., Wallace, C. J., Jacobs, H. E., Eckman, T., & Massel, H. K. (1986). Training skills in the psychiatrically disabled: Learning coping and competence. *Schizophrenia Bulletin, 12,* 631–647.

Lichtenstein, E., & Glasgow, R. E. (1992). Smoking cessation: What have we learned over the past decade? *Journal of Consulting and Clinical Psychology, 60,* 518–527.

Lidz, C. W., Mulvey, E. P., Appelbaum, P. S., & Cleveland, S. (1989). Commitment: The consistency of clinicians and the use of legal standards. *American Journal of Psychiatry, 146,* 176–181.

Lidz, T., Fleck, S., & Cornelison, A. (1965). *Schizophrenia and the family.* New York: International Universities Press.

Lieberman, J. A., Alvir, J. M. J., Woerner, M., Degreef, G., Bilder, R. M., Ashtari, M., Bogerts, B., Mayerhoff, D. I., Geisler, S. H., Loebel, A., Levy, D. L., Hinrichsen, G., Szymanski, S., Chakos, M., Koreen, A., Borenstein, M., & Kane, J. M. (1992). Prospective study of psychobiology in first-episode schizophrenia at Hillside Hospital. *Schizophrenia Bulletin, 18,* 351–372.

Lieberman, M. (1986). Self-help groups and psychiatry. *American Psychiatric Association Annual Review, 5,* 744–760.

Lied, E. R., & Marlatt, G. A. (1979). Modeling as a determinant of alcohol consumption: Effects of subject sex and prior drinking history. *Addictive Behaviors, 4,* 49–54.

Lief, H. I. (1985). Evaluation of inhibited sexual desire: Relational aspects. In H. S. Kaplan (Ed.), *Comprehensive evaluation of disorders of sexual desire.* Washington, DC: American Psychiatric Press.

Liem, J. H. (1980). Family studies of schizophrenia: An update and commentary. *Schizophrenia Bulletin, 6,* 429–455.

Light, K. C., Koepke, J. P., Obrist, P. A., & Willis, P. A. (1983). Psychological stress induces sodium and fluid retention in men at high risk for hypertension. *Science, 220,* 429–431.

Lilienfeld, S. O., & Waldman, I. D. (1990). The relation between childhood attention-deficit hyperactivity disorder and adult antisocial behavior re-examined: The problem of heterogeneity. *Clinical Psychology Review, 10,* 699–725.

Lin, K. (1991). *Cultural influences on the diagnosis of psychotic and organic disorders.* Paper prepared for the National Institute of Mental Health sponsored Conference on Culture and Diagnosis, Pittsburgh, PA.

Lin, K., Lau, J. C., Yamamoto, J., Zheng, Y., Kim, H., Cho, K., & Nakasaki, G. (1992). Hwa-byung: A community study of Korean Americans. *The Journal of Nervous and Mental Disease, 180,* 386–391.

Lin, K., Poland, R. E., Nuccio, I., Matsuda, K., Hathuc, N., Su, T., & Fu, P. (1989). A longitudinal assessment of haloperidol doses and serum concentrations in Asian and Caucasian schizophrenic patients. *American Journal of Psychiatry, 146,* 1307–1311.

Linehan, M. M., Armstrong, H. E., Suarez, A., Allmon, D., & Heard, H. L. (1991). Cognitive-behavioral treatment of chronically parasuicidal borderline patients. *Archives of General Psychiatry, 48,* 1060–1064.

Linehan, M. M., Heard, H. L., & Armstrong, H. E. (1993). Naturalistic follow-up of a behavioral treatment for chronically parasuicidal borderline patients. *Archives of General Psychiatry, 50,* 971–974.

Linehan, M. M., Tutek, D. A., Heard, H. L., & Armstrong, H. E. (1994). Interpersonal outcome of cognitive behavioral treatment for chronically suicidal borderline patients. *American Journal of Psychiatry, 151,* 1771–1776.

Lips, H. M. (1988). *Sex and gender.* Mountain View, CA: Mayfield.

Lipsky, M. J., Kassinove, H., & Miller, N. J. (1980). Effects of rational-emotive therapy, rational role reversal, and rational-emotive imagery on the emotional adjustment of community mental health center patients. *Journal of Consulting and Clinical Psychology, 18,* 366–374.

Lipton, S. T., & Gendelman, H. E. (1995). Dementia associated with the acquired immunodeficiency syndrome. *New England Journal of Medicine, 332,* 934–940.

Lisak, D., & Roth, S. (1988). Motivational factors in nonincarcerated sexually aggressive men. *Journal of Personality and Social Psychology, 55,* 795–802.

Litrownik, A. J., & McInnis, E. T. (1986). Information processing and autism. In R. E. Ingran (Ed.), *Information processing approaches to clinical psychology.* New York: Academic.

Livesley, W., Schroeder, M., Jackson, D., & Jang, K. (1994). Categorical distinctions in the study of personality disorder: Implications for classification. *Journal of Abnormal Psychology, 103,* 6–17.

Lively, W. J., Jackson, D. N., & Schroeder, M. L. (1992). Factorial structure of traits delineating personality disorders in clinical and general population samples. *Journal of Abnormal Psychology, 101(3),* 432–440.

Livingston, R., Witt, A., & Smith, G. R. (1995). Families who somatize. *Journal of Developmental and Behavioral Pediatrics, 16,* 42–46.

Lobo, A., Saz, P., Marcos, G., Dia, J. L., & De-la Camara, C. (1995). The prevalence of dementia and depression in the elderly community in a southern European population: The Zaragoza study. *Archives of General Psychiatry, 52,* 497–506.

Lochman, J. E. (1992). Cognitive-behavioral intervention with aggressive boys: Three-year follow-up and preventive effects. *Journal of Consulting and Clinical Psychology, 60,* 426–432.

Lochman, J. E., White, K. J., & Wayland, K. K. (1991). Cognitive-behavioral assessment and treatment with aggressive children. In P. C. Kendall (Ed.), *Child and adolescent therapy: Cognitive-behavioral procedures.* New York: Guilford Press.

Loeber, M., Van Kammen, W. B., & Maughan, B. (1993). Developmental pathways in disruptive child behavior. *Development and Psychopathology, 5,* 103–133.

Loeber, R. (1985). Patterns and development of child antisocial behavior. In G. J. Whitehurst (Ed.), *Annals of child development* (Vol. 2). New York: JAI Press.

Loeber, R. (1990). Development and risk factors of juvenile antisocial behavior and delinquency. *Clinical Psychology Review, 10,* 1–41.

Loftus, E. (1993). The reality of repressed memories. *American Psychologist, 48,* 518–537.

Lopez, S. R., Grover, K., Holland, D., Johnson, M., Kain, C., Kanel, K., Mellins, C., & Rhyne, M. (1989). Development of culturally sensitive psychotherapists. *Professional Psychology: Research and Practice, 20,* 369–376.

LoPiccolo, J. (1977). Direct treatment of sexual dysfunction in the couple. In J. Money & H. Musaph (Eds.), *Handbook of sexology.* Amsterdam: Excerpta Medica.

LoPiccolo, J. (1990). Treatment of sexual dysfunction. In A. S. Bellak, M. Ersen & A. E. Kazdin (Eds.), *International handbook of behavior modification and therapy* (2nd ed.). New York: Plenum.

LoPiccolo, J., & Friedman, J. R. (1988). Broad spectrum treatment of low sexual desire: Integration of cognitive, behavioral, and systemic treatment. In S. Leiblum & R. Rosen (Eds.), *Sexual desire disorders.* New York: Guilford Press.

LoPiccolo, J., & Stock, W. E. (1987). Sexual function, dysfunction, and counseling in gynecological practice. In Z. Rosenwaks, F. Benjamin & M. L. Stone (Eds.), *Gynecology.* New York: Macmillan.

Loranger, A. W. (1996). Dependent personality disorder: Age, sex, and Axis I comorbidity. *Journal of Nervous and Mental Disease, 184,* 17–21.

Lord, C., & Rutter, M. (1994). Autism and pervasive developmental disorders. In M. Rutter, E. Taylor & L. Hersov (Eds.), *Child and adolescent psychiatry.* Oxford: Blackwell Scientific Publications.

Lovaas, O. I. (1987). Behavioral treatment and normal educational and intellectual functioning in young autistic children. *Journal of Consulting and Clinical Psychology, 55,* 3–9.

Lovaas, O. I., Koegel, R. L., & Schreibman, L. (1979). Stimulus overselectivity in autism: A review of research. *Psychological Bulletin, 86,* 1236–1254.

Lovaas, O. I., Koegel, R. L., Simmons, J. Q., & Long, J. S. (1973). Some generalization and follow-up measures on autistic children in behavior therapy. *Journal of Applied Behavior Analysis, 6,* 131–165.

Lovaas, O. I., Smith, T., & McEachin, J. J. (1989). Clarifying comments on the Young Autism Study: Reply to Schopler, Short, and Mesibov. *Journal of Consulting and Clinical Psychology, 57,* 165–167.

Luborsky, L. (1984). *Principles of psychoanalytic psychotherapy: A manual for supportive-expressive treatment.* New York: Basic.

Luborsky, L., McLellan, A., Woody, G. E., O'Brien, C. P., & Auerbach, A. (1985). Therapist success and its determinants. *Archives of General Psychiatry, 42,* 602–611.

Lucas, A. R., Beard, C. M., O'Fallon, W., & Kurland, L. (1991). Fifty year trends in the incidence of anorexia nervosa in Rochester, Minnesota: A population-based study. *American Journal of Psychiatry, 148,* 917–922.

Ludwig, A. M. (1972). On and off the wagon: Reasons for drinking and abstaining by alcoholics. *Quarterly Journal of Studies on Alcohol, 33,* 91–96.

Ludwig, A. M. (1985). Cognitive processes associated with "spontaneous" recovery from alcoholism. *Journal of Studies on Alcohol, 46,* 53–58.

Luk, S., & Leung, P. W. (1989). Conners' teacher's rating scale: A validity study in Hong Kong. *Journal of Child Psychology and Psychiatry, 30,* 785–794.

Lunn, S., Skyksbjerg, M., Schulsinger, H., Parnas, J., Pedersen, C., & Mathiesen, L. (1991). A preliminary report on the neuropsychologic sequelae of human immunodeficiency virus. *Archives of General Psychiatry, 48,* 139–142.

Luntz, B. K., & Widom, C. S. (1994). Antisocial personality disorder in abused and neglected children grown up. *American Journal of Psychiatry, 151,* 670–674.

Luria, A. R. (1973). *The working brain.* New York: Basic Books.

Lykken, D. T., & Tellegen, A. (1996). Happiness is a stochastic phenomenon. *Psychological Science, 7,* 186–189.

Lykken, D. T. (1957). A study of anxiety in the sociopathic personality. *Journal of Abnormal and Social Psychology, 55,* 6–10.

Lyons, M. J., True, W. R., Eisen, S. A., Goldberg, J., Meyer, J. M., Faraone, S. V., Eaves, L. J., & Tsuang, M. T. (1995). Differential heritability of adult and juvenile antisocial traits. *Archives of General Psychiatry, 52,* 906–915.

Lyons-Ruth, K. (1996). Attachment relationships among children with aggressive behavior problems: The role of disorganized early attachment patterns. *Journal of Consulting and Clinical Psychology, 64,* 64–73.

MacCoun, R. J. (1993). Drugs and the law: A psychological analysis of drug prohibition. *Psychological Bulletin, 113,* 497–512.

MacDonald, M. (1981). *Mystical Bedlam: Madness, anxiety, and healing in seventeenth-century England.* Cambridge: Cambridge University Press.

Mace, F., Kratochwill, T. R., & Fiello, R. A. (1983). Positive treatment of aggressive behavior in a mentally retarded adult: A case study. *Behavior Therapy, 14,* 689–696.

MacLeod, A. K., & Byrne, A. (1996). Anxiety, depression, and the anticipation of future positive and negative experiences. *Journal of Abnormal Psychology, 105,* 286–289.

MacMillan, D. L., Keogh, B., & Jones, R. L. (1986). Special education research on mildly handicapped learners. In M. C. Wittrock (Ed.), *Handbook of research on teaching.* New York: Macmillan.

Madden, P. A. F., Heath, A. C., Rosenthal, N. E., & Martin, N. G. (1996). Seasonal changes in mood and behavior: The role of genetic factors. *Archives of General Psychiatry, 53,* 47–55.

Madle, R. A. (1990). Mental retardation in adulthood. In M. Hersen & C. Last (Eds.), *Handbook of child and adult psychopathology: A longitudinal perspective.* New York: Pergamon Press.

Magee, W. J., Eaton, W., Wittchen, B., Hans-Ulrich, C., McGonagle, K. A., & Kessler, R. C. (1996). Agoraphobia, simple phobia, and social phobia in the national comorbidity survey. *Archives of General Psychiatry, 53,* 159–168.

Magnusson, D., & Ohman, A. (1987). *Psychopathology: An interactional perspective.* New York: Academic Press.

Mahley, R. W., Nathan, B. P., & Pitas, R. E. (1996). Apolipoprotein E: Structure, function, and possible roles in Alzheimer's disease. *Annals of the New York Academy of Sciences, 777,* 139–145.

Mahoney, M. J. (1977). Reflections on the cognitive-learning trend in psychotherapy. *American Psychologist, 32,* 5–13.

Mahoney, M. J. (1980). *Abnormal psychology: Perspectives on human variance.* New York: Harper & Row.

Mahoney, M. J. (1993). Theoretical developments in the cognitive psychotherapies. *Journal of Consulting and Clinical Psychology, 61,* 187–193.

Mahoney, M. J., & Arnkoff, D. B. (1978). Cognitive and self-control therapies. In S. L. Garfield & A. E. Bergin (Eds.), *Handbook of psychotherapy and behavior change* (2nd ed.). New York: Wiley.

Mahoney, M. J., Lyddon, W., & Alford, D. (1989). An evaluation of the rational-emotive theory of psychotherapy. In M. E. Bernard & R. DiGiuseppe (Eds.), *Inside rational-emotive therapy: A critical appraisal of the theory and therapy of Albert Ellis.* New York: Academic Press.

Mai, F. M. (1995). Psychiatrists' attitudes to multiple personality disorder. *Canadian Journal of Psychiatry, 40,* 154–157.

Maier, S. F., & Laudenslager, M. (1985). Stress and health: Exploring the links. *Psychology Today, 19,* 44–49.

Maiuro, R. D., Cahn, T. S., Vitaliano, P. P., Wagner, B. C., & Zegree, J. B. (1988). Anger, hostility, and depression in domestically violent versus generally assaultive men and nonviolent control subjects. *Journal of Consulting and Clinical Psychology, 56,* 17–23.

Mak, Y. T., Chiu, H., Woo, J., Kay, R., Chan, Y. S., Hui, E., Sze, K. H., Lum, C., Kwok, T., & Pang, C. P. (1996). Apolipoprotein E genotype and Alzheimer's disease in Hong Kong elderly Chinese. *Neurology, 46,* 146–149.

Malamuth, N. M. (1986). Predictors of naturalistic sexual aggression. *Journal of Personality & Social Psychology, 50,* 953–962.

Malamuth, N. M., & Check, J. V. P. (1983). Sexual arousal to rape depictions: Individual differences. *Journal of Abnormal Psychology, 92,* 55–67.

Malaspina, D., Quitkin, H. M., & Kaufmann, C. A. (1992). Epidemiology and genetics of neuropsychiatric disorders. In S. C. Yudofsky & R. E. Hales (Eds.), *The American Psychiatric Press*

Textbook of Neuropsychiatry. Washington, DC: American Psychiatric Press.

Malcarne, V. L., Compas, B. E., Epping-Jordan, J. E., & Howell, D. C. (1995). Cognitive factors in adjustment to cancer: attributions to self-blame and perceptions of control. *Journal of Behavioral Medicine, 18,* 401–417.

Male, D., Champion, B., Cooke, A., & Owen, M. (1991). *Advanced immunology.* Philadelphia: Lippincott.

Maletzky, B., & Price, R. (1984). Public masturbation in men: Precursor to exhibitionism? *Journal of Sex Education and Therapy, 10,* 31–36.

Malinosky-Rummell, R., & Hansen, D. J. (1993). Long-term consequences of childhood physical abuse. *Psychological Bulletin, 114,* 68–79.

Manchi, M., & Cohen, P. (1990). Early childhood eating behaviour and adolescent eating disorders. *Journal of the American Academy of Child and Adolescent Psychiatry, 29,* 112–117.

Mann, B. J., & MacKenzie, E. P. (1996). Pathways among marital functioning, parental behaviors, and child behavior problems in school-age boys. *Journal of Consulting and Clinical Psychology, 25,* 183–191.

Mann, J. J., & Kapur, S. (1991). The emergence of suicidal ideation and behavior during antidepressant pharmacotherapy. *Archives of General Psychiatry, 48,* 1027–1033.

Mann, J. J., McBride, P. A., Brown, R. P., Linnoila, M., Leon, A. C., DeMeo, M., Mieczkowski, T., Myers, J. E., Stanley, M. (1992). Relationship between central and peripheral serotonin indexes in depressed and suicidal psychiatric inpatients. *Archives of General Psychiatry, 49,* 442–446.

Mannuzza, S., & Klein, R. (1992). Predictors of outcome of children with attention-deficit hyperactivity disorder. In G. Weiss (Ed.), *Child and adolescent psychiatric clinics of North America: Attention-deficit hyperactivity disorder* (pp. 567–578). Philadelphia: Saunders.

Mannuzza, S., Klein, R. G., Bessler, A., Malloy, P., & LaPadula, M. (1993). Adult outcome of hyperactive boys: Educational achievement, occupational rank, and psychiatric status. *Archives of General Psychiatry, 50,* 565–576.

Mannuzza, S., Klein, R. G., Bonagura, N., Malloy, P., Giampino, T. L., & Addalli, K. A. (1991). Hyperactive boys almost grown up: V. Replication of psychiatric status. *Archives of General Psychiatry, 48,* 77–83.

Mannuzza, S., Klein, R. G., Konig, P. H., & Giampino, T. L. (1989). Hyperactive boys almost grown up: IV. Criminality and its relationship to psychiatric status. *Archives of General Psychiatry, 46,* 1073–1079.

Manuck, S. B., Proietti, J. M., Rader, S. J., & Polefrone, J. M. (1985). Parental hypertension, affect, and cardiovascular response to cognitive challenge. *Psychosomatic Medicine, 47,* 189–200.

Marcus, J., Hans, S. Auerbach, J., & Auerbach, A. (1993). Children at risk for schizophrenia: The Jerusalem Infant Development Study. II. Neurobehavioral deficits at school age. *Archives of General Psychiatry, 50,* 797–809.

Marder, K., Tang, M. X., Cote, L., & Stern, Y. (1995). The frequency and associated risk factors for dementia in patients with Parkinson's disease. *Archives of Neurology, 52,* 695–701.

Marengo, J., Harrow, M., Sands, J., & Galloway, C. (1991). European versus U.S. data on the course of schizophrenia. *American Journal of Psychiatry, 148,* 606–611.

Margolin, G. (1987). Marital therapy: A cognitive-behavioral-affective approach. In N. Jacobson (Ed.), *Psychotherapists in clinical practice: Cognitive and behavioral perspectives.* New York: Guilford Press.

Margolin, G., John, R. S., & Gleberman, L. (1988). Affective responses to conflictual discussions in violent and nonviolent couples. *Journal of Consulting and Clinical Psychology, 56,* 24–33.

Margraf, J., & Ehlers, A. (1989). Etiological models of panic: Medical and biological aspects. In R. Baker (Ed.), *Panic disorder: Theory, research, and therapy.* Chicester, England: Wiley.

Margraf, J., & Schneider, S. (1991). *Outcome and active ingredients of cognitive-behavioral treatments for panic disorder.* Paper presented at the Annual Meeting of the Association for the Advancement of Behavior Therapy, November 26, New York.

Maris, R., Berman, A. L., Maltsberger, J. T., & Yufit, R. I. (Eds.). (1992). *Assessment and prediction of suicide.* New York: Guilford.

Maris, R. W. (1992). Forensic suicidology: Litigation of suicide cases and equivocal deaths. In B. Bongar (Ed.), *Suicide: Guidelines for assessment, management, and treatment.* New York: Oxford University Press.

Maris, R. W. (1992). How are suicides different? In R. Maris, A. L. Berman, J. T. Maltsberger & R. I. Yufit (Eds.), *Assessment and prediction of suicide.* New York, London: Guilford Press.

Markovitz, J. H., Matthews, K. A., Wing, R. R., Kuller, L. H., & Meilahn, E. (1991). Psychological, biological and health behavior predictors of blood pressure changes in middle-aged women. *Journal of Hypertension, 9,* 399–406.

Marks, I. M. (1981). Review of behavioral psychotherapy: Obsessive-compulsive disorders. *American Journal of Psychiatry, 138,* 584–592.

Marks, M. P., Basoglu, M., Alkubaisy, T., Sengun, S., & Marks, I. (1991). Are anxiety symptoms and catastrophic cognitions directly related? *Journal of Anxiety Disorders, 5,* 247–254.

Marlatt, G. A. (1978). Craving for alcohol, loss of control, and relapse: A cognitive-behavioral analysis. In P. E. Nathan, G. A. Marlatt & T. Loberg (Eds.), *Alcoholism: New directions in behavioral research and treatment.* New York: Plenum Press.

Marlatt, G. A., Demming, B., & Reid, J. (1973). Loss of control drinking in alcoholics. *Journal of Abnormal Psychology, 81,* 233–241.

Marlatt, G. A., & Gordon, J. R. (1980). Determinants of relapse: Implications for the maintenance of behavior change. In P. O. Davidson & S. M. Davidson (Eds.), *Behavioral medicine: Changing health lifestyles* (pp. 410–452). New York: Brunner/Mazel.

Marlatt, G. A., & Gordon, J. R. (1985). *Relapse prevention: Maintenance strategies in the treatment of addictive behaviors.* New York: Guilford Press.

Marshall, W. L., & Barbaree, H. E. (1990a). An integrated theory of the etiology of sexual offending. In W. Marshall, D. Laws & H. Barbaree (Eds.), *Handbook of sexual assault: Issues, theories, and treatment of the offender* (pp. 257–275). New York: Plenum Press.

Marshall, W. L., & Barbaree, H. E. (1990b). Outcome of comprehensive cognitive-behavioral treatment programs. In W. Marshall, D. Laws & H. Barbaree (Eds.), *Handbook of sexual assault: Issues, theories, and treatment of the offender.* New York: Plenum.

Marshall, W. L., Jones, R., Ward, T., Johnston, P., & Barbaree, H. E. (1991). Treatment outcome with sex offenders. *Clinical Psychology Review, 11,* 465–485.

Marshall, W. L., Laws, D. R., & Barbaree, H. E. (Eds.). (1990). *Handbook of sexual assault.* London: Plenum Press.

Martin, B., & Hoffman, J. A. (1990). Conduct disorders. In M. Lewis & S. M. Miller (Eds.), *Handbook of developmental psychopathology.* New York: Plenum Press.

Mash, E. J., Terdal, L. G., & Anderson, K. (1973). The Response-Class Matrix: A procedure for recording parent-child interactions. *Journal of Consulting and Clinical Psychology, 40,* 163–164.

Maslow, R. H. (1968). *Toward a psychology of being.* New York: Van Nostrand Rinehold.

Masserman, J. H., & Yum, K. S. (1946). An analysis of the effects of alcohol on experimental neurosis in cats. *Psychosomatic Medicine, 8,* 36–52.

Masten, A. S. (1990, August). Homeless children: Risk, trauma, and adjustment. Paper presented at the annual meeting of the American Psychological Association, Boston, MA.

Masters, J., Burish, T., Hollon, S. D., & Rimm, D. (1987). *Behavior therapy: Techniques and empirical findings.* San Diego: Harcourt Brace Jovanovich.

Masters, W. H., & Johnson, V. E. (1970). *Human sexual inadequacy.* Boston: Little, Brown.

Masters, W. H., & Johnson, V. E. (1966). *Human sexual response.* Boston: Little, Brown.

Masterson, J. (1976). *Psychotherapy of the borderline adult.* New York: Brunner/Mazel.

Mathews, A. M. (1985). Cognitive-behavioral models of anxiety. In E. Karas (Ed.), *Current issues in clinical psychology* (Vol. 2). New York: Plenum Press.

Matson, J., & Barrett, R. (1982). (Eds.), *Psychopathology in the mentally retarded.* New York: Grune & Stratton.

Matthews, K. A. (1988). Coronary heart disease and Type A behaviors: Update on and alternative to the Booth-Kewley and Friedman (1987) quantitative review. *Psychological Bulletin, 104,* 373–380.

Matthews, K. A., & Jennings, J. R. (1984). Cardiovascular responses of boys exhibiting the Type A behavior pattern. *Psychosomatic Medicine, 46,* 484–497.

Mavissakalian, M., Turner, S., Michelson, L., & Jacobs, R. (1985). Tricyclic antidepressants in obsessive-compulsive disorder: Antiobsessional or antidepressant agents? *American Journal of Psychiatry, 142,* 572–576.

Mayerhoff, D. I., Loebel, A. D., Alvir, J. M. J., Szymanski, S. R., Geisler, S. H., Borenstein, M., & Lieberman, J. A. (1994). The deficit state in first-episode schizophrenia. *American Journal of Psychiatry, 151,* 1417–1422.

Mayron, L. M., Ott, J. N., Nations, R., & Mayron, E. L. (1974). Light, radiation, and academic behavior: Initial studies on the effects of full-spectrum lighting and radiation shielding on behavior and academic performance of school children. *Academic Therapy, 10,* 33–47.

Mays, V. M., & Albee, G. W. (1992). Psychotherapy and ethnic minorities. In D. K. Freedheim (Ed.), *History of psychotherapy: A century of change* (pp. 552–570). Washington, DC: American Psychological Association.

Mazur, E., Wolchik, S. A., & Sandler, I. (1992). Negative cognitive errors and positive illusions for negative divorce events: Predictors of children's psychological adjustment. *Journal of Abnormal Child Psychology, 20,* 523–542.

McAdoo, W. G., & DeMeyer, M. K. (1978). Personality characteristics of parents. In M. Rutter & E. Schopler (Eds.), *Autism: A reappraisal of concepts and treatment.* New York: Plenum Press.

McArdle, P., O'Brien, G., & Kolvin, I. (1995). Hyperactivity: Prevalence and relationship with conduct disorder. *Journal of Child Psychology and Psychiatry, 36,* 279–303.

McCord, J. (1988). Identifying developmental paradigms leading to alcoholism. *Journal of Studies on Alcohol, 49,* 357–362.

McCrady, B. S. (1994). Alcoholics anonymous and behavior therapy: Can habits be treated as diseases? Can diseases be treated as habits? *Journal of Consulting and Clinical Psychology, 62,* 1159–1166.

McCubbin, J. A., Surwitt, R. S., & Williams, R. B. (1985). Endogenous opiate peptides, stress reactivity, and risk for hypertension. *Hypertension, 7,* 808–811.

McFall, M. E., & Wollersheim, J. P. (1979). Obsessive-compulsive neurosis: A cognitive-behavioral formulation and approach to treatment. *Cognitive Therapy and Research, 3,* 333–348.

McFarlane, J. W., Allen, L., & Honzik, M. P. (1954). *A developmental study of the behavior problems of normal children between 21 months and 14 years.* Berkeley: University of California Press.

McFarlane, W. R., Lukens, E., Link, B., Dushay, R., Deakins, S. A., Newmark, M., Dunne, E. J., Horen, B., & Toran, J. (1995). Multiple-family groups and psychoeducation in the treatment of schizophrenia. *Archives of General Psychiatry, 52,* 679–687.

McGee, R., Silva, P. A., & Williams, S. (1984). Behavior problems in a population of seven-year-old children: Prevalence, stability, and types of disorder—a research report. *Journal of Child Psychology and Psychiatry, 25,* 251–259.

McGinnies, E. (1949). Emotionality and perceptual defense. *Psychological Review, 56,* 244–251.

McGlashan, T. H., & Fenton, W. S. (1991). Classical subtypes for schizophrenia: Literature review for DSM-IV. *Schizophrenia Bulletin, 17,* 609–623.

McGrath, M. E. (1984). First person account: Where did I go? *Schizophrenia Bulletin, 10,* 638–640.

McGue, M., Pickens, R., & Svikis, D. (1992). Sex and age effects on the inheritance of alcohol problems: A twin study. *Journal of Abnormal Psychology, 101,* 3–17.

McGuffin, P., Katz, R., Watkins, S., & Rutherford, J. (1996). A hospital-based twin register of the heritability of DSM-IV unipolar depression. *Archives of General Psychiatry, 53,* 129–136.

McIntosh, J. L. (1992). Suicide of the elderly. In B. Bonger (Ed.), *Suicide: Guidelines for assessment, management, and treatment.* New York: Oxford University Press.

McKim, W. A. (1986). *Drugs and behavior: An introduction to behavioral pharmacology.* Englewood Cliffs, NJ: Prentice-Hall.

McLaren, J., & Bryson, S. E. (1987). Review of recent epidemiological studies of mental retardation: Prevalence, associated disorders, and etiology. *American Journal of Mental Retardation, 92,* 243–254.

McLennan, J. M., Lord, C., & Schopler, E. (1993). Sex differences in higher functioning people with autism. *Journal of Autism and Developmental Disorders, 23,* 217–228.

McLeod, J. D. (1994). Anxiety disorders and marital quality. *Journal of Abnormal Psychology, 103,* 767–776.

McMahon, R. C. (1980). Genetic etiology in the hyperactive child syndrome: A critical review. *American Journal of Orthopsychiatry, 50,* 145–150.

McNally, R. J., Amir, N., & Lipke, H. J. (1996). Subliminal processing of threat cues in posttraumatic stress disorder? *Journal of Anxiety Disorders, 10,* 115–128.

McNally, R. J., & Eke, M. (1996). Anxiety sensitivity, suffocation fear, and breath-holding duration as predictors of response to carbon dioxide challenge. *Journal of Abnormal Psychology, 105,* 146–149.

McNaughton, M., Smith, L., Patterson, T., & Grant, I. (1990). Stress, social support, coping resources, and immune status in the elderly. *Journal of Nervous and Mental Disease, 178,* 460–461.

McNeal, E. T., & Cimbolic, P. (1986). Antidepressants and biochemical theories of depression. *Psychological Bulletin, 99,* 361–374.

McNeil, D. W., Ries, B. J., Taylor, L. J., Boone, M. L., Carter, L. E., Turk, C. L., & Lewin, M. R. (1995). Comparison of social phobia subtypes using Stroop tests. *Journal of Anxiety Disorders, 9,* 47–57.

McNeill, E. (1967). *The quiet furies.* Englewood Cliffs, NJ: Prentice-Hall.

Mednick, S. A., Gabrielli, W. F., & Hutchings, B. (1984). Genetic influences in criminal convictions: Evidence from an adoption cohort. *Science, 234,* 891–894.

Mednick, S. A., Machon, R. A., Huttunen, M. O., & Bonett, D. (1988). Adult schizophrenia following prenatal exposure to an influenza epidemic. *Archives of General Psychiatry, 45,* 189–192.

Meehan, P. J., Lamb, J. A., Saltzman, L. E., & O'Carroll, P. W. (1992). Attempted suicide among young adults: Progress toward a meaningful estimate of prevalence. *American Journal of Psychiatry, 149,* 41–44.

Meehl, P. E. (1959). Some ruminations on the validation of clinical procedures. *Canadian Journal of Psychology, 13,* 102–128.

Meehl, P. E. (1962). Schizotaxia, schizotypy, schizophrenia. *American Psychologist, 17,* 827–838.

Meehl, P. E., & Rosen, A. (1955). Antecedent probability and the efficiency of psychometric signs, patterns, or cutting scores. *Psychological Bulletin, 52,* 194–216.

Mehlman, P. T., Higley, J. D., Faucher, I., Lilly, A. A., Taub, D. M., Vickers, J., Suomi, S. J., & Linnoila, M. (1994). Low CSF 5-HIAA concentrations and severe aggression and impaired impulse control in nonhuman primates. *American Journal of Psychiatry, 151,* 1485–1491.

Meichenbaum, D. (1971). Examination of model characteristics in reducing avoidance behavior. *Journal of Personality and Social Psychology, 17,* 298–307.

Meichenbaum, D. (1977). *Cognitive behavior modification: An integrative approach.* New York: Plenum Press.

Meichenbaum, D. (1985). *Stress inoculation training.* New York: Pergamon Press.

Meichenbaum, D. (1993). Changing conceptions of cognitive behavior modification: Retrospect and prospect. *Journal of Consulting and Clinical Psychology, 61,* 202–205.

Meichenbaum, D., & Gilmore, J. B. (1982). Resistance from a cognitive-behavioral perspective. In P. L. Wachtel (Ed.), *Resistance: Psychodynamic and behavioral approaches.* New York: Plenum.

Meichenbaum, D., & Turk, D. (1987). *Facilitating treatment adherence: A practitioner's guidebook.* New York: Plenum Press.

Mello, N. K. (1975). A semantic aspect of alcoholism. In H. D. Cappell & A. E. LeBlanc (Eds.), *Biological and behavioral approaches to drug dependence.* Toronto: Addiction Research Foundation.

Melman, A., & Tiefer, L. (1992). Surgery for erectile disorders: Operative procedures and psychological issues. In R. Rosen & S. Leiblum (Eds.), *Erectile disorders: Assessment and treatment.* New York: Guilford Press.

Meltzer, H. Y. (1995). Clozapine: Is another view valid? *American Journal of Psychiatry, 152,* 821–825.

Menzies, R., & Webster, C. D. (1995). Construction and validation of risk assessments in a six-year follow-up of forensic patients: A tridemensional analysis. *Journal of Consulting and Clinical Psychology, 63,* 766–778.

Merckelbach, H., de Jong, P. J., Muris, P., & van den Hout, M. A. (1996). The etiology of specific phobias: A review. *Clinical Psychology Review, 16,* 337–361.

Merikangas, K. R., & Weissman, M. M. (1986). Epidemiology of DSM-III Axis II personality disorders. In A. J. Frances & R. E. Hales (Eds.), *The American Psychiatric Association Annual Review.* Washington, DC: American Psychiatric Press.

Merskey, H. (1994). The artifactual nature of multiple personality disorder: Comments on Charles Barton's "Backstage in psychiatry: The multiple personality disorder controversy." *Dissociation Progress in the Dissociative Disorders, 7,* 173–175.

Merskey, H. (1995). Multiple personality disorder and false memory syndrome. *British Journal of Psychiatry, 166,* 281–283.

Mesibov, G. B., & Shea, V. (1996). Full inclusion and students with autism. *Journal of Autism and Developmental Disorders, 26,* 337–346.

Meyer-Bahlburg, H. F. L., Ehrhardt, A. A., Rosen, L. R., Gruen, R. S., Veridiano, N. P., Vann, F. H., & Neuwalder, H. F. (1995). Prenatal estrogens and the development of homosexual orientation. *Developmental Psychology, 31,* 12–21.

Michelson, L. (1987). Cognitive-behavioral assessment and treatment of agoraphobia. In L. Michelson & M. Ascher (Eds.), *Anxiety and stress disorders: Cognitive-behavioral assessment and treatment.* New York: Guilford Press.

Michelson, L., & Marchione, K. (1989). *Cognitive, behavioral, and physiologically based treatments of agoraphobia: A comparative outcome study.* Paper presented at the Annual Meeting of the Association for the Advancement of Behavior Therapy, November, Washington, DC.

Michelson, L., Mavissakalian, M., & Marchione, K. (1985). Cognitive and behavioral treatments of agoraphobia: Clinical, behavioral, and psychophysiological outcomes. *Journal of Consulting and Clinical Psychology, 53,* 913–925.

Michelson, L., & Ray, W. (1996). (Eds.) *Handbook of dissociation: Theoretical, empirical, and clinical perspectives.* New York: Plenum Press.

Miklowitz, D. J., Goldstein, M., Nuechterlein, K., Snyder, K., & Mintz, J. (1988). Family factors and the course of bipolar affective disorder. *Archives of General Psychiatry, 51,* 48–57.

Miklowitz, D. J., Velligan, D. I., Goldstein, M. J., Nuechterlein, K. H., Gitlin, M. J., Ranlett, G., & Doane, J. A. (1991). Communication deviance in families of schizophrenic and manic patients. *Journal of Abnormal Psychology, 100,* 163–173.

Milich, R., Loney, J., & Landau, S. (1982). The independent dimensions of hyperactivity and aggression: A validation with playroom observation data. *Journal of Abnormal Psychology, 91,* 183–198.

Milich, R., Loney, J., & Roberts, M. (1986). Playroom observations of activity level and sustained attention: Two-year stability. *Journal of Consulting and Clinical Psychology, 54,* 272–274.

Miller, I. W., Norman, W. H., & Keitner, G. I. (1989). Cognitive-behavioral treatment of depressed inpatients: Six- and twelve-month follow-up. *American Journal of Psychiatry, 146,* 1274–1279.

Miller, L. C., Barrett, C. L., & Hampe, E. (1974). Phobias of childhood in a prescientific era. In S. Davids (Ed.), *Child personality and psychopathology.* New York: Wiley.

Miller, T. Q., Smith, T. W., Turner, C. W., Guijarro, M. L., & Hallet, A. J. (1996). A meta-analytic review of research on hostility and physical health. *Psychological Bulletin, 119,* 322–348.

Miller, W., Benefield, G., & Tonigan, J. S. (1993). Enhancing motivation for change in problem drinking: A controlled comparison of two therapist styles. *Journal of Consulting and Clinical Psychology, 61,* 455–461.

Miller, W., Hedrick, K., & Taylor, C. (1983). Addictive behaviors and life problems before and after behavioral treatment of problem drinkers. *Addictive Behaviors, 8,* 403–412.

Miller-Perrin, C. L., & Wurtele, S. K. (1988). The child sexual abuse prevention movement: A critical analysis of primary and secondary approaches. *Clinical Psychology Review, 8,* 313–329.

Millon, T. (1983). An integrative theory of personality and psychopathology. In T. Millon (Ed.), *Theories of personality and psychopathology.* New York: Holt, Rinehart & Winston.

Mineka, S., Davidson, M., Cook, M., & Keir, R. (1984). Observational conditioning of snake fear in rhesus monkeys. *Journal of Abnormal Psychology, 93,* 355–372.

Minshew, N. J. (1996). Brief report: Brain mechanisms in autism— Functional and structural abnormalities. *Journal of Autism and Developmental Disorders, 26,* 205–209.

Mintz, L. I., Lieberman, R. P., Miklowitz, D. J., & Mintz, J. (1987). Expressed emotion: A call for partnership among relatives, patients, and professionals. *Schizophrenia Bulletin, 13,* 227–235.

Minuchin, S., (1974). *Families and family therapy.* Cambridge, MA: Harvard University Press.

Minuchin, S., Lee, W., & Simon, G. M. (1996). *Mastering family therapy: Journeys of growth and transformation.* New York: Wiley.

Minuchin, S., Roseman, B. L., & Baker, L. (1978). *Psychosomatic families: Anorexia nervosa in context.* Cambridge, MA: Harvard University Press.

Mischel, W. (1968). *Personality and assessment.* New York: Wiley.

Mitchell, S. A. (1988). *Relational concepts in psychoanalysis.* Cambridge, MA: Harvard University Press.

Modestin, J. (1992). Multiple personality disorder in Switzerland. *American Journal of Psychiatry, 149,* 88–92.

Moffitt, T. E. (1990). Juvenile delinquency and attention deficit disorder: Boy's developmental trajectories from age 3 to age 5. *Child Development, 61,* 893–910.

Moffitt, T. E. (1993a). Adolescence-limited and life course persistent antisocial behavior: A developmental taxonomy. *Psychological Review, 100,* 674–701.

Moffitt, T. E. (1993b). The neuropsychology of conduct disorder. *Development and Psychopathology, 5,* 135–151.

Moffitt, T. E., Lynam, D. R., & Silva, P. A. (1994). Neuropsychological tests predicting persistent male delinquency. *Criminology, 32,* 277–300.

Mohler, H., & Okada, T. (1977). Benzodiazepine reception: Demonstration in the central nervous system. *Science, 198,* 849–851.

Mohr, D. C., & Beutler, L. E. (1990). Erectile dysfunction: A review of diagnostic and treatment procedures. *Clinical Psychology Review, 10,* 123–150.

Monahan, J. (1993). Limiting therapist exposure to Tarasoff liability: Guidelines for risk containment. *American Psychologist, 48,* 242–250.

Monahan, J., & Steadman, H. J. (1984). *Crime and mental disorder.* Washington, DC: National Institute of Justice.

Moncher, M., Holden, G., & Trimble, J. (1990). Substance abuse among Native-American youth. *Journal of Consulting and Clinical Psychology, 58,* 408–415.

Money, J. (1988). *Gay, straight, and in-between.* New York: Oxford University Press.

Monti, P. M., Rohsenow, D. J., Rubonis, A., Niaura, R., Sirota, A., Colby, S., Goddard, P., & Abrams, D. B. (1993). Cue exposure with coping skills treatment for male alcoholics: A preliminary investigation. *Journal of Consulting and Clinical Psychology, 61,* 1011–1019.

Moos, R. H., Bromet, E., Tsu, V., & Moos, B. (1979). Family characteristics and the outcome of treatment for alcoholics. *Quarterly Journal of Studies on Alcohol, 40,* 78–88.

Moos, R. H., & Moos, B. S. (1986). *Family Environment Scale manual* (rev. ed.). Palo Alto, CA: Consulting Psychologists.

Morbidity and Mortality Weekly Report. (1992, September 11). Vol. 41, No. 136, pp. 664–668.

Morris, R. D. (1988). Classification of learning disabilities: Old problems and new approaches. *Journal of Consulting and Clinical Psychology, 56,* 789–794.

Mortimer, H. (1995). Welcoming young children with special needs into mainstream education. *Support for Learning, 10,* 164–169.

Mosbach, P., & Leventhal, H. (1988). Peer group identification and smoking: Implications for intervention. *Journal of Abnormal Psychology, 97,* 238–245.

Mott, F. L., & Haurin, R. J. (1988). Linkages between sexual activity and alcohol and drug use among American adolescents. *Family Planning Perspectives, 20,* 128–136.

Mudford, O. C. (1995). An intrusive and restrictive alternative to contingent shock. *Behavioral Interventions, 10,* 87–99.

Mueser, K. T., Bellack, A. S., Morrison, R. L., & Wade, J. H. (1990a). Gender, social competence, and symptomatology in schizophrenia: A longitudinal analysis. *Journal of Abnormal Psychology, 99,* 138–147.

Mueser, K. T., Yarnold, P. R., Levinson, D. F., Singh, H., Bellack, A. S., Kee, K., Morrison, R. L., & Yadalam, K. G. (1990b). Prevalence of substance abuse in schizophrenia: Demographic and clinical correlates. *Schizophrenia Bulletin, 16,* 31–56.

Mulatu, M. (1995). Prevalence and risk factors for psychopathology in Ethiopian children. *Journal of the American Academy of Child and Adolescent Psychiatry, 34,* 100–109.

Murphy, C. M., & O'Leary, K. D. (1989). Psychological aggression predicts physical aggression in early marriage. *Journal of Consulting and Clinical Psychology, 57,* 579–582.

Myers, J. K., Weissman, M. M., Tischler, G. L., Holzer, C. E., Leaf, P. J., Orvaschel, H., Anthony, J. C., Boyd, J. H., Burke, J. D.,

Kramer, M., & Stoltzman, R. (1984). Six-month prevalence of psychiatric disorders in three communities: 1980 to 1982. *Archives of General Psychiatry, 41,* 959–967.

Myers, R. H., Schaefer, E. J., Wilson, P. W., D'Ahostino, R., Ordovas, J. M., Espino, A., Au, R., White, R. F., Knoefel, J. E., Cobb, J. L., McNulty, K. A., Beiser, A., & Wolf, P. A. (1996). Apolipoprotein E epsilon 4 association with dementia in a population-based study: The Farmington study. *Neurology, 46,* 673–677.

Myles, B. S., Simpson, R. L., & Johnson, S. (1995). Students with higher functioning autistic disorder: Do we know who they are? *Focus on Autistic Behavior, 9,* 1–12.

Narrow, W. E., Regier, D. A., Rae, D. S., Manderschied, R. W., & Locke, B. Z. (1993). Use of services by persons with mental and addictive disorders: Findings from the National Institute of Mental Health Epidemiologic Catchment Area Program. *Archives of General Psychiatry, 50,* 95–107.

Nathan, P. E. (1988). The addictive personality is the behavior of the addict. *Journal of Consulting and Clinical Psychology, 56,* 183–188.

Nathan, P. E., & McCrady, B. (1987). Bases for the use of abstinence as a goal in the behavioral treatment of alcohol abusers. *Drugs and Society, 2,* 455–476.

Nathan, P. E., & Skinstad, A. (1987). Outcomes of treatment for alcohol problems: Current methods, problems, and results. *Journal of Consulting and Clinical Psychology, 55,* 332–340.

Nathan, S. G. (1986). The epidemiology of the DSM-III psychosexual dysfunctions. *Journal of Sex and Marital Therapy, 12,* 267–281.

National Advisory Mental Health Council (1995). *Basic behavioral science research for mental health: A national investment.* Washington, DC: U.S. Government Printing Office.

National Advisory Mental Health Council. (1990). *National plan for research on child and adolescent mental disorders.* Washington, DC: National Institute of Mental Health.

National Advisory Mental Health Council. (1993). *Health care reform for Americans with severe mental illness: Report of the National Advisory Mental Health Council.* Washington, DC: National Institute of Mental Health.

National Center for Health Statistics. (1992). Advance report of final mortality statistics, 1989. *NCHS Monthly Vital Statistics Report, 40* (8).

National Institute of Drug Abuse. (1992). National Household Survey on Drug Abuse. *Statistical Abstract of the United States 1992* (112th ed.). U.S. Dept. of Commerce, Bureau of the Census.

Neal, A. M., & Knisley, H. (1995). What are African American children afraid of? II. A twelve-month follow-up. *Journal of Anxiety Disorders, 9,* 151–161.

Neal, A. M., Lilly, R. S., & Zakis, S. (1993). What are African-American children afraid of: A preliminary study. *Journal of Anxiety Disorders, 7,* 129–139.

Neal, A. M., & Turner, S. M. (1991). Anxiety disorders research with African Americans: Current status. *Psychological Bulletin, 109,* 400–410.

Nee, L. E., Caine, E. D., & Polinsky, R. J. (1980). Gilles de la Tourette syndrome: Clinical and family study in 50 cases. *Annals of Neurology, 7,* 41–49.

Neisser, U., Boodoo, G., Bouchard, T. J., Boykin, A. W., Brody, N., Ceci, S. J., Halpern, D. F., Loehlin, J. C., Perloff, R., Sternberg, R. J., & Urbina, S. (1996). Intelligence: Knowns and unknowns. *American Psychologist, 51,* 77–101.

Nelson, W. M., & Finch, A. (1995). *"Keeping your cool": The anger-management workbook.* Ardmore, Pa.: Workbook.

Neumann, C. S., Grimes, K., Walker, E. F., & Baum, K. (1995). Developmental pathways to schizophrenia: Behavioral subtypes. *Journal of Abnormal Psychology, 104,* 558–566.

Nevid, J. S., Javier, R. A., & Moulton, J. L. (1996). Factors predicting participant attrition in a community-based, culturally specific smoking-cessation program for Hispanic smokers. *Health Psychology, 15,* 226–229.

Newcomb, M., & Bentler, P. (1988). Impact of adolescent drug use and social support on problems of young adults: A longitudinal study. *Journal of Abnormal Psychology, 97,* 64–75.

Newman, D., Moffitt, T., Caspi, A., Magdol, L., et al. (1996). Psychiatric disorder in a birth cohort of young adults: Prevalence, comorbidity, clinical significance, and new case incidence from ages 11–21. *Journal of Consulting and Clinical Psychology, 64,* 552–562.

Newman, F. L., Griffin, B. P., Black, W., & Page, S. E. (1989). Linking level of care to level of need: Assessing the need for mental health care for nursing home residents. *American Psychologist, 44,* 1315–1325.

Newman, J. P., & Kosson, D. S. (1986). Passive avoidance learning in psychopathic and nonpsychopathic offenders. *Journal of Abnormal Psychology, 95,* 257–263.

Newton, T. L., & Kiecolt-Glaser, J. K. (1995). Hostility and erosion of marital quality during early marriage. *Journal of Behavioral Medicine, 18,* 601–619.

Nezu, A., Nezu, C., & Peri, M. (1989). *Problem-solving therapy for depression: Theory, research, and clinical guidelines.* New York: Wiley.

Ng, V. W. (1990). *Madness in late imperial China: From illness to deviance.* Oklahoma City: University of Oklahoma Press.

Nichols, M. (1984). *Family therapy: Concepts and methods.* Needham, MA: Allyn & Bacon.

Nicholson, R. S., & Kugler, K. E. (1991). Competent and incompetent criminal defendants: A quantitative review of comparative research. *Psychological Bulletin, 109,* 355–370.

Nides, M. A., Rakos, R. F., Gonzales, D., Murray, R. P., Tashkin, D. P., & Bjornson-Benson, W. M. (1995). Predictors of initial smoking cessation and relapse through the first 2 years of the lung health study. *Journal of Consulting and Clinical Psychology, 63,* 60–69.

Nietzel, M. Y., Russell, R. L., Hemmings, K. A., & Gretter, M. L. (1987). Clinical significance of psychotherapy for unipolar depression: A meta-analytic approach to social comparison. *Journal of Consulting and Clinical Psychology, 55,* 156–161.

Nigg, J. T., & Goldsmith, H. H. (1994). Genetics of personality disorders: Perspectives from personality and psychopathology research. *Psychological Bulletin, 115,* 346–380.

Nigg, J. T., Lohr, N. E., Westen, D., Gold, L. J., & Silk, K. R. (1992). Malevolent object representations in borderline personality disorder and major depression. *Journal of Abnormal Psychology, 101,* 61–67.

Nisbet, R. E. (1993). Violence and U.S. regional culture. *American Psychologist, 48,* 441–449.

Nisbett, R. E., & Ross, L. (1980). *Human inference: Strategies and shortcomings of social judgment.* Englewood Cliffs, NJ: Prentice-Hall.

Nobler, M. S., Sackeim, H. A., Prohovnik, I., Moeller, J. R., Mukherjee, S., Schnur, D. B., Prudic, J., & Devanand, D. P. (1994). Regional cerebral blood flow in mood disorders, III. *Archives of General Psychiatry, 51,* 884–897.

Nolen-Hoeksema, S. N. (1987). Sex differences in unipolar depression: Evidence and theory. *Psychological Bulletin, 101,* 259–282.

Nolen-Hoeksema, S. N. (1990). *Sex differences in depression.* Stanford: Stanford University Press.

Nolen-Hoeksema, S. N. (1991). Responses to depression and their effects on the duration of depressive episodes. *Journal of Abnormal Psychology, 100,* 569–582.

Nolen-Hoeksema, S. N., Morrow, J., & Fredrickson, B. L. (1993). Response styles and the duration of episodes of depressed mood. *Journal of Abnormal Psychology, 102,* 20–28.

Nopoulos, P., Torres, I., Flaum, M., Andreasen, N. C., Ehrhardt, J. C., & Yuh, W. T. C. (1995). Brain morphology in first-episode schizophrenia. *American Journal of Psychiatry, 152,* 1721–1723.

Norcross, J. C., & Goldfried, M. (1992). *Handbook of psychotherapy integration.* New York: Basic Books.

Norcross, J. C., & Prochaska, J. (1988). A study of eclectic (and integrative) views revisited. *Professional Psychology: Research and Practice, 19,* 170–174.

Norden, K. A., Klein, D. N., Donaldson, S. K., Pepper, C. M., & Klein, L. (1995). Reports of the early home environment in DSM-III-R personality disorders. *Journal of Personality Disorders, 9,* 213–223.

Norquist, G., & Wells, K. (1991). Mental health needs of the uninsured. *Archives of General Psychiatry, 48,* 475–478.

Norton, G. R., Cox, B. J., Asmundson, G. J. G., & Maser, J. D. (1995). The growth of research on anxiety disorders during the 1980s. *Journal of Anxiety Disorders, 9,* 75–85.

Nuechterlein, K. H., & Dawson, M. E. (1984). Information processing and attentional functioning in the developmental course of schizophrenic disorders. *Schizophrenia Bulletin, 10,* 160–203.

Nuechterlein, K. H., Dawson, M. E., Gitlin, M., Ventura, J., Goldstein, M. J., Snyder, K. S., Yee, C. M., & Mintz, J. (1992). Developmental processes in schizophrenic disorders: Longitudinal studies of vulnerability and stress. *Schizophrenia Bulletin, 18,* 387–426.

Nwaefuna, A. (1981). Anorexia nervosa in a developing country. *British Journal of Psychiatry, 138,* 270–271.

Nye, C. L., Zucker, R. A., & Fitzgerald, H. E. (1995). Early intervention in the path to alcohol problems through conduct problems: Treatment involvement and child behavior change. *Journal of Consulting and Clinical Psychology, 63,* 831–840.

O'Brien, C. P. (1996). Recent developments in the pharmacotherapy of substance abuse. *Journal of Consulting and Clinical Psychology, 64,* 677–686.

O'Connell, R. A., Mayo, J. A., Flatow, J., Cuthbertson, B., & O'Brien, B. E. (1991). Outcome of bipolar disorder on long-term treatment with lithium. *British Journal of Psychiatry, 159,* 123–129.

O'Connor, D. W., Pollitt, P. A., Roth, M., Brook, P. B., & Reiss, B. B. (1990). Memory complaints and impairment in normal, depressed, and demented elderly person identified in a community survey. *Archives of General Psychiatry, 47,* 224–227.

O'Connor, E. A., Carbonari, J. P., & DiClemente, C. C. (1996). Gender and smoking cessation: A factor structure comparison of processes of change. *Journal of Consulting and Clinical Psychology, 64,* 130–138.

O'Connor, N., & Hermelin, B. (1988). Annotation: Low intelligence and special abilities. *Journal of Child Psychology and Psychiatry, 29,* 391–396.

O'Donnell, C. R. (1995). Firearm deaths among children and youth. *American Psychologist, 50,* 771–776.

O'Donnell, J., Hawkins, J. D., & Abbott, R. D. (1995). Predicting serious delinquency and substance use among aggressive boys. *Journal of Consulting and Clinical Psychology, 63,* 529–537.

O'Farrell, T. J., & Murphy, C. M. (1995). Marital violence before and after alcoholism treatment. *Journal of Consulting and Clinical Psychology, 63,* 256–262.

O'Hare, W., Pollard, K., Mann, T., & Kent, M. (1991). African-Americans in the 1990's. *Population Bulletin, 46,* No. 11. Washington, D.C.: Population Reference Bureau, Inc.

O'Leary, K. D. (1980). Pills or skills for hyperactive children. *Journal of Applied Behavior Analysis, 13,* 191–204.

O'Leary, K. D. (1988). Physical aggression between spouses: A social learning theory perspective. In V. B. Van Hasselt, R. L. Morrison, A. S. Bellack & M. Hersen (Eds.), *Handbook of family violence.* New York: Plenum Press.

O'Leary, K. D., Barling, J., Arias, I., Rosenbaum, A., Malone, J., & Tyree, A. (1989). Prevalence and stability of physical aggression between spouses: A longitudinal analysis. *Journal of Consulting and Clinical Psychology, 57,* 263–268.

O'Leary, K. D., Pelham, W. E., Rosenbaum, A., & Price, G. H. (1976). Behavioral treatment of hyperkinetic children: An experimental evaluation of its usefulness. *Clinical Pediatrics, 15,* 510–515.

O'Leary, K. D., Rosenbaum, A., & Hughes, P. C. (1978). Fluorescent lighting: A purported source of hyperactive behavior. *Journal of Abnormal Child Psychology, 6,* 285–289.

O'Leary, K. D., & Wilson, G. T. (1987). *Behavior therapy: Application and outcome* (2nd ed.). Englewood Cliffs, NJ: Prentice-Hall.

Obrist, P. A. (1981). *Cardiovascular psychophysiology: A perspective.* New York: Plenum.

Oetting, E. R., & Beauvais, F. (1990). Adolescent drug use: Findings of national and local surveys. *Journal of Consulting and Clinical Psychology, 58,* 385–394.

Offord, D. R., Boyle, M. C., & Racine, Y. (1991). The epidemiology of antisocial behavior in childhood and adolescence. In D. Pepler & K. H. Rubin (Eds.), *The development and treatment of childhood aggression.* Hillsdale, NJ: Erlbaum.

Ogata, S. N., Silk, K. R., & Goodrich, S. (1990). Childhood sexual and physical abuse in adult patients with borderline personality disorder. *American Journal of Psychiatry, 147,* 1008–1013.

Ohman, A., & Soares, J. J. F. (1994). Unconscious anxiety: Phobic responses to masked stimuli. *Journal of Abnormal Psychology, 103,* 231–240.

Oldham, J. M., Skodol, A. E., Kellman, H. D., Hyler, S. E., Doidge, N., Rosnick, L., & Gallaher, P. E. (1995). Comorbidity of Axis I and Axis II disorders. *American Journal of Psychiatry, 152,* 571–578.

Olfson, M., & Klerman, G. L. (1993). Trends in the prescription of antidepressants by office-based psychiatrists. *American Journal of Psychiatry, 150,* 571–577.

Olichney, J. M., Hansen, L. A., Galasko, D., Saitoh, T., Hofstetter, C. R., Katzman, R., & Thal, L. J. (1996). The apolipoprotein epsilon 4 allele is associated with increased neuritic plaques and cerebral amyloid angiopathy in Alzheimer's disease and Lewy body variant. *Neurology, 47,* 190–196.

Olivardia, R., & Pope, H. G. (1995). Eating disorders in college men. *American Journal of Psychiatry, 152,* 1279–1285.

Oliver, J. E. (1985). Successive generations of child maltreatment: Social, and medical disorders in the parents. *British Journal of Psychiatry, 147,* 484–490.

Oliver, J. E. (1988). Successive generations of child maltreatment: The children. *British Journal of Psychiatry, 153,* 543–553.

Ollendick, T. H., & King, N. (1991). Origins of childhood fears. *Behaviour Research and Therapy, 29,* 117–123.

Ollendick, T. H., & Mayer, J. A. (1984). School phobia. In S. Turner (Ed.), *Behavioral theories and treatment of anxiety.* New York: Plenum Press.

Olson, D., Portner, J., & Lavee, Y. (1985). *Faces III.* Family Social Science, University of Minnesota, St. Paul, MN.

Oquendo, M. A. (1995). Differential diagnosis of ataque de nervios. *American Journal of Orthopsychiatry, 65,* 60–65.

Orlinsky, D. E., & Howard, K. I. (1986). Process and outcome in psychotherapy. In S. Garfield & A. E. Bergin (Eds.), *Handbook of psychotherapy and behavior change* (3rd ed.). New York: Wiley.

Osofsky, J. D. (1995). The effects of exposure to violence on young children. *American Psychologist, 50,* 782–788.

Ossip-Klein, D. J., Giovino, G. A., Megahed, N., Black, P. M., Emont, S. L., Stiggins, J., Shulman, E., & Moore, L. (1991). Effects of a smokers' hotline: Results of a 10-county self-help trial. *Journal of Consulting and Clinical Psychology, 59,* 325–332.

Ost, L. G. (1991). *Cognitive therapy versus applied relaxation in the treatment of panic disorder.* Paper presented at the European

Association of Behavior Therapy Convention, September, Oslo, Norway.

Overmier, J. B., & Seligman, M. E. P. (1967). Effects of inescapable shock upon subsequent escape and avoidance learning. *Journal of Comparative and Physiological Psychology, 63,* 23–33.

Oyama, F., Shimada, H., Oyama, R., & Ihara, Y. (1995). Apolipoprotein E genotype, Alzheimer's pathologies and related gene expression in the aged population. *Brain Research. Molecular Brain Research, 29,* 92–98.

Padesky, C. A. (1987). *Cognitive therapy treatment for avoidant personality disorder.* Unpublished manuscript.

Palace, E. M. (1995). Modification of dysfunctional patterns of sexual response through autonomic arousal and false physiological feedback. *Journal of Consulting and Clinical Psychology, 63,* 604–615.

Pantony, K., & Caplan, P. J. (1991). Delusional dominating personality disorder: A modest proposal for identifying some consequences of rigid masculine socialization. *Canadian Psychology, 32,* 120–135.

Park, S., Holzman, P. S., & Goldman-Rakic, P. S. (1995). Spatial working memory deficits in the relatives of schizophrenic patients. *Archives of General Psychiatry, 52,* 821–828.

Parker, G., Tupling, H., & Brown, L. B. (1979). A parental bonding instrument. *British Journal of Medical Psychology, 52,* 1–10.

Parkes, M. C., Benjamin, B., & Fitzgerald, R. G. (1969). Broken heart: A statistical study of mortality among widowers. *British Medical Journal, 1,* 740–743.

Parnas, J., Cannon, T., Jacobsen, B., Schulsinger, H., Schulsinger, F., & Mednick, S. (1993). Lifetime DSM-III-R diagnostic outcomes in the offspring of schizophrenic mothers. *Archives of General Psychiatry, 50,* 707–714.

Pattatucci, A. M. L., & Hamer, D. H. (1995). Development and familiarity of sexual orientation in females. *Behavior Genetics, 25,* 407–420.

Patterson, C. (1992). Children of lesbian and gay parents. *Child Development, 63,* 1025–1042.

Patterson, G. R. (1974). Interventions for boys with conduct problems: Multiple settings, treatments, and criteria. *Journal of Consulting and Clinical Psychology, 42,* 471–481.

Patterson, G. R. (1982). A social learning approach to family intervention: Vol. 3. *Coercive family process.* Eugene, OR: Castalia.

Patterson, G. R. (1996). Some characteristics of a developmental theory for early-onset delinquency. In M. F. Lenzenweger & J. J. Haugaard (Eds.), *Frontiers of developmental psychopathology* (pp. 81–124). New York: Oxford University Press.

Patterson, G. R., & Bank, L. (1989). Some amplifying mechanisms for pathologic processes in families. In M. Gunnar & E. Thelen (Eds.), *Minnesota symposium on child psychology: Systems and development* (pp. 167–209). Hillsdale, NJ: Erlbaum.

Patterson, G. R., Chamberlain, P., & Reid, J. B. (1982). A comparative evaluation of a parent-training program. *Behavior Therapy, 13,* 638–650.

Patterson, G. R., DeBaryshe, B. D., & Ramsey, E. (1989). A developmental perspective on antisocial behavior. *American Psychologist, 44,* 329–335.

Pattison, E. M. (1976). Nonabstinent drinking goals in the treatment of alcoholism. In R. J. Gibbons, Y. Israel, H. Kalant, R. E. Popharn, W. Schmidt & R. G. Smart (Eds.), *Research advances in alcohol and drug problems* (Vol. 3). New York: Wiley.

Paul, G. L. (1966). Insight vs. desensitization in psychotherapy: An experiment in anxiety reduction. Stanford, CA: Stanford University Press.

Paul, G. L., & Lentz, R. J. (1977). *Psychosocial treatment of chronic mental patients (milieu vs. social learning programs).* Cambridge, MA: Harvard University Press.

Pauls, D. L., Raymond, C. L., Stevenson, J. F., & Leckman, J. F. (1991). A family study of Gilles de la Tourette. *American Journal of Human Genetics, 48,* 154–163.

Pauly, I. B. (1985). Gender identity disorders. In M. Farber (Ed.), *Human sexuality: Psychosexual effects of disease.* New York: Macmillan.

Pavlov, I. P. (1928). *Lectures on conditioned reflexes.* New York: Liveright.

Pelham, W., Carlson, C., Sams, S., Vallano, G., Dixon, M., & Hoza, B. (1993). Separate and combined effects of methylphenidate and behavior modification on boys with attention-deficit hyperactivity disorder in the classroom. *Journal of Consulting and Clinical Psychology, 61,* 506–515.

Pena, J. M., & Koss-Chioino, J. D. (1992). Cultural sensitivity in drug treatment research with African American males. *Drugs and Society, 6,* 157–179.

Penn, D. L., & Mueser, K. T. (1996). Research update on the psychosocial treatment of schizophrenia. *American Journal of Psychiatry, 153,* 607–617.

Pennebaker, J. W., Kiecolt-Glaser, J., & Glaser, R. (1988). Disclosure of traumas and immune function: Health implications for psychotherapy. *Journal of Consulting and Clinical Psychology, 56,* 239–245.

Pepper, C. M., Klein, D. N., Anderson, R. L., Riso, L. P., Ouimette, P. C., & Lizardi, H. (1995). DSM-III-R Axis II comorbidity in dysthymia and major depression. *American Journal of Psychiatry, 152,* 239–247.

Perkins, K. A. (1993). Weight gain following smoking cessation. *Journal of Consulting and Clinical Psychology, 61,* 768–777.

Perris, C. (1989). *Cognitive psychotherapy and the schizophrenic disorders.* New York: Guilford Press.

Perry, S. W. (1990). Organic mental disorders caused by HIV: Update on early diagnosis and treatment. *American Journal of Psychiatry, 147,* 696–710.

Petersen, M. E., & Dickey, R. (1995). Surgical sex reassignment: A comparative survey of international centers. *Archives of Sexual Behavior, 24,* 135–156.

Peterson, C., & Seligman, M. E. P. (1984). Causal explanations as a risk factor for depression: Theory and evidence. *Psychological Review, 91,* 347–374.

Peuskens, J. (1995). Risperidone in the treatment of patients with chronic schizophrenia: A multi-national, multi-centre, double-blind, parallel-group study versus Haloperidol. *British Journal of Psychiatry, 166,* 712–726.

Peyser, C. E., Folstein, M., Chase, G. A., Starkstein, S., Brandt, J., Cockrell, J. R., Bylsma, F., Coyle, J. T., McHugh, P. R., & Folstein, S. E. (1995). Trial of D-a-tocopherol in Huntington's disease. *American Journal of Psychiatry, 152,* 1771–1775.

Pfeiffer, S. I., Norton, J., Nelson, L., & Shott, S. (1995). Efficacy of vitamin B6 and magnesium in the treatment of autism: A methodology review and summary of outcomes. *Journal of Autism and Developmental Disorders, 25,* 481–493.

Phares, V., & Compas, B. E. (1992). The role of fathers in child and adolescent psychopathology: Make room for daddy. *Psychological Bulletin, 111,* 387–412.

Phillips, D. P., & Carstensen, L. L. (1988). The effect of suicide stories on various demographic groups, 1968–1985. *Suicide and Life-Threatening Behavior, 18,* 100–114.

Phillips, E. L. (1968). Achievement place: Token reinforcement procedures in a home-style setting for "predelinquent" boys. *Journal of Applied Behavior Analysis, 1,* 213–223.

Piacentini, J., Gitow, A., Jaffer, M., Graae, F., & Whitaker, A. (1994). Outpatient behavioral treatment of child and adolescent obsessive compulsive disorder. *Journal of Anxiety Disorders, 8,* 277–289.

Pickar, D., Owen, R. R., Litman, R. E., Konicki, E., Gutierrez, R., & Rapaport, M. H. (1992). Clinical and biologic response to clozapine in patients with schizophrenia: Crossover comparison with fluphenazine. *Archives of General Psychiatry, 49,* 345–353.

Pickens, R., Svikis, D., McGue, M., Lykken, D., Heston, L., & Clayton, P. (1991). Heterogeneity in the inheritance of alcoholism: A study of male and female twins. *Archives of General Psychiatry, 48,* 19–28.

Pihl, R. O., & Peterson, J. B. (1992). Etiology. *Annual review of addictions research and treatment.* New York: Pergamon Press.

Pilkonis, P. A., Heape, C. L., Proietti, J. M., Clark, S. W., McDavid, J. D., & Pitts, T. E. (1995). The reliability and validity of two structured diagnostic interviews for personality disorders. *Archives of General Psychiatry, 52,* 1025–1033.

Piper, A. (1995). Treatment for multiple personality disorder. *American Journal of Psychotherapy, 49,* 315–316.

Pitts, F., & McClure, J. (1967). Lactate metabolism in anxiety neurosis. *New England Journal of Medicine, 277,* 1329–36.

Plomin, R. (1989). Environment and genes: Determinants of behavior. *American Psychologist, 42,* 105–111.

Plomin, R., & DeFries, J. C. (1980). Genetics and intelligence: Recent data. *Intelligence, 4,* 15–24.

Plomin, R., Nitz, K., & Rowe, D. C. (1990). Behavioral genetics and aggressive behavior in childhood. In M. Lewis & S. M. Miller (Eds.), *Handbook of developmental psychopathology.* New York: Plenum Press.

Poewe, W., & Wenning, G. (1996). The natural history of Parkinson's disease. *Neurology, 47*(Suppl. 3), 146–152.

Polich, J., Armor, D., & Braiker, H. (1981). *The course of alcoholism: Four years after treatment.* New York: Wiley.

Polivy, J., & Herman, C. P. (1985). Dieting and binging. *American Psychologist, 40,* 193–210.

Polivy, J., & Herman, C. P. (1987). Diagnosis and treatment of normal eating. *Journal of Consulting and Clinical Psychology, 55,* 635–644.

Pollock, V. (1992). Meta-analysis of subjective sensitivity to alcohol in sons of alcoholics. *American Journal of Psychiatry, 149,* 1534–1538.

Pollock, V., Schneider, L., Gabrielli, W., & Goodwin, D. W. (1986). Sex of parent and offspring in the transmission of alcoholism: A meta-analysis. *Journal of Nervous and Mental Disease, 175,* 668–673.

Pope, H. G., Jr., Hudson, J. I., & Yurgelun-Todd, D. (1984). Anorexia nervosa and bulimia among 300 suburban women shoppers. *American Journal of Psychiatry, 141,* 292–294.

Pope, H. G., Mangweth, B., Negrao, A. B., Hudson, J. I., & Cordas, T. A. (1994). Childhood sexual abuse and bulimia nervosa: A comparison of American, Austrian, and Brazilian women. *American Journal of Psychiatry, 151,* 732–737.

Pope, K. S. (1990). Therapist-patient sexual involvement: A review of the research. *Clinical Psychology Review, 10,* 477–490.

Post, R. M. (1987). Mechanisms of action of carbamazepine and related anticonvulsants in affective illness. In H. Y. Meltzer (Ed.), *Psychopharmacology: The third generation of progress.* New York: Raven Press.

Post, R. M. (1988). Time course of clinical effects of carbamazepine: Implications for mechanisms of action. *Journal of Clinical Psychiatry, 49(Suppl.),* 35–48.

Post, R. M. (1992). Transduction of psychosocial stress into the neurobiology of recurrent affective disorder. *American Journal of Psychiatry, 149,* 999–1010.

Post, R. M., Rubinow, D. R., & Ballenger, J. C. (1984). Conditioning, sensitization, and kindling: Implications for the course of affective illness. In R. Post & J. Ballenger (Eds.), *Neurobiology of mood disorders.* Baltimore: Williams & Wilkins.

Poulter, N., Khaw, K. T., Hopwood, B. E., Mugambi, M., Peart, W. S., Rose, G., & Sever, P. S. (1984). Blood pressure and its correlates in an African tribe in urban and rural environments. *Journal of Epidemiology and Community Health, 38,* 181–185.

Powch, I. G., & Houston, B. K. (1996). Hostility, anger, and cardiovascular reactivity in white women. *Health Psychology, 15,* 200–208.

Power, K. G., Simpson, R., Swanson, V., & Wallace, L. (1990). A controlled comparison of cognitive-behavioral therapy, diazepam, and placebo, alone and in combination, for the treatment of generalized anxiety disorder. *Journal of Anxiety Disorders, 4,* 267–292.

Prentky, R. A., Burgess, A. W., Rokous, F., Lee, A., Hartman, C., Ressler, R., & Douglas, J. (1989). The presumptive role of fantasy in serial sexual homicide. *The American Journal of Psychiatry, 146,* 887–891.

Prentky, R. A., & Knight, R. A. (1991). Identifying critical dimensions for discrimination among rapists. *Journal of Consulting and Clinical Psychology, 59,* 643–661.

Price, T. R. P., Goetz, K. L., & Lovell, M. R. (1992). Neuropsychiatric aspects of brain tumors. In S. C. Yudofsky & R. E. Hales (Eds.), *The American Psychiatric Press Textbook of Neuropsychiatry.* Washington, DC: American Psychiatric Press.

Prien, R. F. (1988). Somatic treatment of unipolar depressive disorder. In A. J. Frances & R. E. Hales (Eds.), *Review of psychiatry.* Washington, DC: American Psychiatric Press.

Prigatano, G., Glisky, E., & Konoff, P. (1996). Cognitive rehabilitation after traumatic brain injury. In P. Corrigan & S. Yudofsky (Eds.), *Cognitive rehabilitation for neuropsychiatric disorders* (pp. 223–242). Washington, D.C.: American Psychiatric Press.

Prince, V., & Bentler, P. M. (1972). Survey of 504 cases of transvestism. *Psychological Reports, 31,* 903–917.

Prior, M. (1984). Developing concepts of childhood autism: The influence of experimental cognitive research. *Journal of Consulting and Clinical Psychology, 52,* 4–16.

Prochaska, J. O., DiClemente, C., & Norcross, J. (1992). In search of how people change: Applications to addictive behaviors. *American Psychologist, 47,* 83–107.

Pruchno, R. A., Kleban, M. H., Michaels, J. E., & Dempsey, N. P. (1990). Mental and physical health of caregiving spouses: Development of a causal model. *Journal of Gerontology: Psychological Sciences, 45,* 192–199.

Pruchno, R. A., & Potashnik, S. L. (1989). Caregiving spouses: Physical and mental health in perspective. *Journal of the American Geriatric Society, 37,* 697–705.

Purdon, S. E., Mohr, E., Ilivitsky, V., Jones, B. D., & Barry, D. W. (1994). Huntington's disease: Pathogenesis, diagnosis, and treatment. *Journal of Psychiatry and Neuroscience, 19,* 359–367.

Putnam, F. (1984). The psychophysiological investigation of multiple personality disorder: A review. *Psychiatric Clinics of North America, 7,* 31–39.

Putnam, F. W. (1989). *Diagnosis and treatment of multiple personality disorder.* New York: Guilford Press.

Pynoos, R. S., Fredrick, C., Nader, K., Arroyo, W., Steinberg, A., Eth, S., Nuney, F., & Fairbanks, L. (1987). Life threat and posttraumatic stress in school age children. *Archives of General Psychiatry, 44,* 1057–1063.

Quay, H. C. (1965). Psychopathic personality as pathological stimulus seeking. *American Journal of Psychiatry, 122,* 180–183.

Quay, H. C. (1986). Conduct disorders. In H. C. Quay & J. S. Wherry (Eds.), *Psychopathological disorders of childhood.* New York: Wiley.

Quinn, E. P., Brandon, T. H., & Copeland, A. L. (1996). Is task persistence related to smoking and substance abuse? The application of learned industriousness theory to addictive behaviors. *Experimental and Clinical Psychopharmacology, 4,* 186–190.

Quintana, H., Birmaher, B., Stedge, D., Lennon, S., Freed, J., Bridge, J., & Greenhill, L. (1995). Use of methylphenidate in the treatment of children with autistic disorder. *Journal of Autism and Developmental Disorders, 25,* 283–294.

Rachman, S., & de Silva, P. (1978). Abnormal and normal obsessions. *Behaviour Research and Therapy, 16,* 233–248.

Rachman, S., & Hodgson, R. (1968). Experimentally-induced "sexual fetishism": Replication and development. *Psychological Record, 18,* 25–27.

Rachman, S., & Hodgson, R. (1980). *Obsessions and compulsions.* Englewood Cliffs, NJ: Prentice-Hall.

Radloff, L. S. (1977). The CES-D Scale: A new self-report depression scale for research in the general population. *Applied Psychological Measurement, 1,* 385–401.

Ragland, D. R., & Brand, R. J. (1988). Coronary heart disease mortality in the Western Collaborative Group Study: Follow-up experience of 22 years. *American Journal of Epidemiology, 127,* 462–475.

Ragland, D. R., & Brand, R. J. (1988). Type A behavior and mortality from coronary heart disease. *New England Journal of Medicine, 138,* 65–69.

Raine, A. (1993). Features of borderline personality and violence. *Journal of Clinical Psychology, 49,* 277–281.

Raine, A. (1993). *The psychopathology of crime: Criminal behavior as a clinical disorder.* San Diego, CA: Academic Press.

Raine, A., Brennan, P., & Mednick, S. A. (1994). Birth complications combined with early maternal rejection at age 1 year predispose to violent crime at age 18 years. *Archives of General Psychiatry, 51,* 984–988.

Raine, A., Venables, P. H., & Williams, M. (1990). Relationships between central and autonomic measures of arousal at age 15 years and criminality at age 24 years. *Archives of General Psychiatry, 47,* 1003–1007.

Raine, A., Venables, P. H., & Williams, M. (1995). High autonomic arousal and electrodermal orienting at age 15 years as protective factors against criminal behavior at age 29 years. *American Journal of Psychiatry, 152,* 1595–1600.

Ram, R., Bromet, E. J., Eaton, W. W., Pato, C., & Schwartz, J. E. (1992). The natural course of schizophrenia: A review of first admission studies. *Schizophrenia Bulletin, 18,* 185–208.

Rao, S. M., Huber, S. J., & Bornstein, R. A. (1992). Emotional changes with multiple sclerosis and Parkinson's disease. *Journal of Consulting and Clinical Psychology, 60,* 369–378.

Rapee, R. M. (1991). Generalized anxiety disorder: A review of clinical features and theoretical concepts. *Clinical Psychology Review, 11,* 419–440.

Rapee, R. M., & Barlow, D. H. (1989). Psychological treatment of unexpected panic attacks: Cognitive/behavioral components. In R. Baker (Ed.), *Panic disorder: Theory, research, and therapy.* New York: Wiley.

Rapoport, J. L. (1986). Childhood obsessive-compulsive disorder. *Journal of Child Psychiatry and Psychology, 27,* 289–295.

Rapoport, J. L. (1989). The biology of obsessions and compulsions. *Scientific American, 260,* 83–89.

Rapoport, J. L., Buchsbaum, M. S., Zahn, T. P., Weingartner, H., Ludlow, C., & Mikkelsen, E. J. (1978). Dextroamphetamine: Cognitive and behavioral effects in normal prepubertal boys. *Science, 199,* 560–563.

Rapport, M. D., & Kelly, K. L. (1991). Psychostimulant effects on learning and cognitive function in children with attention deficit hyperactivity disorder: Findings and implications. In J. L. Matson (Ed.), *Hyperactivity in children: A handbook.* New York: Pergamon Press.

Rauschenberger, S., & Lynn, S. J. (1995). Fantasy proneness, DSM-III-R 1 psychopathology and dissociation. *Journal of Abnormal Psychology, 104,* 373–380.

Ravaja, N., Keltikangas-Jarvinen, D., & Keskivaara, P. (1996). Type A factors as predictors of changes in the metabolic syndrome precursors in adolescents and young adults: A 3-year follow-up study. *Health Psychology, 15,* 18–29.

Reardon, G. T., Rifkin, A., Schwartz, A., Myerson, A., & Siris, S. (1989). Changing patterns of neuroleptic dosage over a decade. *American Journal of Psychiatry, 146,* 726–729.

Reed, G. (1985). *Obsessional experience and compulsive behavior: A cognitive-structural approach.* New York: Academic Press.

Regier, D. A., Burke, J., & Burke, K. (1990). Comorbidity of affective and anxiety disorders in the NIMH epidemiological catchment area program. In J. Maser & C. Cloninger (Eds.), *Comorbidity of mood and anxiety disorders.* Washington, DC: American Psychiatric Press.

Regier, D. A., Farmer, M. E., Raye, D. S., Locke, B. Z., Keith, S. J., Judd, L. L., & Goodwin, R. K. (1990). Comorbidity of mental disorders with drug and alcohol abuse: Results from the Epidemiologic Catchment Area (ECA) study. *Journal of the American Medical Association, 264,* 2511–2518.

Reich, J. H., & Green, A. I. (1991). Effect of personality disorders on outcome of treatment. *Journal of Nervous and Mental Disease, 179(2),* 74–82.

Reif, L. V., Patton, M. J., & Gold, P. B. (1995). Bereavement, stress, and social support in members of a self-help group. *Journal of Community Psychology, 23,* 292–306.

Reilly, P. M., Sees, K. L., Shopshire, M. S., Hall, S. M., Delucchi, K. L., Tusel, D. J., Banys, P., Clark, H. W., & Piotrowski, N. A. (1995). Self-efficacy and illicit opioid use in a 180-day methadone detoxification treatment. *Journal of Consulting and Clinical Psychology, 63,* 158–162.

Reiss, D., Hetherington, E. M., Plomin, R., Howe, G. W., Simmens, S. J., Henderson, S. H., O'Connor, T. J., Bussell, D. A., Anderson, E. R., & Law, T. (1995). Genetic questions for environmental studies. *Archives of General Psychiatry, 52,* 925–936.

Reiss, D., Hetherington, E. M., Plomin, R., Howe, G. W., Simmens, S. J., Henderson, S. H., O'Connor, T. J., Bussell, D. A., Anderson, E. R., & Law, T. (1995). Genetic questions for environmental studies: Differential parenting and psychopathology in adolescence. *Archives of General Psychiatry, 52,* 925–936.

Reiss, S., Peterson, R., Gursky, D., McNally, R. (1986). Anxiety sensitivity, anxiety frequency, and the prediction of fearfulness. *Behaviour Research and Therapy, 24,* 1–8.

Reitan, R. M., & Davison, L. A. (1974). *Clinical neuropsychology: Current status and applications.* Washington, DC: V. H. Winston & Sons.

Renneberg, B., Goldstein, A. J., Phillips, D., & Chambless, D. L. (1990). Intensive behavioral group treatment of avoidant personality disorder. *Behavior Therapy, 21,* 363–377.

Repp, A. C., & Deitz, D. E. D. (1983). Mental retardation. In T. Ollendick & M. Hersen (Eds.), *Handbook of child psychopathology.* New York: Plenum Press.

Reppucci, N. D., & Haugaard, J. J. (1989). Prevention of child sexual abuse. *American Psychologist, 44,* 1266–1275.

Rescorla, R. A. (1988). Pavlovian conditioning: It's not what you think it is. *American Psychologist, 43,* 151–160.

Resnicow, K., Ross-Gaddy, D., & Vaughan, R. D. (1995). Structure of problem and positive behaviors in African American youths. *Journal of Consulting and Clinical Psychology, 63,* 594–603.

Retzinger, S. M. (1991). *Violent emotions: Shame and rage in marital quarrels.* Newbury Park, CA: Sage.

Rey, J. M., Morris-Yates, A., Singh, M., Andrews, G., & Stewart, G. W. (1995). Continuities between psychiatric disorders in adolescents and personality disorders in young adults. *American Journal of Psychiatry, 152,* 895–900.

Reynolds, W. M. (1992). The study of internalizing disorders in children and adolescents. In W. M. Reynolds (Ed.), *Internalizing disorders in children and adolescents.* New York: Wiley.

Reznick, J. S., Kagan, J., Snidman, N., Gersten, M., Baak, K., & Rosenberg, A. (1986). Inhibited and uninhibited children: A follow-up study. *Child Development, 57,* 660–680.

Rice, D. P., Kelman, S., Miller, L. S., & Dunmeyer, S. (1990). *The economic costs of alcohol and drug abuse and mental illness: 1985.* Report submitted to the Office of Financing and Coverage Policy of the Alcohol, Drug Abuse, and Mental Health

Administration, U.S. Department of Health and Human Services. San Francisco, CA: Institute for Health and Aging, University of California, 1990.

Rice, M. E., Quinsey, V. L., & Harris, G. T. (1991). Sexual recidivism among child molesters released from a maximum security psychiatric institution. *Journal of Consulting and Clinical Psychology, 59,* 381–386.

Rich, C. L., Young, D., & Fowler, R. C. (1986). San Diego suicide study. I. Young vs. old subjects. *Archives of General Psychiatry, 43,* 577–582.

Rich, C. L., Young, J. G., Fowler, R. C., Wagner, J., & Black, N. A. (1990). Guns and suicide: Possible effects of some specific legislation. *American Journal of Psychiatry, 147,* 342–346.

Richards, R., Kinney, D. K., Lunde, I., Benet, M., & Merzel, A. P. C. (1988). Creativity in manic-depressives, cyclothymes, their normal relatives, and control subjects. *Journal of Abnormal Psychology, 97,* 281–288.

Richardson, M. A., Haugland, G., & Craig, T. J. (1991). Neuroleptic use, Parkinsonian symptoms, tardive dyskinesia, and associated factors in child and adolescent psychiatric patients. *American Journal of Psychiatry, 148,* 1322–1328.

Richardson, S. A., Katz, M., Koller, H., McLaren, L., & Rubinstein, B. (1979). Some characteristics of a population of mentally retarded young adults in a British city: A basis for estimating service needs. *Journal of Mental Deficiency Research, 23,* 275–283.

Rickels, K., Schweizer, E., Case, W., & Greenblatt, D. (1991). Long-term therapeutic use of benzodiazepines: I. Effects of abrupt discontinuation. *Archives of General Psychiatry, 47,* 899–907.

Rickels, K., Schweizer, E., Sanalosi, I., Case, W., & Chung, H. (1988). Long-term treatment of anxiety and risk of withdrawal. *Archives of General Psychiatry, 45,* 444–452.

Rimland, B. (1964). *Infantile autism.* New York: Appleton-Century-Crofts.

Rimland, B. (1974). Infantile autism: Status and research. In A. Davids (Ed.), *Child personality and psychopathology: Current topics.* New York: Wiley.

Rinehart, J. S., & Schiff, I. (1985). Sexuality and the menopause. In M. Farber (Ed.), *Human sexuality: Psychosexual effects of disease.* New York: Macmillan.

Rippere, V. (1977a). "What's the thing to do when you're feeling depressed?" — a pilot study. *Behaviour Research and Therapy, 15,* 185–191.

Rippere, V. (1977b). Commonsense beliefs about depression and antidepressive behaviour: A study of social consensus. *Behaviour Research and Therapy, 15,* 465–473.

Riso, L. P., Klein, D. N., Ferro, T., Kasch, K. L., Pepper, C. M., Schwartz, J. E., & Aronson, T. A. (1996). Understanding the comorbidity between early-onset dysthymia and Cluster B personality disorders: A family study. *American Journal of Psychiatry, 153,* 900–906.

Roberts, L. (1988). Vietnam's psychological toll. *Science, 241,* 159–161.

Roberts, R. E., Lewinsohn, P. M., & Seeley, J. R. (1991). Screening for adolescent depression: A comparison of depression scales. *Journal of the American Academy of Child and Adolescent Psychiatry, 30,* 58–66.

Roberts, W., Penk, W., Gearing, M., Robinowitz, R., Dolan, M., & Patterson, E. (1982). Interpersonal problems of Vietnam combat veterans with symptoms of posttraumatic stress disorder. *Journal of Abnormal Psychology, 91,* 444–450.

Robins, C. J. (1990). Congruence of personality and life events in depression. *Journal of Abnormal Psychology, 99,* 393–397.

Robins, L. N. (1966). *Deviant children grown up.* Baltimore: Williams & Wilkins.

Robins, L. N. (1986). Epidemiology of antisocial personality. In G. L. Klerman, M. M. Weissman, P. S. Appelbaum & L. H. Roth (Eds.), *Psychiatry: Social, epidemiologic, and legal psychiatry* (pp. 231–244). New York: Basic Books.

Robins, L. N., Helzer, J. E., Croughan, J., & Ratcliff, K. S. (1981). National Institute of Mental Health Diagnostic Interview Schedule: Its history, characteristics, and validity. *Archives of General Psychiatry, 38,* 381–389.

Robins, L. N., Helzer, J., Ratcliff, K., & Seyfried, W. (1982). Validity of the Diagnostic Interview Schedule, Version II: DSM-III diagnoses. *Psychological Medicine, 12,* 855–870.

Robins, L. N., Helzer, J. E., Weissman, M. M., Orvaschel, H., Gruenberg, E., Burke, J. K., & Regier, D. A. (1984). Lifetime prevalence of specific psychiatric disorders in three cities. *Archives of General Psychiatry, 41,* 949–958.

Robins, L. N., & Price, R. K. (1991). Adult disorders predicted by childhood conduct problems. Results from the NIMH Epidemiologic Catchment Area project. *Psychiatry, 54,* 116–132.

Robinson, J. L., Kagan, J., Reznick, J. S., & Corley, R. (1992). The heritability of inhibited and uninhibited behavior: A twin study. *Developmental Psychology, 28,* 1030–1037.

Robinson, L. A., Berman, J. S., & Neimeyer, R. A. (1990). Psychotherapy for the treatment of depression: A comprehensive review of controlled outcome research. *Psychological Bulletin, 108,* 30–49.

Robinson, R. G., Bolduc, P. L., & Price, T. R. (1987). Two year longitudinal study of poststroke mood disorders: Diagnosis and outcome at one and two years. *Stroke, 18,* 837–843.

Robinson, R. G., Kubos, K. L., Starr, L. B., et al. (1983). Mood changes in stroke patients: Relationship to lesion location. *Comprehensive Psychiatry, 24,* 555–566.

Rockett, I. R. H., & Smith, G. S. (1989). Homicide, suicide, motor vehicle crash, and fall mortality: United States' experience in comparative perspective. *American Journal of Public Health, 79,* 1396–1400.

Rodin, J., & Ickovics, J. R. (1990). Women's health: Review and research agenda as we approach the 21st century. *American Psychologist, 45,* 1018–1034.

Rogers, C. (1951). *Client-centered therapy.* Boston: Houghton Mifflin.

Rogers, C. (1961). *On becoming a person.* Boston: Houghton Mifflin.

Rogers, C., Gendlin, E. T., Kiesler, D. J., & Truax, C. B. (1967). *The therapeutic relationship and its impact: A study of psychotherapy with schizophrenics.* Madison, WI: University of Wisconsin Press.

Rohrbeck, C. A., & Twentyman, C. T. (1986). A multimodal assessment of impulsiveness in abusing, neglectful, and nonmaltreating mothers and their preschool children. *Journal of Consulting and Clinical Psychology, 54,* 231–236.

Romanczyk, R., & Kistner, J. (1982). Psychosis and mental retardation: Issues of coexistence. In J. Matson & R. Barrett (Eds.), *Psychopathology in the mentally retarded.* New York: Grune & Stratton.

Romme, M., & Escher, A. (1989). Hearing voices. *Schizophrenia Bulletin, 15,* 209–216.

Room, R. (1968). Cultural contingencies of alcoholism: Variations between and within nineteenth century urban ethnic groups in alcohol-related death rates. *Journal of Health and Social Behavior, 9,* 99–113.

Room, R., & Greenfield, T. (1993). Alcoholics anonymous, other 12-step movements and psychotherapy in the U.S. population, 1990. *Addiction, 88,* 555–562.

Rooth, F. G. (1973). Exhibitionism outside Europe and America. *Archives of Sexual Behavior, 2,* 351–363.

Roper Organization (1992). *Unusual personal experiences: An analysis of the data from three national surveys.* Las Vegas, NV: Bigelow Holding.

Rorer, L. G. (1989). Rational-emotive therapy: I. An integrated psychological and philosophical basis. *Cognitive Therapy and Research, 13,* 475–492.

Rorty, M., Yager, J., & Rossotto, E. (1994). Childhood sexual, physical, and psychological abuse in bulimia nervosa. *American Journal of Psychiatry, 151,* 1122–1126.

Rose, D. T., Abramson, L. Y., Hodulik, C. J., Halberstadt, L., & Leff, G. (1994). Heterogeneity of cognitive style among depressed inpatients. *Journal of Abnormal Psychology, 103,* 419–429.

Rose, J. S., Chassin, L., Presson, C. C., & Sherman, S. J. (1996). Prospective predictors of quit attempts and smoking cessation in young adults. *Health Psychology, 15,* 261–268.

Rosen, G. (1968). *Madness in Society: Chapters in the historical sociology of mental illness.* Chicago: University of Chicago Press.

Rosen, G. M. (1987). Self-help treatment books and the commercialization of psychotherapy. *American Psychologist, 42,* 46–51.

Rosen, J. N. (1946). The treatment of schizophrenic psychosis by direct analytic therapy. *The Psychiatric Quarterly, 21.*

Rosen, R. C., & Leiblum, S. R. (1995). Treatment of sexual disorders in the 1990s: An integrated approach. *Journal of Consulting and Clinical Psychology, 63,* 877–890.

Rosenbaum, J. F., Biederman, J., Bolduc-Murphy, E. A., Faraone, S. V., et al. (1993). Behavioral inhibition in childhood: A risk factor for anxiety disorders. *Harvard Review of Psychiatry, 1,* 2–16.

Rosenbaum, J. F., Biederman, J., Gersten, M., Hirshfeld, D. R., Meminger, S. R., Herman, J. R., Kagan, J., Reznick, S., & Snidman, N. (1988). Behavioral inhibition in children of parents with panic disorder and agoraphobia. *Archives of General Psychiatry, 45,* 463–470.

Rosenbaum, M. (1990). The role of depression in couples involved in murder-suicide and homicide. *American Journal of Psychiatry, 147,* 1036–1039.

Rosenberg, H. (1993). Prediction of controlled drinking by alcoholics and problem drinkers. *Psychological Bulletin, 113,* 129–139.

Rosenberg, M. (1988, May). Adult behaviors that reflect childhood incest. *Medical Aspects of Human Sexuality,* pp. 114–124.

Rosenberger, P. H., & Miller, G. A. (1989). Comparing borderline definitions: DSM-III borderline and schizotypal personality disorders. *Journal of Abnormal Psychology, 98,* 161–169.

Rosenfarb, I. S., Goldstein, M. J., Mintz, J., & Nuechterlein, K. H. (1995). Expressed emotion and subclinical psychopathology observable within the transactions between schizophrenic patients and their family members. *Journal of Abnormal Psychology, 104,* 259–267.

Rosenman, R., Brand, R. J., Jenkins, C. D., Friedman, M., Straus, R., & Wurm, M. (1975). Coronary heart disease in the Western Collaborative Group Study: Final follow-up experience of 8 1/2 years. *Journal of the American Medical Association, 233,* 872–877.

Rosenstock, I. M. (1974). Historical origins of the health belief model. *Health Education Monographs, 2,* 328–335.

Rosenthal, R. (1995). Writing meta-analytic reviews. *Psychological Bulletin, 118,* 183–192.

Rosenthal, T., & Bandura, A. (1978). Psychological modeling: Theory and practice. In S. L. Garfield & A. E. Bergin (Eds.), *Handbook of psychotherapy and behavior change* (2nd ed.). New York: Wiley.

Rosenzweig, M. R., Bennett, E. L., & Diamond, M. C. (1972). Brain changes in response to experience. *Scientific American, 226,* 22–29.

Rosenzweig, M. R., Leiman, A. L., & Breedlove, S. M. (1996). *Biological psychology.* Sunderland, MA: Sinauer Associates.

Roses, A. D. (1996). Apolipoprotein E alleles as risk factors in Alzheimer's disease. *Annual Review of Medicine, 47,* 387–400.

Rosnow, R., & Rosenthal, R. (1996). Contrasts and interactions redux: Five easy pieces. *Psychological Science, 7,* 253–257.

Ross, A. O., & Pelham, W. E. (1981). Child psychopathology. *Annual Review of Psychology, 32,* 243–278.

Ross, C. A., Anderson, G., Fleisher, W. P., & Norton, G. R. (1991). The frequency of multiple personality disorder among psychiatric inpatients. *American Journal of Psychiatry, 148,* 1717–1720.

Ross, L. (1977). The intuitive psychologist and his shortcomings: Distortions in the attribution process. In L. Berkowitz (Ed.), *Advances in experimental social psychology* (Vol. 10). New York: Academic Press.

Rost, K. M., Akins, R. N., Brown, F. W., & Smith, G. R. (1992). The comorbidity of DSM-III-R personality disorders in somatization disorder. *General Hospital Psychiatry, 14,* 322–326.

Roth, W. T., Margraf, J., Ehler, A., Taylor, B., Maddock, R. J., Davies, S., & Agras, S. (1992). Stress test reactivity in panic disorder. *Archives of General Psychiatry, 49,* 301–310.

Rothblum, E., Berman, J., Coffey, P., Shantinath, S., & Solomon, S. (1993). Feminist approaches to therapy with depressed women: A discussion. *The Journal of Training and Practice in Professional Psychology, 7,* 100–112.

Rotheram-Borus, M. J., Rosario, M., Reid, H., & Koopman, C. (1995). Predicting patterns of sexual acts among homosexual and bisexual youths. *American Journal of Psychiatry, 152,* 588–595.

Roy, A., DeJong, J., & Linnoila, M. (1989). Cerebrospinal fluid monoamine metabolites and suicidal behavior in depressed patients. *Archives of General Psychiatry, 46,* 609–612.

Rozanski, A., Bairey, C. N., Krantz, D. S., & Friedman, J. (1988). Mental stress and the induction of silent myocardial ischemia in patients with coronary heart disease. *New England Journal of Medicine, 318,* 1005–1012.

Rubenstein, J. L. R., Lotspeich, L., & Ciaranello, R. D. (1990). The neurobiology of developmental disorders. In B. Lahey & A. E. Kazdin (Eds.), *Advances in clinical child psychology* (Vol. 13). New York: Plenum Press.

Rubonis, A. V., & Bickman, L. (1991). Psychological impairment in the wake of disaster: The disaster-psychopathology relationship. *Psychological Bulletin, 109,* 384–399.

Ruocchio, P. (1989). First person account: Fighting the fight—The schizophrenic's nightmare. *Schizophrenia Bulletin, 15,* 163–166.

Rush, A. J., & Weissenburger, J. E. (1994). Melancholic symptom features and DSM-IV. *American Journal of Psychiatry, 151,* 489–498.

Rush, A. J., Beck, A. T., Kovacs, M., & Hollon, S. D. (1977). Comparative efficacy of cognitive therapy and pharmacotherapy in the treatment of depressed outpatients. *Cognitive Therapy and Research, 1,* 17–37.

Rush, B. (1947). *The selected writings of Benjamin Rush* (Ed. D. D. Runes). New York: Philosophical Library.

Russo, D. C., Carr, E. G., & Lovaas, O. I. (1980). Self-injury in pediatric populations. In J. Ferguson & C. B. Taylor (Eds.), *Comprehensive handbook of behavioral medicine.* New York: Spectrum.

Russo, J., Vitaliano, P. P., Brewer, D. D., Katon, W., & Becker, J. (1995). Psychiatric disorders in spouse caregivers of care recipients with Alzheimer's disease and matched controls: A diathesis-stress model of psychopathology. *Journal of Abnormal Psychology, 104,* 197–204.

Rutter, M. (1977). Brain damage syndromes in childhood: Concepts and findings. *Journal of Child Psychology and Psychiatry, 139,* 21–33.

Rutter, M. (1978). Language disorder and infantile autism. In M. Rutter & E. Schopler (Eds.), *Autism: A reappraisal of concepts and treatment.* New York: Plenum Press.

Rutter, M., & Quinton, D. (1984). Parental psychiatric disorder: Effects on children. *Psychological Medicine, 14,* 853–880.

Rutter, M., & Schopler, E. (1987). Autism and pervasive developmental disorders: Concepts and diagnostic issues. *Journal of Autism and Developmental Disabilities, 17,* 159–186.

Rutter, M., Tizard, J., Yule, W., Graham, P., & Whitmore, K. (1976). Research report: Isle of Wight studies, 1964–1974. *Psychological Medicine, 6,* 313–332.

Rybicki, B., Johnson, C., Uman, J., & Gorell, J. (1993). Parkinson's disease mortality and the industrial use of heavy metals in Michigan. *Movement Disorders, 8,* 87–92.

Rzewnicki, R., & Forgays, D. G. (1987). Recidivism and self-cure of smoking and obesity: An attempt to replicate. *American Psychologist, 42,* 97–100.

Sackeim, H. A., & Rush, A. J. (1995). Melancholia and response to ECT. *American Journal of Psychiatry, 152,* 1242–1243.

Safer, D. J., & Krager, J. M. (1988). A survey of medication treatment for hyperactive/inattentive students. *Journal of the American Medical Association, 260,* 2256–2259.

Safran, J. D., & Segal, Z. V. (1990). *Interpersonal process in cognitive therapy.* New York: Basic Books.

Saigh, P. A. (1986). In vitro flooding in the treatment of a 6-year-old boy's posttraumatic stress disorder. *Behaviour Research and Therapy, 24,* 685–688.

Saks, E. R. (1995). The criminal responsibility of people with multiple personality disorder. *Psychiatric Quarterly, 66,* 119–131.

Salkovskis, P. M. (Ed.). (1996). *Frontiers of cognitive therapy.* New York: Guilford Press.

Salkovskis, P. M., & Clark, D. M. (1991). Cognitive therapy for panic attacks. *Journal of Cognitive Psychotherapy, 5,* 215–226.

Salkovskis, P. M., & Harrison, J. (1984). Abnormal and normal obsessions: A replication. *Behaviour Research and Therapy, 22,* 549–552.

Salkovskis, P. M., Jones, D. R., & Clark, D. M. (1986). Respiratory control in the treatment of panic attacks; Replication and extension with concurrent measurement of behavior and CO_2. *British Journal of Psychiatry, 148,* 526–532.

Salkovskis, P. M., & Warwick, H. M. C. (1986). Morbid preoccupations, health anxiety and reassurance: A cognitive-behavioral approach to hypochondriasis. *Behaviour Research and Therapy, 24,* 597–602.

Salter, A. (1949). *Conditional reflex therapy.* New York: Farrar, Straus.

Saltzman, L. E., Mercy, J. A., O'Carroll, P. W., Rosenberg, M. L., & Rhodes, P. H. (1992). Weapon involvement and injury outcomes in family and intimate assaults. *Journal of the American Medical Association, 267,* 3043–3047.

Salzman, C. (1991). Why don't clinical trial results always correspond to clinical experience? *Neuropsychopharmacology, 4,* 265–267.

Sanday, P. (1981). The socio-cultural context of rape: A cross-cultural study. *Journal of Social Issues, 37,* 5–27.

Sandberg, D. E., Meyer-Bahlburg, H. F. L., Ehrhardt, A. A., & Yager, T. J. (1993). The prevalence of gender-atypical behavior in elementary school children. *Journal of the American Academy of Child and Adolescent Psychiatry, 32,* 306–314.

Sanders, B., & Giolas, M. (1991). Dissociation and childhood trauma in psychologically disturbed adolescents. *American Journal of Psychiatry, 148,* 50–54.

Sanders, J. D., Smith, T. W., & Alexander, F. (1991). Type A behavior and marital interaction: Hostile-dominant responses during conflict. *Journal of Behavioral Medicine, 14,* 567–580.

Santrock, J. W., & Warshak, R. A. (1986). Development of father custody relationships and legal/clinical considerations in father-custody families. In M. E. Lamb (Ed.), *The father's role: Applied perspectives.* New York: Wiley.

Sanua, V. D. (1984). Is infantile autism a universal phenomenon? *International Journal of Social Psychiatry, 30,* 163–177.

Sarason, I. G. (1979). Three lacunae of cognitive therapy. *Cognitive Therapy and Research, 3,* 223–235.

Sargeant, J. K., Bruce, M., Florio, L., & Weissman, M. (1990). Factors associated with 1-year outcome of major depression in the community. *Archives of General Psychiatry, 47,* 519–526.

Sartorius, N., Jablensky, A., Korten, A., Ernberg, G., Anker, M., Cooper, J. E., & Day, R. (1986). Early manifestations and first-contact incidence of schizophrenia in different cultures: A preliminary report on the initial evaluation phase of the WHO Collaborative Study on Determinants of Outcome of Severe Mental Disorders. *Psychological Medicine, 16,* 909–928.

Sartorius, N., Ustun, T. B., Korten, A., Cooper, J. E., & van Drimmelen, J. (1995). Progress toward achieving a common language in psychiatry, II: Results from the international field trials of the ICD-10 diagnostic criteria for research for mental and behavioral disorders. *American Journal of Psychiatry, 152,* 1427–1437.

Satir, V. (1964). *Conjoint family therapy.* Palo Alto, CA: Science and Behavior.

Sato, T., Takeichi, M., Shirahama, M., & Fuku, T. (1995). Doctor-shopping patients and users of alternative medicine among Japanese primary-care patients. *General Hospital Psychiatry, 17,* 115–125.

Sattler, J. (1990). *Assessment of Children* (3rd ed.). San Diego, CA: J. Sattler.

Saunders, A. M., Hulette, O., Welsh-Bohmer, K. A., Schmechel, D. E., Crain, B., Burke, J. R., Alberts, M. J., Strittmatter, W. J., Breitner, J. C., Rosenberg, C., et al. (1996). Specificity, sensitivity, and predictive value of apolipoprotein-E genotyping for sporadic Alzheimer's disease. *Lancet, 348,* 90–93.

Saykin, A. J., Gur, R. C., Gur, R. E., Mozley, P. D., Mozley, L. H., Resnick, S. M., Kester, D. B., & Stafiniak, P. (1991). Neuropsychological function in schizophrenia: Selective impairment in memory and learning. *Archives of General Psychiatry, 48,* 618–624.

Saylor, C. F., Finch, Jr., A. J., Baskin, C. H., Furey, W., Kelly, M. M. (1984). Construct validity for measures of childhood depression: Application of multitrait-multimethod methodology. *Journal of Consulting and Clinical Psychology, 52,* 977–985.

Scarr, S., & Weinberg, R. A. (1976). The IQ performance of black children adopted by white families. *American Psychologist, 31,* 726–739.

Schachter, S. (1982). Recidivism and self-cure of smoking and obesity. *American Psychologist, 37,* 436–444.

Schacter, D. L., Kihlstrom, J. F., Kihlstrom, L. C., & Berren, M. B. (1989). Autobiographical memory in a case of multiple personality disorder. *Journal of Abnormal Psychology, 98,* 508–514.

Schaefer, J. M. (1982). Ethnic and racial variations in alcohol use and abuse. In National Institute on Alcohol Abuse and Alcoholism. Special population issues. *Alcohol and Health Monograph No. 4, DHHS Publication No. (ADM) 88–1193.* Washington, DC: U.S. Government Printing Office.

Schafer, J., & Brown, S. A. (1991). Marijuana and cocaine effect expectancies and drug use patterns. *Journal of Consulting and Clinical Psychology, 59,* 558–565.

Schafer, R. B., Keith, P. M., & Schafer, E. (1995). Predicting fat in diets of marital partners using the health belief model. *Journal of Behavioral Medicine, 18,* 419–433.

Schiavi, R. C. (1985). Evaluation of impaired sexual desire: Biological aspects. In H. S. Kaplan (Ed.), *Comprehensive evaluation of disorders of sexual desire* (App. 17–34). Washington, DC: American Psychiatric Press, Inc.

Schiavi, R. C., Schreiner-Engle, P., Mandeli, J., Schanzer, H., & Cohen, E. (1990). Healthy aging and male sexual function. *American Journal of Psychiatry, 147,* 766–771.

Schiavi, R. C., Theilgaard, A., Owen, D. R., & White, D. (1988). Sex chromosome anomalies, hormones, and sexuality. *Archives of General Psychiatry, 45,* 19–24.

Schildkraut, J. J. (1965). The catecholamine hypothesis of affective disorders: A review of supporting evidence. *American Journal of Psychiatry, 122,* 509–522.

Schleifer, S. J., Keller, S. E., Camerino, M., Thornton, J. C., & Stein, M. (1983). Suppression of lymphocyte stimulation following bereavement. *Journal of the American Medical Association, 250,* 374–377.

Schopler, E. (1986). Editorial: Treatment abuse and its reduction. *Journal of Autism and Developmental Disabilities, 16,* 99–103.

Schopler, E., & Hennike, J. M. (1990). Past and present trends in residential treatment. *Journal of Autism and Developmental Disorders, 20,* 291–298.

Schopler, E., Short, A., & Mesibov, G. (1989). Relation of behavioral treatment to "normal functioning": Comment on Lovaas. *Journal of Consulting and Clinical Psychology, 57,* 162–164.

Schott, R. L. (1995). The childhood and family dynamics of transvestites. *Archives of Sexual Behavior, 24,* 309–327.

Schreiber, F. (1974). *Sybil.* New York: Warner.

Schreibman, L. (1988). *Autism.* Newbury Park, CA: Sage.

Schuckit, M. A. (1987). Biological vulnerability to alcoholism. *Journal of Consulting and Clinical Psychology, 55,* 301–309.

Schuckit, M. A. (1996). Recent developments in the pharmacotherapy of alcohol dependence. (1996). *Journal of Consulting and Clinical Psychology, 64,* 669–676.

Schwartz, G. E. (1978). Psychobiological foundations of psychotherapy and behavior change. In S. L. Garfield & A. E. Bergin (Eds.), *Handbook of psychotherapy and behavior change* (2nd ed.). New York: Wiley.

Schwartz, G. E. (1984). Biofeedback as a paradigm for health enhancement and disease prevention: A systems perspective. In J. D. Matarazzo, S. M. Weiss, J. Herd, N. E. Miller & S. M. Weiss (Eds.), *Behavioral health: A handbook of health enhancement and disease prevention.* New York: Wiley Interscience.

Schwartz, J. M., Stoessel, P. W., Baxter, L. R., Martin, K. M., & Phelps, M. E. (1996). Systematic changes in cerebral glucose metabolic rate after successful behavior modification treatment of obsessive-compulsive disorder. *Archives of General Psychiatry, 53,* 109–113.

Schwartz, R. M., & Garamoni, G. L. (1986). Cognitive assessment: A multibehavior-multimethod-multiperspective approach. *Journal of Psychopathology and Behavioral Assessment, 8,* 185–197.

Schweizer, E., Rickels, K., Case, G., & Greenblatt, D. (1990). Long-term therapeutic use of benzodiazepines: II. Effects of gradual taper. *Archives of General Psychiatry, 47,* 908–915.

Schweizer, E., Rickels, K., Weiss, S., & Zavodnick, S. (1993). Maintenance drug treatment of panic disorder. *Archives of General Psychiatry, 50,* 51–60.

Scott, D. W. (1986). Anorexia nervosa: A review of possible genetic factors. *International Journal of Eating Disorders, 5,* 1–20.

Scott, S. (1994). Mental retardation. In M. Rutter, E. Taylor & L. Hersov (Eds.), *Child and adolescent psychiatry.* Oxford: Blackwell.

Searles, J. S. (1988). The role of genetics in the pathogenesis of alcoholism. *Journal of Abnormal Psychology, 97,* 153–167.

Secretary of Health and Human Services, Secretary Report (1993). *Alcohol and health: Eight special reports to the U.S. Congress.*

Seedat, K., Seedat, M., & Hackland, D. (1982). Biosocial factors and hypertension in urban and rural Zulus. *South African Medical Journal, 61,* 999–1002.

Segal, S. P. (1989). Civil commitment standards and patient mix in England/Wales, Italy, and the United States. *American Journal of Psychiatry, 146,* 187–193.

Segal, Z. V., & Ingram, R. E. (1994). Mood priming and construct activation in tests of cognitive vulnerability to unipolar depression. *Clinical Psychology Review, 14,* 663–695.

Seguin, J. R., Pihl, R. O., Harden, P. W., Tremblay, R. E., & Boulerice, B. (1995). Cognitive and neuropsychological characteristics of physically aggressive boys. *Journal of Abnormal Psychology, 104,* 614–624.

Sejnowski, T. J., Koch, C., & Churchland, P. S. (1988). Computational neuroscience. *Science, 99,* 1299–1306.

Seligman, M. E. P. (1971). Phobias and preparedness. *Behaviour Research and Therapy, 2,* 307–320.

Seligman, M. E. P. (1975). *Helplessness, on depression, development, and death.* San Francisco: Freeman.

Selkoe, D. (1992). Aging brains, aging mind. *Scientific American, 267,* 134–142.

Sever, P., Gordon, D., Peart, W., & Beighton, P. (1980). Blood pressure and its correlates in urban and tribal Africa. *Lancet, 11,* 60–64.

Seyle, H. (1956). *The stress of life.* New York: McGraw-Hill.

Shaffer, D. (1977). Enuresis. In M. Rutter & L. Herzov (Eds.), *Child psychiatry: Modern approaches.* Philadelphia: Blackwell.

Shaffer, D. (1994). Enuresis. In M. Rutter, E. Taylor & L. Hersov (Eds.), *Child and adolescent psychiatry.* Oxford: Blackwell.

Shaffer, D., Gould, M. S., Fisher, P., Trautman, P., Moreau, D., Kleinman, M., & Flory, M. (1996). Psychiatric diagnosis in child and adolescent suicide. *Archives of General Psychiatry, 53,* 339–348.

Shapiro, A. K., Shapiro, E. S., Bruun, R. D., & Sweet, R. D. (1978). *Gilles de la Tourette syndrome.* New York: Raven Press.

Shapiro, D. (1965). *Neurotic styles.* New York: Basic Books.

Shapiro, D. (1981). *Autonomy and rigid character.* New York: Basic.

Shaywitz, B. A., Shaywitz, S. E., Byrne, T., Cohen, D. J., & Rothman, S. (1983). Attention deficit disorder: Quantitative analysis of CT. *Neurology, 33,* 1500–1503.

Shea, M. T. (1993). Psychosocial treatment of personality disorders. *Journal of Personality Disorders, 1,* 167–180.

Shea, M. T., Elkin, I., Imber, S. D., Sotsky, S. M., Watkins, J. T., Collins, J. F., Pilkonis, P. A., Beckham, E., Glass, D. R., Dolan, R. T., & Parloff, M. B. (1992). Course of depressive symptoms over follow-up: Findings from the National Institute of Mental Health Treatment of Depression Collaborative Research Program. *Archives of General Psychiatry, 49,* 782–787.

Shedler, J., & Block, J. (1990). Adolescent drug use and psychological health: A longitudinal inquiry. *American Psychologist, 45,* 612–630.

Shedler, J., Mayman, M., & Manis, M. (1993). The *illusion* of mental health. *American Psychologist, 48,* 1117–1131.

Sheley, J., & Brewer, V. (1995). Possession and carrying of firearms among suburban youth. *Public Health Reports, 110,* 18–26.

Sheley, J., & Wright, J. (1993). Motivations for gun possession and carrying among serious juvenile offenders. *Behavioral Sciences and the Law, 11,* 375–388.

Shepperson, B. (1995). The control of sexuality in young people with Down's syndrome. *Child: Care, Health, and Development, 21,* 333–349.

Sherbourne, C. D., Hays, R. D., & Wells, K. B. (1995). Personal and psychosocial risk factors for physical and mental health outcomes and course of depression among depressed patients. *Journal of Consulting and Clinical Psychology, 63,* 345–355.

Sherrington, R., Brynjolfsson, J., Petursson, H., Potter, M. (1988). Localization of a susceptibility locus for schizophrenia on chromosome 5. *Nature, 336,* 164–167.

Sherwood, A., Allen M. T., Obrist, P. A., & Langer, A. W. (1986). Evaluation of Beta-adrenergic influences on cardiovascular and metabolic adjustments to physical and psychological stress. *Psychophysiology, 23,* 89–104.

Shiffman, S. (1993). Smoking cessation treatment: Any progress? *Journal of Consulting and Clinical Psychology, 61,* 718–722.

Shiffman, S., Paty, J. A., Gnys, M., Kassel, J. A., & Hickcox, M. (1996). First lapses to smoking: Within-subjects analysis of real-time reports. *Journal of Consulting and Clinical Psychology, 64,* 366–379.

Shinn, M., Knickman, J. R., & Weitzman, B. C. (1991). Social relationships and vulnerability to becoming homeless among poor families. *American Psychologist, 46,* 1180–1187.

Shioiri, T., Murashita, J., Kato, T., Fujii, K., & Takahashi, S. (1996). Characteristic clinical features and clinical course in 270 Japanese outpatients with panic disorder. *Journal of Anxiety Disorders, 10,* 163–172.

Shirk, S. R., & Russell, R. (1996). *Change processes in child psychotherapy: Revitalizing treatment and research.* New York: Guilford Press.

Shneidman, E. (1987). A psychological approach to suicide. In G. R. VandenBos & B. K. Bryant (Eds.), *Cataclysms, crises, and catastrophes: Psychology in action.* Washington, DC: American Psychological Association.

Shoham-Salomon, V., & Rosenthal, R. (1987). Paradoxical interventions: A meta-analysis. *Journal of Consulting and Clinical Psychology, 55,* 22–28.

Shulman, C., Yirmiya, N., & Greenbaum, C. W. (1995). From categorization to classification: A comparison among individuals with autism, mental retardation, and normal development. *Journal of Abnormal Psychology, 104,* 601–609.

Siegel, J. M., Sorenson, S. B., Golding, J. M., Burnam, M. A., & Stein, J. A. (1987). The prevalence of childhood sexual assault: The Los Angeles Epidemiologic Catchment Area project. *American Journal of Epidemiology, 126,* 1141–1153.

Siegel, S. (1989). Pharmacological conditioning and drug effects. In A. J. Goudie & L. Emmett-Oglesby (Eds.), *Psychoactive drugs: Tolerance and sensitization.* Humana Press.

Siegman, A. W. (1994). From Type A to hostility to anger: Reflections on the history of coronary-prone behavior. In A. W. Siegman & T. W. Smith (Eds.), *Anger, hostility and the heart* (pp. 1–21). Hillsdale, NJ: Erlbaum.

Siever, L. J., & Davis, K. L. (1985). Overview: Toward a dysregulation hypothesis of depression. *American Journal of Psychiatry, 142,* 1017–1031.

Siever, L. J., & Davis, K. L. (1991). A psychobiological perspective on the personality disorders. *American Journal of Psychiatry, 148,* 1647–1658.

Siever, L. J., Rotter, M., Losonczy, M., Guo, S. L., Mitropoulou, V., Trestman, R., Apter, S., Zemishlany, Z., Silverman, J., & Horvath, T. B. (1995). Lateral ventricular enlargement in schizotypal personality disorder. *Psychiatry Research, 57,* 109–118.

Silk, K. R., Eisner, W., Allport, C., DeMars, C., Miller, C., Justice, R. W., & Lewis, M. (1994). Focused time-limited inpatient treatment of borderline personality disorder. *Journal of Personality Disorders, 8,* 268–278.

Silk, K. R., Lee, S., Hill, E. M., & Lohr, N. E. (1995). Borderline personality disorder symptoms and severity of sexual abuse. *American Journal of Psychiatry, 152,* 1059–1064.

Silove, D., Harris, M., Morgan, A., Boyce, P., Manicavasagar, V., Hadzi-Pavlovic, D., & Wilhelm, K. (1995). Is early separation anxiety a specific precursor of panic disorder-agoraphobia? A community study. *Psychological Medicine, 25,* 405–411.

Silver, E. (1995). Punishment or treatment? Comparing the lengths of confinement of successful and unsuccessful insanity defendants. *Law and Human Behavior, 19,* 375–388.

Silver, E., Cirincione, C., & Steadman, H. J. (1994). Demythologizing inaccurate perceptions of the insanity defense. *Law and Human Behavior, 18,* 63–70.

Silver, J. M., Hales, R. E., & Yudofsky, S. C. (1992). Neuropsychiatric aspects of traumatic brain injury. In S. C. Yudofsky & R. E. Hales (Eds.), *The American Psychiatric Press textbook of neuropsychiatry.* Washington, DC: American Psychiatric Press.

Silverstone, T., & Romans-Clarkson, S. (1989). Bipolar affective disorder: Causes and prevention of relapse. *British Journal of Psychiatry, 154,* 321–335.

Simon, G., Ormel, J., VonKorff, M., & Barlow, W. (1995). Health care costs associated with depressive and anxiety disorders in primary care. *American Journal of Psychiatry, 152,* 352–357.

Simon, G. E., Grothaus, L., Durham, M. L., VonKorff, M., & Pabiniak, C. (1996). Impact of visit copayments on outpatient mental health utilization by members of a health maintenance organization. *American Journal of Psychiatry, 153,* 331–338.

Simon, H. (1991). Exercise and human immune function. In R. Ader, D. Felton & N. Cohen (Eds.), *Psychoneuroimmunology.* San Diego: Academic Press.

Singer, M., & Wynne, L. C. (1963). Differentiating characteristics of the parents of childhood schizophrenics. *American Journal of Psychiatry, 120,* 476–487.

Sizemore, C. (1989). *A mind of my own.* New York: Morrow.

Skinner, B. F. (1953). *Science and human behavior.* New York: Macmillan.

Skinner, B. F. (1969). *Contingencies of reinforcement: A theoretical analysis.* New York: Appleton.

Sklar, L. S., & Anisman, H. (1979). Stress and coping factors influence tumor growth. *Science, 205,* 513–515.

Sloan, J. H., Rivara, F. P., Reay, D. T., James, A. F., & Kellermann, A. L. (1990). Firearm regulations and rates of suicide: A comparison of two metropolitan areas. *The New England Journal of Medicine, 322,* 369–373.

Smalley, S. L. (1991). Genetic influences in autism. *Psychiatric Clinics of North America, 14,* 125–139.

Smalley, S. L., & Collins, F. (1996). Brief report: Genetic, prenatal, and immunologic factors. *Journal of Autism and Developmental Disorders, 26,* 195–203.

Smart, R. G. (1975). Spontaneous recovery in alcoholics: A review and analysis of the available research. *Drug and Alcohol Dependence, 1,* 277–285.

Smith, A. L., & Weissman, M. M. (1992). Epidemiology. In E. S. Paykel (Ed.), *Handbook of affective disorders* (pp. 111–129). New York: Guilford Press.

Smith, D. (1982). Trends in counseling and psychotherapy. *American Psychologist, 37,* 802–809.

Smith, G. M. (1980). Perceived effects of substance use: A general theory. In D. J. Lettieri, M. Sayers, & H. W. Pearson (Eds.), *Theories on drug abuse: Selected contemporary perspectives.* National Institute on Drug Abuse, Research Monograph No. 30. DHHS (ADM) 80–967. Washington, DC: U.S. GPO.

Smith, G. R., Rost, K., & Kashner, M. (1995). A trial of the effect of a standardized psychiatric consultation on health outcomes and costs in somatizing patients. *Archives of General Psychiatry, 52,* 238–243.

Smith, G. T., Goldman, M. S., Greenbaum, P. E., & Christiansen, B. A. (1995). Expectancy for social facilitation from drinking: The divergent paths of high-expectancy and low-expectancy adolescents. *Journal of Abnormal Psychology, 104,* 32–40.

Smith, M. L., & Glass, G. V. (1977). Meta-analyses of psychotherapy outcome studies. *American Psychologist, 32,* 752–760.

Smith, R. E., & Winokur, G. (1991). Mood disorders (bipolar). In M. Hersen & S. M. Turner (Eds.), *Adult psychopathology and diagnosis.* New York: Wiley.

Smith, S. D., Pennington, B. F., Kimberling, W. J., & Ing, P. (1990). Familial dyslexia: Use of genetic linkage data to define subtypes. *Journal of the American Academy of Child and Adolescent Psychiatry, 29,* 204–213.

Smith, S. S., & Newman, J. P. (1990). Alcohol and drug abuse-dependence disorders in psychopathic and nonpsychopathic criminal offenders. *Journal of Abnormal Psychology, 99,* 430–439.

Smith, T. W. (1989). Assessment in rational-emotive therapy: Empirical access to the ABCD model. In M. E. Bernard & R. DiGiuseppe (Eds.), *Inside rational emotive therapy: A critical appraisal of the theory and therapy of Albert Ellis.* New York: Academic Press.

Smith, T. W. (1994). Concepts and methods in the study of anger, hostility and health. In A. W. Siegman & T. W. Smith (Eds.), *Anger, hostility and the heart* (pp. 23–42). Hillsdale, NJ: Erlbaum.

Smith, T. W., & Allred, K. D. (1986). Rationality revisited: a reassessment of the empirical support for the rational-emotive model. In P. C. Kendall (Ed.), *Advances in cognitive-behavioral research and therapy* (Vol. 5). New York: Academic Press.

Smith, T. W., & Brown, P. (1991). Cynical hostility, attempts to exert social control, and cardiovascular reactivity in married couples. *Journal of Behavioral Medicine, 14,* 581–592.

Smyer, M. A. (1989). Nursing homes as a setting for psychological practice: Public policy perspectives. *American Psychologist, 44,* 1307–1315.

Smyth, C., Kalsi, G., Brynjolfsson, J., O'Neill, J., Curtis, D., Rifkin, L., Moloney, E., Murphy, P., Sherrington, R., Petursson, H., & Gurling, H. (1996). Further tests for linkage of bipolar affective disorder to the tyrosine hydroxylase gene locus on chromosome 11p15 in a new series of multiplex British affective disorder pedigrees. *American Journal of Psychiatry, 153,* 271–274.

Snowden, L. R., & Cheung, F. K. (1990). Use of inpatient mental health services by members of ethnic minority groups. *American Psychologist, 45,* 347–355.

Sobel, E., Louhija, J., Sulkava, R., Davanipour, Z., Kontula, K., Miettinen, H., Tikkanen, M., Kainulainen, K., & Tilvis, R. (1995). Lack of association of apolipoprotein E allele epsilon 4 with late-onset Alzheimer's disease among Finnish centenarians. *Neurology, 45,* 903–907.

Sobell, M. B., & Sobell, L. C. (1973). Alcoholics treated by individualized behavior therapy: One-year treatment outcome. *Behaviour Research and Therapy, 11,* 599–618.

Sobell, M. B., & Sobell, L. C. (1976). Second-year treatment outcome of alcoholics treated by individualized behavior therapy: Results. *Behaviour Research and Therapy, 14,* 195–214.

Sokol, M. S., & Pfeffer, C. R. (1992). Suicidal behavior of children. In B. Bongar (Ed.), *Suicide: Guidelines for assessment, management, and treatment.* New York: Oxford University Press.

Soloff, P. H. (1989). Psychopharmacologic therapies in borderline personality disorder. In A. Tasman, R. E. Hales & A. J. Frances (Eds.), *Review of psychiatry* (Vol. 8). Washington, DC: American Psychiatric Press.

Solomon, D. A., Keitner, G. I., Miller, I. W., Shea, M. T., et al. (1995). Course of illness and maintenance treatments for patients with bipolar disorder. *Journal of Clinical Psychiatry, 56,* 5–13.

Sommers-Flanagan, J., & Sommers-Flanagan, R. (1996). Efficacy of antidepressant medication with depressed youth: What psychologists should know. *Professional Psychology: Research and Practice, 27,* 145–153.

Sorensen, S., & Siegel, J. (1992). Gender, ethnicity, and sexual assault: Findings from a Los Angeles study. *Journal of Social Issues, 48,* 93–104.

Sorenson, R. (1973). *Adolescent sexuality in contemporary America.* New York: World.

Sorenson, S. B., Stein, J. A., Siegel, J. M., Golding, J. M., & Burnam, M. A. (1987). The prevalence of adult sexual assault: The Los Angeles epidemiologic catchment area project. *American Journal of Epidemiology, 126,* 1154–1164.

Sosa, R., Kennell, J., Klaus, M., Robertson, S., & Urrutia, J. (1980). The effect of a supportive companion on perinatal problems, length of labor, and mother-infant interaction. *New England Journal of Medicine, 303,* 597–600.

Spanos, N. P. (1994). Multiple identity enactments and multiple personality disorder: A sociocognitive perspective. *Psychological Bulletin, 116,* 143–165.

Spector, I. P., & Carey, M. P. (1990). Incidence and prevalence of the sexual dysfunctions: A critical review of the empirical literature. *Archives of Sexual Behavior, 19,* 389–408.

Spencer, D. D., Robbins, R. J., Naftolin, F., Phil, D., Marek, K. L., Vollmer, T., Leranth, C., Roth, R. H., Price, L. H., Gjedde, A., Bunney, B. S., Sass, K. J., Elsworth, J. D., Kier, E. L., Makuch, R., Hoffer, P. B., & Redmond, E. R. (1992). Unilateral transplantation of human fetal mesencephalic tissue into the caudate nucleus of patients with Parkinson's disease. *New England Journal of Medicine, 327,* 1541–1548.

Spencer, T., Biederman, J., Wilens, T., & Faraone, S. (1994). Is attention deficit hyperactivity disorder in adults a valid disorder? *Harvard Review of Psychiatry, 1,* 326–335.

Spencer, T., Biederman, J., Wilens, T., Harding, M., O'Donnell, D., & Griffin, S. (1996). Pharmacotherapy of attention-deficit hyperactivity disorder across the life cycle. *Journal of the American Academy of Child and Adolescent Psychiatry, 35,* 409–432.

Spencer, T., Wilens, T., Biederman, J., Faraone, S. V., Ablon, S., & Lapey, K. (1995). A double-blind crossover comparison of methylphenidate and placebo in adults with childhood-onset attention-deficit hyperactivity disorder. *Archives of General Psychiatry, 52,* 434–443.

Spiegel, D., Bloom, J. R., Kraemer, H. C., & Gottheil, E. (1989). Effect of psychosocial treatment on survival of patients with metastatic breast cancer. *Lancet* (October 14), 888–891.

Spitzer, R. L., First, M. B., Williams, J. B. W., Kendler, K., Pincus, H. A., & Tucker, G. (1992). Now is the time to retire the term "organic mental disorders." *American Journal of Psychiatry, 149,* 240–244.

Spitzer, R. L., Skodol, A. E., Gibbon, M., Williams, J. B. W. (1983). Statue. In R. L. Spitzer, A. E. Skodol, M. Gibbon & J. B. W. Williams (Eds.), *Psychopathology: A case book* (pp. 139–143). New York: McGraw-Hill.

Spitzer, R. L., Williams, J. B. W., Gibbon, M., & First, M. B. (1990). *Structured Clinical Interview for DSM-III-R.* Washington, DC: American Psychiatric Press.

Spitzer, R. L., Williams, J. B. W., Kass, F., & Davies, M. (1989). National field trial of the DSM-III-R diagnostic criteria for self-defeating personality disorder. *American Journal of Psychiatry, 146,* 1561–1567.

Spivack, G., & Shure, M. B. (1982). The cognition of social adjustment: Interpersonal cognitive problem-solving thinking. In B. B. Lahey & A. E. Kazdin (Eds.), *Advances in clinical child psychology* (Vol. 5). New York: Plenum Press.

Sprafka, J. M., Folsom, A. R., Burke, G. L., Hahn, L. P., & Pirie, P. (1990). Type A behavior and its association with cardiovascular disease prevalence in blacks and whites: The Minnesota Heart Study. *Journal of Behavioral Medicine, 13,* 1–14.

Springer, T., Lohr, N. E., Buchtel, H. A., & Silk, K. R. 1995. A preliminary report of short-term cognitive-behavioral group therapy for inpatients with personality disorders. *Journal of Psychotherapy Practice and Research, 5,* 57–71.

Sroufe, A., & Rutter, M. (1984). The domain of developmental psychopathology. *Child Development, 55,* 17–29.

Stanton, M. D., & Todd, T. C. (1982). *The family therapy of drug abuse and addiction.* New York: Guilford Press.

Stark, K. D., Reynolds, W. M., & Kaslow, N. J. (1987). Comparison of the relative efficacy of self-control therapy and a behavioral problem-solving therapy for depression in children. *Journal of Abnormal Child Psychology, 15,* 91–113.

Starkstein, S. E., & Robinson, R. G. (1992). Neuropsychiatric aspects of cerebral vascular disorders. In S. C. Yudofsky & R. E. Hales (Eds.), *The American Psychiatric Press textbook of neuropsychiatry.* Washington, DC: American Psychiatric Press.

Stattin, H., & Magnusson, D. (1989). The role of early aggressive behavior in the frequency, seriousness, and types of later crime. *Journal of Consulting and Clinical Psychology, 57,* 710–718.

Staub, E. (1996). Cultural-societal roots of violence: The examples of genocidal violence and of contemporary youth violence in the United States. *American Psychologist, 51,* 117–132.

Steen, E., & Steen, J. (1989). Controversy concerning parental age effect in 47, =21 Down's syndrome. *Human Genetics, 81,* 300–301.

Stein, D. J., Simeon, D., Frenkel, M., Islam, M. N., & Hollander, E. (1995). An open trial of valproate in borderline personality disorder. *Journal of Clinical Psychology, 56,* 506–510.

Stein, M. B., Heuser, I. J., Juncos, J. L., & Uhde, T. W. (1990). Anxiety disorders in patients with Parkinson's disease. *American Journal of Psychiatry, 147,* 217–220.

Steinberg, L. (1987). Single parents, stepparents, and the susceptibility of adolescents to antisocial peer pressure. *Child Development, 58,* 269–275.

Steinberg, M., Cicchetti, D., Buchanan, J., & Rakfeldt, J. (1994). Distinguishing between multiple personality disorder, dissociative identity disorder and schizophrenia using the structured clinical interview for DSM-IV dissociative disorders. *Journal of Nervous and Mental Disease, 182,* 495–502.

Steinhausen, H. C. (1994). Anorexia and bulimia nervosa. In M. Rutter, E. Taylor & L. Hersov (Eds.), *Child and adolescent psychiatry.* Oxford: Blackwell Scientific Publications.

Steketee, G., & Foa, E. (1987). Rape victims: Post-traumatic stress response and their treatment: A review of the literature. *Journal of Anxiety Disorders, 1,* 69–86.

Stemberger, R. T., Turner, S. M., Beidel, D. C., & Calhoun, D. S. (1995). Social phobia. An analysis of possible developmental factors. *Journal of Abnormal Psychology, 104,* 526–531.

Stephens, R. S., Roffman, R. A., & Simpson, E. E. (1993). Adult marijuana users seeking treatment. *Journal of Consulting and Clinical Psychology, 61,* 1100–1104.

Stern, R. A., & Bachman, D. L. (1991). Depressive symptoms following stroke. *American Journal of Psychiatry, 148,* 351–356.

Stern, Y., Marder, K., Bell, K., Chen, J., Dooneief, G., Goldstein, S., Mindry, D., Richards, M., Sano, M., Williams, J., Gorman, J., Ehrhardt, A., & Mayeux, R. (1991). Multidisciplinary baseline assessment of homosexual men with and without human immunodeficiency virus infection: III. Neurologic and neuropsychological findings. *Archives of General Psychiatry, 48,* 131–138.

Stevenson, J., & Meares, R. (1992). An outcome study of psychotherapy for patients with borderline personality disorder. *American Journal of Psychiatry, 149,* 358–362.

Stewart, S. H. (1996). Alcohol abuse in individuals exposed to trauma: A critical review. *Psychological Bulletin, 120,* 83–112.

Stewart, S. H., Peterson, J. B., & Pihl, R. O. (1995). Anxiety sensitivity and self-reported alcohol consumption rates in university women. *Journal of Anxiety Disorders, 9,* 283–292.

Stokes, A., Bawden, H. N., Camfield, P., Ackman, J., & Dooley, J. M. (1991). Peer problems in Tourette's disorder. *Pediatrics, 87,* 936–942.

Stone, M. H. (1989). The course of borderline personality disorder. In A. Tasman, R. E. Hales & A. J. Frances (Eds.), *Review of Psychiatry.* Washington, DC: American Psychiatric Press.

Stone, M. H. (1993). Long-term outcome in personality disorders. *British Journal of Psychiatry, 162,* 299–313.

Strack, S., & Lorr, M. (Eds.). (1994). *Differentiating normal and abnormal personality.* New York: Springer Publishing Co.

Straus, M. A., & Gelles, R. J. (1986). Societal change and change in family violence from 1975–1985 as revealed by two national surveys. *Journal of Marriage and the Family, 48,* 465–479.

Stravynski, A., Lesage, A., Marcouiller, M., & Elie, R. (1989). A test of the therapeutic mechanism in social skills training with avoidant personality disorder. *Journal of Nervous and Mental Disease, 177,* 739–744.

Stravynski, A., Marks, I., & Yule, W. (1982). Social skills problems in neurotic outpatients: Social skills training with and without cognitive modification. *Archives of General Psychiatry, 39,* 1378–1385.

Streissguth, A. P., Barr, H. M., Sampson, P. D., Darby, B. L., & Martin, D. C. (1989). IQ at age 4 in relation to maternal alcohol use and smoking during pregnancy. *Developmental Psychology, 25,* 3–11.

Strittmatter, W. J., Saunders, A. M., Schmechel, D., Pericak-Vance, M., Enghild, J., Salvesen, G. S., & Roses, A. D. (1993). Apolipoprotein E: High-avidity binding to beta-amyloid and increased frequency of type 4 allele in late-onset familial Alzheimer disease. *Proceedings of the National Academy of Sciences of the United States of America, 90,* 1977–1981.

Strober, M. (1992). Relevance of early age-of-onset in genetic studies of affective disorder. *Journal of the American Academy of Child and Adolescent Psychiatry, 31,* 505–510.

Strober, M., & Katz, J. (1987). Do eating disorders and affective disorders share a common etiology? *International Journal of Eating Disorders, 6,* 171–180.

Stroop, J. R. (1938). Factors affecting speed in serial verbal reactions. *Psychological Monographs, 50,* 38–48.

Strube, M. J. (1988). The decision to leave an abusive relationship: Empirical evidence and theoretical issues. *Psychological Bulletin, 104,* 236–250.

Strupp, H., & Binder, J. (1984). *Psychotherapy in a new key: A guide to time limited dynamic psychotherapy.* New York: Basic Books.

Stuss, D. T., Gow, C. A., & Hetherington, C. R. (1992). "No longer Gage": Frontal lobe dysfunction and emotional changes. *Journal of Consulting and Clinical Psychology, 60,* 349–359.

Suddath, R. L., Christison, G. W., Torrey, E. F., Casanova, M. F., & Weinberger, D. R. (1990). Anatomical abnormalities in the brains of monozygotic twins discordant for schizophrenia. *The New England Journal of Medicine, 322,* 789–794.

Sue, S. (1977). Community mental health services to minority groups: Some optimism, some pessimism. *American Psychologist, 32,* 616–624.

Sue, S. (1992). Ethnicity and mental health: Research and policy issues. *Journal of Social Issues, 48,* 187–205.

Sue, S., Chun, C. A., & Gee, K. (1995). Ethnic minority intervention and treatment research. In J. F. Aponte, R. Y. Rivers, & J. Wohl (Eds.), *Psychological interventions and cultural diversity* (pp. 266–282). Boston: Allyn and Bacon.

Sue, S., Fujino, D. C., Hu, L., Takeuchi, D. T., & Zane, N. W. S. (1991). Community mental health services for ethnic minority groups: A test of the cultural responsiveness hypothesis. *Journal of Consulting and Clinical Psychology, 59,* 533–540.

Sue, S., Zane, N., & Young, K. (1994). Research on psychotherapy with culturally diverse populations. In S. Garfield & A. Bergin (Eds.), *Handbook of psychotherapy and behavior change* (4th ed.). New York: Wiley.

Suematsu, H., Kuboki, T., & Itoh, T. (1985). Statistical studies on the prognosis of anorexia nervosa. *Psychosomatics, 43,* 104–112.

Sugiyama, T., & Abe, T. (1989). The prevalence of autism in Nagoya, Japan: A total population study. *Journal of Autism and Developmental Disorders, 19,* 87–96.

Sundberg, N. D. (1977). *Assessment of persons.* New Jersey: Prentice-Hall.

Susser, E. S., Lin, S. P., Conover, S. A., & Struening, E. L. (1991). Childhood antecedents of homelessness in psychiatric patients. *American Journal of Psychiatry, 148,* 1026–1030.

Susser, E., Neugebauer, R., Hoek, H. W., Brown, A. S., Lin, S., Labovitz, D., & Gorman, J. M. (1996). Schizophrenia after prenatal famine: Further evidence. *Archives of General Psychiatry, 53,* 25–31.

Sussman, S., Dent, C., Stacy, A., Burciaga, C., Raynor, A., Turner, G., Charlin, V., Craig, S., Hansen, W., Burton, D., & Flay, B. (1990). Peer group association and adolescent tobacco use. *Journal of Abnormal Psychology, 99,* 349–352.

Sutker, P. B., Davis, J. M., Uddo, M., & Ditta, S. R. (1995). War zone stress, personal resources, and PTSD in Persian Gulf war returnees. *Journal of Abnormal Psychology, 104,* 444–452.

Sutker, P. B., DeSanto, N. A., & Allain, A. N. (1985). Adjective self-descriptions in antisocial men and women. *Journal of Psychopathology and Behavioral Assessment, 7,* 175–181.

Sutton-Simon, K., & Goldfried, M. R. (1979). Faulty thinking patterns in two types of anxiety. *Cognitive Therapy and Research, 3,* 193–203.

Svartberg, M., & Stiles, T. (1991). Comparative effects of short-term psychodynamic psychotherapy. *Journal of Consulting and Clinical Psychology, 59,* 704–714.

Swanson, J., & Kinsbourne, M. (1980). Artificial color and hyperactive children. In R. M. Knights & D. J. Bakker (Eds.), *Treatment of hyperactive and learning disabled children.* Baltimore: University Park Press.

Swartz, M., Hughes, D., Blazer, D., & George, L. (1987). Somatization disorder in the community: A study of diagnostic concordance among three diagnostic systems. *The Journal of Nervous and Mental Disease, 175,* 26–33.

Swedo, S. E., Pleeter, J. D., Richter, D. M., Hoffman, C. L., Allen, A. J., Hamburger, S. D., Turner, E. H., Yamada, E. M., & Rosenthal, N. E. (1995). Rates of seasonal affective disorder in children and adolescents. *American Journal of Psychiatry, 152,* 1016–1019.

Szatmari, P., Offord, D. R., & Boyle, M. H. (1989). Ontario child health study: Prevalence of attention deficit disorder with hyperactivity. *Journal of Child Psychology and Psychiatry, 30,* 219–230.

Szymanski, S. R., Cannon, T. D., Gallacher, F., Erwin, R. J., & Gur, R. E. (1996). Course of treatment response in first-episode and chronic schizophrenia. *American Journal of Psychiatry, 153,* 519–525.

Szymanski, S. R., Lieberman, J. A., Alvir, J. M., Mayerhoff, D., Loebel, A., Geisler, S., Chakos, M., Koreen, A., Jody, D., Kane, J., Woerner, M., & Cooper, T. (1995). Gender differences in onset of illness, treatment response, course, and biologic indexes in first-episode schizophrenic patients. *American Journal of Psychiatry, 152,* 698–703.

Taller, A. M., Asher, D. M., Pomeroy, K. L., Eldadah, B. A., Godec, M. S., Falkai, P. G., Bogert, B., Kleinman, J. E., Stevens, J. R., & Torrey, E. F. (1996). Search for viral nucleic acid sequences in brain tissues of patients with schizophrenia using nested polymerase chain reaction. *Archives of General Psychiatry, 53,* 32–40.

Tang, M. X., Maestre, G., Tsai, W. Y., Liu, X. H., Feng, L., Chung, W. Y., Chun, M., Schofield, P., Stern, Y., Tycko, B., Mayeux, R. (1996). Relative risk of Alzheimer's disease and age-at-onset distributions, based on APOE genotypes among elderly African Americans, Caucasians, and Hispanics in New York City. *American Journal of Human Genetics, 58,* 574–584.

Tanoue, Y., Oda, S., Asano, F., & Kawashima, K. (1988). Epidemiology of infantile autism in Southern Ibaraki, Japan: Differences in prevalence rates in birth cohorts. *Journal of Autism and Developmental Disorders, 18,* 155–166.

Target, M., & Fonagy, P. (1994). Efficacy of psychoanalysis for children with emotional disorder. *Journal of the American Academy of Child and Adolescent Psychiatry, 33,* 361–371.

Tarnowski, K. J., & Nay, S. M. (1989). Locus of control in children with learning disabilities and hyperactivity: A subgroup analysis. *Journal of Learning Disabilities, 22,* 381–383.

Tarrier, N., Beckett, R., Harwood, S., Baker, A., Yusopoff, L., & Ugareburu, I. (1993). A trial of two cognitive-behavioural methods of treating drug-resistant residual psychotic symptoms in schizophrenic patients, I: Outcome. *British Journal of Psychiatry, 162,* 524–532.

Tasker, F., & Golombok, S. (1995). Adults raised as children in lesbian families. *American Journal of Orthopsychiatry, 65,* 203–215.

Tatai, K. (1983). Japan. In L. A. Headley (Ed.), *Suicide in Asia and the Near East.* Berkeley, CA: University of California Press.

Tate, D. C., Reppucci, N. D., & Mulvey, E. P. (1995). Violent juvenile delinquents: Treatment effectiveness and implications for future action. *American Psychologist, 50,* 777–781.

Tavris, C. (1992). *The mismeasure of woman.* New York: Simon & Schuster.

Taylor, E. (1994). Syndromes of attention deficit and overactivity. In M. Rutter, E. Taylor & L. Hersov (Eds.), *Child and adolescent psychiatry.* Oxford: Blackwell Scientific Publications.

Taylor, H. G. (1989). Learning disabilities. In E. J. Mash & R. A. Barkley (Eds.), *Treatment of childhood disorders.* New York: Guilford Press.

Teasdale, J. D., & Russell, M. L. (1983). Differential effects of induced mood on the recall of positive, negative, and neutral words. *British Journal of Clinical Psychology, 33,* 163–172.

Telch, M. J., Schmidt, N. B., Jaimez, T. L., Jacquin, K. M., & Harrington, P. J. (1995). Impact of cognitive-behavioral treatment on quality of life in panic disorder patients. *Journal of Consulting and Clinical Psychology, 63,* 823–830.

Teplin, L. A., Abram, K. M., & McClelland, G. M. (1996). Prevalence of psychiatric disorders among incarcerated women: Pretrial jail detainees. *Archives of General Psychiatry, 53,* 505–512.

Teri, L., Truax, P., Logsdon, R., Uomoto, J., & Zarit, S. (1992). Assessment of behavioral problems in dementia: The Revised Memory and Behavior Problems Checklist. *Psychology and Aging, 7,* 622–631.

Teri, L., & Wagner, A. (1992). Alzheimer's disease and depression. *Journal of Consulting and Clinical Psychology, 60,* 379–391.

Theorell, T., Lind, E., & Floderus, B. (1975). The relationship of disturbing life-changes and emotions to the early development of myocardial infarction and other serious illnesses. *International Journal of Epidemiology, 4,* 281–293.

Thigpen, C., & Cleckley, H. (1954). *The three faces of Eve.* Kingsport, TN: Kingsport Press.

Thomas, A., & Chess, S. (1977). *Temperament and development.* New York: Brunner/Mazel.

Thomas, A., & Chess, S. (1984). Genesis and evolution of behavioral disorders: From infancy to early adult life. *American Journal of Psychiatry, 141,* 1–9.

Thompson, R. J., & Kronenberger, W. (1990). Behavior problems in children with learning problems. In H. L. Swanson & B. Keogh (Eds.), *Learning disabilities: Theoretical and research issues.* Hillsdale, NJ: Erlbaum.

Thoresen, C., & Powell, L. H. (1992). Type A behavior pattern: New perspectives on theory, assessment, and intervention. *Journal of Consulting and Clinical Psychology, 60,* 595–604.

Thorndike, E. L. (1898). Animal intelligence: An experimental study of the associative processes in animals. *Psychological Monographs, 2* (No. 8).

Thornicroft, G., & Sartorius, N. (1993). The course and outcome of depression in different cultures: 10-year follow-up of the WHO Collaborative Study on the Assessment of Depressive Disorders. *Psychological Medicine, 23,* 1023–1032.

Thurman, P. J., Swaim, R., & Plested, B. (1995). Intervention and treatment of ethnic minority substance abusers. In J. Aponte, R. Rivers, & J. Wohl (Eds.), *Psychological interventions and cultural diversity.* Needham, MA: Allyn & Bacon.

Tienari, P., Sorri, A., Lahti, I., Naarala, M., Wahlberg, K. E., Moring, J., Pohjola, J., & Wynne, L. C. (1987). Genetic and psychosocial factors in schizophrenia: The Finnish Adoptive Family Study. *Schizophrenia Bulletin, 13,* 477–484.

Timmerman, M. G., Wells, L. A., & Chen, S. (1990). Bulimia nervosa and associated alcohol abuse among secondary school students. *Journal of the American Academy of Child and Adolescent Psychiatry, 29,* 118–222.

Tolman, R. M., & Weisz, A. (1995). Coordinated community intervention for domestic violence: The effects of arrest and prosecution on recidivism of woman abuse perpetrators. *Crime and Delinquency, 41,* 481–495.

Tooth, G. C., & Newton, M. P. (1961). *Reports on public health and medical students,* No. 104, Ministry of Health. London: HMSO.

Torgersen, S. (1983). Genetic factors in anxiety disorders. *Archives of General Psychiatry, 40,* 1085–1089.

Torgersen, S. (1986). Genetic factors in moderately severe and mild affective disorders. *Archives of General Psychiatry, 43,* 222–226.

Torgersen, S. (1988). Genetics. In C. Last & M. Hersen (Eds.), *Handbook of anxiety disorders.* New York: Pergamon Press.

Torgesen, J. K. (1977). Memorization processes in reading disabled children. *Journal of Educational Psychology, 69,* 571–578.

Torgesen, J. K. (1979). What shall we do with psychological processes? *Journal of Learning Disabilities, 12,* 6–23.

Torgesen, J. K. (1986). Learning disabilities theory: Its current state and future prospects. *Journal of Learning Disabilities, 19,* 399–407.

Toro, P. A., Weissberg, R. P., Guare, J., & Liebenstein, N. L. (1990). A comparison of children with and without learning disabilities on social cognitive-problem solving skill, social behavior, and family background. *Journal of Learning Disabilities, 23,* 115–120.

Torrey, E. F. (1990). Economic barriers to widespread implementation of model programs for the seriously mentally ill. *Hospital and Community Psychiatry, 41,* 526–531.

Torrey, E. F. (1992). Are we overestimating the genetic contribution to schizophrenia? *Schizophrenia Bulletin, 18,* 159–170.

Touliatos, J., Perlmutter, B. F., & Straus, M. A. (Eds.). (1990). *Handbook of family measurement techniques.* Newbury, CA: Sage.

Tran, G. Q., & Chambless, D. L. (1995). Psychopathology of social phobia: Effects of subtype and of avoidant personality disorder. *Journal of Anxiety Disorders, 9,* 489–501.

Treadwell, K., Flannery, E., & Kendall, P. C. (1995). Ethnicity and gender in relation to adaptive functioning, diagnostic status, and treatment outcome in children from an anxiety clinic. *Journal of Anxiety Disorders, 9,* 373–384.

Treadwell, K., & Kendall, P. C. (1996). Self-talk in anxiety-disordered youth: States-of-mind, content specificity, and treatment outcome. *Journal of Consulting and Clinical Psychology, 64,* 941–950.

Treasure, J., Schmidt, U., Troop, N., & Todd, G. (1996). Sequential treatment for bulimia nervosa incorporating a self-care manual. *British Journal of Psychiatry, 168,* 94–98.

Tremblay, R. E., McCord, J., Boileau, H., LeBlanc, M., Gagnon, C., Charlesbois, P., & Larivee, S. (1990). *The Montreal experiment: School adjustment and self-reported delinquency after three-years of follow-up.* Paper presented at the annual meeting of the American Society of Criminology, Baltimore, Maryland, USA.

Tremblay, R. E., Pagani-Kurtz, L., Masse, L. C., Vitaro, F., & Pihl, R. O. (1995). A bimodal preventive intervention for disruptive kindergarten boys: Its impact through mid-adolescence. *Journal of Consulting and Clinical Psychology, 63,* 560–568.

Tremblay, R. E., Pihl, R. O., Vitaro, F., & Dobkin, P. L. (1994). Predicting early onset of male antisocial behavior from preschool behavior. *Archives of General Psychiatry, 51,* 732–739.

Treml, V. (1982). *Alcohol in the USSR: A statistical study.* Durham, NC: Duke University Press.

Trull, T. J., Widiger, T. A., & Guthrie, P. (1990). Categorical versus dimensional status of borderline personality disorder. *Journal of Abnormal Psychology, 99,* 40–48.

Tuma, J. M. (1989). Mental health services for children: The state of the art. *American Psychologist, 44,* 188–199.

Turner, S. M., & Beidel, D. C. (1988). *Treating obsessive-compulsive disorder.* New York: Pergamon Press.

Turner, S. M., & Beidel, D. C. (1989). Social phobia: Clinical syndrome, diagnosis, and comorbidity. *Clinical Psychology Review, 9,* 3–18.

Turner, S. M., Beidel, D. C., & Townsley, R. M. (1992). Social phobia: A comparison of specific and generalized subtypes and avoidant personality disorder. *Journal of Abnormal Psychology, 101,* 326–331.

Turner, W. M., & Tsuang, M. T. (1990). Impact of substance abuse on the course and outcome of schizophrenia. *Schizophrenia Bulletin, 16,* 87–96.

Tuteur, J. M., Ewigman, B. E., Peterson, L., & Hosokawa, M. C. (1995). The maternal observation matrix and the mother-child interaction scale: Brief observational screening instruments for physically abusive mothers. *Journal of Consulting and Clinical Psychology, 24,* 55–62.

Tutkun, H., Yargic, L. I., & Sar, V. (1995). Dissociative identity disorder: A clinical investigation of 20 cases in Turkey. *Dissociation Progress in the Dissociative Disorders, 8,* 3–9.

Tversky, A., & Kahneman, D. (1973). Availability: A heuristic for judging frequency and probability. *Cognitive Psychology, 5,* 207–232.

Ursano, R. J., Fullerton, C. S., Kao, T. C., & Bhartiya, V. (1995). Longitudinal assessment of posttraumatic stress disorder and depression after exposure to traumatic death. *Journal of Nervous and Mental Disease, 183,* 36–42.

Ussher, J. M., & Dewberry, C. (1995). The nature and long-term effects of childhood sexual abuse: A survey of adult women survivors in Britain. *British Journal of Clinical Psychology, 34,* 177–192.

Uva, J. L. (1995). Autoerotic asphyxiation in the United States. *Journal of Forensic Sciences, 40,* 574–581.

Vaillant, G. E. (1966). Parent-child cultural disparity and drug addiction. *Journal of Nervous and Mental Diseases, 142,* 534–539.

Vaillant, G. E., & Vaillant, C. O. (1990). Natural history of male psychological health, XII: A 45-year study of predictors of successful aging at age 65. *American Journal of Psychiatry, 147,* 31–37.

Valenstein, E. S. (1986). *Great and desperate cures: The rise and decline of psychosurgery and other radical treatments for mental illness.* New York: Basic Books.

Valone, K., Norton, J. P., Goldstein, M. J., & Doane, J. A. (1983). Parental expressed emotion and affective style in an adolescent sample at risk for schizophrenia spectrum disorders. *Journal of Abnormal Psychology, 92,* 399–407.

Van Bourgondien, M. E., & Schopler, E. (1990). Critical issues in the residential care of people with autism. *Journal of Autism and Developmental Disorders, 20,* 291–298.

van den Oord, E. J. C. G., Verhulst, F. C., & Boomsma, D. I. (1996). A genetic study of maternal and paternal ratings of problem behaviors in 3-year-old twins. *Journal of Abnormal Psychology, 105,* 349–357.

Van der Kolk, B. A., Boyd, H., Crystal, J., & Greenburg, M. (1984). Post-traumatic stress disorder as a biologically based disorder: Implications of the animal model of inescapable shock. In B. A. Van der Kolk (Ed.), *Post-traumatic stress disorder: Psychological and biological sequelae.* Washington, DC: American Psychiatric Press.

Van Putten, T., Marder, S. R., & Mintz, J. (1992). Blacks, schizophrenia, and neuroleptic treatment: In reply. *Archives of General Psychiatry, 49,* 165.

Vandenberg, S. G., & Crowe, L. (1989). Genetic factors in childhood psychopathology. In B. Lahey & A. E. Kazdin (Eds.), *Advances in clinical child psychology* (Vol. 12). New York: Plenum Press.

VanHasselt, V. B., Hersen, M., & Null, J. A. (1993). Drug abuse prevention for high-risk African American children and their families: A review and model program. *Addictive Behaviors, 18,* 213–234.

Vaughan, R., McCarthy, J., Armstrong, B., Walter, H., Waterman, P., & Tiezzi, L. (1996). Carrying and using weapons: A survey of minority junior high school students in New York City. *American Journal of Public Health, 86,* 568–572.

Vaz, E. W. (1967). *Middle class juvenile delinquency.* New York: Harper & Row.

Ventura, J., Nuechterlein, K. H., Lukoff, D., & Hardesty, J. P. (1989). A prospective study of stressful life events and schizophrenic relapse. *Journal of Abnormal Psychology, 98,* 407–411.

Vermeulen, A., Rubes, R., & Verdonck, L. (1972). Testos-terone secretion and metabolism in male senescence. *Journal of Endocrinological Metabolism, 37,* 730.

Vernberg, E. M., LaGreca, A. M., Silverman, W. K., & Prinstein, M. J. (1996). Prediction of posttraumatic stress symptoms in children after hurricane Andrew. *Journal of Abnormal Psychology, 105,* 237–248.

Verrier, R. L., DeSilva, R. A., & Lown, B. (1983). Psycho-logical factors in cardiac arrhythmias and sudden death. In D. S. Krantz, A. Baum, & J. E. Singer (Eds.), *Handbook of psychology and health.* Hillsdale, NJ: Erlbaum.

Virkkunen, M., De Jong, J., Bartko, J., Goodwin, M., & Linnoila, M. (1989). Relationship of psychobiological variables to recidivism in violent offenders and impulsive fire setters. *Archives of General Psychiatry, 46,* 600–603.

Virkkunen, M., Eggert, M., Rawlings, R., & Linnoila, M. (1996). A prospective follow-up study of alcoholic violent offenders and fire setters. *Archives of General Psychiatry, 53,* 523–529.

Virkkunen, M., Nuutila, A., Goodwin, F. K., & Linnoila, M. (1987). Cerebrospinal fluid monoamine metabolites in male arsonists. *Archives of General Psychiatry, 44,* 241–247.

Virkkunen, M., Rawlings, R., Tokola, R., Poland, R. E., Guidotti, A., Nemeroff, C., Bissette, G., Kalogeras, K., Karonen, S. L., & Linnoila, M. (1994). CSF biochemistries, glucose metabolism, and diurnal activity rhythms in alcoholic, violent offenders, fire setters, and healthy volunteers. *Archives of General Psychiatry, 51,* 20–27.

Visintainer, M. A., Volpicelli, J. R., & Seligman, M. (1982). Tumor rejection in rats after inescapable or escapable shock. *Science, 216,* 437–439.

Visser, S., & Bouman, T. K. (1992). Cognitive behavioral approaches to the treatment of hypochondriasis: Six single-case crossover studies. *Behaviour Research and Therapy, 30,* 301–306.

Vitaliano. P. P., Russo, J., Carr, J. E., Maiuro, R. D., & Becker, J. (1985). The ways of coping checklist: revision and psychometric properties. *Multivariate Behavioral Research, 20,* 3–26.

Vitousek, K. B., & Orimoto, L. (1993). Cognitive-behavioral models of anorexia nervosa, bulimia nervosa, and obesity. In K. S. Dobson & P. C. Kendall (Eds.), *Psychopathology and cognition.* Orlando, FL: Academic Press.

Volkmar, F. R. (1996). Brief report: Diagnostic issues in autism: Results of the DSM-IV field trial. *Journal of Autism and Developmental Disorders, 26,* 155–157.

Wadden, T. A., Brown, G., Foster, G. D., & Linowitz, J. R. (1991). Salience of weight related worries in adolescent males and females. *International Journal of Eating Disorders, 10,* 407–414.

Wadden, T. A., Luborsky, L., Greer, S., & Crits-Cristoph, P. (1984). The behavioral treatment of essential hypertension: an update and comparison with pharmacological treatment. *Clinical Psychology Review, 4,* 403–429.

Wahler, R. G., & Dumas, J. E. (1989). Attentional problems in dysfunctional mother-child interactions: An interbehavioral model. *Psychological Bulletin, 105,* 116–130.

Wakefield, H., & Underwager, R. (1992). Recovered memories of alleged sexual abuse: Lawsuits against parents. *Behavioral Sciences and the Law, 10,* 483–507.

Walker, E. F., & Lewine, R. J. (1990). Prediction of adult-onset schizophrenia from childhood home movies of the patients. *American Journal of Psychiatry, 147,* 1052–1056.

Walker, E. F., Savoie, T., & Davis, D. (1994). Neuromotor precursors of schizophrenia. *Schizophrenia Bulletin, 20,* 441–451.

Walker, L. E. A. (1989). Psychology and violence against women. *American Psychologist, 44,* 695–702.

Walker, L. S., Garber, J., & Greene, J. W. (1994). Somatic complaints in pediatric patients: A prospective study of the role of negative life events, child social and academic competence, and parental somatic symptoms. *Journal of Consulting and Clinical Psychology, 62,* 1213–1221.

Wallerstein, J. S., & Blakeslee, S. (1989). *Second chances.* New York: Ticknor & Fields.

Wallerstein, J. S., Corbin, S. B., & Lewis, J. M. (1988). Children of divorce: A 10-year study. In E. M. Hetherington & J. D. Arasteh (Eds.), *Impact of divorce, single parenting, and stepparenting on children.* Hillsdale, NJ: Erlbaum.

Wallerstein, J. S., & Kelly, J. (1974). The effects of parental divorce: The adolescent experience. In E. J. Anthony & C. Koupernick (Eds.), *The child in his family,* (Vol. 3). New York: Wiley.

Walsh, D. C., Hingson, R. W., Merrigan, D. M., Morelock Levenson, S., Cupples, A., Heeren, T., Coffman, G. A., Becker, C. A., Barker, T. A., Hamilton, S. K., McGuire, T. G., & Kelly, C. A. (1991). Special article: A randomized trial of treatment options for alcohol-abusing workers. *New England Journal of Medicine, 325,* 775–782.

Wanberg, K. W. (1969). Prevalence of symptoms found among excessive drinkers. *International Journal of the Addictions, 4,* 169–185.

Wanigaratne, S., & Barker, C. (1995). Clients' preferences for styles of therapy. *British Journal of Clinical Psychology, 34,* 215–222.

Warner, L. A., & Kessler, R. C. (1995). Prevalence and correlates of drug use and dependence in the United States. *Archives of General Psychiatry, 52,* 219–229.

Warren, R., & Zgourides, G. D. (1991). *Anxiety disorders: A rational-emotive perspective.* New York: Pergamon Press.

Warwick, H. M. C., & Marks, I. M. (1988). Behavioral treatment of illness phobia and hypochondriasis: A pilot study of 17 cases. *British Journal of Psychiatry, 152,* 239–241.

Watson, J. B., & Rayner, R. (1920). Conditioned emotional reactions. *Journal of Experimental Psychology, 3,* 1–14.

Watt, N. F., & Saiz, C. (1991). Longitudinal studies of premorbid development of adult schizophrenics. In E. F. Walker (Ed.), *Schizophrenia: A life-course in developmental perspective.* San Diego: Academic Press.

Webster, D., Gainer, P., & Champion, H. (1993). Weapon carrying among inner-city junior high school students: Defensive behavior vs. aggressive delinquency. *American Journal of Public Health, 83,* 1604–1608.

Webster's Twentieth Century Dictionary, Unabridged. (1986). New York: Standard Reference Works Publishing Company.

Webster-Stratton, C., & Herbert, M. (1994). *Troubled families— Problem children: Working with parents, a collaborative process.* New York: Wiley.

Wechsler, D. (1981). *Manual for the Wechsler Adult Intelligence Scale: Revised.* New York: Psychological Corporation.

Wechsler, D. (1989). *Wechsler Intelligence Scale for Children: Third Edition.* Psychological Corporation. San Antonio: Harcourt Brace Jovanovich.

Weeks, G. R., & L'Abate, L. (1982). *Paradoxical psychotherapy: Theory and practice with individuals, couples, and families.* New York: Brunner/Mazel.

Wehr, T. A., Sack, D. A., & Rosenthal, N. E. (1987). Sleep reduction as a final common pathway in the genesis of mania. *American Journal of Psychiatry, 144,* 201–204.

Weibel-Orlando, J. (1987). Culture-specific treatment modalities: Assessing client-to-treatment fit in Indian alcoholism programs. In W. M. Cox (Ed.), *Treatment and prevention of alcohol problems: A resource manual.* New York: Academic Press.

Weich, S., Lewis, G., & Mann, A. (1996). Effect of early life experiences and personality on the reporting of psychosocial distress in general practice: A preliminary investigation. *British Journal of Psychiatry, 168,* 116–120.

Weiner, H. (1985). The physiology of eating disorders. *International Journal of Eating Disorders, 4,* 347–388.

Weiner, I. B. (1975). *Principles of psychotherapy.* New York: Wiley.

Weingartner, H., Rapaport, J. L., Buchsbaum, M. S., Bunney, W. E., Ebert, M. H., Mikkelsen, E. J., & Caine, E. D. (1980). Cognitive processes in normal and hyperactive children and their responses to amphetamine treatment. *Journal of Abnormal Psychology, 89,* 25–37.

Weisman, A., Lopez, S., Karno, M., & Jenkins, J. (1993). An attributional analysis of expressed emotion in Mexican-American families with schizophrenia. *Journal of Abnormal Psychology, 102,* 601–606.

Weiss, B., & Weisz, J. (1995). Relative effectiveness of behavioral versus nonbehavioral child psychotherapy. *Journal of Consulting and Clinical Psychology, 63,* 317–320.

Weiss, G., & Hechtman, L. (1986). *Hyperactive children grown up.* New York: Guilford Press.

Weiss, G., Hechtman, L., Milroy, T., & Perlman, T. (1985). Psychiatric status of hyperactivities as adults: A controlled prospective 15-year follow-up of 63 hyperactive children. *Journal of the American Academy of Child and Adolescent Psychiatry, 24,* 211–220.

Weiss, J. M. (1971). Effects of coping behavior in different warning signal conditions on stress pathology in rats. *Journal of Comparative and Physiological Psychology, 77,* 1–13.

Weiss, R. S. (1979). Growing up a little faster: The experience of growing up in a single parent household. *Journal of Social Issues, 35,* 97–111.

Weissberg, R. P., Caplan, M., & Harwood, R. L. (1991). Promoting competent young people in competence-enhancing environments: A systems-based perspective on primary prevention. *Journal of Consulting and Clinical Psychology, 59,* 830–841.

Weissman, M. M. (1993). The epidemiology of personality disorders: A 1990 update. *Journal of Personality Disorders,* (Suppl.), 44–62.

Weissman, M. M., Gammon, G. D., John, K., Merikangas, K. R., Warner, V., Prusoff, B. A., & Sholomkas, D. (1987). Children of depressed parents: Increased psychopathology and early onset of major depression. *Archives of General Psychiatry, 44,* 847–853.

Weissman, M. M., & Klerman, G. L. (1990). Interpersonal psychotherapy for depression. In B. B. Wolman & G. Stricker (Eds.), *Depressive disorders: Facts, theories, and treatment methods.* New York: Wiley.

Weissman, M. M., & Klerman, G. L. (1992). Interpersonal psychotherapy. In E. S. Paykel (Ed.), *Handbook of affective disorders.* New York: Guilford Press.

Weissman, M. M., & Olfson, M. (1995). Depression in women: Implications for health care research. *Science, 269,* 799–801.

Weissman, M. M., Sholomkas, D., & John, K. (1981). The assessment of social adjustment: An update. *Archives of General Psychiatry, 38,* 1250–1258.

Weisz, J., Chaiyasit, W., Weiss, B., Eastman, K., & Jackson, E. (1995). A multimethod study of problem behavior among Thai and American children in school: Teacher reports versus direct observations. *Child Development, 66,* 402–415.

Weisz, J., Sigman, M., Weiss, B., & Mosk, J. (1993). Parent reports of behavioral and emotional problems among children in Kenya, Thailand, and the United States. *Child Development, 64,* 98–109.

Weisz, J., Suwanlert, S., Chaiyasit, W., Weiss, B., Achenbach, T., & Eastman, K. (1993). Behavioral and emotional problems among Thai and American adolescents: Parent reports for ages 12–16. *Journal of Abnormal Psychology, 102,* 395–403.

Weisz, J., Weiss, B., Han, S., Granger, D., & Morton, T. (1995). Effects of psychotherapy with children and adolescents revisited: A

meta-analysis of treatment outcome studies. *Psychological Bulletin, 117,* 450–468.

Weisz, J. R., Martin, S. L., Walter, B. R., & Fernandez, G. A. (1991). Differential prediction of young adult arrests for property and personal crimes: Findings of a cohort follow-up study of violent boys from North Carolina's Willie M. Program. *Journal of Child Psychology and Psychiatry, 32,* 783–792.

Weisz, J. R., Weiss, B., Han, S. S., Granger, D. A., & Morton, T. (1995). Effects of psychotherapy with children and adolescents revisited: A meta-analysis of treatment outcome studies. *Psychological Bulletin, 117,* 450–468.

Wekerle, C., & Wolfe, D. A. (1993). Prevention of child physical abuse and neglect: Promising new directions. *Clinical Psychology Review, 13,* 501–540.

Wells, K. B., Stewart, A., Hays, R. D., Burnam, M. A., Rogers, W., Daniels, M., Berry, S., Greenfield, S., & Ware, J. (1989). The functioning and well being of depressed patients: Results from the medical outcome study. *Journal of the American Medical Association, 262,* 914–919.

Wells, K. C., & Forehand, R. (1985). Conduct and oppositional disorders. In P. H. Bornstein & A. E. Kazdin (Eds.), *Handbook of clinical behavior therapy with children.* Homewood, IL: Dorsey.

Welte, J. W., & Barnes, G. M. (1987). Alcohol use among adolescent minority groups. *Journal of Studies on Alcohol, 48,* 329–336.

Wenar, C. (1982). *Psychopathology from infancy through adolescence: A developmental approach.* New York: Random House.

Wenar, C., Ruttenberg, B. A., Kalish-Weiss, B., & Wolf, E. G. (1986). The development of normal and autistic children: A comparative study. *Journal of Autism and Developmen-tal Disorders, 16,* 317–323.

Wenger, N. K., Speroff, L., & Packard, B. (1993). Cardiovas-cular health in women. *New England Journal of Medicine, 329,* 247–256.

West, D. J. (1982). *Delinquency: Its roots, careers, and prospects.* Cambridge, MA: Harvard University Press.

Westen, D. (1988). Transference and information processing. *Clinical Psychology Review, 8,* 161–179.

Westen, D., Lohr, N., Silk, K. R., Gold, L., & Kerber, K. (1990). Object relations and social cognitions in borderlines, major depressives, and normals: A Thematic Apperception Test analysis. *Journal of Consulting and Clinical Psychology, 58,* 355–364.

Westermeyer, J. F., & Harrow, M. (1986). Predicting outcome in schizophrenics and nonschizophrenics of both sexes: The Zigler-Phillips Social Competence Scale. *Journal of Abnormal Psychology, 95,* 406–409.

Wettstein, R. M., Mulvey, E. P., & Rogers, R. (1991). A prospective comparison of four insanity defense standards. *American Journal of Psychiatry, 148,* 21–27.

Whalen, C. K., & Henker, B. (1991). Therapies for hyperactive children: Comparisons, combinations, and compromises. *Journal of Consulting and Clinical Psychology, 59,* 126–137.

Whitaker, A., Johnson, J., Shaffer, D., Rapoport, J. L., Kalikow, K., Walsh, B. T., Davies, M., Braiman, S., & Dolinsky, A. (1990). Uncommon troubles in young people: prevalence estimates of selected psychiatric disorders in a nonreferred adolescent population. *Archives of General Psychiatry, 47,* 487–496.

Whitehead, W. E. (1992). Behavioral medicine approaches to gastrointestinal disorders. *Journal of Consulting and Clinical Psychology, 60,* 605–612.

Whitehead, W. E., & Schuster, M. M. (1985). *Gastrointes-tinal disorders: Behavioral and physiological basis for treatment.* San Diego: Academic Press.

Whitehouse, P. J., Friedland, R. P., & Strauss, M. E. (1992). Neuropsychiatric aspects of degenerative dementias associated with motor dysfunction. In S. C. Yudofsky & R. E. Hales (Eds.), *The American Psychiatric Press textbook of neuropsychiatry.* Washington, DC: American Psychiatric Press.

Wickizer, T. M., Lessler, D., & Travis, K. M. (1996). Controlling inpatient psychiatric utilization through managed care. *American Journal of Psychiatry, 153*, 339–345.

Wicks-Nelson, R., & Israel, A. C. (1984). *Behavior disorders of childhood.* Englewood Cliffs, NJ: Prentice-Hall.

Wicks-Nelson, R., & Israel, A. C. (1991). *Behavior disorders of childhood* (2nd ed.). Englewood Cliffs, NJ: Prentice-Hall.

Widiger, T., & Costa, P. (1994). Personality and personality disorders. *Journal of Abnormal Psychology, 103*, 78–91.

Widiger, T. A., Cadoret, R., Hare, R., Robins, L., Rutherford, M., Zanarini, M., Alterman, A., Apple, M., Corbitt, E., Forth, A., Hart, S., Kultermann, J., Woody, G., & Frances, A. (1996). DSM-IV antisocial personality disorder field trial. *Journal of Abnormal Psychology, 105*, 3–16.

Widiger, T. A., Frances, A. J., Pincus, H. A., Davis, W. W., & First, M. B. (1991). Toward an empirical classification for the DSM-IV. *Journal of Abnormal Psychology, 100*, 280–288.

Widiger, T. A., Frances, A. J., Warner, L., & Bluhm, C. (1986). Diagnostic criteria for the borderline and schizotypal personality disorders. *Journal of Abnormal Psychology, 95*, 43–51.

Widiger, T. A., & Rogers, J. H. (1989). Prevalence and comorbidity of personality disorders. *Psychiatric Annals, 19*, 132–136.

Widiger, T. A., & Shea, T. (1991). Differentiation of Axis I and Axis II disorders. *Journal of Abnormal Psychology, 100*, 399–406.

Widiger, T. A., & Spitzer, R. (1991). Sex bias in the diagnosis of personality disorders: Conceptual and methodological issues. *Clinical Psychology Review, 11*, 1–22.

Widiger, T. A., Trull, T. J., Hurt, S. W., Clarkin, J., & Frances, A. (1987). A multidimensional scaling of the DSM-III personality disorders. *Archives of General Psychiatry, 44*, 557–563.

Widom, C. S. (1989a). Does violence beget violence? A critical examination of the literature. *Psychological Bulletin, 106*, 3–28.

Widom, C. S. (1989b). The cycle of violence. *Science, 244*, 160–166.

Wiggins, J. S., & Pincus, A. L. (1989). Conceptions of personality disorders and dimensions of personality. *Psycho-logical Assessment: A Journal of Consulting and Clinical Psychology, 1(4)*, 305–316.

Wiist, W. H., & Flack, J. M. (1992). A test of the John Henryism hypothesis: Cholesterol and blood pressure. *Journal of Behavioral Medicine, 15*, 15–30.

Wilfley, D., Agras, W. S., Telch, C., Rossiter, E., Schneider, J., Cole, A., Sifford, L., & Raeburn, S. (1993). Group cognitive-behavioral therapy and group interpersonal psychotherapy for the nonpurging bulimic individual: A controlled comparison. *Journal of Consulting and Clinical Psychology, 61*, 296–305.

Williams, C. L., & Berry, J. W. (1991). Primary prevention of acculturative stress among refugees: Application of psychological theory and practice. *American Psychologist, 46*, 632–641.

Williams, J. M. G., Mathews, A., & MacLeod, C. (1996). The emotional Stroop task and psychopathology. *Psychological Bulletin.*

Williams, L., & Finkelhor, D. (1990). The characteristics of incestuous fathers: A review of recent studies. In W. Marshall, D. Laws & H. Barbaree (Eds.), *Handbook of sexual assault: Issues, theories, and treatment of the offender.* New York: Plenum Press.

Williams, P., & King, M. (1987). The 'epidemic' of anorexia nervosa: another medical myth? *Lancet* (January), 205–208.

Williams, R. B., Barefoot, J., Califf, R., Haney, T., Sanders, W., Pryor, D., Hlatky, M., Siegler, I., & Mark, D. (1992). Prognostic importance of social and economic resources among medically treated patients with angiographically documented coronary heart disease. *Journal of the American Medical Association, 267*, 520–524.

Williams, S., & Rappoport, J. A. (1983). Cognitive treatments in the natural environment for agoraphobics. *Behavior Therapy, 14*, 299–313.

Williamson, D. F., Kahn, H. S., Remington, P. L., & Anda, R. F. (1990). The 10-year incidence of overweight and major weight gain in U.S. adults. *Archives of Internal Medicine, 150*, 665–672.

Wilson, G. T. (1977). Booze, beliefs and behavior: Cognitive processes in alcohol use and abuse. In P. E. Nathan, G. A. Marlatt & T. Loberg (Eds.), *Alcoholism: New directions in behavioral research and treatment.* New York: Plenum Press.

Wilson, G. T., & Lawson, D. M. (1976). Expectancies, alcohol and sexual arousal in male social drinkers. *Journal of Abnormal Psychology, 85*, 587–594.

Wilson, M. N., Phillip, D., Kohn, L. P., & Curry-El, J. (1995). Cultural relativistic approach toward ethnic minorities in family therapy. In J. F. Aponte, R. Y. Rivers, & J. Wohl (Eds.), *Psychological intervention and cultural diversity.* Boston: Allyn and Bacon.

Windle, M. (1990). A longitudinal study of antisocial behaviors in early adolescence as predictors of late adolescent substance use: Gender and ethnic group differences. *Journal of Abnormal Psychology, 99*, 86–91.

Winfield, I., George, L. K., Swartz, M., & Blazer, D. G. (1990). Sexual assault and psychiatric disorders among a community sample of women. *American Journal of Psychiatry, 147*, 335–341.

Winn, R. L., & Newton, N. (1982). Sexuality in aging: A study of 106 cultures. *Archives of Sexual Behavior, 11*, 283–298.

Winnicott, D. (1951). *Transitional objects and transitional phenomena. Through paediatrics to psychoanalysis.* New York: Basic Books.

Winnicott, D. (1971). *Playing and reality.* New York: Basic Books.

Winokur, G., Coryell, W., Keller, M., Endicott, J., & Akiskal, H. (1993). A prospective follow-up of patients with bipolar and primary unipolar affective disorder. *Archives of General Psychiatry, 50*, 457–465.

Winokur, G., Coryell, W., Keller, M., Endicott, J., & Leon, A. (1995). A family study of manic-depressive (bipolar I) disease: Is it a distinct illness separable from primary unipolar depression? *Archives of General Psychiatry, 52*, 367–373.

Wirz-Justice, A., Graw, P., Krauchi, K., Gisin, B., Jochum, A., Arendt, J., Fisch, H. U., Buddeberg, C., & Poldinger, W. (1993). Light therapy in seasonal affective disorder is independent of time of day or circadian phase. *Archives of General Psychiatry, 50*, 929–937.

Wise, M. G., & Brandt, G. T. (1992). Delirium. In S. C. Yudofsky & R. E. Hales (Eds.), *The American Psychiatric Press textbook of neuropsychiatry.* Washington, DC: American Psychiatric Press.

Wohl, J. (1995). Traditional individual psychotherapy and ethnic minorities. In J. F. Aponte, R. Y. Rivers, & J. Wohl (Eds.), *Psychological interventions and cultural diversity.* Boston: Allyn and Bacon.

Wolf, M. M., Risley, T., & Mees, H. (1964). Application of operant conditioning procedures to the behavior problems of an autistic child. *Behaviour Research and Therapy, 1*, 305–312.

Wolf, S., & Wolff, H. G. (1947). *Human gastric function: An experimental study of a man and his stomach.* New York: Oxford University Press.

Wolfe, D. A. (1985). Child-abusive parents: An empirical review and analysis. *Psychological Bulletin, 97*, 462–482.

Wolfe, D. A., & Wekerle, C. (1993). Treatment strategies for child physical abuse and neglect: A critical progress report. *Clinical Psychology Review, 13*, 473–500.

Wolfe, V. V., Finch, A. J., Saylor, C. F., Blount, R. L., Pallmeyer, T. P., & Carek, D. J. (1987). Negative affectivity in children: A multitrait-multimethod investigation. *Journal of Consulting and Clinical Psychology, 55*, 245–250.

Wolkin, A., Sanfilipo, M., Wolf, A. P., Angrist, B., Brodie, J. D., & Rotrosen, J. (1992). Negative symptoms and hypofrontality in chronic schizophrenia. *Archives of General Psychiatry, 49*, 959–965.

Wolpe, J. (1958). *Psychotherapy by reciprocal inhibition.* Stanford, CA: Stanford University Press.

Wolpe, J. (1973). *The practice of behavior therapy* (2nd ed.). New York: Pergamon Press.

Wong, B. Y. L. (1985). Issues in cognitive-behavioral interventions in academic skill areas. *Journal of Abnormal Child Psychology, 13,* 425–442.

Wong, B. Y. L., Harris, K., & Graham, S. (1991). Academic applications of cognitive-behavioral programs with learning disabled students. In P. C. Kendall (Ed.), *Child and adolescent therapy: Cognitive-behavioral procedures.* New York: Guilford Press.

Wong, B. Y. L., & Jones, W. (1982). Increasing metacomprehension in learning disabled and normally achieving students through self-questioning training. *Learning Disabilities Quarterly, 5,* 228–240.

Wood, D. L., Valdez, R. B., Hayashi, T., & Shen, A. (1990). Health of homeless children and housed, poor children. *Pediatrics, 86,* 858–866.

Woods, B. (1994). Management of memory impairment in older people with dementia. *International Review of Psychiatry, 6,* 153–161.

Woody, S. R. (1996). Effects of focus of attention on anxiety levels and social performance of individuals with social phobia. *Journal of Abnormal Psychology, 105,* 61–69.

Wool, C. A., & Barsky, A. J. (1994). Do women somatize more than men? Gender differences in somatization. *Psychosomatics, 35,* 445–452.

World Health Organization (1992). *ICD-10: The ICD-10 classification of mental and behavioral disorders: Clinical descriptions and diagnostic guidelines.* Geneva: World Health Organization.

Worling, J. R. (1995). Sexual abuse histories of adolescent male sex offenders: Differences on the basis of the age and gender of their victims. *Journal of Abnormal Psychology, 104,* 610–613.

Wragg, R. E., & Jeste, D. V. (1989). Overview of depression and psychosis in Alzheimer's disease. *American Journal of Psychiatry, 146,* 577–587.

Wright, P., Takei, N., Rifkin, L., & Murray, R. M. (1995). Maternal influenza, obstetric complications, and schizophrenia. *American Journal of Psychiatry, 152,* 1714–1720.

Wu, J. C., & Bunny, W. E. (1990). The biological basis of an antidepressant response to sleep deprivation and relapse: Review and hypothesis. *American Journal of Psychiatry, 147,* 14–21.

Wyatt, G. E., Guthrie, D., & Notgrass, C. M. (1992). Differential effects of women's child sexual abuse and subsequent sexual revictimization. *Journal of Consulting and Clinical Psychology, 60,* 167–173.

Wyatt, G. E., & Newcomb, M. (1990). Internal and external mediators of women's sexual abuse in childhood. *Journal of Consulting and Clinical Psychology, 58,* 758–767.

Wyatt, R. J. (1991). Neuroleptics and the natural course of schizophrenia. *Schizophrenia Bulletin, 17,* 325–351.

Yates, B. A., & Dowrick, P. W. (1991). Stop the drinking driver: A behavioral school-based prevention program. *Journal of Alcohol and Drug Education, 36,* 12–19.

Yeager, C. A., & Lewis, D. O. (1990). Mortality in a group of formerly incarcerated juvenile delinquents. *American Journal of Psychiatry, 147,* 612–614.

Yeh, M., Takeuchi, D. T., & Sue, S. (1994). Asian-American children treated in the mental health system: A comparison of parallel and mainstream outpatient service centers. *Journal of Clinical Child Psychology, 23,* 5–12.

Young, T. J. (1988). Substance use and abuse among Native Americans. *Clinical Psychology Review, 8,* 125–138.

Yutrzenka, B. A. (1995). Making a case for training in ethnic and cultural diversity in increasing treatment efficacy. *Journal of Consulting and Clinical Psychology, 63,* 197–206.

Zacny, J. C. (1995). A review of the effects of opioids on psychomotor and cognitive functioning in humans. *Experimental and Clinical Psychopharmacology, 3,* 432–466.

Zax, M., & Stricker, G. (1963). *Patterns of psychopathology.* New York: Macmillan.

Zelnik, M., & Kantner, J. F. (1980). Sexual activity, contraceptive use and pregnancy among metropolitan-area teenagers: 1971–1979. *Family Planning Perspectives, 12,* 230–237.

Zettle, R. D., & Hayes, S. C. (1980). Conceptual and empirical status of rational-emotive therapy. In M. Hersen, R. M. Eisler & P. M. Miller (Eds.), *Progress in behavior modification.* (Vol. 9). New York: Academic Press.

Zhu, Shu-Hong, Stretch, V., Balabanis, M., Rosbrook, B., Sadler, G., & Pierce, J. P. (1996). Telephone counseling for smoking cessation: Effects of single-session and multiple-session interventions. *Journal of Consulting and Clinical Psychology, 64,* 202–211.

Zigmond, N., & Baker, J. M. (1995). Concluding comments: current and future practices in inclusive schooling. *Journal of Special Education, 29,* 245–250.

Zill, N. (1988). Behavior, achievement, and health problems among children in stepfamilies: Findings from a national survey of child health. In E. M. Hetherington & J. D. Arasteh (Eds.), *Impact of divorce, single parenting, and stepparenting on children* (pp. 325–368). Hillsdale, NJ: Erlbaum.

Zima, B. T., Wells, K. B., Benjamin, B., & Duan, N. (1996). Mental health problems among homeless mothers: Relationship to service use and child mental health problems. *Archives of General Psychiatry, 53,* 332–338.

Zimbardo, P. G. (1977). *Shyness: What it is, what to do about it.* Reading, MA: Addison-Wesley.

Zimmerman, E. H., Zimmerman, J., & Russell, C. D. (1969). Differential effects of token reinforcement in instruction-following behavior in retarded students instructed in a group. *Journal of Applied Behavior Analysis, 2,* 101–112.

Zimmerman, J. D. (1996). A prosocial media strategy: "Youth against violence: Choose to de-fuse." *American Journal of Orthopsychiatry, 66,* 354–362.

Zinser, M. C., Baker, T. B., Sherman, J., & Cannon, D. (1992). Relation between self-reported affect and drug urges and cravings in continuing and withdrawing smokers. *Journal of Abnormal Psychology, 101,* 617–629.

Zonderman, A. B., Herbst, J. H., Schmidt, C., Costa, P. T., & McCrae, R. R. (1993). Depressive symptoms as a nonspecific, graded risk for psychiatric diagnoses. *Journal of Abnormal Psychology, 102,* 544–552.

Zorc, J. J., Larson, D., Lyons, J., & Beardsley, R. S. (1991). Expenditures for psychotropic medications in the United States in 1985. *American Journal of Psychiatry, 148,* 644–647.

Zucker, R., & Gomberg, E. (1986). Etiology of alcoholism reconsidered: The case for a biopsychosocial process. *American Psychologist, 41,* 783–793.

Zuckerman, M. (1972). *Manual and research report for the Sensation Seeking Scale (SSS).* Newark, DE: University of Delaware Press.

Zuckerman, M. (1978). Sensation seeking and psychopathy. In R. D. Hare & D. Schalling (Eds.), *Psychopathic behavior: Approaches to research.* New York: Wiley.

Zuckerman, M., & Lubin, B. (1965). *Multiple Affect Adjective Check List: Manual.* San Diego: Educational and Industrial Testing Service.

Acknowledgments

PHOTO CREDITS

Chapter 1: p. 2: Jon Riley/TSI; p. 6: Randy Wells/TSI; p. 8: *left,* John Nordell/The Image Works; *right,* Tom Wurl/Stock, Boston, Inc.; p. 10: The Granger Collection; p. 12: Don Smetzer/TSI; p. 13: Stock Montage; p. 14: The Bettmann Archive; p. 15: *top,* Giraudon/Art Resource, New York, *Pinel has the irons removed from the insane at Bicêtre* (French 19th century), Académie de Médecine, Paris, France; *bottom,* Rob Crandall/Stock, Boston, Inc.; p. 18: *top,* Will and Deni McIntyre/Photo Researchers; *bottom,* Charlene Blankenship/Lightwave; p. 24: Steve Starr/Stock, Boston, Inc.; p. 26: Donna Binder/Impact Visuals; p. 27: Deborah Davis/PhotoEdit.

Chapter 2: p. 30: Bob Daemmrich/Stock, Boston, Inc.; p. 35: William Gage/Custom Medical Stock Photos; p. 39: © Sotographs/Liaison International; p. 41: The Bettmann Archive; p. 44: *top,* Ken Heyman/Woodfin Camp & Associates; *bottom,* Lawrence Migdale/Photo Researchers; p. 45: Peter Mikulka; p. 48: *left,* Albert Ellis/The Institute of Rational Emotive Therapy; *right,* Lief Skodgfors/Woodfin Camp & Associates; p. 50: The Bettmann Archive; p. 54: *top left,* Keyston/The Image Works; *top right,* Culver Pictures; *bottom,* Culver Pictures; p. 56: *left,* The Bettmann Archive; *right,* The Bettmann Archive; p. 58: Jim Whitmer/Stock, Boston, Inc.

Chapter 3: p.62: Mark Richards/PhotoEdit; p. 64: © Antman Archives/The Image Works; p. 65: *top,* Photo Researchers; *bottom,* Robin L. Sachs/PhotoEdit; p. 69: Corbis/Bettmann; p. 70: Snark/Art Resource *Dream of one under ether according to the descriptions of a patient of the period* (19th-century engraving) (extract from "Merveilles de la Science" Figuier, Vol. II*)*, Centre d'optique et électricité, Paris, France; p. 77: AP/Wide World Photos; p. 80: Drawing by Cheney; © 1993 The New Yorker Magazine, Inc.; p. 82: Goldberg/Monkmeyer; p. 88: James Wilson/Woodfin Camp & Associates; p. 91: David Joel/TSI.

Chapter 4: p. 96: Laurence Dutton/TSI; p. 102: Bob Daemmrich/The Image Works; p. 109: Bob Daemm-rich/Stock, Boston, Inc.; p. 111: Figure 4.5a, Norman Sundberg; p.113: F. Reischl/Unicorn Stock Photos; p. 115: *left,* Figure 4.7a, Courtesy of Dr. Monte Buchsbaum/Mt. Sinai School of Medicine; *right,* Figure 4.7b, Courtesy of Monte Buchsbaum/Mt. Sinai School of Medicine; p. 117: W.B. Spunbarg/The Picture Cube; p.

125: *left,* Patrick Clark/Monkmeyer; *center,* Georges Merillon/Gamma Liaison; *right,* M. P. Kahl/Photo Researchers.

Chapter 5: p. 128: Carol Lundeen; p. 134: AP/Wide World Photos; p. 136: William Mercer McLeod/*Time* Magazine, © Time, Inc.; p. 137: Michael A. Schwarz/The Image Works; p. 141: Jeff Greenberg/Unicorn Stock Photos; p. 143: Drawing by D. Reilly; © 1993 The New Yorker Magazine, Inc.; p. 150: *top, middle, bottom,* Judy Gelles/Stock, Boston, Inc.; p. 154: AP/Wide World Photos.

Chapter 6: p. 158: Stephen Collins/Photo Researchers; p. 162: Scala/Art Resource *The Scream,* Edvard Munch, National Gallery, Oslo, Norway; p. 164: David Young-Wolff/PhotoEdit; p. 173: K. H. Switak/Photo Researchers; p. 176: cartoon, *Ziggy* © 1992 Ziggy and Friends, Inc. Distributed by Universal Press Syndicate. Reprinted with permission. All rights reserved; p. 177: P. Werner/The Image Works; p. 178: Jonathan Wiggs/The *Boston Globe;* p. 183: cartoon: Drawing by Leo Abbett; p. 186: Corbis/Bettmann; p. 188: Spencer Grant/Photo Researchers; p. 189: Joanna P. Pinneo/Aurora & Quanta Productions.

Chapter 7: p. 192: Robert Llewellyn/Direct Stock; p. 198: Dick Young/Unicorn Stock Photos; p. 199: cartoon, Drawing by Reilly; © 1993 The New Yorker Magazine, Inc.; p. 203: AP/ Wide World Photos; p. 205: Sygma; p. 207: cartoon, Drawing by Leo Abbett; p. 211: AP/Wide World Photos.

Chapter 8: p. 214: Lanpher Productions; p. 219: *left,* Dimitra Lavrakas/The Picture Cube; *right,* SPL/ Custom Medical Stock Photos; p. 222: *left,* UPI/Bettmann; *right,* Chip Hires/Gamma Liaison; p. 226: Laura Dwight/Peter Arnold; p. 227: cartoon, *Peanuts.* Reprinted by permission of United Feature Syndicate, Inc.; p. 229: Andy Sacks/TSI; p. 234: Harlow Primate Lab of Wisconsin; p. 235: J. Griffin/The Image Works; p. 237: cartoon, Drawing by Lorenz; © 1993 The New Yorker Magazine, Inc.; p. 241: *right,* Exley/Gamma Liaison; *left,* A. Knudsen/Sygma; p. 247: UPI/Corbis-Bettmann; p. 250: *left,* AP/Wide World Photos; *right,* AP/Wide World Photos; p. 251: Frank Siteman/The Picture Cube.

Chapter 9: p. 258: Ian Shaw/TSI; p. 260: Culver Pictures; p. 264: A. Ramey/Unicorn Stock Photos; p. 265:

Grunnitus/Monkmeyer Press Photo Service; p. 269: UPI/Corbis-Bettmann; p. 270: Robert Ginn/PhotoEdit; p. 275: Figure 9.6, Nancy C. Andreasen, M.D., Ph.D./University of Iowa; p. 277: Figure 9.8, Karen F. Berman, M. D./NIMH; p. 280: Figure 9.10, Peter M. Witt; p. 285: AP/Wide World Photos; p. 288: *left*, Ann Marie Kuiper; *right*, *Saint-Adolf-Grand-Grand-God-Father* (1915), Adolf Woelffli, case no. 450, inventory no. 4859, photographed by Ingeborg Klinger. Reproduced with permission of the Prinzhorn-Sammlung Collection, Heidelberg.

Chapter 10: p. 296: Ken Straiton/The Stock Market; p. 298: Giraudon/Art Resource, *Influence of the Stars on the Maladies of the Human Body: Tractatus de Pestilentia* (15th century), M. Alnik, Czech manuscript, University Library/Prague, Prague, Czech Republic; p. 302: *left*, *Miami Herald*/Gamma Liaison; *right*, Robert Brenner/PhotoEdit; p. 305: Jim Whitmer/Stock, Boston, Inc.; p. 307: B. Daemmrich/The Image Works; p. 311: Billy Barnes/Stock, Boston, Inc.; p. 315: Pete Saloutos/TSI; p. 317: Dr. A. Liepins/Science Photo Library/Photo Researchers; p. 321: Rick Rickman/MATRIX; p. 324: David Longstreath/AP/Wide World Photos; p. 325: cartoon, © 1997 Bill Lee from The Cartoon Bank. All rights reserved.

Chapter 11: p. 330: Mike McGovern/The Picture Cube; p. 334: F. Fournier/Contact/Woodfin Camp & Associates; p. 336: Dr. Emanuel Rubin/NIAAA; p. 340: Tom Prettyman/PhotoEdit; p. 342: cartoon, Drawing by Leo Abbet; p. 344: A. Glauberman/Science Resource/Photo Researchers; p. 350: Andrew Lichtenstein/Impact Visuals; p. 354: Matthew Neal McVay/Stock, Boston, Inc.; p. 355: Barry Chin/The Boston Globe; p. 362: AP/Wide World Photos; p. 364: AP/Wide World Photos.

Chapter 12: p. 368: S. Tanaka/The Picture Cube; p. 370: Ogust/The Image Works; p. 371: Catherine Leroy/Sipa Press; p. 375: Outline Press © 1997 *Newsweek*, Inc. All rights reserved. Reprinted by permission; p. 377: Barbara Alper/Stock, Boston, Inc.; p. 379: cartoon, Drawing by Mankoff; © 1993 The New Yorker Magazine, Inc.; p. 386: Seth Resnick/Liaison International; p. 387: Marny Malin/SYGMA; p. 389: *top*, AP/Wide World Photos; *bottom*, © 1997 Victoria Roberts from The Cartoon Bank. All rights reserved; p. 393: AP/Wide World Photos; p. 398: *left*, AP/Wide World Photos; *right*, UPI/Corbis-Bettmann; p. 401: Gale Zucker/Stock, Boston, Inc.

Chapter 13: p. 404: Gary Braasch/TSI; p. 407: Barbara Alper/Stock Boston, Inc.; p. 409: Spencer Grant/The Picture Cube, Inc.; p. 410: Gamma/Liaison; p. 411: cartoon: Non Sequitur by Wiley © 1992 The Washington Post Writers' Group 8-12; p. 420: *left*, D. Gorton/*Time* Magazine. © Time, Inc.; *right*, D. Gorton/*Time* Magazine. © Time, Inc.; p. 422: Dr. Jerome Kagan/Harvard University; p. 425: Drawing by Henry Martin © 1993 The New Yorker Magazine, Inc. All rights reserved.

Chapter 14: p. 432: Joe Traver/Gamma Liaison; p. 435: Reuters/Corbis-Bettmann; p. 436: AP/Wide World Photos; p. 438: © 1997 Time Inc. Reprinted by permission; p. 442: *left*, George Kochaniec/SYGMA; *right*, AP/Wide World Photos; p. 444: Dr. Stephen Suomi/NIH/NIHCD; p. 449: Seth Resnick/Stock, Boston, Inc.; p. 451: Anthony Barboza; p. 453: cartoon: Drawing by Mankoff © 1993 The New Yorker Magazine, Inc.; p. 454: Grant LeDuc/Monkmeyer Press Photo Service; p. 459: Shumsky/The Image Works; p. 460: Tom McKitterick/Impact Visuals.

Chapter 15: p. 464: Stephen Simpson/FPG; p. 467: Nancy Richmond/The Image Works; p. 471: cartoon, Dennis the Menace. Used by permission of Hank Ketcham and © North America Syndicate; p. 478: Catherine Ursillo/Photo Researchers, Inc.; p. 479: Dorothy Littell/Stock, Boston, Inc.; p. 481: Frank Pedrick/The Image Works; p. 483: Spencer Grant/Stock, Boston, Inc.; p. 484: cartoon, The Far Side Cartoon by Gary Larson is reprinted by permission of Chronical Features, San Francisco, CA. All rights reserved; p. 487: James Carroll/Stock, Boston, Inc.; p. 491: *People Weekly* © 1992 Marianne Barcelona; p. 492: Reuters/Mike Theiler/Archive Photos.

Chapter 16: p. 498: Bob Daemrich Photography; p. 503: Theresa Frare/NY Times Permissions; p. 504: Figure 16.2, W. B. Saunders & Co./Harcourt Brace & Company. Reprinted with permission; p. 505: *top*, © Lennart Nilsson/Bonnier Alba AB, *A Child Is Born*, Dell Publishing Company; *bottom*, © 1994 George Steinmetz; p. 507: Bob Daemmrich/Stock, Boston, Inc.; p. 509: *left*, Tony Freeman/PhotoEdit; *right*, Laura Dwight/Peter Arnold, Inc.; p. 511: Figure 16.3, Reprinted with permission from *Nadia: A Case of Extraordinary Drawing Ability in an Autistic Child* by Lorna Selfe © Academic Press, Inc. (London) Ltd. 1977; Gamma/Liaison; p. 515: Nancy Pierce/Photo Researchers, Inc.; p. 516: Meri Houtchens Kitchen/The Picture Cube, Inc.

Chapter 17: p. 522: Bill Aron/PhotoEdit; p. 527: *left*, Catherine Karnow/Woodfin Camp & Associates; *right*, Charlie Westerman/Liaison International; p. 528: Evan Agostini/Gamma Liaison; p. 532: Daemmrich/The Image Works; Figure 17.5, Reprinted with permission by Dr. Carl Cottman, Department of Psychobiology, The University of California at Irvine; p. 533: NIH/Science Source/Photo Researchers; p. 534: Catherine Pouedras/Science Photo Library/Photo Researchers, Inc.; p. 537: *left*, AP/Wide World Photos; *right*, AP/Wide World Photos; p. 538: Michael Kaufman/Impact Visuals; p. 541: Alain McLaughlin/Impact Visuals; p. 542: Inga Spence/The Picture Cube, Inc.; p. 544: Martha Tabor/Impact Visuals; p. 545: Kathy Seward-MacKay/Impact Visuals.

Chapter 18: p. 548: Bob Daemmrich/Stock, Boston, Inc.; p. 550: AP/Wide World Photos; p. 556:

Reuters/Barbara L. Johnston/Archive Photos; p. 562: J. P. Laffont/Sygma; p. 564: Nancy Pierce/Photo Researchers; p. 565: *left*, Lawrence Migdale/Photo Researchers; *right*, Donna DeCesare/Impact Visuals; p. 567: cartoon: Drawing by Leo Abbett; p. 570: Lester Sloan/The Gamma Liaison; p. 573: Tony Freeman/PhotoEdit.

TEXT, TABLE, AND LINE ART CREDITS

Chapter 1: p. 7: Figure 1.1, from J. Shedler, M. Mayman & M. Manis (1993), The illusion of mental health, *American Psychologist, 48,* 1117-1131. Copyright © 1993 by the American Psychological Association. Reprinted with permission; p. 19: Figure 1.2, from J. R. Helzer et al., Alcoholism: North America and Asia — A comparison of population surveys with the Diagnostic Interview Schedule, *Archive of General Psychology, 41,* 316. Copyright © 1990, American Medical Association; p. 21: Figure 1.3, from J. Weisz, M. Sigman, B. Weiss & J. Mosk (1993), Parent reports of behavioral and emotional problems among children in Kenya, Thailand, and the United States, *Child Development, 64,* 98-109. Copyright © Society for Research in Child Development, Inc.

Chapter 2: p. 37: Figure 2.5, from L. Lefton, *Psychology* 4/e, 1994, Allyn & Bacon. Reprinted by permission; p. 47: Table 2.3, from A. Ellis (1962), *Reason and emotion in psychotherapy* (New York: Stuart). Copyright © 1962 by The Institute for Rational Living, Inc. Published by arrangement with Carol Publishing Group.

Chapter 3: p. 73: Table 3.3, from E. L. Philips (1968), Achievement place: Token reinforcement procedures in a home-style setting for "predelinquent" boys, *Journal of Applied Behavior Analysis, 1,* 213-223. Used with permission; p. 74: Figure 3.1, from E. L. Philips (1968), Achievement place: Token reinforcement procedures in a home-style setting for "predelinquent" boys, *Journal of Applied Behavior Analysis, 1,* 213-223. Used with permission.

Chapter 4: pp. 104-105: Table 4.1, from M. B. First, R. L. Spitzer, M. Gibbon & J. B. W. Williams (1997), *Structured clinical interview for DSM-IV Axis I Disorders. Patient edition (SCIDI/P,* Version 2.0, 4/97 revision) (Biometrics Research Department, New York State Psychiatric Institutes. 722 West 168th St., New York, NY 10032). Copyright © 1997 Biometrics Research Department; p. 107: Table 4.3, from *Minnesota Multiphasic Personality Inventory-2 (MMPI-2).* Copyright © 1942, 1943 (renewed 1970), 1989 by the Regents of the University of Minnesota. Reproduced by permission of the publisher. "MMPI-2" and "Minnesota Multiphasic Personality Inventory-2" are trademarks owned by the University of Minnesota; p. 108: Figure 4.3, from *Minnesota Multiphasic Personality Inventory (MMPI).* Copyright © by the University of Minnesota 1942, 1943 (renewed 1970). This profile from 1984, 1976, 1982. Reproduced by permission of the University of Minnesota Press; p. 110: Figure 4.4, exhibit "Examples of Neuropsychological Tests," from J. Sattler (1990), *Assessment in Children,* Third Edition (San Diego, CA: J. Sattler), p. 709. Reprinted by permission; p. 120 Table 4.5, Reprinted with permission from *The Diagnostic and Statistical Manual of Mental Disorders,* Fourth Edition. Copyright © 1994 American Psychiatric Association; p. 122: Table 4.6, Reprinted with permission from the *The Diagnostic and Statistical Manual of Mental Disorders,* Fourth Edition. Copyright © 1994 American Psychiatric Association.

Chapter 5: p. 130: Definition of *science.* Copyright © 1996 by Houghton Mifflin Company. Reprinted by permission from *The American Heritage Dictionary of the English Language, Third Edition;* p. 135: Figure 5.3, R. C. Kessler, K. A. McGonagle, S. Zhao, H. U. Wittchen & K. S. Kendler (1994), Lifetime and 12-month prevalence of DSM-III-R psychiatric disorders in the United States, *Archives of General Psychiatry, 51,* 8-19; p. 138: Figure 5.4, illustration by Nancy Doniger from Tamar Lewin, The rise in single parenthood is reshaping the United States, from *The New York Times,* October 5, 1992, pp. B1, B6. Copyright © 1992 by The New York Times Co. Reprinted by permission; p. 144: Figure 5.6, from A. Bandura (1969), *Principles of behavior modification* (New York: Holt, Rinehart, & Winston). Copyright © 1969 by Holt, Rinehart and Winston, reproduced by permission of the publisher; p. 146: Figure 5.7, from Gross & Isaac, Forced arm exercise and DRO in the treatment of bruxism in cerebral palsied children, *Child and Family Behavior Therapy, 4(2/3),* Summer/Fall 1982. Copyright © 1983 by The Haworth Press, Inc.; p. 147: Figure 5.8, from A. Saigh, Changes in ratings of discomfort using a multiple-baseline design, *Behavior Research and Therapy, 24,* 685-688. Copyright © 1986, with permission from Elsevier Science; p. 153: Figure 5.10, from A. E. Kazdin, T. C. Siegel & D. Bass, Cognitive problem-solving skills training and parent management training in the treatment of anti-social behavior in children, *Journal of Consulting and clinical Psychology, 60(5),* 733-747. Copyright © 1992, used with permission from The American Psychological Association.

Chapter 6: p. 160: Table 6.1, reprinted with permission from the *The Diagnostic and Statistical Manual of Mental Disorders,* Fourth Edition. Copyright © 1994 American Psychiatric Association; p. 175: Table 6.4, reprinted with permission from *The Diagnostic and Statistical Manual of Mental Disorders,* Fourth Edition. Copyright © 1994 American Psychiatric Association; p. 179: Figure 6.5, from K. G. Power et al., A controlled comparison of cognitive-behavioral therapy, *Journal of Anxiety Disorders, 4,* 267-292. Copyright © 1990 with kind permission from Elsevier Science Ltd., The Boulevard, Langford Lane, Kidlington OX5 1GB, U.K.; p. 184: Table 6.6, reprinted by permission by G. Reed, *Obsessional Experience and Compulsive Behavior: A Cognitive-Structural Approach*. Copyright © 1985 Academic Press.

Chapter 7: p. 195: Table 7.1, Reprinted with permission from *The Diagnostic and Statistical Manual of Mental Disorders*, Fourth Edition. Copyright © 1994 American Psychiatric Association; p. 197: Figure 7.1, from L. S. Walker, J. Garber & J. W. Greene (1994), Somatic complaints in pediatric patients: A prospective study of the role of negative life events, child and social and academic competence, and parental somatic symptoms, *Journal of Consulting and Clinical Psychology, 62*, 1213-1221. Copyright © 1994 by the American Psychological Association. Reprinted with permission; p. 204: Table 7.2, reprinted with permission from *The Diagnostic and Statistical Manual of Mental Disorders*, Fourth Edition. Copyright © 1994 American Psychiatric Association.

Chapter 8: p. 225: Figure 8.5, from Cross-National Collaborative Group (1992), The changing rate of major depression: Cross-national comparisons, *Journal of the American Medical Association, 268*, 3098-3105. Copyright © 1992, American Medical Association; p. 232: Figure 8.7, from K. S. Kendler, R. C. Kessler, E. E. Walters, C. MacLean, M. C. Neale, A. C. Heath & L. J. Eaves (1995), Stressful life events, genetic liability, and onset of an episode of major depression in women, *American Journal of Psychiatry, 152*, 833-842. Copyright © 1995, the American Psychiatric Association. Reprinted by permission; p. 249: Figure 8.11, from I. Rockett & G. Smith (1989), Homicide, suicide, motor vehicle crash, and fall mortality: United States' experience in comparative perspective, *American Journal of Public Health, 79*, 1396-1400. Copyright © 1989 by American Public Health Association. Reprinted with permission.

Chapter 9: p. 268: Figure 9.2, from S. Arndt, N. C. Andreasen, M. Flaum, D. Miller & P. Nopoulos (1995), A longitudinal study of symptom dimensions in schizophrenia: Predictions and patterns of change, *Archive of General Pyschiatry, 52*, 352-360. Copyright © 1995, American Medical Association; p. 283: Figure 9.12, from I. S. Rosenfarb, M. J. Goldstein, J. Mintz & K. H. Nuechterlein (1995), Expressed emotion and subclinical psychpathology observable within the transactions between schizophrenic patients and their family members, *Journal of Abnormal Psychology, 104*, 259-267. Copyright © 1995 by the American Psychological Association. Reprinted with permission.

Chapter 10: p. 320: Figure 10.10, from R. M. Kaplan, et al. (1993), *Health and Human Behavior*. Copyright © 1993 by the American Cancer Society. Used with permission; p. 326: Figure 10.11, from T. P. Carmosy & J. D. Matarrazzo (1991), Health psychology, in M.

Hersen, A. Kadzin & A. Bellack (Eds.), *The clinical psychology handbook* (2nd ed.) (New York: Pergamon Press). Copyright © 1991 by Allyn & Bacon. Reprinted with permission.

Chapter 11: p. 333: Table 11.1, reprinted with permission from *The Diagnostic and Statistical Manual of Mental Disorders*, Fourth Edition. Copyright © 1994 American Psychiatric Association; p. 352: Figure 11.5, from B. H. Bry, P. McKeon & R. J. Pandina (1982), Extent of drug use as a function of number of risk factors, *Journal of Abnormal Psychology, 91*. Copyright © 1982 by the American Psychological Association. Adapted by permission; p. 357: Figure 11.6, copyright © 1993, *USA Today*. Reprinted with permission; p. 360: Figure 11.7, from G. A. Marlatt & J. R. Gordon (1980), Determinants of relapse: Implications for the maintenance of behavior change, in P. O. Davidson & S. M. Davidson (Eds.), *Behavioral medicine: Changing health lifestyles* (pp. 410-452) (New York: Brunner/Mazel); p. 363: Table 11.4, The Twelve Steps are reprinted with permission of Alcoholics Anonymous World Services, Inc. Permission to reprint this material does not mean that AA has reviewed or approved the contents of this publication or that AA agrees with the views expressed herein. AA is a program of recovery from alcoholism only. Use of the Twelve Steps in connection with programs and activities that are patterned after AA but that address other problems does not imply otherwise.

Chapter 12: pp. 372-373: Figure 12.1, from R. Crooks & K. Baur (1990), *Our sexuality* (4th ed.) (Redwood City, CA: Benjamin Cummings) Copyright © 1993, 1989, 1987, 1983, 1980. The Benjamin Cummings Publishing Co. Copyright © 1995 Brooke/Cole Publishing Co., Pacific Grove, CA 93950, a division of International Thomson Publishing, Inc. By permission of the publisher; p. 374: Figure 12.2, Masters & Johnson Institute. Used with permission; p. 378: Figure 12.3, from M. J. Rotheram-Borus, M. Rosario, H. Reid & C. Koopman (1995), Predicting patterns of sexual acts among homosexual and bisexual youths, *American Journal of Psychiatry, 152*, 588-595. Copyright © 1995, the American Psychiatric Association. Reprinted by permission; p. 381: Figure 12.4, from E. M. Palace (1995), Modification of dysfunctional patterns of sexual response through autonomic arousal and false psychological feedback, *Journal of Consulting and Clinical Psychology, 63*, 604-615. Copyright © 1995 by the American Psychological Association. Reprinted with permission; p. 392: Figure 12.6, from T. C. Chaplin, M. E. Rice & G. T. Harris (1995), Salient victim suffering and the sexual responses of child molesters, *Journal of Consulting and Clinical Psychology, 63*, 249-255. Copyright © 1995 by the American Psychological Association. Reprinted with permission.

Chapter 13: p. 406: Table 13.1, Reprinted with permission from *The Diagnostic and Statistical Manual of Mental Disorders*, Fourth Edition. Copyright © 1994

American Psychiatric Association; p. 409: Table 13.2, from L. J. Chapman, J. P. Chapman & M. L. Raulin, Body-image aberration in schizophrenia, *Journal of Abnormal Psychology, 87,* 399-407. Copyright © 1978 by the American Psychological Association. Reprinted with permission; p. 418: Figure 13.3, from J. S. Wiggins & A. L. Pincus (1989), Conceptions of personality disorders and dimensions of personality, *Psychological Assessment: A Journal of Consulting and Clinical Psychology, 1*(4), 305-316. Copyright © 1989 by the American Psychological Association. Reprinted with permission; p. 423: Figure 13.4, reprinted with permission from J. Kagan, J. S. Reznick & N. Snidman (1988), Biological bases of childhood shyness, *Science, 240,* 167-171. Copyright © 1988 American Association for the Advancement of Science; p. 423: Figure 13.5, reprinted with permission of The Society for Research in Child Development, Inc.

Chapter 14: p. 434: Table 14.1, reprinted with permission from *The Diagnostic and Statistical Manual of Mental Disorders,* Fourth Edition. Copyright © 1994 American Psychiatric Association; p. 436: Table 14.2, from R. Hare, S. Hart & T. Harpur (1991), Psychopathology and the DSM-IV criteria for antisocial personality disorder, *Journal of Abnormal Psychology, 100.* Copyright 1991 by the American Psychological Association. Reprinted by permission; p. 437: Table 14.3, from L. N. Robins (1986), Epidemiology of antisocial personality, in G. L. Klerman, M. M. Weissman, P. S. Applebaum & L. H. Roth (Eds.), *Social, epidemiologic, and legal psychiatry* (Vol. 5, pp. 231-244) (New York: Basic Books). Copyright © 1986 by Basic Books, Lippincott. Used with permission; p. 445: Figure 14.2, from R. Hare, S. Hart, & T. Harpur (1991), Psychopathology and the DSM-IV criteria for antisocial personality disorder, J*ournal of Abnormal Psychology, 100.* Copyright © 1991 by the American Psychological Association. Reprinted by permission; p. 461: Figure 14.5, from E. B. Foa, D. Hearst-Ikeda & K. J. Perry (1995), Evaluation of a brief cognitive-behavioral program for the prevention of chronic PTSD in recent assault victims, *Journal of Consulting and Clinical Psychology, 63,* 948-955. Copyright © 1995 by the American Psychological Association. Reprinted with permission.

Chapter 15: p. 474: Figure 15.2, from J. Kagan, et. al., Reflection-impulsivity: The generality and dynamics of conceptual tempo, *Journal of Abnormal Psychology, 71,* 17-24. Copyright © 1966 by the American Psychological Association. Reprinted by permission; p. 475: Table 15.2, reprinted with permission from *The Diagnostic and Statistical Manual of Mental Disorders,* Fourth Edition. Copyright © 1994 American Psychiatric Association; p. 482: Figure 15.3, from A. E. Kazdin, K. Esveldt-Dawson, N. H. French & A. S. Unis (1987), Problem-solving skills training and relationship therapy in the treatment of antisocial child behavior, *Journal of Consulting and Clinical Psychology, 55*(1), 76-85.

Copyright © 1987 by the American Psychological Association. Reprinted by permission; p. 489: Figure 15.4, from Lewinsohn et al. (1990), Cognitive-behavioral treatment for depressed adolescents, *Behavior Therapy, 21,* 385-401. Copyright © 1990 by the Association for Advancement of Behavior Therapy. Reprinted by permission of the publisher; p. 493: Figure 15.5, from C. G. Fairburn, P. A. Norman, S. L. Welch, M. E. O'Connor, H. A. Doll & R. C. Peveler (1995), A prospective study of outcome in bulimia nervosa and the long-term effects of three psychological treatments, *Archives of General Psychiatry, 52,* 304-312; p. 494: Table 15.5, from What is a healthy weight?, *New York Times,* September 26, 1992, p. 32. Copyright © 1992 by The New York Times Co. Reprinted by permission.

Chapter 16: p. 501: Table 16.2, from *Manual for the Wechsler Intelligence Scale for Children: Third Edition.* Copyright © 1991, 1974, 1971 by The Psychological Corporation. Reproduced by permission. All rights reserved. "Weschsler Intelligence Scale for Children" and "WISC-III" are registered trademarks; p. 512: Table 16.5, reprinted with permission from *The Diagnostic and Statistical Manual of Mental Disorders,* Fourth Edition. Copyright © 1994 American Psychiatric Association.

Chapter 17: p. 525: Table 17.1, reprinted with permission from M. Folstein, S. Folstein & P. McHugh, Mini-mental state: A practical method for grading the cognitive state of patients for the clinician, *Journal of Psychiatric Research, 12,* 189-198. Copyright © 1975 Elsevier Science Ltd., Oxford, England; p. 526: Table 17.2, reprinted by permission, *The Gerontologist, 17,* 315-320, 1977; p. 530: Figure 17.3, from A. Lobo, P. Saz, G. Marcos, J. L. Dia & C. De-la Camara (1995), The prevalence of dementia and depression in the elderly community in a southern European population: The Zaragoza study, *Archives of General Psychiatry, 52,* 497-506. Copyright © 1995, American Medical Association. Reprinted by permission; p. 531: Figure 17.4, from D. Selkoe (1992), Aging brain, aging mind, *Scientific American,* September, 138. Copyright © 1992 by Scientific American, Inc. All rights reserved; p. 535: Figure 17.6, A. S. Kenderson, S. Fasteal, A. F. Jorm, A. J. Mackinnon, A. E. Korten, H. Christensen, L. Croft & P. A. Jacomb (1995), Apolipoprotein E allele epsilon 4, dementia, and cognitive decline in a population sample, *The Lancet, 346,* 1387-1390. © The Lancet Ltd., 1995. Reprinted by permission; p. 543: Table 17.5, from L. Gross & R. Nagy, Neuropsychiatric aspects of poisonous and toxic disorders, in *The American Psychiatric Press Textbook of Neuropsychiatry.* Copyright © 1992. Reprinted by permission of the American Psychiatric Association.

Chapter 18: p. 562: Figure 18.4, from D. Braddock (1992), Community mental health and mental retardation services in the United States: A comparative study of Resource Allocation, *American Journal of Psychiatry,*

149, 175-783. Copyright © 1992, the American Psychiatric Association. Reprinted by permission; p. 572: Table 18.2, from Coie, Watt, West, Hawkins, Asarnow, Markman, Ramey, Shure & Long (1993), The science of prevention: A conceptual framework and some directions for a national research program, *American Psychologist, 48*, 1022. Copyright © 1993 by the American Psychological Association. Reprinted with permission. For classroom use only; p. 574: Figure 18.7, from J. E. Giliham, K. J. Reivich, L. H. Jaycox & M. E. Seligman (1995), Prevention of depressive symptoms in schoolchildren: Two-year follow-up, *Psychological Science, 6*, 343-351. Reprinted with the permission of Cambridge University Press.

Name Index

Subject Index

Abnormal Psychology
Understarding human Problems.

This book is due for return on or before the last date shown below.

21 SEP 2000

0 2 OCT 2015

10 DEC 2003

- 9 OCT 2007

2 9 JAN 2008

21 sep

D.